Key to map pages

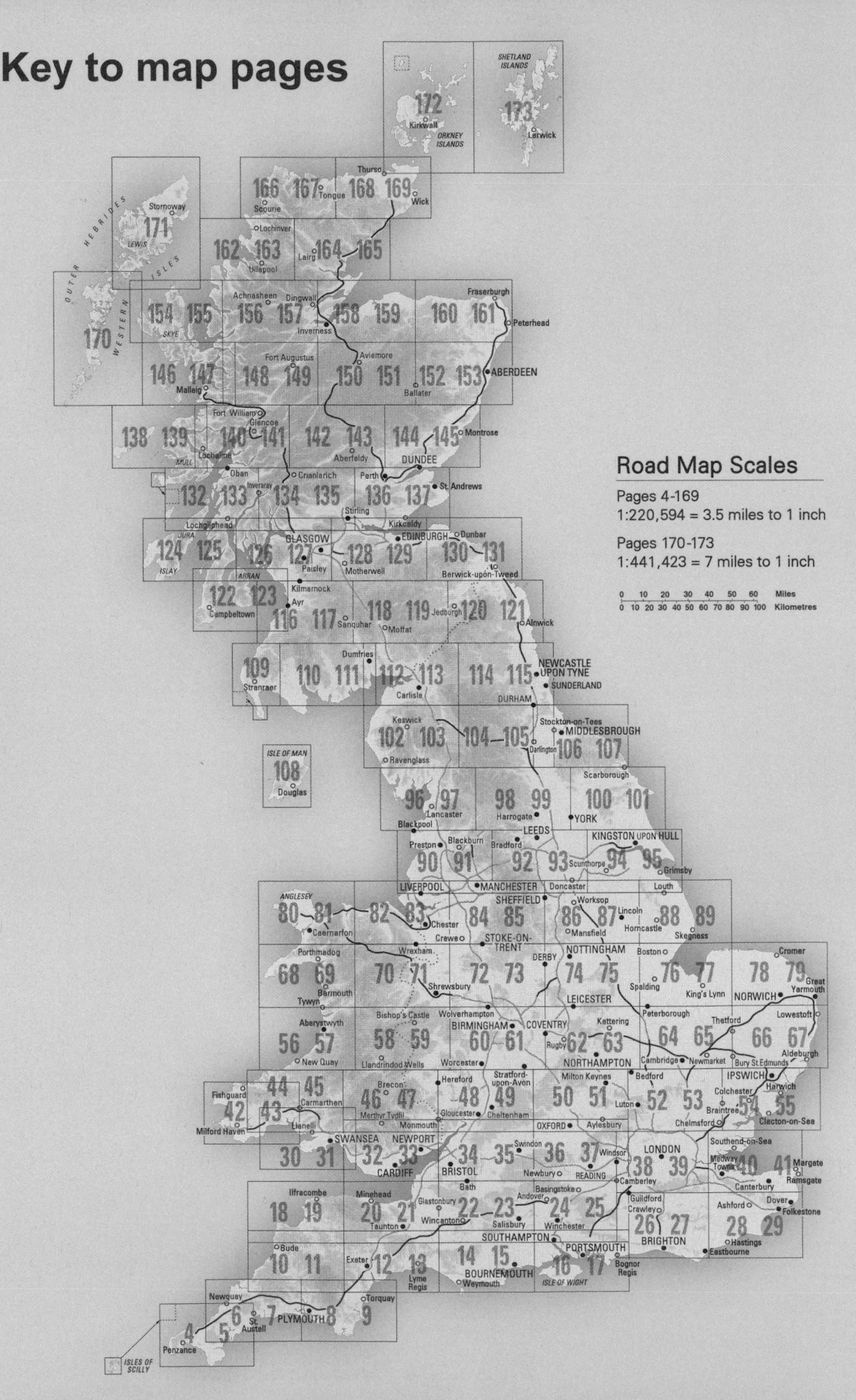

Road Map Scales

Pages 4-169
1:220,594 = 3.5 miles to 1 inch

Pages 170-173
1:441,423 = 7 miles to 1 inch

GREAT BRITAIN
2012

Edition 2012 by Manufacture Française des
Pneumatiques Michelin
Société en commandite par actions au capital de
304 000 000 EUR
Place des Carmes-Déchaux
63 Clermont-Ferrand (France)
R.C.S. Clermont-Ferrand B 855 200 507
© Michelin, Propriétaires-éditeurs 2012.

Cartography supplied by Geographers' A-Z Map
Company Limited.
Copyright © 2011 Geographers' A-Z Map Company Ltd.

Ordnance Survey®   This product includes mapping
data licensed from Ordnance Survey® with the
permission of the Controller of Her Majesty's
Stationery Office. © Crown Copyright 2011. All
rights reserved. Licence Number 100017302.

The Grid in this atlas is the National Grid taken
from Ordnance Survey ® mapping with the
permission of the Controller of Her Majesty's
Stationery Office.

Safety Camera & Fuel Station Databases Copyright
2011 © PocketGPSWorld.com

The Shopmobility logo is a registered symbol of
The National Federation of Shopmobility.

Relief Data within the A-Z Cartography is sourced
from Geo-Innovations.

The representation on the maps of a road, track
or footpath is no evidence of the existence of a
right of way.

All rights reserved.

No part of this publication may be reproduced
or recorded in any form or by any means of
electronic, mechanical, reprographic or other
duplication without the permission of the
Publishers and copyright holders.

While every effort is made to ensure that all
information printed in this publication is correct
and up-to-date, Michelin Maps & Guides accepts
no liability for any direct, indirect or consequential
losses howsoever caused so far as such can be
excluded by law.

In spite of the care taken in the production of this
book, it is possible that a defective copy may have
escaped our attention. If this is so, please return it
to your bookseller, who will exchange it for you,
or contact:

Michelin Maps & Guides
Hannay House - 39 Clarendon Road
WATFORD Herts WD17 1JA
www.ViaMichelin.com

Printed in Italy by Rotolito Lombarda

Cover and title photo:
Fridmar Damm/Photononstop

CONTENTS

II - V   **Route Planning**

2   **Mileage Chart and Journey Times**

3   **Reference Page**

4 - 173   **Britain Road Map Pages**

4 - 169   Main map : 3.5 miles to 1 inch / 2.2 km to 1 cm (1: 220,594)

170 - 173   Northern Isles : 7 miles to 1 inch / 4.4 km to 1 cm (1: 441,423)

174 - 184   **Main Route Maps**

174 - 181   London

182 - 183   Birmingham

184   Manchester

185 - 214   **City & Town Centre Maps**

185 - 186   Reference

187 - 214   City & Town Plans

215 - 216   **Port & Airport Plans**

217 - 275   **Index Pages**

275   Safety Camera Information

276 - 279   **Index to Selected Places of Interest**

280 - 281   **Limited Interchange Motorway Junctions**

282   **Channel Tunnel Plans**
Folkestone & Calais Terminal access maps

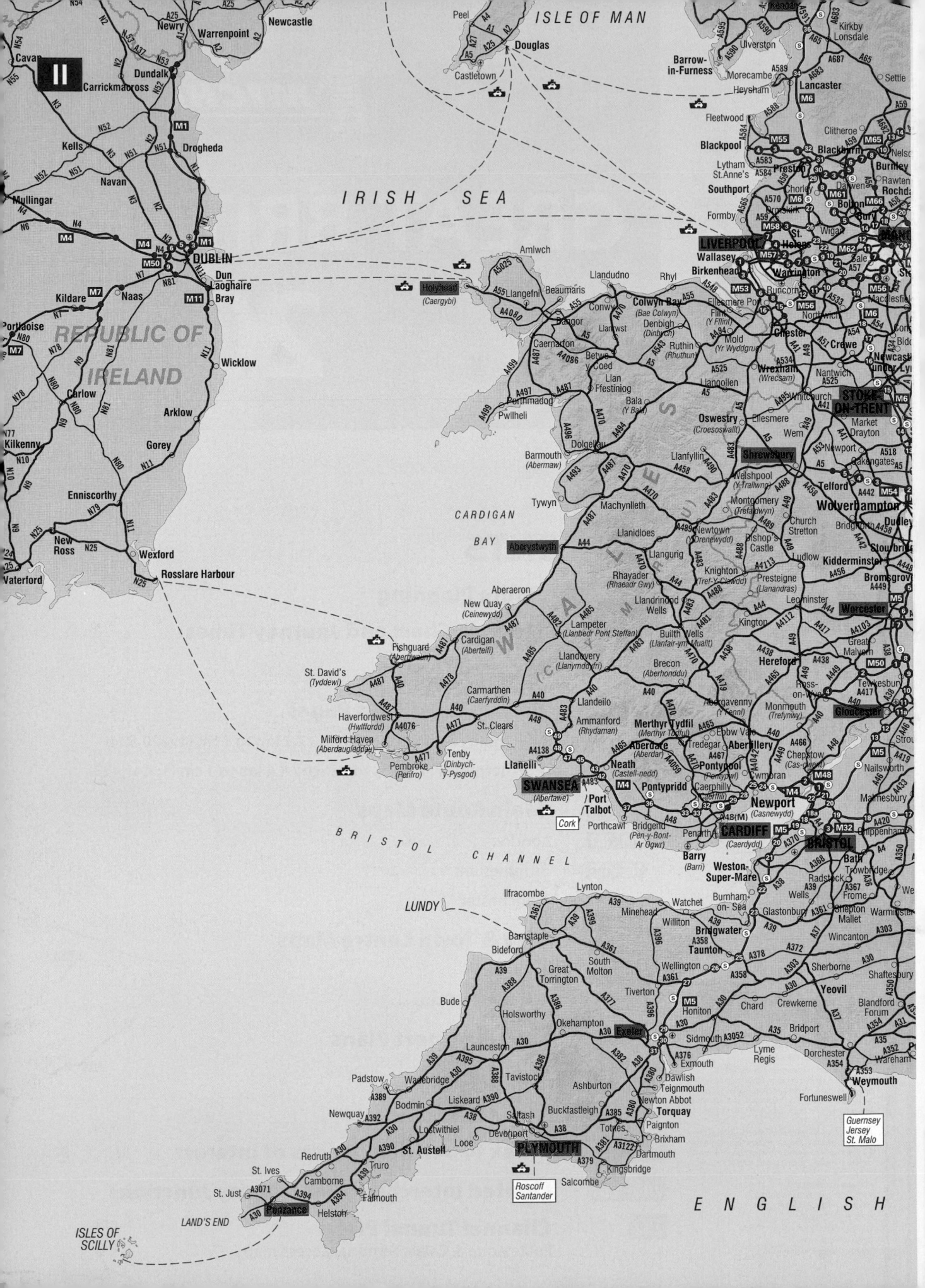

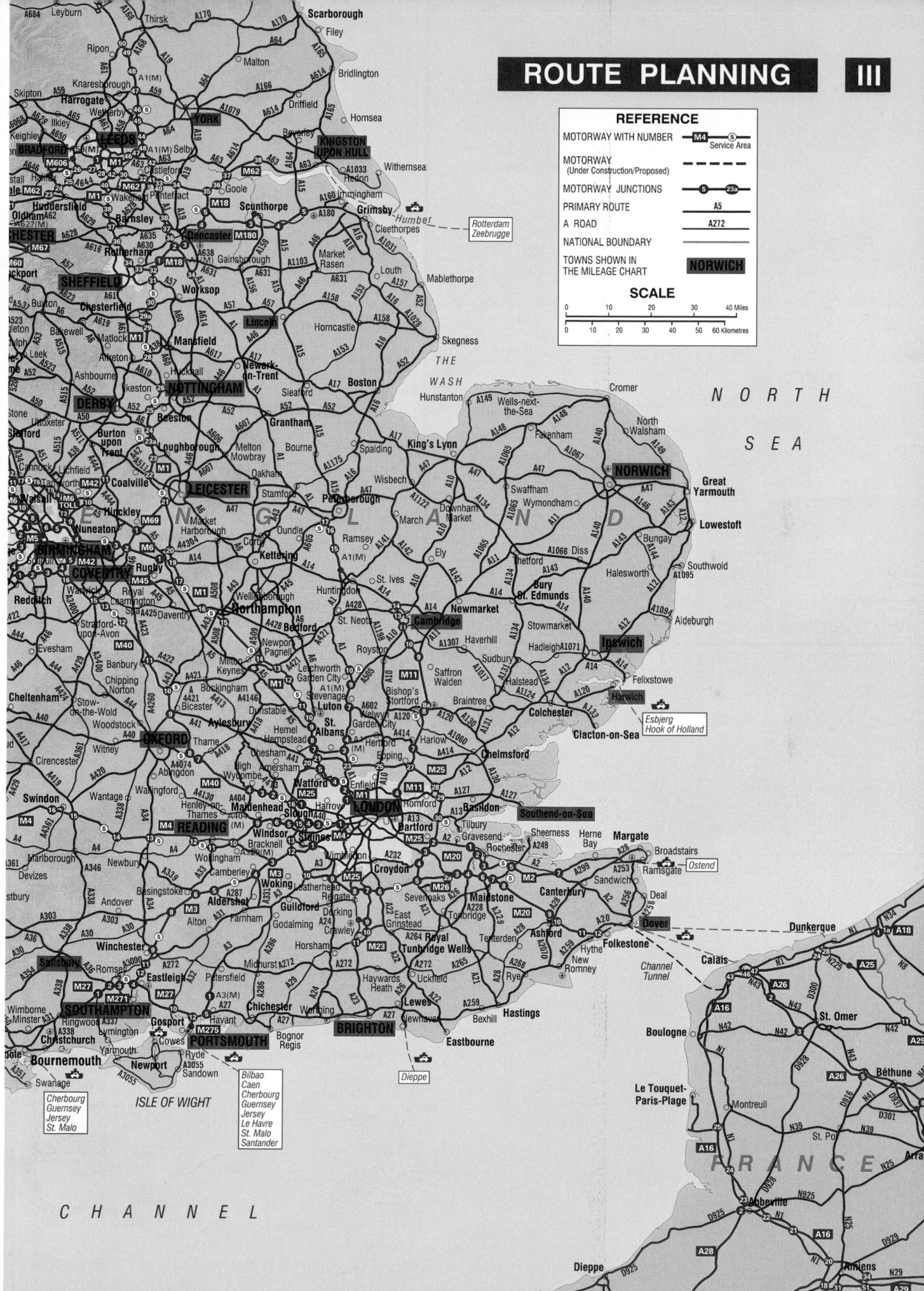

ROUTE PLANNING   III

REFERENCE

MOTORWAY WITH NUMBER	M4 Ⓢ Service Area
MOTORWAY (Under Construction/Proposed)	– – –
MOTORWAY JUNCTIONS	⑤ ㉓ₐ
PRIMARY ROUTE	A5
A ROAD	A272
NATIONAL BOUNDARY	
TOWNS SHOWN IN THE MILEAGE CHART	NORWICH

SCALE

0   10   20   30   40 Miles
0 10 20 30 40 50 60 Kilometres

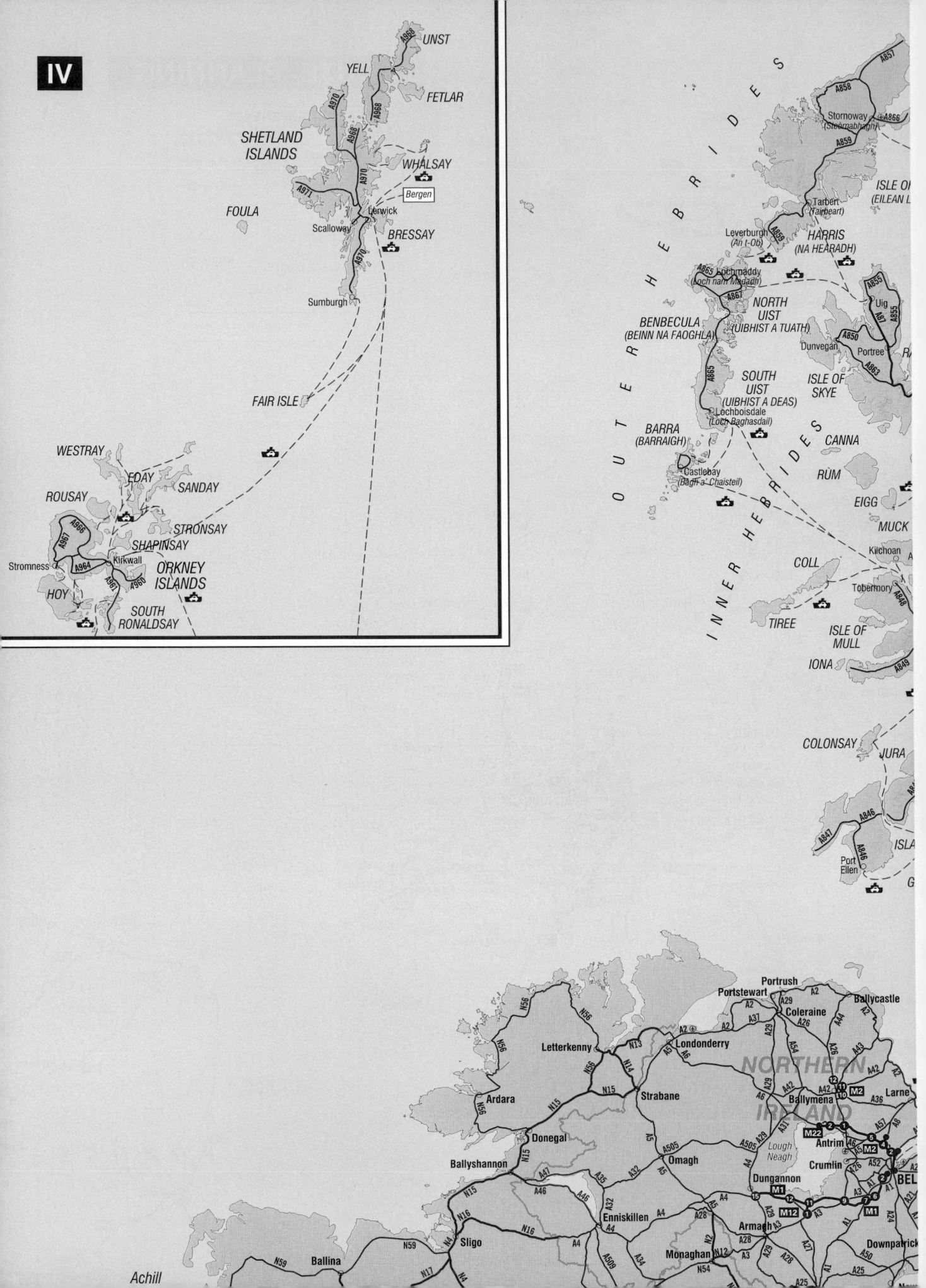

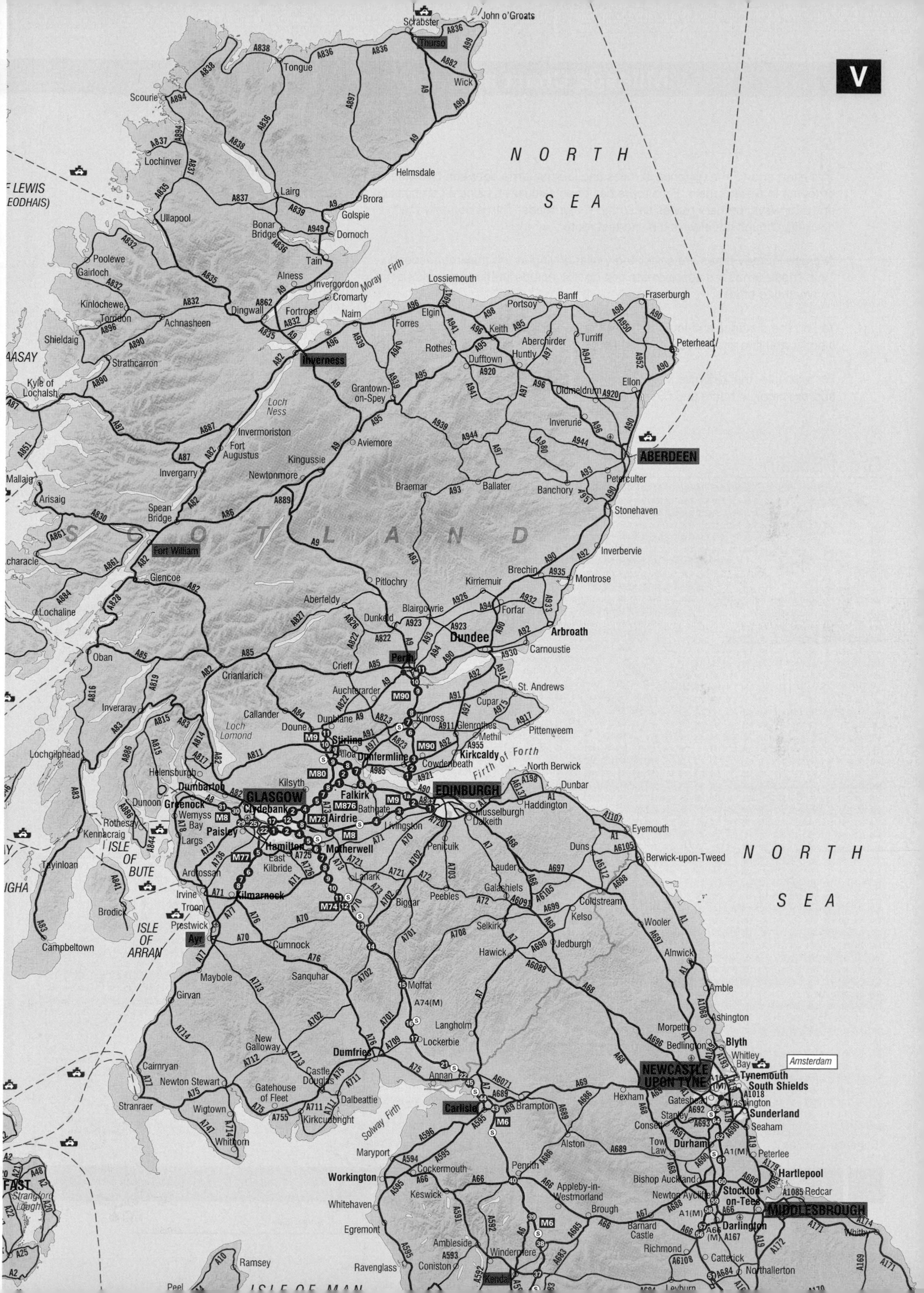

V
NORTH SEA
SCOTLAND
John o'Groats
Scrabster
Thurso
Tongue
Wick
Scourie
Lochinver
Helmsdale
Lairg
Brora
Golspie
Ullapool
Bonar Bridge
Dornoch
Tain
Poolewe
Gairloch
Alness
Invergordon
Moray Firth
Cromarty
Kinlochewe
Torridon
Dingwall
Fortrose
Achnasheen
Shieldaig
Strathcarron
Kyle of Lochalsh
Inverness
Loch Ness
Invermoriston
Fort Augustus
Invergarry
Mallaig
Arisaig
Spean Bridge
Fort William
Glencoe
Lochaline
Oban
Lossiemouth
Nairn
Forres
Elgin
Rothes
Keith
Portsoy
Banff
Fraserburgh
Aberchirder
Turriff
Peterhead
Huntly
Dufftown
Grantown-on-Spey
Oldmeldrum
Ellon
Inverurie
Aviemore
Kingussie
Newtonmore
ABERDEEN
Peterculter
Braemar
Ballater
Banchory
Stonehaven
Inverbervie
Brechin
Montrose
Pitlochry
Kirriemuir
Aberfeldy
Blairgowrie
Forfar
Dunkeld
Arbroath
Dundee
Carnoustie
Perth
Crieff
Crianlarich
St. Andrews
Auchterarder
Cupar
Inveraray
Callander
Dunblane
Kinross
Glenrothes
Pittenweem
Doune
Loch Lomond
Stirling
Methil
Kirkcaldy
Alloa
Firth of Forth
Dunfermline
Cowdenbeath
North Berwick
Lochgilphead
Helensburgh
Kilsyth
Dunbar
Dumbarton
GLASGOW
Falkirk
EDINBURGH
Haddington
Greenock
Clydebank
Bathgate
Musselburgh
Dalkeith
Dunoon
Wemyss Bay
Airdrie
Livingston
Eyemouth
Rothesay
Paisley
Kennacraig
Largs
Hamilton
Motherwell
Penicuik
Duns
Berwick-upon-Tweed
ISLE OF BUTE
East Kilbride
Lauder
Tayinloan
Ardrossan
Lanark
Galashiels
Coldstream
Irvine
Kilmarnock
Peebles
Kelso
Troon
Biggar
Wooler
Brodick
Prestwick
Selkirk
ISLE OF ARRAN
Ayr
Cumnock
Hawick
Jedburgh
Campbeltown
Sanquhar
Alnwick
Maybole
Moffat
Amble
Girvan
Ashington
Langholm
Morpeth
Blyth
New Galloway
Lockerbie
Bedlington
Whitley Bay
Dumfries
Amsterdam
Cairnryan
Annan
Castle Douglas
NEWCASTLE UPON TYNE
Tynemouth
South Shields
Newton Stewart
Gatehouse of Fleet
Hexham
Dalbeattie
Gateshead
Washington
Stranraer
Wigtown
Carlisle
Brampton
Sunderland
Kirkcudbright
Solway Firth
Stanley
Consett
Seaham
Whithorn
Alston
Durham
Maryport
Peterlee
Cockermouth
Penrith
Workington
Bishop Auckland
Hartlepool
Keswick
Appleby-in-Westmorland
Newton Aycliffe
Stockton-on-Tees
Redcar
Whitehaven
Brough
MIDDLESBROUGH
Egremont
Barnard Castle
Darlington
Ambleside
Whitby
Richmond
Ramsey
Windermere
Catterick
Ravenglass
Coniston
Northallerton
Kendal
Peel
ISLE OF MAN
Leyburn
Strangford Lough

This chart shows the distance in miles and journey time between two cities or towns in Great Britain. Each route has been calculated using a combination of motorways, primary routes and other major roads. This is normally the quickest, though not always the shortest route.

Average journey times are calculated whilst driving at the maximum speed limit. These times are approximate and do not include traffic congestion or convenience breaks.

To find the distance and journey time between two cities or towns, follow a horizontal line and vertical column until they meet each other.

For example, the 285 mile journey from London to Penzance is approximately 4 hours and 59 minutes.

Great Britain

Journey times

(Mileage and journey-time matrix — cities listed along the diagonal: Aberdeen, Aberystwyth, Ayr, Birmingham, Bradford, Brighton, Bristol, Cambridge, Cardiff, Carlisle, Coventry, Derby, Doncaster, Dover, Edinburgh, Exeter, Fort William, Glasgow, Gloucester, Harwich, Holyhead, Inverness, Ipswich, Kendal, Kingston upon Hull, Leeds, Leicester, Lincoln, Liverpool, Manchester, Middlesbrough, Newcastle upon Tyne, Norwich, Nottingham, Oxford, Penzance, Perth, Plymouth, Portsmouth, Reading, Salisbury, Sheffield, Shrewsbury, Southampton, Southend-on-Sea, Stoke-on-Trent, Swansea, Thurso, Worcester, York, London.)

Distance in miles

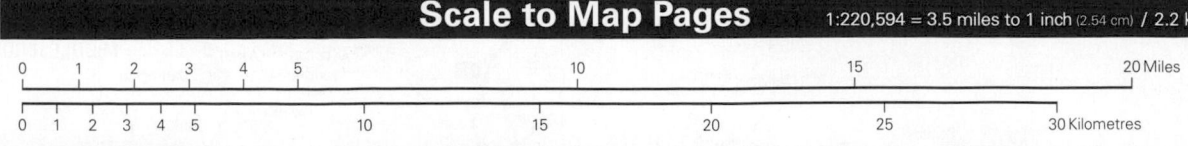

Motorway
Autoroute
Autobahn
`M1`

Motorway Under Construction
Autoroute en construction
Autobahn im Bau

Motorway Proposed
Autoroute prévue
Geplante Autobahn

Motorway Junctions with Numbers
Unlimited Interchange `4`
Limited Interchange `5`

Autoroute échangeur numéroté
Echangeur complet
Echangeur partiel

Autobahnanschlußstelle mit Nummer
Unbeschränkter Fahrtrichtungswechsel
Beschränkter Fahrtrichtungswechsel

Motorway Service Area (with fuel station)
with access from one carriageway only

Aire de services d'autoroute (avec station service)
accessible d'un seul côté

Rastplatz oder Raststätte (mit tankstelle)
Einbahn

Major Road Service Areas
(with fuel station) with 24 hour facilities
`LEEMING` `S` `OLDBURY`

Aire de services sur route prioriataire
(avec station service) Ouverte 24h sur 24

Raststätte
(mit tankstelle) Durchgehend geöffnet

Truckstop (selection of)
Sélection d'aire pour poids lourds
Auswahl von Fernfahrerrastplatz
`T`

Primary Route
Route à grande circulation
Hauptverkehrsstraße
`A41`

Primary Route Junction with Number
Echangeur numéroté
Hauptverkehrsstraßenkreuzung mit Nummer

Primary Route Destination
Route prioritaire, direction
Hauptverkehrsstraße Richtung
`DOVER`

Dual Carriageways (A & B roads)
Route à double chaussées séparées (route A & B)
Zweispurige Schnellstraße (A- und B- Straßen)

Class A Road
Route de type A
A-Straße
`A129`

Class B Road
Route de type B
B-Straße
`B177`

Narrow Major Road (passing places)
Route prioritaire étroite (possibilité de dépassement)
Schmale Hauptverkehrsstaße (mit Überholmöglichkeit)

Major Roads Under Construction
Route prioritaire en construction
Hauptverkehrsstaße im Bau

Major Roads Proposed
Route prioritaire prévue
Geplante Hauptverkehrsstaße

Safety Cameras with Speed Limits
Single Camera
Multiple Cameras located along road
Single & Multiple Variable Speed Cameras

Radars de contrôle de vitesse
Radar simple
Radars multiples situés le long de la route
Radars simples et multiples de contrôle de vitesse variable

Sicherheitskameras mit Tempolimit
Einzelne Kamera
Mehrere Kameras entlang der Straße
Einzelne und mehrere Kameras für variables Tempolimit

Fuel Station
Station service
Tankstelle

Gradient 1:5 (20%) **& steeper**
(ascent in direction of arrow)
Pente égale ou supérieure à 20% (dans le sens de la montée)
20% Steigung und steiler (in Pfeilrichtung)

Toll
Barrière de péage
Gebührenpflichtig
`TOLL`

Mileage between markers
Distence en miles entre les flèches
Strecke zwischen Markierungen in Meilen
`8`

Railway and Station
Voie ferrée et gare
Eisenbahnlinie und Bahnhof

Level Crossing and Tunnel
Passage à niveau et tunnel
Bahnübergang und Tunnel

River or Canal
Rivière ou canal
Fluß oder Kanal

County or Unitary Authority Boundary
Limite de comté ou de division administrative
Grafschafts- oder Verwaltungsbezirksgrenze

National Boundary
Frontière nationale
Landesgrenze

Built-up Area
Agglomération
Geschlossene Ortschaft

Village or Hamlet
Village ou hameau
Dorf oder Weiler

Wooded Area
Zone boisée
Waldgebiet

Spot Height in Feet
Altitude (en pieds)
Höhe in Fuß
• 813

Relief above 400' (122m)
Relief par estompage au-dessus de 400' (122m)
Reliefschattierung über 400' (122m)

National Grid Reference (kilometres)
Coordonnées géographiques nationales (Kilomètres)
Nationale geographische Koordinaten (Kilometer)
100

Page Continuation
Suite à la page indiquée
Seitenfortsetzung
`48`

Area covered by Main Route map
Répartition des cartes des principaux axes routiers
Von Karten mit Hauptverkehrsstrecken
`MAIN ROUTE 180`

Area covered by Town Plan
Ville ayant un plan à la page indiquée
Von Karten mit Stadtplänen erfaßter Bereich
`SEE PAGE 194`

Airport
Aéroport
Flughafen

Airfield
Terrain d'aviation
Flugplatz

Heliport
Héliport
Hubschrauberlandeplatz

Battle Site and Date
Champ de bataille et date
Schlachtfeld und Datum
1066

Castle (open to public)
Château (ouvert au public)
Schloß / Burg (für die Öffentlichkeit zugänglich)

Castle with Garden (open to public)
Château avec parc (ouvert au public)
Schloß mit Garten (für die Öffentlichkeit zugänglich)

Cathedral, Abbey, Church, Friary, Priory
Cathédrale, abbaye, église, monastère, prieuré
Kathedrale, Abtei, Kirche, Mönchskloster, Kloster

Country Park
Parc régional
Landschaftspark

Ferry (vehicular, sea)
(vehicular, river)
(foot only)

Bac (véhicules, mer)
(véhicules, rivière)
(piétons)

Fähre (auto, meer)
(auto, fluß)
(nur für Personen)

Garden (open to public)
Jardin (ouvert au public)
Garten (für die Öffentlichkeit zugänglich)

Golf Course (9 hole) (18 hole)
Terrain de golf (9 trous) (18 trous)
Golfplatz (9 Löcher) (18 Löcher)

Historic Building (open to public)
Monument historique (ouvert au public)
Historisches Gebäude (für die Öffentlichkeit zugänglich)

Historic Building with Garden (open to public)
Monument historique avec jardin (ouvert au public)
Historisches Gebäude mit Garten (für die Öffentlichkeit zugänglich)

Horse Racecourse
Hippodrome
Pferderennbahn

Information Centre
Syndicat d'initiative
Information

Lighthouse
Phare
Leuchtturm

Motor Racing Circuit
Circuit Automobile
Automobilrennbahn

Museum, Art Gallery
Musée
Museum, Galerie

National Trust Property
(National Trust for Scotland)
`NT`
`NTS`

National Trust Property
(National Trust for Scotland)

National Trust- Eigentum
(National Trust for Scotland)

National Park
Parc national
Nationalpark

Nature Reserve or Bird Sanctuary
Réserve naturelle botanique ou ornithologique
Natur- oder Vogelschutzgebiet

Nature Trail or Forest Walk
Chemin forestier, piste verte
Naturpfad oder Waldweg

Place of Interest
Site, curiosité
Sehenswürdigkeit
Monument •

Picnic Site
Lieu pour pique-nique
Picknickplatz

Railway, Steam or Narrow Gauge
Chemin de fer, à vapeur ou à voie étroite
Eisenbahn, Dampf- oder Schmalspurbahn

Theme Park
Centre de loisirs
Vergnügungspark

Viewpoint (360 degrees) (180 degrees)
Vue panoramique (360 degrés) (180 degrés)
Aussichtspunkt (360 Grade) (180 Grade)

Wildlife Park
Réserve de faune
Wildpark

Windmill
Moulin à vent
Windmühle

Zoo or Safari Park
Parc ou réserve zoologique
Zoo oder Safari-Park

Please note: symbols have been enlarged for clarity

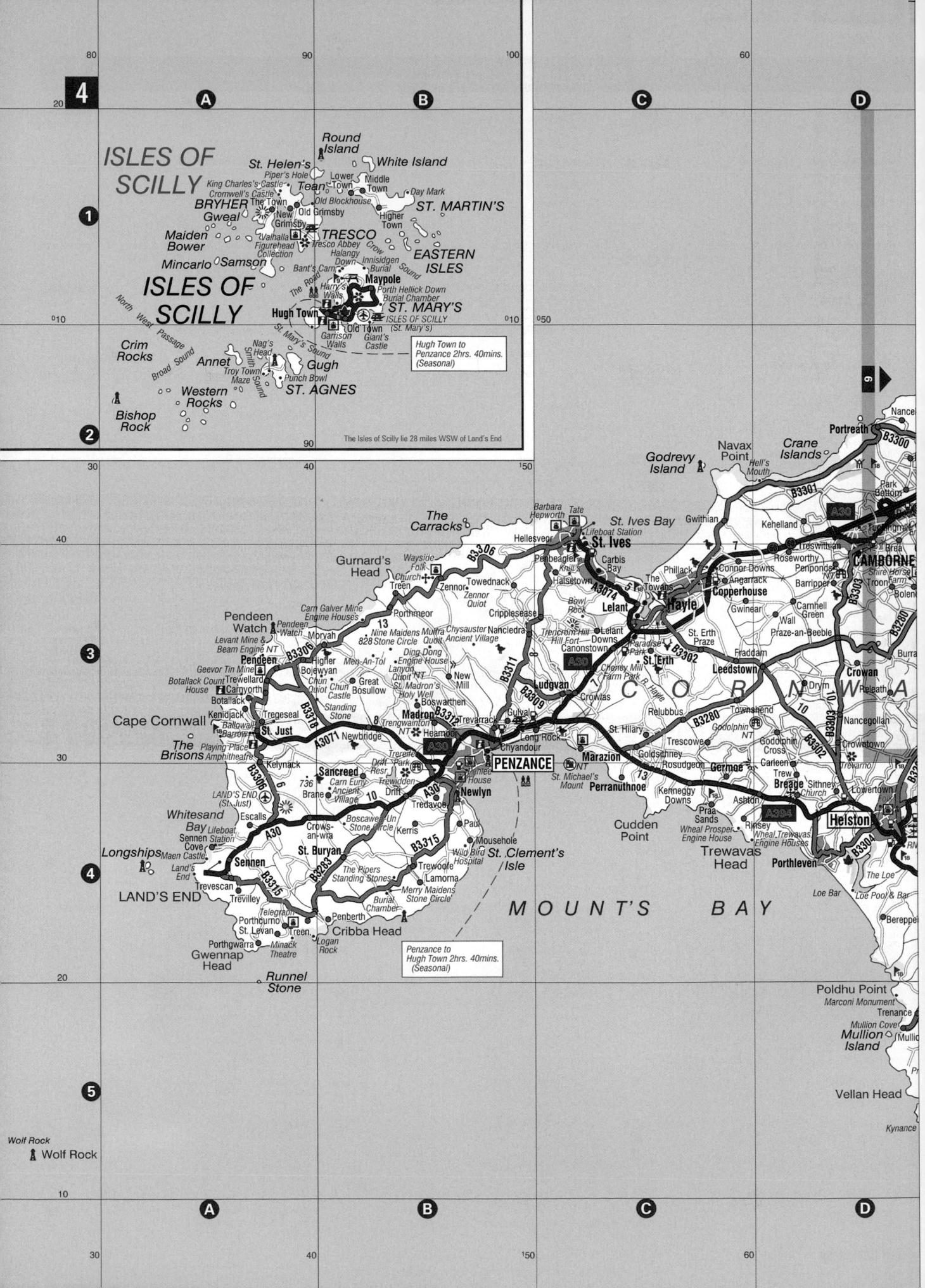

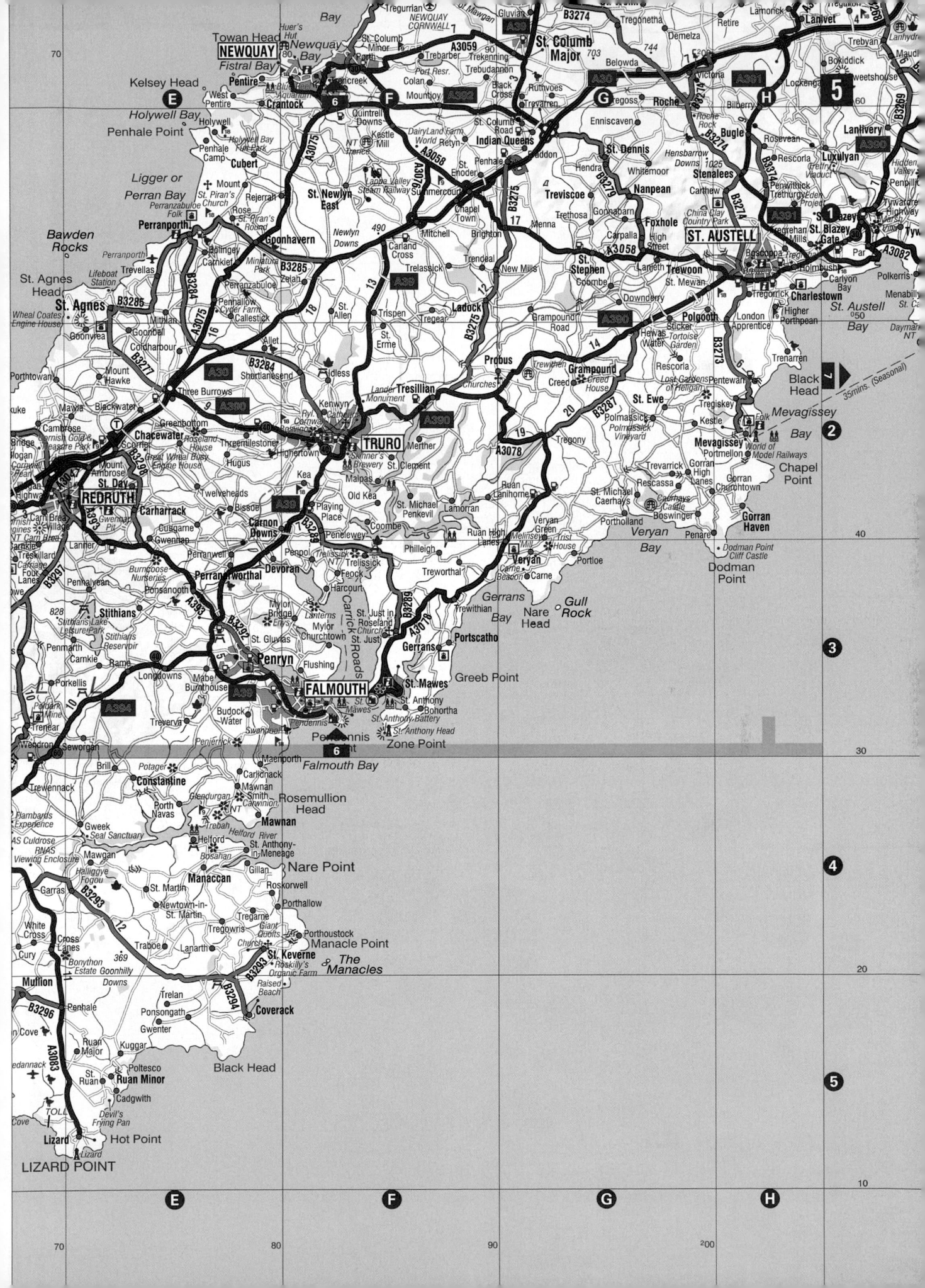

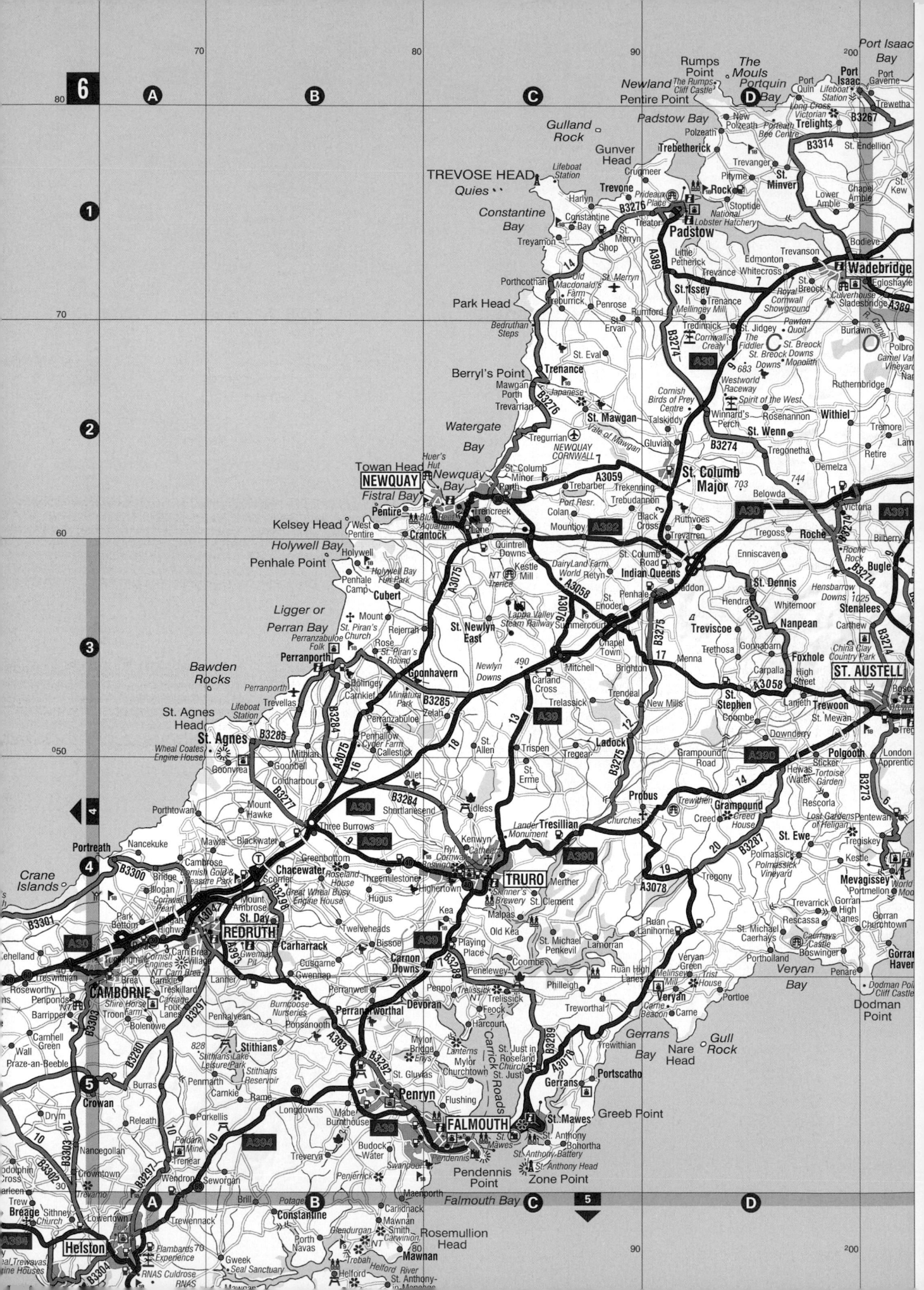

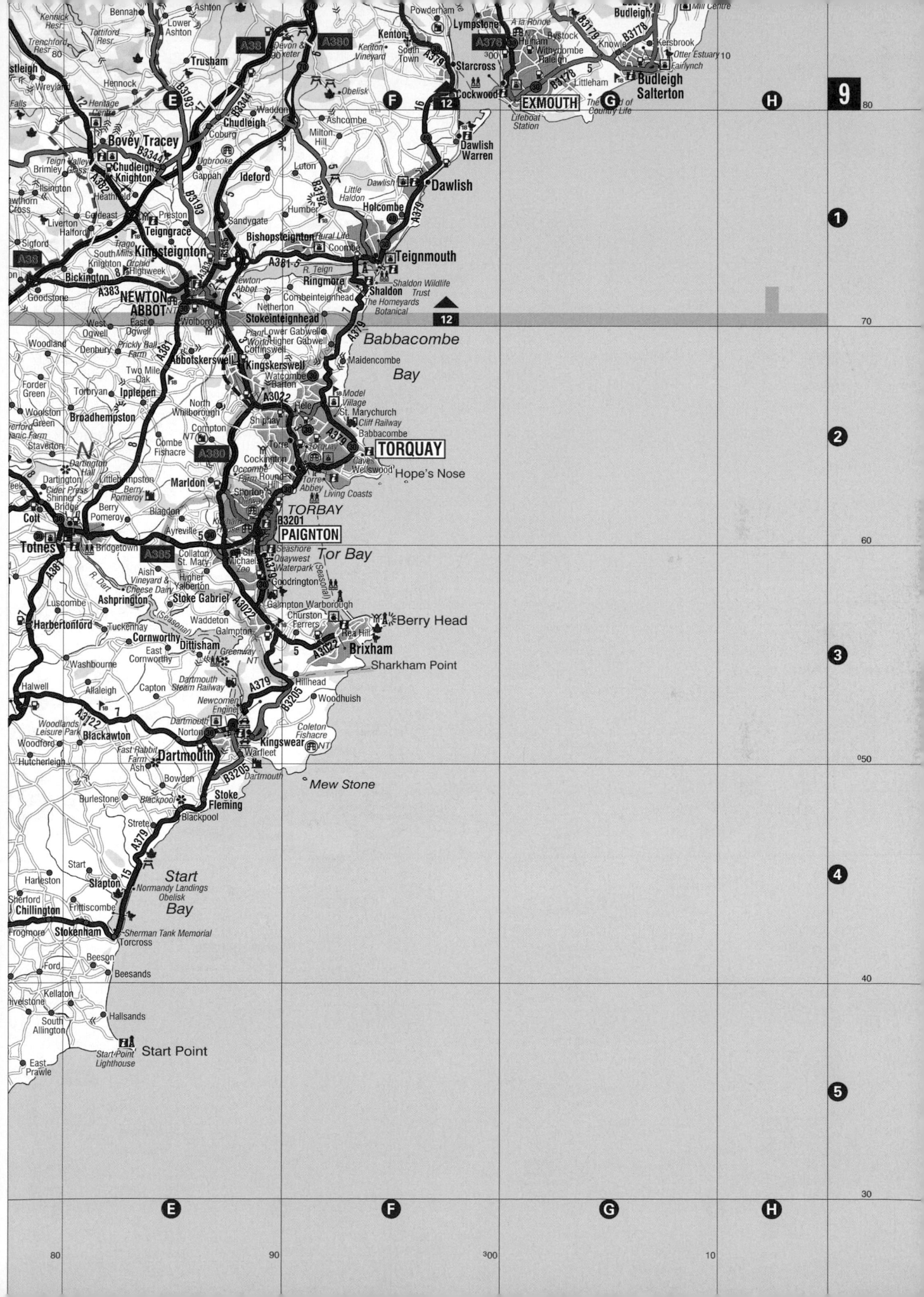

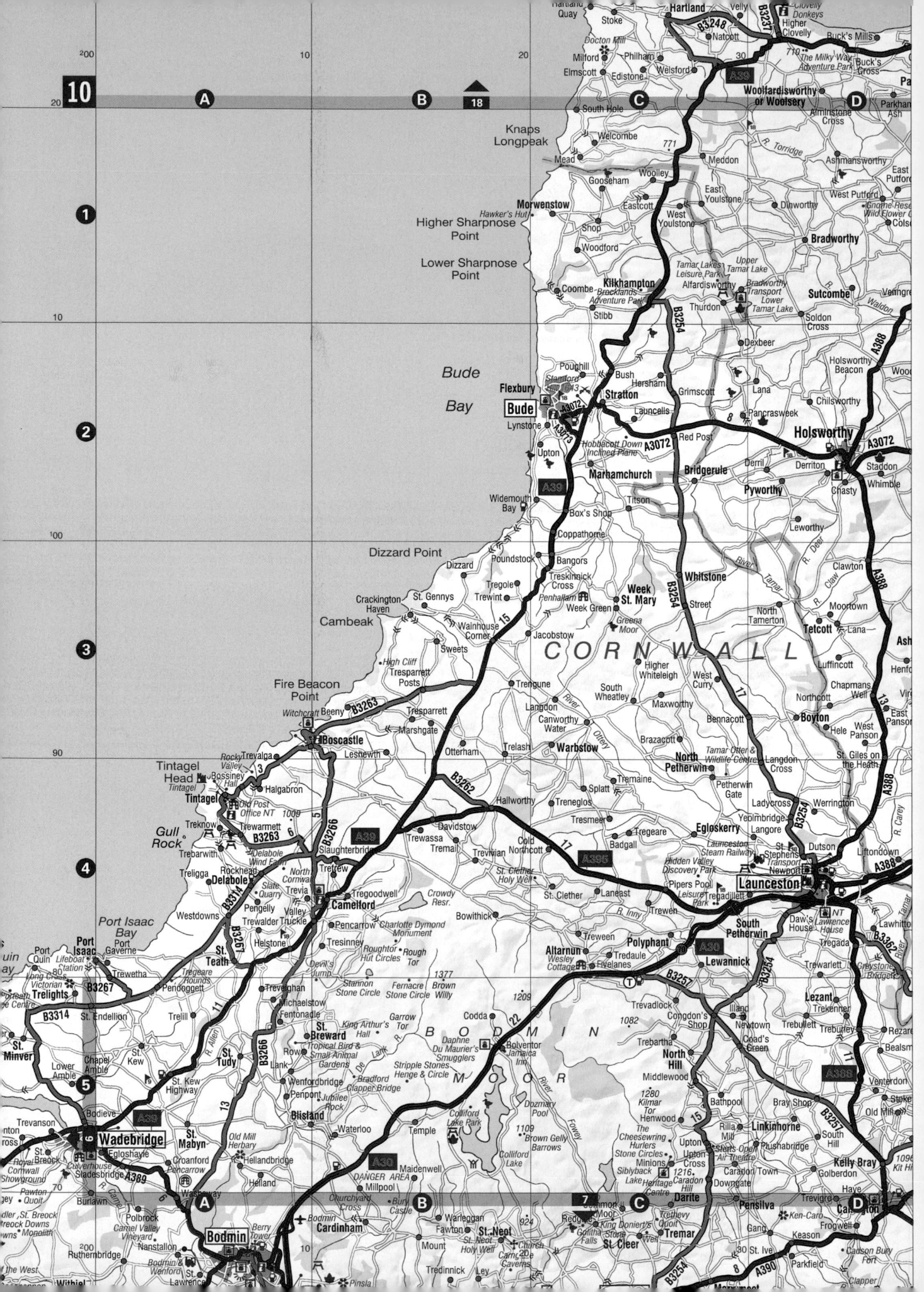

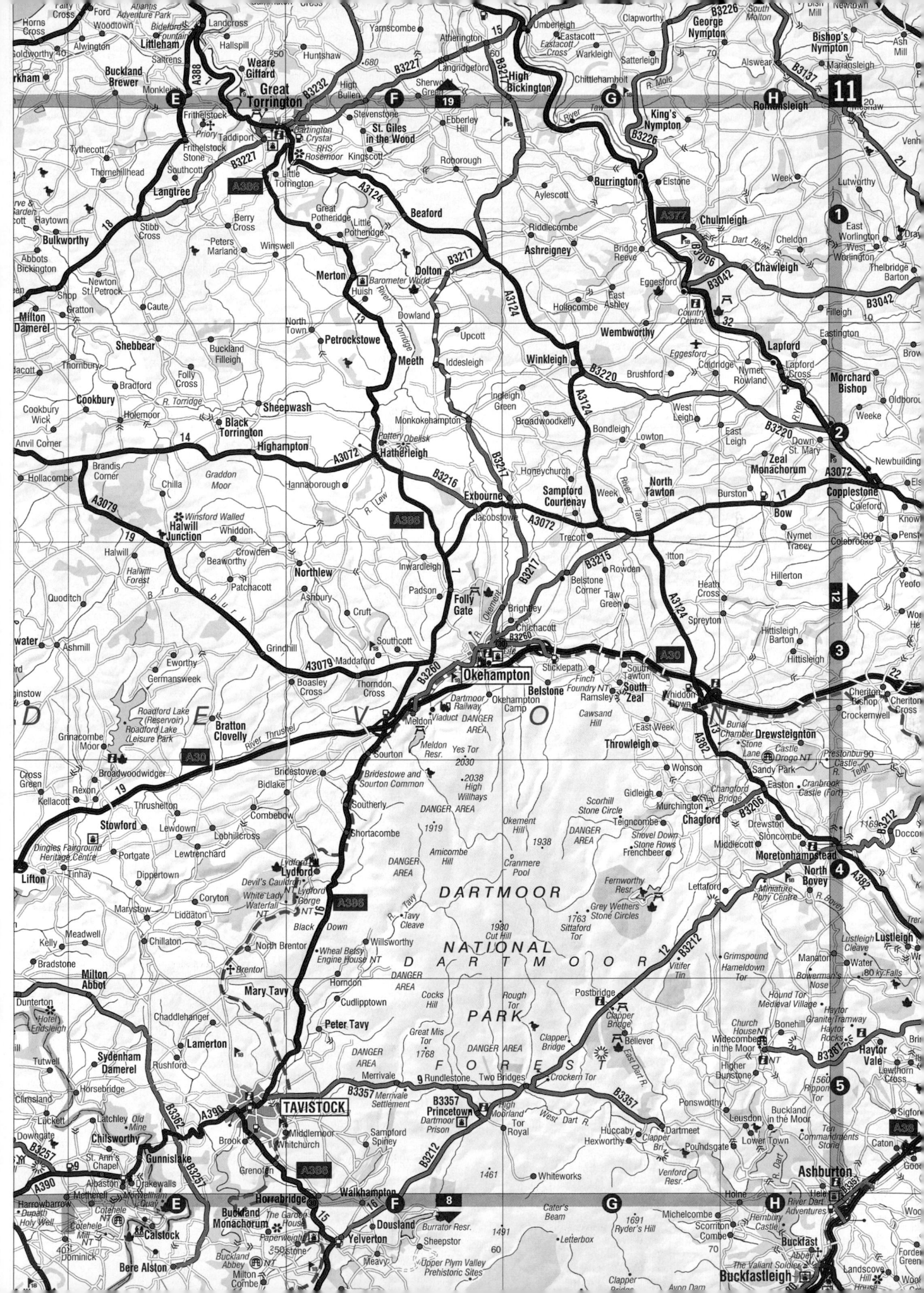

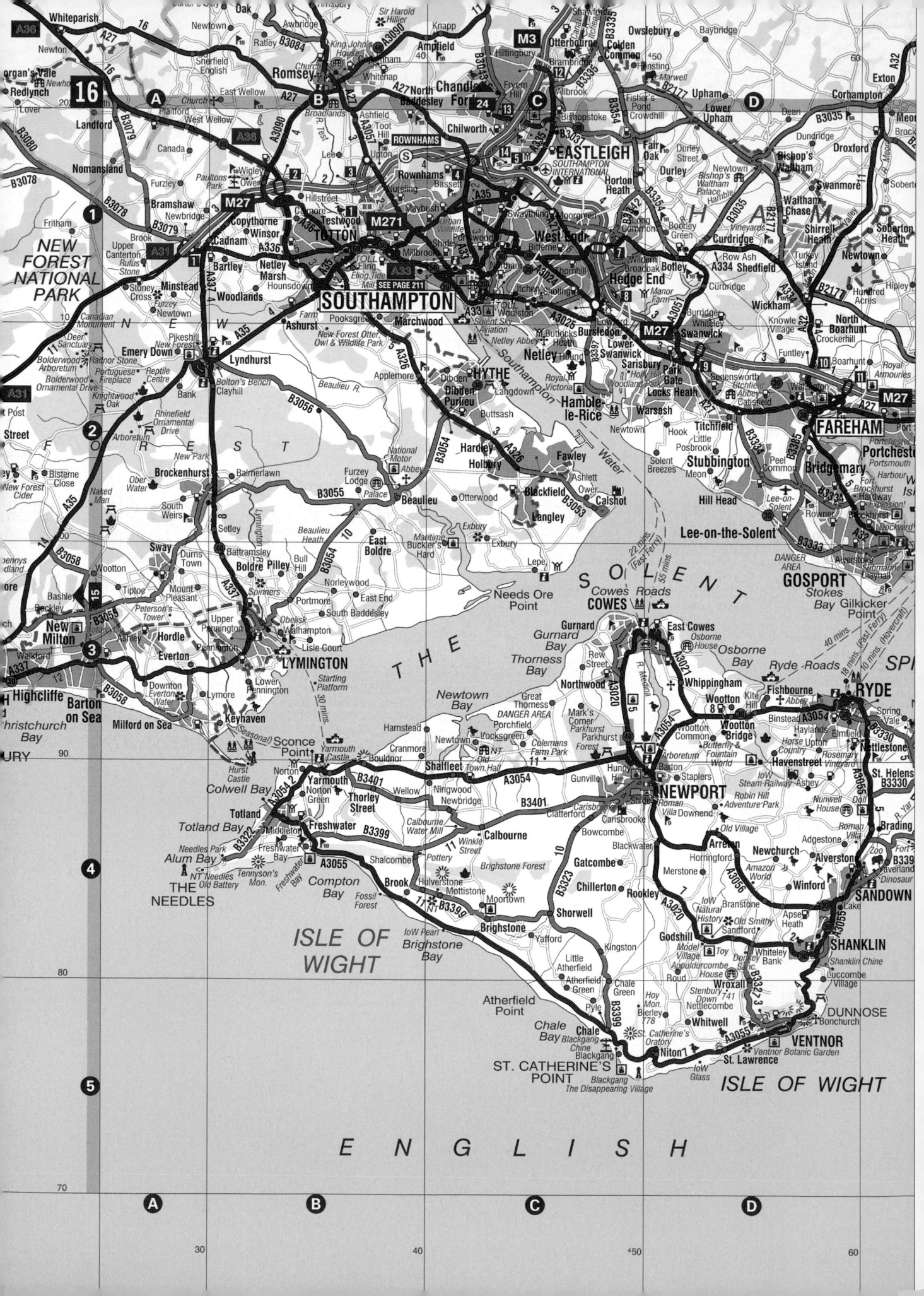

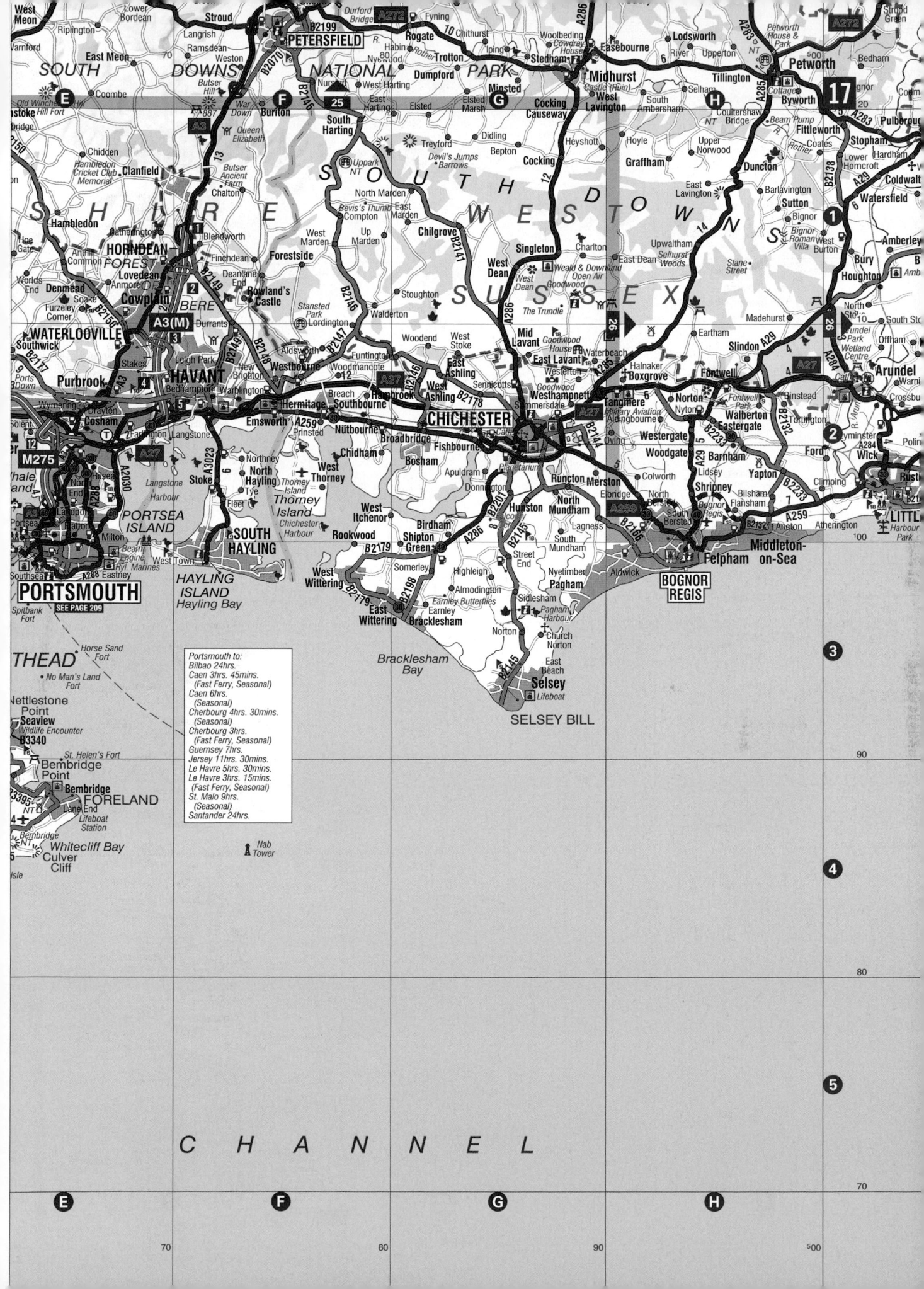

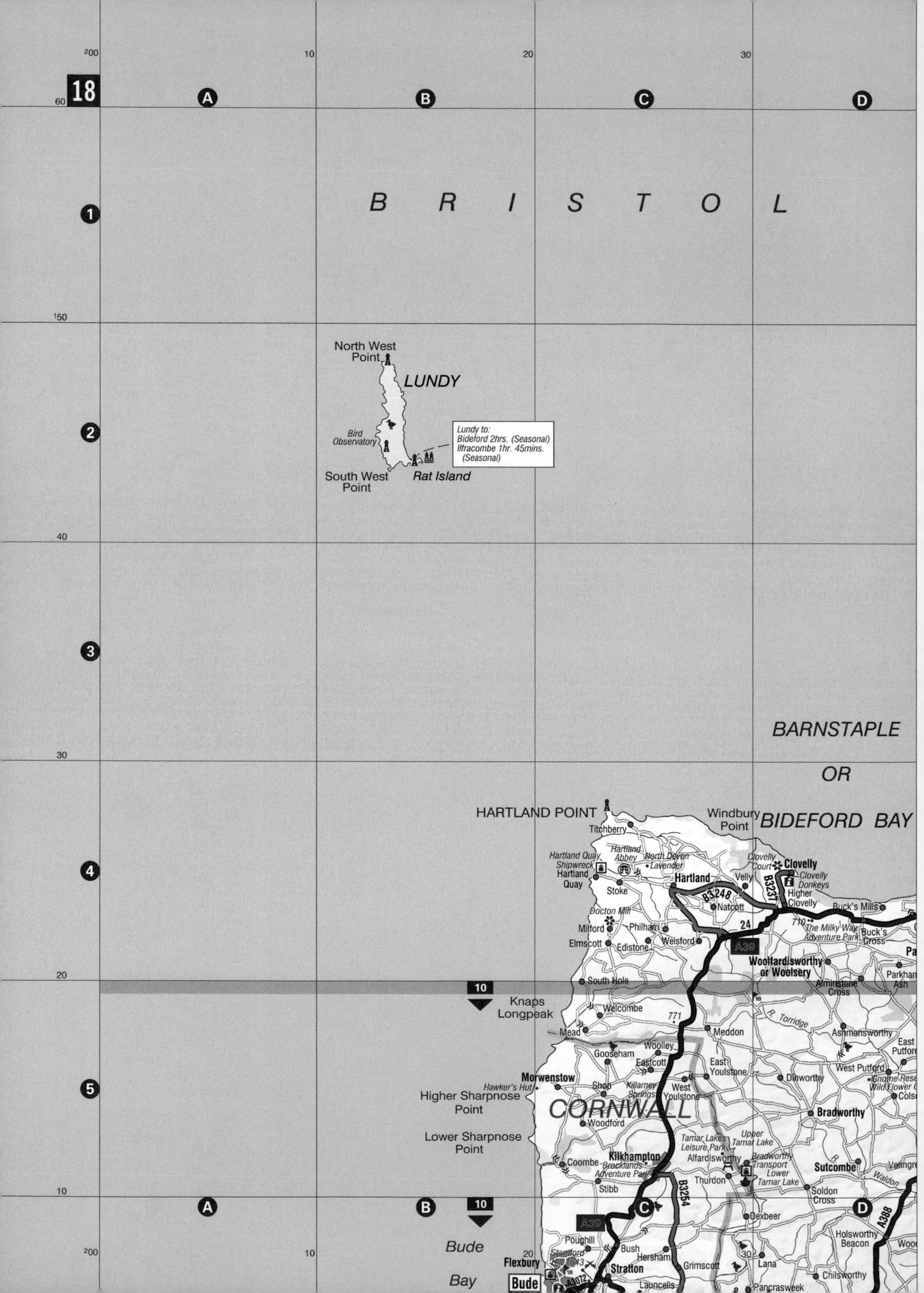

200   10   20   30

60

A   B   C   D

1

150

B R I S T O L

North West
Point

LUNDY

2

*Bird
Observatory*

Lundy to:
Bideford 2hrs. (Seasonal)
Ilfracombe 1hr. 45mins.
(Seasonal)

South West
Point

Rat Island

40

3

BARNSTAPLE

30

OR

HARTLAND POINT   Windbury   **BIDEFORD BAY**
                  Point

Titchberry

4

Hartland Quay   Hartland   North Devon   Clovelly   Clovelly
Shipwreck   Abbey   Lavender   Court
Hartland
*Quay   Stoke   Hartland   Velly   Clovelly
                                Donkeys*
                                        Higher
Docton Mill   B3248   Clovelly   Buck's Mills
Milford   Philham   Natcott   24   710   *The Milky Way   Buck's*
Elmscott   Edistone   Welsford   *Adventure Park*   Cross
                        A39   **Woolfardisworthy   Pa**
                                or Woolsery
20   Alminstone   Parkham
                        South Hole   Cross   Ash

10   Welcome   18

Knaps   Mead   Woolley   Meddon   *R. Torridge*   Ashmansworthy   East
Longpeak   771   Putfor

Gooseham   Eastcott   East   Dinworthy   West Putford   *Gnome Rese
                        Youlstone   Wild Flower C   Colso*

5   Morwenstow   West   Bradworthy
    Hawker's Hut   Shop   *Killarney   Youlstone*
Higher Sharpnose   *Springs*
Point   Woodford   *Tamar Lakes*   *Upper*   Sutcombe
                        Leisure Park   *Tamar Lake*   Venngre

Lower Sharpnose   Bradworthy   *Waldon*
Point   Kilkhampton   Alfardisworthy   *Transport*
    Coombe   *Brocklands*   Lower   Soldon
        Adventure Park   Thurdon   *Tamar Lake*   Cross   D
10   Stibb   B3254   Dexbeer   A388

A   B   10   C   A30   Holsworthy   Woo
                                Beacon

200   10   *Bude*   20   Poughill   Bush   Grimscott   Lana   Chilsworthy

    Flexbury   Stamford   B3   Hersham   Pancrasweek
    Bude   A3072   **Stratton**
Bay   Launcells

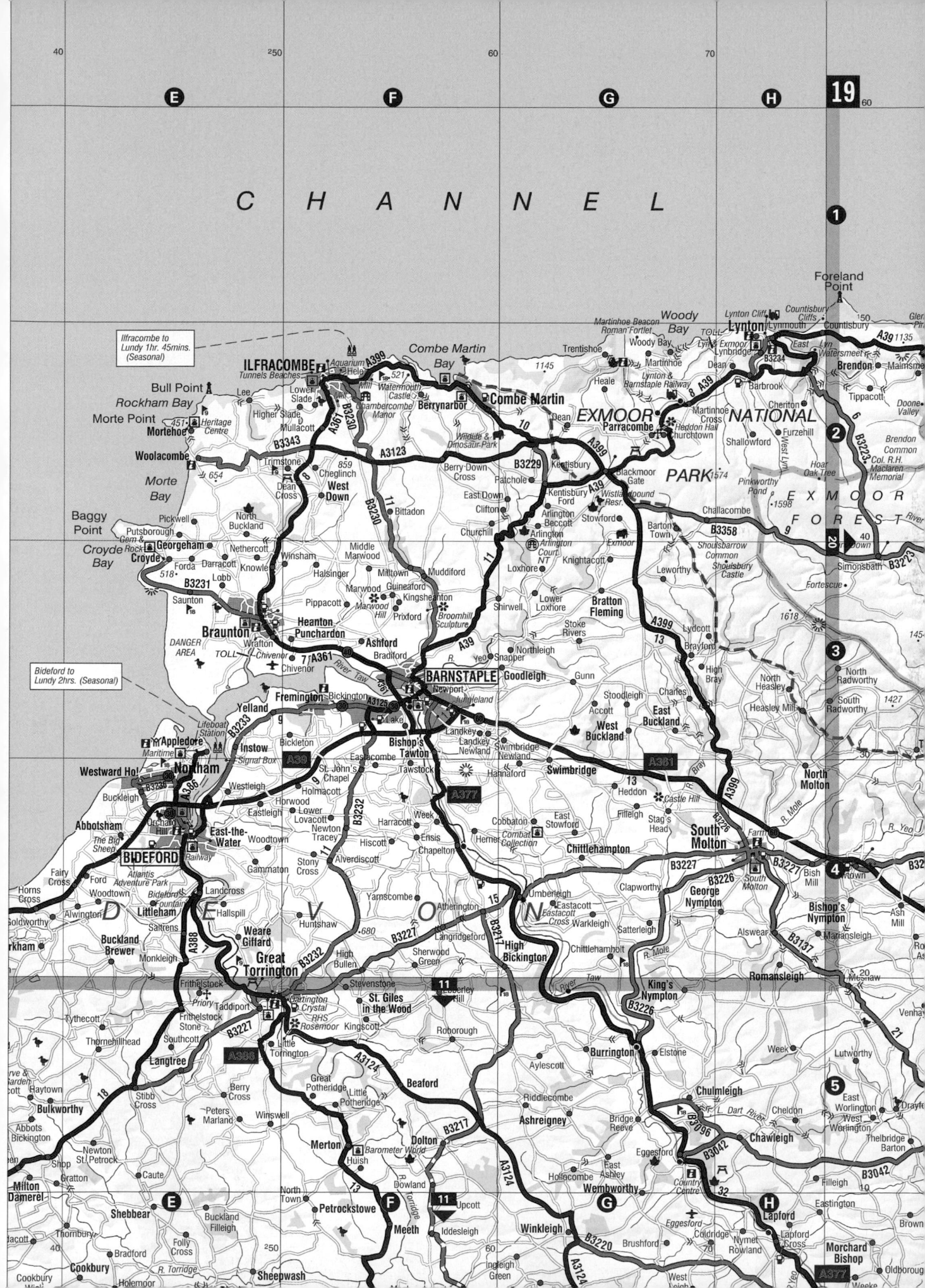

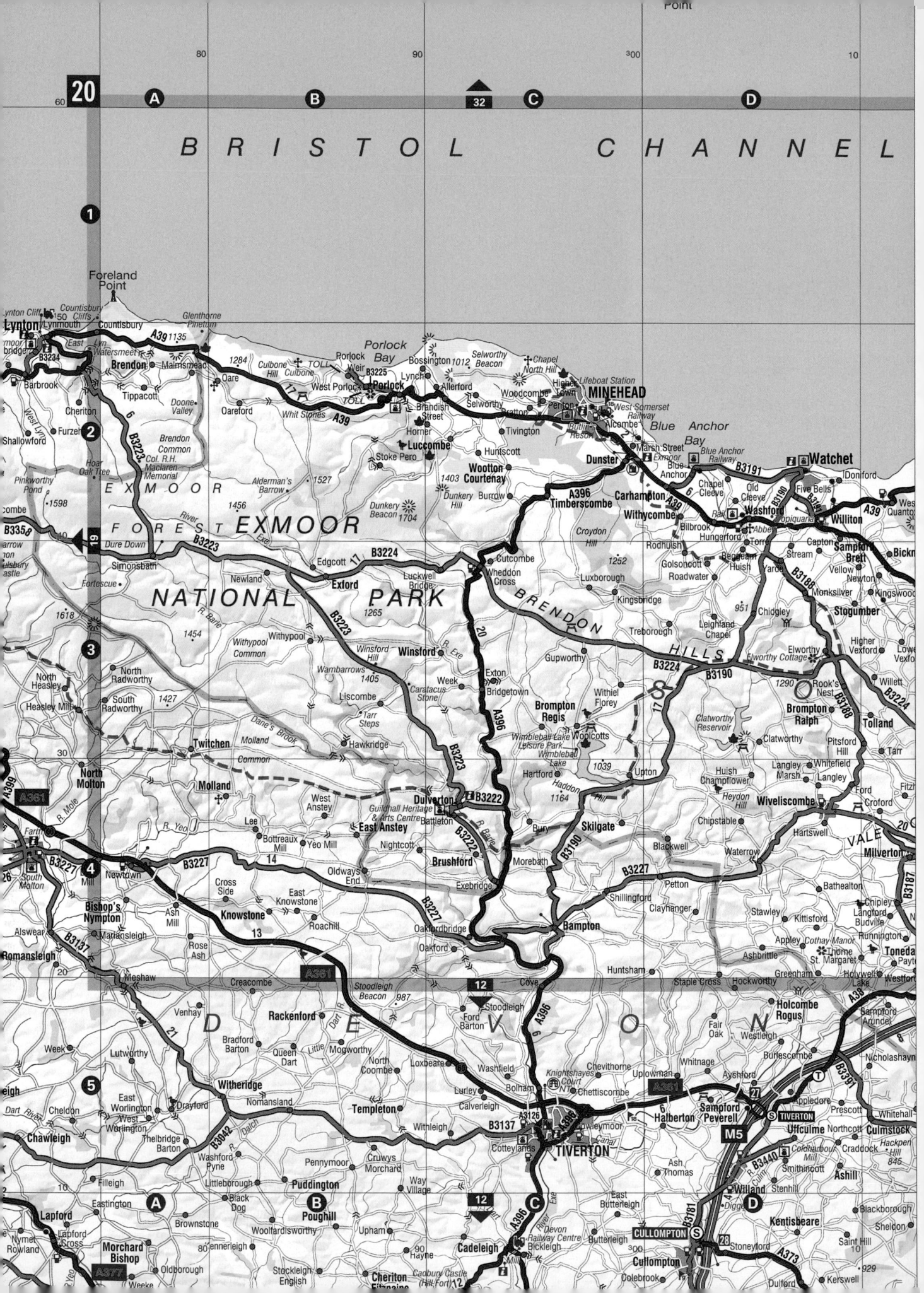

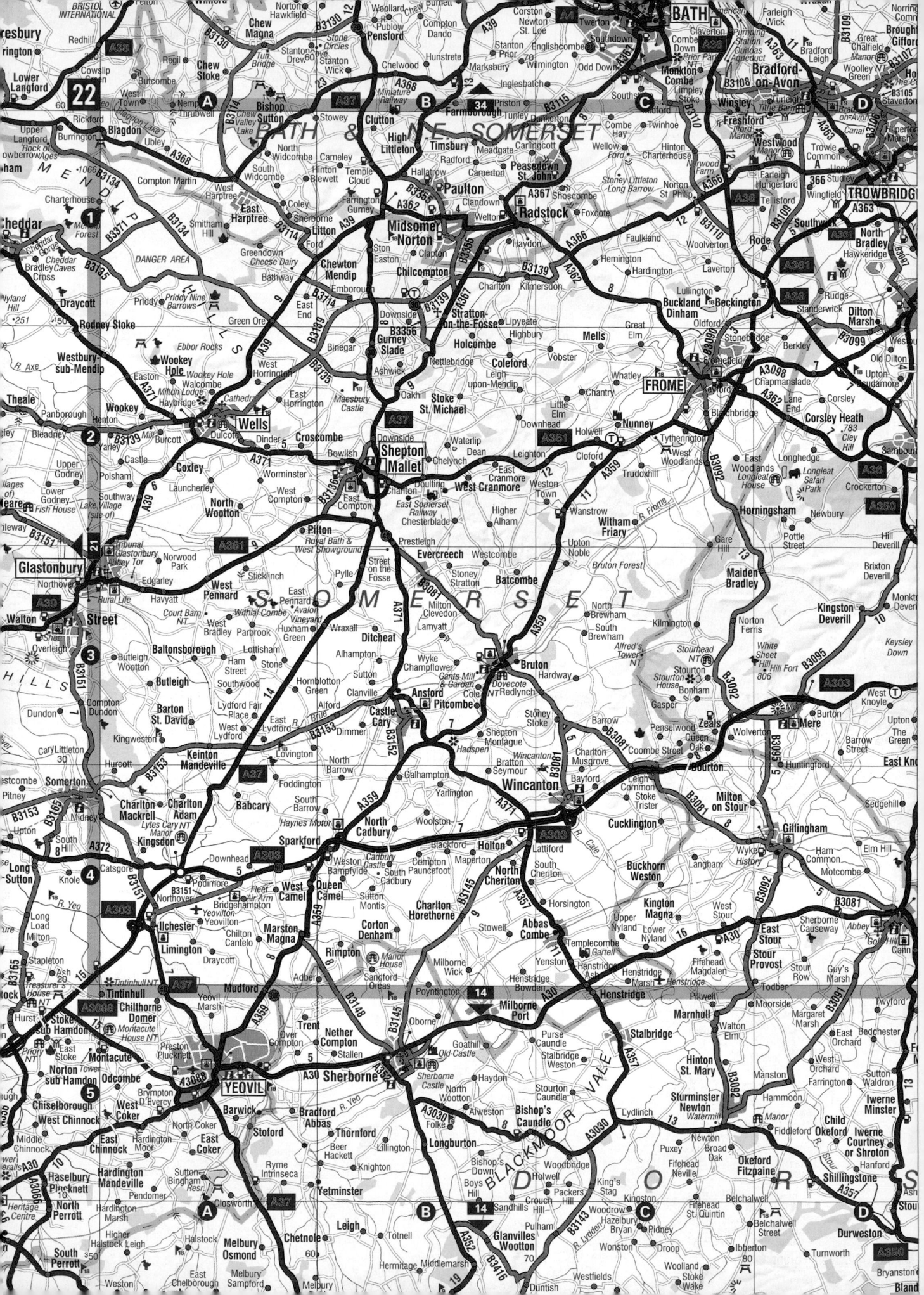

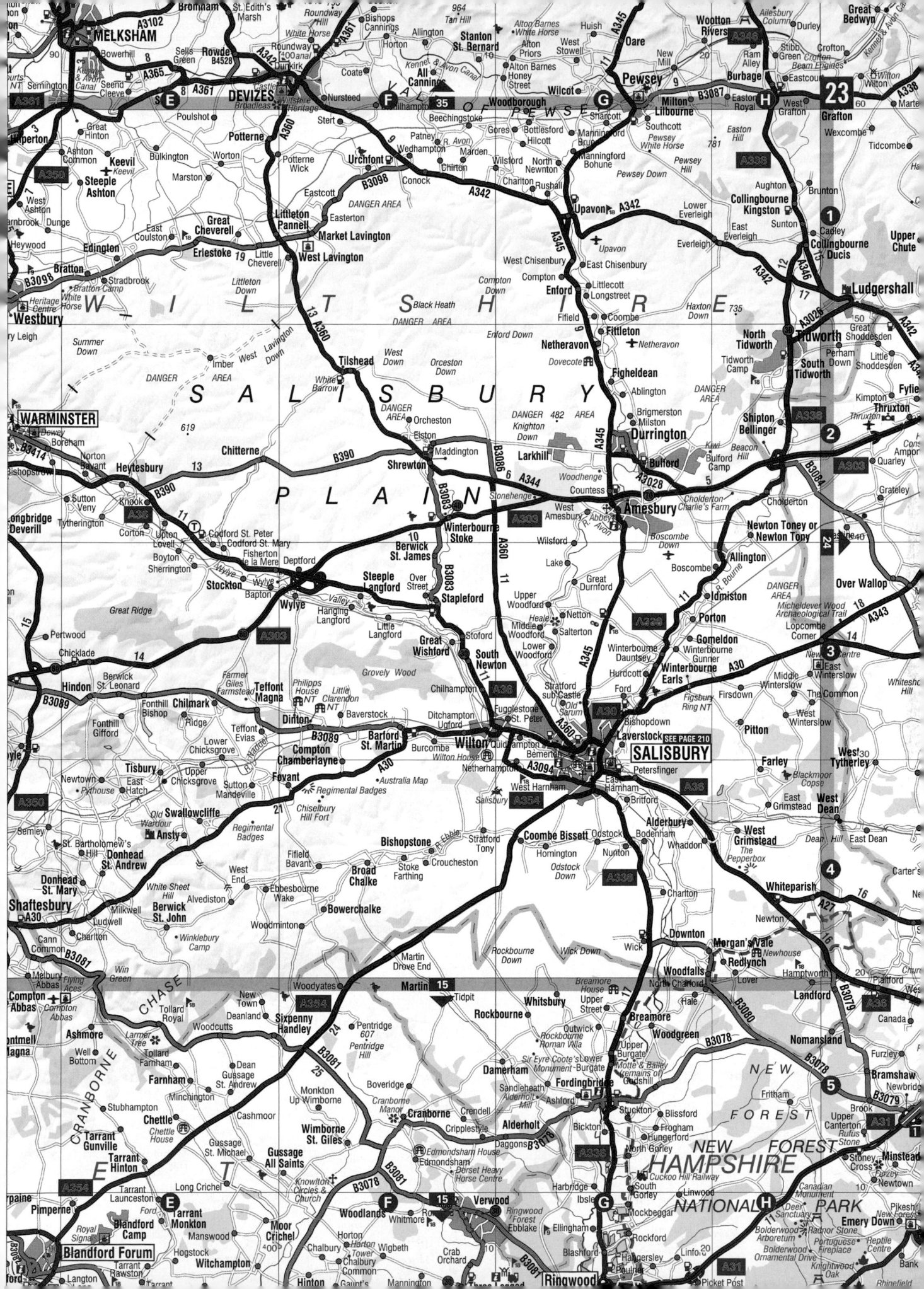

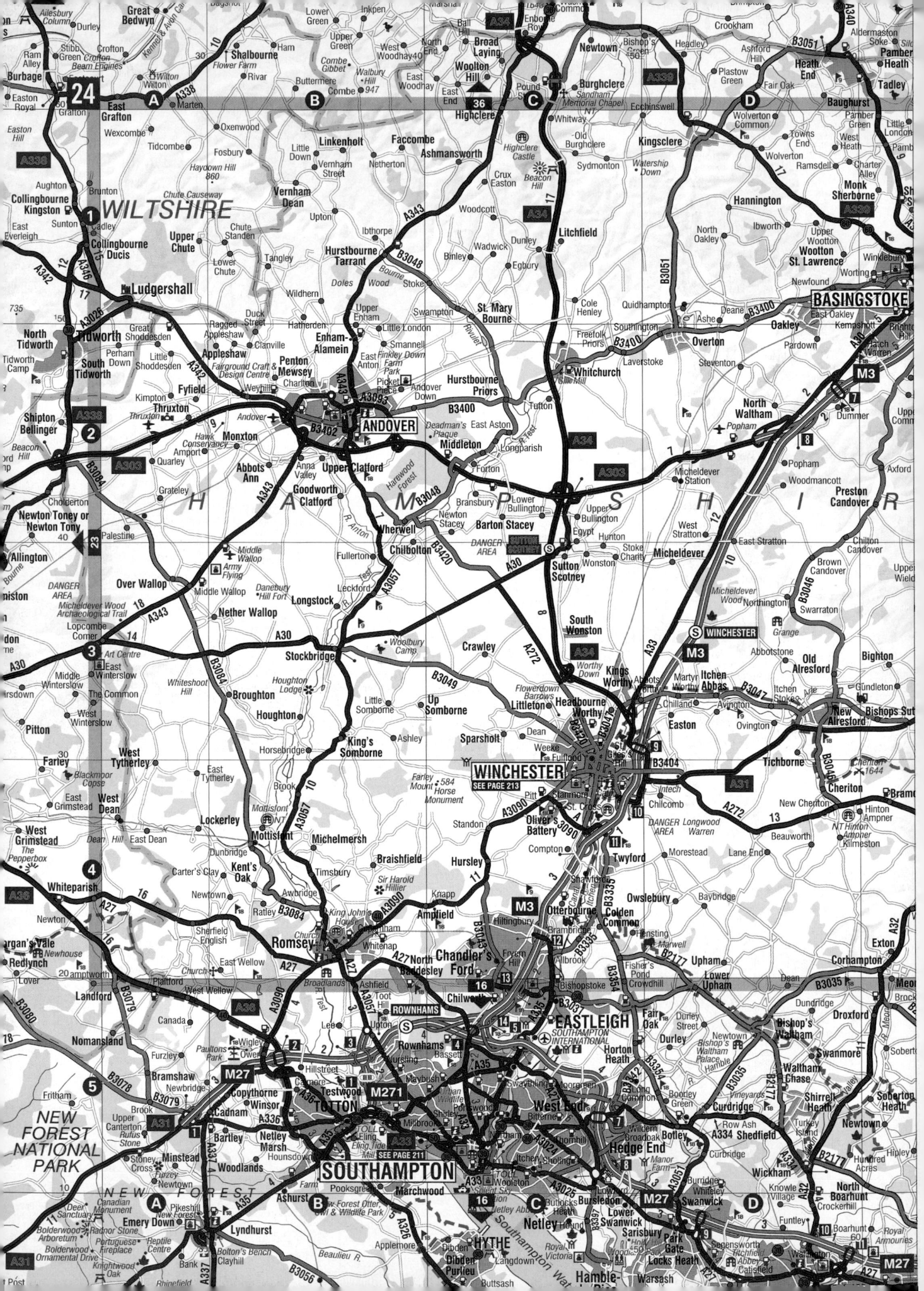

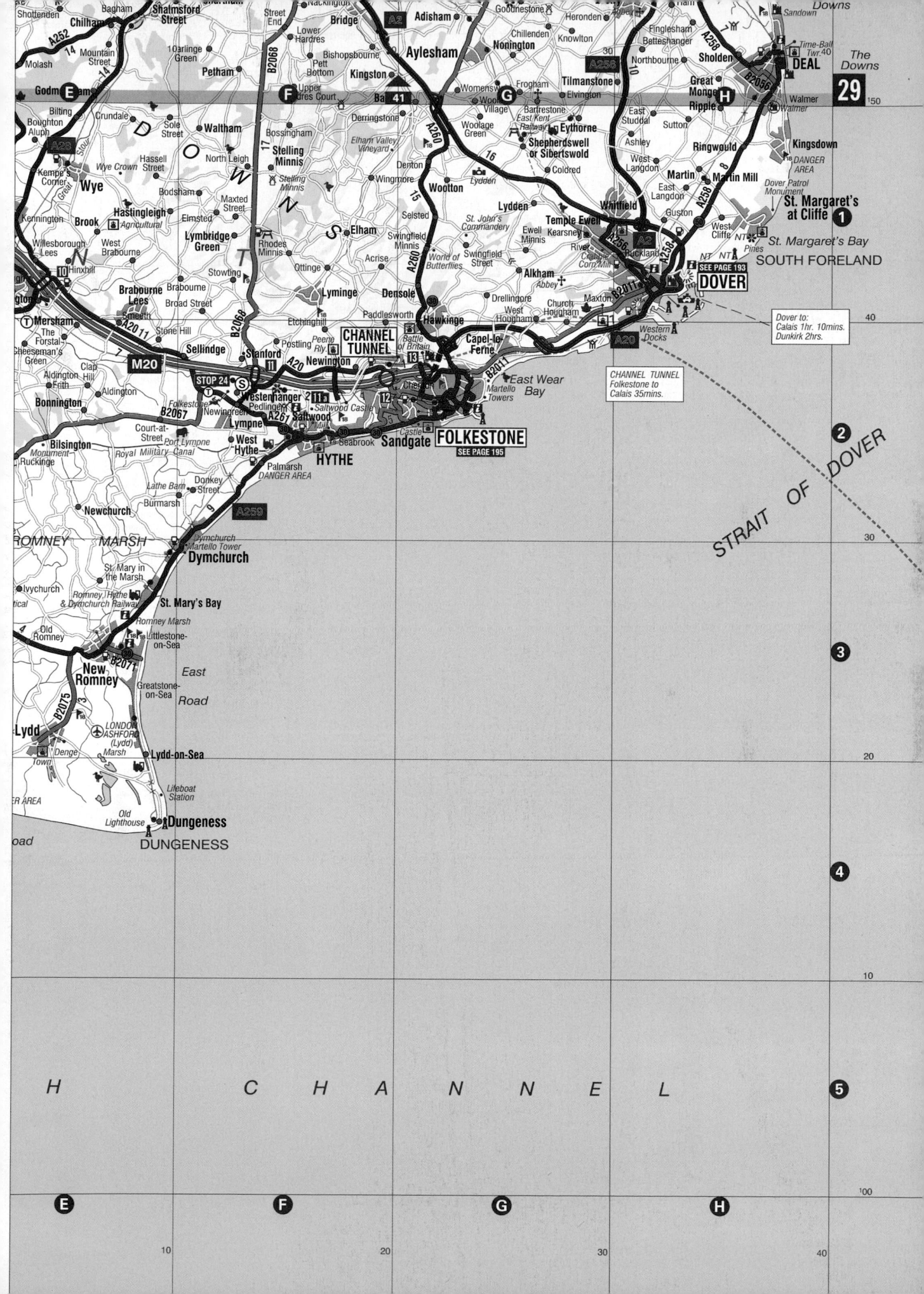

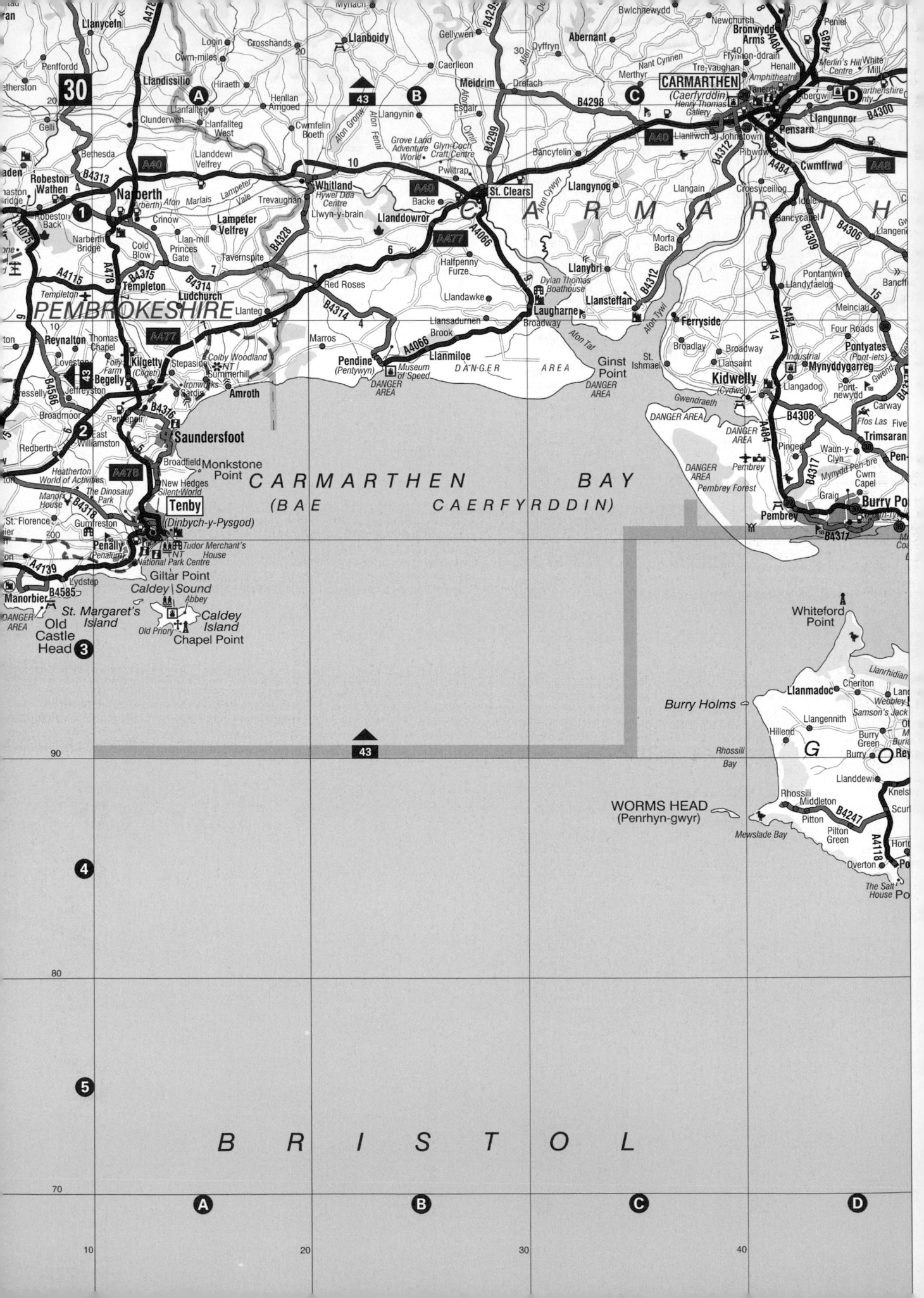

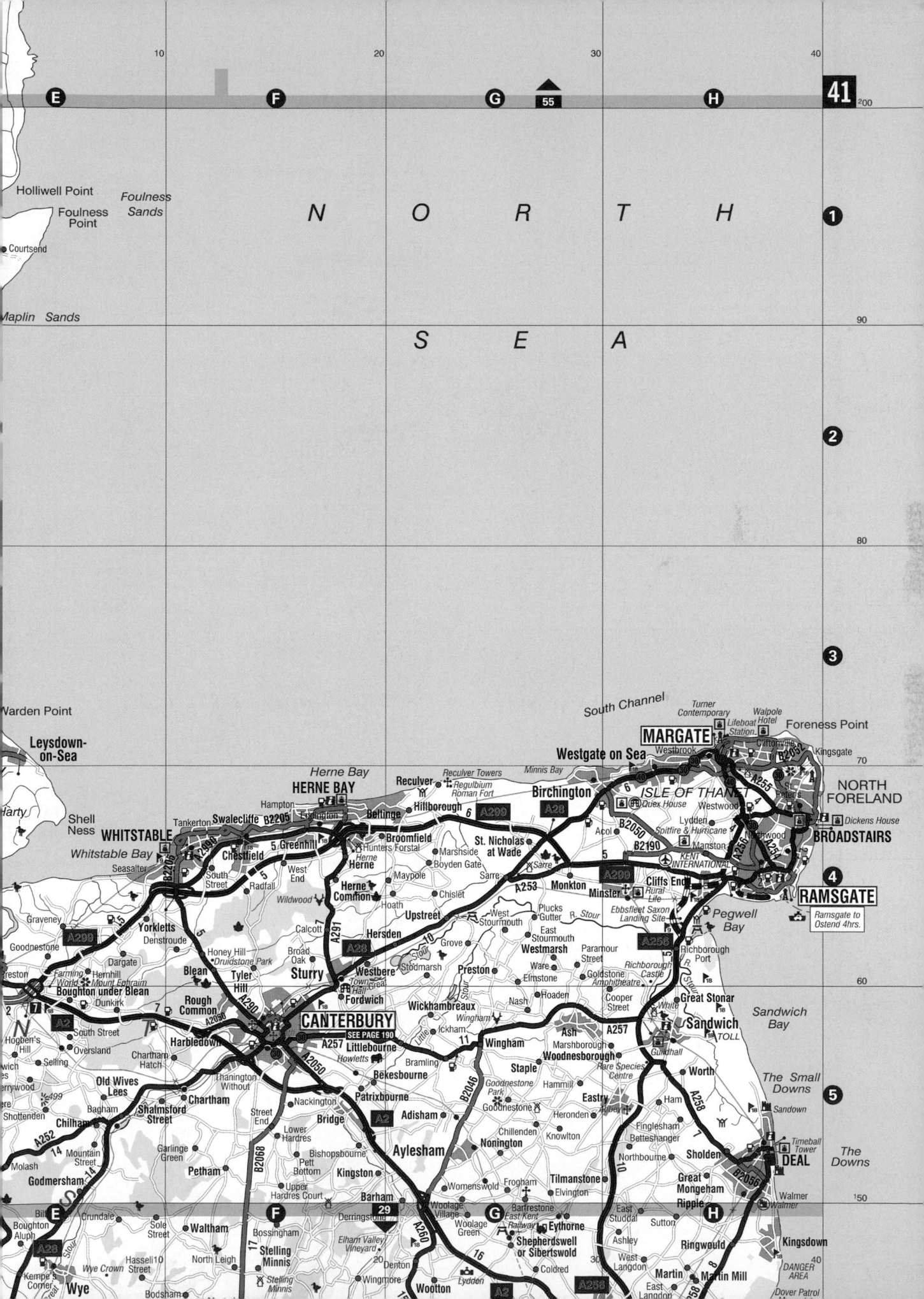

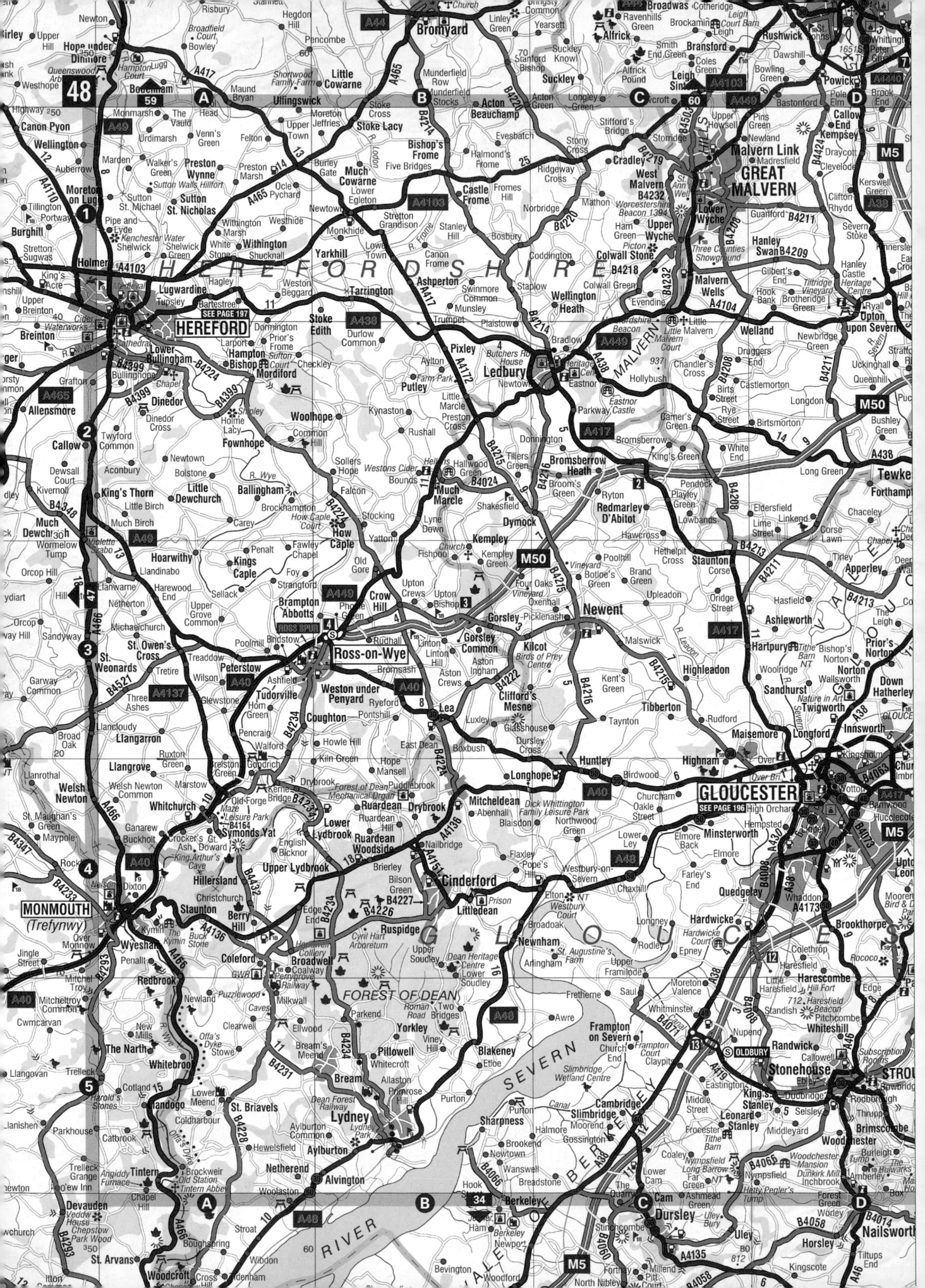

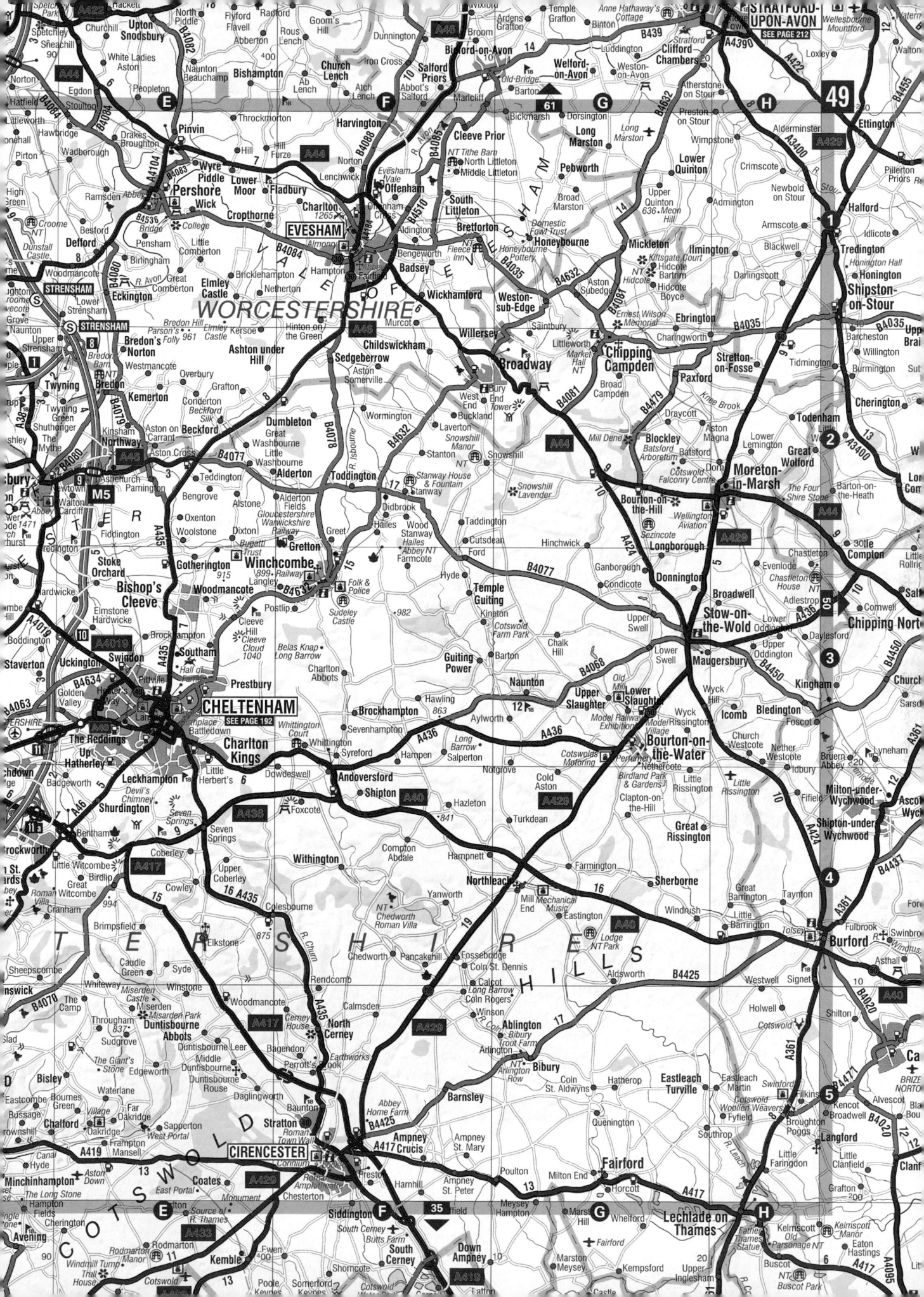

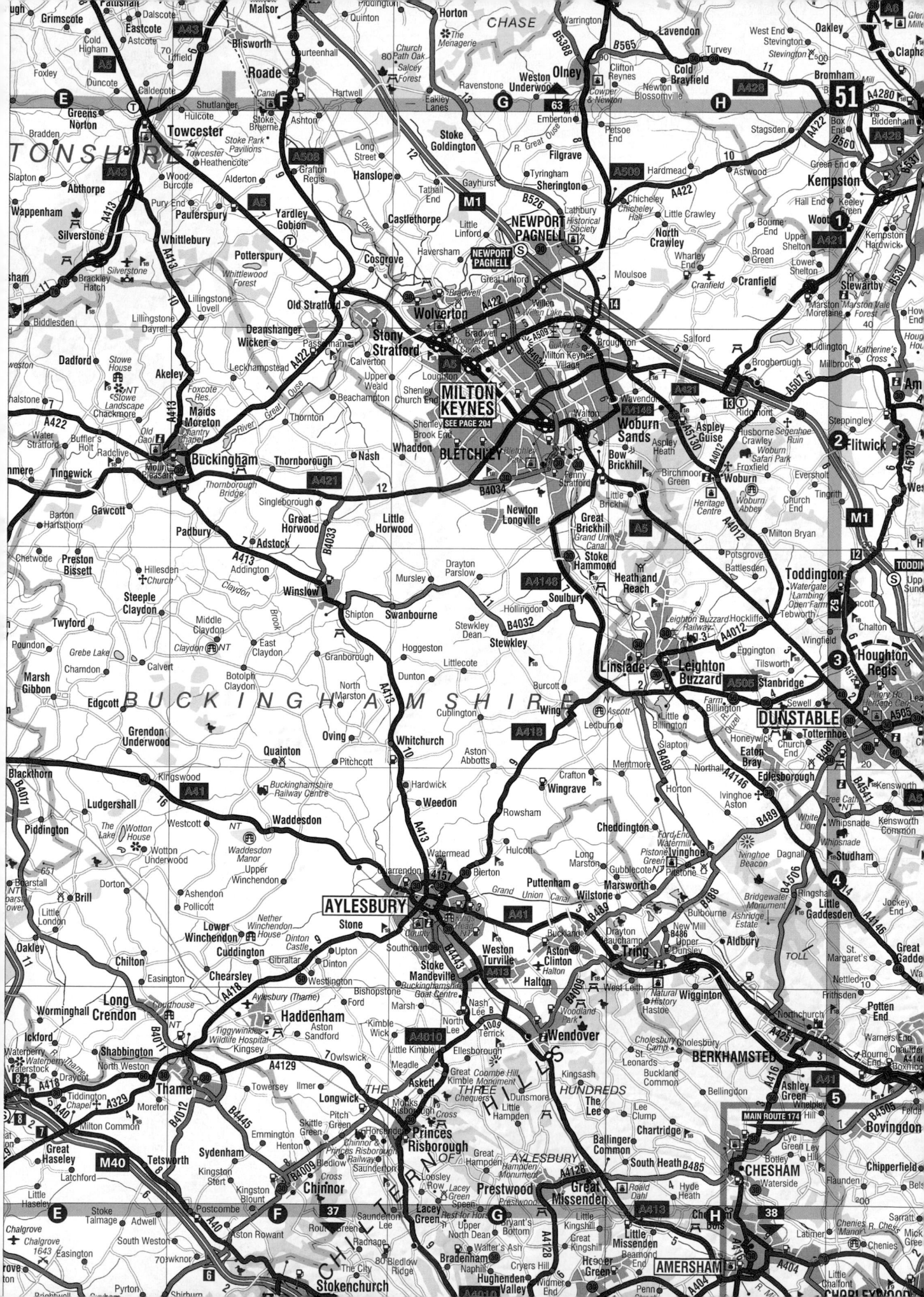

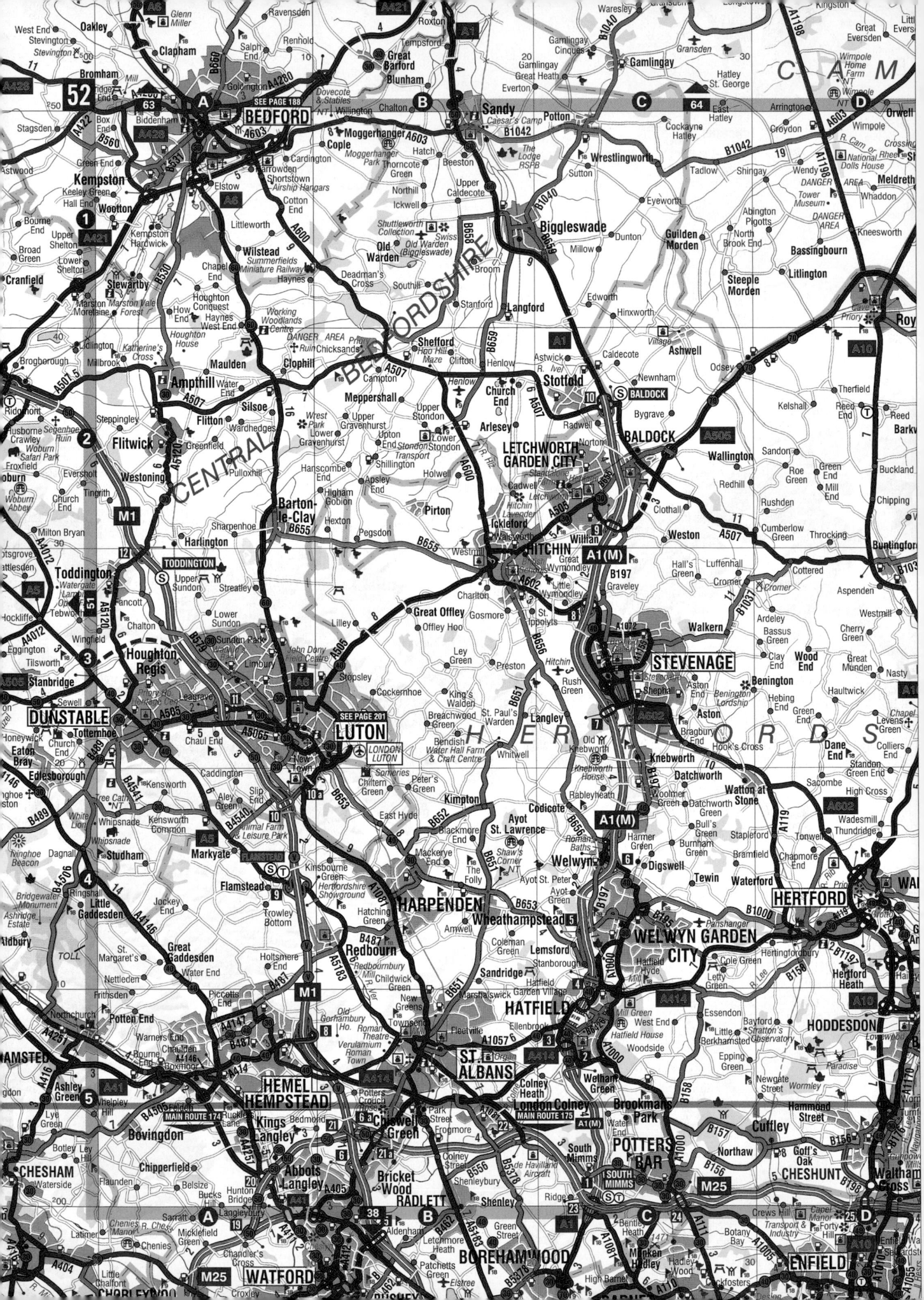

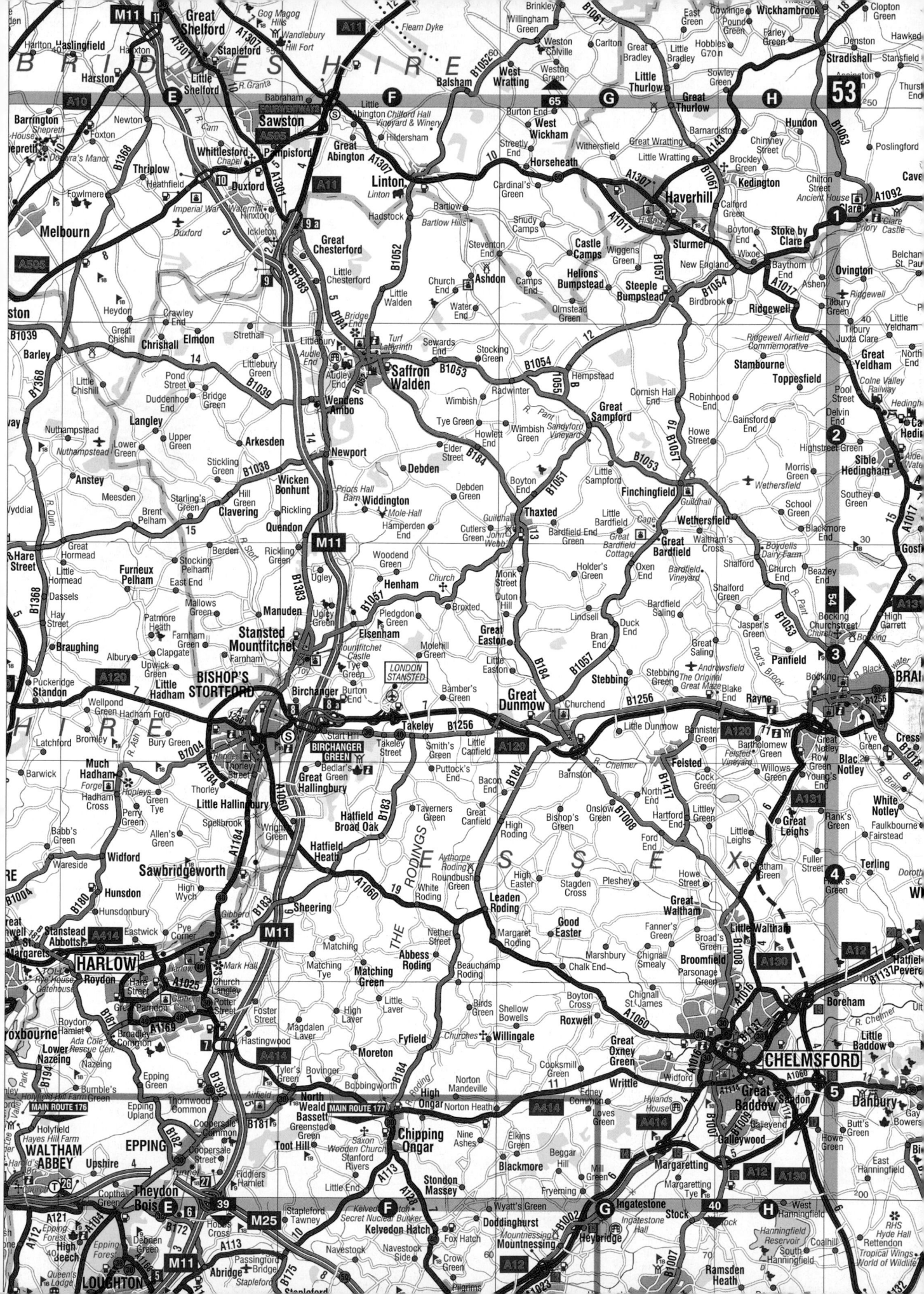

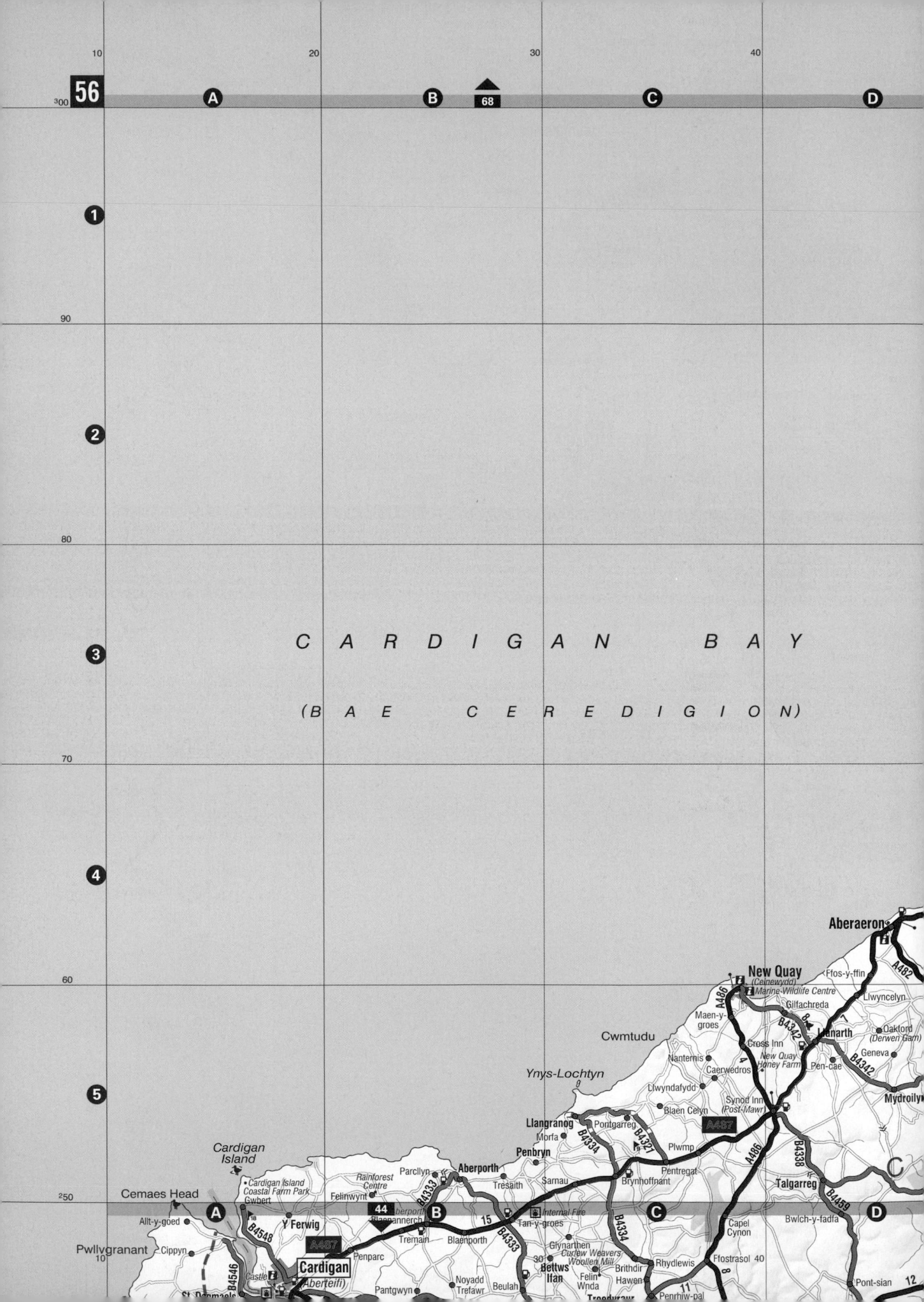

A   B   ▲ 68   C   D

C A R D I G A N   B A Y

(B A E   C E R E D I G I O N)

Aberaeron

New Quay
(Ceinewydd)
Marine Wildlife Centre

Ffos-y-ffin
A482
Llwyncelyn

Maen-y-
groes
Gilfachreda
B4342
Llanarth
Oakford
(Derwen Gam)

Cwmtudu

Cross Inn
New Quay
Honey Farm
Geneva
Pen-cae
B4342

Nanternis
Caerwedros

Ynys-Lochtyn
Llwyndafydd

Synod Inn
(Post-Mawr)
Mydroilyn

Blaen Celyn

Llangranog
Pontgarreg
A487
Morfa
B4334
B4321
Plwmp
A486
B4338
Talgarreg

Penbryn
Pentregat
B4459

Sarnau
Brynhoffnant
C

Cardigan
Island
Cemaes Head

Cardigan Island
Coastal Farm Park
Gwbert
Rainforest
Centre
Parcllyn
Aberporth

Felinwynt
Tresaith

Internal Fire
B4333
Capel
Cynon
Bwlch-y-fadfa

Allt-y-goed
A
44
berporth
Blaenannerch
B
15
Tan-y-groes
B4334
D

Pwllvgranant
Cippyn
Y Ferwig
A487
Tremain
Blaenporth
B4333

Glynarthen
Curlew Weavers
Woollen Mill
Ffostrasol   40

Cardigan
(Aberteifi)
Penparc
30
Bettws
Ifan
Rhydlewis

B4546
Castle
Noyadd
Trefawr
Pantgwyn
Beulah
Felin
Wnda
Hawen
Penrhiw-pal
Pont-sian

St Dogmaels
Troeduraur
12

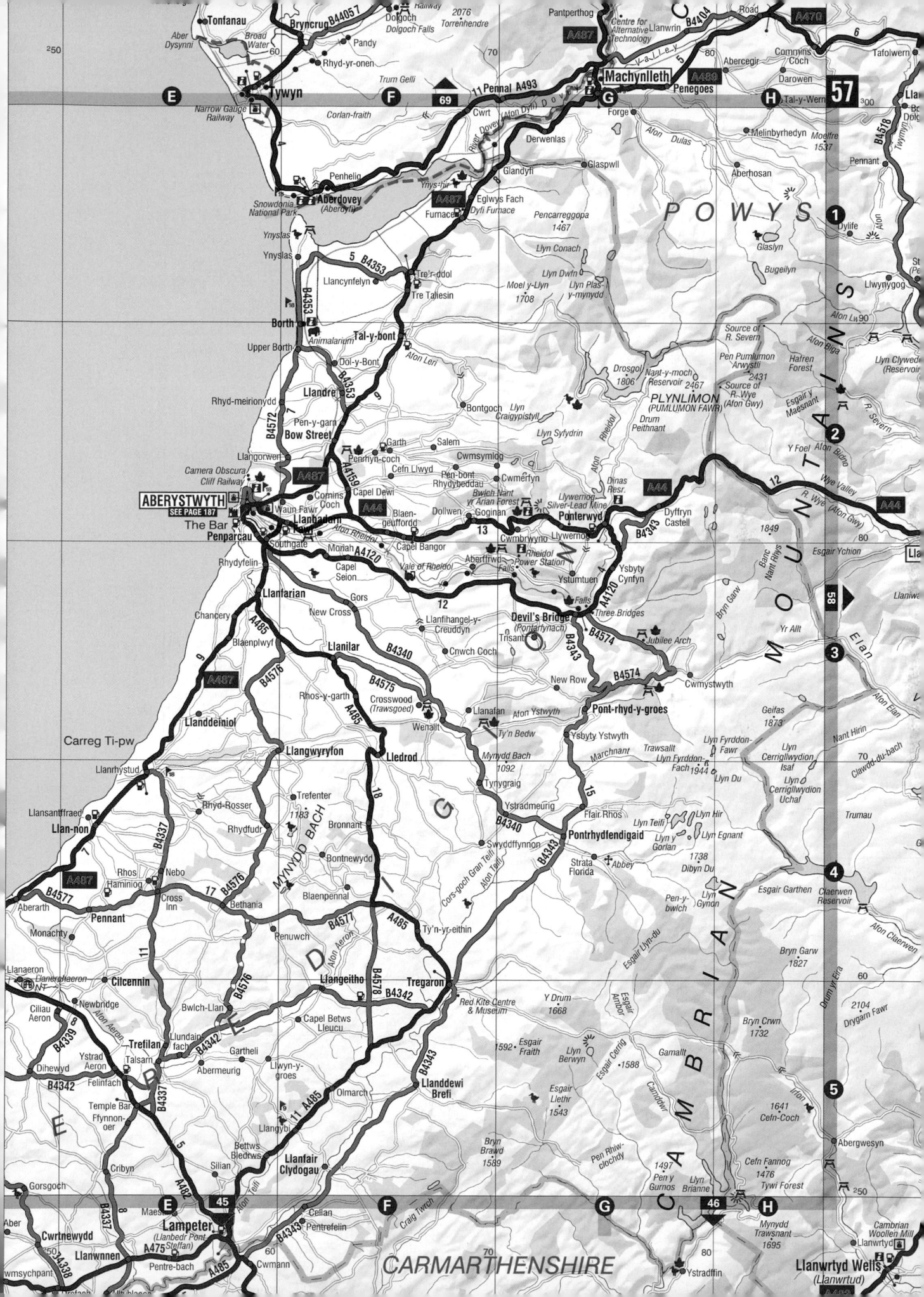

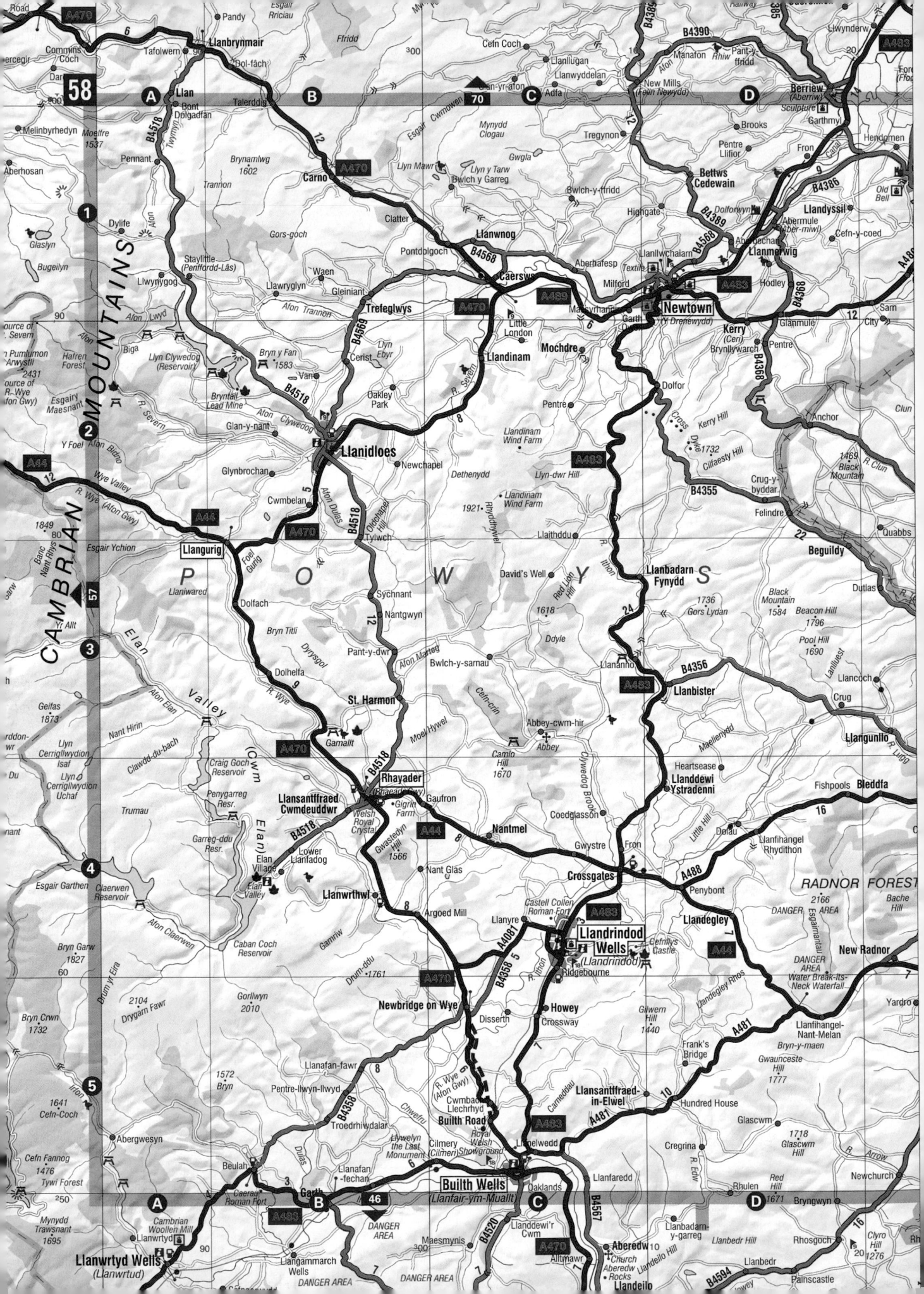

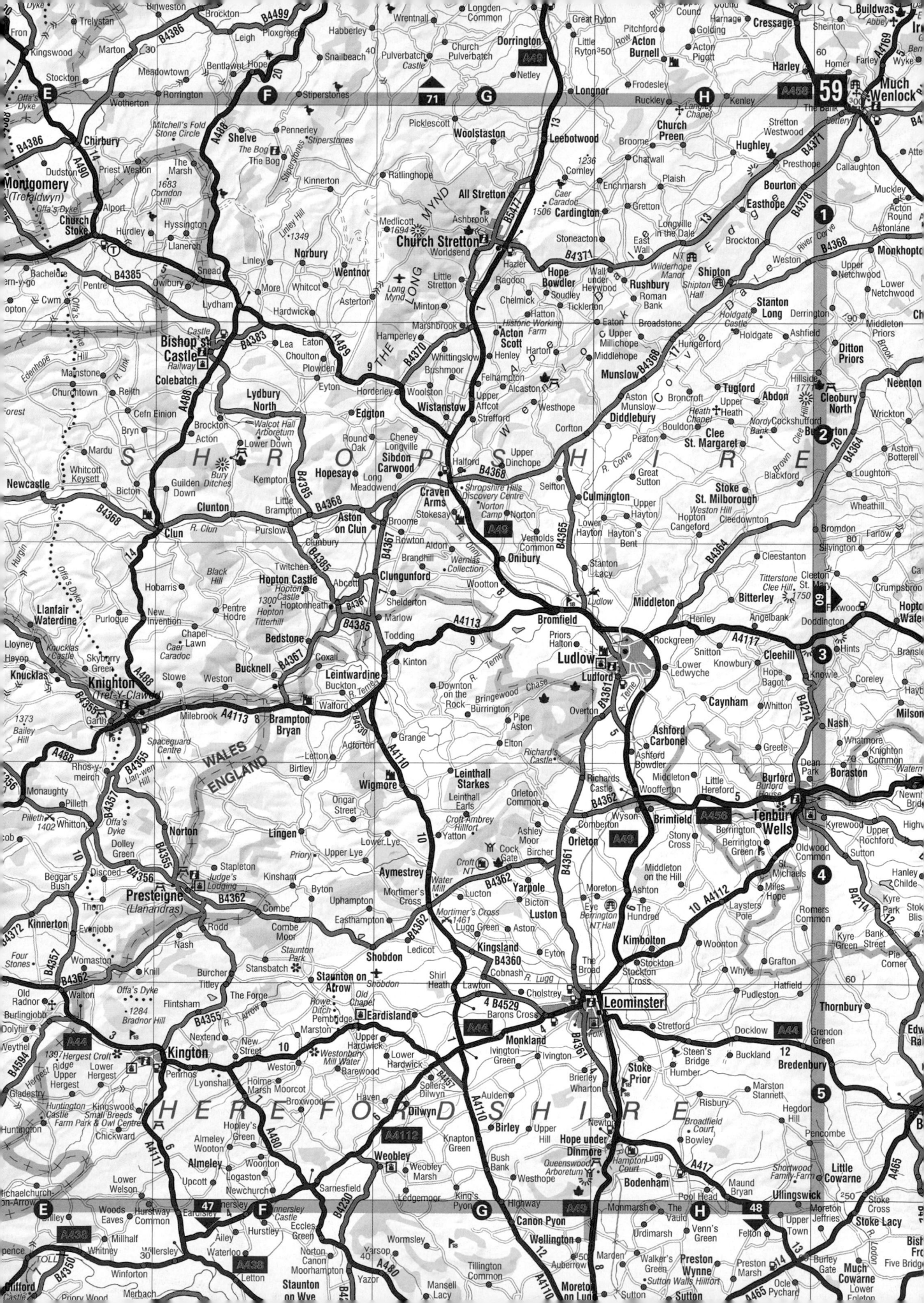

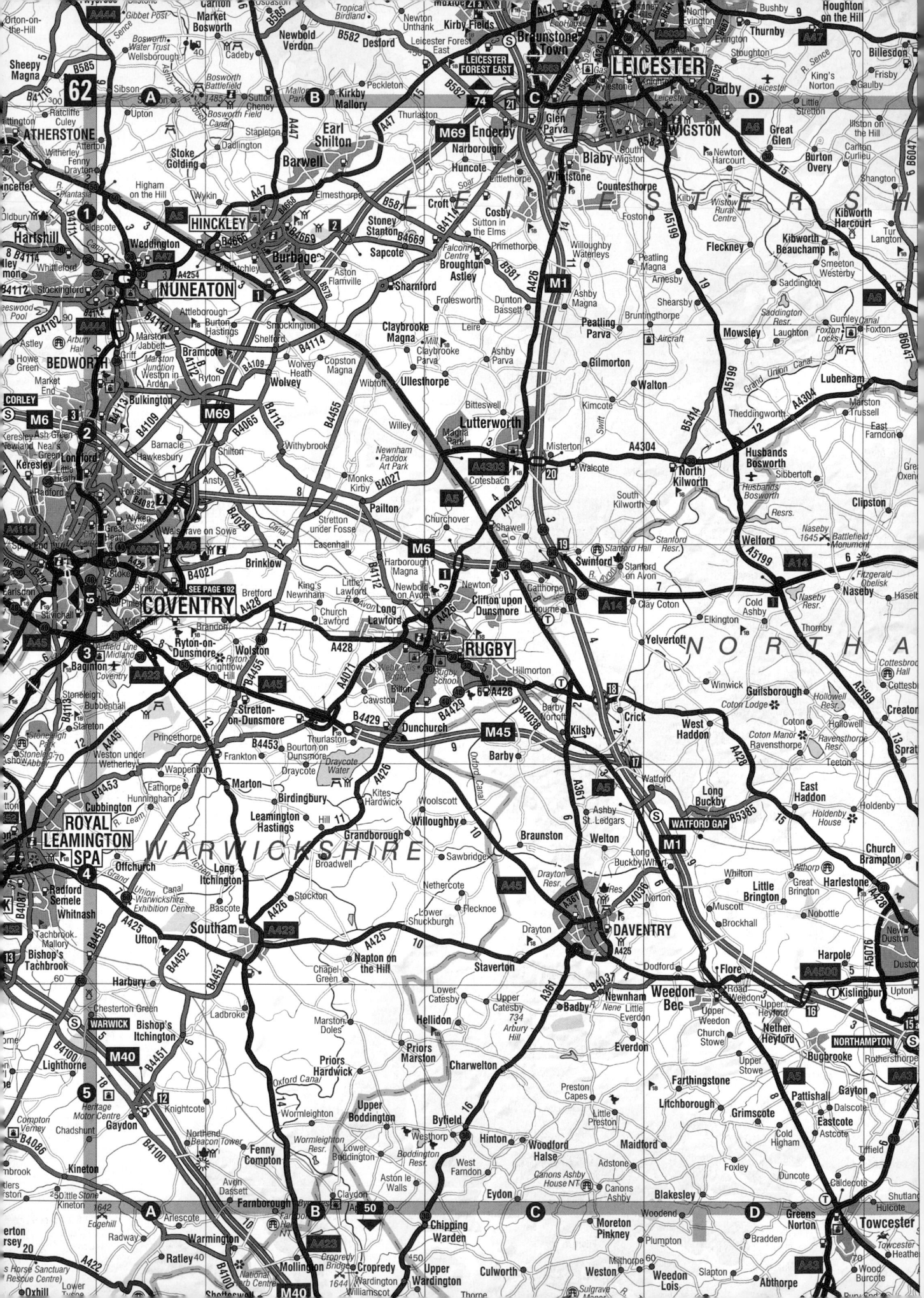

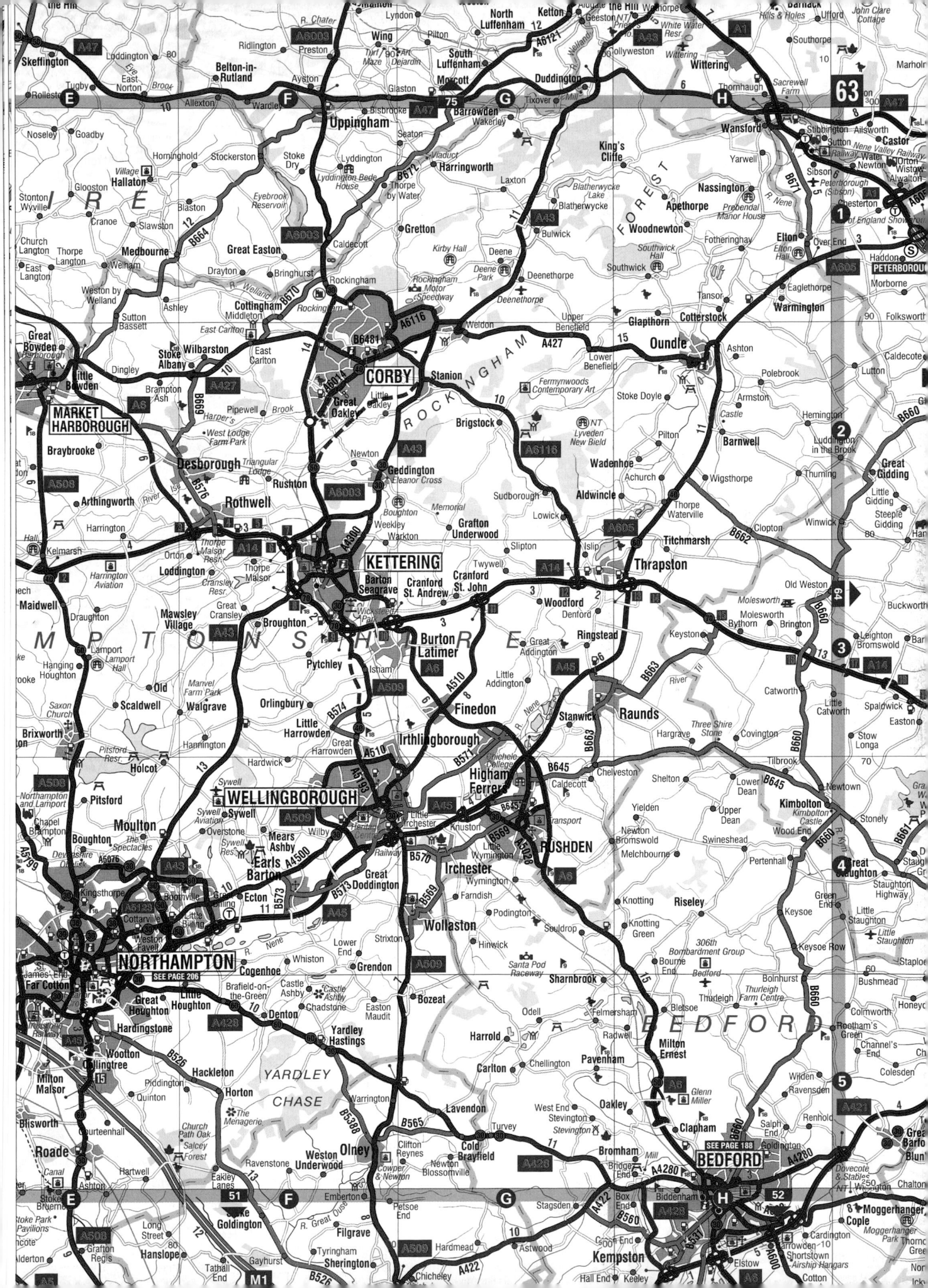

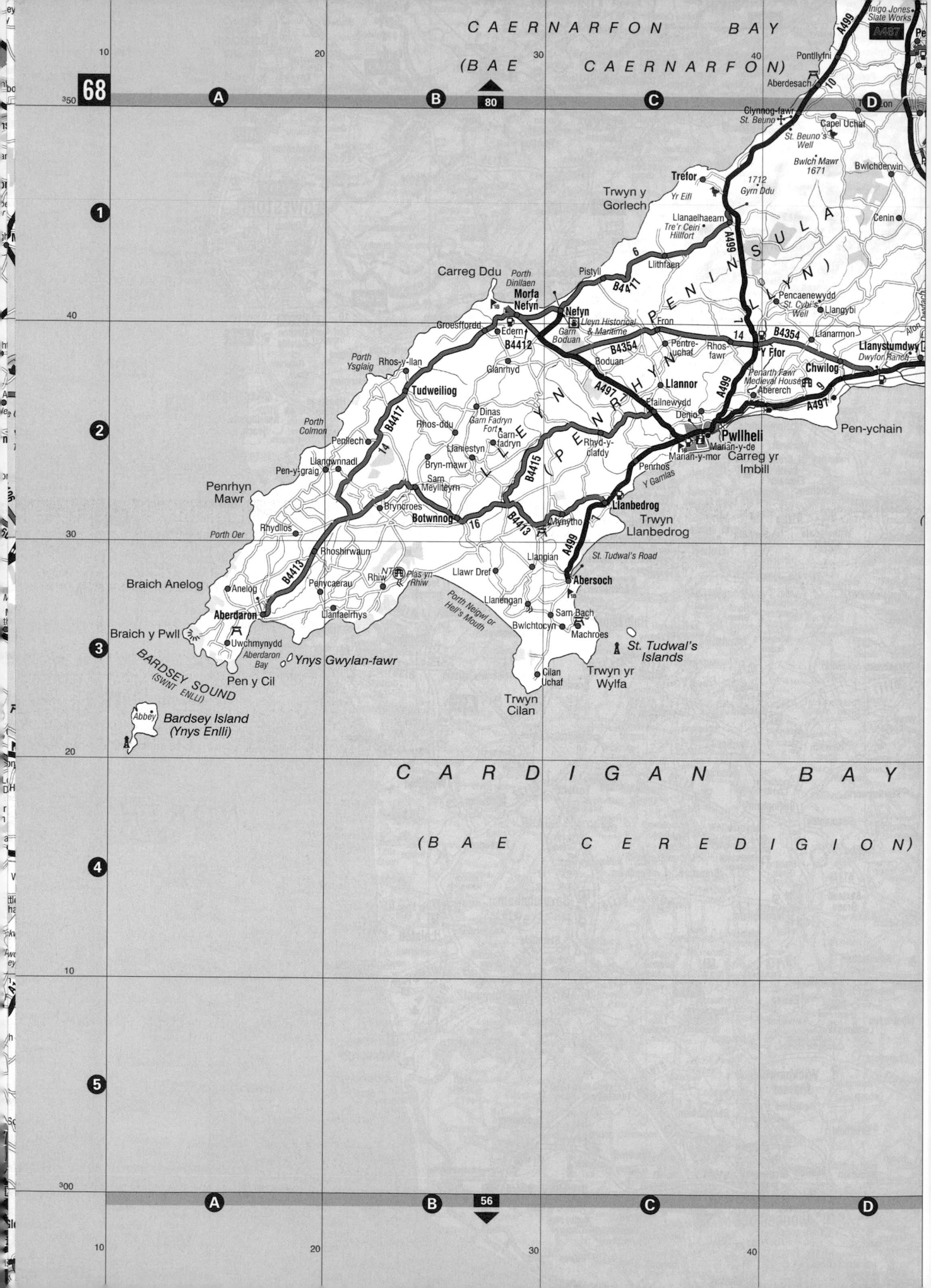

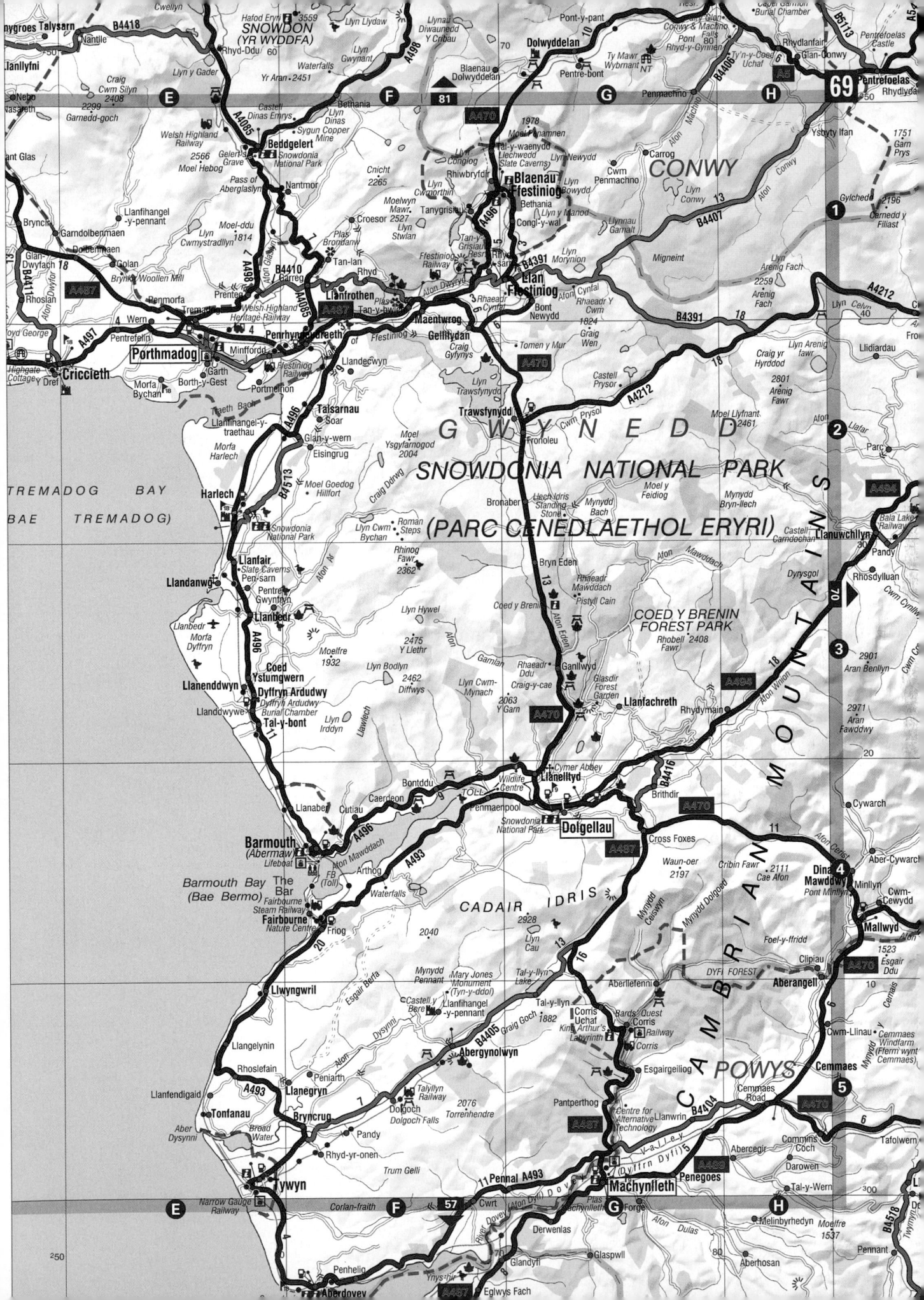

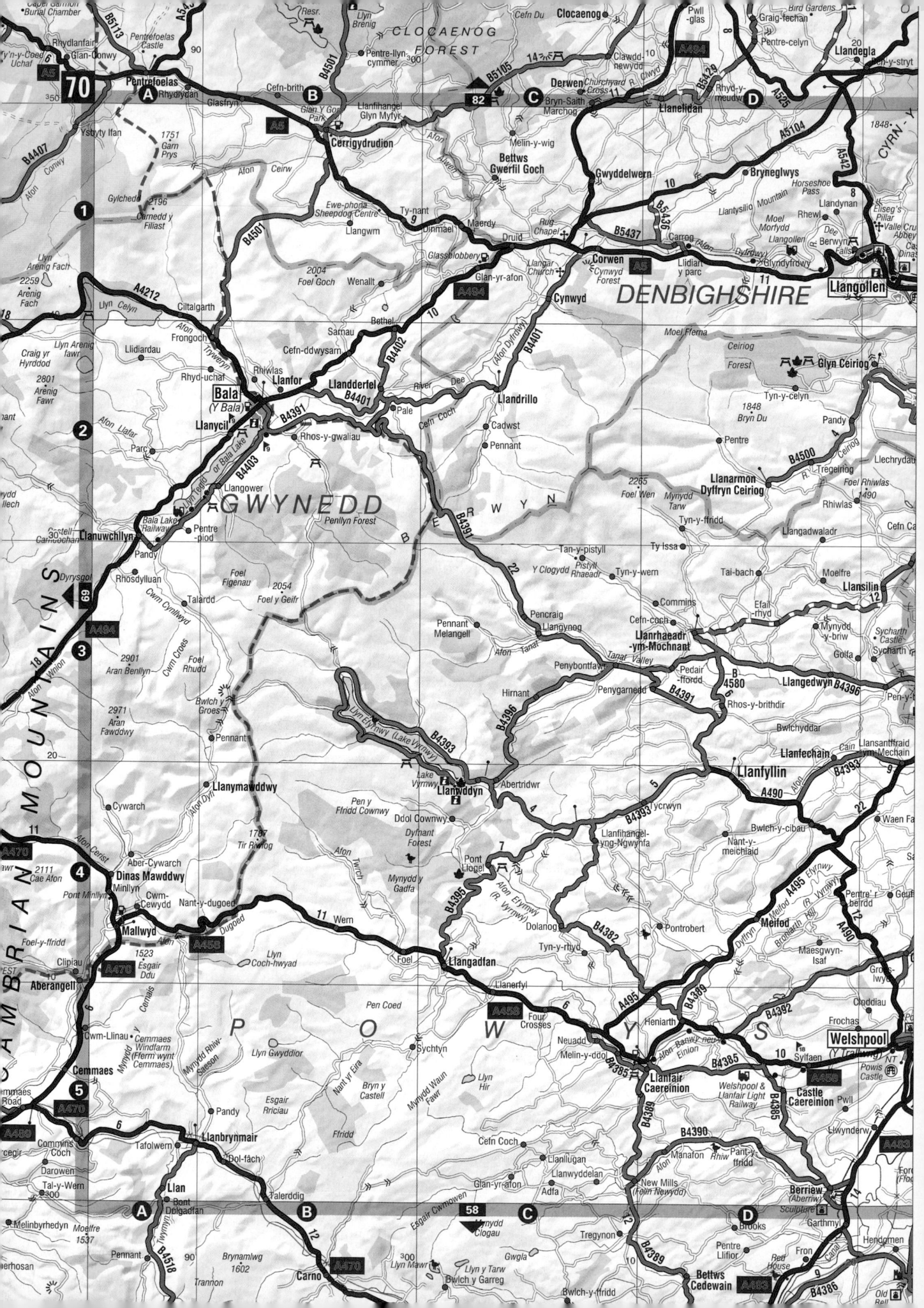

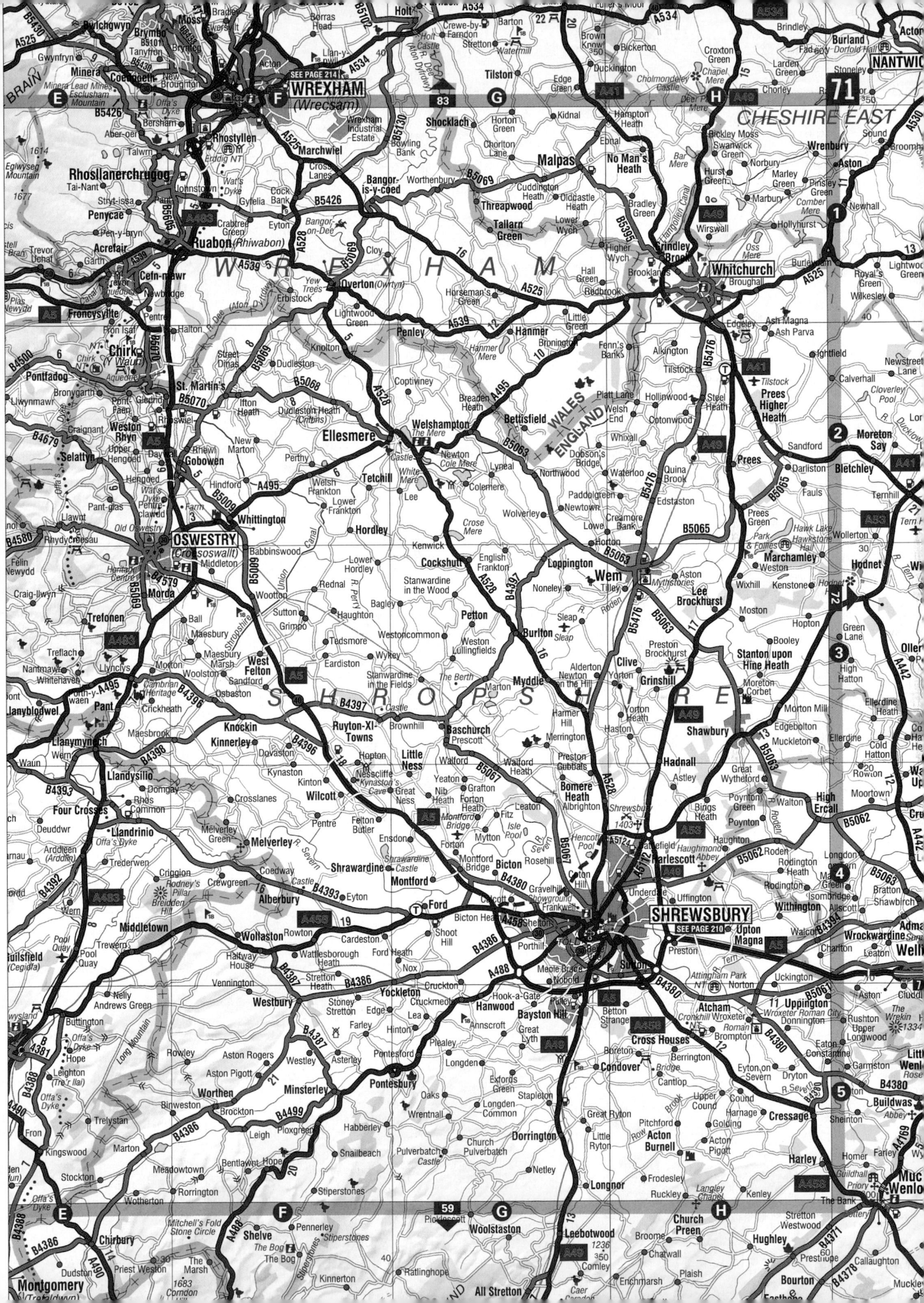

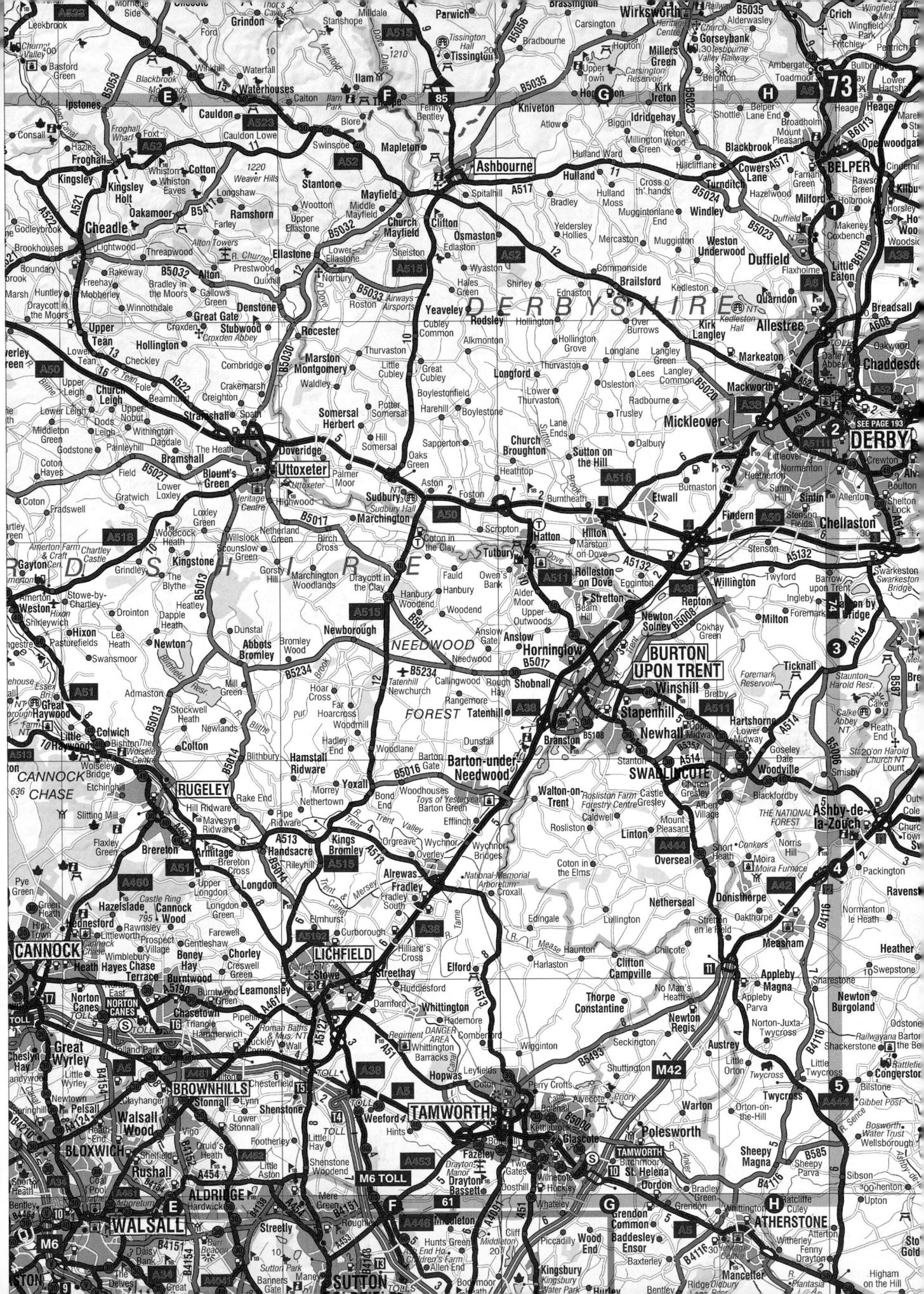

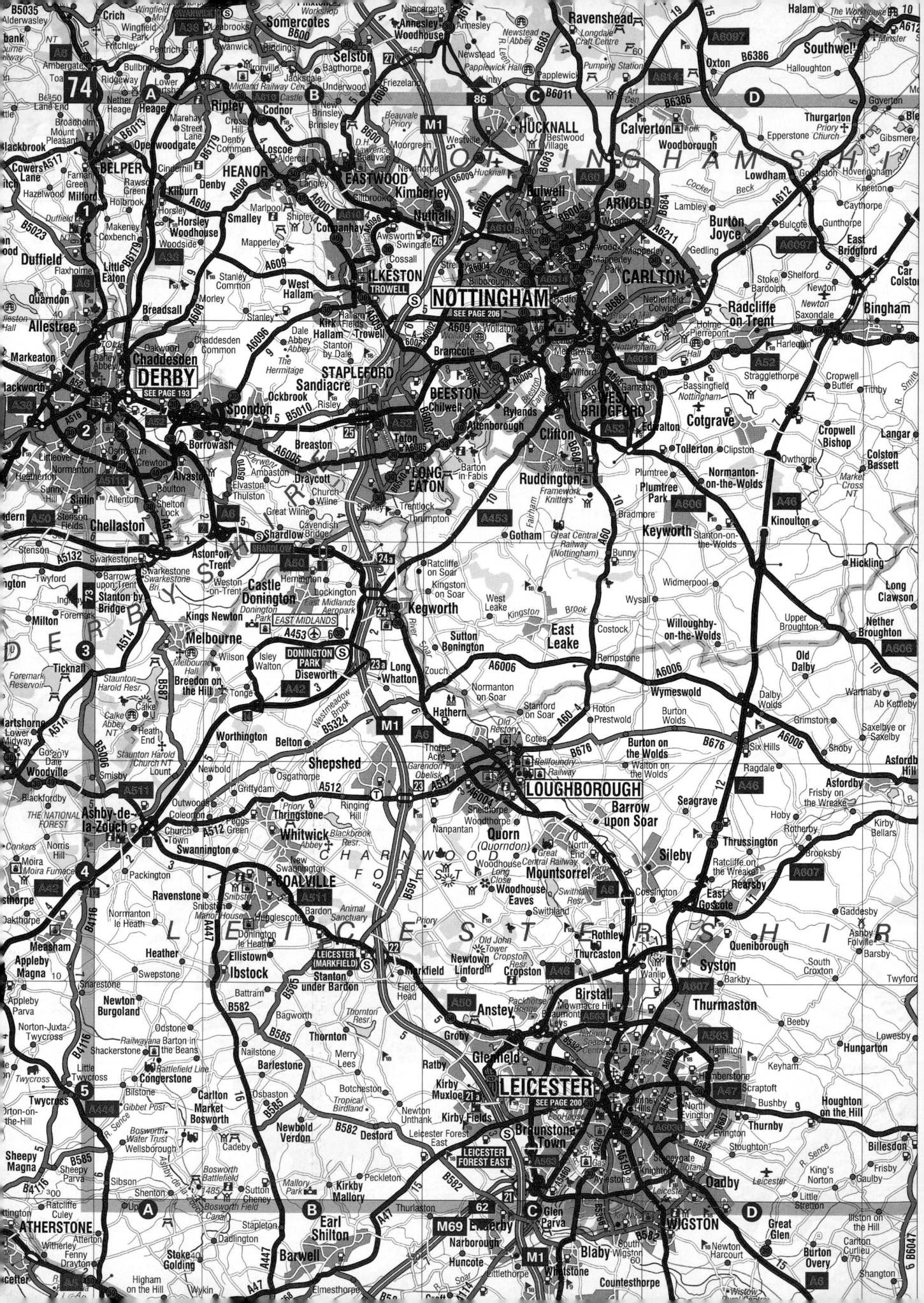

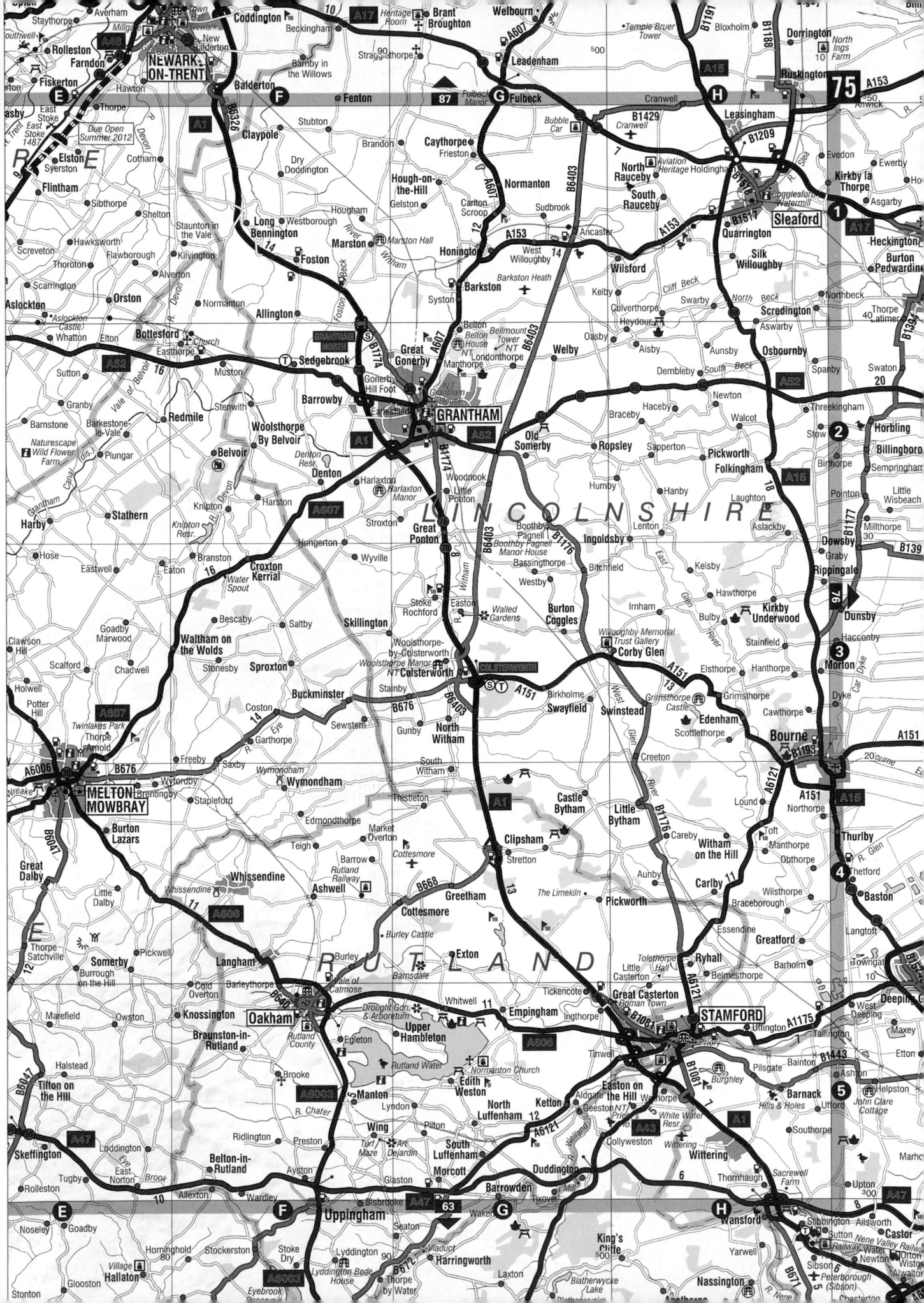

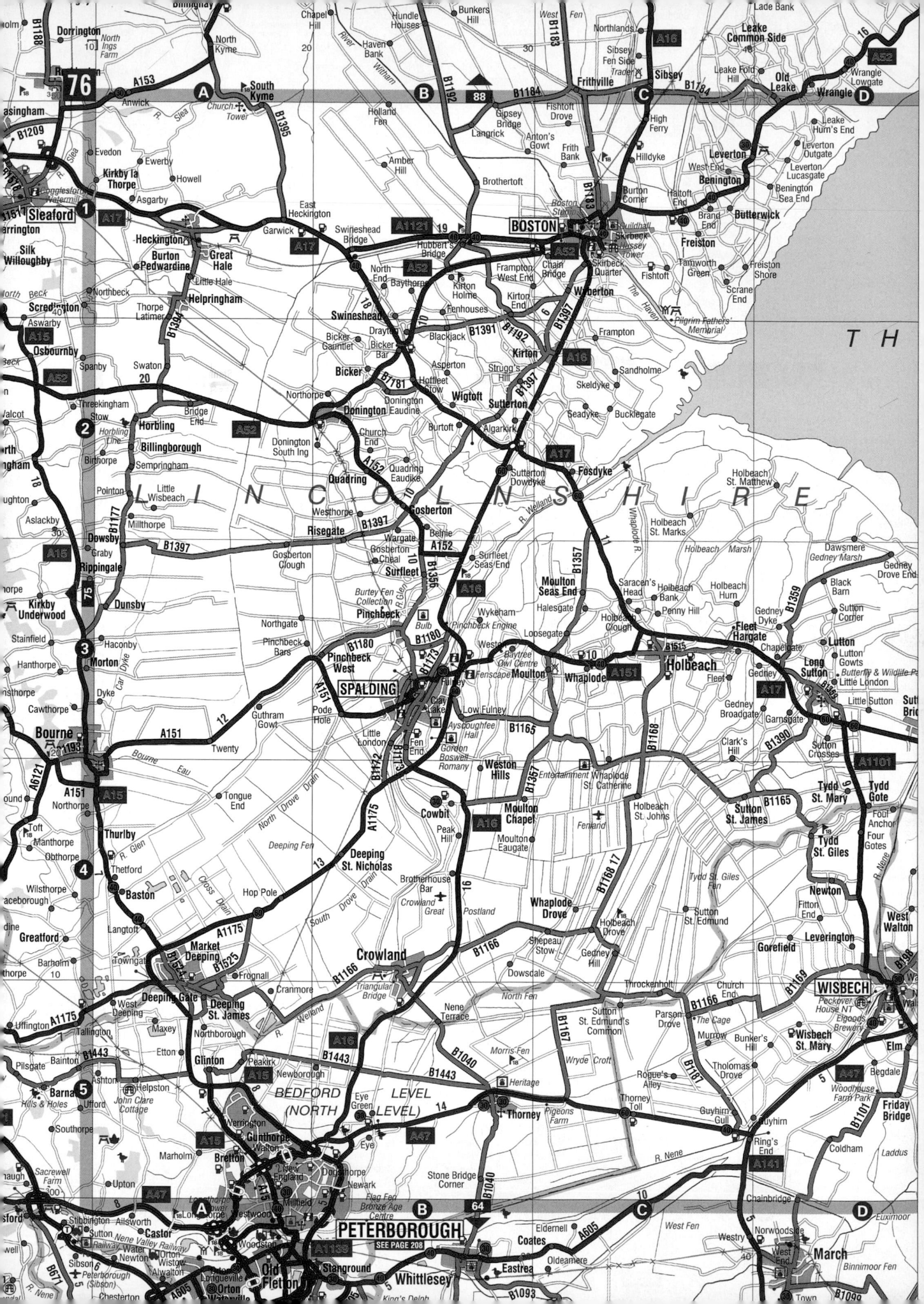

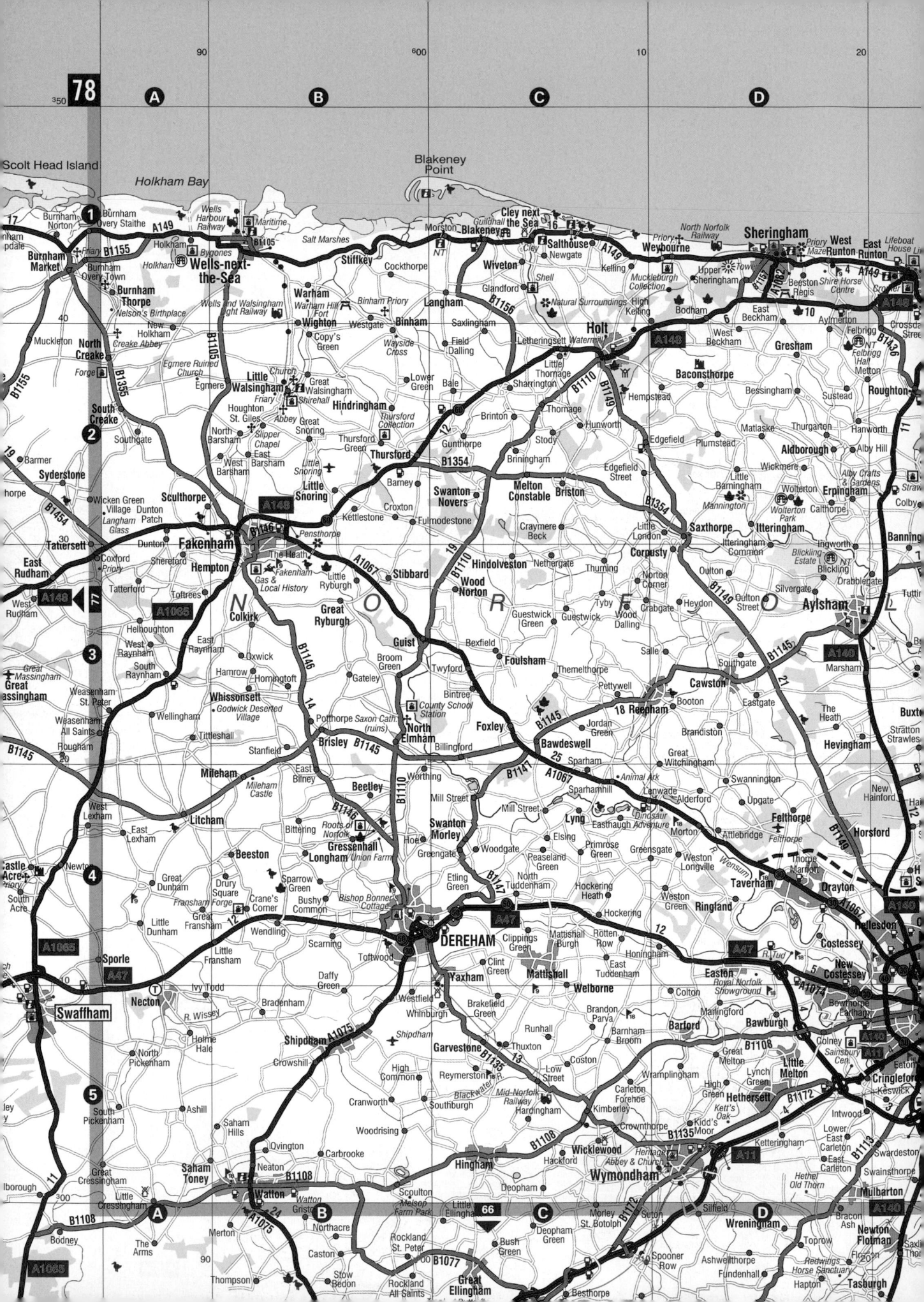

N O R T H

S E A

Theddlethorpe
St. Helen
Seal
Sanctuary

ers
dge

Mablethorpe
Ye Olde
Curiosity
.04 3

Thorpe

3

Trusthorpe

tby
arsh

Sutton on Sea

Sandilands

A52

A1111   Hannah

Markby

6

Thurlby

Huttoft

Anderby
Creek

Drainage

B1449   13

Anderby

hesthorpe

15   **Mumby**

Cumberworth   Authorpe
Row

Helsey   **Chapel
St. Leonards**

Bonthorpe

Hogsthorpe

lloughby

R   E

Slackholme
End

Sloothby

Slackholme
End

*Hardy's
Animal
Farm*

Hasthorpe

Addlethorpe   **Ingoldmells**

Ingoldmells
Point

lton
arsh

Orby   *Orby
Marsh*   *Skegness
(Ingoldmells)*
Water
Leisure Park   *Butlin's
Resort*

Winthorpe   **Seathorne**

n the
arsh

**Burgh
le Marsh**

7

18

A158   Church
Farm   Natureland
Seal Sanctuary

Model Village   **SKEGNESS**

Thorpe
St. Peter

Croft

5

Seacroft

Croft Marsh

emans
ewery
ainfleet
t. Mary
's Toft

Magdalen

**Wainfleet
All Saints**

Gibraltar

A52

5

DANGER AREA

Deeps

Boston

Scolt Head
80 Island

Brancaster Bay

Holkham Bay

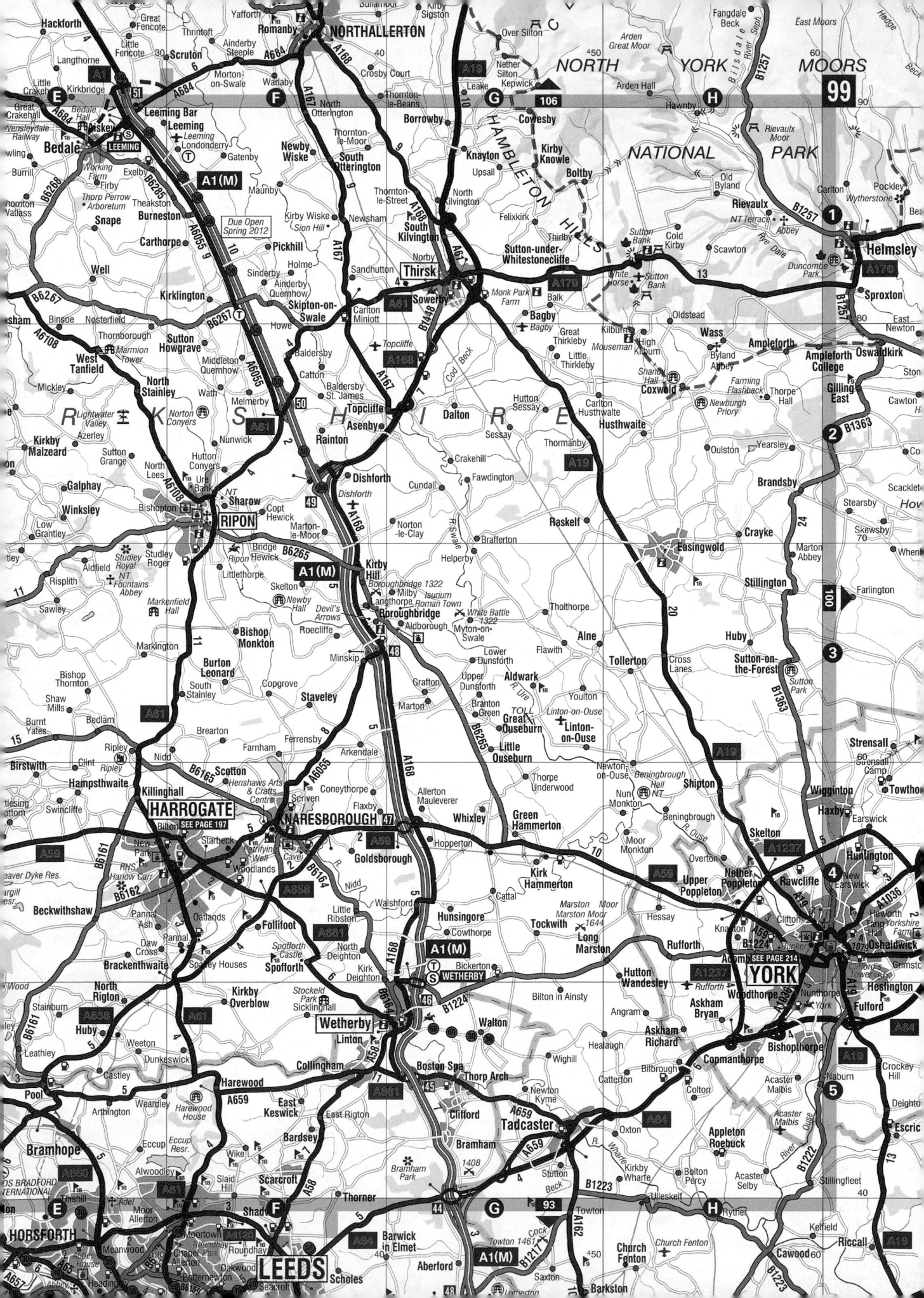

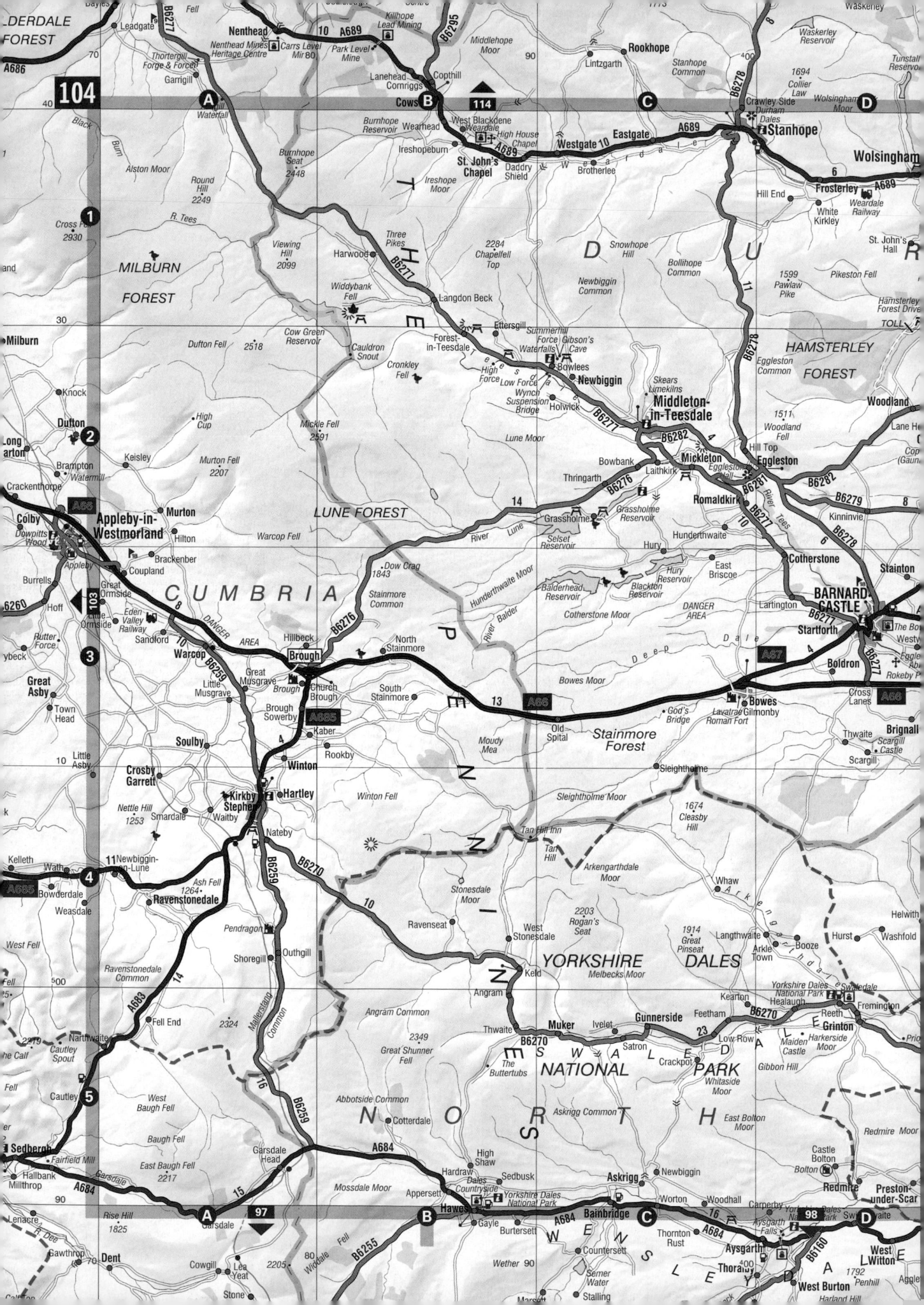

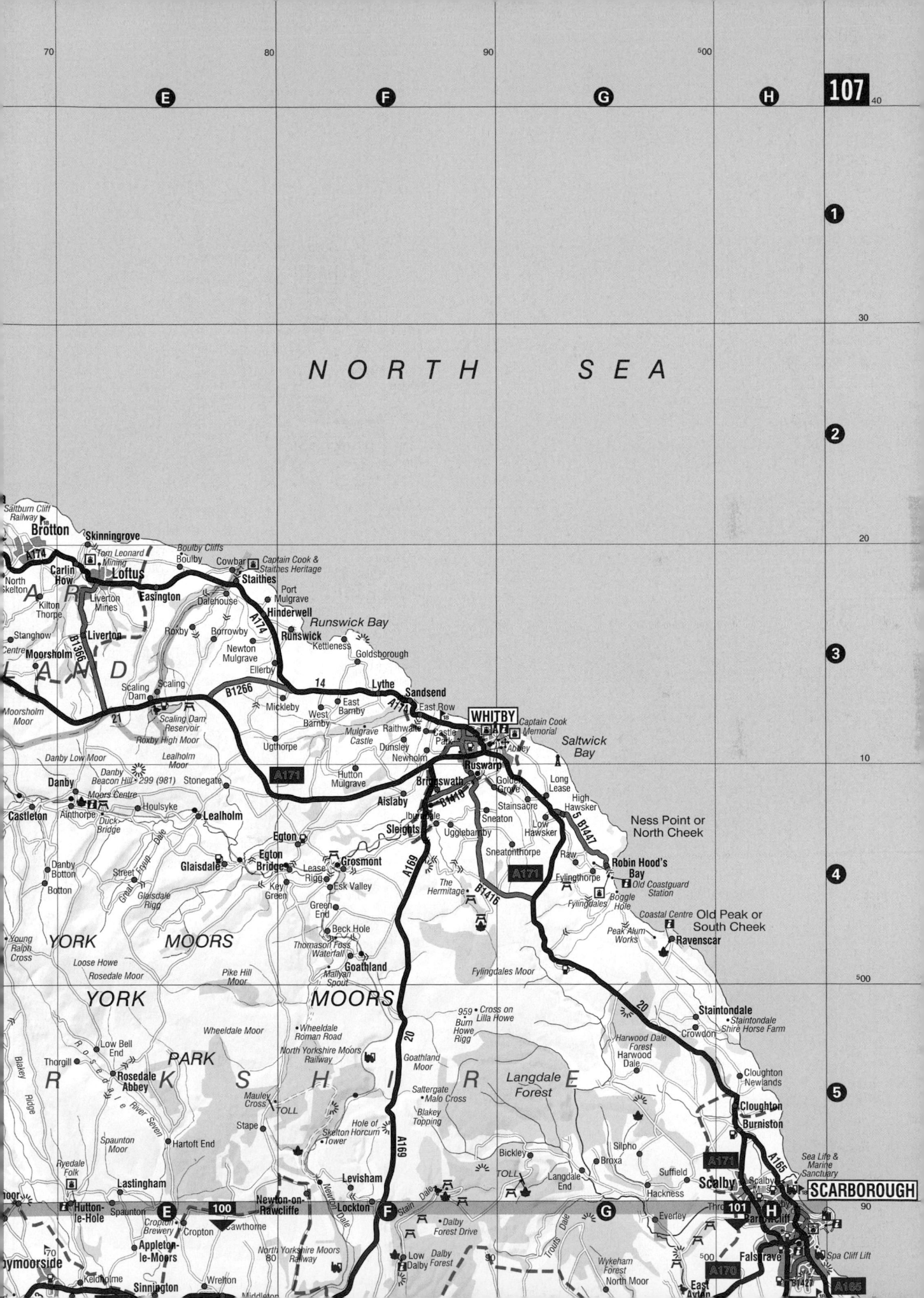

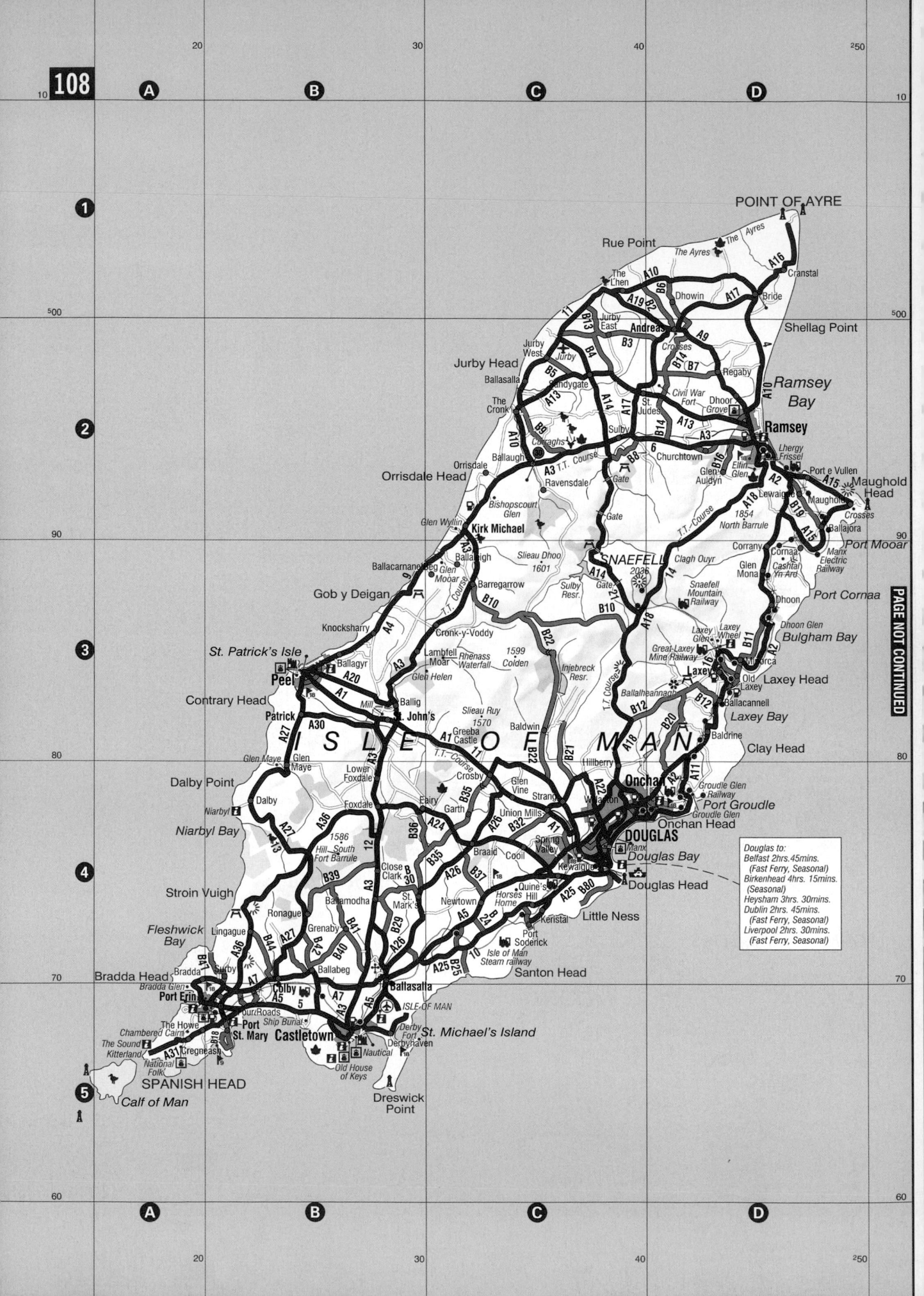

POINT OF AYRE

Rue Point

The Ayres

The Ayres

The Lhen

Cranstal

A10

A16

Dhowin

A17

Bride

A19

B2

B6

Jurby East

B13

A9

Shellag Point

Andreas

Crosses

A10

B3

Jurby West

B14

B7

Regaby

Ramsey Bay

Jurby Head

B5

Sandygate

B4

A13

Ballasalla

St. Judes

Civil War Fort

Dhoor Grove

Ramsey

The Cronk

A10

A14

A17

B14

A13

A3

Lhergy Frissel

A12

B9

Sulby

Churchtown

6

B16

Port e Vullen

Orrisdale

Ballaugh

30

Curraghs

B8

Elfin Glen

Glen Auldyn

A2

A15

Maughold

Orrisdale Head

A3

T.T. Course

Gate

Lewaigue

A18

Maughold Head

Ravensdale

Gate

1854 North Barrule

A19

A15

Crosses

Glen Wyllin

Bishopscourt Glen

Corrany

Cornaa

Ballajora

Manx Electric Railway

Kirk Michael

Clagh Ouyr

Glen Mona

Port Mooar

Ballacarnane Beg

Ballaleigh

Slieau Dhoo 1601

SNAEFELL 2036

Glen Mooar

A14

Gate

14

Snaefell Mountain Railway

Dhoon

Port Cornaa

Barregarrow

Sulby Resr.

B10

Laxey Glen

Laxey Wheel

B11

Bulgham Bay

Gob y Deigan

B10

A18

Great-Laxey Mine Railway

Old Laxey

Laxey Head

Knocksharry

A4

B22

Rhenass Waterfall

1599 Colden

Injebreck Resr.

Laxey

B12

Laxey Bay

St. Patrick's Isle

A3

Lambfell Moar

Ballaheannagh

B12

Ballacannell

Peel

A20

Glen Helen

Slieau Ruy 1570

Baldwin

B22

A18

B20

Baldrine

Contrary Head

A1

Ballig

B21

Clay Head

Patrick

A30

St. John's

A1

Greeba Castle

Hillberry

A22

A11

Onchan

Glen Maye

Glen Maye

T.T. Course

Crosby

Glen Vine

Strang

Willaston

Port Groudle

Dalby Point

Lower Foxdale

B35

Garth

Union Mills

B32

A1

Groudle Glen Railway

Niarbyl

A36

Foxdale

A24

B36

A26

Cooil

Kewaigue

Groudle Glen

Onchan Head

Niarbyl Bay

13

1586 Hill South Fort Barrule

12

A3

B35

Braaid

DOUGLAS

Manx

Douglas Bay

Stroin Vuigh

B39

Ballamodha

St. Mark's

A26

B37

Newtown

Quine's Hill

Horses Hill

A25

B80

Douglas Head

Fleshwick Bay

Lingague

A27

Ronague

Grenaby

B41

B29

A5

Keristal

Little Ness

Bradda Head

B44

Surby

B42

B40

Ballabeg

Port Soderick

Isle of Man Steam railway

Bradda

Bradda Glen

A7

Colby

A7

A3

A5

Ballasalla

A25

B25

10

Santon Head

Port Erin

A5

5

ISLE-OF-MAN

The Howe

Our Roads

Ship Burial

Derby Fort

Derbyhaven

St. Michael's Island

Chambered Cairn

Port St. Mary

B18

Castletown

Nautical

The Sound

A31

Cregneash

Old House of Keys

Kitterland

National Folk

Dreswick Point

SPANISH HEAD

Calf of Man

ISLE OF MAN

PAGE NOT CONTINUED

Douglas to:
Belfast 2hrs.45mins.
(Fast Ferry, Seasonal)
Birkenhead 4hrs. 15mins.
(Seasonal)
Heysham 3hrs. 30mins.
Dublin 2hrs. 45mins.
(Fast Ferry, Seasonal)
Liverpool 2hrs. 30mins.
(Fast Ferry, Seasonal)

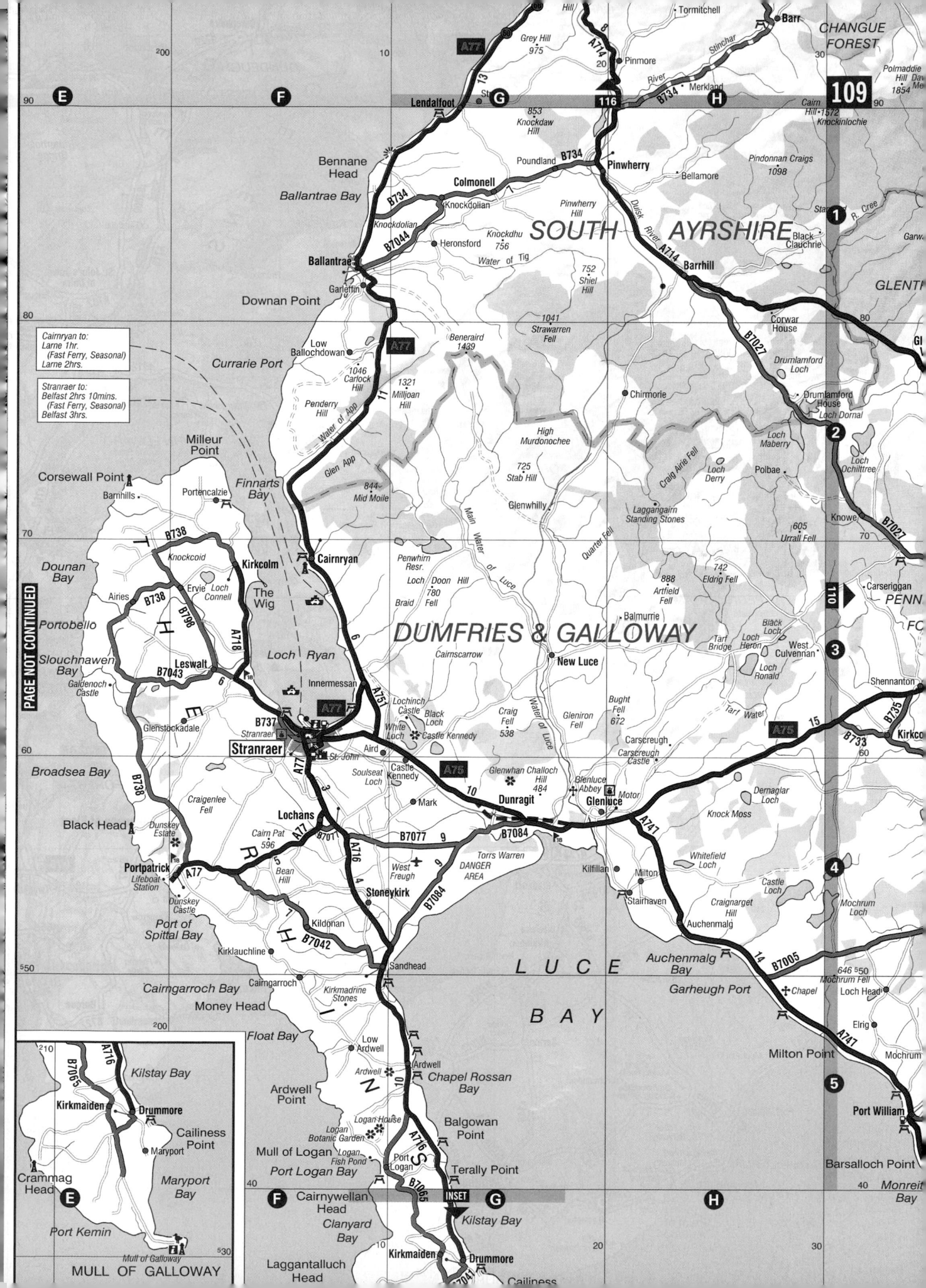

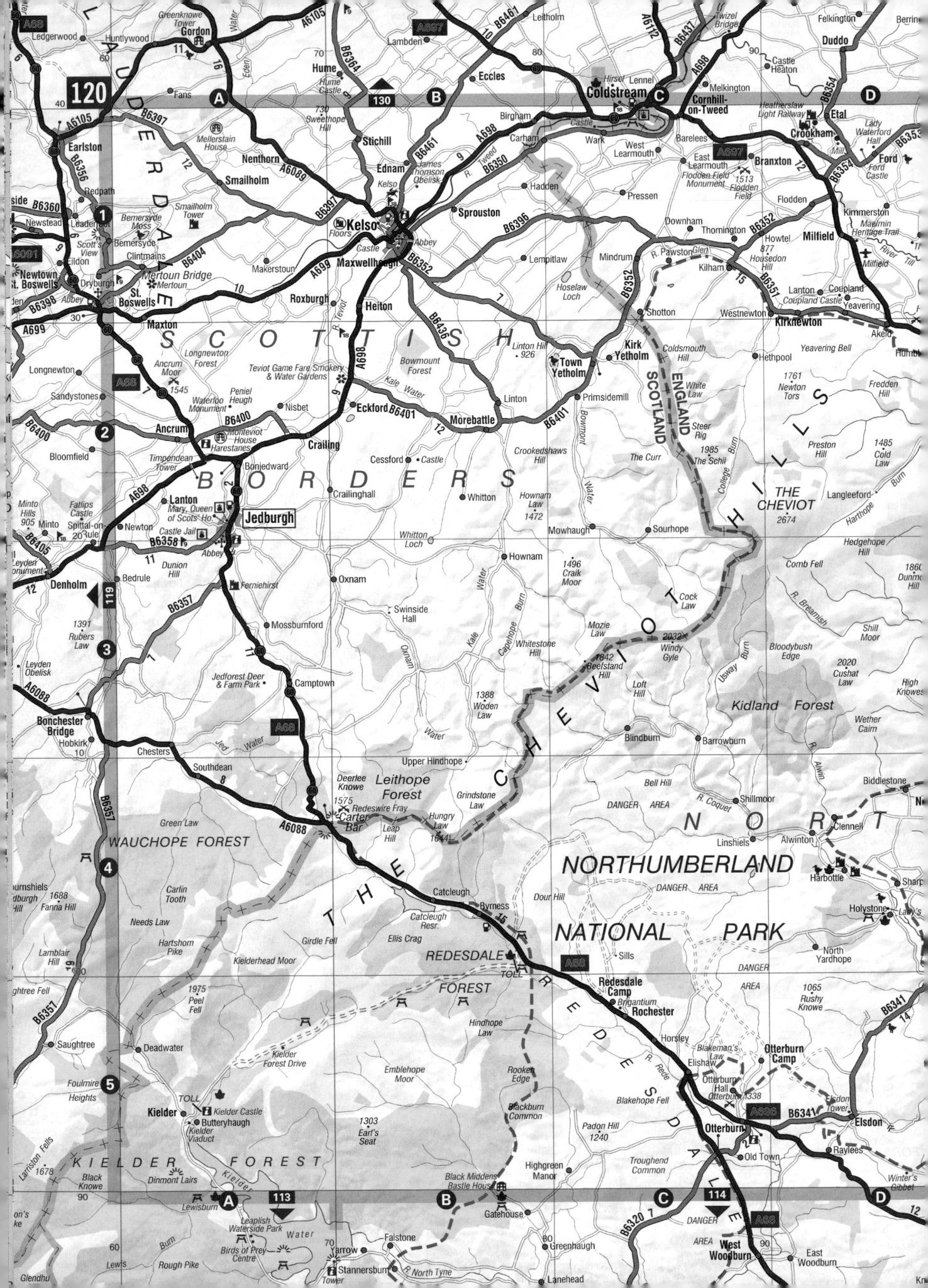

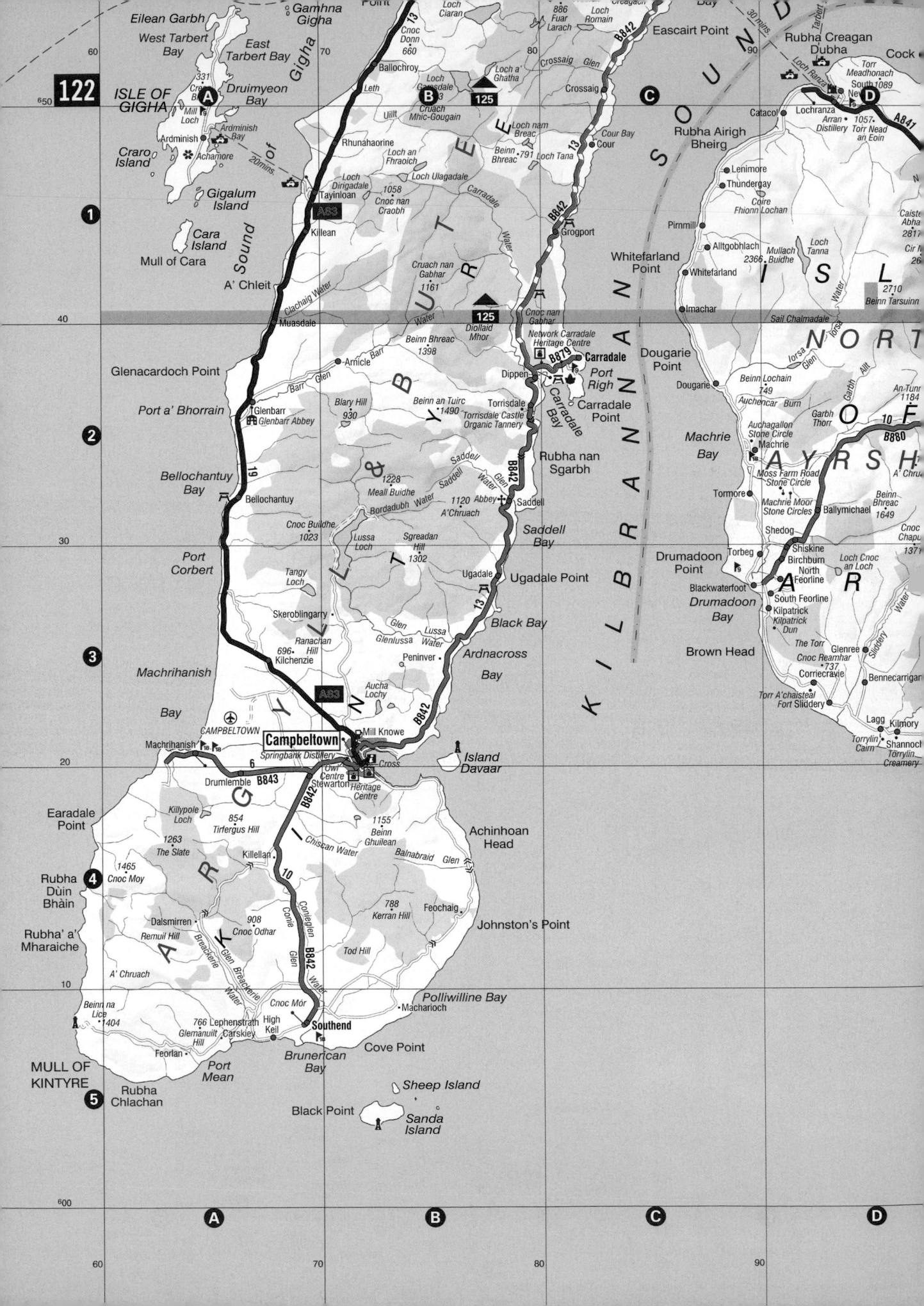

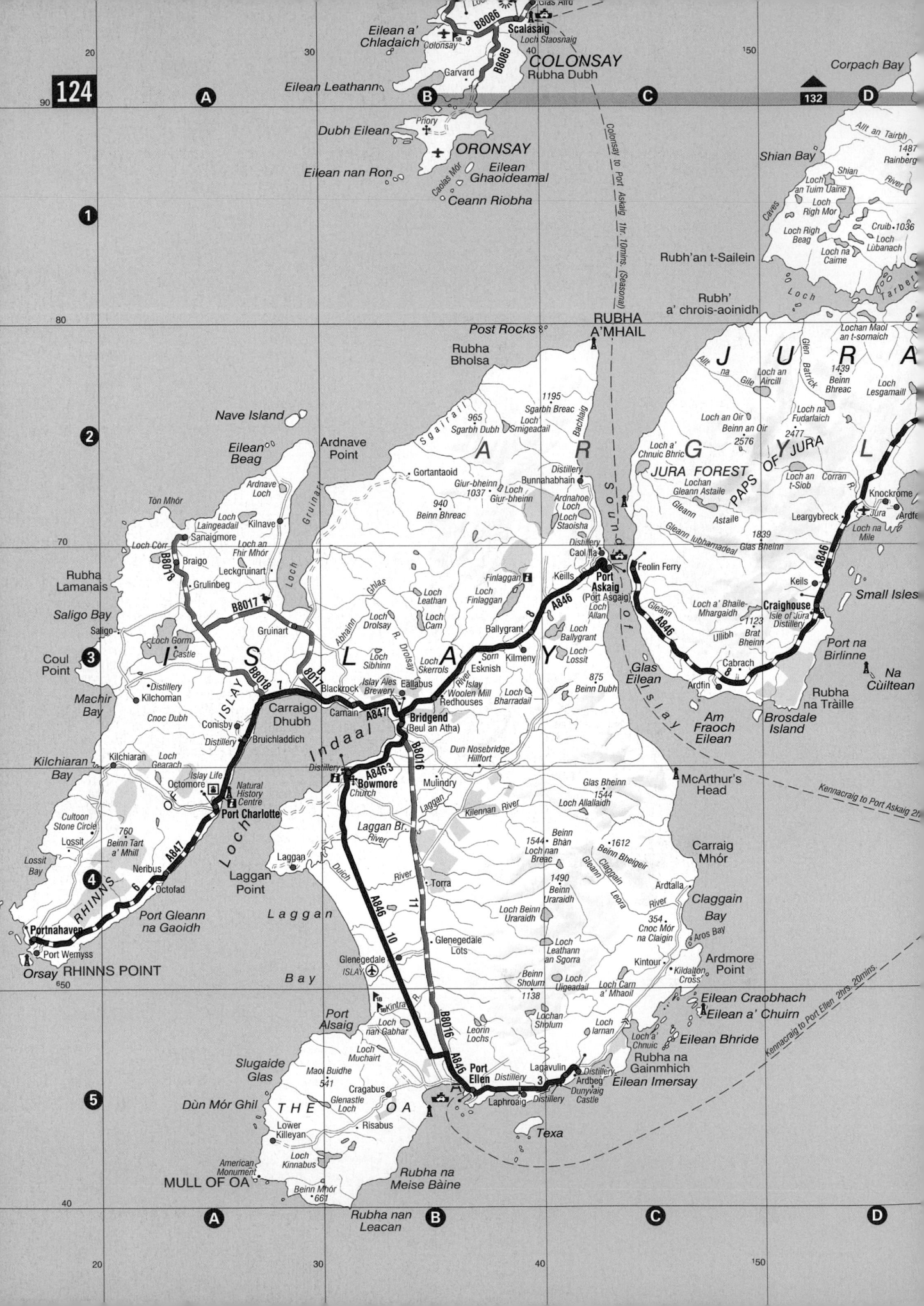

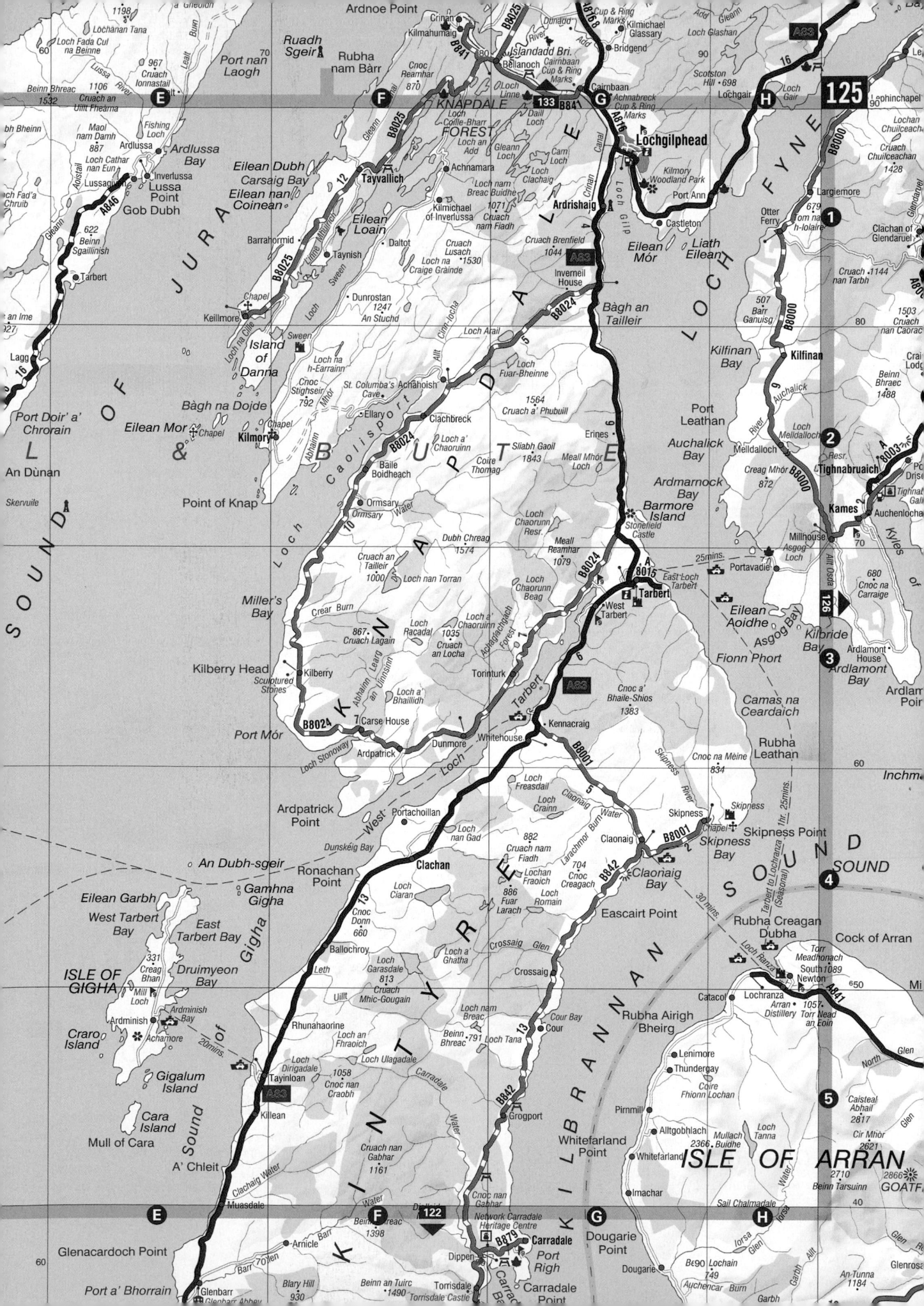

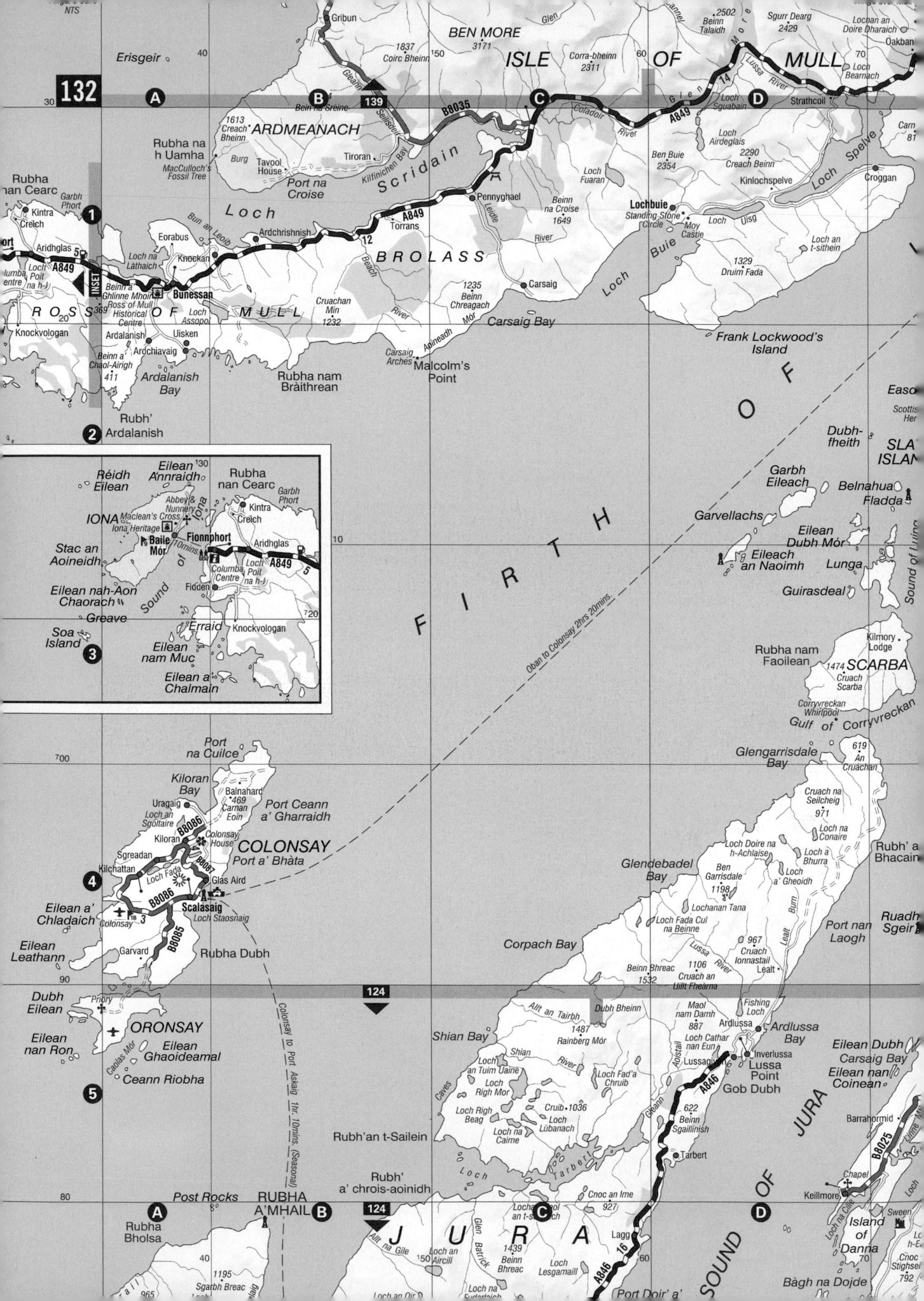

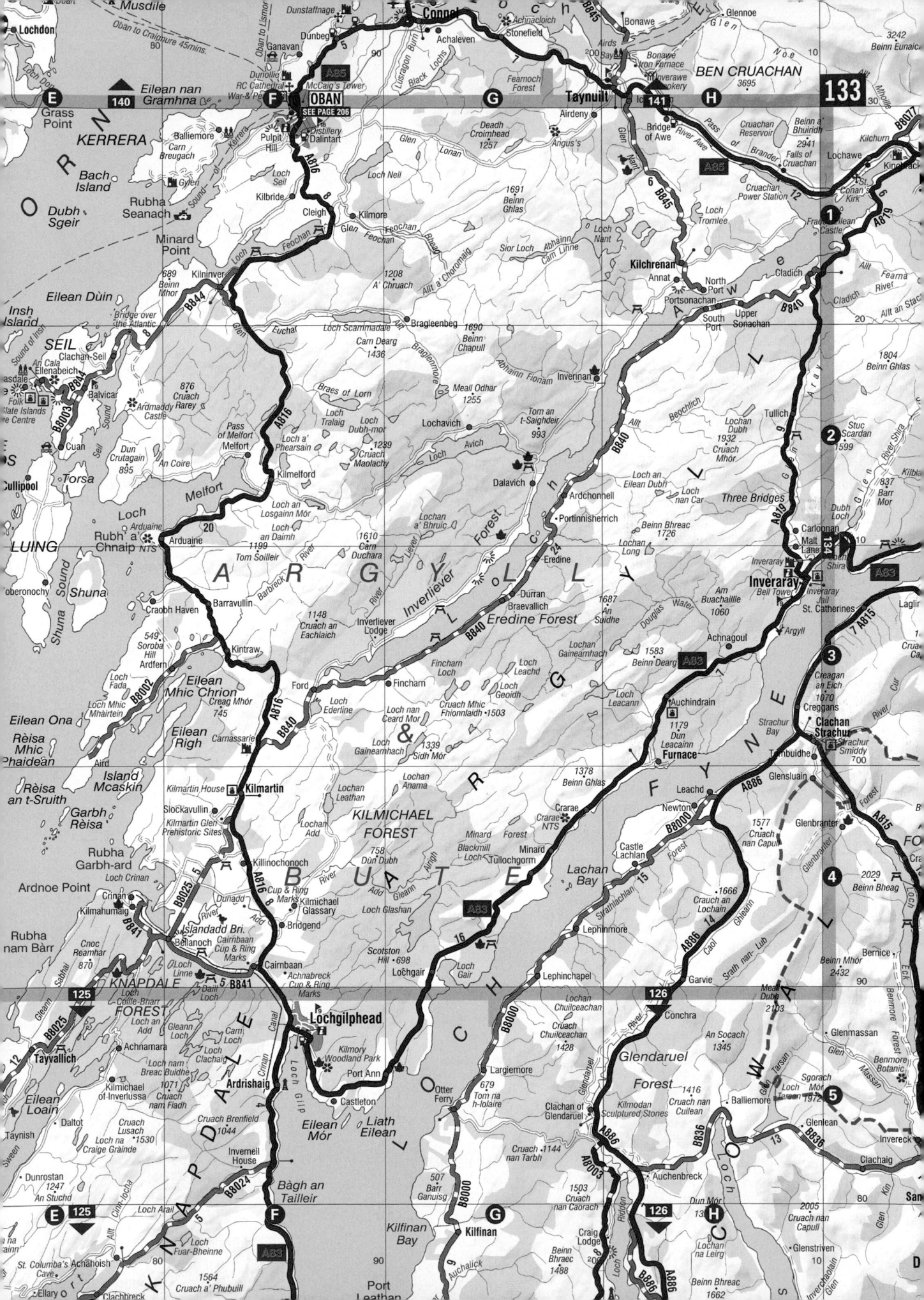

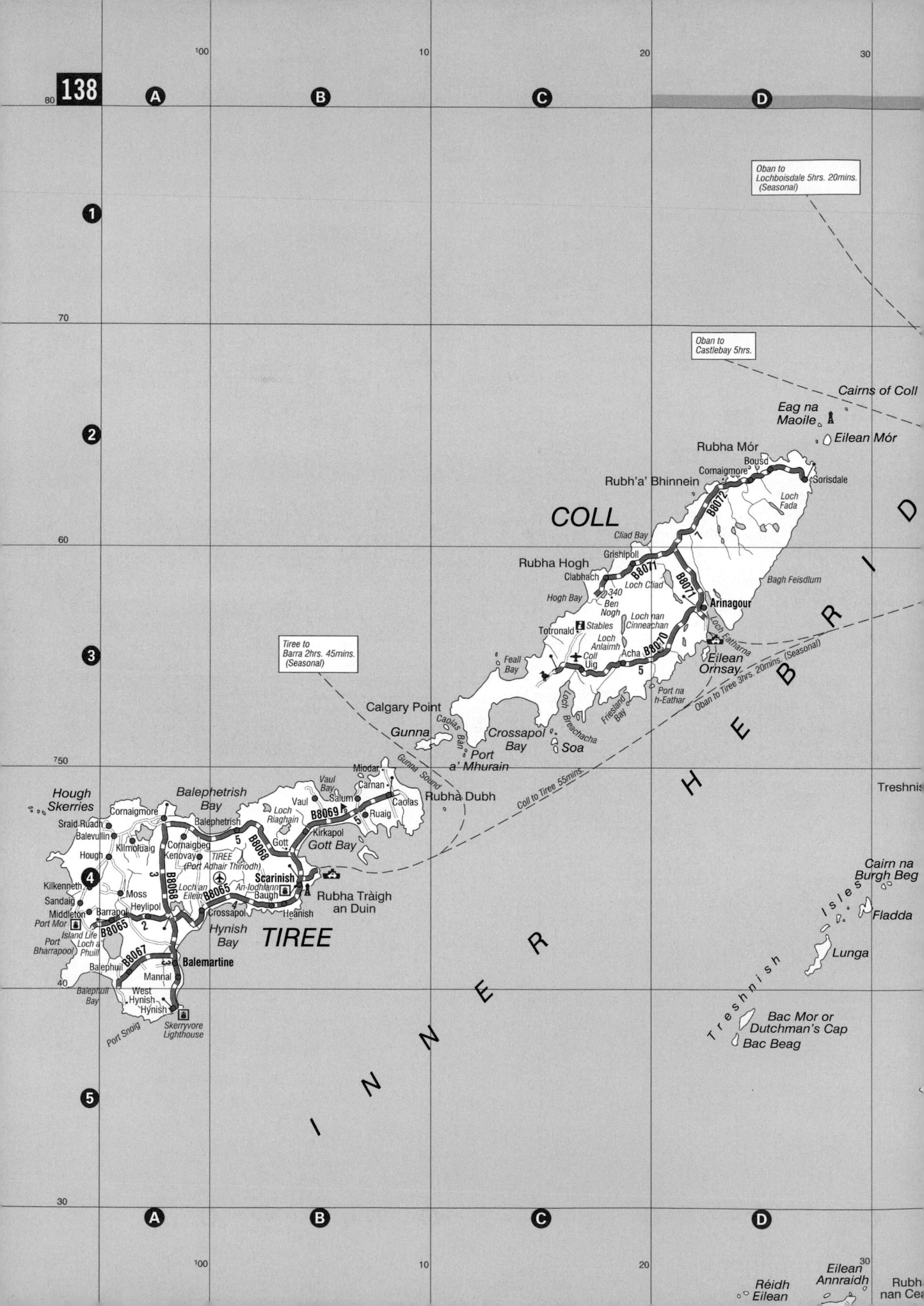

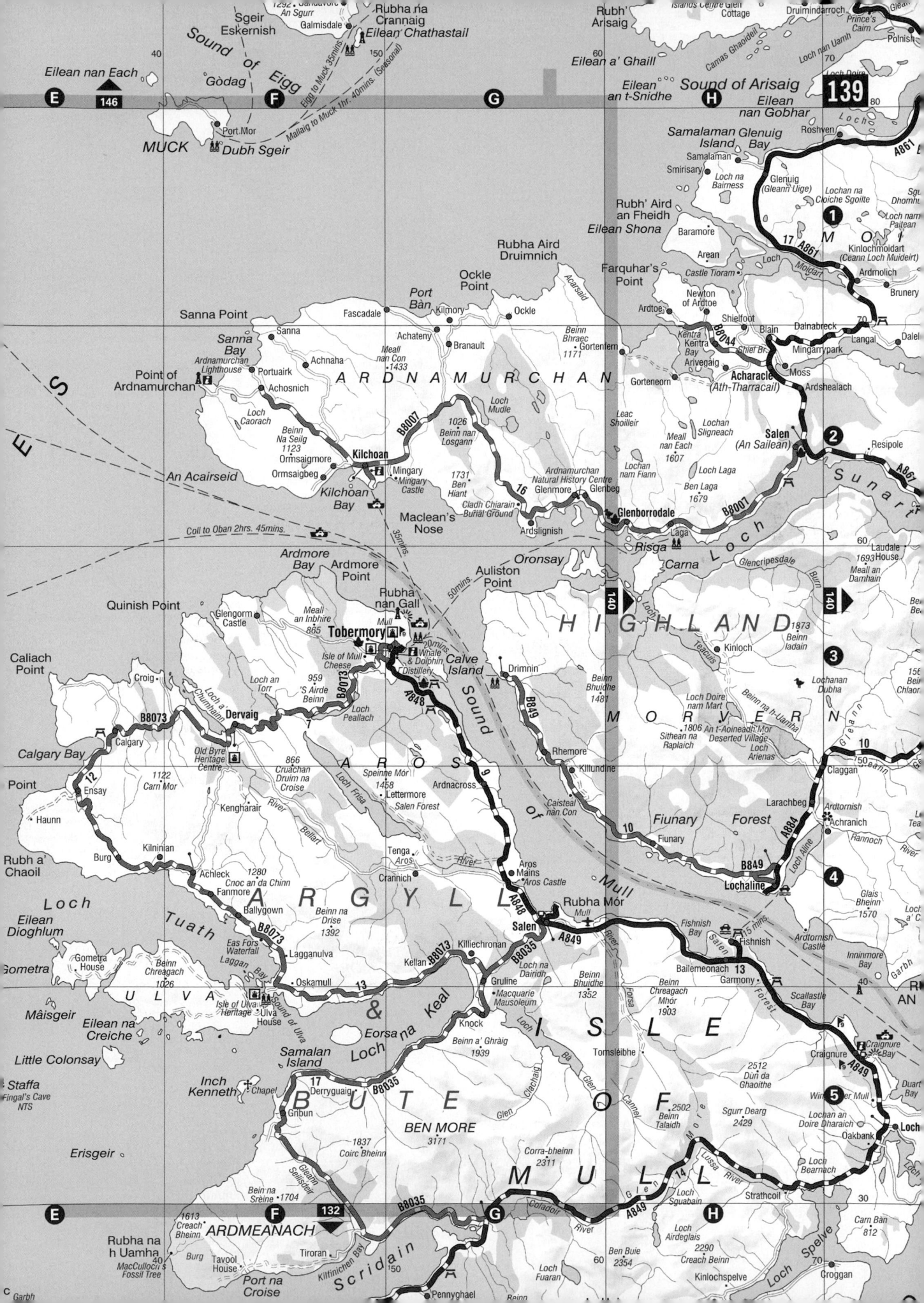

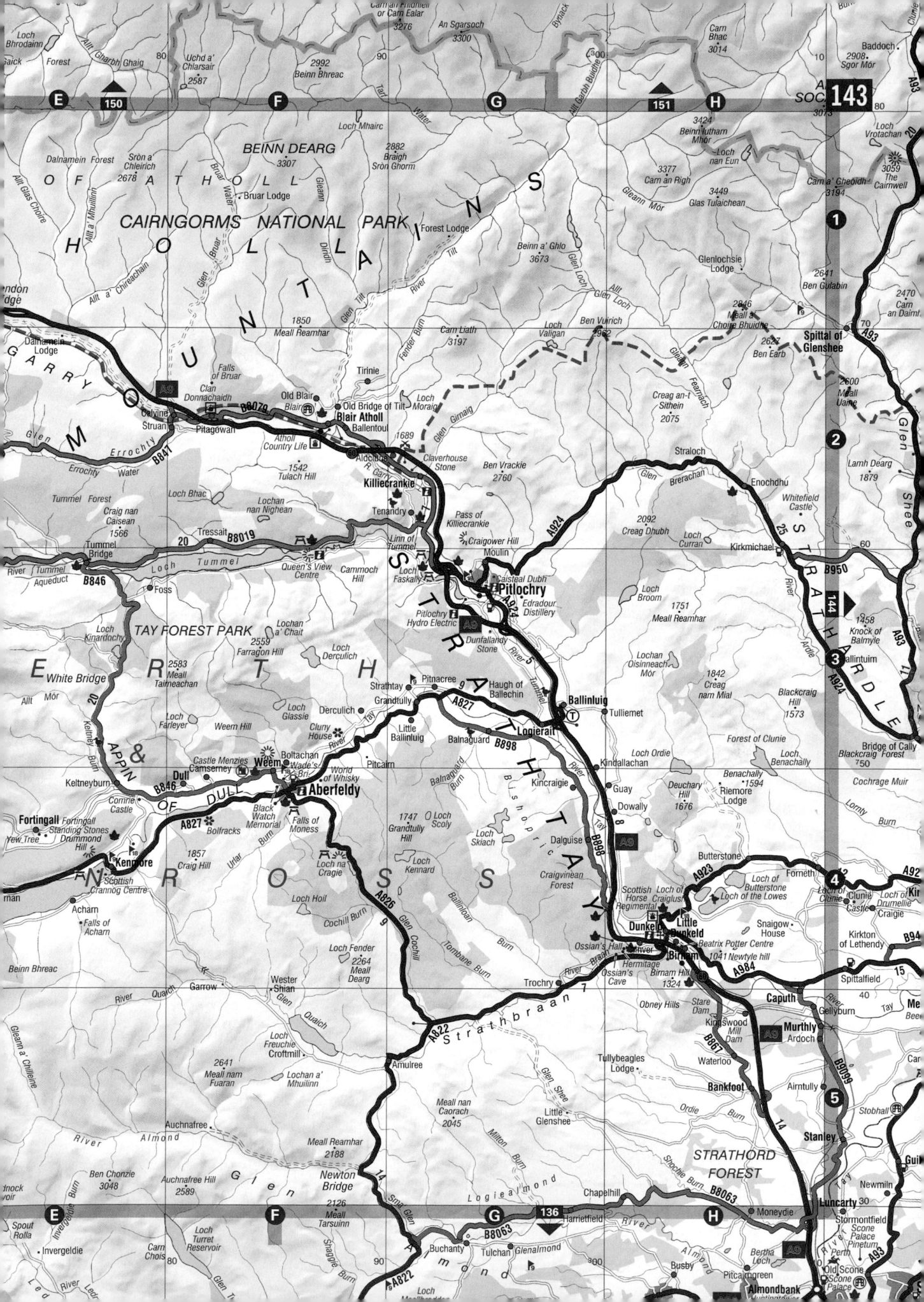

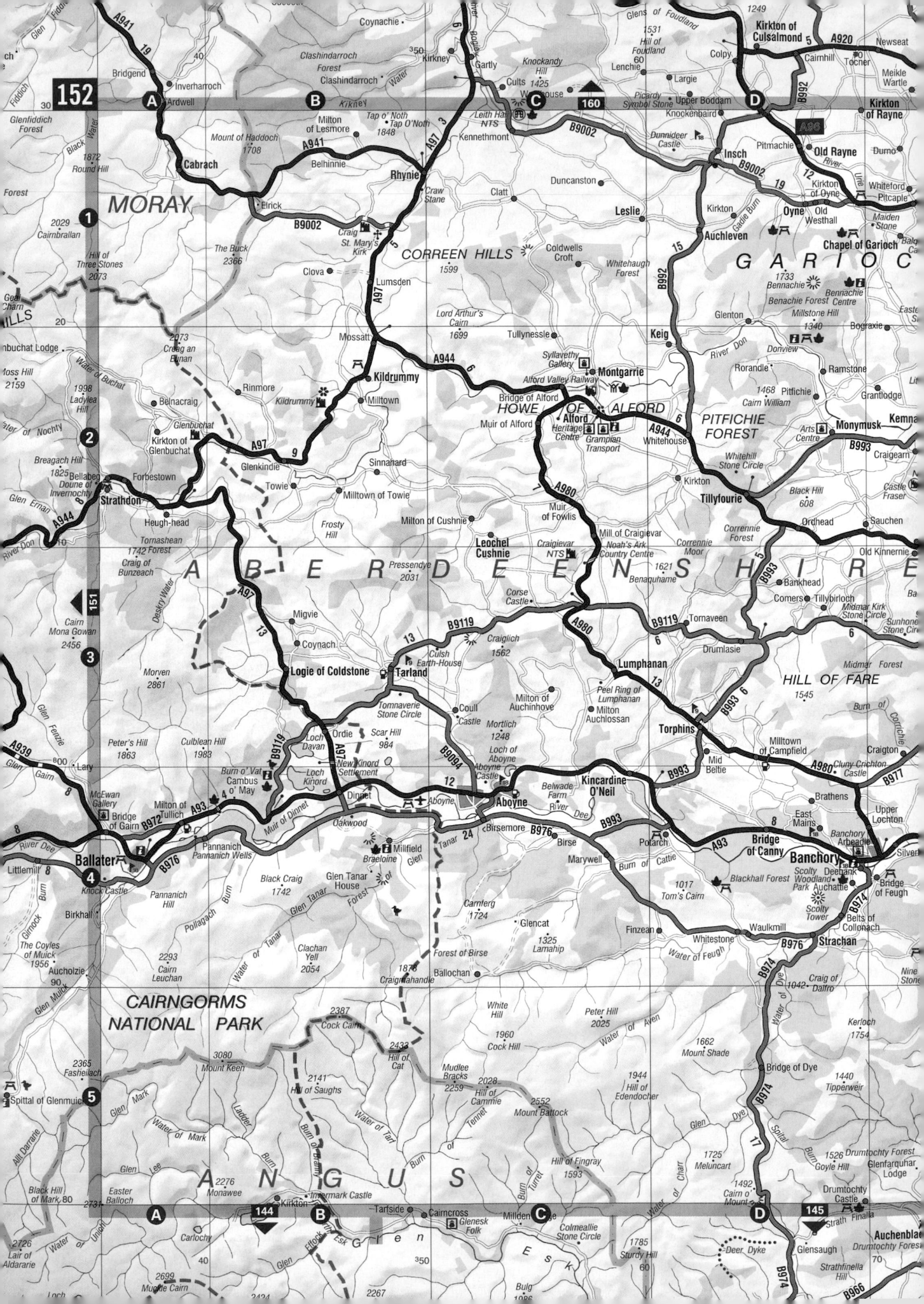

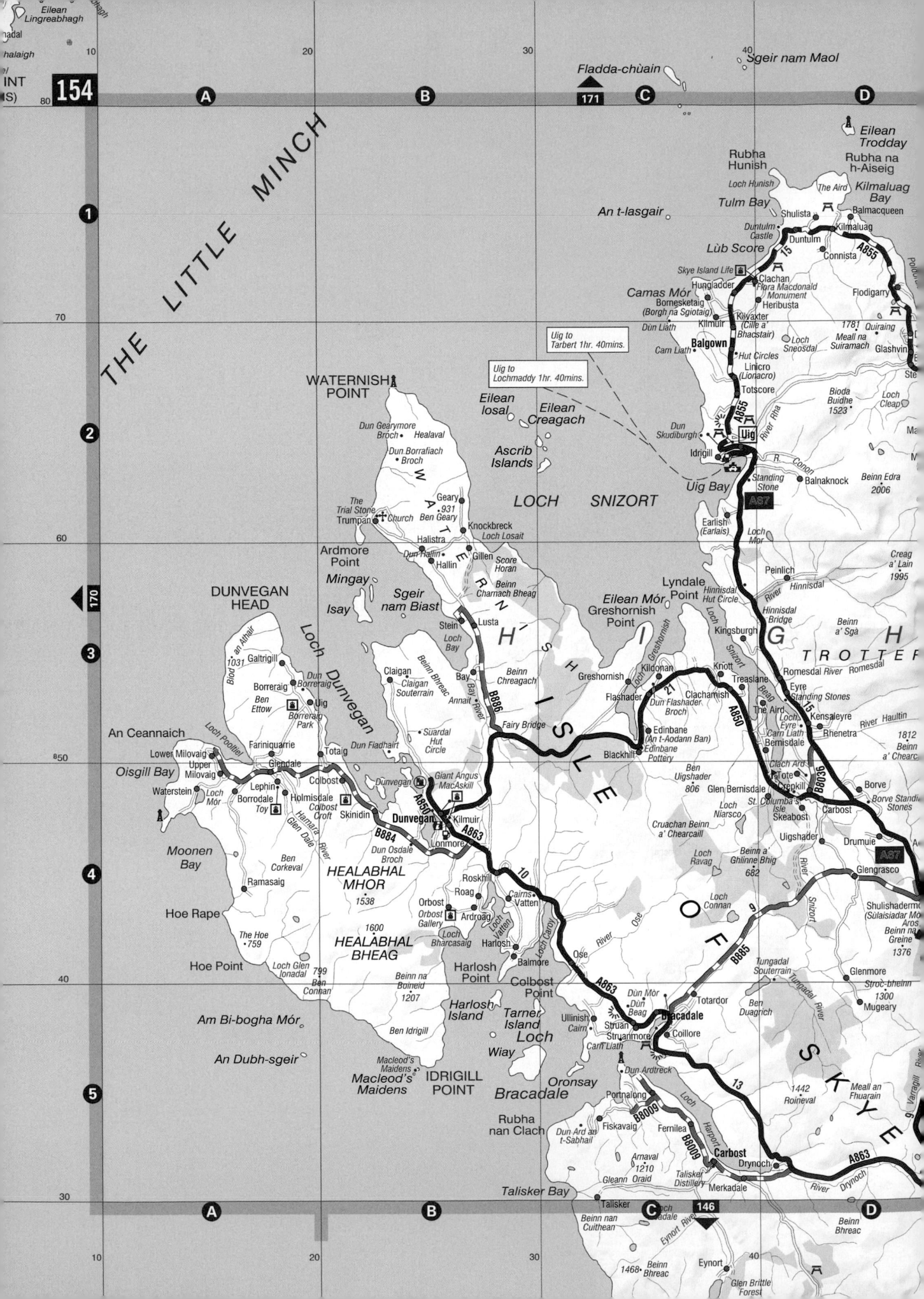

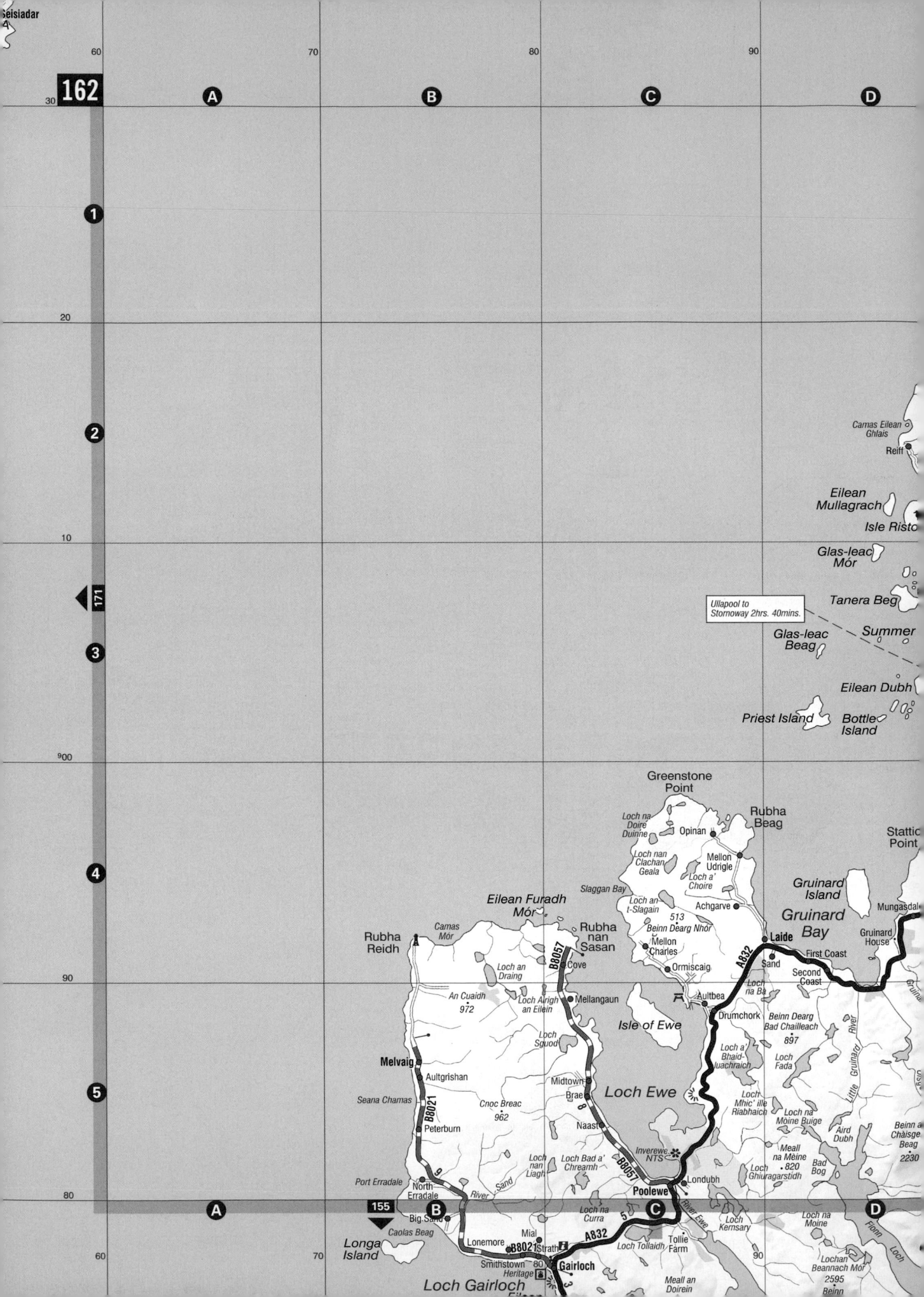

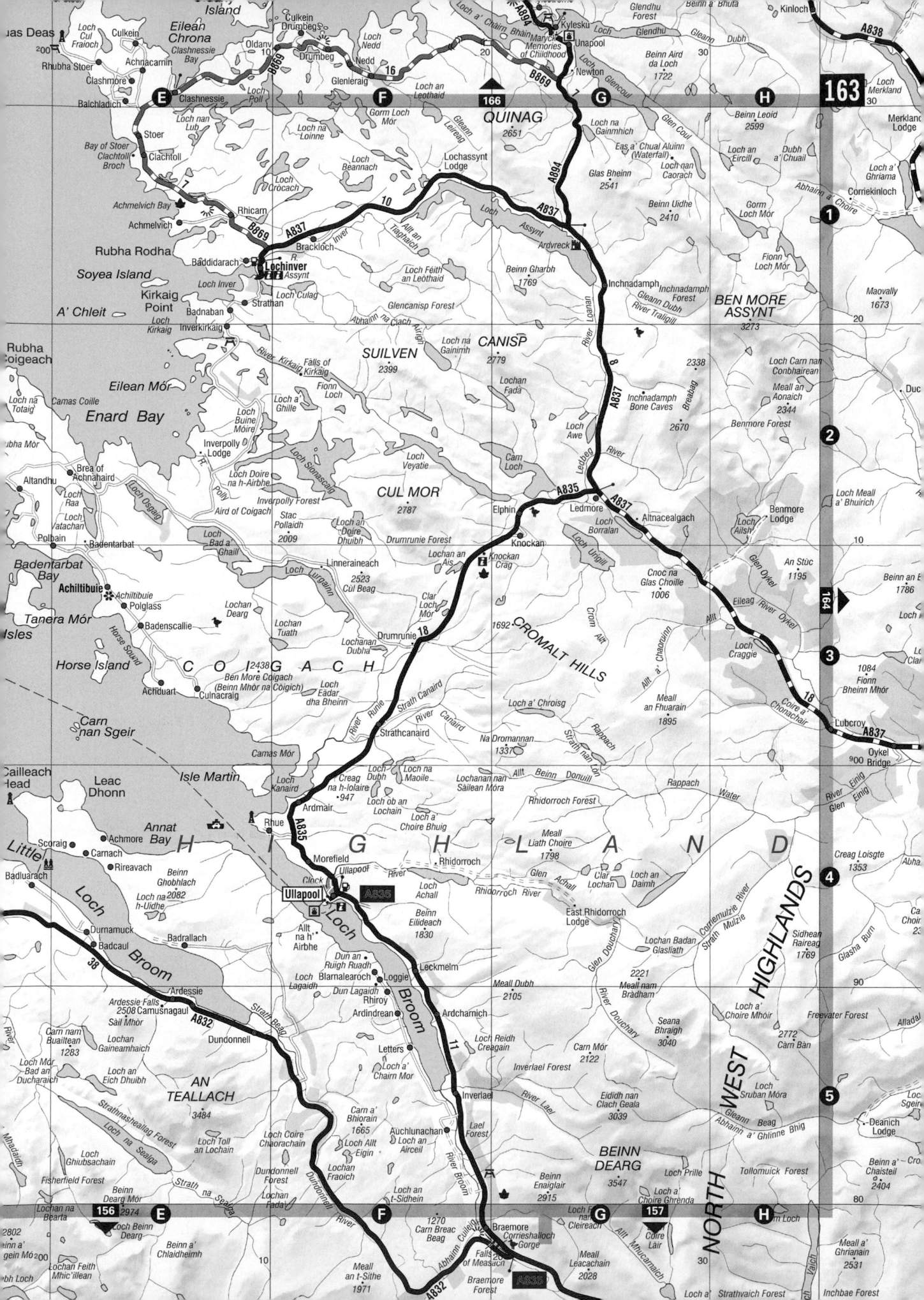

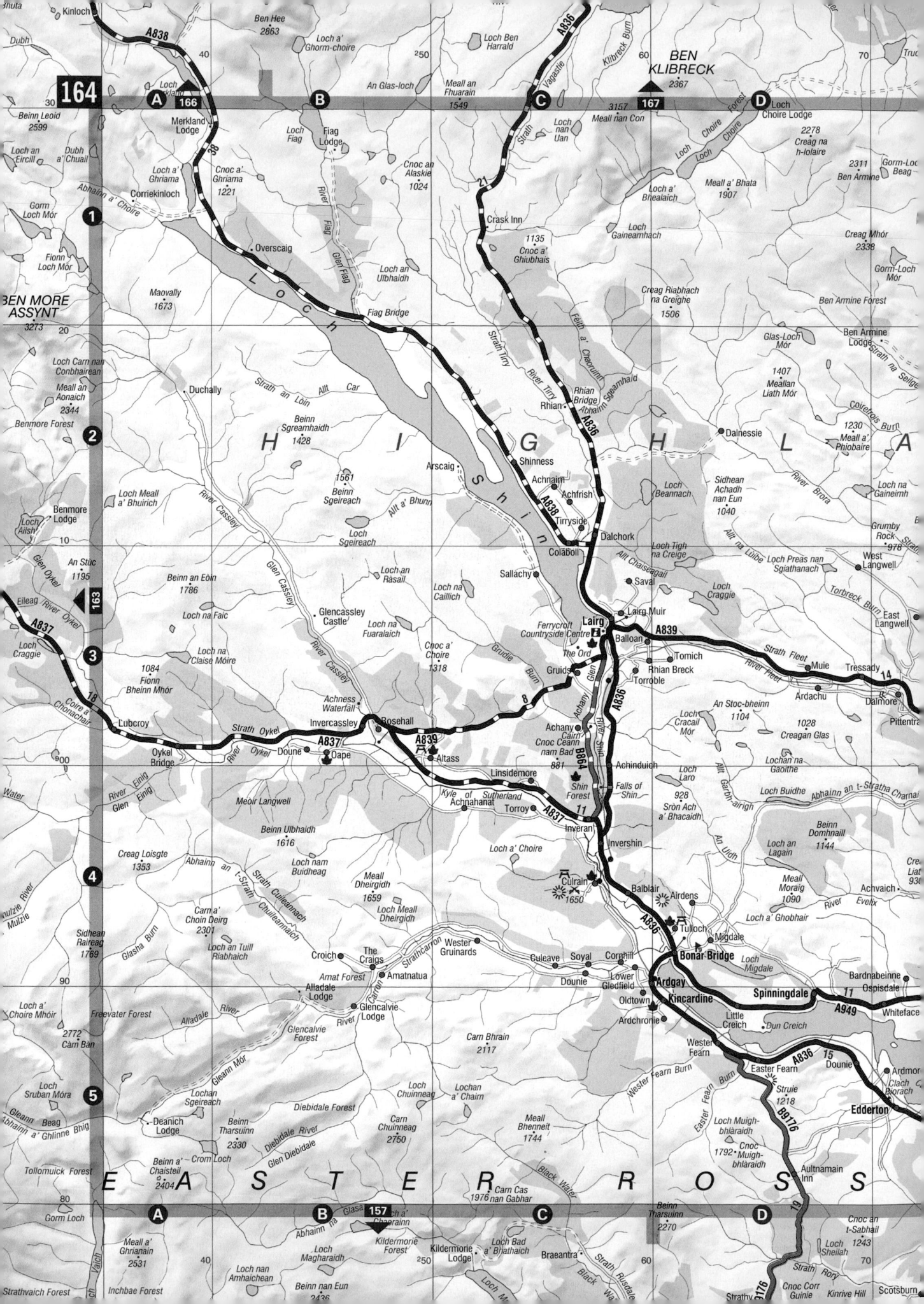

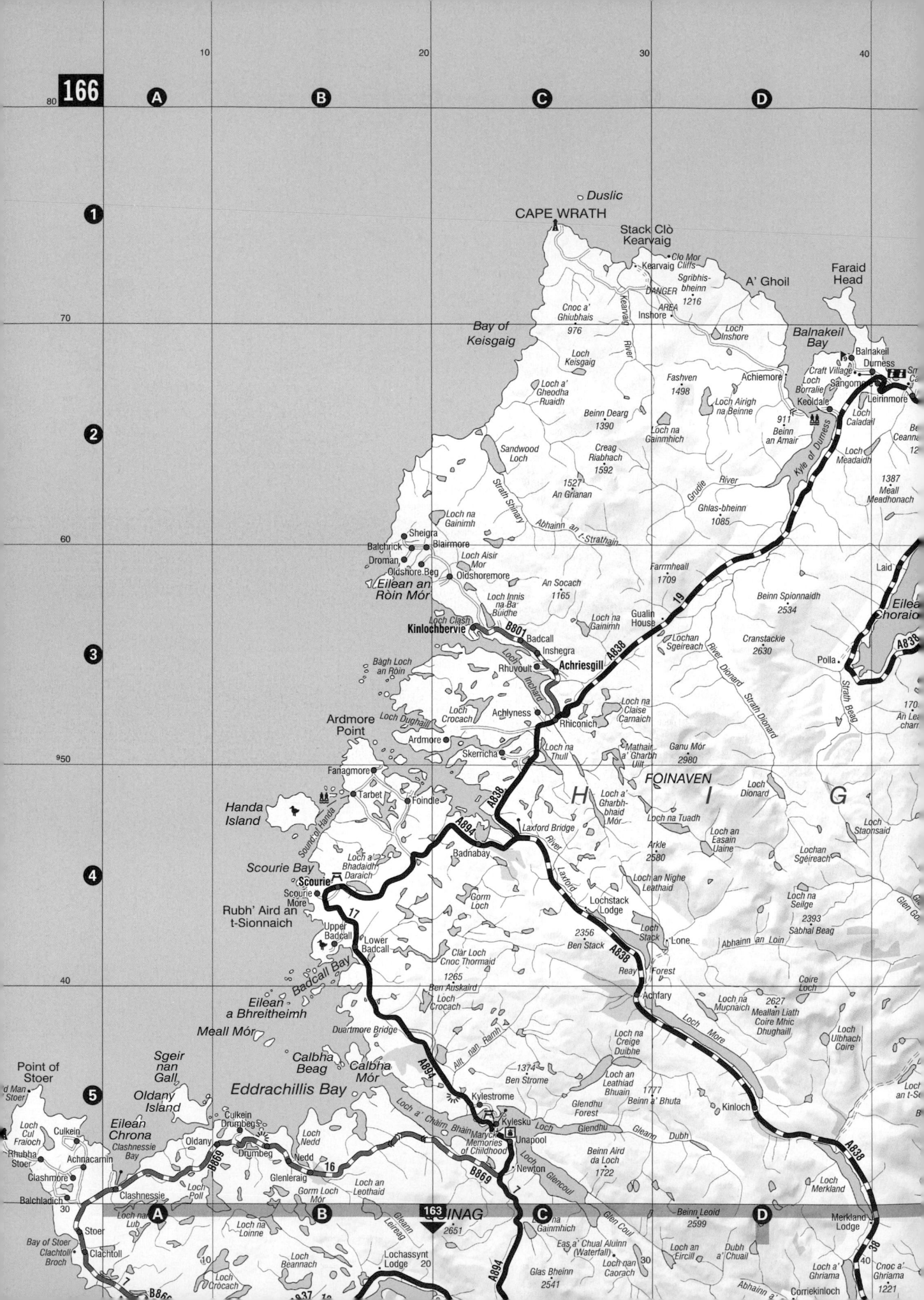

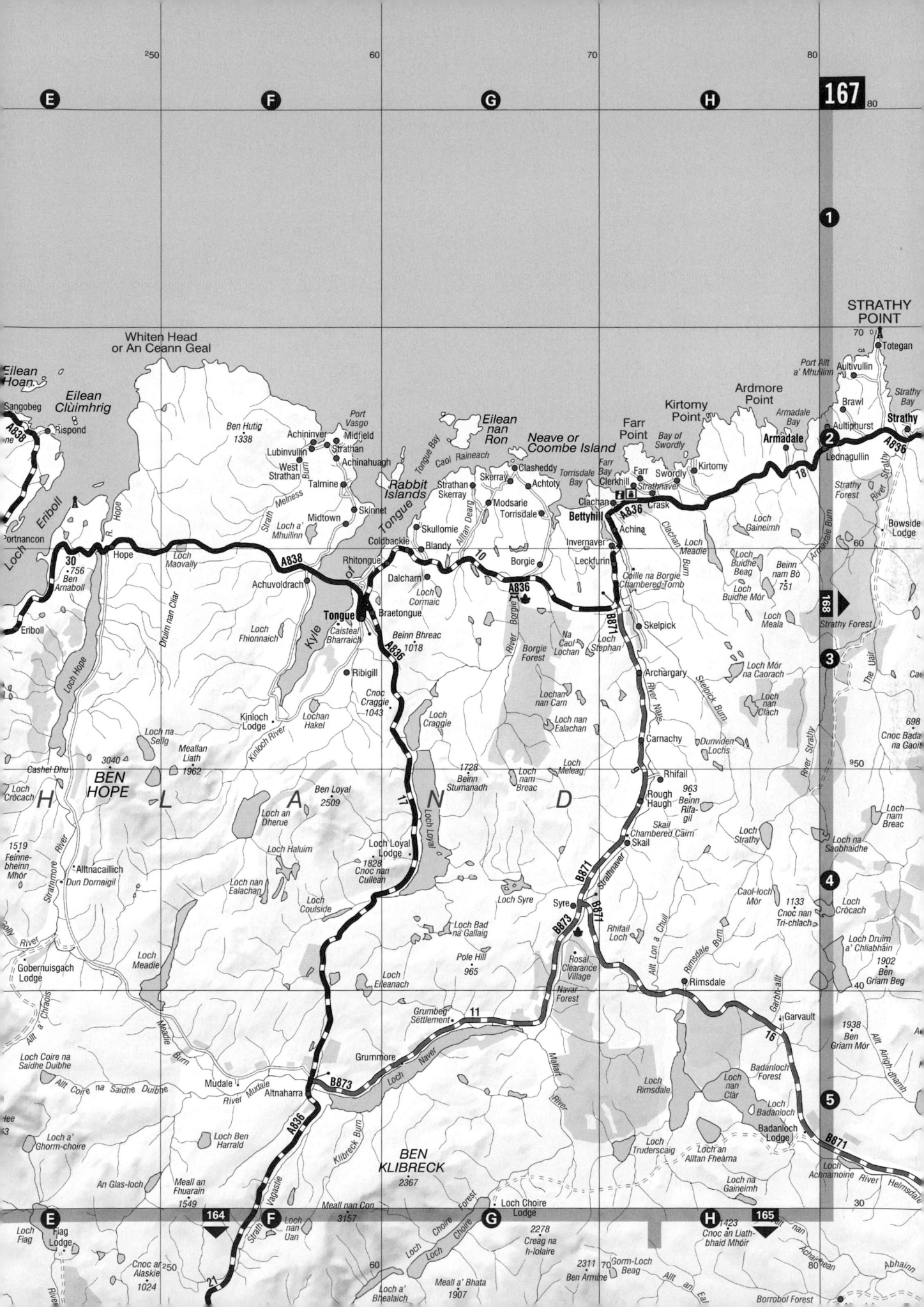

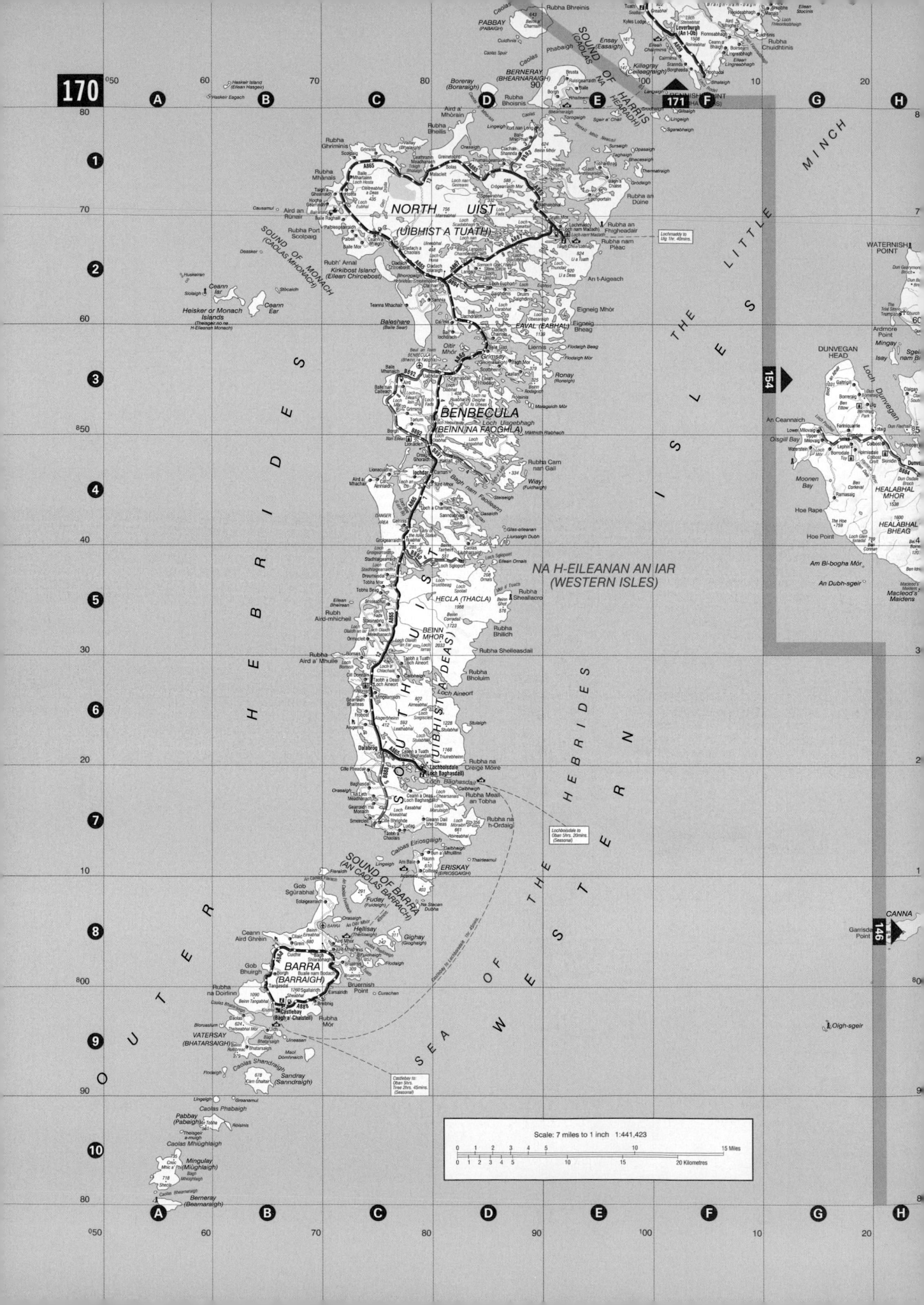

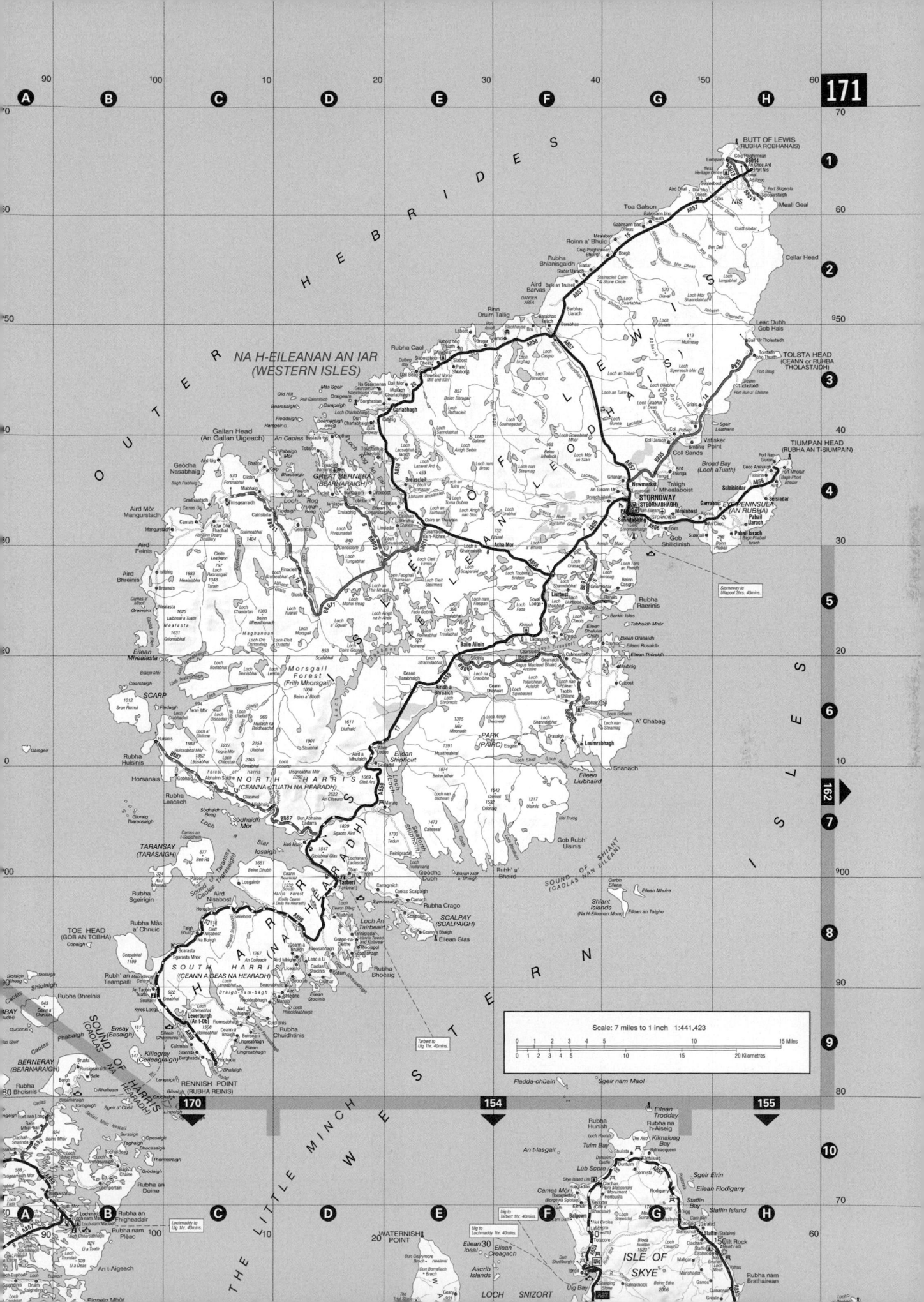

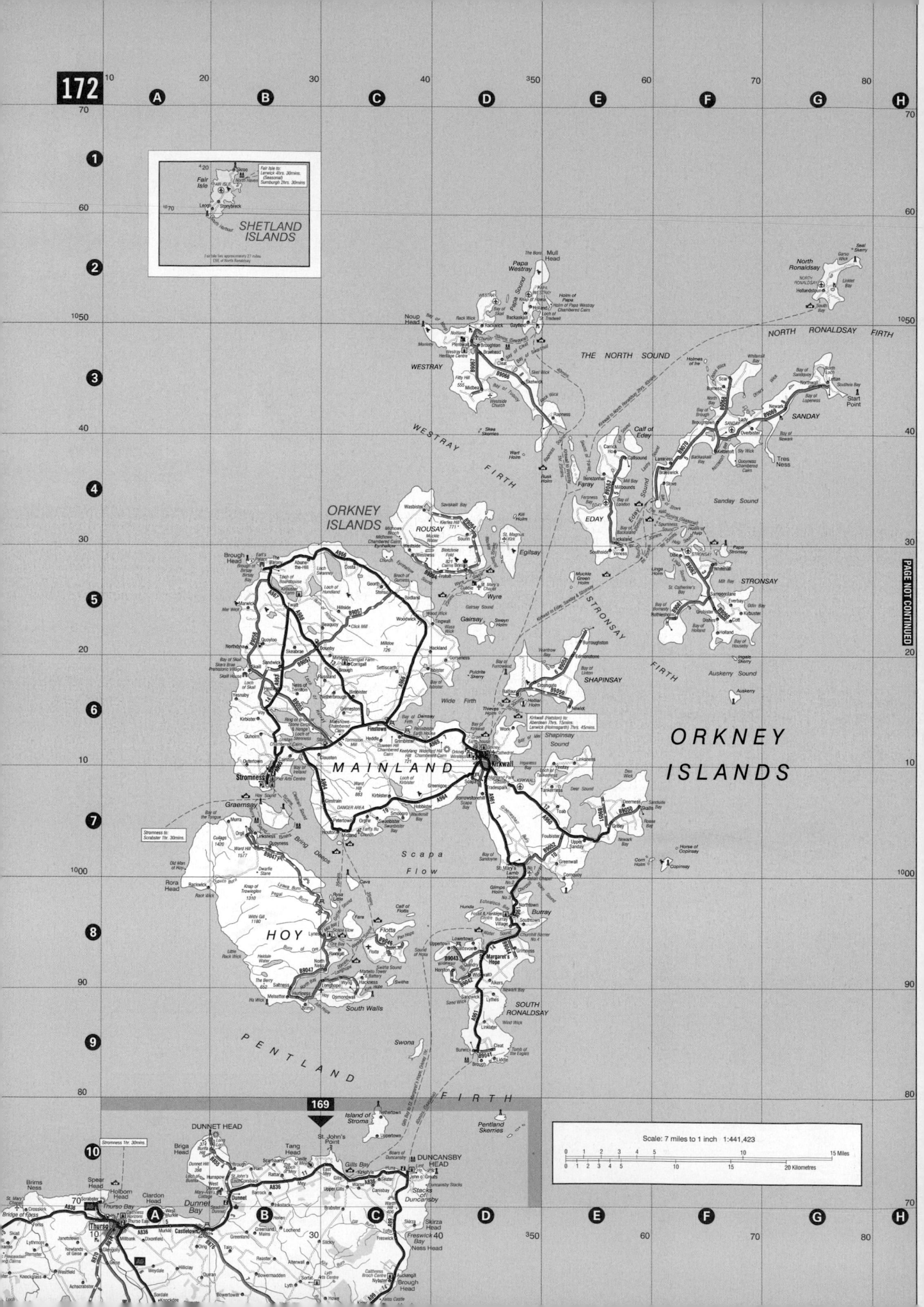

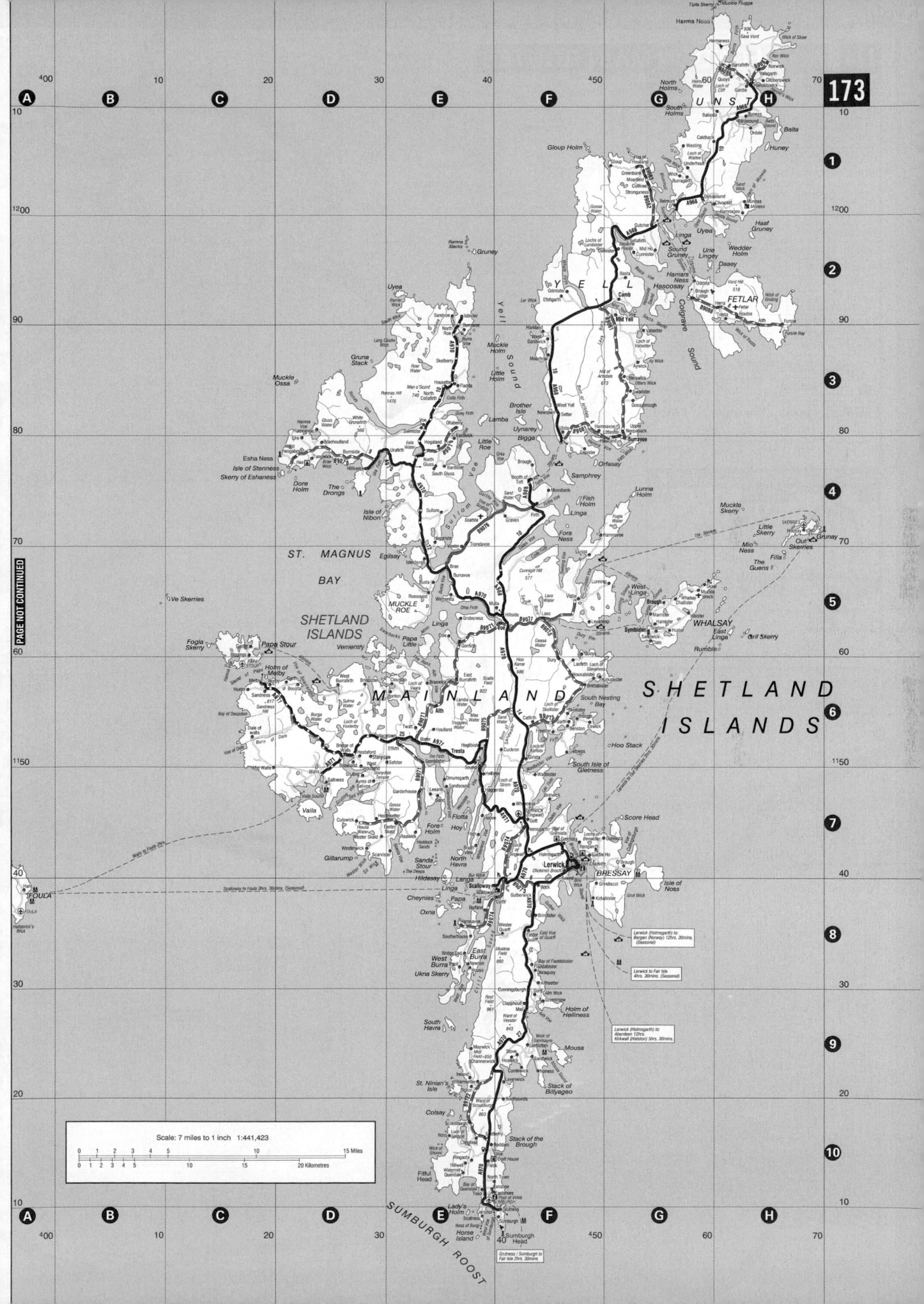

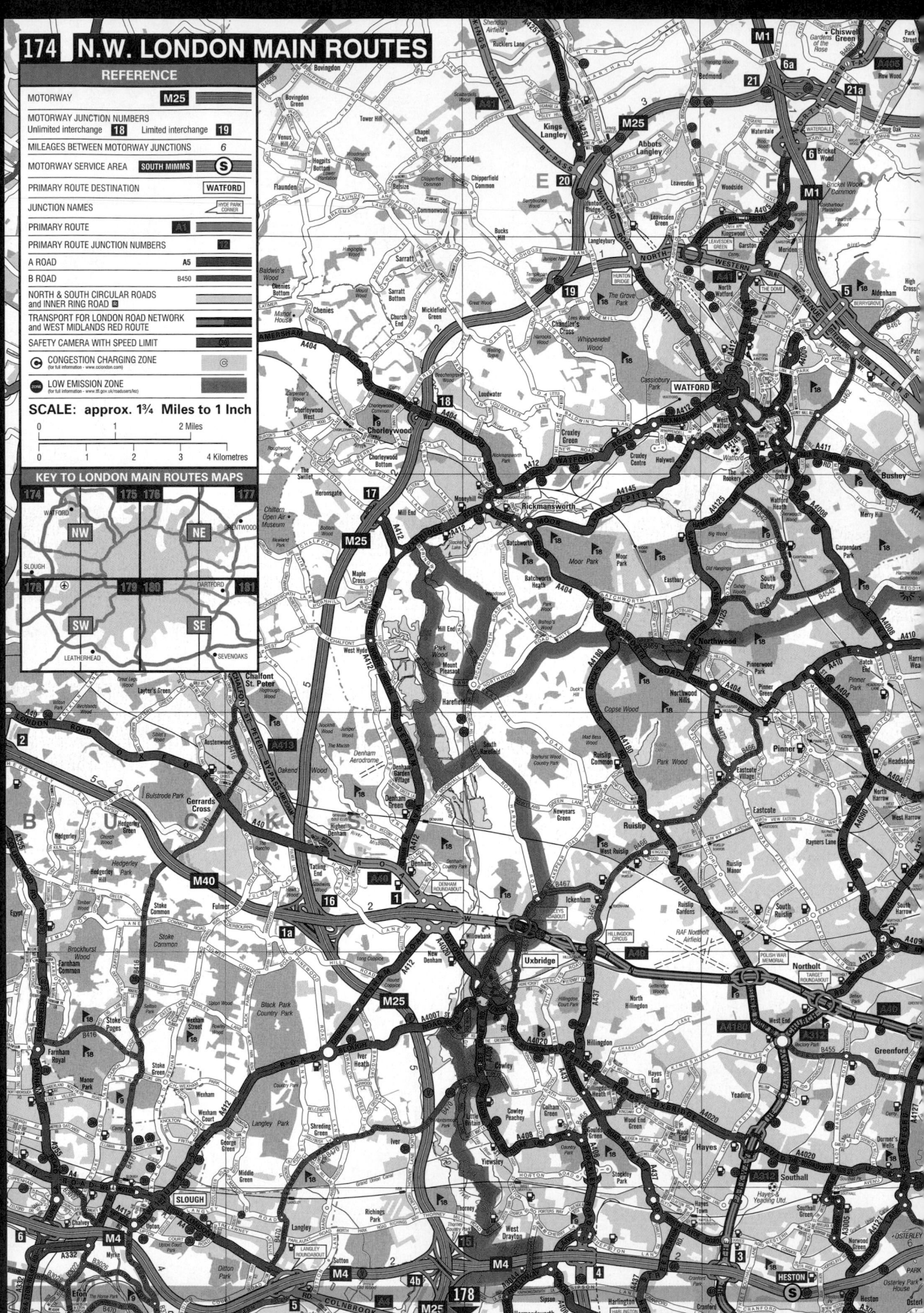

REFERENCE

MOTORWAY	M25
MOTORWAY JUNCTION NUMBERS Unlimited interchange **18** Limited interchange **19**	
MILEAGES BETWEEN MOTORWAY JUNCTIONS	6
MOTORWAY SERVICE AREA	SOUTH MIMMS Ⓢ
PRIMARY ROUTE DESTINATION	WATFORD
JUNCTION NAMES	HYDE PARK CORNER
PRIMARY ROUTE	A1
PRIMARY ROUTE JUNCTION NUMBERS	12
A ROAD	A5
B ROAD	B450
NORTH & SOUTH CIRCULAR ROADS and INNER RING ROAD Ⓡ	
TRANSPORT FOR LONDON ROAD NETWORK and WEST MIDLANDS RED ROUTE	
SAFETY CAMERA WITH SPEED LIMIT	60
Ⓒ CONGESTION CHARGING ZONE (for full information - www.cclondon.com)	Ⓒ
● ZONE LOW EMISSION ZONE (for full information - www.tfl.gov.uk/roadusers/lez)	

SCALE: approx. 1¾ Miles to 1 Inch

0   1   2 Miles

0   1   2   3   4 Kilometres

KEY TO LONDON MAIN ROUTES MAPS

174	175	176	177
WATFORD NW		NE	BRENTWOOD
SLOUGH			
178	179	180	181
SW		SE	DARTFORD
LEATHERHEAD			SEVENOAKS

S.W. LONDON MAIN ROUTES

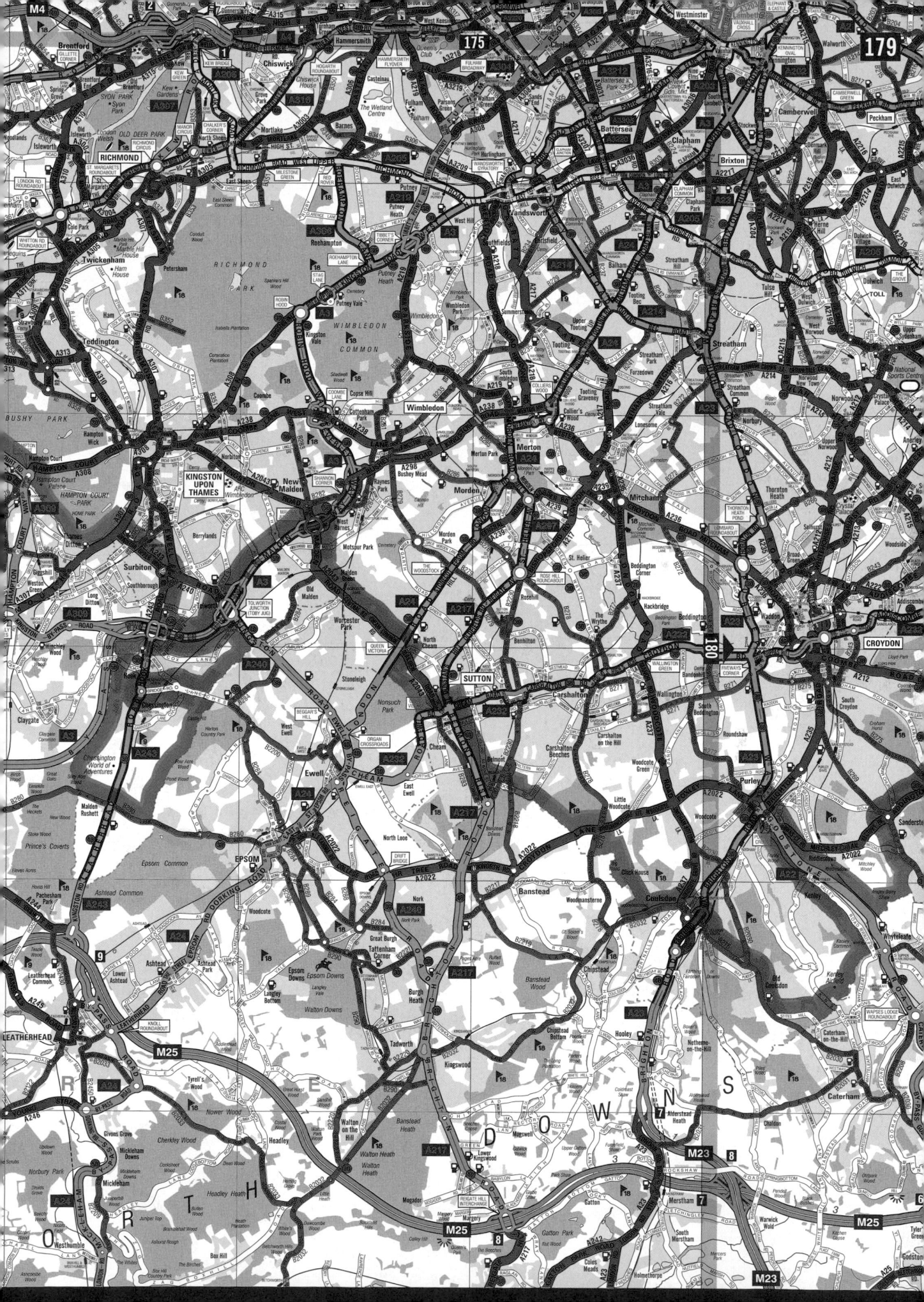

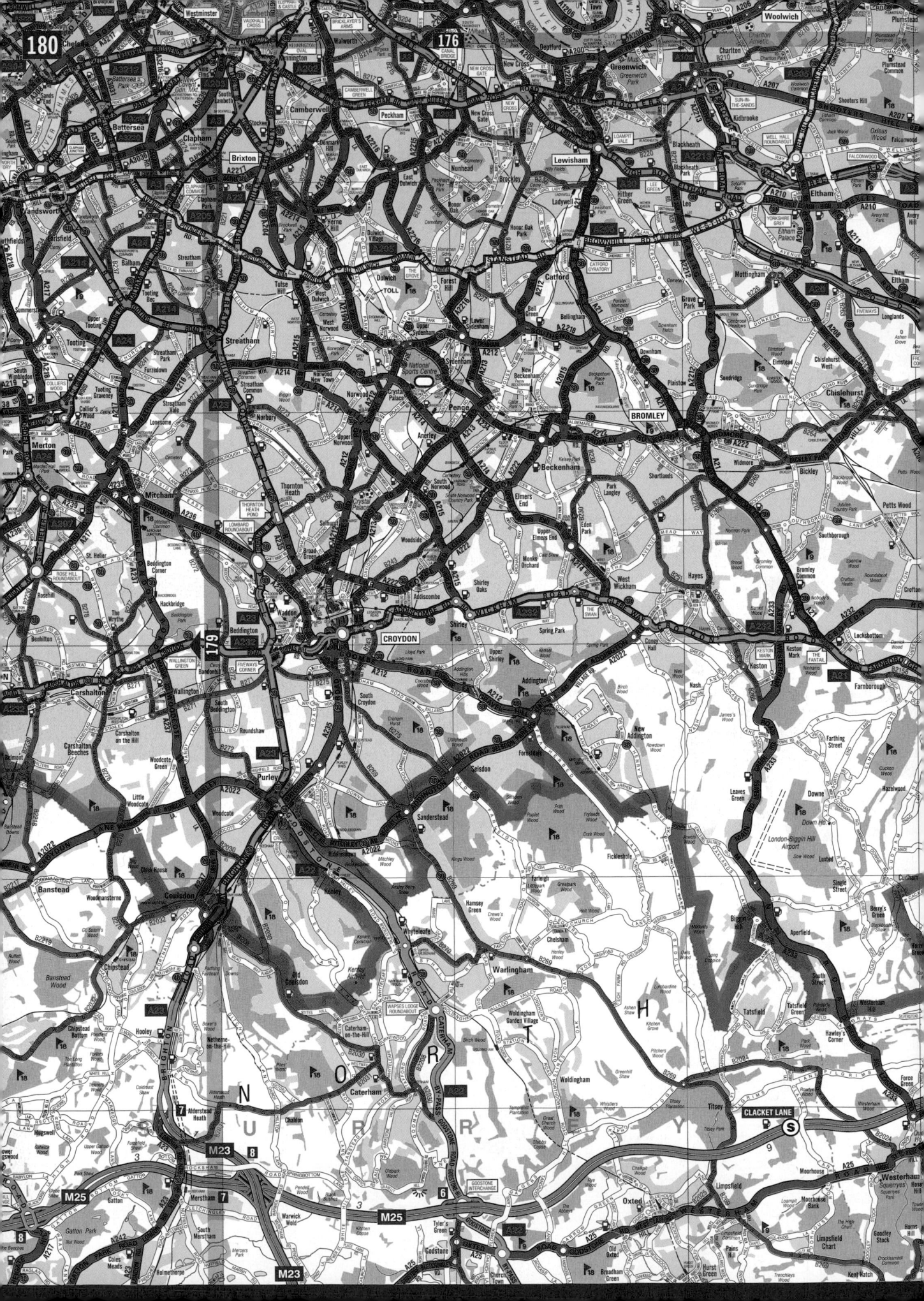

Town Plans

Aberdeen............................187
Aberystwyth.......................187
Ayr.....................................187
Bath...................................187
Bedford..............................188
Birmingham........................188
Blackpool...........................188
Bournemouth......................190
Bradford.............................190
Brighton & Hove.................189
Bristol................................189
Caernarfon.........................190
Cambridge..........................191
Canterbury.........................190
Cardiff (Caerdydd)..............191
Carlisle...............................192
Cheltenham........................192
Chester...............................192
Coventry.............................192
Derby..................................193
Dover..................................193
Dumfries.............................193
Dundee...............................194
Durham...............................194
Eastbourne.........................195
Edinburgh...........................194
Exeter.................................195
Folkestone..........................195
Glasgow..............................196
Gloucester..........................196
Great Yarmouth..................196
Guildford.............................197
Harrogate...........................197
Hereford.............................197
Inverness............................198
Ipswich...............................198
Kilmarnock.........................198
Kingston upon Hull.............199
Leeds..................................199
Leicester.............................200
Lincoln................................198
Liverpool.............................200
London....................202-203
Luton..................................201
Manchester.........................201
Medway Towns....................204
Middlesbrough....................201
Milton Keynes.....................204
Newcastle upon Tyne..........205
Newport (Casnewydd).........205
Northampton.......................206
Norwich..............................205
Nottingham.........................206
Oban...................................206
Oxford.................................207
Paisley................................207
Perth...................................207
Peterborough......................208
Plymouth.............................208
Portsmouth.........................209
Preston...............................208
Reading...............................209
St Andrews.........................209
Salisbury.............................210
Sheffield..............................210
Shrewsbury.........................210
Southampton......................211
Stirling................................211
Stoke-on-Trent....................211
Stratford-upon-Avon............212
Sunderland.........................212
Swansea (Abertawe)...........212
Swindon..............................212
Taunton..............................213
Winchester..........................213
Windsor..............................213
Wolverhampton...................213
Worcester...........................214
Wrexham (Wrecsam)...........214
York....................................214

Port Plans 🛳

Harwich..............................215
Kingston upon Hull..............215
Newcastle upon Tyne...........215
Newhaven...........................215
Pembroke Dock (Doc Penfro).......215
Poole..................................215
Portsmouth.........................215
Weymouth...........................215

Airport Plans ✈

Birmingham International............216
East Midlands.......................216
Glasgow...............................216
London Gatwick.....................216
London Heathrow...................216
London Luton........................216
London Stansted....................216
Manchester International...........216

Motorway Autoroute Autobahn	M1
Motorway Under Construction Autoroute en construction Autobahn im Bau	
Motorway Proposed Autoroute prévue Geplante Autobahn	
Motorway Junctions with Numbers Unlimited Interchange ▣ Limited Interchange ▣ Autoroute échangeur numéroté Echangeur complet Echangeur partiel Autobahnanschlußstelle mit Nummer Unbeschränkter Fahrtrichtungswechsel Beschränkter Fahrtrichtungswechsel	
Primary Route Route à grande circulation Hauptverkehrsstraße	A41
Dual Carriageways (A & B roads) Route à double chaussées séparées (route A & B) Zweispurige Schnellstraße (A- und B- Straßen)	
Class A Road Route de type A A-Straße	A129
Class B Road Route de type B B-Straße	B177
Major Roads Under Construction Route prioritaire en construction Hauptverkehrsstaße im Bau	
Major Roads Proposed Route prioritaire prévue Geplante Hauptverkehrsstaße	
Minor Roads Route secondaire Nebenstraße	
Safety Camera Radars de contrôle de vitesse Sicherheitskamera	
Restricted Access Accès réglementé Beschränkte Zufahrt	
Pedestrianized Road & Main Footway Rue piétonne et chemin réservé aux piétons Fußgängerstraße und Fußweg	
One Way Streets Sens unique Einbahnstraße	
Fuel Station Station service Tankstelle	
Toll Barrière de péage Gebührenpflichtig	TOLL
Railway & Station Voie ferrée et gare Eisenbahnlinie und Bahnhof	
Underground / Metro & DLR Station Station de métro et DLR U-Bahnstation und DLR-Station	DLR
Level Crossing & Tunnel Passage à niveau et tunnel Bahnübergang und Tunnel	
Tram Stop & One Way Tram Stop Arrêt de tramway Straßenbahnhaltestelle	
Built-up Area Agglomération Geschloßene Ortschaft	
Abbey, Cathedral, Priory etc Abbaye, cathédrale, prieuré etc Abtei, Kathedrale, Kloster usw	✝
Airport Aéroport Flughafen	✈

Bus Station Gare routière Bushaltestelle	
Car Park (selection of) Sélection de parkings Auswahl von Parkplatz	P
Church Eglise Kirche	†
City Wall Murs d'enceinte Stadtmauer	
Congestion Charging Zone Zone de péage urbain City-Maut Zone	
Ferry (vehicular) (foot only) Bac (véhicules) (piétons) Fähre (autos) (nur für Personen)	
Golf Course Terrain de golf Golfplatz	⚑9 ⚑18
Heliport Héliport Hubschrauberlandeplatz	
Hospital Hôpital Krankenhaus	H
Lighthouse Phare Leuchtturm	
Market Marché Markt	
National Trust Property (open) NT (restricted opening) NT (National Trust for Scotland) NTS NTS National Trust Property (ouvert) (heures d'ouverture) (National Trust for Scotland) National Trust- Eigentum (geöffnet) (beschränkte Öffnungszeit) (National Trust for Scotland)	
Park & Ride Parking relais Auswahl von Parkplatz	P+
Place of Interest Curiosité Sehenswürdigkeit	■
Police Station Commissariat de police Polizeirevier	▲
Post Office Bureau de poste Postamt	★
Shopping Area (main street & precinct) Quartier commerçant (rue et zone principales) Einkaufsviertel (hauptgeschäftsstraße, fußgängerzone)	
Shopmobility Shopmobility Shopmobility	
Toilet Toilettes Toilette	▽
Tourist Information Centre Syndicat d'initiative Information	𝒊
Viewpoint Vue panoramique Aussichtspunkt	
Visitor Information Centre Centre d'information touristique Besucherzentrum	𝒊

Please note: symbols have been enlarged for clarity

ABERDEEN

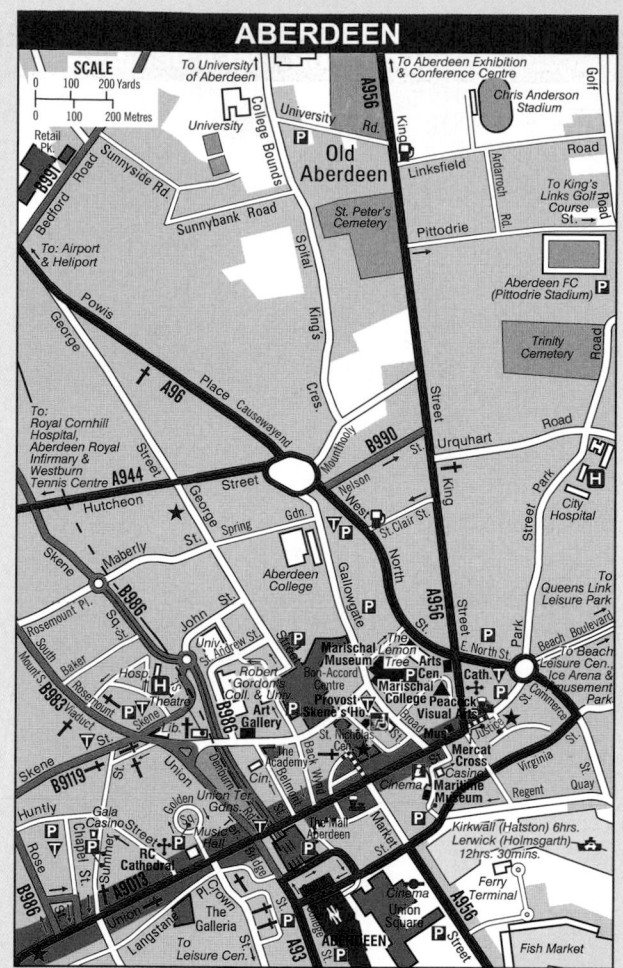

ABERYSTWYTH

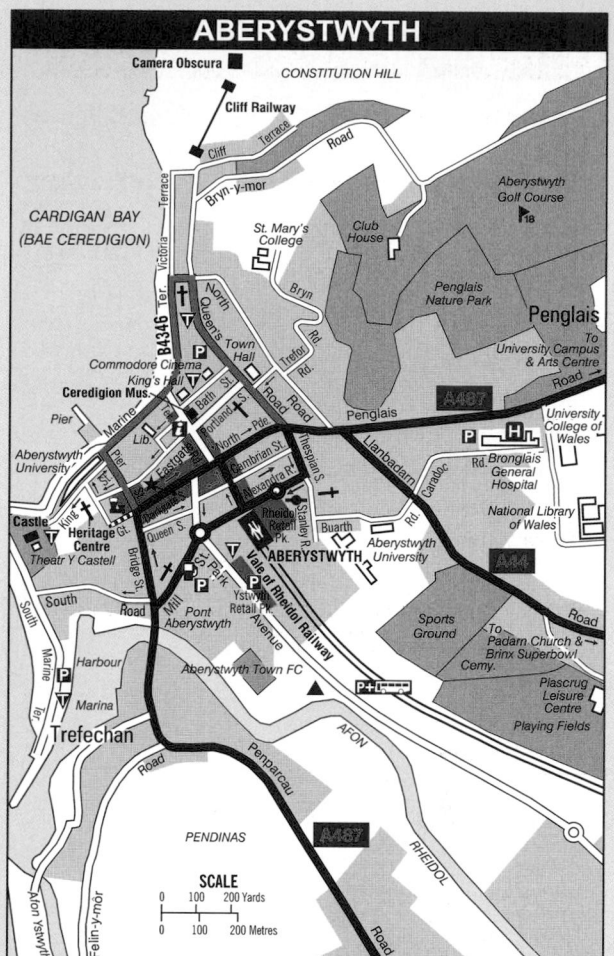

AYR

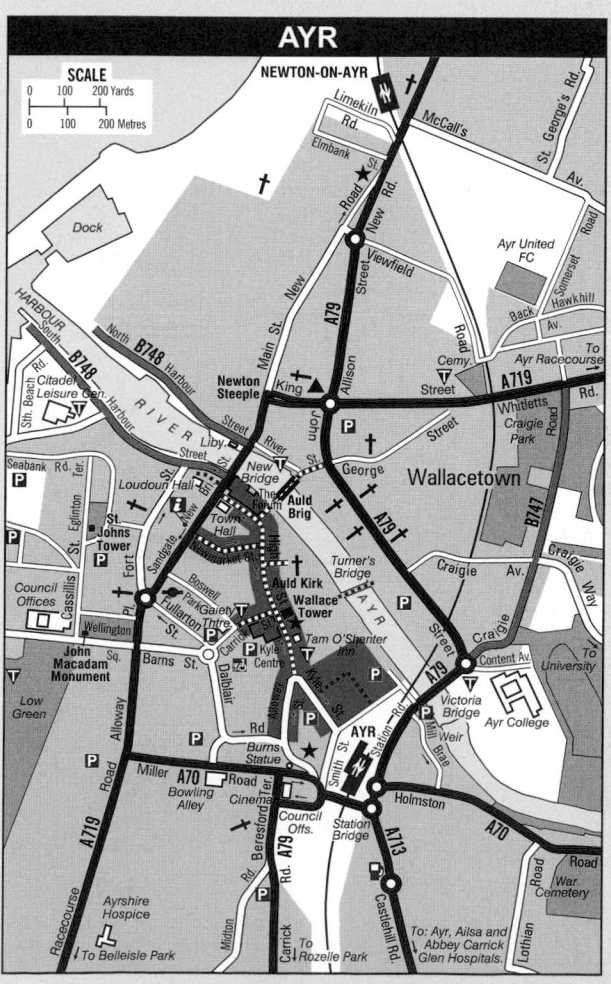

BATH

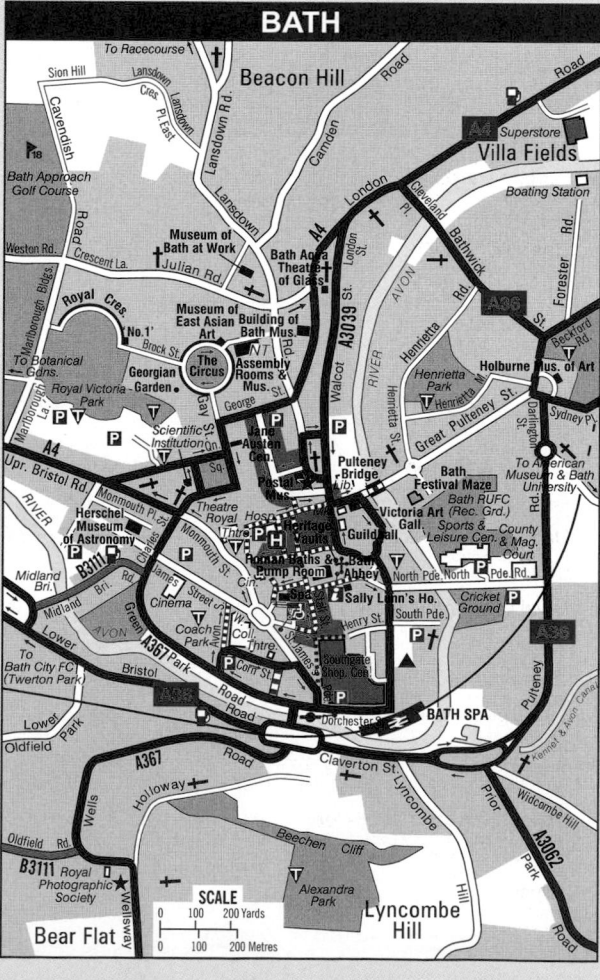

BEDFORD

BLACKPOOL

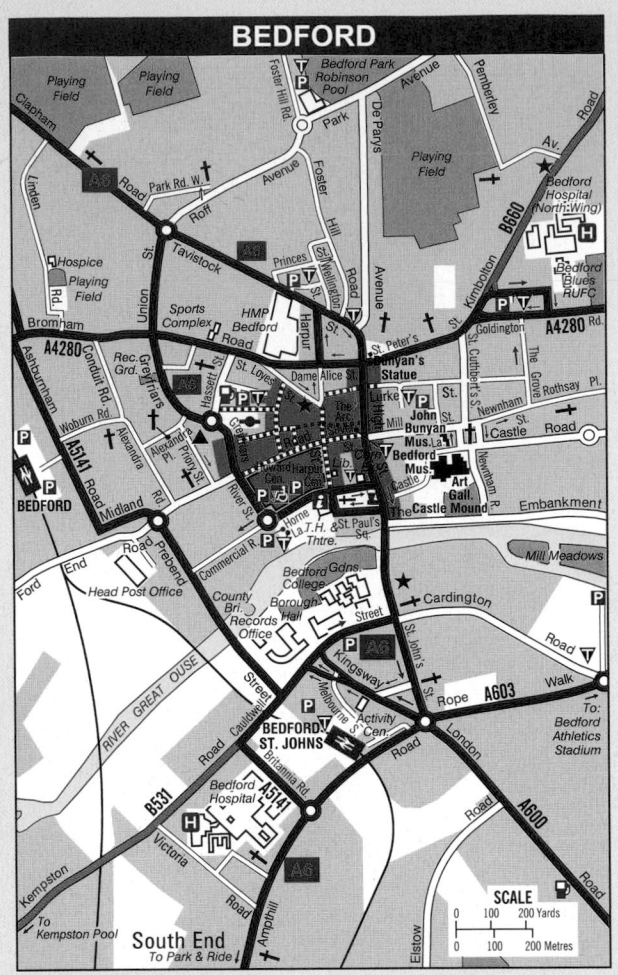

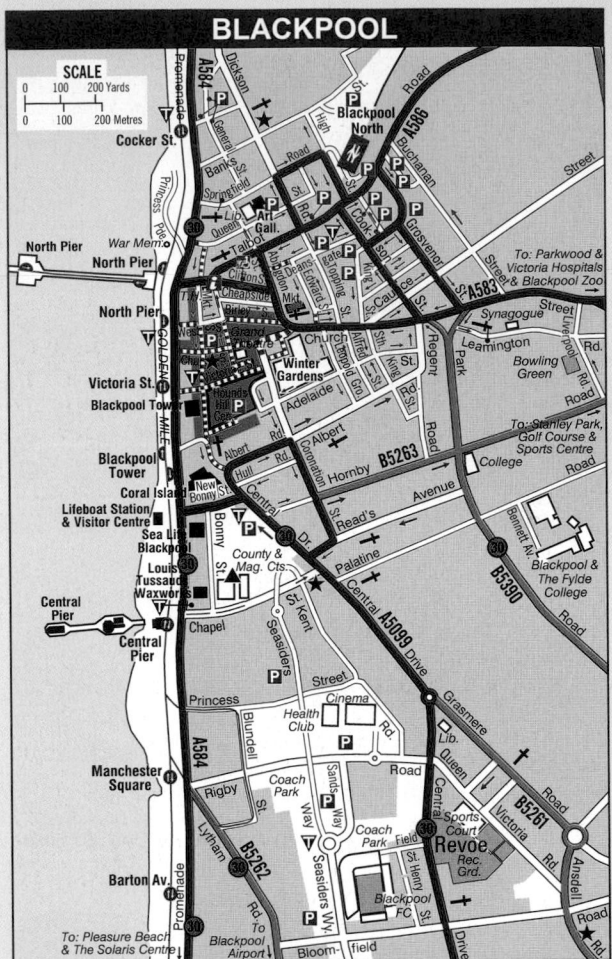

BIRMINGHAM (CITY CENTRE)

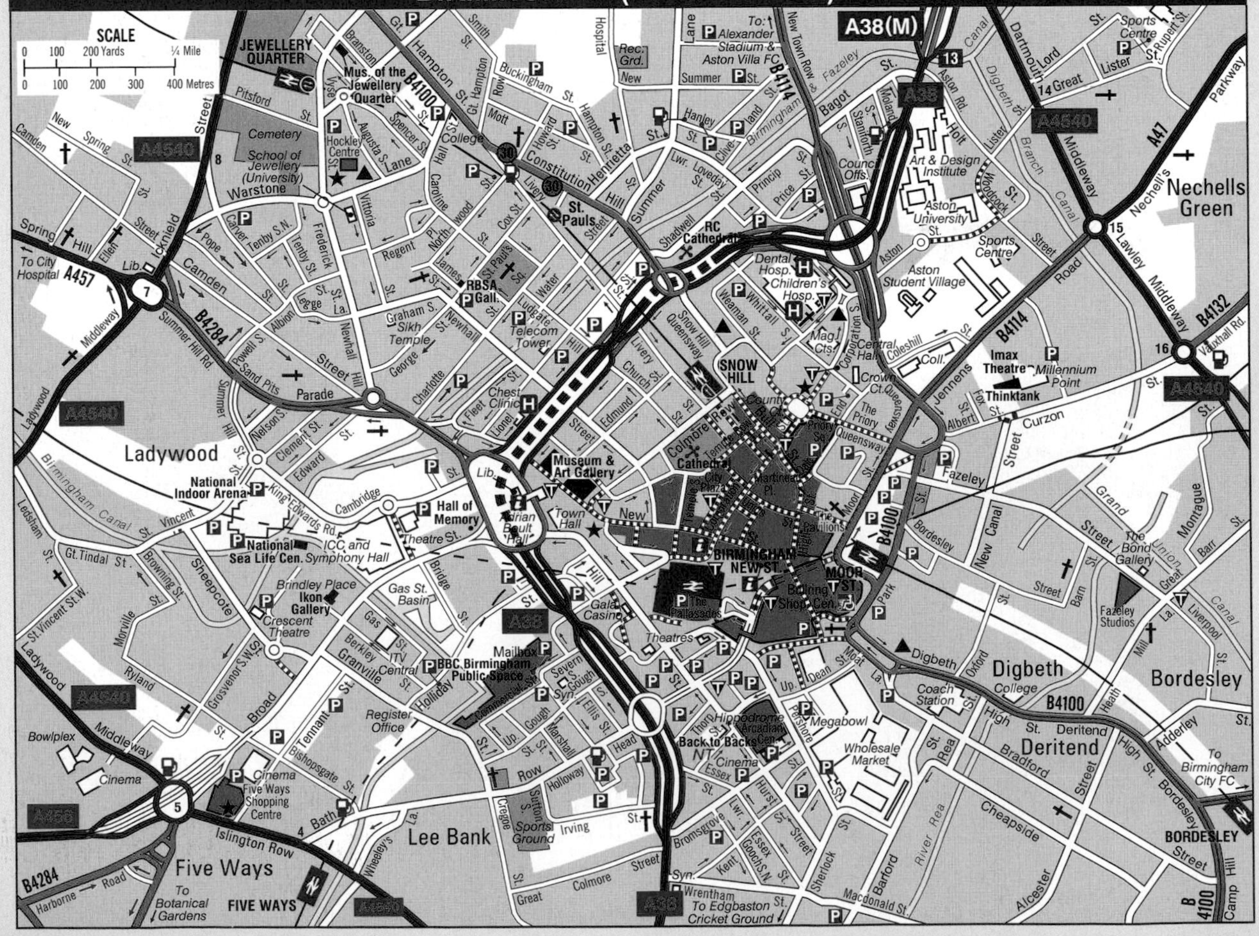

BRIGHTON and HOVE

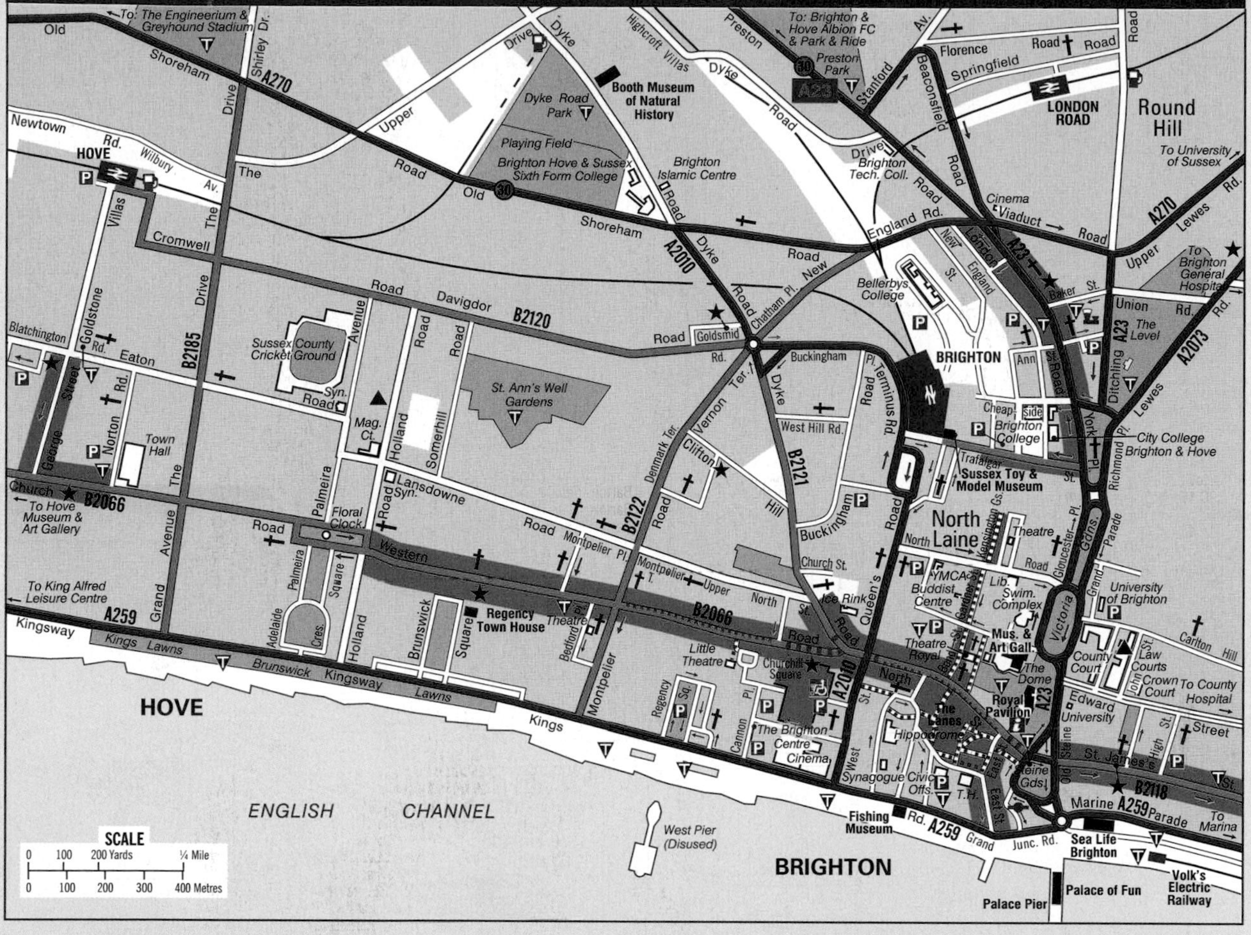

To: The Engineerium & Greyhound Stadium
To: Brighton & Hove Albion FC & Park & Ride
Booth Museum of Natural History
Dyke Road Park
Playing Field
Brighton Hove & Sussex Sixth Form College
Brighton Islamic Centre
Brighton Tech. Coll.
Cinema Viaduct
LONDON ROAD
Round Hill
To University of Sussex
HOVE
Newtown Rd.
Old Shoreham Rd.
Shirley Dr.
Dyke Drive
Highcroft Villas
Preston
Preston Park
Florence Road
Springfield Road
Beaconsfield
Stanford
Wilbury Av.
Davigdor Road
B2120
Goldsmid
Brighton Tech. Coll.
England Rd.
New England Rd.
Booker St.
Upper
Lewes Rd.
A270
To Brighton General Hospital
Sussex County Cricket Ground
Cromwell
Eaton
B2185
B2066
Blatchington Rd.
Goldstone
Norton Rd.
Town Hall
The Drive
Grand Avenue
Palmeira
Adelaide Cres.
Holland Road
Brunswick Square
Regency Square
St. Ann's Well Gardens
Mag. Ct.
Floral Clock
Western Road
B2066
Montpelier Rd.
B2122
B2121
Denmark Terr.
Clifton Hill
West Hill Rd.
Buckingham Road
Church St.
North Laine
Buddhist Centre
YMCA
Lib. Swim. Complex
Bellerbys College
BRIGHTON
Cheapside
Brighton College
City College Brighton & Hove
Trafalgar
Sussex Toy & Model Museum
The Dome
Theatre Royal
Mus. & Art Gall.
University of Brighton
A23
The Level
Ditchling
A2073
Union Road
Richmond
Carlton Hill
Law Courts
Crown to County Court
County Court
Edward Street
Crown to County Hospital
To Hove Museum & Art Gallery
Regency Town House
Little Theatre
Churchill Square
Ice Rink
Queen's Road
The Lanes
Hippodrome
Royal Pavilion
St. James's
B2118
A259
To Marina
HOVE
Kingsway
A259
Kings Lawns
Brunswick Kingsway
Kings
The Brighton Centre Cinema
West St. Synagogue
Civic Offs.
T.H.
Steine Gdns.
Marine Parade
To King Alfred Leisure Centre
ENGLISH CHANNEL
West Pier (Disused)
Fishing Museum
BRIGHTON
Grand Junc. Rd.
Sea Life Brighton
Palace Pier
Palace of Fun
Volk's Electric Railway

SCALE
0 100 200 Yards ¼ Mile
0 100 200 300 400 Metres

BRISTOL

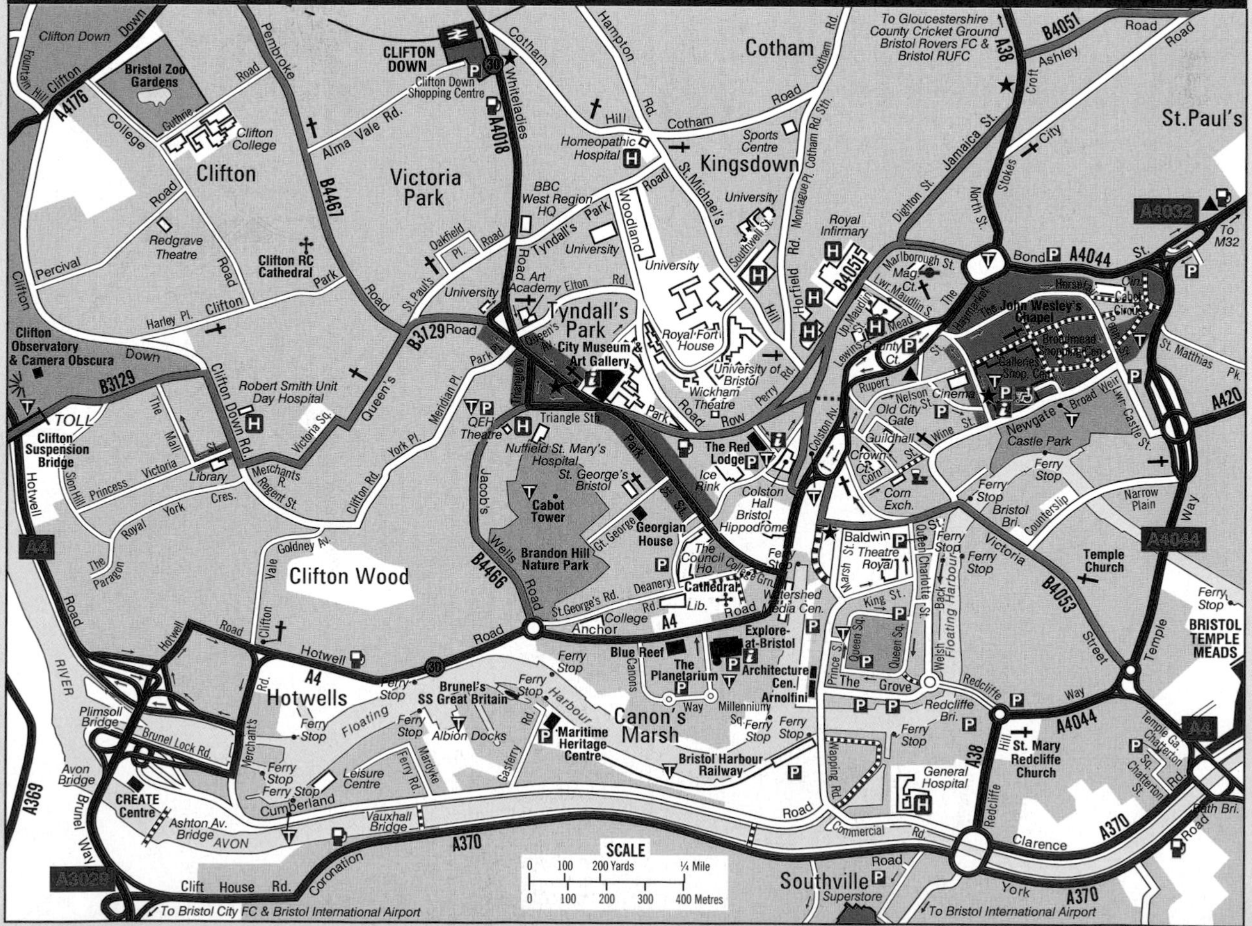

Clifton Down
Bristol Zoo Gardens
CLIFTON DOWN
Clifton Down Shopping Centre
Cotham
To Gloucestershire County Cricket Ground
Bristol Rovers FC & Bristol RUFC
B4051
Ashley Road
A4176
Clifton College
Clifton
Victoria Park
Alma Vale Rd.
Whiteladies Rd.
A4018
Homeopathic Hospital
Sports Centre
Kingsdown
St. Michael's Hill
University
Jamaica St.
St. Paul's
B4467
Redgrave Theatre
Clifton RC Cathedral
Park
St. Paul's Rd.
BBC West Region HQ
Tyndall's Park
University
University
Woodland Rd.
Royal Infirmary
Marlborough St.
A4032
To M32
A4044
Clifton Observatory & Camera Obscura
B3129
Down
Queen's Rd.
Tyndall's Park
City Museum & Art Gallery
University of Bristol
Wickham Theatre
Royal Fort House
John Wesley's Chapel
Broadmead
Shopping Centre
A420
Bristol
Robert Smith Unit Day Hospital
Clifton Suspension Bridge
TOLL
B3129
Hotwell
Princess Victoria
York Royal
The Mall
Merchants Rd.
Regent St.
Library
Meridian Pl.
Oakfield Rd.
QEH Theatre
Triangle Sth.
Park St.
Perry Row
Nelson St.
Old City Gate
Wine St.
Guildhall
Corn Exch.
Newgate
Castle Park
Narrow Plain
Bristol Bri.
Ferry Stop
A4044
Clifton Wood
Nuffield St. Mary's Hospital
St. George's Bristol
The Red Lodge
Ice Rink
Colston Hall
Bristol Hippodrome
Crown Ct.
Baldwin St.
Ferry Stop
Theatre Royal
Temple Church
Temple
BRISTOL TEMPLE MEADS
Brandon Hill Nature Park
Cabot Tower
Georgian House
Brandon Hill
Deanery Rd.
The Council House
Cathedral
Cathedral Lib.
Watershed Media Cen.
King St.
Victoria St.
A4053
B4466
Wells Rd.
St. George's Rd.
College Green
A4
Hotwells
Brunel Lock Rd.
Plimsoll Bridge
CREATE Centre
Brunel Lock Way
Ashton Av. Bridge
AVON
Vauxhall Bridge
Coronation Road
A370
A3029
A369
Avon Bridge
RIVER AVON
Ferry Stop
Floating Harbour
Albion Docks
Leisure Centre
Cumberland Rd.
Maritime Heritage Centre
Brunel's SS Great Britain
Canon's Marsh
Blue Reef
The Planetarium
Explore-at-Bristol
Architecture Cen.
Arnolfini
Bristol Harbour Railway
Prince St.
Queen Sq.
The Grove
Millennium Sq.
Welsh Back
Redcliffe Bri.
General Hospital
A38
Redcliffe Way
St. Mary Redcliffe Church
A4044
Southville
Superstore
York Rd.
Clarence Rd.
A370
Commercial Rd.
To Bristol City FC & Bristol International Airport

SCALE
0 100 200 Yards ¼ Mile
0 100 200 300 400 Metres

BOURNEMOUTH

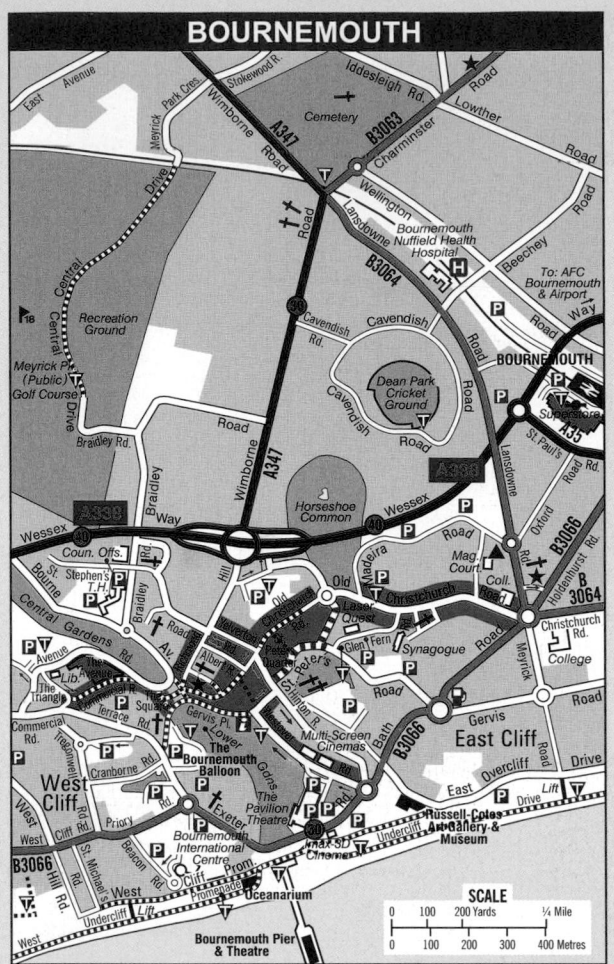

BRADFORD

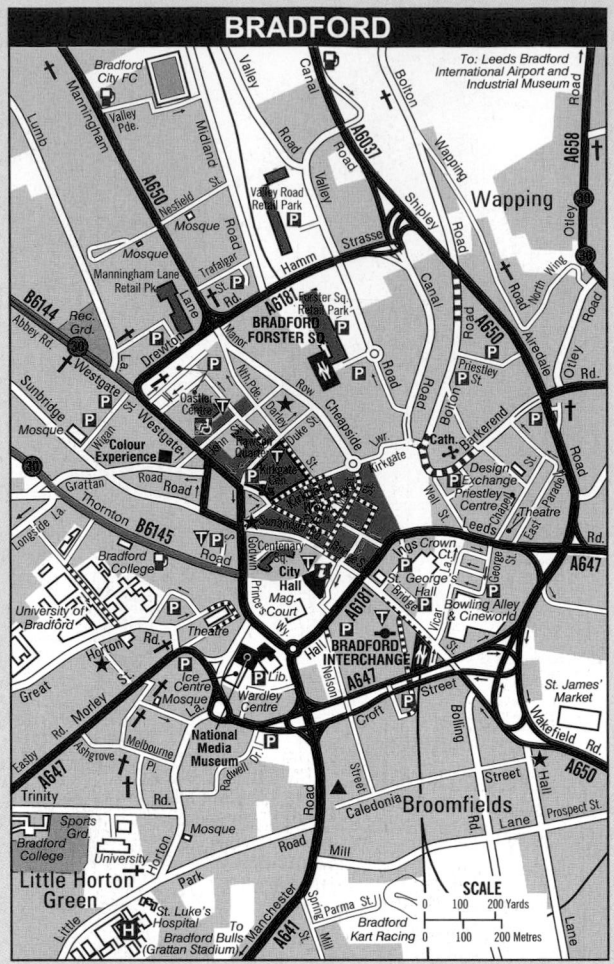

CAERNARFON

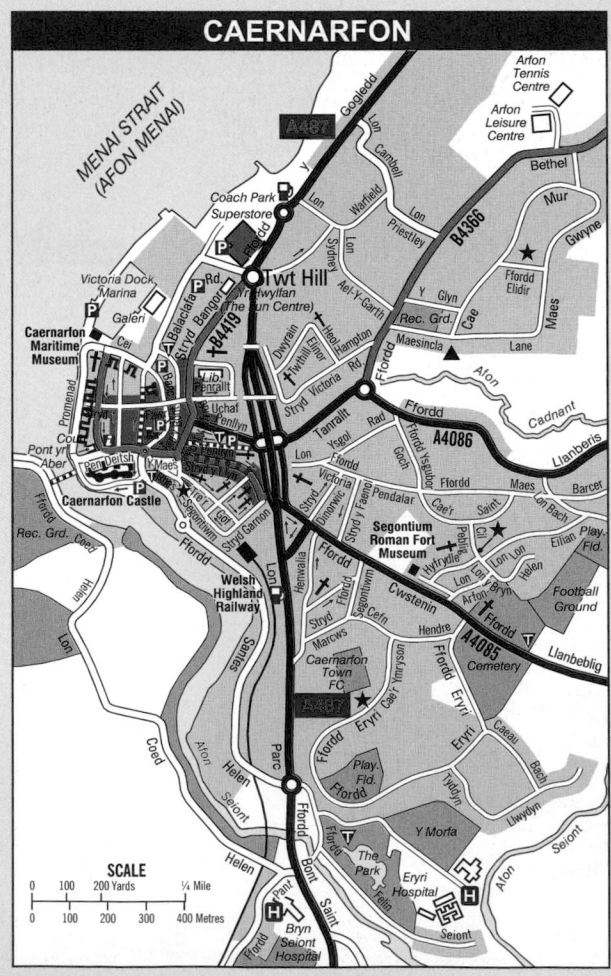

CANTERBURY

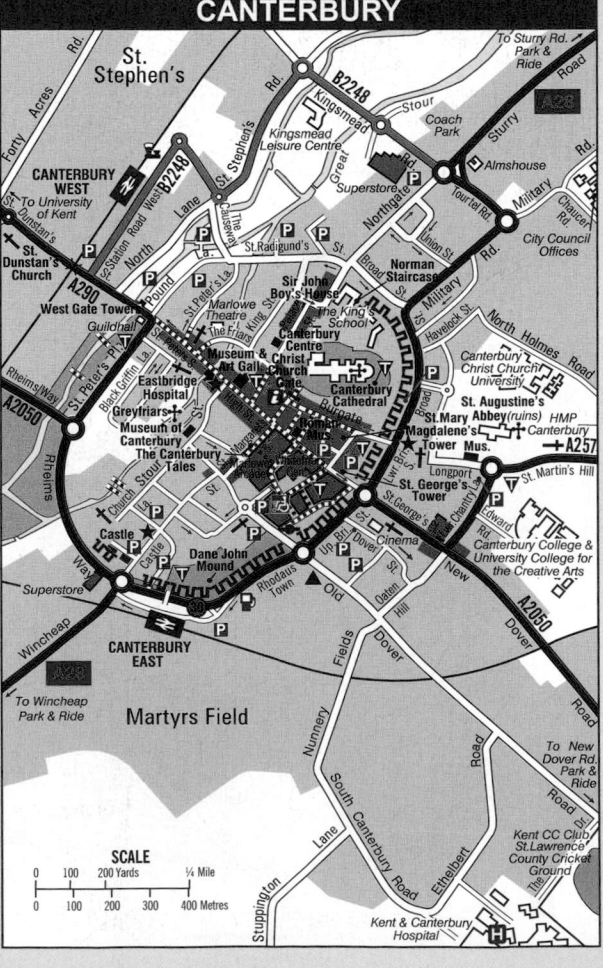

KEY TO COLLEGES

1. Christ's College
2. Churchill College
3. Clare College
4. Clare Hall
5. Corpus Christi College
6. Darwin College
7. Downing College
8. Emmanuel College
9. Fitzwilliam College
10. Gonville & Caius College
11. Hughes Hall
12. Jesus College
13. King's College
14. Lucy Cavendish College
15. Magdalene College
16. Murray Edwards College
17. Newnham College
18. Pembroke College
19. Peterhouse
20. Queens' College
21. Robinson College
22. St.Catharine's College
23. St.Edmund's College
24. St. John's College
25. Selwyn College
26. Sidney Sussex College
27. Trinity College
28. Trinity Hall
29. Wolfson College

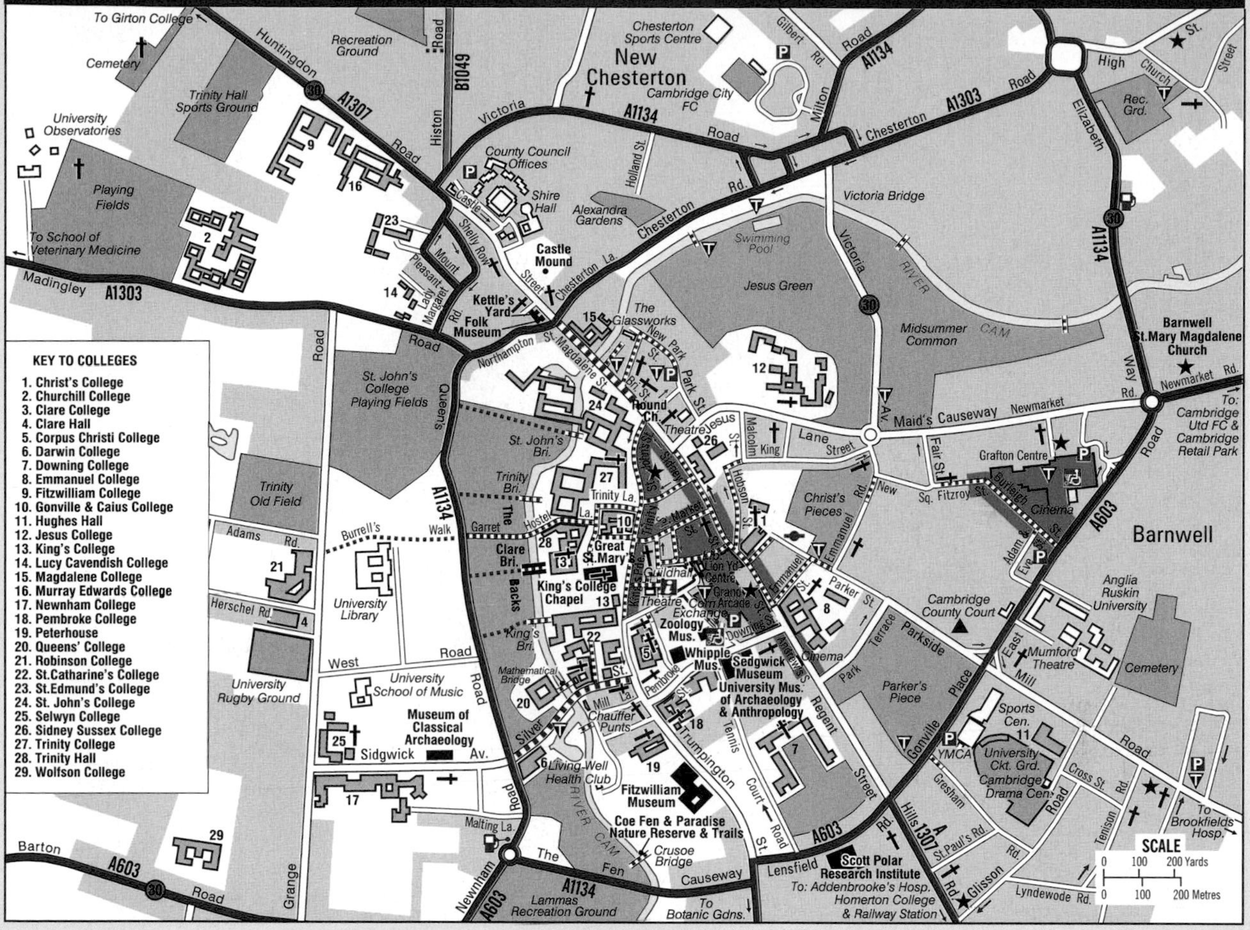

CARDIFF (CAERDYDD)

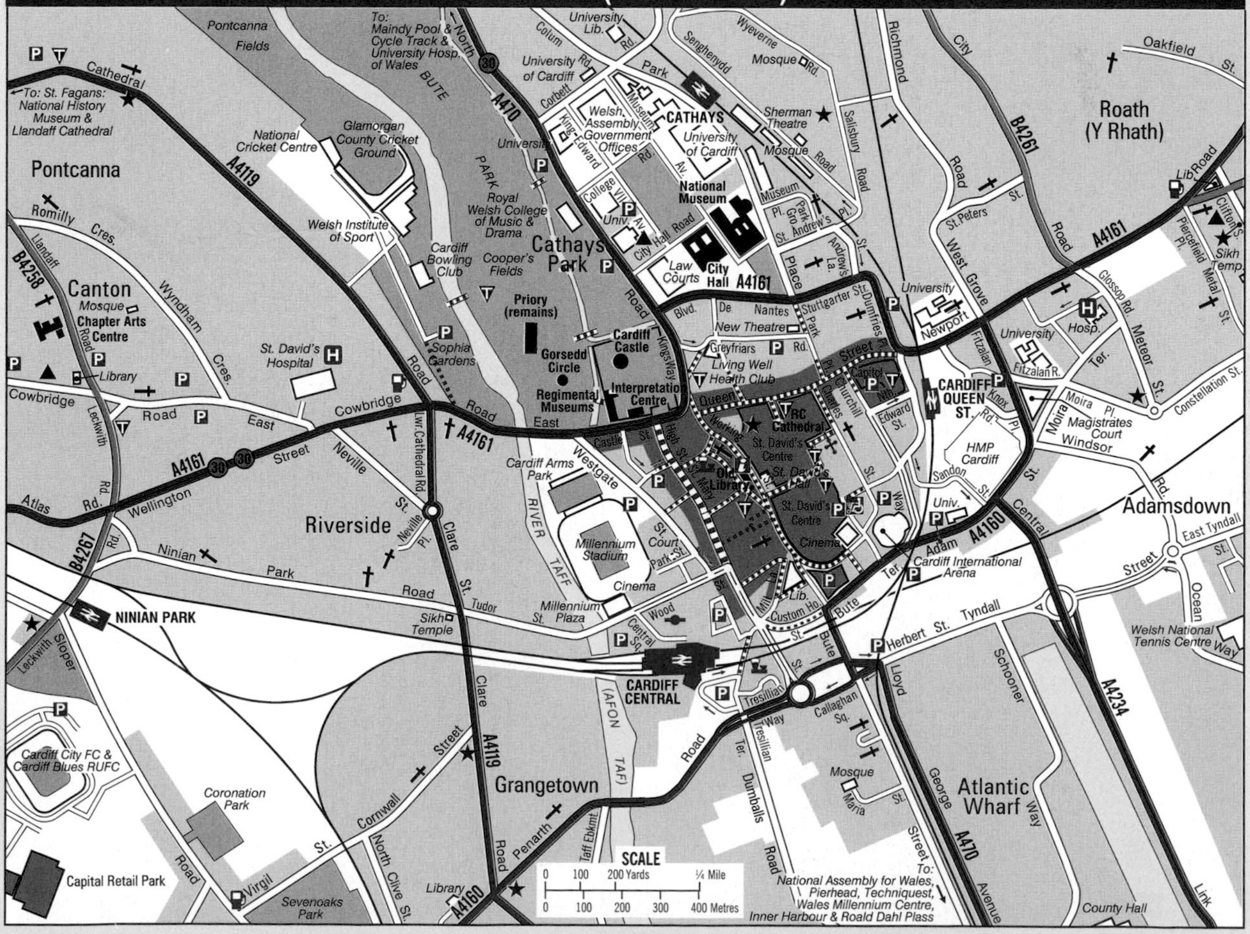

CARLISLE

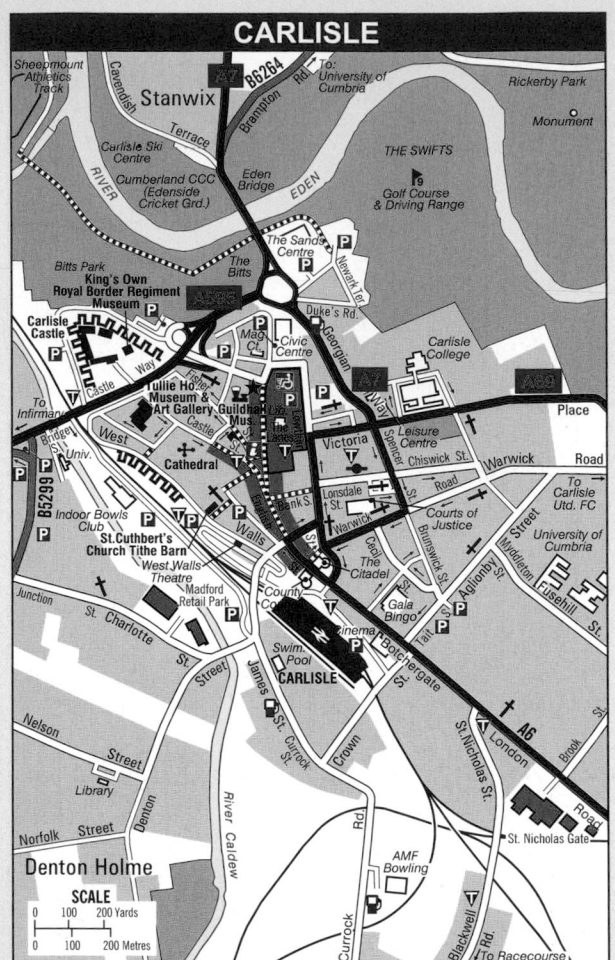

CHELTENHAM

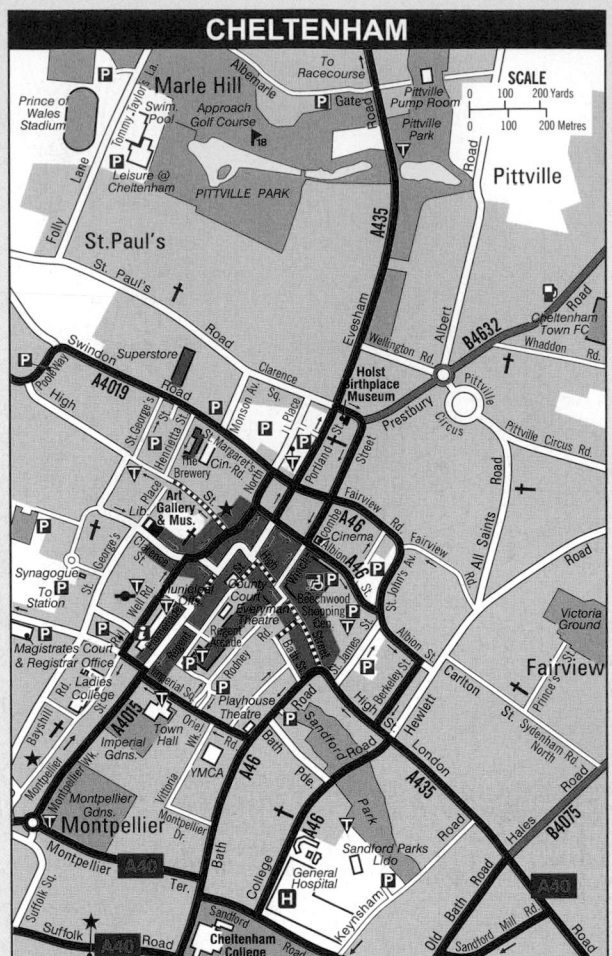

CHESTER

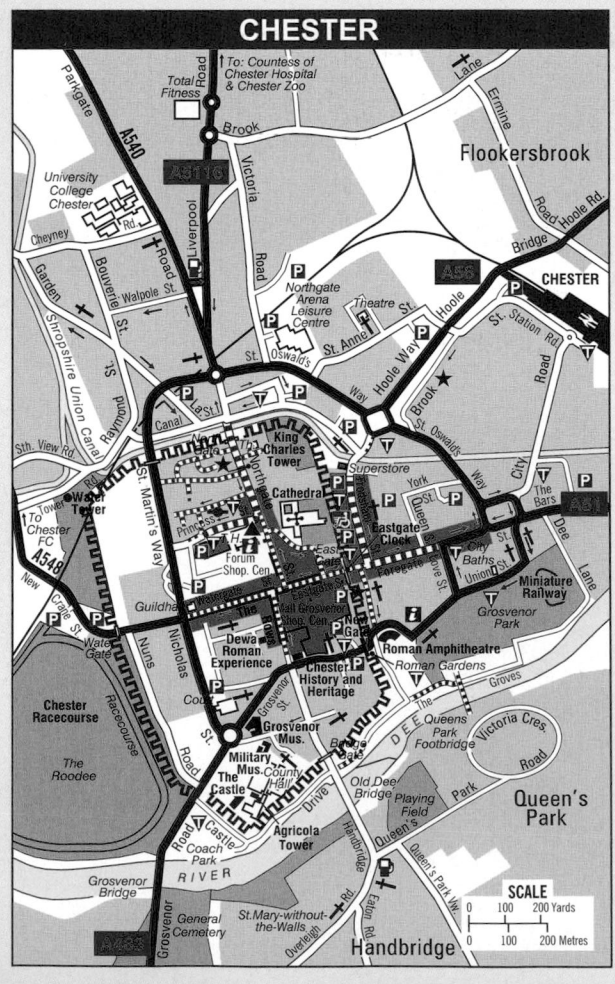

COVENTRY

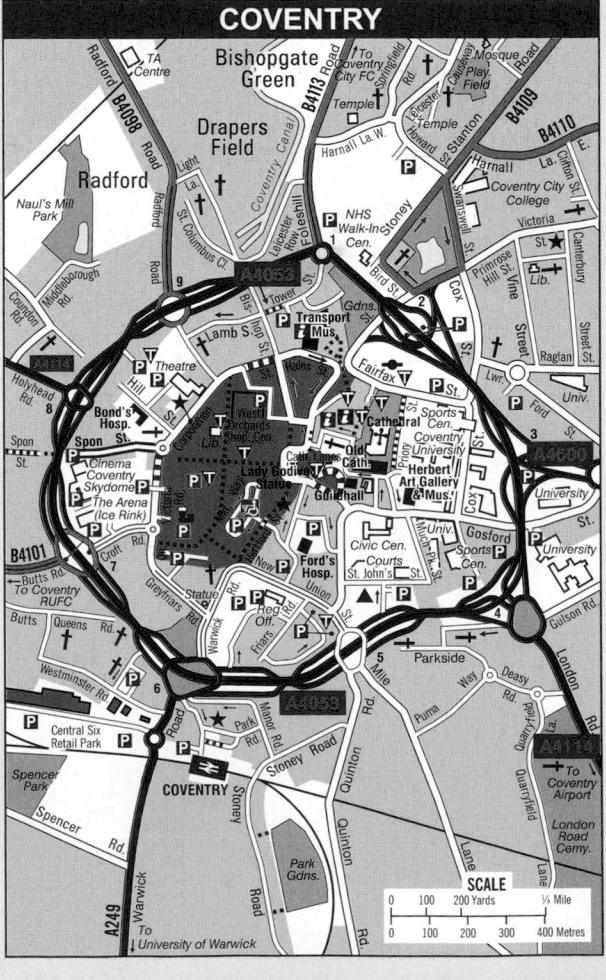

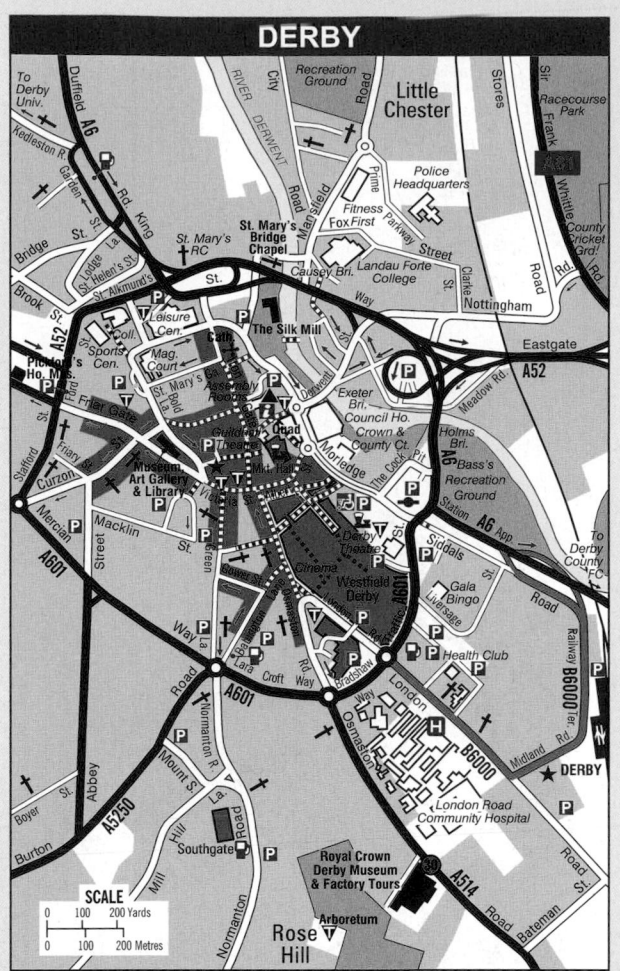

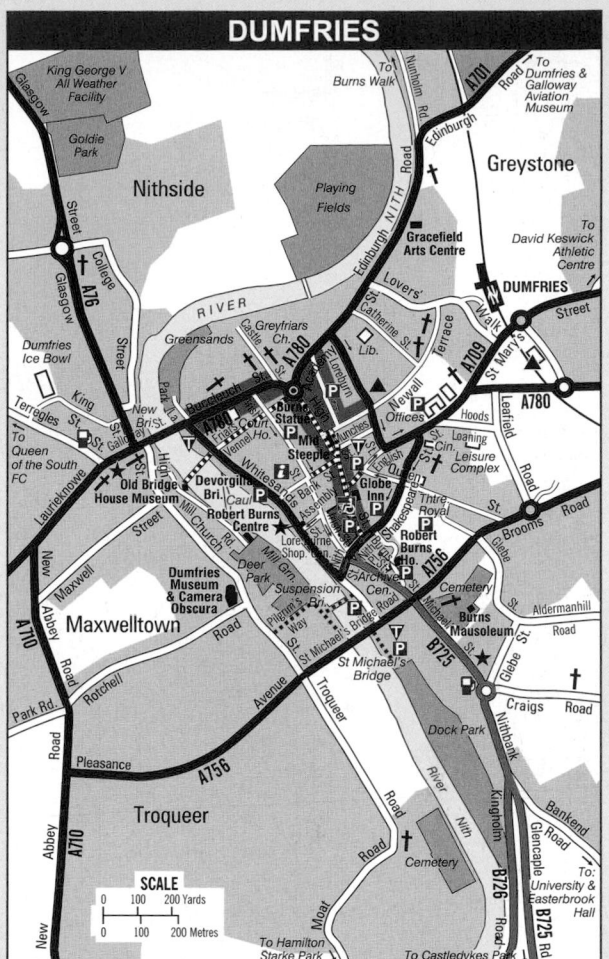

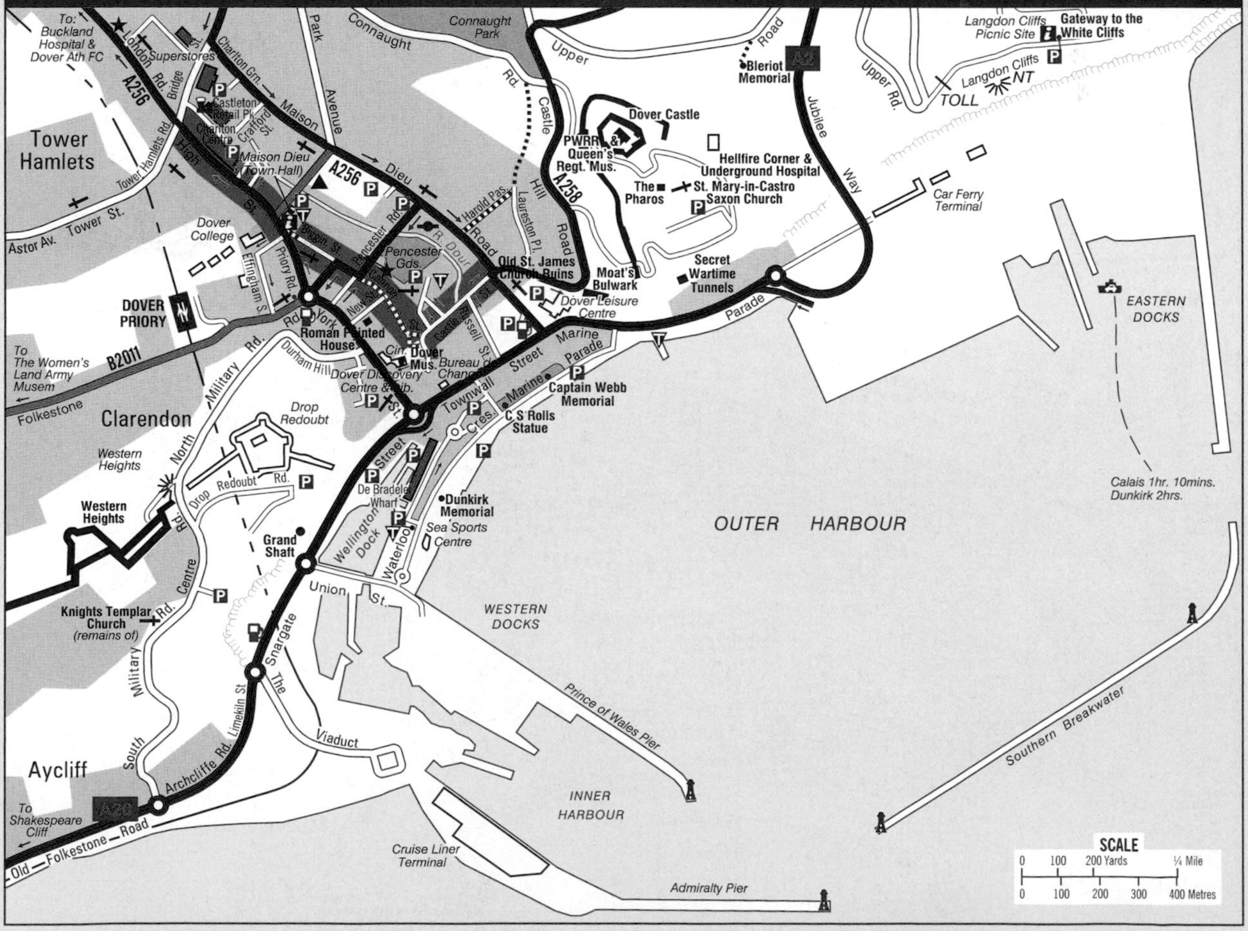

DUNDEE

DURHAM

EDINBURGH

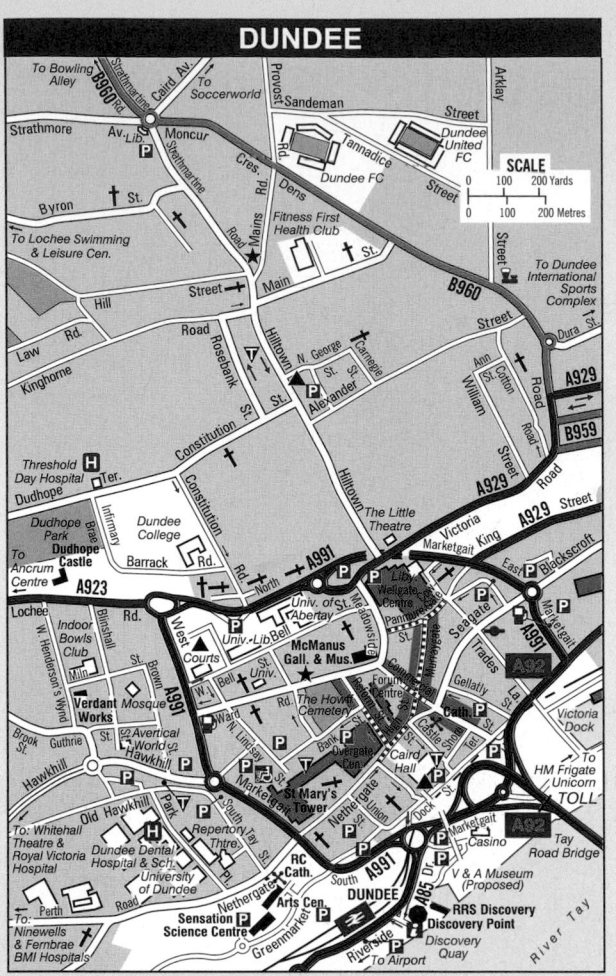

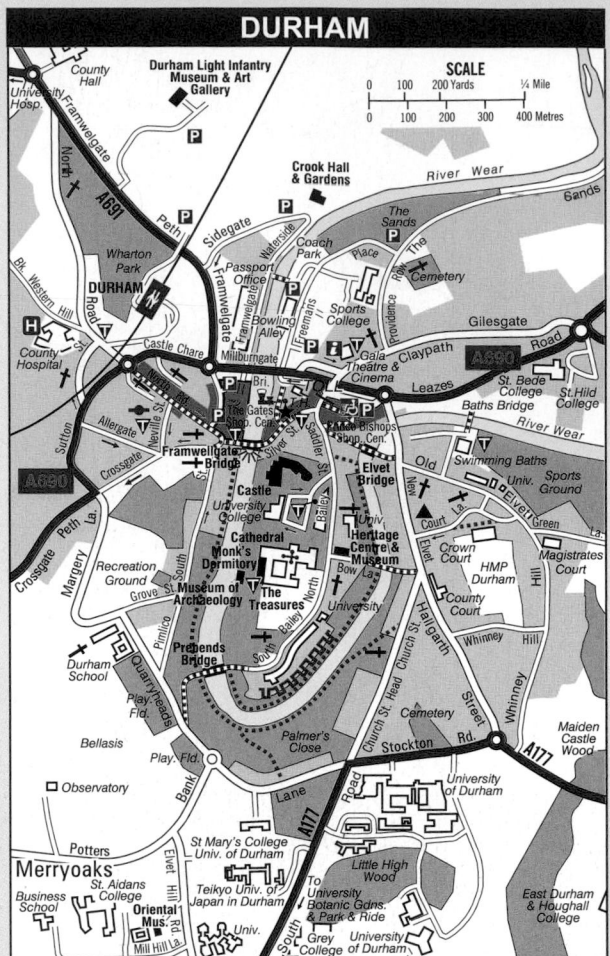

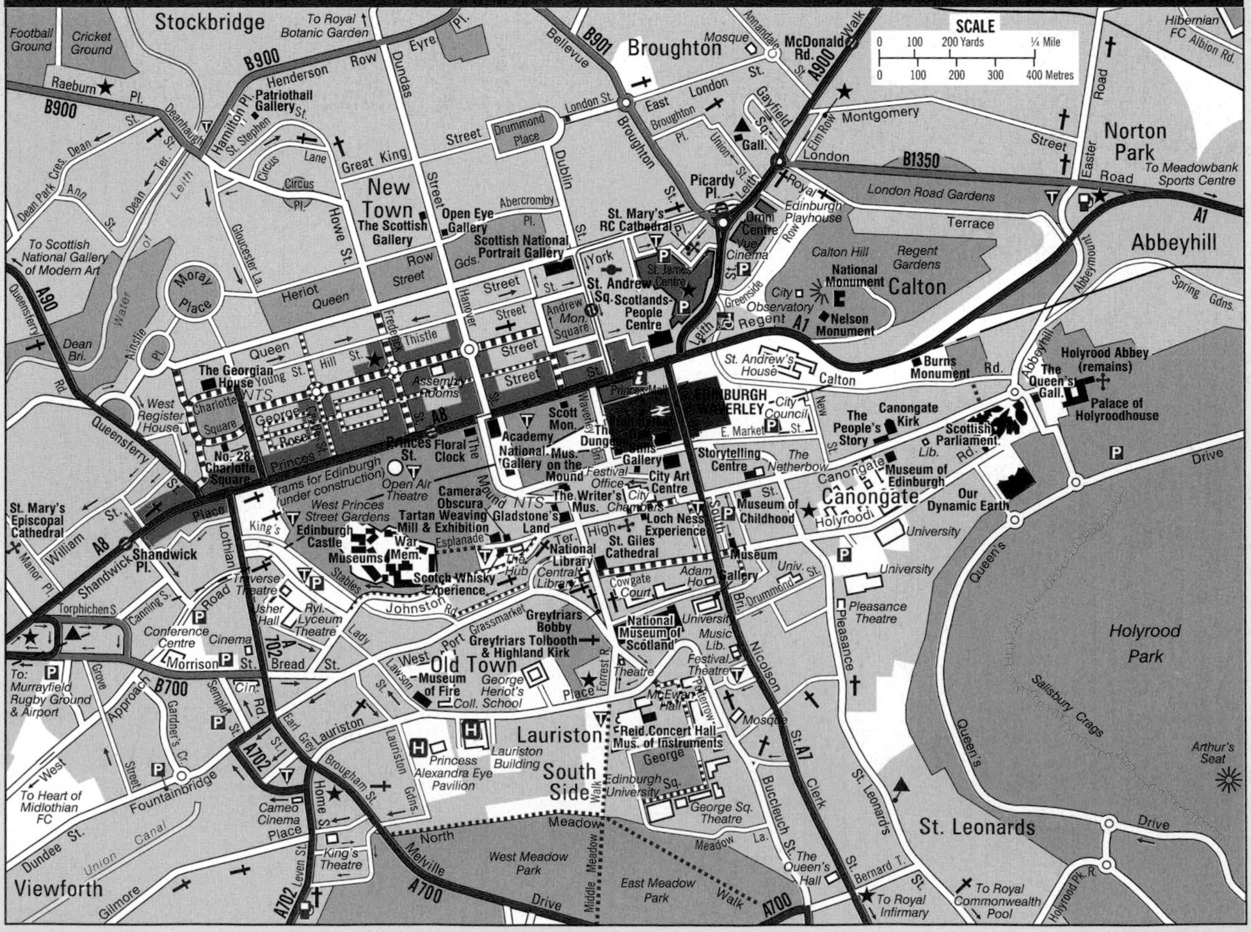

EXETER

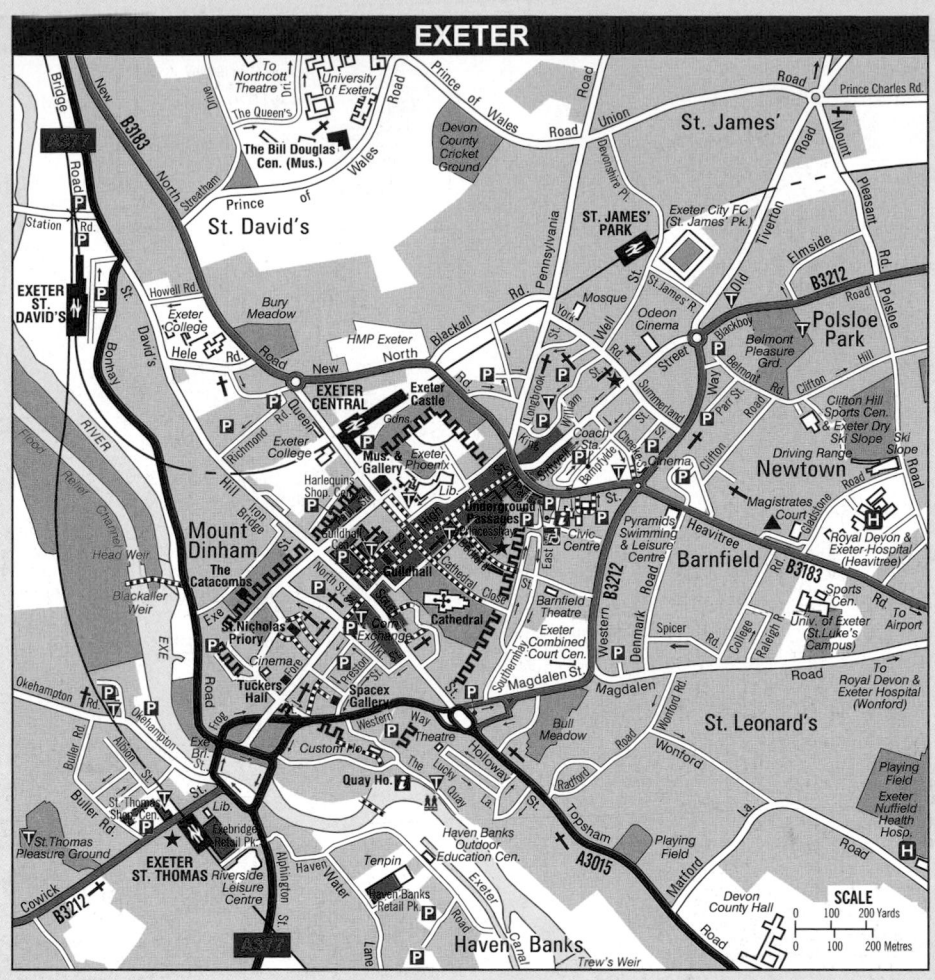

EASTBOURNE

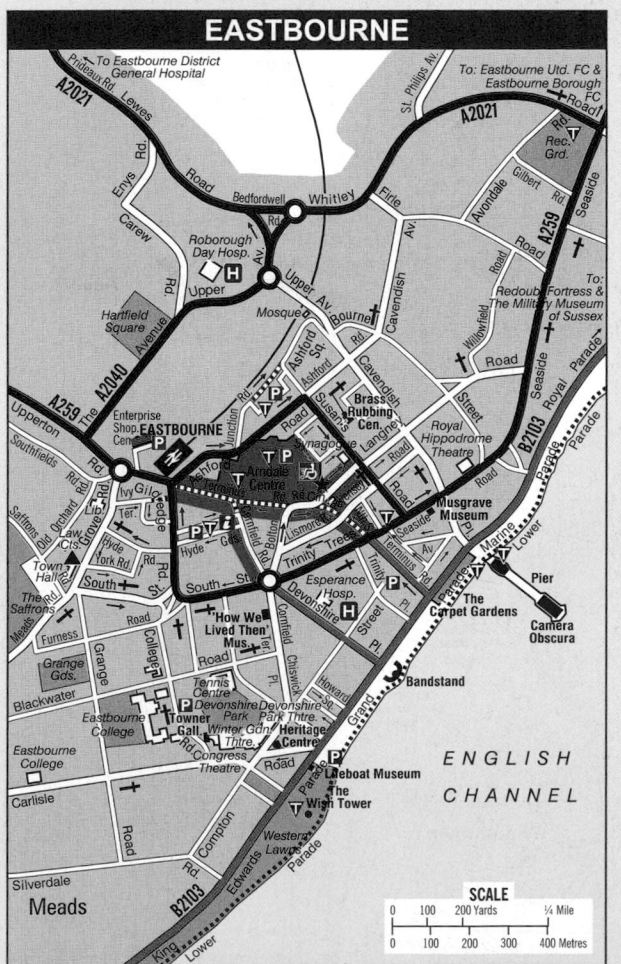

FOLKESTONE

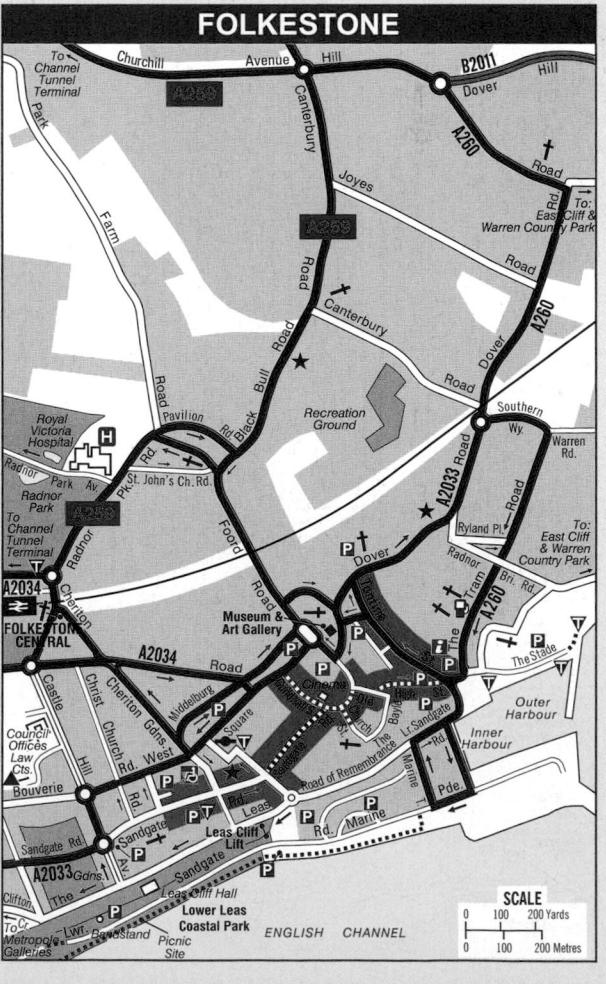

GLASGOW

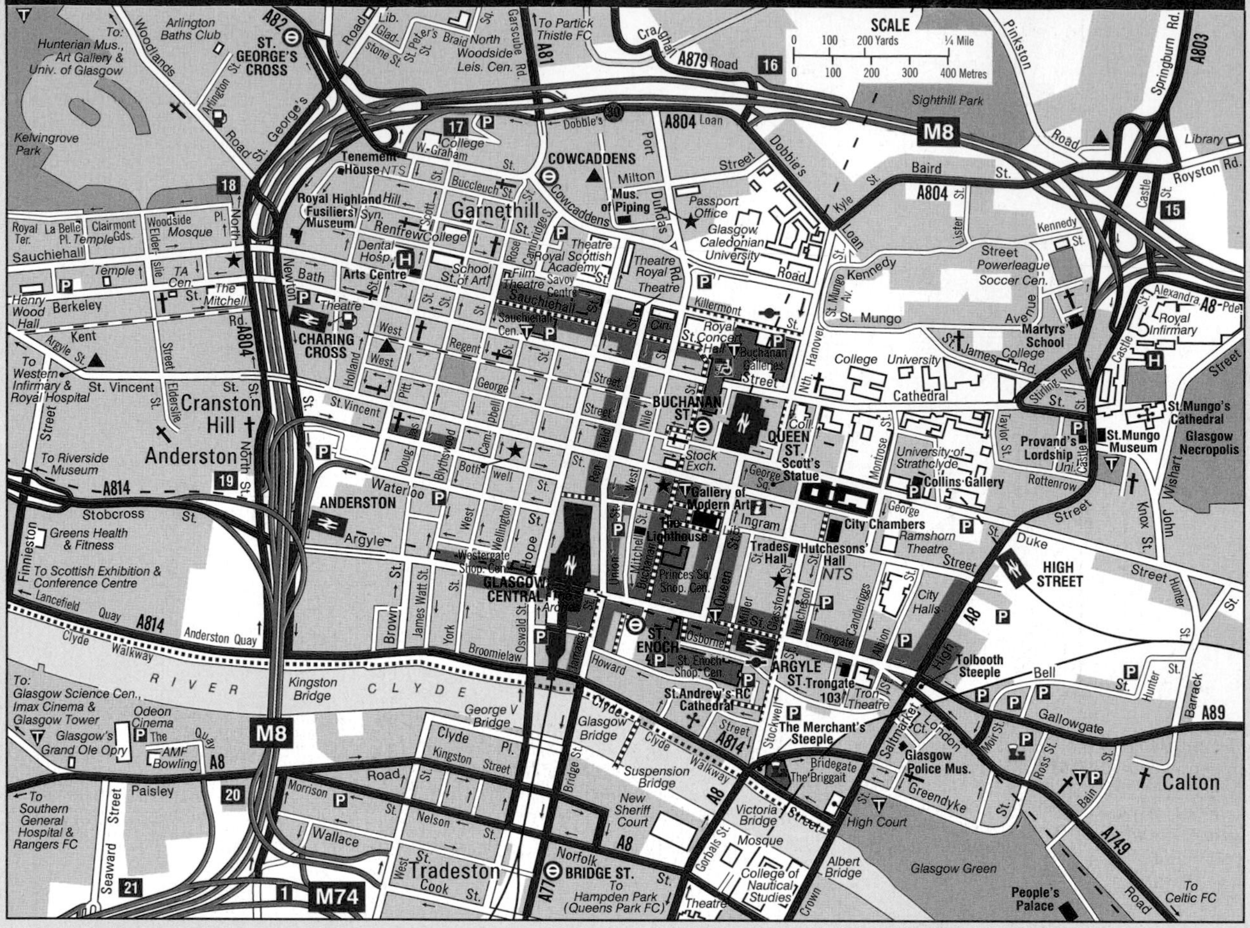

SCALE

0   100   200 Yards   ¼ Mile
0   100   200   300   400 Metres

To: Hunterian Mus., Art Gallery & Univ. of Glasgow

Arlington Baths Club
ST. GEORGE'S CROSS
North Woodside Leis. Cen.
Braid

Kelvingrove Park

Royal La Belle Pl. Temple Gds.
Clairmont
Woodside Pl.
Woodlands
Royal Highland Fusiliers) Museum
Tenement House NTS
College St.
W. Graham St.
Dobble's
Dobbie's Loan
Port Dundas
Sighthill Park
Pinkston Rd.
Royston Rd.
Library
Castle

Kelvinside
Royal Mosque
Synagogue
COWCADDENS
Milton St.
Passport Office
Glasgow Caledonian University
M8
Baird St.
A804
Kennedy St.

Henry Wood Hall
Berkeley
Kent
Sauchiehall
The Mitchell
TA Cen.
Charing Cross
Royal Scottish Academy
Film Theatre
Savoy Cen.
Theatre Royal
Cowcaddens
Garnethill
Dental Hosp.
Royal Highland
School of Art
Arts Centre
Theatre
Buchanan Galleries
St. Mungo
Kennedy
Street Powerleague Soccer Cen.
Alexandra Pde.
A8
Royal Infirmary
Martyrs' School

Western Infirmary & Royal Hospital
Cranston Hill
Anderston
CHARING CROSS
West
Regent
Sauchiehall Cen.
Royal Concert Hall
BUCHANAN ST.
College
University
Cathedral
Collins Gallery
Provand's Lordship
St. Mungo Museum
St. Mungo's Cathedral
Glasgow Necropolis

Stobcross
Greens Health & Fitness
ANDERSTON
Waterloo
Argyle
QUEEN ST.
Scott's Statue
Stock Exch.
Gallery of Modern Art
The Lighthouse
City Chambers
Ramshorn Theatre
University of Strathclyde
Knox
John

To Scottish Exhibition & Conference Centre
A814
Anderston Quay
Clyde
Lancefield

RIVER CLYDE
Kingston Bridge
Walkway
Broomielaw
GLASGOW CENTRAL
St. Enoch Shop. Cen.
Trades Hall
Hutchesons' Hall NTS
City Halls
HIGH STREET
Tolbooth Steeple
Bell
A89

To Glasgow Science Cen., Imax Cinema & Glasgow Tower
Odeon Cinema
AMF Bowling
A8
M8
Clyde Pl.
George V Bridge
Glasgow Bridge
Kingston St.
Suspension Bridge
St. Andrew's RC Cathedral
The Merchant's Steeple
Glasgow Police Mus.
Bridgegate
The Briggait
ARGYLE ST. Trongate
Trades
103
Tron Theatre
Calton

To Southern General Hospital & Rangers FC
Paisley Road
Morrison St.
Wallace St.
Nelson St.
New Sheriff Court
Victoria Bridge
Albert Bridge
Mosque
High Court
Glasgow Green
People's Palace
Greendyke
A749
To Celtic FC

West St.
Tradeston
Cook St.
M74
BRIDGE ST.
Norfolk St.
To Hampden Park (Queens Park FC)
College of Nautical Studies
Theatre
Gorbals St.
Crown St.

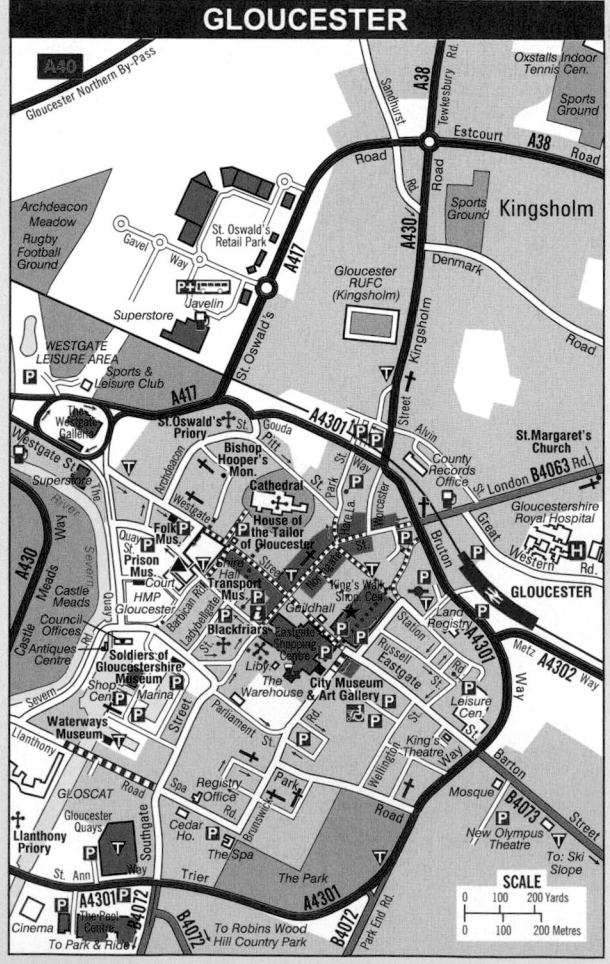

GLOUCESTER

A40
Gloucester Northern By-Pass
Oxstalls Indoor Tennis Cen.
Sports Ground
A38
Tewkesbury Rd.
Estcourt Rd.
A38
Kingsholm
Sandhurst Rd.
Archdeacon Meadow Rugby Football Ground
St. Oswald's Retail Park
Gavel Way
A417
A430
Gloucester RUFC (Kingsholm)
Denmark
Sports Ground
Superstore
Javelin
Westgate Leisure Area
Sports & Leisure Club
A417
A4301
Alvin St.
County Records Office
St.Margaret's Church
B4063
St. Oswald's Priory
Gouda Way
Westgate Gallery
Bishop Hooper's Mon.
Cathedral
Folk Mus.
Prison Mus.
Transport Mus.
House of the Tailor of Gloucester
King's Walk Sh. Cen.
Gloucestershire Royal Hospital
London Rd.
Great Western Rd.
GLOUCESTER
HMP Gloucester
Blackfriars
Station
Eastgate Shopping Centre
Library
Landry Registry
A4302
A4301
Eastgate
Metz Way
Soldiers of Gloucestershire Museum
City Museum & Art Gallery
The Warehouse
Leisure Cen.
Russell St.
Waterways Museum
Marina
Peel Cen.
Parliament St.
King's Theatre
King's Square
Wellington
GLOSCAT
Gloucester Quays
Registry Office
Spa
Cedar Ho.
Park
Barton St.
Mosque
B4073
Llanthony Priory
St. Ann Way
Southgate Way
B4072
The Spa
New Olympus Theatre
To Ski Slope
A4301
Trier Way
The Park
Cinema
A4301
B4072
B4072
To Robins Wood Hill Country Park
To Park & Ride

SCALE

0   100   200 Yards
0   100   200 Metres

GREAT YARMOUTH

To Racecourse
Beaconsfield
North
Crescent Gdns.
North Beach
Rd.
The Waterways
Bure
River
Avenue
Northgate Hospital
Play-Field
Denes
Rec. Grd.
A47
A149
Estcourt Road
New Cemetery
Sandown Road
NORTH SEA
A12
Runham Vauxhall
Acle New Road
Ormond Rd.
Garrison Rd.
Kitchener
Old Cemetery
Nelson Rd.
Euston Rd.
Cinema
North West Tower
GREAT YARMOUTH
North Quay
Mag. Court
Northgate
Coach & Car Park
Rec. Grd.
Britannia Pier
Superstore
A47
Fuller's Hill
B1141
St. Nicholas
Wellesley Rd.
Marine Pde.
Theatre
Joyland Fun Park
North Beach Gardens
Cobholm Island
The Conge
St. George's Rd.
Regent Rd.
Crown Rd.
Louis Tussauds House of Wax
Bowl. Alley
RIVER YARE
Haven Bridge
Market Gates
Elizabethan House Museum NT
St. George's Theatre
Trafalgar Rd.
St. George's Rd.
Marina Leisure & Fitness Centre
Half Quay
Southtown Rd.
A1243
Norfolk Nelson Museum
Old Merchant's House
The Tolhouse Museum
Row 111 House
Hippodrome Circus
The Jetty
Amazonia World of Reptiles
South Beach Gdns.
Pasteur Rd.
Station Rd.
Lichfield Rd.
Nottingham Way
St. Peter's Rd.
Potteries
Time & Tide Mus.
Sea Life Centre
Winter Gardens
Southtown
Pasteur Retail Park
A1243
Friars La.
Queen's Rd.
Stafford Rd.
King's Rd.
To Nelson's Mon.
Wellington Pier
Merrivale Model Village
Pleasure Beach

SCALE

0   100   200 Yards
0   100   200 Metres

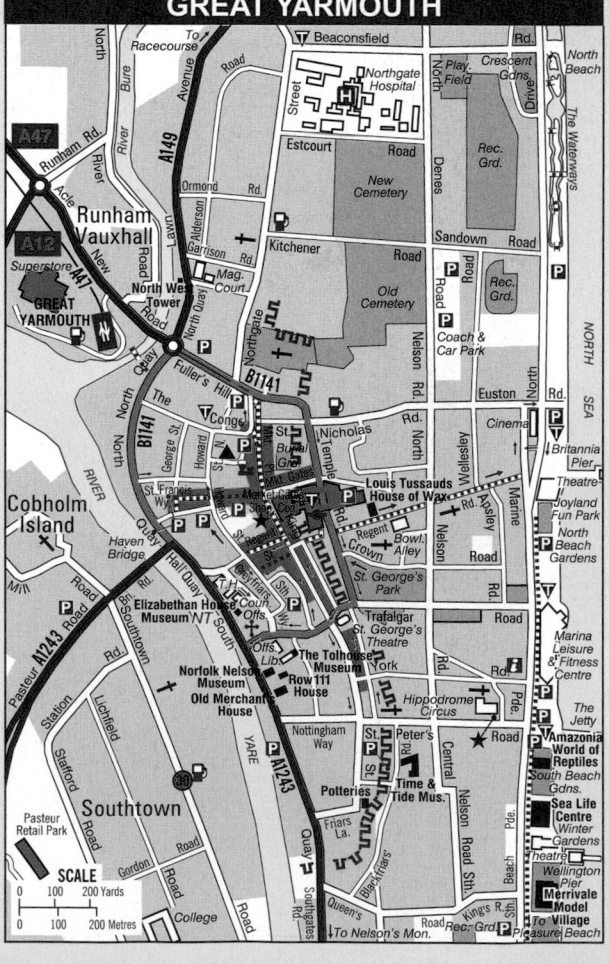

GUILDFORD

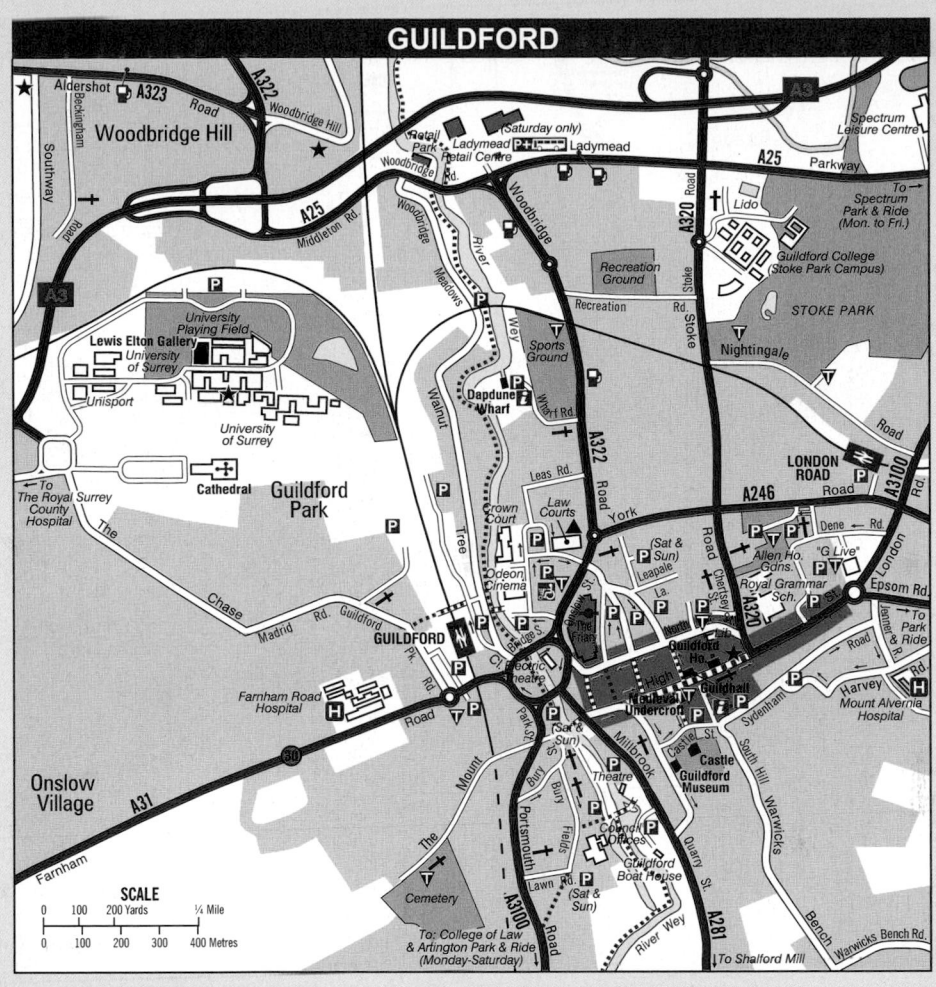

SCALE

0	100	200 Yards		¼ Mile
0	100	200	300	400 Metres

HARROGATE

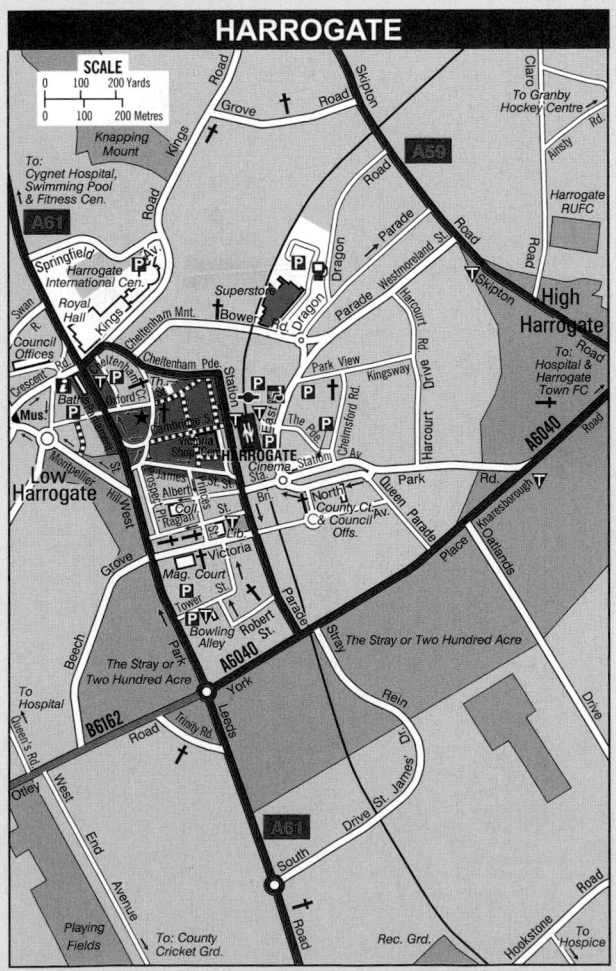

SCALE

0	100	200 Yards
0	100	200 Metres

HEREFORD

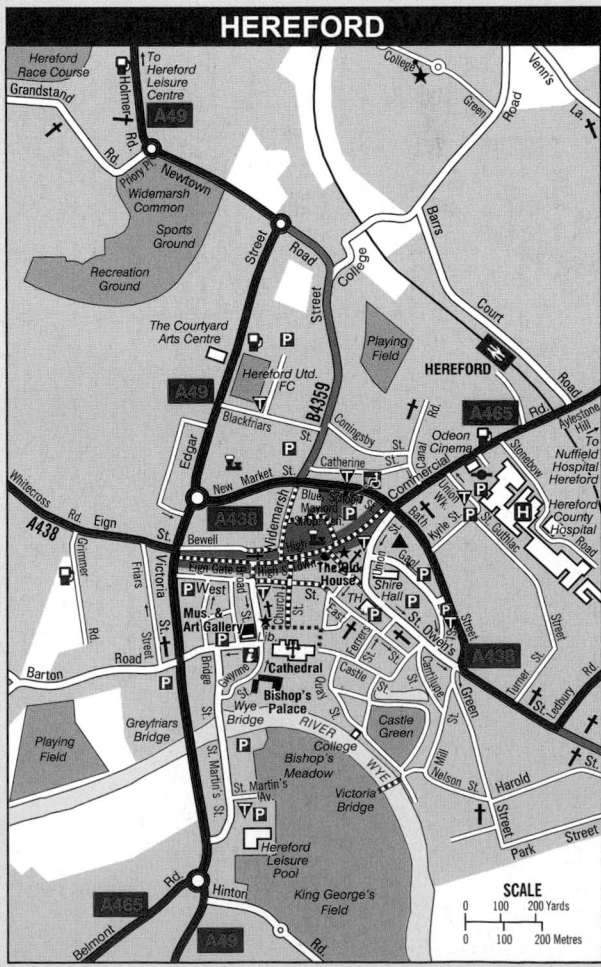

SCALE

0	100	200 Yards
0	100	200 Metres

INVERNESS

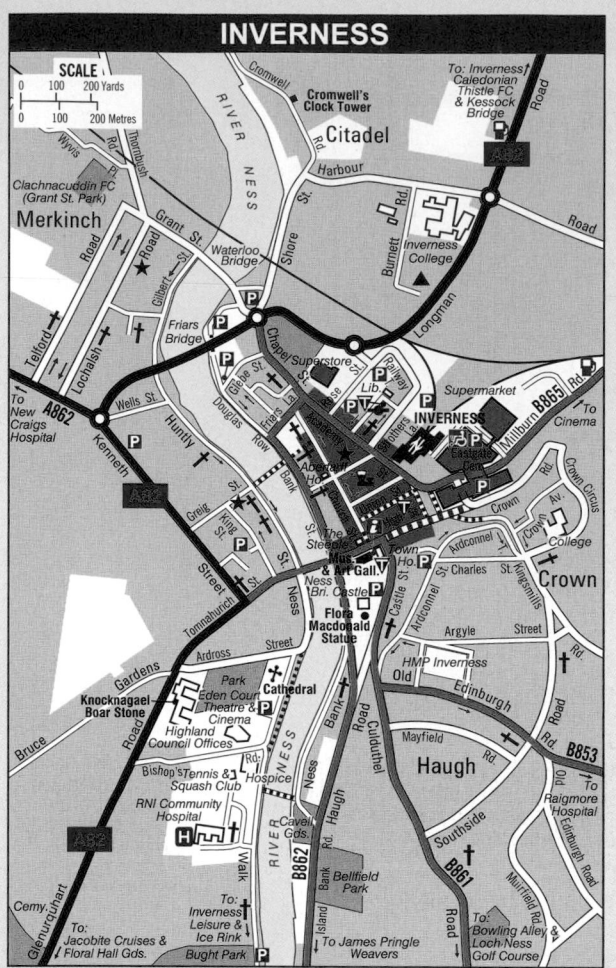

IPSWICH

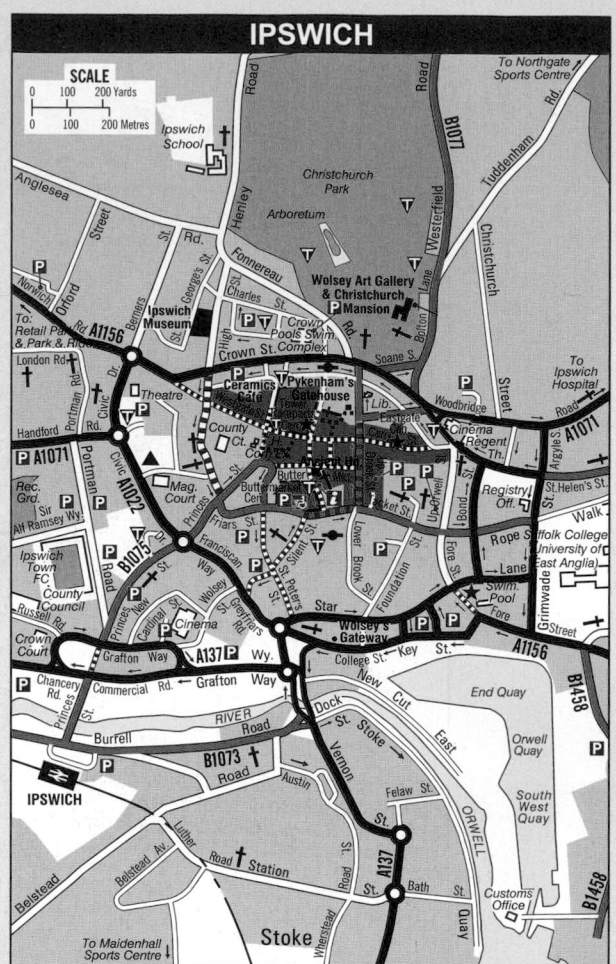

KILMARNOCK

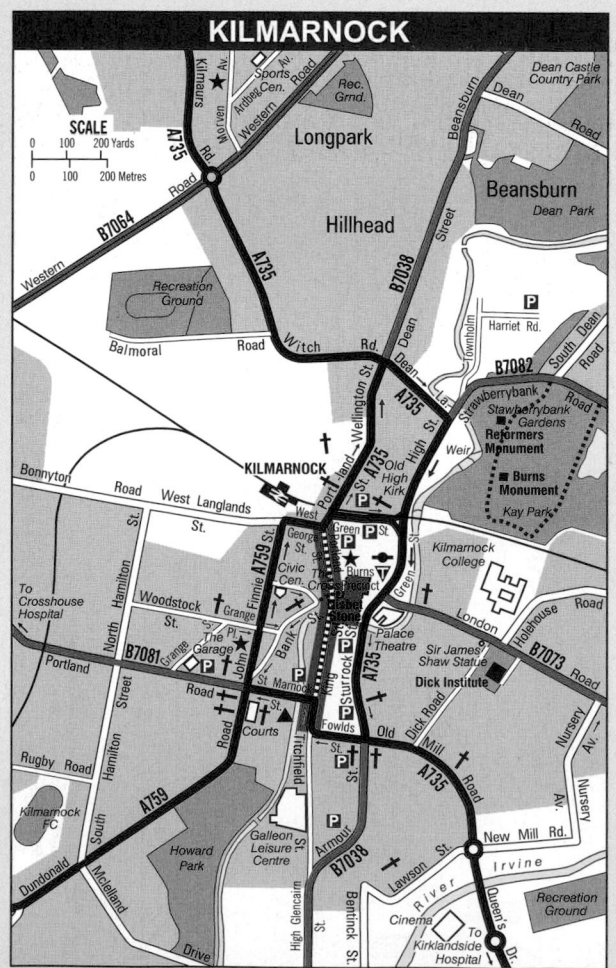

LINCOLN

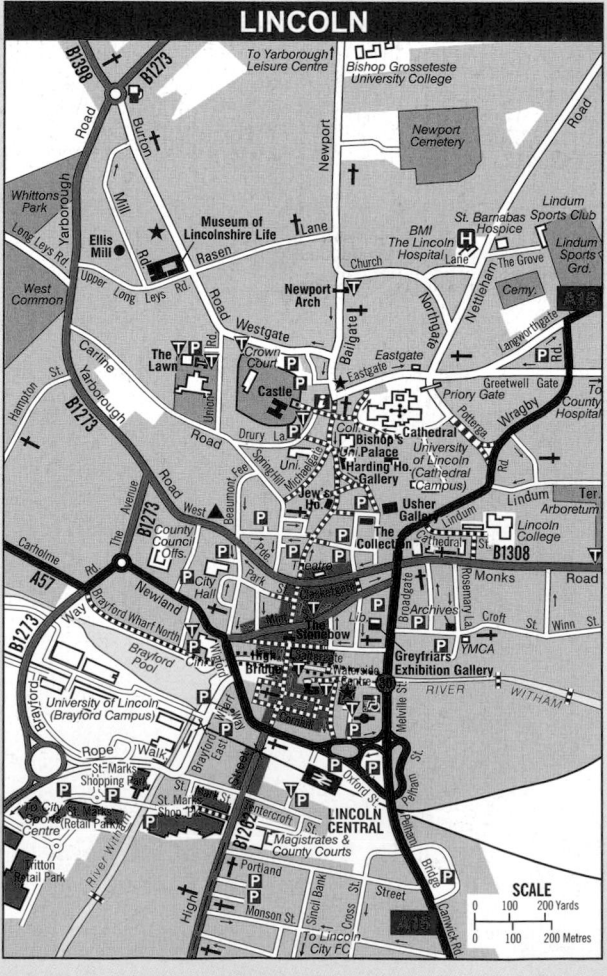

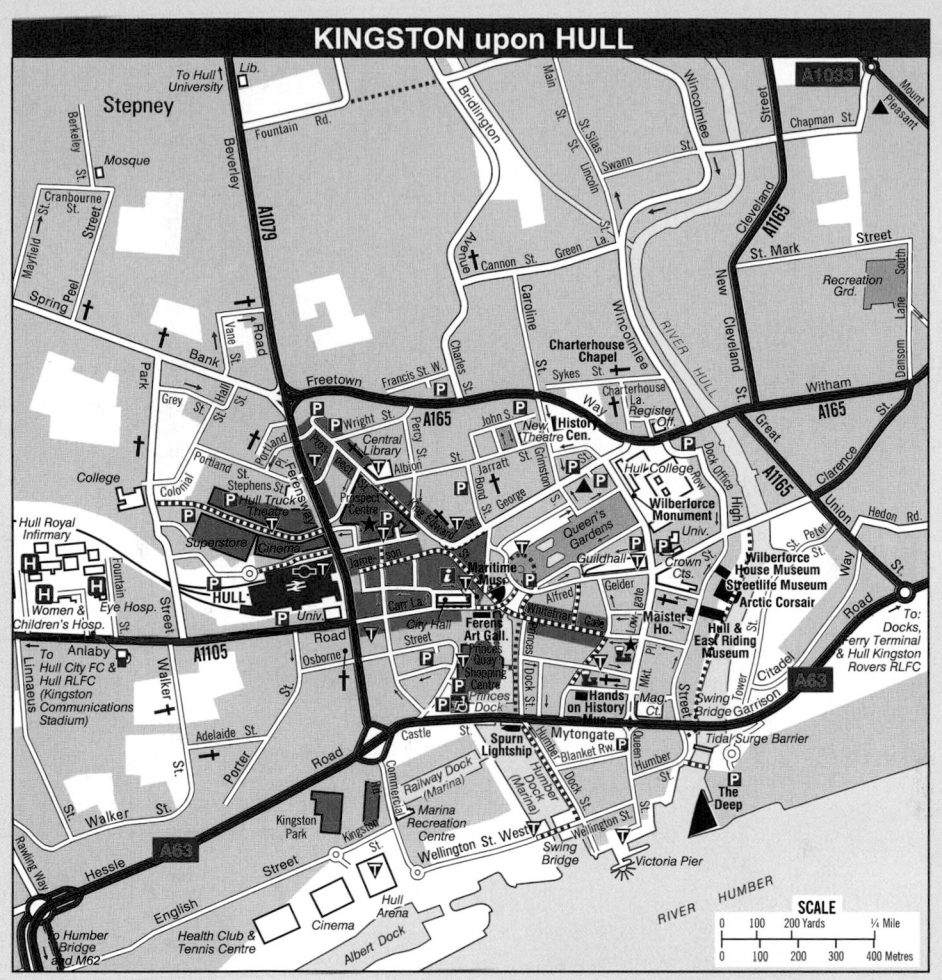

KINGSTON upon HULL

LEEDS

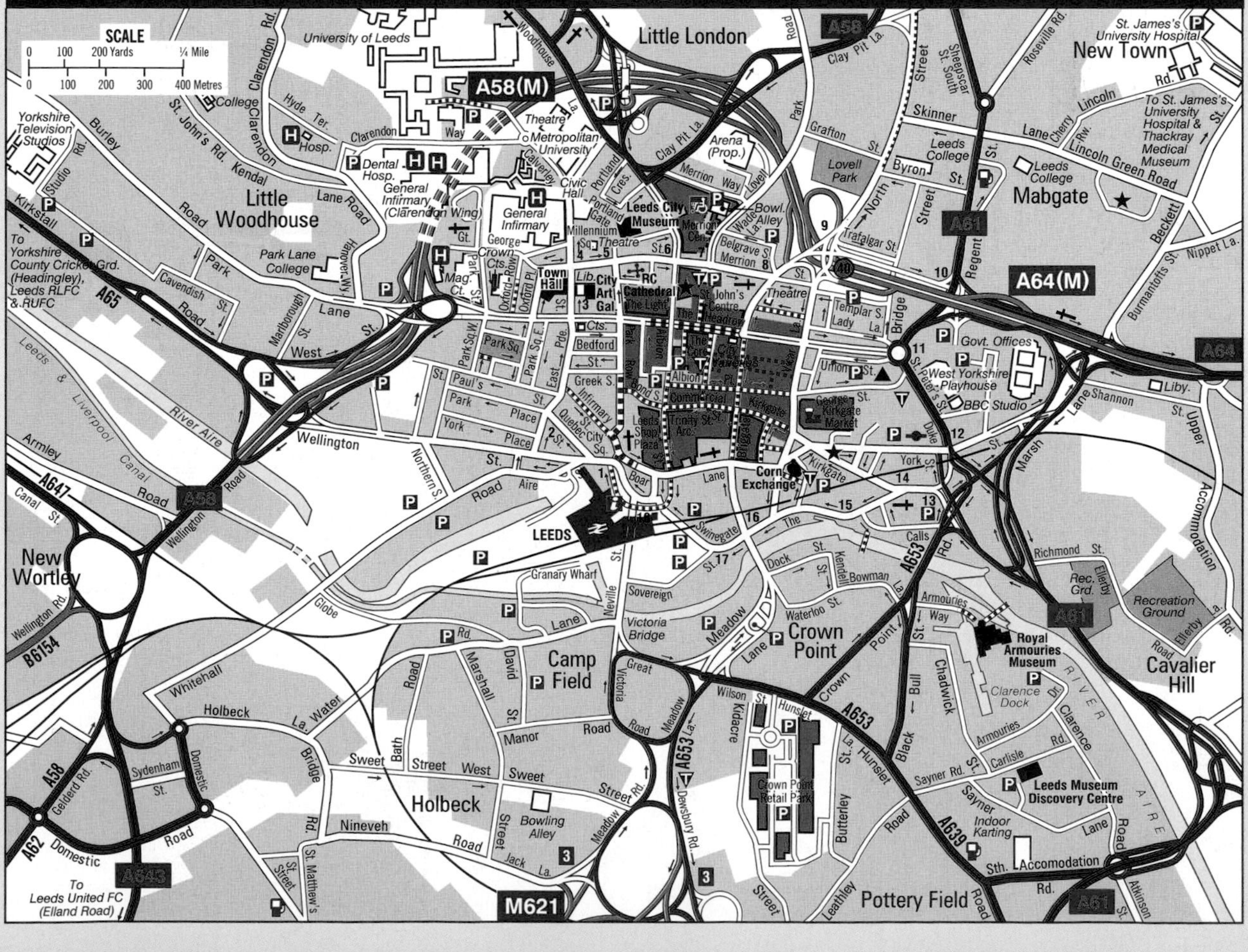

LEICESTER

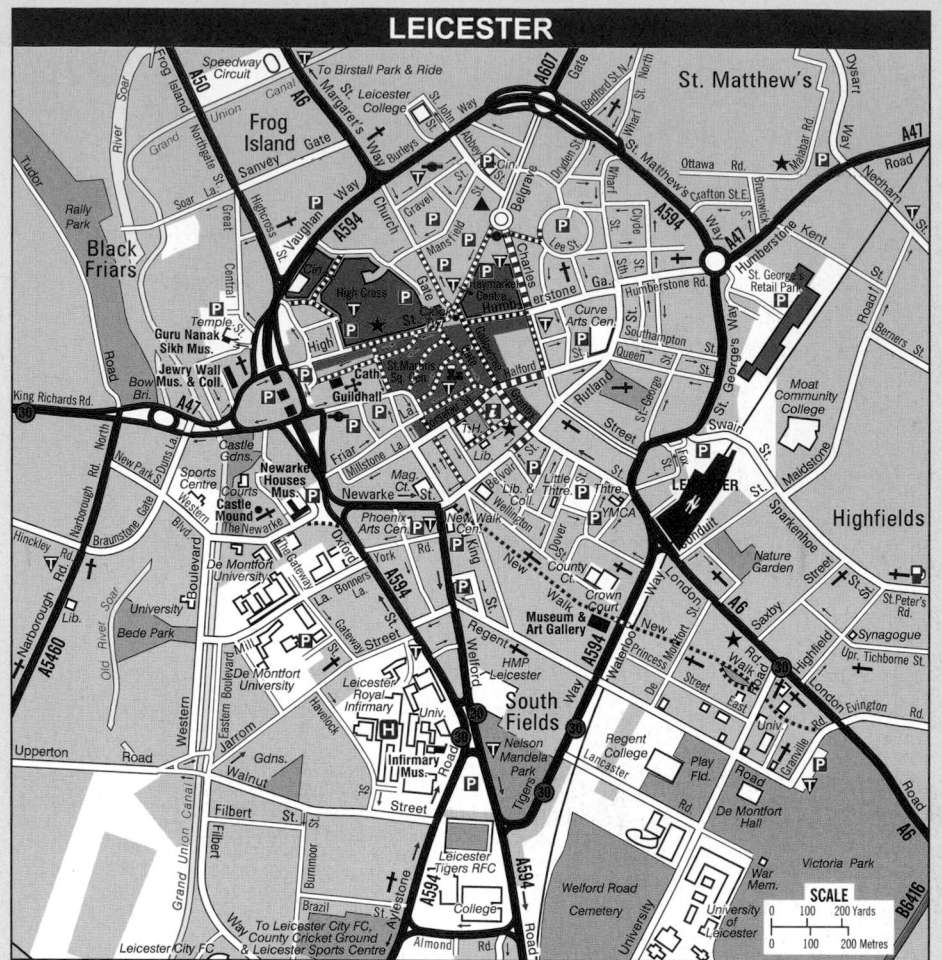

LIVERPOOL

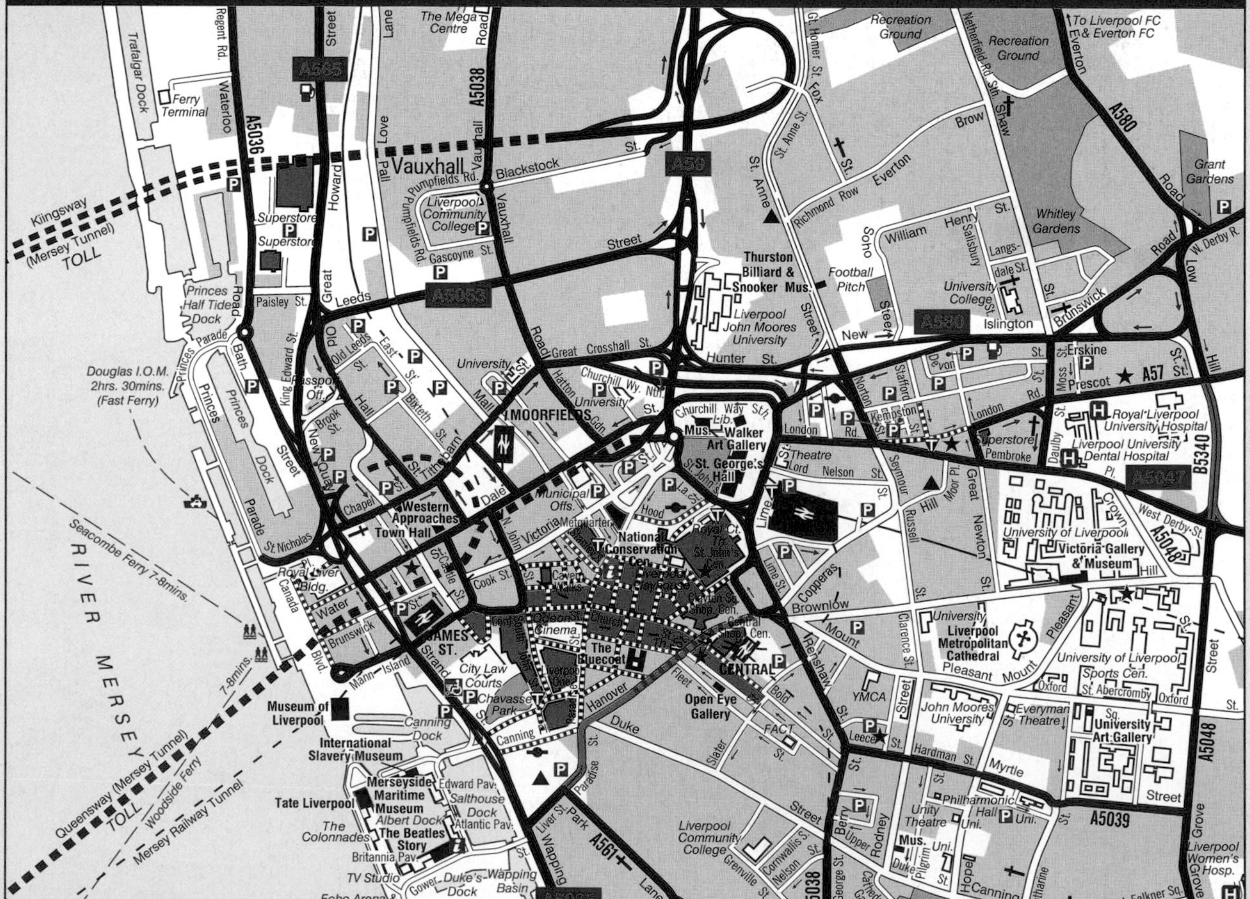

LUTON

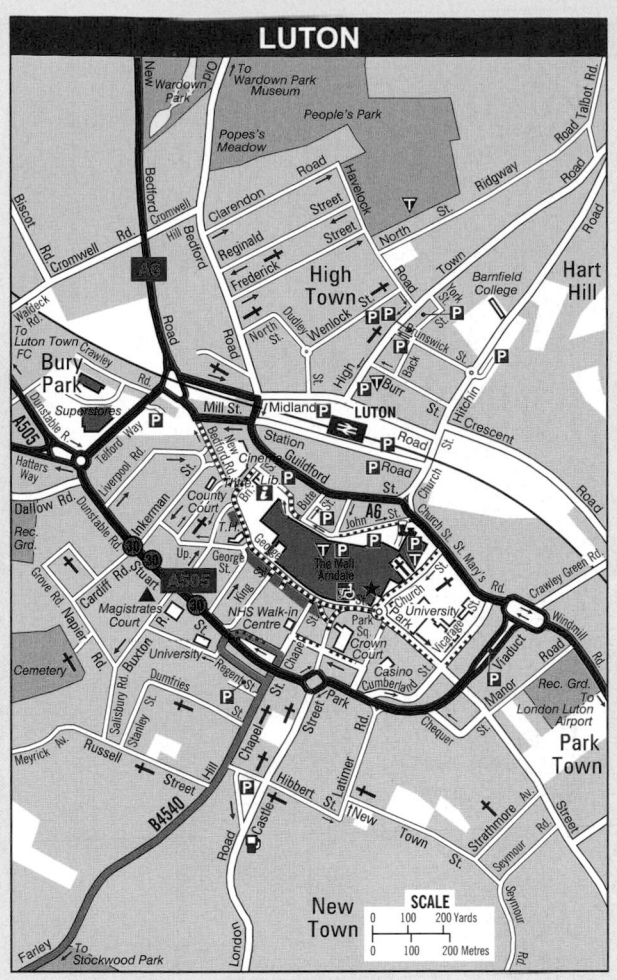

SCALE
| 0 | 100 | 200 Yards |
| 0 | 100 | 200 Metres |

MIDDLESBROUGH

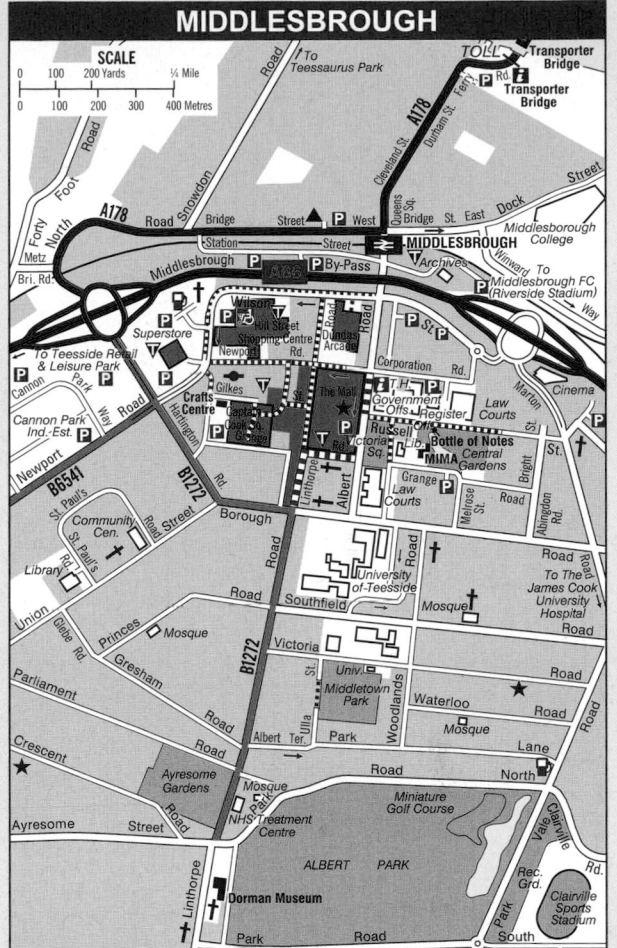

SCALE
| 0 | 100 | 200 Yards | ¼ Mile |
| 0 | 100 | 200 | 300 | 400 Metres |

MANCHESTER (CITY CENTRE)

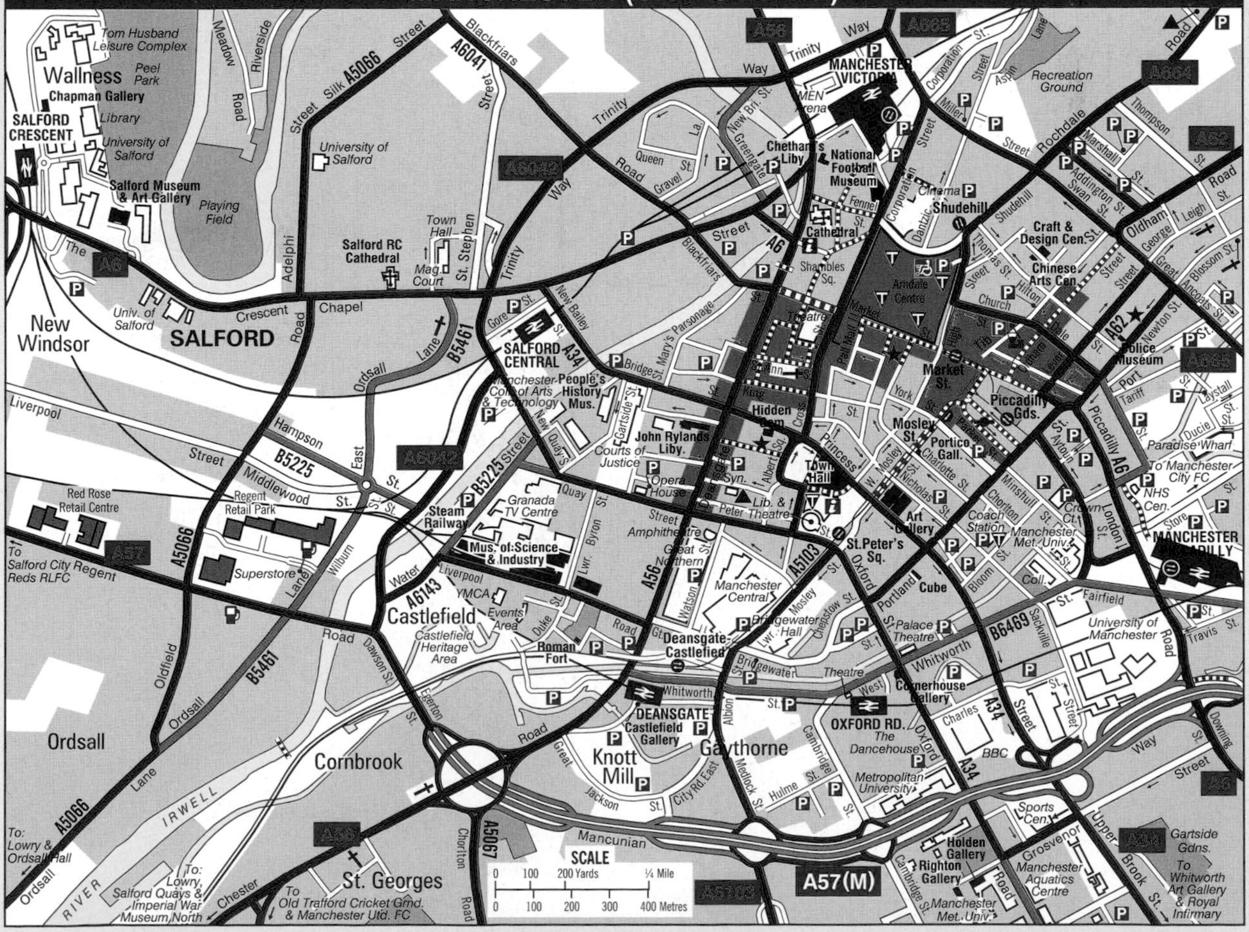

SCALE
| 0 | 100 | 200 Yards | ¼ Mile |
| 0 | 100 | 200 | 300 | 400 Metres |

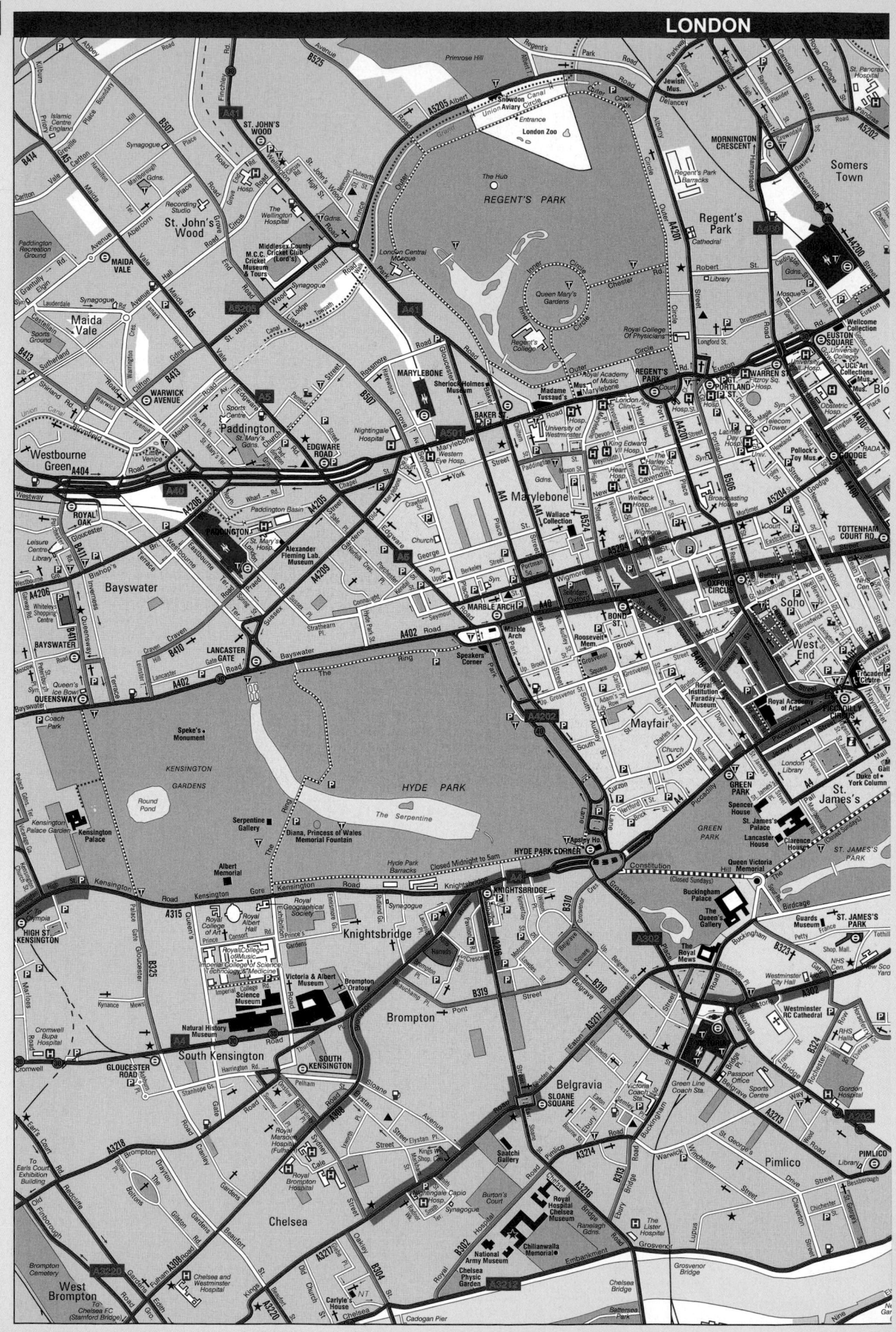

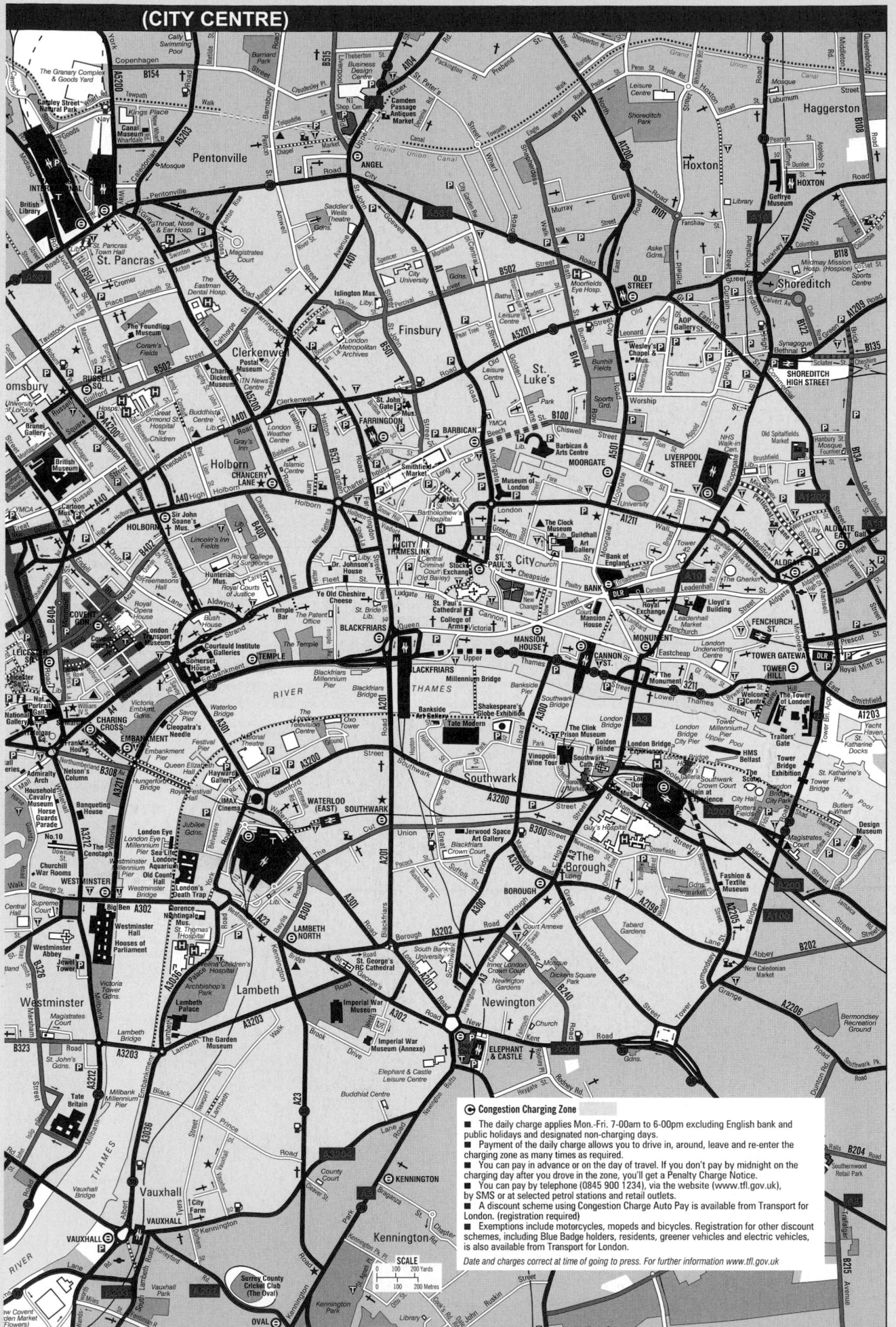

MEDWAY TOWNS

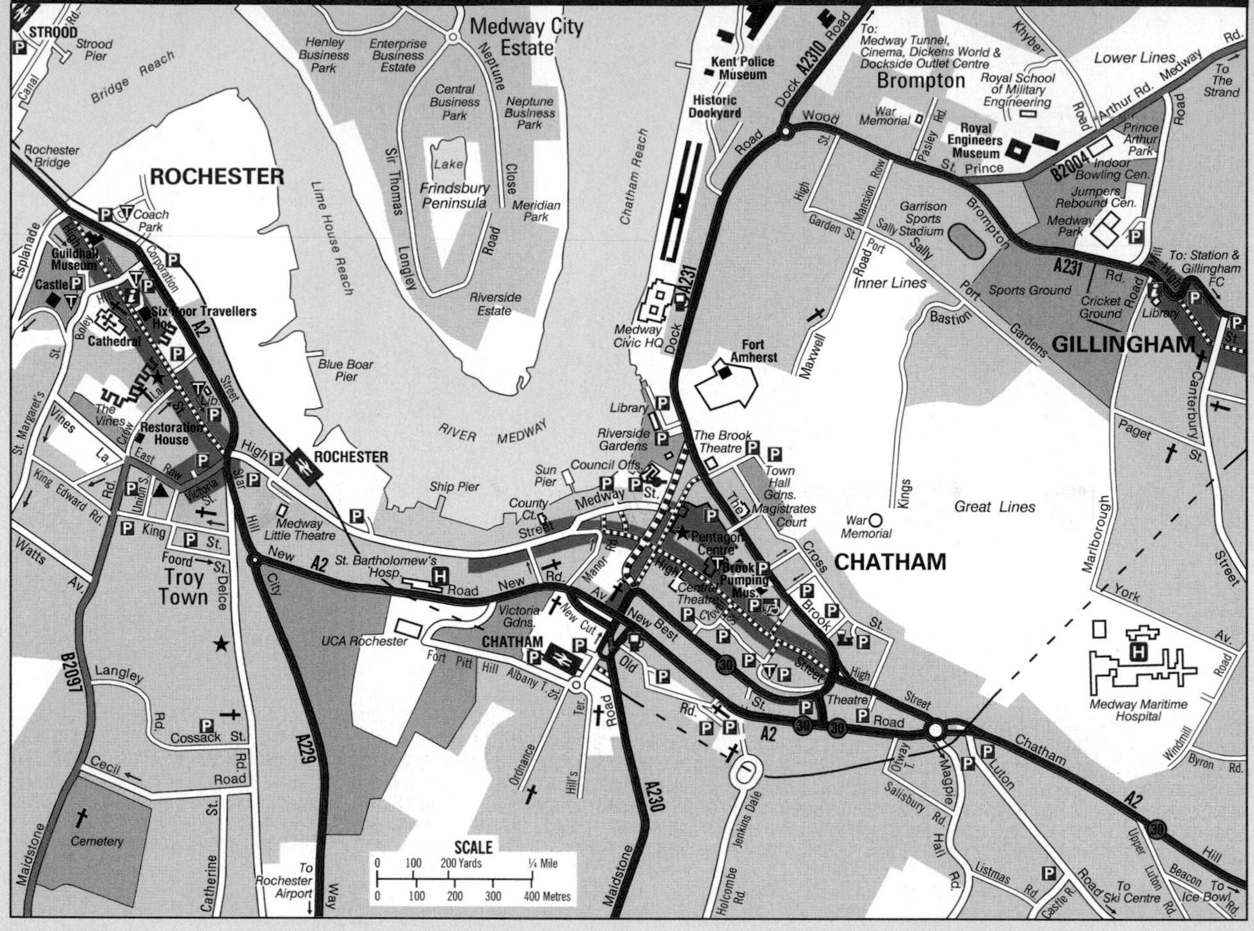

STROOD
ROCHESTER
Medway City Estate
Kent Police Museum
Historic Dockyard
Brompton
GILLINGHAM
CHATHAM
Troy Town
Great Lines
Medway Maritime Hospital
Fort Amherst
Pentagon Centre

SCALE
0 100 200 Yards ¼ Mile
0 100 200 300 400 Metres

MILTON KEYNES

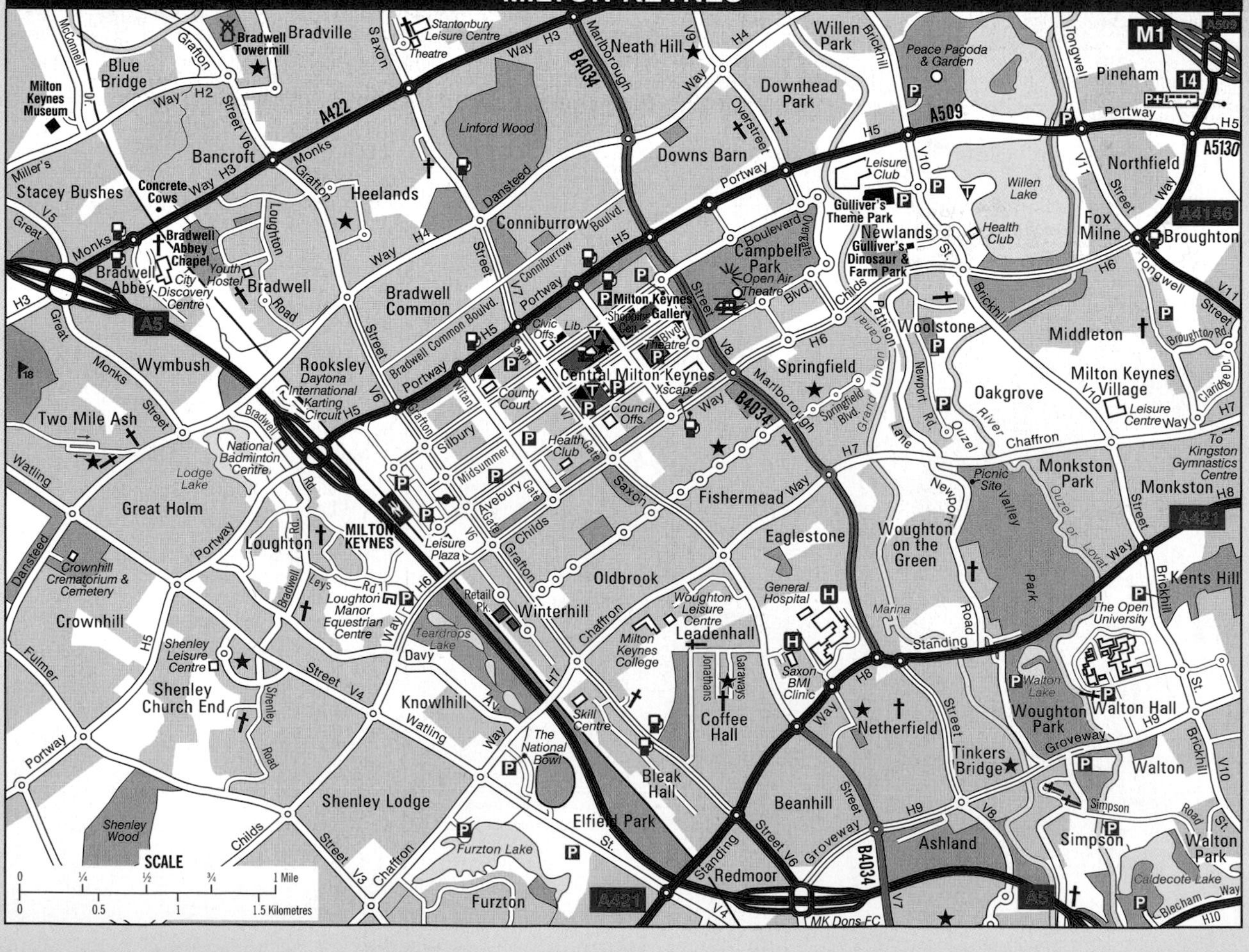

Bradville
Stantonbury
Neath Hill
Willen Park
Pineham
M1
14
Blue Bridge
Milton Keynes Museum
Bancroft
Heelands
Downhead Park
Northfield
Stacey Bushes
Concrete Cows
Conniburrow
Willen Lake
Fox Milne
Broughton
Bradwell Abbey
Bradwell
Bradwell Common
Campbell Park
Newlands
Woolstone
Middleton
Wymbush
Rooksley
Central Milton Keynes
Springfield
Milton Keynes Village
Oakgrove
Two Mile Ash
Silbury
Monkston Park
Monkston
Great Holm
MILTON KEYNES
Loughton
Fishermead
Eaglestone
Woughton on the Green
Kents Hill
Crownhill
Winterhill
Oldbrook
Leadenhall
General Hospital
The Open University
Woughton Park
Walton Hall
Shenley Leisure Centre
Knowlhill
Coffee Hall
Netherfield
Walton
Shenley Church End
Bleak Hall
Beanhill
Tinkers Bridge
Shenley Lodge
Elfield Park
Ashland
Simpson
Walton Park
Furzton
Redmoor
MK Dons FC
Caldecote Lake

SCALE
0 ¼ ½ ¾ 1 Mile
0 0.5 1 1.5 Kilometres

NORWICH

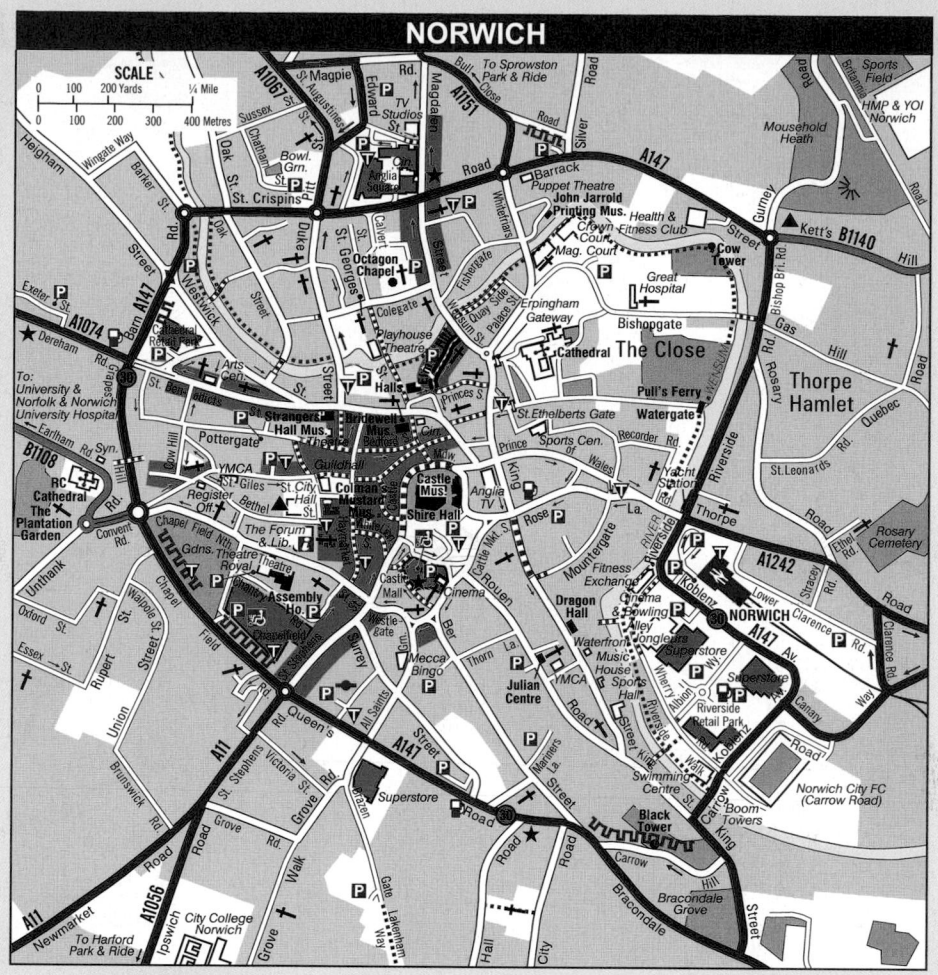

NEWCASTLE UPON TYNE

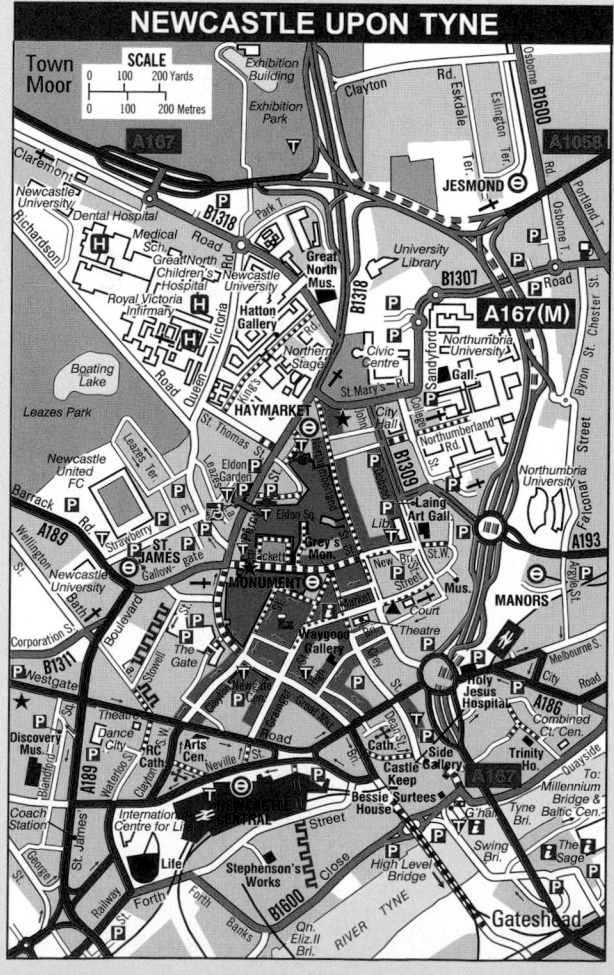

NEWPORT (CASNEWYDD)

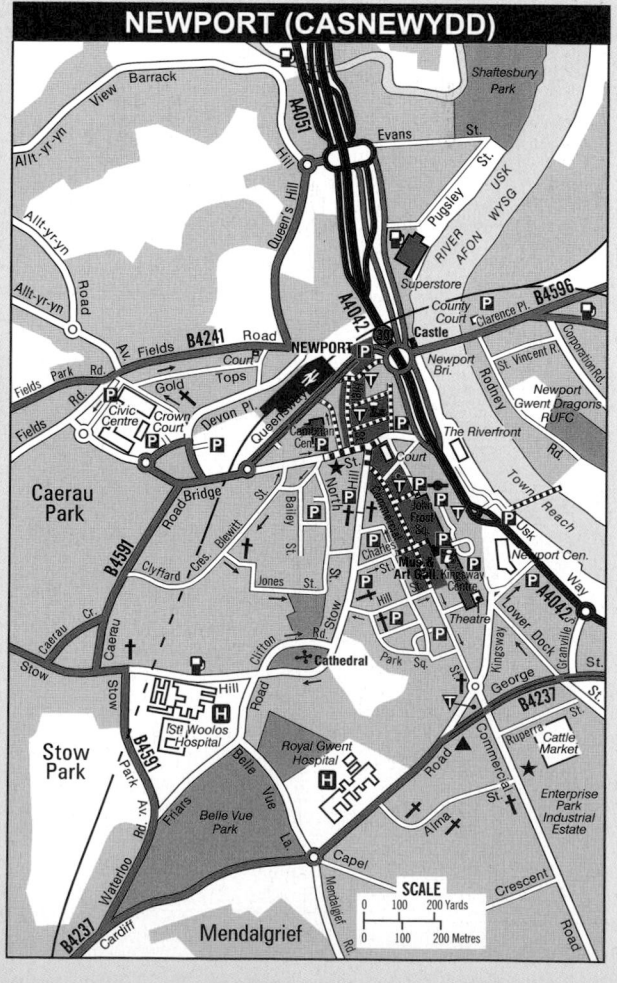

NOTTINGHAM

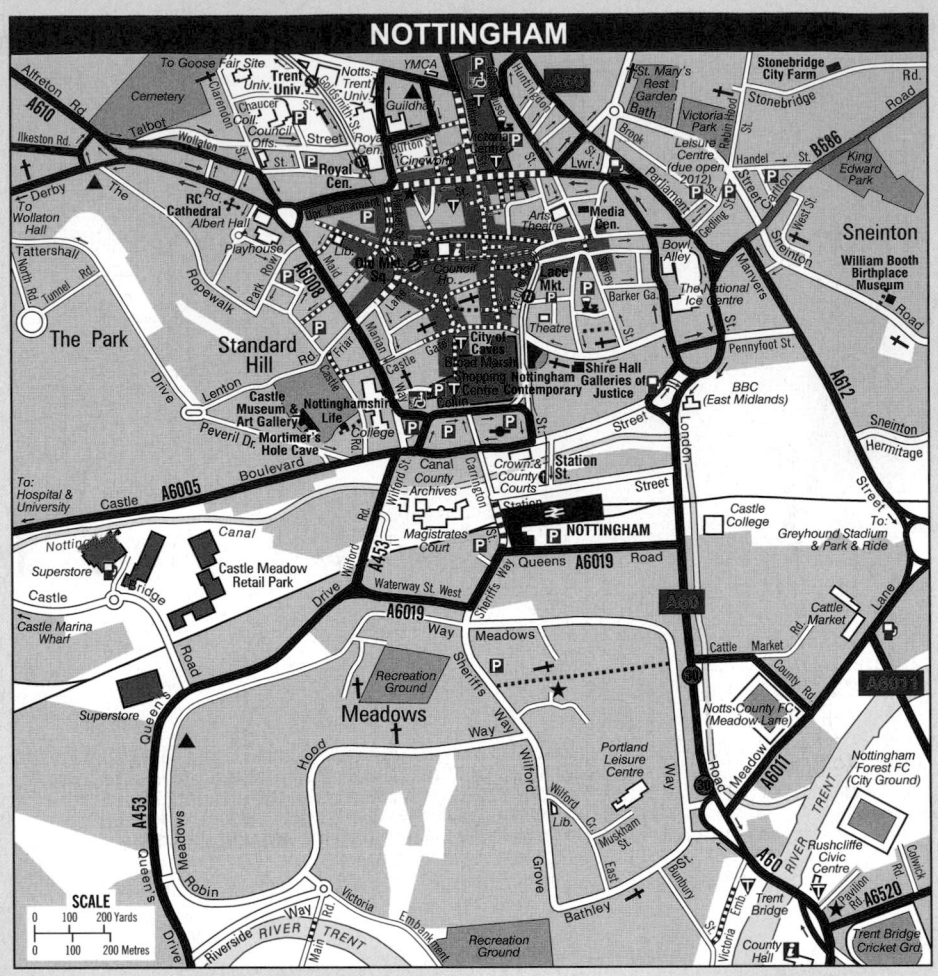

NORTHAMPTON

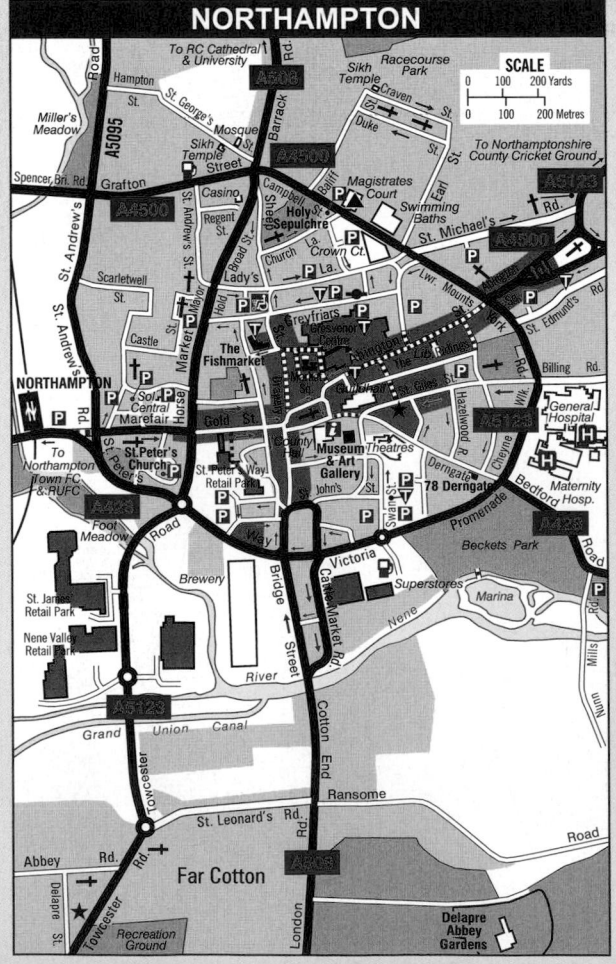

OBAN

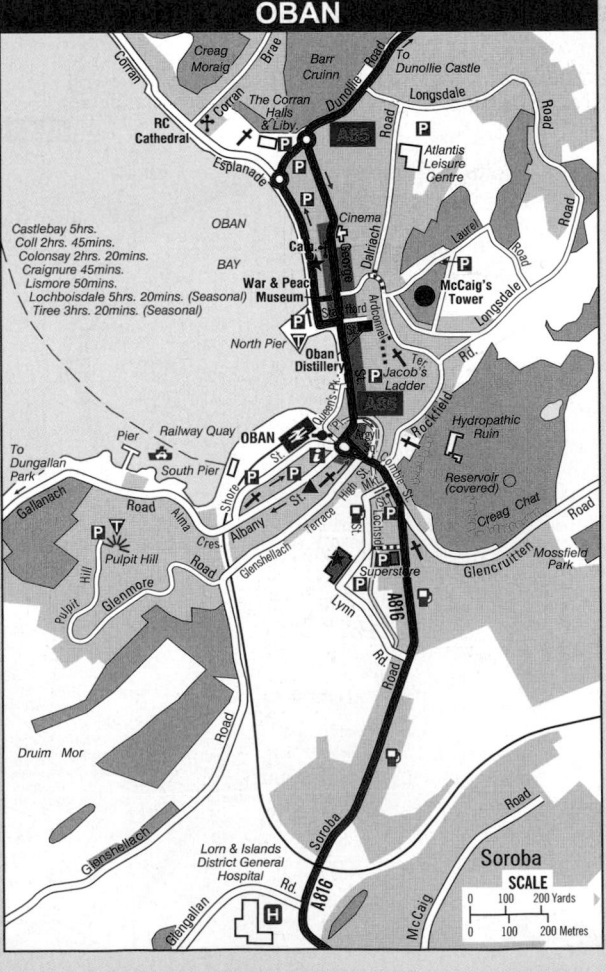

OXFORD

KEY TO COLLEGES
1. All Souls College
2. Balliol College
3. Blackfriars
4. Brasenose College
5. Campion Hall
6. Christ Church
7. Corpus Christi College
8. Examination Schools
9. Exeter College
10. Green Templeton College
11. Harris Manchester College & Chapel
12. Hertford College
13. Jesus College
14. Keble College
15. Kellogg College
16. Lady Margaret Hall
17. Linacre College
18. Lincoln College
19. Magdalen College
20. Mansfield College
21. Merton College
22. New College
23. Nuffield College
24. Oriel College
25. Pembroke College
26. Queen's College, The
27. Regents Park College
28. St. Anne's College
29. St. Antony's College
30. St. Benet's Hall
31. St. Catherine's College
32. St. Cross College
33. St. Edmund Hall
34. St. Hilda's College
35. St. John's College
36. St. Peter's College
37. St. Stephen's House
38. Somerville College
39. Trinity College
40. University College
41. Wadham College
42. Worcester College
43. Wycliffe Hall
SCALE
200 Yards
¼ Mile
400 Metres
Waltham Manor
Norham Manor
Jericho
New Osney
University Parks
Oxford University Cricket Club (The Parks)
Pitt Rivers Museum
University Museum of Natural History
Ashmolean Mus.
Bridge of Sighs
Radcliffe Camera
Carfax Tower
Modern Art Oxford
Botanic Garden
Christ Church Meadow
Deer Park
South Park
Science Oxford
Bate Collection
Folly Bridge
To Seacourt Park & Ride
To Redbridge Park & Ride and Oxford United FC
To: Thornhill Park & Ride & Oxford Brookes University
To Warneford Hospital
To Pear Tree Park & Ride
To: St. Hugh's Coll. & Wolfson Coll.

PAISLEY

Laigh Park
Castlehead
To Glasgow Airport
St. Mirren FC (St. Mirren Park)
Fountain Gardens
PAISLEY GILMOUR ST.
Paisley Museum & Art Galleries
Coats Observatory
Paisley Abbey
Sma' Shot Cotts.
Paisley Thread Mill Museum
PAISLEY CANAL
Saucel Hill
Saucelhill Park
ROYAL ALEXANDRA HOSPITAL
Reid Kerr College
RC Cathedral
To: Elderslie Golf Course & Cinema
To: Dykebar Hospital & Accord Hospice
To: Barshaw Park & Golf Course
To Brodie Park
SCALE
200 Yards
200 Metres

PERTH

SCALE
200 Yards
200 Metres
North Inch
Golf Course
RIVER TAY
Black Watch Regimental Museum (Balhousie Castle)
Bell's Sports Centre
Bowling Greens
St. Catherine's Retail Park
Cathedral
Museum & Art Gall.
Concert Hall
Perth Theatre
St. John's Shop. Cen.
St. John's Kirk
Council Chambers
Queen's Bridge
Perth Leisure Pool
PERTH
Fergusson Gallery
South Inch
King James VI Golf Course
To Perth Racecourse
To Murray Royal Hosp.
To Perth Royal Infirmary
To St. Johnstone FC
To M90
HMP Perth

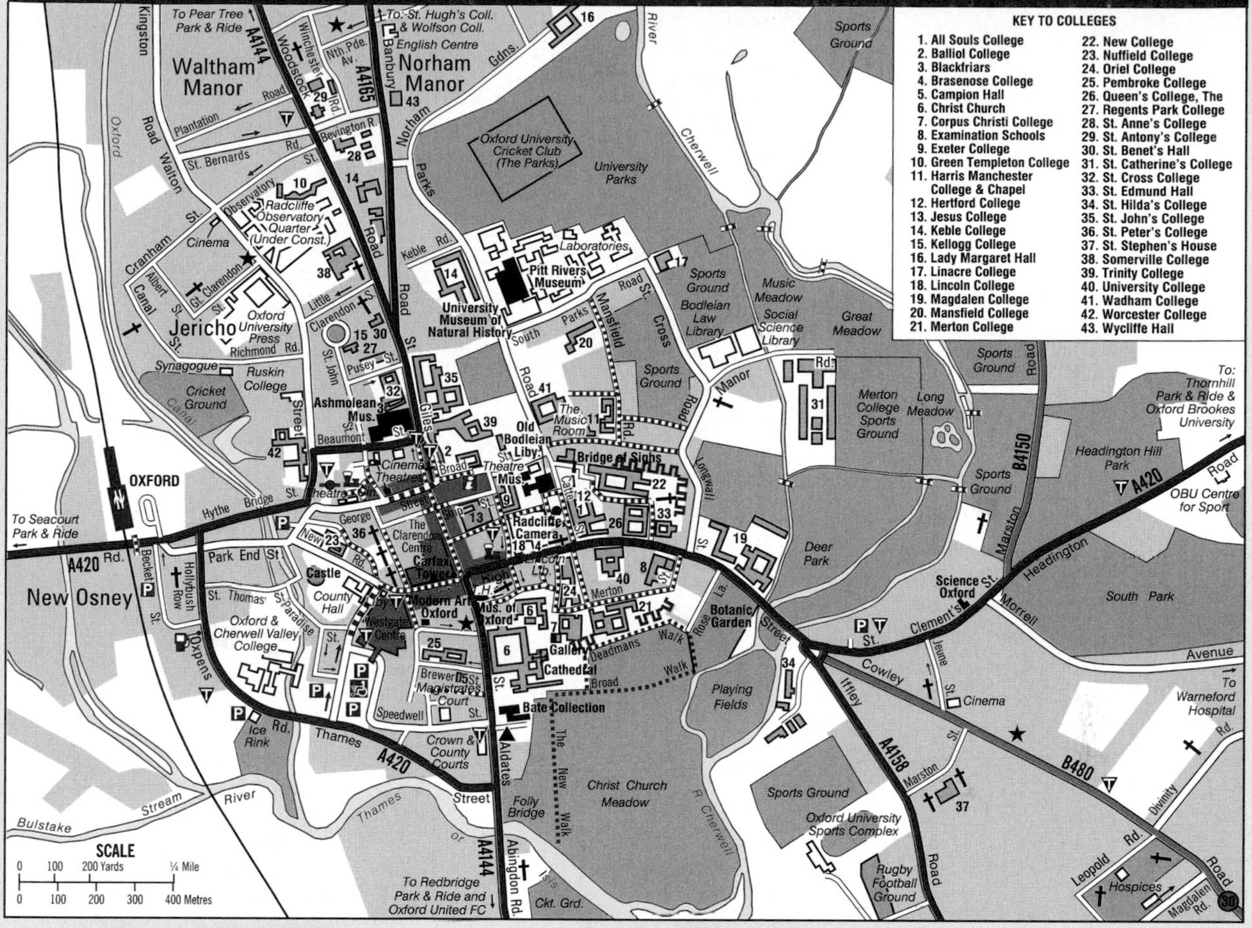

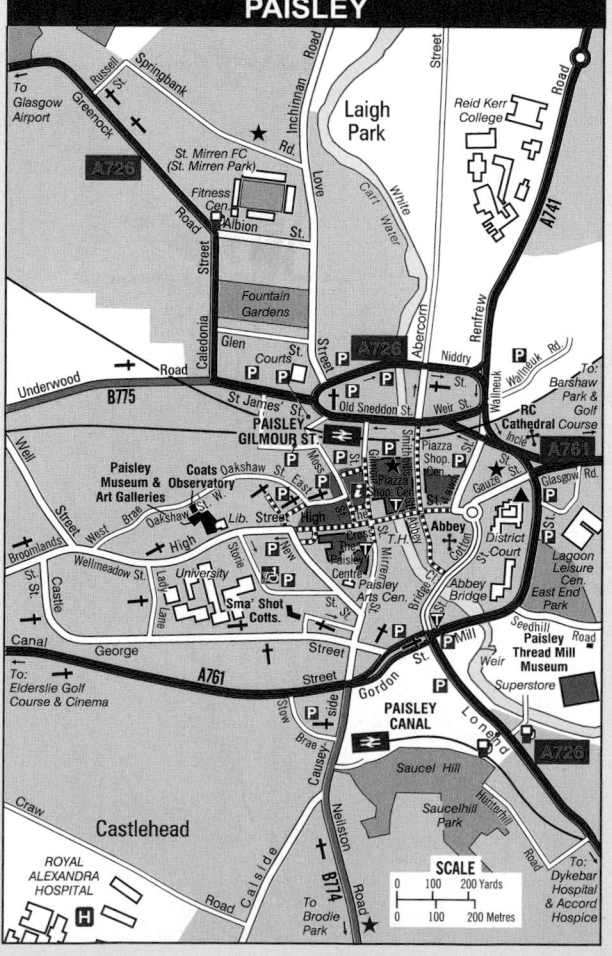

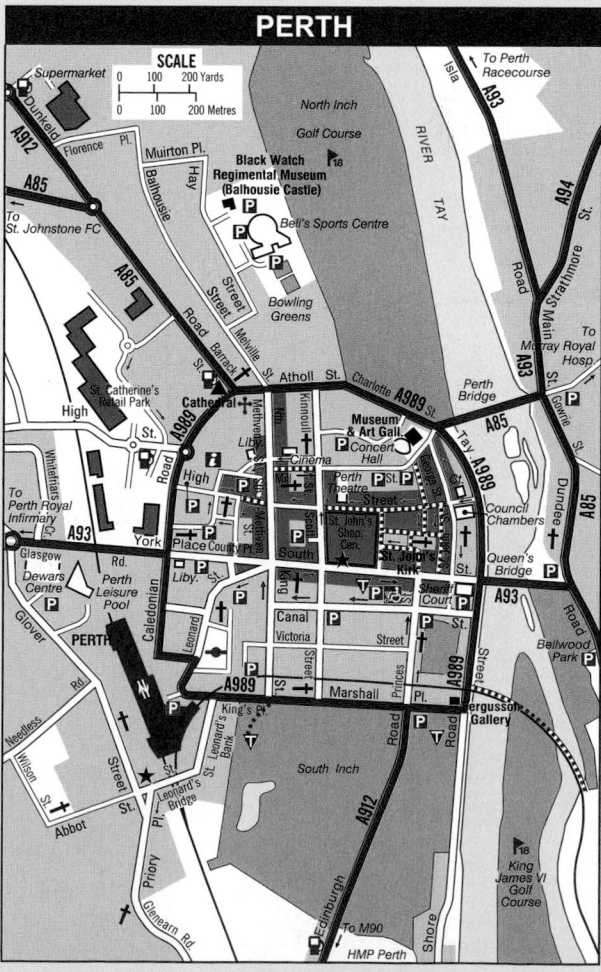

PLYMOUTH

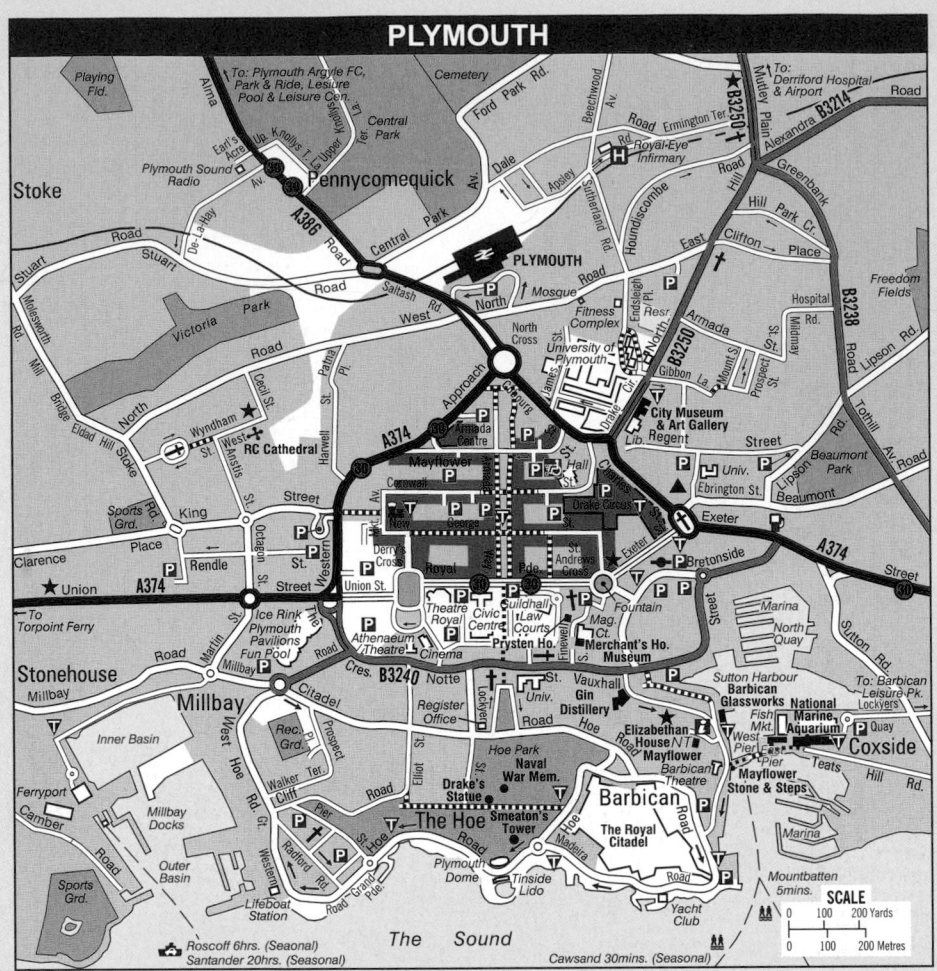

PETERBOROUGH

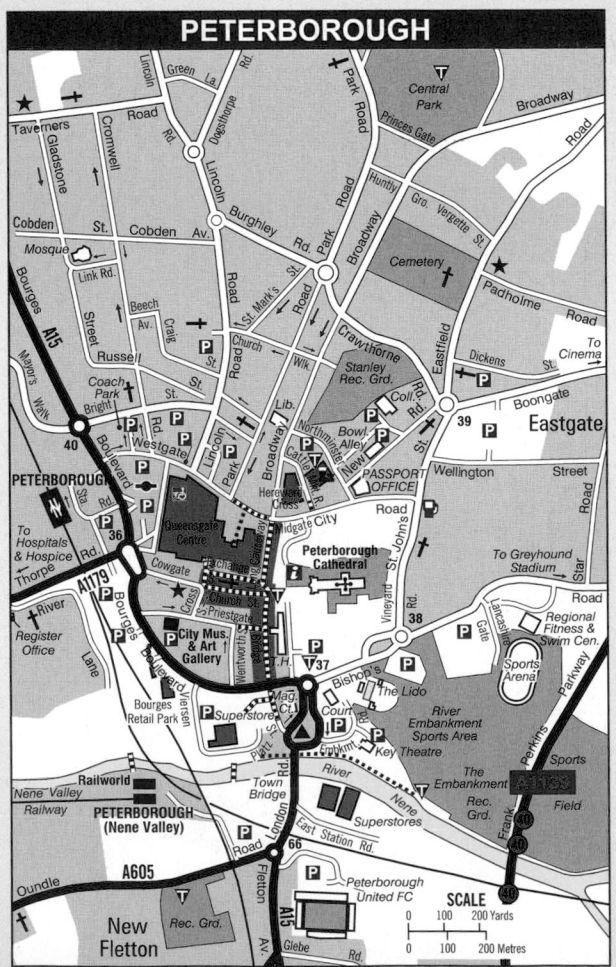

PRESTON

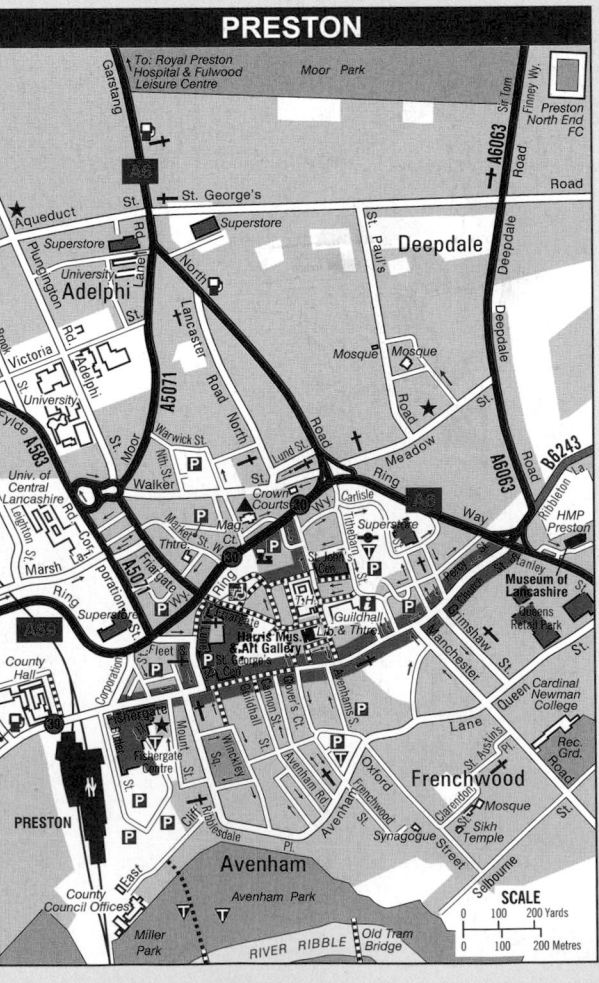

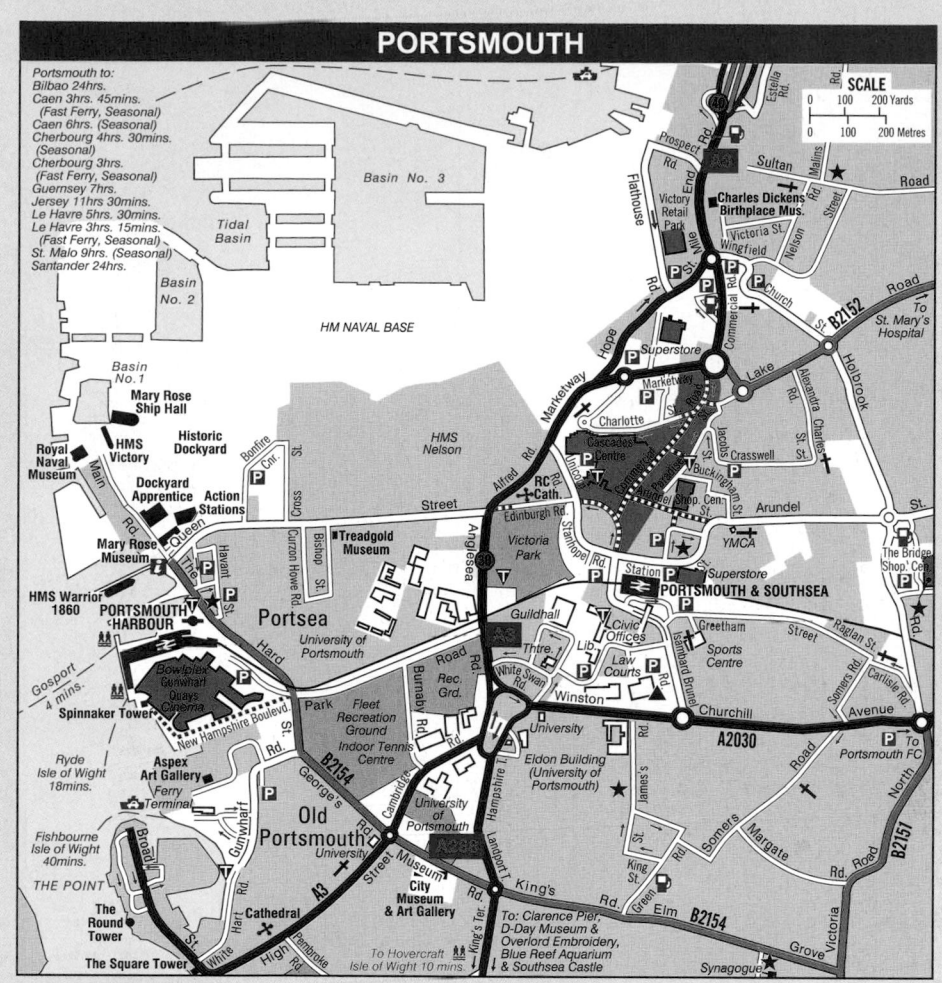

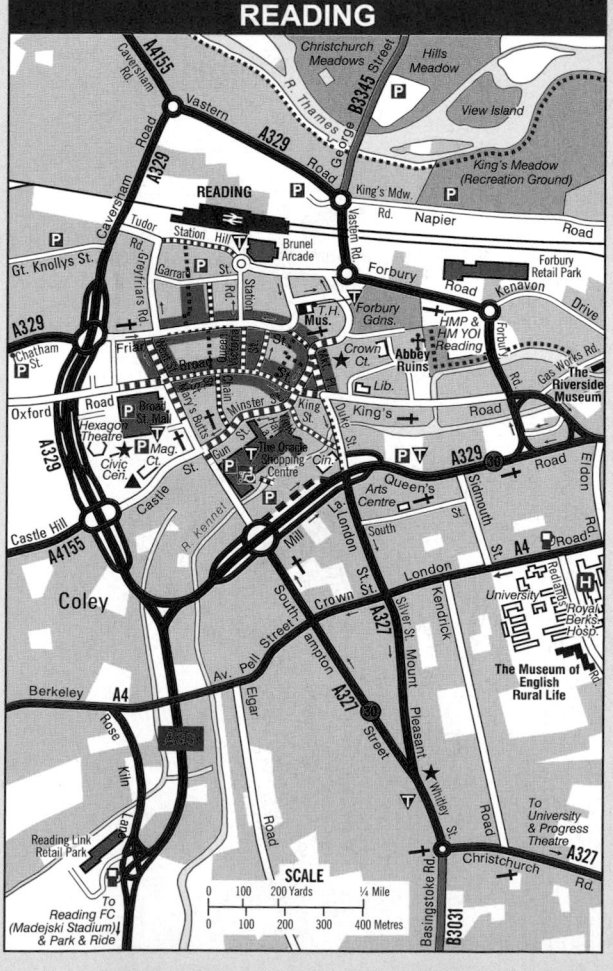

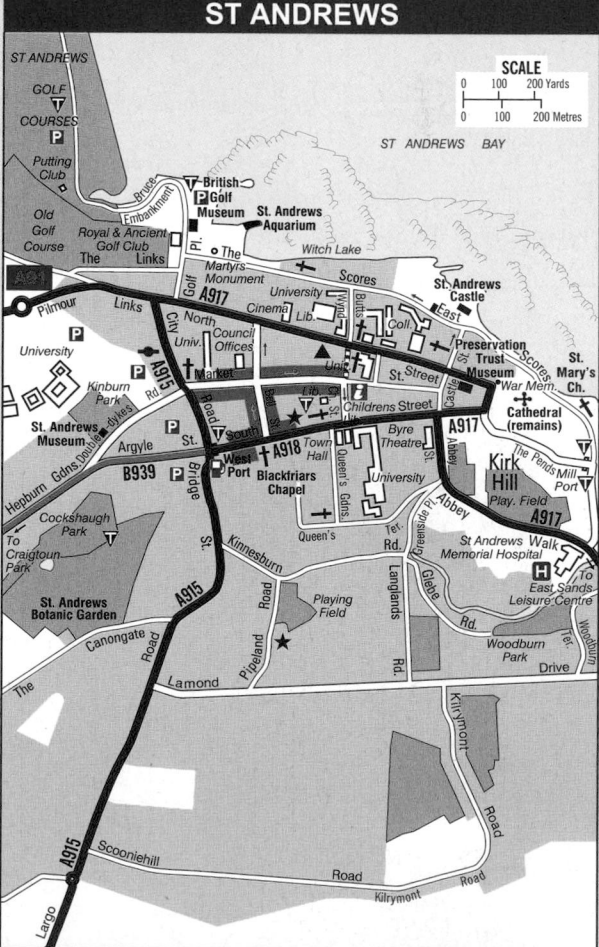

SALISBURY

SHREWSBURY

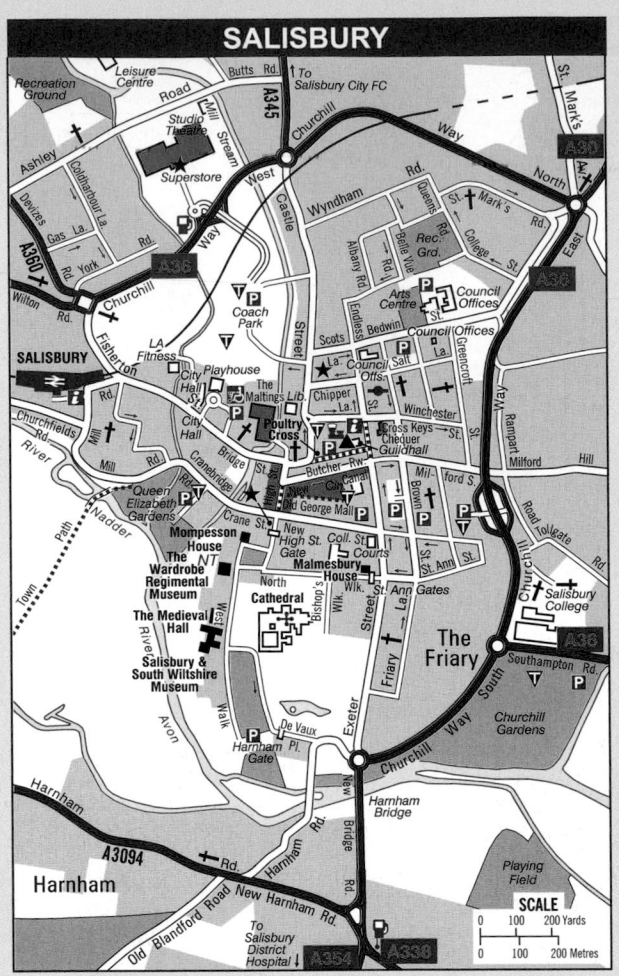

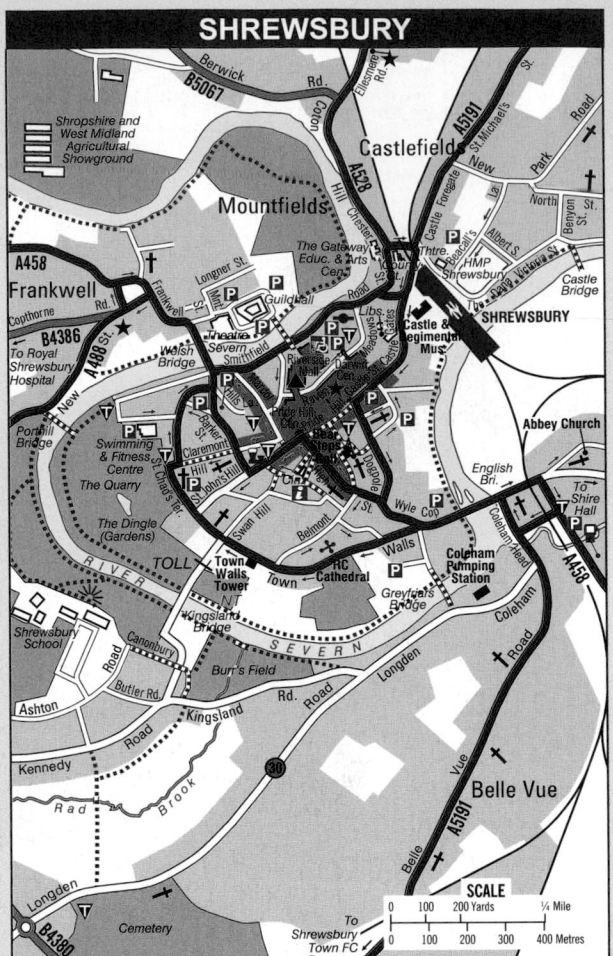

SHEFFIELD

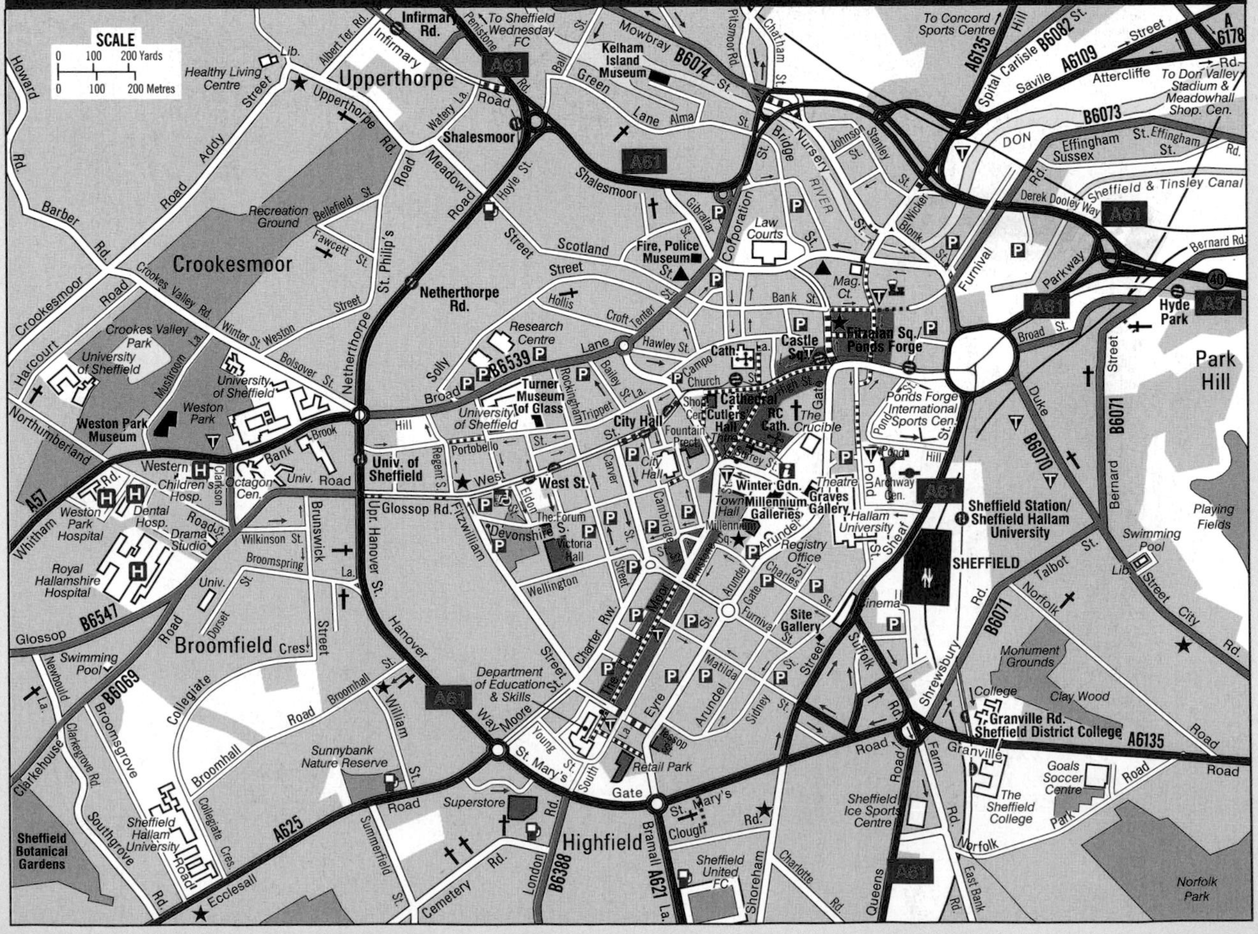

SOUTHAMPTON

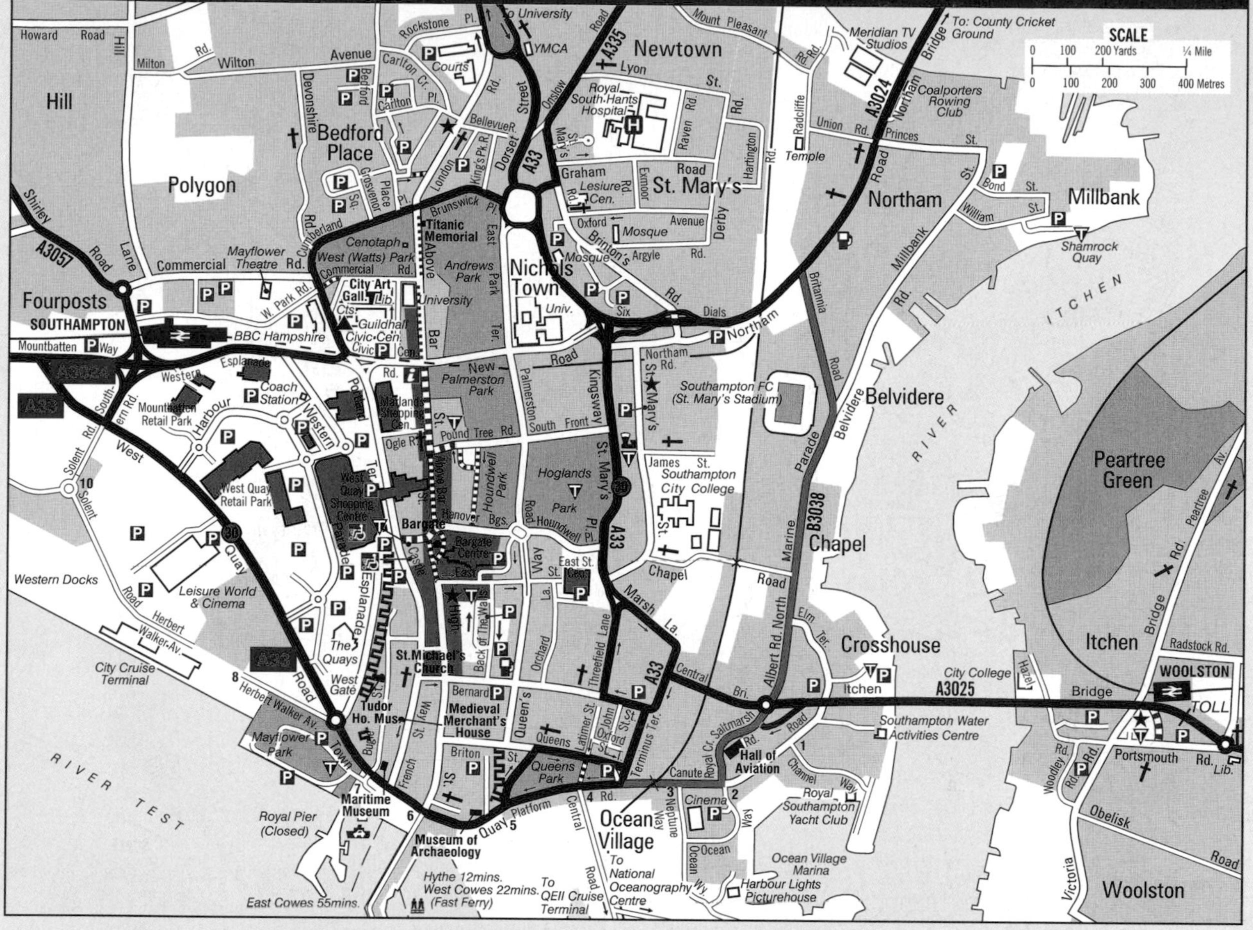

STIRLING

STOKE-ON-TRENT

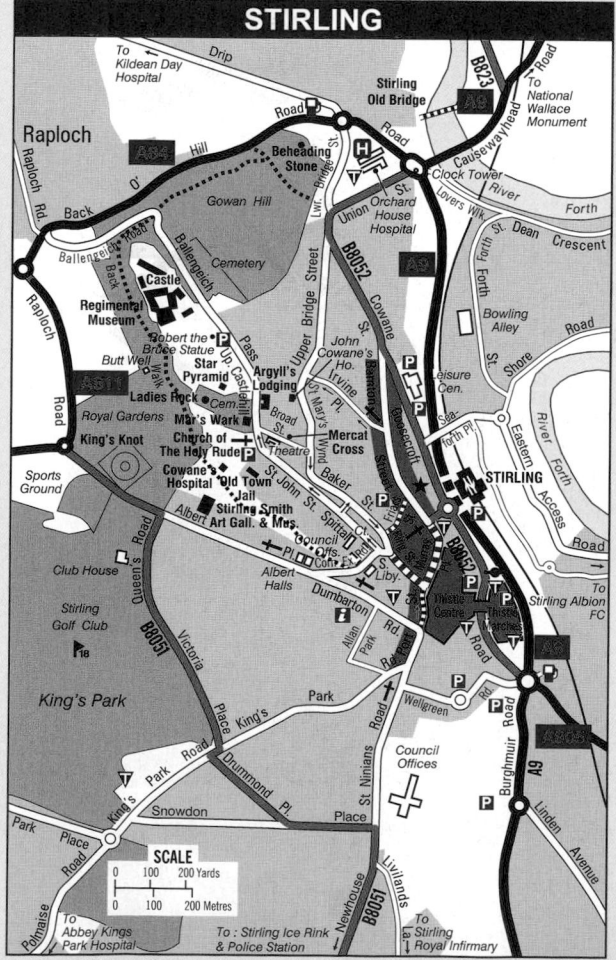

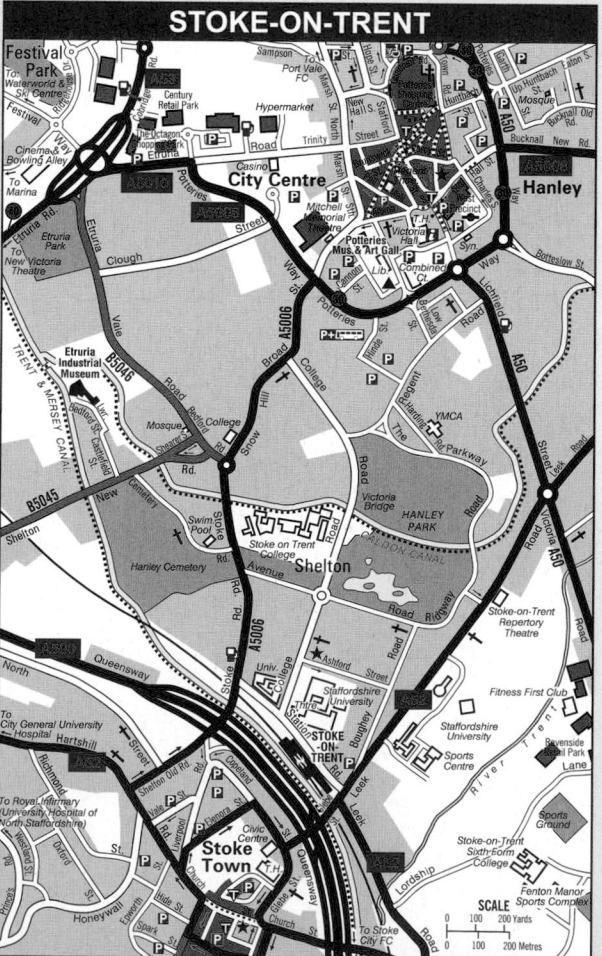

STRATFORD upon AVON

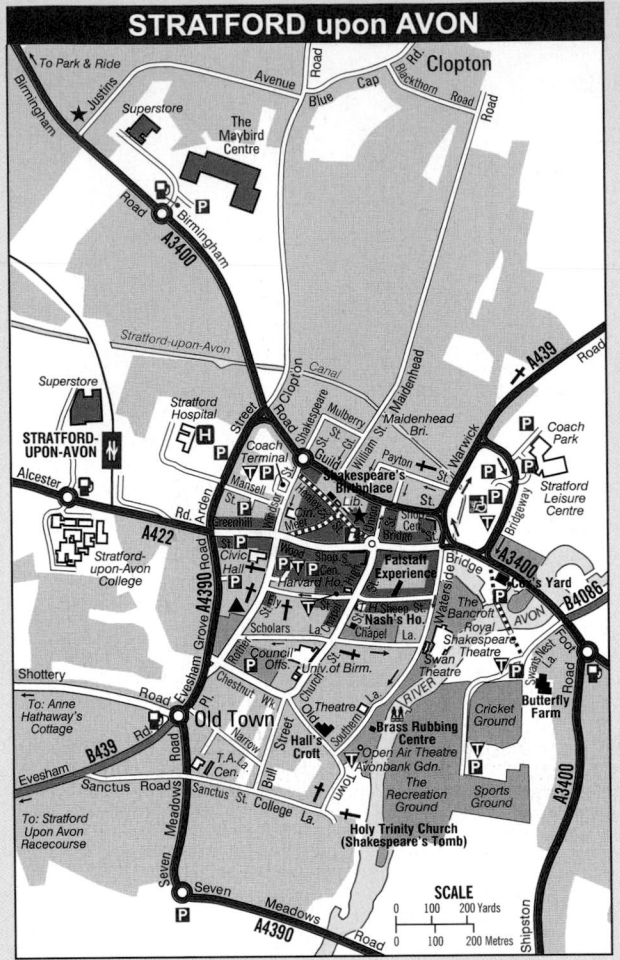

SUNDERLAND

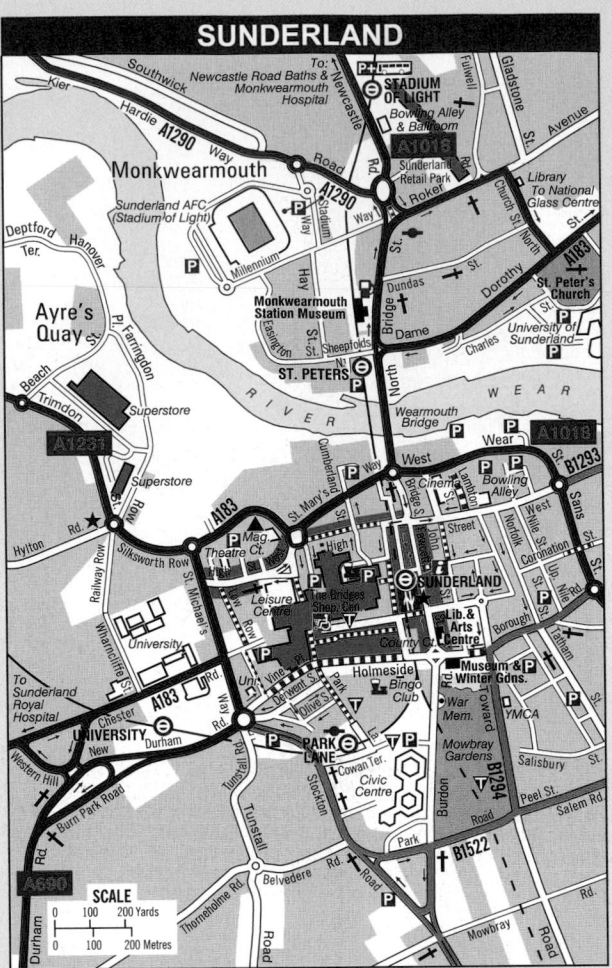

SWANSEA (ABERTAWE)

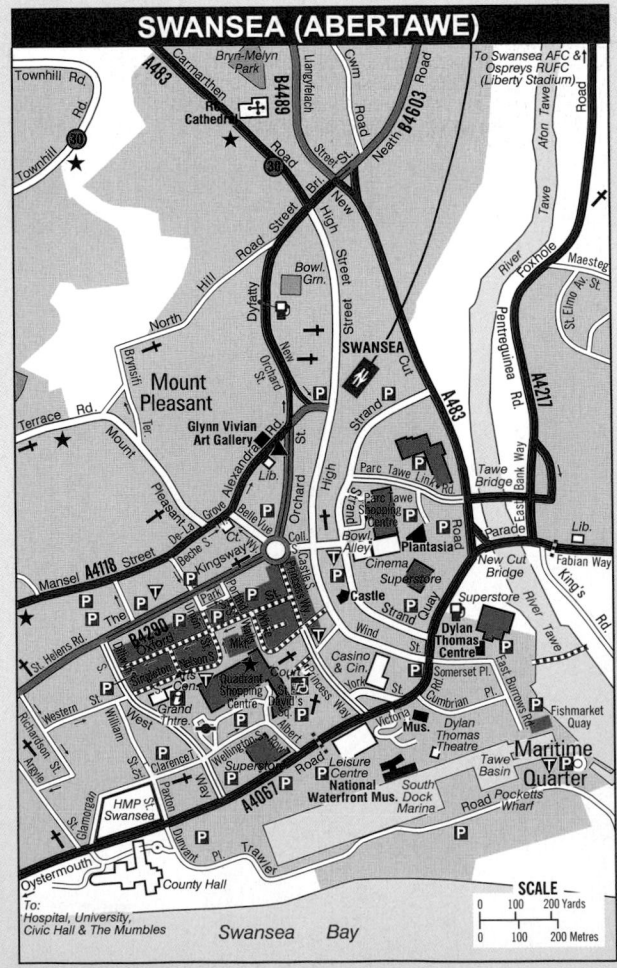

SWINDON

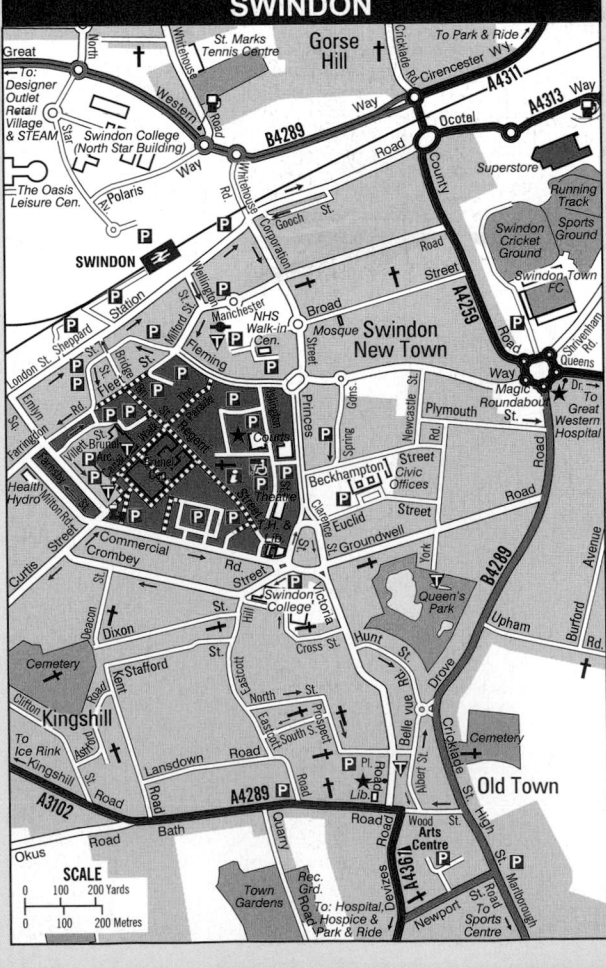

TAUNTON

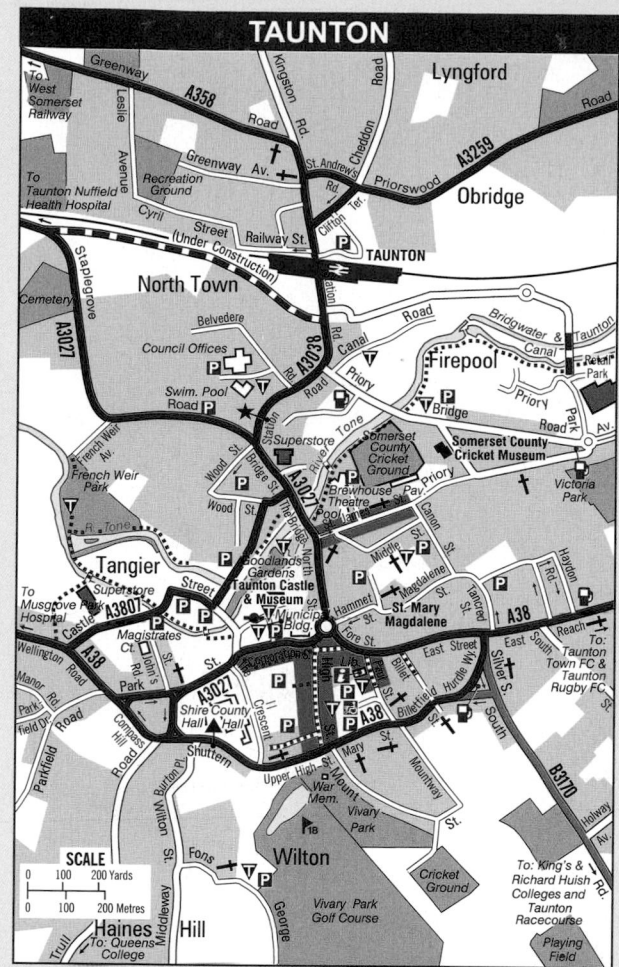

WINCHESTER

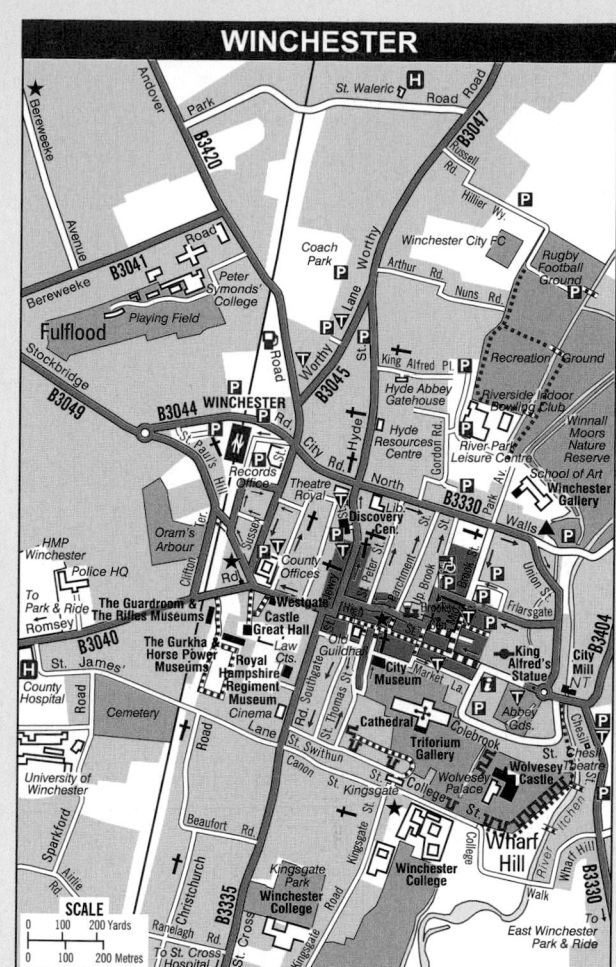

WINDSOR

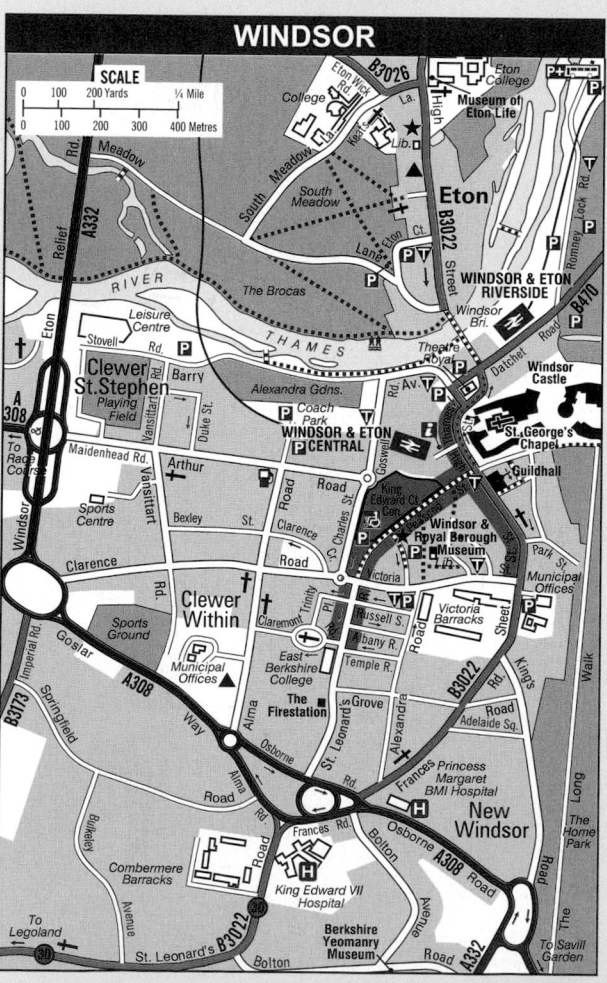

WOLVERHAMPTON

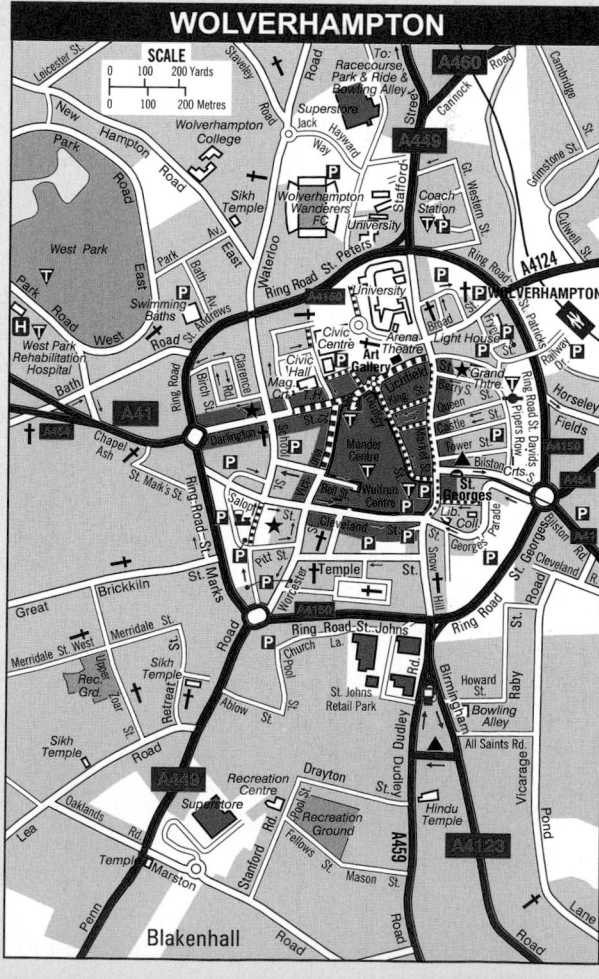

WORCESTER

WREXHAM (WRECSAM)

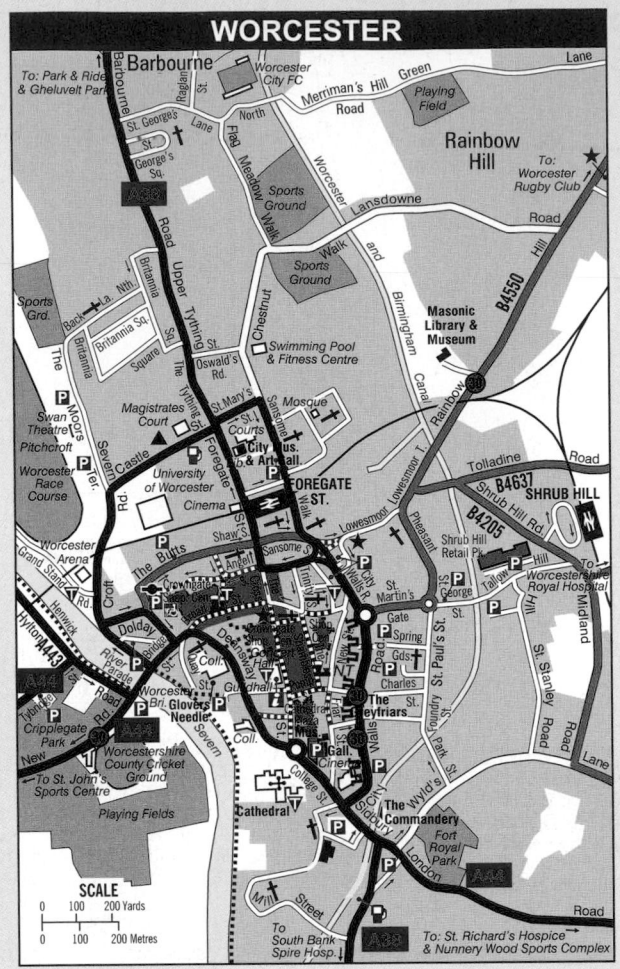

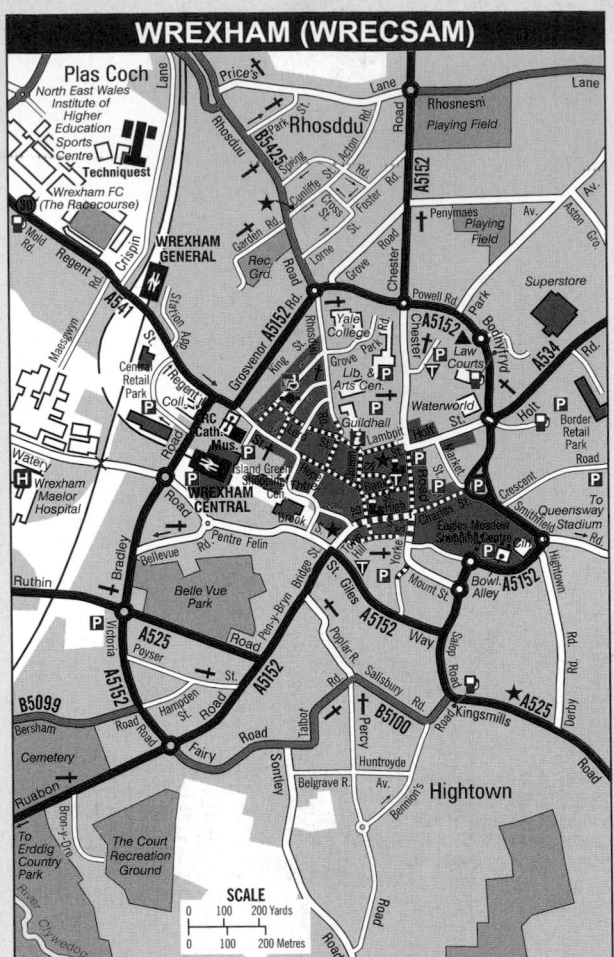

YORK

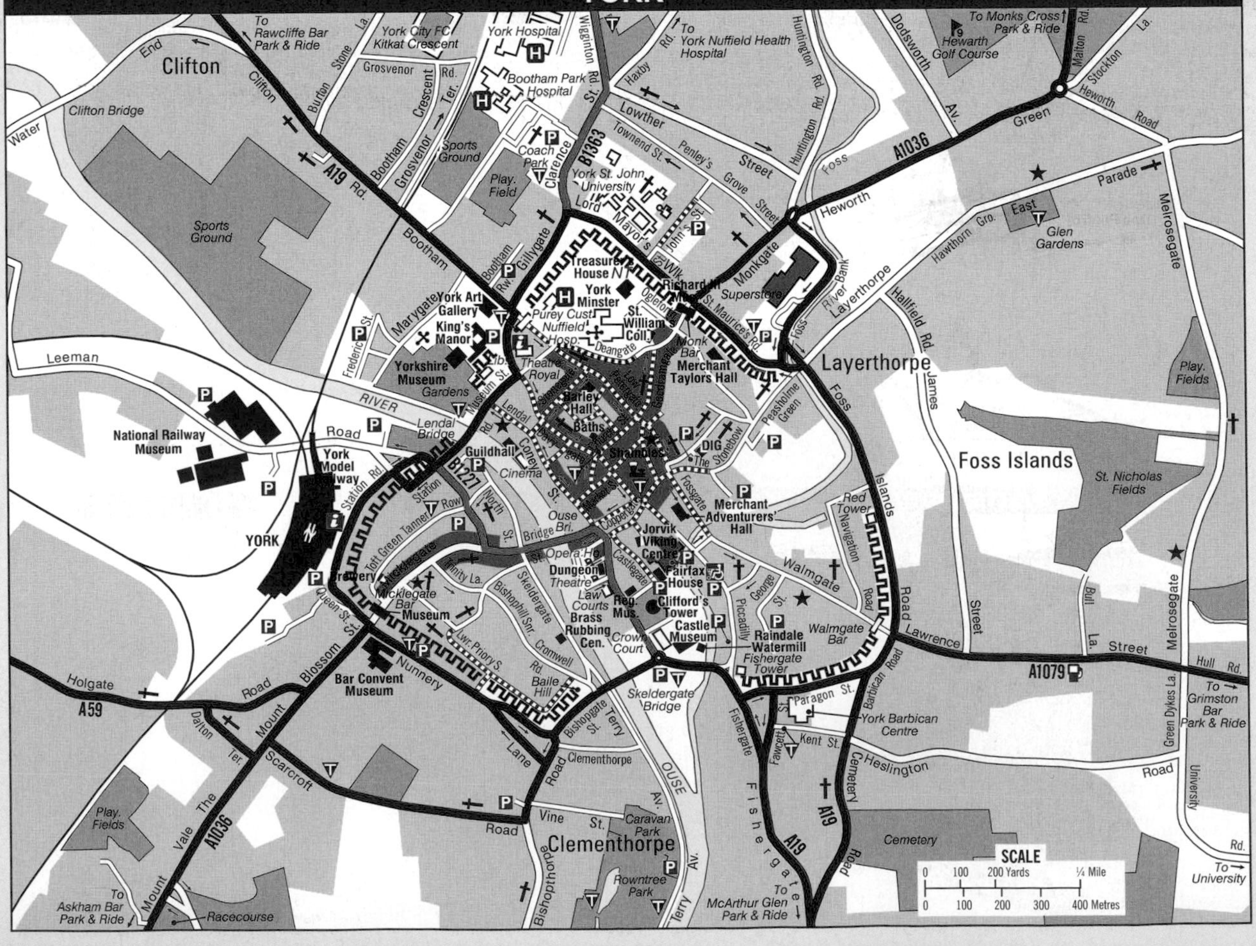

HARWICH

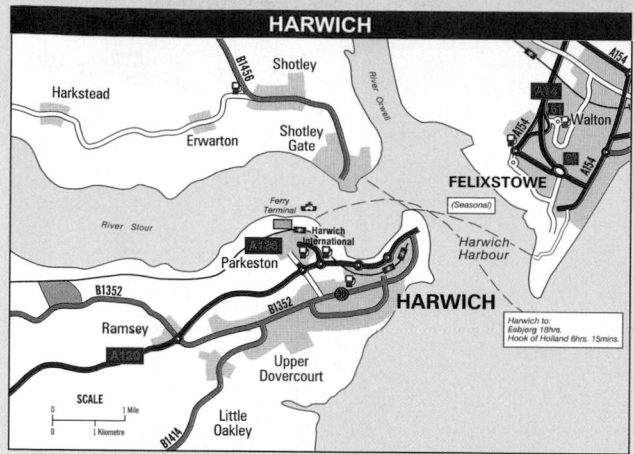

KINGSTON UPON HULL

Hull to:
Rotterdam (Europoort) 10hrs.
Zeebrugge 12hrs. 30mins.

Harwich to:
Esbjerg 18hrs.
Hook of Holland 6hrs. 15mins.

NEWCASTLE UPON TYNE

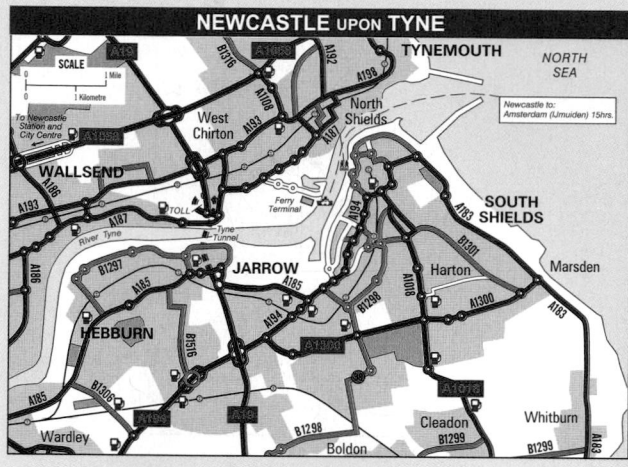

Newcastle to:
Amsterdam (IJmuiden) 15hrs.

NEWHAVEN

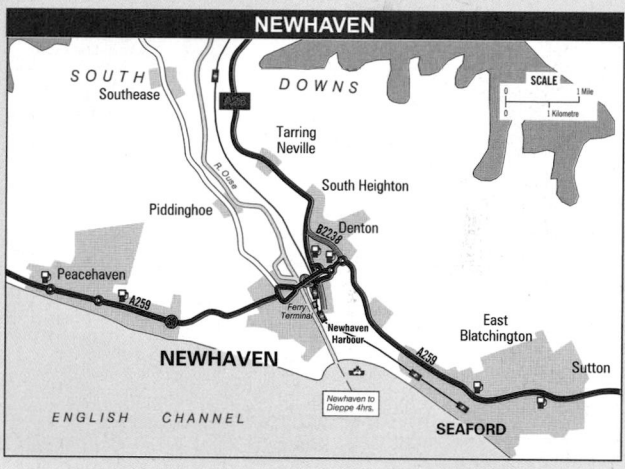

Newhaven to Dieppe 4hrs.

PEMBROKE DOCK (DOC PENFRO)

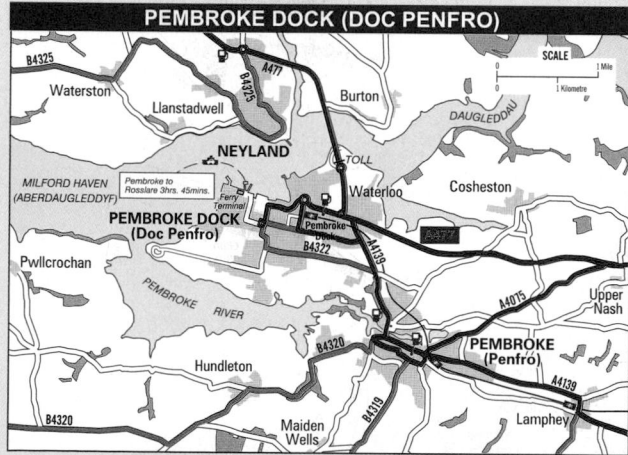

Pembroke to:
Rosslare 3hrs. 45mins.

POOLE

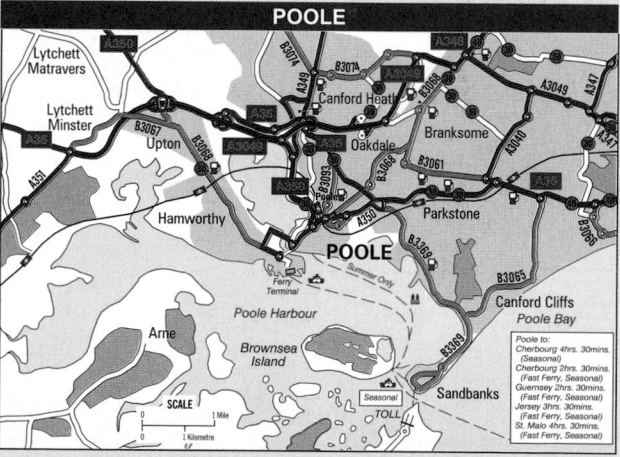

Poole to:
Cherbourg 4hrs. 30mins.
(Seasonal)
Cherbourg 2hrs. 30mins.
(Fast Ferry, Seasonal)
Guernsey 2hrs. 30mins.
(Fast Ferry, Seasonal)
Jersey 3hrs. 30mins.
(Fast Ferry, Seasonal)
St. Malo 4hrs. 30mins.
(Fast Ferry, Seasonal)

PORTSMOUTH

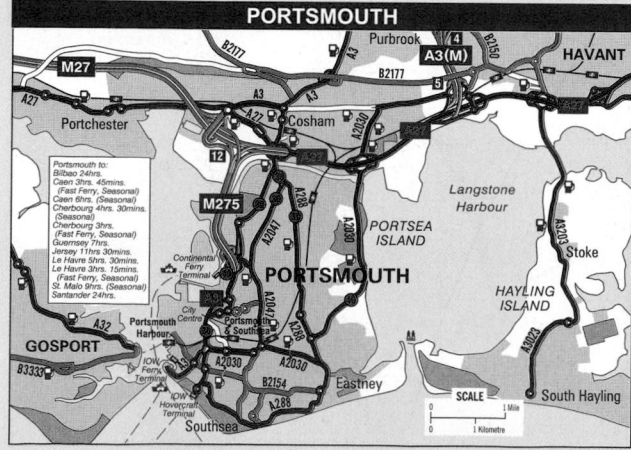

Portsmouth to:
Bilbao 24hrs.
Caen 3hrs. 45mins.
(Fast Ferry, Seasonal)
Caen 6hrs. (Seasonal)
Cherbourg 4hrs. 30mins.
(Seasonal)
Cherbourg 3hrs.
(Fast Ferry, Seasonal)
Guernsey 7hrs.
Jersey 11hrs. 30mins.
Le Havre 3hrs. 30mins.
Le Havre 3hrs. 15mins.
(Fast Ferry, Seasonal)
St. Malo 9hrs. (Seasonal)
Santander 24hrs.

WEYMOUTH

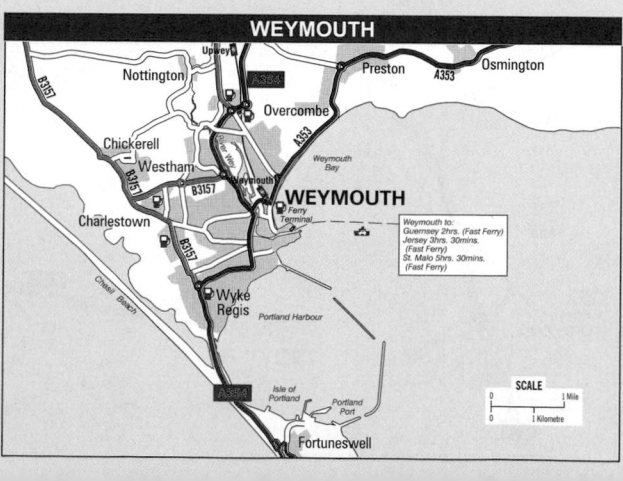

Weymouth to:
Guernsey 2hrs. 30mins.
(Fast Ferry)
Jersey 3hrs. 30mins.
(Fast Ferry)
St. Malo 5hrs. 30mins.
(Fast Ferry)

BIRMINGHAM INTERNATIONAL

EAST MIDLANDS

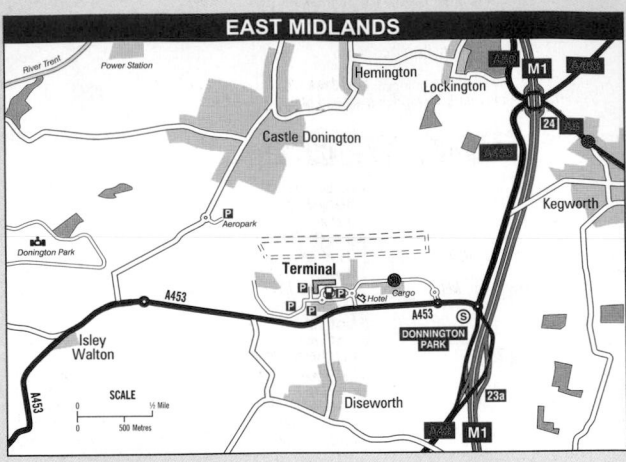

GLASGOW

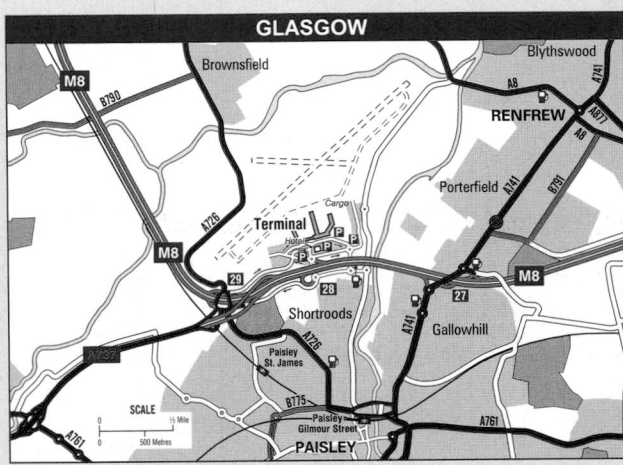

LONDON GATWICK

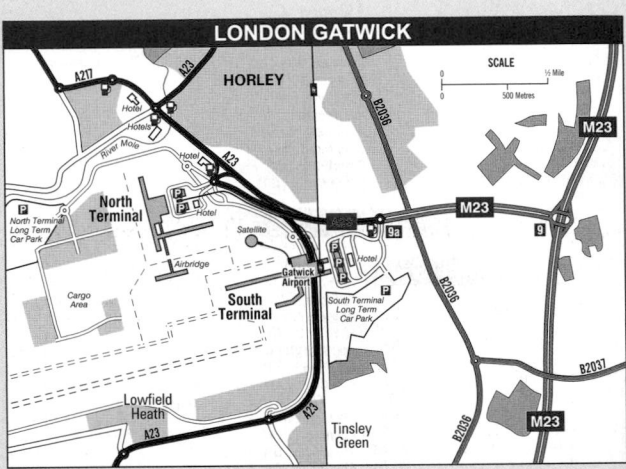

LONDON HEATHROW

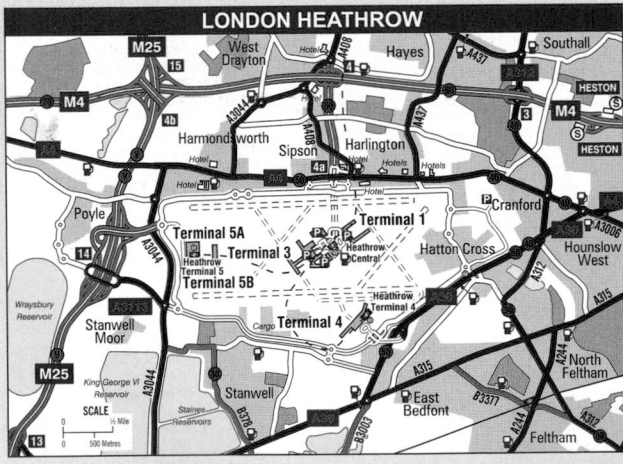

LONDON LUTON

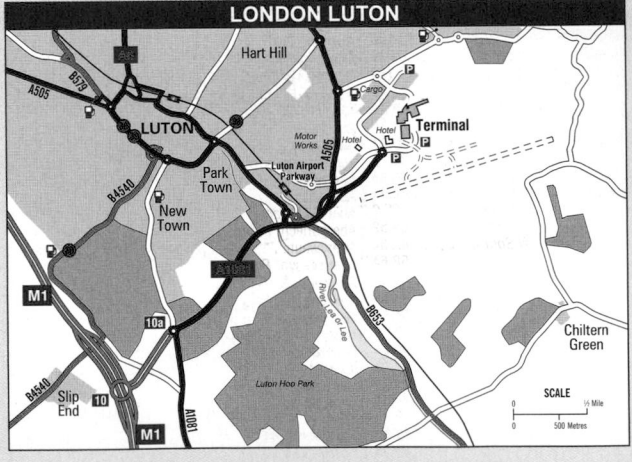

LONDON STANSTED

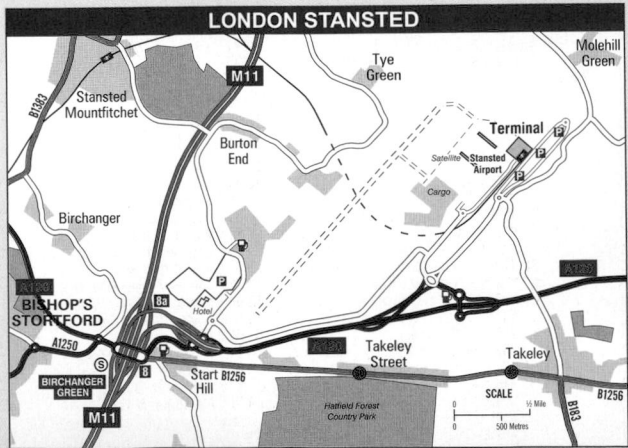

MANCHESTER INTERNATIONAL

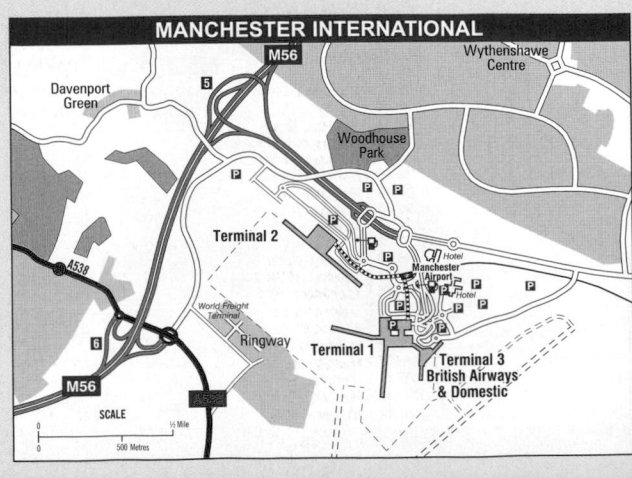

INDEX TO CITIES, TOWNS, VILLAGES, HAMLETS & LOCATIONS & SELECTED PLACES OF INTEREST

(1) A strict alphabetical order is used e.g. An Dùnan follows Andreas but precedes Andwell.

(2) The map reference given refers to the actual map square in which the town spot or built-up area is located and not to the place name.

(3) Major towns are shown in bold, i.e. **Aberdeen**. *Aber* . . . .3G **153** & **187**. Where they appear on a Town Plan a second page reference is given.

(4) Where two or more places of the same name occur in the same County or Unitary Authority, the nearest large town is also given; e.g. Achiemore. *High* . . . .2D **166** (nr. Durness) indicates that Achiemore is located in square 2D on page **166** and is situated near Durness in the Unitary Authority of Highland.

(5) Only one reference is given although due to page overlaps the place may appear on more than one page.

COUNTIES and UNITARY AUTHORITIES with the abbreviations used in this index

Aberdeen : *Aber*
Aberdeenshire : *Abers*
Angus : *Ang*
Argyll & Bute : *Arg*
Bath & N E Somerset : *Bath*
Bedford : *Bed*
Blackburn with Darwen : *Bkbn*
Blackpool : *Bkpl*
Blaenau Gwent : *Blae*
Bournemouth : *Bour*
Bracknell Forest : *Brac*
Bridgend : *B'end*
Brighton & Hove : *Brig*
Bristol : *Bris*
Buckinghamshire : *Buck*
Caerphilly : *Cphy*
Cambridgeshire : *Cambs*
Cardiff : *Card*
Carmarthenshire : *Carm*
Central Bedfordshire : *C Beds*
Ceredigion : *Cdgn*
Cheshire East : *Ches E*
Cheshire West & Chester : *Ches W*
Clackmannanshire : *Clac*
Conwy : *Cnwy*
Cornwall : *Corn*
Cumbria : *Cumb*
Darlington : *Darl*
Denbighshire : *Den*
Derby : *Derb*
Derbyshire : *Derbs*
Devon : *Devn*
Dorset : *Dors*
Dumfries & Galloway : *Dum*
Dundee : *D'dee*
Durham : *Dur*
East Ayrshire : *E Ayr*
East Dunbartonshire : *E Dun*
East Lothian : *E Lot*
East Renfrewshire : *E Ren*
East Riding of Yorkshire : *E Yor*
East Sussex : *E Sus*
Edinburgh : *Edin*
Essex : *Essx*
Falkirk : *Falk*
Fife : *Fife*
Flintshire : *Flin*
Glasgow : *Glas*
Gloucestershire : *Glos*
Greater London : *G Lon*
Greater Manchester : *G Man*
Gwynedd : *Gwyn*
Halton : *Hal*
Hampshire : *Hants*
Hartlepool : *Hart*
Herefordshire : *Here*
Hertfordshire : *Herts*
Highland : *High*
Inverclyde : *Inv*
Isle of Anglesey : *IOA*
Isle of Man : *IOM*
Isle of Wight : *IOW*
Isles of Scilly : *IOS*
Kent : *Kent*
Kingston upon Hull : *Hull*
Lancashire : *Lanc*
Leicester : *Leic*
Leicestershire : *Leics*
Lincolnshire : *Linc*
Luton : *Lutn*
Medway : *Medw*
Merseyside : *Mers*
Merthyr Tydfil : *Mer T*
Middlesbrough : *Midd*
Midlothian : *Midl*
Milton Keynes : *Mil*
Monmouthshire : *Mon*
Moray : *Mor*
Neath Port Talbot : *Neat*
Newport : *Newp*
Norfolk : *Norf*
Northamptonshire : *Nptn*
North Ayrshire : *N Ayr*
North East Lincolnshire : *NE Lin*
North Lanarkshire : *N Lan*
North Lincolnshire : *N Lin*
North Somerset : *N Som*
Northumberland : *Nmbd*
North Yorkshire : *N Yor*
Nottingham : *Nott*
Nottinghamshire : *Notts*
Orkney : *Orkn*
Oxfordshire : *Oxon*
Pembrokeshire : *Pemb*
Perth & Kinross : *Per*
Peterborough : *Pet*
Plymouth : *Plym*
Poole : *Pool*
Portsmouth : *Port*
Powys : *Powy*
Reading : *Read*
Redcar & Cleveland : *Red C*
Renfrewshire : *Ren*
Rhondda Cynon Taff : *Rhon*
Rutland : *Rut*
Scottish Borders : *Bord*
Shetland : *Shet*
Shropshire : *Shrp*
Slough : *Slo*
Somerset : *Som*
Southampton : *Sotn*
South Ayrshire : *S Ayr*
Southend-on-Sea : *S'end*
South Gloucestershire : *S Glo*
South Lanarkshire : *S Lan*
South Yorkshire : *S Yor*
Staffordshire : *Staf*
Stirling : *Stir*
Stockton-on-Tees : *Stoc T*
Stoke-on-Trent : *Stoke*
Suffolk : *Suff*
Surrey : *Surr*
Swansea : *Swan*
Swindon : *Swin*
Telford & Wrekin : *Telf*
Thurrock : *Thur*
Torbay : *Torb*
Torfaen : *Torf*
Tyne & Wear : *Tyne*
Vale of Glamorgan, The : *V Glam*
Warrington : *Warr*
Warwickshire : *Warw*
West Berkshire : *W Ber*
West Dunbartonshire : *W Dun*
Western Isles : *W Isl*
West Lothian : *W Lot*
West Midlands : *W Mid*
West Sussex : *W Sus*
West Yorkshire : *W Yor*
Wiltshire : *Wilts*
Windsor & Maidenhead : *Wind*
Wokingham : *Wok*
Worcestershire : *Worc*
Wrexham : *Wrex*
York : *York*

INDEX

A

Abbas Combe. *Som* 4C **22**
Abberley. *Worc* 4B **60**
Abberley Common. *Worc* 4B **60**
Abberton. *Essx* 4D **54**
Abberton. *Worc* 5D **61**
Abberwick. *Nmbd* 3F **121**
Abbess Roding. *Essx* 4F **53**
Abbey. *Devn* 1E **13**
Abbey-cwm-hir. *Powy* 3C **58**
Abbeydale. *S Yor* 2H **85**
Abbeydale Park. *S Yor* 2H **85**
Abbey Dore. *Here* 2G **47**
Abbey Gate. *Devn* 3F **13**
Abbey Hulton. *Stoke* 1D **72**
Abbey St Bathans. *Bord* 3D **130**
Abbeystead. *Lanc* 4E **97**
Abbeytown. *Cumb* 4C **112**
Abbey Village. *Lanc* 2E **91**
Abbey Wood. *G Lon* 3F **39**
Abbots Ann. *Hants* 2B **24**
Abbots Bickington. *Devn* 1D **11**
Abbots Bromley. *Staf* 3E **73**
Abbotsbury. *Dors* 4A **14**
Abbotsham. *Devn* 4E **19**
Abbotskerswell. *Devn* 2E **9**
Abbots Langley. *Herts* 5A **52**
Abbots Leigh. *N Som* 4A **34**
Abbotsley. *Cambs* 5B **64**
Abbots Morton. *Worc* 5E **61**
Abbots Ripton. *Cambs* 3B **64**
Abbot's Salford. *Warw* 5E **61**
Abbotstone. *Hants* 3D **24**
Abbots Worthy. *Hants* 3C **24**
Abcott. *Shrp* 3F **59**
Abdon. *Shrp* 2H **59**
Abenhall. *Glos* 4B **48**
Aber. *Cdgn* 1E **45**
Aberaeron. *Cdgn* 4D **56**
Aberafan. *Neat* 3G **31**
Aberaman. *Rhon* 5D **46**
Aberangell. *Powy* 4H **69**
Aberarad. *Carm* 1H **43**
Aberarder. *High* 1A **150**
Aberargie. *Per* 2D **136**
Aberarth. *Cdgn* 4D **57**
Aberavon. *Neat* 3G **31**
Aber-banc. *Cdgn* 1D **44**
Aberbargoed. *Cphy* 2E **33**
Aberbechan. *Powy* 1D **58**
Aberbeeg. *Blae* 5F **47**
Aberbowlan. *Carm* 2G **45**
Aberbran. *Powy* 3C **46**
Abercanaid. *Mer T* 5D **46**
Abercarn. *Cphy* 2F **33**
Abercastle. *Pemb* 1C **42**
Abercegir. *Powy* 5H **69**
Aberchalder. *High* 3F **149**
Aberchirder. *Abers* 3D **160**
Abercorn. *W Lot* 2D **129**
Abercraf. *Powy* 4B **46**
Abercregan. *Neat* 2B **32**
Abercrombie. *Fife* 3H **137**
Abercwmboi. *Rhon* 2D **32**
Abercych. *Pemb* 1C **44**
Abercynon. *Rhon* 2D **32**
Aber-Cywarch. *Gwyn* 4A **70**
Aberdalgie. *Per* 1C **136**
Aberdar. *Rhon* 5C **46**
Aberdare. *Rhon* 5C **46**
Aberdaron. *Gwyn* 3A **68**
Aberdaugleddau. *Pemb* 4D **42**
Aberdeen. *Aber* 3G **153** & **187**
Aberdeen (Dyce) Airport. *Aber* 2F **153**
Aberdesach. *Gwyn* 5D **80**
Aberdour. *Fife* 1E **129**
Aberdovey. *Gwyn* 1F **57**
Aberdulais. *Neat* 5A **46**
Aberdyfi. *Gwyn* 1F **57**
Aberedw. *Powy* 1D **46**
Abereiddy. *Pemb* 1B **42**
Abererch. *Gwyn* 2C **68**
Aberfan. *Mer T* 5D **46**
Aberfeldy. *Per* 4F **143**
Aberffraw. *IOA* 4C **80**
Aberffrwd. *Cdgn* 3F **57**
Aberford. *W Yor* 1E **93**
Aberfoyle. *Stir* 3E **135**
Abergarw. *B'end* 3C **32**
Abergarwed. *Neat* 5B **46**
Abergavenny. *Mon* 4G **47**
Abergele. *Cnwy* 3B **82**
Aber-Giar. *Carm* 1F **45**
Abergorlech. *Carm* 2F **45**
Abergwaun. *Pemb* 1D **42**
Abergwesyn. *Powy* 5A **58**
Abergwili. *Carm* 3E **45**
Abergwynfi. *Neat* 2B **32**
Abergwyngregyn. *Gwyn* 3F **81**
Abergynolwyn. *Gwyn* 5F **69**
Aberhafesp. *Powy* 1C **58**
Aberhonddu. *Powy* 3D **46**
Aberhosan. *Powy* 1H **57**
Aberkenfig. *B'end* 3B **32**
Aberlady. *E Lot* 2A **130**
Aberlemno. *Ang* 3E **145**
Aberllefenni. *Gwyn* 5G **69**
Abermaw. *Gwyn* 4F **69**
Abermeurig. *Cdgn* 5E **57**
Aber-miwl. *Powy* 1D **58**
Abermule. *Powy* 1D **58**
Abernant. *Carm* 2H **43**
Abernant. *Rhon* 5D **46**
Abernethy. *Per* 2D **136**
Abernyte. *Per* 5B **144**
Aber-oer. *Wrex* 1E **71**
Aberpennar. *Rhon* 2D **32**
Aberporth. *Cdgn* 5B **56**
Aberriw. *Powy* 5D **70**
Abersoch. *Gwyn* 3C **68**
Abersychan. *Torf* 5F **47**
Abertawe. *Swan* 3F **31** & **Swansea 212**
Aberteifi. *Cdgn* 1B **44**
Aberthin. *V Glam* 4D **32**
Abertillery. *Blae* 5F **47**
Abertridwr. *Cphy* 3E **32**
Abertridwr. *Powy* 4C **70**
Abertyleri. *Blae* 5F **47**
Abertysswg. *Cphy* 5E **47**
Aberuthven. *Per* 2B **136**
Aber Village. *Powy* 3E **46**
Aberyscir. *Powy* 3D **46**
Aberystwyth. *Cdgn* 2E **57** & **187**
Abhainn Suidhe. *W Isl* 7C **171**
Abingdon. *Oxon* 2C **36**
Abinger Common. *Surr* 1C **26**
Abinger Hammer. *Surr* 1B **26**
Abington. *S Lan* 2B **118**
Abington Pigotts. *Cambs* 1D **52**
Ab Kettleby. *Leics* 3E **74**
Ab Lench. *Worc* 5E **61**
Ablington. *Glos* 5G **49**
Ablington. *Wilts* 2G **23**
Abney. *Derbs* 3F **85**
Aboyne. *Abers* 4C **152**
Abram. *G Man* 4E **90**
Abriachan. *High* 5H **157**
Abridge. *Essx* 1F **39**
Abronhill. *N Lan* 2A **128**
Abson. *S Glo* 4C **34**
Abthorpe. *Nptn* 1E **51**
Abune-the-Hill. *Orkn* 5B **172**
Aby. *Linc* 3D **88**
Acairseid. *W Isl* 8C **170**
Acaster Malbis. *York* 5H **99**
Acaster Selby. *N Yor* 5H **99**
Accott. *Devn* 3G **19**
Accrington. *Lanc* 2F **91**
Acha. *Arg* 3C **138**
Achachork. *High* 4D **155**
Achadh a' Chuirn. *High* 1E **147**
Achahoish. *Arg* 2F **125**
Achaleven. *Arg* 5D **140**
Achallader. *Arg* 4H **141**
Acha Mor. *W Isl* 5F **171**
Achanalt. *High* 2E **157**
Achandunie. *High* 1A **158**
Ach'an Todhair. *High* 1E **141**
Achany. *High* 3C **164**
Achaphubuil. *High* 1E **141**
Acharacle. *High* 2A **140**
Acharn. *Ang* 1B **144**
Acharn. *Per* 4E **143**
Acharole. *High* 3E **169**
Achateny. *High* 2G **139**
Achavanich. *High* 4D **169**
Achdalieu. *High* 1E **141**
Achduart. *High* 3E **163**
Achentoul. *High* 5A **168**
Achfary. *High* 5C **166**
Achfrish. *High* 2C **164**
Achgarve. *High* 4C **162**
Achiemore. *High* 2D **166** (nr. Durness)
Achiemore. *High* 3A **168** (nr. Thurso)
A'Chill. *High* 3A **146**
Achiltibuie. *High* 3E **163**
Achina. *High* 2H **167**
Achinahuagh. *High* 2F **167**
Achindarroch. *High* 3E **141**
Achinduich. *High* 3C **164**
Achinduin. *Arg* 5C **140**
Achininver. *High* 2F **167**
Achintee. *High* 4B **156**
Achintraid. *High* 5H **155**
Achleck. *Arg* 4F **139**
Achlorachan. *High* 3F **157**
Achluachrach. *High* 5E **149**
Achlyness. *High* 3C **166**
Achmelvich. *High* 1E **163**
Achmony. *High* 5H **157**
Achmore. *High* 5A **156** (nr. Stromeferry)
Achmore. *High* 4E **163** (nr. Ullapool)
Achnacarnin. *High* 1E **163**
Achnacarry. *High* 5D **148**
Achnaclerach. *High* 2G **157**
Achnacloich. *High* 3D **147**
Ach na Cloiche. *High* 3D **147**
Achnaconeran. *High* 2G **149**
Achnacroish. *Arg* 4C **140**
Achnafalnich. *Arg* 1B **134**
Achnagarron. *High* 1A **158**
Achnaha. *High* 2F **139**
Achnahanat. *High* 4C **164**
Achnahannet. *High* 1D **151**
Achnairn. *High* 2C **164**
Achnamara. *Arg* 1F **125**
Achnanellan. *High* 5C **148**
Achnangoul. *Arg* 3H **133**
Achnasheen. *High* 3D **156**
Achnashellach. *High* 4C **156**
Achosnich. *High* 2F **139**
Achow. *High* 5E **169**
Achranich. *High* 4B **140**
Achreamie. *High* 2C **168**
Achriabhach. *High* 2F **141**
Achriesgill. *High* 3C **166**
Achrimsdale. *High* 3G **165**
Achscrabster. *High* 2C **168**
Achtoty. *High* 2G **167**
Achurch. *Nptn* 2H **63**
Achuvoldrach. *High* 3F **167**
Achvaich. *High* 4E **164**
Achvoan. *High* 3E **165**
Ackenthwaite. *Cumb* 1E **97**
Ackergill. *High* 3F **169**
Ackergillshore. *High* 3F **169**
Acklam. *Midd* 3B **106**
Acklam. *N Yor* 3B **100**
Ackleton. *Shrp* 1B **60**
Acklington. *Nmbd* 4G **121**
Ackton. *W Yor* 2E **93**
Ackworth Moor Top. *W Yor* 3E **93**
Acle. *Norf* 4G **79**
Acocks Green. *W Mid* 2F **61**
Acol. *Kent* 4H **41**
Acomb. *Nmbd* 3C **114**
Acomb. *York* 4H **99**
Aconbury. *Here* 2A **48**
Acre. *G Man* 4H **91**
Acre. *Lanc* 2F **91**
Acrefair. *Wrex* 1E **71**
Acrise. *Kent* 1F **29**
Acton. *Ches E* 5A **84**
Acton. *Dors* 5E **15**
Acton. *G Lon* 2C **38**
Acton. *Shrp* 2F **59**
Acton. *Staf* 1C **72**
Acton. *Suff* 1B **54**
Acton. *Worc* 4C **60**
Acton. *Wrex* 5F **83**
Acton Beauchamp. *Here* 5A **60**
Acton Bridge. *Ches W* 3H **83**
Acton Burnell. *Shrp* 5H **71**
Acton Green. *Here* 5A **60**
Acton Pigott. *Shrp* 5H **71**
Acton Round. *Shrp* 1A **60**
Acton Scott. *Shrp* 2G **59**
Acton Trussell. *Staf* 4D **72**
Acton Turville. *S Glo* 3D **34**
Adabroc. *W Isl* 1H **171**
Adam's Hill. *Worc* 3D **60**
Adbaston. *Staf* 3B **72**
Adber. *Dors* 4B **22**
Adderbury. *Oxon* 2C **50**
Adderley. *Shrp* 2A **72**
Adderstone. *Nmbd* 1F **121**
Addiewell. *W Lot* 3C **128**
Addingham. *W Yor* 5C **98**
Addington. *Buck* 3F **51**
Addington. *G Lon* 4E **39**
Addington. *Kent* 5A **40**
Addinston. *Bord* 4B **130**
Addiscombe. *G Lon* 4E **39**
Addlestone. *Surr* 4B **38**
Addlethorpe. *Linc* 4E **89**
Adeney. *Telf* 4B **72**
Adfa. *Powy* 5C **70**
Adforton. *Here* 3G **59**
Adgestone. *IOW* 4D **16**
Adisham. *Kent* 5G **41**
Adlestrop. *Glos* 3H **49**
Adlingfleet. *E Yor* 2B **94**
Adlington. *Ches E* 2D **84**
Adlington. *Lanc* 3E **90**
Admaston. *Staf* 3E **73**
Admaston. *Telf* 4A **72**
Admington. *Warw* 1G **49**
Adpar. *Cdgn* 1D **44**
Adsborough. *Som* 4F **21**
Adstock. *Buck* 2F **51**
Adstone. *Nptn* 5C **62**
Adversane. *W Sus* 3B **26**
Advie. *High* 5F **159**
Adwalton. *W Yor* 2C **92**
Adwell. *Oxon* 2E **37**
Adwick le Street. *S Yor* 4F **93**
Adwick upon Dearne. *S Yor* 4E **93**
Adziel. *Abers* 3G **161**
Ae. *Dum* 1A **112**
Affleck. *Abers* 1F **153**
Affpuddle. *Dors* 3D **14**
Affric Lodge. *High* 1D **148**
Afon-wen. *Flin* 3D **82**
Agglethorpe. *N Yor* 1C **98**
Aglionby. *Cumb* 4F **113**
Aigburth. *Mers* 2F **83**
Aiginis. *W Isl* 4G **171**
Aike. *E Yor* 5E **101**
Aikers. *Orkn* 8D **172**
Aiketgate. *Cumb* 5F **113**
Aikhead. *Cumb* 5D **112**
Aikton. *Cumb* 4D **112**
Ailey. *Here* 1G **47**
Ailsworth. *Pet* 1A **64**
Ainderby Quernhow. *N Yor* 1F **99**
Ainderby Steeple. *N Yor* 5A **106**
Aingers Green. *Essx* 3E **54**
Ainsdale. *Mers* 3B **90**
Ainsdale-on-Sea. *Mers* 3B **90**
Ainstable. *Cumb* 5G **113**
Ainsworth. *G Man* 3F **91**
Ainthorpe. *N Yor* 4E **107**

Aintree—Ardtalla

Aintree. Mers 1F 83
Aird. Arg 3E 133
Aird. Dum 3F 109
Aird. High 1G 155
(nr. Port Henderson)
Aird. High 3D 147
(nr. Tarskavaig)
Aird. W Isl 3C 170
(on Benbecula)
Aird. W Isl 4H 171
(on Isle of Lewis)
Àird a Bhasair. High 3E 147
Aird a Mhachair. W Isl 4C 170
Aird a Mhulaidh. W Isl 6D 171
Aird Asaig. W Isl 7D 171
Aird Dhail. W Isl 1G 171
Airdens. High 4D 164
Airdeny. Arg 1G 133
Aird Mhidhinis. W Isl 8C 170
Aird Mhighe. W Isl 8D 171
(nr. Ceann a Bhaigh)
Aird Mhighe. W Isl 9C 171
(nr. Fionnsabhagh)
Aird Mhor. W Isl 8C 170
(on Barra)
Aird Mhor. W Isl 4D 170
(on South Uist)
Airdrie. N Lan 3A 128
Aird Shleibhe. W Isl 9D 171
Aird, The. High 3D 154
Aird Thunga. W Isl 4G 171
Aird Uig. W Isl 4C 171
Airedale. W Yor 2E 93
Airidh a Bhruaich. W Isl 6E 171
Airies. Dum 3E 109
Airmyn. E Yor 2H 93
Airntully. Per 5H 143
Airor. High 3F 147
Airth. Falk 1C 128
Airton. N Yor 4B 98
Aisby. Linc 1F 87
(nr. Gainsborough)
Aisby. Linc 2H 75
(nr. Grantham)
Aisgernis. W Isl 6C 170
Aish. Devn 2C 8
(nr. Buckfastleigh)
Aish. Devn 3E 9
(nr. Totnes)
Aisholt. Som 3E 21
Aiskew. N Yor 1E 99
Aislaby. N Yor 1B 100
(nr. Pickering)
Aislaby. N Yor 4F 107
(nr. Whitby)
Aislaby. Stoc T 3B 106
Aisthorpe. Linc 2G 87
Aith. Shet 2H 173
(on Fetlar)
Aith. Shet 6E 173
(on Mainland)
Aithsetter. Shet 8F 173
Akeld. Nmbd 2D 120
Akeley. Buck 2F 51
Akenham. Suff 1E 55
Albaston. Corn 5E 11
Alberbury. Shrp 4F 71
Albert Town. Pemb 3D 42
Albert Village. Leics 4H 73
Albourne. W Sus 4D 26
Albrighton. Shrp 4G 71
(nr. Shrewsbury)
Albrighton. Shrp 5C 72
(nr. Telford)
Alburgh. Norf 2E 67
Albury. Herts 3E 53
Albury. Surr 1B 26
Albyfield. Cumb 4G 113
Alby Hill. Norf 2D 78
Alcaig. High 3H 157
Alcaston. Shrp 2G 59
Alcester. Warw 5E 61
Alciston. E Sus 5G 27
Alcombe. Som 2C 20
Alconbury. Cambs 3A 64
Alconbury Weston. Cambs 3A 64
Aldborough. Norf 2D 78
Aldborough. N Yor 3G 99
Aldbourne. Wilts 4A 36
Aldbrough. E Yor 1F 95
Aldbrough St John. N Yor 3F 105
Aldbury. Herts 4H 51
Aldcliffe. Lanc 3D 96
Aldclune. Per 2G 143
Aldeburgh. Suff 5G 67
Aldeby. Norf 1G 67
Aldenham. Herts 1C 38
Alderbury. Wilts 4G 23
Aldercar. Derbs 1B 74
Alderford. Norf 4D 78
Alderholt. Dors 1G 15
Alderley. Glos 2C 34
Alderley Edge. Ches E 3C 84
Aldermaston. W Ber 5D 36
Aldermaston Stoke. W Ber 5E 36
Aldermaston Wharf. W Ber 5E 36
Alderminster. Warw 1H 49
Alder Moor. Staf 3G 73
Aldersey Green. Ches W 5G 83
Aldershot. Hants 1G 25
Alderton. Glos 2E 49
Alderton. Nptn 1F 51
Alderton. Shrp 3G 71
Alderton. Suff 1G 55
Alderton. Wilts 3D 34
Alderton Fields. Glos 2F 49
Alderwasley. Derbs 5H 85
Aldfield. N Yor 3E 99
Aldford. Ches W 5G 83
Aldgate. Rut 5G 75
Aldham. Essx 3C 54
Aldham. Suff 1D 54
Aldingbourne. W Sus 5A 26
Aldingham. Cumb 2B 96
Aldington. Kent 2E 29
Aldington. Worc 1F 49
Aldington Frith. Kent 2E 29
Aldochlay. Arg 4C 134
Aldon. Shrp 3G 59
Aldoth. Cumb 5C 112
Aldreth. Cambs 3D 64
Aldridge. W Mid 5E 73
Aldringham. Suff 4G 67
Aldsworth. Glos 4G 49
Aldsworth. W Sus 2F 17
Aldwark. Derbs 5G 85
Aldwark. N Yor 3G 99
Aldwick. W Sus 3H 17
Aldwincle. Nptn 2H 63
Aldworth. W Ber 4D 36
Alexandria. W Dun 1E 127
Aley. Som 3E 21
Aley Green. C Beds 4A 52
Alfardisworthy. Devn 1C 10
Alfington. Devn 3E 12
Alfold. Surr 2B 26
Alfold Bars. W Sus 2B 26
Alfold Crossways. Surr 2B 26
Alford. Abers 2C 152
Alford. Linc 3D 88
Alford. Som 3B 22
Alfreton. Derbs 5B 86
Alfrick. Worc 5B 60
Alfrick Pound. Worc 5B 60
Alfriston. E Sus 5G 27
Algarkirk. Linc 2B 76
Alhampton. Som 3B 22
Aline Lodge. W Isl 6D 171
Alkborough. N Lin 2B 94
Alkerton. Oxon 1B 50
Alkham. Kent 1G 29
Alkington. Shrp 2H 71
Alkmonton. Derbs 2F 73
Alladale Lodge. High 5B 164
Allaleigh. Devn 3E 9
Allanbank. N Lan 4B 128
Allanton. N Lan 4B 128
Allanton. Bord 4E 131
Allaston. Glos 5B 48
Allbrook. Hants 4C 24
All Cannings. Wilts 5F 35
Allendale Town. Nmbd 4B 114
Allen End. Warw 1F 61
Allenheads. Nmbd 5B 114
Allensford. Dur 5D 115
Allen's Green. Herts 4E 53
Allensmore. Here 2H 47
Allenton. Derb 2A 74
Aller. Som 4H 21
Allerby. Cumb 1B 102
Allercombe. Devn 3D 12
Allerford. Som 2C 20
Allerston. N Yor 1C 100
Allerthorpe. E Yor 5B 100
Allerton. Mers 2G 83
Allerton. W Yor 1B 92
Allerton Bywater. W Yor 2E 93
Allerton Mauleverer. N Yor 4G 99
Allesley. W Mid 2G 61
Allestree. Derb 2H 73
Allet. Corn 4B 6
Allexton. Leics 5F 75
Allgreave. Ches E 4D 84
Allhallows. Medw 3C 40
Allhallows-on-Sea. Medw 3C 40
Alligin Shuas. High 3H 155
Allimore Green. Staf 4C 72
Allington. Kent 5B 40
Allington. Linc 1F 75
Allington. Wilts 3H 23
(nr. Amesbury)
Allington. Wilts 5F 35
(nr. Devizes)
Allithwaite. Cumb 2C 96
Alloa. Clac 4A 136
Allonby. Cumb 5B 112
Allostock. Ches W 3B 84
Alloway. S Ayr 3C 116
Allowenshay. Som 1G 13
All Saints South Elmham. Suff 2F 67
Allscott. Shrp 1B 60
Allscott. Telf 4A 72
All Stretton. Shrp 1G 59
Allt. Carm 5F 45
Alltami. Flin 4E 83
Alltgobhlach. N Ayr 5G 125
Alltmawr. Powy 1D 46
Alltnacaillich. High 4E 167
Allt na h-Airbhe. High 4F 163
Alltour. High 5E 148
Alltsigh. High 2G 149
Alltwalis. Carm 2E 45
Alltwen. Neat 5H 45
Alltyblacca. Cdgn 1F 45
Allt-y-goed. Pemb 1B 44
Almeley. Here 5F 59
Almeley Wooton. Here 5F 59
Almer. Dors 3E 15
Almholme. S Yor 4F 93
Almington. Staf 2B 72
Alminstone Cross. Devn 4D 18
Almodington. W Sus 3G 17
Almondbank. Per 1C 136
Almondbury. W Yor 3B 92
Almondsbury. S Glo 3B 34
Alne. N Yor 3G 99
Alness. High 2A 158
Alnessferry. High 2A 158
Alnham. Nmbd 3D 121
Alnmouth. Nmbd 3G 121
Alnwick. Nmbd 3F 121
Alphamstone. Essx 2B 54
Alpheton. Suff 5A 66
Alphington. Devn 3C 12
Alpington. Norf 5E 79
Alport. Derbs 4G 85
Alport. Powy 1E 59
Alpraham. Ches E 5H 83
Alresford. Essx 3D 54
Alrewas. Staf 4F 73
Alsager. Ches E 5B 84
Alsagers Bank. Staf 1C 72
Alsop en le Dale. Derbs 5F 85
Alston. Cumb 5A 114
Alston. Devn 2G 13
Alstone. Glos 2E 49
Alstone. Som 2G 21
Alstonefield. Staf 5F 85
Alston Sutton. Som 1H 21
Alswear. Devn 4H 19
Altandhu. High 2D 163
Altanduin. High 1F 165
Altarnun. Corn 4C 10
Altass. High 3B 164
Alterwall. High 2E 169
Altgaltraig. Arg 2B 126
Altham. Lanc 1F 91
Althorne. Essx 1D 40
Althorpe. N Lin 4B 94
Altnabreac. High 4C 168
Altnacealgach. High 2G 163
Altnafeadh. High 3G 141
Altnaharra. High 5F 167
Altofts. W Yor 2D 92
Alton. Derbs 4A 86
Alton. Hants 3F 25
Alton. Staf 1E 73
Alton Barnes. Wilts 5G 35
Altonhill. E Ayr 1D 116
Alton Pancras. Dors 2C 14
Alton Priors. Wilts 5G 35
Altrincham. G Man 2B 84
Altrua. High 4E 149
Alva. Clac 4A 136
Alvanley. Ches W 3G 83
Alvaston. Derb 2A 74
Alvechurch. Worc 3E 61
Alvecote. Warw 5G 73
Alvediston. Wilts 4E 23
Alveley. Shrp 2B 60
Alverdiscott. Devn 4F 19
Alverstoke. Hants 3D 16
Alverstone. IOW 4D 16
Alverthorpe. W Yor 2D 92
Alverton. Notts 1E 75
Alves. Mor 2F 159
Alvescot. Oxon 5A 50
Alveston. S Glo 3B 34
Alveston. Warw 5G 61
Alvie. High 3C 150
Alvingham. Linc 1C 88
Alvington. Glos 5B 48
Alwalton. Cambs 1A 64
Alweston. Dors 1B 14
Alwington. Devn 4E 19
Alwinton. Nmbd 4D 120
Alwoodley. W Yor 5E 99
Alyth. Per 4B 144
Amatnatua. High 4B 164
Am Baile. W Isl 7C 170
Ambaston. Derbs 2B 74
Ambergate. Derbs 5H 85
Amber Hill. Linc 1B 76
Amberley. Glos 5D 48
Amberley. W Sus 4B 26
Amble. Nmbd 4G 121
Amblecote. W Mid 2C 60
Ambler Thorn. W Yor 2A 92
Ambleside. Cumb 4E 103
Ambleston. Pemb 2E 43
Ambrosden. Oxon 4E 50
Amcotts. N Lin 3B 94
Amersham. Buck 1A 38
Amerton. Staf 3D 73
Amesbury. Wilts 2G 23
Amisfield. Dum 1B 112
Amlwch. IOA 1D 80
Amlwch Port. IOA 1D 80
Ammanford. Carm 4G 45
Amotherby. N Yor 2B 100
Ampfield. Hants 4B 24
Ampleforth. N Yor 2H 99
Ampleforth College. N Yor 2H 99
Ampney Crucis. Glos 5F 49
Ampney St Mary. Glos 5F 49
Ampney St Peter. Glos 5F 49
Amport. Hants 2A 24
Ampthill. C Beds 2A 52
Ampton. Suff 3A 66
Amroth. Pemb 4F 43
Amulree. Per 5G 143
Amwell. Herts 4B 52
Anaheilt. High 2C 140
An Àird. High 3D 147
An Camus Darach. High 4E 147
Ancaster. Linc 1G 75
Anchor. Shrp 2D 58
Anchorsholme. Bkpl 5C 96
Anchor Street. Norf 3F 79
An Cnoc. W Isl 4G 171
An Cnoc Ard. W Isl 1H 171
An Coroghon. High 3A 146
Ancroft. Nmbd 5G 131
Ancrum. Bord 2A 120
Ancton. W Sus 5A 26
Anderby. Linc 3E 89
Anderby Creek. Linc 3E 89
Anderson. Dors 3D 15
Anderton. Ches W 3A 84
Andertons Mill. Lanc 3D 90
Andover. Hants 2B 24
Andover Down. Hants 2B 24
Andoversford. Glos 4F 49
Andreas. IOM 2D 108
An Dùnan. High 1D 147
Andwell. Hants 1E 25
Anelog. Gwyn 3A 68
Anfield. Mers 1F 83
Angarrack. Corn 3C 4
Angelbank. Shrp 3H 59
Angersleigh. Som 1F 13
Angerton. Cumb 4D 112
Angle. Pemb 4C 42
An Gleann Ur. W Isl 4G 171
Angmering. W Sus 5B 26
Angmering-on-Sea. W Sus 5B 26
Angram. N Yor 5B 104
(nr. Keld)
Angram. N Yor 5H 99
(nr. York)
Anick. Nmbd 3C 114
Ankerbold. Derbs 4A 86
Ankerville. High 1C 158
Anlaby. E Yor 2D 94
Anlaby Park. Hull 2D 94
An Leth Meadhanach. W Isl 7C 170
Anmer. Norf 3G 77
Anmore. Hants 1E 17
Annan. Dum 3D 112
Annaside. Cumb 1A 96
Annat. Arg 1H 133
Annat. High 3A 156
Annathill. N Lan 2A 128
Anna Valley. Hants 2B 24
Annbank. S Ayr 2D 116
Annesley. Notts 5C 86
Annesley Woodhouse. Notts 5C 86
Annfield Plain. Dur 4E 115
Annscroft. Shrp 5G 71
An Sailean. High 2A 140
Ansdell. Lanc 2B 90
Ansford. Som 3B 22
Ansley. Warw 1G 61
Anslow. Staf 3G 73
Anslow Gate. Staf 3F 73
Ansteadbrook. Surr 2A 26
Anstey. Herts 2E 53
Anstey. Leics 5C 74
Anston. S Lan 5D 128
Anstruther Easter. Fife 3H 137
Anstruther Wester. Fife 3H 137
Ansty. Warw 2A 62
Ansty. W Sus 3D 27
Ansty. Wilts 4E 23
An Taobh Tuath. W Isl 9B 171
An t-Aodann Ban. High 3C 154
An t Ath Leathann. High 1E 147
An Teanga. High 3E 147
Anthill Common. Hants 1E 17
Anthorn. Cumb 4C 112
Antingham. Norf 2E 79
An t-Ob. W Isl 9C 171
Anton's Gowt. Linc 1B 76
Antony. Corn 3A 8
An t-Òrd. High 2E 147
Antrobus. Ches W 3A 84
Anvil Corner. Devn 2D 10
Anwick. Linc 5A 88
Anwoth. Dum 4C 110
Apethorpe. Nptn 1H 63
Apeton. Staf 4C 72
Apley. Linc 3A 88
Apperknowle. Derbs 3A 86
Apperley. Glos 3D 48
Apperley Dene. Nmbd 4D 114
Appersett. N Yor 5B 104
Appin. Arg 4D 140
Appleby. N Lin 3C 94
Appleby-in-Westmorland. Cumb 2H 103
Appleby Magna. Leics 5H 73
Appleby Parva. Leics 5H 73
Applecross. High 4G 155
Appledore. Devn 3E 19
(nr. Bideford)
Appledore. Devn 1D 12
(nr. Tiverton)
Appledore. Kent 3D 28
Appledore Heath. Kent 2D 28
Appleford. Oxon 2D 36
Applegarthtown. Dum 1C 112
Applemore. Hants 2B 16
Appleshaw. Hants 2B 24
Applethwaite. Cumb 2D 102
Appleton. Hal 2H 83
Appleton. Oxon 5C 50
Appleton-le-Moors. N Yor 1B 100
Appleton-le-Street. N Yor 2B 100
Appleton Roebuck. N Yor 5H 99
Appleton Thorn. Warr 2A 84
Appleton Wiske. N Yor 4A 106
Appletree. Nptn 1C 50
Appletreehall. Bord 3H 119
Appletreewick. N Yor 3C 98
Appley. Som 4D 20
Appley Bridge. Lanc 4D 90
Apse Heath. IOW 4D 16
Apsley End. C Beds 2B 52
Apuldram. W Sus 2G 17
Arabella. High 1C 158
Arasaig. High 5E 147
Arbeadie. Abers 4D 152
Arberth. Pemb 3F 43
Arbirlot. Ang 4F 145
Arborfield. Wok 5F 37
Arborfield Cross. Wok 5F 37
Arborfield Garrison. Wok 5F 37
Arbourthorne. S Yor 2A 86
Arbroath. Ang 4F 145
Arbuthnott. Abers 1H 145
Arcan. High 3H 157
Archargary. High 3H 167
Archdeacon Newton. Darl 3F 105
Archiestown. Mor 4G 159
Arclid. Ches E 4B 84
Arclid Green. Ches E 4B 84
Ardachu. High 3D 164
Ardalanish. Arg 2A 132
Ardaneaskan. High 5H 155
Ardarroch. High 5H 155
Ardbeg. Arg 1C 126
(nr. Dunoon)
Ardbeg. Arg 5C 124
(on Islay)
Ardbeg. Arg 3B 126
(on Isle of Bute)
Ardcharnich. High 5F 163
Ardchiavaig. Arg 2A 132
Ardchonnell. Arg 2G 133
Ardchrishnish. Arg 1B 132
Ardchronie. High 5D 164
Ardchullarie. Stir 2E 135
Ardchyle. Stir 1E 135
Ard-dhubh. High 4G 155
Arddleen. Powy 4E 71
Arddlîn. Powy 4E 71
Ardechive. High 4D 148
Ardeley. Herts 3D 52
Ardelve. High 1A 148
Arden. Arg 1E 127
Ardendrain. High 5H 157
Arden Hall. N Yor 5C 106
Ardens Grafton. Warw 5F 61
Ardentinny. Arg 1C 126
Ardeonaig. Stir 5D 142
Ardersier. High 3B 158
Ardery. High 2B 140
Ardessie. High 5E 163
Ardfern. Arg 3F 133
Ardfernal. Arg 2D 124
Ardfin. Arg 3C 124
Ardgartan. Arg 3B 134
Ardgay. High 4C 164
Ardgour. High 2E 141
Ardheslaig. High 3G 155
Ardindrean. High 5F 163
Ardingly. W Sus 3E 27
Ardington. Oxon 3C 36
Ardlamont House. Arg 3A 126
Ardleigh. Essx 3D 54
Ardler. Per 4B 144
Ardley. Oxon 3D 50
Ardlui. Arg 2C 134
Ardlussa. Arg 1E 125
Ardmair. High 4F 163
Ardmay. Arg 3B 134
Ardminish. Arg 5E 125
Ardmolich. High 1B 140
Ardmore. High 3C 166
(nr. Kinlochbervie)
Ardmore. High 5E 164
(nr. Tain)
Ardnacross. Arg 4G 139
Ardnadam. Arg 1C 126
Ardnagrask. High 4H 157
Ardnamurach. High 4G 147
Ardnarff. High 5A 156
Ardnastang. High 2C 140
Ardoch. Per 5H 143
Ardochy House. High 3E 148
Ardpatrick. Arg 3F 125
Ardrishaig. Arg 1G 125
Ardroag. High 4B 154
Ardross. High 1A 158
Ardrossan. N Ayr 5D 126
Ardshealach. High 2A 140
Ardsley. S Yor 4D 93
Ardslignish. High 2G 139
Ardtalla. Arg 4C 124

Ardtalnaig—Badluarach

Ardtalnaig. Per 5E 142
Ardtoe. High 1A 140
Arduaine. Arg 2E 133
Ardullie. High 2H 157
Ardvasar. High 3E 147
Ardvorlich. Per 1F 135
Ardwell. Dum 5G 109
Ardwell. Mor 5A 160
Arean. High 1A 140
Areley Common. Worc 3C 60
Areley Kings. Worc 3B 60
Arford. Hants 3G 25
Argoed. Cphy 2E 33
Argoed Mill. Powy 4B 58
Aridhglas. Arg 2B 132
Arinacrinachd. High 3G 155
Arinagour. Arg 3D 138
Arisaig. High 5E 147
Ariundle. High 2C 140
Arivegaig. High 2A 140
Arkendale. N Yor 3F 99
Arkesden. Essx 2E 53
Arkholme. Lanc 2E 97
Arkle Town. N Yor 4D 104
Arkley. G Lon 1D 38
Arksey. S Yor 4F 93
Arkwright Town. Derbs 3B 86
Arlecdon. Cumb 3B 102
Arlescote. Warw 1B 50
Arlesey. C Beds 2B 52
Arleston. Telf 4A 72
Arley. Ches E 2A 84
Arlingham. Glos 4C 48
Arlington. Devn 2G 19
Arlington. E Sus 5G 27
Arlington. Glos 5G 49
Arlington Beccott. Devn 2G 19
Armadail. High 3E 147
Armadale. High 3E 147
(nr. Isleornsay)
Armadale. High 2H 167
(nr. Strathy)
Armadale. W Lot 3C 128
Armathwaite. Cumb 5G 113
Arminghall. Norf 5E 79
Armitage. Staf 4E 73
Armitage Bridge. W Yor 3B 92
Armley. W Yor 1C 92
Armscote. Warw 1H 49
Arms, The. Norf 1A 66
Armston. Nptn 2H 63
Armthorpe. S Yor 4G 93
Arncliffe. N Yor 2B 98
Arncliffe Cote. N Yor 2B 98
Arncroach. Fife 3H 137
Arne. Dors 4E 15
Arnesby. Leics 1D 62
Arnicle. Arg 2B 122
Arnisdale. High 2G 147
Arnish. High 4E 155
Arniston. Midl 3G 129
Arnol. W Isl 3F 171
Arnold. E Yor 5F 101
Arnold. Notts 1C 74
Arnprior. Stir 4F 135
Arnside. Cumb 2D 96
Aros Mains. Arg 4G 139
Arpafeelie. High 3A 158
Arrad Foot. Cumb 1C 96
Arram. E Yor 5E 101
Arras. E Yor 5D 100
Arrathorne. N Yor 5E 105
Arreton. IOW 4D 16
Arrington. Cambs 5C 64
Arrochar. Arg 3B 134
Arrow. Warw 5E 61
Arscaig. High 2C 164
Artafallie. High 4A 158
Arthington. W Yor 5E 99
Arthingworth. Nptn 2E 63
Arthog. Gwyn 4F 69
Arthrath. Abers 5G 161
Arthurstone. Per 4B 144
Artington. Surr 1A 26
Arundel. W Sus 5B 26
Asby. Cumb 2B 102
Ascog. Arg 3C 126
Ascot. Wind 4A 38
Ascott-under-Wychwood.
Oxon 4B 50
Asenby. N Yor 2F 99
Asfordby. Leics 4E 74
Asfordby Hill. Leics 4E 74
Asgarby. Linc 4C 88
(nr. Horncastle)
Asgarby. Linc 1A 76
(nr. Sleaford)
Ash. Devn 4E 9
Ash. Dors 1D 14
Ash. Kent 5G 41
(nr. Sandwich)
Ash. Kent 4H 39
(nr. Swanley)
Ash. Som 4H 21
Ash. Surr 1G 25
Ashampstead. W Ber 4D 36
Ashbocking. Suff 5D 66
Ashbourne. Derbs 1F 73
Ashbrittle. Som 4D 20
Ashbrook. Shrp 1G 59
Ashburton. Devn 2D 8
Ashbury. Devn 3F 11
Ashbury. Oxon 3A 36
Ashby. N Lin 4B 94
Ashby by Partney. Linc 4D 88
Ashby cum Fenby. NE Lin 4F 95
Ashby de la Launde. Linc 5H 87
Ashby-de-la-Zouch. Leics 4A 74
Ashby Folville. Leics 4E 74
Ashby Magna. Leics 1C 62
Ashby Parva. Leics 2C 62
Ashby Puerorum. Linc 3C 88
Ashby St Ledgars. Nptn 4C 62
Ashby St Mary. Norf 5F 79
Ashchurch. Glos 2E 49
Ashcombe. Devn 5C 12
Ashcott. Som 3H 21
Ashdon. Essx 1F 53
Ashe. Hants 1D 24
Asheldham. Essx 5C 54
Ashen. Essx 1H 53
Ashendon. Buck 4F 51
Ashey. IOW 4D 16
Ashfield. Hants 1B 16
Ashfield. Here 3A 48
Ashfield. Shrp 2H 59
Ashfield. Stir 3G 135
Ashfield. Suff 4E 66
Ashfield Green. Suff 3E 67
Ashfold Crossways. W Sus 3D 26
Ashford. Devn 3F 19
(nr. Barnstaple)
Ashford. Devn 4C 8
(nr. Kingsbridge)
Ashford. Hants 1G 15
Ashford. Kent 1E 28
Ashford. Surr 3B 38
Ashford Bowdler. Shrp 3H 59
Ashford Carbonel. Shrp 3H 59
Ashford Hill. Hants 5D 36
Ashford in the Water. Derbs 4F 85
Ashgill. S Lan 5A 128
Ash Green. Warw 2H 61
Ashgrove. Mor 2G 159
Ashill. Devn 1D 12
Ashill. Norf 5A 78
Ashill. Som 1G 13
Ashingdon. Essx 1C 40
Ashington. Nmbd 1F 115
Ashington. W Sus 4C 26
Ashkirk. Bord 2G 119
Ashlett. Hants 2C 16
Ashleworth. Glos 3D 48
Ashley. Cambs 4F 65
Ashley. Ches E 2B 84
Ashley. Dors 2G 15
Ashley. Glos 2E 35
Ashley. Hants 3A 16
(nr. New Milton)
Ashley. Hants 3B 24
(nr. Winchester)
Ashley. Kent 1H 29
Ashley. Nptn 1E 63
Ashley. Staf 2B 72
Ashley. Wilts 5D 34
Ashley Green. Buck 5H 51
Ashley Heath. Dors 2G 15
Ashley Heath. Staf 2B 72
Ashley Moor. Here 4G 59
Ash Magna. Shrp 2H 71
Ashmanhaugh. Norf 3F 79
Ashmansworth. Hants 1C 24
Ashmansworthy. Devn 1D 10
Ashmead Green. Glos 2C 34
Ashmill. Devn 3D 11
(nr. Holsworthy)
Ash Mill. Devn 4A 20
(nr. South Molton)
Ashmore. Dors 1E 15
Ashmore Green. W Ber 5D 36
Ashover. Derbs 4A 86
Ashow. Warw 3H 61
Ash Parva. Shrp 2H 71
Ashperton. Here 1B 48
Ashprington. Devn 3E 9
Ash Priors. Som 4E 21
Ashreigney. Devn 1G 11
Ash Street. Suff 1D 54
Ashtead. Surr 5C 38
Ash Thomas. Devn 1D 12
Ashton. Corn 4D 4
Ashton. Here 4H 59
Ashton. Inv 2D 126
Ashton. Nptn 2H 63
(nr. Oundle)
Ashton. Nptn 1F 51
(nr. Roade)
Ashton. Pet 5A 76
Ashton Common. Wilts 1E 23
Ashton Hayes. Ches W 4H 83
Ashton-in-Makerfield. G Man 4D 90
Ashton Keynes. Wilts 2F 35
Ashton under Hill. Worc 2E 49
Ashton-under-Lyne. G Man 1D 84
Ashton upon Mersey. G Man 1B 84
Ashurst. Hants 1B 16
Ashurst. Kent 2G 27
Ashurst. Lanc 4C 90
Ashurst. W Sus 4C 26
Ashurst Wood. W Sus 2F 27
Ash Vale. Surr 1G 25
Ashwater. Devn 3D 11
Ashwell. Herts 2C 52
Ashwell. Rut 4F 75
Ashwellthorpe. Norf 1D 66
Ashwick. Som 2B 22
Ashwicken. Norf 4G 77
Ashwood. Staf 2C 60
Askam in Furness. Cumb 2B 96
Askern. S Yor 3F 93
Askerswell. Dors 3A 14
Askett. Buck 5G 51
Askham. Cumb 2G 103
Askham. Notts 3E 87
Askham Bryan. York 5H 99
Askham Richard. York 5H 99
Askrigg. N Yor 5C 104
Askwith. N Yor 5D 98
Aslackby. Linc 2H 75
Aslacton. Norf 1D 66
Aslockton. Notts 1E 75
Aspatria. Cumb 5C 112
Aspenden. Herts 3D 52
Asperton. Linc 2B 76
Aspley Guise. C Beds 2H 51
Aspley Heath. C Beds 2H 51
Aspull. G Man 4E 90
Asselby. E Yor 2H 93
Assington. Suff 2C 54
Assington Green. Suff 5G 65
Astbury. Ches E 4C 84
Astcote. Nptn 5D 62
Asterby. Linc 3B 88
Asterley. Shrp 5F 71
Asterton. Shrp 1F 59
Asthall. Oxon 4A 50
Asthall Leigh. Oxon 4B 50
Astle. High 4E 165
Astley. G Man 4F 91
Astley. Shrp 4H 71
Astley. Warw 2H 61
Astley. Worc 4B 60
Astley Abbotts. Shrp 1B 60
Astley Bridge. G Man 3F 91
Astley Cross. Worc 4C 60
Aston. Ches E 1A 72
Aston. Ches W 3H 83
Aston. Derbs 2F 85
(nr. Hope)
Aston. Derbs 2F 73
(nr. Sudbury)
Aston. Flin 4F 83
Aston. Here 4G 59
Aston. Herts 3C 52
Aston. Oxon 5B 50
Aston. Shrp 1C 60
(nr. Bridgnorth)
Aston. Shrp 3H 71
(nr. Wem)
Aston. S Yor 2B 86
Aston. Staf 1B 72
Aston. Telf 5A 72
Aston. W Mid 1E 61
Aston. Wok 3F 37
Aston Abbotts. Buck 3G 51
Aston Botterell. Shrp 2A 60
Aston-by-Stone. Staf 2D 72
Aston Cantlow. Warw 5F 61
Aston Clinton. Buck 4G 51
Aston Crews. Here 3B 48
Aston Cross. Glos 2E 49
Aston End. Herts 3C 52
Aston Eyre. Shrp 1A 60
Aston Fields. Worc 4D 60
Aston Flamville. Leics 1B 62
Aston Ingham. Here 3B 48
Aston juxta Mondrum.
Ches E 5A 84
Astonlane. Shrp 1A 60
Aston le Walls. Nptn 5B 62
Aston Magna. Glos 2G 49
Aston Munslow. Shrp 2H 59
Aston on Carrant. Glos 2E 49
Aston on Clun. Shrp 2F 59
Aston-on-Trent. Derbs 3B 74
Aston Pigott. Shrp 5F 71
Aston Rogers. Shrp 5F 71
Aston Rowant. Oxon 2F 37
Aston Sandford. Buck 5F 51
Aston Somerville. Worc 2F 49
Aston Subedge. Glos 1G 49
Aston Tirrold. Oxon 3D 36
Aston Upthorpe. Oxon 3D 36
Astrop. Nptn 2D 50
Astwick. C Beds 2C 52
Astwood. Mil 1H 51
Astwood Bank. Worc 4E 61
Aswarby. Linc 2H 75
Aswardby. Linc 3C 88
Atcham. Shrp 5H 71
Atch Lench. Worc 5E 61
Athelhampton. Dors 3C 14
Athelington. Suff 3E 66
Athelney. Som 4G 21
Athelstaneford. E Lot 2B 130
Atherfield Green. IOW 5C 16
Atherington. Devn 4F 19
Atherington. W Sus 5B 26
Athersley. S Yor 4D 92
Atherstone. Warw 1H 61
Atherstone on Stour. Warw 5G 61
Atherton. G Man 4E 91
Ath-Tharracail. High 2A 140
Atlow. Derbs 1G 73
Attadale. High 5B 156
Attenborough. Notts 2C 74
Atterby. Linc 1G 87
Atterley. Shrp 1A 60
Atterton. Leics 1A 62
Attleborough. Norf 1C 66
Attleborough. Warw 1A 62
Attlebridge. Norf 4D 78
Atwick. E Yor 4F 101
Atworth. Wilts 5D 34
Auberrow. Here 1H 47
Aubourn. Linc 4G 87
Aucharnie. Abers 4D 160
Auchattie. Abers 4D 152
Auchavan. Ang 2A 144
Auchbreck. Mor 1G 151
Auchenback. E Ren 4G 127
Auchenblae. Abers 1G 145
Auchenbrack. Dum 5G 117
Auchenbreck. Arg 1B 126
Auchencairn. Dum 4E 111
(nr. Dalbeattie)
Auchencairn. Dum 1A 112
(nr. Dumfries)
Auchencarroch. W Dun 1F 127
Auchencrow. Bord 3E 131
Auchendennan. W Dun 1E 127
Auchendinny. Midl 3F 129
Auchengray. S Lan 4C 128
Auchenhalrig. Mor 2A 160
Auchenheath. S Lan 5B 128
Auchenlochan. Arg 2A 126
Auchenmade. N Ayr 5E 127
Auchenmalg. Dum 4H 109
Auchentiber. N Ayr 5E 127
Auchenvennel. Arg 1D 126
Auchindrain. Arg 3H 133
Auchininna. Abers 4D 160
Auchinleck. Dum 2B 110
Auchinleck. E Ayr 2E 117
Auchinloch. N Lan 2H 127
Auchinstarry. N Lan 2A 128
Auchleven. Abers 1D 152
Auchlochan. S Lan 1H 117
Auchlunachan. High 5F 163
Auchmillan. E Ayr 2E 117
Auchmithie. Ang 4F 145
Auchmuirbridge. Per 3E 136
Auchmull. Ang 1E 145
Auchnacree. Ang 4G 161
Auchnafree. Per 5F 143
Auchnagallin. High 5E 159
Auchnagatt. Abers 4G 161
Aucholzie. Abers 4H 151
Auchreddie. Abers 4F 161
Auchterarder. Per 2B 136
Auchteraw. High 3F 149
Auchterderran. Fife 4E 136
Auchterhouse. Ang 5C 144
Auchtermuchty. Fife 2E 137
Auchterneed. High 3G 157
Auchtertool. Fife 4E 136
Auchtertyre. High 1G 147
Auchtubh. Stir 1E 135
Auckengill. High 2F 169
Auckley. S Yor 4G 93
Audenshaw. G Man 1D 84
Audlem. Ches E 1A 72
Audley. Staf 5B 84
Audley End. Essx 2F 53
Audmore. Staf 3C 72
Auds. Abers 2D 160
Aughertree. Cumb 1D 102
Aughton. E Yor 1H 93
Aughton. Lanc 3E 97
(nr. Lancaster)
Aughton. Lanc 4B 90
(nr. Ormskirk)
Aughton. S Yor 2B 86
Aughton. Wilts 1H 23
Aughton Park. Lanc 4C 90
Auldearn. High 3D 158
Aulden. Here 5G 59
Auldgirth. Dum 1G 111
Auldhouse. S Lan 4H 127
Ault a' chruinn. High 1B 148
Aultbea. High 5C 162
Aultdearg. High 2E 157
Aultgrishan. High 5B 162
Aultguish Inn. High 1F 157
Ault Hucknall. Derbs 4B 86
Aultibea. High 1H 165
Aultiphurst. High 2A 168
Aultivullin. High 2A 168
Aultmore. Mor 3B 160
Aultnamain Inn. High 5D 164
Aunby. Linc 4H 75
Aunsby. Linc 2H 75
Aust. S Glo 3A 34
Austerfield. S Yor 1D 86
Austin Fen. Linc 1C 88
Austrey. Warw 5G 73
Austwick. N Yor 3G 97
Authorpe. Linc 2D 88
Authorpe Row. Linc 3E 89
Avebury. Wilts 5G 35
Avebury Trusloe. Wilts 5F 35
Aveley. Thur 2G 39
Avening. Glos 2D 35
Averham. Notts 5E 87
Aveton Gifford. Devn 4C 8
Avielochan. High 2D 150
Aviemore. High 2C 150
Avington. Hants 3D 24
Avoch. High 3B 158
Avon. Hants 3G 15
Avonbridge. Falk 2C 128
Avon Dassett. Warw 5B 62
Avonmouth. Bris 4A 34
Avonwick. Devn 3D 8
Awbridge. Hants 4B 24
Awliscombe. Devn 2E 13
Awre. Glos 5C 48
Awsworth. Notts 1B 74
Axbridge. Som 1H 21
Axford. Hants 2E 24
Axford. Wilts 5H 35
Axminster. Devn 3F 13
Axmouth. Devn 3F 13
Aycliffe Village. Dur 2F 105
Aydon. Nmbd 3D 114
Aykley Heads. Dur 5F 115
Aylburton. Glos 5B 48
Aylburton Common. Glos 5B 48
Ayle. Nmbd 5A 114
Aylesbeare. Devn 3D 12
Aylesbury. Buck 4G 51
Aylesby. NE Lin 4F 95
Aylescott. Devn 1G 11
Aylesford. Kent 5B 40
Aylesham. Kent 5G 41
Aylestone. Leic 5C 74
Aylmerton. Norf 2D 78
Aylsham. Norf 3D 78
Aylton. Here 2B 48
Aylworth. Glos 3G 49
Aymestrey. Here 4G 59
Aynho. Nptn 2D 50
Ayot Green. Herts 4C 52
Ayot St Lawrence. Herts 4B 52
Ayot St Peter. Herts 4C 52
Ayr. S Ayr 2C 116 & 187
Ayres of Selivoe. Shet 7D 173
Ayreville. Torb 2E 9
Aysgarth. N Yor 1C 98
Ayshford. Devn 1D 12
Ayside. Cumb 1C 96
Ayston. Rut 5F 75
Ayton. Bord 3F 131
Aywick. Shet 3G 173
Azerley. N Yor 2E 99

B

Babbacombe. Torb 2F 9
Babbinswood. Shrp 3F 71
Babb's Green. Herts 4D 53
Babcary. Som 4A 22
Babel. Carm 2B 46
Babell. Flin 3D 82
Babingley. Norf 3F 77
Bablock Hythe. Oxon 5C 50
Babraham. Cambs 5E 65
Babworth. Notts 2D 86
Bac. W Isl 3G 171
Bachau. IOA 2D 80
Bacheldre. Powy 1E 59
Bachymbyd Fawr. Den 4C 82
Backaland. Orkn 4E 172
Backaskaill. Orkn 2D 172
Backbarrow. Cumb 1C 96
Backe. Carm 3G 43
Backfolds. Abers 3H 161
Backford. Ches W 3G 83
Backhill. Abers 5E 161
Backhill of Clackriach. Abers 4G 161
Backies. High 3F 165
Backmuir of New Gilston.
Fife 3G 137
Back of Keppoch. High 5E 147
Back Street. Suff 5G 65
Backwell. N Som 5H 33
Backworth. Tyne 2G 115
Bacon End. Essx 4G 53
Baconsthorpe. Norf 2D 78
Bacton. Here 2G 47
Bacton. Norf 2F 79
Bacton. Suff 4C 66
Bacton Green. Norf 2F 79
Bacup. Lanc 2G 91
Badachonacher. High 1A 158
Badachro. High 1G 155
Badanloch Lodge. High 5H 167
Badavanich. High 3D 156
Badbury. Swin 3G 35
Badby. Nptn 5C 62
Badcall. High 3C 166
Badcaul. High 4E 163
Baddeley Green. Stoke 5D 84
Baddesley Clinton. W Mid 3G 61
Baddesley Ensor. Warw 1G 61
Baddidarach. High 1E 163
Baddoch. Abers 5F 151
Badenscallie. High 3E 163
Badenscoth. Abers 5E 160
Badentarbat. High 2E 163
Badgall. Corn 4C 10
Badgers Mount. Kent 4F 39
Badgeworth. Glos 4E 49
Badgworth. Som 1G 21
Badicaul. High 1F 147
Badingham. Suff 4F 67
Badlesmere. Kent 5E 40
Badlipster. High 4E 169
Badluarach. High 4D 163

Badminton—Batson

Badminton. S Glo 3D 34
Badnaban. High 1E 163
Badnabay. High 4C 166
Badnagie. High 5D 168
Badnellan. High 3F 165
Badninish. High 4E 165
Badrallach. High 4E 163
Badsey. Worc 1F 49
Badshot Lea. Surr 2G 25
Badsworth. W Yor 3E 93
Badwell Ash. Suff 4B 66
Bae Cinmel. Cnwy 2B 82
Bae Colwyn. Cnwy 3A 82
Bae Penrhyn. Cnwy 2H 81
Bagby. N Yor 1G 99
Bag Enderby. Linc 3C 88
Bagendon. Glos 5F 49
Bagginswood. Shrp 2A 60
Bàgh a Chàise. W Isl 1E 170
Bàgh a' Chaisteil. W Isl 9B 170
Bagham. Kent 5E 41
Baghasdal. W Isl 7C 170
Bagh Mor. W Isl 3D 170
Bagh Shiarabhagh. W Isl 8C 170
Bagillt. Flin 3E 83
Baginton. Warw 3H 61
Baglan. Neat 2A 32
Bagley. Shrp 3G 71
Bagley. Som 2H 21
Bagnall. Staf 5D 84
Bagnor. W Ber 5C 36
Bagshot. Surr 4A 38
Bagshot. Wilts 5B 36
Bagstone. S Glo 3B 34
Bagthorpe. Norf 2G 77
Bagthorpe. Notts 5B 86
Bagworth. Leics 5B 74
Bagwy Llydiart. Here 3H 47
Baildon. W Yor 1B 92
Baildon Green. W Yor 1B 92
Baile. W Isl 1E 170
Baile Ailein. W Isl 5E 171
Baile an Truiseil. W Isl 2F 171
Baile Boidheach. Arg 2F 125
Baile Glas. W Isl 3D 170
Bailemeonach. Arg 4A 140
Baile Mhanaich. W Isl 3C 170
Baile Mhartainn. W Isl 1C 170
Baile MhicPhail. W Isl 1D 170
Baile Mor. Arg 2A 132
Baile Mor. W Isl 2C 170
Baile nan Cailleach. W Isl 3C 170
Baile Raghaill. W Isl 2C 170
Bailey Green. Hants 4E 25
Baileyhead. Cumb 1G 113
Bailiesward. Abers 5B 160
Bail' Iochdrach. W Isl 3D 170
Baillieston. Glas 3H 127
Bailrigg. Lanc 4D 97
Bail' Uachdraich. W Isl 2D 170
Bail Ur Tholastaidh. W Isl 3H 171
Bainbridge. N Yor 5C 104
Bainsford. Falk 1B 128
Bainshole. Abers 5D 160
Bainton. E Yor 4D 100
Bainton. Oxon 3D 50
Bainton. Pet 5H 75
Baintown. Fife 3F 137
Baker Street. Thur 2H 39
Bakewell. Derbs 4G 85
Bala. Gwyn 2B 70
Balachuirn. High 4E 155
Balbeg. High 5G 157
(nr. Cannich)
Balbeg. High 1G 149
(nr. Loch Ness)
Balbeggie. Per 1D 136
Balblair. High 4C 164
(nr. Bonar Bridge)
Balblair. High 2B 158
(nr. Invergordon)
Balblair. High 4H 157
(nr. Inverness)
Balby. S Yor 4F 93
Balcathie. Ang 5F 145
Balchladich. High 1E 163
Balchraggan. High 4H 157
Balchrick. High 3B 166
Balcombe. W Sus 2E 27
Balcombe Lane. W Sus 2E 27
Balcurvie. Fife 3F 137
Baldersby. N Yor 2F 99
Baldersby St James. N Yor 2F 99
Balderstone. Lanc 1E 91
Balderton. Ches W 4F 83
Balderton. Notts 5F 87
Baldinnie. Fife 2G 137
Baldock. Herts 2C 52
Baldrine. IOM 3D 108
Baldslow. E Sus 4C 28
Baldwin. IOM 3C 108
Baldwinholme. Cumb 4E 113
Baldwin's Gate. Staf 2B 72
Bale. Norf 2C 78
Balearn. Abers 3H 161
Balemartine. Arg 4A 138
Balephretrish. Arg 4B 138
Balephuil. Arg 4A 138
Balerno. Edin 3E 129
Balevullin. Arg 4A 138
Balfield. Ang 2E 145
Balfour. Orkn 6D 172
Balfron. Stir 1G 127
Balgaveny. Abers 4D 160
Balgonar. Fife 4C 136
Balgowan. High 4A 150
Balgown. High 2C 154
Balgrochan. E Dun 2H 127
Balgy. High 3H 155
Balhalgardy. Abers 1E 153
Baliasta. Shet 1H 173
Baligill. High 2A 168
Balintore. Ang 3B 144
Balintore. High 1C 158
Balintraid. High 1B 158
Balk. N Yor 1G 99
Balkeerie. Ang 4C 144
Balkholme. E Yor 2A 94
Ball. Shrp 3F 71
Ballabeg. IOM 4B 108
Ballacannell. IOM 3D 108
Ballacarnane Beg. IOM 3C 108
Ballachulish. High 3E 141
Ballagyr. IOM 3B 108
Ballajora. IOM 2D 108
Ballaleigh. IOM 3C 108
Ballamodha. IOM 4B 108
Ballantrae. S Ayr 1F 109
Ballards Gore. Essx 1D 40
Ballasalla. IOM 4B 108
(nr. Castletown)
Ballasalla. IOM 2C 108
(nr. Kirk Michael)
Ballater. Abers 4A 152
Ballaugh. IOM 2C 108
Ballencrieff. E Lot 2A 130
Ballencrieff Toll. W Lot 2C 128
Ballentoul. Per 2F 143
Ball Hill. Hants 5C 36
Ballidon. Derbs 5G 85
Balliemore. Arg 1B 126
(nr. Dunoon)
Balliemore. Arg 1F 133
(nr. Oban)
Ballieward. High 5E 159
Ballig. IOM 3B 108
Ballimore. Stir 2E 135
Ballingdon. Suff 1B 54
Ballinger Common. Buck 5H 51
Ballingham. Here 2A 48
Ballingry. Fife 4D 136
Ballinluig. Per 3G 143
Ballintuim. Per 3A 144
Balliveolan. Arg 4C 140
Balloan. High 3C 164
Balloch. High 4B 158
Balloch. N Lan 2A 128
Balloch. Per 2H 135
Balloch. W Dun 1E 127
Ballochan. Abers 4C 152
Ballochgoy. Arg 3B 126
Ballochmyle. E Ayr 2E 117
Ballochroy. Arg 4F 125
Balls Cross. W Sus 3A 26
Ball's Green. E Sus 2F 27
Ballygown. Arg 4F 139
Ballygrant. Arg 3B 124
Ballymichael. N Ayr 2D 122
Balmacara. High 1G 147
Balmaclellan. Dum 2D 110
Balmacqueen. High 1D 154
Balmaha. Stir 4D 134
Balmalcolm. Fife 3F 137
Balmalloch. N Lan 2A 128
Balmeanach. High 5E 155
Balmedie. Abers 2G 153
Balmerino. Fife 1F 137
Balmerlawn. Hants 2B 16
Balmore. E Dun 2H 127
Balmore. High 4B 154
Balmuir. Ang 5D 144
Balmullo. Fife 1G 137
Balmurrie. Dum 3H 109
Balnaboth. Ang 2C 144
Balnabruaich. High 1B 158
Balnabruich. High 5D 168
Balnacoil. High 2F 165
Balnacra. High 4B 156
Balnacroft. Abers 4G 151
Balnageith. Mor 3E 159
Balnaglaic. High 5G 157
Balnagrantach. High 5G 157
Balnaguard. Per 3G 143
Balnahard. Arg 4B 132
Balnain. High 5G 157
Balnakeil. High 2D 166
Balnaknock. High 2D 154
Balnamoon. Abers 3G 161
Balnamoon. Ang 2E 145
Balnapaling. High 2B 158
Balornock. Glas 3H 127
Balquhidder. Stir 1E 135
Balsall. W Mid 3G 61
Balsall Common. W Mid 3G 61
Balscote. Oxon 1B 50
Balsham. Cambs 5E 65
Balstonia. Thur 2A 40
Baltasound. Shet 1H 173
Balterley. Staf 5B 84
Baltersan. Dum 3B 110
Balthangie. Abers 3F 161
Baltonsborough. Som 3A 22
Balvaird. High 3H 157
Balvaird. Per 2D 136
Balvenie. Mor 4H 159
Balvicar. Arg 2E 133
Balvraid. High 2G 147
Balvraid Lodge. High 5C 158
Bamber Bridge. Lanc 2D 90
Bamber's Green. Essx 3F 53
Bamburgh. Nmbd 1F 121
Bamford. Derbs 2G 85
Bamfurlong. G Man 4D 90
Bampton. Cumb 3G 103
Bampton. Devn 4C 20
Bampton. Oxon 5B 50
Bampton Grange. Cumb 3G 103
Banavie. High 1F 141
Banbury. Oxon 1C 50
Bancffosfelen. Carm 4E 45
Banchory. Abers 4D 152
Banchory-Devenick. Abers 3G 153
Bancycapel. Carm 4E 45
Bancyfelin. Carm 3H 43
Banc-y-ffordd. Carm 2E 45
Banff. Abers 2D 160
Bangor. Gwyn 3E 81
Bangor-is-y-coed. Wrex 1F 71
Bangors. Corn 3C 10
Bangor's Green. Lanc 4B 90
Banham. Norf 2C 66
Bank. Hants 2A 16
Bankend. Dum 3B 112
Bankfoot. Per 5H 143
Bankglen. E Ayr 3E 117
Bankhead. Aber 2F 153
Bankhead. Abers 3D 152
Bankhead. S Lan 5B 128
Bankland. Som 4G 21
Bank Newton. N Yor 4B 98
Banknock. Falk 2A 128
Banks. Cumb 3G 113
Banks. Lanc 2B 90
Bankshill. Dum 1C 112
Bank Street. Worc 4A 60
Bank, The. Ches E 5C 84
Bank, The. Shrp 1A 60
Bank Top. Lanc 4D 90
Banners Gate. W Mid 1E 61
Banningham. Norf 3E 78
Banniskirk. High 3D 168
Bannister Green. Essx 3G 53
Bannockburn. Stir 4H 135
Banstead. Surr 5D 38
Bantham. Devn 4C 8
Banton. N Lan 2A 128
Banwell. N Som 1G 21
Banyard's Green. Suff 3F 67
Bapchild. Kent 4D 40
Bapton. Wilts 3E 23
Barabhas. W Isl 2F 171
Barabhas Iarach. W Isl 3F 171
Baramore. High 1A 140
Barassie. S Ayr 1C 116
Baravullin. Arg 4D 140
Barbaraville. High 1B 158
Barber Booth. Derbs 2F 85
Barber Green. Cumb 1C 96
Barbhas Uarach. W Isl 2F 171
Barbieston. S Ayr 3D 116
Barbon. Cumb 1F 97
Barbourne. Worc 5C 60
Barbridge. Ches E 5A 84
Barbrook. Devn 2H 19
Barby. Nptn 3C 62
Barby Nortoft. Nptn 3C 62
Barcaldine. Arg 4D 140
Barcheston. Warw 1A 50
Barclose. Cumb 3F 113
Barcombe. E Sus 4F 27
Barcombe Cross. E Sus 4F 27
Barden. N Yor 5E 105
Barden Scale. N Yor 4C 98
Bardfield End Green. Essx 2G 53
Bardfield Saling. Essx 3G 53
Bardister. Shet 4E 173
Bardnabeinne. High 4E 164
Bardney. Linc 4A 88
Bardon. Leics 4B 74
Bardon Mill. Nmbd 3A 114
Bardowie. E Dun 2G 127
Bardrainney. Inv 2E 127
Bardsea. Cumb 2C 96
Bardsey. W Yor 5F 99
Bardsley. G Man 4H 91
Bardwell. Suff 3B 66
Bare. Lanc 3D 96
Barelees. Nmbd 1C 120
Barewood. Here 5F 59
Barford. Hants 3G 25
Barford. Norf 5D 78
Barford. Warw 4G 61
Barford St John. Oxon 2C 50
Barford St Martin. Wilts 3F 23
Barford St Michael. Oxon 2C 50
Barfrestone. Kent 5G 41
Bargeddie. N Lan 3A 128
Bargod. Cphy 2E 33
Bargoed. Cphy 2E 33
Bargrennan. Dum 2A 110
Barham. Cambs 3A 64
Barham. Kent 5G 41
Barham. Suff 5D 66
Barharrow. Dum 4D 110
Bar Hill. Cambs 4C 64
Barholm. Linc 4H 75
Barkby. Leics 4D 74
Barkestone-le-Vale. Leics 2E 75
Barkham. Wok 5F 37
Barking. G Lon 2F 39
Barking. Suff 5C 66
Barkingside. G Lon 2F 39
Barking Tye. Suff 5C 66
Barkisland. W Yor 3A 92
Barkston. Linc 1G 75
Barkston Ash. N Yor 1E 93
Barkway. Herts 2D 53
Barlanark. Glas 3H 127
Barlaston. Staf 2C 72
Barlavington. W Sus 4A 26
Barlborough. Derbs 3B 86
Barlby. N Yor 1G 93
Barlestone. Leics 5B 74
Barley. Herts 2D 53
Barley. Lanc 5H 97
Barley Mow. Tyne 4F 115
Barleythorpe. Rut 5F 75
Barling. Essx 2D 40
Barlings. Linc 3H 87
Barlow. Derbs 3H 85
Barlow. N Yor 2G 93
Barlow. Tyne 3E 115
Barmby Moor. E Yor 5B 100
Barmby on the Marsh. E Yor 2G 93
Barmer. Norf 2H 77
Barming. Kent 5B 40
Barming Heath. Kent 5B 40
Barmoor. Nmbd 1E 121
Barmouth. Gwyn 4F 69
Barmpton. Darl 3A 106
Barmston. E Yor 4F 101
Barmulloch. Glas 3H 127
Barnack. Pet 5H 75
Barnacle. Warw 2A 62
Barnard Castle. Dur 3D 104
Barnard Gate. Oxon 4C 50
Barnardiston. Suff 1H 53
Barnbarroch. Dum 4F 111
Barnburgh. S Yor 4E 93
Barnby. Suff 2G 67
Barnby Dun. S Yor 4G 93
Barnby in the Willows. Notts 5F 87
Barnby Moor. Notts 2D 86
Barnes. G Lon 3D 38
Barnes Street. Kent 1H 27
Barnet. G Lon 1D 38
Barnetby le Wold. N Lin 4D 94
Barney. Norf 2B 78
Barnham. Suff 3A 66
Barnham. W Sus 5A 26
Barnham Broom. Norf 5C 78
Barnhead. Ang 3F 145
Barnhill. D'dee 5D 145
Barnhill. Mor 3F 159
Barnhill. Per 1D 136
Barnhills. Dum 2E 109
Barningham. Dur 3D 105
Barningham. Suff 3B 66
Barnoldby le Beck. NE Lin 4F 95
Barnoldswick. Lanc 5A 98
Barns Green. W Sus 3C 26
Barnsley. Glos 5F 49
Barnsley. Shrp 1B 60
Barnsley. S Yor 4D 92
Barnstaple. Devn 3F 19
Barnston. Essx 4G 53
Barnston. Mers 2E 83
Barnstone. Notts 2E 75
Barnt Green. Worc 3E 61
Barnton. Ches W 3A 84
Barnwell. Cambs 5D 64
Barnwell. Nptn 2H 63
Barnwood. Glos 4D 48
Barons Cross. Here 5G 59
Barony, The. Orkn 5B 172
Barr. Dum 4G 117
Barr. S Ayr 5B 116
Barra Airport. W Isl 8C 170
Barrachan. Dum 5A 110
Barraglom. W Isl 4D 171
Barrahormid. Arg 1F 125
Barrapol. Arg 4A 138
Barrasford. Nmbd 2C 114
Barravullin. Arg 3F 133
Barregarrow. IOM 3C 108
Barrhead. E Ren 4G 127
Barrhill. S Ayr 1H 109
Barri. V Glam 5E 32
Barrington. Cambs 1D 53
Barrington. Som 1G 13
Barripper. Corn 3D 4
Barrmill. N Ayr 4E 127
Barrock. High 1E 169
Barrow. Lanc 1F 91
Barrow. Rut 4F 75
Barrow. Shrp 5A 72
Barrow. Som 3C 22
Barrow. Suff 4G 65
Barroway Drove. Norf 5E 77
Barrow Bridge. G Man 3E 91
Barrowburn. Nmbd 3C 120
Barrowby. Linc 2F 75
Barrowcliff. N Yor 1E 101
Barrow Common. N Som 5A 34
Barrowden. Rut 5G 75
Barrowford. Lanc 1G 91
Barrow Gurney. N Som 5A 34
Barrow Haven. N Lin 2D 94
Barrow Hill. Derbs 3B 86
Barrow-in-Furness. Cumb 3B 96
Barrow Nook. Lanc 4C 90
Barrows Green. Cumb 1E 97
Barrow's Green. Hal 2H 83
Barrow Street. Wilts 3D 22
Barrow upon Humber. N Lin 2D 94
Barrow upon Soar. Leics 4C 74
Barrow upon Trent. Derbs 3A 74
Barry. Ang 5E 145
Barry. V Glam 5E 32
Barry Island. V Glam 5E 32
Barsby. Leics 4D 74
Barsham. Suff 2F 67
Barston. W Mid 3G 61
Bartestree. Here 1A 48
Barthol Chapel. Abers 5F 161
Bartholomew Green. Essx 3H 53
Barthomley. Ches E 5B 84
Bartley. Hants 1B 16
Bartley Green. W Mid 2E 61
Bartlow. Cambs 1F 53
Barton. Cambs 5D 64
Barton. Ches W 5G 83
Barton. Cumb 2F 103
Barton. Glos 3F 49
Barton. IOW 4D 16
Barton. Lanc 4B 90
(nr. Ormskirk)
Barton. Lanc 1D 90
(nr. Preston)
Barton. N Som 1G 21
Barton. N Yor 4F 105
Barton. Oxon 5D 50
Barton. Torb 2F 9
Barton. Warw 5F 61
Barton Bendish. Norf 5G 77
Barton Gate. Staf 4F 73
Barton Green. Staf 4F 73
Barton Hartsthorn. Buck 2E 51
Barton Hill. N Yor 3B 100
Barton in Fabis. Notts 2C 74
Barton in the Beans. Leics 5A 74
Barton-le-Clay. C Beds 2A 52
Barton-le-Street. N Yor 2B 100
Barton-le-Willows. N Yor 3B 100
Barton Mills. Suff 3G 65
Barton on Sea. Hants 3H 15
Barton-on-the-Heath. Warw 2A 50
Barton St David. Som 3A 22
Barton Seagrave. Nptn 3F 63
Barton Stacey. Hants 2C 24
Barton Town. Devn 2G 19
Barton Turf. Norf 3F 79
Barton-under-Needwood. Staf 4F 73
Barton-upon-Humber. N Lin 2D 94
Barton Waterside. N Lin 2D 94
Barugh Green. S Yor 4D 92
Barway. Cambs 3E 65
Barwell. Leics 1B 62
Barwick. Herts 4D 53
Barwick. Som 1A 14
Barwick in Elmet. W Yor 1D 93
Baschurch. Shrp 3G 71
Bascote. Warw 4B 62
Basford Green. Staf 5D 85
Bashall Eaves. Lanc 5F 97
Bashall Town. Lanc 5G 97
Bashley. Hants 3H 15
Basildon. Essx 2B 40
Basingstoke. Hants 1E 25
Baslow. Derbs 3G 85
Bason Bridge. Som 2G 21
Bassaleg. Newp 3F 33
Bassendean. Bord 5C 130
Bassenthwaite. Cumb 1D 102
Bassett. Sotn 1C 16
Bassingbourn. Cambs 1D 52
Bassingfield. Notts 2D 74
Bassingham. Linc 5G 87
Bassingthorpe. Linc 3G 75
Bassus Green. Herts 3D 52
Basta. Shet 2G 173
Baston. Linc 4A 76
Bastonford. Worc 5C 60
Bastwick. Norf 4G 79
Batchley. Worc 4E 61
Batchworth. Herts 1B 38
Batcombe. Dors 2B 14
Batcombe. Som 3B 22
Bate Heath. Ches E 3A 84
Bath. Bath 5C 34 & 187
Bathampton. Bath 5C 34
Bathealton. Som 4D 20
Batheaston. Bath 5C 34
Bathford. Bath 5C 34
Bathgate. W Lot 3C 128
Bathley. Notts 5E 87
Bathpool. Corn 5C 10
Bathpool. Som 4F 21
Bathville. W Lot 3C 128
Bathway. Som 1A 22
Batley. W Yor 2C 92
Batsford. Glos 2G 49
Batson. Devn 5D 8

Battersby—Bilsby

Battersby. *N Yor* 4C 106
Battersea. *G Lon* 3D 39
Battisborough Cross. *Devn* 4C 8
Battisford. *Suff* 5C 66
Battisford Tye. *Suff* 5C 66
Battle. *E Sus* 4B 28
Battle. *Powy* 2D 46
Battleborough. *Som* 1G 21
Battledown. *Glos* 3E 49
Battlefield. *Shrp* 4H 71
Battlesbridge. *Essx* 1B 40
Battlesden. *C Beds* 3H 51
Battlesea Green. *Suff* 3E 66
Battleton. *Som* 4C 20
Battram. *Leic* 5B 74
Battramsley. *Hants* 3B 16
Batt's Corner. *Surr* 2G 25
Bauds of Cullen. *Mor* 2B 160
Baugh. *Arg* 4B 138
Baughton. *Worc* 1D 49
Baughurst. *Hants* 5D 36
Baulking. *Oxon* 2B 36
Baumber. *Linc* 3B 88
Baunton. *Glos* 5F 49
Baverstock. *Wilts* 3F 23
Bawburgh. *Norf* 5D 78
Bawdeswell. *Norf* 3C 78
Bawdrip. *Som* 3G 21
Bawdsey. *Suff* 1G 55
Bawdsey Manor. *Suff* 2G 55
Bawsey. *Norf* 4F 77
Bawtry. *S Yor* 1D 86
Baxenden. *Lanc* 2F 91
Baxterley. *Warw* 1G 61
Baxter's Green. *Suff* 5G 65
Baybridge. *Hants* 4D 24
Baybridge. *Nmbd* 4C 114
Baycliff. *Cumb* 2B 96
Baydon. *Wilts* 4A 36
Bayford. *Herts* 5D 52
Bayford. *Som* 4C 22
Bayles. *Cumb* 5A 114
Baylham. *Suff* 5D 66
Baynard's Green. *Oxon* 3D 50
Bayston Hill. *Shrp* 5G 71
Baythorn End. *Essx* 1H 53
Baythorpe. *Linc* 1B 76
Bayton. *Worc* 3A 60
Bayton Common. *Worc* 3B 60
Bayworth. *Oxon* 5D 50
Beach. *S Glo* 4C 34
Beachampton. *Buck* 2F 51
Beachamwell. *Norf* 5G 77
Beachley. *Glos* 2A 34
Beacon. *Devn* 2E 13
Beacon End. *Essx* 3C 54
Beacon Hill. *Surr* 3G 25
Beacon's Bottom. *Buck* 2F 37
Beaconsfield. *Buck* 1A 38
Beacontree. *G Lon* 2F 39
Beacrabhaicg. *W Isl* 8D 171
Beadlam. *N Yor* 1A 100
Beadnell. *Nmbd* 2G 121
Beaford. *Devn* 1F 11
Beal. *Nmbd* 5G 131
Beal. *N Yor* 2F 93
Bealsmill. *Corn* 5D 10
Beam Hill. *Staf* 3G 73
Beamhurst. *Staf* 2E 73
Beaminster. *Dors* 2H 13
Beamish. *Dur* 4F 115
Beamond End. *Buck* 1A 38
Beamsley. *N Yor* 4C 98
Bean. *Kent* 3G 39
Beanacre. *Wilts* 5E 35
Beanley. *Nmbd* 3E 121
Beanshanger. *Nptn* 2F 51
Beaquoy. *Orkn* 5C 172
Beardwood. *Bkbn* 2E 91
Beare Green. *Surr* 1C 26
Bearley. *Warw* 4F 61
Bearpark. *Dur* 5F 115
Bearsbridge. *Nmbd* 4A 114
Bearsden. *E Dun* 2G 127
Bearsted. *Kent* 5B 40
Bearstone. *Shrp* 2B 72
Bearwood. *Pool* 3F 15
Bearwood. *W Mid* 2E 61
Beattock. *Dum* 4C 118
Beauchamp Roding. *Essx* 5F 53
Beauchief. *S Yor* 2H 85
Beaufort. *Blae* 4E 47
Beaulieu. *Hants* 2B 16
Beauly. *High* 4H 157
Beaumaris. *IOA* 3F 81
Beaumont. *Cumb* 4E 113
Beaumont. *Essx* 3E 55
Beaumont Hill. *Darl* 3F 105
Beaumont Leys. *Leic* 5C 74
Beausale. *Warw* 3G 61
Beauvale. *Notts* 1B 74
Beauworth. *Hants* 4D 24
Beaworthy. *Devn* 3E 11
Beazley End. *Essx* 3H 53
Bebington. *Mers* 2F 83
Bebside. *Nmbd* 1F 115
Beccles. *Suff* 2G 67
Becconsall. *Lanc* 2C 90
Beckbury. *Shrp* 5B 72
Beckenham. *G Lon* 4E 39
Beckermet. *Cumb* 4B 102
Beckett End. *Norf* 1G 65
Beckfoot. *Cumb* 1A 96
(nr. Broughton in Furness)
Beck Foot. *Cumb* 5H 103
(nr. Kendal)
Beckfoot. *Cumb* 4C 102
(nr. Seascale)
Beckfoot. *Cumb* 5B 112
(nr. Silloth)
Beckford. *Worc* 2E 49
Beckhampton. *Wilts* 5F 35
Beck Hole. *N Yor* 4F 107
Beckingham. *Linc* 5F 87
Beckingham. *Notts* 1E 87
Beckington. *Som* 1D 22
Beckley. *E Sus* 3C 28
Beckley. *Hants* 3H 15
Beckley. *Oxon* 4D 50
Beck Row. *Suff* 3F 65
Beck Side. *Cumb* 1C 96
(nr. Cartmel)
Beckside. *Cumb* 1F 97
(nr. Sedbergh)
Beck Side. *Cumb* 1B 96
(nr. Ulverston)
Beckton. *G Lon* 2F 39
Beckwithshaw. *N Yor* 4E 99
Becontree. *G Lon* 2F 39
Bedale. *N Yor* 1E 99
Bedburn. *Dur* 1E 105
Bedchester. *Dors* 1D 14
Beddau. *Rhon* 3D 32
Beddgelert. *Gwyn* 1E 69
Beddingham. *E Sus* 5F 27
Beddington. *G Lon* 4D 39
Bedfield. *Suff* 4E 66
Bedford. *Bed* 1A 52 & 188
Bedford. *G Man* 4E 91
Bedham. *W Sus* 3B 26
Bedhampton. *Hants* 2F 17
Bedingfield. *Suff* 4D 66
Bedingham Green. *Norf* 1E 67
Bedlam. *N Yor* 3E 99
Bedlar's Green. *Essx* 4F 53
Bedlington. *Nmbd* 1F 115
Bedlinog. *Mer T* 5D 46
Bedminster. *Bris* 4A 34
Bedmond. *Herts* 5A 52
Bednall. *Staf* 4D 72
Bedrule. *Bord* 3A 120
Bedstone. *Shrp* 3F 59
Bedwas. *Cphy* 3E 33
Bedwellty. *Cphy* 5E 47
Bedworth. *Warw* 2A 62
Beeby. *Leics* 5D 74
Beech. *Hants* 3E 25
Beech. *Staf* 2C 72
Beechcliffe. *W Yor* 5C 98
Beech Hill. *W Ber* 5E 37
Beechingstoke. *Wilts* 1F 23
Beedon. *W Ber* 4C 36
Beeford. *E Yor* 4F 101
Beeley. *Derbs* 4G 85
Beelsby. *NE Lin* 4F 95
Beenham. *W Ber* 5D 36
Beeny. *Corn* 3B 10
Beer. *Devn* 4F 13
Beer. *Som* 3H 21
Beercrocombe. *Som* 4G 21
Beer Hackett. *Dors* 1B 14
Beesands. *Devn* 4E 9
Beesby. *Linc* 2D 88
Beeson. *Devn* 4E 9
Beeston. *C Beds* 1B 52
Beeston. *Ches W* 5H 83
Beeston. *Norf* 4B 78
Beeston. *Notts* 2C 74
Beeston. *W Yor* 1C 92
Beeston Regis. *Norf* 1D 78
Beeswing. *Dum* 3F 111
Beetham. *Cumb* 2D 97
Beetham. *Som* 1F 13
Beetley. *Norf* 4B 78
Beffcote. *Staf* 4C 72
Began. *Card* 3F 33
Begbroke. *Oxon* 4C 50
Begdale. *Cambs* 5D 76
Begelly. *Pemb* 4F 43
Beggar Hill. *Essx* 5G 53
Beggar's Bush. *Powy* 4E 59
Beggearn Huish. *Som* 3D 20
Beguildy. *Powy* 3D 58
Beighton. *Norf* 5F 79
Beighton. *S Yor* 2B 86
Beighton Hill. *Derbs* 5G 85
Beinn Casgro. *W Isl* 5G 171
Beith. *N Ayr* 4E 127
Bekesbourne. *Kent* 5F 41
Belaugh. *Norf* 4E 79
Belbroughton. *Worc* 3D 60
Belchalwell. *Dors* 2C 14
Belchalwell Street. *Dors* 2C 14
Belchamp Otten. *Essx* 1B 54
Belchamp St Paul. *Essx* 1A 54
Belchamp Walter. *Essx* 1B 54
Belchford. *Linc* 3B 88
Belfatton. *Abers* 3H 161
Belford. *Nmbd* 1F 121
Belgrano. *Cnwy* 3B 82
Belhaven. *E Lot* 2C 130
Belhelvie. *Abers* 2G 153
Belhinnie. *Abers* 1B 152
Bellabeg. *Abers* 2A 152
Belladrum. *High* 4H 157
Bellamore. *S Ayr* 1H 109
Bellanoch. *Arg* 4F 133
Bell Busk. *N Yor* 4B 98
Belleau. *Linc* 3D 88
Belleheiglash. *Mor* 5F 159
Bell End. *Worc* 3D 60
Bellerby. *N Yor* 5E 105
Bellerby Camp. *N Yor* 5D 105
Bellever. *Devn* 5G 11
Belle Vue. *Cumb* 1C 102
Belle Vue. *Shrp* 4G 71
Bellfield. *S Lan* 1H 117
Belliehill. *Ang* 2E 145
Bellingdon. *Buck* 5H 51
Bellingham. *Nmbd* 1B 114
Bellmount. *Norf* 3E 77
Bellochantuy. *Arg* 2A 122
Bellsbank. *E Ayr* 4D 117
Bell's Cross. *Suff* 5D 66
Bellshill. *N Lan* 4A 128
Bellshill. *Nmbd* 1F 121
Bellside. *N Lan* 4B 128
Bellspool. *Bord* 1D 118
Bellsquarry. *W Lot* 3D 128
Bells Yew Green. *E Sus* 2H 27
Belmaduthy. *High* 3A 158
Belmesthorpe. *Rut* 4H 75
Belmont. *Bkbn* 3E 91
Belmont. *Shet* 1G 173
Belmont. *S Ayr* 3C 116
Belnacraig. *Abers* 2A 152
Belnie. *Linc* 2B 76
Belowda. *Corn* 2D 6
Belper. *Derbs* 1A 74
Belper Lane End. *Derbs* 1H 73
Belph. *Derbs* 3C 86
Belsay. *Nmbd* 2E 115
Belsford. *Devn* 3D 8
Belsize. *Herts* 5A 52
Belstead. *Suff* 1E 55
Belston. *S Ayr* 2C 116
Belstone. *Devn* 3G 11
Belstone Corner. *Devn* 3G 11
Belthorn. *Lanc* 2F 91
Beltinge. *Kent* 4F 41
Beltoft. *N Lin* 4B 94
Belton. *Leics* 3B 74
Belton. *Linc* 2G 75
Belton. *Norf* 5G 79
Belton. *N Lin* 4A 94
Belton-in-Rutland. *Rut* 5F 75
Beltring. *Kent* 1A 28
Belts of Collonach. *Abers* 4D 152
Belvedere. *G Lon* 3F 39
Belvoir. *Leics* 2F 75
Bembridge. *IOW* 4E 17
Bemersyde. *Bord* 1H 119
Bemerton. *Wilts* 3G 23
Bempton. *E Yor* 2F 101
Benacre. *Suff* 2H 67
Ben Alder Lodge. *High* 1C 142
Ben Armine Lodge. *High* 2E 164
Benbecula Airport. *W Isl* 3C 170
Benbuie. *Dum* 5G 117
Benchill. *G Man* 2C 84
Benderloch. *Arg* 5D 140
Bendish. *Herts* 3B 52
Bendronaig Lodge. *High* 5C 156
Benenden. *Kent* 2C 28
Benera. *High* 1G 147
Benfieldside. *Dur* 4D 115
Bengate. *Norf* 3F 79
Bengeworth. *Worc* 1F 49
Bengrove. *Glos* 2E 49
Benhall Green. *Suff* 4F 67
Benholm. *Abers* 2H 145
Beningbrough. *N Yor* 4H 99
Benington. *Herts* 3C 52
Benington. *Linc* 1C 76
Benington Sea End. *Linc* 1D 76
Benllech. *IOA* 2E 81
Benmore Lodge. *High* 2H 163
Bennacott. *Corn* 3D 10
Bennah. *Devn* 4B 12
Bennecarngan. *N Ayr* 3D 122
Bennethead. *Cumb* 2F 103
Benningbrough. *N Yor* 4H 99
Benniworth. *Linc* 2B 88
Benover. *Kent* 1B 28
Benson. *Oxon* 2E 36
Benston. *Shet* 6F 173
Benstonhall. *Orkn* 4E 172
Bent. *Abers* 1F 145
Benthall. *Shrp* 5A 72
Bentham. *Glos* 4E 49
Benthoul. *Aber* 3F 153
Bentlawnt. *Shrp* 5F 71
Bentley. *E Yor* 1D 94
Bentley. *Hants* 2F 25
Bentley. *S Yor* 4F 93
Bentley. *Suff* 2E 54
Bentley. *Warw* 1G 61
Bentley. *W Mid* 1D 61
Bentley Heath. *Herts* 1D 38
Bentley Heath. *W Mid* 3F 61
Bentpath. *Dum* 5F 119
Bents. *W Lot* 3C 128
Bentworth. *Hants* 2E 25
Benvie. *D'dee* 5C 144
Benville. *Dors* 2A 14
Benwell. *Tyne* 3F 115
Benwick. *Cambs* 1C 64
Beoley. *Worc* 4E 61
Beoraidbeg. *High* 4E 147
Bepton. *W Sus* 1G 17
Berden. *Essx* 3E 53
Bere Alston. *Devn* 2A 8
Bere Ferrers. *Devn* 2A 8
Berepper. *Corn* 4D 4
Bere Regis. *Dors* 3D 14
Bergh Apton. *Norf* 5F 79
Berinsfield. *Oxon* 2D 36
Berkeley. *Glos* 2B 34
Berkhamsted. *Herts* 5H 51
Berkley. *Som* 2D 22
Berkswell. *W Mid* 3G 61
Bermondsey. *G Lon* 3E 39
Bernice. *Arg* 4A 134
Bernisdale. *High* 3D 154
Berrick Salome. *Oxon* 2E 36
Berriedale. *High* 1H 165
Berrier. *Cumb* 2F 103
Berriew. *Powy* 5D 70
Berrington. *Nmbd* 5G 131
Berrington. *Shrp* 5H 71
Berrington. *Worc* 4H 59
Berrington Green. *Worc* 4H 59
Berrington Law. *Nmbd* 5F 131
Berrow. *Som* 1G 21
Berrow Green. *Worc* 5B 60
Berry Cross. *Devn* 1E 11
Berry Down Cross. *Devn* 2F 19
Berry Hill. *Glos* 4A 48
Berry Hill. *Pemb* 1A 44
Berryhillock. *Mor* 2C 160
Berrynarbor. *Devn* 2F 19
Berry Pomeroy. *Devn* 2E 9
Berryscaur. *Dum* 5D 118
Berry's Green. *G Lon* 5F 39
Bersham. *Wrex* 1F 71
Berthengam. *Flin* 3D 82
Berwick. *E Sus* 5G 27
Berwick Bassett. *Wilts* 4G 35
Berwick Hill. *Nmbd* 2E 115
Berwick St James. *Wilts* 3F 23
Berwick St John. *Wilts* 4E 23
Berwick St Leonard. *Wilts* 3E 23
Berwick-upon-Tweed. *Nmbd* 4G 131
Berwyn. *Den* 1D 70
Bescaby. *Leics* 3F 75
Bescar. *Lanc* 3B 90
Besford. *Worc* 1E 49
Bessacarr. *S Yor* 4G 93
Bessels Leigh. *Oxon* 5C 50
Bessingby. *E Yor* 3F 101
Bessingham. *Norf* 2D 78
Best Beech Hill. *E Sus* 2H 27
Besthorpe. *Norf* 1C 66
Besthorpe. *Notts* 4F 87
Bestwood Village. *Notts* 1C 74
Beswick. *E Yor* 5E 101
Betchworth. *Surr* 5D 38
Bethania. *Cdgn* 4E 57
Bethania. *Gwyn* 1G 69
(nr. Blaenau Ffestiniog)
Bethania. *Gwyn* 5F 81
(nr. Caernarfon)
Bethel. *Gwyn* 2B 70
(nr. Bala)
Bethel. *Gwyn* 4E 81
(nr. Caernarfon)
Bethel. *IOA* 3C 80
Bethersden. *Kent* 1D 28
Bethesda. *Gwyn* 4F 81
Bethesda. *Pemb* 3E 43
Bethlehem. *Carm* 3G 45
Bethnal Green. *G Lon* 2E 39
Betishill. *N Lan* 3A 128
Betley. *Staf* 1B 72
Betsham. *Kent* 3H 39
Betteshanger. *Kent* 5H 41
Bettiscombe. *Dors* 3H 13
Bettisfield. *Wrex* 2G 71
Betton. *Shrp* 2A 72
Betton Strange. *Shrp* 5H 71
Bettws. *B'end* 3C 32
Bettws. *Newp* 2F 33
Bettws Bledrws. *Cdgn* 5E 57
Bettws Cedewain. *Powy* 1D 58
Bettws Gwerfil Goch. *Den* 1C 70
Bettws Ifan. *Cdgn* 1D 44
Bettws Newydd. *Mon* 5G 47
Bettyhill. *High* 2H 167
Betws. *Carm* 4G 45
Betws Garmon. *Gwyn* 5E 81
Betws-y-Coed. *Cnwy* 5G 81
Betws-yn-Rhos. *Cnwy* 3B 82
Beulah. *Cdgn* 1C 44
Beulah. *Powy* 5B 58
Beul an Atha. *Arg* 3B 124
Bevendean. *Brig* 5E 27
Bevercotes. *Notts* 3E 86
Beverley. *E Yor* 1D 94
Beverston. *Glos* 2D 34
Bevington. *Glos* 2B 34
Bewaldeth. *Cumb* 1D 102
Bewcastle. *Cumb* 2G 113
Bewdley. *Worc* 3B 60
Bewerley. *N Yor* 3D 98
Bewholme. *E Yor* 4F 101
Bexfield. *Norf* 3C 78
Bexhill. *E Sus* 5B 28
Bexley. *G Lon* 3F 39
Bexleyheath. *G Lon* 3F 39
Bexleyhill. *W Sus* 3A 26
Bexwell. *Norf* 5F 77
Beyton. *Suff* 4B 66
Bhalton. *W Isl* 4C 171
Bhatarsaigh. *W Isl* 9B 170
Bibbington. *Derbs* 3E 85
Bibury. *Glos* 5G 49
Bicester. *Oxon* 3D 50
Bickenhall. *Som* 1F 13
Bickenhill. *W Mid* 2F 61
Bicker. *Linc* 2B 76
Bicker Bar. *Linc* 2B 76
Bicker Gauntlet. *Linc* 2B 76
Bickershaw. *G Man* 4E 91
Bickerstaffe. *Lanc* 4C 90
Bickerton. *Ches E* 5H 83
Bickerton. *Nmbd* 4D 121
Bickerton. *N Yor* 4G 99
Bickford. *Staf* 4C 72
Bickington. *Devn* 3F 19
(nr. Barnstaple)
Bickington. *Devn* 5B 12
(nr. Newton Abbot)
Bickleigh. *Devn* 2B 8
(nr. Plymouth)
Bickleigh. *Devn* 2C 12
(nr. Tiverton)
Bickleton. *Devn* 3F 19
Bickley. *N Yor* 5G 107
Bickley Moss. *Ches W* 1H 71
Bickmarsh. *Warw* 5F 61
Bicknacre. *Essx* 5A 54
Bicknoller. *Som* 3E 20
Bicknor. *Kent* 5C 40
Bickton. *Hants* 1G 15
Bicton. *Here* 4G 59
Bicton. *Shrp* 2E 59
(nr. Bishop's Castle)
Bicton. *Shrp* 4G 71
(nr. Shrewsbury)
Bicton Heath. *Shrp* 4G 71
Bidborough. *Kent* 1G 27
Biddenden. *Kent* 2C 28
Biddenden Green. *Kent* 1C 28
Biddenham. *Bed* 1A 52
Biddestone. *Wilts* 4D 34
Biddisham. *Som* 1G 21
Biddlesden. *Buck* 1E 51
Biddlestone. *Nmbd* 4D 120
Biddulph. *Staf* 5C 84
Biddulph Moor. *Staf* 5D 84
Bideford. *Devn* 4E 19
Bidford-on-Avon. *Warw* 5E 61
Bidlake. *Devn* 4F 11
Bidston. *Mers* 2E 83
Bielby. *E Yor* 5B 100
Bieldside. *Aber* 3F 153
Bierley. *IOW* 5D 16
Bierley. *W Yor* 1B 92
Bierton. *Buck* 4G 51
Bigbury. *Devn* 4C 8
Bigbury-on-Sea. *Devn* 4C 8
Bigby. *Linc* 4D 94
Biggar. *Cumb* 3A 96
Biggar. *S Lan* 1C 118
Biggin. *Derbs* 5F 85
(nr. Hartington)
Biggin. *Derbs* 1G 73
(nr. Hulland)
Biggin. *N Yor* 1F 93
Biggings. *Shet* 5C 173
Biggin Hill. *G Lon* 5F 39
Biggleswade. *C Beds* 1B 52
Bighouse. *High* 2A 168
Bighton. *Hants* 3E 24
Biglands. *Cumb* 4D 112
Bignall End. *Staf* 5C 84
Bignor. *W Sus* 4A 26
Bigrigg. *Cumb* 3B 102
Big Sand. *High* 1G 155
Bigton. *Shet* 9E 173
Bilberry. *Corn* 2E 6
Bilborough. *Nott* 1C 74
Bilbrook. *Som* 2D 20
Bilbrook. *Staf* 5C 72
Bilbrough. *N Yor* 5H 99
Bilbster. *High* 3E 169
Bilby. *Notts* 2D 86
Bildershaw. *Dur* 2F 105
Bildeston. *Suff* 1C 54
Billericay. *Essx* 1A 40
Billesdon. *Leics* 5E 74
Billesley. *Warw* 5F 61
Billingborough. *Linc* 2A 76
Billinge. *Mers* 4D 90
Billingford. *Norf* 3C 78
(nr. Dereham)
Billingford. *Norf* 3D 66
(nr. Diss)
Billingham. *Stoc T* 2B 106
Billinghay. *Linc* 5A 88
Billingley. *S Yor* 4E 93
Billingshurst. *W Sus* 3B 26
Billingsley. *Shrp* 2B 60
Billington. *C Beds* 3H 51
Billington. *Lanc* 1F 91
Billington. *Staf* 3C 72
Billockby. *Norf* 4G 79
Billy Row. *Dur* 1E 105
Bilsborrow. *Lanc* 5E 97
Bilsby. *Linc* 3D 88

Bilsham—Bomere Heath

Bilsham. *W Sus* 5A 26
Bilsington. *Kent* 2E 29
Bilson Green. *Glos* 4B 48
Bilsthorpe. *Notts* 4D 86
Bilston. *Midl* 3F 129
Bilston. *W Mid* 1D 60
Bilstone. *Leics* 5A 74
Bilting. *Kent* 1E 29
Bilton. *E Yor* 1E 95
Bilton. *Nmbd* 3G 121
Bilton. *N Yor* 4E 99
Bilton. *Warw* 3B 62
Bilton in Ainsty. *N Yor* 5G 99
Bimbister. *Orkn* 6C 172
Binbrook. *Linc* 1B 88
Binchester. *Dur* 1F 105
Bincombe. *Dors* 4B 14
Bindal. *High* 5G 165
Binegar. *Som* 2B 22
Bines Green. *W Sus* 4C 26
Binfield. *Brac* 4G 37
Binfield Heath. *Oxon* 4F 37
Bingfield. *Nmbd* 2C 114
Bingham. *Notts* 1E 74
Bingham's Melcombe. *Dors* 2C 14
Bingley. *W Yor* 1B 92
Bings Heath. *Shrp* 4H 71
Binham. *Norf* 2B 78
Binley. *Hants* 1C 24
Binley. *W Mid* 3A 62
Binnegar. *Dors* 4D 15
Binniehill. *Falk* 2B 128
Binsoe. *N Yor* 2E 99
Binstead. *IOW* 3D 16
Binstead. *W Sus* 5A 26
Binsted. *Hants* 2F 25
Binton. *Warw* 5F 61
Bintree. *Norf* 3C 78
Binweston. *Shrp* 5F 71
Birch. *Essx* 4C 54
Birchall. *Staf* 5D 85
Bircham Newton. *Norf* 2G 77
Bircham Tofts. *Norf* 2G 77
Birchanger. *Essx* 3F 53
Birchburn. *N Ayr* 3D 122
Birch Cross. *Staf* 2F 73
Bircher. *Here* 4G 59
Birch Green. *Essx* 4C 54
Birchgrove. *Card* 4E 33
Birchgrove. *Swan* 3G 31
Birch Heath. *Ches W* 4H 83
Birch Hill. *Ches W* 3H 83
Birchill. *Devn* 2G 13
Birchington. *Kent* 4G 41
Birch Langley. *G Man* 4G 91
Birchley Heath. *Warw* 1G 61
Birchmoor. *Warw* 5G 73
Birchmoor Green. *C Beds* 2H 51
Birchover. *Derbs* 4G 85
Birch Vale. *Derbs* 2E 85
Birchview. *Mor* 5F 159
Birchwood. *Linc* 4G 87
Birchwood. *Som* 1F 13
Birchwood. *Warr* 1A 84
Bircotes. *Notts* 1D 86
Birdbrook. *Essx* 1H 53
Birdham. *W Sus* 2G 17
Birdholme. *Derbs* 4A 86
Birdingbury. *Warw* 4B 62
Birdlip. *Glos* 4E 49
Birdsall. *N Yor* 3C 100
Birds Edge. *W Yor* 4C 92
Birds Green. *Essx* 5F 53
Birdsgreen. *Shrp* 2B 60
Birdsmoorgate. *Dors* 2G 13
Birdston. *E Dun* 2H 127
Birdwell. *S Yor* 4D 92
Birdwood. *Glos* 4C 48
Birgham. *Bord* 1B 120
Birichen. *High* 4E 165
Birkby. *Cumb* 1B 102
Birkby. *N Yor* 4A 106
Birkdale. *Mers* 3B 90
Birkenhead. *Mers* 2F 83
Birkenhills. *Abers* 4E 161
Birkenshaw. *N Lan* 3H 127
Birkenshaw. *W Yor* 2C 92
Birkhall. *Abers* 4H 151
Birkhill. *Ang* 5C 144
Birkholme. *Linc* 3G 75
Birkin. *N Yor* 2F 93
Birley. *Here* 5G 59
Birling. *Kent* 4A 40
Birling. *Nmbd* 4G 121
Birling Gap. *E Sus* 5G 27
Birlingham. *Worc* 1E 49
Birmingham. *W Mid* 2E 61 & 188
Birmingham International Airport. *W Mid* 2F 61 & 216
Birnam. *Per* 4H 143
Birsay. *Orkn* 5B 172
Birse. *Abers* 4C 152
Birsemore. *Abers* 4C 152
Birstall. *Leics* 5C 74
Birstall. *W Yor* 2C 92
Birstall Smithies. *W Yor* 2C 92
Birstwith. *N Yor* 4E 99
Birthorpe. *Linc* 2A 76
Birtle. *Lanc* 3G 91
Birtley. *Here* 4F 59
Birtley. *Nmbd* 2B 114
Birtley. *Tyne* 4F 115
Birtsmorton. *Worc* 2D 48
Birts Street. *Worc* 2C 48
Bisbrooke. *Rut* 1F 63
Bisham. *Wind* 3G 37
Bishampton. *Worc* 5D 61
Bish Mill. *Devn* 4H 19
Bishop Auckland. *Dur* 2F 105
Bishopbridge. *Linc* 1H 87
Bishopbriggs. *E Dun* 2H 127
Bishop Burton. *E Yor* 1C 94
Bishopdown. *Wilts* 3G 23
Bishop Middleham. *Dur* 1A 106
Bishopmill. *Mor* 2G 159
Bishop Monkton. *N Yor* 3F 99
Bishop Norton. *Linc* 1G 87
Bishopsbourne. *Kent* 5F 41
Bishops Cannings. *Wilts* 5F 35
Bishop's Castle. *Shrp* 2F 59
Bishop's Caundle. *Dors* 1B 14
Bishop's Cleeve. *Glos* 3E 49
Bishop's Down. *Dors* 1B 14
Bishop's Frome. *Here* 1B 48
Bishop's Green. *Essx* 4G 53
Bishop's Green. *Hants* 5D 36
Bishop's Hull. *Som* 4F 21
Bishop's Itchington. *Warw* 5A 62
Bishops Lydeard. *Som* 4E 21
Bishop's Norton. *Glos* 3D 48
Bishop's Nympton. *Devn* 4A 20
Bishop's Offley. *Staf* 3B 72
Bishop's Stortford. *Herts* 3E 53
Bishops Sutton. *Hants* 3E 24
Bishop's Tachbrook. *Warw* 4H 61
Bishop's Tawton. *Devn* 3F 19
Bishopsteignton. *Devn* 5C 12
Bishopstoke. *Hants* 1C 16
Bishopston. *Swan* 4E 31
Bishopstone. *Buck* 4G 51
Bishopstone. *E Sus* 5F 27
Bishopstone. *Here* 1H 47
Bishopstone. *Swin* 3H 35
Bishopstone. *Wilts* 4F 23
Bishopstrow. *Wilts* 2D 23
Bishop Sutton. *Bath* 1A 22
Bishop's Waltham. *Hants* 1D 16
Bishopswood. *Som* 1F 13
Bishops Wood. *Staf* 5C 72
Bishopsworth. *Bris* 5A 34
Bishop Thornton. *N Yor* 3E 99
Bishopthorpe. *York* 5H 99
Bishopton. *Darl* 2A 106
Bishopton. *Dum* 5B 110
Bishopton. *N Yor* 2F 99
Bishopton. *Ren* 2F 127
Bishopton. *Warw* 5F 61
Bishop Wilton. *E Yor* 4B 100
Bishton. *Newp* 3G 33
Bishton. *Staf* 3E 73
Bisley. *Glos* 5E 49
Bisley. *Surr* 5A 38
Bispham. *Bkpl* 5C 96
Bispham Green. *Lanc* 3C 90
Bissoe. *Corn* 4B 6
Bisterne. *Hants* 2G 15
Bisterne Close. *Hants* 2H 15
Bitchfield. *Linc* 3G 75
Bittadon. *Devn* 2F 19
Bittaford. *Devn* 3C 8
Bittering. *Norf* 4B 78
Bitterley. *Shrp* 3H 59
Bitterne. *Sotn* 1C 16
Bitteswell. *Leics* 2C 62
Bitton. *S Glo* 5B 34
Bix. *Oxon* 3F 37
Bixter. *Shet* 6E 173
Blaby. *Leics* 1C 62
Blackawton. *Devn* 3E 9
Black Bank. *Cambs* 2E 65
Black Barn. *Linc* 3D 76
Blackborough. *Devn* 2D 12
Blackborough. *Norf* 4F 77
Blackborough End. *Norf* 4F 77
Black Bourton. *Oxon* 5A 50
Blackboys. *E Sus* 3G 27
Blackbrook. *Derbs* 1H 73
Blackbrook. *Mers* 1H 83
Blackbrook. *Staf* 2B 72
Blackbrook. *Surr* 1C 26
Blackburn. *Abers* 2F 153
Blackburn. *Bkbn* 2E 91
Blackburn. *W Lot* 3C 128
Black Callerton. *Tyne* 3E 115
Black Carr. *Norf* 1C 66
Black Clauchrie. *S Ayr* 1H 109
Black Corries. *High* 3G 141
Black Crofts. *Arg* 5D 140
Black Cross. *Corn* 2D 6
Blackden Heath. *Ches E* 3B 84
Blackditch. *Oxon* 5C 50
Blackdog. *Abers* 2G 153
Black Dog. *Devn* 2B 12
Blackdown. *Dors* 2G 13
Blackdyke. *Cumb* 4C 112
Blacker Hill. *S Yor* 4D 92
Blackfen. *G Lon* 3F 39
Blackfield. *Hants* 2C 16
Blackford. *Cumb* 3E 113
Blackford. *Per* 3A 136
Blackford. *Shrp* 2H 59
Blackford. *Som* 2H 21 (nr. Burnham-on-Sea)
Blackford. *Som* 4B 22 (nr. Wincanton)
Blackfordby. *Leics* 4H 73
Blackgang. *IOW* 5C 16
Blackhall. *Edin* 2F 129
Blackhall. *Ren* 3F 127
Blackhall Colliery. *Dur* 1B 106
Blackhall Mill. *Tyne* 4E 115
Blackhall Rocks. *Dur* 1B 106
Blackham. *E Sus* 2F 27
Blackheath. *Essx* 3D 54
Blackheath. *G Lon* 3E 39
Blackheath. *Suff* 3G 67
Blackheath. *Surr* 1B 26
Blackheath. *W Mid* 2D 61
Black Heddon. *Nmbd* 2D 115
Blackhill. *Abers* 4H 161
Blackhill. *High* 3C 154
Black Hill. *Warw* 5G 61
Blackhills. *Abers* 2G 161
Blackhills. *High* 3D 158
Blackjack. *Linc* 2B 76
Blackland. *Wilts* 5F 35
Black Lane. *G Man* 4F 91
Blackleach. *Lanc* 1C 90
Blackley. *G Man* 4G 91
Blackley. *W Yor* 3B 92
Blacklunans. *Per* 2A 144
Blackmill. *B'end* 3C 32
Blackmoor. *G Man* 4E 91
Blackmoor. *Hants* 3F 25
Blackmoor Gate. *Devn* 2G 19
Blackmore. *Essx* 5G 53
Blackmore End. *Essx* 2H 53
Blackmore End. *Herts* 4B 52
Black Mount. *Arg* 4G 141
Blackness. *Falk* 2D 128
Blacknest. *Hants* 2F 25
Blackney. *Dors* 3H 13
Blacknoll. *Dors* 4D 14
Black Notley. *Essx* 3A 54
Blacko. *Lanc* 5A 98
Black Pill. *Swan* 3F 31
Blackpool. *Bkpl* 1B 90 & 188
Blackpool. *Devn* 4E 9
Blackpool Airport. *Lanc* 1B 90
Blackpool Corner. *Devn* 3G 13
Blackpool Gate. *Cumb* 2G 113
Blackridge. *W Lot* 3C 128
Blackrock. *Arg* 3B 124
Blackrock. *Mon* 4F 47
Blackrod. *G Man* 3E 90
Blackshaw. *Dum* 3B 112
Blackshaw Head. *W Yor* 2H 91
Blacksmith's Green. *Suff* 4D 66
Blacksnape. *Bkbn* 2F 91
Blackstone. *W Sus* 4D 26
Black Street. *Suff* 2H 67
Black Tar. *Pemb* 4D 43
Blackthorn. *Oxon* 4E 50
Blackthorpe. *Suff* 4B 66
Blacktoft. *E Yor* 2B 94
Blacktop. *Aber* 3F 153
Black Torrington. *Devn* 2E 11
Blacktown. *Newp* 3F 33
Blackwall Tunnel. *G Lon* 2E 39
Blackwater. *Corn* 4B 6
Blackwater. *Hants* 1G 25
Blackwater. *IOW* 4D 16
Blackwater. *Som* 1F 13
Blackwaterfoot. *N Ayr* 3C 122
Blackwell. *Darl* 3F 105
Blackwell. *Derbs* 5B 86 (nr. Alfreton)
Blackwell. *Derbs* 3F 85 (nr. Buxton)
Blackwell. *Som* 4D 20
Blackwell. *Warw* 1H 49
Blackwell. *Worc* 3D 61
Blackwood. *Cphy* 2E 33
Blackwood. *Dum* 1G 111
Blackwood. *S Lan* 5A 128
Blackwood Hill. *Staf* 5D 84
Blacon. *Ches W* 4F 83
Bladnoch. *Dum* 4B 110
Bladon. *Oxon* 4C 50
Blaenannerch. *Cdgn* 1C 44
Blaenau Dolwyddelan. *Cnwy* 5F 81
Blaenau Ffestiniog. *Gwyn* 1G 69
Blaenavon. *Torf* 5F 47
Blaenawey. *Mon* 4F 47
Blaen Celyn. *Cdgn* 5C 56
Blaen Clydach. *Rhon* 2C 32
Blaendulais. *Neat* 5B 46
Blaenffos. *Pemb* 1F 43
Blaengarw. *B'end* 2C 32
Blaen-geuffordd. *Cdgn* 2F 57
Blaengwrach. *Neat* 5B 46
Blaengwynfi. *Neat* 2B 32
Blaenllechau. *Rhon* 2D 32
Blaenpennal. *Cdgn* 4F 57
Blaenplwyf. *Cdgn* 3E 57
Blaenporth. *Cdgn* 1C 44
Blaenrhondda. *Rhon* 2C 32
Blaenwaun. *Carm* 2G 43
Blaen-y-coed. *Carm* 2H 43
Blaenycwm. *Rhon* 2C 32
Blagdon. *N Som* 1A 22
Blagdon. *Torb* 2E 9
Blagdon Hill. *Som* 1F 13
Blagill. *Cumb* 5A 114
Blaguegate. *Lanc* 4C 90
Blaich. *High* 1E 141
Blain. *High* 2A 140
Blaina. *Blae* 5F 47
Blair Atholl. *Per* 2F 143
Blair Drummond. *Stir* 4G 135
Blairgowrie. *Per* 4A 144
Blairhall. *Fife* 1D 128
Blairingone. *Per* 4B 136
Blairlogie. *Stir* 4H 135
Blairmore. *Abers* 5B 160
Blairmore. *Arg* 1C 126
Blairmore. *High* 3B 166
Blairquhanan. *W Dun* 1F 127
Blaisdon. *Glos* 4C 48
Blakebrook. *Worc* 3C 60
Blakedown. *Worc* 3C 60
Blake End. *Essx* 3H 53
Blakemere. *Here* 1G 47
Blakeney. *Glos* 5B 48
Blakeney. *Norf* 1C 78
Blakenhall. *Ches E* 1B 72
Blakenhall. *W Mid* 1C 60
Blakeshall. *Worc* 2C 60
Blakesley. *Nptn* 5D 62
Blanchland. *Nmbd* 4C 114
Blandford Camp. *Dors* 2E 15
Blandford Forum. *Dors* 2D 15
Blandford St Mary. *Dors* 2D 15
Bland Hill. *N Yor* 4E 98
Blandy. *High* 3G 167
Blanefield. *Stir* 2G 127
Blankney. *Linc* 4H 87
Blantyre. *S Lan* 4H 127
Blarmachfoldach. *High* 2E 141
Blarnalearoch. *High* 4F 163
Blashford. *Hants* 2G 15
Blaston. *Leics* 1F 63
Blatchbridge. *Som* 2C 22
Blathaisbhal. *W Isl* 1D 170
Blatherwycke. *Nptn* 1G 63
Blawith. *Cumb* 1B 96
Blaxhall. *Suff* 5F 67
Blaxton. *S Yor* 4G 93
Blaydon. *Tyne* 3E 115
Bleadney. *Som* 2H 21
Bleadon. *N Som* 1G 21
Blean. *Kent* 4F 41
Bleasby. *Linc* 2A 88
Bleasby. *Notts* 1E 74
Bleasby Moor. *Linc* 2A 88
Blebocraigs. *Fife* 2G 137
Bleddfa. *Powy* 4E 58
Bledington. *Glos* 3H 49
Bledlow. *Buck* 5F 51
Bledlow Ridge. *Buck* 2F 37
Blencarn. *Cumb* 1H 103
Blencogo. *Cumb* 5C 112
Blendworth. *Hants* 1F 17
Blenheim. *Oxon* 5D 50
Blennerhasset. *Cumb* 5C 112
Bletchingdon. *Oxon* 4D 50
Bletchingley. *Surr* 5E 39
Bletchley. *Mil* 2G 51
Bletchley. *Shrp* 2A 72
Bletherston. *Pemb* 2E 43
Bletsoe. *Bed* 5H 63
Blewbury. *Oxon* 3D 36
Blickling. *Norf* 3D 78
Blidworth. *Notts* 5C 86
Blindburn. *Nmbd* 3C 120
Blindcrake. *Cumb* 1C 102
Blindley Heath. *Surr* 1E 27
Blindmoor. *Som* 1F 13
Blisland. *Corn* 5A 10
Blissford. *Hants* 1G 15
Bliss Gate. *Worc* 3B 60
Blists Hill. *Telf* 5A 72
Blisworth. *Nptn* 5E 63
Blithbury. *Staf* 3E 73
Blitterlees. *Cumb* 4C 112
Blockley. *Glos* 2G 49
Blofield. *Norf* 5F 79
Blofield Heath. *Norf* 4F 79
Blo' Norton. *Norf* 3C 66
Bloomfield. *Bord* 2H 119
Blore. *Staf* 1F 73
Blount's Green. *Staf* 2E 73
Bloxham. *Oxon* 2C 50
Bloxholm. *Linc* 5H 87
Bloxwich. *W Mid* 5E 73
Bloxworth. *Dors* 3D 15
Blubberhouses. *N Yor* 4D 98
Blue Anchor. *Som* 2D 20
Blue Anchor. *Swan* 3E 31
Blue Bell Hill. *Kent* 4B 40
Blue Row. *Essx* 4D 54
Bluetown. *Kent* 5D 40
Blundeston. *Suff* 1H 67
Blunham. *C Beds* 5A 64
Blunsdon St Andrew. *Swin* 3G 35
Bluntington. *Worc* 3C 60
Bluntisham. *Cambs* 3C 64
Blunts. *Corn* 2H 7
Blurton. *Stoke* 1C 72
Blyborough. *Linc* 1G 87
Blyford. *Suff* 3G 67
Blymhill. *Staf* 4C 72
Blymhill Lawns. *Staf* 4C 72
Blyth. *Nmbd* 1G 115
Blyth. *Notts* 2D 86
Blyth. *Bord* 5E 129
Blyth Bank. *Bord* 5E 129
Blyth Bridge. *Bord* 5E 129
Blythburgh. *Suff* 3G 67
Blythe Bridge. *Staf* 1D 72
Blythe Marsh. *Staf* 1D 72
Blythe, The. *Staf* 3E 73
Blyton. *Linc* 1F 87
Boarhills. *Fife* 2H 137
Boarhunt. *Hants* 2E 16
Boarshead. *E Sus* 2G 27
Boar's Head. *G Man* 4D 90
Boars Hill. *Oxon* 5C 50
Boarstall. *Buck* 4E 51
Boasley Cross. *Devn* 3F 11
Boath. *High* 1H 157
Boat of Garten. *High* 2D 150
Bobbing. *Kent* 4C 40
Bobbington. *Staf* 1C 60
Bobbingworth. *Essx* 5F 53
Bocaddon. *Corn* 3F 7
Bocking. *Essx* 3A 54
Bocking Churchstreet. *Essx* 3A 54
Boddam. *Abers* 4H 161
Boddam. *Shet* 10E 173
Boddington. *Glos* 3D 49
Bodedern. *IOA* 2C 80
Bodelwyddan. *Den* 3C 82
Bodenham. *Here* 5H 59
Bodenham. *Wilts* 4G 23
Bodewryd. *IOA* 1C 80
Bodfari. *Den* 3C 82
Bodffordd. *IOA* 3D 80
Bodham. *Norf* 1D 78
Bodiam. *E Sus* 3B 28
Bodicote. *Oxon* 2C 50
Bodieve. *Corn* 1D 6
Bodinnick. *Corn* 3F 7
Bodle Street Green. *E Sus* 4A 28
Bodmin. *Corn* 2E 7
Bodnant. *Cnwy* 3H 81
Bodney. *Norf* 1H 65
Bodorgan. *IOA* 4C 80
Bodrane. *Corn* 2G 7
Bodsham. *Kent* 1F 29
Boduan. *Gwyn* 2C 68
Bodymoor Heath. *Warw* 1F 61
Bogallan. *High* 3A 158
Bogbrae Croft. *Abers* 5H 161
Bogend. *S Ayr* 1C 116
Boghall. *Midl* 3F 129
Boghall. *W Lot* 3C 128
Boghead. *S Lan* 5A 128
Bogindollo. *Ang* 3D 144
Bogmoor. *Mor* 2A 160
Bogniebrae. *Abers* 4C 160
Bognor Regis. *W Sus* 3H 17
Bograxie. *Abers* 2E 152
Bogside. *N Lan* 4B 128
Bog, The. *Shrp* 1F 59
Bogton. *Abers* 3D 160
Bogue. *Dum* 1D 110
Bohenie. *High* 5E 149
Bohortha. *Corn* 5C 6
Boirseam. *W Isl* 9C 171
Bokiddick. *Corn* 2E 7
Bolam. *Dur* 2E 105
Bolam. *Nmbd* 1D 115
Bolberry. *Devn* 5C 8
Bold Heath. *Mers* 2H 83
Boldon. *Tyne* 3G 115
Boldon Colliery. *Tyne* 3G 115
Boldre. *Hants* 3B 16
Boldron. *Dur* 3D 104
Bole. *Notts* 2E 87
Bolehall. *Staf* 5G 73
Bolehill. *Derbs* 5G 85
Bolenowe. *Corn* 5A 6
Boleside. *Bord* 1G 119
Bolham. *Devn* 1C 12
Bolham Water. *Devn* 1E 13
Bolingey. *Corn* 3B 6
Bollington. *Ches E* 3D 84
Bolney. *W Sus* 3D 26
Bolnhurst. *Bed* 5H 63
Bolshan. *Ang* 3F 145
Bolsover. *Derbs* 3B 86
Bolsterstone. *S Yor* 1G 85
Bolstone. *Here* 2A 48
Boltachan. *Per* 3F 143
Boltby. *N Yor* 1G 99
Bolton. *Cumb* 2H 103
Bolton. *E Lot* 2B 130
Bolton. *E Yor* 4B 100
Bolton. *G Man* 4F 91
Bolton. *Nmbd* 3F 121
Bolton Abbey. *N Yor* 4C 98
Bolton-by-Bowland. *Lanc* 5G 97
Boltonfellend. *Cumb* 3F 113
Boltongate. *Cumb* 5D 112
Bolton Green. *Lanc* 3D 90
Bolton-le-Sands. *Lanc* 3D 97
Bolton Low Houses. *Cumb* 5D 112
Bolton New Houses. *Cumb* 5D 112
Bolton-on-Swale. *N Yor* 5F 105
Bolton Percy. *N Yor* 5H 99
Bolton Town End. *Lanc* 3D 97
Bolton upon Dearne. *S Yor* 4E 93
Bolton Wood Lane. *Cumb* 5D 112
Bolventor. *Corn* 5B 10
Bomarsund. *Nmbd* 1F 115
Bomere Heath. *Shrp* 4G 71

Bonar Bridge. High 4D 164
Bonawe. Arg 5E 141
Bonby. N Lin 3D 94
Boncath. Pemb 1G 43
Bonchester Bridge. Bord 3H 119
Bonchurch. IOW 5D 16
Bond End. Staf 4F 73
Bondleigh. Devn 2G 11
Bonds. Lanc 5D 97
Bonehill. Devn 5H 11
Bonehill. Staf 5F 73
Bo'ness. Falk 1C 128
Boney Hay. Staf 4E 73
Bonham. Wilts 3C 22
Bonhill. W Dun 2E 127
Boningale. Shrp 5C 72
Bonjedward. Bord 2A 120
Bonkle. N Lan 4B 128
Bonnington. Ang 5E 145
Bonnington. Edin 3E 129
Bonnington. Kent 2E 29
Bonnybank. Fife 3F 137
Bonnybridge. Falk 1B 128
Bonnykelly. Abers 3F 161
Bonnyrigg. Midl 3G 129
Bonnyton. Ang 5C 144
Bonnytown. Fife 2H 137
Bonsall. Derbs 5G 85
Bont. Mon 4G 47
Bontddu. Gwyn 4F 69
Bont Dolgadfan. Powy 5A 70
Bontgoch. Cdgn 2F 57
Bonthorpe. Linc 3D 89
Bont-newydd. Cdgn 4F 57
Bont-newydd. Cnwy 3C 82
Bontnewydd. Gwyn 4D 81
(nr. Caernarfon)
Bont Newydd. Gwyn 1G 69
(nr. Llan Ffestiniog)
Bontuchel. Den 5C 82
Bonvilston. V Glam 4D 32
Bon-y-maen. Swan 3F 31
Booker. Buck 2G 37
Booley. Shrp 3H 71
Boorley Green. Hants 1D 16
Boosbeck. Red C 3D 106
Boot. Cumb 4C 102
Booth. W Yor 2A 92
Boothby Graffoe. Linc 5G 87
Boothby Pagnell. Linc 2G 75
Booth Green. Ches E 2D 84
Booth of Toft. Shet 4F 173
Boothstown. G Man 4F 91
Boothville. Nptn 4E 63
Booth Wood. W Yor 3A 92
Bootle. Cumb 1A 96
Bootle. Mers 1F 83
Booton. Norf 3D 78
Booze. N Yor 4D 104
Boquhan. Stir 1G 127
Boraston. Shrp 3A 60
Borden. Kent 4C 40
Borden. W Sus 4G 25
Bordlands. Bord 5E 129
Bordley. N Yor 3B 98
Bordon. Hants 3G 25
Boreham. Essx 5A 54
Boreham. Wilts 2D 23
Boreham Street. E Sus 4A 28
Borehamwood. Herts 1C 38
Boreland. Dum 5D 118
Boreston. Devn 3D 8
Borestone Brae. Stir 4H 135
Boreton. Shrp 5H 71
Borgh. W Isl 8B 170
(on Barra)
Borgh. W Isl 3C 170
(on Benbecula)
Borgh. W Isl 1E 170
(on Berneray)
Borgh. W Isl 2G 171
(on Isle of Lewis)
Borghasdal. W Isl 9C 171
Borghastan. W Isl 3D 171
Borgh na Sgiotaig. High 1C 154
Borgie. High 3G 167
Borgue. Dum 5D 110
Borgue. High 1H 165
Borley. Essx 1B 54
Borley Green. Essx 1B 54
Borley Green. Suff 4B 66
Borlum. High 1H 149
Bornais. W Isl 6C 170
Bornesketaig. High 1C 154
Boroughbridge. N Yor 3F 99
Borough Green. Kent 5H 39
Borras Head. Wrex 5F 83
Borreraig. High 3A 154
Borrobol Lodge. High 1F 165
Borrodale. High 4A 154
Borrowash. Derb 2B 74
Borrowby. N Yor 1G 99
(nr. Northallerton)
Borrowby. N Yor 3E 107
(nr. Whitby)
Borrowston. High 4F 169
Borrowstonehill. Orkn 7D 172
Borrowstoun. Falk 1C 128
Borstal. Medw 4B 40
Borth. Cdgn 2F 57
Borthwick. Midl 4G 129
Borth-y-Gest. Gwyn 2E 69

Borve. High 4D 154
Borwick. Lanc 2E 97
Bosbury. Here 1B 48
Boscastle. Corn 3A 10
Boscombe. Bour 3G 15
Boscombe. Wilts 3H 23
Boscoppa. Corn 3E 7
Bosham. W Sus 2G 17
Bosherston. Pemb 5D 42
Bosley. Ches E 4D 84
Bossall. N Yor 3B 100
Bossiney. Corn 4A 10
Bossingham. Kent 1F 29
Bossington. Som 2B 20
Bostadh. W Isl 3D 171
Bostock Green. Ches W 4A 84
Boston. Linc 1C 76
Boston Spa. W Yor 5G 99
Boswarthen. Corn 3B 4
Boswinger. Corn 4D 6
Botallack. Corn 3A 4
Botany Bay. G Lon 1D 39
Botcheston. Leics 5B 74
Botesdale. Suff 3C 66
Bothal. Nmbd 1F 115
Bothampstead. W Ber 4D 36
Bothamsall. Notts 3D 86
Bothel. Cumb 1C 102
Bothenhampton. Dors 3H 13
Bothwell. S Lan 4H 127
Botley. Buck 5H 51
Botley. Hants 1D 16
Botley. Oxon 5C 50
Botloe's Green. Glos 3C 48
Botolph Claydon. Buck 3F 51
Botolphs. W Sus 5C 26
Bottacks. High 2G 157
Bottesford. Leics 2F 75
Bottesford. N Lin 4B 94
Bottisham. Cambs 4E 65
Bottlehill. Wilts 1G 23
Bottomcraig. Fife 1F 137
Bottom o' th' Moor. G Man 3E 91
Botton. N Yor 4D 107
Botton Head. Lanc 3F 97
Bottreaux Mill. Devn 4B 20
Botus Fleming. Corn 2A 8
Botwnnog. Gwyn 2B 68
Bough Beech. Kent 1F 27
Boughrood. Powy 2E 47
Boughspring. Glos 2A 34
Boughton. Norf 5F 77
Boughton. Nptn 4E 63
Boughton. Notts 4D 86
Boughton Aluph. Kent 1E 29
Boughton Green. Kent 5B 40
Boughton Lees. Kent 1E 28
Boughton Malherbe. Kent 1C 28
Boughton Monchelsea. Kent 5B 40
Boughton under Blean. Kent 5E 41
Boulby. Red C 3E 107
Bouldnor. IOW 4B 16
Bouldon. Shrp 2H 59
Boulmer. Nmbd 3G 121
Boulston. Pemb 3D 42
Boultham. Linc 4G 87
Boulton. Derb 2A 74
Boundary. Staf 1D 73
Bounds. Here 2B 48
Bourn. Cambs 5C 64
Bournbrook. W Mid 2E 61
Bourne. Linc 3H 75
Bourne End. Bed 4H 63
Bourne End. Buck 3G 37
Bourne End. C Beds 1H 51
Bourne End. Herts 5A 52
Bournemouth. Bour ....3F 15 & 190
Bournemouth Airport. Dors 3G 15
Bournes Green. Glos 5E 49
Bournes Green. S'end 2D 40
Bournheath. Worc 3D 60
Bournmoor. Dur 4G 115
Bournville. W Mid 2E 61
Bourton. Dors 3C 22
Bourton. N Som 5G 33
Bourton. Oxon 3H 35
Bourton. Shrp 1H 59
Bourton. Wilts 5F 35
Bourton on Dunsmore. Warw 3B 62
Bourton-on-the-Hill. Glos 2G 49
Bourton-on-the-Water. Glos 3G 49
Bousd. Arg 2D 138
Bousta. Shet 6D 173
Boustead Hill. Cumb 4D 112
Bouth. Cumb 1C 96
Bouthwaite. N Yor 2D 98
Boveney. Buck 3A 38
Boveridge. Dors 1F 15
Boverton. V Glam 5C 32
Bovey Tracey. Devn 5B 12
Bovingdon. Herts 5A 52
Bovingdon Green. Buck 3G 37
Bovinger. Essx 5F 53
Bovington Camp. Dors 4D 14
Bow. Devn 2H 11
Bowbank. Dur 2C 104
Bow Brickhill. Mil 2H 51
Bowbridge. Glos 5D 48
Bowburn. Dur 1A 106
Bowcombe. IOW 4C 16
Bowd. Devn 4E 12

Bowden. Devn 4E 9
Bowden. Bord 1H 119
Bowden Hill. Wilts 5E 35
Bowdens. Som 4H 21
Bowderdale. Cumb 4H 103
Bowdon. G Man 2B 84
Bower. Nmbd 1A 114
Bowerchalke. Wilts 4F 23
Bowerhill. Wilts 5E 35
Bower Hinton. Som 1H 13
Bowermadden. High 2E 169
Bowers. Staf 2C 72
Bowers Gifford. Essx 2B 40
Bowershall. Fife 4C 136
Bowertower. High 2E 169
Bowes. Dur 3C 104
Bowgreave. Lanc 5D 97
Bowhousebog. N Lan 4B 128
Bowithick. Corn 4B 10
Bowland Bridge. Cumb 1D 96
Bowlees. Dur 2C 104
Bowley. Here 5H 59
Bowlhead Green. Surr 2A 26
Bowling. W Dun 2F 127
Bowling. W Yor 1B 92
Bowling Bank. Wrex 1F 71
Bowling Green. Worc 5C 60
Bowlish. Som 2B 22
Bowmanstead. Cumb 5E 102
Bowmore. Arg 4B 124
Bowness-on-Solway. Cumb 3D 112
Bowness-on-Windermere.
Cumb 5F 103
Bow of Fife. Fife 2F 137
Bowriefauld. Ang 4E 145
Bowscale. Cumb 1E 103
Bowsden. Nmbd 5F 131
Bowside Lodge. High 2A 168
Bowston. Cumb 5F 103
Bow Street. Cdgn 2F 57
Bowthorpe. Norf 5D 78
Box. Glos 5D 48
Box. Wilts 5D 34
Boxbush. Glos 3B 48
Box End. Bed 1A 52
Boxford. Suff 1C 54
Boxford. W Ber 4C 36
Boxgrove. W Sus 5A 26
Boxley. Kent 5B 40
Boxmoor. Herts 5A 52
Box's Shop. Corn 2C 10
Boxted. Essx 2C 54
Boxted. Suff 5H 65
Boxted Cross. Essx 2D 54
Boxworth. Cambs 4C 64
Boxworth End. Cambs 4C 64
Boyden End. Suff 5G 65
Boyden Gate. Kent 4G 41
Boylestone. Derbs 2F 73
Boylestonfield. Derbs 2F 73
Boyndie. Abers 2D 160
Boynton. E Yor 3F 101
Boys Hill. Dors 1B 14
Boythorpe. Derbs 4A 86
Boyton. Corn 3D 10
Boyton. Suff 1G 55
Boyton. Wilts 3E 23
Boyton Cross. Essx 5G 53
Boyton End. Essx 2G 53
Boyton End. Suff 1H 53
Bozeat. Nptn 5G 63
Braaid. IOM 4C 108
Braal Castle. High 2D 168
Brabling Green. Suff 4E 67
Brabourne. Kent 1F 29
Brabourne Lees. Kent 1E 29
Brabster. High 2F 169
Bracadale. High 5C 154
Bracara. High 4F 147
Braceborough. Linc 4H 75
Bracebridge. Linc 4G 87
Bracebridge Heath. Linc 4G 87
Braceby. Linc 2H 75
Bracewell. Lanc 5A 98
Brackenber. Cumb 3A 104
Brackenfield. Derbs 5A 86
Brackenlands. Cumb 5D 112
Brackenthwaite. Cumb 5D 112
Brackenthwaite. N Yor 4E 99
Brackla. B'end 4C 32
Brackla. High 3C 158
Bracklesham. W Sus 3G 17
Brackletter. High 5D 148
Brackley. Nptn 2D 50
Brackley Hatch. Nptn 1E 51
Brackloch. High 1F 163
Bracknell. Brac 5G 37
Braco. Per 3H 135
Bracobrae. Mor 3C 160
Bracon. N Lin 4A 94
Bracon Ash. Norf 1D 66
Bradbourne. Derbs 5G 85
Bradbury. Dur 2A 106
Bradda. IOM 4A 108
Bradden. Nptn 1E 51
Bradenham. Buck 2G 37
Bradenham. Norf 5B 78
Bradenstoke. Wilts 4F 35
Bradfield. Essx 2E 55
Bradfield. Norf 2E 79
Bradfield. W Ber 4E 36
Bradfield Combust. Suff 5A 66

Bradfield Green. Ches E 5A 84
Bradfield Heath. Essx 3E 55
Bradfield St Clare. Suff 5B 66
Bradfield St George. Suff 4B 66
Bradford. Derbs 4G 85
Bradford. Devn 2E 11
Bradford. W Yor ....1B 92 & 190
Bradford Abbas. Dors 1A 14
Bradford Barton. Devn 1B 12
Bradford Leigh. Wilts 5D 34
Bradford-on-Avon. Wilts 5D 34
Bradford-on-Tone. Som 4E 21
Bradford Peverell. Dors 3B 14
Bradiford. Devn 3F 19
Brading. IOW 4E 16
Bradley. Ches W 3H 83
Bradley. Derbs 1G 73
Bradley. Glos 2C 34
Bradley. Hants 2E 25
Bradley. NE Lin 4F 95
Bradley. N Yor 1C 98
Bradley. Staf 4C 72
Bradley. W Mid 1D 60
Bradley. W Yor 2B 92
Bradley. Wrex 5F 83
Bradley Cross. Som 1H 21
Bradley Green. Ches W 1H 71
Bradley Green. Som 3F 21
Bradley Green. Warw 5G 73
Bradley Green. Worc 4D 61
Bradley in the Moors. Staf 1E 73
Bradley Mount. Ches E 3D 84
Bradley Stoke. S Glo 3B 34
Bradlow. Here 2C 48
Bradmore. Notts 2C 74
Bradmore. W Mid 1C 60
Bradninch. Devn 2D 12
Bradnop. Staf 5E 85
Bradpole. Dors 3H 13
Bradshaw. G Man 3F 91
Bradstone. Devn 4D 11
Bradwall Green. Ches E 4B 84
Bradway. S Yor 2H 85
Bradwell. Derbs 2F 85
Bradwell. Essx 3B 54
Bradwell. Mil 2G 51
Bradwell. Norf 5H 79
Bradwell-on-Sea. Essx 5D 54
Bradwell Waterside. Essx 5C 54
Bradworthy. Devn 1D 10
Brae. High 5C 162
Brae. Shet 5E 173
Braeantra. High 1H 157
Braefield. High 5G 157
Braefindon. High 3A 158
Braegrum. Per 1C 136
Braehead. Ang 3F 145
Braehead. Dum 4B 110
Braehead. Mor 4G 159
Braehead. Orkn 3D 172
Braehead. S Lan 1H 117
(nr. Coalburn)
Braehead. S Lan 4C 128
(nr. Forth)
Braehoulland. Shet 4D 173
Braemar. Abers 4F 151
Braemore. High 5C 168
(nr. Dunbeath)
Braemore. High 1D 156
(nr. Ullapool)
Brae of Achnahaird. High 2E 163
Brae Roy Lodge. High 4F 149
Braeside. Abers 5G 161
Braeside. Inv 2D 126
Braes of Coul. Ang 3B 144
Braeswick. Orkn 4F 172
Braetongue. High 3F 167
Braeval. Stir 3E 135
Braevallich. Arg 3G 133
Braewick. Shet 6E 173
Brafferton. Darl 2F 105
Brafferton. N Yor 2G 99
Brafield-on-the-Green. Nptn 5F 63
Bragar. W Isl 3E 171
Bragbury End. Herts 3C 52
Bragleenbeg. Arg 1G 133
Braichmelyn. Gwyn 4F 81
Braides. Lanc 4D 96
Braidwood. S Lan 5B 128
Braigo. Arg 3A 124
Brailsford. Derbs 1G 73
Braintree. Essx 3A 54
Braiseworth. Suff 3D 66
Braishfield. Hants 4B 24
Braithwaite. Cumb 2D 102
Braithwaite. S Yor 3G 93
Braithwaite. W Yor 5C 98
Braithwell. S Yor 1C 86
Brakefield Green. Norf 5C 78
Bramber. W Sus 4C 26
Brambledown. Kent 3D 40
Brambridge. Hants 4C 24
Bramcote. Notts 2C 74
Bramcote. Warw 2B 62
Bramdean. Hants 4E 24
Bramerton. Norf 5E 79
Bramfield. Herts 4C 52
Bramfield. Suff 3F 67
Bramford. Suff 1E 54
Bramhall. G Man 2C 84
Bramham. W Yor 5G 99

Bramhope. W Yor 5E 99
Bramley. Hants 1E 25
Bramley. S Yor 1B 86
Bramley. Surr 1B 26
Bramley. W Yor 1C 92
Bramley Green. Hants 1E 25
Bramley Head. N Yor 4D 98
Bramley Vale. Derbs 4B 86
Bramling. Kent 5G 41
Brampford Speke. Devn 3C 12
Brampton. Cambs 3B 64
Brampton. Cumb 2H 103
(nr. Appleby-in-Westmorland)
Brampton. Cumb 3G 113
(nr. Carlisle)
Brampton. Linc 3F 87
Brampton. Norf 3E 78
Brampton. S Yor 4E 93
Brampton. Suff 2G 67
Brampton Abbotts. Here 3B 48
Brampton Ash. Nptn 2E 63
Brampton Bryan. Here 3F 59
Brampton en le Morthen.
S Yor 2B 86
Bramshall. Staf 2E 73
Bramshaw. Hants 1A 16
Bramshill. Hants 5F 37
Bramshott. Hants 3G 25
Branault. High 2G 139
Brancaster. Norf 1G 77
Brancaster Staithe. Norf 1G 77
Brancepeth. Dur 1F 105
Branchill. Mor 3E 159
Brand End. Linc 1C 76
Branderburgh. Mor 1G 159
Brandesburton. E Yor 5F 101
Brandeston. Suff 4E 67
Brand Green. Glos 3C 48
Brandhill. Shrp 3G 59
Brandis Corner. Devn 2E 11
Brandish Street. Som 2C 20
Brandiston. Norf 3D 78
Brandon. Dur 1F 105
Brandon. Linc 1G 75
Brandon. Nmbd 3E 121
Brandon. Suff 2G 65
Brandon. Warw 3B 62
Brandon Bank. Cambs 2F 65
Brandon Creek. Norf 1F 65
Brandon Parva. Norf 5C 78
Brandsby. N Yor 2H 99
Brandy Wharf. Linc 1H 87
Brane. Corn 4B 4
Bran End. Essx 3G 53
Branksome. Pool 3F 15
Bransbury. Hants 2C 24
Bransby. Linc 3G 87
Branscombe. Devn 4E 13
Bransford. Worc 5B 60
Bransgore. Hants 3G 15
Bransholme. Hull 1D 94
Bransley. Shrp 3A 60
Branson's Cross. Worc 3E 61
Branston. Leics 3F 75
Branston. Linc 4H 87
Branston. Staf 3G 73
Branston Booths. Linc 4H 87
Branstone. IOW 4D 16
Bransty. Cumb 3A 102
Brant Broughton. Linc 5G 87
Brantham. Suff 2E 54
Branthwaite. Cumb 1D 102
(nr. Caldbeck)
Branthwaite. Cumb 2B 102
(nr. Workington)
Brantingham. E Yor 2C 94
Branton. Nmbd 3E 121
Branton. S Yor 4G 93
Branton Green. N Yor 3G 99
Branxholme. Bord 3G 119
Branxton. Nmbd 1C 120
Brassington. Derbs 5G 85
Brasted. Kent 5F 39
Brasted Chart. Kent 5F 39
Bratch, The. Staf 1C 60
Brathens. Abers 4D 152
Bratoft. Linc 4D 88
Brattleby. Linc 2G 87
Bratton. Som 2C 20
Bratton. Telf 4A 72
Bratton. Wilts 1E 23
Bratton Clovelly. Devn 3E 11
Bratton Fleming. Devn 3G 19
Bratton Seymour. Som 4B 22
Braughing. Herts 3D 53
Braulen Lodge. High 5E 157
Braunston. Nptn 4C 62
Braunstone Town. Leic 5C 74
Braunston-in-Rutland. Rut 5F 75
Braunton. Devn 3E 19
Brawby. N Yor 2B 100
Brawl. High 2A 168
Brawlbin. High 3C 168
Bray. Wind 3A 38
Braybrooke. Nptn 2E 63
Brayford. Devn 3G 19
Bray Shop. Corn 5D 10
Braystones. Cumb 4B 102
Brayton. N Yor 1G 93
Bray Wick. Wind 4G 37
Brazacott. Corn 3C 10
Brea. Corn 4A 6

Breach. W Sus 2F 17
Breachwood Green. Herts 3B 52
Breacleit. W Isl 4D 171
Breaden Heath. Shrp 2G 71
Breadsall. Derbs 1A 74
Breadstone. Glos 5C 48
Breage. Corn 4D 4
Breakachy. High 4G 157
Breakish. High 1E 147
Bream. Glos 5B 48
Breamore. Hants 1G 15
Bream's Meend. Glos 5B 48
Brean. Som 1F 21
Breanais. W Isl 5B 171
Brearton. N Yor 3F 99
Breascleit. W Isl 4E 171
Breaston. Derbs 2B 74
Brecais Àrd. High 1E 147
Brecais Iosal. High 1E 147
Brechfa. Carm 2F 45
Brechin. Ang 3F 145
Breckles. Norf 1B 66
Brecon. Powy 3D 46
Brecon Beacons. Powy 3C 46
Bredbury. G Man 1D 84
Brede. E Sus 4C 28
Bredenbury. Here 5A 60
Breden's Norton. Worc 2E 49
Bredfield. Suff 5E 67
Bredgar. Kent 4C 40
Bredhurst. Kent 4B 40
Bredicot. Worc 5D 60
Bredon. Worc 2E 49
Bredwardine. Here 1G 47
Breedon on the Hill. Leics 3B 74
Breibhig. W Isl .....9B 170 (on Barra)
Breibhig. W Isl .....4G 171 (on Isle of Lewis)
Breich. W Lot 3C 128
Breightmet. G Man 3F 91
Breighton. E Yor 1H 93
Breinton. Here 2H 47
Breinton Common. Here 2H 47
Breiwick. Shet 7F 173
Brelston Green. Here 3A 48
Bremhill. Wilts 4E 35
Brenachie. High 1B 158
Brenchley. Kent 1A 28
Brendon. Devn 2A 20
Brent Cross. G Lon 2D 38
Brent Eleigh. Suff 1C 54
Brentford. G Lon 3C 38
Brentingby. Leics 4E 75
Brent Knoll. Som 1G 21
Brent Pelham. Herts 2E 53
Brentwood. Essx 1H 39
Brenzett. Kent 3E 28
Brereton. Staf 4E 73
Brereton Cross. Staf 4E 73
Brereton Green. Ches E 4B 84
Brereton Heath. Ches E 4C 84
Bressingham. Norf 2C 66
Bretby. Derbs 3G 73
Bretford. Warw 3B 62
Bretforton. Worc 1F 49
Bretherdale Head. Cumb 4G 103
Bretherton. Lanc 2C 90
Brettabister. Shet 6F 173
Brettenham. Norf 2B 66
Brettenham. Suff 5B 66
Bretton. Flin 4F 83
Bretton. Pet 5A 76
Brewer Street. Surr 5E 39
Brewlands Bridge. Ang 2A 144
Brewood. Staf 5C 72
Briantspuddle. Dors 3D 14
Bricket Wood. Herts 5B 52
Brickkilnhampton. Worc 1E 49
Bride. IOM 1D 108
Bridekirk. Cumb 1C 102
Bridell. Pemb 1B 44
Bridestowe. Devn 4F 11
Brideswell. Abers 5C 160
Bridford. Devn 4B 12
Bridfordmills. Devn 4B 12
Bridge. Corn 4A 6
Bridge. Kent 5F 41
Bridge. Som 2G 13
Bridge End. Bed 5H 63
Bridge End. Cumb .....5D 102 (nr. Broughton in Furness)
Bridge End. Cumb .....5E 113 (nr. Dalston)
Bridge End. Linc 2A 76
Bridge End. Shet 8E 173
Bridgefoot. Ang 5C 144
Bridgefoot. Cumb 2B 102
Bridge Green. Essx 2E 53
Bridgehampton. Som 4A 22
Bridge Hewick. N Yor 2F 99
Bridgehill. Dur 4D 115
Bridgemary. Hants 2D 16
Bridgemere. Ches E 1B 72
Bridgemont. Derbs 2E 85
Bridgend. Abers .....5C 160 (nr. Huntly)
Bridgend. Abers .....5H 161 (nr. Peterhead)

Bridgend. Ang .....2E 145 (nr. Brechin)
Bridgend. Ang .....4D 144 (nr. Kirriemuir)
Bridgend. Arg .....4F 133 (nr. Lochgilphead)
Bridgend. Arg .....3B 124 (on Islay)
Bridgend. B'end 3C 32
Bridgend. Cumb 3F 103
Bridgend. Devn 4B 8
Bridgend. Fife 2F 137
Bridgend. High 5A 160
Bridgend. Mor 5A 160
Bridgend. Per 1D 136
Bridgend. W Lot 2D 128
Bridgend of Lintrathen. Ang 3B 144
Bridgeness. Falk 1D 128
Bridge of Alford. Abers 2C 152
Bridge of Allan. Stir 4G 135
Bridge of Avon. Mor 5F 159
Bridge of Awe. Arg 1H 133
Bridge of Balgie. Per 4C 142
Bridge of Brown. High 1F 151
Bridge of Cally. Per 3A 144
Bridge of Canny. Abers 4D 152
Bridge of Dee. Dum 3E 111
Bridge of Don. Aber 2G 153
Bridge of Dun. Ang 3F 145
Bridge of Dye. Abers 5D 152
Bridge of Earn. Per 2D 136
Bridge of Ericht. Per 3C 142
Bridge of Feugh. Abers 4E 152
Bridge of Forss. High 2C 168
Bridge of Gairn. Abers 4A 152
Bridge of Gaur. Per 3C 142
Bridge of Muchalls. Abers 4F 153
Bridge of Oich. High 3F 149
Bridge of Orchy. Arg 5H 141
Bridge of Walls. Shet 6D 173
Bridge of Weir. Ren 3E 127
Bridge Reeve. Devn 1G 11
Bridgerule. Devn 2C 10
Bridge Sollers. Here 1H 47
Bridge Street. Suff 1B 54
Bridgetown. Devn 2E 9
Bridgetown. Som 3C 20
Bridge Town. Warw 5G 61
Bridge Trafford. Ches W 3G 83
Bridgeyate. S Glo 4B 34
Bridgham. Norf 2B 66
Bridgnorth. Shrp 1B 60
Bridgtown. Staf 5D 73
Bridgwater. Som 3G 21
Bridlington. E Yor 3F 101
Bridport. Dors 3H 13
Bridstow. Here 3A 48
Brierfield. Lanc 1G 91
Brierley. Glos 4B 48
Brierley. Here 5G 59
Brierley. S Yor 3E 93
Brierley Hill. W Mid 2D 60
Brierton. Hart 1B 106
Briestfield. W Yor 3C 92
Brigg. N Lin 4D 94
Briggate. Norf 3F 79
Briggswath. N Yor 4F 107
Brigham. Cumb 1B 102
Brigham. E Yor 4E 101
Brighouse. W Yor 2B 92
Brighstone. IOW 4C 16
Brightgate. Derbs 5G 85
Brighthampton. Oxon 5B 50
Brightholmlee. S Yor 1G 85
Brighton. Brig .....5E 27 & 189
Brighton. Corn 3D 6
Brighton Hill. Hants 2E 24
Brightons. Falk 2C 128
Brightwalton. W Ber 4C 36
Brightwalton Green. W Ber 4C 36
Brightwell. Suff 1F 55
Brightwell Baldwin. Oxon 2E 37
Brightwell-cum-Sotwell. Oxon 2D 36
Brigmerston. Wilts 2G 23
Brignall. Dur 3D 104
Brig o'Turk. Stir 3E 135
Brigsley. NE Lin 4F 95
Brigsteer. Cumb 1D 97
Brigstock. Nptn 2G 63
Brill. Buck 4E 51
Brill. Corn 4E 5
Brilley. Here 1F 47
Brimaston. Pemb 2D 42
Brimfield. Here 4H 59
Brimington. Derbs 3B 86
Brimley. Devn 5B 12
Brimpsfield. Glos 4E 49
Brimpton. W Ber 5D 36
Brims. Orkn 9B 172
Brimscombe. Glos 5D 48
Brimstage. Mers 2F 83
Brincliffe. S Yor 2H 85
Brind. E Yor 1H 93
Brindister. Shet 8F 173
Brindle. Lanc 2E 90
Brindley. Ches E 5H 83

Brindley Ford. Stoke 5C 84
Brineton. Staf 4C 72
Bringhurst. Leics 1F 63
Brington. Cambs 3H 63
Brinian. Orkn 5D 172
Briningham. Norf 2C 78
Brinkhill. Linc 3C 88
Brinkley. Cambs 5F 65
Brinklow. Warw 3B 62
Brinkworth. Wilts 3F 35
Brinscall. Lanc 2E 91
Brinscombe. Som 1H 21
Brinsley. Notts 1B 74
Brinsty Common. Here 5A 60
Brinsworth. S Yor 2B 86
Brinton. Norf 2C 78
Brisco. Cumb 4F 113
Brisley. Norf 3B 78
Brislington. Bris 4B 34
Brissenden Green. Kent 2D 28
Bristol. Bris .....4A 34 & 189
Bristol International Airport. N Som 5A 34
Briston. Norf 2C 78
Britannia. Lanc 2G 91
Britford. Wilts 4G 23
Brithdir. Cdgn 1D 44
Brithdir. Gwyn 4G 69
Briton Ferry. Neat 3G 31
Britwell Salome. Oxon 2E 37
Brixham. Torb 3F 9
Brixton. Devn 3B 8
Brixton. G Lon 3E 39
Brixton Deverill. Wilts 3D 22
Brixworth. Nptn 3E 63
Brize Norton. Oxon 5B 50
Broad Alley. Worc 4C 60
Broad Blunsdon. Swin 2G 35
Broadbottom. G Man 1D 85
Broadbridge. W Sus 2G 17
Broadbridge Heath. W Sus 2C 26
Broad Campden. Glos 2G 49
Broad Chalke. Wilts 4F 23
Broadclyst. Devn 3C 12
Broadfield. Inv 2E 127
Broadfield. Pemb 4F 43
Broadfield. W Sus 2D 26
Broadford. High 1E 147
Broadford Bridge. W Sus 3B 26
Broadgate. Cumb 1A 96
Broad Green. Cambs 5F 65
Broad Green. C Beds 1H 51
Broad Green. Worc .....3D 61 (nr. Bromsgrove)
Broad Green. Worc .....5B 60 (nr. Worcester)
Broadhaven. High 3F 169
Broad Haven. Pemb 3C 42
Broadheath. G Man 2B 84
Broad Heath. Staf 3C 72
Broadheath. Worc 4A 60
Broadhembury. Devn 2E 12
Broadhempston. Devn 2E 9
Broad Hill. Cambs 3E 65
Broad Hinton. Wilts 4G 35
Broadholm. Derbs 1A 74
Broadholme. Linc 3F 87
Broadlay. Carm 5D 44
Broad Laying. Hants 5C 36
Broadley. Lanc 3G 91
Broadley. Mor 2A 160
Broadley Common. Essx 5E 53
Broad Marston. Worc 1G 49
Broadmayne. Dors 4C 14
Broadmere. Hants 2E 24
Broadmoor. Pemb 4E 43
Broad Oak. Carm 3F 45
Broad Oak. Cumb 5C 102
Broad Oak. Dors .....3H 13 (nr. Bridport)
Broad Oak. Dors .....1C 14 (nr. Sturminster Newton)
Broad Oak. E Sus .....3B 28 (nr. Hastings)
Broad Oak. E Sus .....3H 27 (nr. Heathfield)
Broadoak. Glos 4B 48
Broadoak. Hants 1C 16
Broadoak. Here 3H 47
Broad Oak. Kent 4F 41
Broadrashes. Mor 3B 160
Broads. Norf 5G 79
Broadsea. Abers 2G 161
Broadshard. Som 1H 13
Broad's Green. Essx 4G 53
Broadstairs. Kent 4H 41
Broadstone. Pool 3F 15
Broadstone. Shrp 2H 59
Broad Street. E Sus 4C 28
Broad Street. Kent .....1F 29 (nr. Ashford)
Broad Street. Kent .....5C 40 (nr. Maidstone)
Broad Street Green. Essx 5B 54
Broad, The. Here 4G 59
Broad Town. Wilts 4F 35
Broadwas. Worc 5B 60
Broadwath. Cumb 4F 113

Broadway. Carm .....5D 45 (nr. Kidwelly)
Broadway. Carm .....3G 43 (nr. Laugharne)
Broadway. Pemb 3C 42
Broadway. Som 1G 13
Broadway. Suff 3F 67
Broadway. Worc 2G 49
Broadwell. Glos .....4A 48 (nr. Cinderford)
Broadwell. Glos .....3H 49 (nr. Stow-on-the-Wold)
Broadwell. Oxon 5A 50
Broadwell. Warw 4B 62
Broadwell House. Nmbd 4C 114
Broadwey. Dors 4B 14
Broadwindsor. Dors 2H 13
Broadwoodkelly. Devn 2G 11
Broadwoodwidger. Devn 4E 11
Broallan. High 4G 157
Brobury. Here 1G 47
Brochel. High 4E 155
Brockamin. Worc 5B 60
Brockbridge. Hants 1E 16
Brockdish. Norf 3E 66
Brockencote. Worc 3C 60
Brockenhurst. Hants 2A 16
Brocketsbrae. S Lan 1H 117
Brockford Street. Suff 4D 66
Brockhall. Nptn 4D 62
Brockham. Surr 1C 26
Brockhampton. Glos .....3E 49 (nr. Bishop's Cleeve)
Brockhampton. Glos .....3F 49 (nr. Sevenhampton)
Brockhampton. Here 2A 48
Brockhill. Bord 2F 119
Brockholes. W Yor 3B 92
Brockhurst. Hants 2D 16
Brocklesby. Linc 3E 95
Brockley. N Som 5H 33
Brockley Corner. Suff 3H 65
Brockley Green. Suff .....1H 53 (nr. Bury St Edmunds)
Brockley Green. Suff .....5H 65 (nr. Haverhill)
Brockleymoor. Cumb 1F 103
Brockmoor. W Mid 2C 60
Brockton. Shrp .....2F 59 (nr. Bishop's Castle)
Brockton. Shrp .....5B 72 (nr. Madeley)
Brockton. Shrp .....1H 59 (nr. Much Wenlock)
Brockton. Shrp .....5F 71 (nr. Pontesbury)
Brockton. Staf 2C 72
Brockton. Telf 4B 72
Brockweir. Glos 5A 48
Brockworth. Glos 4D 49
Brocton. Staf 4D 72
Brodick. N Ayr 2E 123
Brodie. Mor 3D 159
Brodiesord. Abers 3C 160
Brodsworth. S Yor 4F 93
Brogaig. High 2D 154
Brogborough. C Beds 2H 51
Brokenborough. Wilts 3E 35
Broken Cross. Ches E 3C 84
Bromborough. Mers 2F 83
Bromdon. Shrp 2A 60
Brome. Suff 3D 66
Brome Street. Suff 3D 66
Bromeswell. Suff 5F 67
Bromfield. Cumb 5C 112
Bromfield. Shrp 3G 59
Bromford. W Mid 1F 61
Bromham. Bed 5H 63
Bromham. Wilts 5E 35
Bromley. G Lon 4F 39
Bromley. Herts 3E 53
Bromley. Shrp 1B 60
Bromley Cross. G Man 3F 91
Bromley Green. Kent 2D 28
Bromley Wood. Staf 3F 73
Brompton. Medw 4B 40
Brompton. N Yor .....5A 106 (nr. Northallerton)
Brompton. N Yor .....1D 100 (nr. Scarborough)
Brompton. Shrp 5H 71
Brompton-on-Swale. N Yor 5F 105
Brompton Ralph. Som 3D 20
Brompton Regis. Som 3C 20
Bromsash. Here 3B 48
Bromsberrow. Glos 2C 48
Bromsberrow Heath. Glos 2C 48
Bromsgrove. Worc 3D 60
Bromstead Heath. Staf 4B 72
Bromyard. Here 5A 60
Bromyard Downs. Here 5A 60
Bronaber. Gwyn 2G 69
Broncroft. Shrp 2H 59
Brongest. Cdgn 1D 44
Bronington. Wrex 2G 71
Bronllys. Powy 2E 47
Bronnant. Cdgn 4F 57
Bronwydd Arms. Carm 3E 45
Bronydd. Powy 1F 47
Bronygarth. Shrp 2E 71

Brook. Carm 4G 43
Brook. Devn 5E 11
Brook. Hants .....1A 16 (nr. Cadnam)
Brook. Hants .....4B 24 (nr. Romsey)
Brook. IOW 4B 16
Brook. Kent 1E 29
Brook. Surr .....1B 26 (nr. Guildford)
Brook. Surr .....2A 26 (nr. Haslemere)
Brooke. Norf 1E 67
Brooke. Rut 5F 75
Brookend. Glos 5B 48
Brook End. Worc 1D 48
Brookfield. Lanc 1D 90
Brookfield. Ren 3F 127
Brookhouse. Lanc 3E 97
Brookhouse Green. Ches E 4C 84
Brookhouses. Staf 1D 73
Brookhurst. Mers 2F 83
Brookland. Kent 3D 28
Brooklands. G Man 1B 84
Brookmans Park. Herts 5C 52
Brooks. Powy 1D 58
Brooksby. Leics 4D 74
Brooks Green. W Sus 3C 26
Brook Street. Essx 1G 39
Brook Street. Kent 2D 28
Brook Street. W Sus 3E 27
Brookthorpe. Glos 4D 48
Brookville. Norf 1G 65
Brookwood. Surr 5A 38
Broom. C Beds 1B 52
Broom. Fife 3F 137
Broom. Warw 5E 61
Broome. Norf 1F 67
Broome. Shrp .....1H 59 (nr. Cardington)
Broome. Shrp .....2G 59 (nr. Craven Arms)
Broome. Worc 3D 60
Broomedge. Warr 2B 84
Broomend. Abers 2E 153
Broome Park. Nmbd 3F 121
Broomer's Corner. W Sus 3C 26
Broomfield. Abers 5G 161
Broomfield. Essx 4H 53
Broomfield. Kent .....4F 41 (nr. Herne Bay)
Broomfield. Kent .....5C 40 (nr. Maidstone)
Broomfield. Som 3F 21
Broomfleet. E Yor 2B 94
Broom Green. Norf 3B 78
Broomhall. Ches E 1A 72
Broomhall. Wind 4A 38
Broomhaugh. Nmbd 3D 114
Broomhill. Bris 4B 34
Broomhill. Dors 2F 15
Broomhill. High .....1D 151 (nr. Grantown-on-Spey)
Broomhill. High .....1B 158 (nr. Invergordon)
Broomhill. Norf 5F 77
Broomhill. S Yor 4E 93
Broom Hill. Worc 3D 60
Broomhillbank. Dum 5D 118
Broomholm. Norf 2F 79
Broomlands. Dum 4C 118
Broomley. Nmbd 3D 114
Broom of Moy. Mor 3E 159
Broompark. Dur 5F 115
Broom's Green. Glos 2C 48
Brora. High 3G 165
Broseley. Shrp 5A 72
Brotherhouse Bar. Linc 4B 76
Brotheridge Green. Worc 1D 48
Brotherlee. Dur 1C 104
Brothertoft. Linc 1B 76
Brotherton. N Yor 2E 93
Brotton. Red C 2D 107
Broubster. High 2C 168
Brough. Cumb 3A 104
Brough. Derbs 2F 85
Brough. E Yor 2C 94
Brough. High 1E 169
Brough. Notts 5F 87
Brough. Orkn .....6C 172 (nr. Finstown)
Brough. Orkn .....9D 172 (nr. St Margaret's Hope)
Brough. Shet .....6F 173 (nr. Benston)
Brough. Shet .....4G 173 (nr. Booth of Toft)
Brough. Shet .....7G 173 (nr. Bressay)
Brough. Shet .....5G 173 (nr. Whalsay)
Broughall. Shrp 1H 71
Brougham. Cumb 2G 103
Brough Lodge. Shet 2G 173
Brough Sowerby. Cumb 3A 104
Broughton. Cambs 3B 64
Broughton. Flin 4F 83
Broughton. Hants 3B 24
Broughton. Lanc 1D 90
Broughton. Mil 2G 51
Broughton. Nptn 3F 63

Broughton—Butterwick

Broughton. N Lin 4C 94
Broughton. N Yor 2B 100
(nr. Malton)
Broughton. N Yor 4B 98
(nr. Skipton)
Broughton. Orkn 3D 172
Broughton. Oxon 2C 50
Broughton. Bord 1D 118
Broughton. Staf 2B 72
Broughton. V Glam 4C 32
Broughton Astley. Leics 1C 62
Broughton Beck. Cumb 1B 96
Broughton Cross. Cumb 1B 102
Broughton Gifford. Wilts 5D 35
Broughton Green. Worc 4D 60
Broughton Hackett. Worc 5D 60
Broughton in Furness. Cumb 1B 96
Broughton Mills. Cumb 5D 102
Broughton Moor. Cumb 1B 102
Broughton Park. G Man 4G 91
Broughton Poggs. Oxon 5H 49
Broughtown. Orkn 3F 172
Broughty Ferry. D'dee 5D 144
Browland. Shet 6D 173
Brownbread Street. E Sus 4A 28
Brown Candover. Hants 3D 24
Brown Edge. Lanc 3B 90
Brown Edge. Staf 5D 84
Brownhill. Bkbn 1E 91
Brownhill. Shrp 3G 71
Brownhills. Shrp 2A 72
Brownhills. W Mid 5E 73
Brown Knowl. Ches W 5G 83
Brownlow. Ches E 4C 84
Brownlow Heath. Ches E 4C 84
Brown's Green. W Mid 1E 61
Brownshill. Glos 5D 49
Brownston. Devn 3C 8
Brownstone. Devn 2A 12
Browston Green. Norf 5G 79
Broxa. N Yor 5G 107
Broxbourne. Herts 5D 52
Broxburn. E Lot 2C 130
Broxburn. W Lot 2D 129
Broxholme. Linc 3G 87
Broxted. Essx 3F 53
Broxton. Ches W 5G 83
Broxwood. Here 5F 59
Broyle Side. E Sus 4F 27
Brù. W Isl 3F 171
Bruach Mairi. W Isl 4G 171
Bruairnis. W Isl 8C 170
Bruan. High 5F 169
Bruar Lodge. Per 1F 143
Brucehill. W Dun 2E 127
Brucklay. Abers 3G 161
Bruera. Ches W 4G 83
Bruern Abbey. Oxon 3A 50
Bruichladdich. Arg 3A 124
Bruisyard. Suff 4F 67
Bruisyard Street. Suff 4F 67
Brumby. N Lin 4B 94
Brund. Staf 4F 85
Brundall. Norf 5F 79
Brundish. Norf 1F 67
Brundish. Suff 4E 67
Brundish Street. Suff 3E 67
Brunery. High 1B 140
Brunswick Village. Tyne 2F 115
Brunthwaite. W Yor 5C 98
Bruntingthorpe. Leics 1D 62
Brunton. Fife 1F 137
Brunton. Nmbd 2G 121
Brunton. Wilts 1H 23
Brushford. Devn 2G 11
Brushford. Som 4C 20
Brusta. W Isl 1E 170
Bruton. Som 3B 22
Bryanston. Dors 2D 15
Bryant's Bottom. Buck 2G 37
Brydekirk. Dum 2C 112
Brymbo. Cnwy 3H 81
Brymbo. Wrex 5E 83
Brympton D'Evercy. Som 1A 14
Bryn. Carm 5F 45
Bryn. G Man 4D 90
Bryn. Neat 2B 32
Bryn. Shrp 2E 59
Brynamman. Carm 4H 45
Brynberian. Pemb 1F 43
Brynbryddan. Neat 2A 32
Bryncae. Rhon 3C 32
Bryncethin. B'end 3C 32
Bryncir. Gwyn 1D 69
Bryn-coch. Neat 3G 31
Bryncroes. Gwyn 2B 68
Bryncrug. Gwyn 5F 69
Bryn Du. IOA 3C 80
Bryn Eden. Gwyn 3G 69
Bryneglwys. Den 1D 70
Bryn Eglwys. Gwyn 4F 81
Brynford. Flin 3D 82
Bryn Gates. G Man 4D 90
Bryn Golau. Rhon 3D 32
Bryngwran. IOA 3C 80
Bryngwyn. Mon 5G 47
Bryngwyn. Powy 1E 47
Bryn-henllan. Pemb 1E 43
Brynhoffnant. Cdgn 5C 56
Bryn-llwyn. Flin 2C 82
Brynllywarch. Powy 2D 58
Bryn-mawr. Blae 4E 47
Bryn-mawr. Gwyn 2B 68
Brynmenyn. B'end 3C 32
Brynmill. Swan 3F 31
Brynna. Rhon 3C 32
Brynrefail. Gwyn 4E 81
Brynrefail. IOA 2D 81
Brynsadler. Rhon 3D 32
Bryn-Saith Marchog. Den 5C 82
Brynsiencyn. IOA 4D 81
Brynteg. IOA 2D 81
Brynteg. Wrex 5F 83
Brynygwenyn. Mon 4G 47
Bryn-y-maen. Cnwy 3H 81
Buaile nam Bodach. W Isl 8C 170
Bualintur. High 1C 146
Bubbenhall. Warw 3A 62
Bubwith. E Yor 1H 93
Buccleuch. Bord 3F 119
Buchanan Smithy. Stir 1F 127
Buchanhaven. Abers 4H 161
Buchanty. Per 1B 136
Buchany. Stir 3G 135
Buchley. E Dun 2G 127
Buchlyvie. Stir 4E 135
Buckabank. Cumb 5E 113
Buckden. Cambs 4A 64
Buckden. N Yor 2B 98
Buckenham. Norf 5F 79
Buckerell. Devn 2E 13
Buckfast. Devn 2D 8
Buckfastleigh. Devn 2D 8
Buckhaven. Fife 4F 137
Buckholm. Bord 1G 119
Buckholt. Here 4A 48
Buckhorn Weston. Dors 4C 22
Buckhurst Hill. Essx 1F 39
Buckie. Mor 2B 160
Buckingham. Buck 2E 51
Buckland. Buck 4G 51
Buckland. Glos 2F 49
Buckland. Here 5H 59
Buckland. Herts 2D 52
Buckland. Kent 1H 29
Buckland. Oxon 2B 36
Buckland. Surr 5D 38
Buckland Brewer. Devn 4E 19
Buckland Common. Buck 5H 51
Buckland Dinham. Som 1C 22
Buckland Filleigh. Devn 2E 11
Buckland in the Moor. Devn 5H 11
Buckland Monachorum. Devn 2A 8
Buckland Newton. Dors 2B 14
Buckland Ripers. Dors 4B 14
Buckland St Mary. Som 1F 13
Buckland-tout-Saints. Devn 4D 8
Bucklebury. W Ber 4D 36
Bucklegate. Linc 2C 76
Buckleigh. Devn 4E 19
Buckler's Hard. Hants 3C 16
Bucklesham. Suff 1F 55
Buckley. Flin 4E 83
Buckley Green. Warw 4F 61
Buckley Hill. Mers 1F 83
Bucklow Hill. Ches E 2B 84
Buckminster. Leics 3F 75
Bucknall. Linc 4A 88
Bucknall. Stoke 1D 72
Bucknell. Oxon 3D 50
Bucknell. Shrp 3F 59
Buckpool. Mor 2B 160
Bucksburn. Aber 3F 153
Buck's Cross. Devn 4D 18
Bucks Green. W Sus 2B 26
Buckshaw Village. Lanc 2D 90
Bucks Hill. Herts 5A 52
Bucks Horn Oak. Hants 2G 25
Buck's Mills. Devn 4D 18
Buckton. E Yor 2F 101
Buckton. Here 3F 59
Buckton. Nmbd 1E 121
Buckton Vale. G Man 4H 91
Buckworth. Cambs 3A 64
Budby. Notts 4D 86
Bude. Corn 2C 10
Budge's Shop. Corn 3H 7
Budlake. Devn 2C 12
Budle. Nmbd 1F 121
Budleigh Salterton. Devn 4D 12
Budock Water. Corn 5B 6
Buerton. Ches E 1A 72
Buffler's Holt. Buck 2E 51
Bugbrooke. Nptn 5D 62
Buglawton. Ches E 4C 84
Bugle. Corn 3E 6
Bugthorpe. E Yor 4B 100
Buildwas. Shrp 5A 72
Builth Road. Powy 5C 58
Builth Wells. Powy 5C 58
Bulbourne. Herts 4H 51
Bulby. Linc 3H 75
Bulcote. Notts 1D 74
Buldoo. High 2B 168
Bulford. Wilts 2G 23
Bulford Camp. Wilts 2G 23
Bulkeley. Ches E 5H 83
Bulkington. Warw 2A 62
Bulkington. Wilts 1E 23
Bulkworthy. Devn 1D 11
Bullamoor. N Yor 5A 106
Bull Bay. IOA 1D 80
Bullbridge. Derbs 5A 86
Bullgill. Cumb 1B 102
Bull Hill. Hants 3B 16
Bullinghope. Here 2A 48
Bull's Green. Herts 4C 52
Bullwood. Arg 2C 126
Bulmer. Essx 1B 54
Bulmer. N Yor 3A 100
Bulmer Tye. Essx 2B 54
Bulphan. Thur 2H 39
Bulverhythe. E Sus 5B 28
Bulwark. Abers 4G 161
Bulwell. Nott 1C 74
Bulwick. Nptn 1G 63
Bumble's Green. Essx 5E 53
Bun Abhainn Eadarra.
W Isl 7D 171
Bunacaimb. High 5E 147
Bun a' Mhuillinn. W Isl 7C 170
Bunarkaig. High 5D 148
Bunbury. Ches E 5H 83
Bunchrew. High 4A 158
Bundalloch. High 1A 148
Buness. Shet 1H 173
Bunessan. Arg 1A 132
Bungay. Suff 2F 67
Bunkegivie. High 2H 149
Bunker's Hill. Cambs 5D 76
Bunkers Hill. Linc 5B 88
Bunker's Hill. Norf 5H 79
Bunloit. High 1H 149
Bunnahabhain. Arg 2C 124
Bunny. Notts 3C 74
Bunoich. High 3F 149
Bunree. High 2E 141
Bunroy. High 5E 149
Buntait. High 5F 157
Buntingford. Herts 3D 52
Buntings Green. Essx 2B 54
Bunwell. Norf 1D 66
Burbage. Derbs 3E 85
Burbage. Leics 1B 62
Burbage. Wilts 5H 35
Burcher. Here 4F 59
Burchett's Green. Wind 3G 37
Burcombe. Wilts 3F 23
Burcot. Oxon 2D 36
Burcot. Worc 3D 61
Burcote. Shrp 1B 60
Burcott. Buck 4G 51
Burcott. Som 2A 22
Burdale. N Yor 3C 100
Burdrop. Oxon 2B 50
Bures. Suff 2C 54
Burford. Oxon 4A 50
Burford. Shrp 4H 59
Burf, The. Worc 4C 60
Burg. Arg 4E 139
Burgate Great Green. Suff 3C 66
Burgate Little Green. Suff 3C 66
Burgess Hill. W Sus 4E 27
Burgh. Suff 5E 67
Burgh by Sands. Cumb 4E 113
Burgh Castle. Norf 5G 79
Burghclere. Hants 5C 36
Burghead. Mor 2F 159
Burghfield. W Ber 5E 37
Burghfield Common. W Ber 5E 37
Burghfield Hill. W Ber 5E 37
Burgh Heath. Surr 5D 38
Burghill. Here 1H 47
Burgh le Marsh. Linc 4E 89
Burgh Muir. Abers 2E 153
Burgh next Aylsham. Norf 3E 78
Burgh on Bain. Linc 2B 88
Burgh St Margaret. Norf 4G 79
Burgh St Peter. Norf 1G 67
Burghwallis. S Yor 3F 93
Burgie. Mor 3E 159
Burham. Kent 4B 40
Buriton. Hants 4F 25
Burland. Ches E 5A 84
Burland. Shet 8E 173
Burlawn. Corn 2D 6
Burleigh. Brac 3A 38
Burleigh. Glos 5D 48
Burlescombe. Devn 1D 12
Burleston. Dors 3C 14
Burlestone. Devn 4E 9
Burley. Hants 2H 15
Burley. Rut 4F 75
Burley. W Yor 1C 92
Burley Gate. Here 1A 48
Burley in Wharfedale. W Yor 5D 98
Burley Street. Hants 2H 15
Burley Woodhead. W Yor 5D 98
Burlingjobb. Powy 5E 59
Burlington. Shrp 4B 72
Burlton. Shrp 3G 71
Burmantofts. W Yor 1D 92
Burmarsh. Kent 2F 29
Burmington. Warw 2A 50
Burn. N Yor 2F 93
Burnage. G Man 1C 84
Burnaston. Derbs 2G 73
Burnbanks. Cumb 3G 103
Burnby. E Yor 5C 100
Burncross. S Yor 1H 85
Burneside. Cumb 5G 103
Burness. Orkn 3F 172
Burneston. N Yor 1F 99
Burnett. Bath 5B 34
Burnfoot. E Ayr 4D 116
Burnfoot. Per 3B 136
Burnfoot. Bord 3H 119
(nr. Hawick)
Burnfoot. Bord 3G 119
(nr. Roberton)
Burngreave. S Yor 2A 86
Burnham. Buck 2A 38
Burnham. N Lin 3D 94
Burnham Deepdale. Norf 1H 77
Burnham Green. Herts 4C 52
Burnham Market. Norf 1H 77
Burnham Norton. Norf 1H 77
Burnham-on-Crouch. Essx 1D 40
Burnham-on-Sea. Som 2G 21
Burnham Overy Staithe. Norf 1H 77
Burnham Overy Town. Norf 1H 77
Burnham Thorpe. Norf 1A 78
Burnhaven. Abers 4H 161
Burnhead. Dum 5A 118
Burnhervie. Abers 2E 153
Burnhill Green. Staf 5B 72
Burnhope. Dur 5E 115
Burnhouse. N Ayr 4E 127
Burniston. N Yor 5H 107
Burnlee. W Yor 4B 92
Burnley. Lanc 1G 91
Burnleydam. Ches E 1A 72
Burnmouth. Bord 3F 131
Burn Naze. Lanc 5C 96
Burn of Cambus. Stir 3G 135
Burnopfield. Dur 4E 115
Burnsall. N Yor 3C 98
Burnside. Ang 3E 145
Burnside. E Ayr 3E 117
Burnside. Per 3D 136
Burnside. Shet 4D 173
Burnside. S Lan 4H 127
Burnside. W Lot 2D 129
(nr. Broxburn)
Burnside. W Lot 2D 128
(nr. Winchburgh)
Burntcommon. Surr 5B 38
Burntheath. Derbs 2G 73
Burnt Heath. Essx 3D 54
Burnt Hill. W Ber 4D 36
Burnt Houses. Dur 2E 105
Burntisland. Fife 1F 129
Burnt Oak. G Lon 1D 38
Burnton. E Ayr 4D 117
Burntstalk. Norf 2G 77
Burntwood. Staf 5E 73
Burntwood Green. Staf 5E 73
Burnt Yates. N Yor 3E 99
Burnwynd. Edin 3E 129
Burpham. Surr 5B 38
Burpham. W Sus 5B 26
Burradon. Nmbd 4D 121
Burradon. Tyne 2F 115
Burrafirth. Shet 1H 173
Burragarth. Shet 1G 173
Burras. Corn 5A 6
Burraton. Corn 3A 8
Burravoe. Shet 3E 173
(nr. North Roe)
Burravoe. Shet 5E 173
(on Mainland)
Burravoe. Shet 4G 173
(on Yell)
Burray Village. Orkn 8D 172
Burrells. Cumb 3H 103
Burrelton. Per 5A 144
Burridge. Devn 2G 13
Burridge. Hants 1D 16
Burrigill. High 5E 169
Burrill. N Yor 1E 99
Burringham. N Lin 4B 94
Burrington. Devn 1G 11
Burrington. Here 3G 59
Burrington. N Som 1H 21
Burrough End. Cambs 5F 65
Burrough Green. Cambs 5F 65
Burrough on the Hill. Leics 4E 75
Burroughston. Orkn 5E 172
Burrow. Devn 4D 12
Burrow. Som 2C 20
Burrowbridge. Som 4G 21
Burrowhill. Surr 4A 38
Burry. Swan 3D 30
Burry Green. Swan 3D 30
Burry Port. Carm 5E 45
Burscough. Lanc 3C 90
Burscough Bridge. Lanc 3C 90
Bursea. E Yor 1B 94
Burshill. E Yor 5E 101
Bursledon. Hants 2C 16
Burslem. Stoke 1C 72
Burstall. Suff 1D 54
Burstock. Dors 2H 13
Burston. Devn 2H 11
Burston. Norf 2D 66
Burston. Staf 2D 72
Burstow. Surr 1E 27
Burstwick. E Yor 2F 95
Burtersett. N Yor 1A 98
Burtholme. Cumb 3G 113
Burthorpe. Suff 4G 65
Burthwaite. Cumb 5F 113
Burtle. Som 2H 21
Burtoft. Linc 2B 76
Burton. Ches W 4H 83
(nr. Kelsall)
Burton. Ches W 3F 83
(nr. Neston)
Burton. Dors 3G 15
(nr. Christchurch)
Burton. Dors 3B 14
(nr. Dorchester)
Burton. Nmbd 1F 121
Burton. Pemb 4D 43
Burton. Som 2E 21
Burton. Wilts 4D 34
(nr. Chippenham)
Burton. Wilts 3D 22
(nr. Warminster)
Burton. Wrex 5F 83
Burton Agnes. E Yor 3F 101
Burton Bradstock. Dors 4H 13
Burton-by-Lincoln. Linc 3G 87
Burton Coggles. Linc 3G 75
Burton Constable. E Yor 1E 95
Burton Corner. Linc 1C 76
Burton End. Cambs 1G 53
Burton End. Essx 3F 53
Burton Fleming. E Yor 2E 101
Burton Green. W Mid 3G 61
Burton Green. Wrex 5F 83
Burton Hastings. Warw 2B 62
Burton-in-Kendal. Cumb 2E 97
Burton in Lonsdale. N Yor 2F 97
Burton Joyce. Notts 1D 74
Burton Latimer. Nptn 3G 63
Burton Lazars. Leics 4E 75
Burton Leonard. N Yor 3F 99
Burton on the Wolds. Leics 3C 74
Burton Overy. Leics 1D 62
Burton Pedwardine. Linc 1A 76
Burton Pidsea. E Yor 1F 95
Burton Salmon. N Yor 2E 93
Burton's Green. Essx 3B 54
Burton Stather. N Lin 3B 94
Burton upon Stather. N Lin 3B 94
Burton upon Trent. Staf 3G 73
Burton Wolds. Leics 3D 74
Burtonwood. Warr 1H 83
Burwardsley. Ches W 5H 83
Burwarton. Shrp 2A 60
Burwash. E Sus 3A 28
Burwash Common.
E Sus 3H 27
Burwash Weald. E Sus 3A 28
Burwell. Cambs 4E 65
Burwell. Linc 3C 88
Burwen. IOA 1D 80
Burwick. Orkn 9D 172
Bury. Cambs 2B 64
Bury. G Man 3G 91
Bury. Som 4C 20
Bury. W Sus 4B 26
Burybank. Staf 2C 72
Bury End. Worc 2F 49
Bury Green. Herts 3E 53
Bury Hill. S Glo 3C 34
Bury St Edmunds. Suff 4A 66
Burythorpe. N Yor 3B 100
Busbridge. Surr 1A 26
Busby. E Ren 4G 127
Busby. Per 1C 136
Buscot. Oxon 2H 35
Bush. Corn 2C 10
Bush Bank. Here 5G 59
Bushbury. W Mid 5D 72
Bushby. Leics 5D 74
Bushey. Dors 4E 15
Bushey. Herts 1C 38
Bushey Heath. Herts 1C 38
Bush Green. Norf 1C 66
(nr. Attleborough)
Bush Green. Norf 2E 66
(nr. Harleston)
Bush Green. Suff 5B 66
Bushley. Worc 2D 48
Bushley Green. Worc 2D 48
Bushmead. Bed 4A 64
Bushmoor. Shrp 2G 59
Bushton. Wilts 4F 35
Bushy Common. Norf 4B 78
Busk. Cumb 5H 113
Buslingthorpe. Linc 2H 87
Bussage. Glos 5D 49
Bussex. Som 3G 21
Busta. Shet 5E 173
Bustard Green. Essx 3G 53
Butcher's Cross. E Sus 3G 27
Butcombe. N Som 5A 34
Bute Town. Cphy 5E 46
Butleigh. Som 3A 22
Butleigh Wootton. Som 3A 22
Butlers Marston. Warw 5H 61
Butley. Suff 5F 67
Butley High Corner. Suff 1G 55
Butlocks Heath. Hants 2C 16
Butterburn. Cumb 2H 113
Buttercrambe. N Yor 4B 100
Butterknowle. Dur 2E 105
Butterleigh. Devn 2C 12
Buttermere. Cumb 3C 102
Buttermere. Wilts 5B 36
Buttershaw. W Yor 2B 92
Butterstone. Per 4H 143
Butterton. Staf 5E 85
(nr. Leek)
Butterton. Staf 1C 72
(nr. Stoke-on-Trent)
Butterwick. Dur 2A 106
Butterwick. Linc 1C 76

Butterwick. N Yor 2B **100**
(nr. Malton)
Butterwick. N Yor 2D **101**
(nr. Weaverthorpe)
Butteryhaugh. Nmbd 5A **120**
Butt Green. Ches E 5A **84**
Buttington. Powy 5E **71**
Buttonbridge. Shrp 3B **60**
Buttonoak. Shrp 3B **60**
Buttsash. Hants 2C **16**
Butt's Green. Essx 5A **54**
Butt Yeats. Lanc 3E **97**
Buxhall. Suff 5C **66**
Buxted. E Sus 3F **27**
Buxton. Derbs 3E **85**
Buxton. Norf 3E **79**
Buxworth. Derbs 2E **85**
Bwcle. Flin 4E **83**
Bwlch. Powy 3E **47**
Bwlchderwin. Gwyn 1D **68**
Bwlchgwyn. Wrex 5E **83**
Bwlch-Llan. Cdgn 5E **57**
Bwlchnewydd. Carm 3D **44**
Bwlchtocyn. Gwyn 3C **68**
Bwlch-y-cibau. Powy 4D **70**
Bwlchyddar. Powy 3D **70**
Bwlch-y-fadfa. Cdgn 1E **45**
Bwlch-y-ffridd. Powy 1C **58**
Bwlch y Garreg. Powy 1C **58**
Bwlch-y-groes. Pemb 1G **43**
Bwlch-y-haiarn. Cnwy 5G **81**
Bwlch-y-sarnau. Powy 3C **58**
Bybrook. Kent 1E **28**
Byermoor. Tyne 4E **115**
Byers Garth. Dur 5G **115**
Byers Green. Dur 1F **105**
Byfield. Nptn 5C **62**
Byfleet. Surr 4B **38**
Byford. Here 1G **47**
Bygrave. Herts 2C **52**
Byker. Tyne 3F **115**
Byland Abbey. N Yor 2H **99**
Byley. Ches W 4B **84**
Bynea. Carm 3E **31**
Byram. N Yor 2E **93**
Byrness. Nmbd 4B **120**
Bystock. Devn 4D **12**
Bythorn. Cambs 3H **63**
Byton. Here 4F **59**
Bywell. Nmbd 3D **114**
Byworth. W Sus 3A **26**

C

Cabharstadh. W Isl 6F **171**
Cabourne. Linc 4E **95**
Cabrach. Arg 3C **124**
Cabrach. Mor 1A **152**
Cabus. Lanc 5D **97**
Cadbury. Devn 2C **12**
Cadder. E Dun 2H **127**
Caddington. C Beds 4A **52**
Caddonfoot. Bord 1G **119**
Cadeby. Leics 5B **74**
Cadeby. S Yor 4F **93**
Cadeleigh. Devn 2C **12**
Cade Street. E Sus 3H **27**
Cadgwith. Corn 5E **5**
Cadham. Fife 3E **137**
Cadishead. G Man 1B **84**
Cadle. Swan 3F **31**
Cadley. Lanc 1D **90**
Cadley. Wilts 1H **23**
(nr. Ludgershall)
Cadley. Wilts 5H **35**
(nr. Marlborough)
Cadmore End. Buck 2F **37**
Cadnam. Hants 1A **16**
Cadney. N Lin 4D **94**
Cadole. Flin 4E **82**
Cadoxton-Juxta-Neath. Neat . .2A **32**
Cadwell. Herts 2B **52**
Cadwst. Den 2C **70**
Caeathro. Gwyn 4E **81**
Caehopkin. Powy 4B **46**
Caenby. Linc 2H **87**
Caenn-na-Cleithe. W Isl 8D **171**
Caerau. B'end 2B **32**
Caerau. Card 4E **33**
Cae'r-bont. Powy 4B **46**
Cae'r-bryn. Carm 4F **45**
Caerdeon. Gwyn 4F **69**
Caerdydd.
Card . . . . .4E **33** & **Cardiff 191**
Caerfarchell. Pemb 2B **42**
Caerffili. Cphy 3E **33**
Caerfyrddin. Carm 4E **45**
Caergeiliog. IOA 3C **80**
Caergwrle. Flin 5F **83**
Caergybi. IOA 2B **80**
Caerlaverock. Per 2A **136**
Caerleon. Newp 2G **33**
Caerllion. Newp 2G **33**
Caernarfon. Gwyn . . .4D **81** & **190**
Caerphilly. Cphy 3E **33**
Caersws. Powy 1C **58**
Caerwedros. Cdgn 5C **56**
Caerwent. Mon 2H **33**
Caerwys. Flin 3D **82**

Caim. IOA 2F **81**
Caio. Carm 2G **45**
Cairinis. W Isl 2D **170**
Cairisiadar. W Isl 4D **171**
Cairminis. W Isl 9C **171**
Cairnbaan. Arg 4F **133**
Cairnbulg. Abers 2H **161**
Cairncross. Ang 1D **145**
Cairndow. Arg 2A **134**
Cairness. Abers 2H **161**
Cairneyhill. Fife 1D **128**
Cairngarroch. Dum 5F **109**
Cairngorms. High 3D **151**
Cairnhill. Abers 5D **160**
Cairnie. Abers 4B **160**
Cairnorrie. Abers 4F **161**
Cairnryan. Dum 3F **109**
Cairston. Orkn 6B **172**
Caister-on-Sea. Norf 4H **79**
Caistor. Linc 4E **95**
Caistor St Edmund. Norf 5E **79**
Caistron. Nmbd 4D **121**
Cakebole. Worc 3C **60**
Calais Street. Suff 1C **54**
Calanais. W Isl 4E **171**
Calbost. W Isl 6G **171**
Calbourne. IOW 4C **16**
Calceby. Linc 3D **88**
Calcot. Glos 4F **49**
Calcot Row. W Ber 4E **37**
Calcott. Kent 4F **41**
Calcott. Shrp 4G **71**
Caldback. Shet 1H **173**
Caldbeck. Cumb 1E **102**
Caldbergh. N Yor 1C **98**
Caldecote. Cambs 5C **64**
(nr. Cambridge)
Caldecote. Cambs 2A **64**
(nr. Peterborough)
Caldecote. Herts 2C **52**
Caldecote. Warw 1A **62**
Caldecott. Nptn 4G **63**
Caldecott. Oxon 2C **36**
Caldecott. Rut 1F **63**
Calderbank. N Lan 3A **128**
Calder Bridge. Cumb 4B **102**
Calderbrook. G Man 3H **91**
Caldercruix. N Lan 3B **128**
Calder Grove. W Yor 3D **92**
Calder Mains. High 3C **168**
Caldermill. S Lan 5H **127**
Calder Vale. Lanc 5E **97**
Calderwood. S Lan 4H **127**
Caldescote. Nptn 5D **62**
Caldicot. Mon 3H **33**
Caldwell. Derbs 4G **73**
Caldwell. N Yor 3E **105**
Caldy. Mers 2E **83**
Calebrack. Cumb 1E **103**
Caledfwlch. Carm 3G **45**
Calf Heath. Staf 5D **72**
Calford Green. Suff 1G **53**
Calfsound. Orkn 4E **172**
Calgary. Arg 3E **139**
Califer. Mor 3E **159**
California. Cambs 2E **65**
California. Falk 2C **128**
California. Norf 4H **79**
California. Suff 1E **55**
Calke. Derbs 3A **74**
Callakille. High 3F **155**
Callaly. Nmbd 4E **121**
Callander. Stir 3F **135**
Callaughton. Shrp 1A **60**
Callendoun. Arg 1E **127**
Callestick. Corn 3B **6**
Calligarry. High 3E **147**
Callington. Corn 2H **7**
Callingwood. Staf 3F **73**
Callow. Here 2H **47**
Callowell. Glos 5D **48**
Callow End. Worc 1D **48**
Callow Hill. Wilts 3F **35**
Callow Hill. Worc 3B **60**
(nr. Bewdley)
Callow Hill. Worc 4E **61**
(nr. Redditch)
Calmore. Hants 1B **16**
Calmsden. Glos 5F **49**
Calne. Wilts 4E **35**
Calow. Derbs 3B **86**
Calshot. Hants 2C **16**
Calstock. Corn 2A **8**
Calstone Wellington. Wilts 5F **35**
Calthorpe. Norf 2D **78**
Calthorpe Street. Norf 3G **79**
Calthwaite. Cumb 5F **113**
Calton. N Yor 4B **98**
Calton. Staf 5F **85**
Calveley. Ches E 5H **83**
Calver. Derbs 3G **85**
Calverhall. Shrp 2A **72**
Calverleigh. Devn 1C **12**
Calverley. W Yor 1C **92**
Calvert. Buck 3E **51**
Calverton. Mil 2F **51**
Calverton. Notts 1D **74**
Calvine. Per 2F **143**
Calvo. Cumb 4C **112**
Cam. Glos 2C **34**
Camaghael. High 1F **141**
Camas-luinie. High 1B **148**

Camasnacroise. High 3C **140**
Camastianavaig. High 5E **155**
Camasunary. High 2D **146**
Camault Muir. High 4H **157**
Camb. Shet 2G **173**
Camber. E Sus 4D **28**
Camberley. Surr 5G **37**
Camberwell. G Lon 3E **39**
Camblesforth. N Yor 2G **93**
Cambo. Nmbd 1D **114**
Cambois. Nmbd 1G **115**
Camborne. Corn 3D **4**
Cambourne. Cambs 5C **64**
Cambridge. Cambs . . .5D **64** & **191**
Cambridge. Glos 5C **48**
Cambrose. Corn 4A **6**
Cambus. Clac 4A **136**
Cambusbarron. Stir 4G **135**
Cambusnethan. N Lan 4B **128**
Cambuskenneth. Stir 4H **135**
Cambuslang. S Lan 3H **127**
Cambus o'May. Abers 4B **152**
Camden Town. G Lon 2D **39**
Cameley. Bath 1B **22**
Camelford. Corn 4B **10**
Camelon. Falk 1B **128**
Camelsdale. Surr 3A **26**
Camer's Green. Worc 2C **48**
Camerton. Bath 1B **22**
Camerton. Cumb 1B **102**
Camerton. E Yor 2F **95**
Camghouran. Per 3C **142**
Cammachmore. Abers 4G **153**
Cammeringham. Linc 2G **87**
Camore. High 4E **165**
Campbelton. N Ayr 4C **126**
Campbeltown. Arg 3B **122**
Campbeltown Airport. Arg 3A **122**
Cample. Dum 5B **118**
Campmuir. Per 5B **144**
Campsall. S Yor 3F **93**
Campsea Ashe. Suff 5F **67**
Camps End. Cambs 1G **53**
Campton. C Beds 2B **52**
Camptoun. E Lot 2B **130**
Camptown. Bord 3A **120**
Camrose. Pemb 2D **42**
Camserney. Per 4F **143**
Camster. High 4E **169**
Camus Croise. High 2E **147**
Camuscross. High 2E **147**
Camusdarach. High 4E **147**
Camusnagaul. High 1E **141**
(nr. Fort William)
Camusnagaul. High 5E **163**
(nr. Little Loch Broom)
Camusteel. High 4G **155**
Camusterrach. High 4G **155**
Camusvrachan. Per 4D **142**
Canada. Hants 1A **16**
Canadia. E Sus 4B **28**
Canaston Bridge. Pemb 3E **43**
Candlesby. Linc 4D **88**
Candle Street. Suff 3C **66**
Candy Mill. S Lan 5D **128**
Cane End. Oxon 4E **37**
Canewdon. Essx 1C **40**
Canford Cliffs. Pool 4F **15**
Canford Heath. Pool 3F **15**
Canford Magna. Pool 3F **15**
Canham's Green. Suff 4C **66**
Canholes. Derbs 3E **85**
Canisbay. High 1F **169**
Canley. W Mid 3H **61**
Cann. Dors 4D **22**
Cann Common. Dors 4D **23**
Cannich. High 5F **157**
Cannington. Som 3F **21**
Cannock. Staf 4D **73**
Cannock Wood. Staf 4E **73**
Canonbie. Dum 2E **113**
Canon Bridge. Here 1H **47**
Canon Frome. Here 1B **48**
Canon Pyon. Here 1H **47**
Canons Ashby. Nptn 5C **62**
Canonstown. Corn 3C **4**
Canterbury. Kent . . . . .5F **41** & **190**
Cantley. Norf 5F **79**
Cantley. S Yor 4G **93**
Cantlop. Shrp 5H **71**
Canton. Card 4E **33**
Cantray. High 4B **158**
Cantraybruich. High 4B **158**
Cantraywood. High 4B **158**
Cantsdam. Fife 4D **136**
Cantsfield. Lanc 2F **97**
Canvey Island. Essx 2B **40**
Canwick. Linc 4G **87**
Canworthy Water. Corn 3C **10**
Caol. High 1F **141**
Caolas. W Isl 9B **170**
Caolas Liubharsaigh. W Isl . . .4D **170**
Caolas Scalpaigh. W Isl 8E **171**
Caolas Stocinis. W Isl 8D **171**
Caoles. Arg 4B **138**
Caol Ila. Arg 3C **124**
Caol Loch Ailse. High 1F **147**
Caol Reatha. High 1F **147**
Capel. Kent 1H **27**
Capel. Surr 1C **26**

Capel Bangor. Cdgn 2F **57**
Capel Betws Lleucu. Cdgn 5F **57**
Capel Coch. IOA 2D **80**
Capel Curig. Cnwy 5G **81**
Capel Cynon. Cdgn 1D **45**
Capel Dewi. Carm 3E **45**
Capel Dewi. Cdgn 2F **57**
(nr. Aberystwyth)
Capel Dewi. Cdgn 1E **45**
(nr. Llandysul)
Capel Garmon. Cnwy 5H **81**
Capel Green. Suff 1G **55**
Capel Gwyn. IOA 3C **80**
Capel Gwynfe. Carm 3H **45**
Capel Hendre. Carm 4F **45**
Capel Isaac. Carm 3F **45**
Capel Iwan. Carm 1G **43**
Capel-le-Ferne. Kent 2E **29**
Capel Llanilterne. Card 4D **32**
Capel Mawr. IOA 3D **80**
Capel Newydd. Pemb 1G **43**
Capel St Andrew. Suff 1G **55**
Capel St Mary. Suff 2D **54**
Capel Seion. Carm 4F **45**
Capel Seion. Cdgn 3F **57**
Capel Uchaf. Gwyn 1D **68**
Capel-y-ffin. Powy 2F **47**
Capenhurst. Ches W 3F **83**
Capernwray. Lanc 2E **97**
Capheaton. Nmbd 1D **114**
Cappercleuch. Bord 2E **119**
Capplegill. Dum 4D **118**
Capton. Devn 3E **9**
Capton. Som 3D **20**
Caputh. Per 5H **143**
Caradon Town. Corn 5C **10**
Carbis Bay. Corn 3C **4**
Carbost. High 5C **154**
(nr. Loch Harport)
Carbost. High 4D **154**
(nr. Portree)
Carbrook. S Yor 2A **86**
Carbrooke. Norf 5B **78**
Carburton. Notts 3D **86**
Car Colston. Notts 1E **74**
Carcroft. S Yor 3F **93**
Cardenden. Fife 4E **136**
Cardeston. Shrp 4F **71**
Cardewlees. Cumb 4E **113**
Cardiff. Card . . . . .4E **33** & **191**
Cardiff International Airport.
V Glam 5D **32**
Cardigan. Cdgn 1B **44**
Cardinal's Green. Cambs 1G **53**
Cardington. Bed 1A **52**
Cardington. Shrp 1H **59**
Cardinham. Corn 2F **7**
Cardno. Abers 2G **161**
Cardow. Mor 4F **159**
Cardross. Arg 2E **127**
Cardurnock. Cumb 4C **112**
Careby. Linc 4H **75**
Careston. Ang 2E **145**
Carew. Pemb 4E **43**
Carew Cheriton. Pemb 4E **43**
Carew Newton. Pemb 4E **43**
Carey. Here 2A **48**
Carfin. N Lan 4A **128**
Carfrae. Bord 4B **130**
Cargate Green. Norf 4F **79**
Cargenbridge. Dum 2G **111**
Cargill. Per 5A **144**
Cargo. Cumb 4E **113**
Cargreen. Corn 2A **8**
Carham. Nmbd 1B **120**
Carhampton. Som 2D **20**
Carharrack. Corn 4B **6**
Carie. Per 3D **142**
(nr. Loch Rannah)
Carie. Per 5D **142**
(nr. Loch Tay)
Carisbrooke. IOW 4C **16**
Cark. Cumb 2C **96**
Carkeel. Corn 2A **8**
Carlabhagh. W Isl 3E **171**
Carland Cross. Corn 3C **6**
Carlbury. Darl 3F **105**
Carlby. Linc 4H **75**
Carlecotes. S Yor 4B **92**
Carleen. Corn 4D **4**
Carlesmoor. N Yor 2D **98**
Carleton. Cumb 4F **113**
(nr. Carlisle)
Carleton. Cumb 4B **102**
(nr. Egremont)
Carleton. Cumb 2G **103**
(nr. Penrith)
Carleton. Lanc 1B **90**
Carleton. N Yor 5B **98**
Carleton. W Yor 2E **93**
Carleton Forehoe. Norf 5C **78**
Carleton Rode. Norf 1D **66**
Carleton St Peter. Norf 5F **79**
Carlidnack. Corn 4E **5**
Carlin How. Red C 3E **107**
Carlisle. Cumb . . . . .4F **113** & **192**
Carloonan. Arg 2H **133**
Carlops. Bord 4E **129**
Carlton. Bed 5G **63**
Carlton. Cambs 5F **65**

Carlton. Leics 5A **74**
Carlton. N Yor 1A **100**
(nr. Helmsley)
Carlton. N Yor 1C **98**
(nr. Middleham)
Carlton. N Yor 2G **93**
(nr. Selby)
Carlton. Notts 1D **74**
Carlton. S Yor 3D **92**
Carlton. Stoc T 2A **106**
Carlton. Suff 4F **67**
Carlton. W Yor 2D **92**
Carlton Colville. Suff 1H **67**
Carlton Curlieu. Leics 1D **62**
Carlton Husthwaite. N Yor 2G **99**
Carlton in Cleveland. N Yor . . .4C **106**
Carlton in Lindrick. Notts 2C **86**
Carlton-le-Moorland. Linc 5G **87**
Carlton Miniott. N Yor 1F **99**
Carlton-on-Trent. Notts 4F **87**
Carlton Scroop. Linc 1G **75**
Carluke. S Lan 4B **128**
Carlyon Bay. Corn 3E **7**
Carmarthen. Carm 4E **45**
Carmel. Carm 4F **45**
Carmel. Flin 3D **82**
Carmel. Gwyn 5D **81**
Carmel. IOA 2C **80**
Carmichael. S Lan 1B **118**
Carmunnock. Glas 4H **127**
Carmyle. S Lan 3H **127**
Carmyllie. Ang 4E **145**
Carnaby. E Yor 3F **101**
Carnach. High 1C **148**
(nr. Lochcarron)
Carnach. High 4E **163**
(nr. Ullapool)
Carnach. Mor 4E **159**
Carnach. W Isl 8E **171**
Carnachy. High 3H **167**
Carnain. Arg 3B **124**
Carnais. W Isl 4C **171**
Carnan. Arg 4B **138**
Carnan. W Isl 4C **170**
Carnbee. Fife 3H **137**
Carnbo. Per 3C **136**
Carn Brea Village. Corn 4A **6**
Carndu. High 1A **148**
Carne. Corn 5D **6**
Carnell. S Ayr 1D **116**
Carnforth. Lanc 2E **97**
Carn-gorm. High 1B **148**
Carnhedryn. Pemb 2B **42**
Carnhell Green. Corn 3D **4**
Carnie. Abers 3F **153**
Carnkie. Corn 5B **6**
(nr. Falmouth)
Carnkie. Corn 4A **6**
(nr. Redruth)
Carnkief. Corn 3B **6**
Carno. Powy 1B **58**
Carnock. Fife 1D **128**
Carnon Downs. Corn 4B **6**
Carnoustie. Ang 5E **145**
Carntyne. Glas 3H **127**
Carnwath. S Lan 5C **128**
Carnyorth. Corn 3A **4**
Carol Green. W Mid 3G **61**
Carpalla. Corn 3D **6**
Carperby. N Yor 1C **98**
Carradale. Arg 2C **122**
Carragraich. W Isl 8D **171**
Carrbridge. High 1D **150**
Carr Cross. Lanc 3B **90**
Carreglefn. IOA 2C **80**
Carrhouse. N Lin 4A **94**
Carrick Castle. Arg 4A **134**
Carrick Ho. Orkn 4E **172**
Carriden. Falk 1D **128**
Carrington. G Man 1B **84**
Carrington. Linc 5C **88**
Carrington. Midl 3G **129**
Carrog. Cnwy 1G **69**
Carrog. Den 1D **70**
Carron. Falk 1B **128**
Carron. Mor 4G **159**
Carronbridge. Dum 5A **118**
Carronshore. Falk 1B **128**
Carrow Hill. Mon 2H **33**
Carr Shield. Nmbd 5B **114**
Carruth. Ren 4D **4**
Carrutherstown. Dum 2C **112**
Carr Vale. Derbs 4B **86**
Carrville. Dur 5G **115**
Carrycoats Hall. Nmbd 2C **114**
Carsaig. Arg 1C **132**
Carscreugh. Dum 3H **109**
Carsegowan. Dum 4B **110**
Carse House. Arg 3F **125**
Carseriggan. Dum 3A **110**
Carsethorn. Dum 4A **112**
Carshalton. G Lon 4D **38**
Carsington. Derbs 5G **85**
Carskiey. Arg 5A **122**
Carsluith. Dum 4B **110**
Carsphairn. Dum 5E **117**
Carstairs. S Lan 5C **128**
Carstairs Junction. S Lan 5C **128**
Carterhaugh. Ang 4D **144**
Carter's Clay. Hants 4B **24**
Carterton. Oxon 5A **50**
Carterway Heads. Nmbd 4D **114**

Carthew. Corn 3E 6
Carthorpe. N Yor 1F 99
Cartington. Nmbd 4E 121
Cartland. S Lan 5B 128
Cartmel. Cumb 2C 96
Cartmel Fell. Cumb 1D 96
Cartworth. W Yor 4B 92
Carwath. Cumb 5E 112
Carway. Carm 5E 45
Carwinley. Cumb 2F 113
Cascob. Powy 4E 59
Cas-gwent. Mon 2A 34
Cash Feus. Fife 3E 136
Cashlie. Per 4B 142
Cashmoor. Dors 1E 15
Cas-Mael. Pemb 2E 43
Casnewydd.
 Newp ....3G 33 & Newport 205
Cassington. Oxon 4C 50
Cassop. Dur 1A 106
Castell. Cnwy 4G 81
Castell. Den 4D 82
Castell Hendre. Pemb 2E 43
Castell-nedd. Neat 2A 32
Castell Newydd Emlyn. Carm 1D 44
Castell-y-bwch. Torf 2F 33
Casterton. Cumb 2F 97
Castle. Som 2A 22
Castle Acre. Norf 4H 77
Castle Ashby. Nptn 5F 63
Castlebay. W Isl 9B 170
Castle Bolton. N Yor 5D 104
Castle Bromwich. W Mid 2F 61
Castle Bytham. Linc 4G 75
Castlebythe. Pemb 2E 43
Castle Caereinion. Powy 5D 70
Castle Camps. Cambs 1G 53
Castle Carrock. Cumb 4G 113
Castlecary. N Lan 2A 128
Castle Cary. Som 3B 22
Castle Combe. Wilts 4D 34
Castlecraig. High 2C 158
Castle Donington. Leics 3B 74
Castle Douglas. Dum 3E 111
Castle Eaton. Swin 2G 35
Castle Eden. Dur 1B 106
Castleford. W Yor 2E 93
Castle Frome. Here 1B 48
Castle Green. Surr 4A 38
Castle Green. Warw 3G 61
Castle Gresley. Derbs 4G 73
Castle Heaton. Nmbd 5F 131
Castle Hedingham. Essx 2A 54
Castle Hill. Kent 1A 28
Castlehill. Per 5B 144
Castlehill. S Lan 4B 128
Castle Hill. Suff 1E 55
Castlehill. W Dun 2E 127
Castle Kennedy. Dum 4G 109
Castle Lachlan. Arg 4H 133
Castlemartin. Pemb 5D 42
Castlemilk. Glas 4H 127
Castlemorris. Pemb 1D 42
Castlemorton. Worc 2C 48
Castle O'er. Dum 5E 119
Castle Park. N Yor 3F 107
Castlerigg. Cumb 2D 102
Castle Rising. Norf 3F 77
Castleside. Dur 5D 115
Castlethorpe. Mil 1F 51
Castleton. Abers 4F 151
Castleton. Arg 1G 125
Castleton. Derbs 2F 85
Castleton. G Man 3G 91
Castleton. Mor 1F 151
Castleton. Newp 3F 33
Castleton. N Yor 4D 107
Castleton. Per 2B 136
Castletown. Cumb 1G 103
Castletown. Dors 5B 14
Castletown. High 2D 169
Castletown. IOM 5B 108
Castletown. Tyne 4G 115
Castley. N Yor 5E 99
Caston. Norf 1B 66
Castor. Pet 1A 64
Caswell. Swan 4E 31
Catacol. N Ayr 5H 125
Catbrook. Mon 5A 48
Catchems End. Worc 3B 60
Catchgate. Dur 4E 115
Catcleugh. Nmbd 4B 120
Catcliffe. S Yor 2B 86
Catcott. Som 3G 21
Caterham. Surr 5E 39
Catfield. Norf 3F 79
Catfield Common. Norf 3F 79
Catfirth. Shet 6F 173
Catford. G Lon 3E 39
Catforth. Lanc 1C 90
Cathcart. Glas 3G 127
Cathedine. Powy 3E 47
Catherine-de-Barnes. W Mid 2F 61
Catherington. Hants 1E 17
Catherston Leweston. Dors 3G 13
Catherton. Shrp 3A 60
Catisfield. Hants 2D 16
Catlodge. High 4A 150
Catlowdy. Cumb 2F 113
Catmore. W Ber 3C 36
Caton. Devn 5A 12
Caton. Lanc 3E 97

Catrine. E Ayr 2E 117
Cat's Ash. Newp 2G 33
Catsfield. E Sus 4B 28
Catsgore. Som 4A 22
Catshill. Worc 3D 60
Cattal. N Yor 4G 99
Cattawade. Suff 2E 54
Catterall. Lanc 5D 97
Catterick. N Yor 5F 105
Catterick Bridge. N Yor 5F 105
Catterick Garrison. N Yor 5E 105
Catterlen. Cumb 1F 103
Catterline. Abers 1H 145
Catterton. N Yor 5H 99
Catteshall. Surr 1A 26
Catthorpe. Leics 3C 62
Cattistock. Dors 3A 14
Catton. Nmbd 4B 114
Catton. N Yor 2F 99
Catwick. E Yor 5F 101
Catworth. Cambs 3H 63
Caudle Green. Glos 4E 49
Caulcott. Oxon 3D 50
Cauldhame. Stir 4F 135
Cauldmill. Bord 3H 119
Cauldon. Staf 1E 73
Cauldon Lowe. Staf 1E 73
Cauldwells. Abers 3E 161
Caulkerbush. Dum 4G 111
Caulside. Dum 1F 113
Caunsall. Worc 2C 60
Caunton. Notts 4E 87
Causewayend. S Lan 1C 118
Causewayhead. Stir 4H 135
Causey Park. Nmbd 5F 121
Caute. Devn 1E 11
Cautley. Cumb 5H 103
Cavendish. Suff 1B 54
Cavendish Bridge. Derbs 2B 74
Cavenham. Suff 4G 65
Caversfield. Oxon 3D 50
Caversham. Read 4F 37
Caversham Heights. Read 4E 37
Caverswall. Staf 1D 72
Cawdor. High 4C 158
Cawkwell. Linc 2B 88
Cawood. N Yor 1F 93
Cawsand. Corn 3A 8
Cawston. Norf 3D 78
Cawston. Warw 3B 62
Cawthorne. N Yor 1B 100
Cawthorne. S Yor 4C 92
Cawthorpe. Linc 3H 75
Cawton. N Yor 2A 100
Caxton. Cambs 5C 64
Caynham. Shrp 3H 59
Caythorpe. Linc 1G 75
Caythorpe. Notts 1D 74
Cayton. N Yor 1E 101
Ceallan. W Isl 3D 170
Ceann a Bhàigh. W Isl 9C 171
(on Harris)
Ceann a Bhaigh. W Isl 2C 170
(on North Uist)
Ceann a Bhaigh. W Isl 8E 171
(on Scalpay)
Ceann a Bhaigh. W Isl 8E 171
(on South Harris)
Ceannacroc Lodge. High 2E 149
Ceann a Deas Loch Baghasdail.
 W Isl 7C 170
Ceann an Leothaid. High 5E 147
Ceann a Tuath Loch Baghasdail.
 W Isl 6C 170
Ceann Loch Ailleart. High 5F 147
Ceann Loch Muideirt. High 1B 140
Ceann Shiphoirt. W Isl 6E 171
Ceann Tarabhaigh. W Isl 6E 171
Cearsiadar. W Isl 5F 171
Ceathramh Meadhanach.
 W Isl 1C 170
Cefn Berain. Cnwy 4B 82
Cefn-brith. Cnwy 5B 82
Cefn-bryn-brain. Carm 4H 45
Cefn Bychan. Cphy 2F 33
Cefn-bychan. Flin 4D 82
Cefncaeau. Carm 3E 31
Cefn Canol. Powy 2E 71
Cefn Coch. Powy 5C 70
(nr. Llanfair Caereinion)
Cefn-coch. Powy 3D 70
(nr. Llanrhaeadr-ym-Mochnant)
Cefn-coed-y-cymmer. Mer T 5D 46
Cefn Cribwr. B'end 3B 32
Cefn-ddwysarn. Gwyn 2B 70
Cefn Einion. Shrp 2E 59
Cefneithin. Carm 4F 45
Cefn Glas. B'end 3B 32
Cefngorwydd. Powy 1C 46
Cefn Llwyd. Cdgn 2F 57
Cefn-mawr. Wrex 1E 71
Cefn-y-bedd. Flin 5F 83
Cefn-y-coed. Powy 1D 58
Cefn-y-pant. Carm 2F 43
Cegidfa. Powy 4E 70
Ceinewydd. Cdgn 5C 56
Cellan. Cdgn 1G 45
Cellardyke. Fife 3H 137
Cellarhead. Staf 1D 72
Cemaes. IOA 1C 80
Cemmaes. Powy 5H 69
Cemmaes Road. Powy 5H 69

Cenarth. Carm 1C 44
Cenin. Gwyn 1D 68
Ceos. W Isl 5F 171
Cerist. Powy 2B 58
Cerne Abbas. Dors 2B 14
Cerney Wick. Glos 2F 35
Cerrigceinwen. IOA 3D 80
Cerrigydrudion. Cnwy 1B 70
Cess. Norf 4G 79
Cessford. Bord 2B 120
Ceunant. Gwyn 4E 81
Chaceley. Glos 2D 48
Chacewater. Corn 4B 6
Chackmore. Buck 2E 51
Chacombe. Nptn 1C 50
Chadderton. G Man 4H 91
Chaddesden. Derb 2A 74
Chaddesden Common.
 Derb 2A 74
Chaddesley Corbett. Worc 3C 60
Chaddlehanger. Devn 5E 11
Chaddleworth. W Ber 4C 36
Chadlington. Oxon 3B 50
Chadshunt. Warw 5H 61
Chadstone. Nptn 5F 63
Chad Valley. W Mid 2E 61
Chadwell. Leics 3E 75
Chadwell. Shrp 4B 72
Chadwell Heath. G Lon 2F 39
Chadwell St Mary. Thur 3H 39
Chadwick End. W Mid 3G 61
Chadwick Green. Mers 1H 83
Chaffcombe. Som 1G 13
Chafford Hundred. Thur 3H 39
Chagford. Devn 4H 11
Chailey. E Sus 4E 27
Chainbridge. Cambs 5D 76
Chain Bridge. Linc 1C 76
Chainhurst. Kent 1B 28
Chalbury. Dors 2F 15
Chalbury Common. Dors 2F 15
Chaldon. Surr 5E 39
Chaldon Herring. Dors 4C 14
Chale. IOW 5C 16
Chale Green. IOW 5C 16
Chalfont Common. Buck 1B 38
Chalfont St Giles. Buck 1A 38
Chalfont St Peter. Buck 2B 38
Chalford. Glos 5D 49
Chalgrove. Oxon 2E 37
Chalk. Kent 3A 40
Chalk End. Essx 4G 53
Chalk Hill. Glos 3G 49
Challaborough. Devn 4C 8
Challacombe. Devn 2G 19
Challister. Shet 5G 173
Challoch. Dum 3A 110
Challock. Kent 5E 40
Chalton. C Beds 5A 64
(nr. Bedford)
Chalton. C Beds 3A 52
(nr. Luton)
Chalton. Hants 1F 17
Chalvington. E Sus 5G 27
Champany. Falk 2D 128
Chance Inn. Fife 2F 137
Chancery. Cdgn 3E 57
Chandler's Cross. Herts 1B 38
Chandler's Cross. Worc 2C 48
Chandler's Ford. Hants 4C 24
Chanlockfoot. Dum 4G 117
Channel's End. Bed 5A 64
Channel Tunnel. Kent 2F 29
Channerwick. Shet 9F 173
Chantry. Som 2C 22
Chantry. Suff 1E 55
Chapel. Cumb 1D 102
Chapel. Fife 4E 137
Chapel Allerton. Som 1H 21
Chapel Allerton. W Yor 1D 92
Chapel Amble. Corn 1D 6
Chapel Brampton. Nptn 4E 63
Chapelbridge. Cambs 1B 64
Chapel Chorlton. Staf 2C 72
Chapel Cleeve. Som 2D 20
Chapel End. C Beds 1A 52
Chapel-en-le-Frith. Derbs 2E 85
Chapelfield. Abers 2G 145
Chapelgate. Linc 3D 76
Chapel Green. Warw 2G 61
(nr. Coventry)
Chapel Green. Warw 4B 62
(nr. Southam)
Chapel Haddlesey. N Yor 2F 93
Chapelhall. N Lan 3A 128
Chapel Hill. Abers 5H 161
Chapel Hill. Linc 5B 88
Chapel Hill. Mon 5A 48
Chapelhill. Per 1E 136
(nr. Glencarse)
Chapelhill. Per 5H 143
(nr. Harrietfield)
Chapelknowe. Dum 2E 112
Chapel Lawn. Shrp 3F 59
Chapel le Dale. N Yor 2G 97
Chapel Milton. Derbs 2E 85
Chapel of Garioch. Abers 1E 152
Chapel Row. W Ber 5D 36
Chapels. Cumb 1B 96
Chapel St Leonards. Linc 3E 89

Chapel Stile. Cumb 4E 102
Chapelthorne. W Yor 3D 92
Chapelton. Ang 4F 145
Chapelton. Devn 4F 19
Chapelton. High 2D 150
(nr. Grantown-on-Spey)
Chapelton. High 3H 157
(nr. Inverness)
Chapelton. S Lan 5H 127
Chapeltown. Bkbn 3F 91
Chapel Town. Corn 3C 6
Chapeltown. Mor 1G 151
Chapeltown. S Yor 1H 85
Chapmanslade. Wilts 2D 22
Chapmans Well. Devn 3D 10
Chapmore End. Herts 4D 52
Chappel. Essx 3B 54
Chard. Som 2G 13
Chard Junction. Dors 2G 13
Chardstock. Devn 2G 13
Charfield. S Glo 2C 34
Charing. Kent 1D 28
Charing Heath. Kent 1D 28
Charing Hill. Kent 5D 40
Charingworth. Glos 2G 49
Charlbury. Oxon 4B 50
Charlcombe. Bath 5C 34
Charlcutt. Wilts 4E 35
Charlecote. Warw 5G 61
Charles. Devn 3G 19
Charlesfield. Dum 3C 112
Charleshill. Surr 2G 25
Charleston. Ang 4C 144
Charleston. Ren 3F 127
Charlestown. Aber 3G 153
Charlestown. Abers 2H 161
Charlestown. Corn 3E 7
Charlestown. Dors 5B 14
Charlestown. Fife 1D 128
Charlestown. G Man 4G 91
Charlestown. High 1H 155
(nr. Gairloch)
Charlestown. High 4A 158
(nr. Inverness)
Charlestown. W Yor 2H 91
Charlestown of Aberlour.
 Mor 4G 159
Charles Tye. Suff 5C 66
Charlesworth. Derbs 1E 85
Charlton. G Lon 3F 39
Charlton. Hants 2B 24
Charlton. Herts 3B 52
Charlton. Nptn 2D 50
Charlton. Nmbd 1B 114
Charlton. Oxon 3C 36
Charlton. Som 1B 22
(nr. Radstock)
Charlton. Som 2B 22
(nr. Shepton Mallet)
Charlton. Som 4F 21
(nr. Taunton)
Charlton. Telf 4H 71
Charlton. W Sus 1G 17
Charlton. Wilts 1G 23
(nr. Malmesbury)
Charlton. Wilts 1G 23
(nr. Pewsey)
Charlton. Wilts 4G 23
(nr. Salisbury)
Charlton. Wilts 4E 23
(nr. Shaftesbury)
Charlton. Worc 4F 49
(nr. Evesham)
Charlton. Worc 3C 60
(nr. Stourport-on-Severn)
Charlton Abbots. Glos 3F 49
Charlton Adam. Som 4A 22
Charlton Down. Dors 3B 14
Charlton Horethorne. Som 4B 22
Charlton Kings. Glos 3E 49
Charlton Mackrell. Som 4A 22
Charlton Marshall. Dors 2E 15
Charlton Musgrove. Som 4C 22
Charlton-on-Otmoor. Oxon 4D 50
Charlton on the Hill. Dors 2D 15
Charlwood. Hants 3E 25
Charlwood. Surr 1D 26
Charlynch. Som 3F 21
Charminster. Dors 3B 14
Charmouth. Dors 3G 13
Charndon. Buck 3E 51
Charney Bassett. Oxon 2B 36
Charnock Green. Lanc 3D 90
Charnock Richard. Lanc 3D 90
Charsfield. Suff 5E 67
Charterhouse. Som 1H 21
Charter Alley. Hants 1D 24
Charterville Allotments. Oxon 4B 50
Chartham. Kent 5F 41
Chartham Hatch. Kent 5F 41
Chartridge. Buck 5H 51
Chart Sutton. Kent 5B 40
Chart, The. Kent 5F 39
Charvil. W Ber 4F 37
Charwelton. Nptn 5C 62
Chase Terrace. Staf 5E 73
Chasetown. Staf 5E 73
Chastleton. Oxon 3H 49
Chasty. Devn 2D 10
Chatburn. Lanc 5G 97
Chatcull. Staf 2B 72

Chatham.
 Medw ....4B 40 & Medway 204
Chatham Green. Essx 4H 53
Chathill. Nmbd 2F 121
Chatley. Worc 4C 60
Chattenden. Medw 3B 40
Chatteris. Cambs 2C 64
Chattisham. Suff 1D 54
Chatton. Nmbd 2E 121
Chatwall. Shrp 1H 59
Chaulden. Herts 5A 52
Chaul End. C Beds 3A 52
Chawleigh. Devn 1H 11
Chawley. Oxon 5C 50
Chawston. Bed 5A 64
Chawton. Hants 3F 25
Chaxhill. Glos 4C 48
Cheadle. G Man 2C 84
Cheadle. Staf 1E 73
Cheadle Hulme. G Man 2C 84
Cheam. Surr 4D 38
Cheapside. Wind 4A 38
Chearsley. Buck 4F 51
Chebsey. Staf 3C 72
Checkendon. Oxon 3E 37
Checkley. Ches E 1B 72
Checkley. Here 2A 48
Checkley. Staf 2E 73
Chedburgh. Suff 5G 65
Cheddar. Som 1H 21
Cheddington. Buck 4H 51
Cheddleton. Staf 5D 84
Cheddon Fitzpaine. Som 4F 21
Chedglow. Wilts 2E 35
Chedgrave. Norf 1F 67
Chedington. Dors 2H 13
Chediston. Suff 3F 67
Chediston Green. Suff 3F 67
Chedworth. Glos 4F 49
Chedzoy. Som 3G 21
Cheeseman's Green. Kent 2E 29
Cheetham Hill. G Man 4G 91
Cheglinch. Devn 2F 19
Cheldon. Devn 1H 11
Chelford. Ches E 3C 84
Chellaston. Derb 2A 74
Chellington. Bed 5G 63
Chelmarsh. Shrp 2B 60
Chelmick. Shrp 1G 59
Chelmondiston. Suff 2F 55
Chelmorton. Derbs 4F 85
Chelmsford. Essx 5H 53
Chelsea. G Lon 3D 39
Chelsfield. G Lon 4F 39
Chelsham. Surr 5E 39
Chelston. Som 4E 21
Chelsworth. Suff 1C 54
Cheltenham. Glos ....3E 49 & 192
Chelveston. Nptn 4G 63
Chelvey. N Som 5H 33
Chelwood. Bath 5B 34
Chelwood Common. E Sus 3F 27
Chelwood Gate. E Sus 3F 27
Chelworth. Wilts 2E 35
Chelworth Lower Green. Wilts 2F 35
Chelworth Upper Green. Wilts 2F 35
Cheney Longville. Shrp 2G 59
Chenies. Buck 1B 38
Chepstow. Mon 2A 34
Chequerfield. W Yor 2E 93
Chequers Corner. Norf 5D 77
Cherhill. Wilts 4F 35
Cherington. Glos 2E 35
Cherington. Warw 2A 50
Cheriton. Devn 2H 19
Cheriton. Hants 4D 24
Cheriton. Kent 2G 29
Cheriton. Pemb 5D 43
Cheriton. Swan 3D 30
Cheriton Bishop. Devn 3A 12
Cheriton Cross. Devn 3A 12
Cheriton Fitzpaine. Devn 2B 12
Cherrington. Telf 3A 72
Cherrybank. Per 1D 136
Cherry Burton. E Yor 5D 101
Cherry Green. Herts 3D 52
Cherry Hinton. Cambs 5D 65
Cherry Willingham. Linc 3H 87
Chertsey. Surr 4B 38
Cheselbourne. Dors 3C 14
Chesham. Buck 5H 51
Chesham. G Man 3G 91
Chesham Bois. Buck 1A 38
Cheshunt. Herts 5D 52
Cheslyn Hay. Staf 5D 73
Chessetts Wood. Warw 3F 61
Chessington. G Lon 4C 38
Chester. Ches W ....4G 83 & 192
Chesterblade. Som 2B 22
Chesterfield. Derbs 3A 86
Chesterfield. Staf 5F 73
Chesterhope. Nmbd 1C 114
Chester-le-Street. Dur 4F 115
Chester Moor. Dur 5F 115
Chesters. Bord 3A 120
Chesterton. Cambs 4D 64
(nr. Cambridge)
Chesterton. Cambs 1A 64
(nr. Peterborough)
Chesterton. Glos 5F 49
Chesterton. Oxon 3D 50

Chesterton. Shrp 1B 60
Chesterton. Staf 1C 72
Chesterton Green. Warw 5H 61
Chesterwood. Nmbd 3B 114
Chestfield. Kent 4F 41
Cheston. Devn 3C 8
Cheswardine. Shrp 2B 72
Cheswell. Telf 4B 72
Cheswick. Nmbd 5G 131
Cheswick Green. W Mid 3F 61
Chetnole. Dors 2B 14
Chettiscombe. Devn 1C 12
Chettisham. Cambs 2E 65
Chettle. Dors 1E 15
Chetton. Shrp 1A 60
Chetwode. Buck 3E 51
Chetwynd Aston. Telf 4B 72
Cheveley. Cambs 4F 65
Chevening. Kent 5F 39
Chevington. Suff 5G 65
Chevithorne. Devn 1C 12
Chicheley. Mil 1H 51
Chichester. W Sus 2G 17
Chickerell. Dors 4B 14
Chickering. Suff 3E 66
Chicklade. Wilts 3E 23
Chicksands. C Beds 2B 52
Chickward. Here 5E 59
Chidden. Hants 1E 17
Chiddingfold. Surr 2A 26
Chiddingly. E Sus 4G 27
Chiddingstone. Kent 1G 27
Chiddingstone Causeway.
   Kent 1G 27
Chiddingstone Hoath. Kent 1F 27
Chideock. Dors 3H 13
Chidgley. Som 3D 20
Chidham. W Sus 2F 17
Chieveley. W Ber 4C 36
Chignall St James. Essx 5G 53
Chignall Smealy. Essx 4G 53
Chigwell. Essx 1F 39
Chigwell Row. Essx 1F 39
Chilbolton. Hants 2B 24
Chilcomb. Hants 4D 24
Chilcombe. Dors 3A 14
Chilcompton. Som 1B 22
Chilcote. Leics 4G 73
Childer Thornton. Ches W 3F 83
Child Okeford. Dors 1D 14
Childrey. Oxon 3B 36
Child's Ercall. Shrp 3A 72
Childswickham. Worc 2F 49
Childwall. Mers 2G 83
Childwick Green. Herts 4B 52
Chilfrome. Dors 3A 14
Chilgrove. W Sus 1G 17
Chilham. Kent 5E 41
Chilhampton. Wilts 3F 23
Chilla. Devn 2E 11
Chilland. Hants 3D 24
Chillaton. Devn 4E 11
Chillenden. Kent 5G 41
Chillerton. IOW 4C 16
Chillesford. Suff 5F 67
Chillingham. Nmbd 2E 121
Chillington. Devn 4D 9
Chillington. Som 1G 13
Chilmark. Wilts 3E 23
Chilmington Green. Kent 1D 28
Chilson. Oxon 4B 50
Chilsworthy. Corn 5E 11
Chilsworthy. Devn 2D 10
Chiltern Green. C Beds 4B 52
Chilthorne Domer. Som 1A 14
Chilton. Buck 4E 51
Chilton. Devn 2B 12
Chilton. Dur 2F 105
Chilton. Oxon 3C 36
Chilton Candover. Hants 2D 24
Chilton Cantelo. Som 4A 22
Chilton Foliat. Wilts 4B 36
Chilton Lane. Dur 1A 106
Chilton Polden. Som 3G 21
Chilton Street. Suff 1A 54
Chilton Trinity. Som 3F 21
Chilwell. Notts 2C 74
Chilworth. Hants 1C 16
Chilworth. Surr 1B 26
Chimney. Oxon 5B 50
Chimney Street. Suff 1H 53
Chineham. Hants 1E 25
Chingford. G Lon 1E 39
Chinley. Derbs 2E 85
Chinnor. Oxon 5F 51
Chipley. Som 4E 20
Chipnall. Shrp 2B 72
Chippenham. Cambs 4F 65
Chippenham. Wilts 4E 35
Chipperfield. Herts 5A 52
Chipping. Herts 2D 52
Chipping. Lanc 5F 97
Chipping Campden. Glos 2G 49
Chipping Hill. Essx 4B 54
Chipping Norton. Oxon 3B 50
Chipping Ongar. Essx 5F 53

Chipping Sodbury. S Glo 3C 34
Chipping Warden. Nptn 1C 50
Chipstable. Som 4D 20
Chipstead. Kent 5G 39
Chipstead. Surr 5D 38
Chirbury. Shrp 1E 59
Chirk. Wrex 2E 71
Chirmorle. S Ayr 2H 109
Chirnside. Bord 4E 131
Chirnsidebridge. Bord 4E 131
Chirton. Wilts 1F 23
Chisbridge Cross. Buck 3G 37
Chisbury. Wilts 5A 36
Chiselborough. Som 1H 13
Chiselhampton. Swin 4G 35
Chiselhampton. Oxon 2D 36
Chiserley. W Yor 2A 92
Chislehurst. G Lon 4F 39
Chislet. Kent 4G 41
Chiswell. Dors 5B 14
Chiswell Green. Herts 5B 52
Chiswick. G Lon 3D 38
Chisworth. Derbs 1D 85
Chitcombe. E Sus 3C 28
Chithurst. W Sus 4G 25
Chittering. Cambs 4D 65
Chitterley. Devn 2C 12
Chitterne. Wilts 2E 23
Chittlehamholt. Devn 4G 19
Chittlehampton. Devn 4G 19
Chittoe. Wilts 5E 35
Chivelstone. Devn 5D 9
Chivenor. Devn 3F 19
Cholderton. Wilts 2H 23
Cholesbury. Buck 5H 51
Chollerford. Nmbd 2C 114
Chollerton. Nmbd 2C 114
Cholsey. Oxon 3D 36
Cholstrey. Here 5G 59
Chop Gate. N Yor 5C 106
Choppington. Nmbd 1F 115
Chopwell. Tyne 4E 115
Chorley. Ches E 5H 83
Chorley. Lanc 3D 90
Chorley. Shrp 2A 60
Chorley. Staf 4E 73
Chorleywood. Herts 1B 38
Chorlton. Ches E 5B 84
Chorlton-cum-Hardy. G Man 1C 84
Chorlton Lane. Ches W 1G 71
Choulton. Shrp 2F 59
Chrishall. Essx 2E 53
Christchurch. Cambs 1D 65
Christchurch. Dors 3G 15
Christchurch. Glos 4A 48
Christian Malford. Wilts 4E 35
Christleton. Ches W 4G 83
Christmas Common. Oxon 2F 37
Christon. N Som 1G 21
Christon Bank. Nmbd 2G 121
Christow. Devn 4B 12
Chryston. N Lan 2H 127
Chuck Hatch. E Sus 2F 27
Chudleigh. Devn 5B 12
Chudleigh Knighton. Devn 5B 12
Chulmleigh. Devn 1G 11
Chunal. Derbs 1E 85
Church. Lanc 2F 91
Churcham. Glos 4C 48
Church Aston. Telf 4B 72
Church Brampton. Nptn 4E 62
Church Brough. Cumb 3A 104
Church Broughton. Derbs 2G 73
Church Corner. Suff 2G 67
Church Crookham. Hants 1G 25
Churchdown. Glos 4D 48
Church Eaton. Staf 4C 72
Church End. Cambs 5D 65
   (nr. Cambridge)
Church End. Cambs 2B 64
   (nr. Sawtry)
Church End. Cambs 3C 64
   (nr. Willingham)
Church End. Cambs 5C 76
   (nr. Wisbech)
Church End. C Beds 3H 51
   (nr. Dunstable)
Church End. C Beds 2B 52
   (nr. Stotfold)
Church End. C Beds 2H 51
   (nr. Woburn)
Church End. E Yor 4E 101
Church End. Essx 3H 53
   (nr. Braintree)
Church End. Essx 3G 53
   (nr. Great Dunmow)
Church End. Essx 1F 53
   (nr. Saffron Walden)
Churchend. Essx 1E 40
   (nr. Southend-on-Sea)
Church End. Glos 5C 48
Church End. Hants 1E 25
Church End. Linc 2B 76
   (nr. Donington)
Church End. Linc 1D 88
   (nr. North Somercotes)
Church End. Norf 4E 77
Church End. Warw 1G 61
   (nr. Coleshill)
Church End. Warw 1G 61
   (nr. Nuneaton)

Church End. Wilts 4F 35
Church Enstone. Oxon 3B 50
Church Fenton. N Yor 1F 93
Church Green. Devn 3E 13
Church Gresley. Derbs 4G 73
Church Hanborough. Oxon 4C 50
Church Hill. Ches W 4A 84
Church Hill. Worc 4E 61
Church Hougham. Kent 1G 29
Church Houses. N Yor 5D 106
Churchill. Devn 2G 13
   (nr. Axminster)
Churchill. Devn 2F 19
   (nr. Barnstaple)
Churchill. N Som 1H 21
Churchill. Oxon 3A 50
Churchill. Worc 3C 60
   (nr. Kidderminster)
Churchill. Worc 5D 60
   (nr. Worcester)
Churchinford. Som 1F 13
Church Knowle. Dors 4E 15
Church Laneham. Notts 3F 87
Church Langley. Essx 5E 53
Church Langton. Leics 1E 62
Church Lawford. Warw 3B 62
Church Lawton. Ches E 5C 84
Church Leigh. Staf 2E 73
Church Lench. Worc 5E 61
Church Mayfield. Staf 1F 73
Church Minshull. Ches E 4A 84
Church Norton. W Sus 3G 17
Churchover. Warw 2C 62
Church Preen. Shrp 1H 59
Church Pulverbatch. Shrp 5G 71
Churchstanton. Som 1E 13
Church Stoke. Powy 1E 59
Churchstow. Devn 4D 8
Church Stowe. Nptn 5D 62
Church Street. Kent 3B 40
Church Stretton. Shrp 1G 59
Churchthorpe. Linc 1C 88
Churchtown. Cumb 5E 113
Churchtown. Devn 2G 19
Churchtown. IOM 2D 108
Churchtown. Lanc 5D 97
Churchtown. Leics 4A 74
Churchtown. Mers 3B 90
Churchtown. N Lin 4A 94
Churchtown. Shrp 2E 59
Church Village. Rhon 3D 32
Church Warsop. Notts 4C 86
Church Westcote. Glos 3H 49
Church Wilne. Derbs 2B 74
Churnsike Lodge. Nmbd 2H 113
Churston Ferrers. Torb 3F 9
Churt. Surr 3G 25
Churton. Ches W 5G 83
Churwell. W Yor 2C 92
Chute Standen. Wilts 1B 24
Chwilog. Gwyn 2D 68
Chwitffordd. Flin 3D 82
Chyandour. Corn 3B 4
Cilan Uchaf. Gwyn 3B 68
Cilcain. Flin 4D 82
Cilcennin. Cdgn 4E 57
Cilfrew. Neat 5A 46
Cilfynydd. Rhon 2D 32
Cilgerran. Pemb 1B 44
Cilgeti. Pemb 4F 43
Cilgwyn. Carm 3H 45
Cilgwyn. Pemb 1E 43
Ciliau Aeron. Cdgn 5D 57
Cill Amhlaidh. W Isl 4C 170
Cill Donnain. High 1G 165
Cill Donnain. W Isl 6C 170
Cille a' Bhacstair. High 2C 154
Cille Bhrighde. W Isl 7C 170
Cille Pheadair. W Isl 7C 170
Cilmaengwyn. Neat 5H 45
Cilmeri. Powy 5C 58
Cilmery. Powy 5C 58
Cilrhedyn. Pemb 1G 43
Cilsan. Carm 3F 45
Ciltwrch. Powy 1E 47
Cilybebyll. Neat 5H 45
Cilycwm. Carm 2A 46
Cimla. Neat 2A 32
Cinderford. Glos 4B 48
Cinderhill. Derbs 1A 74
Cippenham. Slo 2A 38
Cippyn. Pemb 1B 44
Circebost. W Isl 4D 171
Cirencester. Glos 5F 49
City. Powy 1E 58
City. V Glam 4C 32
City Centre.
   Stoke ....1C 72 & Stoke 211
City Dulas. IOA 2D 80
City (London) Airport. G Lon 2F 39
City, The. Buck 2F 37
Clabhach. Arg 3C 138
Clachaig. Arg 2E 151
Clachaig. High 3F 141
   (nr. Kinlochleven)
Clachaig. High 2E 141
   (nr. Nethy Bridge)
Clachamish. High 3C 154

Clachan. Arg 4F 125
   (on Kintyre)
Clachan. Arg 4C 140
   (on Lismore)
Clachan. High 2H 167
   (nr. Bettyhill)
Clachan. High 2D 155
   (nr. Staffin)
Clachan. High 1C 154
   (nr. Uig)
Clachan. High 5E 155
   (on Raasay)
Clachan Farm. Arg 2A 134
Clachan na Luib. W Isl 2D 170
Clachan of Campsie. E Dun 2H 127
Clachan of Glendaruel. Arg 1A 126
Clachan-Seil. Arg 2E 133
Clachan Shannda. W Isl 1D 170
Clachan Strachur. Arg 3H 133
Clachbreck. Arg 2F 125
Clachnaharry. High 4A 158
Clachtoll. High 1E 163
Clackmannan. Clac 4B 136
Clackmarras. Mor 3G 159
Clacton-on-Sea. Essx 4E 55
Cladach a Chaolais. W Isl 2C 170
Cladach Chairinis. W Isl 3D 170
Cladach Chirceboist. W Isl 2C 170
Cladach Iolaraigh. W Isl 2C 170
Cladich. Arg 1H 133
Cladswell. Worc 5E 61
Claggan. High 1F 141
   (nr. Fort William)
Claggan. High 4A 140
   (nr. Lochaline)
Claigan. High 3B 154
Clandown. Bath 1B 22
Clanfield. Hants 1E 17
Clanfield. Oxon 5A 50
Clanville. Hants 2B 24
Clanville. Som 3B 22
Claonaig. Arg 4G 125
Clapgate. Dors 2F 15
Clapgate. Herts 3E 53
Clapham. Bed 5H 63
Clapham. Devn 4B 12
Clapham. G Lon 3D 39
Clapham. N Yor 3G 97
Clapham. W Sus 5B 26
Clap Hill. Kent 2E 29
Clappers. Bord 4F 131
Clappersgate. Cumb 4E 103
Clapphoull. Shet 9F 173
Clapton. Som 2H 13
   (nr. Crewkerne)
Clapton. Som 1B 22
   (nr. Radstock)
Clapton-in-Gordano. N Som 4H 33
Clapton-on-the-Hill. Glos 4G 49
Clapworthy. Devn 4G 19
Clara Vale. Tyne 3E 115
Clarbeston. Pemb 2E 43
Clarbeston Road. Pemb 2E 43
Clarborough. Notts 2E 87
Clare. Suff 1A 54
Clarebrand. Dum 3E 111
Clarencefield. Dum 3B 112
Clarilaw. Bord 3H 119
Clark's Green. Surr 2C 26
Clark's Hill. Linc 3C 76
Clarkston. E Ren 4G 127
Clasheddy. High 2G 167
Clashindarroch. Abers 5B 160
Clashmore. High 5E 165
   (nr. Dornoch)
Clashmore. High 1E 163
   (nr. Stoer)
Clashnessie. High 5A 166
Clashnoir. Mor 1G 151
Clate. Shet 5G 173
Clathick. Per 1H 135
Clathy. Per 2B 136
Clatt. Abers 1C 152
Clatter. Powy 1B 58
Clatterford. IOW 4C 16
Clatworthy. Som 3D 20
Claughton. Lanc 3E 97
   (nr. Caton)
Claughton. Lanc 5E 97
   (nr. Garstang)
Claughton. Mers 2F 83
Claverdon. Warw 4F 61
Claverham. N Som 5H 33
Clavering. Essx 2E 53
Claverley. Shrp 1B 60
Claverton. Bath 5C 34
Clawdd-coch. V Glam 4D 32
Clawdd-newydd. Den 5C 82
Clawson Hill. Leics 3E 75
Clawton. Devn 3D 10
Claxby. Linc 3D 88
   (nr. Alford)
Claxby. Linc 1A 88
   (nr. Market Rasen)
Claxton. Norf 5F 79
Claxton. N Yor 4A 100
Claybrooke Magna. Leics 2B 62
Claybrooke Parva. Leics 2B 62
Clay Common. Suff 2G 67
Clay Coton. Nptn 3C 62
Clay Cross. Derbs 4A 86
Claydon. Oxon 5B 62

Claydon. Suff 5D 66
Clay End. Herts 3D 52
Claygate. Dum 2E 113
Claygate. Kent 1B 28
Claygate. Surr 4C 38
Claygate Cross. Kent 5H 39
Clayhall. Hants 3E 16
Clayhanger. Devn 4D 20
Clayhanger. W Mid 5E 73
Clayhidon. Devn 1E 13
Clay Hill. Bris 4B 34
Clayhill. E Sus 3C 28
Clayhill. Hants 2B 16
Clayhithe. Cambs 4E 65
Clayholes. Ang 5E 145
Clay Lake. Linc 3B 76
Clayock. High 3D 168
Claypits. Glos 5C 48
Claypole. Linc 1F 75
Claythorpe. Linc 3D 88
Clayton. G Man 1C 84
Clayton. S Yor 4E 93
Clayton. Staf 1C 72
Clayton. W Sus 4E 27
Clayton. W Yor 1B 92
Clayton Green. Lanc 2D 90
Clayton-le-Moors. Lanc 1F 91
Clayton-le-Woods. Lanc 2D 90
Clayton West. W Yor 3C 92
Clayworth. Notts 2E 87
Cleadale. High 5C 146
Cleadon. Tyne 3G 115
Clearbrook. Devn 2B 8
Clearwell. Glos 5A 48
Cleasby. N Yor 3F 105
Cleat. Orkn 3D 172
   (nr. Braehead)
Cleat. Orkn 9D 172
   (nr. St Margaret's Hope)
Cleatlam. Dur 3E 105
Cleator. Cumb 3B 102
Cleator Moor. Cumb 3B 102
Cleckheaton. W Yor 2B 92
Cleedownton. Shrp 2H 59
Cleehill. Shrp 3H 59
Cleekhimin. N Lan 4A 128
Clee St Margaret. Shrp 2H 59
Cleestanton. Shrp 3H 59
Cleethorpes. NE Lin 4G 95
Cleeton St Mary. Shrp 3A 60
Cleeve. N Som 5H 33
Cleeve. Oxon 3E 36
Cleeve Hill. Glos 3E 49
Cleeve Prior. Worc 1F 49
Clehonger. Here 2H 47
Cleigh. Arg 1F 133
Cleish. Per 4C 136
Cleland. N Lan 4B 128
Clench Common. Wilts 5G 35
Clenchwarton. Norf 3E 77
Clennell. Nmbd 4D 120
Clent. Worc 3D 60
Cleobury Mortimer. Shrp 3A 60
Cleobury North. Shrp 2A 60
Clephanton. High 3C 158
Clerkhill. High 2H 167
Clestrain. Orkn 7C 172
Clevancy. Wilts 4F 35
Clevedon. N Som 4H 33
Cleveley. Oxon 3B 50
Cleveleys. Lanc 5C 96
Clevelode. Worc 1D 48
Cleverton. Wilts 3E 35
Clewer. Som 1H 21
Cley next the Sea. Norf 1C 78
Cliaid. W Isl 8B 170
Cliasmol. W Isl 7C 171
Clibberswick. Shet 1H 173
Cliburn. Cumb 2G 103
Cliddesden. Hants 2E 25
Clieves Hills. Lanc 4B 90
Cliff. Warw 1G 61
Cliffburn. Ang 4F 145
Cliffe. Medw 3B 40
Cliffe. N Yor 3F 105
   (nr. Darlington)
Cliffe. N Yor 1G 93
   (nr. Selby)
Cliff End. E Sus 4C 28
Cliffe Woods. Medw 3B 40
Clifford. Here 1F 47
Clifford. W Yor 5G 99
Clifford Chambers. Warw 5F 61
Clifford's Mesne. Glos 3B 48
Cliffs End. Kent 4H 41
Clifton. Bris 4A 34
Clifton. C Beds 2B 52
Clifton. Cumb 2G 103
Clifton. Derbs 1F 73
Clifton. Devn 2G 19
Clifton. G Man 4F 91
Clifton. Lanc 1C 90
Clifton. Nmbd 1F 115
Clifton. N Yor 5D 98
Clifton. Nott 2C 74
Clifton. Oxon 2C 50
Clifton. S Yor 1C 86
Clifton. Stir 5H 141
Clifton. W Yor 2B 92
Clifton. Worc 1D 48
Clifton. York 4H 99
Clifton Campville. Staf 4G 73

Clifton Hampden. *Oxon*	2D	**36**
Clifton Hill. *Worc*	4B	**60**
Clifton Reynes. *Mil*	5G	**63**
Clifton upon Dunsmore.		
Warw	3C	**62**
Clifton upon Teme. *Worc*	4B	**60**
Cliftonville. *Kent*	3H	**41**
Cliftonville. *Norf*	2F	**79**
Climping. *W Sus*	5A	**26**
Climpy. *S Lan*	4C	**128**
Clint. *N Yor*	4E	**99**
Clint Green. *Norf*	4C	**78**
Clintmains. *Bord*	1A	**120**
Cliobh. *W Isl*	4C	**171**
Clipiau. *Gwyn*	4H	**69**
Clippesby. *Norf*	4G	**79**
Clippings Green. *Norf*	4C	**78**
Clipsham. *Rut*	4G	**75**
Clipston. *Nptn*	2E	**62**
Clipston. *Notts*	2D	**74**
Clipstone. *Notts*	4C	**86**
Clitheroe. *Lanc*	5G	**97**
Cliuthar. *W Isl*	8D	**171**
Clive. *Shrp*	3H	**71**
Clivocast. *Shet*	1H	**173**
Clixby. *Linc*	4D	**94**
Clocaenog. *Den*	5C	**82**
Clochan. *Mor*	2B	**160**
Clochforbie. *Abers*	3F	**161**
Clock Face. *Mers*	1H	**83**
Cloddiau. *Powy*	5E	**70**
Cloddymoss. *Mor*	2D	**159**
Clodock. *Here*	3G	**47**
Cloford. *Som*	2C	**22**
Clola. *Abers*	4H	**161**
Clophill. *C Beds*	2A	**52**
Clopton. *Nptn*	2H	**63**
Clopton Corner. *Suff*	5E	**66**
Clopton Green. *Suff*	5G	**65**
Closeburn. *Dum*	5A	**118**
Close Clark. *IOM*	4B	**108**
Closworth. *Som*	1A	**14**
Clothall. *Herts*	2C	**52**
Clotton. *Ches W*	4H	**83**
Clough. *G Man*	3H	**91**
Clough. *W Yor*	3A	**92**
Clough Foot. *W Yor*	2H	**91**
Cloughton. *N Yor*	5H	**107**
Cloughton Newlands. *N Yor*	5H	**107**
Clousta. *Shet*	6E	**173**
Clouston. *Orkn*	6B	**172**
Clova. *Abers*	1B	**152**
Clova. *Ang*	1C	**144**
Clovelly. *Devn*	4D	**18**
Clovenfords. *Bord*	1G	**119**
Clovenstone. *Abers*	2E	**153**
Clovullin. *High*	2E	**141**
Clowne. *Derbs*	3B	**86**
Clows Top. *Worc*	3B	**60**
Cloy. *Wrex*	1F	**71**
Cluanie Inn. *High*	2C	**148**
Cluanie Lodge. *High*	2C	**148**
Cluddley. *Telf*	5A	**72**
Clun. *Shrp*	2F	**59**
Clunas. *High*	4C	**158**
Clunbury. *Shrp*	2F	**59**
Clunderwen. *Pemb*	3F	**43**
Clune. *High*	1B	**150**
Clunes. *High*	5E	**148**
Clungunford. *Shrp*	3F	**59**
Clunie. *Per*	4A	**144**
Clunton. *Shrp*	2F	**59**
Cluny. *Fife*	4E	**137**
Clutton. *Bath*	1B	**22**
Clutton. *Ches W*	5G	**83**
Clwt-y-bont. *Gwyn*	4E	**81**
Clwydfagwyr. *Mer T*	5D	**46**
Clydach. *Mon*	4F	**47**
Clydach. *Swan*	5G	**45**
Clydach Vale. *Rhon*	2C	**32**
Clydebank. *W Dun*	2G	**127**
Clydey. *Pemb*	1G	**43**
Clyffe Pypard. *Wilts*	4F	**35**
Clynder. *Arg*	1D	**126**
Clyne. *Neat*	5B	**46**
Clynelish. *High*	3F	**165**
Clynnog-fawr. *Gwyn*	1D	**68**
Clyro. *Powy*	1F	**47**
Clyst Honiton. *Devn*	3C	**12**
Clyst Hydon. *Devn*	2D	**12**
Clyst St George. *Devn*	4C	**12**
Clyst St Lawrence. *Devn*	2D	**12**
Clyst St Mary. *Devn*	3C	**12**
Clyth. *High*	5E	**169**
Cnip. *W Isl*	4C	**171**
Cnoc Amhlaigh. *W Isl*	4H	**171**
Cnwcau. *Pemb*	1C	**44**
Cnwch Coch. *Cdgn*	3F	**57**
Coad's Green. *Corn*	5C	**10**
Coal Aston. *Derbs*	3A	**86**
Coalbrookdale. *Telf*	5A	**72**
Coalbrookvale. *Blae*	5F	**47**
Coalburn. *S Lan*	1H	**117**
Coalburns. *Tyne*	3E	**115**
Coalcleugh. *Nmbd*	5B	**114**
Coaley. *Glos*	5C	**48**
Coalford. *Abers*	4F	**153**
Coalhall. *E Ayr*	3D	**116**
Coalhill. *Essx*	1B	**40**
Coalpit Heath. *S Glo*	3B	**34**
Coal Pool. *W Mid*	5E	**73**
Coalport. *Telf*	5B	**72**
Coalsnaughton. *Clac*	4B	**136**
Coaltown of Balgonie. *Fife*	4F	**137**
Coaltown of Wemyss. *Fife*	4F	**137**
Coalville. *Leics*	4B	**74**
coalville. *Mil*	5F	**63**
Coalway. *Glos*	4A	**48**
Coanwood. *Nmbd*	4H	**113**
Coat. *Som*	4H	**21**
Coatbridge. *N Lan*	3A	**128**
Coatdyke. *N Lan*	3A	**128**
Coate. *Swin*	3G	**35**
Coate. *Wilts*	5F	**35**
Coates. *Cambs*	1C	**64**
Coates. *Glos*	5E	**49**
Coates. *Linc*	2G	**87**
Coates. *W Sus*	4A	**26**
Coatham. *Red C*	2C	**106**
Coatham Mundeville. *Darl*	2F	**105**
Cobbaton. *Devn*	4G	**19**
Coberley. *Glos*	4E	**49**
Cobhall Common. *Here*	2H	**47**
Cobham. *Kent*	4A	**40**
Cobham. *Surr*	4C	**38**
Cobnash. *Here*	4G	**59**
Coburg. *Devn*	5B	**12**
Cockayne. *N Yor*	5D	**106**
Cockayne Hatley. *C Beds*	1C	**52**
Cock Bank. *Wrex*	1F	**71**
Cock Bridge. *Abers*	3G	**151**
Cockburnspath. *Bord*	2D	**130**
Cock Clarks. *Essx*	5B	**54**
Cockenzie and Port Seton.		
E Lot	2H	**129**
Cockerham. *Lanc*	4D	**96**
Cockermouth. *Cumb*	1C	**102**
Cockernhoe. *Herts*	3B	**52**
Cockfield. *Dur*	2E	**105**
Cockfield. *Suff*	5B	**66**
Cockfosters. *G Lon*	1D	**39**
Cock Gate. *Here*	4G	**59**
Cock Green. *Essx*	4G	**53**
Cocking. *W Sus*	1G	**17**
Cocking Causeway. *W Sus*	1G	**17**
Cockington. *Torb*	2F	**9**
Cocklake. *Som*	2H	**21**
Cocklaw. *Abers*	4H	**161**
Cocklaw. *Nmbd*	2C	**114**
Cockley Beck. *Cumb*	4D	**102**
Cockley Cley. *Norf*	5G	**77**
Cockmuir. *Abers*	3G	**161**
Cockpole Green. *Wind*	3G	**37**
Cockshutford. *Shrp*	2H	**59**
Cockshutt. *Shrp*	3G	**71**
Cockthorpe. *Norf*	1B	**78**
Cockwood. *Devn*	4C	**12**
Cockyard. *Derbs*	3E	**85**
Cockyard. *Here*	2H	**47**
Codda. *Corn*	5B	**10**
Coddenham. *Suff*	5D	**66**
Coddenham Green. *Suff*	5D	**66**
Coddington. *Ches W*	5G	**83**
Coddington. *Here*	1C	**48**
Coddington. *Notts*	5F	**87**
Codford St Mary. *Wilts*	3E	**23**
Codford St Peter. *Wilts*	3E	**23**
Codicote. *Herts*	4C	**52**
Codmore Hill. *W Sus*	3B	**26**
Codnor. *Derbs*	1B	**74**
Codrington. *S Glo*	4C	**34**
Codsall. *Staf*	5C	**72**
Codsall Wood. *Staf*	5C	**72**
Coed Duon. *Cphy*	2E	**33**
Coedely. *Rhon*	3D	**32**
Coedglasson. *Powy*	4C	**58**
Coedkernew. *Newp*	3F	**33**
Coed Morgan. *Mon*	4G	**47**
Coedpoeth. *Wrex*	5E	**83**
Coedway. *Powy*	4F	**71**
Coed-y-bryn. *Cdgn*	1D	**44**
Coed-y-paen. *Mon*	2G	**33**
Coed-yr-ynys. *Powy*	3E	**47**
Coed Ystumgwern. *Gwyn*	3E	**69**
Coelbren. *Powy*	4B	**46**
Coffinswell. *Devn*	2E	**9**
Cofton Hackett. *Worc*	3E	**61**
Cogan. *V Glam*	4E	**33**
Cogenhoe. *Nptn*	4F	**63**
Cogges. *Oxon*	5B	**50**
Coggeshall. *Essx*	3B	**54**
Coggeshall Hamlet. *Essx*	3B	**54**
Coggins Mill. *E Sus*	3G	**27**
Coignafearn Lodge. *High*	2A	**150**
Coig Peighinnean. *W Isl*	1H	**171**
Coig Peighinnean Bhuirgh.		
W Isl	2G	**171**
Coilleag. *W Isl*	7C	**170**
Coillemore. *High*	1A	**158**
Coillore. *High*	5C	**154**
Coire an Fhuarain. *W Isl*	4E	**171**
Coity. *B'end*	3C	**32**
Cokhay Green. *Derbs*	3G	**73**
Col. *W Isl*	3G	**171**
Colaboll. *High*	2C	**164**
Colan. *Corn*	2C	**6**
Colaton Raleigh. *Devn*	4D	**12**
Colbost. *High*	4B	**154**
Colburn. *N Yor*	5E	**105**
Colby. *Cumb*	2H	**103**
Colby. *IOM*	4B	**108**
Colby. *Norf*	2E	**78**
Colchester. *Essx*	3D	**54**
Cold Ash. *W Ber*	5D	**36**
Cold Ashby. *Nptn*	3D	**62**
Cold Ashton. *S Glo*	4C	**34**
Cold Aston. *Glos*	4G	**49**
Coldbackie. *High*	3G	**167**
Cold Blow. *Pemb*	3F	**43**
Cold Brayfield. *Mil*	5G	**63**
Cold Cotes. *N Yor*	2G	**97**
Coldean. *Brig*	5E	**27**
Colden. *W Yor*	2H	**91**
Colden Common. *Hants*	4C	**24**
Coldfair Green. *Suff*	4G	**67**
Coldham. *Cambs*	5D	**76**
Coldham. *Staf*	5C	**72**
Cold Hanworth. *Linc*	2H	**87**
Coldharbour. *Corn*	4B	**6**
Cold Harbour. *Dors*	3E	**15**
Coldharbour. *Glos*	5A	**48**
Coldharbour. *Kent*	5G	**39**
Coldharbour. *Surr*	1C	**26**
Cold Hatton. *Telf*	3A	**72**
Cold Hatton Heath. *Telf*	3A	**72**
Cold Hesledon. *Dur*	5H	**115**
Cold Hiendley. *W Yor*	3D	**92**
Cold Higham. *Nptn*	5D	**62**
Coldingham. *Bord*	3F	**131**
Cold Kirby. *N Yor*	1H	**99**
Coldmeece. *Staf*	2C	**72**
Cold Northcott. *Corn*	4C	**10**
Cold Norton. *Essx*	5B	**54**
Cold Overton. *Leics*	4F	**75**
Coldrain. *Per*	3C	**136**
Coldred. *Kent*	1G	**29**
Coldridge. *Devn*	2G	**11**
Cold Row. *Lanc*	5C	**96**
Coldstream. *Bord*	5E	**131**
Coldwaltham. *W Sus*	4B	**26**
Coldwell. *Here*	2H	**47**
Coldwells. *Abers*	5H	**161**
Coldwells Croft. *Abers*	1C	**152**
Cole. *Shet*	5E	**173**
Cole. *Som*	3B	**22**
Colebatch. *Shrp*	2F	**59**
Colebrook. *Devn*	2D	**12**
Colebrooke. *Devn*	2A	**12**
Coleburn. *Mor*	3G	**159**
Coleby. *Linc*	4G	**87**
Coleby. *N Lin*	3B	**94**
Cole End. *Warw*	2G	**61**
Coleford. *Devn*	2A	**12**
Coleford. *Glos*	4A	**48**
Coleford. *Som*	2B	**22**
Colegate End. *Norf*	2D	**66**
Cole Green. *Herts*	4C	**52**
Cole Henley. *Hants*	1C	**24**
Colehill. *Dors*	2F	**15**
Coleman Green. *Herts*	4B	**52**
Coleman's Hatch. *E Sus*	2F	**27**
Colemere. *Shrp*	2G	**71**
Colemore. *Hants*	3F	**25**
Colemore Green. *Shrp*	1B	**60**
Colenorton. *Leics*	4B	**74**
Colerne. *Wilts*	4D	**34**
Colesbourne. *Glos*	4E	**49**
Colesden. *Bed*	5A	**64**
Coles Green. *Worc*	5B	**60**
Coleshill. *Buck*	1A	**38**
Coleshill. *Oxon*	2H	**35**
Coleshill. *Warw*	2G	**61**
Colestocks. *Devn*	2D	**12**
Colethrop. *Glos*	4D	**48**
Coley. *Bath*	1A	**22**
Colgate. *W Sus*	2D	**26**
Colinsburgh. *Fife*	3G	**137**
Colinton. *Edin*	3F	**129**
Colintraive. *Arg*	2B	**126**
Colkirk. *Norf*	3B	**78**
Collace. *Per*	5B	**144**
Collam. *W Isl*	8D	**171**
Collaton. *Devn*	5D	**8**
Collaton St Mary. *Torb*	2E	**9**
College of Roseisle. *Mor*	2F	**159**
Collessie. *Fife*	2E	**137**
Collier Row. *G Lon*	1F	**39**
Colliers End. *Herts*	3D	**52**
Collier Street. *Kent*	1B	**28**
Colliery Row. *Tyne*	5G	**115**
Collieston. *Abers*	1H	**153**
Collin. *Dum*	2B	**112**
Collingbourne Ducis. *Wilts*	1H	**23**
Collingbourne Kingston.		
Wilts	1H	**23**
Collingham. *Notts*	4F	**87**
Collingham. *W Yor*	5F	**99**
Collingtree. *Nptn*	5E	**63**
Collins Green. *Warr*	1H	**83**
Collins Green. *Worc*	5B	**60**
Colliston. *Ang*	4F	**145**
Colliton. *Devn*	2D	**12**
Collydean. *Fife*	3E	**137**
Collyweston. *Nptn*	5G	**75**
Colmonell. *S Ayr*	1G	**109**
Colmworth. *Bed*	5A	**64**
Colnbrook. *Slo*	3B	**38**
Colne. *Cambs*	3C	**64**
Colne. *Lanc*	5A	**98**
Colne Engaine. *Essx*	2B	**54**
Colney. *Norf*	5D	**78**
Colney Heath. *Herts*	5C	**52**
Colney Street. *Herts*	5B	**52**
Coln Rogers. *Glos*	5F	**49**
Coln St Aldwyns. *Glos*	5G	**49**
Coln St Dennis. *Glos*	4F	**49**
Colpitts Grange. *Nmbd*	4C	**114**
Colpy. *Abers*	5D	**160**
Colscott. *Devn*	1D	**10**
Colsterdale. *N Yor*	1D	**98**
Colsterworth. *Linc*	3G	**75**
Colston Bassett. *Notts*	2D	**74**
Colstoun House. *E Lot*	2B	**130**
Coltfield. *Mor*	2F	**159**
Colthouse. *Cumb*	5E	**103**
Coltishall. *Norf*	4E	**79**
Coltness. *N Lan*	4A	**128**
Colton. *Cumb*	1C	**96**
Colton. *Norf*	5D	**78**
Colton. *N Yor*	5H	**99**
Colton. *Staf*	3E	**73**
Colton. *W Yor*	1D	**92**
Colt's Hill. *Kent*	1H	**27**
Col Uarach. *W Isl*	4G	**171**
Colvend. *Dum*	4F	**111**
Colvister. *Shet*	2G	**173**
Colwall Green. *Here*	1C	**48**
Colwall Stone. *Here*	1C	**48**
Colwell. *Nmbd*	2C	**114**
Colwich. *Staf*	3E	**73**
Colwick. *Notts*	1D	**74**
Colwinston. *V Glam*	4C	**32**
Colworth. *W Sus*	5A	**26**
Colwyn Bay. *Cnwy*	3A	**82**
Colyford. *Devn*	3F	**13**
Colyton. *Devn*	3F	**13**
Combe. *Devn*	2D	**8**
Combe. *Here*	4F	**59**
Combe. *Oxon*	4C	**60**
Combe. *W Ber*	5B	**36**
Combe Almer. *Dors*	3E	**15**
Combebow. *Devn*	4E	**11**
Combe Down. *Bath*	5C	**34**
Combe Fishacre. *Devn*	2E	**9**
Combe Florey. *Som*	3E	**21**
Combe Hay. *Bath*	1C	**22**
Combeinteignhead. *Devn*	5C	**12**
Combe Martin. *Devn*	2F	**19**
Combe Moor. *Here*	4F	**59**
Combe Raleigh. *Devn*	2E	**12**
Comberbach. *Ches W*	3A	**84**
Comberford. *Staf*	5F	**73**
Comberton. *Cambs*	5C	**64**
Comberton. *Here*	4G	**59**
Combe St Nicholas. *Som*	1G	**13**
Combpyne. *Devn*	3F	**13**
Combridge. *Staf*	2E	**73**
Combrook. *Warw*	5H	**61**
Combs. *Derbs*	3E	**85**
Combs. *Suff*	5C	**66**
Combs Ford. *Suff*	5C	**66**
Combwich. *Som*	2F	**21**
Comers. *Abers*	3D	**152**
Comhampton. *Worc*	4C	**60**
Comins Coch. *Cdgn*	2F	**57**
Comley. *Shrp*	1G	**59**
Commercial End. *Cambs*	4E	**65**
Commins. *Powy*	3D	**70**
Commins Coch. *Powy*	5H	**69**
Commondale. *N Yor*	3D	**106**
Commonldale. *Here*	2A	**48**
Common End. *Cumb*	2B	**102**
Common Hill. *Here*	2A	**48**
Common Moor. *Corn*	2G	**7**
Common Platt. *Wilts*	3G	**35**
Commonside. *Ches W*	3H	**83**
Common Side. *Derbs*	3H	**85**
		(nr. Chesterfield)
Commonside. *Derbs*	1G	**73**
		(nr. Derby)
Common, The. *Wilts*	3F	**23**
		(nr. Salisbury)
Common, The. *Wilts*	3F	**35**
		(nr. Swindon)
Compstall. *G Man*	1D	**84**
Compton. *Devn*	2E	**9**
Compton. *Hants*	4C	**24**
Compton. *Staf*	2C	**60**
Compton. *Surr*	1A	**26**
Compton. *W Ber*	3D	**36**
Compton. *W Sus*	1F	**17**
Compton. *Wilts*	1G	**23**
Compton Abbas. *Dors*	1D	**14**
Compton Abdale. *Glos*	4F	**49**
Compton Bassett. *Wilts*	4F	**35**
Compton Beauchamp. *Oxon*	3A	**36**
Compton Bishop. *Som*	1G	**21**
Compton Chamberlayne.		
Wilts	4F	**23**
Compton Dando. *Bath*	5B	**34**
Compton Dundon. *Som*	3H	**21**
Compton Greenfield. *S Glo*	3A	**34**
Compton Martin. *Bath*	1A	**22**
Compton Pauncefoot. *Som*	4B	**22**
Compton Valence. *Dors*	3A	**14**
Comrie. *Fife*	1D	**128**
Comrie. *Per*	1G	**135**
Conaglen. *High*	2E	**141**
Conchra. *Arg*	1B	**126**
Conchra. *High*	1A	**148**
Conder Green. *Lanc*	4D	**96**
Conderton. *Worc*	2E	**49**
Condicote. *Glos*	3G	**49**
Condorrat. *N Lan*	2A	**128**
Condover. *Shrp*	5G	**71**
Coneyhurst Common. *W Sus*	3C	**26**
Coneysthorpe. *N Yor*	2B	**100**
Coneythorpe. *N Yor*	4F	**99**
Coney Weston. *Suff*	3B	**66**
Conford. *Hants*	3G	**25**
Congdon's Shop. *Corn*	5C	**10**
Congerstone. *Leics*	5A	**74**
Congham. *Norf*	3G	**77**
Congleton. *Ches E*	4C	**84**
Congl-y-wal. *Gwyn*	1G	**69**
Congresbury. *N Som*	5H	**33**
Congreve. *Staf*	4D	**72**
Conham. *S Glo*	4B	**34**
Conicaval. *Mor*	3D	**159**
Coningsby. *Linc*	5B	**88**
Conington. *Cambs*	4C	**64**
		(nr. Fenstanton)
Conington. *Cambs*	2A	**64**
		(nr. Sawtry)
Conisbrough. *S Yor*	1C	**86**
Conisby. *Arg*	3A	**124**
Conisholme. *Linc*	1D	**88**
Coniston. *Cumb*	5E	**102**
Coniston. *E Yor*	1E	**95**
Coniston Cold. *N Yor*	4B	**98**
Conistone. *N Yor*	3B	**98**
Connah's Quay. *Flin*	4E	**83**
Connel. *Arg*	5D	**140**
Connel Park. *E Ayr*	3F	**117**
Connista. *High*	1D	**154**
Connor Downs. *Corn*	3C	**4**
Conock. *Wilts*	1F	**23**
Conon Bridge. *High*	3H	**157**
Cononley. *N Yor*	5B	**98**
Cononsyth. *Ang*	4E	**145**
Conordan. *High*	5E	**155**
Consall. *Staf*	1D	**73**
Consett. *Dur*	4E	**115**
Constable Burton. *N Yor*	5E	**105**
Constantine. *Corn*	4E	**5**
Constantine Bay. *Corn*	1C	**6**
Contin. *High*	3G	**157**
Contullich. *High*	1A	**158**
Conwy. *Cnwy*	3G	**81**
Conyer. *Kent*	4D	**40**
Conyer's Green. *Suff*	4A	**66**
Cooden. *E Sus*	5B	**28**
Cooil. *IOM*	4C	**108**
Cookbury. *Devn*	2E	**11**
Cookbury Wick. *Devn*	2D	**11**
Cookham. *Wind*	3G	**37**
Cookham Dean. *Wind*	3G	**37**
Cookham Rise. *Wind*	3G	**37**
Cookhill. *Worc*	5E	**61**
Cookley. *Suff*	3F	**67**
Cookley. *Worc*	2C	**60**
Cookley Green. *Oxon*	2E	**37**
Cookney. *Abers*	4F	**153**
Cooksbridge. *E Sus*	4F	**27**
Cooksey Green. *Worc*	4D	**60**
Cookshill. *Staf*	1D	**72**
Cooksmill Green. *Essx*	5G	**53**
Coolham. *W Sus*	3C	**26**
Cooling. *Medw*	3B	**40**
Cooling Street. *Medw*	3B	**40**
Coombe. *Corn*	1C	**10**
		(nr. Bude)
Coombe. *Corn*	3D	**6**
		(nr. St Austell)
Coombe. *Corn*	4C	**6**
		(nr. Truro)
Coombe. *Devn*	3E	**12**
		(nr. Sidmouth)
Coombe. *Devn*	5C	**12**
		(nr. Teignmouth)
Coombe. *Glos*	2C	**34**
Coombe. *Hants*	4E	**25**
Coombe. *Wilts*	1G	**23**
Coombe Bissett. *Wilts*	4G	**23**
Coombe Hill. *Glos*	3D	**49**
Coombe Keynes. *Dors*	4D	**14**
Coombes. *W Sus*	5C	**26**
Coopersale Common.		
Essx	5E	**53**
Coopersale Street. *Essx*	5E	**53**
Cooper's Corner. *Kent*	1F	**27**
Cooper Street. *Kent*	5H	**41**
Cootham. *W Sus*	4B	**26**
Copalder Corner. *Cambs*	1C	**64**
Copdock. *Suff*	1E	**54**
Copford. *Essx*	3C	**54**
Copford Green. *Essx*	3C	**54**
Copgrove. *N Yor*	3F	**99**
Copister. *Shet*	4F	**173**
Cople. *Bed*	1B	**52**
Copley. *Dur*	2D	**105**
Coplow Dale. *Derbs*	3F	**85**
Copmanthorpe. *York*	5H	**99**
Copp. *Lanc*	1C	**90**
Coppathorne. *Corn*	2C	**10**
Coppenhall. *Ches E*	5B	**84**
Coppenhall. *Staf*	4D	**72**
Coppenhall Moss. *Ches E*	5B	**84**
Copperhouse. *Corn*	3C	**4**
Coppicegate. *Shrp*	2B	**60**
Coppingford. *Cambs*	2A	**64**
Copplestone. *Devn*	2A	**12**
Coppull. *Lanc*	3D	**90**
Coppull Moor. *Lanc*	3D	**90**
Copsale. *W Sus*	3C	**26**
Copster Green. *Lanc*	1E	**91**
Copston Magna. *Warw*	2B	**62**
Copt Green. *Warw*	4F	**61**
Copthall Green. *Essx*	5E	**53**
Copt Heath. *W Mid*	3F	**61**

Copt Hewick—Crockey Hill

Copt Hewick. N Yor 2F 99
Copthill. Dur 5B 114
Copthorne. W Sus 2E 27
Coptiviney. Shrp 2G 71
Copy's Green. Norf 2B 78
Copythorne. Hants 1B 16
Corbridge. Nmbd 3C 114
Corby. Nptn 2F 63
Corby Glen. Linc 3H 75
Cordon. N Ayr 2E 123
Coreley. Shrp 3A 60
Corfe. Som 1F 13
Corfe Castle. Dors 4E 15
Corfe Mullen. Dors 3E 15
Corfton. Shrp 2G 59
Corgarff. Abers 3G 151
Corhampton. Hants 4E 24
Corlae. Dum 5F 117
Corlannau. Neat 2A 32
Corley. Warw 2H 61
Corley Ash. Warw 2G 61
Corley Moor. Warw 2G 61
Cormiston. S Lan 1C 118
Cornaa. IOM 3D 108
Cornaigbeg. Arg 4A 138
Cornaigmore. Arg 2D 138
(on Coll)
Cornaigmore. Arg 4A 138
(on Tiree)
Corner Row. Lanc 1C 90
Corney. Cumb 5C 102
Cornforth. Dur 1A 106
Cornhill. Abers 3C 160
Cornhill. High 4C 164
Cornhill-on-Tweed. Nmbd 1C 120
Cornholme. W Yor 2H 91
Cornish Hall End. Essx 2G 53
Cornquoy. Orkn 7E 172
Cornriggs. Dur 5B 114
Cornsay. Dur 5E 115
Cornsay Colliery. Dur 5E 115
Corntown. High 3H 157
Corntown. V Glam 4C 32
Cornwell. Oxon 3A 50
Cornwood. Devn 3C 8
Cornworthy. Devn 3E 9
Corpach. High 1E 141
Corpusty. Norf 3D 78
Corra. Dum 3F 111
Corran. High 2E 141
(nr. Arnisdale)
Corran. High 3A 148
(nr. Fort William)
Corrany. IOM 3D 108
Corribeg. High 1D 141
Corrie. N Ayr 5B 126
Corrie Common. Dum 1D 112
Corriecravie. N Ayr 3D 122
Corriekinloch. High 1A 164
Corriemoillie. High 2F 157
Corrievarkie Lodge. Per 1C 142
Corrievorrie. High 1B 150
Corrigall. Orkn 6C 172
Corrimony. High 5F 157
Corringham. Linc 1F 87
Corringham. Thur 2B 40
Corris. Gwyn 5G 69
Corris Uchaf. Gwyn 5G 69
Corrour Shooting Lodge.
High 2B 142
Corry. High 1E 147
Corrybrough. High 1C 150
Corrygills. N Ayr 2E 123
Corry of Ardnagrask. High 4H 157
Corsback. High 1E 169
(nr. Dunnet)
Corsback. High 3E 169
(nr. Halkirk)
Corscombe. Dors 2A 14
Corse. Abers 4D 160
Corse. Glos 3C 48
Corsehill. Abers 3G 161
Corse Lawn. Worc 2D 48
Corse of Kinnoir. Abers 4C 160
Corsham. Wilts 4D 34
Corsley. Wilts 2D 22
Corsley Heath. Wilts 2D 22
Corsock. Dum 2E 111
Corston. Bath 5B 34
Corston. Wilts 3E 35
Corstorphine. Edin 2F 129
Cortachy. Ang 3C 144
Corton. Suff 1H 67
Corton. Wilts 2E 23
Corton Denham. Som 4B 22
Corwar House. S Ayr 1H 109
Corwen. Den 1C 70
Coryates. Dors 4B 14
Coryton. Devn 4E 11
Coryton. Thur 2B 40
Cosby. Leics 1C 62
Coscote. Oxon 3D 36
Coseley. W Mid 1D 60
Cosgrove. Nptn 1F 51
Cosham. Port 2E 17
Cosheston. Pemb 4E 43
Coskills. N Lin 3D 94
Cosmeston. V Glam 5E 33
Cossall. Notts 1B 74
Cossington. Leics 4D 74
Cossington. Som 2G 21
Costa. Orkn 5C 172
Costessey. Norf 4D 78
Costock. Notts 3C 74
Coston. Leics 3F 75
Coston. Norf 5C 78
Cote. Oxon 5B 50
Cotebrook. Ches W 4H 83
Cotehill. Cumb 4F 113
Cotes. Cumb 1D 97
Cotes. Leics 3C 74
Cotes. Staf 2C 72
Cotesbach. Leics 2C 62
Cotes Heath. Staf 2C 72
Cotford St Luke. Som 4E 21
Cotgrave. Notts 2D 74
Cothall. Abers 2F 153
Cotham. Notts 1E 75
Cothelstone. Som 3E 21
Cotheridge. Worc 5B 60
Cotherstone. Dur 3D 104
Cothill. Oxon 2C 36
Cotland. Mon 5A 48
Cotleigh. Devn 2F 13
Cotmanhay. Derbs 1B 74
Coton. Cambs 5D 64
Coton. Nptn 3D 62
Coton. Staf 3C 72
(nr. Gnosall)
Coton. Staf 2D 73
(nr. Stone)
Coton. Staf 5F 73
(nr. Tamworth)
Coton Clanford. Staf 3C 72
Coton Hayes. Staf 2D 73
Coton Hill. Shrp 4G 71
Coton in the Clay. Staf 3F 73
Coton in the Elms. Derbs 4G 73
Cotonwood. Shrp 2H 71
Cotonwood. Staf 3C 72
Cott. Devn 2D 9
Cott. Orkn 5F 172
Cottam. E Yor 3D 101
Cottam. Lanc 1D 90
Cottam. Notts 3F 87
Cottartown. High 5E 159
Cottarville. Nptn 4E 63
Cottenham. Cambs 4D 64
Cotterdale. N Yor 5B 104
Cottered. Herts 3D 52
Cotterstock. Nptn 1H 63
Cottesbrooke. Nptn 3E 62
Cottesmore. Rut 4G 75
Cotteylands. Devn 1C 12
Cottingham. E Yor 1D 94
Cottingham. Nptn 1F 63
Cottingley. W Yor 1B 92
Cottisford. Oxon 2D 50
Cotton. Staf 1E 73
Cotton. Suff 4C 66
Cotton End. Bed 1A 52
Cottown. Abers 4F 161
Cotts. Devn 2A 8
Cotwalton. Staf 2D 72
Couch's Mill. Corn 3F 7
Coughton. Here 3A 48
Coughton. Warw 4E 61
Coulags. High 4B 156
Coulby Newham. Midd 3C 106
Coulderton. Cumb 4A 102
Coulin Lodge. High 3C 156
Coull. Abers 3C 152
Coulport. Arg 1D 126
Coulsdon. Surr 5D 39
Coulter. S Lan 1C 118
Coultershaw Bridge. W Sus 4A 26
Coultings. Som 2F 21
Coulton. N Yor 2A 100
Cound. Shrp 5H 71
Coundon. Dur 2F 105
Coundon Grange. Dur 2F 105
Countersett. N Yor 1B 98
Countess. Wilts 2G 23
Countess Cross. Essx 2B 54
Countesthorpe. Leics 1C 62
Countisbury. Devn 2H 19
Coupar Angus. Per 4B 144
Coupe Green. Lanc 2D 90
Coupland. Cumb 3A 104
Coupland. Nmbd 1D 120
Cour. Arg 5G 125
Courance. Dum 5C 118
Court-at-Street. Kent 2E 29
Courteachan. High 4E 147
Courteenhall. Nptn 5E 63
Court Henry. Carm 3F 45
Courtsend. Essx 1E 41
Courtway. Som 3F 21
Cousland. Midl 3G 129
Cousley Wood. E Sus 2A 28
Coustonn. Arg 2B 126
Cove. Arg 1D 126
Cove. Devn 1C 12
Cove. Hants 1G 25
Cove. High 4C 162
Cove. Bord 2D 130
Cove Bay. Aber 3G 153
Covehithe. Suff 2H 67
Coven. Staf 5D 72
Coveney. Cambs 2D 65
Covenham St Bartholomew.
Linc 1C 88
Covenham St Mary. Linc 1C 88
Coven Heath. Staf 5D 72
Coventry. W Mid 3H 61 & 192
Coventry Airport. Warw 3A 62
Coverack. Corn 5E 5
Coverham. N Yor 1D 98
Covesea. Mor 1F 159
Covingham. Swin 3G 35
Covington. Cambs 3H 63
Covington. S Lan 1B 118
Cowan Bridge. Lanc 2F 97
Cowan Head. Cumb 5F 103
Cowbar. Red C 3E 107
Cowbeech. E Sus 4H 27
Cowbit. Linc 4B 76
Cowbridge. V Glam 4C 32
Cowden. Kent 1F 27
Cowdenbeath. Fife 4D 136
Cowdenburn. Bord 4F 129
Cowdenend. Fife 4D 136
Cowers Lane. Derbs 1H 73
Cowes. IOW 3C 16
Cowesby. N Yor 1G 99
Cowfold. W Sus 3D 26
Cowfords. Mor 3H 159
Cowgill. Cumb 1G 97
Cowie. Abers 5F 153
Cowie. Stir 1B 128
Cowlam. E Yor 3D 100
Cowley. Devn 3C 12
Cowley. Glos 4E 49
Cowley. G Lon 2B 38
Cowley. Oxon 5D 50
Cowley. Staf 4C 72
Cowleymoor. Devn 1C 12
Cowling. Lanc 3D 90
Cowling. N Yor 1E 99
(nr. Bedale)
Cowling. N Yor 5B 98
(nr. Glusburn)
Cowlinge. Suff 5G 65
Cowmes. W Yor 3B 92
Cowpe. Lanc 2G 91
Cowpen. Nmbd 1F 115
Cowpen Bewley. Stoc T 2B 106
Cowplain. Hants 1E 17
Cowshill. Dur 5B 114
Cowslip Green. N Som 5H 33
Cowstrandburn. Fife 4C 136
Cowthorpe. N Yor 4G 99
Coxall. Here 3F 59
Coxbank. Ches E 1A 72
Coxbench. Derbs 1A 74
Cox Common. Suff 2G 67
Coxford. Norf 3H 77
Coxgreen. Staf 2C 60
Cox Green. Surr 2B 26
Cox Green. Tyne 4G 115
Coxheath. Kent 5B 40
Coxhoe. Dur 1A 106
Coxley. Som 2A 22
Coxwold. N Yor 2H 99
Coychurch. V Glam 3C 32
Coylton. S Ayr 3D 116
Coylumbridge. High 2D 150
Coynach. Abers 3B 152
Coynachie. Abers 5B 160
Coytrahen. B'end 3B 32
Crabbs Cross. Worc 4E 61
Crabgate. Norf 3C 78
Crab Orchard. Dors 2F 15
Crabtree. W Sus 3D 26
Crabtree Green. Wrex 1F 71
Crackaig. High 2G 165
Crackenthorpe. Cumb 2H 103
Crackington Haven. Corn 3B 10
Crackley. Staf 5C 84
Crackley. Warw 3G 61
Crackleybank. Shrp 4B 72
Crackpot. N Yor 5C 104
Cracoe. N Yor 3B 98
Craddock. Devn 1D 12
Cradhlastadh. W Isl 4C 171
Cradley. Here 1C 48
Cradley. W Mid 2D 60
Cradoc. Powy 2D 46
Crafthole. Corn 3H 7
Crafton. Buck 4G 51
Cragabus. Arg 5B 124
Crag Foot. Lanc 2D 97
Craggan. High 1E 151
Cragganmore. Mor 5F 159
Cragganvallie. High 5H 157
Craggie. High 1F 165
Craggiemore. High 5B 158
Cragg Vale. W Yor 2A 92
Craghead. Dur 4F 115
Crai. Powy 3B 46
Craibstone. Aber 2F 153
Craichie. Ang 4E 145
Craig. Arg 5E 141
Craig. Dum 2D 111
Craig. High 4C 156
(nr. Achnashellach)
Craig. High 2G 155
(nr. Lower Diabaig)
Craig. High 5H 155
(nr. Stromeferry)
Craiganour Lodge. Per 3D 142
Craigbrack. Arg 4A 134
Craig-cefn-parc. Swan 5G 45
Craigdallie. Per 1E 137
Craigdam. Abers 5F 161
Craigdarroch. E Ayr 4F 117
Craigdarroch. High 3G 157
Craigdhu. High 4G 157
Craigearn. Abers 2E 152
Craigellachie. Mor 4G 159
Craigend. Per 1D 136
Craigendoran. Arg 1E 126
Craigends. Ren 3F 127
Craigenputtock. Dum 1E 111
Craigens. E Ayr 3E 117
Craighall. Edin 2E 129
Craighead. Fife 2H 137
Craighouse. Arg 3D 124
Craigie. Abers 2G 153
Craigie. D'dee 5D 144
Craigie. Per 4A 144
(nr. Blairgowrie)
Craigie. Per 1D 136
(nr. Perth)
Craigie. S Ayr 1D 116
Craigielaw. E Lot 2A 130
Craiglemine. Dum 5B 110
Craig-llwyn. Shrp 3E 71
Craiglockhart. Edin 2F 129
Craig Lodge. Arg 2B 126
Craigmalloch. E Ayr 5D 117
Craigmaud. Abers 3F 161
Craigmill. Stir 4H 135
Craigmillar. Edin 2F 129
Craigmore. Arg 3C 126
Craigmuie. Dum 1E 111
Craignair. Dum 3F 111
Craignant. Shrp 2E 71
Craigneuk. N Lan 3A 128
(nr. Airdrie)
Craigneuk. N Lan 4A 128
(nr. Motherwell)
Craignure. Arg 5B 140
Craigo. Abers 2F 145
Craigrory. High 4A 158
Craigrothie. Fife 2F 137
Craigs. Dum 2D 112
Craigshill. W Lot 3D 128
Craigs, The. High 4B 164
Craigton. Aber 3F 153
Craigton. Abers 3E 152
Craigton. Ang 5E 145
(nr. Carnoustie)
Craigton. Ang 3C 144
(nr. Kirriemuir)
Craigton. High 4A 158
Craigtown. High 3A 168
Craig-y-Duke. Neat 5H 45
Craig-y-nos. Powy 4B 46
Craigyloch. Ang 3B 144
Craik. Bord 4F 119
Crail. Fife 3H 137
Crailing. Bord 2A 120
Crailinghall. Bord 2A 120
Crakehill. N Yor 2G 99
Crakemarsh. Staf 2E 73
Crambe. N Yor 3B 100
Crambeck. N Yor 3B 100
Cramlington. Nmbd 2F 115
Cramond. Edin 2E 129
Cramond Bridge. Edin 2E 129
Cranage. Ches E 4B 84
Cranberry. Staf 2C 72
Cranborne. Dors 1F 15
Cranbourne. Brac 3A 38
Cranbrook. Devn 3D 12
Cranbrook. Kent 2B 28
Cranbrook Common. Kent 2B 28
Crane Moor. S Yor 4D 92
Crane's Corner. Norf 4B 78
Cranfield. C Beds 1H 51
Cranford. G Lon 3B 38
Cranford St Andrew. Nptn 3G 63
Cranford St John. Nptn 3G 63
Cranham. Glos 4D 49
Cranham. G Lon 2G 39
Crank. Mers 1H 83
Cranleigh. Surr 2B 26
Cranley. Suff 3D 66
Cranloch. Mor 3G 159
Cranmer Green. Suff 3C 66
Cranmore. IOW 3B 16
Cranmore. Linc 5A 76
Crannich. Arg 4G 139
Crannoch. Mor 3B 160
Cranoe. Leics 1E 63
Cransford. Suff 4F 67
Cranshaws. Bord 3C 130
Cranstal. IOM 1D 108
Crantock. Corn 2B 6
Cranwell. Linc 5H 87
Cranwich. Norf 1G 65
Cranworth. Norf 5B 78
Craobh Haven. Arg 3E 133
Craobhnaclag. High 4G 157
Crapstone. Devn 2B 8
Crarae. Arg 4G 133
Crask. High 2H 167
Crask Inn. High 1C 164
Crask of Aigas. High 4G 157
Craster. Nmbd 3G 121
Cratfield. Suff 3F 67
Crathes. Abers 4E 153
Crathie. Abers 4G 151
Crathie. High 4H 149
Crathorne. N Yor 4B 106
Craven Arms. Shrp 2G 59
Crawcrook. Tyne 3E 115
Crawford. Lanc 4D 90
Crawford. S Lan 2B 118
Crawforddyke. S Lan 4B 128
Crawfordjohn. S Lan 2A 118
Crawick. Dum 3G 117
Crawley. Devn 2F 13
Crawley. Hants 3C 24
Crawley. Oxon 4B 50
Crawley. W Sus 2D 26
Crawley Down. W Sus 2E 27
Crawley Side. Dur 5C 114
Crawshawbooth. Lanc 2G 91
Crawton. Abers 5F 153
Cray. N Yor 2B 98
Cray. Per 2A 144
Crayford. G Lon 3G 39
Crayke. N Yor 2H 99
Craymere Beck. Norf 2C 78
Crays Hill. Essx 1B 40
Cray's Pond. Oxon 3E 37
Crazies Hill. Wok 3F 37
Creacombe. Devn 1B 12
Creagan. Arg 4D 141
Creag Aoil. High 1F 141
Creag Ghoraidh. W Isl 4C 170
Creaguaineach Lodge.
High 2H 141
Creamore Bank. Shrp 2H 71
Creaton. Nptn 3E 62
Creca. Dum 2D 112
Credenhill. Here 1H 47
Crediton. Devn 2B 12
Creebridge. Dum 3B 110
Creech. Dors 4E 15
Creech Heathfield. Som 4F 21
Creech St Michael. Som 4F 21
Creed. Corn 4D 6
Creekmoor. Pool 3E 15
Creekmouth. G Lon 2F 39
Creeting St Mary. Suff 5C 66
Creeting St Peter. Suff 5C 66
Creeton. Linc 3H 75
Creetown. Dum 4B 110
Creggans. Arg 3H 133
Cregneash. IOM 5A 108
Cregrina. Powy 5D 58
Creich. Arg 2B 132
Creich. Fife 1F 137
Creighton. Staf 2E 73
Creigiau. Card 3D 32
Cremyll. Corn 3A 8
Crendell. Dors 1F 15
Crepkill. High 4D 154
Cressage. Shrp 5H 71
Cressbrook. Derbs 3F 85
Cresselly. Pemb 4E 43
Cressing. Essx 3A 54
Cresswell. Nmbd 5G 121
Cresswell. Staf 2D 73
Cresswell Quay. Pemb 4E 43
Creswell. Derbs 3C 86
Creswell Green. Staf 4E 73
Cretingham. Suff 4E 67
Crewe. Ches E 5B 84
Crewe-by-Farndon. Ches W 5G 83
Crewgreen. Powy 4F 71
Crewkerne. Som 2H 13
Crews Hill. G Lon 5D 52
Crewton. Derb 2A 74
Crianlarich. Stir 1C 134
Cribbs Causeway. S Glo 3A 34
Cribyn. Cdgn 5E 57
Criccieth. Gwyn 2D 69
Crich. Derbs 5A 86
Crichton. Midl 3G 129
Crick. Mon 2H 33
Crick. Nptn 3C 62
Crickadarn. Powy 1D 46
Cricket Hill. Hants 5G 37
Cricket Malherbie. Som 1G 13
Cricket St Thomas. Som 2G 13
Crickham. Som 2H 21
Crickheath. Shrp 3E 71
Crickhowell. Powy 4F 47
Cricklade. Wilts 2F 35
Cricklewood. G Lon 2D 38
Cridling Stubbs. N Yor 2F 93
Crieff. Per 1A 136
Criftins. Shrp 2F 71
Criggion. Powy 4E 71
Crigglestone. W Yor 3D 92
Crimchard. Som 2G 13
Crimdon Park. Dur 1B 106
Crimond. Abers 3H 161
Crimonmogate. Abers 3H 161
Crimplesham. Norf 5F 77
Crimscote. Warw 1H 49
Crinan. Arg 4E 133
Cringleford. Norf 5D 78
Crinow. Pemb 3F 43
Cripplesease. Corn 3C 4
Cripplestyle. Dors 1F 15
Cripp's Corner. E Sus 3B 28
Croanford. Corn 5A 10
Crockenhill. Kent 4G 39
Crocker End. Oxon 3F 37
Crockerhill. Hants 2D 16
Crockernwell. Devn 3A 12
Crocker's Ash. Here 4A 48
Crockerton. Wilts 2D 22
Crocketford. Dum 2F 111
Crockey Hill. York 5A 100

Crockham Hill—Dalton

Crockham Hill. *Kent* 5F **39**
Crockhurst Street. *Kent* 1H **27**
Crockleford Heath. *Essx* 3D **54**
Croeserw. *Neat* 2B **32**
Croes-Goch. *Pemb* 1C **42**
Croes Hywel. *Mon* 4G **47**
Croes-lan. *Cdgn* 1D **45**
Croesor. *Gwyn* 1F **69**
Croesoswallt. *Shrp* 3E **71**
Croesyceiliog. *Carm* 4E **45**
Croesyceiliog. *Torf* 2F **33**
Croes-y-mwyalch. *Torf* 2G **33**
Croesywaun. *Gwyn* 5E **81**
Croford. *Som* 4E **20**
Croft. *Leics* 1C **62**
Croft. *Linc* 4E **89**
Croft. *Warr* 1A **84**
Croftamie. *Stir* 1F **127**
Croftfoot. *Glas* 3G **127**
Croftmill. *Per* 5F **143**
Crofton. *Cumb* 4E **112**
Crofton. *W Yor* 3D **93**
Crofton. *Wilts* 5A **36**
Croft-on-Tees. *N Yor* 4F **105**
Crofts. *Dum* 2E **111**
Crofts of Benachielt. *High* 5D **169**
Crofts of Dipple. *Mor* 3H **159**
Crofty. *Swan* 3E **31**
Croggan. *Arg* 1E **132**
Croglin. *Cumb* 5G **113**
Croich. *High* 4B **164**
Croick. *High* 3A **168**
Croig. *Arg* 3E **139**
Cromarty. *High* 2B **158**
Crombie. *Fife* 1D **128**
Cromdale. *High* 1E **151**
Cromer. *Herts* 3C **52**
Cromer. *Norf* 1E **79**
Cromford. *Derbs* 5G **85**
Cromhall. *S Glo* 2B **34**
Cromhall Common. *S Glo* 3B **34**
Cromor. *W Isl* 5G **171**
Cromra. *High* 5H **149**
Cromwell. *Notts* 4E **87**
Cronberry. *E Ayr* 2F **117**
Crondall. *Hants* 2F **25**
Cronk, The. *IOM* 2C **108**
Cronk-y-Voddy. *IOM* 3C **108**
Cronton. *Mers* 2G **83**
Crook. *Cumb* 5F **103**
Crook. *Dur* 1E **105**
Crookdake. *Cumb* 5C **112**
Crooke. *G Man* 4D **90**
Crookedholm. *E Ayr* 1D **116**
Crooked Soley. *Wilts* 4B **36**
Crookes. *S Yor* 2H **85**
Crookgate Bank. *Dur* 4E **115**
Crookhall. *Dur* 4E **115**
Crookham. *Nmbd* 1D **120**
Crookham. *W Ber* 5D **36**
Crookham Village. *Hants* 1F **25**
Crooklands. *Cumb* 1E **97**
Crook of Devon. *Per* 3C **136**
Crookston. *Ren* 3G **127**
Cropredy. *Oxon* 1C **50**
Cropston. *Leics* 4C **74**
Cropthorne. *Worc* 1E **49**
Cropton. *N Yor* 1B **100**
Cropwell Bishop. *Notts* 2D **74**
Cropwell Butler. *Notts* 2D **74**
Cros. *W Isl* 1H **171**
Crosbie. *N Ayr* 5D **126**
Crosbost. *W Isl* 5F **171**
Crosby. *Cumb* 1B **102**
Crosby. *IOM* 4C **108**
Crosby. *Mers* 1F **83**
Crosby. *N Lin* 3B **94**
Crosby Court. *N Yor* 5A **106**
Crosby Garrett. *Cumb* 4A **104**
Crosby Ravensworth. *Cumb* 3H **103**
Crosby Villa. *Cumb* 1B **102**
Croscombe. *Som* 2A **22**
Crosland Moor. *W Yor* 3B **92**
Cross. *Som* 1H **21**
Crossaig. *Arg* 4G **125**
Crossapol. *Arg* 4A **138**
Cross Ash. *Mon* 4H **47**
Cross-at-Hand. *Kent* 1B **28**
Crossbush. *W Sus* 5B **26**
Crosscanonby. *Cumb* 1B **102**
Crossdale Street. *Norf* 2E **79**
Cross End. *Essx* 2B **54**
Crossens. *Mers* 3B **90**
Crossford. *Fife* 1D **128**
Crossford. *S Lan* 5B **128**
Cross Foxes. *Gwyn* 4G **69**
Crossgate. *Orkn* 6D **172**
Crossgate. *Staf* 2D **72**
Crossgatehall. *E Lot* 3G **129**
Crossgates. *Fife* 1E **129**
Crossgates. *N Yor* 1E **101**
Crossgates. *Powy* 4C **58**
Cross Gates. *W Yor* 1D **92**
Crossgill. *Lanc* 3E **97**
Cross Green. *Devn* 4D **11**
Cross Green. *Staf* 5D **72**
Cross Green. *Suff* 5A **66** (nr. Cockfield)
Cross Green. *Suff* 5B **66** (nr. Hitcham)
Cross Hands. *Carm* 4F **45** (nr. Ammanford)
Crosshands. *Carm* 2F **43** (nr. Whitland)
Crosshands. *E Ayr* 1D **117**
Cross Hill. *Derbs* 1B **74**
Crosshill. *E Ayr* 2D **117**
Crosshill. *Fife* 4D **136**
Cross Hill. *Glos* 2A **34**
Crosshill. *S Ayr* 4C **116**
Crosshills. *High* 1A **158**
Cross Hills. *N Yor* 5C **98**
Cross Holme. *N Yor* 5C **106**
Crosshouse. *E Ayr* 1C **116**
Cross Houses. *Shrp* 5H **71**
Crossings. *Cumb* 2G **113**
Cross in Hand. *E Sus* 3G **27**
Cross Inn. *Cdgn* 4E **57** (nr. Aberaeron)
Cross Inn. *Cdgn* 5C **56** (nr. New Quay)
Cross Inn. *Rhon* 3D **32**
Crosskeys. *Cphy* 2F **33**
Crosskirk. *High* 2C **168**
Crosslands. *Cumb* 1C **96**
Cross Lane Head. *Shrp* 1B **60**
Cross Lanes. *Corn* 4D **5**
Cross Lanes. *Dur* 3D **104**
Cross Lanes. *N Yor* 3H **99**
Crosslanes. *Shrp* 4F **71**
Cross Lanes. *Wrex* 1F **71**
Crosslee. *Ren* 3F **127**
Crossmichael. *Dum* 3E **111**
Crossmoor. *Lanc* 1C **90**
Cross Oak. *Powy* 3E **46**
Cross of Jackston. *Abers* 5E **161**
Cross o' th' Hands. *Derbs* 1G **73**
Crossroads. *Abers* 3G **153** (nr. Aberdeen)
Crossroads. *Abers* 4E **153** (nr. Banchory)
Crossroads. *E Ayr* 1D **116**
Cross Side. *Devn* 4B **20**
Cross Street. *Suff* 3D **66**
Crosston. *Ang* 3E **145**
Cross Town. *Ches E* 3B **84**
Crossway. *Mon* 4H **47**
Crossway. *Powy* 5C **58**
Crossway Green. *Mon* 2A **34**
Crossway Green. *Worc* 4C **60**
Crossways. *Dors* 4C **14**
Crosswell. *Pemb* 1F **43**
Crosswood. *Cdgn* 3F **57**
Crosthwaite. *Cumb* 5F **103**
Croston. *Lanc* 3C **90**
Crostwick. *Norf* 4E **79**
Crostwight. *Norf* 3F **79**
Crothair. *W Isl* 4D **171**
Crouch. *Kent* 5H **39**
Croucheston. *Wilts* 4F **23**
Crouch Hill. *Dors* 1C **14**
Croughton. *Nptn* 2D **50**
Crovie. *Abers* 2F **161**
Crow. *Hants* 2G **15**
Crowan. *Corn* 3D **4**
Crowborough. *E Sus* 2G **27**
Crowcombe. *Som* 3E **21**
Crowcroft. *Worc* 5B **60**
Crowdecote. *Derbs* 4F **85**
Crowden. *Derbs* 1E **85**
Crowden. *Devn* 3E **11**
Crowdhill. *Hants* 1C **16**
Crowdon. *N Yor* 5G **107**
Crow Edge. *S Yor* 4B **92**
Crow End. *Cambs* 5C **64**
Crowfield. *Nptn* 1E **50**
Crowfield. *Suff* 5D **66**
Crow Green. *Essx* 1G **39**
Crow Hill. *Here* 3B **48**
Crowhurst. *E Sus* 4B **28**
Crowhurst. *Surr* 1E **27**
Crowhurst Lane End. *Surr* 1E **27**
Crowland. *Linc* 4B **76**
Crowland. *Suff* 3C **66**
Crowlas. *Corn* 3C **4**
Crowle. *N Lin* 3A **94**
Crowle. *Worc* 5D **60**
Crowle Green. *Worc* 5D **60**
Crowmarsh Gifford. *Oxon* 3E **36**
Crown Corner. *Suff* 3E **67**
Crownthorpe. *Norf* 5C **78**
Crowntown. *Corn* 3D **4**
Crows-an-wra. *Corn* 4A **4**
Crowshill. *Norf* 5B **78**
Crowthorne. *Brac* 5G **37**
Crowton. *Ches W* 3H **83**
Croxall. *Staf* 4F **73**
Croxby. *Linc* 1A **88**
Croxdale. *Dur* 1F **105**
Croxden. *Staf* 2E **73**
Croxley Green. *Herts* 1B **38**
Croxton. *Cambs* 4B **64**
Croxton. *Norf* 2B **78** (nr. Fakenham)
Croxton. *Norf* 2A **66** (nr. Thetford)
Croxton. *N Lin* 3D **94**
Croxton. *Staf* 2B **72**
Croxtonbank. *Staf* 2B **72**
Croxton Green. *Ches E* 5H **83**
Croxton Kerrial. *Leics* 3F **75**
Croy. *High* 4B **158**
Croy. *N Lan* 2A **128**
Croyde. *Devn* 3E **19**
Croydon. *Cambs* 1D **52**
Croydon. *G Lon* 4E **39**
Crubenbeg. *High* 4A **150**
Crubenmore Lodge. *High* 4A **150**
Cruckmeore. *Shrp* 5G **71**
Cruckton. *Shrp* 4G **71**
Cruden Bay. *Abers* 5H **161**
Crudgington. *Telf* 4A **72**
Crudie. *Abers* 3E **161**
Crudwell. *Wilts* 2E **35**
Cruft. *Devn* 3F **11**
Crug. *Powy* 3D **58**
Crughywel. *Powy* 4F **47**
Crugmeer. *Corn* 1D **6**
Crugybar. *Carm* 2G **45**
Crug-y-byddar. *Powy* 2D **58**
Crulabhig. *W Isl* 4D **171**
Crumlin. *Cphy* 2F **33**
Crumpsall. *G Man* 4G **91**
Crumpsbrook. *Shrp* 3A **60**
Crundale. *Kent* 1E **29**
Crundale. *Pemb* 3D **42**
Cruwys Morchard. *Devn* 1B **12**
Crux Easton. *Hants* 1C **24**
Cruxton. *Dors* 3B **14**
Crwbin. *Carm* 4E **45**
Cryers Hill. *Buck* 2G **37**
Crymych. *Pemb* 1F **43**
Crynant. *Neat* 5A **46**
Crystal Palace. *G Lon* 3E **39**
Cuaich. *High* 5A **150**
Cuaig. *High* 3G **155**
Cuan. *Arg* 2E **133**
Cubbington. *Warw* 4H **61**
Cubert. *Corn* 3B **6**
Cubley. *S Yor* 4C **92**
Cubley Common. *Derbs* 2F **73**
Cublington. *Buck* 3G **51**
Cublington. *Here* 2H **47**
Cuckfield. *W Sus* 3E **27**
Cucklington. *Som* 4C **22**
Cuckney. *Notts* 3C **86**
Cuckron. *Shet* 6F **173**
Cuddesdon. *Oxon* 5E **50**
Cuddington. *Buck* 4F **51**
Cuddington. *Ches W* 3A **84**
Cuddington Heath. *Ches W* 1G **71**
Cuddy Hill. *Lanc* 1C **90**
Cudham. *G Lon* 5F **39**
Cudlipptown. *Devn* 5F **11**
Cudworth. *Som* 1G **13**
Cudworth. *S Yor* 4D **93**
Cudworth. *Surr* 1D **26**
Cuerdley Cross. *Warr* 2H **83**
Cuffley. *Herts* 5D **52**
Cuidhir. *W Isl* 8B **170**
Cuidhsiadar. *W Isl* 2H **171**
Cuidhtinis. *W Isl* 9C **171**
Culbo. *High* 2A **158**
Culbokie. *High* 3A **158**
Culburnie. *High* 4G **157**
Culcabock. *High* 4A **158**
Culcharry. *High* 3C **158**
Culcheth. *Warr* 1A **84**
Culduie. *High* 4G **155**
Culeave. *High* 4C **164**
Culford. *Suff* 4H **65**
Culgaith. *Cumb* 2H **103**
Culham. *Oxon* 2D **36**
Culkein. *High* 1E **163**
Culkein Drumbeg. *High* 5B **166**
Culkerton. *Glos* 2E **35**
Cullen. *Mor* 2C **160**
Cullercoats. *Tyne* 2G **115**
Cullicudden. *High* 2A **158**
Cullingworth. *W Yor* 1A **92**
Cullipool. *Arg* 2E **133**
Cullivoe. *Shet* 1G **173**
Culloch. *Per* 2G **135**
Culloden. *High* 4B **158**
Cullompton. *Devn* 2D **12**
Culm Davy. *Devn* 1E **13**
Culmington. *Shrp* 2G **59**
Culmstock. *Devn* 1E **12**
Cul na Caepaich. *High* 5E **147**
Culnacnoc. *High* 2E **155**
Culnacraig. *High* 3E **163**
Culrain. *High* 4C **164**
Culross. *Fife* 1C **128**
Culroy. *S Ayr* 3C **116**
Culswick. *Shet* 7D **173**
Cults. *Aber* 3F **153**
Cults. *Abers* 5C **160**
Cults. *Fife* 3F **137**
Cultybraggan Camp. *Per* 1G **135**
Culver. *Devn* 3B **12**
Culverlane. *Devn* 2D **8**
Culverstone Green. *Kent* 4H **39**
Culverthorpe. *Linc* 1H **75**
Culworth. *Nptn* 1D **50**
Culzie Lodge. *High* 1H **157**
Cumberlow Green. *Herts* 2D **52**
Cumbernauld. *N Lan* 2A **128**
Cumbernauld Village. *N Lan* 2A **128**
Cumberworth. *Linc* 3E **89**
Cumdivock. *Cumb* 5E **113**
Cuminestown. *Abers* 3F **161**
Cumledge Mill. *Bord* 4D **130**
Cumlewick. *Shet* 9F **173**
Cummersdale. *Cumb* 4E **113**
Cummertrees. *Dum* 3C **112**
Cummingstown. *Mor* 2F **159**
Cumnock. *E Ayr* 3E **117**
Cumnor. *Oxon* 5C **50**
Cumrew. *Cumb* 4G **113**
Cumwhinton. *Cumb* 4F **113**
Cumwhitton. *Cumb* 4G **113**
Cundall. *N Yor* 2G **99**
Cunninghamhead. *N Ayr* 5E **127**
Cunning Park. *S Ayr* 3C **116**
Cunningsburgh. *Shet* 9F **173**
Cunnister. *Shet* 2G **173**
Cupar. *Fife* 2F **137**
Cupar Muir. *Fife* 2F **137**
Cupernham. *Hants* 4B **24**
Curbar. *Derbs* 3G **85**
Curborough. *Staf* 4F **73**
Curbridge. *Hants* 1D **16**
Curbridge. *Oxon* 5B **50**
Curdridge. *Hants* 1D **16**
Curdworth. *Warw* 1F **61**
Curland. *Som* 1F **13**
Curland Common. *Som* 1F **13**
Curridge. *W Ber* 4C **36**
Currie. *Edin* 3E **129**
Curry Mallet. *Som* 4G **21**
Curry Rivel. *Som* 4G **21**
Curtisden Green. *Kent* 1B **28**
Curtisknowle. *Devn* 3D **8**
Cury. *Corn* 4D **5**
Cusgarne. *Corn* 4B **6**
Cusop. *Here* 1F **47**
Cusworth. *S Yor* 4F **93**
Cutcombe. *Som* 3C **20**
Cuthill. *E Lot* 2G **129**
Cutiau. *Gwyn* 4F **69**
Cutlers Green. *Essx* 2F **53**
Cutmadoc. *Corn* 2E **7**
Cutnall Green. *Worc* 4C **60**
Cutsdean. *Glos* 2F **49**
Cutthorpe. *Derbs* 3H **85**
Cuttiford's Door. *Som* 1G **13**
Cuttivett. *Corn* 2H **7**
Cutts. *Shet* 8F **173**
Cuttybridge. *Pemb* 3D **42**
Cuttyhill. *Abers* 3H **161**
Cuxham. *Oxon* 2E **37**
Cuxton. *Medw* 4B **40**
Cuxwold. *Linc* 4E **95**
Cwm. *Blae* 5E **47**
Cwm. *Den* 3C **82**
Cwm. *Powy* 1E **59**
Cwmafan. *Neat* 2A **32**
Cwmaman. *Rhon* 2C **32**
Cwmann. *Carm* 1F **45**
Cwmbach. *Carm* 2G **43**
Cwmbach. *Powy* 2E **47**
Cwmbach. *Rhon* 5D **46**
Cwmbach Llechryd. *Powy* 5C **58**
Cwmbelan. *Powy* 2B **58**
Cwmbran. *Torf* 2F **33**
Cwmbrwyno. *Cdgn* 2G **57**
Cwm Capel. *Carm* 5E **45**
Cwmcarn. *Cphy* 2F **33**
Cwmcarvan. *Mon* 5H **47**
Cwm-celyn. *Blae* 5F **47**
Cwmcerdinen. *Swan* 5G **45**
Cwm-Cewydd. *Gwyn* 4A **70**
Cwmcoy. *Cdgn* 1C **44**
Cwmcrawnon. *Powy* 4E **47**
Cwmcych. *Pemb* 1G **43**
Cwmdare. *Rhon* 5C **46**
Cwmdu. *Carm* 2G **45**
Cwmdu. *Powy* 3E **47**
Cwmduad. *Carm* 2D **45**
Cwm Dulais. *Swan* 5G **45**
Cwmerfyn. *Cdgn* 2F **57**
Cwmfelin. *B'end* 3B **32**
Cwmfelin Boeth. *Carm* 3F **43**
Cwmfelinfach. *Cphy* 2E **33**
Cwmfelin Mynach. *Carm* 2G **43**
Cwmffrwd. *Carm* 4E **45**
Cwmgiedd. *Powy* 4A **46**
Cwmgors. *Neat* 4H **45**
Cwmgwili. *Carm* 4F **45**
Cwmgwrach. *Neat* 5B **46**
Cwmhiraeth. *Carm* 1H **43**
Cwmifor. *Carm* 3G **45**
Cwmisfael. *Carm* 4E **45**
Cwm-Llinau. *Powy* 5H **69**
Cwmllynfell. *Neat* 4H **45**
Cwm-mawr. *Carm* 4F **45**
Cwm-miles. *Carm* 2F **43**
Cwmorgan. *Carm* 1G **43**
Cwmparc. *Rhon* 2C **32**
Cwm Penmachno. *Cnwy* 1G **69**
Cwmpennar. *Rhon* 5D **46**
Cwm Plysgog. *Pemb* 1B **44**
Cwmrhos. *Powy* 3E **47**
Cwmsychpant. *Cdgn* 1E **45**
Cwmsyfiog. *Cphy* 5E **47**
Cwmsymlog. *Cdgn* 2F **57**
Cwmtillery. *Blae* 5F **47**
Cwm-twrch Isaf. *Powy* 5A **46**
Cwm-twrch Uchaf. *Powy* 4A **46**
Cwmwysg. *Powy* 3B **46**
Cwm-y-glo. *Gwyn* 4E **81**
Cwmyoy. *Mon* 3G **47**
Cwmystwyth. *Cdgn* 3G **57**
Cwrt. *Gwyn* 1F **57**
Cwrtnewydd. *Cdgn* 1E **45**
Cwrt-y-Cadno. *Carm* 1G **45**
Cydweli. *Carm* 5E **45**
Cyffylliog. *Den* 5C **82**
Cymau. *Flin* 5E **83**
Cymer. *Neat* 2B **32**
Cymmer. *Neat* 2B **32**
Cymmer. *Rhon* 2D **32**
Cyncoed. *Card* 3E **33**
Cynghordy. *Carm* 2B **46**
Cynghordy. *Swan* 5G **45**
Cynheidre. *Carm* 5E **45**
Cynonville. *Neat* 2B **32**
Cynwyd. *Den* 1C **70**
Cynwyl Elfed. *Carm* 3D **44**
Cywarch. *Gwyn* 4A **70**

D

Dacre. *Cumb* 2F **103**
Dacre. *N Yor* 3D **98**
Dacre Banks. *N Yor* 3D **98**
Daddry Shield. *Dur* 1B **104**
Dadford. *Buck* 2E **51**
Dadlington. *Leics* 1B **62**
Dafen. *Carm* 5F **45**
Daffy Green. *Norf* 5B **78**
Dagdale. *Staf* 2E **73**
Dagenham. *G Lon* 2F **39**
Daggons. *Dors* 1G **15**
Daglingworth. *Glos* 5E **49**
Dagnall. *Buck* 4H **51**
Dagtail End. *Worc* 4E **61**
Dail. *Arg* 5E **141**
Dail Beag. *W Isl* 3E **171**
Dail bho Dheas. *W Isl* 1G **171**
Dailly. *S Ayr* 4B **116**
Dail Mor. *W Isl* 3E **171**
Dairsie. *Fife* 2G **137**
Daisy Bank. *W Mid* 1E **61**
Daisy Hill. *G Man* 4E **91**
Daisy Hill. *W Yor* 1B **92**
Dalabrog. *W Isl* 6C **170**
Dalavich. *Arg* 2G **133**
Dalbeattie. *Dum* 3F **111**
Dalblair. *E Ayr* 3F **117**
Dalbury. *Derbs* 2G **73**
Dalby. *IOM* 4B **108**
Dalby Wolds. *Leics* 3D **74**
Dalchalm. *High* 3G **165**
Dalcharn. *High* 3G **167**
Dalchork. *High* 2C **164**
Dalchreichart. *High* 2E **149**
Dalchruin. *Per* 2G **135**
Dalcross. *High* 4B **158**
Dalderby. *Linc* 4B **88**
Dale. *Cumb* 5G **113**
Dale. *Pemb* 4C **42**
Dale Abbey. *Derbs* 2B **74**
Dalebank. *Derbs* 4A **86**
Dale Bottom. *Cumb* 2D **102**
Dale Head. *Cumb* 3F **103**
Dalehouse. *N Yor* 3E **107**
Dalelia. *High* 2B **140**
Dale of Walls. *Shet* 6C **173**
Dalgarven. *N Ayr* 5D **126**
Dalgety Bay. *Fife* 1E **129**
Dalginross. *Per* 1G **135**
Dalguise. *Per* 4G **143**
Dalhalvaig. *High* 3A **168**
Dalham. *Suff* 4G **65**
Dalintart. *Arg* 1F **133**
Dalkeith. *Midl* 3G **129**
Dallas. *Mor* 3F **159**
Dalleagles. *E Ayr* 3E **117**
Dall House. *Per* 3C **142**
Dallinghoo. *Suff* 5E **67**
Dallington. *E Sus* 4A **28**
Dallow. *N Yor* 2D **98**
Dalmally. *Arg* 1A **134**
Dalmarnock. *Glas* 3H **127**
Dalmellington. *E Ayr* 4D **117**
Dalmeny. *Edin* 2E **129**
Dalmigavie. *High* 2B **150**
Dalmilling. *S Ayr* 2C **116**
Dalmore. *High* 2A **158** (nr. Alness)
Dalmore. *High* 3E **164** (nr. Rogart)
Dalmuir. *W Dun* 2F **127**
Dalmunach. *Mor* 4G **159**
Dalnabreck. *High* 2B **140**
Dalnacardoch Lodge. *Per* 1E **142**
Dalnamein Lodge. *Per* 2E **143**
Dalnaspidal Lodge. *Per* 1D **142**
Dalnatrat. *High* 3D **140**
Dalnavie. *High* 1A **158**
Dalnawillan Lodge. *High* 4C **168**
Dalness. *High* 3F **141**
Dalnessie. *High* 2D **164**
Dalqueich. *Per* 3C **136**
Dalquhairn. *S Ayr* 5C **116**
Dalreavoch. *High* 3E **165**
Dalreoch. *Per* 2C **136**
Dalry. *Edin* 2F **129**
Dalry. *N Ayr* 5D **126**
Dalrymple. *E Ayr* 3C **116**
Dalscote. *Nptn* 5D **62**
Dalserf. *S Lan* 4A **128**
Dalsmirren. *Arg* 4A **122**
Dalston. *Cumb* 4E **113**
Dalswinton. *Dum* 1G **111**
Dalton. *Dum* 2C **112**

Dalton. *Lanc* 4C **90**
Dalton. *Nmbd* 4C **114**
(nr. Hexham)
Dalton. *Nmbd* 2E **115**
(nr. Ponteland)
Dalton. *N Yor* 4E **105**
(nr. Richmond)
Dalton. *N Yor* 2G **99**
(nr. Thirsk)
Dalton. *S Lan* 4H **127**
Dalton. *S Yor* 1B **86**
Dalton-in-Furness. *Cumb* ...2B **96**
Dalton-le-Dale. *Dur* 5H **115**
Dalton Magna. *S Yor* 1B **86**
Dalton-on-Tees. *N Yor* 4F **105**
Dalton Piercy. *Hart* 1B **106**
Daltot. *Arg* 1F **125**
Dalvey. *High* 5F **159**
Dalwhinnie. *High* 5A **150**
Dalwood. *Devn* 2F **13**
Damerham. *Hants* 1G **15**
Damgate. *Norf* 5G **79**
(nr. Acle)
Damgate. *Norf* 4G **79**
(nr. Martham)
Dam Green. *Norf* 2C **66**
Damhead. *Mor* 3E **159**
Danaway. *Kent* 4C **40**
Danbury. *Essx* 5A **54**
Danby. *N Yor* 4E **107**
Danby Botton. *N Yor* 4D **107**
Danby Wiske. *N Yor* 5A **106**
Danderhall. *Midl* 3G **129**
Danebank. *Ches E* 2D **85**
Danebridge. *Ches E* 4D **84**
Dane End. *Herts* 3D **52**
Danehill. *E Sus* 3F **27**
Danesford. *Shrp* 1B **60**
Daneshill. *Hants* 1E **25**
Danesmoor. *Derbs* 4A **86**
Danestone. *Aber* 2G **153**
Dangerous Corner. *Lanc* ...3D **90**
Daniel's Water. *Kent* 1D **28**
Dan's Castle. *Dur* 1E **105**
Danzey Green. *Warw* 4F **61**
Dapple Heath. *Staf* 3E **73**
Daren. *Powy* 4F **47**
Darenth. *Kent* 3G **39**
Daresbury. *Hal* 2H **83**
Darfield. *S Yor* 4E **93**
Dargate. *Kent* 4E **41**
Dargill. *Per* 2A **136**
Darite. *Corn* 2G **7**
Darlaston. *W Mid* 1D **60**
Darley. *N Yor* 4E **98**
Darley Abbey. *Derb* 2A **74**
Darley Bridge. *Derbs* 4G **85**
Darley Dale. *Derbs* 4G **85**
Darley Head. *N Yor* 4D **98**
Darlingscott. *Warw* 1H **49**
Darlington. *Darl* 3F **105**
Darliston. *Shrp* 2H **71**
Darlton. *Notts* 3E **87**
Darmsden. *Suff* 5C **66**
Darnall. *S Yor* 2A **86**
Darnford. *Abers* 4E **153**
Darnford. *Staf* 5F **73**
Darnhall. *Ches W* 4A **84**
Darnick. *Bord* 1H **119**
Darowen. *Powy* 5H **69**
Darra. *Abers* 4E **161**
Darracott. *Devn* 3E **19**
Darras Hall. *Nmbd* 2E **115**
Darrington. *W Yor* 3E **93**
Darrow Green. *Norf* 2F **67**
Darsham. *Suff* 4G **67**
Dartfield. *Abers* 3H **161**
Dartford. *Kent* 3G **39**
Dartford-Thurrock River Crossing.
Kent 3G **39**
Dartington. *Devn* 2D **9**
Dartmeet. *Devn* 5G **11**
Dartmoor. *Devn* 4F **11**
Dartmouth. *Devn* 3E **9**
Darton. *S Yor* 3D **92**
Darvel. *E Ayr* 1E **117**
Darwen. *Bkbn* 2E **91**
Dassels. *Herts* 3D **53**
Datchet. *Wind* 3A **38**
Datchworth. *Herts* 4C **52**
Datchworth Green.
Herts 4C **52**
Daubhill. *G Man* 4F **91**
Dauntsey. *Wilts* 3E **35**
Dauntsey Green. *Wilts* 3E **35**
Dauntsey Lock. *Wilts* 3E **35**
Dava. *Mor* 5E **159**
Davenham. *Ches W* 3A **84**
Daventry. *Nptn* 4C **62**
Davidson's Mains. *Edin* ...2F **129**
Davidston. *High* 2B **158**
Davidstow. *Corn* 4B **10**
David's Well. *Powy* 3C **58**
Davington. *Dum* 4E **119**
Daviot. *Abers* 1E **153**
Daviot. *High* 5B **158**
Davyhulme. *G Man* 1B **84**
Daw Cross. *N Yor* 4E **99**
Dawdon. *Dur* 5H **115**
Dawesgreen. *Surr* 1D **26**
Dawley. *Telf* 5A **72**
Dawlish. *Devn* 5C **12**

Dawlish Warren. *Devn* 5C **12**
Dawn. *Cnwy* 3A **82**
Daws Heath. *Essx* 2C **40**
Dawshill. *Worc* 5C **60**
Daw's House. *Corn* 4D **10**
Dawsmere. *Linc* 2D **76**
Dayhills. *Staf* 2D **72**
Dayhouse Bank. *Worc* 3D **60**
Daylesford. *Glos* 3H **49**
Daywall. *Shrp* 2E **71**
Ddol. *Flin* 3D **82**
Ddol Cownwy. *Powy* 4C **70**
Deadman's Cross.
C Beds 1B **52**
Deadwater. *Nmbd* 5A **120**
Deaf Hill. *Dur* 1A **106**
Deal. *Kent* 5H **41**
Dean. *Cumb* 2B **102**
Dean. *Devn* 2G **19**
(nr. Combe Martin)
Dean. *Devn* 2H **19**
(nr. Lynton)
Dean. *Dors* 1E **15**
Dean. *Hants* 1D **16**
(nr. Bishop's Waltham)
Dean. *Hants* 3C **24**
(nr. Winchester)
Dean. *Oxon* 3B **50**
Dean. *Som* 2B **22**
Dean Bank. *Dur* 1F **105**
Deanburnhaugh. *Bord* 3F **119**
Dean Cross. *Devn* 2F **19**
Deane. *Hants* 1D **24**
Deanich Lodge. *High* 5A **164**
Deanland. *Dors* 1E **15**
Deanlane End. *W Sus* 1F **17**
Dean Park. *Shrp* 4H **59**
Dean Prior. *Devn* 2D **8**
Dean Row. *Ches E* 2C **84**
Deans. *W Lot* 3D **128**
Deanscales. *Cumb* 2B **102**
Deanshanger. *Nptn* 2F **51**
Deanston. *Stir* 3G **135**
Dearham. *Cumb* 1B **102**
Dearne. *S Yor* 4E **93**
Dearne Valley. *S Yor* 4D **93**
Debach. *Suff* 5E **67**
Debden. *Essx* 2F **53**
Debden Green. *Essx* 2F **53**
(nr. Loughton)
Debden Green. *Essx* 2F **53**
(nr. Saffron Walden)
Debenham. *Suff* 4D **66**
Dechmont. *W Lot* 2D **128**
Deddington. *Oxon* 2C **50**
Dedham. *Essx* 2D **54**
Dedham Heath. *Essx* 2D **54**
Deebank. *Abers* 4D **152**
Deene. *Nptn* 1G **63**
Deenethorpe. *Nptn* 1G **63**
Deepcar. *S Yor* 1G **85**
Deepcut. *Surr* 5A **38**
Deepdale. *Cumb* 1G **97**
Deepdale. *N Lin* 3D **94**
Deepdale. *N Yor* 2A **98**
Deeping Gate. *Pet* 5A **76**
Deeping St James. *Linc* ...5A **76**
Deeping St Nicholas.
Linc 4B **76**
Deerhill. *Mor* 3B **160**
Deerhurst. *Glos* 3D **48**
Deerhurst Walton. *Glos* ...3D **49**
Deerness. *Orkn* 7E **172**
Defford. *Worc* 1E **49**
Defynnog. *Powy* 3C **46**
Deganwy. *Cnwy* 3G **81**
Deighton. *N Yor* 5A **106**
Deighton. *W Yor* 3B **92**
Deighton. *York* 5A **100**
Deiniolen. *Gwyn* 4E **81**
Delabole. *Corn* 4A **10**
Delamere. *Ches W* 4H **83**
Delfour. *High* 3C **150**
Dellieture. *High* 5E **159**
Dell, The. *Suff* 1G **67**
Delly End. *Oxon* 4B **50**
Delny. *High* 1B **158**
Delph. *G Man* 4H **91**
Delves. *Dur* 5E **115**
Delves, The. *W Mid* 1E **61**
Delvin End. *Essx* 2A **54**
Dembleby. *Linc* 2H **75**
Denaby Main. *S Yor* 1B **86**
Denbeath. *Fife* 4F **137**
Denbigh. *Den* 4C **82**
Denbury. *Devn* 2E **9**
Denby. *Derbs* 1A **74**
Denby Common. *Derbs* ...1B **74**
Denby Dale. *W Yor* 4C **92**
Denchworth. *Oxon* 2B **36**
Dendron. *Cumb* 2B **96**
Deneside. *Dur* 5H **115**
Denford. *Nptn* 3G **63**
Dengie. *Essx* 5C **54**
Denham. *Buck* 2B **38**
Denham. *Suff* 4G **65**
(nr. Bury St Edmunds)
Denham. *Suff* 3D **66**
(nr. Eye)
Denham Green. *Buck* 2B **38**
Denham Street. *Suff* 3D **66**

Denhead. *Abers* 5G **161**
(nr. Ellon)
Denhead. *Abers* 3G **161**
(nr. Strichen)
Denhead. *Fife* 2G **137**
Denholm. *Bord* 3H **119**
Denholme. *W Yor* 1A **92**
Denholme Clough. *W Yor* .1A **92**
Denholme Gate. *W Yor* ...1A **92**
Denio. *Gwyn* 2C **68**
Denmead. *Hants* 1E **17**
Dennington. *Suff* 4E **67**
Denny. *Falk* 1B **128**
Denny End. *Cambs* 4D **65**
Dennyloanhead. *Falk* 1B **128**
Den of Lindores. *Fife* 2E **137**
Denshaw. *G Man* 3H **91**
Denside. *Abers* 4F **153**
Densole. *Kent* 1G **29**
Denston. *Suff* 5G **65**
Denstone. *Staf* 1F **73**
Denstroude. *Kent* 4F **41**
Dent. *Cumb* 1G **97**
Denton. *Cambs* 2A **64**
Denton. *Darl* 3F **105**
Denton. *E Sus* 5F **27**
Denton. *G Man* 1D **84**
Denton. *Kent* 1G **29**
Denton. *Linc* 2F **75**
Denton. *Norf* 2E **67**
Denton. *Nptn* 5F **63**
Denton. *N Yor* 5D **98**
Denton. *Oxon* 5D **50**
Denver. *Norf* 5F **77**
Denwick. *Nmbd* 3G **121**
Deopham. *Norf* 5C **78**
Deopham Green. *Norf* 1C **66**
Depden. *Suff* 5G **65**
Depden Green. *Suff* 5G **65**
Deptford. *G Lon* 3E **39**
Deptford. *Wilts* 3F **23**
Derby. *Derb* ...2A **74** & **193**
Derbyhaven. *IOM* 5B **108**
Derculich. *Per* 3F **143**
Dereham. *Norf* 4B **78**
Deri. *Cphy* 5E **47**
Derril. *Devn* 2D **10**
Derringstone. *Kent* 1G **29**
Derrington. *Shrp* 1A **60**
Derrington. *Staf* 3C **72**
Derriton. *Devn* 2D **10**
Derryguaig. *Arg* 5F **139**
Derry Hill. *Wilts* 4E **35**
Derrythorpe. *N Lin* 4B **94**
Dersingham. *Norf* 2F **77**
Dervaig. *Arg* 3F **139**
Derwen. *Den* 5C **82**
Derwen Gam. *Cdgn* 5D **56**
Derwenlas. *Powy* 1G **57**
Desborough. *Nptn* 2F **63**
Desford. *Leics* 5B **74**
Detchant. *Nmbd* 1E **121**
Dethick. *Derbs* 5H **85**
Detling. *Kent* 5B **40**
Deuchar. *Ang* 2D **144**
Deuddwr. *Powy* 4E **71**
Devauden. *Mon* 2H **33**
Devil's Bridge. *Cdgn* 3G **57**
Devitts Green. *Warw* 1G **61**
Devizes. *Wilts* 5F **35**
Devonport. *Plym* 3A **8**
Devonside. *Clac* 4B **136**
Devoran. *Corn* 5B **6**
Dewartown. *Midl* 3G **129**
Dewlish. *Dors* 3C **14**
Dewsbury. *W Yor* 2C **92**
Dewshall Court. *Here* 2H **47**
Dexbeer. *Devn* 2C **10**
Dhoon. *IOM* 3D **108**
Dhoor. *IOM* 2D **108**
Dhowin. *IOM* 1D **108**
Dial Green. *W Sus* 3A **26**
Dial Post. *W Sus* 4C **26**
Dibberford. *Dors* 2H **13**
Dibden. *Hants* 2C **16**
Dibden Purlieu. *Hants* 2C **16**
Dickleburgh. *Norf* 2D **66**
Didbrook. *Glos* 2F **49**
Didcot. *Oxon* 2D **36**
Diddington. *Cambs* 4A **64**
Diddlebury. *Shrp* 2H **59**
Didley. *Here* 2H **47**
Didling. *W Sus* 1G **17**
Didmarton. *Glos* 3D **34**
Didsbury. *G Man* 1C **84**
Didworthy. *Devn* 2C **8**
Digby. *Linc* 5H **87**
Digg. *High* 2D **154**
Diggle. *G Man* 4A **92**
Digmoor. *Lanc* 4C **90**
Digswell. *Herts* 4C **52**
Dihewyd. *Cdgn* 5D **57**
Dilham. *Norf* 3F **79**
Dilhorne. *Staf* 1D **72**
Dillarburn. *S Lan* 5B **128**
Dillington. *Cambs* 4A **64**
Dilston. *Nmbd* 3C **114**
Dilton Marsh. *Wilts* 2D **22**
Dilwyn. *Here* 5G **59**
Dimmer. *Som* 3B **22**
Dimple. *G Man* 3F **91**

Dinas. *Carm* 1G **43**
Dinas. *Gwyn* 5D **81**
(nr. Caernarfon)
Dinas. *Gwyn* 2B **68**
(nr. Tudweiliog)
Dinas Cross. *Pemb* 1E **43**
Dinas Dinlle. *Gwyn* 5D **80**
Dinas Mawddwy. *Gwyn* ...4A **70**
Dinas Powys. *V Glam* 4E **33**
Dinbych. *Den* 4C **82**
Dinbych-y-Pysgod. *Pemb* .4F **43**
Dinckley. *Lanc* 1E **91**
Dinder. *Som* 2A **22**
Dinedor. *Here* 2A **48**
Dinedor Cross. *Here* 2A **48**
Dingestow. *Mon* 4H **47**
Dingle. *Mers* 2F **83**
Dingleden. *Kent* 2C **28**
Dingleton. *Bord* 1H **119**
Dingley. *Nptn* 2E **63**
Dingwall. *High* 3H **157**
Dinmael. *Cnwy* 1C **70**
Dinnet. *Abers* 4B **152**
Dinnington. *Som* 1H **13**
Dinnington. *S Yor* 2C **86**
Dinnington. *Tyne* 2F **115**
Dinorwic. *Gwyn* 4E **81**
Dinton. *Buck* 4F **51**
Dinton. *Wilts* 3F **23**
Dinworthy. *Devn* 1D **10**
Dipley. *Hants* 1F **25**
Dippen. *Arg* 2B **122**
Dippenhall. *Surr* 2G **25**
Dippertown. *Devn* 4E **11**
Dippin. *N Ayr* 3E **123**
Dipple. *S Ayr* 4B **116**
Diptford. *Devn* 3D **8**
Dipton. *Dur* 4E **115**
Dirleton. *E Lot* 1B **130**
Dirt Pot. *Nmbd* 5B **114**
Discoed. *Powy* 4E **59**
Diseworth. *Leics* 3B **74**
Dishes. *Orkn* 5F **172**
Dishforth. *N Yor* 2F **99**
Disley. *Ches E* 2D **85**
Diss. *Norf* 3D **66**
Disserth. *Powy* 5C **58**
Distington. *Cumb* 2B **102**
Ditchampton. *Wilts* 3F **23**
Ditcheat. *Som* 3B **22**
Ditchingham. *Norf* 1F **67**
Ditchling. *E Sus* 4E **27**
Ditteridge. *Wilts* 5D **34**
Dittisham. *Devn* 3E **9**
Ditton. *Hal* 2G **83**
Ditton. *Kent* 5B **40**
Ditton Green. *Cambs* 5F **65**
Ditton Priors. *Shrp* 2A **60**
Divach. *High* 1G **149**
Dixonfield. *High* 2D **168**
Dixton. *Glos* 2E **49**
Dixton. *Mon* 4A **48**
Dizzard. *Corn* 3B **10**
Dobcross. *G Man* 4H **91**
Dobs Hill. *Flin* 4F **83**
Dobson's Bridge. *Shrp* ...2G **71**
Doccombe. *Devn* 4A **12**
Dochgarroch. *High* 4A **158**
Docking. *Norf* 2G **77**
Docklow. *Here* 5H **59**
Dockray. *Cumb* 2E **103**
Doc Penfro. *Pemb* ....4D **42** & **215**
Dodbrooke. *Devn* 4D **8**
Doddenham. *Worc* 5B **60**
Doddinghurst. *Essx* 1G **39**
Doddington. *Cambs* 1C **64**
Doddington. *Kent* 5D **40**
Doddington. *Linc* 4G **87**
Doddington. *Nmbd* 1D **121**
Doddington. *Shrp* 3A **60**
Doddiscombsleigh. *Devn* ..4B **12**
Doddshill. *Norf* 2G **77**
Dodford. *Nptn* 4D **62**
Dodford. *Worc* 3D **60**
Dodington. *Som* 2E **21**
Dodington. *S Glo* 4C **34**
Dodleston. *Ches W* 4F **83**
Dods Leigh. *Staf* 2E **73**
Dodworth. *S Yor* 4D **92**
Doe Lea. *Derbs* 4B **86**
Dogdyke. *Linc* 5B **88**
Dogmersfield. *Hants* 1F **25**
Dogsthorpe. *Pet* 5B **76**
Dog Village. *Devn* 3C **12**
Dolanog. *Powy* 4C **70**
Dolau. *Powy* 4D **58**
Dolau. *Rhon* 3D **32**
Dolbenmaen. *Gwyn* 1E **69**
Doley. *Staf* 3B **72**
Dol-fach. *Powy* 5B **70**
(nr. Llanbrynmair)
Dolfach. *Powy* 3B **58**
(nr. Llanidloes)
Dolfor. *Powy* 2D **58**
Dolgarrog. *Cnwy* 4G **81**
Dolgellau. *Gwyn* 4G **69**
Dolgoch. *Gwyn* 5F **69**
Dol-gran. *Carm* 2E **45**
Dolhelfa. *Powy* 3B **58**
Doll. *High* 3F **165**
Dollar. *Clac* 4B **136**

Dolley Green. *Powy* 4E **59**
Dollwen. *Cdgn* 2F **57**
Dolphin. *Flin* 3D **82**
Dolphingstone. *E Lot* 2G **129**
Dolphinholme. *Lanc* 4E **97**
Dolphinton. *S Lan* 5E **129**
Dolton. *Devn* 1F **11**
Dolwen. *Cnwy* 3A **82**
Dolwyddelan. *Cnwy* 5G **81**
Dol-y-Bont. *Cdgn* 2F **57**
Domgay. *Powy* 4E **71**
Doncaster. *S Yor* 4F **93**
Donhead St Andrew. *Wilts* .4E **23**
Donhead St Mary. *Wilts* ...4E **23**
Doniford. *Som* 2D **20**
Donington. *Linc* 2B **76**
Donington. *Shrp* 5C **72**
Donington Eaudike. *Linc* ..2B **76**
Donington le Heath. *Leics* .4B **74**
Donington on Bain. *Linc* ..2B **88**
Donington South Ing. *Linc* .2B **76**
Donisthorpe. *Leics* 4H **73**
Donkey Street. *Kent* 2F **29**
Donkey Town. *Surr* 4A **38**
Donna Nook. *Linc* 1D **88**
Donnington. *Glos* 3G **49**
Donnington. *Here* 2C **48**
Donnington. *Shrp* 5H **71**
Donnington. *Telf* 4B **72**
Donnington. *W Ber* 5C **36**
Donnington. *W Sus* 2G **17**
Donyatt. *Som* 1G **13**
Doomsday Green. *W Sus* ..2C **26**
Doonfoot. *S Ayr* 3C **116**
Doonholm. *S Ayr* 3C **116**
Dorback Lodge. *High* 2E **151**
Dorchester. *Dors* 3B **14**
Dorchester on Thames. *Oxon* ..2D **36**
Dordon. *Warw* 5G **73**
Dores. *High* 5H **157**
Dorking. *Surr* 1C **26**
Dorking Tye. *Suff* 2C **54**
Dormansland. *Surr* 1F **27**
Dormans Park. *Surr* 1E **27**
Dormanstown. *Red C* 2C **106**
Dormington. *Here* 1A **48**
Dormston. *Worc* 5D **61**
Dorn. *Glos* 2H **49**
Dorney. *Buck* 3A **38**
Dornie. *High* 1A **148**
Dornoch. *High* 5E **165**
Dornock. *Dum* 3D **112**
Dorrery. *High* 3C **168**
Dorridge. *W Mid* 3F **61**
Dorrington. *Linc* 5H **87**
Dorrington. *Shrp* 5G **71**
Dorsington. *Warw* 1G **49**
Dorstone. *Here* 1G **47**
Dorton. *Buck* 4E **51**
Dotham. *IOA* 3C **80**
Dottery. *Dors* 3H **13**
Doublebois. *Corn* 2F **7**
Dougarie. *N Ayr* 2C **122**
Doughton. *Glos* 2D **35**
Douglas. *S Lan* 1H **117**
Douglastown. *Ang* 4D **144**
Douglas Water. *S Lan* 1A **118**
Doulting. *Som* 2B **22**
Dounby. *Orkn* 5B **172**
Doune. *High* 3C **150**
(nr. Kingussie)
Doune. *High* 3B **164**
(nr. Lairg)
Doune. *Stir* 3G **135**
Dounie. *High* 4C **164**
(nr. Bonar Bridge)
Dounie. *High* 5D **164**
(nr. Tain)
Dounreay. *High* 2B **168**
Doura. *N Ayr* 5E **127**
Dousland. *Devn* 2B **8**
Dovaston. *Shrp* 3F **71**
Dove Holes. *Derbs* 3E **85**
Dovenby. *Cumb* 1B **102**
Dover. *Kent* ....1H **29** & **193**
Dovercourt. *Essx* 2F **55**
Doverdale. *Worc* 4C **60**
Doveridge. *Derbs* 2F **73**
Doversgreen. *Surr* 1D **26**
Dowally. *Per* 4H **143**
Dowbridge. *Lanc* 1C **90**
Dowdeswell. *Glos* 4F **49**
Dowlais. *Mer T* 5D **46**
Dowland. *Devn* 1F **11**
Dowlands. *Devn* 3F **13**
Dowles. *Worc* 3B **60**
Dowlesgreen. *Wok* 5G **37**
Dowlish Wake. *Som* 1G **13**
Downall Green. *Mers* 4D **90**
Down Ampney. *Glos* 2F **35**
Downderry. *Corn* 3H **7**
(nr. Looe)
Downderry. *Corn* 3D **6**
(nr. St Austell)
Downe. *G Lon* 4F **39**
Downend. *IOW* 4D **16**
Downend. *S Glo* 4B **34**
Downend. *W Ber* 4C **36**
Down Field. *Cambs* 3F **65**

Downfield. *D'dee* 5C 144
Downgate. *Corn* 5D 10
(nr. Kelly Bray)
Downgate. *Corn* 5C 10
(nr. Upton Cross)
Downham. *Essx* 1B 40
Downham. *Lanc* 5G 97
Downham. *Nmbd* 1C 120
Downham Market. *Norf* 5F 77
Down Hatherley. *Glos* 3D 48
Downhead. *Som* 2B 22
(nr. Frome)
Downhead. *Som* 4A 22
(nr. Yeovil)
Downholland Cross. *Lanc* 4B 90
Downholme. *N Yor* 5E 105
Downies. *Abers* 4G 153
Downley. *Buck* 2G 37
Down St Mary. *Devn* 2H 11
Downside. *Som* 1B 22
(nr. Chilcompton)
Downside. *Som* 2B 22
(nr. Shepton Mallet)
Downside. *Surr* 5C 38
Down, The. *Shrp* 1A 60
Down Thomas. *Devn* 3B 8
Downton. *Hants* 3A 16
Downton. *Wilts* 4G 23
Downton on the Rock. *Here* . .3G 59
Dowsby. *Linc* 3A 76
Dowsdale. *Linc* 4B 76
Dowthwaitehead. *Cumb* 2E 103
Doxey. *Staf* 3D 72
Doxford. *Nmbd* 2F 121
Doynton. *S Glo* 4C 34
Drabblegate. *Norf* 3E 78
Draethen. *Cphy* 3F 33
Draffan. *S Lan* 5A 128
Dragonby. *N Lin* 3C 94
Dragons Green. *W Sus* 3C 26
Drakelow. *Worc* 2C 60
Drakemyre. *N Ayr* 4D 126
Drakes Broughton. *Worc* 1E 49
Drakes Cross. *Worc* 3E 61
Drakewalls. *Corn* 5E 11
Draughton. *Nptn* 3E 63
Draughton. *N Yor* 4C 98
Drax. *N Yor* 2G 93
Draycot. *Oxon* 5E 51
Draycote. *Warw* 4B 62
Draycot Foliat. *Swin* 4G 35
Draycott. *Derbs* 2B 74
Draycott. *Glos* 2G 49
Draycott. *Shrp* 1C 60
Draycott. *Som* 1H 21
(nr. Cheddar)
Draycott. *Som* 4A 22
(nr. Yeovil)
Draycott. *Worc* 1D 48
Draycott in the Clay. *Staf* 3F 73
Draycott in the Moors. *Staf* . .1D 73
Drayford. *Devn* 1A 12
Drayton. *Leics* 1F 63
Drayton. *Linc* 2B 76
Drayton. *Norf* 4D 78
Drayton. *Nptn* 4C 62
Drayton. *Oxon* 2C 36
(nr. Abingdon)
Drayton. *Oxon* 1C 50
(nr. Banbury)
Drayton. *Port* 2E 17
Drayton. *Som* 4H 21
Drayton. *Warw* 5F 61
Drayton. *Worc* 3D 60
Drayton Bassett. *Staf* 5F 73
Drayton Beauchamp. *Buck* . . .4H 51
Drayton Parslow. *Buck* 3G 51
Drayton St Leonard. *Oxon* . . .2D 36
Drebley. *N Yor* 4C 98
Dreenhill. *Pemb* 3D 42
Drefach. *Carm* 4F 45
(nr. Meidrim)
Drefach. *Carm* 2D 44
(nr. Newcastle Emlyn)
Drefach. *Carm* 2G 43
(nr. Tumble)
Drefach. *Cdgn* 1E 45
Dreghorn. *N Ayr* 1C 116
Drellingore. *Kent* 1G 29
Drem. *E Lot* 2B 130
Dreumasdal. *W Isl* 5C 170
Drewsteignton. *Devn* 3H 11
Drewston. *Devn* 4H 11
Driby. *Linc* 3C 88
Driffield. *E Yor* 4E 101
Driffield. *Glos* 2F 35
Drift. *Corn* 4B 4
Drigg. *Cumb* 5B 102
Drighlington. *W Yor* 2C 92
Drimnin. *High* 3G 139
Drimpton. *Dors* 2H 13
Dringhoe. *E Yor* 4F 101
Drinisiadar. *W Isl* 8D 171
Drinkstone. *Suff* 4B 66
Drinkstone Green. *Suff* 4B 66
Drointon. *Staf* 3E 73
Droitwich Spa. *Worc* 4C 60
Droman. *High* 3B 166
Dron. *Per* 2D 136
Dronfield. *Derbs* 3A 86
Dronfield Woodhouse. *Derbs* .3H 85
Drongan. *E Ayr* 3D 116

Dronley. *Ang* 5C 144
Droop. *Dors* 2C 14
Drope. *V Glam* 4E 32
Droxford. *Hants* 1E 16
Droylsden. *G Man* 1C 84
Druggers End. *Worc* 2C 48
Druid. *Den* 1C 70
Druid's Heath. *W Mid* 5E 73
Druidston. *Pemb* 3C 42
Druim. *High* 3D 158
Druimarbin. *High* 1E 141
Druim Fhearna. *High* 2E 147
Druimindarroch. *High* 5E 147
Druim Saighdinis. *W Isl* 2D 170
Drum. *Per* 3C 136
Drumbeg. *High* 5B 166
Drumblade. *Abers* 4C 160
Drumbuie. *Dum* 1C 110
Drumbuie. *High* 5G 155
Drumburgh. *Cumb* 4D 112
Drumburn. *Dum* 3A 112
Drumchapel. *Glas* 2G 127
Drumchardine. *High* 4H 157
Drumchork. *High* 5C 162
Drumclog. *S Lan* 1F 117
Drumeldrie. *Fife* 3G 137
Drumelzier. *Bord* 1D 118
Drumfearn. *High* 2E 147
Drumgask. *High* 4A 150
Drumgelloch. *N Lan* 3A 128
Drumgley. *Ang* 3D 144
Drumguish. *High* 4B 150
Drumin. *Mor* 5F 159
Drumindorsair. *High* 4G 157
Drumlamford House. *S Ayr* . . .2H 109
Drumlasie. *Abers* 3D 152
Drumlemble. *Arg* 4A 122
Drumlithie. *Abers* 5E 153
Drummoddie. *Dum* 5A 110
Drummond. *High* 2A 158
Drummore. *Dum* 5E 109
Drummuir. *Mor* 4A 160
Drumnadrochit. *High* 5H 157
Drumnagorrach. *Mor* 3C 160
Drumoak. *Abers* 4E 153
Drumrunie. *High* 3F 163
Drumry. *W Dun* 2G 127
Drums. *Abers* 1G 153
Drumsleet. *Dum* 2G 111
Drumsmittal. *High* 4A 158
Drums of Park. *Abers* 3C 160
Drumsturdy. *Ang* 5D 145
Drumtochty Castle. *Abers* 5D 152
Drumuie. *High* 4D 154
Drumuillie. *High* 1D 150
Drumvaich. *Stir* 3F 135
Drumwhindle. *Abers* 5G 161
Drunkendub. *Ang* 4F 145
Drury. *Flin* 4E 83
Drury Square. *Norf* 4B 78
Drybeck. *Cumb* 3H 103
Drybridge. *Mor* 2B 160
Drybridge. *N Ayr* 1C 116
Drybrook. *Glos* 4B 48
Drybrook. *Here* 4A 48
Dryburgh. *Bord* 1H 119
Dry Doddington. *Linc* 1F 75
Dry Drayton. *Cambs* 4C 64
Drym. *Corn* 3D 4
Drymen. *Stir* 1F 127
Drymuir. *Abers* 4G 161
Drynachan Lodge. *High* 5C 158
Drynie Park. *High* 3H 157
Drynoch. *High* 5D 154
Dry Sandford. *Oxon* 5C 50
Dryslwyn. *Carm* 3F 45
Dry Street. *Essx* 2A 40
Dryton. *Shrp* 5H 71
Dubford. *Abers* 2E 161
Dubton. *Abers* 3D 160
Dubton. *Ang* 3E 145
Duchally. *High* 2A 164
Duck End. *Essx* 3G 53
Duckington. *Ches W* 5G 83
Ducklington. *Oxon* 5B 50
Duckmanton. *Derbs* 3B 86
Duck Street. *Hants* 2B 24
Dudbridge. *Glos* 5D 48
Duddenhoe End. *Essx* 2E 53
Duddingston. *Edin* 2F 129
Duddington. *Nptn* 5G 75
Duddleswell. *E Sus* 3F 27
Duddo. *Nmbd* 5F 131
Duddon. *Ches W* 4H 83
Duddon Bridge. *Cumb* 1A 96
Dudleston. *Shrp* 2F 71
Dudleston Heath. *Shrp* 2F 71
Dudley. *Tyne* 2F 115
Dudley. *W Mid* 2D 60
Dudston. *Shrp* 1E 59
Dudwells. *Pemb* 2D 42
Duffield. *Derbs* 1H 73
Duffryn. *Neat* 2B 32
Dufftown. *Mor* 4H 159
Duffus. *Mor* 2F 159
Dufton. *Cumb* 2H 103
Duggleby. *N Yor* 3C 100
Duirinish. *High* 5G 155
Duisdalemore. *High* 2E 147
Duisdeil Mòr. *High* 2E 147
Duisky. *High* 1E 141
Dukesfield. *Nmbd* 4C 114

Dukestown. *Blae* 5E 47
Dukinfield. *G Man* 1D 84
Dulas. *IOA* 2D 81
Dulcote. *Som* 2A 22
Dulford. *Devn* 2D 12
Dull. *Per* 4F 143
Dullingham. *Cambs* 5F 65
Dullingham Ley. *Cambs* 5F 65
Dulnain Bridge. *High* 1D 151
Duloe. *Bed* 4A 64
Duloe. *Corn* 3G 7
Dulverton. *Som* 4C 20
Dulwich. *G Lon* 3E 39
Dumbarton. *W Dun* 2F 127
Dumbleton. *Glos* 2F 49
Dumfin. *Arg* 1E 127
Dumfries. *Dum* . . . . .2A 112 & 193
Dumgoyne. *Stir* 1G 127
Dummer. *Hants* 2D 24
Dumpford. *W Sus* 4G 25
Dun. *Ang* 2F 145
Dunagoil. *Arg* 4B 126
Dunalastair. *Per* 3E 142
Dunan. *High* 1D 147
Dunball. *Som* 2G 21
Dunbar. *E Lot* 2C 130
Dunbeath. *High* 5D 168
Dunbeg. *Arg* 5C 140
Dunblane. *Stir* 3G 135
Dunbog. *Fife* 2E 137
Dunbridge. *Hants* 4B 24
Duncanston. *Abers* 1C 152
Duncanston. *High* 3H 157
Dun Charlabhaigh. *W Isl* 3D 171
Dunchideock. *Devn* 4B 12
Dunchurch. *Warw* 3B 62
Duncote. *Nptn* 5D 62
Duncow. *Dum* 1A 112
Duncrievie. *Per* 3D 136
Duncton. *W Sus* 4A 26
Dundee. *D'dee* . . . . . .5D 144 & 194
Dundee Airport. *D'dee* 1F 137
Dundon. *Som* 3H 21
Dundonald. *S Ayr* 1C 116
Dundonnell. *High* 5E 163
Dundraw. *Cumb* 5D 112
Dundreggan. *High* 2F 149
Dundrennan. *Dum* 5E 111
Dundridge. *Hants* 1D 16
Dundry. *N Som* 5A 34
Dunecht. *Abers* 3E 153
Dunfermline. *Fife* 1D 129
Dunford Bridge. *S Yor* 4B 92
Dungate. *Kent* 5D 40
Dunge. *Wilts* 1D 23
Dungeness. *Kent* 4E 29
Dungworth. *S Yor* 2G 85
Dunham-on-the-Hill. *Ches W* . .3G 83
Dunham-on-Trent. *Notts* 3F 87
Dunhampton. *Worc* 4C 60
Dunham Town. *G Man* 2B 84
Dunham Woodhouses.
G Man 2B 84
Dunholme. *Linc* 3H 87
Dunino. *Fife* 2H 137
Dunipace. *Falk* 1B 128
Dunira. *Per* 1G 135
Dunkeld. *Per* 4H 143
Dunkerton. *Bath* 1C 22
Dunkeswell. *Devn* 2E 13
Dunkeswick. *N Yor* 5F 99
Dunkirk. *Kent* 5E 41
Dunkirk. *S Glo* 3C 34
Dunkirk. *Staf* 5C 84
Dunkirk. *Wilts* 5E 35
Dunk's Green. *Kent* 5H 39
Dunlappie. *Ang* 2E 145
Dunley. *Hants* 1C 24
Dunley. *Worc* 4B 60
Dunlichity Lodge. *High* 5A 158
Dunlop. *E Ayr* 5F 127
Dunmaglass Lodge. *High* 1H 149
Dunmore. *Arg* 3F 125
Dunmore. *Falk* 1B 128
Dunmore. *High* 4H 157
Dunnet. *High* 1E 169
Dunnichen. *Ang* 4E 145
Dunnington. *E Yor* 4F 101
Dunnington. *Warw* 5E 61
Dunnington. *York* 4A 100
Dunningwell. *Cumb* 1A 96
Dunnockshaw. *Lanc* 2G 91
Dunoon. *Arg* 2C 126
Dunphail. *Mor* 4E 159
Dunragit. *Dum* 4G 109
Dunrostan. *Arg* 1F 125
Duns. *Bord* 4D 130
Dunsby. *Linc* 3A 76
Dunscar. *G Man* 3F 91
Dunscore. *Dum* 1F 111
Dunscroft. *S Yor* 4G 93
Dunsdale. *Red C* 3D 106
Dunsden Green. *Oxon* 4F 37
Dunsfold. *Surr* 2B 26
Dunsford. *Devn* 4B 12
Dunshalt. *Fife* 2E 137
Dunshillock. *Abers* 4G 161
Dunsley. *N Yor* 3F 107
Dunsley. *Staf* 2C 60
Dunsmore. *Buck* 5G 51

Dunsop Bridge. *Lanc* 4F 97
Dunstable. *C Beds* 3A 52
Dunstall. *Staf* 3F 73
Dunstall. *Staf* 3F 73
Dunstall Green. *Suff* 4G 65
Dunstall Hill. *W Mid* 1D 60
Dunstan. *Nmbd* 3G 121
Dunster. *Som* 2C 20
Dunston. *Linc* 4H 87
Dunston. *Norf* 5E 79
Dunston. *Staf* 4D 72
Dunston. *Tyne* 3F 115
Dunstone. *Devn* 3B 8
Dunston Heath. *Staf* 4D 72
Dunsville. *S Yor* 4G 93
Dunswell. *E Yor* 1D 94
Dunsyre. *S Lan* 5D 128
Dunterton. *Devn* 5D 11
Duntisbourne Abbots. *Glos* . . .5E 49
Duntisbourne Leer. *Glos* 5E 49
Duntisbourne Rouse. *Glos* 5E 49
Duntish. *Dors* 2B 14
Duntocher. *W Dun* 2F 127
Dunton. *Buck* 3G 51
Dunton. *C Beds* 1C 52
Dunton. *Norf* 2A 78
Dunton Bassett. *Leics* 1C 62
Dunton Green. *Kent* 5G 39
Dunton Patch. *Norf* 2A 78
Duntulm. *High* 1D 154
Dunure. *S Ayr* 3B 116
Dunvant. *Swan* 3E 31
Dunvegan. *High* 4B 154
Dunwich. *Suff* 3G 67
Dunwood. *Staf* 5D 84
Durdar. *Cumb* 4F 113
Durgates. *E Sus* 2H 27
Durham. *Dur* . . . . . . .5F 115 & 194
Durham Tees Valley Airport.
Darl 3A 106
Durisdeer. *Dum* 4A 118
Durisdeermill. *Dum* 4A 118
Durkar. *W Yor* 3D 92
Durleigh. *Som* 3F 21
Durley. *Hants* 1D 16
Durley. *Wilts* 5H 35
Durley Street. *Hants* 1D 16
Durlow Common. *Here* 2B 48
Durnamuck. *High* 4E 163
Durness. *High* 2E 166
Durno. *Abers* 1E 152
Duror. *High* 3D 141
Durran. *Arg* 3G 133
Durran. *High* 2D 169
Durrant Green. *Kent* 2C 28
Durrants. *Hants* 1F 17
Durrington. *W Sus* 5C 26
Durrington. *Wilts* 2G 23
Dursley. *Glos* 2C 34
Dursley Cross. *Glos* 4B 48
Durston. *Som* 4F 21
Durweston. *Dors* 2D 14
Dury. *Shet* 6F 173
Duston. *Nptn* 4E 62
Duthil. *High* 1D 150
Dutlas. *Powy* 3E 58
Dutson. *Corn* 4D 10
Dutton. *Ches W* 3H 83
Duxford. *Cambs* 1E 53
Duxford. *Oxon* 2B 36
Dwygyfylchi. *Cnwy* 3G 81
Dwyran. *IOA* 4D 80
Dyce. *Aber* 2F 153
Dyffryn. *B'end* 2B 32
Dyffryn. *Carm* 2H 43
Dyffryn. *Pemb* 1D 42
Dyffryn. *V Glam* 4D 32
Dyffryn Ardudwy. *Gwyn* 3E 69
Dyffryn Castell. *Cdgn* 2G 57
Dyffryn Ceidrych. *Carm* 3H 45
Dyffryn Cellwen. *Neat* 5B 46
Dyke. *Linc* 3A 76
Dyke. *Mor* 3D 159
Dykehead. *Ang* 2C 144
Dykehead. *N Lan* 3B 128
Dykehead. *Stir* 4E 135
Dykend. *Ang* 3B 144
Dykesfield. *Cumb* 4E 112
Dylife. *Powy* 1A 58
Dymchurch. *Kent* 3F 29
Dymock. *Glos* 2C 48
Dyrham. *S Glo* 4C 34
Dysart. *Fife* 4F 137
Dyserth. *Den* 3C 82

E

Eachwick. *Nmbd* 2E 115
Eadar Dha Fhadhail. *W Isl* 4C 171
Eagland Hill. *Lanc* 5D 96
Eagle. *Linc* 4F 87
Eagle Barnsdale. *Linc* 4F 87
Eagle Moor. *Linc* 4F 87
Eaglescliffe. *Stoc T* 3B 106
Eaglesfield. *Cumb* 2B 102
Eaglesfield. *Dum* 2D 112
Eaglesham. *E Ren* 4G 127
Eaglethorpe. *Nptn* 1H 63

Eagley. *G Man* 3F 91
Eairy. *IOM* 4B 108
Eakley Lanes. *Mil* 5F 63
Eakring. *Notts* 4D 86
Ealand. *N Lin* 3A 94
Ealing. *G Lon* 2C 38
Eallabus. *Arg* 3B 124
Eals. *Nmbd* 4H 113
Eamont Bridge. *Cumb* 2G 103
Earby. *Lanc* 5B 98
Earcroft. *Bkbn* 2E 91
Eardington. *Shrp* 1B 60
Eardisland. *Here* 5G 59
Eardisley. *Here* 1G 47
Eardiston. *Shrp* 3F 71
Eardiston. *Worc* 4A 60
Earith. *Cambs* 3C 64
Earlais. *High* 2C 154
Earle. *Nmbd* 2D 121
Earlesfield. *Linc* 2G 75
Earlestown. *Mers* 1H 83
Earley. *Wok* 4F 37
Earlham. *Norf* 5D 78
Earlish. *High* 2C 154
Earls Barton. *Nptn* 4F 63
Earls Colne. *Essx* 3B 54
Earls Common. *Worc* 5D 60
Earl's Croome. *Worc* 1D 48
Earlsdon. *W Mid* 3H 61
Earlsferry. *Fife* 3G 137
Earlsford. *Abers* 5F 161
Earl's Green. *Suff* 4C 66
Earlsheaton. *W Yor* 2C 92
Earl Shilton. *Leics* 1B 62
Earl Soham. *Suff* 4E 67
Earl Sterndale. *Derbs* 4E 85
Earlston. *E Ayr* 1D 116
Earlston. *Bord* 1H 119
Earl Stonham. *Suff* 5D 66
Earlswood. *Mon* 2H 33
Earlswood. *Warw* 3F 61
Earlyvale. *Bord* 4F 129
Earnley. *W Sus* 3G 17
Earsairidh. *W Isl* 9C 170
Earsdon. *Tyne* 2G 115
Earsham. *Norf* 2F 67
Earsham Street. *Suff* 3E 67
Earswick. *York* 4A 100
Eartham. *W Sus* 5A 26
Earthcott Green. *S Glo* 3B 34
Easby. *N Yor* 4C 106
(nr. Great Ayton)
Easby. *N Yor* 4E 105
(nr. Richmond)
Easdale. *Arg* 2E 133
Easebourne. *W Sus* 4G 25
Easenhall. *Warw* 3B 62
Eashing. *Surr* 1A 26
Easington. *Buck* 4E 51
Easington. *Dur* 5H 115
Easington. *E Yor* 3G 95
Easington. *Nmbd* 1F 121
Easington. *Oxon* 2C 50
(nr. Banbury)
Easington. *Oxon* 2E 37
(nr. Watlington)
Easington. *Red C* 3E 107
Easington Colliery. *Dur* 5H 115
Easington Lane. *Tyne* 5G 115
Easingwold. *N Yor* 3H 99
Easole Street. *Kent* 5G 41
Eassie. *Ang* 4C 144
Eassie and Nevay. *Ang* 4C 144
East Aberthaw. *V Glam* 5D 32
Eastacombe. *Devn* 4F 19
Eastacott. *Devn* 4G 19
East Allington. *Devn* 4D 8
East Anstey. *Devn* 4B 20
East Anton. *Hants* 2B 24
East Appleton. *N Yor* 5F 105
East Ardsley. *W Yor* 2D 92
East Ashley. *Devn* 1G 11
East Ashling. *W Sus* 2G 17
East Aston. *Hants* 2C 24
East Ayton. *N Yor* 1D 101
East Barkwith. *Linc* 2A 88
East Barnby. *N Yor* 3F 107
East Barnet. *G Lon* 1D 39
East Barns. *E Lot* 2D 130
East Barsham. *Norf* 2B 78
East Beach. *W Sus* 3G 17
East Beckham. *Norf* 1D 78
East Bedfont. *G Lon* 3B 38
East Bennan. *N Ayr* 3D 123
East Bergholt. *Suff* 2D 54
East Bierley. *W Yor* 2B 92
East Blatchington. *E Sus* 5F 27
East Bliney. *Norf* 4B 78
East Bloxworth. *Dors* 3D 15
East Boldre. *Hants* 2B 16
East Bolton. *Nmbd* 3F 121
Eastbourne. *Darl* 3F 105
Eastbourne. *E Sus* . . . . .5H 27 & 195
East Brent. *Som* 1G 21
East Bridge. *Suff* 4G 67
East Bridgford. *Notts* 1D 74
East Briscoe. *Dur* 3C 104
East Buckland. *Devn* 3G 19
(nr. Barnstaple)
East Buckland. *Devn* 4C 8
(nr. Thurlestone)

East Budleigh. Devn 4D 12
Eastburn. W Yor 5C 98
East Burnham. Buck 2A 38
East Burrafirth. Shet 6E 173
East Burton. Dors 4D 14
Eastbury. Herts 1B 38
Eastbury. W Ber 4B 36
East Butsfield. Dur 5E 115
East Butterleigh. Devn 2C 12
East Butterwick. N Lin 4B 94
Eastby. N Yor 4C 98
East Calder. W Lot 3D 129
East Carleton. Norf 5D 78
East Carlton. Nptn 2F 63
East Carlton. W Yor 5E 98
East Chaldon. Dors 4C 14
East Challow. Oxon 3B 36
East Charleton. Devn 4D 8
East Chelborough. Dors 2A 14
East Chiltington. E Sus 4E 27
East Chinnock. Som 1H 13
East Chisenbury. Wilts 1G 23
Eastchurch. Kent 3D 40
East Clandon. Surr 5B 38
East Claydon. Buck 3F 51
East Clevedon. N Som 4H 33
East Clyne. High 3F 165
East Clyth. High 5E 169
East Coker. Som 1A 14
Eastcombe. Glos 5D 49
East Combe. Som 3E 21
East Common. N Yor 1G 93
East Compton. Som 2B 22
East Cornworthy. Devn 3E 9
Eastcote. G Lon 2C 38
Eastcote. Nptn 5D 62
Eastcote. W Mid 3F 61
Eastcott. Corn 1C 10
Eastcott. Wilts 1F 23
East Cottingwith. E Yor 5B 100
East Coulston. Wilts 1E 23
Eastcourt. Wilts 5H 35
(nr. Pewsey)
Eastcourt. Wilts 2E 35
(nr. Tetbury)
East Cowes. IOW 3D 16
East Cowick. E Yor 2G 93
East Cowton. N Yor 4A 106
East Cramlington. Nmbd 2F 115
East Cranmore. Som 2B 22
East Creech. Dors 4E 15
East Croachy. High 1A 150
East Dean. E Sus 5G 27
East Dean. Glos 3B 48
East Dean. Hants 4A 24
East Dean. W Sus 4A 26
East Down. Devn 2G 19
East Drayton. Notts 3E 87
East Dundry. N Som 5A 34
East Ella. Hull 2D 94
East End. Cambs 3C 64
East End. Dors 3E 15
East End. E Yor 4F 101
(nr. Ulrome)
East End. E Yor 2F 95
(nr. Withernsea)
East End. Hants 3B 16
(nr. Lymington)
East End. Hants 5C 36
(nr. Newbury)
East End. Herts 3E 53
East End. Kent 3D 40
(nr. Minster)
East End. Kent 2C 28
(nr. Tenterden)
East End. N Som 4H 33
East End. Oxon 4B 50
East End. Som 1A 22
East End. Suff 2E 54
Easter Ardross. High 1A 158
Easter Balgedie. Per 3D 136
Easter Balmoral. Abers 4G 151
Easter Brae. High 2A 158
Easter Buckieburn. Stir 1A 128
Easter Bush. Midl 3F 129
Easter Compton. S Glo 3A 34
Easter Fearn. High 5D 164
Easter Galcantray. High 4C 158
Eastergate. W Sus 5A 26
Easterhouse. Glas 3H 127
Easter Howgate. Midl 3F 129
Easter Kinkell. High 3H 157
Easter Lednathie. Ang 2C 144
Easter Ogil. Ang 2D 144
Easter Ord. Abers 3F 153
Easter Quarff. Shet 8F 173
Easter Rhynd. Per 2D 136
Easter Skeld. Shet 7E 173
Easter Suddie. High 3A 158
Easterton. Wilts 1F 23
Eastertown. Som 1G 21
Easter Tulloch. Abers 1G 145
East Everleigh. Wilts 1H 23
East Farleigh. Kent 5B 40
East Farndon. Nptn 2E 62
East Ferry. Linc 1F 87
Eastfield. N Lan 3B 128
(nr. Caldercruix)
Eastfield. N Lan 3B 128
(nr. Harthill)
Eastfield. N Yor 1E 101
Eastfield. S Lan 3H 127

Eastfield Hall. Nmbd 4G 121
East Fortune. E Lot 2B 130
East Garforth. W Yor 1E 93
East Garston. W Ber 4B 36
Eastgate. Dur 1C 104
Eastgate. Norf 3D 78
East Ginge. Oxon 3C 36
East Gores. Essx 3B 54
East Goscote. Leics 4D 74
East Grafton. Wilts 5A 36
East Green. Suff 5F 65
East Grimstead. Wilts 4H 23
East Grinstead. W Sus 2E 27
East Guldeford. E Sus 3D 28
East Haddon. Nptn 4D 62
East Hagbourne. Oxon 3D 36
East Halton. N Lin 2E 95
East Ham. G Lon 2F 39
Eastham. Mers 2F 83
Eastham. Worc 4A 60
Eastham Ferry. Mers 2F 83
Easthampstead. Brac 5G 37
Easthampton. Here 4G 59
East Hanney. Oxon 2C 36
East Hanningfield. Essx 5A 54
East Hardwick. W Yor 3E 93
East Harling. Norf 2B 66
East Harlsey. N Yor 5B 106
East Harnham. Wilts 4G 23
East Harptree. Bath 1A 22
East Hartford. Nmbd 2F 115
East Harting. W Sus 1G 17
East Hatch. Wilts 4E 23
East Hatley. Cambs 5B 64
Easthaugh. Norf 4C 78
East Hauxwell. N Yor 5E 105
East Haven. Ang 5E 145
Eastheath. Wok 5G 37
East Heckington. Linc 1A 76
East Hedleyhope. Dur 5E 115
East Helmsdale. High 2H 165
East Hendred. Oxon 3C 36
East Heslerton. N Yor 2D 100
East Hoathly. E Sus 4G 27
East Holme. Dors 4D 15
Easthope. Shrp 1H 59
East Horrington. Som 2A 22
East Horsley. Surr 5B 38
East Horton. Nmbd 1E 121
Easthouses. Midl 3G 129
East Howe. Bour 3F 15
East Huntspill. Som 2G 21
East Hyde. C Beds 4B 52
East Ilsley. W Ber 3C 36
Eastington. Devn 2H 11
Eastington. Glos 4G 49
(nr. Northleach)
Eastington. Glos 5C 48
(nr. Stonehouse)
East Keal. Linc 4C 88
East Kennett. Wilts 5G 35
East Keswick. W Yor 5F 99
East Kilbride. S Lan 4H 127
East Kirkby. Linc 4C 88
East Knapton. N Yor 2C 100
East Knighton. Dors 4D 14
East Knowstone. Devn 4B 20
East Knoyle. Wilts 3D 23
East Kyloe. Nmbd 1E 121
East Lambrook. Som 1H 13
East Langdon. Kent 1H 29
East Langton. Leics 1E 63
East Langwell. High 3E 164
East Lavant. W Sus 2G 17
East Lavington. W Sus 4A 26
East Layton. N Yor 4E 105
Eastleach Martin. Glos 5H 49
Eastleach Turville. Glos 5G 49
East Leake. Notts 3C 74
East Learmouth. Nmbd 1C 120
Eastleigh. Devn 4E 19
(nr. Bideford)
East Leigh. Devn 2H 11
(nr. Crediton)
East Leigh. Devn 3C 8
(nr. Modbury)
Eastleigh. Hants 1C 16
East Lexham. Norf 4A 78
East Lilburn. Nmbd 2E 121
Eastling. Kent 5D 40
East Linton. E Lot 2B 130
East Liss. Hants 4F 25
East Lockinge. Oxon 3C 36
East Looe. Corn 3G 7
East Lound. N Lin 1E 87
East Lulworth. Dors 4D 14
East Lutton. N Yor 3D 100
East Lydford. Som 3A 22
East Lyng. Som 4G 21
East Mains. Abers 4D 152
East Malling. Kent 5B 40
East Marden. W Sus 1G 17
East Markham. Notts 3E 87
East Marton. N Yor 4B 98
East Meon. Hants 4E 25
East Mersea. Essx 4D 54
East Mey. High 1F 169
East Midlands Airport.
Leics ....3B 74 & 216
East Molesey. Surr 4C 38

Eastmoor. Norf 5G 77
East Morden. Dors 3E 15
East Morton. W Yor 5D 98
East Ness. N Yor 2A 100
East Newton. E Yor 1F 95
East Newton. N Yor 2A 100
Eastney. Port 3E 17
Eastnor. Here 2C 48
East Norton. Leics 5E 75
East Nynehead. Som 4E 21
East Oakley. Hants 1D 24
East Ogwell. Devn 5B 12
Easton. Cambs 3A 64
Easton. Cumb 4D 112
(nr. Burgh by Sands)
Easton. Cumb 2F 113
(nr. Longtown)
Easton. Devn 4H 11
Easton. Dors 5B 14
Easton. Hants 3D 24
Easton. Linc 3G 75
Easton. Norf 4D 78
Easton. Som 2A 22
Easton. Suff 5E 67
Easton. Wilts 4D 35
Easton Grey. Wilts 3D 35
Easton-in-Gordano. N Som 4A 34
Easton Maudit. Nptn 5F 63
Easton on the Hill. Nptn 5H 75
Easton Royal. Wilts 5H 35
East Orchard. Dors 1D 14
East Ord. Nmbd 4F 131
East Panson. Devn 3D 10
East Peckham. Kent 1A 28
East Pennard. Som 3A 22
East Perry. Cambs 4A 64
East Pitcorthie. Fife 3H 137
East Portlemouth. Devn 5D 8
East Prawle. Devn 5D 9
East Preston. W Sus 5B 26
East Putford. Devn 1D 10
East Quantoxhead. Som 2E 21
East Rainton. Tyne 5G 115
East Ravendale. NE Lin 1B 88
East Raynham. Norf 3A 78
Eastrea. Cambs 1B 64
East Rhidorroch Lodge.
High 4G 163
Eastriggs. Dum 3D 112
East Rigton. W Yor 5F 99
East Rounton. N Yor 4B 106
East Row. N Yor 3F 107
East Rudham. Norf 3H 77
East Runton. Norf 1D 78
East Ruston. Norf 3F 79
Eastry. Kent 5H 41
East Saltoun. E Lot 3A 130
East Shaws. Dur 3D 105
East Shefford. W Ber 4B 36
Eastshore. Shet 10E 173
East Sleekburn. Nmbd 1F 115
East Somerton. Norf 4G 79
East Stockwith. Linc 1E 87
East Stoke. Dors 4D 14
East Stoke. Notts 1E 75
East Stoke. Som 1H 13
East Stour. Dors 4D 22
East Stourmouth. Kent 4G 41
East Stowford. Devn 4G 19
East Stratton. Hants 2D 24
East Studdal. Kent 1H 29
East Taphouse. Corn 2F 7
East-the-Water. Devn 4E 19
East Thirston. Nmbd 5F 121
East Tilbury. Thur 3A 40
East Tisted. Hants 3F 25
East Torrington. Linc 2A 88
East Tuddenham. Norf 4C 78
East Tytherley. Hants 4A 24
East Tytherton. Wilts 4E 35
East Village. Devn 2B 12
Eastville. Linc 5D 88
East Wall. Shrp 1H 59
East Walton. Norf 4G 77
East Week. Devn 3G 11
Eastwell. Leics 3E 75
East Wellow. Hants 4B 24
East Wemyss. Fife 4F 137
East Whitburn. W Lot 3C 128
Eastwick. Herts 4E 53
Eastwick. Shet 4E 173
East Williamston. Pemb 4E 43
East Winch. Norf 4F 77
East Winterslow. Wilts 3H 23
East Wittering. W Sus 3F 17
East Witton. N Yor 1D 98
Eastwood. Notts 1B 74
Eastwood. S'end 2C 40
East Woodburn. Nmbd 1C 114
Eastwood End. Cambs 1D 64
East Woodhay. Hants 5C 36
East Woodlands. Som 2C 22
East Worldham. Hants 3F 25
East Worlington. Devn 1A 12
East Wretham. Norf 1B 66
East Youlstone. Devn 1C 10

Eaton. Norf 2F 77
(nr. Heacham)
Eaton. Norf 5E 78
(nr. Norwich)
Eaton. Notts 3E 86
Eaton. Oxon 5C 50
Eaton. Shrp 2F 59
(nr. Bishop's Castle)
Eaton. Shrp 1H 59
(nr. Church Stretton)
Eaton Bishop. Here 2H 47
Eaton Bray. C Beds 3H 51
Eaton Constantine. Shrp 5H 71
Eaton Hastings. Oxon 2A 36
Eaton Socon. Cambs 5A 64
Eaton upon Tern. Shrp 3A 72
Eau Brink. Norf 4E 77
Eaves Green. W Mid 2G 61
Ebberley Hill. Devn 1F 11
Ebberston. N Yor 1C 100
Ebbesbourne Wake. Wilts 4E 23
Ebblake. Dors 2G 15
Ebbsfleet. Kent 3H 39
Ebbw Vale. Blae 5E 47
Ebchester. Dur 4E 115
Ebernoe. W Sus 3A 26
Ebford. Devn 4C 12
Ebley. Glos 5D 48
Ebnal. Ches W 1G 71
Ebrington. Glos 1G 49
Ecchinswell. Hants 1D 24
Ecclefechan. Dum 2C 112
Eccles. G Man 1B 84
Eccles. Kent 4B 40
Eccles. Bord 5D 130
Ecclesall. S Yor 2H 85
Ecclesfield. S Yor 1A 86
Eccles Green. Here 1G 47
Eccleshall. Staf 3C 72
Eccleshill. W Yor 1B 92
Ecclesmachan. W Lot 2D 128
Eccles on Sea. Norf 3G 79
Eccles Road. Norf 1C 66
Eccleston. Ches W 4G 83
Eccleston. Lanc 3D 90
Eccleston. Mers 1G 83
Eccup. W Yor 5E 99
Echt. Abers 3E 153
Eckford. Bord 2B 120
Eckington. Derbs 3B 86
Eckington. Worc 1E 49
Ecton. Nptn 4F 63
Edale. Derbs 2F 85
Eday Airport. Orkn 4E 172
Edburton. W Sus 4D 26
Edderside. Cumb 5C 112
Edderton. High 5E 164
Eddington. Kent 4F 41
Eddington. W Ber 5B 36
Eddleston. Bord 5F 129
Eddlewood. S Lan 4A 128
Edenbridge. Kent 1F 27
Edendonich. Arg 1A 134
Edenfield. Lanc 3G 91
Edenhall. Cumb 1G 103
Edenham. Linc 3H 75
Edensor. Derbs 4G 85
Edentaggart. Arg 4C 134
Edenthorpe. S Yor 4G 93
Eden Vale. Dur 1B 106
Edern. Gwyn 2B 68
Edgarley. Som 3A 22
Edgbaston. W Mid 2E 61
Edgcott. Buck 3E 51
Edgcott. Som 3B 20
Edge. Glos 5D 48
Edge. Shrp 5F 71
Edgebolton. Shrp 3H 71
Edge End. Glos 4A 48
Edgefield. Norf 2C 78
Edgefield Street. Norf 2C 78
Edge Green. Ches W 5G 83
Edgehead. Midl 3G 129
Edgeley. Shrp 1H 71
Edgeside. Lanc 2G 91
Edgeworth. Glos 5E 49
Edgiock. Worc 4E 61
Edgmond. Telf 4B 72
Edgmond Marsh. Telf 3B 72
Edgton. Shrp 2F 59
Edgware. G Lon 1C 38
Edgworth. Bkbn 3F 91
Edinbane. High 3C 154
Edinburgh. Edin ....2F 129 & 194
Edinburgh Airport. Edin 2E 129
Edingale. Staf 4G 73
Edingley. Notts 5D 86
Edingthorpe. Norf 2F 79
Edington. Som 3G 21
Edington. Wilts 1E 23
Edingworth. Som 1G 21
Edistone. Devn 4C 18
Edithmead. Som 2G 21
Edith Weston. Rut 5G 75
Edlaston. Derbs 1F 73
Edlesborough. Buck 4H 51
Edlingham. Nmbd 4F 121
Edlington. Linc 3B 88
Edmondsham. Dors 1F 15
Edmondsley. Dur 5F 115
Edmondthorpe. Leics 4F 75
Edmonstone. Orkn 5E 172

Edmonton. Corn 1D 6
Edmonton. G Lon 1E 39
Edmundbyers. Dur 4D 114
Ednam. Bord 1B 120
Ednaston. Derbs 1G 73
Edney Common. Essx 5G 53
Edrom. Bord 4E 131
Edstaston. Shrp 2H 71
Edstone. Warw 4F 61
Edwalton. Notts 2D 74
Edwardstone. Suff 1C 54
Edwardsville. Mer T 2D 32
Edwinsford. Carm 2G 45
Edwinstowe. Notts 4D 86
Edworth. C Beds 1C 52
Edwyn Ralph. Here 5A 60
Edzell. Ang 2F 145
Efail-fach. Neat 2A 32
Efail Isaf. Rhon 3D 32
Efailnewydd. Gwyn 2C 68
Efail-rhyd. Powy 3D 70
Efailwen. Carm 2F 43
Efenechtyd. Den 5D 82
Effingham. Surr 5C 38
Effingham Common. Surr 5C 38
Effirth. Shet 6E 173
Efflinch. Staf 4F 73
Efford. Devn 2B 12
Efstigarth. Shet 2F 173
Egbury. Hants 1C 24
Egdon. Worc 5D 60
Egerton. G Man 3F 91
Egerton. Kent 1D 28
Egerton Forstal. Kent 1C 28
Eggborough. N Yor 2F 93
Eggbuckland. Plym 3A 8
Eggesford. Devn 1G 11
Eggington. C Beds 3H 51
Eggington. Derbs 3G 73
Egglescliffe. Stoc T 3B 106
Eggleston. Dur 2C 104
Egham. Surr 3B 38
Egham Hythe. Surr 3B 38
Egleton. Rut 5F 75
Eglingham. Nmbd 3F 121
Egloshayle. Corn 5A 10
Egloskerry. Corn 4C 10
Eglwysbach. Cnwy 3H 81
Eglwys Brewis. V Glam 5D 32
Eglwys Fach. Cdgn 1F 57
Eglwyswrw. Pemb 1F 43
Egmanton. Notts 4E 87
Egmere. Norf 2B 78
Egremont. Cumb 3B 102
Egremont. Mers 1F 83
Egton. N Yor 4F 107
Egton Bridge. N Yor 4F 107
Egypt. Buck 2A 38
Egypt. Hants 2C 24
Eight Ash Green. Essx 3C 54
Eight Mile Burn. Midl 4E 129
Eignaig. High 4B 140
Eilanreach. High 2G 147
Eildon. Bord 1H 119
Eileanach Lodge. High 2H 157
Eilean Fhlodaigh. W Isl 3D 170
Eilean Iarmain. High 2F 147
Einacleit. W Isl 5D 171
Eisgein. W Isl 6F 171
Eisingrug. Gwyn 2F 69
Elan Village. Powy 4B 58
Elberton. S Glo 3B 34
Elbridge. W Sus 5A 26
Elburton. Plym 3B 8
Elcho. Per 1D 136
Elcombe. Swin 3G 35
Elcot. W Ber 5B 36
Eldernell. Cambs 1C 64
Eldersfield. Worc 2D 48
Elderslie. Ren 3F 127
Elder Street. Essx 2F 53
Eldon. Dur 2F 105
Eldroth. N Yor 3G 97
Eldwick. W Yor 5D 98
Elfhowe. Cumb 5F 103
Elford. Nmbd 1F 121
Elford. Staf 4F 73
Elford Closes. Cambs 3D 65
Elgin. Mor 2G 159
Elgol. High 2D 146
Elham. Kent 1F 29
Elie. Fife 3G 137
Eling. Hants 1B 16
Eling. W Ber 4D 36
Elishaw. Nmbd 5C 120
Elizafield. Dum 2B 112
Elkesley. Notts 3D 86
Elkington. Nptn 3D 62
Elkins Green. Essx 5G 53
Elkstone. Glos 4E 49
Ellan. High 1C 150
Elland. W Yor 2B 92
Ellary. Arg 2F 125
Ellastone. Staf 1F 73
Ellbridge. Corn 2A 8
Ellel. Lanc 4D 97
Ellemford. Bord 3D 130
Ellenabeich. Arg 2E 133
Ellenborough. Cumb 1B 102
Ellenbrook. Herts 5C 52
Ellenhall. Staf 3C 72
Ellen's Green. Surr 2B 26

Ellerbec—Felbridge

Ellerbec. N Yor 5B 106
Ellerburn. N Yor 1C 100
Ellerby. N Yor 3E 107
Ellerdine. Telf 3A 72
Ellerdine Heath. Telf 3A 72
Ellerhayes. Devn 2C 12
Elleric. Arg 4E 141
Ellerker. E Yor 2C 94
Ellerton. E Yor 1H 93
Ellerton. N Yor 5F 105
Ellerton. Shrp 3B 72
Ellesborough. Buck 5G 51
Ellesmere. Shrp 2F 71
Ellesmere Port. Ches W 3G 83
Ellingham. Hants 2G 15
Ellingham. Norf 1F 67
Ellingham. Nmbd 2F 121
Ellingstring. N Yor 1D 98
Ellington. Cambs 3A 64
Ellington. Nmbd 5G 121
Ellington Thorpe. Cambs 3A 64
Elliot. Ang 5F 145
Ellisfield. Hants 2E 25
Ellishadder. High 2E 155
Ellistown. Leics 4B 74
Ellon. Abers 5G 161
Ellonby. Cumb 1F 103
Ellough. Suff 2G 67
Elloughton. E Yor 2C 94
Ellwood. Glos 5A 48
Elm. Cambs 5D 76
Elmbridge. Glos 4D 48
Elmbridge. Worc 4D 60
Elmdon. Essx 2E 53
Elmdon. W Mid 2F 61
Elmdon Heath. W Mid 2F 61
Elmesthorpe. Leics 1B 62
Elmfield. IOW 3D 16
Elm Hill. Dors 4D 22
Elmhurst. Staf 4F 73
Elmley Castle. Worc 1E 49
Elmley Lovett. Worc 4C 60
Elmore. Glos 4C 48
Elmore Back. Glos 4C 48
Elm Park. G Lon 2G 39
Elmscott. Devn 4C 18
Elmsett. Suff 1D 54
Elmstead. Essx 3D 54
Elmstead Heath. Essx 3D 54
Elmstead Market. Essx 3D 54
Elmsted. Kent 1F 29
Elmstone. Kent 4G 41
Elmstone Hardwicke. Glos 3E 49
Elmswell. E Yor 4D 101
Elmswell. Suff 4B 66
Elmton. Derbs 3C 86
Elphin. High 2G 163
Elphinstone. E Lot 2G 129
Elrick. Abers 3F 153
Elrick. Mor 1B 152
Elrig. Dum 5A 110
Elsdon. Nmbd 5D 120
Elsecar. S Yor 1A 86
Elsenham. Essx 3F 53
Elsfield. Oxon 4D 50
Elsham. N Lin 3D 94
Elsing. Norf 4C 78
Elslack. N Yor 5B 98
Elsrickle. S Lan 5D 128
Elstead. Surr 1A 26
Elsted. W Sus 1G 17
Elsted Marsh. W Sus 4G 25
Elsthorpe. Linc 3H 75
Elstob. Dur 2A 106
Elston. Devn 2A 12
Elston. Lanc 1E 90
Elston. Notts 1E 75
Elston. Wilts 2F 23
Elstone. Devn 1G 11
Elstow. Bed 1A 52
Elstree. Herts 1C 38
Elstronwick. E Yor 1F 95
Elswick. Lanc 1C 90
Elswick. Tyne 3F 115
Elsworth. Cambs 4C 64
Elterwater. Cumb 4E 103
Eltham. G Lon 3F 39
Eltisley. Cambs 5B 64
Elton. Cambs 1H 63
Elton. Ches W 3G 83
Elton. Derbs 4G 85
Elton. Glos 4C 48
Elton. G Man 3F 91
Elton. Here 3G 59
Elton. Notts 2E 75
Elton. Stoc T 3B 106
Elton Green. Ches W 3G 83
Eltringham. Nmbd 3D 115
Elvanfoot. S Lan 3B 118
Elvaston. Derbs 2B 74
Elveden. Suff 3H 65
Elvetham Heath. Hants 1F 25
Elvingston. E Lot 2A 130
Elvington. Kent 5G 41
Elvington. York 5B 100
Elwick. Hart 1B 106
Elwick. Nmbd 1F 121
Elworth. Ches E 4B 84
Elworth. Dors 4A 14
Elworthy. Som 3D 20
Ely. Cambs 2E 65
Ely. Card 4E 33
Emberton. Mil 1G 51
Embleton. Cumb 1C 102
Embleton. Dur 2B 106
Embleton. Nmbd 2G 121
Embo. High 4F 165
Emborough. Som 1B 22
Embo Street. High 4F 165
Embsay. N Yor 4C 98
Emery Down. Hants 2A 16
Emley. W Yor 3C 92
Emmbrook. Wok 5F 37
Emmer Green. Read 4F 37
Emmington. Oxon 5F 51
Emneth. Norf 5D 77
Emneth Hungate. Norf 5E 77
Empingham. Rut 5G 75
Empshott. Hants 3F 25
Emsworth. Hants 2F 17
Enborne. W Ber 5C 36
Enborne Row. W Ber 5C 36
Enchmarsh. Shrp 1H 59
Enderby. Leics 1C 62
Endmoor. Cumb 1E 97
Endon. Staf 5D 84
Endon Bank. Staf 5D 84
Enfield. G Lon 1E 39
Enfield Wash. G Lon 1E 39
Enford. Wilts 1G 23
Engine Common. S Glo 3B 34
Englefield. W Ber 4E 36
Englefield Green. Surr 3A 38
Engleseabrook. Ches E 5B 84
English Bicknor. Glos 4A 48
Englishcombe. Bath 5C 34
English Frankton. Shrp 3G 71
Enham Alamein. Hants 2B 24
Enmore. Som 3F 21
Ennerdale Bridge. Cumb 3B 102
Enniscaven. Corn 3D 6
Enoch. Dum 4A 118
Enochdhu. Per 2H 143
Ensay. Arg 4E 139
Ensbury. Bour 3F 15
Ensdon. Shrp 4G 71
Ensis. Devn 4F 19
Enson. Staf 3D 72
Enstone. Oxon 3B 50
Enterkinfoot. Dum 4A 118
Enville. Staf 2C 60
Eolaigearraidh. W Isl 8C 170
Eorabus. Arg 1A 132
Eoropaidh. W Isl 1H 171
Epney. Glos 4C 48
Epperstone. Notts 1D 74
Epping. Essx 5E 53
Epping Green. Essx 5E 53
Epping Green. Herts 5C 52
Epping Upland. Essx 5E 53
Eppleby. N Yor 3E 105
Eppleworth. E Yor 1D 94
Epsom. Surr 4D 38
Epwell. Oxon 1B 50
Epworth. N Lin 4A 94
Epworth Turbary. N Lin 4A 94
Erbistock. Wrex 1F 71
Erbusaig. High 1F 147
Erchless Castle. High 4G 157
Erdington. W Mid 1F 61
Eredine. Arg 3G 133
Eriboll. High 3E 167
Ericstane. Dum 3C 118
Eridge Green. E Sus 2G 27
Erines. Arg 2G 125
Eriswell. Suff 3G 65
Erith. G Lon 3G 39
Erlestoke. Wilts 1E 23
Ermine. Linc 3G 87
Ermington. Devn 3C 8
Ernesettle. Plym 3A 8
Erpingham. Norf 2D 78
Erriottwood. Kent 5D 40
Errogie. High 1H 149
Errol. Per 1E 137
Errol Station. Per 1E 137
Erskine. Ren 2F 127
Erskine Bridge. Ren 2F 127
Ervie. Dum 3F 109
Erwarton. Suff 2F 55
Erwood. Powy 1D 46
Eryholme. N Yor 4A 106
Eryrys. Den 5E 82
Escalls. Corn 4A 4
Escomb. Dur 1E 105
Escrick. N Yor 5A 100
Esgair. Carm 3D 45
(nr. Carmarthen)
Esgair. Carm 3G 43
(nr. St Clears)
Esgairgeiliog. Powy 5G 69
Esh. Dur 5E 115
Esher. Surr 4C 38
Esholt. W Yor 5D 98
Eshott. Nmbd 5G 121
Eshton. N Yor 4B 98
Esh Winning. Dur 5E 115
Eskadale. High 5G 157
Eskbank. Midl 3G 129
Eskdale Green. Cumb 4C 102
Eskdalemuir. Dum 5E 119
Eskham. Linc 1C 88
Esknish. Arg 3B 124
Esk Valley. N Yor 4F 107
Eslington Hall. Nmbd 3E 121
Espley Hall. Nmbd 5F 121
Esprick. Lanc 1C 90
Essendine. Rut 4H 75
Essendon. Herts 5C 52
Essich. High 5A 158
Essington. Staf 5D 72
Eston. Red C 3C 106
Estover. Plym 3B 8
Eswick. Shet 6F 173
Etal. Nmbd 1D 120
Etchilhampton. Wilts 5F 35
Etchingham. E Sus 3B 28
Etchinghill. Kent 2F 29
Etchinghill. Staf 4E 73
Etherley Dene. Dur 2E 105
Ethie Haven. Ang 4F 145
Etling Green. Norf 4C 78
Etloe. Glos 5B 48
Eton. Wind 3A 38
Eton Wick. Wind 3A 38
Etteridge. High 4A 150
Ettersgill. Dur 2B 104
Ettiley Heath. Ches E 4B 84
Ettington. Warw 1A 50
Etton. E Yor 5D 101
Etton. Pet 5A 76
Ettrick. Bord 3E 119
Ettrickbridge. Bord 2F 119
Etwall. Derbs 2G 73
Eudon Burnell. Shrp 2B 60
Eudon George. Shrp 2A 60
Euston. Suff 3A 66
Euxton. Lanc 3D 90
Evanstown. B'end 3C 32
Evanton. High 2A 158
Evedon. Linc 1H 75
Evelix. High 4E 165
Evendine. Here 1C 48
Evenjobb. Powy 4E 59
Evenley. Nptn 2D 50
Evenlode. Glos 3H 49
Even Swindon. Swin 3G 35
Evenwood. Dur 2E 105
Evenwood Gate. Dur 2E 105
Everbay. Orkn 5F 172
Evercreech. Som 3B 22
Everdon. Nptn 5C 62
Everingham. E Yor 5C 100
Everleigh. Wilts 1H 23
Everley. N Yor 1D 100
Eversholt. C Beds 2H 51
Evershot. Dors 2A 14
Eversley. Hants 5F 37
Eversley Centre. Hants 5F 37
Eversley Cross. Hants 5F 37
Everthorpe. E Yor 1C 94
Everton. C Beds 5B 64
Everton. Hants 3A 16
Everton. Mers 1F 83
Everton. Notts 1D 86
Evertown. Dum 2E 113
Evesbatch. Here 1B 48
Evesham. Worc 1F 49
Evington. Leic 5D 74
Ewden Village. S Yor 1G 85
Ewdness. Shrp 1B 60
Ewell. Surr 4D 38
Ewell Minnis. Kent 1G 29
Ewelme. Oxon 2E 37
Ewen. Glos 2F 35
Ewenny. V Glam 4C 32
Ewerby. Linc 1A 76
Ewes. Dum 5F 119
Ewesley. Nmbd 5E 121
Ewhurst. Surr 1B 26
Ewhurst Green. E Sus 3B 28
Ewhurst Green. Surr 2B 26
Ewlo. Flin 4F 83
Ewloe. Flin 4F 83
Ewood Bridge. Lanc 2F 91
Eworthy. Devn 3E 11
Ewshot. Hants 1G 25
Ewyas Harold. Here 3G 47
Exbourne. Devn 2G 11
Exbury. Hants 2C 16
Exceat. E Sus 5G 27
Exebridge. Som 4C 20
Exelby. N Yor 1E 99
Exeter. Devn 3C 12 & 195
Exeter International Airport.
Devn 3D 12
Exford. Som 3B 20
Exfords Green. Shrp 5G 71
Exhall. Warw 5F 61
Exlade Street. Oxon 3E 37
Exminster. Devn 4C 12
Exmoor. Som 3B 20
Exmouth. Devn 4D 12
Exnaboe. Shet 10E 173
Exning. Suff 4F 65
Exton. Devn 4C 12
Exton. Hants 4E 24
Exton. Rut 4G 75
Exton. Som 3C 20
Exwick. Devn 3C 12
Eyam. Derbs 3G 85
Eydon. Nptn 5C 62
Eye. Here 4G 59
Eye. Pet 5B 76
Eye. Suff 3D 66
Eye Green. Pet 5B 76
Eyemouth. Bord 3F 131
Eyeworth. C Beds 1C 52
Eyhorne Street. Kent 5C 40
Eyke. Suff 5F 67
Eynesbury. Cambs 5A 64
Eynort. High 1B 146
Eynsford. Kent 4G 39
Eynsham. Oxon 5C 50
Eyre. High 3D 154
(on Isle of Skye)
Eyre. High 5E 155
(on Raasay)
Eythorne. Kent 1G 29
Eyton. Here 4G 59
Eyton. Shrp 2F 59
(nr. Bishop's Castle)
Eyton. Shrp 4F 71
(nr. Shrewsbury)
Eyton. Wrex 1F 71
Eyton on Severn. Shrp 5H 71
Eyton upon the Weald Moors.
Telf 4A 72

F

Faccombe. Hants 1B 24
Faceby. N Yor 4B 106
Faddiley. Ches E 5H 83
Fadmoor. N Yor 1A 100
Fagwyr. Swan 5G 45
Faichem. High 3E 149
Faifley. W Dun 2G 127
Fail. S Ayr 2D 116
Failand. N Som 4A 34
Failford. S Ayr 2D 116
Failsworth. G Man 4H 91
Fairbourne. Gwyn 4F 69
Fairbourne Heath. Kent 5C 40
Fairburn. N Yor 2E 93
Fairfield. Derbs 3E 85
Fairfield. Kent 3D 28
Fairfield. Worc 3D 60
(nr. Bromsgrove)
Fairfield. Worc 1F 49
(nr. Evesham)
Fairford. Glos 5G 49
Fair Green. Norf 4F 77
Fair Hill. Cumb 1G 103
Fairhill. S Lan 4A 128
Fair Isle Airport. Shet 1B 172
Fairlands. Surr 5A 38
Fairlie. N Ayr 4D 126
Fairlight. E Sus 4C 28
Fairlight Cove. E Sus 4C 28
Fairmile. Devn 3D 12
Fairmile. Surr 4C 38
Fairmilehead. Edin 3F 129
Fair Oak. Devn 1D 12
Fair Oak. Hants 1C 16
(nr. Eastleigh)
Fair Oak. Hants 5D 36
(nr. Kingsclere)
Fairoak. Staf 2B 72
Fair Oak Green. Hants 5E 37
Fairseat. Kent 4H 39
Fairstead. Essx 4A 54
Fairstead. Norf 4F 77
Fairwarp. E Sus 3F 27
Fairwater. Card 4E 33
Fairy Cross. Devn 4E 19
Fakenham. Norf 3B 78
Fakenham Magna. Suff 3B 66
Fala. Midl 3H 129
Fala Dam. Midl 3H 129
Falcon. Here 2B 48
Faldingworth. Linc 2H 87
Falfield. S Glo 2B 34
Falkenham. Suff 2F 55
Falkirk. Falk 2B 128
Falkland. Fife 3E 137
Fallin. Stir 4H 135
Fallowfield. G Man 1C 84
Falmer. E Sus 5E 27
Falmouth. Corn 5C 6
Falsgrave. N Yor 1E 101
Falstone. Nmbd 1A 114
Fanagmore. High 4B 166
Fancott. C Beds 3A 52
Fanellan. High 4G 157
Fangdale Beck. N Yor 5C 106
Fangfoss. E Yor 4B 100
Fankerton. Falk 1A 128
Fanmore. Arg 4F 139
Fanner's Green. Essx 4G 53
Fannich Lodge. High 2E 156
Fans. Bord 5C 130
Farcet. Cambs 1B 64
Far Cotton. Nptn 5E 63
Fareham. Hants 2D 16
Farewell. Staf 4E 73
Far Forest. Worc 3B 60
Farforth. Linc 3C 88
Far Green. Glos 5C 48
Far Hoarcross. Staf 3F 73
Faringdon. Oxon 2A 36
Farington. Lanc 2D 90
Farlam. Cumb 4G 113
Farleigh. N Som 5H 33
Farleigh. Surr 4E 39
Farleigh Hungerford. Som 1D 22
Farleigh Wallop. Hants 2E 24
Farleigh Wick. Wilts 5D 34
Farlesthorpe. Linc 3D 88
Farleton. Cumb 1E 97
Farleton. Lanc 3E 97
Farley. High 4G 157
Farley. N Som 4H 33
Farley. Shrp 5F 71
(nr. Shrewsbury)
Farley. Shrp 5A 72
(nr. Telford)
Farley. Staf 1E 73
Farley. Wilts 4H 23
Farley Green. Suff 5G 65
Farley Green. Surr 1B 26
Farley Hill. Wok 5F 37
Farley's End. Glos 4C 48
Farlington. N Yor 3A 100
Farlington. Port 2E 17
Farlow. Shrp 2A 60
Farmborough. Bath 5B 34
Farmcote. Glos 3F 49
Farmcote. Shrp 1B 60
Farmington. Glos 4G 49
Far Moor. G Man 4D 90
Farmoor. Oxon 5C 50
Farmtown. Mor 3C 160
Farnah Green. Derbs 1H 73
Farnborough. G Lon 4F 39
Farnborough. Hants 1G 25
Farnborough. Warw 1C 50
Farnborough. W Ber 3C 36
Farncombe. Surr 1A 26
Farndish. Bed 4G 63
Farndon. Ches W 5G 83
Farndon. Notts 5E 87
Farnell. Ang 3F 145
Farnham. Dors 1E 15
Farnham. Essx 3E 53
Farnham. N Yor 3F 99
Farnham. Suff 4F 67
Farnham. Surr 2G 25
Farnham Common. Buck 2A 38
Farnham Green. Essx 3E 53
Farnham Royal. Buck 2A 38
Farnhill. N Yor 5C 98
Farningham. Kent 4G 39
Farnley. N Yor 5E 98
Farnley Tyas. W Yor 3B 92
Farnsfield. Notts 5D 86
Farnworth. G Man 4F 91
Farnworth. Hal 2H 83
Far Oakridge. Glos 5E 49
Farr. High 2H 167
(nr. Bettyhill)
Farr. High 5A 158
(nr. Inverness)
Farr. High 3C 150
(nr. Kingussie)
Farraline. High 1H 149
Farringdon. Devn 3D 12
Farrington. Dors 1D 14
Farrington Gurney. Bath 1B 22
Far Sawrey. Cumb 5E 103
Farsley. W Yor 1C 92
Farthinghoe. Nptn 2D 50
Farthingstone. Nptn 5D 62
Farthorpe. Linc 3B 88
Fartown. W Yor 3B 92
Farway. Devn 3E 13
Fasag. High 3A 156
Fascadale. High 1G 139
Fasnacloich. Arg 4E 141
Fassfern. High 1E 141
Fatfield. Tyne 4G 115
Faugh. Cumb 4G 113
Fauld. Staf 3F 73
Fauldhouse. W Lot 3C 128
Faulkbourne. Essx 4A 54
Faulkland. Som 1C 22
Fauls. Shrp 2H 71
Faverdale. Darl 3F 105
Faversham. Kent 4E 40
Fawdington. N Yor 2G 99
Fawfieldhead. Staf 4E 85
Fawkham Green. Kent 4G 39
Fawler. Oxon 4B 50
Fawley. Buck 3F 37
Fawley. Hants 2C 16
Fawley. W Ber 3B 36
Fawley Chapel. Here 3A 48
Fawton. Corn 2F 7
Faxfleet. E Yor 2B 94
Faygate. W Sus 2D 26
Fazakerley. Mers 1F 83
Fazeley. Staf 5F 73
Feabuie. High 4B 158
Feagour. High 4H 149
Fearann Dhomhnaill. High 3E 147
Fearby. N Yor 1D 98
Fearn. High 1C 158
Fearnan. Per 4E 142
Fearnbeg. High 3G 155
Fearnhead. Warr 1A 84
Fearnmore. High 2G 155
Featherstone. Staf 5D 72
Featherstone. W Yor 2E 93
Featherstone Castle. Nmbd 3H 113
Feckenham. Worc 4E 61
Feering. Essx 3B 54
Feetham. N Yor 5C 104
Feizor. N Yor 3G 97
Felbridge. Surr 2E 27

Felbrigg. *Norf* 2E 78
Felcourt. *Surr* 1E 27
Felden. *Herts* 5A 52
Felhampton. *Shrp* 2G 59
Felindre. *Carm* . . . .3F 45 (nr. Llandeilo)
Felindre. *Carm* . . . .2G 45 (nr. Llandovery)
Felindre. *Carm* . . . .2D 44 (nr. Newcastle Emlyn)
Felindre. *Powy* 2D 58
Felindre. *Swan* 5G 45
Felindre Farchog. *Pemb* 1F 43
Felinfach. *Cdgn* 5E 57
Felinfach. *Powy* 2D 46
Felinfoel. *Carm* 5F 45
Felingwmisaf. *Carm* 3F 45
Felingwmuchaf. *Carm* 3F 45
Felin Newydd. *Powy* . . . .5C 70 (nr. Newtown)
Felin Newydd. *Powy* . . . .3E 70 (nr. Oswestry)
Felin Wnda. *Cdgn* 1D 44
Felinwynt. *Cdgn* 5B 56
Felixkirk. *N Yor* 1G 99
Felixstowe. *Suff* 2F 55
Felixstowe Ferry. *Suff* 2G 55
Felkington. *Nmbd* 5F 131
Fell End. *Cumb* 5A 104
Felling. *Tyne* 3F 115
Fell Side. *Cumb* 1E 102
Felmersham. *Bed* 5G 63
Felmingham. *Norf* 3E 79
Felpham. *W Sus* 3H 17
Felsham. *Suff* 5B 66
Felsted. *Essx* 3G 53
Feltham. *G Lon* 3C 38
Felthamhill. *Surr* 3B 38
Felthorpe. *Norf* 4D 78
Felton. *Here* 1A 48
Felton. *N Som* 5A 34
Felton. *Nmbd* 4F 121
Felton Butler. *Shrp* 4F 71
Feltwell. *Norf* 1G 65
Fenay Bridge. *W Yor* 3B 92
Fence. *Lanc* 1G 91
Fence Houses. *Tyne* 4G 115
Fencott. *Oxon* 4D 50
Fen Ditton. *Cambs* 4D 65
Fen Drayton. *Cambs* 4C 64
Fen End. *Linc* 3B 76
Fen End. *W Mid* 3G 61
Fenham. *Nmbd* 5G 131
Fenham. *Tyne* 3F 115
Fenhouses. *Linc* 1B 76
Feniscowles. *Bkbn* 2E 91
Feniton. *Devn* 3D 12
Fenn Green. *Shrp* 2B 60
Fenn's Bank. *Wrex* 2H 71
Fenn Street. *Medw* 3B 40
Fenny Bentley. *Derbs* 5F 85
Fenny Bridges. *Devn* 3E 12
Fenny Compton. *Warw* 5B 62
Fenny Drayton. *Leics* 1A 62
Fenny Stratford. *Mil* 2G 51
Fenrother. *Nmbd* 5F 121
Fenstanton. *Cambs* 4C 64
Fen Street. *Norf* 1C 66
Fenton. *Cambs* 3C 64
Fenton. *Cumb* 4G 113
Fenton. *Linc* . . . .5F 87 (nr. Caythorpe)
Fenton. *Linc* . . . .3F 87 (nr. Saxilby)
Fenton. *Nmbd* 1D 120
Fenton. *Notts* 2E 87
Fenton. *Stoke* 1C 72
Fentonadle. *Corn* 5A 10
Fenton Barns. *E Lot* 1B 130
Fenwick. *E Ayr* 5F 127
Fenwick. *Nmbd* . . . .5G 131 (nr. Berwick-upon-Tweed)
Fenwick. *Nmbd* . . . .2D 114 (nr. Hexham)
Fenwick. *S Yor* 3F 93
Feochaig. *Arg* 4B 122
Feock. *Corn* 5C 6
Feolin Ferry. *Arg* 3C 124
Feorlan. *Arg* 5A 122
Ferindonald. *High* 3E 147
Feriniquarrie. *High* 3A 154
Fern. *Ang* 2D 145
Ferndale. *Rhon* 2C 32
Ferndown. *Dors* 2F 15
Ferness. *High* 4D 158
Fernham. *Oxon* 2A 36
Fernhill. *W Sus* 1D 27
Fernhill Heath. *Worc* 5C 60
Fernhurst. *W Sus* 4G 25
Fernieflatt. *Abers* 1H 145
Ferniegair. *S Lan* 4A 128
Fernilea. *High* 5C 154
Fernilee. *Derbs* 3E 85
Ferrensby. *N Yor* 3F 99
Ferriby Sluice. *N Lin* 2C 94
Ferring. *W Sus* 5C 26
Ferryden. *Ang* 3G 145
Ferryhill. *Aber* 3G 153
Ferry Hill. *Cambs* 2C 64
Ferryhill. *Dur* 1F 105
Ferryhill Station. *Dur* 1F 105

Ferryside. *Carm* 4D 44
Ferryton. *High* 2A 158
Fersfield. *Norf* 2C 66
Fersit. *High* 1A 142
Feshiebridge. *High* 3C 150
Fetcham. *Surr* 5C 38
Fetterangus. *Abers* 3G 161
Fettercairn. *Abers* 1F 145
Fewcott. *Oxon* 3D 50
Fewston. *N Yor* 4D 98
Ffairfach. *Carm* 3G 45
Ffair Rhos. *Cdgn* 4G 57
Ffaldybrenin. *Carm* 1G 45
Ffarmers. *Carm* 1G 45
Ffawyddog. *Powy* 4F 47
Ffodun. *Powy* 5E 71
Fforest. *Carm* 5F 45
Fforest-fach. *Swan* 3F 31
Fforest Goch. *Neat* 5H 45
Ffostrasol. *Cdgn* 1D 44
Ffos-y-ffin. *Cdgn* 4D 56
Ffrith. *Flin* 5E 83
Ffrwdgrech. *Powy* 3D 46
Ffwl-y-mwn. *V Glam* 5D 32
Ffynnon-ddrain. *Carm* 3E 45
Ffynnongroyw. *Flin* 2D 82
Ffynnon Gynydd. *Powy* 1E 47
Ffynnonoer. *Cdgn* 5E 57
Fiag Lodge. *High* 1B 164
Fidden. *Arg* 2B 132
Fiddington. *Glos* 2E 49
Fiddington. *Som* 2F 21
Fiddleford. *Dors* 1D 14
Fiddlers Hamlet. *Essx* 5E 53
Field. *Staf* 2E 73
Field Assarts. *Oxon* 4B 50
Field Broughton. *Cumb* 1C 96
Field Dalling. *Norf* 2C 78
Fieldhead. *Cumb* 1F 103
Field Head. *Leics* 5B 74
Fifehead Magdalen. *Dors* 4C 22
Fifehead Neville. *Dors* 1C 14
Fifehead St Quintin. *Dors* 1C 14
Fife Keith. *Mor* 3B 160
Fifield. *Oxon* 4H 49
Fifield. *Wilts* 1G 23
Fifield. *Wind* 3A 38
Fifield Bavant. *Wilts* 4F 23
Figheldean. *Wilts* 2G 23
Filby. *Norf* 4G 79
Filey. *N Yor* 1F 101
Filford. *Dors* 3H 13
Filgrave. *Mil* 1G 51
Filkins. *Oxon* 5H 49
Filleigh. *Devn* . . . .1H 11 (nr. Crediton)
Filleigh. *Devn* . . . .4G 19 (nr. South Molton)
Fillingham. *Linc* 2G 87
Fillongley. *Warw* 2G 61
Filton. *S Glo* 4B 34
Fimber. *E Yor* 3C 100
Finavon. *Ang* 3D 145
Fincham. *Norf* 5F 77
Finchampstead. *Wok* 5F 37
Finchdean. *Hants* 1F 17
Finchingfield. *Essx* 2G 53
Finchley. *G Lon* 1D 38
Findern. *Derbs* 2H 73
Findhorn. *Mor* 2E 159
Findhorn Bridge. *High* 1C 150
Findochty. *Mor* 2B 160
Findo Gask. *Per* 1C 136
Findon. *Abers* 4G 153
Findon. *W Sus* 5C 26
Findon Mains. *High* 2A 158
Findon Valley. *W Sus* 5C 26
Finedon. *Nptn* 3G 63
Fingal Street. *Suff* 3E 66
Fingest. *Buck* 2F 37
Finghall. *N Yor* 1D 98
Fingland. *Cumb* 4D 112
Fingland. *Dum* 3G 117
Finglesham. *Kent* 5H 41
Fingringhoe. *Essx* 3D 54
Finiskaig. *High* 4A 148
Finmere. *Oxon* 2E 51
Finnart. *Per* 3C 142
Finningham. *Suff* 4C 66
Finningley. *S Yor* 1D 86
Finnygaud. *Abers* 3D 160
Finsbury. *G Lon* 2E 39
Finstall. *Worc* 3D 61
Finsthwaite. *Cumb* 1C 96
Finstock. *Oxon* 4B 50
Finstown. *Orkn* 6C 172
Fintry. *Abers* 3E 161
Fintry. *D'dee* 5D 144
Fintry. *Stir* 1H 127
Finwood. *Warw* 4F 61
Finzean. *Abers* 4D 152
Fionnphort. *Arg* 2B 132
Fionnsabhagh. *W Isl* 9C 171
Firbeck. *S Yor* 2C 86
Firby. *N Yor* . . . .1E 99 (nr. Bedale)
Firby. *N Yor* . . . .3B 100 (nr. Malton)
Firgrove. *G Man* 3H 91
Firsdown. *Wilts* 3H 23

First Coast. *High* 4D 162
Firth. *Shet* 4F 173
Fir Tree. *Dur* 1E 105
Fishbourne. *IOW* 3D 16
Fishbourne. *W Sus* 2G 17
Fishburn. *Dur* 1A 106
Fishcross. *Clac* 4B 136
Fisherford. *Abers* 5D 160
Fisher's Pond. *Hants* 4C 24
Fisher's Row. *Lanc* 5D 96
Fisherstreet. *W Sus* 2A 26
Fisherton. *High* 3B 158
Fisherton. *S Ayr* 3B 116
Fisherton de la Mere. *Wilts* 3E 23
Fishguard. *Pemb* 1D 42
Fishlake. *S Yor* 3G 93
Fishley. *Norf* 4G 79
Fishnish. *Arg* 4A 140
Fishpond Bottom. *Dors* 3G 13
Fishponds. *Bris* 4B 34
Fishpool. *Glos* 3B 48
Fishpool. *G Man* 4G 91
Fishpools. *Powy* 4D 58
Fishtoft. *Linc* 1C 76
Fishtoft Drove. *Linc* 1C 76
Fishwick. *Bord* 4F 131
Fiskavaig. *High* 5C 154
Fiskerton. *Linc* 3H 87
Fiskerton. *Notts* 5E 87
Fitch. *Shet* 7E 173
Fitling. *E Yor* 1F 95
Fittleton. *Wilts* 2G 23
Fittleworth. *W Sus* 4B 26
Fitton End. *Cambs* 4D 76
Fitz. *Shrp* 4G 71
Fitzhead. *Som* 4E 20
Fitzwilliam. *W Yor* 3E 93
Fiunary. *High* 4A 140
Five Ash Down. *E Sus* 3F 27
Five Ashes. *E Sus* 3G 27
Five Bells. *Som* 2D 20
Five Bridges. *Here* 1B 48
Fivehead. *Som* 4G 21
Five Lane Ends. *Lanc* 4E 97
Fivelanes. *Corn* 4C 10
Five Oak Green. *Kent* 1H 27
Five Oaks. *W Sus* 3B 26
Five Roads. *Carm* 5E 45
Five Ways. *Warw* 3G 61
Flack's Green. *Essx* 4A 54
Flackwell Heath. *Buck* 3G 37
Fladbury. *Worc* 1E 49
Fladda. *Shet* 3E 173
Fladdabister. *Shet* 8F 173
Flagg. *Derbs* 4F 85
Flamborough. *E Yor* 2G 101
Flamstead. *Herts* 4A 52
Flansham. *W Sus* 5A 26
Flasby. *N Yor* 4B 98
Flash. *Staf* 4E 85
Flashader. *High* 3C 154
Flatt, The. *Cumb* 2G 113
Flaunden. *Herts* 5A 52
Flawborough. *Notts* 1E 75
Flawith. *N Yor* 3G 99
Flax Bourton. *N Som* 5A 34
Flaxby. *N Yor* 4F 99
Flaxholme. *Derbs* 1H 73
Flaxley. *Glos* 4B 48
Flaxley Green. *Staf* 4E 73
Flaxpool. *Som* 3E 21
Flaxton. *N Yor* 3A 100
Fleck. *Shet* 10E 173
Fleckney. *Leics* 1D 62
Flecknoe. *Warw* 4C 62
Fledborough. *Notts* 3F 87
Fleet. *Dors* 4B 14
Fleet. *Hants* . . . .1G 25 (nr. Farnborough)
Fleet. *Hants* . . . .2F 17 (nr. South Hayling)
Fleet. *Linc* 3C 76
Fleet Hargate. *Linc* 3C 76
Fleetville. *Herts* 5B 52
Fleetwood. *Lanc* 5C 96
Fleggburgh. *Norf* 4G 79
Fleisirin. *W Isl* 4H 171
Flemingston. *V Glam* 4D 32
Flemington. *S Lan* . . . .3H 127 (nr. Glasgow)
Flemington. *S Lan* . . . .5A 128 (nr. Strathaven)
Flempton. *Suff* 4H 65
Fleoideabhagh. *W Isl* 9C 171
Fletcher's Green. *Kent* 1G 27
Fletchertown. *Cumb* 5D 112
Fletching. *E Sus* 3F 27
Fleuchary. *High* 4E 165
Flexbury. *Corn* 2C 10
Flexford. *Surr* 5A 38
Flimby. *Cumb* 1B 102
Flimwell. *E Sus* 2B 28
Flint. *Flin* 3E 83
Flintham. *Notts* 1E 75
Flint Mountain. *Flin* 3E 83
Flinton. *E Yor* 1F 95
Flintsham. *Here* 5F 59
Flishinghurst. *Kent* 2B 28
Flitcham. *Norf* 3G 77
Flitton. *C Beds* 2A 52
Flitwick. *C Beds* 2A 52

Flixborough. *N Lin* 3B 94
Flixton. *G Man* 1B 84
Flixton. *N Yor* 2E 101
Flixton. *Suff* 2F 67
Flockton. *W Yor* 3C 92
Flodden. *Nmbd* 1D 120
Flodigarry. *High* 1D 154
Flood's Ferry. *Cambs* 1C 64
Flookburgh. *Cumb* 2C 96
Flordon. *Norf* 1D 66
Flore. *Nptn* 4D 62
Flotterton. *Nmbd* 4E 121
Flowton. *Suff* 1D 54
Flushing. *Abers* 4H 161
Flushing. *Corn* 5C 6
Fluxton. *Devn* 3D 12
Flyford Flavell. *Worc* 5D 61
Fobbing. *Thur* 2B 40
Fochabers. *Mor* 3H 159
Fochriw. *Cphy* 5E 46
Fockerby. *N Lin* 3B 94
Fodderty. *High* 3H 157
Foddington. *Som* 4A 22
Foel. *Powy* 4B 70
Foffarty. *Ang* 4D 144
Foggathorpe. *E Yor* 1A 94
Fogo. *Bord* 5D 130
Fogorig. *Bord* 5D 130
Foindle. *High* 4B 166
Folda. *Ang* 2A 144
Fole. *Staf* 2E 73
Foleshill. *W Mid* 2A 62
Foley Park. *Worc* 3C 60
Folke. *Dors* 1B 14
Folkestone. *Kent* . . . .2G 29 & 195
Folkingham. *Linc* 2H 75
Folkington. *E Sus* 5G 27
Folksworth. *Cambs* 1A 64
Folkton. *N Yor* 2E 101
Folla Rule. *Abers* 5E 161
Follifoot. *N Yor* 4F 99
Folly Cross. *Devn* 2E 11
Folly Gate. *Devn* 3F 11
Folly, The. *Herts* 4B 52
Folly, The. *W Ber* 5C 36
Fonmon. *V Glam* 5D 32
Fonthill Bishop. *Wilts* 3E 23
Fonthill Gifford. *Wilts* 3E 23
Fontmell Magna. *Dors* 1D 14
Fontwell. *W Sus* 5A 26
Font-y-gary. *V Glam* 5D 32
Foodieash. *Fife* 2F 137
Foolow. *Derbs* 3F 85
Footdee. *Aber* 3G 153
Footherley. *Staf* 5F 73
Foots Cray. *G Lon* 3F 39
Forbestown. *Abers* 2A 152
Force Forge. *Cumb* 5E 103
Force Mills. *Cumb* 5E 103
Forcett. *N Yor* 3E 105
Ford. *Arg* 3F 133
Ford. *Buck* 5F 51
Ford. *Derbs* 2B 86
Ford. *Devn* . . . .3C 8 (nr. Bideford)
Ford. *Devn* . . . .4D 9 (nr. Holberton)
Ford. *Devn* . . . .4D 9 (nr. Salcombe)
Ford. *Glos* 3F 49
Ford. *Nmbd* 1D 120
Ford. *Plym* 3A 8
Ford. *Shrp* 4G 71
Ford. *Som* . . . .1A 22 (nr. Wells)
Ford. *Som* . . . .4D 20 (nr. Wiveliscombe)
Ford. *Staf* 5E 85
Ford. *W Sus* 5B 26
Ford. *Wilts* . . . .4D 34 (nr. Chippenham)
Ford. *Wilts* . . . .4G 23 (nr. Salisbury)
Forda. *Devn* 3E 19
Ford Barton. *Devn* 1C 12
Fordcombe. *Kent* 1G 27
Fordell. *Fife* 1E 129
Forden. *Powy* 5E 71
Ford End. *Essx* 4G 53
Forder Green. *Devn* 2D 9
Ford Green. *Lanc* 5D 97
Fordham. *Cambs* 3F 65
Fordham. *Essx* 3C 54
Fordham. *Norf* 1F 65
Fordham Heath. *Essx* 3C 54
Ford Heath. *Shrp* 4G 71
Fordhouses. *W Mid* 5D 72
Fordie. *Per* 1G 135
Fordingbridge. *Hants* 1G 15
Fordington. *Linc* 3D 88
Fordon. *E Yor* 2E 101
Fordoun. *Abers* 1G 145
Ford Street. *Essx* 3C 54
Ford Street. *Som* 1E 13
Fordwells. *Oxon* 4B 50
Fordwich. *Kent* 5F 41
Fordyce. *Abers* 2C 160
Forebridge. *Staf* 3D 72
Foremark. *Derbs* 3H 73
Forest. *N Yor* 4F 105
Forestburn Gate. *Nmbd* 5E 121

Foresterseat. *Mor* 3F 159
Forest Green. *Glos* 2D 34
Forest Green. *Surr* 1C 26
Forest Hall. *Cumb* 4G 103
Forest Head. *Cumb* 4G 113
Forest Hill. *Oxon* 5D 50
Forest-in-Teesdale. *Dur* 2B 104
Forest Lodge. *Per* 1G 143
Forest Mill. *Clac* 4B 136
Forest Row. *E Sus* 2F 27
Forestside. *W Sus* 1F 17
Forest Town. *Notts* 4C 86
Forfar. *Ang* 3D 144
Forgandenny. *Per* 2C 136
Forge. *Powy* 1G 57
Forge Side. *Torf* 5F 47
Forge, The. *Here* 5F 59
Forgewood. *N Lan* 4A 128
Forgie. *Mor* 3A 160
Forglen. *Abers* 4D 160
Formby. *Mers* 4A 90
Forncett End. *Norf* 1D 66
Forncett St Mary. *Norf* 1D 66
Forncett St Peter. *Norf* 1D 66
Forneth. *Per* 4H 143
Fornham All Saints. *Suff* 4H 65
Fornham St Martin. *Suff* 4A 66
Forres. *Mor* 3E 159
Forrestfield. *N Lan* 3B 128
Forrest Lodge. *Dum* 1C 110
Forsbrook. *Staf* 1D 72
Forse. *High* 5E 169
Forsinard. *High* 4A 168
Forss. *High* 2C 168
Forstal, The. *Kent* 2E 29
Forston. *Dors* 3B 14
Fort Augustus. *High* 3F 149
Forteviot. *Per* 2C 136
Fort George. *High* 3B 158
Forth. *S Lan* 4C 128
Forthampton. *Glos* 2D 48
Forthay. *Glos* 2C 34
Forth Road Bridge. *Fife* 2E 129
Fortingall. *Per* 4E 143
Fort Matilda. *Inv* 2D 126
Forton. *Hants* 2C 24
Forton. *Lanc* 4D 97
Forton. *Shrp* 4G 71
Forton. *Som* 2G 13
Forton. *Staf* 3B 72
Forton Heath. *Shrp* 4G 71
Fortrie. *Abers* 4D 160
Fortrose. *High* 3B 158
Fortuneswell. *Dors* 5B 14
Fort William. *High* 1F 141
Forty Green. *Buck* 1A 38
Forty Hill. *G Lon* 1E 39
Forward Green. *Suff* 5C 66
Fosbury. *Wilts* 1B 24
Foscot. *Oxon* 3H 49
Fosdyke. *Linc* 2C 76
Foss. *Per* 3E 143
Fossebridge. *Glos* 4F 49
Foster Street. *Essx* 5E 53
Foston. *Derbs* 2F 73
Foston. *Leics* 1D 62
Foston. *Linc* 1F 75
Foston. *N Yor* 3A 100
Foston on the Wolds. *E Yor* 4F 101
Fotherby. *Linc* 1C 88
Fothergill. *Cumb* 1B 102
Fotheringhay. *Nptn* 1H 63
Foubister. *Orkn* 7E 172
Foula Airport. *Shet* 8A 173
Foul Anchor. *Cambs* 4D 76
Foulbridge. *Cumb* 5F 113
Foulden. *Norf* 1G 65
Foulden. *Bord* 4F 131
Foul Mile. *E Sus* 4H 27
Foulridge. *Lanc* 5A 98
Foulsham. *Norf* 3C 78
Fountainhall. *Bord* 5H 129
Four Alls, The. *Shrp* 2A 72
Four Ashes. *Staf* . . . .5D 72 (nr. Cannock)
Four Ashes. *Staf* . . . .2C 60 (nr. Kinver)
Four Ashes. *Suff* 3C 66
Four Crosses. *Powy* . . . .5C 70 (nr. Llanerfyl)
Four Crosses. *Powy* . . . .4E 71 (nr. Llanymynech)
Four Crosses. *Staf* 5D 72
Four Elms. *Kent* 1F 27
Four Forks. *Som* 3F 21
Four Gotes. *Cambs* 4D 76
Four Lane End. *S Yor* 4C 92
Four Lane Ends. *Lanc* 4E 97
Four Lanes. *Corn* 5A 6
Fourlanes End. *Ches E* 5B 84
Four Marks. *Hants* 3E 25
Four Mile Bridge. *IOA* 3B 80
Four Oaks. *E Sus* 3C 28
Four Oaks. *Glos* 3B 48
Four Oaks. *W Mid* 2G 61
Four Roads. *Carm* 5E 45
Four Roads. *IOM* 5B 108
Fourstones. *Nmbd* 3B 114
Four Throws. *Kent* 3B 28
Fovant. *Wilts* 4F 23
Foveran. *Abers* 1G 153
Fowey. *Corn* 3F 7

Fowlershill. *Abers* 2G 153
Fowley Common. *Warr* 1A 84
Fowlis. *Ang* 5C 144
Fowlis Wester. *Per* 1B 136
Fowlmere. *Cambs* 1E 53
Fownhope. *Here* 2A 48
Foxcombe Hill. *Oxon* 5C 50
Fox Corner. *Surr* 5A 38
Foxcote. *Glos* 4F 49
Foxcote. *Som* 1C 22
Foxdale. *IOM* 4B 108
Foxearth. *Essx* 1B 54
Foxfield. *Cumb* 1B 96
Foxham. *Wilts* 4E 35
Fox Hatch. *Essx* 1G 39
Foxhole. *Corn* 3D 6
Foxholes. *N Yor* 2E 101
Foxhunt Green. *E Sus* 4G 27
Fox Lane. *Hants* 1G 25
Foxley. *Norf* 3C 78
Foxley. *Nptn* 5D 62
Foxley. *Wilts* 3D 35
Foxlydiate. *Worc* 4E 61
Fox Street. *Essx* 3D 54
Foxt. *Staf* 1E 73
Foxton. *Cambs* 1E 53
Foxton. *Dur* 2A 106
Foxton. *Leics* 2D 62
Foxton. *N Yor* 5B 106
Foxup. *N Yor* 2A 98
Foxwist Green. *Ches W* 4A 84
Foxwood. *Shrp* 3A 60
Foy. *Here* 3A 48
Foyers. *High* 1G 149
Foynesfield. *High* 3C 158
Fraddam. *Corn* 3C 4
Fraddon. *Corn* 3D 6
Fradley. *Staf* 4F 73
Fradley South. *Staf* 4F 73
Fradswell. *Staf* 2D 73
Fraisthorpe. *E Yor* 3F 101
Framfield. *E Sus* 3F 27
Framingham Earl. *Norf* 5E 79
Framingham Pigot. *Norf* 5E 79
Framlingham. *Suff* 4E 67
Frampton. *Dors* 3B 14
Frampton. *Linc* 2C 76
Frampton Cotterell. *S Glo* . . .3B 34
Frampton Mansell. *Glos* 5E 49
Frampton on Severn. *Glos* . . .5C 48
Frampton West End. *Linc* . . .1B 76
Framsden. *Suff* 5D 66
Framwellgate Moor. *Dur* 5F 115
Franche. *Worc* 3C 60
Frandley. *Ches W* 3A 84
Frankby. *Mers* 2E 83
Frankfort. *Norf* 3F 79
Frankley. *Worc* 2D 61
Frank's Bridge. *Powy* 5D 58
Frankton. *Warw* 3B 62
Frankwell. *Shrp* 4G 71
Frant. *E Sus* 2G 27
Fraserburgh. *Abers* 2G 161
Frating Green. *Essx* 3D 54
Fratton. *Port* 2E 17
Freathy. *Corn* 3A 8
Freckenham. *Suff* 3F 65
Freckleton. *Lanc* 2C 90
Freeby. *Leics* 3F 75
Freefolk Priors. *Hants* 2C 24
Freehay. *Staf* 1E 73
Freeland. *Oxon* 4C 50
Freester. *Shet* 6F 173
Freiston. *Linc* 1C 76
Freiston Shore. *Linc* 1C 76
Fremington. *Devn* 3F 19
Fremington. *N Yor* 5D 104
Frenchbeer. *Devn* 4G 11
French Street. *Kent* 5F 39
Frenich. *Stir* 3D 134
Frensham. *Surr* 2G 25
Frenze. *Norf* 2D 66
Fresgoe. *High* 2B 168
Freshfield. *Mers* 4A 90
Freshford. *Bath* 5C 34
Freshwater. *IOW* 4B 16
Freshwater Bay. *IOW* 4B 16
Freshwater East. *Pemb* 5E 43
Fressingfield. *Suff* 3E 67
Freston. *Suff* 2E 55
Freswick. *High* 2F 169
Frethern. *Glos* 5C 48
Frettenham. *Norf* 4E 79
Freuchie. *Fife* 3E 137
Freystrop. *Pemb* 3D 43
Friar's Gate. *E Sus* 2F 27
Friar Waddon. *Dors* 4B 14
Friday Bridge. *Cambs* 5D 76
Friday Street. *E Sus* 5G 27
Friday Street. *Surr* 1C 26
Fridaythorpe. *E Yor* 4C 100
Friden. *Derbs* 4F 85
Friern Barnet. *G Lon* 1D 39
Friesthorpe. *Linc* 2H 87
Frieston. *Linc* 1G 75
Frieth. *Buck* 2F 37
Friezeland. *Notts* 5B 86
Frilford. *Oxon* 2C 36
Frilsham. *W Ber* 4D 36
Frimley. *Surr* 1G 25
Frimley Green. *Surr* 1G 25

Frindsbury. *Medw* 4B 40
Fring. *Norf* 2G 77
Fringford. *Oxon* 3E 50
Frinsted. *Kent* 5C 40
Frinton-on-Sea. *Essx* 4F 55
Friockheim. *Ang* 4E 145
Friog. *Gwyn* 4F 69
Frisby. *Leics* 5E 74
Frisby. *Linc* 4D 88
Frisby on the Wreake. *Leics* . .4D 74
Friskney. *Linc* 5D 88
Friskney Eaudyke. *Linc* 5D 88
Friston. *E Sus* 5G 27
Friston. *Suff* 4G 67
Fritchley. *Derbs* 5A 86
Fritham. *Hants* 1H 15
Frith Bank. *Linc* 1C 76
Frith Common. *Worc* 4A 60
Frithelstock. *Devn* 1E 11
Frithelstock Stone. *Devn* 1E 11
Frithenden. *Herts* 5A 52
Frithville. *Linc* 5C 88
Frittenden. *Kent* 1C 28
Frittiscombe. *Devn* 4E 9
Fritton. *Norf* 5G 79
        (nr. Great Yarmouth)
Fritton. *Norf* 1E 67
        (nr. Long Stratton)
Fritwell. *Oxon* 3D 50
Frizinghall. *W Yor* 1B 92
Frizington. *Cumb* 3B 102
Frobost. *W Isl* 6C 170
Frocester. *Glos* 5C 48
Frochas. *Powy* 5D 70
Frodesley. *Shrp* 5H 71
Frodingham. *N Lin* 3C 94
Frodsham. *Ches W* 3H 83
Froggatt. *Derbs* 3G 85
Froghall. *Staf* 1E 73
Frogham. *Hants* 1G 15
Frogham. *Kent* 5G 41
Frogmore. *Devn* 4D 8
Frogmore. *Hants* 5G 37
Frogmore. *Herts* 5B 52
Frognall. *Linc* 4A 76
Frogwell. *Corn* 2H 7
Frolesworth. *Leics* 1C 62
Frome. *Som* 2C 22
Fromefield. *Som* 2C 22
Frome St Quintin. *Dors* 2A 14
Fromes Hill. *Here* 1B 48
Fron. *Carm* 2A 46
Fron. *Gwyn* 5E 81
        (nr. Caernarfon)
Fron. *Gwyn* 2C 68
        (nr. Pwllheli)
Fron. *Powy* 4C 58
        (nr. Llandrindod Wells)
Fron. *Powy* 1D 58
        (nr. Newtown)
Fron. *Powy* 2G 27
        (nr. Welshpool)
Froncysyllte. *Wrex* 1E 71
Frongoch. *Gwyn* 2B 70
Fron Isaf. *Wrex* 1E 71
Fronoleu. *Gwyn* 2G 69
Frosterley. *Dur* 1D 104
Frotoft. *Orkn* 5D 172
Froxfield. *C Beds* 2H 51
Froxfield. *Wilts* 5A 36
Froxfield Green. *Hants* 4F 25
Fryern Hill. *Hants* 4C 24
Fryerning. *Essx* 5G 53
Fryton. *N Yor* 2A 100
Fugglestone St Peter. *Wilts* . .3G 23
Fulbeck. *Linc* 5G 87
Fulbourn. *Cambs* 5E 65
Fulbrook. *Oxon* 4A 50
Fulflood. *Hants* 3C 24
Fulford. *Som* 4F 21
Fulford. *Staf* 2D 72
Fulford. *York* 5A 100
Fulham. *G Lon* 3D 38
Fulking. *W Sus* 4D 26
Fuller's Moor. *Ches W* 5G 83
Fuller Street. *Essx* 4H 53
Fullerton. *Hants* 3B 24
Fulletby. *Linc* 3B 88
Full Sutton. *E Yor* 4B 100
Fullwood. *E Ayr* 4F 127
Fulmer. *Buck* 2A 38
Fulmodestone. *Norf* 2B 78
Fulnetby. *Linc* 3H 87
Fulney. *Linc* 3B 76
Fulstow. *Linc* 1C 88
Fulthorpe. *Stoc T* 2B 106
Fulwell. *Tyne* 4G 115
Fulwood. *Lanc* 1D 90
Fulwood. *Notts* 5B 86
Fulwood. *Som* 1F 13
Fulwood. *S Yor* 2G 85
Fundenhall. *Norf* 1D 66
Funtington. *W Sus* 2G 17
Funtley. *Hants* 2D 16
Funzie. *Shet* 2H 173
Furley. *Devn* 2F 13
Furnace. *Arg* 3H 133
Furnace. *Carm* 5F 45
Furnace. *Cdgn* 1F 57
Furner's Green. *E Sus* 3F 27
Furness Vale. *Derbs* 2E 85

Furneux Pelham. *Herts* 3E 53
Furzebrook. *Dors* 4E 15
Furzehill. *Devn* 2H 19
Furzehill. *Dors* 2F 15
Furzeley Corner. *Hants* 1E 17
Furzey Lodge. *Hants* 2B 16
Furzley. *Hants* 1A 16
Fyfield. *Essx* 5F 53
Fyfield. *Glos* 5H 49
Fyfield. *Hants* 2A 24
Fyfield. *Oxon* 2C 36
Fyfield. *Wilts* 5G 35
Fylde, The. *Lanc* 1B 90
Fylingthorpe. *N Yor* 4G 107
Fyning. *W Sus* 4G 25
Fyvie. *Abers* 5E 161

G

Gabhsann bho Dheas. *W Isl* . . .2G 171
Gabhsann bho Thuath.
        W Isl 2G 171
Gabroc Hill. *E Ayr* 4F 127
Gadbrook. *Surr* 1D 26
Gaddesby. *Leics* 4D 74
Gadfa. *IOA* 2D 80
Gadgirth. *S Ayr* 2D 116
Gaer. *Powy* 3E 47
Gaerwen. *IOA* 3D 81
Gagingwell. *Oxon* 3C 50
Gaick Lodge. *High* 5B 150
Gailey. *Staf* 4D 72
Gainford. *Dur* 3E 105
Gainsborough. *Linc* 1F 87
Gainsborough. *Suff* 1E 55
Gainsford End. *Essx* 2H 53
Gairletter. *Arg* 1C 126
Gairloch. *Abers* 3E 153
Gairloch. *High* 1H 155
Gairlochy. *High* 5D 148
Gairney Bank. *Per* 4D 136
Gairnshiel Lodge. *Abers* 3G 151
Gaisgill. *Cumb* 4H 103
Gaitsgill. *Cumb* 5E 113
Galashiels. *Bord* 1G 119
Galgate. *Lanc* 4D 97
Galhampton. *Som* 4B 22
Gallatown. *Fife* 4E 137
Galley Common. *Warw* 1H 61
Galleyend. *Essx* 5H 53
Galleywood. *Essx* 5H 53
Gallin. *Per* 4C 142
Gallowfauld. *Ang* 4D 144
Gallowhill. *E Dun* 2H 127
Gallowhill. *Per* 5A 144
Gallowhill. *Ren* 3F 127
Gallowhills. *Abers* 3H 161
Gallows Green. *Staf* 1E 73
Gallows Green. *Worc* 4D 60
Gallowstree Common. *Oxon* . .3E 37
Galltair. *High* 1G 147
Gallt Melyd. *Den* 2C 82
Galmington. *Som* 4F 21
Galmisdale. *High* 5C 146
Galmpton. *Devn* 4C 8
Galmpton. *Torb* 3E 9
Galmpton Warborough. *Torb* . .3E 9
Galphay. *N Yor* 2E 99
Galston. *E Ayr* 1D 117
Galton. *Dors* 4C 14
Galtrigill. *High* 3A 154
Gamblesby. *Cumb* 1H 103
Gamelsby. *Cumb* 4D 112
Gamesley. *Derbs* 1E 85
Gamlingay. *Cambs* 5B 64
Gamlingay Cinques. *Cambs* . . .5B 64
Gamlingay Great Heath.
        C Beds 5B 64
Gammaton. *Devn* 4E 19
Gammersgill. *N Yor* 1C 98
Gamston. *Notts* 2D 72
        (nr. Nottingham)
Gamston. *Notts* 3E 86
        (nr. Retford)
Ganarew. *Here* 4A 48
Ganavan. *Arg* 5C 140
Ganborough. *Glos* 3G 49
Gang. *Corn* 2H 7
Ganllwyd. *Gwyn* 3G 69
Gannochy. *Ang* 1E 145
Gannochy. *Per* 1D 136
Gansclet. *High* 4F 169
Ganstead. *E Yor* 1E 95
Ganthorpe. *N Yor* 2A 100
Ganton. *N Yor* 2D 101
Gants Hill. *G Lon* 2F 39
Gappah. *Devn* 5B 12
Garafad. *High* 2D 155
Garboldisham. *Norf* 2C 66
Garden City. *Flin* 4F 83
Gardeners Green. *Wok* 5G 37
Gardenstown. *Abers* 2F 161
Garden Village. *S Yor* 1G 85
Garden Village. *Swan* 3E 31
Garderhouse. *Shet* 7E 173
Gardham. *E Yor* 5D 100
Gardie. *Shet* 1D 173
        (on Papa Stour)
Gardie. *Shet* 1H 173
        (on Unst)
Gardie Ho. *Shet* 7F 173

Gare Hill. *Som* 2C 22
Garelochhead. *Arg* 4B 134
Garford. *Oxon* 2C 36
Garforth. *W Yor* 1E 93
Gargrave. *N Yor* 4B 98
Gargunnock. *Stir* 4G 135
Garleffin. *S Ayr* 1F 109
Garlieston. *Dum* 5B 110
Garlinge Green. *Kent* 5F 41
Garlogie. *Abers* 3E 153
Garmelow. *Staf* 3B 72
Garmond. *Abers* 3F 161
Garmondsway. *Dur* 1A 106
Garmony. *Arg* 4A 140
Garmouth. *Mor* 2H 159
Garmston. *Shrp* 5A 72
Garnant. *Carm* 4G 45
Garndiffaith. *Torf* 5F 47
Garndolbenmaen. *Gwyn* 1D 69
Garnett Bridge. *Cumb* 5G 103
Garnfadryn. *Gwyn* 2B 68
Garnkirk. *N Lan* 3H 127
Garnlydan. *Blae* 4E 47
Garnsgate. *Linc* 3D 76
Garnswllt. *Swan* 5G 45
Garn-yr-erw. *Torf* 4F 47
Garrabost. *W Isl* 4H 171
Garrallan. *E Ayr* 3E 117
Garras. *Corn* 4E 5
Garreg. *Gwyn* 1F 69
Garrigill. *Cumb* 5A 114
Garriston. *N Yor* 5E 105
Garrogie Lodge. *High* 2H 149
Garros. *High* 2D 155
Garrow. *Per* 4F 143
Garsdale. *Cumb* 1G 97
Garsdale Head. *Cumb* 5A 104
Garsdon. *Wilts* 3E 35
Garshall Green. *Staf* 2D 72
Garsington. *Oxon* 5D 50
Garstang. *Lanc* 5D 97
Garston. *Mers* 2G 83
Garswood. *Mers* 1H 83
Gartcosh. *N Lan* 3H 127
Garth. *B'end* 2B 32
Garth. *Cdgn* 2F 57
Garth. *Gwyn* 2E 69
Garth. *IOM* 4C 108
Garth. *Powy* 1C 46
        (nr. Builth Wells)
Garth. *Powy* 3E 59
        (nr. Knighton)
Garth. *Shet* 6D 173
        (nr. Sandness)
Garth. *Shet* 6F 173
        (nr. Skellister)
Garth. *Wrex* 1E 71
Garthamlock. *Glas* 3H 127
Garthbrengy. *Powy* 2D 46
Gartheli. *Cdgn* 5E 57
Garthmyl. *Powy* 1D 58
Garthorpe. *Leics* 3F 75
Garthorpe. *N Lin* 3B 94
Garth Owen. *Powy* 1D 58
Garth Row. *Cumb* 5G 103
Gartly. *Abers* 5C 160
Gartmore. *Stir* 4E 135
Gartness. *N Lan* 3A 128
Gartness. *Stir* 1G 127
Gartocharn. *W Dun* 1F 127
Garton. *E Yor* 1F 95
Garton-on-the-Wolds. *E Yor* . .4D 101
Gartsherrie. *N Lan* 3A 128
Gartymore. *High* 2H 165
Garvald. *E Lot* 2B 130
Garvamore. *High* 4H 149
Garvard. *Arg* 4A 132
Garvault. *High* 5H 167
Garve. *High* 2F 157
Garvestone. *Norf* 5C 78
Garvie. *Arg* 4H 133
Garvock. *Abers* 1G 145
Garvock. *Inv* 2D 126
Garway. *Here* 3H 47
Garway Common. *Here* 3H 47
Garway Hill. *Here* 3H 47
Garwick. *Linc* 1A 76
Gaskan. *High* 1C 140
Gasper. *Wilts* 3C 22
Gastard. *Wilts* 5D 35
Gasthorpe. *Norf* 2B 66
Gatcombe. *IOW* 4C 16
Gateacre. *Mers* 2G 83
Gatebeck. *Cumb* 1E 97
Gate Burton. *Linc* 2F 87
Gateforth. *N Yor* 2F 93
Gatehead. *E Ayr* 1C 116
Gate Helmsley. *N Yor* 4A 100
Gatehouse. *Nmbd* 1A 114
Gatehouse of Fleet. *Dum* 4D 110
Gatelawbridge. *Dum* 5B 118
Gateley. *Norf* 3B 78
Gatenby. *N Yor* 1F 99
Gatesgarth. *Cumb* 3C 102
Gateshead. *Tyne* 3F 115
Gatesheath. *Ches W* 4G 83
Gateside. *Ang* 4D 144
        (nr. Forfar)
Gateside. *Ang* 4C 144
        (nr. Kirriemuir)
Gateside. *Fife* 3D 136
Gateside. *N Ayr* 4E 127

Gathurst. *G Man* 4D 90
Gatley. *G Man* 2C 84
Gatton. *Surr* 5D 39
Gattonside. *Bord* 1H 119
Gatwick (London) Airport.
        W Sus . . . . .1D 27 & 216
Gaufron. *Powy* 4B 58
Gaulby. *Leics* 5D 74
Gauldry. *Fife* 1F 137
Gaultree. *Norf* 5D 77
Gaunt's Common. *Dors* 2F 15
Gaunt's Earthcott. *S Glo* 3B 34
Gautby. *Linc* 3A 88
Gavinton. *Bord* 4D 130
Gawber. *S Yor* 4D 92
Gawcott. *Buck* 2E 51
Gawsworth. *Ches E* 4C 84
Gawthorpe. *W Yor* 2C 92
Gawthrop. *Cumb* 1F 97
Gawthwaite. *Cumb* 1B 96
Gay Bowers. *Essx* 5A 54
Gaydon. *Warw* 5A 62
Gayfield. *Orkn* 2D 172
Gayhurst. *Mil* 1G 51
Gayle. *N Yor* 1A 98
Gayles. *N Yor* 4E 105
Gay Street. *W Sus* 3B 26
Gayton. *Mers* 2E 83
Gayton. *Norf* 4G 77
Gayton. *Nptn* 5E 62
Gayton. *Staf* 3D 73
Gayton le Marsh. *Linc* 2D 88
Gayton le Wold. *Linc* 2B 88
Gayton Thorpe. *Norf* 4G 77
Gaywood. *Norf* 3F 77
Gazeley. *Suff* 4G 65
Geanies. *High* 1C 158
Gearraidh Bhailteas. *W Isl* . . .6C 170
Gearraidh Bhaird. *W Isl* 6F 171
Gearraidh ma Monadh.
        W Isl 7C 170
Gearraidh na h-Aibhne.
        W Isl 4E 171
Geary. *High* 2B 154
Geddes. *High* 3C 158
Gedding. *Suff* 5B 66
Geddington. *Nptn* 2F 63
Gedintailor. *High* 5E 155
Gedling. *Notts* 1D 74
Gedney. *Linc* 3D 76
Gedney Broadgate. *Linc* 3D 76
Gedney Drove End. *Linc* 3D 76
Gedney Dyke. *Linc* 3D 76
Gedney Hill. *Linc* 4C 76
Gee Cross. *G Man* 1D 84
Geeston. *Rut* 5G 75
Geilston. *Arg* 2E 127
Geirinis. *W Isl* 4C 170
Geise. *High* 2D 168
Geisiadar. *W Isl* 4D 171
Gelder Shiel. *Abers* 5G 151
Geldeston. *Norf* 1F 67
Gell. *Cnwy* 4A 82
Gelli. *Pemb* 3E 43
Gelli. *Rhon* 2C 32
Gellifor. *Den* 4D 82
Gelligaer. *Cphy* 2E 33
Gellilydan. *Gwyn* 2F 69
Gellinudd. *Neat* 5H 45
Gellyburn. *Per* 5H 143
Gellywen. *Carm* 2G 43
Gelston. *Dum* 4E 111
Gelston. *Linc* 1G 75
Gembling. *E Yor* 4F 101
Gentleshaw. *Staf* 4E 73
Geocrab. *W Isl* 8D 171
George Green. *Buck* 2A 38
Georgeham. *Devn* 3E 19
George Nympton. *Devn* 4H 19
Georgetown. *Blae* 5E 47
Georgetown. *Ren* 3F 127
Georth. *Orkn* 5C 172
Gerlan. *Gwyn* 4F 81
Germansweek. *Devn* 3E 11
Germoe. *Corn* 4C 4
Gerrans. *Corn* 5C 6
Gerrard's Bromley. *Staf* 2B 72
Gerrards Cross. *Buck* 2A 38
Gerston. *High* 3D 168
Gestingthorpe. *Essx* 2B 54
Gethsemane. *Pemb* 1A 44
Geuffordd. *Powy* 4E 70
Gibraltar. *Buck* 4F 51
Gibraltar. *Linc* 5E 89
Gibraltar. *Suff* 5D 66
Gibsmere. *Notts* 1E 74
Giddeahall. *Wilts* 4D 34
Gidea Park. *G Lon* 2G 39
Gidleigh. *Devn* 4G 11
Giffnock. *E Ren* 4G 127
Gifford. *E Lot* 3B 130
Giffordtown. *Fife* 2E 137
Giggetty. *Staf* 1C 60
Giggleswick. *N Yor* 3H 97
Gignog. *Pemb* 2C 42
Gilberdyke. *E Yor* 2B 94
Gilbert's End. *Worc* 1D 48
Gilbert's Green. *Warw* 3F 61
Gilchriston. *E Lot* 3A 130
Gilcrux. *Cumb* 1C 102
Gildersome. *W Yor* 2C 92

Gildingwells—Great Ashfield

Gildingwells. S Yor 2C 86
Gilesgate Moor. Dur 5F 115
Gileston. V Glam 5D 32
Gilfach. Cphy 2E 33
Gilfach Goch. Rhon 2C 32
Gilfachreda. Cdgn 5D 56
Gilgarran. Cumb 2B 102
Gillamoor. N Yor 5D 107
Gillan. Corn 4E 5
Gillar's Green. Mers 1G 83
Gillen. High 3B 154
Gilling East. N Yor 2A 100
Gillingham. Dors 4D 22
Gillingham.
Medw 4B 40 & Medway 204
Gillingham. Norf 1G 67
Gilling West. N Yor 4E 105
Gillock. High 3E 169
Gillow Heath. Staf 5C 84
Gills. High 1F 169
Gill's Green. Kent 2B 28
Gilmanscleuch. Bord 2F 119
Gilmerton. Edin 3F 129
Gilmerton. Per 1A 136
Gilmonby. Dur 3C 104
Gilmorton. Leics 2C 62
Gilsland. Nmbd 3H 113
Gilsland Spa. Cumb 3H 113
Gilston. Midl 4H 129
Giltbrook. Notts 1B 74
Gilwern. Mon 4F 47
Gimingham. Norf 2E 79
Giosla. W Isl 5D 171
Gipping. Suff 4C 66
Gipsey Bridge. Linc 1B 76
Gipton. W Yor 1D 92
Girdle Toll. N Ayr 5E 127
Girlsta. Shet 6F 173
Girsby. N Yor 4A 106
Girthon. Dum 4D 110
Girton. Cambs 4D 64
Girton. Notts 4F 87
Girvan. S Ayr 5A 116
Gisburn. Lanc 5H 97
Gisleham. Suff 2H 67
Gislingham. Suff 3C 66
Gissing. Norf 2D 66
Gittisham. Devn 3E 13
Gladestry. Powy 5E 59
Gladsmuir. E Lot 2A 130
Glaichbea. High 5H 157
Glais. Swan 5H 45
Glaisdale. N Yor 4E 107
Glame. High 4E 155
Glamis. Ang 4C 144
Glamisdale. High 5C 146
Glanaman. Carm 4G 45
Glan-Conwy. Cnwy 5H 81
Glandford. Norf 1C 78
Glan Duar. Carm 1F 45
Glandwr. Blae 5F 47
Glandwr. Pemb 2F 43
Glan-Dwyfach. Gwyn 1D 69
Glandy Cross. Carm 2F 43
Glandyfi. Cdgn 1F 57
Glangrwyney. Powy 4F 47
Glanmule. Powy 1D 58
Glanrhyd. Gwyn 2B 68
Glanrhyd. Pemb 1B 44
(nr. Cardigan)
Glan-rhyd. Pemb 1F 43
(nr. Crymych)
Glan-rhyd. Powy 5A 46
Glanton. Nmbd 3E 121
Glanton Pyke. Nmbd 3E 121
Glanvilles Wootton. Dors 2B 14
Glan-y-don. Flin 3D 82
Glan-y-nant. Powy 2B 58
Glan-yr-afon. Gwyn 1C 70
Glan-yr-afon. IOA 2F 81
Glan-yr-afon. Powy 5C 70
Glan-y-wern. Gwyn 2F 69
Glapthorn. Nptn 1H 63
Glapwell. Derbs 4B 86
Glas Aird. Arg 4A 132
Glas-allt Shiel. Abers 5G 151
Glasbury. Powy 2E 47
Glaschoil. Mor 5E 159
Glascoed. Den 3B 82
Glascoed. Mon 5G 47
Glascote. Staf 5G 73
Glascwm. Powy 5D 58
Glasfryn. Cnwy 5B 82
Glasgow. Glas 3G 127 & 196
Glasgow Airport.
Ren 3F 127 & 216
Glasgow Prestwick
International Airport.
S Ayr 2C 116
Glashvin. High 2D 154
Glasinfryn. Gwyn 4E 81
Glas na Cardaich. High 4E 147
Glasnacardoch. High 4E 147
Glasnakille. High 2D 146
Glaspwll. Cdgn 1G 57
Glassburn. High 5F 157
Glassenbury. Kent 2B 28
Glasserton. Dum 5B 110
Glassford. S Lan 5A 128
Glassgreen. Mor 2G 159
Glasshouse. Glos 3C 48
Glasshouses. N Yor 3D 98
Glasson. Cumb 3D 112
Glasson. Lanc 4D 96
Glassonby. Cumb 1G 103
Glasterlaw. Ang 3E 145
Glaston. Rut 5F 75
Glastonbury. Som 3H 21
Glatton. Cambs 2A 64
Glazebrook. Warr 1A 84
Glazebury. Warr 1A 84
Glazeley. Shrp 2B 60
Gleadless. S Yor 2A 86
Gleadsmoss. Ches E 4C 84
Gleann Dail bho Dheas.
W Isl 7C 170
Gleann Tholastaidh. W Isl 3H 171
Gleann Uige. High 1A 140
Gleaston. Cumb 2B 96
Glecknabae. Arg 3B 126
Gledrid. Shrp 2E 71
Gleiniant. Powy 1B 58
Glemsford. Suff 1B 54
Glen. Dum 4C 110
Glenancross. High 4E 147
Glen Audlyn. IOM 2D 108
Glenbarr. Arg 2A 122
Glenbeg. High 2G 139
Glen Bernisdale. High 4D 154
Glenbervie. Abers 5E 153
Glenboig. N Lan 3A 128
Glenborrodale. High 2A 140
Glenbranter. Arg 4A 134
Glenbreck. Bord 2C 118
Glenbrein Lodge. High 2G 149
Glenbrittle. High 1C 146
Glenbuchat Lodge. Abers 2H 151
Glenbuck. E Ayr 2G 117
Glenburn. Ren 3F 127
Glencalvie Lodge. High 5B 164
Glencaple. Dum 3A 112
Glencarron Lodge. High 3C 156
Glencarse. Per 1D 136
Glencassley Castle. High 3B 164
Glencat. Abers 4C 152
Glencoe. High 3F 141
Glen Cottage. High 5E 147
Glencraig. Fife 4D 136
Glendale. High 4A 154
Glendevon. Per 3B 136
Glendoebeg. High 3G 149
Glendoick. Per 1E 136
Glendoune. S Ayr 5A 116
Glenduckie. Fife 2E 137
Gleneagles. Per 3B 136
Glenegedale. Arg 4B 124
Glenegedale Lots. Arg 4B 124
Glenelg. High 2G 147
Glenernie. Mor 4E 159
Glenesslin. Dum 1F 111
Glenfarg. Per 2D 136
Glenfarquhar Lodge. Abers 5E 152
Glenferness Mains. High 4D 158
Glenfeshie Lodge. High 4C 150
Glenfiddich Lodge. Mor 5H 159
Glenfield. Leics 5C 74
Glenfinnan. High 5B 148
Glenfintaig Lodge. High 5E 149
Glenfoot. Per 2D 136
Glenfyne Lodge. Arg 2B 134
Glengap. Dum 4D 110
Glengarnock. N Ayr 4E 126
Glengolly. High 2D 168
Glengorm Castle. Arg 3F 139
Glengrasco. High 4D 154
Glenhead Farm. Ang 2B 144
Glenholm. Bord 1D 118
Glen House. Bord 1E 119
Glenhurich. High 2C 140
Glenkerry. Bord 3E 119
Glenkiln. Dum 2F 111
Glenkindle. Abers 2B 152
Glenkinglass Lodge. Arg 5F 141
Glenkirk. Bord 2C 118
Glenlean. Arg 1B 126
Glenlee. Dum 1D 110
Glenleraig. High 5B 166
Glenlichorn. Per 2G 135
Glenlivet. Mor 1F 151
Glenlochar. Dum 3E 111
Glenlochsie Lodge. Per 1H 143
Glenluce. Dum 4G 109
Glenmarskie. High 3F 157
Glenmassan. Arg 1C 126
Glenmavis. N Lan 3A 128
Glen Maye. IOM 4B 108
Glenmazeran Lodge. High 1B 150
Glenmidge. Dum 1F 111
Glen Mona. IOM 3D 108
Glenmore. High 2G 139
(nr. Glenborrodale)
Glenmore. High 3D 151
(nr. Kingussie)
Glenmore. High 4D 154
(on Isle of Skye)
Glenmoy. Ang 2D 144
Glennoe. Arg 5E 141
Glen of Coachford. Abers 4B 160
Glenogil. Ang 2D 144
Glen Parva. Leics 1C 62
Glenprosen Village. Ang 2C 144
Glenree. N Ayr 3D 122
Glenridding. Cumb 3E 103
Glenrosa. N Ayr 2E 123
Glenrothes. Fife 3E 137
Glensanda. High 4C 140
Glensaugh. Abers 1F 145
Glenshero Lodge. High 4H 149
Glensluain. Arg 4H 133
Glenstockadale. Dum 3F 109
Glenstriven. Arg 2B 126
Glen Tanar House. Abers 4B 152
Glentham. Linc 1H 87
Glenton. Abers 1D 152
Glentress. Bord 1E 119
Glentromie Lodge. High 4B 150
Glentrool Lodge. Dum 1B 110
Glentrool Village. Dum 2A 110
Glentruim House. High 4A 150
Glentworth. Linc 2G 87
Glenuig. High 1A 140
Glen Village. Falk 2B 128
Glen Vine. IOM 4C 108
Glenwhilly. Dum 2G 109
Glenzierfoot. Dum 2E 113
Glespin. S Lan 2H 117
Gletness. Shet 6F 173
Glewstone. Here 3A 48
Glib Cheois. W Isl 5F 171
Glinton. Pet 5A 76
Glooston. Leics 1E 63
Glossop. Derbs 1E 85
Gloster Hill. Nmbd 4G 121
Gloucester. Glos 4D 48 & 196
Gloucestershire Airport. Glos 3D 49
Gloup. Shet 1G 173
Glusburn. N Yor 5C 98
Glutt Lodge. High 5B 168
Glutton Bridge. Staf 4E 85
Gluvian. Corn 2D 6
Glympton. Oxon 3C 50
Glyn. Cnwy 3A 82
Glynarthen. Cdgn 1D 44
Glynbrochan. Powy 2B 58
Glyn Ceiriog. Wrex 2E 70
Glyncoch. Rhon 2D 32
Glyncorrwg. Neat 2B 32
Glynde. E Sus 5F 27
Glyndebourne. E Sus 4F 27
Glyndyfrdwy. Den 1D 70
Glyn Ebwy. Blae 5E 47
Glynllan. B'end 3C 32
Glyn-neath. Neat 5B 46
Glynogwr. B'end 3C 32
Glyntaff. Rhon 3D 32
Glyntawe. Powy 4B 46
Glynteg. Carm 2D 44
Gnosall. Staf 3C 72
Gnosall Heath. Staf 3C 72
Goadby. Leics 1E 63
Goadby Marwood. Leics 3E 75
Goatacre. Wilts 4F 35
Goathill. Dors 1B 14
Goathland. N Yor 4F 107
Goathurst. Som 3F 21
Goathurst Common. Kent 5F 39
Goat Lees. Kent 1E 28
Gobernuisgach Lodge. High 4E 167
Gobernuisgeach. High 5B 168
Gobhaig. W Isl 7C 171
Gobowen. Shrp 2F 71
Godalming. Surr 1A 26
Goddard's Corner. Suff 4E 67
Goddard's Green. Kent 2C 28
(nr. Benenden)
Goddard's Green. Kent 2B 28
(nr. Cranbrook)
Goddards Green. W Sus 3D 27
Godford Cross. Devn 2E 13
Godleybrook. Staf 1D 73
Godmanchester. Cambs 3B 64
Godmanstone. Dors 3B 14
Godmersham. Kent 5E 41
Godolphin Cross. Corn 3D 4
Godre'r-graig. Neat 5A 46
Godshill. Hants 1G 15
Godshill. IOW 4D 16
Godstone. Staf 2E 73
Godstone. Surr 5E 39
Goetre. Mon 5G 47
Goff's Oak. Herts 5D 52
Gogar. Edin 2E 129
Goginan. Cdgn 2F 57
Golan. Gwyn 1E 69
Golant. Corn 3F 7
Golberdon. Corn 5D 10
Golborne. G Man 1A 84
Golcar. W Yor 3A 92
Goldcliff. Newp 3G 33
Golden Cross. E Sus 4G 27
Golden Green. Kent 1H 27
Golden Grove. Carm 4F 45
Golden Grove. N Yor 4F 107
Golden Hill. Pemb 2D 43
Goldenhill. Stoke 5C 84
Golden Pot. Hants 2F 25
Golden Valley. Glos 3E 49
Golders Green. G Lon 2D 38
Goldhanger. Essx 5C 54
Gold Hill. Norf 1E 65
Golding. Shrp 5H 71
Goldington. Bed 5H 63
Goldsborough. N Yor 4F 99
(nr. Harrogate)
Goldsborough. N Yor 3F 107
(nr. Whitby)
Goldsithney. Corn 3C 4
Goldstone. Kent 4G 41
Goldstone. Shrp 3B 72
Goldthorpe. S Yor 4E 93
Goldworthy. Devn 4D 19
Golfa. Powy 3D 70
Gollanfield. High 3C 158
Gollinglith Foot. N Yor 1D 98
Golsoncott. Som 3D 20
Golspie. High 4F 165
Gomeldon. Wilts 3G 23
Gomersal. W Yor 2C 92
Gometra House. Arg 4E 139
Gomshall. Surr 1B 26
Gonalston. Notts 1D 74
Gonerby Hill Foot. Linc 2G 75
Gonfirth. Shet 5E 173
Gonnabarn. Corn 3D 6
Good Easter. Essx 4G 53
Gooderstone. Norf 5G 77
Goodleigh. Devn 3G 19
Goodmanham. E Yor 5C 100
Goodmayes. G Lon 2F 39
Goodnestone. Kent 5G 41
(nr. Aylesham)
Goodnestone. Kent 4E 41
(nr. Faversham)
Goodrich. Here 4A 48
Goodrington. Torb 3E 9
Goodshaw. Lanc 2G 91
Goodshaw Fold. Lanc 2G 91
Goodstone. Devn 5A 12
Goodwick. Pemb 1D 42
Goodworth Clatford. Hants 2B 24
Goole. E Yor 2H 93
Goom's Hill. Worc 5E 61
Goonbell. Corn 4B 6
Goonhavern. Corn 3B 6
Goonvrea. Corn 4B 6
Goose Green. Cumb 1E 97
Goose Green. S Glo 3C 34
Gooseham. Corn 1C 10
Goosewell. Plym 3B 8
Goosey. Oxon 2B 36
Goosnargh. Lanc 1D 90
Goostrey. Ches E 3B 84
Gorcott Hill. Warw 4E 61
Gord. Shet 9F 173
Gordon. Bord 5C 130
Gordonbush. High 3F 165
Gordonstown. Abers 3C 160
(nr. Cornhill)
Gordonstown. Abers 5E 160
(nr. Fyvie)
Gorebridge. Midl 3G 129
Gorefield. Cambs 4D 76
Gores. Wilts 1G 23
Gorgie. Edin 2F 129
Goring. Oxon 3E 36
Goring-by-Sea. W Sus 5C 26
Goring Heath. Oxon 4E 37
Gorleston-on-Sea. Norf 5H 79
Gornalwood. W Mid 1D 60
Gorran Churchtown. Corn 4D 6
Gorran Haven. Corn 4E 6
Gorran High Lanes. Corn 4D 6
Gors. Cdgn 3F 57
Gorsedd. Flin 3D 82
Gorseinon. Swan 3E 31
Gorseness. Orkn 6D 172
Gorseybank. Derbs 5G 85
Gorsgoch. Cdgn 5D 57
Gorslas. Carm 4F 45
Gorsley. Glos 3B 48
Gorsley Common. Here 3B 48
Gorstan. High 2F 157
Gorstella. Ches W 4F 83
Gorsty Common. Here 2H 47
Gorsty Hill. Staf 3E 73
Gortantaoid. Arg 2B 124
Gorteneorn. High 2A 140
Gortenfern. High 2A 140
Gorton. G Man 1C 84
Gosbeck. Suff 5D 66
Gosberton. Linc 2B 76
Gosberton Cheal. Linc 3B 76
Gosberton Clough. Linc 3A 76
Goseley Dale. Derbs 3H 73
Gosfield. Essx 3A 54
Gosford. Oxon 4D 50
Gosforth. Cumb 4B 102
Gosforth. Tyne 3F 115
Gosmore. Herts 3B 52
Gospel End Village. Staf 1C 60
Gosport. Hants 2E 16
Gossabrough. Shet 3G 173
Gossington. Glos 5C 48
Gossops Green. W Sus 2D 26
Goswick. Nmbd 5G 131
Gotham. Notts 2C 74
Gotherington. Glos 3E 49
Gott. Arg 4B 138
Gott. Shet 7F 173
Goudhurst. Kent 2B 28
Goulceby. Linc 3B 88
Gourdon. Abers 1H 145
Gourock. Inv 2D 126
Govan. Glas 3G 127
Govanhill. Glas 3G 127
Goverton. Notts 1E 74
Goveton. Devn 4D 8
Govilon. Mon 4F 47
Gowanhill. Abers 2H 161
Gowdall. E Yor 2G 93
Gowerton. Swan 3E 31
Gowkhall. Fife 1D 128
Gowthorpe. E Yor 4B 100
Goxhill. E Yor 5F 101
Goxhill. N Lin 2E 94
Goxhill Haven. N Lin 2E 94
Goytre. Neat 3A 32
Grabhair. W Isl 6F 171
Graby. Linc 3H 75
Graffham. W Sus 4A 26
Grafham. Cambs 4A 64
Grafham. Surr 1B 26
Grafton. Here 2H 47
Grafton. N Yor 3G 99
Grafton. Oxon 5A 50
Grafton. Shrp 4G 71
Grafton. Worc 2E 49
(nr. Evesham)
Grafton. Worc 4H 59
(nr. Leominster)
Grafton Flyford. Worc 5D 60
Grafton Regis. Nptn 1F 51
Grafton Underwood. Nptn 2G 63
Grafty Green. Kent 1C 28
Graianrhyd. Den 5E 82
Graig. Carm 5E 45
Graig. Cnwy 3H 81
Graig. Den 3C 82
Graig-fechan. Den 5D 82
Graig Penllyn. V Glam 4C 32
Grain. Medw 3C 40
Grainsby. Linc 1B 88
Grainthorpe. Linc 1C 88
Grainthorpe Fen. Linc 1C 88
Graiselound. N Lin 1E 87
Gramasdail. W Isl 3D 170
Grampound. Corn 4D 6
Grampound Road. Corn 3D 6
Granborough. Buck 3F 51
Granby. Notts 2E 75
Grandborough. Warw 4B 62
Grandpont. Oxon 5D 50
Grandtully. Per 3G 143
Grange. Cumb 3D 102
Grange. E Ayr 1D 116
Grange. Here 3G 59
Grange. Mers 2E 83
Grange. Per 1E 137
Grange Crossroads. Mor 3B 160
Grange Hill. G Lon 1F 39
Grangemill. Derbs 5G 85
Grange Moor. W Yor 3C 92
Grangemouth. Falk 1C 128
Grange of Lindores. Fife 2E 137
Grange-over-Sands. Cumb 2D 96
Grangepans. Falk 1D 128
Grange, The. N Yor 5C 106
Grangetown. Card 4E 33
Grangetown. Red C 2C 106
Grange Villa. Dur 4F 115
Granish. High 2C 150
Gransmoor. E Yor 4F 101
Granston. Pemb 1C 42
Grantchester. Cambs 5D 64
Grantham. Linc 2G 75
Grantley. N Yor 3E 99
Grantlodge. Abers 2E 152
Granton. Edin 2F 129
Grantown-on-Spey. High 1E 151
Grantshouse. Bord 3E 130
Grappenhall. Warr 2A 84
Grasby. Linc 4D 94
Grasmere. Cumb 4E 103
Grasscroft. G Man 4H 91
Grassendale. Mers 2F 83
Grassgarth. Cumb 5E 113
Grassholme. Dur 2C 104
Grassington. N Yor 3C 98
Grassmoor. Derbs 4B 86
Grassthorpe. Notts 4E 87
Grateley. Hants 2A 24
Gratton. Devn 1D 11
Gratton. Staf 5D 84
Gratwich. Staf 2E 73
Graveley. Cambs 4B 64
Graveley. Herts 3C 52
Gravelhill. Shrp 4G 71
Gravel Hole. G Man 4H 91
Gravelly Hill. W Mid 1F 61
Graven. Shet 4F 173
Graveney. Kent 4E 41
Gravesend. Kent 3H 39
Grayingham. Linc 1G 87
Grayrigg. Cumb 5G 103
Grays. Thur 3H 39
Grayshott. Hants 3G 25
Grayson Green. Cumb 2A 102
Grayswood. Surr 2A 26
Graythorp. Hart 2C 106
Grazeley. Wok 5E 37
Grealin. High 2E 155
Greasbrough. S Yor 1B 86
Greasby. Mers 2E 83
Great Abington. Cambs 1F 53
Great Addington. Nptn 3G 63
Great Alne. Warw 5F 61
Great Altcar. Lanc 4B 90
Great Amwell. Herts 4D 52
Great Asby. Cumb 3H 103
Great Ashfield. Suff 4B 66

Great Ayton—Hackness

Great Ayton. *N Yor* 3C 106
Great Baddow. *Essx* 5H 53
Great Bardfield. *Essx* 2G 53
Great Barford. *Bed* 5A 64
Great Barr. *W Mid* 1E 61
Great Barrington. *Glos* 4H 49
Great Barrow. *Ches W* 4G 83
Great Barton. *Suff* 4A 66
Great Barugh. *N Yor* 2B 100
Great Bavington. *Nmbd* 1C 114
Great Bealings. *Suff* 1F 55
Great Bedwyn. *Wilts* 5A 36
Great Bentley. *Essx* 3E 54
Great Billing. *Nptn* 4F 63
Great Bircham. *Norf* 2G 77
Great Blakenham. *Suff* 5D 66
Great Blencow. *Cumb* 1F 103
Great Bolas. *Telf* 3A 72
Great Bookham. *Surr* 5C 38
Great Bosullow. *Corn* 3B 4
Great Bourton. *Oxon* 1C 50
Great Bowden. *Leics* 2E 63
Great Bradley. *Suff* 5F 65
Great Braxted. *Essx* 4B 54
Great Bricett. *Suff* 5C 66
Great Brickhill. *Buck* 2H 51
Great Bridgeford. *Staf* 3C 72
Great Brington. *Nptn* 4D 62
Great Bromley. *Essx* 3D 54
Great Broughton. *Cumb* 1B 102
Great Broughton. *N Yor* 4C 106
Great Budworth. *Ches W* 3A 84
Great Burdon. *Darl* 3A 106
Great Burstead. *Essx* 1A 40
Great Busby. *N Yor* 4C 106
Great Canfield. *Essx* 4F 53
Great Carlton. *Linc* 2D 88
Great Casterton. *Rut* 5H 75
Great Chalfield. *Wilts* 5D 34
Great Chart. *Kent* 1D 28
Great Chatwell. *Staf* 4B 72
Great Chesterford. *Essx* 1F 53
Great Cheverell. *Wilts* 1E 23
Great Chilton. *Dur* 1F 105
Great Chishill. *Cambs* 2E 53
Great Clacton. *Essx* 4E 55
Great Cliff. *W Yor* 3D 92
Great Clifton. *Cumb* 2B 102
Great Coates. *NE Lin* 3F 95
Great Comberton. *Worc* 1E 49
Great Corby. *Cumb* 4F 113
Great Cornard. *Suff* 1B 54
Great Cowden. *E Yor* 5G 101
Great Coxwell. *Oxon* 2A 36
Great Crakehall. *N Yor* 1E 99
Great Cransley. *Nptn* 3F 63
Great Cressingham. *Norf* 5H 77
Great Crosby. *Mers* 1F 83
Great Cubley. *Derbs* 2F 73
Great Dalby. *Leics* 4E 75
Great Doddington. *Nptn* 4F 63
Great Doward. *Here* 4A 48
Great Dunham. *Norf* 4A 78
Great Dunmow. *Essx* 3G 53
Great Durnford. *Wilts* 3G 23
Great Easton. *Essx* 3G 53
Great Easton. *Leics* 1F 63
Great Eccleston. *Lanc* 5D 96
Great Edstone. *N Yor* 1B 100
Great Ellingham. *Norf* 1C 66
Great Elm. *Som* 2C 22
Great Eppleton. *Tyne* 5G 115
Great Eversden. *Cambs* 5C 64
Great Fencote. *N Yor* 5F 105
Great Finborough. *Suff* 5C 66
Greatford. *Linc* 4H 75
Great Fransham. *Norf* 4A 78
Great Gaddesden. *Herts* 4A 52
Great Gate. *Staf* 1E 73
Great Gidding. *Cambs* 2A 64
Great Givendale. *E Yor* 4C 100
Great Glemham. *Suff* 4F 67
Great Glen. *Leics* 1D 62
Great Gonerby. *Linc* 2G 75
Great Gransden. *Cambs* 5B 64
Great Green. *Norf* 2E 67
Great Green. *Suff* 5B 66
(nr. Lavenham)
Great Green. *Suff* 3D 66
(nr. Palgrave)
Great Habton. *N Yor* 2B 100
Great Hale. *Linc* 1A 76
Great Hallingbury. *Essx* 4F 53
Greatham. *Hants* 3F 25
Greatham. *Hart* 2B 106
Greatham. *W Sus* 4B 26
Great Hampden. *Buck* 5G 51
Great Harrowden. *Nptn* 3F 63
Great Harwood. *Lanc* 1F 91
Great Haseley. *Oxon* 5E 51
Great Hatfield. *E Yor* 5F 101
Great Haywood. *Staf* 3D 73
Great Heath. *W Mid* 2H 61
Great Heck. *N Yor* 2F 93
Great Henny. *Essx* 2B 54
Great Hinton. *Wilts* 1E 23
Great Hockham. *Norf* 1B 66
Great Holland. *Essx* 4F 55
Great Horkesley. *Essx* 2C 54
Great Hormead. *Herts* 2E 53
Great Horton. *W Yor* 1B 92
Great Horwood. *Buck* 2F 51
Great Houghton. *Nptn* 5E 63
Great Houghton. *S Yor* 4E 93
Great Hucklow. *Derbs* 3F 85
Great Kelk. *E Yor* 4F 101
Great Kendale. *E Yor* 3E 101
Great Kimble. *Buck* 5G 51
Great Kingshill. *Buck* 2G 37
Great Langdale. *Cumb* 4D 102
Great Langton. *N Yor* 5F 105
Great Leighs. *Essx* 4H 53
Great Limber. *Linc* 4E 95
Great Linford. *Mil* 1G 51
Great Livermere. *Suff* 3A 66
Great Longstone. *Derbs* 3G 85
Great Lumley. *Dur* 5F 115
Great Lyth. *Shrp* 5G 71
Great Malvern. *Worc* 1C 48
Great Maplestead. *Essx* 2B 54
Great Marton. *Bkpl* 1B 90
Great Massingham. *Norf* 3G 77
Great Melton. *Norf* 5D 78
Great Milton. *Oxon* 5E 51
Great Missenden. *Buck* 5G 51
Great Mitton. *Lanc* 1F 91
Great Mongeham. *Kent* 5H 41
Great Moulton. *Norf* 1D 66
Great Munden. *Herts* 3D 52
Great Musgrave. *Cumb* 3A 104
Great Ness. *Shrp* 4F 71
Great Notley. *Essx* 3H 53
Great Oak. *Mon* 5G 47
Great Oakley. *Essx* 3E 55
Great Oakley. *Nptn* 2F 63
Great Offley. *Herts* 3B 52
Great Ormside. *Cumb* 3A 104
Great Orton. *Cumb* 4E 113
Great Ouseburn. *N Yor* 3G 99
Great Oxendon. *Nptn* 2E 63
Great Oxney Green. *Essx* 5G 53
Great Parndon. *Essx* 5E 53
Great Paxton. *Cambs* 4B 64
Great Plumpton. *Lanc* 1B 90
Great Plumstead. *Norf* 4F 79
Great Ponton. *Linc* 2G 75
Great Potheridge. *Devn* 1F 11
Great Preston. *W Yor* 2E 93
Great Raveley. *Cambs* 2B 64
Great Rissington. *Glos* 4G 49
Great Rollright. *Oxon* 2B 50
Great Ryburgh. *Norf* 3B 78
Great Ryle. *Nmbd* 3E 121
Great Ryton. *Shrp* 5G 71
Great Saling. *Essx* 3G 53
Great Salkeld. *Cumb* 1G 103
Great Sampford. *Essx* 2G 53
Great Sankey. *Warr* 2H 83
Great Saredon. *Staf* 5D 72
Great Saxham. *Suff* 4G 65
Great Shefford. *W Ber* 4B 36
Great Shelford. *Cambs* 5D 64
Great Shoddesden. *Hants* 2A 24
Great Smeaton. *N Yor* 4A 106
Great Snoring. *Norf* 2B 78
Great Somerford. *Wilts* 3E 35
Great Stainton. *Darl* 2A 106
Great Stambridge. *Essx* 1C 40
Great Staughton. *Cambs* 4A 64
Great Steeping. *Linc* 4D 88
Great Stonar. *Kent* 5H 41
Greatstone-on-Sea. *Kent* 3E 29
Great Strickland. *Cumb* 2G 103
Great Stukeley. *Cambs* 3B 64
Great Sturton. *Linc* 3B 88
Great Sutton. *Ches W* 3F 83
Great Sutton. *Shrp* 2H 59
Great Swinburne. *Nmbd* 2C 114
Great Tew. *Oxon* 3B 50
Great Tey. *Essx* 3B 54
Great Thirkleby. *N Yor* 2G 99
Great Thorness. *IOW* 3C 16
Great Thurlow. *Suff* 5F 65
Great Torr. *Devn* 4C 8
Great Torrington. *Devn* 1E 11
Great Tosson. *Nmbd* 4E 121
Great Totham North. *Essx* 4B 54
Great Totham South. *Essx* 4B 54
Great Tows. *Linc* 1B 88
Great Urswick. *Cumb* 2B 96
Great Wakering. *Essx* 2D 40
Great Waldingfield. *Suff* 1C 54
Great Walsingham. *Norf* 2B 78
Great Waltham. *Essx* 4G 53
Great Warley. *Essx* 1G 39
Great Washbourne. *Glos* 2E 49
Great Wenham. *Suff* 2D 54
Great Whelnetham. *Suff* 5A 66
Great Whittington. *Nmbd* 2D 114
Great Wigborough. *Essx* 4C 54
Great Wilbraham. *Cambs* 5E 65
Great Wilne. *Derbs* 2B 74
Great Wishford. *Wilts* 3F 23
Great Witchingham. *Norf* 3D 78
Great Witcombe. *Glos* 4E 49
Great Witley. *Worc* 4B 60
Great Wolford. *Warw* 2H 49
Greatworth. *Nptn* 1D 50
Great Wratting. *Suff* 1G 53
Great Wymondley. *Herts* 3C 52
Great Wyrley. *Staf* 5D 73
Great Wytheford. *Shrp* 4H 71
Great Yarmouth. *Norf* 5H 79 & 196
Great Yeldham. *Essx* 2A 54
Grebby. *Linc* 4D 88
Greeba Castle. *IOM* 3C 108
Greenbank. *Shet* 1G 173
Greenbottom. *Corn* 4B 6
Greenburn. *W Lot* 3C 128
Greencroft. *Dur* 4E 115
Greencroft Park. *Dur* 5E 115
Greendown. *Som* 1A 22
Greendykes. *Nmbd* 2E 121
Green End. *Bed* 1A 52
(nr. Bedford)
Green End. *Bed* 4A 64
(nr. St Neots)
Green End. *Herts* 2D 52
(nr. Buntingford)
Green End. *Herts* 3D 52
(nr. Stevenage)
Green End. *N Yor* 4F 107
Green End. *Warw* 2G 61
Greenfield. *Arg* 4B 134
Greenfield. *C Beds* 2A 52
Greenfield. *Flin* 3D 82
Greenfield. *G Man* 4H 91
Greenfield. *Oxon* 2F 37
Greenfoot. *N Lan* 3A 128
Greenford. *G Lon* 2C 38
Greengairs. *N Lan* 2A 128
Greengate. *Norf* 4C 78
Greengill. *Cumb* 1C 102
Greenhalgh. *Lanc* 1C 90
Greenham. *Dors* 2H 13
Greenham. *Som* 4D 20
Greenham. *W Ber* 5C 36
Green Hammerton. *N Yor* 4G 99
Greenhaugh. *Nmbd* 1A 114
Greenhead. *Nmbd* 3H 113
Green Heath. *Staf* 4D 73
Greenhill. *Dum* 2C 112
Greenhill. *Falk* 2B 128
Greenhill. *Kent* 4F 41
Greenhill. *S Yor* 2H 85
Greenhill. *Worc* 3C 60
Greenhills. *N Ayr* 4E 127
Greenhithe. *Kent* 3G 39
Greenholm. *E Ayr* 1E 117
Greenhow Hill. *N Yor* 3D 98
Greenigoe. *Orkn* 7D 172
Greenland. *High* 2E 169
Greenland Mains. *High* 2E 169
Greenlands. *Worc* 4E 61
Green Lane. *Shrp* 3A 72
Green Lane. *Warw* 4E 61
Greenlaw. *Bord* 5D 130
Greenlea. *Dum* 2B 112
Greenloaning. *Per* 3H 135
Greenmount. *G Man* 3F 91
Greenmow. *Shet* 9F 173
Greenock. *Inv* 2D 126
Greenock Mains. *E Ayr* 2F 117
Greenodd. *Cumb* 1C 96
Green Ore. *Som* 1A 22
Greenrow. *Cumb* 4C 112
Greens. *Abers* 4F 161
Greensgate. *Norf* 4D 78
Greenside. *Tyne* 3E 115
Greensidehill. *Nmbd* 3D 121
Greens Norton. *Nptn* 1E 51
Greenstead Green. *Essx* 3B 54
Greensted Green. *Essx* 5F 53
Green Street. *Herts* 1C 38
Green Street. *Suff* 3D 66
Green Street Green. *G Lon* 4F 39
Green Street Green. *Kent* 3G 39
Greenstreet Green. *Suff* 1D 54
Green, The. *Cumb* 1A 96
Green, The. *Wilts* 3D 22
Green Tye. *Herts* 4E 53
Greenwall. *Orkn* 7E 172
Greenway. *Pemb* 2E 43
Greenway. *V Glam* 4D 32
Greenwell. *Cumb* 4G 113
Greenwich. *G Lon* 3E 39
Greet. *Glos* 2F 49
Greete. *Shrp* 3H 59
Greetham. *Linc* 3C 88
Greetham. *Rut* 4G 75
Greetland. *W Yor* 2A 92
Gregson Lane. *Lanc* 2D 90
Grein. *W Isl* 8B 170
Greinetobht. *W Isl* 1D 170
Greinton. *Som* 3H 21
Gremista. *Shet* 7F 173
Grenaby. *IOM* 4B 108
Grendon. *Nptn* 4F 63
Grendon. *Warw* 1G 61
Grendon Common. *Warw* 1G 61
Grendon Green. *Here* 5H 59
Grendon Underwood. *Buck* 3E 51
Grenofen. *Devn* 5E 11
Grenoside. *S Yor* 1H 85
Greosabhagh. *W Isl* 8D 171
Gresford. *Wrex* 5F 83
Gresham. *Norf* 2D 78
Greshornish. *High* 3C 154
Gressenhall. *Norf* 4B 78
Gressingham. *Lanc* 2E 97
Greta Bridge. *Dur* 3D 105
Gretna. *Dum* 3E 112
Gretna Green. *Dum* 3E 112
Gretton. *Glos* 2F 49
Gretton. *Nptn* 1G 63
Gretton. *Shrp* 1H 59
Grewelthorpe. *N Yor* 2E 99
Greygarth. *N Yor* 2D 98
Grey Green. *N Lin* 4A 94
Greylake. *Som* 3G 21
Greysouthen. *Cumb* 2B 102
Greystoke. *Cumb* 1F 103
Greystoke Gill. *Cumb* 2F 103
Greystone. *Ang* 4E 145
Greystones. *S Yor* 2H 85
Greywell. *Hants* 1F 25
Griais. *W Isl* 3G 171
Grianan. *W Isl* 4G 171
Gribthorpe. *E Yor* 1A 94
Gribun. *Arg* 5F 139
Griff. *Warw* 2A 62
Griffithstown. *Torf* 2F 33
Griffydam. *Leics* 4B 74
Griggs Green. *Hants* 3G 25
Grimbister. *Orkn* 6C 172
Grimeford Village. *Lanc* 3E 90
Grimeston. *Orkn* 6C 172
Grimethorpe. *S Yor* 4E 93
Griminis. *W Isl* 3C 170
(on Benbecula)
Griminis. *W Isl* 1C 170
(on North Uist)
Grimister. *Shet* 2F 173
Grimley. *Worc* 4C 60
Grimness. *Orkn* 8D 172
Grimoldby. *Linc* 2C 88
Grimpo. *Shrp* 3F 71
Grimsargh. *Lanc* 1D 90
Grimsbury. *Oxon* 1C 50
Grimsby. *NE Lin* 3F 95
Grimscote. *Nptn* 5D 62
Grimscott. *Corn* 2C 10
Grimshaw. *Bkbn* 2F 91
Grimshaw Green. *Lanc* 3C 90
Grimsthorpe. *Linc* 3H 75
Grimston. *E Yor* 1F 95
Grimston. *Leics* 3D 74
Grimston. *Norf* 3G 77
Grimston. *York* 4A 100
Grimstone. *Dors* 3B 14
Grimstone End. *Suff* 4B 66
Grinacombe Moor. *Devn* 3E 11
Grindale. *E Yor* 2F 101
Grindhill. *Devn* 3E 11
Grindiscol. *Shet* 8F 173
Grindle. *Shrp* 5B 72
Grindleford. *Derbs* 3G 85
Grindleton. *Lanc* 5G 97
Grindley. *Staf* 3E 73
Grindley Brook. *Shrp* 1H 71
Grindlow. *Derbs* 3F 85
Grindon. *Nmbd* 5F 131
Grindon. *Staf* 5E 85
Gringley on the Hill. *Notts* 1E 87
Grinsdale. *Cumb* 4E 113
Grinshill. *Shrp* 3H 71
Grinton. *N Yor* 5D 104
Griomsidar. *W Isl* 5G 171
Grishipoll. *Arg* 3C 138
Grisling Common. *E Sus* 3F 27
Gristhorpe. *N Yor* 1E 101
Griston. *Norf* 1B 66
Gritley. *Orkn* 7E 172
Grittenham. *Wilts* 3F 35
Grittleton. *Wilts* 4D 34
Grizebeck. *Cumb* 1B 96
Grizedale. *Cumb* 5E 103
Grobister. *Orkn* 5F 172
Grobsness. *Shet* 5E 173
Groby. *Leics* 5C 74
Groes. *Cnwy* 4C 82
Groes. *Neat* 3A 32
Groes-faen. *Rhon* 3D 32
Groesffordd. *Gwyn* 2B 68
Groesffordd. *Powy* 3D 46
Groeslon. *Gwyn* 5D 81
Groes-lwyd. *Powy* 4E 70
Groes-wen. *Cphy* 3E 33
Grogport. *Arg* 5G 125
Groigearraidh. *W Isl* 4C 170
Gromford. *Suff* 5F 67
Gronant. *Flin* 2C 82
Groombridge. *E Sus* 2G 27
Grosmont. *Mon* 3H 47
Grosmont. *N Yor* 4F 107
Groton. *Suff* 1C 54
Grove. *Dors* 5C 14
Grove. *Kent* 4G 41
Grove. *Notts* 3E 87
Grove. *Oxon* 2B 36
Grovehill. *E Yor* 1D 94
Grove Park. *G Lon* 3F 39
Grovesend. *Swan* 5F 45
Grove, The. *Dum* 2A 112
Grove, The. *Worc* 1D 48
Grub Street. *Staf* 3B 72
Grudie. *High* 2F 157
Gruids. *High* 3C 164
Gruinard House. *High* 4D 162
Gruinart. *Arg* 3A 124
Grulinbeg. *Arg* 3A 124
Gruline. *Arg* 4G 139
Grummore. *High* 5G 167
Grundisburgh. *Suff* 5E 66
Gruting. *Shet* 7D 173
Grutness. *Shet* 10F 173
Gualachulain. *High* 4F 141
Gualin House. *High* 3D 166
Guardbridge. *Fife* 2G 137
Guarlford. *Worc* 1D 48
Guay. *Per* 4H 143
Gubblecote. *Herts* 4H 51
Guestling Green. *E Sus* 4C 28
Guestling Thorn. *E Sus* 4C 28
Guestwick. *Norf* 3C 78
Guestwick Green. *Norf* 3C 78
Guide. *Bkbn* 2F 91
Guide Post. *Nmbd* 1F 115
Guilden Down. *Shrp* 2F 59
Guilden Morden. *Cambs* 1C 52
Guilden Sutton. *Ches W* 4G 83
Guildford. *Surr* 1A 26 & 197
Guildtown. *Per* 5A 144
Guilsborough. *Nptn* 3D 62
Guilsfield. *Powy* 4E 70
Guineaford. *Devn* 3F 19
Guisborough. *Red C* 3D 106
Guiseley. *W Yor* 5D 98
Guist. *Norf* 3B 78
Guiting Power. *Glos* 3F 49
Gulberwick. *Shet* 8F 173
Gullane. *E Lot* 1A 130
Gulling Green. *Suff* 5H 65
Gulval. *Corn* 3B 4
Gumfreston. *Pemb* 4F 43
Gumley. *Leics* 1D 62
Gunby. *E Yor* 1H 93
Gunby. *Linc* 3G 75
Gundleton. *Hants* 3E 24
Gun Green. *Kent* 2B 28
Gun Hill. *E Sus* 4G 27
Gunn. *Devn* 3G 19
Gunnerside. *N Yor* 5C 104
Gunnerton. *Nmbd* 2C 114
Gunness. *N Lin* 3B 94
Gunnislake. *Corn* 5E 11
Gunnista. *Shet* 7F 173
Gunsgreenhill. *Bord* 3F 131
Gunstone. *Staf* 5C 72
Gunthorpe. *Norf* 2C 78
Gunthorpe. *N Lin* 1F 87
Gunthorpe. *Notts* 1D 74
Gunthorpe. *Pet* 5A 76
Gunville. *IOW* 4C 16
Gupworthy. *Som* 3C 20
Gurnard. *IOW* 3C 16
Gurney Slade. *Som* 2B 22
Gurnos. *Powy* 5A 46
Gussage All Saints. *Dors* 1F 15
Gussage St Andrew. *Dors* 1E 15
Gussage St Michael. *Dors* 1E 15
Guston. *Kent* 1H 29
Gutcher. *Shet* 2G 173
Guthram Gowt. *Linc* 3A 76
Guthrie. *Ang* 3E 145
Guyhirn. *Cambs* 5D 76
Guyhirn Gull. *Cambs* 5C 76
Guy's Head. *Linc* 3D 77
Guy's Marsh. *Dors* 4D 22
Guyzance. *Nmbd* 4G 121
Gwaelod-y-garth. *Card* 3E 32
Gwaenynog Bach. *Den* 4C 82
Gwaenysgor. *Flin* 2C 82
Gwalchmai. *IOA* 3C 80
Gwastad. *Pemb* 2E 43
Gwaun-Cae-Gurwen. *Neat* 4H 45
Gwaun-y-bara. *Cphy* 3E 33
Gwbert. *Cdgn* 1B 44
Gweek. *Corn* 4E 5
Gwehelog. *Mon* 5G 47
Gwenddwr. *Powy* 1D 46
Gwennap. *Corn* 4B 6
Gwenter. *Corn* 5E 5
Gwernaffield. *Flin* 4E 82
Gwernesney. *Mon* 5H 47
Gwernogle. *Carm* 2F 45
Gwern-y-go. *Powy* 1E 58
Gwernymynydd. *Flin* 4E 82
Gwersyllt. *Wrex* 5F 83
Gwespyr. *Flin* 2D 82
Gwinear. *Corn* 3C 4
Gwithian. *Corn* 2C 4
Gwredog. *IOA* 2D 80
Gwyddelwern. *Den* 1C 70
Gwyddgrug. *Carm* 2E 45
Gwynfryn. *Wrex* 5E 83
Gwystre. *Powy* 4C 58
Gwytherin. *Cnwy* 4A 82
Gyfelia. *Wrex* 1F 71
Gyffin. *Cnwy* 3G 81

H

Haa of Houlland. *Shet* 1G 173
Habberley. *Shrp* 5F 71
Habblesthorpe. *Notts* 2E 87
Habergham. *Lanc* 1G 91
Habin. *W Sus* 4G 25
Habrough. *NE Lin* 3E 95
Haceby. *Linc* 2H 75
Hacheston. *Suff* 5F 67
Hackenthorpe. *S Yor* 2B 86
Hackford. *Norf* 5C 78
Hackforth. *N Yor* 5F 105
Hackland. *Orkn* 5C 172
Hackleton. *Nptn* 5F 63
Hackman's Gate. *Worc* 3C 60
Hackness. *N Yor* 5G 107
Hackness. *Orkn* 8C 172

Hackney. *G Lon* 2E **39**	Hallin. *High* 3B **154**	Hampstead Norreys. *W Ber* 4D **36**	Hardingham. *Norf* 5C **78**	Harrapool. *High* 1E **147**
Hackthorn. *Linc* 2G **87**	Halling. *Medw* 4B **40**	Hampsthwaite. *N Yor* 4E **99**	Hardingstone. *Nptn* 5E **63**	Harrapul. *High* 1E **147**
Hackthorpe. *Cumb* 2G **103**	Hallington. *Linc* 2C **88**	Hampton. *Devn* 3F **13**	Hardings Wood. *Ches E* 5C **84**	Harrietfield. *Per* 1B **136**
Haclait. *W Isl* 4D **170**	Hallington. *Nmbd* 2C **114**	Hampton. *G Lon* 3C **38**	Hardington. *Som* 1C **22**	Harrietsham. *Kent* 5C **40**
Haconby. *Linc* 3A **76**	Halloughton. *Notts* 5D **86**	Hampton. *Kent* 4F **41**	Hardington Mandeville. *Som* . .1A **14**	Harrington. *Cumb* 2A **102**
Hadden. *Bord* 1B **120**	Hallow. *Worc* 5C **60**	Hampton. *Shrp* 2B **60**	Hardington Marsh. *Som* 2A **14**	Harrington. *Linc* 3C **88**
Haddenham. *Buck* 5F **51**	Hallow Heath. *Worc* 5C **60**	Hampton. *Swin* 2G **35**	Hardington Moor. *Som* 1A **14**	Harrington. *Nptn* 2E **63**
Haddenham. *Cambs* 3D **64**	Hallsands. *Devn* 5E **9**	Hampton. *Worc* 1F **49**	Hardley. *Hants* 2C **16**	Harringworth. *Nptn* 1G **63**
Haddenham End. *Cambs* . . .3D **64**	Hall's Green. *Herts* 3C **52**	Hampton Bishop. *Here* 2A **48**	Hardley Street. *Norf* 5F **79**	Harriseahead. *Staf* 5C **84**
Haddington. *E Lot* 2B **130**	Hallspill. *Devn* 4E **19**	Hampton Fields. *Glos* 2D **35**	Hardmead. *Mil* 1H **51**	Harriston. *Cumb* 5C **112**
Haddington. *Linc* 4G **87**	Halltoft End. *Linc* 1C **76**	Hampton Hargate. *Pet* 1A **64**	Hardstoft. *Derbs* 4B **86**	**Harrogate**. *N Yor* . . . . .4F **99** & **197**
Haddiscoe. *Norf* 1G **67**	Halltree. *Bord* 4A **130**	Hampton Heath. *Ches W* . . .1H **71**	Hardway. *Hants* 2E **16**	Harrold. *Bed* 5G **63**
Haddo. *Abers* 5F **161**	Hallwood Green. *Glos* 2B **48**	Hampton in Arden. *W Mid* . .2G **61**	Hardway. *Som* 3C **22**	Harrop Dale. *G Man* 4A **92**
Haddon. *Cambs* 1A **64**	Hallworthy. *Corn* 4B **10**	Hampton Loade. *Shrp* 2B **60**	Hardwick. *Buck* 4G **51**	**Harrow**. *G Lon* 2C **38**
Hademore. *Staf* 5F **73**	Hallyne. *Bord* 5E **129**	Hampton Lovett. *Worc* 4C **60**	Hardwick. *Cambs* 5C **64**	Harrowbarrow. *Corn* 2H **7**
Hadfield. *Derbs* 1E **85**	Halmer End. *Staf* 1C **72**	Hampton Lucy. *Warw* 5G **61**	Hardwick. *Norf* 2E **66**	Harrowden. *Bed* 1A **52**
Hadham Cross. *Herts* 4E **53**	Halmond's Frome. *Here* 1B **48**	Hampton Magna. *Warw* 4G **61**	Hardwick. *Nptn* 4F **63**	Harrowgate Hill. *Darl* 3F **105**
Hadham Ford. *Herts* 3E **53**	Halmore. *Glos* 5B **48**	Hampton on the Hill. *Warw* . .4G **61**	Hardwick. *Oxon* 3D **50**	Harrow on the Hill. *G Lon* . . .2C **38**
Hadleigh. *Essx* 2C **40**	Halnaker. *W Sus* 5A **26**	Hampton Poyle. *Oxon* 4D **50**	(nr. Bicester)	Harrow Weald. *G Lon* 1C **38**
Hadleigh. *Suff* 1D **54**	Halsall. *Lanc* 3B **90**	Hampton Wick. *G Lon* 4C **38**	Hardwick. *Oxon* 5B **50**	Harry Stoke. *S Glo* 4B **34**
Hadleigh Heath. *Suff* 1C **54**	Halse. *Nptn* 1D **50**	Hamptworth. *Wilts* 1H **15**	(nr. Witney)	Harston. *Cambs* 5D **64**
Hadley. *Telf* 4A **72**	Halse. *Som* 4E **21**	Hamrow. *Norf* 3B **78**	Hardwick. *Shrp* 1F **59**	Harston. *Leics* 2F **75**
Hadley. *Worc* 4C **60**	Halsetown. *Corn* 3C **4**	Hamsey. *E Sus* 4F **27**	Hardwick. *S Yor* 2B **86**	Harswell. *E Yor* 5C **100**
Hadley End. *Staf* 3F **73**	Halsham. *E Yor* 2F **95**	Hamsey Green. *Surr* 5E **39**	Hardwick. *Stoc T* 2B **106**	Hart. *Hart* 1B **106**
Hadlow. *Kent* 1H **27**	Halsinger. *Devn* 3F **19**	Hamstall Ridware. *Staf* 4F **73**	Hardwick. *W Mid* 1E **61**	Hartburn. *Nmbd* 1D **115**
Hadlow Down. *E Sus* 3G **27**	Halstead. *Essx* 2B **54**	Hamstead. *IOW* 3C **16**	Hardwick. *Glos* 3E **49**	Hartburn. *Stoc T* 3B **106**
Hadnall. *Shrp* 3H **71**	Halstead. *Kent* 4F **39**	Hamstead. *W Mid* 1E **61**	(nr. Cheltenham)	Hartest. *Suff* 5H **65**
Hadstock. *Essx* 1F **53**	Halstead. *Leics* 5E **75**	Hamstead Marshall. *W Ber* . .5C **36**	Hardwicke. *Glos* 4C **48**	Hartfield. *E Sus* 2F **27**
Hadston. *Nmbd* 5G **121**	Halstock. *Dors* 2A **14**	Hamsterley. *Dur* 4E **115**	(nr. Gloucester)	Hartford. *Cambs* 3B **64**
Hady. *Derbs* 3A **86**	Halsway. *Som* 3E **21**	(nr. Consett)	Hardwicke. *Here* 1F **47**	Hartford. *Ches W* 3A **84**
Hadzor. *Worc* 4D **60**	Haltcliff Bridge. *Cumb* 1E **103**	Hamsterley. *Dur* 1E **105**	Hardwick Village. *Notts* 3D **86**	Hartfordbridge. *Hants* 1F **25**
Haffenden Quarter. *Kent* . . .1C **28**	Haltham. *Linc* 4B **88**	(nr. Wolsingham)	Hardy's Green. *Essx* 3C **54**	Hartford End. *Essx* 4G **53**
Haggate. *Lanc* 1G **91**	Haltoft End. *Linc* 1C **76**	Hamsterley Mill. *Dur* 4E **115**	Hare. *Som* 1F **13**	Harthill. *Ches W* 5H **83**
Haggbeck. *Cumb* 2F **113**	Halton. *Buck* 5G **51**	Hamstreet. *Kent* 2E **28**	Hareby. *Linc* 4C **88**	Harthill. *N Lan* 3C **128**
Haggersta. *Shet* 7E **173**	Halton. *Hal* 2H **83**	Ham Street. *Som* 3A **22**	Hareden. *Lanc* 4F **97**	Harthill. *S Yor* 2B **86**
Haggerston. *Nmbd* 5G **131**	Halton. *Lanc* 3E **97**	Hamworthy. *Pool* 3E **15**	Harefield. *G Lon* 1B **38**	Hartington. *Derbs* 4F **85**
Haggrister. *Shet* 4E **173**	Halton. *Nmbd* 3C **114**	Hanbury. *Staf* 3F **73**	Hare Green. *Essx* 3D **54**	Hartland. *Devn* 4C **18**
Hagley. *Here* 1A **48**	Halton. *W Yor* 1D **92**	Hanbury. *Worc* 4D **60**	Hare Hatch. *Wok* 4G **37**	Hartland Quay. *Devn* 4C **18**
Hagley. *Worc* 2D **60**	Halton. *Wrex* 2F **71**	Hanbury Woodend. *Staf* 3F **73**	Harehill. *Derbs* 2F **73**	Hartle. *Worc* 3D **60**
Hagnaby. *Linc* 4C **88**	Halton East. *N Yor* 4C **98**	Hanby. *Linc* 2H **75**	Harehills. *W Yor* 1D **92**	Hartlebury. *Worc* 3C **60**
Hagworthingham. *Linc* 4C **88**	Halton Fenside. *Linc* 4D **88**	Hanchurch. *Staf* 1C **72**	Harehope. *Nmbd* 2E **121**	**Hartlepool**. *Hart* 1C **106**
Haigh. *G Man* 4E **90**	Halton Gill. *N Yor* 2A **98**	Hand and Pen. *Devn* 3D **12**	Harelaw. *Dum* 2F **113**	Hartley. *Cumb* 4A **104**
Haigh Moor. *W Yor* 2C **92**	Halton Holegate. *Linc* 4D **88**	Handbridge. *Ches W* 4G **83**	Harelaw. *Dur* 4E **115**	Hartley. *Kent* 2B **28**
Haighton Green. *Lanc* 1D **90**	Halton Lea Gate. *Nmbd* 4H **113**	Handcross. *W Sus* 3D **26**	Hareplain. *Kent* 2C **28**	(nr. Cranbrook)
Haile. *Cumb* 4B **102**	Halton Moor. *W Yor* 1D **92**	Handforth. *Ches E* 2C **84**	Harescombe. *Glos* 4D **48**	Hartley. *Kent* 4H **39**
Hailes. *Glos* 2F **49**	Halton Shields. *Nmbd* 3D **114**	Handley. *Ches W* 5G **83**	Haresfield. *Glos* 4D **48**	(nr. Dartford)
Hailey. *Herts* 4D **52**	Halton West. *N Yor* 4H **97**	Handley. *Derbs* 4A **86**	Harestock. *Hants* 3C **24**	Hartley. *Nmbd* 2G **115**
Hailey. *Oxon* 4B **50**	Haltwhistle. *Nmbd* 3A **114**	Handsacre. *Staf* 4E **73**	Hareswell. *Hants*	Hartley Green. *Staf* 2D **73**
Hailsham. *E Sus* 5G **27**	Halvergate. *Norf* 5G **79**	Handsworth. *S Yor* 2B **86**	Harewood. *W Yor* 5F **99**	Hartley Mauditt. *Hants* 3F **25**
Hail Weston. *Cambs* 4A **64**	Halwell. *Devn* 3D **9**	Handsworth. *W Mid* 1E **61**	Harewood End. *Here* 3A **48**	Hartley Wespall. *Hants* 1E **25**
Hainault. *G Lon* 1F **39**	Halwill. *Devn* 3E **11**	Handy Cross. *Buck* 2G **37**	Harford. *Devn* 3C **8**	Hartley Wintney. *Hants* 1F **25**
Hainford. *Norf* 4E **78**	Halwill Junction. *Devn* 3E **11**	Hanford. *Dors* 1D **14**	Hargate. *Norf* 1D **66**	Hartlip. *Kent* 4C **40**
Hainton. *Linc* 2A **88**	Ham. *Devn* 2F **13**	Hanford. *Stoke* 1C **72**	Hargatewall. *Derbs* 3F **85**	Hartmount. *High* 1B **158**
Hainworth. *W Yor* 1A **92**	Ham. *Glos* 2B **34**	Hangersley. *Hants* 2G **15**	Hargrave. *Ches W* 4G **83**	Hartoft End. *N Yor* 5E **107**
Haisthorpe. *E Yor* 3F **101**	Ham. *G Lon* 3C **38**	Hanging Houghton. *Nptn* . . .3E **63**	Hargrave. *Nptn* 3H **63**	Harton. *N Yor* 3B **100**
Hakin. *Pemb* 4C **42**	Ham. *High* 1E **169**	Hanging Langford. *Wilts* 3F **23**	Hargrave. *Suff* 5G **65**	Harton. *Shrp* 2G **59**
Halam. *Notts* 5D **86**	Ham. *Kent* 5H **41**	Hangleton. *Brig* 5D **26**	Harker. *Cumb* 3E **113**	Harton. *Tyne* 3G **115**
Halbeath. *Fife* 1E **129**	Ham. *Plym* 3A **8**	Hangleton. *W Sus* 5B **26**	Harkland. *Shet* 2E **35**	Hartpury. *Glos* 3C **48**
Halberton. *Devn* 1D **12**	Ham. *Shet* 8A **173**	Hanham. *S Glo* 4B **34**	Harkstead. *Suff* 2E **55**	Hartshead. *W Yor* 2B **92**
Halcro. *High* 2E **169**	Ham. *Som* 1F **13**	Hanham Green. *S Glo* 4B **34**	Harlaston. *Staf* 4G **73**	**Hartshill**. *Warw* 1H **61**
Hale. *Cumb* 2E **97**	(nr. Ilminster)	Hankelow. *Ches E* 1A **72**	Harlaxton. *Linc* 2F **75**	Hartshorne. *Derbs* 3H **73**
Hale. *G Man* 2B **84**	Ham. *Som* 4F **21**	Hankerton. *Wilts* 2E **35**	Harlech. *Gwyn* 2E **69**	Hartsop. *Cumb* 3F **103**
Hale. *Hal* 2G **83**	(nr. Taunton)	Hankham. *E Sus* 5H **27**	Harlequin. *Notts* 2D **74**	Hart Station. *Hart* 1B **106**
Hale. *Hants* 1G **15**	Ham. *Som* 4E **21**	**Hanley**. *Stoke* . . . .1C **72** & **Stoke 211**	Harlescott. *Shrp* 4H **71**	Hartswell. *Som* 4D **20**
Hale Bank. *Hal* 2G **83**	(nr. Wellington)	Hanley Castle. *Worc* 1D **48**	Harleston. *Devn* 4D **9**	Hartwell. *Nptn* 5E **63**
Halebarns. *G Man* 2B **84**	Ham. *Wilts* 5B **36**	Hanley Childe. *Worc* 4A **60**	Harleston. *Norf* 2E **67**	Hartwood. *Lanc* 3D **90**
Hales. *Norf* 1F **67**	Hambleden. *Buck* 3F **37**	Hanley Swan. *Worc* 1D **48**	Harleston. *Suff* 4C **66**	Hartwood. *N Lan* 4B **128**
Hales. *Staf* 2B **72**	Hambledon. *Hants* 1E **17**	Hanley William. *Worc* 4A **60**	Harlestone. *Nptn* 4E **62**	Harvel. *Kent* 4A **40**
Halesgate. *Linc* 3C **76**	Hambledon. *Surr* 2A **26**	Hanlith. *N Yor* 3B **98**	Harley. *Shrp* 5H **71**	Harvington. *Worc* 1F **49**
Hales Green. *Derbs* 1F **73**	Hamble-le-Rice. *Hants* 2C **16**	Hanmer. *Wrex* 2G **71**	Harley. *S Yor* 1A **86**	(nr. Evesham)
Halesowen. *W Mid* 2D **60**	Hambleton. *Lanc* 5C **96**	Hannaborough. *Devn* 2F **11**	Harling Road. *Norf* 2B **66**	Harvington. *Worc* 3C **60**
Hale Street. *Kent* 1A **28**	Hambleton. *N Yor* 1F **93**	Hannaford. *Devn* 4G **19**	Harlington. *C Beds* 2A **52**	(nr. Kidderminster)
Halesworth. *Suff* 3F **67**	Hambrook. *S Glo* 4B **34**	Hannah. *Linc* 3E **89**	Harlington. *G Lon* 3B **38**	**Harwich**. *Essx* . . . . . .2F **55** & **215**
Halewood. *Mers* 2G **83**	Hambrook. *W Sus* 2F **17**	Hannington. *Hants* 1D **24**	Harlington. *S Yor* 4E **93**	Harwood. *Dur* 1B **104**
Halford. *Devn* 5B **12**	Ham Common. *Dors* 4D **22**	Hannington. *Nptn* 3F **63**	Harlosh. *High* 4B **154**	Harwood. *G Man* 3F **91**
Halford. *Shrp* 2G **59**	Hameringham. *Linc* 4C **88**	Hannington. *Swin* 2G **35**	**Harlow**. *Essx* 5E **53**	Harwood Dale. *N Yor* 5G **107**
Halford. *Warw* 1A **50**	Hamerton. *Cambs* 3A **64**	Hannington Wick. *Swin* 2G **35**	Harlow Hill. *Nmbd* 3D **115**	Harworth. *Notts* 1D **86**
Halfpenny. *Cumb* 1E **97**	Ham Green. *Here* 1C **48**	Hanscombe End. *C Beds* 2B **52**	Harlsey Castle. *N Yor* 5B **106**	Hascombe. *Surr* 2A **26**
Halfpenny Furze. *Carm* 3G **43**	Ham Green. *Kent* 4C **40**	Hanslope. *Mil* 1G **51**	Harlthorpe. *E Yor* 1H **93**	Haselbech. *Nptn* 3E **62**
Halfpenny Green. *Shrp* 1C **60**	Ham Green. *N Som* 4A **34**	Hanthorpe. *Linc* 3H **75**	Harlton. *Cambs* 5C **64**	Haselbury Plucknett. *Som* . . .1H **13**
Halfway. *Carm* 2G **45**	Ham Green. *Worc* 4E **61**	**Hanwell**. *G Lon* 2C **38**	Harlyn. *Corn* 1C **6**	Haseley. *Warw* 4G **61**
Halfway. *Powy* 2B **46**	Ham Hill. *Kent* 4A **40**	Hanwell. *Oxon* 1C **50**	Harman's Cross. *Dors* 4E **15**	Haselor. *Warw* 5F **61**
Halfway. *S Yor* 2B **86**	Hamilton. *Leics* 5D **74**	Hanwood. *Shrp* 5G **71**	Harmby. *N Yor* 1D **98**	Hasfield. *Glos* 3D **48**
Halfway. *W Ber* 5C **36**	**Hamilton**. *S Lan* 4A **128**	Hanworth. *G Lon* 3C **38**	Harmer Green. *Herts* 4C **52**	Hasguard. *Pemb* 4C **42**
Halfway House. *Shrp* 4F **71**	Hamister. *Shet* 5G **173**	Hanworth. *Norf* 2D **78**	Harmer Hill. *Shrp* 3G **71**	Haskayne. *Lanc* 4B **90**
Halfway Houses. *Kent* 3D **40**	**Hammersmith**. *G Lon* . . .3D **38**	Happas. *Ang* 4D **144**	Harmondsworth. *G Lon* 3B **38**	Hasketon. *Suff* 5E **67**
Halgabron. *Corn* 4A **10**	Hammerwich. *Staf* 5E **73**	Happendon. *S Lan* 1A **118**	Harmston. *Linc* 4G **87**	Hasland. *Derbs* 4A **86**
Halifax. *W Yor* 2A **92**	Hammerwood. *E Sus* 2F **27**	Happisburgh. *Norf* 2F **79**	Harnage. *Shrp* 5H **71**	Haslemere. *Surr* 2A **26**
Halistra. *High* 3B **154**	**Hammersmith**. *G Lon* . . .3D **38**	Happisburgh Common. *Norf* . .3F **79**	Harnham. *Nmbd* 1D **115**	**Haslingden**. *Lanc* 2F **91**
Halket. *E Ayr* 4F **127**	Hammill. *Kent* 5G **41**	Hapsford. *Ches W* 3G **83**	Harnhill. *Glos* 5F **49**	Haslingden Grane. *Lanc* 2F **91**
Halkirk. *High* 3D **168**	Hammond Street. *Herts* 5D **52**	Hapton. *Lanc* 1F **91**	Harold Hill. *G Lon* 1G **39**	Haslingfield. *Cambs* 5D **64**
Halkyn. *Flin* 3E **82**	Hammoon. *Dors* 1D **14**	Hapton. *Norf* 1D **66**	Haroldston West. *Pemb* 3C **42**	Haslington. *Ches E* 5B **84**
Hall. *E Ren* 4F **127**	Hamnavoe. *Shet* 3D **173**	Harberton. *Devn* 3D **9**	Haroldswick. *Shet* 1H **173**	Hassall. *Ches E* 5B **84**
Hallam Fields. *Derbs* 1B **74**	(nr. Braehoulland)	Harbertonford. *Devn* 3D **9**	Harold Wood. *G Lon* 1G **39**	Hassall Green. *Ches E* 5B **84**
Halland. *E Sus* 4G **27**	Hamnavoe. *Shet* 4E **173**	Harbledown. *Kent* 5F **41**	Harome. *N Yor* 1A **100**	Hassell Street. *Kent* 1E **29**
Hallands, The. *N Lin* 2D **94**	(nr. Burland)	Harborne. *W Mid* 2E **61**	**Harpenden**. *Herts* 4B **52**	Hassendean. *Bord* 2H **119**
Hallaton. *Leics* 1E **63**	Hamnavoe. *Shet* 4F **173**	Harborough Magna. *Warw* . .3B **62**	Harpford. *Devn* 3D **12**	Hassingham. *Norf* 5F **79**
Hallatrow. *Bath* 1B **22**	(nr. Lunna)	Harbottle. *Nmbd* 4D **120**	Harpham. *E Yor* 3E **101**	Hassocks. *W Sus* 4E **27**
Hallbank. *Cumb* 5H **103**	Hamnavoe. *Shet* 3F **173**	Harbourneford. *Devn* 2D **8**	Harpley. *Norf* 3G **77**	Hassop. *Derbs* 3G **85**
Hallbankgate. *Cumb* 4G **113**	(on Yell)	Harbours Hill. *Worc* 4D **60**	Harpley. *Worc* 4A **60**	Haster. *High* 3F **169**
Hall Dunnerdale. *Cumb* 5D **102**	Hamp. *Som* 3G **21**	Harbridge. *Hants* 1G **15**	Harpole. *Nptn* 4D **62**	Hasthorpe. *Linc* 4D **89**
Hallen. *S Glo* 3A **34**	Hampden Park. *E Sus* 5H **27**	Harbury. *Warw* 4A **62**	Harpsdale. *High* 3D **168**	Hastigrow. *High* 2E **169**
Hall End. *Bed* 1A **52**	Hampden End. *Essx* 2F **53**	Harby. *Leics* 2E **75**	Harpsden. *Oxon* 3F **37**	Hastingleigh. *Kent* 1E **29**
Hallgarth. *Dur* 5G **115**	Hampen. *Glos* 3F **49**	Harby. *Notts* 3F **87**	Harpswell. *Linc* 2G **87**	**Hastings**. *E Sus* 5C **28**
Hall Green. *Ches E* 5C **84**	Hamperden End. *Essx* 2F **53**	Harcombe. *Devn* 3E **13**	Harden. *W Yor* 1A **92**	Hastingwood. *Essx* 5E **53**
Hall Green. *Norf* 2D **66**	Hampnett. *Glos* 4F **49**	Harcombe Bottom. *Devn* 3G **13**	Hardenhuish. *Wilts* 4E **35**	Hastoe. *Herts* 5H **51**
Hall Green. *W Mid* 2F **61**	Hampole. *S Yor* 3F **93**	Harcourt. *Corn* 5C **6**	Hardgate. *Abers* 3E **153**	Haston. *Shrp* 3H **71**
Hall Green. *W Yor* 3D **92**	Hampreston. *Dors* 3F **15**	Hardam. *W Sus* 4B **26**	Hardgate. *Dum* 3F **111**	Haswell. *Dur* 5G **115**
Hall Green. *Wrex* 1G **71**	**Hampstead**. *G Lon* 2D **38**	Hardham. *W Sus* 4B **26**	Harracott. *Devn* 4F **19**	Haswell. *Dur* 5G **115**
Halliburton. *Bord* 5C **130**				

Haswell Plough. *Dur* 5G 115
Hatch. *C Beds* 1B 52
Hatch Beauchamp. *Som* 4G 21
Hatch End. *G Lon* 1C 38
Hatching Green. *Herts* 4B 52
Hatchmere. *Ches W* 3H 83
Hatch Warren. *Hants* 2E 24
Hatcliffe. *NE Lin* 4F 95
Hatfield. *Here* 5H 59
Hatfield. *Herts* 5C 52
Hatfield. *S Yor* 4G 93
Hatfield. *Worc* 5C 60
Hatfield Broad Oak. *Essx* 4F 53
Hatfield Garden Village. *Herts* .5C 52
Hatfield Heath. *Essx* 4F 53
Hatfield Hyde. *Herts* 4C 52
Hatfield Peverel. *Essx* 4A 54
Hatfield Woodhouse. *S Yor* . . .4G 93
Hatford. *Oxon* 2B 36
Hatherden. *Hants* 1B 24
Hatherleigh. *Devn* 2F 11
Hathern. *Leics* 3C 74
Hatherop. *Glos* 5G 49
Hathersage. *Derbs* 2G 85
Hathersage Booths. *Derbs* . . .2G 85
Hatherton. *Ches E* 1A 72
Hatherton. *Staf* 4D 72
Hatley St George. *Cambs* 5B 64
Hatt. *Corn* 2H 7
Hattersley. *G Man* 1D 85
Hattingley. *Hants* 3E 25
Hatton. *Abers* 5H 161
Hatton. *Derbs* 2G 73
Hatton. *G Lon* 3B 38
Hatton. *Linc* 3A 88
Hatton. *Shrp* 1G 59
Hatton. *Warr* 2H 83
Hatton. *Warw* 4G 61
Hattoncrook. *Abers* 1F 153
Hatton Heath. *Ches W* 4G 83
Hatton of Fintray. *Abers* 2F 153
Haugh. *E Ayr* 2D 117
Haugh. *Linc* 3D 88
Haugham. *Linc* 2C 88
Haugh Head. *Nmbd* 2E 121
Haughley. *Suff* 4C 66
Haughley Green. *Suff* 4C 66
Haugh of Ballechin. *Per* 3G 143
Haugh of Glass. *Mor* 5B 160
Haugh of Urr. *Dum* 3F 111
Haughton. *Ches E* 5H 83
Haughton. *Notts* 3D 86
Haughton. *Shrp* 1A 60
     (nr. Bridgnorth)
Haughton. *Shrp* 3F 71
     (nr. Oswestry)
Haughton. *Shrp* 5B 72
     (nr. Shifnal)
Haughton. *Shrp* 4H 71
    (nr. Shrewsbury)
Haughton. *Staf* 3C 72
Haughton Green. *G Man* 1D 84
Haughton le Skerne. *Darl* . . .3A 106
Haultwick. *Herts* 3D 52
Haunn. *Arg* 4E 139
Haunn. *W Isl* 7C 170
Haunton. *Staf* 4G 73
Hauxton. *Cambs* 5D 64
Havannah. *Ches E* 4C 84
Havant. *Hants* 2F 17
Haven. *Here* 5G 59
Haven Bank. *Linc* 5B 88
Havenside. *E Yor* 2E 95
Havenstreet. *IOW* 3D 16
Haven, The. *W Sus* 2B 26
Havercroft. *W Yor* 3D 93
Haverfordwest. *Pemb* 3D 42
Haverhill. *Suff* 1G 53
Haverigg. *Cumb* 2A 96
Havering-atte-Bower. *G Lon* . .1G 39
Havering's Grove. *Essx* 1A 40
Haversham. *Mil* 1G 51
Haverthwaite. *Cumb* 1C 96
Haverton Hill. *Stoc T* 2B 106
Havyatt. *Som* 3A 22
Hawarden. *Flin* 4F 83
Hawbridge. *Worc* 1E 49
Hawcoat. *Cumb* 2B 96
Hawcross. *Glos* 2C 48
Hawen. *Cdgn* 1D 44
Hawes. *N Yor* 1A 98
Hawes Green. *Norf* 1E 67
Hawick. *Bord* 3H 119
Hawkchurch. *Devn* 2G 13
Hawkedon. *Suff* 5G 65
Hawkenbury. *Kent* 1C 28
Hawkeridge. *Wilts* 1D 22
Hawkerland. *Devn* 4D 12
Hawkesbury. *S Glo* 3C 34
Hawkesbury. *W Mid* 2A 62
Hawkesbury Upton. *S Glo* 3C 34
Hawkes End. *W Mid* 2G 61
Hawk Green. *G Man* 2D 84
Hawkhurst. *Kent* 2B 28
Hawkhurst Common. *E Sus* . . .4G 27
Hawkinge. *Kent* 1G 29
Hawkley. *Hants* 4F 25
Hawkridge. *Som* 3B 20
Hawksdale. *Cumb* 5E 113
Hawkshaw. *G Man* 3F 91
Hawkshead. *Cumb* 5E 103

Hawkshead Hill. *Cumb* 5E 103
Hawkswick. *N Yor* 2B 98
Hawksworth. *Notts* 1E 75
Hawksworth. *W Yor* 5D 98
Hawkwell. *Essx* 1C 40
Hawley. *Hants* 1G 25
Hawley. *Kent* 3G 39
Hawling. *Glos* 3F 49
Hawnby. *N Yor* 1H 99
Haworth. *W Yor* 1A 92
Hawstead. *Suff* 5A 66
Hawthorn. *Dur* 5H 115
Hawthorn Hill. *Brac* 4G 37
Hawthorn Hill. *Linc* 5B 88
Hawthorpe. *Linc* 3H 75
Hawton. *Notts* 5E 87
Haxby. *York* 4A 100
Haxey. *N Lin* 1E 87
Haybridge. *Shrp* 3A 60
Haybridge. *Som* 2A 22
Haydock. *Mers* 1H 83
Haydon. *Bath* 1B 22
Haydon. *Dors* 1B 14
Haydon. *Som* 4F 21
Haydon Bridge. *Nmbd* 3B 114
Haydon Wick. *Swin* 3G 35
Haye. *Corn* 2H 7
Hayes. *G Lon* 4F 39
     (nr. Bromley)
Hayes. *G Lon* 2B 38
     (nr. Uxbridge)
Hayfield. *Derbs* 2E 85
Hay Green. *Norf* 4E 77
Hayhill. *E Ayr* 3D 116
Haylands. *IOW* 3D 16
Hayle. *Corn* 3C 4
Hayley Green. *W Mid* 2D 60
Hayne. *Devn* 2B 12
Haynes. *C Beds* 1A 52
Haynes West End. *C Beds* . . .1A 52
Hay-on-Wye. *Powy* 1F 47
Hayscastle. *Pemb* 2C 42
Hayscastle Cross. *Pemb* 2D 42
Haysden. *Kent* 1G 27
Hayshead. *Ang* 4F 145
Hay Street. *Herts* 3D 53
Hayton. *Aber* 3G 153
Hayton. *Cumb* 5C 112
     (nr. Aspatria)
Hayton. *Cumb* 4G 113
     (nr. Brampton)
Hayton. *E Yor* 5C 100
Hayton. *Notts* 2E 87
Hayton's Bent. *Shrp* 2H 59
Haytor Vale. *Devn* 5A 12
Haytown. *Devn* 1D 11
Haywards Heath. *W Sus* . . .3E 27
Haywood. *S Lan* 4C 128
Hazelbank. *S Lan* 5B 128
Hazelbury Bryan. *Dors* 2C 14
Hazeleigh. *Essx* 5B 54
Hazeley. *Hants* 1F 25
Hazel Grove. *G Man* 2D 84
Hazelhead. *S Yor* 4B 92
Hazelslade. *Staf* 4E 73
Hazel Street. *Kent* 2A 28
Hazelton Walls. *Fife* 1F 137
Hazelwood. *Derbs* 1H 73
Hazlemere. *Buck* 2G 37
Hazler. *Shrp* 1G 59
Hazlerigg. *Tyne* 2F 115
Hazles. *Staf* 1E 73
Hazleton. *Glos* 4F 49
Hazon. *Nmbd* 4F 121
Heacham. *Norf* 2F 77
Headbourne Worthy. *Hants* . . .3C 24
Headcorn. *Kent* 1C 28
Headingley. *W Yor* 1C 92
Headington. *Oxon* 5D 50
Headlam. *Dur* 3E 105
Headless Cross. *Worc* 4E 61
Headley. *Hants* 3G 25
    (nr. Haslemere)
Headley. *Hants* 5D 36
    (nr. Kingsclere)
Headley. *Surr* 5D 38
Headley Down. *Hants* 3G 25
Headley Heath. *Worc* 3E 61
Headley Park. *Bris* 5A 34
Head of Muir. *Falk* 1B 128
Headon. *Notts* 3E 87
Heads Nook. *Cumb* 4F 113
Heage. *Derbs* 5A 86
Healaugh. *N Yor* 5D 104
     (nr. Grinton)
Healaugh. *N Yor* 5H 99
     (nr. York)
Heald Green. *G Man* 2C 84
Heale. *Devn* 2G 19
Healey. *G Man* 3G 91
Healey. *Nmbd* 4D 114
Healey. *N Yor* 1D 98
Healeyfield. *Dur* 5D 114
Healey Hall. *Nmbd* 4D 114
Healing. *NE Lin* 3F 95
Heamoor. *Corn* 3B 4
Heanish. *Arg* 4B 138
Heanor. *Derbs* 1B 74
Heanton Punchardon. *Devn* . .3F 19
Heapham. *Linc* 2F 87
Heartsease. *Powy* 4D 58

Heasley Mill. *Devn* 3H 19
Heaste. *High* 2E 147
Heath. *Derbs* 4B 86
Heath and Reach. *C Beds* 3H 51
Heath Common. *W Sus* 4C 26
Heathcote. *Derbs* 4F 85
Heath Cross. *Devn* 3H 11
Heathencote. *Nptn* 1F 51
Heath End. *Derbs* 3A 74
Heath End. *Hants* 5D 36
Heath End. *W Mid* 5E 73
Heather. *Leics* 4A 74
Heatherfield. *High* 4D 155
Heatherton. *Derb* 2H 73
Heathfield. *Cambs* 1E 53
Heathfield. *Cumb* 5C 112
Heathfield. *Devn* 5B 12
Heathfield. *E Sus* 3G 27
Heathfield. *Ren* 3E 126
Heathfield. *Som* 3E 21
   (nr. Lydeard St Lawrence)
Heathfield. *Som* 4E 21
    (nr. Norton Fitzwarren)
Heath Green. *Worc* 3E 61
Heathhall. *Dum* 2A 112
Heath Hayes. *Staf* 4E 73
Heath Hill. *Shrp* 4B 72
Heath House. *Som* 2H 21
Heathrow (London) Airport.
    G Lon . . . . .3B 38 & 216
Heathstock. *Devn* 2F 13
Heath, The. *Norf* 3E 79
     (nr. Buxton)
Heath, The. *Norf* 2D 78
     (nr. Fakenham)
Heath, The. *Norf* 3D 78
     (nr. Hevingham)
Heath, The. *Staf* 2E 73
Heath, The. *Suff* 2E 55
Heathton. *Shrp* 1C 60
Heathtop. *Derbs* 2F 73
Heath Town. *W Mid* 1D 60
Heatley. *G Man* 2B 84
Heatley. *Staf* 3E 73
Heaton. *Lanc* 3D 96
Heaton. *Staf* 4D 84
Heaton. *Tyne* 3F 115
Heaton. *W Yor* 1B 92
Heaton Moor. *G Man* 1C 84
Heaton's Bridge. *Lanc* 3C 90
Heaverham. *Kent* 5G 39
Heavitree. *Devn* 3C 12
Hebburn. *Tyne* 3G 115
Hebden. *N Yor* 3C 98
Hebden Bridge. *W Yor* 2H 91
Hebden Green. *Ches W* 4A 84
Hebing End. *Herts* 3D 52
Hebron. *Carm* 2F 43
Hebron. *Nmbd* 1E 115
Heck. *Dum* 1B 112
Heckdyke. *Notts* 1E 87
Heckfield. *Hants* 5F 37
Heckfield Green. *Suff* 3D 66
Heckington. *Linc* 1A 76
Heckmondwike. *W Yor* 2C 92
Heckmondwike. *W Yor* 2C 92
Heddington. *Wilts* 5E 35
Heddle. *Orkn* 6C 172
Heddon. *Devn* 4G 19
Heddon-on-the-Wall. *Nmbd* . . .3E 115
Hedenham. *Norf* 1F 67
Hedge End. *Hants* 1C 16
Hedgerley. *Buck* 2A 38
Hedging. *Som* 4G 21
Hedley on the Hill. *Nmbd* 4D 115
Hednesford. *Staf* 4E 73
Hedon. *E Yor* 2E 95
Hegdon Hill. *Here* 5H 59
Heglibister. *Shet* 6E 173
Heighington. *Darl* 2F 105
Heighington. *Linc* 4H 87
Heightington. *Worc* 3B 60
Heights of Brae. *High* 2H 157
Heights of Fodderty. *High* 2H 157
Heights of Kinlochewe. *High* . .2C 156
Heiton. *Bord* 1B 120
Hele. *Devn* 5H 11
     (nr. Ashburton)
Hele. *Devn* 2C 12
     (nr. Exeter)
Hele. *Devn* 3D 10
     (nr. Holsworthy)
Hele. *Devn* 2F 19
     (nr. Ilfracombe)
Hele. *Torb* 2F 9
Helensburgh. *Arg* 1D 126
Helford. *Corn* 4E 5
Hellhoughton. *Norf* 3A 78
Helions Bumpstead. *Essx* 1G 53
Helland. *Corn* 5A 10
Helland. *Som* 4G 21
Hellandbridge. *Corn* 5A 10
Hellesdon. *Norf* 4E 78
Hellesveor. *Corn* 2C 4
Hellidon. *Nptn* 5C 62
Hellifield. *N Yor* 4A 98
Hellingly. *E Sus* 4G 27
Helmdon. *Nptn* 1D 50
Helmingham. *Suff* 5D 66
Helmington Row. *Dur* 1E 105

Helmsdale. *High* 2H 165
Helmshore. *Lanc* 2F 91
Helmsley. *N Yor* 1A 100
Helperby. *N Yor* 3G 99
Helperthorpe. *N Yor* 2D 100
Helpringham. *Linc* 1A 76
Helpston. *Pet* 5A 76
Helsby. *Ches W* 3G 83
Helsey. *Linc* 3E 89
Helston. *Corn* 4D 4
Helstone. *Corn* 4A 10
Helton. *Cumb* 2G 103
Helwith. *N Yor* 4D 105
Helwith Bridge. *N Yor* 3H 97
Helygain. *Flin* 3E 82
Hemblington. *Norf* 4F 79
Hemerdon. *Devn* 3B 8
Hemingbrough. *N Yor* 1G 93
Hemingby. *Linc* 3B 88
Hemingfield. *S Yor* 4D 93
Hemingford Abbots. *Cambs* . . .3B 64
Hemingford Grey. *Cambs* 3B 64
Hemingstone. *Suff* 5D 66
Hemington. *Leics* 3B 74
Hemington. *Nptn* 2H 63
Hemington. *Som* 1C 22
Hemley. *Suff* 1F 55
Hemlington. *Midd* 3B 106
Hempholme. *E Yor* 4E 101
Hempnall. *Norf* 1E 67
Hempnall Green. *Norf* 1E 67
Hempriggs. *High* 4F 169
Hemp's Green. *Essx* 3C 54
Hempstead. *Essx* 2G 53
Hempstead. *Medw* 4B 40
Hempstead. *Norf* 2D 78
     (nr. Holt)
Hempstead. *Norf* 3G 79
     (nr. Stalham)
Hempsted. *Glos* 4D 48
Hempton. *Norf* 3B 78
Hempton. *Oxon* 2C 50
Hemsby. *Norf* 4G 79
Hemswell. *Linc* 1G 87
Hemswell Cliff. *Linc* 2G 87
Hemsworth. *Dors* 2E 15
Hemsworth. *W Yor* 3E 93
Hem, The. *Shrp* 5B 72
Hemyock. *Devn* 1E 13
Henallt. *Carm* 3E 45
Henbury. *Bris* 4A 34
Henbury. *Ches E* 3C 84
Hendomen. *Powy* 1E 58
Hendon. *G Lon* 2D 38
Hendon. *Tyne* 4H 115
Hendra. *Corn* 3D 6
Hendre. *B'end* 3C 32
Hendreforgan. *Rhon* 3C 32
Hendy. *Carm* 5F 45
Heneglwys. *IOA* 3D 80
Henfeddau Fawr. *Pemb* 1G 43
Henfield. *S Glo* 4B 34
Henfield. *W Sus* 4D 26
Henford. *Devn* 3D 10
Hengoed. *Cphy* 2E 33
Hengoed. *Shrp* 2E 71
Hengrave. *Suff* 4H 65
Henham. *Essx* 3F 53
Heniarth. *Powy* 5D 70
Henlade. *Som* 4F 21
Henley. *Dors* 2B 14
Henley. *Shrp* 2G 59
    (nr. Church Stretton)
Henley. *Shrp* 3H 59
     (nr. Ludlow)
Henley. *Som* 3H 21
Henley. *Suff* 5D 66
Henley. *W Sus* 4G 25
Henley-in-Arden. *Warw* 4F 61
Henley-on-Thames. *Oxon* 3F 37
Henley's Down. *E Sus* 4B 28
Henley Street. *Kent* 4A 40
Henllan. *Cdgn* 1D 44
Henllan. *Den* 4C 82
Henllan. *Mon* 3F 47
Henllan Amgoed. *Carm* 3F 43
Henllys. *Torf* 2F 33
Henlow. *C Beds* 2B 52
Hennock. *Devn* 4B 12
Henny Street. *Essx* 2B 54
Henryd. *Cnwy* 3G 81
Henry's Moat. *Pemb* 2E 43
Hensall. *N Yor* 2F 93
Henshaw. *Nmbd* 3A 114
Hensingham. *Cumb* 3A 102
Henstead. *Suff* 2G 67
Hensting. *Hants* 4C 24
Henstridge. *Som* 1C 14
Henstridge Ash. *Som* 4C 22
Henstridge Bowden. *Som* 4B 22
Henstridge Marsh. *Som* 4C 22
Henton. *Oxon* 5F 51
Henton. *Som* 2H 21
Henwood. *Corn* 5C 10
Heogan. *Shet* 7F 173
Heol Senni. *Powy* 3C 46
Heol-y-Cyw. *B'end* 3C 32
Hepburn. *Nmbd* 2E 121
Hepple. *Nmbd* 4D 121
Hepscott. *Nmbd* 1F 115
Heptonstall. *W Yor* 2H 91

Hepworth. *Suff* 3B 66
Hepworth. *W Yor* 4B 92
Herbrandston. *Pemb* 4C 42
Hereford. *Here* . . . . .2A 48 & 197
Heribusta. *High* 1D 154
Heriot. *Bord* 4H 129
Hermiston. *Edin* 2E 129
Hermitage. *Dors* 2B 14
Hermitage. *Bord* 5H 119
Hermitage. *W Ber* 4D 36
Hermitage. *W Sus* 2F 17
Hermon. *Carm* 3G 45
     (nr. Llandeilo)
Hermon. *Carm* 2D 44
    (nr. Newcastle Emlyn)
Hermon. *IOA* 4C 80
Hermon. *Pemb* 1G 43
Herne. *Kent* 4F 41
Herne Bay. *Kent* 4F 41
Herne Common. *Kent* 4F 41
Herne Pound. *Kent* 5A 40
Herner. *Devn* 4F 19
Hernhill. *Kent* 4E 41
Herodsfoot. *Corn* 2G 7
Heronden. *Kent* 5G 41
Herongate. *Essx* 1H 39
Heronsford. *S Ayr* 1G 109
Heronsgate. *Herts* 1B 38
Heron's Ghyll. *E Sus* 3F 27
Herra. *Shet* 2H 173
Herriard. *Hants* 2E 25
Herringfleet. *Suff* 1G 67
Herringswell. *Suff* 4G 65
Herrington. *Tyne* 4G 115
Hersden. *Kent* 4G 41
Hersham. *Corn* 2C 10
Hersham. *Surr* 4C 38
Herstmonceux. *E Sus* 4H 27
Herston. *Dors* 5F 15
Herston. *Orkn* 8D 172
Hertford. *Herts* 4D 52
Hertford Heath. *Herts* 4D 52
Hertingfordbury. *Herts* 4D 52
Hesketh. *Lanc* 2C 90
Hesketh Bank. *Lanc* 2C 90
Hesketh Lane. *Lanc* 5F 97
Hesket Newmarket. *Cumb* . . .1E 103
Heskin Green. *Lanc* 3D 90
Hesleden. *Dur* 1B 106
Hesleyside. *Nmbd* 1B 114
Heslington. *York* 4A 100
Hessay. *York* 4H 99
Hessenford. *Corn* 3H 7
Hessett. *Suff* 4B 66
Hessilhead. *N Ayr* 4E 127
Hessle. *Hull* 2D 94
Hestaford. *Shet* 6D 173
Hest Bank. *Lanc* 3D 96
Hester's Way. *Glos* 3E 49
Hestinsetter. *Shet* 7D 173
Heston. *G Lon* 3C 38
Hestwall. *Orkn* 6B 172
Heswall. *Mers* 2E 83
Hethe. *Oxon* 3D 50
Hethelpit Cross. *Glos* 3C 48
Hethersett. *Norf* 5D 78
Hethersgill. *Cumb* 3F 113
Hetherside. *Cumb* 3F 113
Hethpool. *Nmbd* 2C 120
Hett. *Dur* 1F 105
Hetton. *N Yor* 4B 98
Hetton-le-Hole. *Tyne* 5G 115
Hetton Steads. *Nmbd* 1E 121
Heugh. *Nmbd* 2D 115
Heugh-head. *Abers* 2A 152
Heveningham. *Suff* 3F 67
Hever. *Kent* 1F 27
Heversham. *Cumb* 1D 97
Hevingham. *Norf* 3D 78
Hewas Water. *Corn* 4D 6
Hewelsfield. *Glos* 5A 48
Hewish. *N Som* 5G 33
Hewish. *Som* 2H 13
Hewood. *Dors* 2G 13
Heworth. *York* 4A 100
Hexham. *Nmbd* 3C 114
Hextable. *Kent* 3G 39
Hexton. *Herts* 2B 52
Hexworthy. *Devn* 5G 11
Heybridge. *Essx* 1H 39
     (nr. Brentwood)
Heybridge. *Essx* 5B 54
     (nr. Maldon)
Heybridge Basin. *Essx* 5B 54
Heybrook Bay. *Devn* 4A 8
Heydon. *Cambs* 1E 53
Heydon. *Norf* 3D 78
Heydour. *Linc* 2H 75
Heylipol. *Arg* 4A 138
Heyop. *Powy* 3E 59
Heysham. *Lanc* 3D 96
Heyshott. *W Sus* 1G 17
Heytesbury. *Wilts* 2E 23
Heythrop. *Oxon* 3B 50
Heywood. *G Man* 3G 91
Heywood. *Wilts* 1D 22
Hibaldstow. *N Lin* 4C 94
Hickleton. *S Yor* 4E 93
Hickling. *Norf* 3G 79
Hickling. *Notts* 3D 74
Hickling Green. *Norf* 3G 79
Hickling Heath. *Norf* 3G 79

Hickstead—Holt End

Hickstead. *W Sus* 3D 26
Hidcote Bartrim. *Glos* 1G 49
Hidcote Boyce. *Glos* 1G 49
Higford. *Shrp* 5B 72
High Ackworth. *W Yor* 3E 93
Higham. *Derbs* 5A 86
Higham. *Kent* 3B 40
Higham. *Lanc* 1G 91
Higham. *S Yor* 4D 92
Higham. *Suff* 2D 54
(nr. Ipswich)
Higham. *Suff* 4G 65
(nr. Newmarket)
Higham Dykes. *Nmbd* 2E 115
Higham Ferrers. *Nptn* 4G 63
Higham Gobion. *C Beds* 2B 52
Higham on the Hill. *Leics* 1A 62
Highampton. *Devn* 2E 11
Higham Wood. *Kent* 1G 27
High Angerton. *Nmbd* 1D 115
High Auldgirth. *Dum* 1G 111
High Bankhill. *Cumb* 5G 113
High Banton. *N Lan* 1A 128
High Barnet. *G Lon* 1D 38
High Beech. *Essx* 1F 39
High Bentham. *N Yor* 3F 97
High Bickington. *Devn* 4G 19
High Biggins. *Cumb* 2F 97
High Birkwith. *N Yor* 2H 97
High Blantyre. *S Lan* 4H 127
High Bonnybridge. *Falk* 2B 128
High Borrans. *Cumb* 4F 103
High Bradfield. *S Yor* 1G 85
High Bray. *Devn* 3G 19
Highbridge. *Cumb* 5E 113
Highbridge. *High* 5D 148
Highbridge. *Som* 2G 21
Highbrook. *W Sus* 2E 27
High Brooms. *Kent* 1G 27
High Bullen. *Devn* 4F 19
Highburton. *W Yor* 3B 92
Highbury. *Som* 2B 22
High Buston. *Nmbd* 4G 121
High Callerton. *Nmbd* 2E 115
High Carlingill. *Cumb* 4H 103
High Catton. *E Yor* 4B 100
High Church. *Nmbd* 1E 115
Highclere. *Hants* 5C 36
Highcliffe. *Dors* 3H 15
High Cogges. *Oxon* 5B 50
High Common. *Norf* 5B 78
High Coniscliffe. *Darl* 3F 105
High Crosby. *Cumb* 4F 113
High Cross. *Hants* 4F 25
High Cross. *Herts* 4D 52
High Dougarie. *N Ayr* 2C 122
High Easter. *Essx* 4G 53
High Eggborough. *N Yor* 2F 93
High Ellington. *N Yor* 1D 98
Higher Alham. *Som* 2B 22
Higher Ansty. *Dors* 2C 14
Higher Ashton. *Devn* 4B 12
Higher Ballam. *Lanc* 1B 90
Higher Bartle. *Lanc* 1D 90
Higher Bockhampton. *Dors* 3C 14
Higher Bojewyan. *Corn* 3A 4
High Ercall. *Telf* 4H 71
Higher Cheriton. *Devn* 2E 12
Higher Clovelly. *Devn* 4D 18
Higher Compton. *Plym* 3A 8
Higher Dean. *Devn* 2D 8
Higher Dinting. *Derbs* 1E 85
Higher Dunstone. *Devn* 5H 11
Higher End. *G Man* 4D 90
Higher Gabwell. *Devn* 2F 9
Higher Halstock Leigh. *Dors* 2A 14
Higher Heysham. *Lanc* 3D 96
Higher Hurdsfield. *Ches E* 3D 84
Higher Kingcombe. *Dors* 3A 14
Higher Kinnerton. *Flin* 4F 83
Higher Melcombe. *Dors* 2C 14
Higher Penwortham. *Lanc* 2D 90
Higher Porthpean. *Corn* 3E 7
Higher Poynton. *Ches E* 2D 84
Higher Shotton. *Flin* 4F 83
Higher Shurlach. *Ches W* 3A 84
Higher Slade. *Devn* 2F 19
Higher Tale. *Devn* 2D 12
Highertown. *Corn* 4C 6
Higher Town. *IOS* 1B 4
Higher Town. *Som* 2C 20
Higher Vexford. *Som* 3E 20
Higher Walton. *Lanc* 2D 90
Higher Walton. *Warr* 2H 83
Higher Whatcombe. *Dors* 2D 14
Higher Wheelton. *Lanc* 2E 90
Higher Whiteleigh. *Corn* 3C 10
Higher Whitley. *Ches W* 3A 84
Higher Wincham. *Ches W* 3A 84
Higher Wraxall. *Dors* 2A 14
Higher Wych. *Wrex* 1G 71
Higher Yalberton. *Torb* 3E 9
High Etherley. *Dur* 2E 105
High Ferry. *Linc* 1C 76
Highfield. *E Yor* 1H 93
Highfield. *N Ayr* 4E 126
Highfield. *Tyne* 4E 115
Highfields Caldecote. *Cambs* 5C 64
High Garrett. *Essx* 3A 54
Highgate. *G Lon* 2D 39
Highgate. *N Ayr* 4E 127
Highgate. *Powy* 1D 58
High Grange. *Dur* 1E 105
High Green. *Cumb* 4F 103
High Green. *Norf* 5D 78
High Green. *Shrp* 2B 60
High Green. *S Yor* 1H 85
High Green. *W Yor* 3B 92
High Green. *Worc* 1D 49
Highgreen Manor. *Nmbd* 5C 120
High Halden. *Kent* 2C 28
High Halstow. *Medw* 3B 40
High Ham. *Som* 3H 21
High Harrington. *Cumb* 2B 102
High Haswell. *Dur* 5G 115
High Hatton. *Shrp* 3A 72
High Hawkser. *N Yor* 4G 107
High Hesket. *Cumb* 5F 113
High Hesleden. *Dur* 1B 106
High Hoyland. *S Yor* 3C 92
High Hunsley. *E Yor* 1C 94
High Hurstwood. *E Sus* 3F 27
High Hutton. *N Yor* 3B 100
High Ireby. *Cumb* 1D 102
High Keil. *Arg* 5A 122
High Kelling. *Norf* 1D 78
High Kilburn. *N Yor* 2H 99
High Knipe. *Cumb* 3G 103
High Lands. *Dur* 2E 105
Highlands, The. *Shrp* 2A 60
Highlane. *Ches E* 4C 84
Highlane. *Derbs* 2B 86
High Lane. *G Man* 2D 84
High Lane. *Here* 4A 60
High Laver. *Essx* 5F 53
Highlaws. *Cumb* 5C 112
Highleadon. *Glos* 3C 48
High Legh. *Ches E* 2A 84
Highleigh. *W Sus* 3G 17
High Leven. *Stoc T* 3B 106
Highley. *Shrp* 2B 60
High Littleton. *Bath* 1B 22
High Longthwaite. *Cumb* 5D 112
High Lorton. *Cumb* 2C 102
High Marishes. *N Yor* 2C 100
High Marnham. *Notts* 3F 87
High Melton. *S Yor* 4F 93
High Mickley. *Nmbd* 3D 115
Highmoor. *Cumb* 5D 112
High Moor. *Lanc* 3D 90
Highmoor. *Oxon* 3F 37
Highmoor Cross. *Oxon* 3F 37
Highmoor Hill. *Mon* 3H 33
High Mowthorpe. *N Yor* 3C 100
Highnam. *Glos* 4C 48
High Newport. *Tyne* 4G 115
High Newton. *Cumb* 1D 96
High Newton-by-the-Sea.
Nmbd 2G 121
High Nibthwaite. *Cumb* 1B 96
High Offley. *Staf* 3B 72
High Ongar. *Essx* 5F 53
High Onn. *Staf* 4C 72
High Orchard. *Glos* 4D 48
High Park. *Mers* 3B 90
High Roding. *Essx* 4G 53
High Row. *Cumb* 1E 103
High Salvington. *W Sus* 5C 26
High Scales. *Cumb* 5C 112
High Shaw. *N Yor* 5B 104
High Shincliffe. *Dur* 5F 115
High Side. *Cumb* 1D 102
High Spen. *Tyne* 3E 115
Highsted. *Kent* 4D 40
High Stoop. *Dur* 5E 115
High Street. *Corn* 3D 6
High Street. *Suff* 5G 67
(nr. Aldeburgh)
High Street. *Suff* 2F 67
(nr. Bungay)
High Street. *Suff* 3G 67
(nr. Yoxford)
Highstreet Green. *Essx* 2A 54
High Street Green. *Suff* 5C 66
Highstreet Green. *Surr* 2A 26
Hightae. *Dum* 2B 112
High Throston. *Hart* 1B 106
Hightown. *Ches E* 4C 84
Hightown. *Mers* 4A 90
High Town. *Staf* 4D 73
Hightown Green. *Suff* 5B 66
High Toynton. *Linc* 4B 88
High Trewhitt. *Nmbd* 4E 121
High Valleyfield. *Fife* 1D 128
Highway. *Here* 1H 47
Highweek. *Devn* 5B 12
High Westwood. *Dur* 4E 115
Highwood. *Staf* 2E 73
Highwood. *Worc* 4A 60
High Worsall. *N Yor* 4A 106
Highworth. *Swin* 2H 35
High Wray. *Cumb* 5E 103
High Wych. *Herts* 4E 53
High Wycombe. *Buck* 2G 37
Hilborough. *Norf* 5H 77
Hilcott. *Wilts* 1G 23
Hildenborough. *Kent* 1G 27
Hildersham. *Cambs* 1F 53
Hilderstone. *Staf* 2D 72
Hilderthorpe. *E Yor* 3F 101
Hilfield. *Dors* 2B 14
Hilgay. *Norf* 1F 65
Hill. *S Glo* 2B 34
Hill. *Warw* 4B 62
Hill. *Worc* 1E 49
Hillam. *N Yor* 2F 93
Hillbeck. *Cumb* 3A 104
Hillberry. *IOM* 4C 108
Hillborough. *Kent* 4G 41
Hillbourne. *Pool* 3F 15
Hillbrae. *Abers* 4D 160
(nr. Aberchirder)
Hillbrae. *Abers* 1E 153
(nr. Inverurie)
Hillbrae. *Abers* 5F 161
(nr. Methlick)
Hill Brow. *Hants* 4F 25
Hillbutts. *Dors* 2E 15
Hillclifflane. *Derbs* 1G 73
Hillcommon. *Som* 4E 21
Hill Deverill. *Wilts* 2D 22
Hilldyke. *Linc* 1C 76
Hill End. *Dur* 1D 104
Hillend. *Fife* 1E 129
(nr. Inverkeithing)
Hill End. *Fife* 4C 136
(nr. Saline)
Hillend. *N Lan* 3B 128
Hill End. *N Yor* 4C 98
Hillend. *Shrp* 1C 60
Hillend. *Swan* 3D 30
Hillersland. *Glos* 4A 48
Hillerton. *Devn* 3H 11
Hillesden. *Buck* 3E 51
Hillesley. *Glos* 3C 34
Hillfarrance. *Som* 4E 21
Hill Furze. *Worc* 1E 49
Hill Gate. *Here* 3H 47
Hill Green. *Essx* 2E 53
Hillgreen. *W Ber* 4C 36
Hillhead. *Abers* 5C 160
Hill Head. *Hants* 2D 16
Hillhead. *S Ayr* 3D 116
Hillhead. *Torb* 3F 9
Hillhead of Auchentumb.
Abers 3G 161
Hilliard's Cross. *Staf* 4F 73
Hilliclay. *High* 2D 168
Hillingdon. *G Lon* 2B 38
Hillington. *Norf* 3G 77
Hillington. *Ren* 3G 127
Hillmorton. *Warw* 3C 62
Hill of Beath. *Fife* 4D 136
Hill of Fearn. *High* 1C 158
Hill of Fiddes. *Abers* 1G 153
Hill of Keillor. *Ang* 4B 144
Hill of Overbrae. *Abers* 2F 161
Hill Ridware. *Staf* 4E 73
Hillsborough. *S Yor* 1H 85
Hillside. *Abers* 4G 153
Hillside. *Ang* 2G 145
Hillside. *Devn* 2D 8
Hillside. *Mers* 3B 90
Hillside. *Orkn* 5C 172
Hillside. *Shet* 5F 173
Hillside. *Shrp* 2A 60
Hill Side. *W Yor* 3B 92
Hillside. *Worc* 4B 60
Hillside of Prieston. *Ang* 5C 144
Hill Somersal. *Derbs* 2F 73
Hillstown. *Derbs* 4B 86
Hillstreet. *Hants* 1B 16
Hillswick. *Shet* 4D 173
Hill, The. *Cumb* 1A 96
Hill Top. *Dur* 2C 104
(nr. Barnard Castle)
Hill Top. *Dur* 5F 115
(nr. Durham)
Hill Top. *Dur* 4E 115
(nr. Stanley)
Hill Top. *Hants* 2C 16
Hill View. *Dors* 3E 15
Hillwell. *Shet* 10E 173
Hill Wootton. *Warw* 4H 61
Hillyland. *Per* 1C 136
Hilmarton. *Wilts* 4F 35
Hilperton. *Wilts* 1D 22
Hilperton Marsh. *Wilts* 1D 22
Hilsea. *Port* 2E 17
Hilston. *E Yor* 1F 95
Hiltingbury. *Hants* 4C 24
Hilton. *Cambs* 4B 64
Hilton. *Cumb* 2A 104
Hilton. *Derbs* 2G 73
Hilton. *Dors* 2C 14
Hilton. *Dur* 2E 105
Hilton. *High* 5E 165
Hilton. *Shrp* 1B 60
Hilton. *Staf* 5E 73
Hilton. *Stoc T* 3B 106
Hilton of Cadboll. *High* 1C 158
Himbleton. *Worc* 5D 60
Himley. *Staf* 1C 60
Hincaster. *Cumb* 1E 97
Hinchcliffe Mill. *W Yor* 4B 92
Hinchwick. *Glos* 2G 49
Hinckley. *Leics* 1B 62
Hinderclay. *Suff* 3C 66
Hinderwell. *N Yor* 3E 107
Hindford. *Shrp* 2F 71
Hindhead. *Surr* 3G 25
Hindley. *G Man* 4E 90
Hindley. *Nmbd* 4D 114
Hindley Green. *G Man* 4E 91
Hindlip. *Worc* 5C 60
Hindolveston. *Norf* 3C 78
Hindon. *Wilts* 3E 23
Hindringham. *Norf* 2B 78
Hingham. *Norf* 5C 78
Hinksford. *Staf* 2C 60
Hinstock. *Shrp* 3A 72
Hintlesham. *Suff* 1D 54
Hinton. *Hants* 3H 15
Hinton. *Here* 2G 47
Hinton. *Nptn* 5C 62
Hinton. *Shrp* 5G 71
Hinton. *S Glo* 4C 34
Hinton Ampner. *Hants* 4D 24
Hinton Blewett. *Bath* 1A 22
Hinton Charterhouse. *Bath* 1C 22
Hinton-in-the-Hedges. *Nptn* 2D 50
Hinton Martell. *Dors* 2F 15
Hinton on the Green. *Worc* 1F 49
Hinton Parva. *Swin* 3H 35
Hinton St George. *Som* 1H 13
Hinton St Mary. *Dors* 1C 14
Hinton Waldrist. *Oxon* 2B 36
Hints. *Shrp* 3A 60
Hints. *Staf* 5F 73
Hinwick. *Bed* 4G 63
Hinxhill. *Kent* 1E 29
Hinxton. *Cambs* 1E 53
Hinxworth. *Herts* 1C 52
Hipley. *Hants* 1E 16
Hipperholme. *W Yor* 2B 92
Hipsburn. *Nmbd* 3G 121
Hipswell. *N Yor* 5E 105
Hiraeth. *Carm* 2F 43
Hirn. *Abers* 3E 153
Hirnant. *Powy* 3C 70
Hirst. *N Lan* 3B 128
Hirst. *Nmbd* 1F 115
Hirst Courtney. *N Yor* 2G 93
Hirwaen. *Den* 4D 82
Hirwaun. *Rhon* 5C 46
Hiscott. *Devn* 4F 19
Histon. *Cambs* 4D 64
Hitcham. *Suff* 5B 66
Hitchin. *Herts* 3B 52
Hittisleigh. *Devn* 3H 11
Hittisleigh Barton. *Devn* 3H 11
Hive. *E Yor* 1B 94
Hixon. *Staf* 3E 73
Hoaden. *Kent* 5G 41
Hoar Cross. *Staf* 3F 73
Hoarwithy. *Here* 3A 48
Hoath. *Kent* 4G 41
Hobarris. *Shrp* 3F 59
Hobbister. *Orkn* 7C 172
Hobbles Green. *Suff* 5G 65
Hobbs Cross. *Essx* 1F 39
Hobkirk. *Bord* 3H 119
Hobson. *Dur* 4E 115
Hoby. *Leics* 4D 74
Hockering. *Norf* 4C 78
Hockering Heath. *Norf* 4C 78
Hockerton. *Notts* 5E 86
Hockley. *Essx* 1C 40
Hockley. *Staf* 5G 73
Hockley. *W Mid* 3G 61
Hockley Heath. *W Mid* 3F 61
Hockliffe. *C Beds* 3H 51
Hockwold cum Wilton. *Norf* 2G 65
Hockworthy. *Devn* 1D 12
Hoddesdon. *Herts* 5D 52
Hoddlesden. *Bkbn* 2F 91
Hoddomcross. *Dum* 2C 112
Hodgeston. *Pemb* 5E 43
Hodley. *Powy* 1D 58
Hodnet. *Shrp* 3A 72
Hodsoll Street. *Kent* 4H 39
Hodson. *Swin* 3G 35
Hodthorpe. *Derbs* 3C 86
Hoe. *Norf* 4B 78
Hoe Gate. *Hants* 1E 17
Hoe, The. *Plym* 3A 8
Hoff. *Cumb* 3H 103
Hoffleet Stow. *Linc* 2B 76
Hogaland. *Shet* 4E 173
Hogben's Hill. *Kent* 5E 41
Hoggard's Green. *Suff* 5A 66
Hoggeston. *Buck* 3G 51
Hoggrill's End. *Warw* 1G 61
Hogha Gearraidh. *W Isl* 1C 170
Hoghton. *Lanc* 2E 90
Hoghton Bottoms. *Lanc* 2E 91
Hognaston. *Derbs* 5G 85
Hogsthorpe. *Linc* 3E 89
Hogstock. *Dors* 2E 15
Holbeach. *Linc* 3C 76
Holbeach Bank. *Linc* 3C 76
Holbeach Clough. *Linc* 3C 76
Holbeach Drove. *Linc* 4C 76
Holbeach Hurn. *Linc* 3C 76
Holbeach St Johns. *Linc* 4C 76
Holbeach St Marks. *Linc* 2C 76
Holbeach St Matthew. *Linc* 2D 76
Holbeck. *Notts* 3C 86
Holbeck. *W Yor* 1C 92
Holbeck Woodhouse. *Notts* 3C 86
Holberrow Green. *Worc* 5E 61
Holbeton. *Devn* 3C 8
Holborn. *G Lon* 2E 39
Holbrook. *Derbs* 1A 74
Holbrook. *S Yor* 2B 86
Holbrook. *Suff* 2E 55
Holburn. *Nmbd* 1E 121
Holbury. *Hants* 2C 16
Holcombe. *Devn* 5C 12
Holcombe. *G Man* 3F 91
Holcombe. *Som* 2B 22
Holcombe Brook. *G Man* 3F 91
Holcombe Rogus. *Devn* 1D 12
Holcot. *Nptn* 4E 63
Holden. *Lanc* 5G 97
Holdenby. *Nptn* 4D 62
Holder's Green. *Essx* 3G 53
Holdgate. *Shrp* 2H 59
Holdingham. *Linc* 1H 75
Holditch. *Dors* 2G 13
Holemoor. *Devn* 2E 11
Hole Street. *W Sus* 4C 26
Holford. *Som* 2E 21
Holker. *Cumb* 2C 96
Holkham. *Norf* 1A 78
Hollacombe. *Devn* 2D 11
Holland. *Orkn* 2D 172
(on Papa Westray)
Holland. *Orkn* 5F 172
(on Stronsay)
Holland Fen. *Linc* 1B 76
Holland Lees. *Lanc* 4D 90
Holland-on-Sea. *Essx* 4F 55
Holland Park. *W Mid* 5E 73
Hollandstoun. *Orkn* 2G 172
Hollesley. *Suff* 1G 55
Hollinfare. *Warr* 1A 84
Hollingbourne. *Kent* 5C 40
Hollingbury. *Brig* 5E 27
Hollingdon. *Buck* 3G 51
Hollingrove. *E Sus* 3A 28
Hollington. *Derbs* 1G 73
Hollington. *E Sus* 4B 28
Hollington. *Staf* 2E 73
Hollington Grove. *Derbs* 2G 73
Hollingworth. *G Man* 1E 85
Hollins. *Derbs* 3H 85
Hollins. *G Man* 4G 91
(nr. Bury)
Hollins. *G Man* 4G 91
(nr. Middleton)
Hollinsclough. *Staf* 4E 85
Hollinswood. *Telf* 5A 72
Hollinthorpe. *W Yor* 1D 93
Hollinwood. *G Man* 4H 91
Hollinwood. *Shrp* 2H 71
Hollocombe. *Devn* 1G 11
Holloway. *Derbs* 5H 85
Hollow Court. *Worc* 5D 61
Hollowell. *Nptn* 3D 62
Hollow Meadows. *S Yor* 2G 85
Hollows. *Dum* 2E 113
Hollybush. *Cphy* 5E 47
Hollybush. *E Ayr* 3C 116
Hollybush. *Worc* 2C 48
Holly End. *Norf* 5D 77
Holly Hill. *N Yor* 4E 105
Hollyhurst. *Ches E* 1H 71
Hollym. *E Yor* 2G 95
Hollywood. *Worc* 3E 61
Holmacott. *Devn* 4F 19
Holmbridge. *W Yor* 4B 92
Holmbury St Mary. *Surr* 1C 26
Holmbush. *Corn* 3E 7
Holmcroft. *Staf* 3D 72
Holme. *Cambs* 2A 64
Holme. *Cumb* 2E 97
Holme. *N Lin* 4C 94
Holme. *N Yor* 1F 99
Holme. *Notts* 5F 87
Holme. *W Yor* 4B 92
Holmebridge. *Dors* 4D 15
Holme Chapel. *Lanc* 2G 91
Holme Hale. *Norf* 5A 78
Holme Lacy. *Here* 2A 48
Holme Marsh. *Here* 5F 59
Holmend. *Dum* 4C 118
Holme next the Sea. *Norf* 1G 77
Holme-on-Spalding-Moor.
E Yor 1B 94
Holme on the Wolds. *E Yor* 5D 100
Holme Pierrepont. *Notts* 2D 74
Holmer. *Here* 1A 48
Holmer Green. *Buck* 1A 38
Holmes. *Lanc* 3C 90
Holme St Cuthbert. *Cumb* 5C 112
Holmes Chapel. *Ches E* 4B 84
Holmesfield. *Derbs* 3H 85
Holmeswood. *Lanc* 3C 90
Holmewood. *Derbs* 4B 86
Holmfirth. *W Yor* 4B 92
Holmhead. *E Ayr* 2E 117
Holmisdale. *High* 4A 154
Holm of Drumlanrig. *Dum* 5H 117
Holmpton. *E Yor* 2G 95
Holmrook. *Cumb* 5B 102
Holmsgarth. *Shet* 7F 173
Holmside. *Dur* 5F 115
Holmwrangle. *Cumb* 5G 113
Holne. *Devn* 2D 8
Holsworthy. *Devn* 2D 10
Holsworthy Beacon. *Devn* 2D 10
Holt. *Dors* 2F 15
Holt. *Norf* 2C 78
Holt. *Wilts* 5D 34
Holt. *Worc* 4C 60
Holt. *Wrex* 5G 83
Holtby. *York* 4A 100
Holt End. *Hants* 3E 25
Holt End. *Worc* 4E 61

Holt Fleet—Huxham

Holt Fleet. *Worc* 4C **60**
Holt Green. *Lanc* 4B **90**
Holt Heath. *Dors* 2F **15**
Holt Heath. *Worc* 4C **60**
Holton. *Oxon* 5E **50**
Holton. *Som* 4B **22**
Holton. *Suff* 3F **67**
Holton cum Beckering. *Linc* 2A **88**
Holton Heath. *Dors* 3E **15**
Holton le Clay. *Linc* 4F **95**
Holton le Moor. *Linc* 1H **87**
Holton St Mary. *Suff* 2D **54**
Holt Pound. *Hants* 2G **25**
Holtsmere End. *Herts* 4A **52**
Holtye. *E Sus* 2F **27**
Holwell. *Dors* 1C **14**
Holwell. *Herts* 2B **52**
Holwell. *Leics* 3E **75**
Holwell. *Oxon* 5H **49**
Holwell. *Som* 2C **22**
Holwick. *Dur* 2C **104**
Holworth. *Dors* 4C **14**
Holybourne. *Hants* 2F **25**
Holy City. *Devn* 2G **13**
Holy Cross. *Worc* 3D **60**
Holyfield. *Essx* 5D **53**
Holyhead. *IOA* 2B **80**
Holy Island. *Nmbd* 5H **131**
Holymoorside. *Derbs* 4H **85**
Holyport. *Wind* 4G **37**
Holystone. *Nmbd* 4D **120**
Holytown. *N Lan* 3A **128**
Holywell. *Cambs* 3C **64**
Holywell. *Corn* 3B **6**
Holywell. *Dors* 2A **14**
Holywell. *Flin* 3D **82**
Holywell. *Glos* 2C **34**
Holywell. *Nmbd* 2G **115**
Holywell. *Warw* 4F **61**
Holywell Green. *W Yor* 3A **92**
Holywell Lake. *Som* 4E **20**
Holywell Row. *Suff* 3G **65**
Holywood. *Dum* 1G **111**
Homer. *Shrp* 5A **72**
Homer Green. *Mers* 4B **90**
Homersfield. *Suff* 2E **67**
Hom Green. *Here* 3A **48**
Homington. *Wilts* 4G **23**
Honeyborough. *Pemb* 4D **42**
Honeybourne. *Worc* 1G **49**
Honeychurch. *Devn* 2G **11**
Honeydon. *Bed* 5A **64**
Honey Hill. *Kent* 4F **41**
Honey Street. *Wilts* 5G **35**
Honey Tye. *Suff* 2C **54**
Honeywick. *C Beds* 3H **51**
Honiley. *Warw* 3G **61**
Honing. *Norf* 3F **79**
Honingham. *Norf* 4D **78**
Honington. *Linc* 1G **75**
Honington. *Suff* 3B **66**
Honington. *Warw* 1A **50**
Honiton. *Devn* 2E **13**
Honley. *W Yor* 3B **92**
Honnington. *Telf* 4B **72**
Hoo. *Suff* 5E **67**
Hoobrook. *Worc* 3C **60**
Hood Green. *S Yor* 4D **92**
Hooe. *E Sus* 5A **28**
Hooe. *Plym* 3B **8**
Hooe Common. *E Sus* 4A **28**
Hoohill. *Bkpl* 1B **90**
Hook. *Cambs* 1D **64**
Hook. *E Yor* 2A **94**
Hook. *G Lon* 4C **38**
Hook. *Hants* 1F **25**
(nr. Basingstoke)
Hook. *Hants* 2D **16**
(nr. Fareham)
Hook. *Pemb* 3D **43**
Hook. *Wilts* 3F **35**
Hook-a-Gate. *Shrp* 5G **71**
Hook Bank. *Worc* 1D **48**
Hooke. *Dors* 2A **14**
Hooker Gate. *Tyne* 4E **115**
Hookgate. *Staf* 2B **72**
Hook Green. *Kent* 2A **28**
(nr. Lamberhurst)
Hook Green. *Kent* 3H **39**
(nr. Longfield)
Hook Green. *Kent* 4H **39**
(nr. Meopham)
Hook Norton. *Oxon* 2B **50**
Hook's Cross. *Herts* 3C **52**
Hook Street. *Glos* 2B **34**
Hookway. *Devn* 3B **12**
Hookwood. *Surr* 1D **26**
Hoole. *Ches W* 4G **83**
Hooley. *Surr* 5D **39**
Hooley Bridge. *G Man* 3G **91**
Hooley Brow. *G Man* 3G **91**
Hoo St Werburgh. *Medw* 3B **40**
Hooton. *Ches W* 3F **83**
Hooton Levitt. *S Yor* 1C **86**
Hooton Pagnell. *S Yor* 4E **93**
Hooton Roberts. *S Yor* 1B **86**
Hoove. *Shet* 7E **173**
Hope. *Derbs* 2F **85**
Hope. *Flin* 5F **83**
Hope. *High* 2E **167**
Hope. *Powy* 5E **71**
Hope. *Shrp* 5F **71**
Hope. *Staf* 5F **85**
Hope Bagot. *Shrp* 3H **59**
Hope Bowdler. *Shrp* 1G **59**
Hopedale. *Staf* 5F **85**
Hope Green. *Ches E* 2D **84**
Hopeman. *Mor* 2F **159**
Hope Mansell. *Here* 4B **48**
Hopesay. *Shrp* 2F **59**
Hope's Green. *Essx* 2B **40**
Hopetown. *W Yor* 2D **93**
Hope under Dinmore. *Here* 5H **59**
Hopley's Green. *Here* 5F **59**
Hopperton. *N Yor* 4G **99**
Hop Pole. *Linc* 4A **76**
Hopstone. *Shrp* 1B **60**
Hopton. *Derbs* 5G **85**
Hopton. *Powy* 1E **59**
Hopton. *Shrp* 3F **71**
(nr. Oswestry)
Hopton. *Shrp* 3H **71**
(nr. Wem)
Hopton. *Staf* 3D **72**
Hopton. *Suff* 3B **66**
Hopton Cangeford. *Shrp* 2H **59**
Hopton Castle. *Shrp* 3F **59**
Hoptonheath. *Shrp* 3F **59**
Hopton Heath. *Staf* 3D **72**
Hopton on Sea. *Norf* 5H **79**
Hopton Wafers. *Shrp* 3A **60**
Hopwas. *Staf* 5F **73**
Hopwood. *Worc* 3E **61**
Horam. *E Sus* 4G **27**
Horbling. *Linc* 2A **76**
Horbury. *W Yor* 3C **92**
Horcott. *Glos* 5G **49**
Horden. *Dur* 5H **115**
Horderley. *Shrp* 2G **59**
Hordle. *Hants* 3A **16**
Hordley. *Shrp* 2F **71**
Horeb. *Carm* 3F **45**
(nr. Brechfa)
Horeb. *Carm* 5E **45**
(nr. Llanelli)
Horeb. *Cdgn* 1D **45**
Horfield. *Bris* 4B **34**
Horgabost. *W Isl* 8C **171**
Horham. *Suff* 3E **66**
Horkesley Heath. *Essx* 3C **54**
Horkstow. *N Lin* 3C **94**
Horley. *Oxon* 1C **50**
Horley. *Surr* 1D **27**
Horn Ash. *Dors* 2G **13**
Hornblotton Green. *Som* 3A **22**
Hornby. *Lanc* 3E **97**
Hornby. *N Yor* 4A **106**
(nr. Appleton Wiske)
Hornby. *N Yor* 5F **105**
(nr. Catterick Garrison)
Horncastle. *Linc* 4B **88**
Hornchurch. *G Lon* 2G **39**
Horncliffe. *Nmbd* 5F **131**
Horndean. *Hants* 1E **17**
Horndean. *Bord* 5E **131**
Horndon. *Devn* 4F **11**
Horndon on the Hill. *Thur* 2A **40**
Horne. *Surr* 1E **27**
Horner. *Som* 2C **20**
Horning. *Norf* 4F **79**
Horninghold. *Leics* 1F **63**
Horninglow. *Staf* 3G **73**
Horningsea. *Cambs* 4D **65**
Horningsham. *Wilts* 2D **22**
Horningtoft. *Norf* 3B **78**
Hornsbury. *Som* 1G **13**
Hornsby. *Cumb* 4G **113**
Hornsbygate. *Cumb* 4G **113**
Horns Corner. *Kent* 3B **28**
Horns Cross. *Devn* 4D **19**
Hornsea. *E Yor* 5G **101**
Hornsea Burton. *E Yor* 5G **101**
Hornsey. *G Lon* 2E **39**
Hornton. *Oxon* 1B **50**
Horpit. *Swin* 3H **35**
Horrabridge. *Devn* 2B **8**
Horringer. *Suff* 4H **65**
Horringford. *IOW* 4D **16**
Horrocks Fold. *G Man* 3F **91**
Horrocksford. *Lanc* 5G **97**
Horsbrugh Ford. *Bord* 1E **119**
Horsebridge. *Devn* 5E **11**
Horsebridge. *Hants* 3B **24**
Horse Bridge. *Staf* 5D **84**
Horsebrook. *Staf* 4C **72**
Horsecastle. *N Som* 5H **33**
Horsehay. *Telf* 5A **72**
Horseheath. *Cambs* 1G **53**
Horsehouse. *N Yor* 1C **98**
Horsell. *Surr* 5A **38**
Horseman's Green. *Wrex* 1G **71**
Horsenden. *Buck* 5F **51**
Horseway. *Cambs* 2D **64**
Horsey. *Norf* 3G **79**
Horsey. *Som* 3G **21**
Horsford. *Norf* 4D **78**
Horsforth. *W Yor* 1C **92**
Horsham. *W Sus* 2C **26**
Horsham. *Worc* 5B **60**
Horsham St Faith. *Norf* 4E **78**
Horsington. *Linc* 4A **88**
Horsington. *Som* 4C **22**
Horsley. *Derbs* 1A **74**
Horsley. *Glos* 2D **34**
Horsley. *Nmbd* 3D **115**
(nr. Prudhoe)
Horsley. *Nmbd* 5C **120**
(nr. Rochester)
Horsley Cross. *Essx* 3E **54**
Horsleycross Street. *Essx* 3E **54**
Horsleyhill. *Bord* 3H **119**
Horsleyhope. *Dur* 5D **114**
Horsley Woodhouse. *Derbs* 1A **74**
Horsmonden. *Kent* 1A **28**
Horspath. *Oxon* 5D **50**
Horstead. *Norf* 4E **79**
Horsted Keynes. *W Sus* 3E **27**
Horton. *Buck* 4H **51**
Horton. *Dors* 2F **15**
Horton. *Lanc* 4A **98**
Horton. *Nptn* 5F **63**
Horton. *Shrp* 2G **71**
Horton. *Som* 1G **13**
Horton. *S Glo* 3C **34**
Horton. *Staf* 5D **84**
Horton. *Swan* 4D **30**
Horton. *Wilts* 5F **35**
Horton. *Wind* 3B **38**
Horton Cross. *Som* 1G **13**
Horton-cum-Studley. *Oxon* 4D **50**
Horton Grange. *Nmbd* 2F **115**
Horton Green. *Ches W* 1G **71**
Horton Heath. *Hants* 1C **16**
Horton in Ribblesdale. *N Yor* 2H **97**
Horton Kirby. *Kent* 4G **39**
Hortonwood. *Telf* 4A **72**
Horwich. *G Man* 3E **91**
Horwich End. *Derbs* 2E **85**
Horwood. *Devn* 4F **19**
Hoscar. *Lanc* 3C **90**
Hose. *Leics* 3E **75**
Hosh. *Per* 1A **136**
Hosta. *W Isl* 1C **170**
Hoswick. *Shet* 9F **173**
Hotham. *E Yor* 1B **94**
Hothfield. *Kent* 1D **28**
Hoton. *Leics* 3C **74**
Houbie. *Shet* 2H **173**
Hough. *Arg* 4A **138**
Hough. *Ches E* 5B **84**
(nr. Crewe)
Hough. *Ches E* 3C **84**
(nr. Wilmslow)
Hougham. *Linc* 1F **75**
Hough Green. *Hal* 2G **83**
Hough-on-the-Hill. *Linc* 1G **75**
Houghton. *Cambs* 3B **64**
Houghton. *Cumb* 4F **113**
Houghton. *Hants* 3B **24**
Houghton. *Nmbd* 3E **115**
Houghton. *Pemb* 4D **43**
Houghton. *W Sus* 4B **26**
Houghton Bank. *Darl* 2F **105**
Houghton Conquest. *C Beds* 1A **52**
Houghton Green. *E Sus* 3D **28**
Houghton-le-Side. *Darl* 2F **105**
Houghton-le-Spring. *Tyne* 5G **115**
Houghton on the Hill. *Leics* 5D **74**
Houghton Regis. *C Beds* 3A **52**
Houghton St Giles. *Norf* 2B **78**
Houlland. *Shet* 6E **173**
(on Mainland)
Houlland. *Shet* 4G **173**
(on Yell)
Houlsyke. *N Yor* 4E **107**
Hound. *Hants* 2C **16**
Hound Green. *Hants* 1F **25**
Houndslow. *Bord* 5C **130**
Houndsmoor. *Som* 4E **21**
Houndwood. *Bord* 3E **131**
Hounsdown. *Hants* 1B **16**
Hounslow. *G Lon* 3C **38**
Housabister. *Shet* 6F **173**
Housay. *Shet* 4H **173**
Househill. *High* 3C **158**
Housetter. *Shet* 3E **173**
Houss. *Shet* 8E **173**
Houston. *Ren* 3F **127**
Housty. *High* 5D **168**
Houton. *Orkn* 7C **172**
Hove. *Brig* 5D **27** & **189**
Hoveringham. *Notts* 1E **74**
Hoveton. *Norf* 4F **79**
Hovingham. *N Yor* 2A **100**
How. *Cumb* 4G **113**
How Caple. *Here* 2B **48**
Howden. *E Yor* 2H **93**
Howden-le-Wear. *Dur* 1E **105**
Howe. *High* 2F **169**
Howe. *Norf* 5E **79**
Howe. *N Yor* 1F **99**
Howe Green. *Essx* 5H **53**
(nr. Chelmsford)
Howegreen. *Essx* 5B **54**
(nr. Maldon)
Howe Green. *Warw* 2H **61**
Howell. *Linc* 1A **76**
How End. *C Beds* 1A **52**
Howe of Teuchar. *Abers* 4E **161**
Howes. *Dum* 3C **112**
Howe Street. *Essx* 4G **53**
(nr. Chelmsford)
Howe Street. *Essx* 2G **53**
(nr. Finchingfield)
Howe, The. *Cumb* 1D **96**
Howe, The. *IOM* 5A **108**
Howey. *Powy* 5C **58**
Howgate. *Midl* 4F **129**
Howgill. *Lanc* 5H **97**
Howgill. *N Yor* 4C **98**
How Green. *Kent* 1F **27**
How Hill. *Norf* 4F **79**
Howick. *Nmbd* 3G **121**
Howle. *Telf* 3A **72**
Howle Hill. *Here* 3B **48**
Howleigh. *Som* 1F **13**
Howlett End. *Essx* 2F **53**
Howley. *Som* 2F **13**
Howley. *Warr* 2A **84**
Hownam. *Bord* 3B **120**
Howsham. *N Lin* 4D **94**
Howsham. *N Yor* 3B **100**
Howtel. *Nmbd* 1C **120**
Howt Green. *Kent* 4C **40**
Howton. *Here* 3H **47**
Howwood. *Ren* 3E **127**
Hoxne. *Suff* 3D **66**
Hoylake. *Mers* 2E **82**
Hoyland. *S Yor* 4D **92**
Hoylandswaine. *S Yor* 4C **92**
Hoyle. *W Sus* 4A **26**
Hubberholme. *N Yor* 2B **98**
Hubberston. *Pemb* 4C **42**
Hubbert's Bridge. *Linc* 1B **76**
Huby. *N Yor* 5E **99**
(nr. Harrogate)
Huby. *N Yor* 3H **99**
(nr. York)
Huccaby. *Devn* 5G **11**
Hucclecote. *Glos* 4D **48**
Hucking. *Kent* 5C **40**
Hucknall. *Notts* 1C **74**
Huddersfield. *W Yor* 3B **92**
Huddington. *Worc* 5D **60**
Huddlesford. *Staf* 5F **73**
Hudswell. *N Yor* 4E **105**
Huggate. *E Yor* 4C **100**
Hugglescote. *Leics* 4B **74**
Hughenden Valley. *Buck* 2G **37**
Hughley. *Shrp* 1H **59**
Hughton. *High* 4G **157**
Hugh Town. *IOS* 1B **4**
Hugus. *Corn* 4B **6**
Huish. *Devn* 1F **11**
Huish. *Wilts* 5G **35**
Huish Champflower. *Som* 4D **20**
Huish Episcopi. *Som* 4H **21**
Huisinis. *W Isl* 6B **171**
Hulcote. *Nptn* 5E **62**
Hulcott. *Buck* 4G **51**
Hulham. *Devn* 4D **12**
Hull. *Hull* 2D **94** & **199**
Hulland. *Derbs* 1G **73**
Hulland Moss. *Derbs* 1G **73**
Hulland Ward. *Derbs* 1G **73**
Hullavington. *Wilts* 3D **35**
Hullbridge. *Essx* 1C **40**
Hulme. *G Man* 1C **84**
Hulme. *Staf* 1D **72**
Hulme End. *Staf* 5F **85**
Hulme Walfield. *Ches E* 4C **84**
Hulverstone. *IOW* 4B **16**
Hulver Street. *Suff* 2G **67**
Humber. *Devn* 5C **12**
Humber. *Here* 5H **59**
Humber Bridge. *N Lin* 2D **94**
Humberside International Airport.
N Lin 3D **94**
Humberston. *NE Lin* 4G **95**
Humberstone. *Leic* 5D **74**
Humbie. *E Lot* 3A **130**
Humbleton. *E Yor* 1F **95**
Humbleton. *Nmbd* 2D **121**
Humby. *Linc* 2H **75**
Hume. *Bord* 5D **130**
Humshaugh. *Nmbd* 2C **114**
Huna. *High* 1F **169**
Huncoat. *Lanc* 1F **91**
Huncote. *Leics* 1C **62**
Hundall. *Derbs* 3A **86**
Hunderthwaite. *Dur* 2C **104**
Hundleby. *Linc* 4C **88**
Hundle Houses. *Linc* 5B **88**
Hundleton. *Pemb* 4D **42**
Hundon. *Suff* 1H **53**
Hundred Acres. *Hants* 1D **16**
Hundred House. *Powy* 5D **58**
Hundred, The. *Here* 4H **59**
Hungarton. *Leics* 5D **74**
Hungerford. *Hants* 1G **15**
Hungerford. *Shrp* 2H **59**
Hungerford. *Som* 2D **20**
Hungerford. *W Ber* 5B **36**
Hungerford Newtown. *W Ber* 4B **36**
Hunger Hill. *G Man* 4E **91**
Hungerton. *Linc* 2F **75**
Hungladder. *High* 1C **154**
Hungryhatton. *Shrp* 3A **72**
Hunmanby. *N Yor* 2E **101**
Hunmanby Sands. *N Yor* 2F **101**
Hunningham. *Warw* 4A **62**
Hunnington. *Worc* 2D **60**
Hunny Hill. *IOW* 4C **16**
Hunsdon. *Herts* 4E **53**
Hunsdonbury. *Herts* 4E **53**
Hunsingore. *N Yor* 4G **99**
Hunslet. *W Yor* 1D **92**
Hunslet Carr. *W Yor* 2D **92**
Hunsonby. *Cumb* 1G **103**
Hunspow. *High* 1E **169**
Hunstanton. *Norf* 1F **77**
Hunstanworth. *Dur* 5C **114**
Hunston. *Suff* 4B **66**
Hunston. *W Sus* 2G **17**
Hunstrete. *Bath* 5B **34**
Hunt End. *Worc* 4E **61**
Hunterfield. *Midl* 3G **129**
Hunters Forstal. *Kent* 4F **41**
Hunter's Quay. *Arg* 2C **126**
Huntham. *Som* 4G **21**
Hunthill Lodge. *Ang* 1D **144**
Huntingdon. *Cambs* 3B **64**
Huntingfield. *Suff* 3F **67**
Huntingford. *Wilts* 3D **22**
Huntington. *Ches W* 4G **83**
Huntington. *E Lot* 2A **130**
Huntington. *Here* 5E **59**
Huntington. *Staf* 4D **72**
Huntington. *Telf* 5A **72**
Huntington. *York* 4A **100**
Huntingtower. *Per* 1C **136**
Huntley. *Glos* 4C **48**
Huntley. *Staf* 1E **73**
Huntly. *Abers* 4C **160**
Huntlywood. *Bord* 5C **130**
Hunton. *Hants* 3C **24**
Hunton. *Kent* 1B **28**
Hunton. *N Yor* 5E **105**
Hunton Bridge. *Herts* 5A **52**
Hunt's Corner. *Norf* 2C **66**
Huntscott. *Som* 2C **20**
Hunt's Cross. *Mers* 2G **83**
Hunts Green. *Warw* 1F **61**
Huntsham. *Devn* 4D **20**
Huntshaw. *Devn* 4F **19**
Huntspill. *Som* 2G **21**
Huntstile. *Som* 3F **21**
Huntstrete. *Bath* 5B **34**
Huntworth. *Som* 3G **21**
Hunwick. *Dur* 1E **105**
Hunworth. *Norf* 2C **78**
Hurcott. *Som* 1G **13**
(nr. Ilminster)
Hurcott. *Som* 4A **22**
(nr. Somerton)
Hurdcott. *Wilts* 3G **23**
Hurdley. *Powy* 1E **59**
Hurdsfield. *Ches E* 3D **84**
Hurlet. *Glas* 3G **127**
Hurley. *Warw* 1G **61**
Hurley. *Wind* 3G **37**
Hurlford. *E Ayr* 1D **116**
Hurliness. *Orkn* 9B **172**
Hurlston Green. *Lanc* 3B **90**
Hurn. *Dors* 3G **15**
Hursey. *Dors* 2H **13**
Hursley. *Hants* 4C **24**
Hurst. *G Man* 4H **91**
Hurst. *N Yor* 4D **104**
Hurst. *Som* 1H **13**
Hurst. *Wok* 4F **37**
Hurstbourne Priors. *Hants* 2C **24**
Hurstbourne Tarrant. *Hants* 1B **24**
Hurst Green. *Ches E* 1H **71**
Hurst Green. *E Sus* 3B **28**
Hurst Green. *Essx* 4D **54**
Hurst Green. *Lanc* 1E **91**
Hurst Green. *Surr* 5E **39**
Hurstley. *Here* 1G **47**
Hurstpierpoint. *W Sus* 4D **27**
Hurstway Common. *Here* 1F **47**
Hurst Wickham. *W Sus* 4D **27**
Hurstwood. *Lanc* 1G **91**
Hurtmore. *Surr* 1A **26**
Hurworth-on-Tees. *Darl* 3A **106**
Hurworth Place. *Darl* 3F **105**
Hury. *Dur* 3C **104**
Husbands Bosworth. *Leics* 2D **62**
Husborne Crawley. *C Beds* 2H **51**
Husthwaite. *N Yor* 2H **99**
Hutcherleigh. *Devn* 3D **9**
Hut Green. *N Yor* 2F **93**
Huthwaite. *Notts* 5B **86**
Huttoft. *Linc* 3E **89**
Hutton. *Cumb* 2F **103**
Hutton. *E Yor* 4E **101**
Hutton. *Essx* 1H **39**
Hutton. *Lanc* 2C **90**
Hutton. *N Som* 1G **21**
Hutton. *Bord* 4F **131**
Hutton Bonville. *N Yor* 4A **106**
Hutton Buscel. *N Yor* 1D **100**
Hutton Conyers. *N Yor* 2F **99**
Hutton Cranswick. *E Yor* 4E **101**
Hutton End. *Cumb* 1F **103**
Hutton Gate. *Red C* 3C **106**
Hutton Henry. *Dur* 1B **106**
Hutton-le-Hole. *N Yor* 1B **100**
Hutton Magna. *Dur* 3E **105**
Hutton Mulgrave. *N Yor* 4F **107**
Hutton Roof. *Cumb* 2E **97**
(nr. Kirkby Lonsdale)
Hutton Roof. *Cumb* 1E **103**
(nr. Penrith)
Hutton Rudby. *N Yor* 4B **106**
Huttons Ambo. *N Yor* 3B **100**
Hutton Sessay. *N Yor* 2G **99**
Hutton Village. *Red C* 3D **106**
Hutton Wandesley. *N Yor* 4H **99**
Huxham. *Devn* 3C **12**

Huxham Green. Som 3A 22
Huxley. Ches W 4H 83
Huxter. Shet 6C 173
(on Mainland)
Huxter. Shet 5G 173
(on Whalsay)
Huyton. Mers 1G 83
Hwlffordd. Pemb 3D 42
Hycemoor. Cumb 1A 96
Hyde. Glos 5D 49
(nr. Stroud)
Hyde. Glos 3F 49
(nr. Winchcombe)
Hyde. G Man 1D 84
Hyde Heath. Buck 5H 51
Hyde Lea. Staf 3D 72
Hyde Park. S Yor 4F 93
Hydestile. Surr 1A 26
Hyndford Bridge. S Lan 5C 128
Hynish. Arg 5A 138
Hyssington. Powy 1F 59
Hythe. Hants 2C 16
Hythe. Kent 2F 29
Hythe End. Wind 3B 38
Hythie. Abers 3H 161
Hyton. Cumb 1A 96

I

Ianstown. Mor 2B 160
Iarsiadar. W Isl 4D 171
Ibberton. Dors 2C 14
Ible. Derbs 5G 85
Ibrox. Glas 3G 127
Ibsley. Hants 2G 15
Ibstock. Leics 4B 74
Ibstone. Buck 2F 37
Ibthorpe. Hants 1B 24
Iburndale. N Yor 4F 107
Ibworth. Hants 1D 24
Icelton. N Som 5G 33
Ichrachan. Arg 5E 141
Ickburgh. Norf 1H 65
Ickenham. G Lon 2B 38
Ickenthwaite. Cumb 1C 96
Ickford. Buck 5E 51
Ickham. Kent 5G 41
Ickleford. Herts 2B 52
Icklesham. E Sus 4C 28
Ickleton. Cambs 1E 53
Icklingham. Suff 3G 65
Ickwell. C Beds 1B 52
Icomb. Glos 3H 49
Idbury. Oxon 3H 49
Iddesleigh. Devn 2F 11
Ide. Devn 3B 12
Ideford. Devn 5B 12
Iden. E Sus 3D 28
Iden Green. Kent 2C 28
(nr. Benenden)
Iden Green. Kent 2B 28
(nr. Goudhurst)
Idle. W Yor 1B 92
Idless. Corn 4C 6
Idlicote. Warw 1A 50
Idmiston. Wilts 3G 23
Idole. Carm 4E 45
Idridgehay. Derbs 1G 73
Idrigill. High 2C 154
Idstone. Oxon 3A 36
Iffley. Oxon 5D 50
Ifield. W Sus 2D 26
Ifieldwood. W Sus 2D 26
Ifold. W Sus 2B 26
Iford. E Sus 5F 27
Ifton Heath. Shrp 2F 71
Ightfield. Shrp 2H 71
Ightham. Kent 5G 39
Iken. Suff 5G 67
Ilam. Staf 5F 85
Ilchester. Som 4A 22
Ilderton. Nmbd 2E 121
Ilford. G Lon 2F 39
Ilford. Som 1G 13
Ilfracombe. Devn 2F 19
Ilkeston. Derbs 1B 74
Ilketshall St Andrew. Suff 2F 67
Ilketshall St Lawrence. Suff 2F 67
Ilketshall St Margaret. Suff 2F 67
Ilkley. W Yor 5D 98
Illand. Corn 5C 10
Illey. W Mid 2D 61
Illidge Green. Ches E 4B 84
Illington. Norf 2B 66
Illingworth. W Yor 2A 92
Illogan. Corn 4A 6
Illogan Highway. Corn 4A 6
Illston on the Hill. Leics 1E 62
Ilmer. Buck 5F 51
Ilmington. Warw 1H 49
Ilminster. Som 1G 13
Ilsington. Devn 5A 12
Ilsington. Dors 3C 14
Ilston. Swan 3E 31
Ilton. N Yor 2D 98
Ilton. Som 1G 13
Imachar. N Ayr 5G 125
Imber. Wilts 2E 23
Immingham. NE Lin 3E 95
Immingham Dock. NE Lin 3E 95

Impington. Cambs 4D 64
Ince. Ches W 3G 83
Ince Blundell. Mers 4B 90
Ince-in-Makerfield. G Man 4D 90
Inchbae Lodge. High 2G 157
Inchbare. Ang 2F 145
Inchberry. Mor 3H 159
Inchbraoch. Ang 3G 145
Inchbrook. Glos 5D 48
Incheril. High 2C 156
Inchinnan. Ren 3F 127
Inchlaggan. High 3D 148
Inchmichael. Per 1E 137
Inchnadamph. High 1G 163
Inchree. High 2E 141
Inchture. Per 1E 137
Inchyra. Per 1D 136
Indian Queens. Corn 3D 6
Ingatestone. Essx 1H 39
Ingbirchworth. S Yor 4C 92
Ingestre. Staf 3D 73
Ingham. Linc 2G 87
Ingham. Norf 3F 79
Ingham. Suff 3A 66
Ingham Corner. Norf 3F 79
Ingleborough. Norf 4D 76
Ingleby. Derbs 3H 73
Ingleby Arncliffe. N Yor 4B 106
Ingleby Barwick. Stoc T 3B 106
Ingleby Greenhow. N Yor 4C 106
Ingleigh Green. Devn 2G 11
Inglemire. Hull 1D 94
Inglesbatch. Bath 5C 34
Ingleton. Dur 2E 105
Ingleton. N Yor 2F 97
Inglewhite. Lanc 5E 97
Ingoe. Nmbd 2D 114
Ingol. Lanc 1D 90
Ingoldisthorpe. Norf 2F 77
Ingoldmells. Linc 4E 89
Ingoldsby. Linc 2H 75
Ingon. Warw 5G 61
Ingram. Nmbd 3E 121
Ingrave. Essx 1H 39
Ingrow. W Yor 1A 92
Ings. Cumb 5F 103
Ingst. S Glo 3A 34
Ingthorpe. Rut 5G 75
Ingworth. Norf 3D 78
Inkberrow. Worc 5E 61
Inkford. Worc 3E 61
Inkpen. W Ber 5B 36
Inkstack. High 1E 169
Innellan. Arg 3C 126
Inner Hope. Devn 5C 8
Innerleith. Fife 2E 137
Innerleithen. Bord 1F 119
Innerleven. Fife 3F 137
Innermessan. Dum 3F 109
Innerwick. E Lot 2D 130
Innerwick. Per 4C 142
Innsworth. Glos 3D 48
Insch. Abers 1D 152
Insh. High 3C 150
Inshegra. High 3C 166
Inshore. High 1D 166
Inskip. Lanc 1C 90
Instow. Devn 3E 19
Intwood. Norf 5D 78
Inver. Abers 4G 151
Inver. High 5F 165
Inver. Per 4H 143
Inverailort. High 5F 147
Inveralligin. High 3H 155
Inverallochy. Abers 2H 161
Inveramsay. Abers 1E 153
Inveran. High 4C 164
Inveraray. Arg 3H 133
Inverarish. High 5E 155
Inverarity. Ang 4D 144
Inverarnan. Arg 2C 134
Inverarnie. High 5A 158
Inverbeg. Arg 4C 134
Inverbervie. Abers 1H 145
Inverboyndie. Abers 2D 160
Invercassley. High 3B 164
Invercharnan. High 4F 141
Inverchoran. High 3E 157
Invercreran. Arg 4E 141
Inverdruie. High 2D 150
Inverebrie. Abers 5G 161
Invereck. Arg 1C 126
Inveresk. E Lot 2G 129
Inveresragan. Arg 5D 141
Inverey. Abers 5E 151
Inverfarigaig. High 1H 149
Invergarry. High 3F 149
Invergeldie. Per 1G 135
Invergordon. High 2B 158
Invergowrie. Per 5C 144
Inverguseran. High 3F 147
Inverharroch. Mor 5A 160
Inverie. High 3F 147
Inverinan. Arg 2G 133
Inverinate. High 1B 148
Inverkeilor. Ang 4F 145
Inverkeithing. Fife 1E 129
Inverkeithny. Abers 4D 160
Inverkip. Inv 2D 126
Inverkirkaig. High 2E 163
Inverlael. High 5F 163
Inverliever Lodge. Arg 3F 133

Inverliver. Arg 5E 141
Inverloch. High 1F 141
Inverlochlarig. Stir 2D 134
Inverlussa. Arg 1E 125
Inver Mallie. High 5D 148
Invermarkie. Abers 5B 160
Invermoriston. High 2G 149
Invernaver. High 2H 167
Inverneil House. Arg 1G 125
Inverness. High . . . . . .4A 158 & 198
Inverness Airport. High 3B 158
Invernettie. Abers 4H 161
Inverpolly Lodge. High 2E 163
Inverquharity. Abers 4H 161
Inverroy. High 5E 149
Inversanda. High 3D 140
Invershiel. High 2B 148
Invershin. High 4C 164
Invershore. High 5E 169
Inversnaid. Stir 3C 134
Inverugie. Abers 4H 161
Inveruglas. Arg 3C 134
Inverurie. Abers 1E 153
Invervar. Per 4D 142
Inverythan. Abers 4E 161
Inwardleigh. Devn 3F 11
Inworth. Essx 4B 54
Iochdar. W Isl 4C 170
Iping. W Sus 4G 25
Ipplepen. Devn 2E 9
Ipsden. Oxon 3E 37
Ipstones. Staf 1E 73
Ipswich. Suff . . . . .1E 55 & 198
Irby. Mers 2E 83
Irby in the Marsh. Linc 4D 88
Irby upon Humber. NE Lin 4E 95
Irchester. Nptn 4G 63
Ireby. Cumb 1D 102
Ireby. Lanc 2F 97
Ireland. Shet 9E 173
Ireleth. Cumb 2B 96
Ireshopeburn. Dur 1B 104
Ireton Wood. Derbs 1G 73
Irlam. G Man 1B 84
Irnham. Linc 3H 75
Iron Acton. S Glo 3B 34
Iron Bridge. Cambs 1D 65
Ironbridge. Telf 5A 72
Iron Cross. Warw 5E 61
Ironville. Derbs 5B 86
Irstead. Norf 3F 79
Irthington. Cumb 3F 113
Irthlingborough. Nptn 3G 63
Irton. N Yor 1E 101
Irvine. N Ayr 1C 116
Irvine Mains. N Ayr 1C 116
Isabella Pit. Nmbd 1G 115
Isauld. High 2B 168
Isbister. Orkn 6C 172
Isbister. Shet 2E 173
(on Mainland)
Isbister. Shet 5G 173
(on Whalsay)
Isfield. E Sus 4F 27
Isham. Nptn 3F 63
Island Carr. N Lin 4C 94
Islay Airport. Arg 4B 124
Isle Abbotts. Som 4G 21
Isle Brewers. Som 4G 21
Isleham. Cambs 3F 65
Isle of Man Airport. IOM 5B 108
Isle of Thanet. Kent 4H 41
Isle of Whithorn. Dum 5B 110
Isleornsay. High 2F 147
Islesburgh. Shet 5E 173
Isles of Scilly (St Mary's) Airport.
IOS 1B 4
Islesteps. Dum 2A 112
Isleworth. G Lon 3C 38
Isley Walton. Leics 3B 74
Islibhig. W Isl 5B 171
Islington. G Lon 2E 39
Islington. Telf 3B 72
Islip. Nptn 3G 63
Islip. Oxon 4D 50
Islwyn. Cphy 2F 33
Isombridge. Telf 4A 72
Istead Rise. Kent 4H 39
Itchen. Sotn 1C 16
Itchen Abbas. Hants 3D 24
Itchen Stoke. Hants 3D 24
Itchingfield. W Sus 3C 26
Itchington. S Glo 3B 34
Itlaw. Abers 3D 160
Itteringham. Norf 2D 78
Itteringham Common. Norf 3D 78
Itton. Devn 3G 11
Itton Common. Mon 2H 33
Ivegill. Cumb 5F 113
Ivelet. N Yor 5C 104
Iverchaolain. Arg 2B 126
Iver Heath. Buck 2B 38
Iveston. Dur 4E 115
Ivetsey Bank. Staf 4C 72
Ivinghoe. Buck 4H 51
Ivinghoe Aston. Buck 4H 51
Ivington. Here 5G 59
Ivington Green. Here 5G 59
Ivybridge. Devn 3C 8
Ivychurch. Kent 3E 29
Ivy Hatch. Kent 5G 39
Ivy Todd. Norf 5A 78

Iwade. Kent 4D 40
Iwerne Courtney. Dors 1D 14
Iwerne Minster. Dors 1D 14
Ixworth. Suff 3B 66
Ixworth Thorpe. Suff 3B 66

J

Jackfield. Shrp 5A 72
Jack Hill. N Yor 4E 98
Jacksdale. Notts 5B 86
Jackton. S Lan 4G 127
Jacobstow. Corn 3B 10
Jacobstowe. Devn 2F 11
Jacobswell. Surr 5A 38
Jameston. Pemb 5E 43
Jamestown. Dum 5F 119
Jamestown. Fife 1E 129
Jamestown. High 3G 157
Jamestown. W Dun 1E 127
Janetstown. High 2C 168
(nr. Thurso)
Janetstown. High 3F 169
(nr. Wick)
Jarrow. Tyne 3G 115
Jarvis Brook. E Sus 3G 27
Jasper's Green. Essx 3H 53
Jaywick. Essx 4E 55
Jedburgh. Bord 2A 120
Jeffreyston. Pemb 4E 43
Jemimaville. High 2B 158
Jenkins Park. High 3F 149
Jersey Marine. Neat 3G 31
Jesmond. Tyne 3F 115
Jevington. E Sus 5G 27
Jingle Street. Mon 4H 47
Jockey End. Herts 4A 52
Jodrell Bank. Ches E 3B 84
Johnby. Cumb 1F 103
John o' Gaunts. W Yor 2D 92
John o' Groats. High 1F 169
John's Cross. E Sus 3B 28
Johnshaven. Abers 2G 145
Johnson Street. Norf 4F 79
Johnston. Pemb 3D 42
Johnstone. Ren 3F 127
Johnstonebridge. Dum 5C 118
Johnstown. Carm 4D 45
Johnstown. Wrex 1F 71
Joppa. Edin 2G 129
Joppa. S Ayr 3D 116
Jordan Green. Norf 3C 78
Jordans. Buck 1A 38
Jordanston. Pemb 1D 42
Jump. S Yor 4D 93
Jumpers Common. Dors 3G 15
Juniper. Nmbd 4C 114
Juniper Green. Edin 3E 129
Jurby East. IOM 2C 108
Jurby West. IOM 2C 108
Jury's Gap. E Sus 4D 28

K

Kaber. Cumb 3A 104
Kaimend. S Lan 5C 128
Kaimes. Edin 3F 129
Kaimrig End. Bord 5D 129
Kames. Arg 2A 126
Kames. E Ayr 2F 117
Kea. Corn 4C 6
Keadby. N Lin 3B 94
Keal Cotes. Linc 4C 88
Kearsney. G Man 4F 91
Kearsney. Kent 1G 29
Kearstwick. Cumb 1F 97
Kearton. N Yor 5C 104
Kearvaig. High 1C 166
Keasden. N Yor 3G 97
Keason. Corn 2H 7
Keckwick. Hal 2H 83
Keddington. Linc 2C 88
Keddington Corner. Linc 2C 88
Kedington. Suff 1H 53
Kedleston. Derbs 1H 73
Kedlock Feus. Fife 2F 137
Keekle. Cumb 3B 102
Keelby. Linc 3E 95
Keele. Staf 1C 72
Keeley Green. Bed 1A 52
Keeston. Pemb 3D 42
Keevil. Wilts 1E 23
Kegworth. Leics 3B 74
Kehelland. Corn 2D 4
Keig. Abers 2D 152
Keighley. W Yor 5C 98
Keilarsbrae. Clac 4A 136
Keillmore. Arg 1E 125
Keillor. Per 4B 144
Keillour. Per 1B 136
Keills. Arg 3C 124
Keiloch. Abers 4F 151
Keils. Arg 3D 124
Keinton Mandeville. Som 3A 22
Keir Mill. Dum 5A 118
Keirsleywell Row. Nmbd 4A 114
Keisby. Linc 3H 75
Keisley. Cumb 2A 104
Keiss. High 2F 169
Keith. Mor 3B 160

Keith Inch. Abers 4H 161
Kelbrook. Lanc 5B 98
Kelby. Linc 1H 75
Keld. Cumb 3G 103
Keld. N Yor 4B 104
Keldholme. N Yor 1B 100
Kelfield. N Lin 4B 94
Kelfield. N Yor 1F 93
Kelham. Notts 5E 87
Kellacott. Devn 4E 11
Kellan. Arg 4G 139
Kellas. Ang 5D 144
Kellas. Mor 3F 159
Kellaton. Devn 5E 9
Kelleth. Cumb 4H 103
Kelling. Norf 1C 78
Kellingley. N Yor 2F 93
Kellington. N Yor 2F 93
Kelloe. Dur 1A 106
Kelloholm. Dum 3G 117
Kells. Cumb 3A 102
Kelly. Devn 4D 11
Kelly Bray. Corn 5D 10
Kelmarsh. Nptn 3E 63
Kelmscott. Oxon 2A 36
Kelsale. Suff 4F 67
Kelsall. Ches W 4H 83
Kelshall. Herts 2D 52
Kelsick. Cumb 4C 112
Kelso. Bord 1B 120
Kelstedge. Derbs 4H 85
Kelstern. Linc 1B 88
Kelsterton. Flin 3E 83
Kelston. Bath 5C 34
Keltneyburn. Per 4E 143
Kelton. Dur 2A 112
Kelton Hill. Dum 4E 111
Kelty. Fife 4D 136
Kelvedon. Essx 4B 54
Kelvedon Hatch. Essx 1G 39
Kelvinside. Glas 3G 127
Kelynack. Corn 3A 4
Kemback. Fife 2G 137
Kemberton. Shrp 5B 72
Kemble. Glos 2E 35
Kemerton. Worc 2E 49
Kemeys Commander.
Mon 5G 47
Kemnay. Abers 2E 153
Kempe's Corner. Kent 1E 29
Kempley. Glos 3B 48
Kempley Green. Glos 3B 48
Kempsey. Worc 1D 48
Kempsford. Glos 2G 35
Kemps Green. Warw 3F 61
Kempshott. Hants 1E 24
Kempston. Bed 1A 52
Kempston Hardwick. Bed 1A 52
Kempton. Shrp 2F 59
Kemp Town. Brig 5E 27
Kemsing. Kent 5G 39
Kemsley. Kent 4D 40
Kenardington. Kent 2D 28
Kenchester. Here 1H 47
Kencot. Oxon 5A 50
Kendal. Cumb 5G 103
Kendleshire. S Glo 4B 34
Kendray. S Yor 4D 92
Kenfig. B'end 3B 32
Kenfig Hill. B'end 3B 32
Kengharair. Arg 4F 139
Kenidjack. Corn 3A 4
Kenilworth. Warw 3G 61
Kenknock. Stir 5B 142
Kenley. G Lon 5E 39
Kenley. Shrp 5H 71
Kenmore. High 3G 155
Kenmore. Per 4E 143
Kenn. Devn 4C 12
Kenn. Som 5H 33
Kennacraig. Arg 3G 125
Kenneggy Downs. Corn 4C 4
Kennerleigh. Devn 2B 12
Kennet. Clac 4B 136
Kennethmont. Abers 1C 152
Kennett. Cambs 4G 65
Kennford. Devn 4C 12
Kenninghall. Norf 2C 66
Kennington. Kent 1E 29
Kennington. Oxon 5D 50
Kennoway. Fife 3F 137
Kennyhill. Suff 3F 65
Kennythorpe. N Yor 3B 100
Kenovay. Arg 4A 138
Kensaleyre. High 3D 154
Kensington. G Lon 3D 38
Kenstone. Shrp 3H 71
Kensworth. C Beds 4A 52
Kensworth Common. C Beds . . .4A 52
Kentallen. High 3E 141
Kentchurch. Here 3H 47
Kentford. Suff 4G 65
Kent International Airport.
Kent 4H 41
Kentisbeare. Devn 2D 12
Kentisbury. Devn 2G 19
Kentisbury Ford. Devn 2G 19
Kentmere. Cumb 4F 103
Kenton. Devn 4C 12
Kenton. G Lon 2C 38
Kenton. Suff 4D 66
Kenton Bankfoot. Tyne 3F 115

Kentra—Kirkham

Kentra. High 2A 140
Kentrigg. Cumb 5G 103
Kents Bank. Cumb 2C 96
Kent's Green. Glos 3C 48
Kent's Oak. Hants 4B 24
Kent Street. E Sus 4B 28
Kent Street. Kent 5A 40
Kent Street. W Sus 3D 26
Kenwick. Shrp 2G 71
Kenwyn. Corn 4C 6
Kenyon. Warr 1A 84
Keoldale. High 2D 166
Keppoch. High 1B 148
Kepwick. N Yor 5B 106
Keresley. W Mid 2H 61
Keresley Newland. Warw 2H 61
Keristal. IOM 4C 108
Kerne Bridge. Here 4A 48
Kerridge. Ches E 3D 84
Kerris. Corn 4B 4
Kerrow. High 5F 157
Kerry. Powy 2D 58
Kerrycroy. Arg 3C 126
Kerry's Gate. Here 2G 47
Kersall. Notts 4E 86
Kersbrook. Devn 4D 12
Kerse. Ren 4E 127
Kersey. Suff 1D 54
Kershopefoot. Cumb 1F 113
Kersoe. Worc 2E 49
Kerswell. Devn 2D 12
Kerswell Green. Worc 1D 48
Kesgrave. Suff 1F 55
Kessingland. Suff 2H 67
Kessingland Beach. Suff 2H 67
Kestle. Corn 4D 6
Kestle Mill. Corn 3C 6
Keston. G Lon 4F 39
Keswick. Cumb 2D 102
Keswick. Norf 2F 79
(nr. North Walsham)
Keswick. Norf 5E 78
(nr. Norwich)
Ketsby. Linc 3C 88
Kettering. Nptn 3F 63
Ketteringham. Norf 5D 78
Kettins. Per 5B 144
Kettlebaston. Suff 5B 66
Kettlebridge. Fife 3F 137
Kettlebrook. Staf 5G 73
Kettleburgh. Suff 4E 67
Kettleholm. Dum 2C 112
Kettleness. N Yor 3F 107
Kettleshulme. Ches E 3D 85
Kettlesing. N Yor 4E 99
Kettlesing Bottom. N Yor 4E 99
Kettlestone. Norf 2B 78
Kettlethorpe. Linc 3F 87
Kettletoft. Orkn 4F 172
Kettlewell. N Yor 2B 98
Ketton. Rut 5G 75
Kew. G Lon 3C 38
Kewaigue. IOM 4C 108
Kewstoke. N Som 5G 33
Kexbrough. S Yor 4D 92
Kexby. Linc 2F 87
Kexby. York 4B 100
Keyford. Som 2C 22
Key Green. Ches E 4C 84
Key Green. N Yor 4F 107
Keyham. Leics 5D 74
Keyhaven. Hants 3B 16
Keyhead. Abers 3H 161
Keyingham. E Yor 2F 95
Keymer. W Sus 4E 27
Keynsham. Bath 5B 34
Keysoe. Bed 4H 63
Keysoe Row. Bed 4H 63
Key's Toft. Linc 5D 89
Keyston. Cambs 3H 63
Key Street. Kent 4C 40
Keyworth. Notts 2D 74
Kibblesworth. Tyne 4F 115
Kibworth Beauchamp. Leics 1D 62
Kibworth Harcourt. Leics 1D 62
Kidbrooke. G Lon 3F 39
Kidburngill. Cumb 2B 102
Kiddemore Green. Staf 5C 72
Kidderminster. Worc 3C 60
Kiddington. Oxon 3C 50
Kidd's Moor. Norf 5D 78
Kidlington. Oxon 4C 50
Kidmore End. Oxon 4E 37
Kidnal. Ches W 1G 71
Kidsgrove. Staf 5C 84
Kidstones. N Yor 1B 98
Kidwelly. Carm 5E 45
Kiel Crofts. Arg 5D 140
Kielder. Nmbd 5A 120
Kilbagie. Fife 4B 136
Kilbarchan. Ren 3F 127
Kilbeg. High 3E 147
Kilberry. Arg 3F 125
Kilbirnie. N Ayr 4E 126
Kilbride. Arg 1F 133
Kilbride. High 1C 147
Kilbucho Place. Bord 1C 118
Kilburn. Derbs 1A 74
Kilburn. G Lon 2D 38
Kilburn. N Yor 2H 99
Kilby. Leics 1D 62
Kilchattan. Arg 4A 132
(on Colonsay)
Kilchattan. Arg 4C 126
(on Isle of Bute)
Kilchattan Bay. Arg 4B 126
Kilchenzie. Arg 3A 122
Kilcheran. Arg 5C 140
Kilchiaran. Arg 3A 124
Kilchoan. High 4F 147
(nr. Inverie)
Kilchoan. High 2F 139
(nr. Tobermory)
Kilchoman. Arg 3A 124
Kilchrenan. Arg 1H 133
Kilconquhar. Fife 3G 137
Kilcot. Glos 3B 48
Kilcoy. High 3H 157
Kilcreggan. Arg 1D 126
Kildale. N Yor 4D 106
Kildary. High 1B 158
Kildermorie Lodge. High 1H 157
Kildonan. Dum 4F 109
Kildonan. High 1G 165
(nr. Helmsdale)
Kildonan. High 3C 154
(on Isle of Skye)
Kildonan. N Ayr 3E 123
Kildonnan. High 5C 146
Kildrummy. Abers 2B 152
Kildwick. N Yor 5C 98
Kilfillan. Dum 4H 109
Kilfinan. Arg 2H 125
Kilfinnan. High 4E 149
Kilgetty. Pemb 4F 43
Kilgour. Fife 3E 136
Kilgrammie. S Ayr 4B 116
Kilham. E Yor 3E 101
Kilham. Nmbd 1C 120
Kilkenneth. Arg 4A 138
Kilkhampton. Corn 1C 10
Killamarsh. Derbs 2B 86
Killandrist. Arg 4C 140
Killay. Swan 3F 31
Killean. Arg 5E 125
Killearn. Stir 1G 127
Killellan. Arg 4A 122
Killen. High 3A 158
Killerby. Darl 3E 105
Killichonan. Per 3C 142
Killiechronan. Arg 4G 139
Killiecrankie. Per 2G 143
Killilan. High 5B 156
Killimster. High 3F 169
Killin. Stir 5C 142
Killinghall. N Yor 4E 99
Killinghurst. Surr 2A 26
Killington. Cumb 1F 97
Killingworth. Tyne 2F 115
Killin Lodge. High 3H 149
Killinochonoch. Arg 4F 133
Killochyett. Bord 5A 130
Killundine. High 4G 139
Kilmacolm. Inv 3E 127
Kilmahog. Stir 3F 135
Kilmahumaig. Arg 4E 133
Kilmalieu. High 3C 140
Kilmaluag. High 1D 154
Kilmany. Fife 1F 137
Kilmarie. High 2D 146
Kilmarnock. E Ayr 1D 116 & 198
Kilmaron. Fife 2F 137
Kilmartin. Arg 4F 133
Kilmaurs. E Ayr 5F 127
Kilmelford. Arg 2F 133
Kilmeny. Arg 3B 124
Kilmersdon. Som 1B 22
Kilmeston. Hants 4D 24
Kilmichael Glassary. Arg 4F 133
Kilmichael of Inverlussa. Arg 1F 125
Kilmington. Devn 3F 13
Kilmington. Wilts 3C 22
Kilmoluag. Arg 4A 138
Kilmorack. High 4G 157
Kilmore. Arg 1F 133
Kilmore. High 3E 147
Kilmory. Arg 2F 125
Kilmory. High 1G 139
(nr. Kilchoan)
Kilmory. High 3B 146
(on Rùm)
Kilmory. N Ayr 3D 122
Kilmory Lodge. Arg 3E 132
Kilmote. High 2G 165
Kilmuir. High 4B 154
(nr. Dunvegan)
Kilmuir. High 1B 158
(nr. Invergordon)
Kilmuir. High 4A 158
(nr. Inverness)
Kilmuir. High 1C 154
(nr. Uig)
Kilmun. Arg 1C 126
Kilnave. Arg 2A 124
Kilncadzow. S Lan 5B 128
Kilndown. Kent 2B 28
Kiln Green. Here 4B 48
Kiln Green. Wind 4G 37
Kilnhill. Cumb 1D 102
Kilnhurst. S Yor 1B 86
Kilninian. Arg 4E 139
Kilninver. Arg 1F 133
Kiln Pit Hill. Nmbd 4D 114
Kilnsea. E Yor 3H 95
Kilnsey. N Yor 3B 98
Kilnwick. E Yor 5D 101
Kiloran. Arg 4A 132
Kilpatrick. N Ayr 3D 122
Kilpeck. Here 2H 47
Kilpin. E Yor 2A 94
Kilpin Pike. E Yor 2A 94
Kilrenny. Fife 3H 137
Kilsby. Nptn 3C 62
Kilspindie. Per 1E 136
Kilsyth. N Lan 2A 128
Kiltarlity. High 4H 157
Kilton. Som 2E 21
Kilton Thorpe. Red C 3D 107
Kilvaxter. High 2C 154
Kilve. Som 2E 21
Kilvington. Notts 1F 75
Kilwinning. N Ayr 5D 126
Kimberley. Norf 5C 78
Kimberley. Notts 1B 74
Kimblesworth. Dur 5F 115
Kimble Wick. Buck 5G 51
Kimbolton. Cambs 4H 63
Kimbolton. Here 4H 59
Kimcote. Leics 2C 62
Kimmeridge. Dors 5E 15
Kimmerston. Nmbd 1D 120
Kimpton. Hants 2A 24
Kimpton. Herts 4B 52
Kinbeachie. High 2A 158
Kinbrace. High 5A 168
Kinbuck. Stir 3G 135
Kincaple. Fife 2G 137
Kincardine. Fife 1C 128
Kincardine. High 5D 164
Kincardine Bridge. Fife 1C 128
Kincardine O'Neil. Abers 4C 152
Kinchrackine. Arg 1A 134
Kincorth. Aber 3G 153
Kincraig. High 3C 150
Kincraigie. Per 4G 143
Kindallachan. Per 3G 143
Kineton. Glos 3F 49
Kineton. Warw 5H 61
Kinfauns. Per 1D 136
Kingairloch. High 3C 140
Kingarth. Arg 4B 126
Kingcoed. Mon 5H 47
King Edward. Abers 3E 160
Kingerby. Linc 1H 87
Kingham. Oxon 3A 50
Kingholm Quay. Dum 2A 112
Kinghorn. Fife 1F 129
Kingie. High 3D 148
Kinglassie. Fife 4E 137
Kingledores. Bord 2D 118
Kingodie. Per 1F 137
King o' Muirs. Clac 4A 136
King's Acre. Here 1H 47
Kingsand. Corn 3A 8
Kingsash. Buck 5G 51
Kingsbarns. Fife 2H 137
Kingsbridge. Devn 4D 8
Kingsbridge. Som 3C 20
King's Bromley. Staf 4F 73
Kingsburgh. High 3C 154
Kingsbury. G Lon 2C 38
Kingsbury. Warw 1G 61
Kingsbury Episcopi. Som 4H 21
Kings Caple. Here 3A 48
Kingscavil. W Lot 2D 128
Kingsclere. Hants 1D 24
King's Cliffe. Nptn 1H 63
Kingscote. Glos 2D 34
Kingscott. Devn 1F 11
Kings Coughton. Warw 5E 61
Kingscross. N Ayr 3E 123
Kingsdon. Som 4A 22
Kingsdown. Kent 1H 29
Kingsdown. Swin 3G 35
Kingsdown. Wilts 5D 34
Kingseat. Fife 4D 136
Kingsey. Buck 5F 51
Kingsfold. Lanc 2D 90
Kingsfold. W Sus 2C 26
Kingsford. E Ayr 5F 127
Kingsford. Worc 2C 60
Kingsforth. N Lin 3D 94
Kingsgate. Kent 3H 41
King's Green. Glos 2C 48
Kingshall Street. Suff 4B 66
Kingsheanton. Devn 3F 19
King's Heath. W Mid 2E 61
Kings Hill. Kent 5A 40
Kingsholm. Glos 4D 48
Kingshouse. High 3G 141
Kingshouse. Stir 1E 135
Kingshurst. W Mid 2F 61
Kingskerswell. Devn 2E 9
Kingskettle. Fife 3F 137
Kingsland. Here 4G 59
Kingsland. IOA 2B 80
Kings Langley. Herts 5A 52
Kingsley. Ches W 3H 83
Kingsley. Hants 3F 25
Kingsley. Staf 1E 73
Kingsley Green. W Sus 3G 25
Kingsley Holt. Staf 1E 73
King's Lynn. Norf 3F 77
King's Meaburn. Cumb 2H 103
Kings Moss. Mers 4D 90
Kingsmuir. Ang 4D 145
Kingsmuir. Fife 3H 137
Kings Muir. Bord 1E 119
King's Newnham. Warw 3B 62
Kings Newton. Derbs 3A 74
Kingsnorth. Kent 2E 28
Kingsnorth. Medw 3C 40
King's Norton. Leics 5D 74
King's Norton. W Mid 3E 61
King's Nympton. Devn 1G 11
King's Pyon. Here 5G 59
Kings Ripton. Cambs 3B 64
King's Somborne. Hants 3B 24
King's Stag. Dors 1C 14
King's Stanley. Glos 5D 48
King's Sutton. Nptn 2C 50
Kingstanding. W Mid 1E 61
Kingsteignton. Devn 5B 12
Kingsteps. High 3D 158
King Sterndale. Derbs 3E 85
King's Thorn. Here 2A 48
Kingsthorpe. Nptn 4E 63
Kingston. Cambs 5C 64
Kingston. Devn 4C 8
Kingston. Dors 2C 14
(nr. Sturminster Newton)
Kingston. Dors 5E 15
(nr. Swanage)
Kingston. E Lot 1B 130
Kingston. Hants 2G 15
Kingston. IOW 4C 16
Kingston. Kent 5F 41
Kingston. Mor 2H 159
Kingston. W Sus 5B 26
Kingston Bagpuize. Oxon 2C 36
Kingston Blount. Oxon 2F 37
Kingston by Sea. W Sus 5D 26
Kingston Deverill. Wilts 3D 22
Kingstone. Here 2H 47
Kingstone. Som 1G 13
Kingstone. Staf 3E 73
Kingston Lisle. Oxon 3B 36
Kingston Maurward. Dors 3C 14
Kingston near Lewes. E Sus 5E 27
Kingston on Soar. Notts 3C 74
Kingston Russell. Dors 3A 14
Kingston St Mary. Som 4F 21
Kingston Seymour. N Som 5H 33
Kingston Stert. Oxon 5F 51
Kingston upon Hull. Hull 2D 94 & 199
Kingston upon Thames. G Lon 4C 38
King's Walden. Herts 3B 52
Kingswear. Devn 3E 9
Kingswells. Aber 3F 153
Kingswinford. W Mid 2C 60
Kingswood. Buck 4E 51
Kingswood. Glos 2C 34
Kingswood. Here 5E 59
Kingswood. Kent 5C 40
Kingswood. Per 5H 143
Kingswood. Powy 5E 71
Kingswood. Som 3E 20
Kingswood. S Glo 4B 34
Kingswood. Surr 5D 38
Kingswood. Warw 3F 61
Kingswood Common. Staf 5C 72
Kings Worthy. Hants 3C 24
Kingthorpe. Linc 3A 88
Kington. Here 5F 59
Kington. S Glo 2B 34
Kington. Worc 5D 61
Kington Langley. Wilts 4E 35
Kington Magna. Dors 4C 22
Kington St Michael. Wilts 4E 35
Kingussie. High 3B 150
Kingweston. Som 3A 22
Kinharrachie. Abers 5G 161
Kinhrive. High 1B 158
Kinkell Bridge. Per 2B 136
Kinknockie. Abers 4H 161
Kinkry Hill. Cumb 2G 113
Kinlet. Shrp 2B 60
Kinloch. High 5D 166
(nr. Loch More)
Kinloch. High 3A 140
(nr. Lochaline)
Kinloch. High 4C 146
(on Rùm)
Kinloch. Per 4A 144
Kinlochard. Stir 3D 134
Kinlochbervie. High 3C 166
Kinlocheil. High 1D 141
Kinlochewe. High 2C 156
Kinloch Hourn. High 3B 148
Kinloch Laggan. High 5H 149
Kinlochleven. High 2F 141
Kinloch Lodge. High 3F 167
Kinlochmoidart. High 1B 140
Kinlochmore. High 2F 141
Kinloch Rannoch. Per 3D 142
Kinlochspelve. Arg 1D 132
Kinloid. High 5E 147
Kinloss. Mor 2E 159
Kinmel Bay. Cnwy 2B 82
Kinmuck. Abers 2F 153
Kinnadie. Abers 4G 161
Kinnaird. Per 1E 137
Kinneff. Abers 1H 145
Kinnelhead. Dum 4C 118
Kinnell. Ang 3F 145
Kinnerley. Shrp 3F 71
Kinnernie. Abers 2E 152
Kinnersley. Here 1G 47
Kinnersley. Worc 1D 48
Kinnerton. Powy 4E 59
Kinnerton. Shrp 1F 59
Kinnesswood. Per 3D 136
Kinninvie. Dur 2D 104
Kinnordy. Ang 3C 144
Kinoulton. Notts 2D 74
Kinross. Per 3D 136
Kinrossie. Per 5A 144
Kinsbourne Green. Herts 4B 52
Kinsey Heath. Ches E 1A 72
Kinsham. Here 4F 59
Kinsham. Worc 2E 49
Kinsley. W Yor 3E 93
Kinson. Bour 3F 15
Kintbury. W Ber 5B 36
Kintessack. Mor 2E 159
Kintillo. Per 2D 136
Kinton. Here 3G 59
Kinton. Shrp 4F 71
Kintore. Abers 2E 153
Kintour. Arg 4C 124
Kintra. Arg 2B 132
Kintraw. Arg 3F 133
Kinveachy. High 2D 150
Kinver. Staf 2C 60
Kinwarton. Warw 5F 61
Kiplingcotes. E Yor 5D 100
Kippax. W Yor 1E 93
Kippen. Stir 4F 135
Kippford. Dum 4F 111
Kipping's Cross. Kent 1H 27
Kirbister. Orkn 7C 172
(nr. Hobbister)
Kirbister. Orkn 6B 172
(nr. Quholm)
Kirbuster. Orkn 5F 172
Kirby Bedon. Norf 5E 79
Kirby Bellars. Leics 4E 74
Kirby Cane. Norf 1F 67
Kirby Cross. Essx 3F 55
Kirby Fields. Leics 5C 74
Kirby Grindalythe. N Yor 3D 100
Kirby Hill. N Yor 4E 105
(nr. Richmond)
Kirby Hill. N Yor 3F 99
(nr. Ripon)
Kirby Knowle. N Yor 1G 99
Kirby-le-Soken. Essx 3F 55
Kirby Misperton. N Yor 2B 100
Kirby Muxloe. Leics 5C 74
Kirby Row. Norf 1F 67
Kirby Sigston. N Yor 5B 106
Kirby Underdale. E Yor 4C 100
Kirby Wiske. N Yor 1F 99
Kirdford. W Sus 3B 26
Kirk. High 3E 169
Kirkabister. Shet 8F 173
(on Bressay)
Kirkabister. Shet 6F 173
(on Mainland)
Kirkandrews. Dum 5D 110
Kirkandrews-on-Eden. Cumb 4E 113
Kirkapol. Arg 4B 138
Kirkbampton. Cumb 4E 112
Kirkbean. Dum 4A 112
Kirk Bramwith. S Yor 3G 93
Kirkbride. Cumb 4D 112
Kirkbridge. N Yor 5F 105
Kirkbuddo. Ang 4E 145
Kirkburn. E Yor 4D 101
Kirkburton. W Yor 3B 92
Kirkby. Linc 1H 87
Kirkby. Mers 1G 83
Kirkby. N Yor 4C 106
Kirkby Fenside. Linc 4C 88
Kirkby Fleetham. N Yor 5F 105
Kirkby Green. Linc 5H 87
Kirkby-in-Ashfield. Notts 5C 86
Kirkby Industrial Estate. Mers 1G 83
Kirkby-in-Furness. Cumb 1B 96
Kirkby la Thorpe. Linc 1A 76
Kirkby Lonsdale. Cumb 2F 97
Kirkby Malham. N Yor 3A 98
Kirkby Mallory. Leics 5B 74
Kirkby Malzeard. N Yor 2E 99
Kirkby Mills. N Yor 1B 100
Kirkbymoorside. N Yor 1A 100
Kirkby on Bain. Linc 4B 88
Kirkby Overblow. N Yor 5F 99
Kirkby Stephen. Cumb 4A 104
Kirkby Thore. Cumb 2H 103
Kirkby Underwood. Linc 3H 75
Kirkby Wharfe. N Yor 5H 99
Kirkcaldy. Fife 4E 137
Kirkcambeck. Cumb 3G 113
Kirkcolm. Dum 3F 109
Kirkconnel. Dum 3G 117
Kirkconnell. Dum 3A 112
Kirkcowan. Dum 3A 110
Kirkcudbright. Dum 4D 111
Kirkdale. Mers 1F 83
Kirk Deighton. N Yor 4F 99
Kirk Ella. E Yor 2D 94
Kirkfieldbank. S Lan 5B 128
Kirkforthar Feus. Fife 3E 137
Kirkgunzeon. Dum 3F 111
Kirk Hallam. Derbs 1B 74
Kirkham. Lanc 1C 90

Kirkham—Larport

Kirkham. *N Yor* 3B **100**
Kirkhamgate. *W Yor* 2C **92**
Kirk Hammerton. *N Yor* 4G **99**
Kirkharle. *Nmbd* 1D **114**
Kirkheaton. *Nmbd* 2D **114**
Kirkheaton. *W Yor* 3B **92**
Kirkhill. *Ang* 2F **145**
Kirkhill. *High* 4H **157**
Kirkhope. *S Lan* 4B **118**
Kirkhouse. *Bord* 1F **119**
Kirkibost. *High* 2D **146**
Kirkinch. *Ang* 4C **144**
Kirkinner. *Dum* 4B **110**
Kirkintilloch. *E Dun* 2H **127**
Kirk Ireton. *Derbs* 5G **85**
Kirkland. *Cumb* 3B **102** (nr. Cleator Moor)
Kirkland. *Cumb* 1H **103** (nr. Penrith)
Kirkland. *Cumb* 5D **112** (nr. Wigton)
Kirkland. *Dum* 3G **117** (nr. Kirkconnel)
Kirkland. *Dum* 5H **117** (nr. Moniaive)
Kirkland Guards. *Cumb* 5C **112**
Kirk Langley. *Derbs* 2G **73**
Kirklauchline. *Dum* 4F **109**
Kirkleatham. *Red C* 2C **106**
Kirklevington. *Stoc T* 4B **106**
Kirkley. *Suff* 1H **67**
Kirklington. *N Yor* 1F **99**
Kirklington. *Notts* 5D **86**
Kirklinton. *Cumb* 3F **113**
Kirkliston. *Edin* 2E **129**
Kirkmabreck. *Dum* 4B **110**
Kirkmaiden. *Dum* 5E **109**
Kirk Merrington. *Dur* 1F **105**
Kirk Michael. *IOM* 2C **108**
Kirkmichael. *Per* 2H **143**
Kirkmichael. *S Ayr* 4C **116**
Kirkmuirhill. *S Lan* 5A **128**
Kirknewton. *Nmbd* 1D **120**
Kirknewton. *W Lot* 3E **129**
Kirkney. *Abers* 5C **160**
Kirk of Shotts. *N Lan* 3B **128**
Kirkoswald. *Cumb* 5G **113**
Kirkoswald. *S Ayr* 4B **116**
Kirkpatrick. *Dum* 5B **118**
Kirkpatrick Durham. *Dum* 2E **111**
Kirkpatrick-Fleming. *Dum* 2D **112**
Kirk Sandall. *S Yor* 4G **93**
Kirksanton. *Cumb* 1A **96**
Kirk Smeaton. *N Yor* 3F **93**
Kirkstall. *W Yor* 1C **92**
Kirkstile. *Dum* 5F **119**
Kirkstyle. *High* 1F **169**
Kirkthorpe. *W Yor* 2D **92**
Kirkton. *Abers* 2D **152** (nr. Alford)
Kirkton. *Abers* 1D **152** (nr. Insch)
Kirkton. *Abers* 4F **161** (nr. Turriff)
Kirkton. *Ang* 5D **144** (nr. Dundee)
Kirkton. *Ang* 4D **144** (nr. Forfar)
Kirkton. *Ang* 5B **152** (nr. Tarfside)
Kirkton. *Dum* 1A **112**
Kirkton. *Fife* 1F **137**
Kirkton. *High* 4E **165** (nr. Golspie)
Kirkton. *High* 1G **147** (nr. Kyle of Lochalsh)
Kirkton. *High* 4B **156** (nr. Lochcarron)
Kirkton. *Bord* 3H **119**
Kirkton. *S Lan* 2B **118**
Kirktonhill. *W Dun* 2E **127**
Kirkton Manor. *Bord* 1E **118**
Kirkton of Airlie. *Ang* 3C **144**
Kirkton of Auchterhouse. *Ang* 5C **144**
Kirkton of Bourtie. *Abers* 1F **153**
Kirkton of Collace. *Per* 5A **144**
Kirkton of Craig. *Ang* 3G **145**
Kirkton of Culsalmond. *Abers* 5D **160**
Kirkton of Durris. *Abers* 4E **153**
Kirkton of Glenbuchat. *Abers* 2A **152**
Kirkton of Glenisla. *Ang* 2B **144**
Kirkton of Kingoldrum. *Ang* 3C **144**
Kirkton of Largo. *Fife* 3G **137**
Kirkton of Lethendy. *Per* 4A **144**
Kirkton of Logie Buchan. *Abers* 1G **153**
Kirkton of Maryculter. *Abers* 4F **153**
Kirkton of Menmuir. *Ang* 2E **145**
Kirkton of Monikie. *Ang* 5E **145**
Kirkton of Oyne. *Abers* 1D **152**
Kirkton of Rayne. *Abers* 5D **160**
Kirkton of Skene. *Abers* 3F **153**
Kirktown. *Abers* 2G **161** (nr. Fraserburgh)
Kirktown. *Abers* 3H **161** (nr. Peterhead)
Kirktown of Alvah. *Abers* 2D **160**
Kirktown of Auchterless. *Abers* 4E **160**
Kirktown of Deskford. *Mor* 2C **160**
Kirktown of Fetteresso. *Abers* 5F **153**
Kirktown of Mortlach. *Mor* 5H **159**
Kirktown of Slains. *Abers* 1H **153**
Kirkurd. *Bord* 5E **129**
Kirkwall. *Orkn* 6D **172**
Kirkwall Airport. *Orkn* 7D **172**
Kirkwhelpington. *Nmbd* 1C **114**
Kirk Yetholm. *Bord* 2C **120**
Kirmington. *N Lin* 3E **94**
Kirmond le Mire. *Linc* 1A **88**
Kirn. *Arg* 2C **126**
Kirriemuir. *Ang* 3C **144**
Kirstead Green. *Norf* 1E **67**
Kirtlebridge. *Dum* 2D **112**
Kirtleton. *Dum* 2D **112**
Kirtling. *Cambs* 5F **65**
Kirtling Green. *Cambs* 5F **65**
Kirtlington. *Oxon* 4D **50**
Kirtomy. *High* 2H **167**
Kirton. *Linc* 2C **76**
Kirton. *Notts* 4D **86**
Kirton. *Suff* 2F **55**
Kirton End. *Linc* 1B **76**
Kirton Holme. *Linc* 1B **76**
Kirton in Lindsey. *N Lin* 1G **87**
Kishorn. *High* 4H **155**
Kislingbury. *Nptn* 5D **62**
Kite Hill. *IOW* 3D **16**
Kites Hardwick. *Warw* 4B **62**
Kittisford. *Som* 4D **20**
Kittle. *Swan* 4E **31**
Kittybrewster. *Aber* 3G **153**
Kitwood. *Hants* 3E **25**
Kivernoll. *Here* 2H **47**
Kiveton Park. *S Yor* 2B **86**
Knaith. *Linc* 2F **87**
Knaith Park. *Linc* 2F **87**
Knaphill. *Surr* 5A **38**
Knapp. *Hants* 4C **24**
Knapp. *Per* 5B **144**
Knapp. *Som* 4G **21**
Knapperfield. *High* 3E **169**
Knapton. *Norf* 2F **79**
Knapton. *York* 4H **99**
Knapton Green. *Here* 5G **59**
Knapwell. *Cambs* 4C **64**
Knaresborough. *N Yor* 4F **99**
Knarsdale. *Nmbd* 4H **113**
Knatts Valley. *Kent* 4G **39**
Knaven. *Abers* 4F **161**
Knayton. *N Yor* 1G **99**
Knebworth. *Herts* 3C **52**
Knedlington. *E Yor* 2H **93**
Kneesall. *Notts* 4E **86**
Kneesworth. *Cambs* 1D **52**
Kneeton. *Notts* 1E **74**
Knelston. *Swan* 4D **30**
Knenhall. *Staf* 2D **72**
Knightacott. *Devn* 3G **19**
Knightcote. *Warw* 5B **62**
Knightcott. *N Som* 1G **21**
Knightley. *Staf* 3C **72**
Knightley Dale. *Staf* 3C **72**
Knightlow Hill. *Warw* 3B **62**
Knighton. *Devn* 4B **8**
Knighton. *Dors* 1B **14**
Knighton. *Leic* 5D **74**
Knighton. *Powy* 3E **59**
Knighton. *Som* 2E **21**
Knighton. *Staf* 3B **72** (nr. Eccleshall)
Knighton. *Staf* 1B **72** (nr. Woore)
Knighton. *Warw* 5H **61**
Knighton. *Wilts* 4A **36**
Knighton. *Worc* 5E **61**
Knighton Common. *Worc* 3A **60**
Knight's End. *Cambs* 1D **64**
Knightswood. *Glas* 3G **127**
Knightwick. *Worc* 5B **60**
Knill. *Here* 4E **59**
Knipton. *Leics* 2F **75**
Knitsley. *Dur* 5E **115**
Kniveton. *Derbs* 5G **85**
Knock. *Arg* 5G **139**
Knock. *Cumb* 2H **103**
Knock. *Mor* 3C **160**
Knockally. *High* 5D **168**
Knockan. *Arg* 1B **132**
Knockan. *High* 2G **163**
Knockandhu. *Mor* 1G **151**
Knockando. *Mor* 4F **159**
Knockarthur. *High* 3E **165**
Knockbain. *High* 3A **158**
Knockbreck. *High* 2B **154**
Knockdee. *High* 2D **168**
Knockdolian. *S Ayr* 1G **109**
Knockdon. *S Ayr* 3C **116**
Knockdown. *Glos* 3D **34**
Knockenbaird. *Abers* 1D **152**
Knockenkelly. *N Ayr* 3E **123**
Knockentiber. *E Ayr* 1C **116**
Knockfarrel. *High* 3H **157**
Knockglass. *High* 2C **168**
Knockholt. *Kent* 5F **39**
Knockholt Pound. *Kent* 5F **39**
Knockie Lodge. *High* 2G **149**
Knockin. *Shrp* 3F **71**
Knockinlaw. *E Ayr* 1D **116**
Knockinnon. *High* 5D **169**
Knockrome. *Arg* 2D **124**
Knocksharry. *IOM* 3B **108**
Knockshinnoch. *E Ayr* 3D **116**
Knockvennie. *Dum* 2E **111**
Knockvologan. *Arg* 3B **132**
Knodishall. *Suff* 4G **67**
Knole. *Som* 4H **21**
Knollbury. *Mon* 3H **33**
Knolls Green. *Ches E* 3C **84**
Knolton. *Wrex* 2F **71**
Knook. *Wilts* 2E **23**
Knossington. *Leics* 5F **75**
Knott. *High* 3C **154**
Knott End-on-Sea. *Lanc* 5C **96**
Knotting. *Bed* 4H **63**
Knotting Green. *Bed* 4H **63**
Knottingley. *W Yor* 2E **93**
Knotts. *Cumb* 2F **103**
Knotty Ash. *Mers* 1G **83**
Knotty Green. *Buck* 1A **38**
Knowbury. *Shrp* 3H **59**
Knowe. *Dum* 2A **110**
Knowefield. *Cumb* 4F **113**
Knowehead. *Dum* 5F **117**
Knowes. *E Lot* 2C **130**
Knowesgate. *Nmbd* 1C **114**
Knoweside. *S Ayr* 3B **116**
Knowle. *Bris* 4A **34**
Knowle. *Devn* 3E **19** (nr. Braunton)
Knowle. *Devn* 4D **12** (nr. Budleigh Salterton)
Knowle. *Devn* 2A **12** (nr. Crediton)
Knowle. *Shrp* 3H **59**
Knowle. *W Mid* 3F **61**
Knowle Green. *Lanc* 1E **91**
Knowle St Giles. *Som* 1G **13**
Knowlesands. *Shrp* 1B **60**
Knowles of Elrick. *Abers* 3D **160**
Knowle Village. *Hants* 2D **16**
Knowl Hill. *Wind* 4G **37**
Knowlton. *Kent* 5G **41**
Knowsley. *Mers* 1G **83**
Knowstone. *Devn* 4B **20**
Knucklas. *Powy* 3E **59**
Knuston. *Nptn* 4G **63**
Knutsford. *Ches E* 3B **84**
Knypersley. *Staf* 5C **84**
Krumlin. *W Yor* 3A **92**
Kuggar. *Corn* 5E **5**
Kyleakin. *High* 1F **147**
Kyle of Lochalsh. *High* 1F **147**
Kylerhea. *High* 1F **147**
Kylesku. *High* 5C **166**
Kyles Lodge. *W Isl* 9B **171**
Kylesmorar. *High* 4G **147**
Kylestrome. *High* 5C **166**
Kymin. *Mon* 4A **48**
Kynaston. *Here* 2B **48**
Kynaston. *Shrp* 3F **71**
Kynnersley. *Telf* 4A **72**
Kyre Green. *Worc* 4A **60**
Kyre Park. *Worc* 4A **60**
Kyrewood. *Worc* 4A **60**

L

Labost. *W Isl* 3E **171**
Lacasaidh. *W Isl* 5F **171**
Lacasdail. *W Isl* 4G **171**
Laceby. *NE Lin* 4F **95**
Lacey Green. *Buck* 5G **51**
Lach Dennis. *Ches W* 3B **84**
Lache. *Ches W* 4F **83**
Lackford. *Suff* 3G **65**
Lacock. *Wilts* 5E **35**
Ladbroke. *Warw* 5B **62**
Laddingford. *Kent* 1A **28**
Lade Bank. *Linc* 5C **88**
Ladock. *Corn* 3C **6**
Lady. *Orkn* 3F **172**
Ladybank. *Fife* 2F **137**
Ladycross. *Corn* 4D **10**
Lady Green. *Mers* 4B **90**
Lady Hall. *Cumb* 1A **96**
Ladykirk. *Bord* 5E **131**
Ladysford. *Abers* 2G **161**
Ladywood. *W Mid* 2E **61**
Ladywood. *Worc* 4C **60**
Laga. *High* 2A **140**
Lagavulin. *Arg* 5C **124**
Lagg. *Arg* 2D **125**
Lagg. *N Ayr* 3D **122**
Laggan. *Arg* 4A **124**
Laggan. *High* 4E **149** (nr. Fort Augustus)
Laggan. *High* 4A **150** (nr. Newtonmore)
Laggan. *Mor* 5H **159**
Lagganlia. *High* 3C **150**
Lagganulva. *Arg* 4F **139**
Laglingarten. *Arg* 3A **134**
Lagness. *W Sus* 2G **17**
Laid. *High* 3E **166**
Laide. *High* 4D **162**
Laigh Fenwick. *E Ayr* 5F **127**
Laindon. *Essx* 2A **40**
Lairg. *High* 3C **164**
Lairg Muir. *High* 3C **164**
Laithes. *Cumb* 1F **103**
Laithkirk. *Dur* 2C **104**
Lake. *Devn* 3F **19**
Lake. *IOW* 4D **16**
Lake. *Wilts* 3G **23**
Lake District. *Cumb* 3E **103**
Lakenham. *Norf* 5E **79**
Lakenheath. *Suff* 2G **65**
Lakesend. *Norf* 1E **65**
Lakeside. *Cumb* 1C **96**
Laleham. *Surr* 4B **38**
Laleston. *B'end* 3B **32**
Lamancha. *Bord* 4F **129**
Lamarsh. *Essx* 2B **54**
Lamas. *Norf* 3E **79**
Lamb Corner. *Essx* 2D **54**
Lambden. *Bord* 5D **130**
Lamberhead Green. *G Man* 4D **90**
Lamberhurst. *Kent* 2A **28**
Lamberhurst Quarter. *Kent* 2A **28**
Lamberton. *Bord* 4F **131**
Lambeth. *G Lon* 3E **39**
Lambfell Moar. *IOM* 3B **108**
Lambhill. *Glas* 3G **127**
Lambley. *Nmbd* 4H **113**
Lambley. *Notts* 1D **74**
Lambourn. *W Ber* 4B **36**
Lambourne End. *Essx* 1F **39**
Lambourn Woodlands. *W Ber* 4B **36**
Lambrook. *Som* 4F **21**
Lambs Green. *Dors* 3E **15**
Lambs Green. *W Sus* 2D **26**
Lambston. *Pemb* 3D **42**
Lamellion. *Corn* 2G **7**
Lamerton. *Devn* 5E **11**
Lamesley. *Tyne* 4F **115**
Laminess. *Orkn* 4F **172**
Lamington. *High* 1B **158**
Lamington. *S Lan* 1B **118**
Lamlash. *N Ayr* 2E **123**
Lamonby. *Cumb* 1F **103**
Lamorick. *Corn* 2E **7**
Lamorna. *Corn* 4B **4**
Lamorran. *Corn* 4C **6**
Lampeter. *Cdgn* 1F **45**
Lampeter Velfrey. *Pemb* 3F **43**
Lamphey. *Pemb* 4E **43**
Lamplugh. *Cumb* 2B **102**
Lamport. *Nptn* 3E **63**
Lamyatt. *Som* 3B **22**
Lana. *Devn* 3D **10** (nr. Ashwater)
Lana. *Devn* 2D **10** (nr. Holsworthy)
Lanark. *S Lan* 5B **128**
Lanarth. *Corn* 4E **5**
Lancaster. *Lanc* 3D **97**
Lanchester. *Dur* 5E **115**
Lancing. *W Sus* 5C **26**
Landbeach. *Cambs* 4D **64**
Landcross. *Devn* 4E **19**
Landerberry. *Abers* 3E **153**
Landford. *Wilts* 1A **16**
Land Gate. *G Man* 4D **90**
Landhallow. *High* 5D **169**
Landimore. *Swan* 3D **30**
Landkey. *Devn* 3F **19**
Landkey Newland. *Devn* 3F **19**
Landore. *Swan* 3F **31**
Landport. *Port* 2E **17**
Landrake. *Corn* 2H **7**
Landscove. *Devn* 2D **9**
Land's End (St Just) Airport. *Corn* 4A **4**
Landshipping. *Pemb* 3E **43**
Landulph. *Corn* 2A **8**
Landywood. *Staf* 5D **73**
Lane. *Corn* 2C **6**
Laneast. *Corn* 4C **10**
Lane Bottom. *Lanc* 1G **91**
Lane End. *Buck* 2G **37**
Lane End. *Hants* 4D **24**
Lane End. *IOW* 4E **17**
Lane End. *Wilts* 2D **22**
Lane Ends. *Derbs* 2G **73**
Lane Ends. *Dur* 1E **105**
Lane Ends. *Lanc* 4G **97**
Laneham. *Notts* 3F **87**
Lanehead. *Dur* 5B **114** (nr. Cowshill)
Lane Head. *Dur* 3E **105** (nr. Hutton Magna)
Lane Head. *Dur* 2D **105** (nr. Woodland)
Lane Head. *G Man* 1A **84**
Lanehead. *Nmbd* 1A **114**
Lane Head. *W Yor* 4B **92**
Lane Heads. *Lanc* 1C **90**
Lanercost. *Cumb* 3G **113**
Laneshaw Bridge. *Lanc* 5B **98**
Laney Green. *Staf* 5D **72**
Langais. *W Isl* 2D **170**
Langal. *High* 2B **140**
Langar. *Notts* 2E **74**
Langbank. *Ren* 2E **127**
Langbar. *N Yor* 4C **98**
Langburnshiels. *Bord* 4H **119**
Langcliffe. *N Yor* 3H **97**
Langdale End. *N Yor* 5G **107**
Langdon. *Corn* 3C **10**
Langdon Beck. *Dur* 1B **104**
Langdon Cross. *Corn* 4D **10**
Langdon Hills. *Essx* 2A **40**
Langdown. *Hants* 2C **16**
Langdyke. *Fife* 3F **137**
Langenhoe. *Essx* 4D **54**
Langford. *C Beds* 1B **52**
Langford. *Devn* 2D **12**
Langford. *Essx* 5B **54**
Langford. *Notts* 5F **87**
Langford. *Oxon* 5H **49**
Langford. *Som* 4F **21**
Langford Budville. *Som* 4E **20**
Langham. *Dors* 4C **22**
Langham. *Essx* 2D **54**
Langham. *Norf* 1C **78**
Langham. *Rut* 4F **75**
Langham. *Suff* 4B **66**
Langho. *Lanc* 1F **91**
Langholm. *Dum* 1E **113**
Langland. *Swan* 4F **31**
Langleeford. *Nmbd* 2D **120**
Langley. *Ches E* 3D **84**
Langley. *Derbs* 1B **74**
Langley. *Essx* 2E **53**
Langley. *Glos* 3F **49**
Langley. *Hants* 2C **16**
Langley. *Herts* 3C **52**
Langley. *Kent* 5C **40**
Langley. *Nmbd* 3B **114**
Langley. *Slo* 3B **38**
Langley. *Som* 4D **20**
Langley. *Warw* 4F **61**
Langley. *W Sus* 4G **25**
Langley Burrell. *Wilts* 4E **35**
Langleybury. *Herts* 5A **52**
Langley Common. *Derbs* 2G **73**
Langley Green. *Derbs* 2G **73**
Langley Green. *Norf* 5F **79**
Langley Green. *Warw* 4F **61**
Langley Green. *W Sus* 2D **26**
Langley Heath. *Kent* 5C **40**
Langley Marsh. *Som* 4D **20**
Langley Moor. *Dur* 5F **115**
Langley Park. *Dur* 5F **115**
Langley Street. *Norf* 5F **79**
Langney. *E Sus* 5H **27**
Langold. *Notts* 2C **86**
Langore. *Corn* 4D **10**
Langport. *Som* 4H **21**
Langrick. *Linc* 1B **76**
Langridge. *Bath* 5C **34**
Langridgeford. *Devn* 4F **19**
Langrigg. *Cumb* 5C **112**
Langrish. *Hants* 4F **25**
Langsett. *S Yor* 4C **92**
Langshaw. *Bord* 1H **119**
Langstone. *Hants* 2F **17**
Langthorne. *N Yor* 5F **105**
Langthorpe. *N Yor* 3F **99**
Langthwaite. *N Yor* 4D **104**
Langtoft. *E Yor* 3E **101**
Langtoft. *Linc* 4A **76**
Langton. *Dur* 3E **105**
Langton. *Linc* 4B **88** (nr. Horncastle)
Langton. *Linc* 3C **88** (nr. Spilsby)
Langton. *N Yor* 3B **100**
Langton by Wragby. *Linc* 3A **88**
Langton Green. *Kent* 2G **27**
Langton Herring. *Dors* 4B **14**
Langton Long Blandford. *Dors* 2E **15**
Langton Matravers. *Dors* 5F **15**
Langtree. *Devn* 1E **11**
Langwathby. *Cumb* 1G **103**
Langwith. *Derbs* 4C **86**
Langworth. *Linc* 3H **87**
Lanivet. *Corn* 2E **7**
Lanjeth. *Corn* 3D **6**
Lank. *Corn* 5A **10**
Lanlivery. *Corn* 3E **7**
Lanner. *Corn* 5B **6**
Lanreath. *Corn* 3F **7**
Lansallos. *Corn* 3F **7**
Lansdown. *Bath* 5C **34**
Lansdown. *Glos* 3E **49**
Lanteglos Highway. *Corn* 3F **7**
Lanton. *Nmbd* 1D **120**
Lanton. *Bord* 2A **120**
Lapford. *Devn* 2H **11**
Lapford Cross. *Devn* 2H **11**
Laphroaig. *Arg* 5B **124**
Lapley. *Staf* 4C **72**
Lapworth. *Warw* 3F **61**
Larachbeg. *High* 4A **140**
Larbert. *Falk* 1B **128**
Larden Green. *Ches E* 5H **83**
Larel. *High* 3D **169**
Largie. *Abers* 5D **160**
Largiemore. *Arg* 1H **125**
Largoward. *Fife* 3G **137**
Largs. *N Ayr* 4D **126**
Largue. *Abers* 4D **160**
Largybeg. *N Ayr* 3E **123**
Largymeanoch. *N Ayr* 3E **123**
Largymore. *N Ayr* 3E **123**
Larkfield. *Inv* 2D **126**
Larkfield. *Kent* 5A **40**
Larkhall. *Bath* 5C **34**
Larkhall. *S Lan* 4A **128**
Larkhill. *Wilts* 2G **23**
Larling. *Norf* 2B **66**
Larport. *Here* 2A **48**

Lartington—Little Bognor

Lartington. *Dur* 3D **104**
Lary. *Abers* 3H **151**
Lasham. *Hants* 2E **25**
Lashenden. *Kent* 1C **28**
Lassodie. *Fife* 4D **136**
Lasswade. *Midl* 3G **129**
Lastingham. *N Yor* 5E **107**
Latchford. *Herts* 3D **53**
Latchford. *Oxon* 5E **51**
Latchingdon. *Essx* 5B **54**
Latchley. *Corn* 5E **11**
Latchmere Green. *Hants* 5E **37**
Lathbury. *Mil* 1G **51**
Latheron. *High* 5D **169**
Latheronwheel. *High* 5D **169**
Lathom. *Lanc* 4C **90**
Lathones. *Fife* 3G **137**
Latimer. *Buck* 1B **38**
Latteridge. *S Glo* 3B **34**
Lattiford. *Som* 4B **22**
Latton. *Wilts* 2F **35**
Laudale House. *High* 3B **140**
Lauder. *Bord* 5B **130**
Laugharne. *Carm* 3H **43**
Laughterton. *Linc* 3F **87**
Laughton. *E Sus* 4G **27**
Laughton. *Leics* 2D **62**
Laughton. *Linc* 1F **87**
(nr. Gainsborough)
Laughton. *Linc* 2H **75**
(nr. Grantham)
Laughton Common. *S Yor* 2C **86**
Laughton en le Morthen. *S Yor* 2C **86**
Launcells. *Corn* 2C **10**
Launceston. *Corn* 4D **10**
Launcherley. *Som* 2A **22**
Launton. *Oxon* 3E **50**
Laurencekirk. *Abers* 1G **145**
Laurieston. *Dum* 3D **111**
Laurieston. *Falk* 2C **128**
Lavendon. *Mil* 5G **63**
Lavenham. *Suff* 1C **54**
Laverhay. *Dum* 5D **118**
Laversdale. *Cumb* 3F **113**
Laverstock. *Wilts* 3G **23**
Laverstoke. *Hants* 2C **24**
Laverton. *Glos* 2F **49**
Laverton. *N Yor* 2E **99**
Laverton. *Som* 1C **22**
Lavister. *Wrex* 5F **83**
Law. *S Lan* 4B **128**
Lawers. *Per* 5D **142**
Lawford. *Essx* 2D **54**
Lawhitton. *Corn* 4D **10**
Lawkland. *N Yor* 3G **97**
Lawley. *Shrp* 5A **72**
Lawnhead. *Staf* 3C **72**
Lawrenny. *Pemb* 4E **43**
Lawshall. *Suff* 5A **66**
Lawton. *Here* 5G **59**
Laxey. *IOM* 3D **108**
Laxfield. *Suff* 3E **67**
Laxfirth. *Shet* 6F **173**
Laxo. *Shet* 5F **173**
Laxton. *E Yor* 2A **94**
Laxton. *Nptn* 1G **63**
Laxton. *Notts* 4E **86**
Laycock. *W Yor* 5C **98**
Layer Breton. *Essx* 4C **54**
Layer-de-la-Haye. *Essx* 3C **54**
Layer Marney. *Essx* 4C **54**
Layland's Green. *W Ber* 5B **36**
Laymore. *Dors* 2G **13**
Laysters Pole. *Here* 4H **59**
Layter's Green. *Buck* 1A **38**
Laytham. *E Yor* 1H **93**
Lazenby. *Red C* 3C **106**
Lazonby. *Cumb* 1G **103**
Lea. *Derbs* 5H **85**
Lea. *Here* 3B **48**
Lea. *Linc* 2F **87**
Lea. *Shrp* 2F **59**
(nr. Bishop's Castle)
Lea. *Shrp* 5G **71**
(nr. Shrewsbury)
Lea. *Wilts* 3E **35**
Leabrooks. *Derbs* 5B **86**
Leac a Li. *W Isl* 8D **171**
Leachd. *Arg* 4H **133**
Leachkin. *High* 4A **158**
Leachpool. *Pemb* 3D **42**
Leadburn. *Midl* 4F **129**
Leadenham. *Linc* 5G **87**
Leaden Roding. *Essx* 4F **53**
Leaderfoot. *Bord* 1H **119**
Leadgate. *Cumb* 5A **114**
Leadgate. *Dur* 4E **115**
Leadgate. *Nmbd* 4E **115**
Leadhills. *S Lan* 3A **118**
Leadingcross Green. *Kent* 5C **40**
Lea End. *Worc* 3E **61**
Leafield. *Oxon* 4B **50**
Leagrave. *Lutn* 3A **52**
Lea Hall. *W Mid* 2F **61**
Lea Heath. *Staf* 3E **73**
Leake. *N Yor* 5B **106**
Leake Common Side. *Linc* 5C **88**
Leake Fold Hill. *Linc* 5D **88**
Leake Hurn's End. *Linc* 1D **76**
Lealholm. *N Yor* 4E **107**
Lealt. *Arg* 4D **132**
Lealt. *High* 2E **155**
Leam. *Derbs* 3G **85**
Lea Marston. *Warw* 1G **61**
Leamington Hastings. *Warw* 4B **62**
Leamington Spa, Royal. *Warw* 4H **61**
Leamonsley. *Staf* 5F **73**
Leamside. *Dur* 5G **115**
Leargybreck. *Arg* 2D **124**
Lease Rigg. *N Yor* 4F **107**
Leasgill. *Cumb* 1D **97**
Leasingham. *Linc* 1H **75**
Leasingthorne. *Dur* 1F **105**
Leasowe. *Mers* 1E **83**
Leatherhead. *Surr* 5C **38**
Leathley. *N Yor* 5E **99**
Leaths. *Dum* 3E **111**
Leaton. *Shrp* 4G **71**
Leaton. *Telf* 4A **72**
Lea Town. *Lanc* 1C **90**
Leaveland. *Kent* 5E **40**
Leavenheath. *Suff* 2C **54**
Leavening. *N Yor* 3B **100**
Leaves Green. *G Lon* 4F **39**
Lea Yeat. *Cumb* 1G **97**
Leazes. *Dur* 4E **115**
Lebberston. *N Yor* 1E **101**
Lechlade on Thames. *Glos* 2H **35**
Leck. *Lanc* 2F **97**
Leckford. *Hants* 3B **24**
Leckfurin. *High* 3H **167**
Leckgruinart. *Arg* 3A **124**
Leckhampstead. *Buck* 2F **51**
Leckhampstead. *W Ber* 4C **36**
Leckhampstead Street. *W Ber* 4C **36**
Leckhampton. *Glos* 4E **49**
Leckmelm. *High* 4F **163**
Leckwith. *V Glam* 4E **33**
Leconfield. *E Yor* 5E **101**
Ledaig. *Arg* 5D **140**
Ledburn. *Buck* 3H **51**
Ledbury. *Here* 2C **48**
Ledgemoor. *Here* 5G **59**
Ledgowan. *High* 3D **156**
Ledicot. *Here* 4G **59**
Ledmore. *High* 2G **163**
Lednabirichen. *High* 4E **165**
Lednagullin. *High* 2A **168**
Ledsham. *Ches W* 3F **83**
Ledsham. *W Yor* 2E **93**
Ledston. *W Yor* 2E **93**
Ledstone. *Devn* 4D **8**
Ledwell. *Oxon* 3C **50**
Lee. *Devn* 2E **19**
(nr. Ilfracombe)
Lee. *Devn* 4B **20**
(nr. South Molton)
Lee. *G Lon* 3F **39**
Lee. *Hants* 1B **16**
Lee. *Lanc* 4E **97**
Lee. *Shrp* 2G **71**
Leeans. *Shet* 7E **173**
Leebotten. *Shet* 9F **173**
Leebotwood. *Shrp* 1G **59**
Lee Brockhurst. *Shrp* 3H **71**
Leece. *Cumb* 3B **96**
Leechpool. *Mon* 3A **34**
Lee Clump. *Buck* 5H **51**
Leeds. *Kent* 5C **40**
Leeds. *W Yor* 1C **92** & **199**
Leeds Bradford International Airport. *W Yor* 5E **98**
Leedstown. *Corn* 3D **4**
Leegomery. *Telf* 4A **72**
Lee Head. *Derbs* 1E **85**
Leek. *Staf* 5D **85**
Leekbrook. *Staf* 5D **85**
Leek Wootton. *Warw* 4G **61**
Lee Mill. *Devn* 3B **8**
Leeming. *N Yor* 1E **99**
Leeming Bar. *N Yor* 5F **105**
Lee Moor. *Devn* 2B **8**
Lee Moor. *W Yor* 2D **92**
Lee-on-the-Solent. *Hants* 2D **16**
Lees. *Derbs* 2G **73**
Lees. *G Man* 4H **91**
Lees. *W Yor* 1A **92**
Lees, The. *Kent* 5E **40**
Leeswood. *Flin* 4E **83**
Lee, The. *Buck* 5H **51**
Leetown. *Per* 1E **136**
Leftwich. *Ches W* 3A **84**
Legbourne. *Linc* 2C **88**
Legburthwaite. *Cumb* 3E **102**
Legerwood. *Bord* 5B **130**
Legsby. *Linc* 2A **88**
Leicester. *Leic* 5C **74** & **200**
Leicester Forest East. *Leics* 5C **74**
Leigh. *Dors* 2B **14**
Leigh. *G Man* 4E **91**
Leigh. *Kent* 1G **27**
Leigh. *Shrp* 5F **71**
Leigh. *Surr* 1D **26**
Leigh. *Wilts* 2F **35**
Leigh. *Worc* 5B **60**
Leigham. *Plym* 3B **8**
Leigh Beck. *Essx* 2C **40**
Leigh Common. *Som* 4C **22**
Leigh Delamere. *Wilts* 4D **35**
Leigh Green. *Kent* 2D **28**
Leighland Chapel. *Som* 3D **20**
Leigh-on-Sea. *S'end* 2C **40**
Leigh Park. *Hants* 2F **17**
Leigh Sinton. *Worc* 5B **60**
Leighterton. *Glos* 2D **34**
Leigh, The. *Glos* 3D **48**
Leighton. *N Yor* 2D **98**
Leighton. *Powy* 5E **71**
Leighton. *Shrp* 5A **72**
Leighton. *Som* 2C **22**
Leighton Bromswold. *Cambs* 3A **64**
Leighton Buzzard. *C Beds* 3H **51**
Leigh-upon-Mendip. *Som* 2B **22**
Leinthall Earls. *Here* 4G **59**
Leinthall Starkes. *Here* 4G **59**
Leintwardine. *Here* 3G **59**
Leire. *Leics* 1C **62**
Leirinmore. *High* 2E **166**
Leishmore. *High* 4G **157**
Leiston. *Suff* 4G **67**
Leitfie. *Per* 4B **144**
Leith. *Edin* 2F **129**
Leitholm. *Bord* 5D **130**
Lelant. *Corn* 3C **4**
Lelant Downs. *Corn* 3C **4**
Lelley. *E Yor* 1F **95**
Lem Hill. *Worc* 3B **60**
Lemington. *Tyne* 3E **115**
Lemmington Hall. *Nmbd* 3F **121**
Lempitlaw. *Bord* 1B **120**
Lemsford. *Herts* 4C **52**
Lenacre. *Cumb* 1F **97**
Lenchie. *Abers* 5C **160**
Lenchwick. *Worc* 1F **49**
Lendalfoot. *S Ayr* 5A **116**
Lendrick. *Stir* 3E **135**
Lenham. *Kent* 5C **40**
Lenham Heath. *Kent* 1D **28**
Lenimore. *N Ayr* 5G **125**
Lennel. *Bord* 5E **131**
Lennoxtown. *E Dun* 2H **127**
Lenton. *Linc* 2H **75**
Lentran. *High* 4H **157**
Lenwade. *Norf* 4C **78**
Lenzie. *E Dun* 2H **127**
Leochel Cushnie. *Abers* 2C **152**
Leogh. *Shet* 1B **172**
Leominster. *Here* 5G **59**
Leonard Stanley. *Glos* 5D **48**
Lepe. *Hants* 3C **16**
Lephenstrath. *Arg* 5A **122**
Lephin. *High* 4A **154**
Lephinchapel. *Arg* 4G **133**
Lephinmore. *Arg* 4G **133**
Leppington. *N Yor* 3B **100**
Lepton. *W Yor* 3C **92**
Lerryn. *Corn* 3F **7**
Lerwick. *Shet* 7F **173**
Lerwick (Tingwall) Airport. *Shet* 7F **173**
Lesbury. *Nmbd* 3G **121**
Leslie. *Abers* 1C **152**
Leslie. *Fife* 3E **137**
Lesmahagow. *S Lan* 1H **117**
Lesnewth. *Corn* 3B **10**
Lessingham. *Norf* 3F **79**
Lessonhall. *Cumb* 4D **112**
Leswalt. *Dum* 3F **109**
Letchmore Heath. *Herts* 1C **38**
Letchworth Garden City. *Herts* 2C **52**
Letcombe Bassett. *Oxon* 3B **36**
Letcombe Regis. *Oxon* 3B **36**
Letham. *Ang* 4E **145**
Letham. *Falk* 1B **128**
Letham. *Fife* 2F **137**
Lethanhill. *E Ayr* 3D **116**
Lethenty. *Abers* 4F **161**
Letheringham. *Suff* 5E **67**
Letheringsett. *Norf* 2C **78**
Lettaford. *Devn* 4H **11**
Lettan. *Orkn* 3G **172**
Letter. *Abers* 2E **153**
Letterewe. *High* 1B **156**
Letterfearn. *High* 1A **148**
Lettermore. *Arg* 4F **139**
Letters. *High* 5F **163**
Letterston. *Pemb* 2D **42**
Letton. *Here* 1G **47**
(nr. Kington)
Letton. *Here* 3F **59**
(nr. Leintwardine)
Letty Green. *Herts* 4C **52**
Letwell. *S Yor* 2C **86**
Leuchars. *Fife* 1G **137**
Leumrabhagh. *W Isl* 6F **171**
Leusdon. *Devn* 5H **11**
Levaneap. *Shet* 5F **173**
Levedale. *Staf* 4C **72**
Leven. *E Yor* 5F **101**
Leven. *Fife* 3F **137**
Levencorroch. *N Ayr* 3E **123**
Levenhall. *E Lot* 2G **129**
Levens. *Cumb* 1D **97**
Levens Green. *Herts* 3D **52**
Levenshulme. *G Man* 1C **84**
Levenwick. *Shet* 9F **173**
Leverburgh. *W Isl* 9C **171**
Leverington. *Cambs* 4D **76**
Leverton. *Linc* 1C **76**
Leverton. *W Ber* 4B **36**
Leverton Lucasgate. *Linc* 1D **76**
Leverton Outgate. *Linc* 1D **76**
Levington. *Suff* 2F **55**
Levisham. *N Yor* 5F **107**
Levishie. *High* 2G **149**
Lew. *Oxon* 5B **50**
Lewaigue. *IOM* 2D **108**
Lewannick. *Corn* 4C **10**
Lewdown. *Devn* 4E **11**
Lewes. *E Sus* 4F **27**
Leweston. *Pemb* 2D **42**
Lewisham. *G Lon* 3E **39**
Lewiston. *High* 1H **149**
Lewistown. *B'end* 3C **32**
Lewknor. *Oxon* 2F **37**
Leworthy. *Devn* 3G **19**
(nr. Barnstaple)
Leworthy. *Devn* 2D **10**
(nr. Holsworthy)
Lewson Street. *Kent* 4D **40**
Lewthorn Cross. *Devn* 5A **12**
Lewtrenchard. *Devn* 4E **11**
Ley. *Corn* 2F **7**
Leybourne. *Kent* 5A **40**
Leyburn. *N Yor* 5E **105**
Leycett. *Staf* 1B **72**
Leyfields. *Staf* 5G **73**
Ley Green. *Herts* 3B **52**
Ley Hill. *Buck* 5H **51**
Leyland. *Lanc* 2D **90**
Leylodge. *Abers* 2E **153**
Leymoor. *W Yor* 3B **92**
Leys. *Per* 5B **144**
Leysdown-on-Sea. *Kent* 3E **41**
Leysmill. *Ang* 4F **145**
Leyton. *G Lon* 2E **39**
Leytonstone. *G Lon* 2F **39**
Lezant. *Corn* 5D **10**
Leziate. *Norf* 4F **77**
Lhanbryde. *Mor* 2G **159**
Lhen, The. *IOM* 1C **108**
Liatrie. *High* 5E **157**
Libanus. *Powy* 3C **46**
Libberton. *S Lan* 5C **128**
Libbery. *Worc* 5D **60**
Liberton. *Edin* 3F **129**
Liceasto. *W Isl* 8D **171**
Lichfield. *Staf* 5F **73**
Lickey. *Worc* 3D **61**
Lickey End. *Worc* 3D **61**
Lickfold. *W Sus* 3A **26**
Liddaton. *Devn* 4E **11**
Liddington. *Swin* 3H **35**
Liddle. *Orkn* 9D **172**
Lidgate. *Suff* 5G **65**
Lidgett. *Notts* 4D **86**
Lidham Hill. *E Sus* 4C **28**
Lidlington. *C Beds* 2H **51**
Lidsey. *W Sus* 5A **26**
Lidstone. *Oxon* 3B **50**
Lienassie. *High* 1B **148**
Liff. *Ang* 5C **144**
Lifford. *W Mid* 2E **61**
Lifton. *Devn* 4D **11**
Liftondown. *Devn* 4D **10**
Lighthorne. *Warw* 5H **61**
Light Oaks. *Staf* 5D **84**
Lightwater. *Surr* 4A **38**
Lightwood. *Staf* 1E **73**
Lightwood. *Stoke* 1D **72**
Lightwood Green. *Ches E* 1A **72**
Lightwood Green. *Wrex* 1F **71**
Lilbourne. *Nptn* 3C **62**
Lilburn Tower. *Nmbd* 2E **121**
Lillesdon. *Som* 4G **21**
Lilleshall. *Telf* 4B **72**
Lilley. *Herts* 3B **52**
Lilliesleaf. *Bord* 2H **119**
Lillingstone Dayrell. *Buck* 2F **51**
Lillingstone Lovell. *Buck* 1F **51**
Lillington. *Dors* 1B **14**
Lilstock. *Som* 2E **21**
Lilybank. *Inv* 2E **126**
Lilyhurst. *Shrp* 4B **72**
Limbrick. *Lanc* 3E **90**
Limbury. *Lutn* 3A **52**
Limekilnburn. *S Lan* 4A **128**
Limekilns. *Fife* 1D **129**
Limerigg. *Falk* 2B **128**
Limestone Brae. *Nmbd* 5A **114**
Lime Street. *Worc* 2D **48**
Limington. *Som* 4A **22**
Limpenhoe. *Norf* 5F **79**
Limpley Stoke. *Wilts* 5C **34**
Limpsfield. *Surr* 5E **39**
Limpsfield Chart. *Surr* 5F **39**
Linburn. *W Lot* 3E **129**
Linby. *Notts* 5C **86**
Linchmere. *W Sus* 3G **25**
Lincluden. *Dum* 2A **112**
Lincoln. *Linc* 3G **87** & **198**
Lincomb. *Worc* 4C **60**
Lindale. *Cumb* 1D **96**
Lindal in Furness. *Cumb* 2B **96**
Lindean. *Bord* 1G **119**
Linden. *Glos* 4D **48**
Lindfield. *W Sus* 3E **27**
Lindford. *Hants* 3G **25**
Lindores. *Fife* 2E **137**
Lindridge. *Worc* 4A **60**
Lindsell. *Essx* 3G **53**
Lindsey. *Suff* 1C **54**
Lindsey Tye. *Suff* 1C **54**
Linford. *Hants* 2G **15**
Linford. *Thur* 3A **40**
Lingague. *IOM* 4B **108**
Lingdale. *Red C* 3D **106**
Lingen. *Here* 4F **59**
Lingfield. *Surr* 1E **27**
Lingoed. *Mon* 3G **47**
Lingreabhagh. *W Isl* 9C **171**
Ling, The. *Norf* 1F **67**
Lingwood. *Norf* 5F **79**
Lingy Close. *Cumb* 4E **113**
Linicro. *High* 2C **154**
Linkend. *Worc* 2D **48**
Linkenholt. *Hants* 1B **24**
Linkinhorne. *Corn* 5D **10**
Linklater. *Orkn* 9D **172**
Linksness. *Orkn* 7B **172**
(on Hoy)
Linksness. *Orkn* 6E **172**
(on Mainland)
Linktown. *Fife* 4E **137**
Linkwood. *Mor* 2G **159**
Linley. *Shrp* 1F **59**
(nr. Bishop's Castle)
Linley. *Shrp* 1A **60**
(nr. Bridgnorth)
Linley Green. *Here* 5A **60**
Linlithgow. *W Lot* 2C **128**
Linlithgow Bridge. *Falk* 2C **128**
Linneraineach. *High* 3F **163**
Linshiels. *Nmbd* 4C **120**
Linsiadar. *W Isl* 4E **171**
Linsidemore. *High* 4C **164**
Linslade. *C Beds* 3H **51**
Linstead Parva. *Suff* 3F **67**
Linstock. *Cumb* 4F **113**
Linthwaite. *W Yor* 3B **92**
Lintlaw. *Bord* 4E **131**
Lintmill. *Mor* 2C **160**
Linton. *Cambs* 1F **53**
Linton. *Derbs* 4G **73**
Linton. *Here* 3B **48**
Linton. *Kent* 5B **40**
Linton. *N Yor* 3B **98**
Linton. *Bord* 2B **120**
Linton. *W Yor* 5F **99**
Linton Colliery. *Nmbd* 5G **121**
Linton Hill. *Here* 3B **48**
Linton-on-Ouse. *N Yor* 3G **99**
Lintzford. *Tyne* 4E **115**
Lintzgarth. *Dur* 5C **114**
Linwood. *Hants* 2G **15**
Linwood. *Linc* 2A **88**
Linwood. *Ren* 3F **127**
Lionacleit. *W Isl* 4C **170**
Lionacro. *High* 2C **154**
Lionacuidhe. *W Isl* 4C **170**
Lional. *W Isl* 1H **171**
Liphook. *Hants* 3G **25**
Lipley. *Shrp* 2B **72**
Lipyeate. *Som* 1B **22**
Liquo. *N Lan* 4B **128**
Liscard. *Mers* 1F **83**
Liscombe. *Som* 3B **20**
Liskeard. *Corn* 2G **7**
Lisle Court. *Hants* 3B **16**
Liss. *Hants* 4F **25**
Lissett. *E Yor* 4F **101**
Liss Forest. *Hants* 4F **25**
Lissington. *Linc* 2A **88**
Liston. *Essx* 1B **54**
Lisvane. *Card* 3E **33**
Liswerry. *Newp* 3G **33**
Litcham. *Norf* 4A **78**
Litchard. *B'end* 3C **32**
Litchborough. *Nptn* 5D **62**
Litchfield. *Hants* 1C **24**
Litherland. *Mers* 1F **83**
Litlington. *Cambs* 1D **52**
Litlington. *E Sus* 5G **27**
Littemill. *Nmbd* 3G **121**
Litterty. *Abers* 3E **161**
Little Abington. *Cambs* 1F **53**
Little Addington. *Nptn* 3G **63**
Little Airmyn. *N Yor* 2H **93**
Little Alne. *Warw* 4F **61**
Little Ardo. *Abers* 5F **161**
Little Asby. *Cumb* 4H **103**
Little Aston. *Staf* 5E **73**
Little Atherfield. *IOW* 4C **16**
Little Ayton. *N Yor* 3C **106**
Little Baddow. *Essx* 5A **54**
Little Badminton. *S Glo* 3D **34**
Little Ballinluig. *Per* 3G **143**
Little Bampton. *Cumb* 4D **112**
Little Bardfield. *Essx* 2G **53**
Little Barford. *Bed* 5A **64**
Little Barningham. *Norf* 2D **78**
Little Barrington. *Glos* 4H **49**
Little Barrow. *Ches W* 4G **83**
Little Barugh. *N Yor* 2B **100**
Little Bavington. *Nmbd* 2C **114**
Little Bealings. *Suff* 1F **55**
Littlebeck. *Cumb* 3H **103**
Little Bedwyn. *Wilts* 5A **36**
Little Bentley. *Essx* 3E **54**
Little Berkhamsted. *Herts* 5C **52**
Little Billing. *Nptn* 4F **63**
Little Billington. *C Beds* 3H **51**
Little Birch. *Here* 2A **48**
Little Bispham. *Bkpl* 5C **96**
Little Blakenham. *Suff* 1E **54**
Little Blencow. *Cumb* 1F **103**
Little Bognor. *W Sus* 3B **26**

Little Bolas. Shrp 3A 72
Little Bollington. Ches E 2B 84
Little Bookham. Surr 5C 38
Littleborough. Devn 1B 12
Littleborough. G Man 3H 91
Littleborough. Notts 2F 87
Littlebourne. Kent 5G 41
Little Bourton. Oxon 1C 50
Little Bowden. Leics 2E 63
Little Bradley. Suff 5F 65
Little Brampton. Shrp 2F 59
Little Brechin. Ang 2E 145
Littlebredy. Dors 4A 14
Little Brickhill. Mil 2H 51
Little Bridgeford. Staf 3C 72
Little Brington. Nptn 4D 62
Little Bromley. Essx 3D 54
Little Broughton. Cumb 1B 102
Little Budworth. Ches W 4H 83
Little Burstead. Essx 1A 40
Little Burton. E Yor 5F 101
Littlebury. Essx 2F 53
Littlebury Green. Essx 2E 53
Little Bytham. Linc 4H 75
Little Canfield. Essx 3F 53
Little Canford. Dors 3F 15
Little Carlton. Linc 2C 88
Little Carlton. Notts 5E 87
Little Casterton. Rut 5H 75
Little Catwick. E Yor 5F 101
Little Catworth. Cambs 3A 64
Little Cawthorpe. Linc 2C 88
Little Chalfont. Buck 1A 38
Little Chart. Kent 1D 28
Little Chesterford. Essx 1F 53
Little Cheverell. Wilts 1E 23
Little Chishill. Cambs 2E 53
Little Clacton. Essx 4E 55
Little Clanfield. Oxon 5A 50
Little Clifton. Cumb 2B 102
Little Coates. NE Lin 4F 95
Little Comberton. Worc 1E 49
Little Common. E Sus 5B 28
Little Compton. Warw 2A 50
Little Cornard. Suff 2B 54
Littlecote. Buck 3G 51
Littlecott. Wilts 1G 23
Little Cowarne. Here 5A 60
Little Coxwell. Oxon 2A 36
Little Crakehall. N Yor 5F 105
Little Crawley. Mil 1H 51
Little Creich. High 5D 164
Little Cressingham. Norf 5A 78
Little Crosby. Mers 4B 90
Little Crosthwaite. Cumb 2D 102
Little Cubley. Derbs 2F 73
Little Dalby. Leics 4E 75
Little Dawley. Telf 5A 72
Littledean. Glos 4B 48
Little Dens. Abers 4H 161
Little Dewchurch. Here 2A 48
Little Ditton. Cambs 5F 65
Littledown. Dors 4B 14
Little Down. Hants 1B 24
Little Downham. Cambs 2E 65
Little Drayton. Shrp 2A 72
Little Driffield. E Yor 4E 101
Little Dunham. Norf 4A 78
Little Dunkeld. Per 4H 143
Little Dunmow. Essx 3G 53
Little Easton. Essx 3G 53
Little Eaton. Derbs 1A 74
Little Eccleston. Lanc 5D 96
Little Ellingham. Norf 1C 66
Little Elm. Som 2C 22
Little End. Essx 5F 53
Little Everdon. Nptn 5C 62
Little Eversden. Cambs 5C 64
Little Faringdon. Oxon 5H 49
Little Fencote. N Yor 5F 105
Little Fenton. N Yor 1F 93
Littleferry. High 4F 165
Little Fransham. Norf 4B 78
Little Gaddesden. Herts 4H 51
Little Garway. Here 3H 47
Little Gidding. Cambs 2A 64
Little Glemham. Suff 5F 67
Little Glenshee. Per 5G 143
Little Gransden. Cambs 5B 64
Little Green. Suff 3C 66
Little Green. Wrex 1G 71
Little Grimsby. Linc 1C 88
Little Habton. N Yor 2B 100
Little Hadham. Herts 3E 53
Little Hale. Linc 1A 76
Little Hallingbury. Essx 4E 53
Littleham. Devn 4E 19
(nr. Bideford)
Littleham. Devn 4D 12
(nr. Exmouth)
Little Hampden. Buck 5G 51
Littlehampton. W Sus 5B 26
Little Haresfield. Glos 5D 48
Little Harrowden. Nptn 3F 63
Little Haseley. Oxon 5E 51
Little Hatfield. E Yor 5F 101
Little Hautbois. Norf 3E 79
Little Haven. Pemb 3C 42
Little Hay. Staf 5F 73
Little Hayfield. Derbs 2E 85
Little Haywood. Staf 3E 73
Little Heath. W Mid 2H 61
Little Heck. N Yor 2F 93

Littlehempston. Devn 2E 9
Little Herbert's. Glos 3E 49
Little Hereford. Here 4H 59
Little Horkesley. Essx 2C 54
Little Hormead. Herts 3E 53
Little Horsted. E Sus 4F 27
Little Horton. W Yor 1B 92
Little Horwood. Buck 2F 51
Little Houghton. Nptn 5F 63
Little Houghton. S Yor 4E 93
Little Hucklow. Derbs 3F 85
Little Hulton. G Man 4F 91
Little Irchester. Nptn 4G 63
Little Kelk. E Yor 3E 101
Little Kimble. Buck 5G 51
Little Kineton. Warw 5H 61
Little Kingshill. Buck 2G 37
Little Langdale. Cumb 4E 102
Little Langford. Wilts 3F 23
Little Laver. Essx 5F 53
Little Lawford. Warw 3B 62
Little Leigh. Ches W 3A 84
Little Leighs. Essx 4H 53
Little Leven. E Yor 5E 101
Little Lever. G Man 4F 91
Little Linford. Mil 1G 51
Little London. Buck 4E 51
Little London. E Sus 4G 27
Little London. Hants 2B 24
(nr. Andover)
Little London. Hants 1E 24
(nr. Basingstoke)
Little London. Linc 3D 76
(nr. Long Sutton)
Little London. Linc 3B 76
(nr. Spalding)
Little London. Norf 2E 79
(nr. North Walsham)
Little London. Norf 1G 65
(nr. Northwold)
Little London. Norf 2D 78
(nr. Saxthorpe)
Little London. Norf 1F 65
(nr. Southery)
Little London. Powy 2C 58
Little Longstone. Derbs 3F 85
Little Malvern. Worc 1C 48
Little Maplestead. Essx 2B 54
Little Marcle. Here 2B 48
Little Marlow. Buck 3G 37
Little Massingham. Norf 3G 77
Little Melton. Norf 5D 78
Littlemill. Abers 4H 151
Littlemill. E Ayr 3D 116
Littlemill. High 4D 158
Little Mill. Mon 5G 47
Little Milton. Oxon 5E 50
Little Missenden. Buck 1A 38
Littlemoor. Derbs 4A 86
Littlemoor. Dors 4B 14
Littlemore. Oxon 5D 50
Little Mountain. Flin 4E 83
Little Musgrave. Cumb 3A 104
Little Ness. Shrp 4G 71
Little Neston. Ches W 3F 83
Little Newcastle. Pemb 2D 43
Little Newsham. Dur 3E 105
Little Oakley. Essx 3F 55
Little Oakley. Nptn 2F 63
Little Onn. Staf 4C 72
Little Ormside. Cumb 3A 104
Little Orton. Cumb 4E 113
Little Orton. Leics 5H 73
Little Ouse. Norf 2F 65
Little Ouseburn. N Yor 3G 99
Littleover. Derb 2H 73
Little Packington. Warw 2G 61
Little Paxton. Cambs 4A 64
Little Petherick. Corn 1D 6
Little Plumpton. Lanc 1B 90
Little Plumstead. Norf 4F 79
Little Ponton. Linc 2G 75
Littleport. Cambs 2E 65
Little Posbrook. Hants 2D 16
Little Potheridge. Devn 1F 11
Little Preston. Nptn 5C 62
Little Raveley. Cambs 3B 64
Little Reynoldston. Swan 4D 31
Little Ribston. N Yor 4F 99
Little Rissington. Glos 4G 49
Little Rogart. High 3E 165
Little Rollright. Oxon 2A 50
Little Ryburgh. Norf 3B 78
Little Ryle. Nmbd 3E 121
Little Ryton. Shrp 5G 71
Little Salkeld. Cumb 1G 103
Little Sampford. Essx 2G 53
Little Sandhurst. Brac 5G 37
Little Saredon. Staf 5D 72
Little Saxham. Suff 4G 65
Little Scatwell. High 3F 157
Little Shelford. Cambs 5D 64
Little Shoddesden. Hants 2A 24
Little Singleton. Lanc 1B 90
Little Smeaton. N Yor 3F 93
Little Snoring. Norf 2B 78
Little Sodbury. S Glo 3C 34
Little Somborne. Hants 3B 24
Little Somerford. Wilts 3E 35
Little Soudley. Shrp 3B 72
Little Stainforth. N Yor 3H 97

Little Stainton. Darl 2A 106
Little Stanney. Ches W 3G 83
Little Staughton. Bed 4A 64
Little Steeping. Linc 4D 88
Littlester. Shet 3G 173
Little Stoke. Staf 2D 72
Littlestone-on-Sea. Kent 3E 29
Little Stonham. Suff 4D 66
Little Stretton. Leics 5D 74
Little Stretton. Shrp 1G 59
Little Strickland. Cumb 3G 103
Little Stukeley. Cambs 3B 64
Little Sugnall. Staf 2C 72
Little Sutton. Ches W 3F 83
Little Sutton. Linc 3D 76
Little Swinburne. Nmbd 2C 114
Little Tew. Oxon 3B 50
Little Tey. Essx 3B 54
Little Thetford. Cambs 3E 65
Little Thirkleby. N Yor 2G 99
Little Thornage. Norf 2C 78
Little Thornton. Lanc 5C 96
Littlethorpe. Leics 1C 62
Littlethorpe. N Yor 3F 99
Little Thorpe. W Yor 2B 92
Little Thurlow. Suff 5F 65
Little Thurrock. Thur 3H 39
Littleton. Ches W 4G 83
Littleton. Hants 3C 24
Littleton. Som 3H 21
Littleton. Surr 1A 26
(nr. Guildford)
Littleton. Surr 4B 38
(nr. Staines)
Littleton Drew. Wilts 3D 34
Littleton Pannell. Wilts 1E 23
Littleton-upon-Severn. S Glo . . .3A 34
Little Torboll. High 4E 165
Little Torrington. Devn 1E 11
Little Totham. Essx 4B 54
Little Town. Cumb 3D 102
Littletown. Dur 5G 115
Littletown. High 5E 165
Little Twycross. Leics 5H 73
Little Urswick. Cumb 2B 96
Little Wakering. Essx 2D 40
Little Walden. Essx 1F 53
Little Waldingfield. Suff 1C 54
Little Walsingham. Norf 2B 78
Little Waltham. Essx 4H 53
Little Warley. Essx 1H 39
Little Washbourne. Glos 2E 49
Little Weighton. E Yor 1C 94
Little Wenham. Suff 2D 54
Little Wenlock. Telf 5A 72
Little Whelnetham. Suff 5A 66
Little Whittingham Green.
Suff 3E 67
Littlewick Green. Wind 4G 37
Little Wilbraham. Cambs 5E 65
Littlewindsor. Dors 2H 13
Little Wisbeach. Linc 2A 76
Little Witcombe. Glos 4E 49
Little Witley. Worc 4B 60
Little Wittenham. Oxon 2D 36
Little Wolford. Warw 2A 50
Littleworth. Bed 1A 52
Littleworth. Glos 2G 49
Littleworth. Oxon 2B 36
Littleworth. Staf 4E 73
(nr. Cannock)
Littleworth. Staf 3B 72
(nr. Eccleshall)
Littleworth. Staf 3D 72
(nr. Stafford)
Littleworth. W Sus 3C 26
Littleworth. Worc 4D 61
(nr. Redditch)
Littleworth. Worc 1D 49
(nr. Worcester)
Little Wratting. Suff 1G 53
Little Wymington. Nptn 4G 63
Little Wymondley. Herts 3C 52
Little Wyrley. Staf 5E 73
Little Yeldham. Essx 2A 54
Litton. Derbs 3F 85
Litton. N Yor 2B 98
Litton. Som 1A 22
Litton Cheney. Dors 3A 14
Liurbost. W Isl 5F 171
Liverpool. Mers . . . . . .1F 83 & 200
Liverpool John Lennon Airport.
Mers 2G 83
Liversedge. W Yor 2B 92
Liverton. Devn 5B 12
Liverton. Red C 3E 107
Liverton Mines. Red C 3E 107
Livingston. W Lot 3D 128
Livingston Village. W Lot 3D 128
Lixwm. Flin 3D 82
Lizard. Corn 5E 5
Llaingoch. IOA 2B 80
Llaithddu. Powy 2C 58
Llampha. V Glam 4C 32
Llan. Powy 5A 70
Llanaber. Gwyn 4F 69
Llanaelhaearn. Gwyn 1C 68
Llanaeron. Cdgn 4D 57
Llanafan. Cdgn 3F 57
Llanafan-fawr. Powy 5B 58

Llanafan-fechan. Powy 5B 58
Llanallgo. IOA 2D 81
Llanandras. Powy 4F 59
Llananno. Powy 3C 58
Llanarmon. Gwyn 2D 68
Llanarmon Dyffryn Ceiriog.
Wrex 2D 70
Llanarmon-yn-Ial. Den 5D 82
Llanarth. Cdgn 5D 56
Llanarth. Mon 4G 47
Llanarthne. Carm 3F 45
Llanasa. Flin 2D 82
Llanbabo. IOA 2C 80
Llanbadarn Fawr. Cdgn 2F 57
Llanbadarn Fynydd. Powy 3C 58
Llanbadarn-y-garreg. Powy 1E 46
Llanbadoc. Mon 5G 47
Llanbadrig. IOA 1C 80
Llanbeder. Newp 2G 33
Llanbedr. Gwyn 3E 69
Llanbedr. Powy 3F 47
(nr. Crickhowell)
Llanbedr. Powy 1E 47
(nr. Hay-on-Wye)
Llanbedr-Dyffryn-Clwyd. Den . .5D 82
Llanbedrgoch. IOA 2E 81
Llanbedrog. Gwyn 2C 68
Llanbedr Pont Steffan. Cdgn . . .1F 45
Llanbedr-y-cennin. Cnwy 4G 81
Llanberis. Gwyn 4E 81
Llanbethery. V Glam 5D 32
Llanbister. Powy 3D 58
Llanblethian. V Glam 4C 32
Llanboidy. Carm 2G 43
Llanbradach. Cphy 2E 33
Llanbrynmair. Powy 5A 70
Llanbydderi. V Glam 5D 32
Llancadle. V Glam 5D 32
Llancarfan. V Glam 4D 32
Llancatal. V Glam 5D 32
Llancayo. Mon 5G 47
Llancloudy. Here 3H 47
Llancoch. Powy 3E 58
Llancynfelyn. Cdgn 1F 57
Llandaff. Card 4E 33
Llandanwg. Gwyn 3E 69
Llandarcy. Neat 3G 31
Llandawke. Carm 3G 43
Llanddaniel-Fab. IOA 3D 81
Llanddarog. Carm 4F 45
Llanddeiniol. Cdgn 3E 57
Llanddeiniolen. Gwyn 4E 81
Llandderfel. Gwyn 2B 70
Llanddeusant. Carm 3A 46
Llanddeusant. IOA 2C 80
Llanddew. Powy 2D 46
Llanddewi. Swan 4D 30
Llanddewi Brefi. Cdgn 5F 57
Llanddewi'r Cwm. Powy 1D 46
Llanddewi Rhydderch. Mon 4G 47
Llanddewi Velfrey. Pemb 3F 43
Llanddewi Ystradenni. Powy . . .4D 58
Llanddoged. Cnwy 4H 81
Llanddona. IOA 3E 81
Llanddowror. Carm 3G 43
Llanddulas. Cnwy 3B 82
Llanddwywe. Gwyn 3E 69
Llanddyfnan. IOA 3E 81
Llandecwyn. Gwyn 2F 69
Llandefaelog Fach. Powy 2D 46
Llandefaelog-tre'r-graig.
Powy 2E 47
Llandefalle. Powy 2E 46
Llandegai. Gwyn 3E 81
Llandegfan. IOA 3E 81
Llandegla. Den 5D 82
Llandegley. Powy 4D 58
Llandegveth. Mon 2G 33
Llandeilo. Carm 3G 45
Llandeilo Graban. Powy 1D 46
Llandeilo'r Fan. Powy 2B 46
Llandeloy. Pemb 2C 42
Llandenny. Mon 5H 47
Llandevaud. Newp 2H 33
Llandevenny. Mon 3H 33
Llandilo. Pemb 2F 43
Llandinabo. Here 3A 48
Llandinam. Powy 2C 58
Llandissilio. Pemb 2F 43
Llandogo. Mon 5A 48
Llandough. V Glam 4C 32
(nr. Cowbridge)
Llandough. V Glam 4E 33
(nr. Penarth)
Llandovery. Carm 2A 46
Llandow. V Glam 4C 32
Llandre. Cdgn 2F 57
Llandrillo. Den 2C 70
Llandrillo-yn-Rhos. Cnwy 2H 81
Llandrindod. Powy 4C 58
Llandrindod Wells. Powy 4C 58
Llandrinio. Powy 4E 71
Llandsadwrn. Carm 2G 45
Llandudno. Cnwy 2G 81
Llandudno Junction. Cnwy 3G 81
Llandudoch. Pemb 1B 44
Llandw. V Glam 4C 32
Llandwrog. Gwyn 5D 80
Llandybie. Carm 4G 45
Llandyfaelog. Carm 4E 45
Llandyfan. Carm 4G 45
Llandyfriog. Cdgn 1D 44

Llandyfrydog. IOA 2D 80
Llandygwydd. Cdgn 1C 44
Llandynan. Den 1D 70
Llandyrnog. Den 4D 82
Llandysilio. Powy 4E 71
Llandyssil. Powy 1D 58
Llandysul. Cdgn 1E 45
Llanedeyrn. Card 3F 33
Llaneglwys. Powy 2D 46
Llanegryn. Gwyn 5F 69
Llanegwad. Carm 3F 45
Llaneilian. IOA 1D 80
Llanelian-yn-Rhos. Cnwy 3A 82
Llanelidan. Den 5D 82
Llanelieu. Powy 2E 47
Llanellen. Mon 4G 47
Llanelli. Carm 3E 31
Llanelltyd. Gwyn 4G 69
Llanelly. Mon 4F 47
Llanelly Hill. Mon 4F 47
Llanelwedd. Powy 5C 58
Llanelwy. Den 3C 82
Llanenddwyn. Gwyn 3E 69
Llanengan. Gwyn 3B 68
Llanerch. Powy 1F 59
Llanerchymedd. IOA 2D 80
Llanerfyl. Powy 5C 70
Llaneuddog. IOA 2D 80
Llanfachraeth. IOA 2C 80
Llanfaelog. IOA 3C 80
Llanfaelrhys. Gwyn 3B 68
Llanfaenor. Mon 4H 47
Llanfaes. IOA 3F 81
Llanfaes. Powy 3D 46
Llanfaethlu. IOA 2C 80
Llanfaglan. Gwyn 4D 80
Llanfair. Gwyn 3E 69
Llanfair. Here 1F 47
Llanfair Caereinion. Powy 5D 70
Llanfair Clydogau. Cdgn 5F 57
Llanfair Dyffryn Clwyd. Den . . .5D 82
Llanfairfechan. Cnwy 3F 81
Llanfair-Nant-Gwyn. Pemb 1F 43
Llanfair Pwllgwyngyll. IOA 3E 81
Llanfair Talhaiarn. Cnwy 3B 82
Llanfair Waterdine. Shrp 3E 59
Llanfair-ym-Muallt. Powy 5C 58
Llanfairyneubwll. IOA 3C 80
Llanfairynghornwy. IOA 1C 80
Llanfallteg. Carm 3F 43
Llanfallteg West. Carm 3F 43
Llanfaredd. Powy 5C 58
Llanfarian. Cdgn 3E 57
Llanfechain. Powy 3D 70
Llanfechell. IOA 1C 80
Llanfechreth. Gwyn 3G 69
Llanfendigaid. Gwyn 5E 69
Llanferres. Den 4D 82
Llan Ffestiniog. Gwyn 1G 69
Llanflewyn. IOA 2C 80
Llanfihangel Glyn Myfyr.
Cnwy 1B 70
Llanfihangel Nant Bran. Powy . .2C 46
Llanfihangel-Nant-Melan.
Powy 5D 58
Llanfihangel Rhydithon.
Powy 4D 58
Llanfihangel Rogiet. Mon 3H 33
Llanfihangel Tal-y-llyn. Powy . . .3E 46
Llanfihangel-uwch-Gwili.
Carm 3E 45
Llanfihangel-yng-Ngwynfa.
Powy 4C 70
Llanfihangel yn Nhowyn. IOA . .3C 80
Llanfihangel-y-pennant. Gwyn . .1E 69
(nr. Golan)
Llanfihangel-y-pennant. Gwyn . .5F 69
(nr. Tywyn)
Llanfilo. Powy 2E 46
Llanfinhangel-ar-Arth. Carm . . .2E 45
Llanfinhangel-y-Creuddyn.
Cdgn 3F 57
Llanfinhangel-y-traethau.
Gwyn 2E 69
Llanfleiddan. V Glam 4C 32
Llanfoist. Mon 4F 47
Llanfor. Gwyn 2B 70
Llanfrechfa. Torf 2G 33
Llanfrothen. Gwyn 1F 69
Llanfrynach. Powy 3D 46
Llanfwrog. Den 5D 82
Llanfwrog. IOA 2C 80
Llanfyllin. Powy 3D 70
Llanfynydd. Carm 3F 45
Llanfynydd. Flin 5E 83
Llanfyrnach. Pemb 1G 43
Llangadfan. Powy 4C 70
Llangadog. Carm 3H 45
(nr. Llandovery)
Llangadog. Carm 5E 45
(nr. Llanelli)
Llangadwaladr. IOA 4C 80
Llangadwaladr. Powy 2D 70
Llangaffo. IOA 4D 80
Llangain. Carm 4D 44
Llangammarch Wells. Powy 1C 46
Llangan. V Glam 4C 32
Llangarron. Here 3A 48
Llangasty-Talyllyn. Powy 3E 47
Llangathen. Carm 3F 45
Llangattock. Powy 4F 47
Llangattock Lingoed. Mon 3G 47

Llangattock-Vibon-Avel. Mon . . .4H 47
Llangedwyn. Powy 3D 70
Llangefni. IOA 3D 80
Llangeinor. B'end 3C 32
Llangeitho. Cdgn 5F 57
Llangeler. Carm 2D 44
Llangelynin. Gwyn 5E 69
Llangendeirne. Carm 4E 45
Llangennech. Carm 5F 45
Llangennith. Swan 3D 30
Llangenny. Powy 4F 47
Llangernyw. Cnwy 4A 82
Llangian. Gwyn 3B 68
Llangiwg. Neat 5H 45
Llangloffan. Pemb 1D 42
Llanglydwen. Carm 2F 43
Llangoed. IOA 3F 81
Llangoedmor. Cdgn 1B 44
Llangollen. Den 1E 70
Llangolman. Pemb 2F 43
Llangorse. Powy 3E 47
Llangorwen. Cdgn 2F 57
Llangovan. Mon 5H 47
Llangower. Gwyn 2B 70
Llangranog. Cdgn 5C 56
Llangristiolus. IOA 3D 80
Llangrove. Here 4A 48
Llangua. Mon 3G 47
Llangunllo. Powy 3E 58
Llangunnor. Carm 3E 45
Llangurig. Powy 3B 58
Llangwm. Cnwy 1B 70
Llangwm. Mon 5H 47
Llangwm. Pemb 4D 43
Llangwm-isaf. Mon 5H 47
Llangwnnadl. Gwyn 2B 68
Llangwyfan. Den 4D 82
Llangwyfan-isaf. IOA 4C 80
Llangwyllog. IOA 3D 80
Llangwyryfon. Cdgn 3E 57
Llangybi. Cdgn 5F 57
Llangybi. Gwyn 1D 68
Llangybi. Mon 2G 33
Llangyfelach. Swan 3F 31
Llangynhafal. Den 4D 82
Llangynidr. Powy 4E 47
Llangynin. Carm 3G 43
Llangynog. Carm 3H 43
Llangynog. Powy 3C 70
Llangynwyd. B'end 3B 32
Llanhamlach. Powy 3D 46
Llanharan. Rhon 3D 32
Llanharry. Rhon 3D 32
Llanhennock. Mon 2G 33
Llanhilleth. Blae 5F 47
Llanidloes. Powy 2B 58
Llaniestyn. Gwyn 2B 68
Llanigon. Powy 1F 47
Llanilar. Cdgn 3F 57
Llanilid. Rhon 3C 32
Llanilltud Fawr. V Glam 5C 32
Llanishen. Card 3E 33
Llanishen. Mon 5H 47
Llanllawddog. Carm 3E 45
Llanllechid. Gwyn 4F 81
Llanllowell. Mon 2G 33
Llanllugan. Powy 5C 70
Llanllwch. Carm 4D 45
Llanllwchaiarn. Powy 1D 58
Llanllwni. Carm 2E 45
Llanllyfni. Gwyn 5D 80
Llanmadoc. Swan 3D 30
Llanmaes. V Glam 5C 32
Llanmartin. Newp 3G 33
Llanmerwig. Powy 1D 58
Llanmihangel. V Glam 4C 32
Llan-mill. Pemb 3F 43
Llanmiloe. Carm 4G 43
Llanmorlais. Swan 3E 31
Llannefydd. Cnwy 3B 82
Llannon. Carm 5F 45
Llan-non. Cdgn 4E 57
Llannor. Gwyn 2C 68
Llanpumsaint. Carm 3E 45
Llanrhaeadr. Den 4C 82
Llanrhaeadr-ym-Mochnant.
    Powy 3D 70
Llanrhidian. Swan 3D 31
Llanrhos. Cnwy 2G 81
Llanrhyddlad. IOA 2C 80
Llanrhystud. Cdgn 4E 57
Llanrian. Pemb 1C 42
Llanrothal. Here 4H 47
Llanrug. Gwyn 4E 81
Llanrumney. Card 3F 33
Llanrwst. Cnwy 4G 81
Llansadurnen. Carm 3G 43
Llansadwrn. IOA 3E 81
Llansaint. Carm 5D 45
Llansamlet. Swan 3F 31
Llansanffraid Glan Conwy.
    Cnwy 3H 81
Llansannan. Cnwy 4B 82
Llansannor. V Glam 4C 32
Llansantffraed. Cdgn 4E 57
Llansantffraed. Powy 3E 46
Llansantffraed Cwmdeuddwr.
    Powy 4B 58
Llansantffraed in Elwel. Powy . .5C 58
Llansantffraid-ym-Mechain.
    Powy 3E 70
Llansawel. Carm 2G 45

Llansawel. Neat 3G 31
Llansilin. Powy 3E 70
Llansoy. Mon 5H 47
Llanspyddid. Powy 3D 46
Llanstadwell. Pemb 4D 42
Llansteffan. Carm 3H 43
Llanstephan. Powy 1E 46
Llantarnam. Torf 2F 33
Llanteg. Pemb 3F 43
Llanthony. Mon 3F 47
Llantilio Crossenny. Mon 4G 47
Llantilio Pertholey. Mon 4G 47
Llantood. Pemb 1B 44
Llantrisant. Mon 2G 33
Llantrisant. Rhon 3D 32
Llantrithyd. V Glam 4D 32
Llantwit Fardre. Rhon 3D 32
Llantwit Major. V Glam 5C 32
Llanuwchllyn. Gwyn 2A 70
Llanvaches. Newp 2H 33
Llanvair Discoed. Mon 2H 33
Llanvapley. Mon 4G 47
Llanvetherine. Mon 4G 47
Llanveynoe. Here 2G 47
Llanvihangel Crucorney.
    Mon 3G 47
Llanvihangel Gobion. Mon 5G 47
Llanvihangel Ystern-Llewern.
    Mon 4H 47
Llanwarne. Here 3A 48
Llanwddyn. Powy 4C 70
Llanwenarth. Mon 4F 47
Llanwenog. Cdgn 1E 45
Llanwern. Newp 3G 33
Llanwinio. Carm 2G 43
Llanwnda. Gwyn 5D 81
Llanwnda. Pemb 1D 42
Llanwnnen. Cdgn 1F 45
Llanwnog. Powy 1C 58
Llanwrda. Carm 2H 45
Llanwrin. Powy 5G 69
Llanwrthwl. Powy 4B 58
Llanwrtud. Powy 1B 46
Llanwrtyd. Powy 1B 46
Llanwrtyd Wells. Powy 1B 46
Llanwyddelan. Powy 5C 70
Llanyblodwel. Shrp 3E 71
Llanybri. Carm 3H 43
Llanybydder. Carm 1F 45
Llanycefn. Pemb 2E 43
Llanychaer. Pemb 1D 43
Llanycil. Gwyn 2B 70
Llanymawddwy. Gwyn 4B 70
Llanymddyfri. Carm 2A 46
Llanymynech. Shrp 3E 71
Llanynghenedl. IOA 2C 80
Llanynys. Den 4D 82
Llan-y-pwll. Wrex 5F 83
Llanyrafon. Torf 2G 33
Llanyre. Powy 4C 58
Llanystumdwy. Gwyn 2D 68
Llanywern. Powy 3E 46
Llawhaden. Pemb 3E 43
Llawndy. Flin 2D 82
Llawnt. Shrp 2E 71
Llawr Dref. Gwyn 3B 68
Llawryglyn. Powy 1B 58
Llay. Wrex 5F 83
Llechfaen. Powy 3D 46
Llechryd. Cphy 5E 46
Llechryd. Cdgn 1C 44
Llechrydau. Wrex 2E 71
Lledrod. Cdgn 3F 57
Llethrid. Swan 3E 31
Llidiad-Nenog. Carm 2F 45
Llidiardau. Gwyn 2A 70
Llidiart y Parc. Den 1D 70
Llithfaen. Gwyn 1C 68
Lloc. Flin 3D 82
Llong. Flin 4E 83
Llowes. Powy 1E 47
Lloyney. Powy 3E 59
Llundain-fach. Cdgn 5E 57
Llwydcoed. Rhon 5C 46
Llwyncelyn. Cdgn 5D 56
Llwyncelyn. Swan 5G 45
Llwyndaffydd. Cdgn 5C 56
Llwynderw. Powy 5E 70
Llwyn-du. Mon 4F 47
Llwyngwril. Gwyn 5E 69
Llwynhendy. Carm 3E 31
Llwynmawr. Wrex 2E 71
Llwyn-on Village. Mer T 4D 46
Llwyn-teg. Carm 5F 45
Llwyn-y-brain. Carm 3F 43
Llwyngog. Powy 1A 58
Llwyn-y-groes. Cdgn 5E 57
Llwynypia. Rhon 2C 32
Llynclys. Shrp 3E 71
Llynfaes. IOA 3D 80
Llysfaen. Cnwy 3A 82
Llyswen. Powy 2E 47
Llysworney. V Glam 4C 32
Llys-y-fran. Pemb 2E 43
Llywel. Powy 3B 46
Llywernog. Cdgn 2G 57
Loan. Falk 2C 128
Loanend. Nmbd 4F 131
Loanhead. Midl 3F 129
Loaningfoot. Dum 4A 112
Loanreoch. High 1A 158
Loans. S Ayr 1C 116

Loansdean. Nmbd 1F 115
Lobb. Devn 3E 19
Lobhillcross. Devn 4E 11
Lochaber. Mor 3E 159
Loch a Charnain. W Isl 4D 170
Loch a Ghainmhich. W Isl 5E 171
Lochailort. High 5F 147
Lochaline. High 4A 140
Lochans. Dum 4F 109
Locharbriggs. Dum 1A 112
Lochardil. High 4A 158
Lochassynt Lodge. High 1F 163
Lochavich. Arg 2G 133
Lochawe. Arg 1A 134
Loch Baghasdail. W Isl 7C 170
Lochboisdale. W Isl 7C 170
Lochbuie. Arg 1D 132
Lochcarron. High 5A 156
Loch Choire Lodge. High 5G 167
Lochdochart House. Stir 1D 134
Lochdon. Arg 5B 140
Lochearnhead. Stir 1E 135
Lochee. D'dee 5C 144
Lochend. High 5H 157
    (nr. Inverness)
Lochend. High 2E 169
    (nr. Thurso)
Locherben. Dum 5B 118
Lochfoot. Dum 2F 111
Lochgair. Arg 4G 133
Lochgarthside. High 2H 149
Lochgelly. Fife 4D 136
Lochgilphead. Arg 1G 125
Lochgoilhead. Arg 3A 134
Loch Head. Dum 5A 110
Lochhill. Mor 2G 159
Lochindorb Lodge. High 5D 158
Lochlane. Per 1H 135
Loch Lomond. Arg 3C 134
Loch Loyal Lodge. High 4G 167
Lochluichart. High 2F 157
Lochmaben. Dum 1B 112
Lochmaddy. W Isl 2D 170
Loch nam Madadh. W Isl 2E 170
Lochore. Fife 4D 136
Lochportain. W Isl 1E 170
Lochranza. N Ayr 4H 125
Loch Sgioport. W Isl 5D 170
Lochside. Abers 2G 145
Lochside. High 5A 168
    (nr. Achentoul)
Lochside. High 3C 158
    (nr. Nairn)
Lochslin. High 5F 165
Lochstack Lodge. High 4C 166
Lochton. Abers 4E 153
Lochty. Fife 3H 137
Lochuisge. High 3B 140
Lochussie. High 3G 157
Lochwinnoch. Ren 4E 127
Lochyside. High 1F 141
Lockengate. Corn 2E 7
Lockerbie. Dum 1C 112
Lockeridge. Wilts 5G 35
Lockerley. Hants 4A 24
Lockhills. Cumb 5G 113
Locking. N Som 1G 21
Lockington. E Yor 5D 101
Lockington. Leics 3B 74
Lockleywood. Shrp 3A 72
Locksgreen. IOW 3C 16
Locks Heath. Hants 2D 16
Lockton. N Yor 5F 107
Loddington. Leics 5E 75
Loddington. Nptn 3F 63
Loddiswell. Devn 4D 8
Loddon. Norf 1F 67
Lode. Cambs 4E 65
Loders. Dors 3H 13
Lodsworth. W Sus 3A 26
Lofthouse. N Yor 2D 98
Lofthouse. W Yor 2D 92
Lofthouse Gate. W Yor 2D 92
Loftus. Red C 3E 107
Logan. E Ayr 2E 117
Loganlea. W Lot 3C 128
Logaston. Here 5F 59
Loggerheads. Staf 2B 72
Loggie. High 4F 163
Logie. Ang 2F 145
Logie. Fife 1G 137
Logie. Mor 3E 159
Logie Coldstone. Abers 3B 152
Logie Pert. Ang 2F 145
Logierait. Per 3G 143
Login. Carm 2F 43
Lolworth. Cambs 4C 64
Londesborough. E Yor 5C 100
London. G Lon . . . . . .2E 39 & 202-203
London Apprentice. Corn 3E 6
London Ashford (Lydd) Airport.
    Kent 3E 29
London City Airport. G Lon 2F 39
London Colney. Herts 5B 52
Londonderry. N Yor 1F 99
London Gatwick Airport.
    W Sus . . . . .1D 27 & 216
London Heathrow Airport.
    G Lon . . . . .3B 38 & 216

London Luton Airport.
    Lutn . . . . .3B 52 & 216
London Southend Airport.
    Essx 2C 40
London Stansted Airport.
    Essx . . . . .3F 53 & 216
Londonthorpe. Linc 2G 75
Londubh. High 5C 162
Lonemore. High 5E 165
    (nr. Dornoch)
Lonemore. High 1G 155
    (nr. Gairloch)
Long Ashton. N Som 4A 34
Long Bank. Worc 3B 60
Longbar. N Ayr 4E 127
Long Bennington. Linc 1F 75
Longbenton. Tyne 3F 115
Longborough. Glos 3G 49
Long Bredy. Dors 3A 14
Longbridge. Warw 4G 61
Longbridge. W Mid 3E 61
Longbridge Deverill. Wilts 2D 22
Long Buckby. Nptn 4D 62
Long Buckby Wharf. Nptn 4D 62
Longburgh. Cumb 4E 112
Longburton. Dors 1B 14
Long Clawson. Leics 3E 74
Longcliffe. Derbs 5G 85
Long Common. Hants 1D 16
Long Compton. Staf 3C 72
Long Compton. Warw 2A 50
Longcot. Oxon 2A 36
Long Crendon. Buck 5E 51
Long Crichel. Dors 1E 15
Longcroft. Cumb 4D 112
Longcroft. Falk 2A 128
Longcross. Surr 4A 38
Longdale. Cumb 4H 103
Longdales. Cumb 5G 113
Longden. Shrp 5G 71
Longden Common. Shrp 5G 71
Long Ditton. Surr 4C 38
Longdon. Staf 4E 73
Longdon. Worc 2D 48
Longdon Green. Staf 4E 73
Longdon on Tern. Telf 4A 72
Longdown. Devn 3B 12
Longdowns. Corn 5B 6
Long Drax. N Yor 2G 93
Long Duckmanton. Derbs 3B 86
Long Eaton. Derbs 2B 74
Longfield. Kent 4H 39
Longfield. Shet 10E 173
Longfield Hill. Kent 4H 39
Longford. Derbs 2G 73
Longford. Glos 3D 48
Longford. G Lon 3B 38
Longford. Shrp 2A 72
Longford. Telf 4B 72
Longford. W Mid 2H 61
Longforgan. Per 1F 137
Longformacus. Bord 4C 130
Longframlington. Nmbd 4F 121
Long Gardens. Essx 2B 54
Long Green. Ches W 3G 83
Long Green. Worc 2D 48
Longham. Dors 3F 15
Longham. Norf 4B 78
Long Hanborough. Oxon 4C 50
Longhedge. Wilts 2D 22
Longhill. Abers 3H 161
Longhirst. Nmbd 1F 115
Longhope. Glos 4B 48
Longhope. Orkn 8C 172
Longhorsley. Nmbd 5F 121
Longhoughton. Nmbd 3G 121
Long Itchington. Warw 4B 62
Long Lane. Telf 4A 72
Long Lawford. Warw 3B 62
Long Lease. N Yor 4G 107
Longley Green. Worc 5B 60
Long Load. Som 4H 21
Longmanhill. Abers 2E 161
Long Marston. Herts 4G 51
Long Marston. N Yor 4H 99
Long Marston. Warw 1G 49
Long Marton. Cumb 2H 103
Long Meadow. Cambs 4E 65
Long Meadowend. Shrp 2G 59
Long Melford. Suff 1B 54
Longmoor Camp. Hants 3F 25
Longmorn. Mor 3G 159
Longmoss. Ches E 3C 84
Long Newnton. Glos 2E 35
Long Newton. Stoc T 3A 106
Longney. Glos 4C 48
Longniddry. E Lot 2H 129
Longnor. Shrp 5G 71
Longnor. Staf 4E 85
    (nr. Leek)
Longnor. Staf 4C 72
    (nr. Stafford)
Longparish. Hants 2C 24
Longpark. Cumb 3F 113
Long Preston. N Yor 4H 97
Longridge. Lanc 1E 90
Longridge. Staf 4D 72

Longridge. W Lot 3C 128
Longriggend. N Lan 2B 128
Long Riston. E Yor 5F 101
Long Rock. Corn 3C 4
Longsdon. Staf 5D 84
Longshaw. G Man 4D 90
Longshaw. Staf 1E 73
Longside. Abers 4H 161
Longslow. Shrp 2A 72
Longstanton. Cambs 4C 64
Longstock. Hants 3B 24
Longstowe. Cambs 5C 64
Long Stratton. Norf 1D 66
Long Street. Mil 1F 51
Longstreet. Wilts 1G 23
Long Sutton. Hants 2F 25
Long Sutton. Linc 3D 76
Long Sutton. Som 4H 21
Longthorpe. Pet 1A 64
Long Thurlow. Suff 4C 66
Longthwaite. Cumb 2F 103
Longton. Lanc 2C 90
Longton. Stoke 1D 72
Longtown. Cumb 3E 113
Longtown. Here 3G 47
Longville in the Dale. Shrp 1H 59
Long Whatton. Leics 3B 74
Longwick. Buck 5F 51
Long Wittenham. Oxon 2D 36
Longwitton. Nmbd 1D 115
Longworth. Oxon 2B 36
Longyester. E Lot 3B 130
Lonmore. High 4B 154
Looe. Corn 3G 7
Loose. Kent 5B 40
Loosegate. Linc 3C 76
Loosley Row. Buck 5G 51
Lopcombe Corner. Wilts 3A 24
Lopen. Som 1H 13
Loppington. Shrp 3G 71
Lorbottle. Nmbd 4E 121
Lorbottle Hall. Nmbd 4E 121
Lordington. W Sus 2F 17
Loscoe. Derbs 1B 74
Loscombe. Dors 3A 14
Losgaintir. W Isl 8C 171
Lossiemouth. Mor 2G 159
Lossit. Arg 4A 124
Lostock Gralam. Ches W 3A 84
Lostock Green. Ches W 3A 84
Lostock Hall. Lanc 2D 90
Lostock Junction. G Man 4E 91
Lostwithiel. Corn 3F 7
Lothbeg. High 2G 165
Lothersdale. N Yor 5B 98
Lothianbridge. Midl 3G 129
Lothianburn. Edin 3F 129
Lothmore. High 2G 165
Lottisham. Som 3A 22
Loudwater. Buck 1A 38
Loughborough. Leics 4C 74
Loughor. Swan 3E 31
Loughton. Essx 1F 39
Loughton. Mil 2G 51
Loughton. Shrp 2A 60
Lound. Linc 4H 75
Lound. Notts 2D 86
Lound. Suff 1H 67
Lount. Leics 4A 74
Louth. Linc 2C 88
Love Clough. Lanc 2G 91
Lovedean. Hants 1E 17
Lover. Wilts 4H 23
Loversall. S Yor 1C 86
Loves Green. Essx 5G 53
Loveston. Pemb 4E 43
Lovington. Som 3A 22
Low Ackworth. W Yor 3E 93
Low Angerton. Nmbd 1D 115
Low Ardwell. Dum 5F 109
Low Ballochdoan. S Ayr 2F 109
Lowbands. Glos 2C 48
Low Barlings. Linc 3H 87
Low Bell End. N Yor 5E 107
Low Bentham. N Yor 3F 97
Low Borrowbridge. Cumb 4H 103
Low Bradfield. S Yor 1G 85
Low Bradley. N Yor 5C 98
Low Braithwaite. Cumb 5F 113
Low Brunton. Nmbd 2C 114
Low Burnham. N Lin 4A 94
Lowca. Cumb 2A 102
Low Catton. E Yor 4B 100
Low Coniscliffe. Darl 3F 105
Low Coylton. S Ayr 3D 116
Low Crosby. Cumb 4F 113
Low Dalby. N Yor 1C 100
Lowdham. Notts 1D 74
Low Dinsdale. Darl 3A 106
Lowe. Shrp 2G 71
Low Ellington. N Yor 1E 98
Lower Amble. Corn 1D 6
Lower Ansty. Dors 2C 14
Lower Arboll. High 5F 165
Lower Arncott. Oxon 4E 50
Lower Ashton. Devn 4B 12
Lower Assendon. Oxon 3F 37
Lower Auchenreath. Mor 2A 160
Lower Badcall. High 4B 166
Lower Ballam. Lanc 1B 90
Lower Basildon. W Ber 4E 36
Lower Beeding. W Sus 3D 26

Lower Benefield—Manmoel

Lower Benefield. *Nptn* 2G **63**
Lower Bentley. *Worc* 4D **61**
Lower Beobridge. *Shrp* 1B **60**
Lower Bockhampton. *Dors* 3C **14**
Lower Boddington. *Nptn* 5B **62**
Lower Bordean. *Hants* 4E **25**
Lower Brailes. *Warw* 2B **50**
Lower Breakish. *High* 1E **147**
Lower Broadheath. *Worc* 5C **60**
Lower Brynamman. *Neat* 4H **45**
Lower Bullingham. *Here* 2A **48**
Lower Bullington. *Hants* 2C **24**
Lower Burgate. *Hants* 1G **15**
Lower Cam. *Glos* 5C **48**
Lower Catesby. *Nptn* 5C **62**
Lower Chapel. *Powy* 2D **46**
Lower Cheriton. *Devn* 2E **12**
Lower Chicksgrove. *Wilts* 3E **23**
Lower Chute. *Wilts* 1B **24**
Lower Clopton. *Warw* 5F **61**
Lower Common. *Hants* 2E **25**
Lower Cumberworth. *W Yor* 4C **92**
Lower Darwen. *Bkbn* 2E **91**
Lower Dean. *Bed* 4H **63**
Lower Dean. *Devn* 2D **8**
Lower Diabaig. *High* 2G **155**
Lower Dicker. *E Sus* 4G **27**
Lower Dounreay. *High* 2B **168**
Lower Down. *Shrp* 2F **59**
Lower Dunsforth. *N Yor* 3G **99**
Lower East Carleton. *Norf* 5D **78**
Lower Egleton. *Here* 1B **48**
Lower Ellastone. *Derbs* 1F **73**
Lower End. *Nptn* 4F **63**
Lower Everleigh. *Wilts* 1G **23**
Lower Eype. *Dors* 3H **13**
Lower Failand. *N Som* 4A **34**
Lower Faintree. *Shrp* 2A **60**
Lower Farringdon. *Hants* 3F **25**
Lower Foxdale. *IOM* 4B **108**
Lower Frankton. *Shrp* 2F **71**
Lower Froyle. *Hants* 2F **25**
Lower Gabwell. *Devn* 2F **9**
Lower Gledfield. *High* 4C **164**
Lower Godney. *Som* 2H **21**
Lower Gravenhurst. *C Beds* 2B **52**
Lower Green. *Essx* 2E **53**
Lower Green. *Norf* 2B **78**
Lower Green. *Staf* 5D **72**
Lower Green. *W Ber* 5B **36**
Lower Halstow. *Kent* 4C **40**
Lower Hardres. *Kent* 5F **41**
Lower Hardwick. *Here* 5G **59**
Lower Hartshay. *Derbs* 5A **86**
Lower Hawthwaite. *Cumb* 1B **96**
Lower Hayton. *Shrp* 2H **59**
Lower Hergest. *Here* 5E **59**
Lower Heyford. *Oxon* 3C **50**
Lower Heysham. *Lanc* 3D **96**
Lower Higham. *Kent* 3B **40**
Lower Holbrook. *Suff* 2E **55**
Lower Holditch. *Dors* 2G **13**
Lower Hordley. *Shrp* 3F **71**
Lower Horncroft. *W Sus* 4B **26**
Lower Horsebridge. *E Sus* 4G **27**
Lower Kilcott. *Glos* 3C **34**
Lower Killeyan. *Arg* 5A **124**
Lower Kingcombe. *Dors* 3A **14**
Lower Kingswood. *Surr* 5D **38**
Lower Kinnerton. *Ches W* 4F **83**
Lower Langford. *N Som* 5H **33**
Lower Largo. *Fife* 3G **137**
Lower Layham. *Suff* 1D **54**
Lower Ledwyche. *Shrp* 3H **59**
Lower Leigh. *Staf* 2E **73**
Lower Lemington. *Glos* 2H **49**
Lower Lenie. *High* 1H **149**
Lower Ley. *Glos* 4C **48**
Lower Llanfadog. *Powy* 4B **58**
Lower Lode. *Glos* 2D **49**
Lower Lovacott. *Devn* 4F **19**
Lower Loxhore. *Devn* 3G **19**
Lower Loxley. *Staf* 2E **73**
Lower Lydbrook. *Glos* 4A **48**
Lower Lye. *Here* 4G **59**
Lower Machen. *Newp* 3F **33**
Lower Maes-coed. *Here* 2G **47**
Lower Meend. *Glos* 5A **48**
Lower Milovaig. *High* 3A **154**
Lower Moor. *Worc* 1E **49**
Lower Morton. *S Glo* 2B **34**
Lower Mountain. *Flin* 5F **83**
Lower Nazeing. *Essx* 5D **53**
Lower Netchwood. *Shrp* 1A **60**
Lower Nyland. *Dors* 4C **22**
Lower Oakfield. *Fife* 4D **136**
Lower Oddington. *Glos* 3H **49**
Lower Ollach. *High* 5E **155**
Lower Penarth. *V Glam* 5E **33**
Lower Penn. *Staf* 1C **60**
Lower Pennington. *Hants* 3B **16**
Lower Peover. *Ches W* 3B **84**
Lower Pilsley. *Derbs* 4B **86**
Lower Pitkerrie. *High* 1C **158**
Lower Place. *G Man* 3H **91**
Lower Quinton. *Warw* 1G **49**
Lower Rainham. *Medw* 4C **40**
Lower Raydon. *Suff* 2D **54**
Lower Seagry. *Wilts* 3E **35**
Lower Shelton. *C Beds* 1H **51**
Lower Shiplake. *Oxon* 4F **37**
Lower Shuckburgh. *Warw* 4B **62**
Lower Sketty. *Swan* 3F **31**
Lower Slade. *Devn* 2F **19**
Lower Slaughter. *Glos* 3G **49**
Lower Soudley. *Glos* 4B **48**
Lower Stanton St Quintin.
Wilts 3E **35**
Lower Stoke. *Medw* 3C **40**
Lower Stondon. *C Beds* 2B **52**
Lower Stonnall. *Staf* 5E **73**
Lower Stow Bedon. *Norf* 1B **66**
Lower Street. *Norf* 2E **79**
Lower Strensham. *Worc* 1E **49**
Lower Sundon. *C Beds* 3A **52**
Lower Swanwick. *Hants* 2C **16**
Lower Swell. *Glos* 3G **49**
Lower Tale. *Devn* 2D **12**
Lower Tean. *Staf* 2E **73**
Lower Thurlton. *Norf* 1G **67**
Lower Thurnham. *Lanc* 4D **96**
Lower Thurvaston. *Derbs* 2G **73**
Lowertown. *Corn* 4D **4**
Lower Town. *Devn* 5H **11**
Lower Town. *Here* 1B **48**
Lower Town. *IOS* 1B **4**
Lowertown. *Orkn* 8D **172**
Lower Town. *Pemb* 1D **42**
Lower Tysoe. *Warw* 1B **50**
Lower Upham. *Hants* 1D **16**
Lower Upnor. *Medw* 3B **40**
Lower Vexford. *Som* 3E **20**
Lower Walton. *Warr* 2A **84**
Lower Wear. *Devn* 4C **12**
Lower Weare. *Som* 1H **21**
Lower Welson. *Here* 5E **59**
Lower Whatcombe. *Dors* 2D **14**
Lower Whitley. *Ches W* 3A **84**
Lower Wield. *Hants* 2E **25**
Lower Winchendon. *Buck* 4F **51**
Lower Withington. *Ches E* 4C **84**
Lower Woodend. *Buck* 3G **37**
Lower Woodford. *Wilts* 3G **23**
Lower Wraxall. *Dors* 2A **14**
Lower Wych. *Ches W* 1G **71**
Lower Wyche. *Worc* 1C **48**
Lowesby. *Leics* 5E **74**
Lowestoft. *Suff* 1H **67**
Loweswater. *Cumb* 2C **102**
Low Etherley. *Dur* 2E **105**
Lowfield Heath. *W Sus* 1D **26**
Lowford. *Hants* 1C **16**
Low Fulney. *Linc* 3B **76**
Low Gate. *Nmbd* 3C **114**
Lowgill. *Cumb* 5H **103**
Lowgill. *Lanc* 3F **97**
Low Grantley. *N Yor* 2E **99**
Low Green. *N Yor* 4E **98**
Low Habberley. *Worc* 3C **60**
Low Ham. *Som* 4H **21**
Low Hameringham. *Linc* 4C **88**
Low Hawkser. *N Yor* 4G **107**
Low Hesket. *Cumb* 5F **113**
Low Hesleyhurst. *Nmbd* 5E **121**
Lowick. *Cumb* 1B **96**
Lowick. *Nptn* 2G **63**
Lowick. *Nmbd* 1E **121**
Lowick Bridge. *Cumb* 1B **96**
Lowick Green. *Cumb* 1B **96**
Low Knipe. *Cumb* 3G **103**
Low Leighton. *Derbs* 2E **85**
Low Lorton. *Cumb* 2C **102**
Low Marishes. *N Yor* 2C **100**
Low Marnham. *Notts* 4F **87**
Low Mill. *N Yor* 5D **106**
Low Moor. *Lanc* 5G **97**
Low Moor. *W Yor* 2B **92**
Low Moorsley. *Tyne* 5G **115**
Low Newton-by-the-Sea.
Nmbd 2G **121**
Lownie Moor. *Ang* 4D **145**
Lowood. *Bord* 1H **119**
Low Row. *Cumb* 3G **113**
(nr. Brampton)
Low Row. *Cumb* 5C **112**
(nr. Wigton)
Low Row. *N Yor* 5C **104**
Lowsonford. *Warw* 4F **61**
Low Street. *Norf* 5C **78**
Lowther. *Cumb* 2G **103**
Lowthorpe. *E Yor* 3E **101**
Lowton. *Devn* 2G **11**
Lowton. *G Man* 1A **84**
Lowton. *Som* 1E **13**
Lowton Common. *G Man* 1A **84**
Low Torry. *Fife* 1D **128**
Low Toynton. *Linc* 3B **88**
Low Valleyfield. *Fife* 1C **128**
Low Westwood. *Dur* 4E **115**
Low Whinnow. *Cumb* 4E **112**
Low Wood. *Cumb* 1C **96**
Low Worsall. *N Yor* 4A **106**
Low Wray. *Cumb* 4E **103**
Loxbeare. *Devn* 1C **12**
Loxhill. *Surr* 2B **26**
Loxhore. *Devn* 3G **19**
Loxley. *S Yor* 2H **85**
Loxley. *Warw* 5G **61**
Loxley Green. *Staf* 2E **73**
Loxton. *N Som* 1G **21**
Loxwood. *W Sus* 2B **26**
Lubcroy. *High* 3A **164**
Lubenham. *Leics* 2E **62**
Lubinvullin. *High* 2F **167**
Luccombe. *Som* 2C **20**
Luccombe Village. *IOW* 4D **16**
Lucker. *Nmbd* 1F **121**
Luckett. *Corn* 5D **11**
Luckington. *Wilts* 3D **34**
Lucklawhill. *Fife* 1G **137**
Luckwell Bridge. *Som* 3C **20**
Lucton. *Here* 4G **59**
Ludag. *W Isl* 7C **170**
Ludborough. *Linc* 1B **88**
Ludchurch. *Pemb* 3F **43**
Luddenden. *W Yor* 2A **92**
Luddenden Foot. *W Yor* 2A **92**
Luddenham. *Kent* 4D **40**
Ludderburn. *Cumb* 5F **103**
Luddesdown. *Kent* 4A **40**
Luddington. *N Lin* 3B **94**
Luddington. *Warw* 5F **61**
Luddington in the Brook.
Nptn 2A **64**
Ludford. *Linc* 2A **88**
Ludford. *Shrp* 3H **59**
Ludgershall. *Buck* 4E **51**
Ludgershall. *Wilts* 1A **24**
Ludgvan. *Corn* 3C **4**
Ludham. *Norf* 4F **79**
Ludlow. *Shrp* 3H **59**
Ludstone. *Shrp* 1C **60**
Ludwell. *Wilts* 4E **23**
Ludworth. *Dur* 5G **115**
Luffenhall. *Herts* 3C **52**
Luffincott. *Devn* 3D **10**
Lugar. *E Ayr* 2E **117**
Luggate Burn. *E Lot* 2C **130**
Lugg Green. *Here* 4G **59**
Luggiebank. *N Lan* 2A **128**
Lugton. *E Ayr* 4F **127**
Lugwardine. *Here* 1A **48**
Luib. *High* 1D **146**
Luib. *Stir* 1D **135**
Lulham. *Here* 1H **47**
Lullington. *Derbs* 4G **73**
Lullington. *E Sus* 5G **27**
Lullington. *Som* 1C **22**
Lulsgate Bottom. *N Som* 5A **34**
Lulsley. *Worc* 5B **60**
Lulworth Camp. *Dors* 4D **14**
Lumb. *Lanc* 2G **91**
Lumb. *W Yor* 2A **92**
Lumby. *N Yor* 1E **93**
Lumphanan. *Abers* 3C **152**
Lumphinnans. *Fife* 4D **136**
Lumsdaine. *Bord* 3E **131**
Lumsden. *Abers* 1B **152**
Lunan. *Ang* 3F **145**
Lunanhead. *Ang* 3D **145**
Luncarty. *Per* 1C **136**
Lund. *E Yor* 5D **100**
Lund. *N Yor* 1G **93**
Lundie. *Ang* 5B **144**
Lundin Links. *Fife* 3G **137**
Lundy Green. *Norf* 1E **67**
Lunna. *Shet* 5F **173**
Lunning. *Shet* 5G **173**
Lunnon. *Swan* 4E **31**
Lunsford. *Kent* 5B **40**
Lunsford's Cross. *E Sus* 4B **28**
Lunt. *Mers* 4B **90**
Luppitt. *Devn* 2E **13**
Lupridge. *Devn* 3D **8**
Lupset. *W Yor* 3D **92**
Lupton. *Cumb* 1E **97**
Lurgashall. *W Sus* 3A **26**
Lurley. *Devn* 1C **12**
Lusby. *Linc* 4C **88**
Luscombe. *Devn* 3D **9**
Luson. *Devn* 4C **8**
Luss. *Arg* 4C **134**
Lussagiven. *Arg* 1E **125**
Lusta. *High* 3B **154**
Lustleigh. *Devn* 4A **12**
Luston. *Here* 4G **59**
Luthermuir. *Abers* 2F **145**
Luthrie. *Fife* 2F **137**
Lutley. *Staf* 2C **60**
Luton. *Devn* 2D **12**
(nr. Honiton)
Luton. *Devn* 5C **12**
(nr. Teignmouth)
Luton. *Lutn* 3A **52 & 201**
Luton (London) Airport.
Lutn 3B **52 & 216**
Lutterworth. *Leics* 2C **62**
Lutton. *Devn* 3B **8**
(nr. Ivybridge)
Lutton. *Devn* 2C **8**
(nr. South Brent)
Lutton. *Linc* 3D **76**
Lutton. *Nptn* 2A **64**
Lutton Gowts. *Linc* 3D **76**
Lutworthy. *Devn* 1A **12**
Luxborough. *Som* 3C **20**
Luxley. *Glos* 3B **48**
Luxulyan. *Corn* 3E **7**
Lybster. *High* 5E **169**
Lydbury North. *Shrp* 2F **59**
Lydcott. *Devn* 3G **19**
Lydd. *Kent* 3E **29**
Lydden. *Kent* 1G **29**
(nr. Dover)
Lydden. *Kent* 4H **41**
(nr. Margate)
Lyddington. *Rut* 1F **63**
Lydd (London Ashford) Airport.
Kent 3E **29**
Lydd-on-Sea. *Kent* 3E **29**
Lydeard St Lawrence. *Som* 3E **21**
Lyde Green. *Hants* 1F **25**
Lydford. *Devn* 4F **11**
Lydford Fair Place. *Som* 3A **22**
Lydgate. *G Man* 4H **91**
Lydgate. *W Yor* 2H **91**
Lydham. *Shrp* 1F **59**
Lydiard Millicent. *Wilts* 3F **35**
Lydiate. *Mers* 4B **90**
Lydiate Ash. *Worc* 3D **61**
Lydlinch. *Dors* 1C **14**
Lydmarsh. *Som* 2G **13**
Lydney. *Glos* 5B **48**
Lydstep. *Pemb* 5E **43**
Lye. *W Mid* 2D **60**
Lye Green. *Buck* 5H **51**
Lye Green. *E Sus* 2G **27**
Lye Head. *Worc* 3B **60**
Lye, The. *Shrp* 1A **60**
Lyford. *Oxon* 2B **36**
Lyham. *Nmbd* 1E **121**
Lylestone. *N Ayr* 5E **127**
Lymbridge Green. *Kent* 1F **29**
Lyme Regis. *Dors* 3G **13**
Lyminge. *Kent* 1F **29**
Lymington. *Hants* 3B **16**
Lyminster. *W Sus* 5B **26**
Lymm. *Warr* 2A **84**
Lymore. *Hants* 3A **16**
Lympne. *Kent* 2F **29**
Lympsham. *Som* 1G **21**
Lympstone. *Devn* 4C **12**
Lynaberack Lodge. *High* 4B **150**
Lynbridge. *Devn* 2H **19**
Lynch. *Som* 2C **20**
Lynchat. *High* 3B **150**
Lynch Green. *Norf* 5D **78**
Lyndhurst. *Hants* 2B **16**
Lyndon. *Rut* 5G **75**
Lyne. *Bord* 5F **129**
Lyne. *Surr* 4B **38**
Lyneal. *Shrp* 2G **71**
Lyne Down. *Here* 2B **48**
Lyneham. *Oxon* 3A **50**
Lyneham. *Wilts* 4F **35**
Lyneholmeford. *Cumb* 2G **113**
Lynemouth. *Nmbd* 5G **121**
Lyne of Gorthleck. *High* 1H **149**
Lyne of Skene. *Abers* 2E **153**
Lynesack. *Dur* 2D **105**
Lyness. *Orkn* 8C **172**
Lyng. *Norf* 4C **78**
Lyngate. *Norf* 2E **79**
(nr. North Walsham)
Lyngate. *Norf* 3F **79**
(nr. Worstead)
Lynmouth. *Devn* 2H **19**
Lynn. *Staf* 5E **73**
Lynn. *Telf* 4B **72**
Lynsted. *Kent* 4D **40**
Lynstone. *Corn* 2C **10**
Lynton. *Devn* 2H **19**
Lynwilg. *High* 2C **150**
Lyon's Gate. *Dors* 2B **14**
Lyonshall. *Here* 5F **59**
Lytchett Matravers. *Dors* 3E **15**
Lytchett Minster. *Dors* 3E **15**
Lyth. *High* 2E **169**
Lytham. *Lanc* 2B **90**
Lytham St Anne's. *Lanc* 2B **90**
Lythe. *N Yor* 3F **107**
Lythes. *Orkn* 9D **172**
Lythmore. *High* 2C **168**

M

Mabe Burnthouse. *Corn* 5B **6**
Mabie. *Dum* 2A **112**
Mablethorpe. *Linc* 2E **89**
Macbiehill. *Bord* 4E **129**
Macclesfield. *Ches E* 3D **84**
Macclesfield Forest. *Ches E* 3D **85**
Macduff. *Abers* 2E **160**
Machan. *S Lan* 4A **128**
Macharioch. *Arg* 5B **122**
Machen. *Cphy* 3F **33**
Machrie. *N Ayr* 2C **122**
Machrihanish. *Arg* 3A **122**
Machroes. *Gwyn* 3C **68**
Machynlleth. *Powy* 5G **69**
Mackerye End. *Herts* 4B **52**
Mackworth. *Derb* 2H **73**
Macmerry. *E Lot* 2H **129**
Maddaford. *Devn* 3F **11**
Madderty. *Per* 1B **136**
Maddington. *Wilts* 2F **23**
Maddiston. *Falk* 2C **128**
Madehurst. *W Sus* 4A **26**
Madeley. *Staf* 1B **72**
Madeley. *Telf* 5A **72**
Madeley Heath. *Staf* 1B **72**
Madeley Heath. *Worc* 3D **60**
Madford. *Devn* 1E **13**
Madingley. *Cambs* 4C **64**
Madley. *Here* 2H **47**
Madresfield. *Worc* 1D **48**
Madron. *Corn* 3B **4**
Maenaddwyn. *IOA* 2D **80**
Maenclochog. *Pemb* 2E **43**
Maendy. *V Glam* 4D **32**
Maenporth. *Corn* 4E **5**
Maentwrog. *Gwyn* 1F **69**
Maen-y-groes. *Cdgn* 5C **56**
Maer. *Staf* 2B **72**
Maerdy. *Carm* 3G **45**
Maerdy. *Cnwy* 1C **70**
Maerdy. *Rhon* 2C **32**
Maesbrook. *Shrp* 3F **71**
Maesbury. *Shrp* 3F **71**
Maesbury Marsh. *Shrp* 3F **71**
Maes-glas. *Flin* 3D **82**
Maesgwyn-Isaf. *Powy* 4D **70**
Maeshafn. *Den* 4E **82**
Maes Llyn. *Cdgn* 1D **44**
Maesmynis. *Powy* 1D **46**
Maesteg. *B'end* 2B **32**
Maestir. *Cdgn* 1F **45**
Maesybont. *Carm* 4F **45**
Maesycrugiau. *Carm* 1E **45**
Maesycwmmer. *Cphy* 2E **33**
Maesyrhandir. *Powy* 1C **58**
Magdalen Laver. *Essx* 5F **53**
Maggieknockater. *Mor* 4H **159**
Magham Down. *E Sus* 4H **27**
Maghull. *Mers* 4B **90**
Magna Park. *Leics* 2C **62**
Magor. *Mon* 3H **33**
Magpie Green. *Suff* 3C **66**
Magwyr. *Mon* 3H **33**
Maidenbower. *W Sus* 2D **27**
Maiden Bradley. *Wilts* 3D **22**
Maidencombe. *Torb* 2F **9**
Maidenhayne. *Devn* 3F **13**
Maidenhead. *Wind* 3G **37**
Maiden Law. *Dur* 5E **115**
Maiden Newton. *Dors* 3A **14**
Maidens. *S Ayr* 4B **116**
Maiden's Green. *Brac* 4G **37**
Maidensgrove. *Oxon* 3F **37**
Maidenwell. *Corn* 5B **10**
Maidenwell. *Linc* 3C **88**
Maiden Wells. *Pemb* 5D **42**
Maidford. *Nptn* 5D **62**
Maids Moreton. *Buck* 2F **51**
Maidstone. *Kent* 5B **40**
Maidwell. *Nptn* 3E **63**
Mail. *Shet* 9F **173**
Maindee. *Newp* 3G **33**
Mainsforth. *Dur* 1A **106**
Mains of Auchindachy. *Mor* 4B **160**
Mains of Auchnagatt. *Abers* 4G **161**
Mains of Drum. *Abers* 4F **153**
Mains of Edingight. *Mor* 3C **160**
Mainsriddle. *Dum* 4G **111**
Mainstone. *Shrp* 2E **59**
Maisemore. *Glos* 3D **48**
Major's Green. *Worc* 3F **61**
Makeney. *Derbs* 1A **74**
Makerstoun. *Bord* 1A **120**
Malacleit. *W Isl* 1C **170**
Malaig. *High* 4E **147**
Malaig Bheag. *High* 4E **147**
Malborough. *Devn* 5D **8**
Malcoff. *Derbs* 2E **85**
Malcolmburn. *Mor* 3A **160**
Malden Rushett. *G Lon* 4C **38**
Maldon. *Essx* 5B **54**
Malham. *N Yor* 3B **98**
Maligar. *High* 2D **155**
Malinslee. *Telf* 5A **72**
Mallaig. *High* 4E **147**
Malleny Mills. *Edin* 3E **129**
Mallows Green. *Essx* 3E **53**
Malltraeth. *IOA* 4D **80**
Mallwyd. *Gwyn* 4A **70**
Malmesbury. *Wilts* 3E **35**
Malmsmead. *Devn* 2A **20**
Malpas. *Ches W* 1G **71**
Malpas. *Corn* 4C **6**
Malpas. *Newp* 2F **33**
Malswick. *Glos* 3C **48**
Maltby. *S Yor* 1C **86**
Maltby. *Stoc T* 3B **106**
Maltby le Marsh. *Linc* 2D **88**
Malt Lane. *Arg* 3H **133**
Maltman's Hill. *Kent* 1D **28**
Malton. *N Yor* 2B **100**
Malvern Link. *Worc* 1C **48**
Malvern Wells. *Worc* 1C **48**
Mamble. *Worc* 3A **60**
Mamhilad. *Mon* 5G **47**
Manaccan. *Corn* 4E **5**
Manafon. *Powy* 5D **70**
Manais. *W Isl* 9D **171**
Manaton. *Devn* 4A **12**
Manby. *Linc* 2C **88**
Mancetter. *Warw* 1H **61**
Manchester. *G Man* 1C **84 & 201**
Manchester International Airport.
G Man 2C **84 & 216**
Mancot. *Flin* 4F **83**
Manea. *Cambs* 2D **65**
Maney. *W Mid* 1F **61**
Manfield. *N Yor* 3F **105**
Mangotsfield. *S Glo* 4B **34**
Mangurstadh. *W Isl* 4C **171**
Mankinholes. *W Yor* 2H **91**
Manley. *Ches W* 3H **83**
Manmoel. *Cphy* 5E **47**

Mannal—Methwold

Mannal. *Arg* 4A **138**
Mannerston. *Falk* 2D **128**
Manningford Bohune. *Wilts* 1G **23**
Manningford Bruce. *Wilts* 1G **23**
Manningham. *W Yor* 1B **92**
Mannings Heath. *W Sus* 3D **26**
Mannington. *Dors* 2F **15**
Manningtree. *Essx* 2E **54**
Mannofield. *Aber* 3G **153**
Manorbier. *Pemb* 5E **43**
Manorbier Newton. *Pemb* 5E **43**
Manorowen. *Pemb* 1D **42**
Manor Park. *G Lon* 2F **39**
Mansell Gamage. *Here* 1G **47**
Mansell Lacy. *Here* 1H **47**
Mansergh. *Cumb* 1F **97**
Mansewood. *Glas* 3G **127**
Mansfield. *E Ayr* 3F **117**
Mansfield. *Notts* 4C **86**
Mansfield Woodhouse. *Notts* 4C **86**
Mansriggs. *Cumb* 1B **96**
Manston. *Dors* 1D **14**
Manston. *Kent* 4H **41**
Manston. *W Yor* 1D **92**
Manswood. *Dors* 2E **15**
Manthorpe. *Linc* 4H **75**
(nr. Bourne)
Manthorpe. *Linc* 2G **75**
(nr. Grantham)
Manton. *N Lin* 4C **94**
Manton. *Notts* 3C **86**
Manton. *Rut* 5F **75**
Manton. *Wilts* 5G **35**
Manuden. *Essx* 3E **53**
Maperton. *Som* 4B **22**
Maplebeck. *Notts* 4E **86**
Maple Cross. *Herts* 1B **38**
Mapledurham. *Oxon* 4E **37**
Mapledurwell. *Hants* 1E **25**
Maplehurst. *W Sus* 3C **26**
Maplescombe. *Kent* 4G **39**
Mapperley. *Derbs* 1B **74**
Mapperley. *Notts* 1C **74**
Mapperley Park. *Notts* 1C **74**
Mapperton. *Dors* 3A **14**
(nr. Beaminster)
Mapperton. *Dors* 3E **15**
(nr. Poole)
Mappleborough Green. *Warw* 4E **61**
Mappleton. *Derbs* 1F **73**
Mappleton. *E Yor* 5G **101**
Mapplewell. *S Yor* 4D **92**
Mappowder. *Dors* 2C **14**
Maraig. *W Isl* 7E **171**
Marazion. *Corn* 3C **4**
Marbhig. *W Isl* 6G **171**
Marbury. *Ches E* 1H **71**
March. *Cambs* 1D **64**
Marcham. *Oxon* 2C **36**
Marchamley. *Shrp* 3H **71**
Marchington. *Staf* 2F **73**
Marchington Woodlands. *Staf* 3F **73**
Marchwiel. *Wrex* 1F **71**
Marchwood. *Hants* 1B **16**
Marcross. *V Glam* 5C **32**
Marden. *Here* 1A **48**
Marden. *Kent* 1B **28**
Marden. *Wilts* 1F **23**
Marden Beech. *Kent* 1B **28**
Marden Thorn. *Kent* 1B **28**
Mardu. *Shrp* 2E **59**
Mardy. *Mon* 4G **47**
Marefield. *Leics* 5E **75**
Mareham le Fen. *Linc* 4B **88**
Mareham on the Hill. *Linc* 4B **88**
Marehay. *Derbs* 1A **74**
Marehill. *W Sus* 4B **26**
Maresfield. *E Sus* 3F **27**
Marfleet. *Hull* 2E **95**
Marford. *Wrex* 5F **83**
Margam. *Neat* 3A **32**
Margaret Marsh. *Dors* 1D **14**
Margaret Roding. *Essx* 4F **53**
Margaretting. *Essx* 5G **53**
Margaretting Tye. *Essx* 5G **53**
Margate. *Kent* 3H **41**
Margery. *Surr* 5D **38**
Margnaheglish. *N Ayr* 2E **123**
Marham. *Norf* 5G **77**
Marhamchurch. *Corn* 2C **10**
Marholm. *Pet* 5A **76**
Marian Cwm. *Den* 3C **82**
Mariandyrys. *IOA* 2F **81**
Marian-glas. *IOA* 2E **81**
Mariansleigh. *Devn* 4H **19**
Marian-y-de. *Gwyn* 2C **68**
Marine Town. *Kent* 3D **40**
Marion-y-mor. *Gwyn* 2C **68**
Marishader. *High* 2D **155**
Marjoriebanks. *Dum* 1B **112**
Mark. *Dum* 4G **109**
Mark. *Som* 2G **21**
Markbeech. *Kent* 1F **27**
Markby. *Linc* 3D **89**
Mark Causeway. *Som* 2G **21**
Mark Cross. *E Sus* 2G **27**
Markeaton. *Derb* 2H **73**
Market Bosworth. *Leics* 5B **74**
Market Deeping. *Linc* 4A **76**
Market Drayton. *Shrp* 2A **72**
Market End. *Warw* 2H **61**
Market Harborough. *Leics* 2E **63**
Markethill. *Per* 5B **144**
Market Lavington. *Wilts* 1F **23**
Market Overton. *Rut* 4F **75**
Market Rasen. *Linc* 2A **88**
Market Stainton. *Linc* 2B **88**
Market Weighton. *E Yor* 5C **100**
Market Weston. *Suff* 3B **66**
Markfield. *Leics* 4B **74**
Markham. *Cphy* 5E **47**
Markinch. *Fife* 3E **137**
Markington. *N Yor* 3E **99**
Marksbury. *Bath* 5B **34**
Mark's Corner. *IOW* 3C **16**
Marks Tey. *Essx* 3C **54**
Markwell. *Corn* 3H **7**
Markyate. *Herts* 4A **52**
Marlborough. *Wilts* 5G **35**
Marlcliff. *Warw* 5E **61**
Marldon. *Devn* 2E **9**
Marle Green. *E Sus* 4G **27**
Marlesford. *Suff* 5F **67**
Marley Green. *Ches E* 1H **71**
Marley Hill. *Tyne* 4F **115**
Marlingford. *Norf* 5D **78**
Mar Lodge. *Abers* 5E **151**
Marloes. *Pemb* 4B **42**
Marlow. *Buck* 3G **37**
Marlow. *Here* 3G **59**
Marlow Bottom. *Buck* 3G **37**
Marlow Common. *Buck* 3G **37**
Marlpit Hill. *Kent* 1F **27**
Marlpits. *E Sus* 3F **27**
Marlpool. *Derbs* 1B **74**
Marnhull. *Dors* 1C **14**
Marnoch. *Abers* 3C **160**
Marnock. *N Lan* 3A **128**
Marple. *G Man* 2D **84**
Marr. *S Yor* 4F **93**
Marrel. *High* 2H **165**
Marrick. *N Yor* 5D **105**
Marrister. *Shet* 5G **173**
Marros. *Carm* 4G **43**
Marsden. *Tyne* 3G **115**
Marsden. *W Yor* 3A **92**
Marsett. *N Yor* 1B **98**
Marsh. *Buck* 5G **51**
Marsh. *Devn* 1F **13**
Marshall Meadows. *Nmbd* 4F **131**
Marshalsea. *Dors* 2G **13**
Marshalswick. *Herts* 5B **52**
Marsham. *Norf* 3D **78**
Marshaw. *Lanc* 4E **97**
Marsh Baldon. *Oxon* 2D **36**
Marsh Benham. *W Ber* 5C **36**
Marshborough. *Kent* 5H **41**
Marshbrook. *Shrp* 2G **59**
Marshbury. *Essx* 4G **53**
Marshchapel. *Linc* 1C **88**
Marshfield. *Newp* 3F **33**
Marshfield. *S Glo* 4C **34**
Marshgate. *Corn* 3B **10**
Marsh Gibbon. *Buck* 3E **51**
Marsh Green. *Devn* 3D **12**
Marsh Green. *Kent* 1F **27**
Marsh Green. *Staf* 5C **84**
Marsh Green. *Telf* 4A **72**
Marsh Lane. *Derbs* 3B **86**
Marshside. *Kent* 4G **41**
Marshside. *Mers* 3B **90**
Marsh Side. *Norf* 1G **77**
Marsh Street. *Som* 2C **20**
Marsh, The. *Powy* 1F **59**
Marsh, The. *Shrp* 3A **72**
Marshwood. *Dors* 3G **13**
Marske. *N Yor* 4E **105**
Marske-by-the-Sea. *Red C* 2D **106**
Marston. *Ches W* 3A **84**
Marston. *Here* 5F **59**
Marston. *Linc* 1F **75**
Marston. *Oxon* 5D **50**
Marston. *Staf* 3D **72**
(nr. Stafford)
Marston. *Staf* 4C **72**
(nr. Wheaton Aston)
Marston. *Warw* 1G **61**
Marston. *Wilts* 1E **23**
Marston Doles. *Warw* 5B **62**
Marston Green. *W Mid* 2F **61**
Marston Hill. *Glos* 2G **35**
Marston Jabbett. *Warw* 2A **62**
Marston Magna. *Som* 4A **22**
Marston Meysey. *Wilts* 2G **35**
Marston Montgomery. *Derbs* 2F **73**
Marston Moretaine. *C Beds* 1H **51**
Marston on Dove. *Derbs* 3G **73**
Marston St Lawrence. *Nptn* 1D **50**
Marston Stannett. *Here* 5H **59**
Marston Trussell. *Nptn* 2D **62**
Marstow. *Here* 4A **48**
Marsworth. *Buck* 4H **51**
Marten. *Wilts* 5A **36**
Marthall. *Ches E* 3C **84**
Martham. *Norf* 4G **79**
Marthwaite. *Cumb* 5H **103**
Martin. *Hants* 1F **15**
Martin. *Kent* 1H **29**
Martin. *Linc* 4B **88**
(nr. Horncastle)
Martin. *Linc* 5A **88**
(nr. Metheringham)
Martindale. *Cumb* 3F **103**
Martin Dales. *Linc* 4A **88**
Martin Drove End. *Hants* 4F **23**
Martinhoe. *Devn* 2G **19**
Martinhoe Cross. *Devn* 2G **19**
Martin Hussingtree. *Worc* 4C **60**
Martin Mill. *Kent* 1H **29**
Martinscroft. *Warr* 2A **84**
Martin's Moss. *Ches E* 4C **84**
Martinstown. *Dors* 4B **14**
Martlesham. *Suff* 1F **55**
Martlesham Heath. *Suff* 1F **55**
Martletwy. *Pemb* 3E **43**
Martley. *Worc* 5B **60**
Martock. *Som* 1H **13**
Marton. *Ches E* 4C **84**
Marton. *Cumb* 2B **96**
Marton. *E Yor* 3G **101**
(nr. Bridlington)
Marton. *E Yor* 1E **95**
(nr. Hull)
Marton. *Linc* 2F **87**
Marton. *Midd* 3C **106**
Marton. *N Yor* 3G **99**
(nr. Boroughbridge)
Marton. *N Yor* 1B **100**
(nr. Pickering)
Marton. *Shrp* 3G **71**
(nr. Myddle)
Marton. *Shrp* 5E **71**
(nr. Worthen)
Marton. *Warw* 4B **62**
Marton Abbey. *N Yor* 3H **99**
Marton-le-Moor. *N Yor* 2F **99**
Martyr's Green. *Surr* 5B **38**
Martyr Worthy. *Hants* 3D **24**
Marwick. *Orkn* 5B **172**
Marwood. *Devn* 3F **19**
Marybank. *High* 3G **157**
(nr. Dingwall)
Marybank. *High* 1B **158**
(nr. Invergordon)
Maryburgh. *High* 3H **157**
Maryfield. *Corn* 3A **8**
Maryhill. *Glas* 3G **127**
Marykirk. *Abers* 2F **145**
Marylebone. *G Lon* 2D **39**
Marylebone. *G Man* 4D **90**
Marypark. *Mor* 5F **159**
Maryport. *Cumb* 1B **102**
Maryport. *Dum* 5E **109**
Marystow. *Devn* 4E **11**
Mary Tavy. *Devn* 5F **11**
Maryton. *Ang* 3C **144**
(nr. Kirriemuir)
Maryton. *Ang* 3F **145**
(nr. Montrose)
Marywell. *Abers* 4C **152**
Marywell. *Ang* 4F **145**
Masham. *N Yor* 1E **98**
Mashbury. *Essx* 4G **53**
Masongill. *N Yor* 2F **97**
Masons Lodge. *Abers* 3F **153**
Mastin Moor. *Derbs* 3B **86**
Mastrick. *Aber* 3G **153**
Matching. *Essx* 4F **53**
Matching Green. *Essx* 4F **53**
Matching Tye. *Essx* 4F **53**
Matfen. *Nmbd* 2D **114**
Matfield. *Kent* 1A **28**
Mathern. *Mon* 2A **34**
Mathon. *Here* 1C **48**
Mathry. *Pemb* 1C **42**
Matlaske. *Norf* 2D **78**
Matlock. *Derbs* 4G **85**
Matlock Bath. *Derbs* 5G **85**
Matterdale End. *Cumb* 2E **103**
Mattersey. *Notts* 2D **86**
Mattersey Thorpe. *Notts* 2D **86**
Mattingley. *Hants* 1F **25**
Mattishall. *Norf* 4C **78**
Mattishall Burgh. *Norf* 4C **78**
Mauchline. *E Ayr* 2D **117**
Maud. *Abers* 4G **161**
Maudlin. *Corn* 2E **7**
Maugersbury. *Glos* 3G **49**
Maughold. *IOM* 2D **108**
Maulden. *C Beds* 2A **52**
Maulds Meaburn. *Cumb* 3H **103**
Maunby. *N Yor* 1F **99**
Maund Bryan. *Here* 5H **59**
Mautby. *Norf* 4G **79**
Mavesyn Ridware. *Staf* 4E **73**
Mavis Enderby. *Linc* 4C **88**
Mawbray. *Cumb* 5B **112**
Mawdesley. *Lanc* 3C **90**
Mawdlam. *B'end* 3B **32**
Mawgan. *Corn* 4E **5**
Mawgan Porth. *Corn* 2C **6**
Maw Green. *Ches E* 5B **84**
Mawla. *Corn* 4B **6**
Mawnan. *Corn* 4E **5**
Mawnan Smith. *Corn* 4E **5**
Mawsley Village. *Nptn* 3F **63**
Mawthorpe. *Linc* 3D **88**
Maxey. *Pet* 5A **76**
Maxstoke. *Warw* 2G **61**
Maxted Street. *Kent* 1F **29**
Maxton. *Kent* 1G **29**
Maxton. *Bord* 1A **120**
Maxwellheugh. *Bord* 1B **120**
Maxwelltown. *Dum* 2A **112**
Maxworthy. *Corn* 3C **10**
Mayals. *Swan* 4F **31**
Maybole. *S Ayr* 4C **116**
Maybush. *Sotn* 1B **16**
Mayes Green. *Surr* 2C **26**
Mayfield. *E Sus* 3G **27**
Mayfield. *Midl* 3G **129**
Mayfield. *Per* 1C **136**
Mayfield. *Staf* 1F **73**
Mayford. *Surr* 5A **38**
Mayhill. *Swan* 3F **31**
Mayland. *Essx* 5C **54**
Maylandsea. *Essx* 5C **54**
Maynard's Green. *E Sus* 4G **27**
Maypole. *IOS* 1B **4**
Maypole. *Kent* 4G **41**
Maypole. *Mon* 4H **47**
Maypole Green. *Norf* 1G **67**
Maypole Green. *Suff* 5B **66**
Mayshill. *S Glo* 3B **34**
Maywick. *Shet* 9E **173**
Mead. *Devn* 1C **10**
Meadgate. *Bath* 1B **22**
Meadle. *Buck* 5G **51**
Meadowbank. *Ches W* 4A **84**
Meadowfield. *Dur* 1F **105**
Meadow Green. *Here* 5B **60**
Meadowmill. *E Lot* 2H **129**
Meadows. *Nott* 2C **74**
Meadowtown. *Shrp* 5F **71**
Meadwell. *Devn* 4E **11**
Meaford. *Staf* 2C **72**
Mealabost. *W Isl* 2G **171**
(nr. Borgh)
Mealabost. *W Isl* 4G **171**
(nr. Stornoway)
Mealasta. *W Isl* 5B **171**
Meal Bank. *Cumb* 5G **103**
Mealrigg. *Cumb* 5C **112**
Mealsgate. *Cumb* 5D **112**
Meanwood. *W Yor* 1C **92**
Mearbeck. *N Yor* 3H **97**
Meare. *Som* 2H **21**
Meare Green. *Som* 4F **21**
(nr. Curry Mallet)
Meare Green. *Som* 4G **21**
(nr. Stoke St Gregory)
Mears Ashby. *Nptn* 4F **63**
Measham. *Leics* 4H **73**
Meath Green. *Surr* 1D **27**
Meathop. *Cumb* 1D **96**
Meaux. *E Yor* 1D **94**
Meavy. *Devn* 2B **8**
Medbourne. *Leics* 1E **63**
Medburn. *Nmbd* 2E **115**
Meddon. *Devn* 1C **10**
Meden Vale. *Notts* 4C **86**
Medlam. *Linc* 5C **88**
Medlicott. *Shrp* 1G **59**
Medmenham. *Buck* 3G **37**
Medomsley. *Dur* 4E **115**
Medstead. *Hants* 3E **25**
Medway Towns. *Medw* 4B **40** & **204**
Meerbrook. *Staf* 4D **85**
Meer End. *W Mid* 3G **61**
Meers Bridge. *Linc* 2D **89**
Meesden. *Herts* 2E **53**
Meeson. *Telf* 3A **72**
Meeth. *Devn* 2F **11**
Meeting Green. *Suff* 5G **65**
Meeting House Hill. *Norf* 3F **79**
Meidrim. *Carm* 2G **43**
Meifod. *Powy* 4D **70**
Meigle. *Per* 4B **144**
Meikle Earnock. *S Lan* 4A **128**
Meikle Kilchattan Butts. *Arg* 4B **126**
Meikleour. *Per* 5A **144**
Meikle Tarty. *Abers* 1G **153**
Meikle Wartle. *Abers* 5E **160**
Meinciau. *Carm* 4E **45**
Meir. *Stoke* 1D **72**
Meir Heath. *Staf* 1D **72**
Melbourn. *Cambs* 1D **53**
Melbourne. *Derbs* 3A **74**
Melbourne. *E Yor* 5B **100**
Melbury Abbas. *Dors* 4D **23**
Melbury Bubb. *Dors* 2A **14**
Melbury Osmond. *Dors* 2A **14**
Melbury Sampford. *Dors* 2A **14**
Melby. *Shet* 6C **173**
Melchbourne. *Bed* 4H **63**
Melcombe Bingham. *Dors* 2C **14**
Melcombe Regis. *Dors* 4B **14**
Meldon. *Devn* 3F **11**
Meldon. *Nmbd* 1E **115**
Meldreth. *Cambs* 1D **53**
Melfort. *Arg* 2F **133**
Melgarve. *High* 4G **149**
Meliden. *Den* 2C **82**
Melinbyrhedyn. *Powy* 1H **57**
Melincourt. *Neat* 5B **46**
Melin-y-coed. *Cnwy* 4H **81**
Melin-y-ddol. *Powy* 5C **70**
Melin-y-wig. *Den* 1C **70**
Melkington. *Nmbd* 5E **131**
Melkinthorpe. *Cumb* 2G **103**
Melkridge. *Nmbd* 3A **114**
Melksham. *Wilts* 5E **35**
Mellangaun. *High* 5C **162**
Melldalloch. *Arg* 2H **125**
Mellguards. *Cumb* 5F **113**
Melling. *Lanc* 2E **97**
Melling. *Mers* 4B **90**
Melling Mount. *Mers* 4C **90**
Mellis. *Suff* 3C **66**
Mellon Charles. *High* 4C **162**
Mellon Udrigle. *High* 4C **162**
Mellor. *G Man* 2D **85**
Mellor. *Lanc* 1E **91**
Mellor Brook. *Lanc* 1E **91**
Mells. *Som* 2C **22**
Melmerby. *Cumb* 1H **103**
Melmerby. *N Yor* 1C **98**
(nr. Middleham)
Melmerby. *N Yor* 2F **99**
(nr. Ripon)
Melplash. *Dors* 3H **13**
Melrose. *Bord* 1H **119**
Melsetter. *Orkn* 9B **172**
Melsonby. *N Yor* 4E **105**
Meltham. *W Yor* 3A **92**
Meltham Mills. *W Yor* 3B **92**
Melton. *E Yor* 2C **94**
Melton. *Suff* 5E **67**
Meltonby. *E Yor* 4B **100**
Melton Constable. *Norf* 2C **78**
Melton Mowbray. *Leics* 4E **75**
Melton Ross. *N Lin* 3D **94**
Melvaig. *High* 5B **162**
Melverley. *Shrp* 4F **71**
Melverley Green. *Shrp* 4F **71**
Melvich. *High* 2A **168**
Membury. *Devn* 2F **13**
Memsie. *Abers* 2G **161**
Memus. *Ang* 3D **144**
Menabilly. *Corn* 3E **7**
Menai Bridge. *IOA* 3E **81**
Mendham. *Suff* 2E **67**
Mendlesham. *Suff* 4D **66**
Mendlesham Green. *Suff* 4C **66**
Menethorpe. *N Yor* 3B **100**
Menheniot. *Corn* 2G **7**
Menithwood. *Worc* 4B **60**
Menna. *Corn* 3D **6**
Mennock. *Dum* 4H **117**
Menston. *W Yor* 5D **98**
Menstrie. *Clac* 4H **135**
Menthorpe. *N Yor* 1H **93**
Mentmore. *Buck* 4H **51**
Meole Brace. *Shrp* 4G **71**
Meols. *Mers* 2E **83**
Meon. *Hants* 2D **16**
Meonstoke. *Hants* 4E **24**
Meopham. *Kent* 4H **39**
Meopham Green. *Kent* 4H **39**
Meopham Station. *Kent* 4H **39**
Mepal. *Cambs* 2D **64**
Meppershall. *C Beds* 2B **52**
Merbach. *Here* 1G **47**
Mercaston. *Derbs* 1G **73**
Merchiston. *Edin* 2F **129**
Mere. *Ches E* 2B **84**
Mere. *Wilts* 3D **22**
Mere Brow. *Lanc* 3C **90**
Mereclough. *Lanc* 1G **91**
Mere Green. *W Mid* 1F **61**
Mere Green. *Worc* 4D **60**
Mere Heath. *Ches W* 3A **84**
Mereside. *Bkpl* 1B **90**
Meretown. *Staf* 3B **72**
Mereworth. *Kent* 5A **40**
Meriden. *W Mid* 2G **61**
Merkadale. *High* 5C **154**
Merkland. *S Ayr* 5B **116**
Merkland Lodge. *High* 1A **164**
Merley. *Pool* 3F **15**
Merlin's Bridge. *Pemb* 3D **42**
Merridge. *Som* 3F **21**
Merrington. *Shrp* 3G **71**
Merrion. *Pemb* 5D **42**
Merriott. *Som* 1H **13**
Merrivale. *Devn* 5F **11**
Merrow. *Surr* 5B **38**
Merrybent. *Darl* 3F **105**
Merry Lees. *Leics* 5B **74**
Merrymeet. *Corn* 2G **7**
Mersham. *Kent* 2E **29**
Merstham. *Surr* 5D **39**
Merston. *W Sus* 2G **17**
Merstone. *IOW* 4D **16**
Merther. *Corn* 4C **6**
Merthyr. *Carm* 3D **44**
Merthyr Cynog. *Powy* 2C **46**
Merthyr Dyfan. *V Glam* 4E **32**
Merthyr Mawr. *B'end* 4B **32**
Merthyr Tudful. *Mer T* 5D **46**
Merthyr Tydfil. *Mer T* 5D **46**
Merthyr Vale. *Mer T* 5D **46**
Merton. *Devn* 1F **11**
Merton. *G Lon* 4D **38**
Merton. *Norf* 1B **66**
Merton. *Oxon* 4D **50**
Meshaw. *Devn* 1A **12**
Messing. *Essx* 4B **54**
Messingham. *N Lin* 4B **94**
Metcombe. *Devn* 3D **12**
Metfield. *Suff* 2E **67**
Metherell. *Corn* 2A **8**
Metheringham. *Linc* 4H **87**
Methil. *Fife* 4F **137**
Methilhill. *Fife* 4F **137**
Methley. *W Yor* 2D **93**
Methley Junction. *W Yor* 2D **93**
Methlick. *Abers* 5F **161**
Methven. *Per* 1C **136**
Methwold. *Norf* 1G **65**

Methwold Hythe. Norf 1G 65
Mettingham. Suff 1F 67
Metton. Norf 2D 78
Mevagissey. Corn 4E 6
Mexborough. S Yor 4E 93
Mey. High 1E 169
Meysey Hampton. Glos 2G 35
Miabhag. W Isl 8D 171
Miabhaig. W Isl 7C 171
(nr. Cliasmol)
Miabhaig. W Isl 4C 171
(nr. Timsgearraidh)
Mial. High 1G 155
Michaelchurch. Here 3A 48
Michaelchurch Escley. Here 2G 47
Michaelchurch-on-Arrow.
Powy 5E 59
Michaelston-le-Pit. V Glam 4E 33
Michaelston-y-Fedw. Newp 3F 33
Michaelstow. Corn 5A 10
Michelcombe. Devn 2C 8
Micheldever. Hants 3D 24
Micheldever Station.
Hants 2D 24
Michelmersh. Hants 4B 24
Mickfield. Suff 4D 66
Micklebring. S Yor 1C 86
Mickleby. N Yor 3F 107
Micklefield. W Yor 1E 93
Micklefield Green. Herts 1B 38
Mickleham. Surr 5C 38
Mickleover. Derb 2H 73
Micklethwaite. Cumb 4D 112
Micklethwaite. W Yor 5D 98
Mickleton. Dur 2C 104
Mickleton. Glos 1G 49
Mickletown. W Yor 2D 93
Mickle Trafford. Ches W 4G 83
Mickley. N Yor 2E 99
Mickley Green. Suff 5H 65
Mickley Square. Nmbd 3D 115
Mid Ardlaw. Abers 2G 161
Midbea. Orkn 3D 172
Mid Beltie. Abers 3D 152
Mid Calder. W Lot 3D 129
Mid Clyth. High 5E 169
Middle Assendon. Oxon 3F 37
Middle Aston. Oxon 3C 50
Middle Barton. Oxon 3C 50
Middlebie. Dum 2D 112
Middle Chinnock. Som 1H 13
Middle Claydon. Buck 3F 51
Middlecliffe. S Yor 4E 93
Middlecott. Devn 4H 11
Middle Drums. Ang 3E 145
Middle Duntisbourne. Glos 5E 49
Middle Essie. Abers 3H 161
Middleforth Green. Lanc 2D 90
Middleham. N Yor 1D 98
Middle Handley. Derbs 3B 86
Middle Harling. Norf 2B 66
Middlehope. Shrp 2G 59
Middle Littleton. Worc 1F 49
Middle Maes-coed. Here 2G 47
Middlemarsh. Dors 2B 14
Middle Marwood. Devn 3F 19
Middle Mayfield. Staf 1F 73
Middlemoor. Devn 5E 11
Middlemuir. Abers 4F 161
(nr. New Deer)
Middlemuir. Abers 3G 161
(nr. Strichen)
Middle Rainton. Tyne 5G 115
Middle Rasen. Linc 2H 87
Middlesbrough.
Midd . . . . .3B 106 & 201
Middlesceugh. Cumb 5E 113
Middleshaw. Cumb 1E 97
Middlesmoor. N Yor 2C 98
Middles, The. Dur 4F 115
Middlestone. Dur 1F 105
Middlestone Moor. Dur 1F 105
Middle Stoughton. Som 2H 21
Middlestown. W Yor 3C 92
Middle Street. Glos 5C 48
Middle Taphouse. Corn 2F 7
Middleton. Ang 4E 145
Middleton. Arg 4A 138
Middleton. Cumb 1F 97
Middleton. Derbs 4F 85
(nr. Bakewell)
Middleton. Derbs 5G 85
(nr. Wirksworth)
Middleton. Essx 2B 54
Middleton. G Man 4G 91
Middleton. Hants 2C 24
Middleton. Hart 1C 106
Middleton. Here 4H 59
Middleton. IOW 4B 16
Middleton. Lanc 4D 96
Middleton. Midl 4G 129
Middleton. Norf 4F 77
Middleton. Nptn 1F 63
Middleton. Nmbd 1F 121
(nr. Belford)
Middleton. Nmbd 1D 114
(nr. Morpeth)
Middleton. N Yor 5D 98
(nr. Ilkley)
Middleton. N Yor 1B 100
(nr. Pickering)
Middleton. Per 3D 136

Middleton. Shrp 3H 59
(nr. Ludlow)
Middleton. Shrp 3F 71
(nr. Oswestry)
Middleton. Suff 4G 67
Middleton. Swan 4D 30
Middleton. Warw 1F 61
Middleton. W Yor 2D 92
Middleton Cheney. Nptn 1D 50
Middleton Green. Staf 2D 73
Middleton Hall. Nmbd 2D 121
Middleton-in-Teesdale. Dur 2C 104
Middleton One Row. Darl 3A 106
Middleton-on-Leven. N Yor 4B 106
Middleton-on-Sea. W Sus 5A 26
Middleton on the Hill. Here 4H 59
Middleton-on-the-Wolds.
E Yor 5D 100
Middleton Priors. Shrp 1A 60
Middleton Quernhow.
N Yor 2F 99
Middleton St George. Darl 3A 106
Middleton Scriven. Shrp 2A 60
Middleton Stoney. Oxon 3D 50
Middleton Tyas. N Yor 4F 105
Middletown. Cumb 4A 102
Middle Town. IOS 1B 4
Middletown. Powy 4F 71
Middle Tysoe. Warw 1B 50
Middle Wallop. Hants 3A 24
Middlewich. Ches E 4B 84
Middle Winterslow. Wilts 3H 23
Middlewood. Corn 5C 10
Middlewood. S Yor 1H 85
Middle Woodford. Wilts 3G 23
Middlewood Green. Suff 4C 66
Middleyard. Glos 5D 48
Middlezoy. Som 3G 21
Middridge. Dur 2F 105
Midelney. Som 4H 21
Midfield. High 2F 167
Midford. Bath 5C 34
Mid Garrary. Dum 2C 110
Midge Hall. Lanc 2D 90
Midgeholme. Cumb 4H 113
Midgham. W Ber 5D 36
Midgley. W Yor 2A 92
(nr. Halifax)
Midgley. W Yor 3C 92
(nr. Horbury)
Mid Ho. Shet 2G 173
Midhopestones. S Yor 1G 85
Midhurst. W Sus 4G 25
Mid Kirkton. N Ayr 4C 126
Mid Lambrook. Som 1H 13
Midland. Orkn 7C 172
Mid Lavant. W Sus 2G 17
Midlem. Bord 2H 119
Midney. Som 4A 22
Midsomer Norton. Bath 1B 22
Midton. Inv 2D 126
Midtown. High 5C 162
(nr. Poolewe)
Midtown. High 2F 167
(nr. Tongue)
Midville. Linc 5C 88
Mid Walls. Shet 7C 173
Midway. Derbs 3H 73
Mid Yell. Shet 2G 173
Migdale. High 4D 164
Migvie. Abers 3B 152
Milber. Devn 5B 12
Milborne Port. Som 1B 14
Milborne St Andrew. Dors 3D 14
Milborne Wick. Som 4B 22
Milbourne. Nmbd 2E 115
Milbourne. Wilts 3E 35
Milburn. Cumb 2H 103
Milbury Heath. S Glo 2B 34
Milby. N Yor 3G 99
Milcombe. Oxon 2C 50
Milden. Suff 1C 54
Mildenhall. Suff 3G 65
Mildenhall. Wilts 5H 35
Milebrook. Powy 3F 59
Milebush. Kent 1B 28
Mile End. Cambs 2F 65
Mile End. Essx 3C 54
Mileham. Norf 4B 78
Mile Oak. Brig 5D 26
Miles Green. Staf 5C 84
Miles Hope. Here 4H 59
Milesmark. Fife 1D 128
Mile Town. Kent 3D 40
Milfield. Nmbd 1D 120
Milford. Derbs 1A 74
Milford. Devn 4C 18
Milford. Powy 1C 58
Milford. Staf 3D 72
Milford. Surr 1A 26
Milford Haven. Pemb 4D 42
Milford on Sea. Hants 3A 16
Milkwall. Glos 5A 48
Milkwell. Wilts 4E 23
Milland. W Sus 4G 25
Millbank. High 2D 168
Mill Bank. W Yor 2A 92
Millbeck. Cumb 2D 102
Millbounds. Orkn 4E 172
Millbreck. Abers 3H 161
Millbridge. Surr 2G 25
Millbrook. C Beds 2A 52
Millbrook. Corn 3A 8

Millbrook. G Man 1D 85
Millbrook. Sotn 1B 16
Mill Common. Suff 2G 67
Mill Corner. E Sus 3C 28
Milldale. Staf 5F 85
Millden Lodge. Ang 1E 145
Milldens. Ang 3E 145
Mill End. Buck 3F 37
Mill End. Cambs 4E 65
Millend. Glos 2C 34
(nr. Dursley)
Mill End. Glos 4G 49
(nr. Northleach)
Mill End. Herts 2D 52
Millerhill. Midl 3G 129
Miller's Dale. Derbs 3F 85
Millers Green. Derbs 5G 85
Millerston. N Lan 3H 127
Millfield. Abers 4B 152
Millfield. Pet 1A 64
Millgate. Lanc 3G 91
Mill Green. Essx 5G 53
Mill Green. Norf 2D 66
Mill Green. Shrp 3A 72
Mill Green. Staf 3E 73
Mill Green. Suff 1C 54
Millhalf. Here 1F 47
Millhall. E Ren 4G 127
Millhayes. Devn 2F 13
(nr. Honiton)
Millhayes. Devn 1E 13
(nr. Wellington)
Millhead. Lanc 2D 97
Millheugh. S Lan 4A 128
Mill Hill. Bkbn 2E 91
Mill Hill. G Lon 1D 38
Millholme. Cumb 5G 103
Millhouse. Arg 2A 126
Millhouse. Cumb 1E 103
Millhousebridge. Dum 1C 112
Millhouses. S Yor 2H 85
Millikenpark. Ren 3F 127
Millington. E Yor 4C 100
Millington Green. Derbs 1G 73
Mill Knowe. Arg 3B 122
Mill Lane. Hants 1F 25
Millmeece. Staf 2C 72
Mill of Craigievar. Abers 2C 152
Mill of Fintray. Abers 2F 153
Mill of Haldane. W Dun 1F 127
Millom. Cumb 1A 96
Millow. C Beds 1C 52
Millpool. Corn 5B 10
Millport. N Ayr 4C 126
Mill Side. Cumb 1D 96
Mill Street. Norf 4C 78
(nr. Lyng)
Mill Street. Norf 4E 20
(nr. Swanton Morley)
Millthorpe. Derbs 3H 85
Millthorpe. Linc 2A 76
Millthrop. Cumb 5H 103
Milltimber. Aber 3F 153
Milltown. Abers 3G 151
(nr. Corgarff)
Milltown. Abers 2B 152
(nr. Lumsden)
Milltown. Corn 3F 7
Milltown. Derbs 4A 86
Milltown. Devn 3F 19
Milltown. Dum 2E 113
Milltown. Mor 4C 160
Milltown of Aberdalgie. Per 1C 136
Milltown of Auchindoun.
Mor 4A 160
Milltown of Campfield.
Abers 3D 152
Milltown of Edinville. Mor 4G 159
Milltown of Towie. Abers 2B 152
Milnacraig. Ang 3B 144
Milnathort. Per 3D 136
Milngavie. E Dun 2G 127
Milnholm. Stir 1A 128
Milnrow. G Man 3H 91
Milnthorpe. Cumb 1D 97
Milnthorpe. W Yor 3D 92
Milson. Shrp 3A 60
Milstead. Kent 5D 40
Milston. Wilts 2G 23
Milthorpe. Nptn 1D 50
Milton. Ang 4C 144
Milton. Cambs 4D 65
Milton. Cumb 2C 50
(nr. Banbury)
Milton. Cumb 3G 113
(nr. Brampton)
Milton. Cumb 1E 97
(nr. Crooklands)
Milton. Derbs 3H 73
Milton. Dum 2F 111
(nr. Crocketford)
Milton. Dum 4H 109
(nr. Glenluce)
Milton. E Ayr 2D 116
Milton. Glas 2G 127
Milton. High 3F 157
(nr. Achnasheen)
Milton. High 4G 155
(nr. Applecross)
Milton. High 5G 157
(nr. Drumnadrochit)

Milton. High 1B 158
(nr. Invergordon)
Milton. High 4H 157
(nr. Inverness)
Milton. High 3F 169
(nr. Wick)
Milton. Mor 2C 160
(nr. Cullen)
Milton. Mor 2F 151
(nr. Tomintoul)
Milton. N Som 5G 33
Milton. Notts 3E 86
Milton. Oxon 2C 36
Milton. Pemb 4E 43
Milton. Port 3E 17
Milton. Som 4H 21
Milton. Stir 3E 135
(nr. Aberfoyle)
Milton. Stir 4D 134
(nr. Drymen)
Milton. Stoke 5D 84
Milton. W Dun 2F 127
Milton Abbas. Dors 2D 14
Milton Abbot. Devn 5E 11
Milton Auchlossan. Abers 3C 152
Milton Bridge. Midl 3F 129
Milton Bryan. C Beds 2H 51
Milton Clevedon. Som 3B 22
Milton Coldwells. Abers 5G 161
Milton Combe. Devn 2A 8
Milton Common. Oxon 5E 51
Milton Damerel. Devn 1D 11
Milton End. Glos 5G 49
Milton Ernest. Bed 5H 63
Milton Green. Ches W 5G 83
Milton Hill. Devn 5C 12
Milton Hill. Oxon 2C 36
Milton Keynes. Mil . . . . . .2G 51 & 204
Milton Keynes Village. Mil 2G 51
Milton Lilbourne. Wilts 5G 35
Milton Malsor. Nptn 5E 63
Milton Morenish. Per 5D 142
Milton of Auchinhove. Abers 3C 152
Milton of Balgonie. Fife 3F 137
Milton of Barras. Abers 1H 145
Milton of Campsie. E Dun 2H 127
Milton of Cultoquhey. Per 1A 136
Milton of Cushnie. Abers 2C 152
Milton of Finavon. Ang 3D 145
Milton of Gollanfield. High 3B 158
Milton of Lesmore. Abers 1B 152
Milton of Tullich. Abers 4A 152
Milton on Stour. Dors 4C 22
Milton Regis. Kent 4C 40
Milton Street. E Sus 5G 27
Milton-under-Wychwood.
Oxon 4A 50
Milverton. Som 4E 20
Milverton. Warw 4H 61
Milwich. Staf 2D 72
Mimbridge. Surr 4A 38
Minard. Arg 4G 133
Minchington. Dors 1E 15
Minchinhampton. Glos 5D 49
Mindrum. Nmbd 1C 120
Minehead. Som 2C 20
Minera. Wrex 5E 83
Minety. Wilts 2F 35
Minffordd. Gwyn 2E 69
Mingarrypark. High 2A 140
Mingary. High 2G 139
Mingearraidh. W Isl 6C 170
Miningsby. Linc 4C 88
Minions. Corn 5C 10
Minishant. S Ayr 3C 116
Minllyn. Gwyn 4A 70
Minnigaff. Dum 3B 110
Minorca. IOM 3D 108
Minskip. N Yor 3F 99
Minstead. Hants 1A 16
Minsted. W Sus 4G 25
Minster. Kent 4H 41
(nr. Ramsgate)
Minster. Kent 3D 40
(nr. Sheerness)
Minsteracres. Nmbd 4D 114
Minsterley. Shrp 5F 71
Minster Lovell. Oxon 4B 50
Minsterworth. Glos 4C 48
Minterne Magna. Dors 2B 14
Minterne Parva. Dors 2B 14
Minting. Linc 3A 88
Mintlaw. Abers 4H 161
Minto. Bord 2H 119
Minton. Shrp 1G 59
Minwear. Pemb 3E 43
Minworth. W Mid 1F 61
Miodar. Arg 4B 138
Mirbister. Orkn 5C 172
Mireland. High 2F 169
Mirehouse. Cumb 3A 102
Mireland. High 2F 169
Mirfield. W Yor 3C 92
Miserden. Glos 5E 49
Miskin. Rhon 3D 32
Misson. Notts 1D 86
Misterton. Leics 2C 62
Misterton. Notts 1E 87
Misterton. Som 2H 13
Mistley. Essx 2E 55
Mistley Heath. Essx 2E 55
Mitcham. G Lon 4D 39

Mitcheldean. Glos 4B 48
Mitchell. Corn 3C 6
Mitchel Troy. Mon 4H 47
Mitcheltroy Common. Mon 5H 47
Mitford. Nmbd 1E 115
Mithian. Corn 3B 6
Mitton. Staf 4C 72
Mixbury. Oxon 2E 50
Mixenden. W Yor 2A 92
Mixon. Staf 5E 85
Moarfield. Shet 1G 173
Moat. Cumb 2F 113
Moats Tye. Suff 5C 66
Mobberley. Ches E 3B 84
Mobberley. Staf 1E 73
Moccas. Here 1G 47
Mochdre. Cnwy 3H 81
Mochdre. Powy 2C 58
Mochrum. Dum 5A 110
Mockbeggar. Hants 2G 15
Mockerkin. Cumb 2B 102
Modbury. Devn 3C 8
Moddershall. Staf 2D 72
Modsarie. High 2G 167
Moelfre. Cnwy 3B 82
Moelfre. IOA 2E 81
Moelfre. Powy 3D 70
Moffat. Dum 4C 118
Moggerhanger. C Beds 1B 52
Mogworthy. Devn 1B 12
Moira. Leics 4H 73
Molash. Kent 5E 41
Mol-chlach. High 2C 146
Mold. Flin 4E 83
Molehill Green. Essx 3F 53
Molescroft. E Yor 5E 101
Molesden. Nmbd 1E 115
Molesworth. Cambs 3H 63
Moll. High 5E 155
Molland. Devn 4B 20
Mollington. Ches W 3F 83
Mollington. Oxon 1C 50
Mollinsburn. N Lan 2A 128
Monachty. Cdgn 4E 57
Monachyle. Stir 2D 134
Monar Lodge. High 4E 156
Monaughty. Powy 4E 59
Monewden. Suff 5E 67
Moneydie. Per 1C 136
Moneyrow Green. Wind 4G 37
Moniaive. Dum 5G 117
Monifieth. Ang 5E 145
Monikie. Ang 5E 145
Monimail. Fife 2E 137
Monington. Pemb 1B 44
Monk Bretton. S Yor 4D 92
Monken Hadley. G Lon 1D 38
Monk Fryston. N Yor 2F 93
Monk Hesleden. Dur 1B 106
Monkhide. Here 1B 48
Monkhill. Cumb 4E 113
Monkhopton. Shrp 1A 60
Monkland. Here 5G 59
Monkleigh. Devn 4E 19
Monknash. V Glam 4C 32
Monkokehampton. Devn 2F 11
Monkseaton. Tyne 2G 115
Monks Eleigh. Suff 1C 54
Monk's Gate. W Sus 3D 26
Monk's Heath. Ches E 3C 84
Monk Sherborne. Hants 1E 24
Monkshill. Abers 4E 161
Monksilver. Som 3D 20
Monks Kirby. Warw 2B 62
Monk Soham. Suff 4E 66
Monk Soham Green. Suff 4E 66
Monkspath. W Mid 3F 61
Monks Risborough. Buck 5G 51
Monksthorpe. Linc 4D 88
Monk Street. Essx 3G 53
Monkswood. Mon 5G 47
Monkton. Devn 2E 13
Monkton. Kent 4G 41
Monkton. Pemb 4D 42
Monkton. S Ayr 2C 116
Monkton Combe. Bath 5C 34
Monkton Deverill. Wilts 3D 22
Monkton Farleigh. Wilts 5D 34
Monkton Heathfield. Som 4F 21
Monktonhill. S Ayr 2C 116
Monkton Up Wimborne. Dors . . .1F 15
Monkton Wyld. Dors 3G 13
Monkwearmouth. Tyne 4H 115
Monkwood. Dors 3H 13
Monkwood. Hants 3E 25
Monmarsh. Here 1A 48
Monmouth. Mon 4A 48
Monnington on Wye. Here 1G 47
Monreith. Dum 5A 110
Montacute. Som 1H 13
Montford. Arg 3C 126
Montford. Shrp 4G 71
Montford Bridge. Shrp 4G 71
Montgarrie. Abers 2C 152
Montgarswood. E Ayr 2E 117
Montgomery. Powy 1E 58
Montgreenan. N Ayr 5E 127
Montrave. Fife 3F 137
Montrose. Ang 3G 145
Monxton. Hants 2B 24
Monyash. Derbs 4F 85
Monymusk. Abers 2D 152

Monzie. Per 1A 136
Moodiesburn. N Lan 2H 127
Moon's Green. Kent 3C 28
Moonzie. Fife 2F 137
Moor. Som 1H 13
Moor Allerton. W Yor 1C 92
Moorbath. Dors 3H 13
Moorbrae. Shet 3F 173
Moorcot. Here 5F 59
Moor Crichel. Dors 2E 15
Moor Cross. Devn 3C 8
Moordown. Bour 3F 15
Moore. Hal 2H 83
Moorend. Dur 2D 112
Moor End. E Yor 1B 94
Moorend. Glos 5C 48
(nr. Dursley)
Moorend. Glos 4D 48
(nr. Gloucester)
Moorends. S Yor 3G 93
Moorgate. S Yor 1B 86
Moorgreen. Hants 1C 16
Moorgreen. Notts 1B 74
Moor Green. Wilts 5D 34
Moorhaigh. Notts 4C 86
Moorhall. Derbs 3H 85
Moorhampton. Here 1G 47
Moorhouse. Cumb 4E 113
(nr. Carlisle)
Moorhouse. Cumb 4D 112
(nr. Wigton)
Moorhouse. Notts 4E 87
Moorhouse. Surr 5F 39
Moorhouses. Linc 5B 88
Moorland. Som 3G 21
Moorlinch. Som 3H 21
Moor Monkton. N Yor 4H 99
Moor of Granary. Mor 3E 159
Moor Row. Cumb 3B 102
(nr. Whitehaven)
Moor Row. Cumb 5D 112
(nr. Wigton)
Moorsholm. Red C 3D 107
Moorside. Dors 1C 14
Moorside. G Man 4H 91
Moor, The. Kent 3B 28
Moortown. Devn 3D 10
Moortown. Hants 2G 15
Moortown. IOW 4C 16
Moortown. Linc 1H 87
Moortown. Telf 4A 72
Moortown. W Yor 1D 92
Morangie. High 5E 165
Morar. High 4E 147
Morborne. Cambs 1A 64
Morchard Bishop. Devn 2A 12
Morcombelake. Dors 3H 13
Morcott. Rut 5G 75
Morda. Shrp 3E 71
Morden. G Lon 4D 38
Mordiford. Here 2A 48
Mordon. Dur 2A 106
More. Shrp 1F 59
Morebath. Devn 4C 20
Morebattle. Bord 2B 120
Morecambe. Lanc 3D 96
Morefield. High 4F 163
Moreleigh. Devn 3D 8
Morenish. Per 5C 142
Moresby Parks. Cumb 3A 102
Morestead. Hants 4D 24
Moreton. Dors 4D 14
Moreton. Essx 5F 53
Moreton. Here 4H 59
Moreton. Mers 1E 83
Moreton. Oxon 5E 51
Moreton. Staf 4B 72
Moreton Corbet. Shrp 3H 71
Moretonhampstead. Devn 4A 12
Moreton-in-Marsh. Glos 2H 49
Moreton Jeffries. Here 1B 48
Moreton Morrell. Warw 5H 61
Moreton on Lugg. Here 1A 48
Moreton Pinkney. Nptn 1D 50
Moreton Say. Shrp 2A 72
Moreton Valence. Glos 5C 48
Morfa. Cdgn 5C 56
Morfa Bach. Carm 4D 44
Morfa Bychan. Gwyn 2E 69
Morfa Glas. Neat 5B 46
Morfa Nefyn. Gwyn 1B 68
Morganstown. Card 3E 33
Morgan's Vale. Wilts 4G 23
Morham. E Lot 2B 130
Moriah. Cdgn 3F 57
Morland. Cumb 2G 103
Morley. Ches E 2C 84
Morley. Derbs 1A 74
Morley. Dur 2E 105
Morley. W Yor 2C 92
Morley St Botolph. Norf 1C 66
Morningside. Edin 2F 129
Morningside. N Lan 4B 128
Morningthorpe. Norf 1E 66
Morpeth. Nmbd 1F 115
Morrey. Staf 4F 73
Morridge Side. Staf 5E 85
Morridge Top. Staf 4E 85
Morrington. Dum 1F 111
Morris Green. Essx 2H 53
Morriston. Swan 3F 31

Morston. Norf 1C 78
Mortehoe. Devn 2E 19
Morthen. S Yor 2B 86
Mortimer. W Ber 5E 37
Mortimer's Cross. Here 4G 59
Mortimer West End.
Hants 5E 37
Mortomley. S Yor 1H 85
Morton. Cumb 1F 103
(nr. Calthwaite)
Morton. Cumb 4E 113
(nr. Carlisle)
Morton. Derbs 4B 86
Morton. Linc 3H 75
(nr. Bourne)
Morton. Linc 1F 87
(nr. Gainsborough)
Morton. Linc 4D 78
(nr. Lincoln)
Morton. Norf 4D 78
Morton. Notts 5E 87
Morton. Shrp 3E 71
Morton. S Glo 2B 34
Morton Bagot. Warw 4F 61
Morton Mill. Shrp 3H 71
Morton-on-Swale.
N Yor 5A 106
Morton Tinmouth. Dur 2E 105
Morvah. Corn 3B 4
Morval. Corn 3G 7
Morvich. High 3E 165
(nr. Golspie)
Morvich. High 1B 148
(nr. Shiel Bridge)
Morvil. Pemb 1E 43
Morville. Shrp 1A 60
Morwenstow. Corn 1C 10
Morwick Hall. Nmbd 4G 121
Mosborough. S Yor 2B 86
Moscow. E Ayr 5F 127
Mose. Shrp 1B 60
Mosedale. Cumb 1E 103
Moseley. W Mid 2E 61
(nr. Birmingham)
Moseley. W Mid 5D 72
(nr. Wolverhampton)
Moseley. Worc 5C 60
Moss. Arg 4A 138
Moss. High 2A 140
Moss. S Yor 3F 93
Moss. Wrex 5F 83
Mossatt. Abers 2B 152
Moss Bank. Mers 1H 83
Mossbank. Shet 4F 173
Mossblown. S Ayr 2D 116
Mossbrow. G Man 2B 84
Mossburnford. Bord 3A 120
Mossdale. Dum 2D 110
Mossedge. Cumb 3F 113
Mossend. N Lan 3A 128
Mossgate. Staf 2D 72
Moss Lane. Ches E 3D 84
Mossley. Ches E 4C 84
Mossley. G Man 4H 91
Mossley Hill. Mers 2F 83
Moss of Barmuckity. Mor 2G 159
Mosspark. Glas 3G 127
Mosspaul. Bord 5G 119
Moss Side. Cumb 4C 112
Moss Side. G Man 1C 84
Moss-side. High 3C 158
Moss Side. Lanc 1B 90
(nr. Blackpool)
Moss Side. Lanc 2D 90
(nr. Preston)
Moss Side. Mers 4B 90
Moss-side of Cairness.
Abers 2H 161
Mosstodloch. Mor 2H 159
Mosswood. Nmbd 4D 114
Mossy Lea. Lanc 3D 90
Mosterton. Dors 2H 13
Moston. Shrp 3H 71
Moston Green. Ches E 4B 84
Mostyn. Flin 2D 82
Mostyn Quay. Flin 2D 82
Motcombe. Dors 4D 22
Motherby. Cumb 2F 103
Motherwell. N Lan 4A 128
Mottingham. G Lon 3F 39
Mottisfont. Hants 4B 24
Mottistone. IOW 4C 16
Mottram in Longdendale.
G Man 1D 85
Mottram St Andrew. Ches E 3C 84
Mott's Mill. E Sus 2G 27
Mouldsworth. Ches W 3H 83
Moulin. Per 3G 143
Moulsecoomb. Brig 5E 27
Moulsford. Oxon 3D 36
Moulsoe. Mil 1H 51
Moulton. Ches W 4A 84
Moulton. Linc 3C 76
Moulton. Nptn 4E 63
Moulton. N Yor 4F 105
Moulton. Suff 4F 65
Moulton. V Glam 4D 32
Moulton Chapel. Linc 4B 76
Moulton Eugate. Linc 4B 76
Moulton St Mary. Norf 5F 79
Moulton Seas End. Linc 3C 76

Mount. Corn 2F 7
(nr. Bodmin)
Mount. Corn 3B 6
(nr. Newquay)
Mountain Ash. Rhon 2D 32
Mountain Cross. Bord 5E 129
Mountain Street. Kent 5E 41
Mountain Water. Pemb 2D 42
Mount Ambrose. Corn 4B 6
Mountbenger. Bord 2F 119
Mountblow. W Dun 2F 127
Mount Bures. Essx 2C 54
Mountfield. E Sus 3B 28
Mountgerald. High 2H 157
Mount Hawke. Corn 4B 6
Mount High. High 2A 158
Mountjoy. Corn 2C 6
Mount Lothian. Midl 4F 129
Mountnessing. Essx 1H 39
Mounton. Mon 2A 34
Mount Pleasant. Buck 2E 51
Mount Pleasant. Ches E 5C 84
Mount Pleasant. Derbs 1H 73
(nr. Derby)
Mount Pleasant. Derbs 4G 73
(nr. Swadlincote)
Mount Pleasant. E Sus 4F 27
Mount Pleasant. Fife 2E 137
Mount Pleasant. Hants 3A 16
Mount Pleasant. Norf 1B 66
Mount Skippett. Oxon 4B 50
Mountsorrel. Leics 4C 74
Mount Stuart. Arg 4C 126
Mousehole. Corn 4B 4
Mouswald. Dum 2B 112
Mow Cop. Ches E 5C 84
Mowden. Darl 3F 105
Mowhaugh. Bord 2C 120
Mowmacre Hill. Leic 5C 74
Mowsley. Leics 2D 62
Moy. High 5B 158
Moylgrove. Pemb 1B 44
Moy Lodge. High 5G 149
Muasdale. Arg 5E 125
Muchalls. Abers 4G 153
Much Birch. Here 2A 48
Much Cowarne. Here 1B 48
Much Dewchurch. Here 2H 47
Muchelney. Som 4H 21
Muchelney Ham. Som 4H 21
Much Hadham. Herts 4E 53
Much Hoole. Lanc 2C 90
Muchlarnick. Corn 3G 7
Much Marcle. Here 2B 48
Muchrachd. High 5E 157
Much Wenlock. Shrp 1A 60
Mucking. Thur 2A 40
Muckle Breck. Shet 5G 173
Muckleford. Dors 3B 14
Mucklestone. Staf 2B 72
Muckleton. Norf 2H 77
Muckleton. Shrp 3H 71
Muckley. Shrp 1A 60
Muckley Corner. Staf 5E 73
Muckton. Linc 2C 88
Mudale. High 5F 167
Muddiford. Devn 3F 19
Mudeford. Dors 3G 15
Mudford. Som 1A 14
Mudgley. Som 2H 21
Mugdock. Stir 2G 127
Mugeary. High 5D 154
Muggington. Derbs 1G 73
Muggintonlane End. Derbs 1G 73
Muggleswick. Dur 4D 114
Mugswell. Surr 5D 38
Muie. High 3D 164
Muirden. Abers 3E 160
Muirdrum. Ang 5E 145
Muiredge. Per 1E 137
Muirend. Glas 3G 127
Muirhead. Ang 5C 144
Muirhead. Fife 3E 137
Muirhead. N Lan 3H 127
Muirhouses. Falk 1D 128
Muirkirk. E Ayr 2F 117
Muir of Alford. Abers 2C 152
Muir of Fairburn. High 3G 157
Muir of Fowlis. Abers 2C 152
Muir of Miltonduff. Mor 3F 159
Muir of Ord. High 3H 157
Muir of Tarradale. High 3H 157
Muirshearlich. High 5D 148
Muirtack. Abers 5G 161
Muirton. High 2B 158
Muirton. Per 1D 136
Muirton of Ardblair. Per 4A 144
Muirtown. Per 2B 136
Muiryfold. Abers 3E 161
Muker. N Yor 5C 104
Mulbarton. Norf 5D 78
Mulben. Mor 3A 160
Mulindry. Arg 4B 124
Mulla. Shet 5F 173
Mullach Charlabhaigh. W Isl 3E 171
Mullacott. Devn 2F 19
Mullion. Corn 5D 4
Mullion Cove. Corn 5D 4
Mumbles. Swan 4F 31
Mumby. Linc 3E 89
Munderfield Row. Here 5A 60
Munderfield Stocks. Here 5A 60

Mundesley. Norf 2F 79
Mundford. Norf 1H 65
Mundham. Norf 1F 67
Mundon. Essx 5B 54
Munerigie. High 3E 149
Mungasdale. High 4D 162
Mungrisdale. Cumb 1E 103
Munlochy. High 3A 158
Munsley. Here 1B 48
Munslow. Shrp 2H 59
Murchington. Devn 4G 11
Murcot. Worc 1F 49
Murcott. Oxon 4D 50
Murdishaw. Hal 2H 83
Murieston. W Lot 3D 128
Murkle. High 2D 168
Murlaggan. High 4C 148
Murra. Orkn 7B 172
Murray, The. S Lan 4H 127
Murrayfield. Edin 2F 129
Murrell Green. Hants 1F 25
Murroes. Ang 5D 144
Murrow. Cambs 5C 76
Mursley. Buck 3G 51
Murthly. Per 5H 143
Murton. Cumb 2A 104
Murton. Dur 5G 115
Murton. Nmbd 5F 131
Murton. Swan 4E 31
Murton. York 4A 100
Musbury. Devn 3F 13
Muscoates. N Yor 1A 100
Muscott. Nptn 4D 62
Musselburgh. E Lot 2G 129
Muston. Leics 2F 75
Muston. N Yor 2E 101
Mustow Green. Worc 3C 60
Muswell Hill. G Lon 2D 39
Mutehill. Dum 5D 111
Mutford. Suff 2G 67
Muthill. Per 2A 136
Mutterton. Devn 2D 12
Muxton. Telf 4B 72
Mwmbwls. Swan 4F 31
Mybster. High 3D 168
Myddfai. Carm 2A 46
Myddle. Shrp 3G 71
Mydroilyn. Cdgn 5D 56
Myerscough. Lanc 1C 90
Mylor Bridge. Corn 5C 6
Mylor Churchtown. Corn 5C 6
Mynachlog-ddu. Pemb 1F 43
Mynydd-bach. Mon 2H 33
Mynydd Isa. Flin 4E 83
Mynyddislwyn. Cphy 2E 33
Mynydd Llandegai. Gwyn 4F 81
Mynydd Mechell. IOA 1C 80
Mynydd-y-briw. Powy 3D 70
Mynyddygarreg. Carm 5E 45
Mynytho. Gwyn 2C 68
Myrebird. Abers 4E 153
Myrelandhorn. High 3E 169
Mytchett. Surr 1G 25
Mythe, The. Glos 2D 49
Mytholmroyd. W Yor 2A 92
Myton-on-Swale. N Yor 3G 99
Mytton. Shrp 4G 71

N

Naast. High 5C 162
Na Buirgh. W Isl 8C 171
Naburn. York 5H 99
Nab Wood. W Yor 1B 92
Nackington. Kent 5F 41
Nacton. Suff 1F 55
Nafferton. E Yor 4E 101
Na Gearrannan. W Isl 3D 171
Nailbridge. Glos 4B 48
Nailsbourne. Som 4F 21
Nailsea. N Som 4H 33
Nailstone. Leics 5B 74
Nailsworth. Glos 2D 34
Nairn. High 3C 158
Nalderswood. Surr 1D 26
Nancegollan. Corn 3D 4
Nancekuke. Corn 4A 6
Nancledra. Corn 3B 4
Nangreaves. G Man 3G 91
Nanhyfer. Pemb 1E 43
Nannerch. Flin 4D 82
Nanpantan. Leics 4C 74
Nanpean. Corn 3D 6
Nanstallon. Corn 2E 7
Nant-ddu. Powy 4D 46
Nanternis. Cdgn 5C 56
Nantgaredig. Carm 3E 45
Nantgarw. Rhon 3E 33
Nant Glas. Powy 4B 58
Nantglyn. Den 4C 82
Nantgwyn. Powy 3B 58
Nantlle. Gwyn 5E 81
Nantmawr. Shrp 3E 71
Nantmel. Powy 4C 58
Nantmor. Gwyn 1F 69
Nant Peris. Gwyn 5F 81
Nantwich. Ches E 5A 84
Nant-y-bai. Carm 1A 46
Nant-y-bwch. Blae 4E 47
Nant-y-Derry. Mon 5G 47

Nant-y-dugoed. Powy 4B 70
Nant-y-felin. Cnwy 3F 81
Nantyffyllon. B'end 2B 32
Nantyglo. Blae 4E 47
Nant-y-meichiaid. Powy 4D 70
Nant-y-moel. B'end 2C 32
Nant-y-Pandy. Cnwy 3F 81
Naphill. Buck 2G 37
Nappa. Lanc 4A 98
Napton on the Hill. Warw 4B 62
Narberth. Pemb 3F 43
Narberth Bridge. Pemb 3F 43
Narborough. Leics 1C 62
Narborough. Norf 4G 77
Narkurs. Corn 3H 7
Narth, The. Mon 5A 48
Narthwaite. Cumb 5A 104
Nasareth. Gwyn 1D 68
Naseby. Nptn 3D 62
Nash. Buck 2F 51
Nash. Here 4F 59
Nash. Kent 5G 41
Nash. Newp 3G 33
Nash. Shrp 3A 60
Nash Lee. Buck 5G 51
Nassington. Nptn 1H 63
Nasty. Herts 3D 52
Natcott. Devn 4C 18
Nateby. Cumb 4A 104
Nateby. Lanc 5D 96
Nately Scures. Hants 1F 25
Natland. Cumb 1E 97
Naughton. Suff 1D 54
Naunton. Glos 3G 49
Naunton. Worc 2D 49
Naunton Beauchamp. Worc 5D 60
Navenby. Linc 5G 87
Navestock Heath. Essx 1G 39
Navestock Side. Essx 1G 39
Navidale. High 2H 165
Nawton. N Yor 1A 100
Nayland. Suff 2C 54
Nazeing. Essx 5E 53
Nealhouse. Cumb 4E 113
Neal's Green. W Mid 2H 61
Neap House. N Lin 3B 94
Near Sawrey. Cumb 5E 103
Neasden. G Lon 2D 38
Neasham. Darl 3A 106
Neath. Neat 2A 32
Neath Abbey. Neat 3G 31
Neatishead. Norf 3F 79
Neaton. Norf 5B 78
Nebo. Cdgn 4E 57
Nebo. Cnwy 5H 81
Nebo. Gwyn 5D 81
Nebo. IOA 1D 80
Necton. Norf 5A 78
Nedd. High 5B 166
Nedderton. Nmbd 1F 115
Nedging. Suff 1D 54
Nedging Tye. Suff 1D 54
Needham. Norf 2E 67
Needham Market. Suff 5C 66
Needham Street. Suff 4G 65
Needingworth. Cambs 3C 64
Needwood. Staf 3F 73
Neen Savage. Shrp 3A 60
Neen Sollars. Shrp 3A 60
Neenton. Shrp 2A 60
Nefyn. Gwyn 1C 68
Neilston. E Ren 4F 127
Neithrop. Oxon 1C 50
Nelly Andrews Green. Powy 5E 71
Nelson. Cphy 2E 32
Nelson. Lanc 1G 91
Nelson Village. Nmbd 2F 115
Nemphlar. S Lan 5B 128
Nempnett Thrubwell. Bath 5A 34
Nene Terrace. Linc 5B 76
Nenthall. Cumb 5A 114
Nenthead. Cumb 5A 114
Nenthorn. Bord 1A 120
Nercwys. Flin 4E 83
Neribus. Arg 4A 124
Nerston. S Lan 4H 127
Nesbit. Nmbd 1D 121
Nesfield. N Yor 5C 98
Ness. Ches W 3F 83
Nesscliffe. Shrp 4F 71
Ness of Tenston. Orkn 6B 172
Neston. Ches W 3E 83
Neston. Wilts 5D 34
Nethanfoot. S Lan 5B 128
Nether Alderley. Ches E 3C 84
Netheravon. Wilts 2G 23
Nether Blainslie. Bord 5B 130
Netherbrae. Abers 3E 161
Netherbrough. Orkn 6C 172
Nether Broughton. Leics 3D 74
Netherburn. S Lan 5B 128
Nether Burrow. Lanc 2F 97
Netherbury. Dors 3H 13
Netherby. Cumb 2E 113
Nether Careston. Ang 3E 145
Nether Cerne. Dors 3B 14
Nether Compton. Dors 1A 14
Nethercote. Glos 3G 49
Nethercote. Warw 4C 62
Nethercott. Devn 3E 19
Nethercott. Oxon 3C 50

Nether Dallachy—Newtown

Nether Dallachy. *Mor* 2A 160
Nether Durdie. *Per* 1E 136
Nether End. *Derbs* 3G 85
Netherend. *Glos* 5A 48
Nether Exe. *Devn* 2C 12
Netherfield. *E Sus* 4B 28
Netherfield. *Notts* 1D 74
Nethergate. *Norf* 3C 78
Netherhampton. *Wilts* 4G 23
Nether Handley. *Derbs* 3B 86
Nether Haugh. *S Yor* 1B 86
Nether Heage. *Derbs* 5A 86
Nether Heyford. *Nptn* 5D 62
Netherhouses. *Cumb* 1B 96
Nether Howcleugh. *Dum* 3C 118
Nether Kellet. *Lanc* 3E 97
Nether Kinmundy. *Abers* 4H 161
Netherland Green. *Staf* 2F 73
Nether Langwith. *Notts* 3C 86
Netherlaw. *Dum* 5E 111
Netherley. *Abers* 4F 153
Nethermill. *Dum* 1B 112
Nethermills. *Mor* 3C 160
Nether Moor. *Derbs* 4A 86
Nether Padley. *Derbs* 3G 85
Netherplace. *E Ren* 4G 127
Nether Poppleton. *York* 4H 99
Netherseal. *Derbs* 4G 73
Nether Silton. *N Yor* 5B 106
Nether Stowey. *Som* 3E 21
Nether Street. *Essx* 4F 53
Netherstreet. *Wilts* 5E 35
Netherthird. *E Ayr* 3E 117
Netherthong. *W Yor* 4B 92
Netherton. *Ang* 3E 145
Netherton. *Cumb* 1B 102
Netherton. *Devn* 5B 12
Netherton. *Hants* 1B 24
Netherton. *Here* 3A 48
Netherton. *Mers* 1F 83
Netherton. *N Lan* 4A 128
Netherton. *Nmbd* 4D 121
Netherton. *Per* 3A 144
Netherton. *Shrp* 2B 60
Netherton. *Stir* 2G 127
Netherton. *W Mid* 2D 60
Netherton. *W Yor* 3C 92 (nr. Horbury)
Netherton. *W Yor* 3B 92 (nr. Huddersfield)
Netherton. *Worc* 1E 49
Nethertown. *Cumb* 4A 102
Nethertown. *High* 1F 169
Nethertown. *Staf* 4F 73
Nether Urquhart. *Fife* 3D 136
Nether Wallop. *Hants* 3B 24
Nether Wasdale. *Cumb* 4C 102
Nether Welton. *Cumb* 5E 113
Nether Westcote. *Glos* 3H 49
Nether Whitacre. *Warw* 1G 61
Netherwhitton. *Nmbd* 5F 121
Nether Worton. *Oxon* 2C 50
Nethy Bridge. *High* 1E 151
Netley. *Hants* 2C 16
Netley. *Shrp* 5G 71
Netley Marsh. *Hants* 1B 16
Nettlebed. *Oxon* 3F 37
Nettlebridge. *Som* 2B 22
Nettlecombe. *Dors* 3A 14
Nettlecombe. *IOW* 5D 16
Nettleden. *Herts* 4A 52
Nettleham. *Linc* 3H 87
Nettlestead. *Kent* 5A 40
Nettlestead Green. *Kent* 5A 40
Nettlestone. *IOW* 3E 16
Nettlesworth. *Dur* 5F 115
Nettleton. *Linc* 4E 94
Nettleton. *Wilts* 4D 34
Netton. *Devn* 4B 8
Netton. *Wilts* 3G 23
Neuadd. *Carm* 3H 45
Neuadd. *Powy* 5C 70
Neuk, The. *Abers* 4E 153
Nevendon. *Essx* 1B 40
Nevern. *Pemb* 1A 44
New Abbey. *Dum* 3A 112
New Aberdour. *Abers* 2F 161
New Addington. *G Lon* 4E 39
Newall. *W Yor* 5D 98
New Alresford. *Hants* 3D 24
New Alyth. *Per* 4B 144
Newark. *Orkn* 3G 172
Newark. *Pet* 5B 76
Newark-on-Trent. *Notts* 5E 87
New Arley. *Warw* 2G 61
Newarthill. *N Lan* 4A 128
New Ash Green. *Kent* 4H 39
New Balderton. *Notts* 5F 87
New Barn. *Kent* 4H 39
New Barnetby. *N Lin* 3D 94
Newbattle. *Midl* 3G 129
New Bewick. *Nmbd* 2E 121
Newbie. *Dum* 3C 112
Newbiggin. *Cumb* 2H 103 (nr. Appleby)
Newbiggin. *Cumb* 3B 96 (nr. Barrow-in-Furness)
Newbiggin. *Cumb* 5G 113 (nr. Cumrew)
Newbiggin. *Cumb* 2F 103 (nr. Penrith)
Newbiggin. *Cumb* 5B 102 (nr. Seascale)
Newbiggin. *Dur* 5E 115 (nr. Consett)
Newbiggin. *Dur* 2C 104 (nr. Holwick)
Newbiggin. *Nmbd* 5C 114
Newbiggin. *N Yor* 5C 104 (nr. Askrigg)
Newbiggin. *N Yor* 1F 101 (nr. Filey)
Newbiggin. *N Yor* 1B 98 (nr. Thoralby)
Newbiggin-by-the-Sea. *Nmbd* 1G 115
Newbigging. *Ang* 5D 145 (nr. Monikie)
Newbigging. *Ang* 4B 144 (nr. Newtyle)
Newbigging. *Ang* 5D 144 (nr. Tealing)
Newbigging. *Edin* 2E 129
Newbigging. *S Lan* 5D 128
Newbiggin-on-Lune. *Cumb* 4A 104
Newbold. *Derbs* 3A 86
Newbold. *Leics* 4B 74
Newbold on Avon. *Warw* 3B 62
Newbold on Stour. *Warw* 1H 49
Newbold Pacey. *Warw* 5G 61
Newbold Verdon. *Leics* 5B 74
New Bolingbroke. *Linc* 5C 88
Newborough. *IOA* 4D 80
Newborough. *Pet* 5B 76
Newborough. *Staf* 3F 73
Newbottle. *Nptn* 2D 50
Newbottle. *Tyne* 4G 115
New Boultham. *Linc* 3G 87
Newbourne. *Suff* 1F 55
New Brancepeth. *Dur* 5F 115
Newbridge. *Cphy* 2F 33
Newbridge. *Cdgn* 5E 57
Newbridge. *Corn* 3B 4
New Bridge. *Dum* 2G 111
Newbridge. *Edin* 2E 129
Newbridge. *Hants* 1A 16
Newbridge. *IOW* 4C 16
Newbridge. *N Yor* 1C 100
Newbridge. *Pemb* 1D 42
Newbridge. *Wrex* 1E 71
Newbridge Green. *Worc* 2D 48
Newbridge-on-Usk. *Mon* 2G 33
Newbridge on Wye. *Powy* 5C 58
New Brighton. *Flin* 4E 83
New Brighton. *Hants* 2F 17
New Brighton. *Mers* 1F 83
New Brinsley. *Notts* 5B 86
Newbrough. *Nmbd* 3B 114
New Broughton. *Wrex* 5F 83
New Buckenham. *Norf* 1C 66
Newbuildings. *Devn* 2A 12
Newburgh. *Abers* 1G 153
Newburgh. *Fife* 2E 137
Newburgh. *Lanc* 3C 90
Newburn. *Tyne* 3E 115
Newbury. *W Ber* 5C 36
Newbury. *Wilts* 2D 22
Newby. *Cumb* 2G 103
Newby. *N Yor* 2G 97 (nr. Ingleton)
Newby. *N Yor* 1E 101 (nr. Scarborough)
Newby. *N Yor* 3C 106 (nr. Stokesley)
Newby Bridge. *Cumb* 1C 96
Newby Cote. *N Yor* 2G 97
Newby East. *Cumb* 4F 113
Newby Head. *Cumb* 2G 103
New Byth. *Abers* 3F 161
Newby West. *Cumb* 4E 113
Newby Wiske. *N Yor* 1F 99
Newcastle. *B'end* 3B 32
Newcastle. *Mon* 4H 47
Newcastle. *Shrp* 2E 59
Newcastle Emlyn. *Carm* 1D 44
Newcastle International Airport. *Tyne* 2E 115
Newcastleton. *Bord* 1F 113
Newcastle-under-Lyme. *Staf* 1C 72
Newcastle Upon Tyne. *Tyne* 3F 115 & 205
Newchapel. *Pemb* 1G 43
Newchapel. *Powy* 2B 58
Newchapel. *Staf* 5C 84
Newchapel. *Surr* 1E 27
New Cheriton. *Hants* 4D 24
Newchurch. *Carm* 3D 45
Newchurch. *Here* 5F 59
Newchurch. *IOW* 4D 16
Newchurch. *Kent* 2E 29
Newchurch. *Lanc* 1G 91 (nr. Nelson)
Newchurch. *Lanc* 2G 91 (nr. Rawtenstall)
Newchurch. *Mon* 2H 33
Newchurch. *Powy* 5E 58
Newchurch. *Staf* 3F 73
New Costessey. *Norf* 4D 78
Newcott. *Devn* 2F 13
New Cowper. *Cumb* 5C 112
Newcraighall. *Edin* 2G 129
New Crofton. *W Yor* 3D 93
New Cross. *Cdgn* 3F 57
New Cross. *Som* 1H 13
New Cumnock. *E Ayr* 3F 117
New Deer. *Abers* 4F 161
New Denham. *Buck* 2B 38
Newdigate. *Surr* 1C 26
New Duston. *Nptn* 4E 62
New Earswick. *York* 4A 100
New Edlington. *S Yor* 1C 86
New Elgin. *Mor* 2G 159
New Ellerby. *E Yor* 1E 95
Newell Green. *Brac* 4G 37
New Eltham. *G Lon* 3F 39
New End. *Warw* 4F 61
New End. *Worc* 5E 61
Newenden. *Kent* 3C 28
New England. *Essx* 1H 53
New England. *Pet* 5A 76
Newent. *Glos* 3C 48
New Ferry. *Mers* 2F 83
Newfield. *Dur* 4F 115 (nr. Chester-le-Street)
Newfield. *Dur* 1F 105 (nr. Willington)
New Forest. *Hants* 1H 15
Newfound. *Hants* 1D 24
New Fryston. *W Yor* 2E 93
New Galloway. *Dum* 2D 110
Newgate. *Norf* 1C 78
Newgate. *Pemb* 2C 42
Newgate Street. *Herts* 5D 52
New Greens. *Herts* 5B 52
New Grimsby. *IOS* 1A 4
New Hainford. *Norf* 4E 78
Newhall. *Ches E* 1A 72
Newhall. *Staf* 3G 73
Newham. *Nmbd* 2F 121
New Hartley. *Nmbd* 2G 115
Newhaven. *Derbs* 4F 85
Newhaven. *E Sus* 5F 27 & 215
Newhaven. *Edin* 2F 129
New Haw. *Surr* 4B 38
New Hedges. *Pemb* 4F 43
New Herrington. *Tyne* 4G 115
Newhey. *G Man* 3H 91
New Holkham. *Norf* 2A 78
New Holland. *N Lin* 2D 94
Newholm. *N Yor* 3F 107
New Houghton. *Derbs* 4C 86
New Houghton. *Norf* 3G 77
Newhouse. *N Lan* 3A 128
New Houses. *N Yor* 2H 97
New Hutton. *Cumb* 5G 103
New Hythe. *Kent* 5B 40
Newick. *E Sus* 3F 27
Newingreen. *Kent* 2F 29
Newington. *Edin* 2F 129
Newington. *Kent* 2F 29 (nr. Folkestone)
Newington. *Kent* 4C 40 (nr. Sittingbourne)
Newington. *Notts* 1D 86
Newington. *Oxon* 2E 36
Newington Bagpath. *Glos* 2D 34
New Inn. *Carm* 2E 45
New Inn. *Mon* 5H 47
New Inn. *N Yor* 2H 97
New Inn. *Torf* 5G 47
New Invention. *Shrp* 3E 59
New Kelso. *High* 4B 156
New Lanark. *S Lan* 5B 128
Newland. *Glos* 5A 48
Newland. *Hull* 1D 94
Newland. *N Yor* 2G 93
Newland. *Som* 3B 20
Newland. *Worc* 1C 48
Newlandrig. *Midl* 3G 129
Newlands. *Cumb* 1E 103
Newlands. *Essx* 2C 40
Newlands. *High* 4B 158
Newlands. *Nmbd* 4D 115
Newlands. *Notts* 4C 86
Newlands. *Staf* 3E 73
Newlands of Geise. *High* 2C 168
Newlands of Tynet. *Mor* 2A 160
Newlands Park. *IOA* 2B 80
New Lane. *Lanc* 3C 90
New Lane End. *Warr* 1A 84
New Langholm. *Dum* 1E 113
New Leake. *Linc* 5D 88
New Leeds. *Abers* 3G 161
New Lenton. *Nott* 2C 74
New Longton. *Lanc* 2D 90
Newlot. *Orkn* 6E 172
New Luce. *Dum* 3G 109
Newlyn. *Corn* 4B 4
Newmachar. *Abers* 2F 153
Newmains. *N Lan* 4B 128
New Mains of Ury. *Abers* 5F 153
New Malden. *G Lon* 4D 38
Newman's Green. *Suff* 1B 54
Newmarket. *Suff* 4F 65
Newmarket. *W Isl* 4G 171
New Marske. *Red C* 2D 106
New Marton. *Shrp* 2F 71
New Micklefield. *W Yor* 1E 93
New Mill. *Abers* 4E 160
New Mill. *Corn* 3B 4
New Mill. *Herts* 4H 51
Newmill. *Mor* 3B 160
Newmill. *Bord* 3G 119
New Mill. *W Yor* 4B 92
New Mill. *Wilts* 5G 35
Newmillerdam. *W Yor* 3D 92
New Mills. *Corn* 3C 6
New Mills. *Derbs* 2E 85
Newmills. *Fife* 1D 128
Newmills. *High* 2A 158
New Mills. *Mon* 5A 48
New Mills. *Powy* 5C 70
Newmiln. *Per* 5A 144
Newmilns. *E Ayr* 1E 117
New Milton. *Hants* 3H 15
New Mistley. *Essx* 2E 54
New Moat. *Pemb* 2E 43
Newmore. *High* 3H 157 (nr. Dingwall)
Newmore. *High* 1A 158 (nr. Invergordon)
Newnham. *Cambs* 5D 64
Newnham. *Glos* 4B 48
Newnham. *Hants* 1F 25
Newnham. *Herts* 2C 52
Newnham. *Kent* 5D 40
Newnham. *Nptn* 5C 62
Newnham. *Warw* 4F 61
Newnham Bridge. *Worc* 4A 60
New Ollerton. *Notts* 4D 86
New Oscott. *W Mid* 1F 61
Newpark. *Fife* 2G 137
New Park. *N Yor* 4E 99
New Pitsligo. *Abers* 3F 161
New Polzeath. *Corn* 1D 6
Newport. *Corn* 4D 10
Newport. *Devn* 3F 19
Newport. *E Yor* 1B 94
Newport. *Essx* 2F 53
Newport. *Glos* 2B 34
Newport. *High* 1H 165
Newport. *IOW* 4D 16
Newport. *Newp* 3G 33 & 205
Newport. *Norf* 4H 79
Newport. *Pemb* 1E 43
Newport. *Som* 4G 21
Newport. *Telf* 4B 72
Newport-on-Tay. *Fife* 1G 137
Newport Pagnell. *Mil* 1G 51
Newpound Common. *W Sus* 3B 26
New Prestwick. *S Ayr* 2C 116
New Quay. *Cdgn* 5C 56
Newquay. *Corn* 2C 6
Newquay Cornwall Airport. *Corn* 2C 6
New Rackheath. *Norf* 4E 79
New Radnor. *Powy* 4E 58
New Rent. *Cumb* 1F 103
New Ridley. *Nmbd* 4D 114
New Romney. *Kent* 3E 29
New Rossington. *S Yor* 1D 86
New Row. *Cdgn* 3G 57
New Row. *Lanc* 1E 91
New Row. *N Yor* 3D 106
New Sauchie. *Clac* 4A 136
Newsbank. *Ches E* 4C 84
Newseat. *Abers* 5E 160
Newsham. *Lanc* 1D 90
Newsham. *Nmbd* 2G 115
Newsham. *N Yor* 3E 105 (nr. Richmond)
Newsham. *N Yor* 1F 99 (nr. Thirsk)
New Sharlston. *W Yor* 3D 93
Newsholme. *E Yor* 2H 93
Newsholme. *Lanc* 4H 97
New Shoreston. *Nmbd* 1F 121
New Springs. *G Man* 4D 90
Newstead. *Notts* 5C 86
Newstead. *Bord* 1H 119
New Stevenston. *N Lan* 4A 128
New Street. *Here* 5F 59
Newstreet Lane. *Shrp* 2A 72
New Swanage. *Dors* 4F 15
New Swannington. *Leics* 4B 74
Newthorpe. *N Yor* 1E 93
Newthorpe. *Notts* 1B 74
Newton. *Arg* 4H 133
Newton. *B'end* 4B 32
Newton. *Cambs* 1E 53 (nr. Cambridge)
Newton. *Cambs* 4D 76 (nr. Wisbech)
Newton. *Ches W* 4G 83 (nr. Chester)
Newton. *Ches W* 5H 83 (nr. Tattenhall)
Newton. *Cumb* 2B 96
Newton. *Derbs* 5B 86
Newton. *Dors* 1C 14
Newton. *Dum* 2D 112 (nr. Annan)
Newton. *Dum* 5D 118 (nr. Moffat)
Newton. *G Man* 1D 84
Newton. *Here* 2G 47 (nr. Ewyas Harold)
Newton. *Here* 5H 59 (nr. Leominster)
Newton. *High* 2B 158 (nr. Cromarty)
Newton. *High* 4B 158 (nr. Inverness)
Newton. *High* 5C 166 (nr. Kylestrome)
Newton. *High* 4F 169 (nr. Wick)
Newton. *Lanc* 2E 97 (nr. Carnforth)
Newton. *Lanc* 4F 97 (nr. Clitheroe)
Newton. *Lanc* 1C 90 (nr. Kirkham)
Newton. *Linc* 2H 75
Newton. *Mers* 2E 83
Newton. *Mor* 2F 159
Newton. *Norf* 4H 77
Newton. *Nptn* 2F 63
Newton. *Nmbd* 3D 114
Newton. *Notts* 1D 74
Newton. *Bord* 2A 120
Newton. *Shet* 8E 173
Newton. *Shrp* 1B 60 (nr. Bridgnorth)
Newton. *Shrp* 2G 71 (nr. Wem)
Newton. *Som* 3E 20
Newton. *S Lan* 3H 127 (nr. Glasgow)
Newton. *S Lan* 1B 118 (nr. Lanark)
Newton. *Staf* 3E 73
Newton. *Suff* 1C 54
Newton. *Swan* 4F 31
Newton. *Warw* 3C 62
Newton. *W Lot* 2D 129
Newton. *Wilts* 4H 23
Newton Abbot. *Devn* 5B 12
Newtonairds. *Dum* 1F 111
Newton Arlosh. *Cumb* 4D 112
Newton Aycliffe. *Dur* 2F 105
Newton Bewley. *Hart* 2B 106
Newton Blossomville. *Mil* 5G 63
Newton Bromswold. *Bed* 4G 63
Newton Burgoland. *Leics* 5A 74
Newton by Toft. *Linc* 2H 87
Newton Ferrers. *Devn* 4B 8
Newton Flotman. *Norf* 1E 66
Newtongrange. *Midl* 3G 129
Newton Green. *Mon* 2A 34
Newton Hall. *Dur* 5F 115
Newton Hall. *Nmbd* 3D 114
Newton Harcourt. *Leics* 1D 62
Newton Heath. *G Man* 4G 91
Newtonhill. *Abers* 4G 153
Newtonhill. *High* 4H 157
Newton Hill. *W Yor* 2D 92
Newton Ketton. *Darl* 2A 106
Newton Kyme. *N Yor* 5G 99
Newton-le-Willows. *Mers* 1H 83
Newton-le-Willows. *N Yor* 1E 98
Newton Longville. *Buck* 2G 51
Newton Mearns. *E Ren* 4G 127
Newtonmore. *High* 4B 150
Newton Morrell. *N Yor* 4F 105
Newton Mulgrave. *N Yor* 3E 107
Newton of Ardtoe. *High* 1A 140
Newton of Balcanquhal. *Per* 2D 136
Newton of Beltrees. *Ren* 4E 127
Newton of Falkland. *Fife* 3E 137
Newton of Mountblairy. *Abers* 3E 160
Newton of Pitcairns. *Per* 2C 136
Newton-on-Ouse. *N Yor* 4H 99
Newton-on-Rawcliffe. *N Yor* 5F 107
Newton on the Hill. *Shrp* 3G 71
Newton-on-the-Moor. *Nmbd* 4F 121
Newton on Trent. *Linc* 3F 87
Newton Poppleford. *Devn* 4D 12
Newton Purcell. *Oxon* 2E 51
Newton Regis. *Warw* 5G 73
Newton Reigny. *Cumb* 1F 103
Newton Rigg. *Cumb* 1F 103
Newton St Cyres. *Devn* 3B 12
Newton St Faith. *Norf* 4E 78
Newton St Loe. *Bath* 5C 34
Newton St Petrock. *Devn* 1E 11
Newton Solney. *Derbs* 3G 73
Newton Stacey. *Hants* 2C 24
Newton Stewart. *Dum* 3B 110
Newton Toney. *Wilts* 2H 23
Newton Tony. *Wilts* 2H 23
Newton Tracey. *Devn* 4F 19
Newton under Roseberry. *Red C* 3C 106
Newton Unthank. *Leics* 5B 74
Newton upon Ayr. *S Ayr* 2C 116
Newton upon Derwent. *E Yor* 5B 100
Newton Valence. *Hants* 3F 25
Newton-with-Scales. *Lanc* 1B 90
Newtown. *Abers* 2E 160
Newtown. *Cambs* 4H 63
Newtown. *Corn* 5C 10
Newtown. *Cumb* 5B 112 (nr. Aspatria)
Newtown. *Cumb* 3G 113 (nr. Brampton)
Newtown. *Cumb* 2G 103 (nr. Penrith)
Newtown. *Derbs* 2D 85
Newtown. *Devn* 4A 20

Newtown—Nuttall

Newtown. *Dors* 2H **13**
(nr. Beaminster)
New Town. *Dors* 1E **15**
(nr. Sixpenny Handley)
New Town. *E Lot* 2H **129**
Newtown. *Falk* 1C **128**
Newtown. *Glos* 5B **48**
(nr. Lydney)
Newtown. *Glos* 2E **49**
(nr. Tewkesbury)
Newtown. *Hants* 1D **16**
(nr. Bishop's Waltham)
Newtown. *Hants* 3G **25**
(nr. Liphook)
Newtown. *Hants* 1A **16**
(nr. Lyndhurst)
Newtown. *Hants* 5C **36**
(nr. Newbury)
Newtown. *Hants* 4B **24**
(nr. Romsey)
Newtown. *Hants* 2C **16**
(nr. Warsash)
Newtown. *Hants* 1E **16**
(nr. Wickham)
Newtown. *Here* 2B **48**
(nr. Ledbury)
Newtown. *Here* 2A **48**
(nr. Little Dewchurch)
Newtown. *Here* 1B **48**
(nr. Stretton Grandison)
Newtown. *High* 3F **149**
Newtown. *IOM* 4C **108**
Newtown. *IOW* 3C **16**
Newtown. *Lanc* 3D **90**
New Town. *Lutn* 3A **52**
Newtown. *Nmbd* 4E **121**
(nr. Rothbury)
Newtown. *Nmbd* 2E **121**
(nr. Wooler)
Newtown. *Pool* 3F **15**
Newtown. *Powy* 1D **58**
Newtown. *Rhon* 2D **32**
Newtown. *Shet* 3F **173**
Newtown. *Shrp* 2G **71**
Newtown. *Som* 1F **13**
Newtown. *Staf* 4D **84**
(nr. Biddulph)
Newtown. *Staf* 5D **73**
(nr. Cannock)
Newtown. *Staf* 4E **85**
(nr. Longnor)
New Town. *W Yor* 2E **93**
Newtown. *Wilts* 4E **23**
Newtown-in-St Martin. *Corn* 4E **5**
Newtown Linford. *Leics* 4C **74**
Newtown St Boswells. *Bord* 1H **119**
New Tredegar. *Cphy* 5E **47**
Newtyle. *Ang* 4B **144**
New Village. *E Yor* 1D **94**
New Village. *S Yor* 4F **93**
New Walsoken. *Cambs* 5D **76**
New Waltham. *NE Lin* 4F **95**
New Winton. *E Lot* 2H **129**
New World. *Cambs* 1C **64**
New Yatt. *Oxon* 4B **50**
Newyears Green. *G Lon* 2B **38**
New York. *Linc* 5B **88**
New York. *Tyne* 2G **115**
Nextend. *Here* 5F **59**
Neyland. *Pemb* 4D **42**
Nib Heath. *Shrp* 4G **71**
Nicholashayne. *Devn* 1E **12**
Nicholaston. *Swan* 4E **31**
Nidd. *N Yor* 3F **99**
Niddrie. *Edin* 2F **129**
Niddry. *Edin* 2D **129**
Nigg. *Aber* 3G **153**
Nigg. *High* 1C **158**
Nigg Ferry. *High* 2B **158**
Nightcott. *Som* 4B **20**
Nimmer. *Som* 1G **13**
Nine Ashes. *Essx* 5F **53**
Ninebanks. *Nmbd* 4A **114**
Nine Elms. *Swin* 3G **35**
Ninemile Bar. *Dum* 2F **111**
Nine Mile Burn. *Midl* 4E **129**
Ninfield. *E Sus* 4B **28**
Ningwood. *IOW* 4C **16**
Nisbet. *Bord* 2A **120**
Nisbet Hill. *Bord* 4D **130**
Niton. *IOW* 5D **16**
Nitshill. *E Ren* 4G **127**
Niwbwrch. *IOA* 4D **80**
Noak Hill. *G Lon* 1G **39**
Nobold. *Shrp* 4G **71**
Nobottle. *Nptn* 4D **62**
Nocton. *Linc* 4H **87**
Nogdam End. *Norf* 5F **79**
Noke. *Oxon* 4D **50**
Nolton. *Pemb* 3C **42**
Nolton Haven. *Pemb* 3C **42**
No Man's Heath. *Ches W* 1H **71**
No Man's Heath. *Warw* 5G **73**
Nomansland. *Devn* 1B **12**
Nomansland. *Wilts* 1A **16**
Noneley. *Shrp* 3G **71**
Noness. *Shet* 9F **173**
Nonikiln. *High* 1A **158**
Nonington. *Kent* 5G **41**
Nook. *Cumb* 2F **113**
(nr. Longtown)
Nook. *Cumb* 1E **97**
(nr. Milnthorpe)
Noranside. *Ang* 2D **144**
Norbreck. *Bkpl* 5C **96**
Norbridge. *Here* 1C **48**
Norbury. *Ches E* 1H **71**
Norbury. *Derbs* 1F **73**
Norbury. *Shrp* 1F **59**
Norbury. *Staf* 3B **72**
Norby. *N Yor* 1G **99**
Norby. *Shet* 6C **173**
Norcross. *Lanc* 5C **96**
Nordelph. *Norf* 5E **77**
Norden. *G Man* 3G **91**
Nordley. *Shrp* 1A **60**
Norfolk Broads. *Norf* 5G **79**
Norham. *Nmbd* 5F **131**
Norland Town. *W Yor* 2A **92**
Norley. *Ches W* 3H **83**
Norleywood. *Hants* 3B **16**
Normanby. *N Lin* 3B **94**
Normanby. *N Yor* 1B **100**
Normanby. *Red C* 3C **106**
Normanby-by-Spital. *Linc* 2H **87**
Normanby le Wold. *Linc* 1A **88**
Norman Cross. *Cambs* 1A **64**
Normandy. *Surr* 5A **38**
Norman's Bay. *E Sus* 5A **28**
Norman's Green. *Devn* 2D **12**
Normanton. *Derb* 2H **73**
Normanton. *Leics* 1F **75**
Normanton. *Linc* 1G **75**
Normanton. *Notts* 5E **86**
Normanton. *W Yor* 2D **93**
Normanton le Heath. *Leics* 4A **74**
Normanton on Soar. *Notts* 3C **74**
Normanton-on-the-Wolds. *Notts* 2D **74**
Normanton on Trent. *Notts* 4E **87**
Normoss. *Lanc* 1B **90**
Norrington Common. *Wilts* 5D **35**
Norris Green. *Mers* 1F **83**
Norris Hill. *Leics* 4H **73**
Norristhorpe. *W Yor* 2C **92**
Northacre. *Norf* 1B **66**
Northall. *Buck* 3H **51**
Northallerton. *N Yor* 5A **106**
Northam. *Devn* 4E **19**
Northam. *Sotn* 1C **16**
Northampton. *Nptn* 4E **63** & **206**
North Anston. *S Yor* 2C **86**
North Ascot. *Brac* 4A **38**
North Aston. *Oxon* 3C **50**
Northaw. *Herts* 5C **52**
Northay. *Som* 1F **13**
North Baddesley. *Hants* 4B **24**
North Balfern. *Dum* 4B **110**
North Ballachulish. *High* 2E **141**
North Barrow. *Som* 4B **22**
North Barsham. *Norf* 2B **78**
Northbeck. *Linc* 1H **75**
North Benfleet. *Essx* 2B **40**
North Bersted. *W Sus* 5A **26**
North Berwick. *E Lot* 1B **130**
North Bitchburn. *Dur* 1E **105**
North Blyth. *Nmbd* 1G **115**
North Boarhunt. *Hants* 1E **16**
North Bockhampton. *Dors* 3G **15**
Northborough. *Pet* 5A **76**
Northbourne. *Kent* 5H **41**
Northbourne. *Oxon* 3D **36**
North Bovey. *Devn* 4H **11**
North Bowood. *Dors* 3H **13**
North Bradley. *Wilts* 1D **22**
North Brentor. *Devn* 4E **11**
North Brewham. *Som* 3C **22**
Northbrook. *Oxon* 3C **50**
North Brook End. *Cambs* 1C **52**
North Broomhill. *Nmbd* 4G **121**
North Buckland. *Devn* 2E **19**
North Burlingham. *Norf* 4F **79**
North Cadbury. *Som* 4B **22**
North Carlton. *Linc* 3G **87**
North Cave. *E Yor* 1B **94**
North Cerney. *Glos* 5F **49**
North Chailey. *E Sus* 3E **27**
Northchapel. *W Sus* 3A **26**
North Charford. *Hants* 1G **15**
North Charlton. *Nmbd* 2F **121**
North Cheriton. *Som* 4B **22**
North Chideock. *Dors* 3H **13**
Northchurch. *Herts* 5H **51**
North Cliffe. *E Yor* 1B **94**
North Clifton. *Notts* 3F **87**
North Close. *Dur* 1F **105**
North Cockerington. *Linc* 1C **88**
North Coker. *Som* 1A **14**
North Collafirth. *Shet* 3E **173**
North Common. *E Sus* 3E **27**
North Commonty. *Abers* 4F **161**
North Coombe. *Devn* 1B **12**
North Cornelly. *B'end* 3B **32**
North Cotes. *Linc* 4G **95**
Northcott. *Devn* 3D **10**
(nr. Boyton)
Northcott. *Devn* 1D **12**
(nr. Culmstock)
Northcourt. *Oxon* 2D **36**
North Cove. *Suff* 2G **67**
North Cowton. *N Yor* 4F **105**
North Craigo. *Ang* 2F **145**
North Crawley. *Mil* 1H **51**
North Cray. *G Lon* 3F **39**
North Creake. *Norf* 2A **78**
North Curry. *Som* 4G **21**
North Dalton. *E Yor* 4D **100**
North Deighton. *N Yor* 4F **99**
North Dronley. *Ang* 5C **144**
North Duffield. *N Yor* 1G **93**
Northdyke. *Orkn* 5B **172**
Northedge. *Derbs* 4A **86**
North Elkington. *Linc* 1B **88**
North Elmham. *Norf* 3B **78**
North Elmsall. *W Yor* 3E **93**
Northend. *Buck* 2F **37**
North End. *E Yor* 1F **95**
North End. *Essx* 4G **53**
(nr. Great Dunmow)
North End. *Essx* 2A **54**
(nr. Great Yeldham)
North End. *Hants* 5C **36**
North End. *Leics* 4C **74**
North End. *Linc* 1B **76**
North End. *Norf* 1B **66**
North End. *N Som* 5H **33**
North End. *Port* 2E **17**
Northend. *Warw* 5A **62**
North End. *W Sus* 5C **26**
North End. *Wilts* 2F **35**
North Erradale. *High* 5B **162**
North Evington. *Leic* 5D **74**
North Fambridge. *Essx* 1C **40**
North Fearns. *High* 5E **155**
North Featherstone. *W Yor* 2E **93**
North Feorline. *N Ayr* 3D **122**
North Ferriby. *E Yor* 2C **94**
Northfield. *Aber* 3F **153**
Northfield. *Hull* 2D **94**
Northfield. *Som* 3F **21**
Northfield. *W Mid* 3E **61**
Northfleet. *Kent* 3H **39**
North Frodingham. *E Yor* 4F **101**
Northgate. *Linc* 3A **76**
North Gluss. *Shet* 4E **173**
North Gorley. *Hants* 1G **15**
North Green. *Norf* 2E **66**
North Green. *Suff* 4F **67**
(nr. Framlingham)
North Green. *Suff* 3F **67**
(nr. Halesworth)
North Green. *Suff* 4F **67**
(nr. Saxmundham)
North Greetwell. *Linc* 3H **87**
North Grimston. *N Yor* 3C **100**
North Halling. *Medw* 4B **40**
North Hayling. *Hants* 2F **17**
North Hazelrigg. *Nmbd* 1E **121**
North Heasley. *Devn* 3H **19**
North Heath. *W Sus* 3B **26**
North Hill. *Corn* 5C **10**
North Hinksey Village. *Oxon* 5C **50**
North Holmwood. *Surr* 1C **26**
North Huish. *Devn* 3D **8**
North Hykeham. *Linc* 4G **87**
Northiam. *E Sus* 3C **28**
Northill. *C Beds* 1B **52**
Northington. *Hants* 3D **24**
North Kelsey. *Linc* 4D **94**
North Kelsey Moor. *Linc* 4D **94**
North Kessock. *High* 4A **158**
North Killingholme. *N Lin* 3E **95**
North Kilvington. *N Yor* 1G **99**
North Kilworth. *Leics* 2D **62**
North Kyme. *Linc* 5A **88**
North Lancing. *W Sus* 5C **26**
Northlands. *Linc* 5C **88**
Northleach. *Glos* 4G **49**
North Lee. *Buck* 5G **51**
North Lees. *N Yor* 2E **99**
Northleigh. *Devn* 3G **19**
(nr. Barnstaple)
Northleigh. *Devn* 3E **13**
(nr. Honiton)
North Leigh. *Kent* 1F **29**
North Leigh. *Oxon* 4B **50**
North Leverton. *Notts* 2E **87**
Northlew. *Devn* 3F **11**
North Littleton. *Worc* 1F **49**
North Lopham. *Norf* 2C **66**
North Luffenham. *Rut* 5G **75**
North Marden. *W Sus* 1G **17**
North Marston. *Buck* 3F **51**
North Middleton. *Midl* 4G **129**
North Middleton. *Nmbd* 2E **121**
North Molton. *Devn* 4H **19**
North Moor. *N Yor* 1D **100**
Northmoor. *Oxon* 5C **50**
Northmoor Green. *Som* 3G **21**
North Moreton. *Oxon* 3D **36**
Northmuir. *Ang* 3C **144**
North Mundham. *W Sus* 2G **17**
North Murie. *Per* 1E **137**
North Muskham. *Notts* 5E **87**
North Ness. *Orkn* 8C **172**
North Newbald. *E Yor* 1C **94**
North Newington. *Oxon* 2C **50**
North Newnton. *Wilts* 1G **23**
North Newton. *Som* 3F **21**
Northney. *Hants* 2F **17**
North Nibley. *Glos* 2C **34**
North Oakley. *Hants* 1D **24**
North Ockendon. *G Lon* 2G **39**
Northolt. *G Lon* 2C **38**
Northop. *Flin* 4E **83**
Northop Hall. *Flin* 4E **83**
North Ormesby. *Midd* 3C **106**
North Ormsby. *Linc* 1B **88**
Northorpe. *Linc* 4H **75**
(nr. Bourne)
Northorpe. *Linc* 2B **76**
(nr. Donington)
Northorpe. *Linc* 1F **87**
(nr. Gainsborough)
North Otterington. *N Yor* 1F **99**
Northover. *Som* 3H **21**
(nr. Glastonbury)
Northover. *Som* 4A **22**
(nr. Yeovil)
North Owersby. *Linc* 1H **87**
Northowram. *W Yor* 2B **92**
North Perrott. *Som* 2H **13**
North Petherton. *Som* 3F **21**
North Petherwin. *Corn* 4C **10**
North Pickenham. *Norf* 5A **78**
North Piddle. *Worc* 5D **60**
North Poorton. *Dors* 3A **14**
North Port. *Arg* 1H **133**
Northport. *Dors* 4E **15**
North Queensferry. *Fife* 1E **129**
North Radworthy. *Devn* 3A **20**
North Rauceby. *Linc* 1H **75**
Northrepps. *Norf* 2E **79**
North Rigton. *N Yor* 5E **99**
North Rode. *Ches E* 4C **84**
North Roe. *Shet* 3E **173**
North Ronaldsay Airport. *Orkn* 2G **172**
North Row. *Cumb* 1D **102**
North Runcton. *Norf* 4F **77**
North Sannox. *N Ayr* 5B **126**
North Scale. *Cumb* 2A **96**
North Scarle. *Linc* 4F **87**
North Seaton. *Nmbd* 1F **115**
North Seaton Colliery. *Nmbd* 1F **115**
North Sheen. *G Lon* 3C **38**
North Shian. *Arg* 4D **140**
North Shields. *Tyne* 3G **115**
North Shoebury. *S'end* 2D **40**
North Shore. *Bkpl* 1B **90**
North Side. *Cumb* 2B **102**
North Skelton. *Red C* 3D **106**
North Somercotes. *Linc* 1D **88**
North Stainley. *N Yor* 2E **99**
North Stainmore. *Cumb* 3B **104**
North Stifford. *Thur* 2H **39**
North Stoke. *Bath* 5C **34**
North Stoke. *Oxon* 3E **36**
North Stoke. *W Sus* 4B **26**
Northstowe. *Cambs* 4D **64**
North Street. *Hants* 3E **25**
North Street. *Kent* 5E **40**
North Street. *Medw* 3C **40**
North Street. *W Ber* 4E **37**
North Sunderland. *Nmbd* 1G **121**
North Tamerton. *Corn* 3D **10**
North Tawton. *Devn* 2G **11**
North Thoresby. *Linc* 1B **88**
North Town. *Devn* 2F **11**
Northtown. *Orkn* 8D **172**
North Town. *Shet* 10E **173**
North Tuddenham. *Norf* 4C **78**
North Walbottle. *Tyne* 3E **115**
Northwall. *Orkn* 3G **172**
North Walney. *Cumb* 3A **96**
North Walsham. *Norf* 2E **79**
North Waltham. *Hants* 2D **24**
North Warnborough. *Hants* 1F **25**
North Water Bridge. *Ang* 2F **145**
North Watten. *High* 3E **169**
Northway. *Glos* 2E **49**
Northway. *Swan* 4E **31**
North Weald Bassett. *Essx* 5F **53**
North Weston. *N Som* 4H **33**
North Weston. *Oxon* 5E **51**
North Wheatley. *Notts* 2E **87**
North Whilborough. *Devn* 2E **9**
Northwich. *Ches W* 3A **84**
North Wick. *Bath* 5A **34**
Northwick. *Som* 2G **21**
Northwick. *S Glo* 3A **34**
North Widcombe. *Bath* 1A **22**
North Willingham. *Linc* 2A **88**
North Wingfield. *Derbs* 4B **86**
North Witham. *Linc* 3G **75**
Northwold. *Norf* 1G **65**
Northwood. *Derbs* 4G **85**
Northwood. *G Lon* 1B **38**
Northwood. *IOW* 3C **16**
Northwood. *Kent* 4H **41**
Northwood. *Shrp* 2G **71**
Northwood. *Stoke* 1C **72**
Northwood Green. *Glos* 4C **48**
North Wootton. *Dors* 1B **14**
North Wootton. *Norf* 3F **77**
North Wootton. *Som* 2A **22**
North Wraxall. *Wilts* 4D **34**
North Wroughton. *Swin* 3G **35**
North Yardhope. *Nmbd* 4D **120**
North York Moors. *N Yor* 5D **107**
Norton. *Devn* 3E **9**
Norton. *Glos* 3D **48**
Norton. *Hal* 2H **83**
Norton. *Herts* 2C **52**
Norton. *IOW* 4B **16**
Norton. *Mon* 3H **47**
Norton. *Nptn* 4D **62**
Norton. *Notts* 3C **86**
Norton. *Powy* 4F **59**
Norton. *Shrp* 2G **59**
(nr. Ludlow)
Norton. *Shrp* 5B **72**
(nr. Madeley)
Norton. *Shrp* 5H **71**
(nr. Shrewsbury)
Norton. *S Yor* 3F **93**
(nr. Askern)
Norton. *S Yor* 2A **86**
(nr. Sheffield)
Norton. *Stoc T* 2B **106**
Norton. *Suff* 4B **66**
Norton. *Swan* 4F **31**
Norton. *W Sus* 5A **26**
(nr. Arundel)
Norton. *W Sus* 3G **17**
(nr. Selsey)
Norton. *Wilts* 3D **35**
Norton. *Worc* 1F **49**
(nr. Evesham)
Norton. *Worc* 5C **60**
(nr. Worcester)
Norton Bavant. *Wilts* 2E **23**
Norton Bridge. *Staf* 2C **72**
Norton Canes. *Staf* 5E **73**
Norton Canon. *Here* 1G **47**
Norton Corner. *Norf* 3C **78**
Norton Disney. *Linc* 5F **87**
Norton East. *Staf* 5E **73**
Norton Ferris. *Wilts* 3C **22**
Norton Fitzwarren. *Som* 4F **21**
Norton Green. *IOW* 4B **16**
Norton Green. *Stoke* 5D **84**
Norton Hawkfield. *Bath* 5A **34**
Norton Heath. *Essx* 5G **53**
Norton in Hales. *Shrp* 2B **72**
Norton in the Moors. *Stoke* 5C **84**
Norton-Juxta-Twycross. *Leics* 5H **73**
Norton-le-Clay. *N Yor* 2G **99**
Norton Lindsey. *Warw* 4G **61**
Norton Little Green. *Suff* 4B **66**
Norton Malreward. *Bath* 5B **34**
Norton Mandeville. *Essx* 5F **53**
Norton-on-Derwent. *N Yor* 2B **100**
Norton St Philip. *Som* 1C **22**
Norton Subcourse. *Norf* 1G **67**
Norton sub Hamdon. *Som* 1H **13**
Norton Woodseats. *S Yor* 2A **86**
Norwell. *Notts* 4E **87**
Norwell Woodhouse. *Notts* 4E **87**
Norwich. *Norf* 5E **79** & **205**
Norwich International Airport. *Norf* 4E **79**
Norwick. *Shet* 1H **173**
Norwood. *Derbs* 2B **86**
Norwood Green. *W Yor* 2B **92**
Norwood Hill. *Surr* 1D **26**
Norwood Park. *Som* 3A **22**
Norwoodside. *Cambs* 1D **64**
Noseley. *Leics* 1E **63**
Noss. *Shet* 10E **173**
Noss Mayo. *Devn* 4B **8**
Nosterfield. *N Yor* 1E **99**
Nostie. *High* 1A **148**
Notgrove. *Glos* 3G **49**
Nottage. *B'end* 4B **32**
Nottingham. *Nott* 1C **74** & **206**
Nottington. *Dors* 4B **14**
Notton. *Dors* 3B **14**
Notton. *W Yor* 3D **92**
Notton. *Wilts* 5E **35**
Nounsley. *Essx* 4A **54**
Noutard's Green. *Worc* 4B **60**
Nox. *Shrp* 4G **71**
Noyadd Trefawr. *Cdgn* 1C **44**
Nuffield. *Oxon* 3E **37**
Nunburnholme. *E Yor* 5C **100**
Nuncargate. *Notts* 5B **86**
Nunclose. *Cumb* 5F **113**
Nuneaton. *Warw* 1A **62**
Nuneham Courtenay. *Oxon* 2D **36**
Nun Monkton. *N Yor* 4H **99**
Nunnerie. *S Lan* 3B **118**
Nunney. *Som* 2C **22**
Nunnington. *N Yor* 2A **100**
Nunnykirk. *Nmbd* 5E **121**
Nunsthorpe. *NE Lin* 4F **95**
Nunthorpe. *Red C* 3C **106**
Nunthorpe. *York* 5H **99**
Nunton. *Wilts* 4G **23**
Nunwick. *Nmbd* 2B **114**
Nunwick. *N Yor* 2F **99**
Nupend. *Glos* 5C **48**
Nursling. *Hants* 1B **16**
Nursted. *W Sus* 4F **25**
Nursteed. *Wilts* 5F **35**
Nurston. *V Glam* 5D **32**
Nutbourne. *W Sus* 2F **17**
(nr. Chichester)
Nutbourne. *W Sus* 4B **26**
(nr. Pulborough)
Nutfield. *Surr* 5E **39**
Nuthall. *Notts* 1C **74**
Nuthampstead. *Herts* 2E **53**
Nuthurst. *Warw* 3F **61**
Nuthurst. *W Sus* 3C **26**
Nutley. *E Sus* 3F **27**
Nuttall. *G Man* 3F **91**

Nutwell. S Yor 4G 93
Nybster. High 2F 169
Nyetimber. W Sus 3G 17
Nyewood. W Sus 4G 25
Nymet Rowland. Devn 2H 11
Nymet Tracey. Devn 2H 11
Nympsfield. Glos 5D 48
Nynehead. Som 4E 21
Nyton. W Sus 5A 26

O

Oadby. Leics 5D 74
Oad Street. Kent 4C 40
Oakamoor. Staf 1E 73
Oakbank. Arg 5B 140
Oakbank. W Lot 3D 129
Oakdale. Cphy 2E 33
Oakdale. Pool 3F 15
Oake. Som 4E 21
Oaken. Staf 5C 72
Oakenclough. Lanc 5E 97
Oakengates. Telf 4B 72
Oakenholt. Flin 3E 83
Oakenshaw. Dur 1F 105
Oakenshaw. W Yor 2B 92
Oakerthorpe. Derbs 5A 86
Oakford. Cdgn 5D 56
Oakford. Devn 4C 20
Oakfordbridge. Devn 4C 20
Oakgrove. Ches E 4D 84
Oakham. Rut 5F 75
Oakhanger. Ches E 5B 84
Oakhanger. Hants 3F 25
Oakhill. Som 2B 22
Oakington. Cambs 4D 64
Oaklands. Powy 5C 58
Oakle Street. Glos 4C 48
Oakley. Bed 5H 63
Oakley. Buck 4E 51
Oakley. Fife 1D 128
Oakley. Hants 1D 24
Oakley. Suff 3D 66
Oakley Green. Wind 3A 38
Oakley Park. Powy 2B 58
Oakmere. Ches W 4H 83
Oakridge. Glos 5E 49
Oaks. Shrp 5G 71
Oaksey. Wilts 2E 35
Oaks Green. Derbs 2F 73
Oakshaw Ford. Cumb 2G 113
Oakshott. Hants 4F 25
Oakthorpe. Leics 4H 73
Oak Tree. Darl 3A 106
Oakwood. Derb 2A 74
Oakwood. W Yor 1D 92
Oakwoodhill. Surr 2C 26
Oakworth. W Yor 1A 92
Oape. High 3B 164
Oare. Kent 4E 40
Oare. Som 2B 20
Oare. W Ber 4D 36
Oare. Wilts 5G 35
Oareford. Som 2B 20
Oasby. Linc 2H 75
Oath. Som 4G 21
Oathlaw. Ang 3D 145
Oatlands. N Yor 4F 99
Oban. Arg ....1F 133 & 206
Oban. W Isl 7D 171
Oborne. Dors 1B 14
Obsdale. High 2A 158
Obthorpe. Linc 4H 75
Occlestone Green. Ches W 4A 84
Occold. Suff 3D 66
Ochiltree. E Ayr 2E 117
Ochtermuthill. Per 2H 135
Ochtertyre. Per 1H 135
Ockbrook. Derbs 2B 74
Ockeridge. Worc 4B 60
Ockham. Surr 5B 38
Ockle. High 1G 139
Ockley. Surr 1C 26
Ocle Pychard. Here 1A 48
Octofad. Arg 4A 124
Octomore. Arg 4A 124
Octon. E Yor 3E 101
Odcombe. Som 1A 14
Odd Down. Bath 5C 34
Oddingley. Worc 5D 60
Oddington. Oxon 4E 50
Oddsta. Shet 2G 173
Odell. Bed 5F 63
Odie. Orkn 5F 172
Odiham. Hants 1F 25
Odsey. Cambs 2C 52
Odstock. Wilts 4G 23
Odstone. Leics 5A 74
Offchurch. Warw 4A 62
Offenham. Worc 1F 49
Offenham Cross. Worc 1F 49
Offerton. G Man 2D 84
Offerton. Tyne 4G 115
Offham. E Sus 4F 27
Offham. Kent 5A 40
Offham. W Sus 5B 26
Offleyhay. Staf 3C 72
Offley Hoo. Herts 3B 52
Offleymarsh. Staf 3B 72
Offord Cluny. Cambs 4B 64
Offord D'Arcy. Cambs 4B 64

Offton. Suff 1D 54
Offwell. Devn 3E 13
Ogbourne Maizey. Wilts 4G 35
Ogbourne St Andrew. Wilts 4G 35
Ogbourne St George. Wilts 4H 35
Ogden. G Man 3H 91
Ogle. Nmbd 2E 115
Ogmore. V Glam 4B 32
Ogmore-by-Sea. V Glam 4B 32
Ogmore Vale. B'end 2C 32
Okeford Fitzpaine. Dors 1D 14
Okehampton. Devn 3F 11
Okehampton Camp. Devn 3F 11
Okraquoy. Shet 8F 173
Okus. Swin 3G 35
Old. Nptn 3E 63
Old Aberdeen. Aber 3G 153
Old Alresford. Hants 3D 24
Oldany. High 5B 166
Old Arley. Warw 1G 61
Old Basford. Nott 1C 74
Old Basing. Hants 1E 25
Oldberrow. Warw 4F 61
Old Bewick. Nmbd 2E 121
Old Bexley. G Lon 3F 39
Old Blair. Per 2F 143
Old Bolingbroke. Linc 4C 88
Oldborough. Devn 2A 12
Old Brampton. Derbs 3H 85
Old Bridge of Tilt. Per 2F 143
Old Bridge of Urr. Dum 3E 111
Old Buckenham. Norf 1C 66
Old Burghclere. Hants 1C 24
Oldbury. Shrp 1B 60
Oldbury. Warw 1H 61
Oldbury. W Mid 2D 61
Oldbury-on-Severn. S Glo 2B 34
Oldbury on the Hill. Glos 3D 34
Old Byland. N Yor 1H 99
Old Cassop. Dur 1A 106
Oldcastle. Mon 3G 47
Oldcastle Heath. Ches W 1G 71
Old Catton. Norf 4E 79
Old Clee. NE Lin 4F 95
Old Cleeve. Som 2D 20
Old Clipstone. Notts 4D 86
Old Colwyn. Cnwy 3A 82
Oldcotes. Notts 2C 86
Old Coulsdon. G Lon 5E 39
Old Dailly. S Ayr 5B 116
Old Dalby. Leics 3D 74
Old Dam. Derbs 3F 85
Old Deer. Abers 4G 161
Old Dilton. Wilts 2D 22
Old Down. S Glo 3B 34
Oldeamere. Cambs 1C 64
Old Edlington. S Yor 1C 86
Old Eldon. Dur 2F 105
Old Ellerby. E Yor 1E 95
Old Fallings. W Mid 5D 72
Oldfallow. Staf 4D 72
Old Felixstowe. Suff 2G 55
Oldfield. Shrp 2A 60
Oldfield. Worc 4C 60
Old Fletton. Pet 1A 64
Oldford. Som 1C 22
Old Forge. Here 4A 48
Old Glossop. Derbs 1E 85
Old Goole. E Yor 2H 93
Old Gore. Here 3B 48
Old Graitney. Dum 3E 112
Old Grimsby. IOS 1A 4
Oldhall. High 3E 169
Old Hall Street. Norf 2F 79
Oldham. G Man 4H 91
Oldhamstocks. E Lot 2D 130
Old Heathfield. E Sus 3G 27
Old Hill. W Mid 2D 60
Old Hunstanton. Norf 1F 77
Old Hurst. Cambs 3B 64
Old Hutton. Cumb 1E 97
Old Kea. Corn 4C 6
Old Kilpatrick. W Dun 2F 127
Old Kinnernie. Abers 3E 152
Old Knebworth. Herts 3C 52
Oldland. S Glo 4B 34
Old Laxey. IOM 3D 108
Old Leake. Linc 5D 88
Old Lenton. Nott 2C 74
Old Llanberis. Gwyn 5F 81
Old Malton. N Yor 2B 100
Oldmeldrum. Abers 1F 153
Old Micklefield. W Yor 1E 93
Old Mill. Corn 5D 10
Oldmixon. N Som 1G 21
Old Monkland. N Lan 3A 128
Old Newton. Suff 4C 66
Old Park. Telf 5A 72
Old Pentland. Midl 3F 129
Old Philpstoun. W Lot 2D 128
Old Quarrington. Dur 1A 106
Old Radnor. Powy 5E 59
Old Rayne. Abers 1D 152
Oldridge. Devn 3B 12
Old Romney. Kent 3E 29
Old Scone. Per 1D 136
Oldshore Beg. High 3C 166
Oldshoremore. High 3C 166
Old Snydale. W Yor 2E 93
Old Sodbury. S Glo 3C 34
Old Somerby. Linc 2G 75
Old Spital. Dur 3C 104

Oldstead. N Yor 1H 99
Old Stratford. Nptn 1F 51
Old Swan. Mers 1F 83
Old Swarland. Nmbd 4F 121
Old Tebay. Cumb 4H 103
Old Town. Cumb 5F 113
Old Town. E Sus 5G 27
Oldtown. High 5C 164
Old Town. IOS 1B 4
Oldtown of Ord. Abers 3D 160
Old Trafford. G Man 1C 84
Old Tupton. Derbs 4A 86
Oldwall. Cumb 3F 113
Oldwalls. Swan 3D 31
Old Warden. C Beds 1B 52
Oldways End. Som 4B 20
Old Westhall. Abers 1D 152
Old Weston. Cambs 3H 63
Oldwhat. Abers 3F 161
Old Windsor. Wind 3A 38
Old Wives Lees. Kent 5E 41
Old Woking. Surr 5B 38
Oldwood Common. Worc 4H 59
Old Woodstock. Oxon 4C 50
Olgrinmore. High 3C 168
Oliver's Battery. Hants 4C 24
Ollaberry. Shet 3E 173
Ollerton. Ches E 3B 84
Ollerton. Notts 4D 86
Ollerton. Shrp 3A 72
Olmarch. Cdgn 5F 57
Olmstead Green. Cambs 1G 53
Olney. Mil 5F 63
Olrig. High 2D 169
Olton. W Mid 2F 61
Olveston. S Glo 3B 34
Ombersley. Worc 4C 60
Ompton. Notts 4D 86
Onchan. IOM 4D 108
Onecote. Staf 5E 85
Onehouse. Suff 5C 66
Onen. Mon 4H 47
Ongar Hill. Norf 3E 77
Ongar Street. Here 4F 59
Onibury. Shrp 3G 59
Onich. High 2E 141
Onllwyn. Neat 4B 46
Onneley. Shrp 1B 72
Onslow Green. Essx 4G 53
Onslow Village. Surr 1A 26
Onthank. E Ayr 1D 116
Openwoodgate. Derbs 1A 74
Opinan. High 1G 155
(nr. Gairloch)
Opinan. High 4C 162
(nr. Laide)
Orasaigh. W Isl 6F 171
Orbost. High 4B 154
Orby. Linc 4D 89
Orchard Hill. Devn 4E 19
Orchard Portman. Som 4F 21
Orcheston. Wilts 2F 23
Orcop. Here 3H 47
Orcop Hill. Here 3H 47
Ord. High 2E 147
Ordale. Shet 1H 173
Ordhead. Abers 2D 152
Ordie. Abers 3B 152
Ordiquish. Mor 3H 159
Ordley. Nmbd 4C 114
Ordsall. Notts 3E 86
Ore. E Sus 4C 28
Oreham Common. W Sus 4D 26
Oreton. Shrp 2A 60
Orford. Linc 1B 88
Orford. Suff 1H 55
Orford. Warr 1A 84
Organford. Dors 3E 15
Orgil. Orkn 7B 172
Orgreave. Staf 4F 73
Oridge Street. Glos 3C 48
Orlestone. Kent 2D 28
Orleton. Here 4G 59
Orleton. Worc 4A 60
Orleton Common. Here 4G 59
Orlingbury. Nptn 3F 63
Ormacleit. W Isl 5C 170
Ormathwaite. Cumb 2D 102
Ormesby. Midd 3C 106
Ormesby St Margaret. Norf 4G 79
Ormesby St Michael. Norf 4G 79
Ormiscaig. High 4C 162
Ormiston. E Lot 3H 129
Ormsaigbeg. High 2F 139
Ormsaigmore. High 2F 139
Ormsary. Arg 2F 125
Ormsgill. Cumb 2A 96
Ormskirk. Lanc 4C 90
Orphir. Orkn 7C 172
Orpington. G Lon 4F 39
Orrell. Lanc 4D 90
Orrell. Mers 1F 83
Orrisdale. IOM 2C 108
Orsett. Thur 2H 39
Orslow. Staf 4C 72
Orston. Notts 1E 75
Orthwaite. Cumb 1D 102
Orton. Cumb 4H 103
Orton. Mor 3H 159
Orton. Nptn 3F 63

Orton. Staf 1C 60
Orton Longueville. Pet 1A 64
Orton-on-the-Hill. Leics 5H 73
Orton Waterville. Pet 1A 64
Orton Wistow. Pet 1A 64
Orwell. Cambs 5C 64
Osbaldeston. Lanc 1E 91
Osbaldwick. York 4A 100
Osbaston. Leics 5B 74
Osbaston. Shrp 3F 71
Osbournby. Linc 2H 75
Osclay. High 5E 169
Oscroft. Ches W 4H 83
Ose. High 4C 154
Osgathorpe. Leics 4B 74
Osgodby. Linc 1H 87
Osgodby. N Yor 1E 101
(nr. Scarborough)
Osgodby. N Yor 1G 93
(nr. Selby)
Oskaig. High 5E 155
Oskamull. Arg 4F 139
Osleston. Derb 2G 73
Osmaston. Derb 2A 74
Osmaston. Derbs 1G 73
Osmington. Dors 4C 14
Osmington Mills. Dors 4C 14
Osmondthorpe. W Yor 1D 92
Osmondwall. Orkn 9C 172
Osmotherley. N Yor 5B 106
Osnaburgh. Fife 2G 137
Ospisdale. High 5E 164
Ospringe. Kent 4E 40
Ossett. W Yor 2C 92
Ossington. Notts 4E 87
Ostend. Essx 1D 40
Ostend. Norf 2F 79
Osterley. G Lon 3C 38
Oswaldkirk. N Yor 2A 100
Oswaldtwistle. Lanc 2F 91
Oswestry. Shrp 3E 71
Otby. Linc 1A 88
Otford. Kent 5G 39
Otham. Kent 5B 40
Otherton. Staf 4D 72
Othery. Som 3G 21
Otley. Suff 5E 66
Otley. W Yor 5E 98
Otterbourne. Hants 4C 24
Otterburn. Nmbd 5C 120
Otterburn. N Yor 4A 98
Otterburn Camp. Nmbd 5C 120
Otterburn Hall. Nmbd 5C 120
Otter Ferry. Arg 1H 125
Otterford. Som 1F 13
Otterham. Corn 3B 10
Otterhampton. Som 2F 21
Otterham Quay. Kent 4C 40
Ottershaw. Surr 4B 38
Otterspool. Mers 2F 83
Otterswick. Shet 3G 173
Otterton. Devn 4D 12
Otterwood. Hants 2C 16
Ottery St Mary. Devn 3E 12
Ottinge. Kent 1F 29
Ottringham. E Yor 2F 95
Oughterby. Cumb 4D 112
Oughtershaw. N Yor 1A 98
Oughterside. Cumb 5C 112
Oughtibridge. S Yor 1H 85
Oughtrington. Warr 2A 84
Oulston. N Yor 2H 99
Oulton. Cumb 4D 112
Oulton. Norf 3D 78
Oulton. Staf 3B 72
(nr. Gnosall Heath)
Oulton. Staf 2D 72
(nr. Stone)
Oulton. Suff 1H 67
Oulton. W Yor 2D 92
Oulton Broad. Suff 1H 67
Oulton Street. Norf 3D 78
Oundle. Nptn 2H 63
Ousby. Cumb 1H 103
Ousdale. High 1H 165
Ousden. Suff 5G 65
Ousefleet. E Yor 2B 94
Ouston. Dur 4F 115
Ouston. Nmbd 4A 114
(nr. Bearsbridge)
Ouston. Nmbd 2D 114
(nr. Stamfordham)
Outer Hope. Devn 4C 8
Outertown. Orkn 6B 172
Outgate. Cumb 5E 103
Outhgill. Cumb 4A 104
Outlands. Staf 2B 72
Outlane. W Yor 3A 92
Out Newton. E Yor 2G 95
Out Rawcliffe. Lanc 5D 96
Outwell. Norf 5E 77
Outwick. Hants 1G 15
Outwood. Surr 1E 27
Outwood. W Yor 2D 92
Outwood. Worc 3D 60
Outwoods. Leics 4B 74
Outwoods. Staf 4B 72
Ouzlewell Green. W Yor 2D 92
Ovenden. W Yor 2A 92
Over. Cambs 3C 64
Over. Ches W 4A 84
Over. Glos 4D 48

Over. S Glo 3A 34
Overbister. Orkn 3F 172
Over Burrows. Derbs 2G 73
Overbury. Worc 2E 49
Overcombe. Dors 4B 14
Over Compton. Dors 1A 14
Over End. Cambs 1H 63
Over Finlarg. Ang 4D 144
Overgreen. Derbs 3H 85
Over Green. W Mid 1F 61
Over Haddon. Derbs 4G 85
Over Hulton. G Man 4E 91
Over Kellet. Lanc 2E 97
Over Kiddington. Oxon 3C 50
Overleigh. Som 3H 21
Overley. Staf 4F 73
Over Monnow. Mon 4A 48
Over Norton. Oxon 3B 50
Over Peover. Ches E 3B 84
Overpool. Ches W 3F 83
Overscaig. High 1B 164
Overseal. Derbs 4G 73
Over Silton. N Yor 5B 106
Oversland. Kent 5E 41
Overstone. Nptn 4F 63
Over Stowey. Som 3E 21
Overstrand. Norf 1E 79
Over Stratton. Som 1H 13
Over Street. Wilts 3F 23
Overthorpe. Nptn 1C 50
Overton. Aber 2F 153
Overton. Ches W 3H 83
Overton. Hants 2D 24
Overton. High 5E 169
Overton. Lanc 4D 96
Overton. N Yor 4H 99
Overton. Shrp 2A 60
(nr. Bridgnorth)
Overton. Shrp 3H 59
(nr. Ludlow)
Overton. Swan 4D 30
Overton. W Yor 3C 92
Overton. Wrex 1F 71
Overtown. Lanc 2F 97
Overtown. N Lan 4B 128
Overtown. Swin 4G 35
Over Wallop. Hants 3A 24
Over Whitacre. Warw 1G 61
Over Worton. Oxon 3C 50
Oving. Buck 3F 51
Oving. W Sus 5A 26
Ovingdean. Brig 5E 27
Ovingham. Nmbd 3D 115
Ovington. Dur 3E 105
Ovington. Essx 1A 54
Ovington. Hants 3D 24
Ovington. Norf 5B 78
Ovington. Nmbd 3D 114
Owen's Bank. Staf 3G 73
Ower. Hants 2C 16
(nr. Holbury)
Ower. Hants 1B 16
(nr. Totton)
Owermoigne. Dors 4C 14
Owlbury. Shrp 1F 59
Owler Bar. Derbs 3G 85
Owlerton. S Yor 2H 85
Owlsmoor. Brac 5G 37
Owlswick. Buck 5F 51
Owmby. Linc 4D 94
Owmby-by-Spital. Linc 2H 87
Ownham. W Ber 4C 36
Owrytn. Wrex 1F 71
Owslebury. Hants 4D 24
Owston. Leics 5E 75
Owston. S Yor 3F 93
Owston Ferry. N Lin 4B 94
Owstwick. E Yor 1F 95
Owthorne. E Yor 2G 95
Owthorpe. Notts 2D 74
Owton Manor. Hart 2B 106
Oxborough. Norf 5G 77
Oxbridge. Dors 3H 13
Oxcombe. Linc 3C 88
Oxen End. Essx 3G 53
Oxenhall. Glos 3C 48
Oxenholme. Cumb 5G 103
Oxenhope. W Yor 1A 92
Oxen Park. Cumb 1C 96
Oxenpill. Som 2H 21
Oxenton. Glos 2E 49
Oxenwood. Wilts 1B 24
Oxford. Oxon ....5D 50 & 207
Oxgangs. Edin 3F 129
Oxhey. Herts 1C 38
Oxhill. Warw 1B 50
Oxley. W Mid 5C 72
Oxley Green. Essx 4C 54
Oxley's Green. E Sus 3A 28
Oxlode. Cambs 2D 65
Oxnam. Bord 3B 120
Oxshott. Surr 4C 38
Oxspring. S Yor 4C 92
Oxted. Surr 5E 39
Oxton. Mers 2F 83
Oxton. N Yor 5H 99
Oxton. Notts 5D 86
Oxton. Bord 4A 130
Oxwich. Swan 4D 31
Oxwich Green. Swan 4D 31
Oxwick. Norf 3B 78
Oykel Bridge. High 3A 164

Oyne. *Abers* 1D 152
Oystermouth. *Swan* 4F 31
Ozleworth. *Glos* 2C 34

P

Pabail Iarach. *W Isl* 4H 171
Pabail Uarach. *W Isl* 4H 171
Pachesham. *Surr* 5C 38
Packers Hill. *Dors* 1C 14
Packington. *Leics* 4A 74
Packmoor. *Stoke* 5C 84
Packmores. *Warw* 4G 61
Packwood. *W Mid* 3F 61
Packwood Gullet. *W Mid* . . .3F 61
Padanaram. *Ang* 3D 144
Padbury. *Buck* 2F 51
Paddington. *G Lon* 2D 38
Paddington. *Warr* 2A 84
Paddlesworth. *Kent* 2F 29
Paddock. *Kent* 5D 40
Paddockhole. *Dum* 1D 112
Paddock Wood. *Kent* 1A 28
Paddolgreen. *Shrp* 2H 71
Padeswood. *Flin* 4E 83
Padiham. *Lanc* 1F 91
Padside. *N Yor* 4D 98
Padson. *Devn* 3F 11
Padstow. *Corn* 1D 6
Padworth. *W Ber* 5E 36
Page Bank. *Dur* 1F 105
Pagham. *W Sus* 3G 17
Paglesham Churchend. *Essx* . .1D 40
Paglesham Eastend. *Essx* . . .1D 40
Paibeil. *W Isl* 2C 170
(on North Uist)
Paibeil. *W Isl* 8C 171
(on Taransay)
Paiblesgearraidh. *W Isl* 2C 170
Paignton. *Torb* 2E 9
Pailton. *Warw* 2B 62
Paine's Corner. *E Sus* 3H 27
Painleyhill. *Staf* 2E 73
Painscastle. *Powy* 1E 47
Painshawfield. *Nmbd* 3D 114
Painsthorpe. *E Yor* 4C 100
Painswick. *Glos* 5D 48
Painter's Forstal. *Kent* 5D 40
Painthorpe. *W Yor* 3D 92
Pairc Shiaboist. *W Isl* 3E 171
Paisley. *Ren* . . . . . .3F **127** & **207**
Pakefield. *Suff* 1H 67
Pakenham. *Suff* 4B 66
Pale. *Gwyn* 2B 70
Palehouse Common. *E Sus* . . .4F 27
Palestine. *Hants* 2A 24
Paley Street. *Wind* 4G 37
Palgowan. *Dum* 1A 110
Palgrave. *Suff* 3D 66
Pallington. *Dors* 3C 14
Palmarsh. *Kent* 2F 29
Palmer Moor. *Derbs* 2F 73
Palmers Cross. *W Mid* 5C 72
Palmerstown. *V Glam* 5E 33
Palnackie. *Dum* 4F 111
Palnure. *Dum* 3B 110
Palterton. *Derbs* 4B 86
Pamber End. *Hants* 1E 24
Pamber Green. *Hants* 1E 24
Pamber Heath. *Hants* 5E 36
Pamington. *Glos* 2E 49
Pamphill. *Dors* 2E 15
Pampisford. *Cambs* 1E 53
Panborough. *Som* 2H 21
Panbride. *Ang* 5E 145
Pancakehill. *Glos* 4F 49
Pancrasweek. *Devn* 2C 10
Pandy. *Gwyn* 3A 70
(nr. Bala)
Pandy. *Gwyn* 5F 69
(nr. Tywyn)
Pandy. *Mon* 3G 47
Pandy. *Powy* 5B 70
Pandy. *Wrex* 2D 70
Pandy Tudur. *Cnwy* 4A 82
Panfield. *Essx* 3H 53
Pangbourne. *W Ber* 4E 37
Pannal. *N Yor* 4F 99
Pannal Ash. *N Yor* 4E 99
Pannanich. *Abers* 4A 152
Pant. *Shrp* 3E 71
Pant. *Wrex* 1F 71
Pantasaph. *Flin* 3D 82
Pant Glas. *Gwyn* 1D 68
Pant-glas. *Shrp* 2E 71
Pantgwyn. *Carm* 3F 45
Pantgwyn. *Cdgn* 1C 44
Pant-lasau. *Swan* 3F 31
Panton. *Linc* 3A 88
Pant-pastynog. *Den* 4C 82
Pantperthog. *Gwyn* 5G 69
Pant-teg. *Carm* 3E 45
Pant-y-Caws. *Carm* 2F 43
Pant-y-dwr. *Powy* 3B 58
Pant-y-ffridd. *Powy* 5D 70
Pantyffynnon. *Carm* 4G 45
Pant-y-llyn. *Carm* 4G 45
Pant-yr-awel. *B'end* 3C 32
Pant y Wacco. *Flin* 3D 82
Panxworth. *Norf* 4F 79

Papa Stour Airport. *Shet* 6C 173
Papa Westray Airport. *Orkn* . .2D 172
Papcastle. *Cumb* 1C 102
Papigoe. *High* 3F 169
Papil. *Shet* 8E 173
Papple. *E Lot* 2B 130
Pappleton. *Notts* 5C 86
Papworth Everard. *Cambs* . . .4B 64
Papworth St Agnes. *Cambs* . .4B 64
Par. *Corn* 3E 7
Paramour Street. *Kent* 4G 41
Parbold. *Lanc* 3C 90
Parbrook. *Som* 3A 22
Parbrook. *W Sus* 3B 26
Parc. *Gwyn* 2A 70
Parclllyn. *Cdgn* 5B 56
Pardown. *Hants* 2D 24
Pardshaw. *Cumb* 2B 102
Parham. *Suff* 4F 67
Park. *Abers* 4E 153
Park. *Arg* 4D 140
Park. *Dum* 5B 118
Park Bottom. *Corn* 4A 6
Park Corner. *E Sus* 2G 27
Park Corner. *Oxon* 3E 37
Parkend. *Glos* 5B 48
Park End. *Nmbd* 2B 114
Parkeston. *Essx* 2F 55
Parkfield. *Corn* 2H 7
Parkgate. *Ches W* 3E 83
Parkgate. *Cumb* 5D 112
Parkgate. *Dum* 1B 112
Park Gate. *Hants* 2D 16
Parkgate. *Surr* 1D 26
Park Gate. *Worc* 3D 60
Parkhall. *W Dun* 2F 127
Parkham. *Devn* 4D 19
Parkham Ash. *Devn* 4D 18
Parkhead. *Cumb* 5E 113
Parkhead. *Glas* 3H 127
Park Hill. *Mers* 4C 90
Parkhouse. *Mon* 5H 47
Parkhurst. *IOW* 3C 16
Park Lane. *G Man* 4F 91
Park Lane. *Staf* 5C 72
Parkmill. *Swan* 4E 31
Park Mill. *W Yor* 3C 92
Parkneuk. *Abers* 1G 145
Parkside. *N Lan* 4B 128
Parkstone. *Pool* 3F 15
Park Street. *Herts* 5B 52
Park Street. *W Sus* 2C 26
Park Town. *Oxon* 5D 50
Park Village. *Nmbd* 3H 113
Parkway. *Here* 2C 48
Parley Cross. *Dors* 3F 15
Parmoor. *Buck* 3F 37
Parr. *Mers* 1H 83
Parracombe. *Devn* 2G 19
Parrog. *Pemb* 1E 43
Parsonage Green. *Essx* 4H 53
Parsonby. *Cumb* 1C 102
Parson Cross. *S Yor* 1A 86
Parson Drove. *Cambs* 5C 76
Partick. *Glas* 3G 127
Partington. *G Man* 1B 84
Partney. *Linc* 4D 88
Parton. *Cumb* 2A 102
(nr. Whitehaven)
Parton. *Cumb* 4D 112
(nr. Wigton)
Parton. *Dum* 2D 111
Partridge Green. *W Sus* 4C 26
Parwich. *Derbs* 5F 85
Passenham. *Nptn* 2F 51
Passfield. *Hants* 3G 25
Passingford Bridge. *Essx* 1G 39
Paston. *Norf* 2F 79
Pasturefields. *Staf* 3D 73
Patchacott. *Devn* 3E 11
Patcham. *Brig* 5E 27
Patchetts Green. *Herts* 1C 38
Patching. *W Sus* 5B 26
Patchole. *Devn* 2G 19
Patchway. *S Glo* 3B 34
Pateley Bridge. *N Yor* 3D 98
Pathe. *Som* 3G 21
Pathfinder Village. *Devn* 3B 12
Pathhead. *Abers* 2G 145
Pathhead. *E Ayr* 3F 117
Pathhead. *Fife* 4E 137
Pathhead. *Midl* 3G 129
Pathlow. *Warw* 5F 61
Path of Condie. *Per* 2C 136
Pathstruie. *Per* 2C 136
Patmore Heath. *Herts* 3E 53
Patna. *E Ayr* 3D 116
Patney. *Wilts* 1F 23
Patrick. *IOM* 3B 108
Patrick Brompton. *N Yor* 5F 105
Patrington. *E Yor* 2G 95
Patrington Haven. *E Yor* 2G 95
Patrixbourne. *Kent* 5F 41
Patterdale. *Cumb* 3E 103
Pattiesmuir. *Fife* 1D 129
Pattingham. *Staf* 1C 60
Pattishall. *Nptn* 5D 62
Pattiswick. *Essx* 3B 54
Patton Bridge. *Cumb* 5G 103
Paul. *Corn* 4B 4

Paulerspury. *Nptn* 1F 51
Paull. *E Yor* 2E 95
Paulton. *Bath* 1B 22
Pauperhaugh. *Nmbd* 5F 121
Pave Lane. *Telf* 4B 72
Pavenham. *Bed* 5G 63
Pawlett. *Som* 2G 21
Pawston. *Nmbd* 1C 120
Paxford. *Glos* 2G 49
Paxton. *Bord* 4F 131
Payhembury. *Devn* 2D 12
Paythorne. *Lanc* 4H 97
Peacehaven. *E Sus* 5F 27
Peak Dale. *Derbs* 3E 85
Peak District. *Derbs* 2F 85
Peak Forest. *Derbs* 3F 85
Peak Hill. *Linc* 4B 76
Peakirk. *Pet* 5A 76
Pearsie. *Ang* 3C 144
Peasedown St John. *Bath* . . .1C 22
Peaseland Green. *Norf* 4C 78
Peasemore. *W Ber* 4C 36
Peasenhall. *Suff* 4F 67
Pease Pottage. *W Sus* 2D 26
Peaslake. *Surr* 1B 26
Peasley Cross. *Mers* 1H 83
Peasmarsh. *E Sus* 3C 28
Peasmarsh. *Som* 1G 13
Peasmarsh. *Surr* 1A 26
Peaston. *E Lot* 3H 129
Peastonbank. *E Lot* 3H 129
Peathill. *Abers* 2G 161
Peat Inn. *Fife* 3G 137
Peatling Magna. *Leics* 1C 62
Peatling Parva. *Leics* 2C 62
Peaton. *Arg* 1D 126
Peaton. *Shrp* 2H 59
Peats Corner. *Suff* 4D 66
Pebmarsh. *Essx* 2B 54
Pebworth. *Worc* 1G 49
Pecket Well. *W Yor* 2H 91
Peckforton. *Ches E* 5H 83
Peckham Bush. *Kent* 5A 40
Peckleton. *Leics* 5B 74
Pedair-ffordd. *Powy* 3D 70
Pedham. *Norf* 4F 79
Pedlinge. *Kent* 2F 29
Pedmore. *W Mid* 2D 60
Pedwell. *Som* 3H 21
Peebles. *Bord* 5F 129
Peel. *IOM* 3B 108
Peel. *Bord* 1G 119
Peel Common. *Hants* 2D 16
Peening Quarter. *Kent* 3C 28
Peggs Green. *Leics* 4B 74
Pegsdon. *C Beds* 2B 52
Pegswood. *Nmbd* 1F 115
Peinchorran. *High* 5E 155
Peinlich. *High* 3D 154
Pelaw. *Tyne* 3G 115
Pelcomb Bridge. *Pemb* 3D 42
Pelcomb Cross. *Pemb* 3D 42
Peldon. *Essx* 4C 54
Pelsall. *W Mid* 5E 73
Pelton. *Dur* 4F 115
Pelutho. *Cumb* 5C 112
Pelynt. *Corn* 3G 7
Pemberton. *Carm* 5F 45
Pembrey. *Carm* 5E 45
Pembridge. *Here* 5F 59
Pembroke. *Pemb* 4D 43
Pembroke Dock.
Pemb . . . . .4D **42** & **215**
Pembroke Ferry. *Pemb* 4D 43
Pembury. *Kent* 1H 27
Penallt. *Mon* 4A 48
Penally. *Pemb* 5F 43
Penalt. *Here* 3A 48
Penalum. *Pemb* 5F 43
Penare. *Corn* 4D 6
Penarth. *V Glam* 4E 33
Penbeagle. *Corn* 3C 4
Penberth. *Corn* 4B 4
Pen-bont Rhydybeddau. *Cdgn* . .2F 57
Penbryn. *Cdgn* 5B 56
Pencader. *Carm* 2E 45
Pen-cae. *Cdgn* 5D 56
Pencaenewydd. *Gwyn* 1D 68
Pencaerau. *Neat* 3G 31
Pencaitland. *E Lot* 3H 129
Pencarnisiog. *IOA* 3C 80
Pencarreg. *Carm* 1F 45
Pencarrow. *Corn* 4B 10
Pencelli. *Powy* 3D 46
Pen-clawdd. *Swan* 3E 31
Pencoed. *B'end* 3C 32
Pencombe. *Here* 5H 59
Pencraig. *Here* 3A 48
Pencraig. *Powy* 3C 70
Pendeen. *Corn* 3A 4
Penderyn. *Rhon* 5C 46
Pendine. *Carm* 4G 43
Pendlebury. *G Man* 4F 91
Pendleton. *G Man* 1C 84
Pendleton. *Lanc* 1F 91
Pendock. *Worc* 2C 48
Pendoggett. *Corn* 5A 10
Pendomer. *Som* 1A 14
Pendoylan. *V Glam* 4D 32
Pendre. *B'end* 3C 32

Penegoes. *Powy* 5G 69
Penelewey. *Corn* 4C 6
Penffordd. *Pemb* 2E 43
Penffordd-Lâs. *Powy* 1A 58
Penfro. *Pemb* 4D 43
Pengam. *Cphy* 2E 33
Pengam. *Card* 4F 33
Penge. *G Lon* 3E 39
Pengelly. *Corn* 4A 10
Pengenffordd. *Powy* 2E 47
Pengorffwysfa. *IOA* 1D 80
Pengover Green. *Corn* 2G 7
Pengwern. *Den* 3C 82
Penhale. *Corn* 5D 5
(nr. Mullion)
Penhale. *Corn* 3D 6
(nr. St Austell)
Penhale Camp. *Corn* 3B 6
Penhallow. *Corn* 3B 6
Penhalvean. *Corn* 5B 6
Penhelig. *Gwyn* 1F 57
Penhill. *Swin* 3G 35
Penhow. *Newp* 2H 33
Penhurst. *E Sus* 4A 28
Peniarth. *Gwyn* 5F 69
Penicuik. *Midl* 3F 129
Peniel. *Carm* 3E 45
Penifiler. *High* 4D 155
Peninver. *Arg* 3B 122
Penisa'r Waun. *Gwyn* 4E 81
Penistone. *S Yor* 4C 92
Penketh. *Warr* 2H 83
Penkill. *S Ayr* 5B 116
Penkridge. *Staf* 4D 72
Penley. *Wrex* 2G 71
Penllech. *Gwyn* 2B 68
Penllergaer. *Swan* 3F 31
Pen-llyn. *IOA* 2C 80
Penmachno. *Cnwy* 5G 81
Penmaen. *Swan* 4E 31
Penmaenmawr. *Cnwy* 3G 81
Penmaenpool. *Gwyn* 4F 69
Penmaen Rhos. *Cnwy* 3A 82
Pen-marc. *V Glam* 5D 32
Penmark. *V Glam* 5D 32
Penmarth. *Corn* 5B 6
Penmon. *IOA* 2F 81
Penmorfa. *Gwyn* 1E 69
Penmynydd. *IOA* 3E 81
Penn. *Buck* 1A 38
Penn. *Dors* 3G 13
Penn. *W Mid* 1C 60
Pennal. *Gwyn* 5G 69
Pennan. *Abers* 2F 161
Pennant. *Cdgn* 4E 57
Pennant. *Den* 2C 70
Pennant. *Gwyn* 3B 70
Pennant. *Powy* 1A 58
Pennant Melangell. *Powy* 3C 70
Pennar. *Pemb* 4D 42
Pennard. *Swan* 4E 31
Pennerley. *Shrp* 1F 59
Pennington. *Cumb* 2B 96
Pennington. *G Man* 1A 84
Pennington. *Hants* 3B 16
Pennorth. *Powy* 3E 46
Penn Street. *Buck* 1A 38
Pennsylvania. *Devn* 3C 12
Pennsylvania. *S Glo* 4C 34
Penny Bridge. *Cumb* 1C 96
Pennycross. *Plym* 3A 8
Pennygate. *Norf* 3F 79
Pennyghael. *Arg* 1C 132
Penny Hill. *Linc* 3C 76
Pennylands. *Lanc* 4C 90
Pennymoor. *Devn* 1B 12
Pennyvenie. *E Ayr* 4D 117
Pennywell. *Tyne* 4G 115
Penparc. *Cdgn* 1C 44
Penparcau. *Cdgn* 2E 57
Penpedairheol. *Cphy* 2E 33
Penperlleni. *Mon* 5G 47
Penpillick. *Corn* 3E 7
Penpol. *Corn* 5C 6
Penpoll. *Corn* 3F 7
Penponds. *Corn* 3D 4
Penpont. *Corn* 5A 10
Penpont. *Dum* 5H 117
Penpont. *Powy* 3C 46
Penprysg. *B'end* 3C 32
Penquit. *Devn* 3C 8
Penrherber. *Carm* 1G 43
Penrhiw. *Pemb* 1C 44
Penrhiwceiber. *Rhon* 2D 32
Pen Rhiwfawr. *Neat* 4H 45
Penrhiw-llan. *Cdgn* 1D 44
Penrhiw-pal. *Cdgn* 1D 44
Penrhos. *Gwyn* 2C 68
Penrhos. *Here* 5F 59
Penrhos. *IOA* 2B 80
Penrhos. *Mon* 4H 47
Penrhos. *Powy* 4B 46
Penrhos Garnedd. *Gwyn* 3E 81
Penrhyn. *IOA* 1C 80
Penrhyn Bay. *Cnwy* 2H 81
Penrhyn-coch. *Cdgn* 2F 57
Penrhyndeudraeth. *Gwyn* 2F 69
Penrhyn Side. *Cnwy* 2H 81
Penrice. *Swan* 4D 31
Penrith. *Cumb* 2G 103
Penrose. *Corn* 1C 6
Penruddock. *Cumb* 2F 103

Penryn. *Corn* 5B 6
Pensarn. *Carm* 4E 45
Pen-sarn. *Gwyn* 3E 69
Pensax. *Worc* 4B 60
Pensby. *Mers* 2E 83
Penselwood. *Som* 3C 22
Pensford. *Bath* 5B 34
Pensham. *Worc* 1E 49
Penshaw. *Tyne* 4G 115
Penshurst. *Kent* 1G 27
Pensilva. *Corn* 2G 7
Pensnett. *W Mid* 2D 60
Penston. *E Lot* 2H 129
Penstone. *Devn* 2A 12
Pente-tafarn-y-fedw.
Cnwy 4H 81
Pentewan. *Corn* 4E 6
Pentir. *Gwyn* 4E 81
Pentire. *Corn* 2B 6
Pentlepoir. *Pemb* 4F 43
Pentlow. *Essx* 1B 54
Pentney. *Norf* 4G 77
Penton Mewsey. *Hants* 2B 24
Pentraeth. *IOA* 3E 81
Pentre. *Powy* 1E 59
(nr. Church Stoke)
Pentre. *Powy* 2D 58
(nr. Kerry)
Pentre. *Powy* 2C 58
(nr. Mochdre)
Pentre. *Rhon* 2C 32
Pentre. *Shrp* 4F 71
Pentre. *Wrex* 2D 70
(nr. Llanfyllin)
Pentre. *Wrex* 1E 71
(nr. Rhosllanerchrugog)
Pentrebach. *Carm* 2B 46
Pentre-bach. *Cdgn* 1F 45
Pentrebach. *Mer T* 5D 46
Pentre-bach. *Powy* 2C 46
Pentrebach. *Swan* 5G 45
Pentre Berw. *IOA* 3D 80
Pentre-bont. *Cnwy* 5G 81
Pentrecagal. *Carm* 1D 44
Pentre-celyn. *Den* 5D 82
Pentre-clawdd. *Shrp* 2E 71
Pentreclwydau. *Neat* 5B 46
Pentre-cwrt. *Carm* 2D 45
Pentre Dolau Honddu.
Powy 1C 46
Pentre-du. *Cnwy* 5G 81
Pentre-dwr. *Swan* 3F 31
Pentrefelin. *Carm* 3F 45
Pentrefelin. *Cdgn* 1G 45
Pentrefelin. *Cnwy* 3H 81
Pentrefelin. *Gwyn* 2E 69
Pentrefoelas. *Cnwy* 5A 82
Pentre Galar. *Pemb* 1F 43
Pentregat. *Cdgn* 5C 56
Pentre Gwenlais. *Carm* 4G 45
Pentre Gwynfryn. *Gwyn* 3E 69
Pentre Halkyn. *Flin* 3E 82
Pentre Hodre. *Shrp* 3F 59
Pentre-Llanrhaeadr. *Den* 4C 82
Pentre Llifior. *Powy* 1D 58
Pentrellwyn. *IOA* 2E 81
Pentre-llwyn-llwyd. *Powy* 5B 58
Pentre-llyn-cymmer.
Cnwy 5B 82
Pentre Meyrick. *V Glam* 4C 32
Pentre-piod. *Gwyn* 2A 70
Pentre-poeth. *Newp* 3F 33
Pentre'r Beirdd. *Powy* 4D 70
Pentre'r-felin. *Powy* 2C 46
Pentre-ty-gwyn. *Carm* 2B 46
Pentre-uchaf. *Gwyn* 2C 68
Pentrich. *Derbs* 5A 86
Pentridge. *Dors* 1F 15
Pen-twyn. *Cphy* 5F 47
(nr. Oakdale)
Pentwyn. *Cphy* 5E 46
(nr. Rhymney)
Pentwyn. *Card* 3F 33
Pentyrch. *Card* 3E 32
Pentywyn. *Carm* 4G 43
Penuwch. *Cdgn* 4E 57
Penwithick. *Corn* 3E 7
Penwyllt. *Powy* 4B 46
Penybanc. *Carm* 4G 45
(nr. Ammanford)
Penybanc. *Carm* 3G 45
(nr. Llandeilo)
Pen-y-bont. *Carm* 2H 43
Penybont. *Powy* 4D 58
(nr. Llandrindod Wells)
Pen-y-bont. *Powy* 3E 70
(nr. Llanfyllin)
Pen-y-Bont Ar Ogwr. *B'end* . . .3C 32
Penybontfawr. *Powy* 3C 70
Pen-y-bryn. *Cphy* 2E 33
Pen-y-bryn. *Pemb* 1B 44
Pen-y-bryn. *Wrex* 1E 71
Pen-y-cae. *Powy* 4B 46
Penycae. *Wrex* 1E 71
Pen-y-cae-mawr. *Mon* 2H 33
Penycwm. *Pemb* 2C 42
Pen-y-Darren. *Mer T* 5D 46
Pen-y-cefn. *Flin* 3D 82
Pen-y-clawdd. *Mon* 5H 47
Pen-y-coedcae. *Rhon* 3D 32
Penycwm. *Pemb* 2C 42
Pen-y-Darren. *Mer T* 5D 46
Pen-y-fai. *B'end* 3B 32

Penyffordd. Flin 4F 83
(nr. Mold)
Pen-y-ffordd. Flin 2D 82
(nr. Prestatyn)
Pen-y-garn. Cdgn 2F 57
Pen-y-garn. Gwyn 5E 81
Pen-y-garnedd. IOA 3E 81
Penygarnedd. Powy 3D 70
Pen-y-graig. Gwyn 2B 68
Penygraig. Rhon 2C 32
Penygraigwen. IOA 2D 80
Pen-y-groes. Carm 4F 45
Penygroes. Gwyn 5D 80
Penygroes. Pemb 1F 43
Pen-y-Mynydd. Carm 5E 45
Penymynydd. Flin 4F 83
Penyrheol. Cphy 3E 33
Pen-yr-heol. Mon 4H 47
Penyrheol. Swan 3E 31
Pen-yr-Heolgerrig. Mer T 5D 46
Penysarn. IOA 1D 80
Pen-y-stryt. Den 5E 82
Penywaun. Rhon 5C 46
Penzance. Corn 3B 4
Peopleton. Worc 5D 60
Peover Heath. Ches E 3B 84
Peper Harow. Surr 1A 26
Peplow. Shrp 3A 72
Pepper Arden. N Yor 4F 105
Perceton. N Ayr 5E 127
Percyhorner. Abers 2G 161
Perham Down. Wilts 2A 24
Periton. Som 2C 20
Perkinsville. Dur 4F 115
Perlethorpe. Notts 3D 86
Perranarworthal. Corn 5B 6
Perranporth. Corn 3B 6
Perranuthnoe. Corn 4C 4
Perranwell. Corn 5B 6
Perranzabuloe. Corn 3B 6
Perrott's Brook. Glos 5F 49
Perry. W Mid 1E 61
Perry Barr. W Mid 1E 61
Perry Crofts. Staf 5G 73
Perry Green. Essx 3B 54
Perry Green. Herts 4E 53
Perry Green. Wilts 3E 35
Perry Street. Kent 3H 39
Perry Street. Som 2G 13
Perrywood. Kent 5E 41
Pershall. Staf 3C 72
Pershore. Worc 1E 49
Pertenhall. Bed 4H 63
Perth. Per . . . . .1D 136 & 207
Perthy. Shrp 2F 71
Perton. Staf 1C 60
Pertwood. Wilts 3D 23
Peterborough. Pet . . . . . . .1A 64 & 208
Peterburn. High 5B 162
Peterchurch. Here 2G 47
Peterculter. Aber 3F 153
Peterhead. Abers 4H 161
Peterlee. Dur 5H 115
Petersfield. Hants 4F 25
Petersfinger. Wilts 4G 23
Peter's Green. Herts 4B 52
Peters Marland. Devn 1E 11
Peterstone Wentlooge. Newp . . .3F 33
Peterston-super-Ely. V Glam . . .4D 32
Peterstow. Here 3A 48
Peter Tavy. Devn 5F 11
Petertown. Orkn 7C 172
Petham. Kent 5F 41
Petherwin Gate. Corn 4C 10
Petrockstowe. Devn 2F 11
Petsoe End. Mil 1G 51
Pett. E Sus 4C 28
Pettaugh. Suff 5D 66
Pett Bottom. Kent 5F 41
Petteridge. Kent 1A 28
Pettinain. S Lan 5C 128
Pettistree. Suff 5E 67
Petton. Devn 4D 20
Petton. Shrp 3G 71
Petts Wood. G Lon 4F 39
Pettycur. Fife 1F 129
Pettywell. Norf 3C 78
Petworth. W Sus 3A 26
Pevensey. E Sus 5A 28
Pevensey Bay. E Sus 5A 28
Pewsey. Wilts 5G 35
Pheasants Hill. Buck 3F 37
Philadelphia. Tyne 4G 115
Philham. Devn 4C 18
Philiphaugh. Bord 2G 119
Phillack. Corn 3C 4
Philleigh. Corn 5C 6
Philpstoun. W Lot 2D 128
Phocle Green. Here 3B 48
Phoenix Green. Hants 1F 25
Pibsbury. Som 4H 21
Pibwrlwyd. Carm 4E 45
Pica. Cumb 2B 102
Piccadilly. Warw 1G 61
Piccadilly Corner. Norf 2E 67
Piccotts End. Herts 5A 52
Pickering. N Yor 1B 100
Picket Piece. Hants 2B 24
Picket Post. Hants 2G 15
Pickford. W Mid 2G 61
Pickhill. N Yor 1F 99
Picklenash. Glos 3C 48

Picklescott. Shrp 1G 59
Pickletillem. Fife 1G 137
Pickmere. Ches E 3A 84
Pickstock. Telf 3B 72
Pickwell. Devn 2E 19
Pickwell. Leics 4E 75
Pickworth. Linc 2H 75
Pickworth. Rut 4G 75
Picton. Ches W 3G 83
Picton. Flin 2D 82
Picton. N Yor 4B 106
Pict's Hill. Som 4H 21
Pidsford. Nptn 4E 63
Pidsford Hill. Som 3E 20
Pitsmoor. S Yor 2A 86
Piddinghoe. E Sus 5F 27
Piddington. Buck 2G 37
Piddington. Nptn 5F 63
Piddington. Oxon 4E 51
Piddlehinton. Dors 3C 14
Piddletrenthide. Dors 2C 14
Pidley. Cambs 3C 64
Pidney. Dors 2C 14
Pie Corner. Here 4A 60
Piercebridge. Darl 3F 105
Pierowall. Orkn 3D 172
Pigdon. Nmbd 1E 115
Pightley. Som 3F 21
Pikehall. Derbs 5F 85
Pikeshill. Hants 2A 16
Pilford. Dors 2F 15
Pilgrims Hatch. Essx 1G 39
Pilham. Linc 1F 87
Pill. N Som 4A 34
Pillaton. Corn 2H 7
Pillaton. Staf 4D 72
Pillerton Hersey. Warw 1A 50
Pillerton Priors. Warw 1A 50
Pilleth. Powy 4E 59
Pilley. Hants 3B 16
Pilley. S Yor 4D 92
Pillgwenlly. Newp 3G 33
Pilling. Lanc 5D 96
Pilling Lane. Lanc 5C 96
Pillowell. Glos 5B 48
Pill, The. Mon 3H 33
Pillwell. Dors 1C 14
Pilning. S Glo 3A 34
Pilsbury. Derbs 4F 85
Pilsdon. Dors 3H 13
Pilsgate. Pet 5H 75
Pilsley. Derbs 3G 85
(nr. Bakewell)
Pilsley. Derbs 4B 86
(nr. Clay Cross)
Pilson Green. Norf 4F 79
Piltdown. E Sus 3F 27
Pilton. Edin 2F 129
Pilton. Nptn 2H 63
Pilton. Rut 5G 75
Pilton. Som 2A 22
Pilton Green. Swan 4D 30
Pimperne. Dors 2E 15
Pinchbeck. Linc 3B 76
Pinchbeck Bars. Linc 3A 76
Pinchbeck West. Linc 3B 76
Pincock. Lanc 3D 90
Pinford End. Suff 5H 65
Pinged. Carm 5E 45
Pinhoe. Devn 3C 12
Pinkerton. E Lot 2D 130
Pinkneys Green. Wind 3G 37
Pinley. W Mid 3A 62
Pinley Green. Warw 4G 61
Pinmill. Suff 2F 55
Pinmore. S Ayr 5B 116
Pins Green. Worc 1C 48
Pinsley Green. Ches E 1H 71
Pinvin. Worc 1E 49
Pinwherry. S Ayr 1G 109
Pipe and Lyde. Here 1A 48
Pipe Aston. Here 3G 59
Pipe Gate. Shrp 1B 72
Pipehill. Staf 5E 73
Piperhill. High 3C 158
Pipe Ridware. Staf 4E 73
Pipers Pool. Corn 4C 10
Pipewell. Nptn 2F 63
Pippacott. Devn 3F 19
Pipton. Powy 2E 47
Pirbright. Surr 5A 38
Pirnmill. N Ayr 5G 125
Pirton. Herts 2B 52
Pirton. Worc 1D 49
Pisgah. Stir 3G 135
Pishill. Oxon 3F 37
Pistyll. Gwyn 1C 68
Pitagowan. Per 2F 143
Pitcairn. Per 3F 143
Pitcairngreen. Per 1C 136
Pitcalnie. High 1C 158
Pitcaple. Abers 1E 152
Pitchcombe. Glos 5D 48
Pitchcott. Buck 3F 51
Pitchford. Shrp 5H 71
Pitch Green. Buck 5F 51
Pitch Place. Surr 5A 38
Pitcombe. Som 3B 22
Pitcox. E Lot 2C 130
Pitcur. Per 5B 144
Pitfichie. Abers 2D 152
Pitgrudy. High 4E 165
Pitkennedy. Ang 3E 145

Pitlessie. Fife 3F 137
Pitlochry. Per 3G 143
Pitmachie. Abers 1D 152
Pitmaduthy. High 1B 158
Pitmedden. Abers 1F 153
Pitminster. Som 1F 13
Pitnacree. Per 3G 143
Pitney. Som 4H 21
Pitroddie. Per 1E 136
Pitscottie. Fife 2G 137
Pitsea. Essx 2B 40
Pitsford. Nptn 4E 63
Pitsford Hill. Som 3E 20
Pitsmoor. S Yor 2A 86
Pitstone. Buck 4H 51
Pitt. Hants 4C 24
Pitt Court. Glos 2C 34
Pittentrail. High 3E 164
Pittenweem. Fife 3H 137
Pittington. Dur 5G 115
Pitton. Swan 4D 30
Pitton. Wilts 3H 23
Pittswood. Kent 1H 27
Pittulie. Abers 2G 161
Pittville. Glos 3E 49
Pitversie. Per 2D 136
Pityme. Corn 1D 6
Pity Me. Dur 5F 115
Pixey Green. Suff 3E 67
Pixley. Here 2B 48
Place Newton. N Yor 2C 100
Plaidy. Abers 3E 161
Plaidy. Corn 3G 7
Plain Dealings. Pemb 3E 43
Plains. N Lan 3A 128
Plainsfield. Som 3E 21
Plaish. Shrp 1H 59
Plaistow. Here 2B 48
Plaistow. W Sus 2B 26
Plaitford. Wilts 1A 16
Plas Llwyd. Cnwy 3B 82
Plastow Green. Hants 5D 36
Plas yn Cefn. Den 3C 82
Platt. Kent 5H 39
Platt Bridge. G Man 4E 90
Platt Lane. Shrp 2H 71
Platts Common. S Yor 4D 92
Platt's Heath. Kent 5C 40
Platt, The. E Sus 2G 27
Plawsworth. Dur 5F 115
Plaxtol. Kent 5H 39
Playden. E Sus 3D 28
Playford. Suff 1F 55
Play Hatch. Oxon 4F 37
Playing Place. Corn 4C 6
Playley Green. Glos 2C 48
Plealey. Shrp 5G 71
Plean. Stir 1B 128
Pleasington. Bkbn 2E 91
Pleasley. Derbs 4C 86
Pledgdon Green. Essx 3F 53
Plenmeller. Nmbd 3A 114
Pleshey. Essx 4G 53
Plockton. High 5H 155
Plocrapol. W Isl 8D 171
Ploughfield. Here 1G 47
Plowden. Shrp 2F 59
Ploxgreen. Shrp 5F 71
Pluckley. Kent 1D 28
Plucks Gutter. Kent 4G 41
Plumbland. Cumb 1C 102
Plumgarths. Cumb 5F 103
Plumley. Ches E 3B 84
Plummers Plain. W Sus 3D 26
Plumpton. Cumb 1F 103
Plumpton. E Sus 4E 27
Plumpton. Nptn 1D 50
Plumpton Foot. Cumb 1F 103
Plumpton Green. E Sus 4E 27
Plumpton Head. Cumb 1G 103
Plumstead. G Lon 3F 39
Plumstead. Norf 2D 78
Plumtree. Notts 2D 74
Plumtree Park. Notts 2D 74
Plungar. Leics 2E 75
Plush. Dors 2C 14
Plushabridge. Corn 5D 10
Plwmp. Cdgn 5C 56
Plymouth. Plym . . . . .3A 8 & 208
Plymouth City Airport. Plym 3B 8
Plympton. Plym 3B 8
Plymstock. Plym 3B 8
Plymtree. Devn 2D 12
Pockley. N Yor 1A 100
Pocklington. E Yor 5C 100
Pode Hole. Linc 3B 76
Podimore. Som 4A 22
Podington. Bed 4G 63
Podmore. Staf 2B 72
Poffley End. Oxon 4B 50
Point Clear. Essx 4D 54
Pointon. Linc 2A 76
Pokesdown. Bour 3G 15
Polbae. Dum 2H 109
Polbain. High 3E 163
Polbathic. Corn 3H 7
Polbeth. W Lot 3D 128
Polbrock. Corn 2E 6
Polchar. High 3C 150
Polebrook. Nptn 2H 63
Pole Elm. Worc 1D 48
Polegate. E Sus 5G 27

Pole Moor. W Yor 3A 92
Poles. High 4E 165
Polesworth. Warw 5G 73
Polglass. High 3E 163
Polgooth. Corn 3D 6
Poling. W Sus 5B 26
Poling Corner. W Sus 5B 26
Polio. High 1B 158
Polkerris. Corn 3E 7
Polla. High 3D 166
Pollard Street. Norf 2F 79
Pollicott. Buck 4F 51
Pollington. E Yor 3G 93
Polloch. High 2B 140
Pollok. Glas 3G 127
Pollokshaws. Glas 3G 127
Pollokshields. Glas 3G 127
Polmaily. High 5G 157
Polmassick. Corn 4D 6
Polmont. Falk 2C 128
Polnessan. E Ayr 3D 116
Polnish. High 5F 147
Polperro. Corn 3G 7
Polruan. Corn 3F 7
Polscoe. Corn 2F 7
Polsham. Som 2A 22
Polskeoch. Dum 4F 117
Polstead. Suff 2C 54
Polstead Heath. Suff 1C 54
Poltesco. Corn 5E 5
Poltimore. Devn 3C 12
Polton. Midl 3G 129
Polwarth. Bord 4D 130
Polyphant. Corn 4C 10
Polzeath. Corn 1D 6
Ponde. Powy 2E 46
Pondersbridge. Cambs 1B 64
Ponders End. G Lon 1E 39
Pond Street. Essx 2E 53
Pondtail. Hants 1G 25
Ponsanooth. Corn 5B 6
Ponsongath. Corn 5E 5
Ponsworthy. Devn 5H 11
Pontamman. Carm 4G 45
Pontantwn. Carm 4E 45
Pontardawe. Neat 5H 45
Pontarddulais. Swan 5F 45
Pontarfynach. Cdgn 3G 57
Pont-ar-gothi. Carm 3F 45
Pont ar Hydfer. Powy 3B 46
Pontarllechau. Carm 3H 45
Pontarsais. Carm 3E 45
Pontblyddyn. Flin 4E 83
Pontbren Llwyd. Rhon 5C 46
Pont Cyfyng. Cnwy 5G 81
Pontdolgoch. Powy 1C 58
Pontefract. W Yor 2E 93
Ponteland. Nmbd 2E 115
Ponterwyd. Cdgn 2G 57
Pontesbury. Shrp 5G 71
Pontesford. Shrp 5G 71
Pontfadog. Wrex 2E 71
Pontfaen. Pemb 1E 43
Pont-faen. Powy 2C 46
Pont-Faen. Shrp 2E 71
Pontgarreg. Cdgn 5C 56
Pont-Henri. Carm 5E 45
Ponthir. Torf 2G 33
Ponthirwaun. Cdgn 1C 44
Pont-iets. Carm 5E 45
Pontllanfraith. Cphy 2E 33
Pontlliw. Swan 5G 45
Pont Llogel. Powy 4C 70
Pontllyfni. Gwyn 5D 80
Pontlottyn. Cphy 5E 46
Pontneddfechan. Neat 5C 46
Pont-newydd. Carm 5E 45
Pont-newydd. Flin 4D 82
Pontnewydd. Torf 2F 33
Ponton. Shet 6E 173
Pont Pen-y-benglog. Gwyn 4F 81
Pontrhydfendigaid. Cdgn 4G 57
Pont Rhyd-y-cyff. B'end 3B 32
Pont-rhyd-y-fen. Neat 2A 32
Pont-rhyd-y-groes. Cdgn 3G 57
Pontrhydyrun. Torf 2F 33
Pont Rhythallt. Gwyn 4E 81
Pontrilas. Here 3G 47
Pontrilas Road. Here 3G 47
Pontrobert. Powy 4D 70
Pont-rug. Gwyn 4E 81
Ponts Green. E Sus 4A 28
Pontshill. Here 3B 48
Pont-Sian. Cdgn 1E 45
Pontsticill. Mer T 4D 46
Pont-Walby. Neat 5B 46
Pontwelly. Carm 2E 45
Pontwgan. Cnwy 3G 81
Pontyates. Carm 5E 45
Pontyberem. Carm 4F 45
Pontybodkin. Flin 5E 83
Pontyclun. Rhon 3D 32
Pontycymer. B'end 2C 32
Pontyglazier. Pemb 1F 43
Pontygwaith. Rhon 2D 32
Pont-y-pant. Cnwy 5G 81
Pontypool. Torf 2F 33
Pontypridd. Rhon 2D 32
Pontypwl. Torf 2F 33
Pontywaun. Cphy 2F 33
Pooksgreen. Hants 1B 16
Pool. Corn 4A 6

Pool. W Yor 5E 99
Poole. N Yor 2E 93
Poole. Pool . . . . .3F 15 & 215
Poole. Som 4E 21
Poole Keynes. Glos 2E 35
Poolend. Staf 5D 84
Poolewe. High 5C 162
Pooley Bridge. Cumb 2F 103
Poolfold. Staf 5C 84
Pool Head. Here 5H 59
Pool Hey. Lanc 3B 90
Poolhill. Glos 3C 48
Poolmill. Here 3A 48
Pool o' Muckhart. Clac 3C 136
Pool Quay. Powy 4E 71
Poolsbrook. Derbs 3B 86
Pool Street. Essx 2A 54
Pootings. Kent 1F 27
Pope Hill. Pemb 3D 42
Pope's Hill. Glos 4B 48
Popeswood. Brac 5G 37
Popham. Hants 2D 24
Poplar. G Lon 2E 39
Popley. Hants 1E 25
Porchfield. IOW 3C 16
Porin. High 3F 157
Poringland. Norf 5E 79
Porkellis. Corn 5A 6
Porlock. Som 2B 20
Porlock Weir. Som 2B 20
Portachoillan. Arg 4F 125
Port Adhair Bheinn na Faoghla.
W Isl 3C 170
Port Adhair Thirlodh. Arg 4B 138
Port Ann. Arg 1H 125
Port Appin. Arg 4D 140
Port Asgaig. Arg 3C 124
Port Askaig. Arg 3C 124
Portavadie. Arg 3H 125
Port Bannatyne. Arg 3B 126
Portbury. N Som 4A 34
Port Carlisle. Cumb 3D 112
Port Charlotte. Arg 4A 124
Portchester. Hants 2E 16
Port Clarence. Stoc T 2B 106
Port Dinorwig. Gwyn 4E 81
Port Driseach. Arg 2A 126
Port Dundas. Glas 3H 127
Port Ellen. Arg 5B 124
Port Elphinstone. Abers 1E 153
Portencalzie. Dum 2F 109
Portencross. N Ayr 5C 126
Port Erin. IOM 5A 108
Port Erroll. Abers 5H 161
Porter's Fen Corner. Norf 5E 77
Portesham. Dors 4B 14
Portessie. Mor 2B 160
Port e Vullen. IOM 2D 108
Port-Eynon. Swan 4D 30
Portfield. Som 4H 21
Portfield Gate. Pemb 3D 42
Portgate. Devn 4E 11
Port Gaverne. Corn 4A 10
Port Glasgow. Inv 2E 127
Portgordon. Mor 2A 160
Portgower. High 2H 165
Porth. Corn 2C 6
Porth. Rhon 2D 32
Porthaethwy. IOA 3E 81
Porthallow. Corn 3G 7
(nr. Looe)
Porthallow. Corn 4E 5
(nr. St Keverne)
Porthalong. High 5C 154
Porthcawl. B'end 4B 32
Porthceri. V Glam 5D 32
Porthcothan. Corn 1C 6
Porthcurno. Corn 4A 4
Port Henderson. High 1G 155
Porthgain. Pemb 1C 42
Porthgwarra. Corn 4A 4
Porthill. Shrp 4G 71
Porthkerry. V Glam 5D 32
Porthleven. Corn 4D 4
Porthllechog. IOA 1D 80
Porthmadog. Gwyn 2E 69
Porthmeirion. Gwyn 2E 69
Porthmeor. Corn 3B 4
Porth Navas. Corn 4E 5
Portholland. Corn 4D 6
Porthoustock. Corn 4F 5
Porthtowan. Corn 4A 6
Porth Tywyn. Carm 5E 45
Porth-y-felin. IOA 2B 80
Porthyrhyd. Carm 4F 45
(nr. Carmarthen)
Porthyrhyd. Carm 2A 46
(nr. Llandovery)
Porth-y-waen. Shrp 3E 71
Portincaple. Arg 4B 134
Portington. E Yor 1A 94
Portinnisherrich. Arg 2G 133
Portinscale. Cumb 2D 102
Port Isaac. Corn 1D 6
Portishead. N Som 4H 33
Portknockie. Mor 2B 160
Port Lamont. Arg 2B 126
Portlethen. Abers 4G 153
Portlethen Village. Abers 4G 153
Portling. Dum 4F 111
Port Lion. Pemb 4D 43
Portloe. Corn 5D 6

Port Logan—Ravenstonedale

Port Logan. *Dum* 5F 109
Portmahomack. *High* 5G 165
Port Mead. *Swan* 3F 31
Portmellon. *Corn* 4E 6
Port Mholair. *W Isl* 4H 171
Port Mor. *High* 1F 139
Portmore. *Hants* 3B 16
Port Mulgrave. *N Yor* 3E 107
Portnacroish. *Arg* 4D 140
Portnahaven. *Arg* 4A 124
Portnalong. *High* 5C 154
Portnaluchaig. *High* 5E 147
Portnancon. *High* 2E 167
Port Nan Giuran. *W Isl* 4H 171
Port nan Long. *W Isl* 1D 170
Port Nis. *W Isl* 1H 171
Portobello. *Edin* 2G 129
Portobello. *W Yor* 3D 92
Port of Menteith. *Stir* 3E 135
Porton. *Wilts* 3G 23
Portormin. *High* 5D 168
Portpatrick. *Dum* 4F 109
Port Quin. *Corn* 1D 6
Port Ramsay. *Arg* 4C 140
Portreath. *Corn* 4A 6
Portree. *High* 4D 155
Port Righ. *High* 4D 155
Port St Mary. *IOM* 5B 108
Portscatho. *Corn* 5C 6
Portsea. *Port* 2E 17
Portskerra. *High* 2A 168
Portskewett. *Mon* 3A 34
Portslade-by-Sea. *Brig* 5D 26
Portsmouth. *Port* 3E 17 & 209
Portsmouth. *W Yor* 2H 91
Port Soderick. *IOM* 4C 108
Port Solent. *Port* 2E 17
Portsonachan. *Arg* 1H 133
Portsoy. *Abers* 2C 160
Port Sunlight. *Mers* 2F 83
Portswood. *Sotn* 1C 16
Port Talbot. *Neat* 4G 31
Porttannachy. *Mor* 2A 160
Port Tennant. *Swan* 3F 31
Portuairk. *High* 2F 139
Portway. *Here* 1H 47
Portway. *Worc* 3E 61
Port Wemyss. *Arg* 4A 124
Port William. *Dum* 5A 110
Portwrinkle. *Corn* 3H 7
Poslingford. *Suff* 1A 54
Postbridge. *Devn* 5G 11
Postcombe. *Oxon* 2F 37
Post Green. *Dors* 3E 15
Posthill. *Staf* 5G 73
Postling. *Kent* 2F 29
Postlip. *Glos* 3F 49
Post-Mawr. *Cdgn* 5D 56
Postwick. *Norf* 5E 79
Potarch. *Abers* 4D 152
Potsgrove. *C Beds* 3H 51
Potten End. *Herts* 5A 52
Potter Brompton. *N Yor* 2D 101
Pottergate Street. *Norf* 1D 66
Potterhanworth. *Linc* 4H 87
Potterhanworth Booths. *Linc* 4H 87
Potter Heigham. *Norf* 4G 79
Potter Hill. *Leics* 3E 75
Potteries, The. *Stoke* 1C 72
Potterne. *Wilts* 1E 23
Potterne Wick. *Wilts* 1E 23
Potternewton. *W Yor* 1D 92
Potters Bar. *Herts* 5C 52
Potters Brook. *Lanc* 4D 97
Potter's Cross. *Staf* 2C 60
Potters Crouch. *Herts* 5B 52
Potter Somersal. *Derbs* 2F 73
Potterspury. *Nptn* 1F 51
Potter Street. *Essx* 5E 53
Potterton. *Abers* 2G 153
Potthorpe. *Norf* 3B 78
Pottle Street. *Wilts* 2D 22
Potto. *N Yor* 4B 106
Potton. *C Beds* 1C 52
Pott Row. *Norf* 3G 77
Pott Shrigley. *Ches E* 3D 84
Poughill. *Corn* 2C 10
Poughill. *Devn* 2B 12
Poulner. *Hants* 2G 15
Poulshot. *Wilts* 1E 23
Poulton. *Glos* 5G 49
Poulton-le-Fylde. *Lanc* 1B 90
Pound Bank. *Worc* 3B 60
Poundbury. *Dors* 3B 14
Poundfield. *E Sus* 2G 27
Poundgate. *E Sus* 3F 27
Pound Green. *E Sus* 3G 27
Pound Green. *Suff* 5G 65
Pound Hill. *W Sus* 2D 27
Poundland. *S Ayr* 1G 109
Poundon. *Buck* 3E 51
Poundsgate. *Devn* 5H 11
Poundstock. *Corn* 3C 10
Pound Street. *Hants* 5C 36
Pounsley. *E Sus* 3G 27
Powburn. *Nmbd* 3E 121
Powderham. *Devn* 4C 12
Powerstock. *Dors* 3A 14
Powfoot. *Dum* 3C 112
Powick. *Worc* 5C 60
Powmill. *Per* 4C 136
Poxwell. *Dors* 4C 14
Poyle. *Slo* 3B 38
Poynings. *W Sus* 4D 26
Poyntington. *Dors* 4B 22
Poynton. *Ches E* 2D 84
Poynton. *Telf* 4H 71
Poynton Green. *Telf* 4H 71
Poystreet Green. *Suff* 5B 66
Praa Sands. *Corn* 4C 4
Pratt's Bottom. *G Lon* 4F 39
Praze-an-Beeble. *Corn* 3D 4
Prees. *Shrp* 2H 71
Preesall. *Lanc* 5C 96
Preesall Park. *Lanc* 5C 96
Prees Green. *Shrp* 2H 71
Prees Higher Heath. *Shrp* 2H 71
Prendergast. *Pemb* 3D 42
Prendwick. *Nmbd* 3E 121
Pren-gwyn. *Cdgn* 1E 45
Prenteg. *Gwyn* 1E 69
Prenton. *Mers* 2F 83
Prescot. *Mers* 1G 83
Prescott. *Devn* 1D 12
Prescott. *Shrp* 3G 71
Preshute. *Wilts* 5G 35
Pressen. *Nmbd* 1C 120
Prestatyn. *Den* 2C 82
Prestbury. *Ches E* 3D 84
Prestbury. *Glos* 3E 49
Presteigne. *Powy* 4F 59
Presthope. *Shrp* 1H 59
Prestleigh. *Som* 2B 22
Preston. *Brig* 5E 27
Preston. *Devn* 5B 12
Preston. *Dors* 4C 14
Preston. *E Lot* 2B 130
(nr. East Linton)
Preston. *E Lot* 2G 129
(nr. Prestonpans)
Preston. *E Yor* 1E 95
Preston. *Glos* 5F 49
Preston. *Herts* 3B 52
Preston. *Kent* 4G 41
(nr. Canterbury)
Preston. *Kent* 4E 40
(nr. Faversham)
Preston. *Lanc* 2D 90 & 208
Preston. *Nmbd* 2F 121
Preston. *Rut* 5F 75
Preston. *Bord* 4D 130
Preston. *Shrp* 4H 71
Preston. *Suff* 5B 66
Preston. *Wilts* 4A 36
(nr. Aldbourne)
Preston. *Wilts* 4F 35
(nr. Lyneham)
Preston Bagot. *Warw* 4F 61
Preston Bissett. *Buck* 3E 51
Preston Bowyer. *Som* 4E 21
Preston Brockhurst. *Shrp* 3H 71
Preston Brook. *Hal* 3H 83
Preston Candover. *Hants* 2E 24
Preston Capes. *Nptn* 5C 62
Preston Cross. *Glos* 2B 48
Preston Gubbals. *Shrp* 4G 71
Preston-le-Skerne. *Dur* 2A 106
Preston Marsh. *Here* 1A 48
Prestonmill. *Dum* 4A 112
Preston on Stour. *Warw* 5G 61
Preston on the Hill. *Hal* 2H 83
Preston on Wye. *Here* 1G 47
Prestonpans. *E Lot* 2G 129
Preston Plucknett. *Som* 1A 14
Preston-under-Scar. *N Yor* 5D 104
Preston upon the Weald Moors.
Telf 4A 72
Preston Wynne. *Here* 1A 48
Prestwich. *G Man* 4G 91
Prestwick. *Nmbd* 2E 115
Prestwick. *S Ayr* 2C 116
Prestwold. *Leics* 3C 74
Prestwood. *Buck* 5G 51
Prestwood. *Staf* 1E 73
Price Town. *B'end* 2C 32
Prickwillow. *Cambs* 2E 65
Priddy. *Som* 1A 22
Priestcliffe. *Derbs* 3F 85
Priesthill. *Glas* 3G 127
Priest Hutton. *Lanc* 2E 97
Priestland. *E Ayr* 1E 117
Priest Weston. *Shrp* 1E 59
Priestwood. *Brac* 4G 37
Priestwood. *Kent* 4A 40
Primethorpe. *Leics* 1C 62
Primrose Green. *Norf* 4C 78
Primrose Hill. *Derbs* 5B 86
Primrose Hill. *Glos* 5B 48
Primrose Hill. *Lanc* 4B 90
Primrose Valley. *N Yor* 2F 101
Primsidemill. *Bord* 2C 120
Princes Gate. *Pemb* 3F 43
Princes Risborough. *Buck* 5G 51
Princethorpe. *Warw* 3B 62
Princetown. *Devn* 5F 11
Prinsted. *W Sus* 2F 17
Prion. *Den* 4C 82
Prior Muir. *Fife* 2H 137
Prior's Frome. *Here* 2A 48
Priors Halton. *Shrp* 3G 59
Priors Hardwick. *Warw* 5B 62
Priorslee. *Telf* 4B 72
Priors Marston. *Warw* 5B 62
Prior's Norton. *Glos* 3D 48
Priory, The. *W Ber* 5B 36
Priory Wood. *Here* 1F 47
Priston. *Bath* 5B 34
Pristow Green. *Norf* 2D 66
Prittlewell. *S'end* 2C 40
Privett. *Hants* 4E 25
Prixford. *Devn* 3F 19
Probus. *Corn* 4D 6
Prospect. *Cumb* 5C 112
Prospect Village. *Staf* 4E 73
Provanmill. *Glas* 3H 127
Prudhoe. *Nmbd* 3D 115
Publow. *Bath* 5B 34
Puckeridge. *Herts* 3D 53
Puckington. *Som* 1G 13
Pucklechurch. *S Glo* 4B 34
Puckrup. *Glos* 2D 49
Puddinglake. *Ches W* 4B 84
Puddington. *Ches W* 3F 83
Puddington. *Devn* 1B 12
Puddlebrook. *Glos* 4B 48
Puddledock. *Norf* 1C 66
Puddletown. *Dors* 3C 14
Pudleston. *Here* 5H 59
Pudsey. *W Yor* 1C 92
Pulborough. *W Sus* 4B 26
Puleston. *Telf* 3B 72
Pulford. *Ches W* 5F 83
Pulham. *Dors* 2C 14
Pulham Market. *Norf* 2D 66
Pulham St Mary. *Norf* 2E 66
Pulley. *Shrp* 5G 71
Pulloxhill. *C Beds* 2A 52
Pulpit Hill. *Arg* 1F 133
Pulverbatch. *Shrp* 5G 71
Pumpherston. *W Lot* 3D 128
Pumsaint. *Carm* 1G 45
Puncheston. *Pemb* 2E 43
Puncknowle. *Dors* 4A 14
Punnett's Town. *E Sus* 3H 27
Purbrook. *Hants* 2E 17
Purfleet. *Thur* 3G 39
Puriton. *Som* 2G 21
Purleigh. *Essx* 5B 54
Purley. *G Lon* 4E 39
Purley on Thames. *W Ber* 4E 37
Purlogue. *Shrp* 3E 59
Purl's Bridge. *Cambs* 2D 65
Purse Caundle. *Dors* 1B 14
Purslow. *Shrp* 2F 59
Purston Jaglin. *W Yor* 3E 93
Purtington. *Som* 2G 13
Purton. *Glos* 5B 48
(nr. Lydney)
Purton. *Glos* 5B 48
(nr. Sharpness)
Purton. *Wilts* 3F 35
Purton Stoke. *Wilts* 2F 35
Pury End. *Nptn* 1F 51
Pusey. *Oxon* 2B 36
Putley. *Here* 2B 48
Putney. *G Lon* 3D 38
Putsborough. *Devn* 2E 19
Puttenham. *Herts* 4G 51
Puttenham. *Surr* 1A 26
Puttock End. *Essx* 1B 54
Puttock's End. *Essx* 4F 53
Puxey. *Dors* 1C 14
Puxton. *N Som* 5H 33
Pwll. *Carm* 5E 45
Pwll. *Powy* 5D 70
Pwllcrochan. *Pemb* 4D 42
Pwll-glas. *Den* 5D 82
Pwllgloyw. *Powy* 2D 46
Pwllheli. *Gwyn* 2C 68
Pwllmeyric. *Mon* 2A 34
Pwlltrap. *Carm* 3G 43
Pwll-y-glaw. *Neat* 2A 32
Pyecombe. *W Sus* 4D 27
Pye Corner. *Herts* 4E 53
Pye Corner. *Newp* 3G 33
Pye Green. *Staf* 4D 73
Pyewipe. *NE Lin* 3F 95
Pyle. *B'end* 3B 32
Pyle. *IOW* 5C 16
Pylle. *Som* 3B 22
Pymoor. *Cambs* 2D 65
Pymoor. *Dors* 3H 13
Pyrford. *Surr* 5B 38
Pyrford Village. *Surr* 5B 38
Pyrton. *Oxon* 2E 37
Pytchley. *Nptn* 3F 63
Pyworthy. *Devn* 2D 10

Q

Quabbs. *Shrp* 2E 58
Quadring. *Linc* 2B 76
Quadring Eaudike. *Linc* 2B 76
Quainton. *Buck* 3F 51
Quaking Houses. *Dur* 4E 115
Quarley. *Hants* 2A 24
Quarndon. *Derbs* 1H 73
Quarrendon. *Buck* 4G 51
Quarrier's Village. *Inv* 3E 127
Quarrington. *Linc* 1H 75
Quarrington Hill. *Dur* 1A 106
Quarry Bank. *W Mid* 2D 60
Quarry, The. *Glos* 2C 34
Quarrywood. *Mor* 2F 159
Quartalehouse. *Abers* 4G 161
Quarter. *N Ayr* 3C 126
Quarter. *S Lan* 4A 128
Quatford. *Shrp* 1B 60
Quatt. *Shrp* 2B 60
Quebec. *Dur* 5E 115
Quedgeley. *Glos* 4D 48
Queen Adelaide. *Cambs* 2E 65
Queenborough. *Kent* 3D 40
Queen Camel. *Som* 4A 22
Queen Charlton. *Bath* 5B 34
Queen Dart. *Devn* 1B 12
Queenhill. *Worc* 2D 48
Queen Oak. *Dors* 3C 22
Queensbury. *W Yor* 2B 92
Queensferry. *Flin* 4F 83
Queenstown. *Bkpl* 1B 90
Queen Street. *Kent* 1A 28
Queenzieburn. *N Lan* 2H 127
Quemerford. *Wilts* 5F 35
Quendale. *Shet* 10E 173
Quendon. *Essx* 2F 53
Queniborough. *Leics* 4D 74
Quenington. *Glos* 5G 49
Quernmore. *Lanc* 3E 97
Quethiock. *Corn* 2H 7
Quholm. *Orkn* 6B 172
Quick's Green. *W Ber* 4D 36
Quidenham. *Norf* 2C 66
Quidhampton. *Hants* 1D 24
Quidhampton. *Wilts* 3G 23
Quilquox. *Abers* 5G 161
Quina Brook. *Shrp* 2H 71
Quindry. *Orkn* 8D 172
Quine's Hill. *IOM* 4C 108
Quinton. *Nptn* 5E 63
Quinton. *W Mid* 2D 61
Quintrell Downs. *Corn* 2C 6
Quixhill. *Staf* 1F 73
Quoditch. *Devn* 3E 11
Quorn. *Leics* 4C 74
Quorndon. *Leics* 4C 74
Quothquan. *S Lan* 1B 118
Quoyloo. *Orkn* 5B 172
Quoyness. *Orkn* 7B 172
Quoys. *Shet* 5F 173
(on Mainland)
Quoys. *Shet* 1H 173
(on Unst)

R

Rableyheath. *Herts* 4C 52
Raby. *Cumb* 4C 112
Raby. *Mers* 3F 83
Rachan Mill. *Bord* 1D 118
Rachub. *Gwyn* 4F 81
Rack End. *Oxon* 5C 50
Rackenford. *Devn* 1B 12
Rackham. *W Sus* 4B 26
Rackheath. *Norf* 4E 79
Racks. *Dum* 2B 112
Rackwick. *Orkn* 8A 172
(on Hoy)
Rackwick. *Orkn* 3D 172
(on Westray)
Radbourne. *Derbs* 2G 73
Radcliffe. *G Man* 4F 91
Radcliffe. *Nmbd* 4G 121
Radcliffe on Trent. *Notts* 2D 74
Radclive. *Buck* 2E 51
Radernie. *Fife* 2G 137
Radfall. *Kent* 4F 41
Radford. *Bath* 1B 22
Radford. *Nott* 1C 74
Radford. *Oxon* 3C 50
Radford. *W Mid* 2H 61
Radford. *Worc* 5E 61
Radford Semele. *Warw* 4H 61
Radipole. *Dors* 4B 14
Radlett. *Herts* 1C 38
Radley. *Oxon* 2D 36
Radnage. *Buck* 2F 37
Radstock. *Bath* 1B 22
Radstone. *Nptn* 1D 50
Radway. *Warw* 1B 50
Radway Green. *Ches E* 5B 84
Radwell. *Bed* 5H 63
Radwell. *Herts* 2C 52
Radwinter. *Essx* 2G 53
Radyr. *Card* 3E 33
RAF Coltishall. *Norf* 3E 79
Rafford. *Mor* 3E 159
Ragdale. *Leics* 4D 74
Ragdon. *Shrp* 1G 59
Ragged Appleshaw. *Hants* 2B 24
Raggra. *High* 4F 169
Raglan. *Mon* 5H 47
Ragnall. *Notts* 3F 87
Raigbeg. *High* 1C 150
Rainford. *Mers* 4C 90
Rainford Junction. *Mers* 4C 90
Rainham. *G Lon* 2G 39
Rainham. *Medw* 4C 40
Rainhill. *Mers* 1G 83
Rainow. *Ches E* 3D 84
Rainton. *N Yor* 2F 99
Rainworth. *Notts* 5C 86
Raisbeck. *Cumb* 4H 103
Raise. *Cumb* 5A 114
Rait. *Per* 1E 137
Raithby. *Linc* 2C 88
Raithby by Spilsby. *Linc* 4C 88
Raithwaite. *N Yor* 3F 107
Rake. *W Sus* 4G 25
Rake End. *Staf* 4E 73
Rakeway. *Staf* 1E 73
Rakewood. *G Man* 3H 91
Ralia. *High* 4B 150
Ram Alley. *Wilts* 5H 35
Ramasaig. *High* 4A 154
Rame. *Corn* 4A 8
(nr. Millbrook)
Rame. *Corn* 5B 6
(nr. Penryn)
Ram Lane. *Kent* 1D 28
Ramnageo. *Shet* 1H 173
Rampisham. *Dors* 2A 14
Rampside. *Cumb* 3B 96
Rampton. *Cambs* 4D 64
Rampton. *Notts* 3E 87
Ramsbottom. *G Man* 3F 91
Ramsburn. *Mor* 3C 160
Ramsbury. *Wilts* 4A 36
Ramscraigs. *High* 1H 165
Ramsdean. *Hants* 4F 25
Ramsdell. *Hants* 1D 24
Ramsden. *Oxon* 4B 50
Ramsden. *Worc* 1E 49
Ramsden Bellhouse. *Essx* 1B 40
Ramsden Heath. *Essx* 1B 40
Ramsey. *Cambs* 2B 64
Ramsey. *Essx* 2F 55
Ramsey. *IOM* 2D 108
Ramsey Forty Foot. *Cambs* 2C 64
Ramsey Heights. *Cambs* 2B 64
Ramsey Island. *Essx* 5C 54
Ramsey Mereside. *Cambs* 2B 64
Ramsey St Mary's. *Cambs* 2B 64
Ramsgate. *Kent* 4H 41
Ramsgill. *N Yor* 2D 98
Ramshaw. *Dur* 5C 114
Ramshorn. *Staf* 1E 73
Ramsley. *Devn* 3G 11
Ramsnest Common. *Surr* 2A 26
Ramstone. *Abers* 2D 152
Ranais. *W Isl* 5G 171
Ranby. *Linc* 3B 88
Ranby. *Notts* 2D 86
Rand. *Linc* 3A 88
Randwick. *Glos* 5D 48
Ranfurly. *Ren* 3E 127
Rangag. *High* 4D 168
Rangemore. *Staf* 3F 73
Rangeworthy. *S Glo* 3B 34
Rankinston. *E Ayr* 3D 116
Rank's Green. *Essx* 4H 53
Ranmore Common. *Surr* 5C 38
Rannoch Station. *Per* 3B 142
Ranochan. *High* 5G 147
Ranskill. *Notts* 2D 86
Ranton. *Staf* 3C 72
Ranton Green. *Staf* 3C 72
Ranworth. *Norf* 4F 79
Raploch. *Stir* 4G 135
Rapness. *Orkn* 3E 172
Rapps. *Som* 1G 13
Rascal Moor. *E Yor* 1B 94
Rascarrel. *Dum* 5E 111
Rashfield. *Arg* 1C 126
Rashwood. *Worc* 4D 60
Raskelf. *N Yor* 2G 99
Rassau. *Blae* 4E 47
Rastrick. *W Yor* 2B 92
Ratagan. *High* 2B 148
Ratby. *Leics* 5C 74
Ratcliffe Culey. *Leics* 1H 61
Ratcliffe on Soar. *Notts* 3B 74
Ratcliffe on the Wreake.
Leics 4D 74
Rathen. *Abers* 2H 161
Rathillet. *Fife* 1F 137
Rathmell. *N Yor* 4H 97
Ratho. *Edin* 2E 129
Ratho Station. *Edin* 2E 129
Rathven. *Mor* 2B 160
Ratley. *Hants* 4B 24
Ratley. *Warw* 1B 50
Ratlinghope. *Shrp* 1G 59
Rattar. *High* 1E 169
Ratten Row. *Cumb* 5E 113
Ratten Row. *Lanc* 5D 96
Rattery. *Devn* 2D 8
Rattlesden. *Suff* 5B 66
Ratton Village. *E Sus* 5G 27
Rattray. *Abers* 3H 161
Rattray. *Per* 4A 144
Raughton. *Cumb* 5E 113
Raughton Head. *Cumb* 5E 113
Raunds. *Nptn* 3G 63
Ravenfield. *S Yor* 1B 86
Ravenglass. *Cumb* 5B 102
Ravenhills Green. *Worc* 5B 60
Raveningham. *Norf* 1F 67
Ravenscar. *N Yor* 4G 107
Ravensdale. *IOM* 2C 108
Ravensden. *Bed* 5H 63
Ravenseat. *N Yor* 4B 104
Ravenshead. *Notts* 5C 86
Ravensmoor. *Ches E* 5A 84
Ravensthorpe. *Nptn* 3D 62
Ravensthorpe. *W Yor* 2C 92
Ravenstone. *Leics* 4B 74
Ravenstonedale. *Cumb* 4A 104

Ravenstown. *Cumb* 2C **96**
Ravenstruther. *S Lan* 5C **128**
Ravensworth. *N Yor* 4E **105**
Raw. *N Yor* 4G **107**
Rawcliffe. *E Yor* 2G **93**
Rawcliffe. *York* 4H **99**
Rawcliffe Bridge. *E Yor* 2G **93**
Rawdon. *W Yor* 1C **92**
Rawgreen. *Nmbd* 4C **114**
Rawmarsh. *S Yor* 1B **86**
Rawnsley. *Staf* 4E **73**
Rawreth. *Essx* 1B **40**
Rawridge. *Devn* 2F **13**
Rawson Green. *Derbs* 1A **74**
Rawtenstall. *Lanc* 2F **91**
Raydon. *Suff* 2D **54**
Raylees. *Nmbd* 5D **120**
Rayleigh. *Essx* 1C **40**
Raymond's Hill. *Devn* 3G **13**
Rayne. *Essx* 3H **53**
Rayners Lane. *G Lon* 2C **38**
Reach. *Cambs* 4E **65**
Read. *Lanc* 1F **91**
Reading. *Read* . . . . . . .4F **37** & **209**
Reading Green. *Suff* 3D **66**
Reading Street. *Kent* 2D **28**
Readymoney. *Corn* 3F **7**
Reagill. *Cumb* 3H **103**
Rea Hill. *Torb* 3F **9**
Rearquhar. *High* 4E **165**
Rearsby. *Leics* 4D **74**
Reasby. *Linc* 3H **87**
Reaseheath. *Ches E* 5A **84**
Reaster. *High* 2E **169**
Reawick. *Shet* 7E **173**
Reay. *High* 2B **168**
Rechullin. *High* 3A **156**
Reculver. *Kent* 4G **41**
Redberth. *Pemb* 4E **43**
Redbourn. *Herts* 4B **52**
Redbourne. *N Lin* 4C **94**
Redbrook. *Glos* 4A **48**
Redbrook. *Wrex* 1H **71**
Redburn. *Nmbd* 4D **158**
Redburn. *Nmbd* 3A **114**
Redcar. *Red C* 2D **106**
Redcastle. *High* 4H **157**
Redcliff Bay. *N Som* 4H **33**
Red Dial. *Cumb* 5D **112**
Redding. *Falk* 2C **128**
Reddingmuirhead. *Falk* 2C **128**
Reddings, The. *Glos* 3E **49**
Reddish. *G Man* 1C **84**
Redditch. *Worc* 4E **61**
Rede. *Suff* 5H **65**
Redenhall. *Norf* 2E **67**
Redesdale Camp. *Nmbd* 5C **120**
Redesmouth. *Nmbd* 1B **114**
Redford. *Ang* 4E **145**
Redford. *Dur* 1D **105**
Redford. *W Sus* 4G **25**
Redfordgreen. *Bord* 3F **119**
Redgate. *Corn* 2G **7**
Redgrave. *Suff* 3C **66**
Redhill. *Abers* 3E **153**
Redhill. *Herts* 2C **52**
Redhill. *N Som* 5H **33**
Redhill. *Shrp* 4B **72**
Redhill. *Surr* 5D **39**
Red Hill. *Warw* 5F **61**
Red Hill. *W Yor* 2E **93**
Redhouses. *Arg* 3B **124**
Redisham. *Suff* 2G **67**
Redland. *Bris* 4A **34**
Redland. *Orkn* 5C **172**
Redlingfield. *Suff* 3D **66**
Red Lodge. *Suff* 3F **65**
Redlynch. *Som* 3C **22**
Redlynch. *Wilts* 4H **23**
Redmain. *Cumb* 1C **102**
Redmarley. *Worc* 4B **60**
Redmarley D'Abitot. *Glos* 2C **48**
Redmarshall. *Stoc T* 2A **106**
Redmile. *Leics* 2E **75**
Redmire. *N Yor* 5D **104**
Rednal. *Shrp* 3F **71**
Redpath. *Bord* 1H **119**
Redpoint. *High* 2G **155**
Red Post. *Corn* 2C **10**
Red Rock. *G Man* 4D **90**
Red Roses. *Carm* 3G **43**
Red Row. *Nmbd* 5G **121**
Redruth. *Corn* 4B **6**
Red Street. *Staf* 5C **84**
Redvales. *G Man* 4F **91**
Red Wharf Bay. *IOA* 2E **81**
Redwick. *Newp* 3H **33**
Redwick. *S Glo* 3A **34**
Redworth. *Darl* 2F **105**
Reed. *Herts* 2D **52**
Reed End. *Herts* 2D **52**
Reedham. *Linc* 5B **88**
Reedham. *Norf* 5G **79**
Reedness. *E Yor* 2B **94**
Reeds Beck. *Linc* 4B **88**
Reemshill. *Abers* 4E **161**
Reepham. *Linc* 3H **87**
Reepham. *Norf* 3C **78**
Reeth. *N Yor* 5D **104**
Regaby. *IOM* 2D **108**
Regil. *N Som* 5A **34**
Regoul. *High* 3C **158**

Reiff. *High* 2D **162**
Reigate. *Surr* 5D **38**
Reighton. *N Yor* 2F **101**
Reilth. *Shrp* 2E **59**
Reinigeadal. *W Isl* 7E **171**
Reisque. *Abers* 1F **153**
Reiss. *High* 3F **169**
Rejerrah. *Corn* 3B **6**
Releath. *Corn* 5A **6**
Relubbus. *Corn* 3C **4**
Relugas. *Mor* 4D **159**
Remenham. *Wok* 3F **37**
Remenham Hill. *Wok* 3F **37**
Rempstone. *Notts* 3C **74**
Rendcomb. *Glos* 5F **49**
Rendham. *Suff* 4F **67**
Rendlesham. *Suff* 5F **67**
Renfrew. *Ren* 3G **127**
Renhold. *Bed* 5H **63**
Renishaw. *Derbs* 3B **86**
Rennington. *Nmbd* 3G **121**
Renton. *W Dun* 2E **127**
Renwick. *Cumb* 5G **113**
Repps. *Norf* 4G **79**
Repton. *Derbs* 3H **73**
Rescassa. *Corn* 4D **6**
Rescobie. *Ang* 3E **145**
Rescorla. *Corn* 3E **7**
(nr. Rosevean)
Rescorla. *Corn* 4D **6**
(nr. St Ewe)
Resipole. *High* 2B **140**
Resolfen. *Neat* 5B **46**
Resolis. *High* 2A **158**
Resolven. *Neat* 5B **46**
Rest and be thankful. *Arg* . . .3B **134**
Reston. *Bord* 3E **131**
Restrop. *Wilts* 3F **35**
Retire. *Corn* 2E **6**
Retford. *Notts* 2E **86**
Rettendon. *Essx* 1B **40**
Retyn. *Corn* 3C **6**
Revesby. *Linc* 4C **88**
Rew. *Devn* 5D **8**
Rew. *Devn* 3C **12**
Rew Street. *IOW* 3C **16**
Rexon. *Devn* 4E **11**
Reybridge. *Wilts* 5E **35**
Reydon. *Suff* 3H **67**
Reymerston. *Norf* 5C **78**
Reynalton. *Pemb* 4E **43**
Reynoldston. *Swan* 4D **31**
Rezare. *Corn* 5D **10**
Rhadyr. *Mon* 5G **47**
Rhaeadr Gwy. *Powy* 4B **58**
Rhandirmwyn. *Carm* 1A **46**
Rhayader. *Powy* 4B **58**
Rheindown. *High* 4H **157**
Rhemore. *High* 3G **139**
Rhenetra. *High* 3D **154**
Rhewl. *Den* 1D **70**
(nr. Llangollen)
Rhewl. *Den* 4D **82**
(nr. Ruthin)
Rhewl. *Shrp* 2F **71**
Rhewl-Mostyn. *Flin* 3D **82**
Rhian. *High* 2C **164**
Rhian Breck. *High* 3C **164**
Rhicarn. *High* 1E **163**
Rhiconich. *High* 3C **166**
Rhicullen. *High* 1A **158**
Rhidorroch. *High* 4F **163**
Rhifail. *High* 4H **167**
Rhigos. *Rhon* 5C **46**
Rhilochan. *High* 3E **165**
Rhiroy. *High* 5F **163**
Rhitongue. *High* 3G **167**
Rhiw. *Gwyn* 3B **68**
Rhiwabon. *Wrex* 1F **71**
Rhiwbina. *Card* 3E **33**
Rhiwbryfdir. *Gwyn* 1F **69**
Rhiwderin. *Newp* 3F **33**
Rhiwlas. *Gwyn* 2B **70**
(nr. Bala)
Rhiwlas. *Gwyn* 4E **81**
(nr. Bangor)
Rhiwlas. *Powy* 2D **70**
Rhodes. *G Man* 4G **91**
Rhodesia. *Notts* 2C **86**
Rhodes Minnis. *Kent* 1F **29**
Rhodiad-y-Brenin. *Pemb* 2B **42**
Rhondda. *Rhon* 2C **32**
Rhonehouse. *Dum* 4E **111**
Rhoose. *V Glam* 5D **32**
Rhos. *Carm* 2D **45**
Rhos. *Neat* 5A **46**
Rhosaman. *Carm* 4H **45**
Rhoscefnhir. *IOA* 3E **81**
Rhoscolyn. *IOA* 3B **80**
Rhos Common. *Powy* 4E **71**
Rhoscrowther. *Pemb* 4D **42**
Rhos-ddu. *Gwyn* 2B **68**
Rhosdylluan. *Gwyn* 3A **70**
Rhosesmor. *Flin* 4E **83**
Rhos-fawr. *Gwyn* 2C **68**
Rhosgadfan. *Gwyn* 5E **81**
Rhosgoch. *IOA* 2D **80**
Rhosgoch. *Powy* 1E **47**
Rhos Haminiog. *Cdgn* 4E **57**
Rhos-hill. *Pemb* 1B **44**
Rhoshirwaun. *Gwyn* 3A **68**

Rhoslan. *Gwyn* 1D **69**
Rhoslefain. *Gwyn* 5E **69**
Rhosllanerchrugog. *Wrex* . . .1E **71**
Rhos Lligwy. *IOA* 2D **81**
Rhosmaen. *Carm* 3G **45**
Rhosmeirch. *IOA* 3D **80**
Rhosneigr. *IOA* 3C **80**
Rhos-on-Sea. *Cnwy* 2H **81**
Rhossili. *Swan* 4D **30**
Rhosson. *Pemb* 2B **42**
Rhos, The. *Pemb* 3E **43**
Rhostrenwfa. *IOA* 3D **80**
Rhostryfan. *Gwyn* 5D **81**
Rhostyllen. *Wrex* 1F **71**
Rhoswiel. *Shrp* 2E **71**
Rhosybol. *IOA* 2D **81**
Rhos-y-brithdir. *Powy* 3D **70**
Rhos-y-garth. *Cdgn* 3F **57**
Rhos-y-gwaliau. *Gwyn* 2B **70**
Rhos-y-llan. *Gwyn* 2B **68**
Rhos-y-meirch. *Powy* 4E **59**
Rhu. *Arg* 1D **126**
Rhuallt. *Den* 3C **82**
Rhubha Stoer. *High* 1E **163**
Rhuddall Heath. *Ches W* 4H **83**
Rhuddlan. *Cdgn* 1E **45**
Rhuddlan. *Den* 3C **82**
Rhue. *High* 4E **163**
Rhulen. *Powy* 1E **47**
Rhunahaorine. *Arg* 5F **125**
Rhuthun. *Den* 5D **82**
Rhuvoult. *High* 3C **166**
Rhyd. *Gwyn* 1F **69**
Rhydaman. *Carm* 4G **45**
Rhydargaeau. *Carm* 3E **45**
Rhydcymerau. *Carm* 2F **45**
Rhydd. *Worc* 1D **48**
Rhyd-Ddu. *Gwyn* 5E **81**
Rhydding. *Neat* 3G **31**
Rhydfudr. *Cdgn* 4E **57**
Rhydlanfair. *Cnwy* 5H **81**
Rhydlewis. *Cdgn* 1D **44**
Rhydlios. *Gwyn* 2A **68**
Rhydlydan. *Cnwy* 5A **82**
Rhyd-meirionydd. *Cdgn* 2F **57**
Rhydowen. *Cdgn* 1E **45**
Rhyd-Rosser. *Cdgn* 4E **57**
Rhydspence. *Powy* 1F **47**
Rhydtalog. *Flin* 5E **83**
Rhyd-uchaf. *Gwyn* 2B **70**
Rhydwyn. *IOA* 2C **80**
Rhyd-y-clafdy. *Gwyn* 2C **68**
Rhydycroesau. *Shrp* 2E **71**
Rhydyfelin. *Cdgn* 3E **57**
Rhydyfelin. *Rhon* 3D **32**
Rhyd-y-foel. *Cnwy* 3B **82**
Rhyd-y-fro. *Neat* 5H **45**
Rhydymain. *Gwyn* 3H **69**
Rhyd-y-meirch. *Mon* 5G **47**
Rhyd-y-meudwy. *Den* 5D **82**
Rhydymwyn. *Flin* 4E **82**
Rhyd-yr-onen. *Gwyn* 5F **69**
Rhyd-y-sarn. *Gwyn* 1F **69**
Rhyl. *Den* 2C **82**
Rhymney. *Cphy* 5E **46**
Rhymni. *Cphy* 5E **46**
Rhynd. *Per* 1D **136**
Rhynie. *Abers* 1B **152**
Ribbesford. *Worc* 3B **60**
Ribbleton. *Lanc* 1D **90**
Ribby. *Lanc* 1C **90**
Ribchester. *Lanc* 1E **91**
Riber. *Derbs* 5H **85**
Ribigill. *High* 3F **167**
Riby. *Linc* 4E **95**
Riccall. *N Yor* 1G **93**
Riccarton. *E Ayr* 1D **116**
Richards Castle. *Here* 4G **59**
Richborough Port. *Kent* 4H **41**
Richings Park. *Buck* 3B **38**
Richmond. *G Lon* 3C **38**
Richmond. *N Yor* 4E **105**
Rickarton. *Abers* 5F **153**
Rickerby. *Cumb* 4F **113**
Rickerscote. *Staf* 3D **72**
Rickford. *N Som* 1H **21**
Rickham. *Devn* 5D **8**
Rickinghall. *Suff* 3C **66**
Rickleton. *Tyne* 4F **115**
Rickling. *Essx* 2E **53**
Rickling Green. *Essx* 3F **53**
Rickmansworth. *Herts* 1B **38**
Riddings. *Derbs* 5B **86**
Riddlecombe. *Devn* 1G **11**
Riddlesden. *W Yor* 5C **98**
Ridge. *Dors* 4E **15**
Ridge. *Herts* 5C **52**
Ridge. *Wilts* 3E **23**
Ridgebourne. *Powy* 4C **58**
Ridge Lane. *Warw* 1G **61**
Ridgeway. *Derbs* 2B **86**
(nr. Alfreton)
Ridgeway. *Derbs* 2B **86**
(nr. Sheffield)
Ridgeway. *Staf* 5C **84**
Ridgeway Cross. *Here* 1C **48**
Ridgeway Moor. *Derbs* 2B **86**
Ridgewell. *Essx* 1H **53**
Ridgewood. *E Sus* 3F **27**
Ridgmont. *C Beds* 2H **51**
Ridgwardine. *Shrp* 2A **72**

Riding Mill. *Nmbd* 3D **114**
Ridley. *Kent* 4H **39**
Ridley. *Nmbd* 3A **114**
Ridlington. *Norf* 2F **79**
Ridlington. *Rut* 5F **75**
Ridsdale. *Nmbd* 1C **114**
Riemore Lodge. *Per* 4H **143**
Rievaulx. *N Yor* 1H **99**
Rift House. *Hart* 1B **106**
Rigg. *Dum* 3D **112**
Riggend. *N Lan* 2A **128**
Rigsby. *Linc* 3D **88**
Rigside. *S Lan* 1A **118**
Riley Green. *Lanc* 2E **90**
Rileyhill. *Staf* 4F **73**
Rilla Mill. *Corn* 5C **10**
Rillington. *N Yor* 2C **100**
Rimington. *Lanc* 5H **97**
Rimpton. *Som* 4B **22**
Rimsdale. *High* 4H **167**
Rimswell. *E Yor* 2G **95**
Ringasta. *Shet* 10E **173**
Ringford. *Dum* 4D **111**
Ringing Hill. *Leics* 4B **74**
Ringinglow. *S Yor* 2G **85**
Ringland. *Norf* 4D **78**
Ringlestone. *Kent* 5C **40**
Ringmer. *E Sus* 4F **27**
Ringmore. *Devn* 4C **8**
(nr. Kingsbridge)
Ringmore. *Devn* 5C **12**
(nr. Teignmouth)
Ring o' Bells. *Lanc* 3C **90**
Ring's End. *Cambs* 5C **76**
Ringsfield. *Suff* 2G **67**
Ringsfield Corner. *Suff* 2G **67**
Ringshall. *Buck* 4H **51**
Ringshall. *Suff* 5C **66**
Ringshall Stocks. *Suff* 5C **66**
Ringstead. *Norf* 1G **77**
Ringstead. *Nptn* 3G **63**
Ringwood. *Hants* 2G **15**
Ringwould. *Kent* 1H **29**
Rinmore. *Abers* 2B **152**
Rinnigill. *Orkn* 8C **172**
Rinsey. *Corn* 4C **4**
Riof. *W Isl* 4D **171**
Ripe. *E Sus* 4G **27**
Ripley. *Derbs* 1B **74**
Ripley. *Hants* 3G **15**
Ripley. *N Yor* 3E **99**
Ripley. *Surr* 5B **38**
Riplingham. *E Yor* 1C **94**
Riplington. *Hants* 4E **25**
Ripon. *N Yor* 2F **99**
Rippingale. *Linc* 3H **75**
Ripple. *Kent* 1H **29**
Ripple. *Worc* 2D **48**
Ripponden. *W Yor* 3A **92**
Rireavach. *High* 4E **163**
Risabus. *Arg* 5B **124**
Risbury. *Here* 5H **59**
Risby. *E Yor* 1D **94**
Risby. *N Lin* 3C **94**
Risby. *Suff* 4G **65**
Risca. *Cphy* 2F **33**
Rise. *E Yor* 5F **101**
Riseden. *E Sus* 2H **27**
Riseden. *Kent* 2B **28**
Rise End. *Derbs* 5G **85**
Risegate. *Linc* 2B **76**
Riseholme. *Linc* 3G **87**
Riseley. *Bed* 4H **63**
Riseley. *Wok* 5F **37**
Rishangles. *Suff* 4D **66**
Rishton. *Lanc* 1F **91**
Rishworth. *W Yor* 3A **92**
Risley. *Derbs* 2B **74**
Risley. *Warr* 1A **84**
Risplith. *N Yor* 3E **99**
Rispond. *High* 2E **167**
Rivar. *Wilts* 5B **36**
Rivenhall. *Essx* 4B **54**
Rivenhall End. *Essx* 4B **54**
River. *Kent* 1G **29**
River. *W Sus* 3A **26**
River Bank. *Cambs* 4E **65**
Riverhead. *Kent* 5G **39**
Rivington. *Lanc* 3E **91**
Roach Bridge. *Lanc* 2D **90**
Roachill. *Devn* 4B **20**
Roade. *Nptn* 5E **63**
Road Green. *Norf* 1E **67**
Roadhead. *Cumb* 2G **113**
Roadmeetings. *S Lan* 5B **128**
Roadside. *High* 2D **168**
Roadside of Catterline.
   Abers 1H **145**
Roadside of Kinneff. *Abers* . . .1H **145**
Roadwater. *Som* 3D **20**
Road Weedon. *Nptn* 5D **62**
Roag. *High* 4B **154**
Roa Island. *Cumb* 3B **96**
Roath. *Card* 4E **33**
Roberton. *Bord* 3G **119**
Roberton. *S Lan* 2B **118**
Robertsbridge. *E Sus* 3B **28**
Robertstown. *Mor* 4G **159**
Robertstown. *Rhon* 5C **46**
Roberttown. *W Yor* 2C **92**
Robeston Back. *Pemb* 3E **43**
Robeston Wathen. *Pemb* 3E **43**

Robeston West. *Pemb* 4C **42**
Robin Hood. *Lanc* 3D **90**
Robin Hood. *W Yor* 2D **92**
Robin Hood Airport
   Doncaster Sheffield.
   S Yor 1D **86**
Robinhood End. *Essx* 2H **53**
Robin Hood's Bay. *N Yor* 4G **107**
Roborough. *Devn* 1F **11**
(nr. Great Torrington)
Roborough. *Devn* 2B **8**
(nr. Plymouth)
Rob Roy's House. *Arg* 2A **134**
Roby. *Mers* 1G **83**
Roby Mill. *Lanc* 4D **90**
Rocester. *Staf* 2F **73**
Roch. *Pemb* 2C **42**
Rochdale. *G Man* 3G **91**
Roche. *Corn* 2D **6**
Rochester.
   Medw . . . . . .4B **40** & **Medway 204**
Rochester. *Nmbd* 5C **120**
Rochford. *Essx* 1C **40**
Rock. *Corn* 1D **6**
Rock. *Nmbd* 2G **121**
Rock. *W Sus* 4C **26**
Rock. *Worc* 3B **60**
Rockbeare. *Devn* 3D **12**
Rockbourne. *Hants* 1G **15**
Rockcliffe. *Cumb* 3E **113**
Rockcliffe. *Dum* 4F **111**
Rockcliffe Cross. *Cumb* 3E **113**
Rock Ferry. *Mers* 2F **83**
Rockfield. *High* 5G **165**
Rockfield. *Mon* 4H **47**
Rockford. *Hants* 2G **15**
Rockgreen. *Shrp* 3H **59**
Rockhampton. *S Glo* 2B **34**
Rockhead. *Corn* 4A **10**
Rockingham. *Nptn* 1F **63**
Rockland All Saints. *Norf* 1B **66**
Rockland St Mary. *Norf* 5F **79**
Rockland St Peter. *Norf* 1B **66**
Rockley. *Wilts* 4G **35**
Rockwell End. *Buck* 3F **37**
Rockwell Green. *Som* 1E **13**
Rodborough. *Glos* 5D **48**
Rodbourne. *Wilts* 3E **35**
Rodd. *Here* 4F **59**
Roddam. *Nmbd* 2E **121**
Rodden. *Dors* 4B **14**
Roddenloft. *E Ayr* 2D **117**
Roddymoor. *Dur* 1E **105**
Rode. *Som* 1D **22**
Rodeheath. *Ches E* 4C **84**
(nr. Congleton)
Rode Heath. *Ches E* 5C **84**
(nr. Kidsgrove)
Roden. *Telf* 4H **71**
Rodhuish. *Som* 3D **20**
Rodington. *Telf* 4H **71**
Rodington Heath. *Telf* 4H **71**
Rodley. *Glos* 4C **48**
Rodmarton. *Glos* 2E **35**
Rodmell. *E Sus* 5F **27**
Rodmersham. *Kent* 4D **40**
Rodmersham Green. *Kent* 4D **40**
Rodney Stoke. *Som* 2H **21**
Rodsley. *Derbs* 1G **73**
Rodway. *Som* 2F **21**
Rodway. *Telf* 4A **72**
Rodwell. *Dors* 5B **14**
Roecliffe. *N Yor* 3F **99**
Roe Green. *Herts* 2D **52**
Roehampton. *G Lon* 3D **38**
Roesound. *Shet* 5E **173**
Roffey. *W Sus* 2C **26**
Rogart. *High* 3E **165**
Rogate. *W Sus* 4G **25**
Roger Ground. *Cumb* 5E **103**
Rogerstone. *Newp* 3F **33**
Roghadal. *W Isl* 9C **171**
Rogiet. *Mon* 3H **33**
Rogue's Alley. *Cambs* 5C **76**
Roke. *Oxon* 2E **37**
Rokemarsh. *Oxon* 2E **36**
Roker. *Tyne* 4H **115**
Rollesby. *Norf* 4G **79**
Rolleston. *Leics* 5E **75**
Rolleston. *Notts* 5E **87**
Rolleston on Dove. *Staf* 3G **73**
Rolston. *E Yor* 5G **101**
Rolvenden. *Kent* 2C **28**
Rolvenden Layne. *Kent* 2C **28**
Romaldkirk. *Dur* 2C **104**
Roman Bank. *Shrp* 1H **59**
Romanby. *N Yor* 5A **106**
Roman Camp. *W Lot* 2D **129**
Romannobridge. *Bord* 5E **129**
Romansleigh. *Devn* 4H **19**
Romers Common. *Worc* 4H **59**
Romesdal. *High* 3D **154**
Romford. *Dors* 2F **15**
Romford. *G Lon* 2G **39**
Romiley. *G Man* 1D **84**
Romsey. *Hants* 4B **24**
Romsley. *Shrp* 2B **60**
Romsley. *Worc* 3D **60**
Ronague. *IOM* 4B **108**
Ronaldsvoe. *Orkn* 8D **172**
Rookby. *Cumb* 3B **104**
Rookhope. *Dur* 5C **114**
Rooking. *Cumb* 3F **103**

Rookley—St Peter The Great

Rookley. *IOW* 4D **16**
Rooks Bridge. *Som* 1G **21**
Rooksey Green. *Suff* 5B **66**
Rook's Nest. *Som* 3D **20**
Rookwood. *W Sus* 3F **17**
Roos. *E Yor* 1F **95**
Roosebeck. *Cumb* 3B **96**
Roosecote. *Cumb* 3B **96**
Rootfield. *High* 3H **157**
Rootham's Green. *Bed* 5A **64**
Rootpark. *S Lan* 4C **128**
Ropley. *Hants* 3E **25**
Ropley Dean. *Hants* 3E **25**
Ropsley. *Linc* 2G **75**
Rora. *Abers* 3H **161**
Rorandle. *Abers* 2D **152**
Rorrington. *Shrp* 5F **71**
Rose. *Corn* 3B **6**
Roseacre. *Lanc* 1C **90**
Rose Ash. *Devn* 4A **20**
Rosebank. *S Lan* 5B **128**
Rosebush. *Pemb* 2E **43**
Rosedale Abbey. *N Yor* 5E **107**
Roseden. *Nmbd* 2E **121**
Rose Green. *Essx* 3C **54**
Rose Green. *Suff* 1C **54**
Rosehall. *High* 3B **164**
Rosehearty. *Abers* 2G **161**
Rose Hill. *E Sus* 4F **27**
Rose Hill. *Lanc* 1G **91**
Rosehill. *Shrp* 2A **72**
(nr. Market Drayton)
Rosehill. *Shrp* 4G **71**
(nr. Shrewsbury)
Roseisle. *Mor* 2F **159**
Rosemarket. *Pemb* 4D **42**
Rosemarkie. *High* 3B **158**
Rosemary Lane. *Devn* 1E **13**
Rosemount. *Per* 4A **144**
Rosenannon. *Corn* 2D **6**
Roser's Cross. *E Sus* 3G **27**
Rosevean. *Corn* 3E **6**
Rosewell. *Midl* 3F **129**
Roseworth. *Stoc T* 2B **106**
Roseworthy. *Corn* 3D **4**
Rosgill. *Cumb* 3G **103**
Roshven. *High* 1B **140**
Roskhill. *High* 4B **154**
Roskorwell. *Corn* 4E **5**
Rosley. *Cumb* 5E **112**
Roslin. *Midl* 3F **129**
Rosliston. *Derbs* 4G **73**
Rosneath. *Arg* 1D **126**
Ross. *Dum* 5D **110**
Ross. *Nmbd* 1F **121**
Ross. *Per* 1G **135**
Ross. *Bord* 3F **131**
Rossendale. *Lanc* 2F **91**
Rossett. *Wrex* 5F **83**
Rossington. *S Yor* 1D **86**
Rosskeen. *High* 2A **158**
Rossland. *Ren* 2F **127**
Ross-on-Wye. *Here* 3B **48**
Roster. *High* 4E **169**
Rostherne. *Ches E* 2B **84**
Rostholme. *S Yor* 4F **93**
Rosthwaite. *Cumb* 3D **102**
Roston. *Derbs* 1F **73**
Rosudgeon. *Corn* 4C **4**
Rosyth. *Fife* 1E **129**
Rothbury. *Nmbd* 4E **121**
Rotherby. *Leics* 4D **74**
Rotherfield. *E Sus* 3G **27**
Rotherfield Greys. *Oxon* 3F **37**
Rotherfield Peppard. *Oxon* 3F **37**
Rotherham. *S Yor* 1B **86**
Rothersthorpe. *Nptn* 5E **62**
Rotherwick. *Hants* 1F **25**
Rothes. *Mor* 4G **159**
Rothesay. *Arg* 3B **126**
Rothienorman. *Abers* 5E **160**
Rothiesholm. *Orkn* 5F **172**
Rothley. *Leics* 4C **74**
Rothley. *Nmbd* 1D **114**
Rothwell. *Linc* 1A **88**
Rothwell. *Nptn* 2F **63**
Rothwell. *W Yor* 2D **92**
Rothwell Haigh. *W Yor* 2D **92**
Rotsea. *E Yor* 4E **101**
Rottal. *Ang* 2C **144**
Rotten End. *Suff* 4F **67**
Rotten Row. *Norf* 4C **78**
Rotten Row. *W Ber* 4D **36**
Rotten Row. *W Mid* 3F **61**
Rottingdean. *Brig* 5E **27**
Rottington. *Cumb* 3A **102**
Roud. *IOW* 4D **16**
Rougham. *Norf* 3H **77**
Rougham. *Suff* 4B **66**
Rough Close. *Staf* 2D **72**
Rough Common. *Kent* 5F **41**
Roughcote. *Staf* 1D **72**
Rough Haugh. *High* 4H **167**
Rough Hay. *Staf* 3G **73**
Roughlee. *Lanc* 5H **97**
Roughley. *W Mid* 1F **61**
Roughsike. *Cumb* 2G **113**
Roughton. *Linc* 4B **88**
Roughton. *Norf* 2E **78**
Roughton. *Shrp* 1B **60**
Roundbush Green. *Essx* 4F **53**
Roundham. *Som* 2H **13**
Roundhay. *W Yor* 1D **92**
Round Hill. *Torb* 2F **9**
Roundhurst. *W Sus* 2A **26**
Round Maple. *Suff* 1C **54**
Round Oak. *Shrp* 2F **59**
Roundstreet Common.
W Sus 3B **26**
Roundthwaite. *Cumb* 4H **103**
Roundway. *Wilts* 5F **35**
Roundyhill. *Ang* 3C **144**
Rousdon. *Devn* 3F **13**
Rousham. *Oxon* 3C **50**
Rous Lench. *Worc* 5E **61**
Routh. *E Yor* 5E **101**
Rout's Green. *Buck* 2F **37**
Row. *Corn* 5A **10**
Row. *Cumb* 1D **96**
(nr. Kendal)
Row. *Cumb* 1H **103**
(nr. Penrith)
Rowanburn. *Dum* 2F **113**
Rowanhill. *Abers* 3H **161**
Rowardennan. *Stir* 4C **134**
Rowarth. *Derbs* 2E **85**
Row Ash. *Hants* 1D **16**
Rowberrow. *Som* 1H **21**
Rowde. *Wilts* 5E **35**
Rowden. *Devn* 3G **11**
Rowden Hill. *Wilts* 4E **35**
Rowen. *Cnwy* 3G **81**
Rowfoot. *Nmbd* 3H **113**
Row Green. *Essx* 3H **53**
Row Heath. *Essx* 4E **55**
Rowhedge. *Essx* 3D **54**
Rowhook. *W Sus* 2C **26**
Rowington. *Warw* 4G **61**
Rowland. *Derbs* 3G **85**
Rowland's Castle. *Hants* 1F **17**
Rowlands Gill. *Tyne* 4E **115**
Rowledge. *Surr* 2G **25**
Rowley. *Dur* 5D **115**
Rowley. *E Yor* 1C **94**
Rowley. *Shrp* 5F **71**
Rowley Hill. *W Yor* 3B **92**
Rowley Regis. *W Mid* 2D **60**
Rowlstone. *Here* 3G **47**
Rowly. *Surr* 1B **26**
Rowner. *Hants* 2D **16**
Rowney Green. *Worc* 3E **61**
Rownhams. *Hants* 1B **16**
Rowrah. *Cumb* 3B **102**
Rowsham. *Buck* 4G **51**
Rowsley. *Derbs* 4G **85**
Rowstock. *Oxon* 3C **36**
Rowston. *Linc* 5H **87**
Row, The. *Lanc* 2D **96**
Rowthorne. *Derbs* 4B **86**
Rowton. *Ches W* 4G **83**
Rowton. *Shrp* 2G **59**
(nr. Ludlow)
Rowton. *Shrp* 4F **71**
(nr. Shrewsbury)
Rowton. *Telf* 4A **72**
Row Town. *Surr* 4B **38**
Roxburgh. *Bord* 1B **120**
Roxby. *N Lin* 3C **94**
Roxby. *N Yor* 3E **107**
Roxton. *Bed* 5A **64**
Roxwell. *Essx* 5G **53**
Royal Leamington Spa.
Warw 4H **61**
Royal Oak. *Darl* 2F **105**
Royal Oak. *Lanc* 4C **90**
Royal Oak. *N Yor* 2F **101**
Royal's Green. *Ches E* 1A **72**
Royal Tunbridge Wells. *Kent* 2G **27**
Royal Wootton Bassett. *Wilts* 3F **35**
Roybridge. *High* 5E **149**
Roydon. *Essx* 4E **53**
Roydon. *Norf* 2C **66**
(nr. Diss)
Roydon. *Norf* 3G **77**
(nr. King's Lynn)
Roydon Hamlet. *Essx* 5E **53**
Royston. *Herts* 1D **52**
Royston. *S Yor* 3D **92**
Royston Water. *Som* 1F **13**
Royton. *G Man* 4H **91**
Ruabon. *Wrex* 1F **71**
Ruaig. *Arg* 4B **138**
Ruan High Lanes. *Corn* 5D **6**
Ruan Lanihorne. *Corn* 4C **6**
Ruan Major. *Corn* 5E **5**
Ruan Minor. *Corn* 5E **5**
Ruarach. *High* 1B **148**
Ruardean. *Glos* 4B **48**
Ruardean Hill. *Glos* 4B **48**
Ruardean Woodside. *Glos* 4B **48**
Rubery. *W Mid* 3D **61**
Ruchazie. *Glas* 3H **127**
Ruckcroft. *Cumb* 5G **113**
Ruckinge. *Kent* 2E **29**
Ruckland. *Linc* 3C **88**
Rucklers Lane. *Herts* 5A **52**
Ruckley. *Shrp* 5H **71**
Rudbaxton. *Pemb* 2D **42**
Rudby. *N Yor* 4B **106**
Ruddington. *Notts* 2C **74**
Rudford. *Glos* 3C **48**
Rudge. *Shrp* 1C **60**
Rudge. *Wilts* 1D **22**
Rudge Heath. *Shrp* 1B **60**
Rudgeway. *S Glo* 3B **34**
Rudgwick. *W Sus* 2B **26**
Rudhall. *Here* 3B **48**
Rudheath. *Ches W* 3A **84**
Rudley Green. *Essx* 5B **54**
Rudloe. *Wilts* 4D **34**
Rudry. *Cphy* 3E **33**
Rudston. *E Yor* 3E **101**
Rudyard. *Staf* 5D **84**
Rufford. *Lanc* 3C **90**
Rufforth. *York* 4H **99**
Rugby. *Warw* 3C **62**
Rugeley. *Staf* 4E **73**
Ruglen. *S Ayr* 4B **116**
Ruilick. *High* 4H **157**
Ruisaurie. *High* 4G **157**
Ruishton. *Som* 4F **21**
Ruisigearraidh. *W Isl* 1E **170**
Ruislip. *G Lon* 2B **38**
Ruislip Common. *G Lon* 2B **38**
Rumbling Bridge. *Per* 4C **136**
Rumburgh. *Suff* 2F **67**
Rumford. *Corn* 1C **6**
Rumford. *Falk* 2C **128**
Rumney. *Card* 4F **33**
Rumwell. *Som* 4E **21**
Runcorn. *Hal* 2H **83**
Runcton. *W Sus* 2G **17**
Runcton Holme. *Norf* 5F **77**
Rundlestone. *Devn* 5F **11**
Runfold. *Surr* 2G **25**
Runhall. *Norf* 5C **78**
Runham. *Norf* 4G **79**
Runnington. *Som* 4E **20**
Runshaw Moor. *Lanc* 3D **90**
Runswick. *N Yor* 3F **107**
Runtaleave. *Ang* 2B **144**
Runwell. *Essx* 1B **40**
Ruscombe. *Wok* 4F **37**
Rushall. *Here* 2B **48**
Rushall. *Norf* 2D **66**
Rushall. *W Mid* 5E **73**
Rushall. *Wilts* 1G **23**
Rushbrooke. *Suff* 4A **66**
Rushbury. *Shrp* 1H **59**
Rushden. *Herts* 2D **52**
Rushden. *Nptn* 4G **63**
Rushenden. *Kent* 3D **40**
Rushford. *Devn* 5E **11**
Rushford. *Suff* 2B **66**
Rush Green. *Herts* 3C **52**
Rushlake Green. *E Sus* 4H **27**
Rushmere. *Suff* 2G **67**
Rushmere St Andrew. *Suff* 1E **55**
Rushmoor. *Surr* 2G **25**
Rushock. *Worc* 3C **60**
Rusholme. *G Man* 1C **84**
Rushton. *Ches W* 4H **83**
Rushton. *Nptn* 2F **63**
Rushton. *Shrp* 5A **72**
Rushton Spencer. *Staf* 4D **84**
Rushwick. *Worc* 5C **60**
Rushyford. *Dur* 2F **105**
Ruskie. *Stir* 3F **135**
Ruskington. *Linc* 5H **87**
Rusland. *Cumb* 1C **96**
Rusper. *W Sus* 2D **26**
Ruspidge. *Glos* 4B **48**
Russell's Water. *Oxon* 3F **37**
Russel's Green. *Suff* 3E **67**
Russ Hill. *Surr* 1D **26**
Russland. *Orkn* 6C **172**
Rusthall. *Kent* 2G **27**
Rustington. *W Sus* 5B **26**
Ruston. *N Yor* 1D **100**
Ruston Parva. *E Yor* 3E **101**
Ruswarp. *N Yor* 4F **107**
Rutherglen. *S Lan* 3H **127**
Ruthernbridge. *Corn* 2E **6**
Ruthin. *Den* 5D **82**
Ruthin. *V Glam* 4C **32**
Ruthrieston. *Aber* 3G **153**
Ruthven. *Abers* 4C **160**
Ruthven. *Ang* 4B **144**
Ruthven. *High* 5C **158**
(nr. Inverness)
Ruthven. *High* 4B **150**
(nr. Kingussie)
Ruthvoes. *Corn* 2D **6**
Ruthwaite. *Cumb* 1D **102**
Ruthwell. *Dum* 3C **112**
Ruxton Green. *Here* 4A **48**
Ruyton-XI-Towns. *Shrp* 3F **71**
Ryal. *Nmbd* 2D **114**
Ryall. *Dors* 3H **13**
Ryall. *Worc* 1D **48**
Ryarsh. *Kent* 5A **40**
Rychraggan. *High* 5G **157**
Rydal. *Cumb* 4E **103**
Ryde. *IOW* 3D **16**
Rye. *E Sus* 3D **28**
Ryecroft Gate. *Staf* 4D **84**
Ryeford. *Here* 3B **48**
Rye Foreign. *E Sus* 3D **28**
Rye Harbour. *E Sus* 4D **28**
Ryehill. *E Yor* 2F **95**
Rye Street. *Worc* 2C **48**
Ryhall. *Rut* 4H **75**
Ryhill. *W Yor* 3D **93**
Ryhope. *Tyne* 4H **115**
Ryhope Colliery. *Tyne* 4H **115**
Rylands. *Notts* 2C **74**
Rylstone. *N Yor* 4B **98**
Ryme Intrinseca. *Dors* 1A **14**
Ryther. *N Yor* 1F **93**
Ryton. *Glos* 2C **48**
Ryton. *N Yor* 2B **100**
Ryton. *Shrp* 5B **72**
Ryton. *Tyne* 3E **115**
Ryton. *Warw* 2A **62**
Ryton-on-Dunsmore. *Warw* 3A **62**
Ryton Woodside. *Tyne* 3E **115**

S

Saasaig. *High* 3E **147**
Sabden. *Lanc* 1F **91**
Sacombe. *Herts* 4D **52**
Sacriston. *Dur* 5F **115**
Sadberge. *Darl* 3A **106**
Saddell. *Arg* 2B **122**
Saddington. *Leics* 1D **62**
Saddle Bow. *Norf* 4F **77**
Saddlescombe. *W Sus* 4D **26**
Saddleworth. *G Man* 4H **91**
Sadgill. *Cumb* 4F **103**
Saffron Walden. *Essx* 2F **53**
Sageston. *Pemb* 4E **43**
Saham Hills. *Norf* 5B **78**
Saham Toney. *Norf* 5A **78**
Saighdinis. *W Isl* 2D **170**
Saighton. *Ches W* 4G **83**
Sain Dunwyd. *V Glam* 5C **32**
Sain Hilari. *V Glam* 4D **32**
St Abbs. *Bord* 3F **131**
St Agnes. *Corn* 3B **6**
St Albans. *Herts* 5B **52**
St Allen. *Corn* 3C **6**
St Andrews. *Fife* 2H **137** & **209**
St Andrews Major. *V Glam* 4E **33**
St Anne's. *Lanc* 2B **90**
St Ann's. *Dum* 5C **118**
St Ann's Chapel. *Corn* 5E **11**
St Ann's Chapel. *Devn* 4C **8**
St Anthony. *Corn* 5C **6**
St Anthony-in-Meneage. *Corn* 4E **5**
St Arvans. *Mon* 2A **34**
St Asaph. *Den* 3C **82**
St Athan. *V Glam* 5D **32**
Sain Tathan. *V Glam* 5D **32**
St Austell. *Corn* 3E **6**
St Bartholomew's Hill. *Wilts* 4E **23**
St Bees. *Cumb* 3A **102**
St Blazey. *Corn* 3E **7**
St Blazey Gate. *Corn* 3E **7**
St Boswells. *Bord* 1A **120**
St Breock. *Corn* 1D **6**
St Breward. *Corn* 5A **10**
St Briavels. *Glos* 5A **48**
St Brides. *Pemb* 3B **42**
St Bride's Major. *V Glam* 4B **32**
St Bride's Netherwent. *Mon* 3H **33**
St Bride's-super-Ely. *V Glam* 4D **32**
St Brides Wentlooge. *Newp* 3F **33**
St Budeaux. *Plym* 3A **8**
Saintbury. *Glos* 2G **49**
St Buryan. *Corn* 4B **4**
St Catherine. *Bath* 4C **34**
St Catherines. *Arg* 3A **134**
St Clears. *Carm* 3G **43**
St Cleer. *Corn* 2G **7**
St Clement. *Corn* 4C **6**
St Clether. *Corn* 4C **10**
St Colmac. *Arg* 3B **126**
St Columb Major. *Corn* 2D **6**
St Columb Minor. *Corn* 2C **6**
St Columb Road. *Corn* 3D **6**
St Combs. *Abers* 2H **161**
St Cross. *Hants* 4C **24**
St Cross South Elmham. *Suff* 2E **67**
St Cyrus. *Abers* 2G **145**
St David's. *Pemb* 2B **42**
St David's. *Per* 1B **136**
St Day. *Corn* 4B **6**
St Dennis. *Corn* 3D **6**
St Dogmaels. *Pemb* 1B **44**
St Dominick. *Corn* 2H **7**
St Donat's. *V Glam* 5C **32**
St Edith's Marsh. *Wilts* 5E **35**
St Endellion. *Corn* 1D **6**
St Enoder. *Corn* 3C **6**
St Erme. *Corn* 4C **6**
St Erney. *Corn* 3H **7**
St Erth. *Corn* 3C **4**
St Erth Praze. *Corn* 3C **4**
St Ervan. *Corn* 1C **6**
St Eval. *Corn* 2C **6**
St Ewe. *Corn* 4D **6**
St Fagans. *Card* 4E **32**
St Fergus. *Abers* 3H **161**
St Fillans. *Per* 1F **135**
St Florence. *Pemb* 4E **43**
St Gennys. *Corn* 3B **10**
St George. *Cnwy* 3B **82**
St Georges. *N Som* 5G **33**
St Georges. *V Glam* 4D **32**
St George's Hill. *Surr* 4B **38**
St Germans. *Corn* 3H **7**
St Giles in the Wood. *Devn* 1F **11**
St Giles on the Heath. *Devn* 3D **10**
St Giles's Hill. *Hants* 4C **24**
St Gluvias. *Corn* 5B **6**
St Harmon. *Powy* 3B **58**
St Helena. *Warw* 5G **73**
St Helen Auckland. *Dur* 2E **105**
St Helens. *Cumb* 1B **102**
St Helens. *E Sus* 4C **28**
St Helens. *IOW* 4E **17**
St Helens. *Mers* 1G **83**
St Hilary. *Corn* 3C **4**
St Hilary. *V Glam* 4D **32**
Saint Hill. *Devn* 2D **12**
Saint Hill. *W Sus* 2E **27**
St Illtyd. *Blae* 5F **47**
St Ippolyts. *Herts* 3B **52**
St Ishmael. *Carm* 5D **44**
St Ishmael's. *Pemb* 4C **42**
St Issey. *Corn* 1D **6**
St Ive. *Corn* 2H **7**
St Ives. *Cambs* 3C **64**
St Ives. *Corn* 2C **4**
St Ives. *Dors* 2G **15**
St James' End. *Nptn* 4E **63**
St James South Elmham. *Suff* 2F **67**
St Jidgey. *Corn* 2D **6**
St John. *Corn* 3A **8**
St John's. *IOM* 3B **108**
St Johns. *Worc* 5C **60**
St John's Chapel. *Devn* 4F **19**
St John's Chapel. *Dur* 1B **104**
St John's Fen End. *Norf* 4E **77**
St John's Hall. *Dur* 1D **104**
St John's Town of Dalry.
Dum 1D **110**
St Judes. *IOM* 2C **108**
St Just. *Corn* 5C **6**
(nr. Falmouth)
St Just. *Corn* 3A **4**
(nr. Penzance)
St Just in Roseland. *Corn* 5C **6**
St Katherines. *Abers* 5E **161**
St Keverne. *Corn* 4E **5**
St Kew. *Corn* 5A **10**
St Kew Highway. *Corn* 5A **10**
St Keyne. *Corn* 2G **7**
St Lawrence. *Corn* 2E **7**
St Lawrence. *Essx* 5C **54**
St Lawrence. *IOW* 5D **16**
St Leonards. *Buck* 5H **51**
St Leonards. *Dors* 2G **15**
St Leonards. *E Sus* 5B **28**
St Levan. *Corn* 4A **4**
St Lythans. *V Glam* 4E **32**
St Mabyn. *Corn* 5A **10**
St Madoes. *Per* 1D **136**
St Margarets. *Here* 2G **47**
St Margaret's. *Herts* 4A **52**
(nr. Hemel Hempstead)
St Margarets. *Herts* 4D **53**
(nr. Hoddesdon)
St Margaret's. *Wilts* 5G **35**
St Margaret's at Cliffe. *Kent* 1H **29**
St Margaret's Hope. *Orkn* 8D **172**
St Margaret South Elmham.
Suff 2F **67**
St Mark's. *IOM* 4B **108**
St Martin. *Corn* 4E **5**
(nr. Helston)
St Martin. *Corn* 3G **7**
(nr. Looe)
St Martins. *Per* 5A **144**
St Martin's. *Shrp* 2F **71**
St Mary Bourne. *Hants* 1C **24**
St Marychurch. *Torb* 2F **9**
St Mary Church. *V Glam* 4D **32**
St Mary Cray. *G Lon* 4F **39**
St Mary Hill. *V Glam* 4C **32**
St Mary Hoo. *Medw* 3C **40**
St Mary in the Marsh. *Kent* 3E **29**
St Mary's. *Orkn* 7D **172**
St Mary's Bay. *Kent* 3E **29**
St Maughan's Green. *Mon* 4H **47**
St Mawes. *Corn* 5C **6**
St Mawgan. *Corn* 2C **6**
St Mellion. *Corn* 2H **7**
St Mellons. *Card* 3F **33**
St Merryn. *Corn* 1C **6**
St Mewan. *Corn* 3D **6**
St Michael Caerhays. *Corn* 4D **6**
St Michael Penkevil. *Corn* 4C **6**
St Michaels. *Kent* 2C **28**
St Michaels. *Torb* 3E **9**
St Michaels. *Worc* 4H **59**
St Michael's on Wyre. *Lanc* 5D **96**
St Michael South Elmham.
Suff 2F **67**
St Minver. *Corn* 1D **6**
St Monans. *Fife* 3H **137**
St Neot. *Corn* 2F **7**
St Neots. *Cambs* 4A **64**
St Newlyn East. *Corn* 3C **6**
St Nicholas. *Pemb* 1D **42**
St Nicholas. *V Glam* 4D **32**
St Nicholas at Wade. *Kent* 4G **41**
St Nicholas South Elmham.
Suff 2F **67**
St Ninians. *Stir* 4H **135**
St Olaves. *Norf* 1G **67**
St Osyth. *Essx* 4E **54**
St Osyth Heath. *Essx* 4E **55**
St Owen's Cross. *Here* 3A **48**
St Paul's Cray. *G Lon* 4F **39**
St Paul's Walden. *Herts* 3B **52**
St Peter's. *Kent* 4H **41**
St Peter The Great. *Worc* 5C **60**

St Petrox. Pemb 5D 42
St Pinnock. Corn 2G 7
St Quivox. S Ayr 2C 116
St Ruan. Corn 5E 5
St Stephen. Corn 3D 6
St Stephens. Corn 4D 10
(nr. Launceston)
St Stephens. Corn 3A 8
(nr. Saltash)
St Teath. Corn 4A 10
St Thomas. Devn 3C 12
St Thomas. Swan 3F 31
St Tudy. Corn 5A 10
St Twynnells. Pemb 5D 42
St Veep. Corn 3F 7
St Vigeans. Ang 4F 145
St Wenn. Corn 2D 6
St Weonards. Here 3H 47
St Winnolls. Corn 3H 7
St Winnow. Corn 3F 7
Salcombe. Devn 5D 8
Salcombe Regis. Devn 4E 13
Salcott. Essx 4C 54
Sale. G Man 1B 84
Saleby. Linc 3D 88
Sale Green. Worc 5D 60
Salehurst. E Sus 3B 28
Salem. Carm 3G 45
Salem. Cdgn 2F 57
Salem. Gwyn 5E 81
Salen. Arg 4G 139
Salen. High 2A 140
Salesbury. Lanc 1E 91
Saleway. Worc 5D 60
Salford. C Beds 2H 51
Salford. G Man
.......1C 84 & Manchester 201
Salford. Oxon 3A 50
Salford Priors. Warw 5E 61
Salfords. Surr 1D 27
Salhouse. Norf 4F 79
Saligo. Arg 3A 124
Saline. Fife 4C 136
Salisbury. Wilts .....3G 23 & 210
Salkeld Dykes. Cumb 1G 103
Sallachan. High 2D 141
Sallachy. High 3C 164
(nr. Lairg)
Sallachy. High 5B 156
(nr. Stromeferry)
Salle. Norf 3D 78
Salmonby. Linc 3C 88
Salmond's Muir. Ang 5E 145
Salperton. Glos 3F 49
Salph End. Bed 5H 63
Salsburgh. N Lan 3B 128
Salt. Staf 3D 72
Salta. Cumb 5B 112
Saltaire. W Yor 1B 92
Saltash. Corn 3A 8
Saltburn. High 2B 158
Saltburn-by-the-Sea. Red C 2D 106
Saltby. Leics 3F 75
Saltcoats. Cumb 5B 102
Saltcoats. N Ayr 5D 126
Saltdean. Brig 5E 27
Salt End. E Yor 2E 95
Salter. Lanc 3F 97
Salterforth. Lanc 5A 98
Salters Lode. Norf 5E 77
Salterswall. Ches W 4A 84
Salterton. Wilts 3G 23
Saltfleet. Linc 1D 88
Saltfleetby All Saints. Linc 1D 88
Saltfleetby St Clements. Linc 1D 88
Saltfleetby St Peter. Linc 2D 88
Saltford. Bath 5B 34
Salthouse. Norf 1C 78
Saltmarshe. E Yor 2A 94
Saltmead. Card 4E 33
Saltness. Orkn 9B 172
Saltness. Shet 7D 173
Saltney. Flin 4F 83
Salton. N Yor 2B 100
Saltrens. Devn 4E 19
Saltwick. Nmbd 2E 115
Saltwood. Kent 2F 29
Salum. Arg 4B 138
Salwarpe. Worc 4C 60
Salwayash. Dors 3H 13
Samalaman. High 1A 140
Sambourne. Warw 4E 61
Sambourne. Wilts 2D 22
Sambrook. Telf 3B 72
Samhla. W Isl 2C 170
Samlesbury. Lanc 1D 90
Samlesbury Bottoms. Lanc 2E 90
Sampford Arundel. Som 1E 12
Sampford Brett. Som 2D 20
Sampford Courtenay. Devn 2G 11
Sampford Peverell. Devn 1D 12
Sampford Spiney. Devn 5F 11
Samsonlane. Orkn 5F 172
Samuelston. E Lot 2A 130
Sanaigmore. Arg 2A 124
Sancreed. Corn 4B 4
Sancton. E Yor 1C 94
Sand. High 4D 162
Sand. Shet 7E 173
Sand. Som 2H 21
Sandaig. Arg 4A 138
Sandaig. High 3F 147

Sandale. Cumb 5D 112
Sandal Magna. W Yor 3D 92
Sandavore. High 5C 146
Sanday Airport. Orkn 3F 172
Sandbach. Ches E 4B 84
Sandbank. Arg 1C 126
Sandbanks. Pool 4F 15
Sandend. Abers 2C 160
Sanderstead. G Lon 4E 39
Sandford. Cumb 3A 104
Sandford. Devn 2B 12
Sandford. Dors 4D 15
Sandford. Hants 2G 15
Sandford. IOW 4D 16
Sandford. N Som 1H 21
Sandford. Shrp 3F 71
(nr. Oswestry)
Sandford. Shrp 2H 71
(nr. Whitchurch)
Sandford. S Lan 5A 128
Sandfordhill. Abers 4H 161
Sandford-on-Thames. Oxon 5D 50
Sandford Orcas. Dors 4B 22
Sandford St Martin. Oxon 3C 50
Sandgate. Kent 2F 29
Sandgreen. Dum 4C 110
Sandhaven. Abers 2G 161
Sandhead. Dum 4F 109
Sandhill. Cambs 2E 65
Sandhills. Dors 1B 14
Sandhills. Oxon 5D 50
Sandhills. Surr 2A 26
Sandhoe. Nmbd 3C 114
Sand Hole. E Yor 1B 94
Sandholme. E Yor 2A 94
Sandholme. Linc 2C 76
Sandhurst. Brac 5G 37
Sandhurst. Glos 3D 48
Sandhurst. Kent 3B 28
Sandhurst Cross. Kent 3B 28
Sandhutton. N Yor 1F 99
(nr. Thirsk)
Sand Hutton. N Yor 4A 100
(nr. York)
Sandiacre. Derbs 2B 74
Sandilands. Linc 2E 89
Sandiway. Ches W 3A 84
Sandleheath. Hants 1G 15
Sandling. Kent 5B 40
Sandlow Green. Ches E 4B 84
Sandness. Shet 6C 173
Sandon. Essx 5H 53
Sandon. Herts 2D 52
Sandon. Staf 3D 72
Sandonbank. Staf 3D 72
Sandown. IOW 4D 16
Sandplace. Corn 3G 7
Sandridge. Herts 4B 52
Sandridge. Wilts 5E 35
Sandringham. Norf 3F 77
Sandsend. N Yor 3F 107
Sandside. Cumb 2C 96
Sandsound. Shet 7E 173
Sands, The. Surr 2G 25
Sandtoft. N Lin 4H 93
Sandvoe. Shet 2E 173
Sandway. Kent 5C 40
Sandwell Green. Suff 3D 66
Sandwich. Kent 5H 41
Sandwick. Cumb 3F 103
Sandwick. Orkn 6B 172
(on Mainland)
Sandwick. Orkn 9D 172
(on South Ronaldsay)
Sandwick. Shet 9F 173
(on Mainland)
Sandwick. Shet 5G 173
(on Whalsay)
Sandwith. Cumb 3A 102
Sandy. Carm 5E 45
Sandy. C Beds 1B 52
Sandy Bank. Linc 5B 88
Sandycroft. Flin 4F 83
Sandy Cross. Here 5A 60
Sandygate. Devn 5B 12
Sandygate. IOM 2C 108
Sandy Haven. Pemb 4C 42
Sandyhills. Dum 4F 111
Sandylands. Lanc 3D 96
Sandylane. Swan 4E 31
Sandy Lane. Wilts 5E 35
Sandy Park. Devn 4H 11
Sandystones. Bord 2H 119
Sandyway. Here 3H 47
Sangobeg. High 2E 167
Sangomore. High 2E 166
Sankyn's Green. Worc 4B 60
Sanna. High 2F 139
Sanndabhaig. W Isl 4G 171
(on Isle of Lewis)
Sanndabhaig. W Isl 4D 170
(on South Uist)
Sannox. N Ayr 5B 126
Sanquhar. Dum 3G 117
Santon. Cumb 4B 102
Santon Bridge. Cumb 4C 102
Santon Downham. Suff 2H 65
Sapcote. Leics 1B 62
Sapey Common. Here 4B 60
Sapiston. Suff 3B 66
Sapley. Cambs 3B 64

Sapperton. Derbs 2F 73
Sapperton. Glos 5E 49
Sapperton. Linc 2H 75
Saracen's Head. Linc 3C 76
Sarclet. High 4F 169
Sardis. Carm 5F 45
Sardis. Pemb 4D 42
(nr. Milford Haven)
Sardis. Pemb 4F 43
(nr. Tenby)
Sarisbury. Hants 2D 16
Sarn. B'end 3C 32
Sarn. Powy 1E 58
Sarnau. Carm 3E 45
Sarnau. Cdgn 5C 56
Sarnau. Gwyn 2B 70
Sarnau. Powy 2D 46
(nr. Brecon)
Sarnau. Powy 4E 71
(nr. Welshpool)
Sarn Bach. Gwyn 3C 68
Sarnesfield. Here 5F 59
Sarn Meyllteyrn. Gwyn 2B 68
Saron. Carm 4G 45
(nr. Ammanford)
Saron. Carm 2D 45
(nr. Newcastle Emlyn)
Saron. Gwyn 4E 81
(nr. Bethel)
Saron. Gwyn 5D 80
(nr. Bontnewydd)
Sarratt. Herts 1B 38
Sarre. Kent 4G 41
Sarsden. Oxon 3A 50
Satley. Dur 5E 115
Satron. N Yor 5C 104
Satterleigh. Devn 4G 19
Satterthwaite. Cumb 5E 103
Satwell. Oxon 3F 37
Sauchen. Abers 2D 152
Saucher. Per 5A 144
Saughall. Ches W 4F 83
Saughtree. Bord 5H 119
Saul. Glos 5C 48
Saundby. Notts 2E 87
Saundersfoot. Pemb 4F 43
Saunderton. Buck 5F 51
Saunderton Lee. Buck 2G 37
Saunton. Devn 3E 19
Sausthorpe. Linc 4C 88
Saval. High 3C 164
Saverley Green. Staf 2D 72
Sawbridge. Warw 4C 62
Sawbridgeworth. Herts 4E 53
Sawdon. N Yor 1D 100
Sawley. Derbs 2B 74
Sawley. Lanc 5G 97
Sawley. N Yor 3E 99
Sawston. Cambs 1E 53
Sawtry. Cambs 2A 64
Saxby. Leics 3F 75
Saxby. Linc 2H 87
Saxby All Saints. N Lin 3C 94
Saxelby. Leics 3D 74
Saxelbye. Leics 3D 74
Saxham Street. Suff 4C 66
Saxilby. Linc 3F 87
Saxlingham. Norf 2C 78
Saxlingham Green. Norf 1E 67
Saxlingham Nethergate. Norf 1E 67
Saxlingham Thorpe. Norf 1E 66
Saxmundham. Suff 4F 67
Saxondale. Notts 1D 74
Saxon Street. Cambs 5F 65
Saxtead. Suff 4E 67
Saxtead Green. Suff 4E 67
Saxthorpe. Norf 2D 78
Saxton. N Yor 1E 93
Sayers Common. W Sus 4D 26
Scackleton. N Yor 2A 100
Scadabhagh. W Isl 8D 171
Scaftworth. Notts 1D 86
Scagglethorpe. N Yor 2C 100
Scaitcliffe. Lanc 2F 91
Scaladal. W Isl 6D 171
Scalasaig. Arg 4A 132
Scalby. E Yor 2B 94
Scalby. N Yor 5H 107
Scalby Mills. N Yor 5H 107
Scaldwell. Nptn 3E 63
Scaleby. Cumb 3F 113
Scaleby Hill. Cumb 3F 113
Scale Houses. Cumb 5G 113
Scales. Cumb 2B 96
(nr. Barrow-in-Furness)
Scales. Cumb 2E 103
(nr. Keswick)
Scalford. Leics 3E 75
Scaling. Red C 3E 107
Scaling Dam. Red C 3E 107
Scalloway. Shet 8F 173
Scalpaigh. W Isl 8E 171
Scalpay House. High 1E 147
Scamblesby. Linc 3B 88
Scamodale. High 1C 140
Scampston. N Yor 2C 100
Scampton. Linc 3G 87
Scaniport. High 5A 158
Scapa. Orkn 7D 172
Scapegoat Hill. W Yor 3A 92
Scar. Orkn 3F 172
Scarasta. W Isl 8C 171

Scarborough. N Yor 1E 101
Scarcliffe. Derbs 4B 86
Scarcroft. W Yor 5F 99
Scardroy. High 3E 156
Scarfskerry. High 1E 169
Scargill. Dur 3D 104
Scarinish. Arg 4B 138
Scarisbrick. Lanc 3B 90
Scarning. Norf 4B 78
Scarrington. Notts 1E 75
Scarth Hill. Lanc 4C 90
Scartho. NE Lin 4F 95
Scarvister. Shet 7E 173
Scatness. Shet 10E 173
Scatwell. High 3F 157
Scawby. N Lin 4C 94
Scawby Brook. N Lin 4C 94
Scawsby. S Yor 4F 93
Scawton. N Yor 1H 99
Scayne's Hill. W Sus 3E 27
Scethrog. Powy 3E 46
Scholar Green. Ches E 5C 84
Scholes. G Man 4D 90
Scholes. W Yor 2B 92
(nr. Bradford)
Scholes. W Yor 4B 92
(nr. Holmfirth)
Scholes. W Yor 1D 93
(nr. Leeds)
Scholey Hill. W Yor 2D 93
School Aycliffe. Dur 2F 105
School Green. Ches W 4A 84
School Green. Essx 2H 53
Scissett. W Yor 3C 92
Scleddau. Pemb 1D 42
Scofton. Notts 2D 86
Scole. Norf 3D 66
Scolpaig. W Isl 1C 170
Scolton. Pemb 2D 43
Scone. Per 1D 136
Sconser. High 5E 155
Scoonie. Fife 3F 137
Scopwick. Linc 5H 87
Scoraig. High 4E 163
Scorborough. E Yor 5E 101
Scorriton. Devn 2D 8
Scorton. Lanc 5E 97
Scorton. N Yor 4F 105
Sco Ruston. Norf 3E 79
Scotbheinn. W Isl 3D 170
Scotby. Cumb 4F 113
Scotch Corner. N Yor 4F 105
Scotforth. Lanc 3D 97
Scot Hay. Staf 1C 72
Scothern. Linc 3H 87
Scotland End. Oxon 2B 50
Scotlandwell. Per 3D 136
Scot Lane End. G Man 4E 91
Scotsburn. High 1B 158
Scotsburn. Mor 2G 159
Scotsdike. Cumb 2E 113
Scots Gap. Nmbd 1D 114
Scotstown. Glas 3G 127
Scotstown. High 2C 140
Scotswood. Tyne 3F 115
Scottas. High 3F 147
Scotter. Linc 4B 94
Scotterthorpe. Linc 4B 94
Scottlethorpe. Linc 3H 75
Scotton. Linc 1F 87
Scotton. N Yor 5E 105
(nr. Catterick Garrison)
Scotton. N Yor 4F 99
(nr. Harrogate)
Scottow. Norf 3E 79
Scoulton. Norf 5B 78
Scounslow Green. Staf 3E 73
Scourie. High 4B 166
Scourie More. High 4B 166
Scousburgh. Shet 10E 173
Scout Green. Cumb 4G 103
Scouthead. G Man 4H 91
Scrabster. High 1C 168
Scrafield. Linc 4C 88
Scrainwood. Nmbd 4D 121
Scrane End. Linc 1C 76
Scraptoft. Leic 5D 74
Scrayingham. N Yor 3B 100
Scredington. Linc 1H 75
Scremby. Linc 4D 88
Scremerston. Nmbd 5G 131
Screveton. Notts 1E 75
Scrivelsby. Linc 4B 88
Scriven. N Yor 4F 99
Scronkey. Lanc 5D 96
Scrooby. Notts 1D 86
Scropton. Derbs 2F 73
Scrub Hill. Linc 5B 88
Scruton. N Yor 5F 105
Scuggate. Cumb 2F 113
Sculamus. High 1E 147
Sculcoates. Hull 1D 94
Sculthorpe. Norf 2A 78
Scunthorpe. N Lin 3B 94
Scurlage. Swan 4D 30
Sea. Som 1G 13
Seaborough. Dors 2H 13
Seabridge. Staf 1C 72
Seabrook. Kent 2F 29

Seaburn. Tyne 3H 115
Seacombe. Mers 1F 83
Seacroft. Linc 4E 89
Seacroft. W Yor 1D 92
Seadyke. Linc 2C 76
Seafield. High 5G 165
Seafield. Midl 3F 129
Seafield. S Ayr 2C 116
Seafield. W Lot 3D 128
Seaford. E Sus 5F 27
Seaforth. Mers 1F 83
Seagrave. Leics 4D 74
Seaham. Dur 5H 115
Seahouses. Nmbd 1G 121
Seal. Kent 5G 39
Sealand. Flin 4F 83
Seale. Surr 2G 25
Seamer. N Yor 1E 101
(nr. Scarborough)
Seamer. N Yor 3B 106
(nr. Stokesley)
Seamill. N Ayr 5C 126
Sea Mills. Bris 4A 34
Sea Palling. Norf 3G 79
Searby. Linc 4D 94
Seasalter. Kent 4E 41
Seascale. Cumb 4B 102
Seaside. Per 1E 137
Seater. High 1F 169
Seathorne. Linc 4E 89
Seathwaite. Cumb 3D 102
(nr. Buttermere)
Seathwaite. Cumb 5D 102
(nr. Ulpha)
Seatle. Cumb 1C 96
Seatoller. Cumb 3D 102
Seaton. Corn 3H 7
Seaton. Cumb 1B 102
Seaton. Devn 3F 13
Seaton. Dur 4G 115
Seaton. E Yor 5F 101
Seaton. Nmbd 2G 115
Seaton. Rut 1G 63
Seaton Burn. Tyne 2F 115
Seaton Carew. Hart 2C 106
Seaton Delaval. Nmbd 2G 115
Seaton Junction. Devn 3F 13
Seaton Ross. E Yor 5B 100
Seaton Sluice. Nmbd 2G 115
Seatown. Abers 2C 160
Seatown. Dors 3H 13
Seatown. Mor 2C 160
(nr. Cullen)
Seatown. Mor 1G 159
(nr. Lossiemouth)
Seave Green. N Yor 4C 106
Seaview. IOW 3E 17
Seaville. Cumb 4C 112
Seavington St Mary. Som 1H 13
Seavington St Michael. Som 1H 13
Seawick. Essx 4E 55
Sebastopol. Torf 2F 33
Sebergham. Cumb 5E 113
Seckington. Warw 5G 73
Second Coast. High 4D 162
Sedbergh. Cumb 5H 103
Sedbury. Glos 2A 34
Sedbusk. N Yor 5B 104
Sedgeberrow. Worc 2F 49
Sedgebrook. Linc 2F 75
Sedgefield. Dur 2A 106
Sedgeford. Norf 2G 77
Sedgehill. Wilts 4D 22
Sedgley. W Mid 1D 60
Sedgwick. Cumb 1E 97
Sedlescombe. E Sus 4B 28
Seend. Wilts 5E 35
Seend Cleeve. Wilts 5E 35
Seer Green. Buck 1A 38
Seething. Norf 1F 67
Sefster. Shet 6E 173
Sefton. Mers 4B 90
Sefton Park. Mers 2F 83
Segensworth. Hants 2D 16
Seggat. Abers 4E 161
Seghill. Nmbd 2F 115
Seifton. Shrp 2G 59
Seighford. Staf 3C 72
Seilebost. W Isl 8C 171
Seisdon. Staf 1C 60
Seisiadar. W Isl 4H 171
Selattyn. Shrp 2E 71
Selborne. Hants 3F 25
Selby. N Yor 1G 93
Selham. W Sus 3A 26
Selkirk. Bord 2G 119
Sellack. Here 3A 48
Sellafirth. Shet 2G 173
Sellick's Green. Som 1F 13
Sellindge. Kent 2F 29
Selling. Kent 5E 41
Sells Green. Wilts 5E 35
Selly Oak. W Mid 2E 61
Selmeston. E Sus 5G 27
Selsdon. G Lon 4E 39
Selsey. W Sus 3G 17
Selsfield Common. W Sus 2E 27
Selside. Cumb 5G 103
Selside. N Yor 2G 97
Selsley. Glos 5D 48
Selsted. Kent 1G 29
Selston. Notts 5B 86

Selworthy. *Som* 2C 20
Semblister. *Shet* 6E 173
Semer. *Suff* 1D 54
Semington. *Wilts* 5D 35
Semley. *Wilts* 4D 23
Sempringham. *Linc* 2A 76
Send. *Surr* 5B 38
Send Marsh. *Surr* 5B 38
Senghenydd. *Cphy* 2E 32
Sennen. *Corn* 4A 4
Sennen Cove. *Corn* 4A 4
Sennicotts. *W Sus* 2G 17
Sennybridge. *Powy* 3C 46
Serlby. *Notts* 2D 86
Sessay. *N Yor* 2G 99
Setchey. *Norf* 4F 77
Setley. *Hants* 2B 16
Setter. *Shet* 3F 173
Settiscarth. *Orkn* 6C 172
Settle. *N Yor* 3H 97
Settrington. *N Yor* 2C 100
Seven Ash. *Som* 3E 21
Sevenhampton. *Glos* 3F 49
Sevenhampton. *Swin* 2H 35
Sevenoaks. *Kent* 5G 39
Sevenoaks Weald. *Kent* 5G 39
Seven Sisters. *Neat* 5B 46
Seven Springs. *Glos* 4E 49
Severn Beach. *S Glo* 3A 34
Severn Stoke. *Worc* 1D 48
Sevington. *Kent* 1E 29
Sewards End. *Essx* 2F 53
Sewardstone. *Essx* 1E 39
Sewell. *C Beds* 3H 51
Sewerby. *E Yor* 3G 101
Seworgan. *Corn* 5B 6
Sewstern. *Leics* 3F 75
Sgallairidh. *W Isl* 9B 170
Sgarasta Mhor. *W Isl* 8C 171
Sgiogarstaigh. *W Isl* 1H 171
Sgreadan. *Arg* 4A 132
Shabbington. *Buck* 5E 51
Shackerley. *Shrp* 5C 72
Shackerstone. *Leics* 5A 74
Shackleford. *Surr* 1A 26
Shadforth. *Dur* 5G 115
Shadingfield. *Suff* 2G 67
Shadoxhurst. *Kent* 2D 28
Shadsworth. *Bkbn* 2E 91
Shadwell. *Norf* 2B 66
Shadwell. *W Yor* 1D 92
Shaftesbury. *Dors* 4D 22
Shafton. *S Yor* 3D 93
Shafton Two Gates. *S Yor* . . .3D 93
Shaggs. *Dors* 4D 14
Shakesfield. *Glos* 2B 48
Shalbourne. *Wilts* 5B 36
Shalcombe. *IOW* 4B 16
Shalden. *Hants* 2E 25
Shaldon. *Devn* 5C 12
Shalfleet. *IOW* 4C 16
Shalford. *Essx* 3H 53
Shalford. *Surr* 1B 26
Shalford Green. *Essx* 3H 53
Shallowford. *Devn* 2H 19
Shallowford. *Staf* 3C 72
Shalmsford Street. *Kent* 5E 41
Shalstone. *Buck* 2E 51
Shamley Green. *Surr* 1B 26
Shandon. *Arg* 1D 126
Shandwick. *High* 1C 158
Shangton. *Leics* 1E 62
Shankhouse. *Nmbd* 2F 115
Shanklin. *IOW* 4D 16
Shannochie. *N Ayr* 3D 122
Shap. *Cumb* 3G 103
Shapwick. *Dors* 2E 15
Shapwick. *Som* 3H 21
Sharcott. *Wilts* 1G 23
Shardlow. *Derbs* 2B 74
Shareshill. *Staf* 5D 72
Sharlston. *W Yor* 3D 93
Sharlston Common. *W Yor* . . .3D 93
Sharnal Street. *Medw* 3B 40
Sharnbrook. *Bed* 5G 63
Sharneyford. *Lanc* 2G 91
Sharnford. *Leics* 1B 62
Sharnhill Green. *Dors* 2C 14
Sharow. *N Yor* 2F 99
Sharpe Green. *Lanc* 1D 90
Sharpenhoe. *C Beds* 2A 52
Sharperton. *Nmbd* 4D 120
Sharpness. *Glos* 5B 48
Sharp Street. *Norf* 3F 79
Sharpthorne. *W Sus* 2E 27
Sharrington. *Norf* 2C 78
Shatterford. *Worc* 2B 60
Shatton. *Derbs* 2G 85
Shaugh Prior. *Devn* 2B 8
Shavington. *Ches E* 5B 84
Shaw. *G Man* 4H 91
Shaw. *W Ber* 5C 36
Shaw. *Wilts* 5D 35
Shawbirch. *Telf* 4A 72
Shawbury. *Shrp* 3H 71
Shawdon Hall. *Nmbd* 3E 121
Shawell. *Leics* 2C 62
Shawford. *Hants* 4C 24
Shaw Green. *Lanc* 3D 90
Shawhead. *Dum* 2F 111
Shaw Mills. *N Yor* 3E 99

Shawwood. *E Ayr* 2E 117
Shearington. *Dum* 3B 112
Shearsby. *Leics* 1D 62
Shearston. *Som* 3F 21
Shebbear. *Devn* 2E 11
Shebdon. *Staf* 3B 72
Shebster. *High* 2C 168
Sheddocksley. *Aber* 3F 153
Shedfield. *Hants* 1D 16
Shedog. *N Ayr* 2D 122
Sheen. *Staf* 4F 85
Sheepbridge. *Derbs* 3A 86
Sheep Hill. *Tyne* 4E 115
Sheepscar. *W Yor* 1D 92
Sheepscombe. *Glos* 4D 49
Sheepstor. *Devn* 2B 8
Sheepwash. *Devn* 2E 11
Sheepwash. *Nmbd* 1F 115
Sheepway. *N Som* 4H 33
Sheepy Magna. *Leics* 5H 73
Sheepy Parva. *Leics* 5H 73
Sheering. *Essx* 4F 53
Sheerness. *Kent* 3D 40
Sheerwater. *Surr* 4B 38
Sheet. *Hants* 4F 25
Sheffield. *S Yor* . . . .2H **85** & **210**
Sheffield Bottom. *W Ber* 5E 37
Sheffield Green. *E Sus* 3F 27
Shefford. *C Beds* 2B 52
Shefford Woodlands.
   W Ber 4B 36
Sheigra. *High* 2B 166
Sheinton. *Shrp* 5A 72
Shelderton. *Shrp* 3G 59
Sheldon. *Derbs* 4F 85
Sheldon. *Devn* 2E 12
Sheldon. *W Mid* 2F 61
Sheldwich. *Kent* 5E 40
Sheldwich Lees. *Kent* 5E 40
Shelf. *W Yor* 2B 92
Shelfanger. *Norf* 2D 66
Shelfield. *Warw* 4F 61
Shelfield. *W Mid* 5E 73
Shelford. *Notts* 1D 74
Shelford. *Warw* 2B 62
Shell. *Worc* 5D 60
Shelley. *Suff* 2D 54
Shelley. *W Yor* 3C 92
Shell Green. *Hal* 2H 83
Shellingford. *Oxon* 2B 36
Shellow Bowells. *Essx* 5G 53
Shelsley Beauchamp. *Worc* . .4B 60
Shelsley Walsh. *Worc* 4B 60
Shelthorpe. *Leics* 4C 74
Shelton. *Bed* 4H 63
Shelton. *Norf* 1E 67
Shelton. *Notts* 1E 75
Shelton. *Shrp* 4G 71
Shelton Green. *Norf* 1E 67
Shelton Lock. *Derb* 2A 74
Shelve. *Shrp* 1F 59
Shelwick. *Here* 1A 48
Shelwick Green. *Here* 1A 48
Shenfield. *Essx* 1H 39
Shenington. *Oxon* 1B 50
Shenley. *Herts* 5B 52
Shenley Brook End. *Mil* 2G 51
Shenleybury. *Herts* 5B 52
Shenley Church End. *Mil* 2G 51
Shenmore. *Here* 2G 47
Shennanton. *Dum* 3A 110
Shenstone. *Staf* 5F 73
Shenstone Woodend. *Staf* . . .5F 73
Shenton. *Leics* 5A 74
Shenval. *Mor* 1G 151
Shepeau Stow. *Linc* 4C 76
Shephall. *Herts* 3C 52
Shepherd's Bush. *G Lon* 2D 38
Shepherd's Gate. *Norf* 4E 77
Shepherd's Green. *Oxon* 3F 37
Shepherd's Port. *Norf* 2F 77
Shepherdswell. *Kent* 1G 29
Shepley. *W Yor* 4B 92
Sheppardstown. *High* 4D 169
Shepperdine. *S Glo* 2B 34
Shepperton. *Surr* 4B 38
Shepreth. *Cambs* 1D 53
Shepshed. *Leics* 4B 74
Shepton Beauchamp. *Som* . . .1H 13
Shepton Mallet. *Som* 2B 22
Shepton Montague. *Som* 3B 22
Shepway. *Kent* 5B 40
Sheraton. *Dur* 1B 106
Sherborne. *Bath* 1A 22
Sherborne. *Dors* 1B 14
Sherborne. *Glos* 4G 49
Sherborne Causeway. *Dors* . .4D 22
Sherborne St John. *Hants* . . .1E 24
Sherbourne. *Warw* 4G 61
Sherburn. *Dur* 5G 115
Sherburn. *N Yor* 2D 100
Sherburn Hill. *Dur* 5G 115
Sherburn in Elmet. *N Yor* 1E 93
Shere. *Surr* 1B 26
Shereford. *Norf* 3A 78
Sherfield English. *Hants* 4A 24
Sherfield on Loddon. *Hants* . .1E 25
Sherford. *Devn* 4D 9
Sherford. *Dors* 3E 15
Sheriffhales. *Shrp* 4B 72
Sheriff Hutton. *N Yor* 3A 100

Sheriffston. *Mor* 2G 159
Sheringham. *Norf* 1D 78
Sherington. *Mil* 1G 51
Shermanbury. *W Sus* 4D 26
Shernal Green. *Worc* 4D 60
Shernborne. *Norf* 2G 77
Sherrington. *Wilts* 3E 23
Sherston. *Wilts* 3D 34
Sherwood. *Nott* 1C 74
Sherwood Green. *Devn* 4F 19
Shettleston. *Glas* 3H 127
Shevington. *G Man* 4D 90
Shevington Moor.
   G Man 3D 90
Shevington Vale. *G Man* 4D 90
Sheviock. *Corn* 3H 7
Shide. *IOW* 4D 16
Shiel Bridge. *High* 2B 148
Shieldaig. *High* 3H 155
   (nr. Charlestown)
Shieldaig. *High* 4H 155
   (nr. Torridon)
Shieldhill. *Dum* 1B 112
Shieldhill. *Falk* 2B 128
Shieldhill. *S Lan* 5D 128
Shieldmuir. *N Lan* 4A 128
Shielfoot. *High* 2A 140
Shielhill. *Abers* 3H 161
Shielhill. *Ang* 3D 144
Shifnal. *Shrp* 5B 72
Shilbottle. *Nmbd* 4F 121
Shilbottle Grange. *Nmbd* 4G 121
Shildon. *Dur* 2F 105
Shillford. *E Ren* 4F 127
Shillingford. *Devn* 4C 20
Shillingford. *Oxon* 2D 36
Shillingford St George.
   Devn 4C 12
Shillingstone. *Dors* 1D 14
Shillington. *C Beds* 2B 52
Shillmoor. *Nmbd* 4C 120
Shilton. *Oxon* 5A 50
Shilton. *Warw* 2B 62
Shilvinghampton. *Dors* 4B 14
Shilvington. *Nmbd* 1E 115
Shimpling. *Norf* 2D 66
Shimpling. *Suff* 5A 66
Shimpling Street. *Suff* 5A 66
Shincliffe. *Dur* 5F 115
Shiney Row. *Tyne* 4G 115
Shinfield. *Wok* 5F 37
Shingay. *Cambs* 1D 52
Shingham. *Norf* 5G 77
Shingle Street. *Suff* 1G 55
Shinner's Bridge. *Devn* 2D 9
Shinness. *High* 2C 164
Shipbourne. *Kent* 5G 39
Shipdham. *Norf* 5B 78
Shipham. *Som* 1H 21
Shiphay. *Torb* 2E 9
Shiplake. *Oxon* 4F 37
Shipley. *Derbs* 1B 74
Shipley. *Nmbd* 3F 121
Shipley. *Shrp* 1C 60
Shipley. *W Sus* 3C 26
Shipley. *W Yor* 1B 92
Shipley Bridge. *Surr* 1E 27
Shipmeadow. *Suff* 1F 67
Shippon. *Oxon* 2C 36
Shipston-on-Stour. *Warw* 1A 50
Shipton. *Buck* 3F 51
Shipton. *Glos* 4F 49
Shipton. *N Yor* 4H 99
Shipton. *Shrp* 1H 59
Shipton Bellinger. *Hants* 2H 23
Shipton Gorge. *Dors* 3H 13
Shipton Green. *W Sus* 3G 17
Shipton Moyne. *Glos* 3D 35
Shipton-on-Cherwell. *Oxon* . . .4C 50
Shiptonthorpe. *E Yor* 5C 100
Shipton-under-Wychwood.
   Oxon 4A 50
Shirburn. *Oxon* 2E 37
Shirdley Hill. *Lanc* 3B 90
Shire. *Cumb* 1H 103
Shirebrook. *Derbs* 4C 86
Shiregreen. *S Yor* 1A 86
Shirehampton. *Bris* 4A 34
Shiremoor. *Tyne* 2G 115
Shirenewton. *Mon* 2H 33
Shireoaks. *Notts* 2C 86
Shires Mill. *Fife* 1C 128
Shirkoak. *Kent* 2D 28
Shirland. *Derbs* 5A 86
Shirley. *Derbs* 1G 73
Shirley. *Sotn* 1C 16
Shirley. *W Mid* 3F 61
Shirleywich. *Staf* 3D 73
Shirl Heath. *Here* 5G 59
Shirrell Heath. *Hants* 1D 16
Shirwell. *Devn* 3F 19
Shiskine. *N Ayr* 3D 122
Shobdon. *Here* 4F 59
Shobnall. *Staf* 3G 73
Shobrooke. *Devn* 2B 12
Shoby. *Leics* 3D 74
Shocklach. *Ches W* 1G 71
Shoeburyness. *S'end* 2D 40
Sholden. *Kent* 5H 41
Sholing. *Sotn* 1C 16
Sholver. *G Man* 4H 91
Shoot Hill. *Shrp* 4G 71

Shop. *Corn* 1C 10
   (nr. Bude)
Shop. *Corn* 1C 6
   (nr. Padstow)
Shop. *Devn* 1D 11
Shopford. *Cumb* 2G 113
Shoreditch. *G Lon* 2E 39
Shoreditch. *Som* 4F 21
Shoregill. *Cumb* 4A 104
Shoreham. *Kent* 4G 39
Shoreham Airport. *W Sus* 5D 26
Shoreham-by-Sea. *W Sus* . .5D 26
Shoresdean. *Nmbd* 5F 131
Shoreswood. *Nmbd* 5F 131
Shore, The. *Fife* 2E 137
Shorncote. *Glos* 2F 35
Shorne. *Kent* 3A 40
Shorne Ridgeway. *Kent* 3A 40
Shortacombe. *Devn* 4F 11
Shortbridge. *E Sus* 3F 27
Shortgate. *E Sus* 4F 27
Short Green. *Norf* 2C 66
Shortheath. *Surr* 2F 55
Short Heath. *Leics* 4H 73
Short Heath. *W Mid* 1E 61
   (nr. Erdington)
Short Heath. *W Mid* 5D 73
   (nr. Wednesfield)
Shortlanesend. *Corn* 4C 6
Shorton. *Torb* 2E 9
Shortstown. *Bed* 1A 52
Shortwood. *S Glo* 4B 34
Shorwell. *IOW* 4C 16
Shoscombe. *Bath* 1C 22
Shotesham. *Norf* 1E 67
Shotgate. *Essx* 1B 40
Shotley. *Suff* 2F 55
Shotley Bridge. *Dur* 4D 115
Shotleyfield. *Nmbd* 4D 114
Shotley Gate. *Suff* 2F 55
Shottenden. *Kent* 5E 41
Shottermill. *Surr* 3G 25
Shottery. *Warw* 5F 61
Shotteswell. *Warw* 1C 50
Shottisham. *Suff* 1G 55
Shottle. *Derbs* 1H 73
Shotton. *Dur* 1B 106
   (nr. Peterlee)
Shotton. *Dur* 2A 106
   (nr. Sedgefield)
Shotton. *Flin* 4E 83
Shotton. *Nmbd* 2F 115
   (nr. Morpeth)
Shotton. *Nmbd* 1C 120
   (nr. Town Yetholm)
Shotton Colliery. *Dur* 5G 115
Shotts. *N Lan* 3B 128
Shotwick. *Ches W* 3F 83
Shouldham. *Norf* 5F 77
Shouldham Thorpe. *Norf* 5F 77
Shoulton. *Worc* 5C 60
Shrawardine. *Shrp* 4F 71
Shrawley. *Worc* 4C 60
Shreding Green. *Buck* 2B 38
Shrewley. *Warw* 4G 61
Shrewsbury. *Shrp* . . .4G 71 & **210**
Shrewton. *Wilts* 2F 23
Shripney. *W Sus* 5A 26
Shrivenham. *Oxon* 3H 35
Shropham. *Norf* 1B 66
Shroton. *Dors* 1D 14
Shrub End. *Essx* 3C 54
Shucknall. *Here* 1A 48
Shudy Camps. *Cambs* 1G 53
Shulishadermor. *High* 4D 155
Shulista. *High* 1D 154
Shurdington. *Glos* 4E 49
Shurlock Row. *Wind* 4G 37
Shurrery. *High* 3C 168
Shurton. *Som* 2F 21
Shustoke. *Warw* 1G 61
Shute. *Devn* 3F 13
   (nr. Axminster)
Shute. *Devn* 2B 12
   (nr. Crediton)
Shutford. *Oxon* 1B 50
Shut Heath. *Staf* 3C 72
Shuthonger. *Glos* 2D 49
Shutlanehead. *Staf* 1C 72
Shutlanger. *Nptn* 1F 51
Shutt Green. *Staf* 5C 72
Shuttington. *Warw* 5G 73
Shuttlewood. *Derbs* 3B 86
Shuttleworth. *G Man* 3G 91
Siabost. *W Isl* 3E 171
Siabost bho Dheas. *W Isl* . . .3E 171
Siabost bho Thuath. *W Isl* . . .3E 171
Siadar. *W Isl* 2F 171
Siadar Uarach. *W Isl* 2F 171
Sibbaldbie. *Dum* 1C 112
Sibbertoft. *Nptn* 2D 62
Sibdon Carwood. *Shrp* 2G 59
Sibertswold. *Kent* 1G 29
Sibford Ferris. *Oxon* 2B 50
Sibford Gower. *Oxon* 2B 50
Sible Hedingham. *Essx* 2A 54
Sibsey. *Linc* 5C 88
Sibsey Fen Side. *Linc* 5C 88
Sibson. *Cambs* 1H 63
Sibson. *Leics* 5A 74
Sibster. *High* 3F 169
Sibthorpe. *Notts* 1E 75

Sibton. *Suff* 4F 67
Sicklesmere. *Suff* 4A 66
Sicklinghall. *N Yor* 5F 99
Sid. *Devn* 4E 13
Sidbury. *Devn* 3E 13
Sidbury. *Shrp* 2A 60
Sidcot. *N Som* 1H 21
Sidcup. *G Lon* 3F 39
Siddick. *Cumb* 1B 102
Siddington. *Ches E* 3C 84
Siddington. *Glos* 2F 35
Side of the Moor. *G Man* 3F 91
Sidestrand. *Norf* 2E 79
Sidford. *Devn* 3E 13
Sidlesham. *W Sus* 3G 17
Sidley. *E Sus* 5B 28
Sidlow. *Surr* 1D 26
Sidmouth. *Devn* 4E 13
Sigford. *Devn* 5A 12
Sigglesthorne. *E Yor* 5F 101
Sighthill. *Edin* 2E 129
Signingstone. *V Glam* 4C 32
Signet. *Oxon* 4H 49
Silchester. *Hants* 5E 37
Sildinis. *W Isl* 6E 171
Sileby. *Leics* 4D 74
Silecroft. *Cumb* 1A 96
Silfield. *Norf* 1D 66
Silian. *Cdgn* 5E 57
Silkstone. *S Yor* 4C 92
Silkstone Common. *S Yor* . . .4C 92
Silksworth. *Tyne* 4G 115
Silk Willoughby. *Linc* 1H 75
Silloth. *Cumb* 4C 112
Sills. *Nmbd* 4C 120
Sillyearn. *Mor* 3C 160
Silpho. *N Yor* 5G 107
Silsden. *W Yor* 5C 98
Silsoe. *C Beds* 2A 52
Silverbank. *Abers* 4E 152
Silverburn. *Midl* 3F 129
Silverdale. *Lanc* 2D 96
Silverdale. *Staf* 1C 72
Silverdale Green. *Lanc* 2D 96
Silver End. *Essx* 4B 54
Silver End. *W Mid* 2D 60
Silvergate. *Norf* 3D 78
Silver Green. *Norf* 1E 67
Silverhillocks. *Abers* 2E 161
Silverley's Green. *Suff* 3E 67
Silverstone. *Nptn* 1E 51
Silverton. *Devn* 2C 12
Silverton. *W Dun* 2F 127
Silvington. *Shrp* 3A 60
Simm's Cross. *Hal* 2H 83
Simm's Lane End. *Mers* 1H 83
Simonburn. *Nmbd* 2B 114
Simonsbath. *Som* 3A 20
Simonstone. *Lanc* 1F 91
Simprim. *Bord* 5E 131
Simpson. *Pemb* 3C 42
Simpson Cross. *Pemb* 3C 42
Sinclairston. *E Ayr* 3D 116
Sinclairtown. *Fife* 4E 137
Sinderby. *N Yor* 1F 99
Sinderhope. *Nmbd* 4B 114
Sindlesham. *Wok* 5F 37
Sinfin. *Derb* 2A 74
Singleborough. *Buck* 2F 51
Singleton. *Kent* 1D 28
Singleton. *Lanc* 1B 90
Singleton. *W Sus* 1G 17
Singlewell. *Kent* 3A 40
Sinkhurst Green. *Kent* 1C 28
Sinnahard. *Abers* 2B 152
Sinnington. *N Yor* 1B 100
Sinton Green. *Worc* 4C 60
Sipson. *G Lon* 3B 38
Sirhowy. *Blae* 4E 47
Sisland. *Norf* 1F 67
Sissinghurst. *Kent* 2B 28
Siston. *S Glo* 4B 34
Sithney. *Corn* 4D 4
Sittingbourne. *Kent* 4D 40
Six Ashes. *Staf* 2B 60
Six Bells. *Blae* 5F 47
Six Hills. *Leics* 3D 74
Sixhills. *Linc* 2A 88
Six Mile Bottom. *Cambs* 5E 65
Sixpenny Handley. *Dors* 1E 15
Sizewell. *Suff* 4G 67
Skail. *High* 4H 167
Skaill. *Orkn* 6B 172
Skaills. *Orkn* 7E 172
Skares. *E Ayr* 3E 117
Skateraw. *E Lot* 2D 130
Skaw. *Shet* 5G 173
Skeabost. *High* 4D 154
Skeabrae. *Orkn* 5B 172
Skeeby. *N Yor* 4E 105
Skeffington. *Leics* 5E 75
Skeffling. *E Yor* 3G 95
Skegby. *Notts* 4B 86
   (nr. Mansfield)
Skegby. *Notts* 3E 87
   (nr. Tuxford)
Skegness. *Linc* 4E 89
Skelberry. *Shet* 10E 173
   (nr. Boddam)
Skelberry. *Shet* 3E 173
   (nr. Housetter)
Skelbo. *High* 4E 165

Skelbo Street. *High* 4E 165
Skelbrooke. *S Yor* 3F 93
Skeldyke. *Linc* 2C 76
Skelfhill. *Bord* 4G 119
Skellingthorpe. *Linc* 3G 87
Skellister. *Shet* 6F 173
Skellorn Green. *Ches E* 2D 84
Skellow. *S Yor* 3F 93
Skelmanthorpe. *W Yor* 3C 92
Skelmersdale. *Lanc* 4C 90
Skelmorlie. *N Ayr* 3C 126
Skelpick. *High* 3H 167
Skelton. *Cumb* 1F 103
Skelton. *E Yor* 2A 94
Skelton. *N Yor* 4D 105
 (nr. Richmond)
Skelton. *N Yor* 3F 99
 (nr. Ripon)
Skelton. *Red C* 3D 106
Skelton Green. *Red C* 3D 106
Skelwick. *Orkn* 3D 172
Skelwith Bridge. *Cumb* 4E 103
Skendleby. *Linc* 4D 88
Skendleby Psalter. *Linc* 3D 88
Skenfrith. *Mon* 3H 47
Skerne. *E Yor* 4E 101
Skeroblingarry. *Arg* 3B 122
Skerray. *High* 2G 167
Skerricha. *High* 3C 166
Skerries Airport. *Shet* 4H 173
Skerton. *Lanc* 3D 97
Sketchley. *Leics* 1B 62
Sketty. *Swan* 3F 31
Skewen. *Neat* 3G 31
Skewsby. *N Yor* 2A 100
Skeyton. *Norf* 3E 79
Skeyton Corner. *Norf* 3E 79
Skiall. *High* 2C 168
Skidbrooke. *Linc* 1D 88
Skidbrooke North End. *Linc* . . .1D 88
Skidby. *E Yor* 1D 94
Skilgate. *Som* 4C 20
Skillington. *Linc* 3F 75
Skinburness. *Cumb* 4C 112
Skinflats. *Falk* 1C 128
Skinidin. *High* 4B 154
Skinnet. *High* 2F 167
Skinningrove. *Red C* 2E 107
Skipness. *Arg* 4G 125
Skippool. *Lanc* 5C 96
Skiprigg. *Cumb* 5E 113
Skipsea. *E Yor* 4F 101
Skipsea Brough. *E Yor* 4F 101
Skipton. *N Yor* 4B 98
Skipton-on-Swale. *N Yor* 2F 99
Skipwith. *N Yor* 1G 93
Skirbeck. *Linc* 1C 76
Skirbeck Quarter. *Linc* 1C 76
Skirlaugh. *E Yor* 1E 95
Skirling. *Bord* 1C 118
Skirmett. *Buck* 2F 37
Skirpenbeck. *E Yor* 4B 100
Skirwith. *Cumb* 1H 103
Skirwith. *N Yor* 2G 97
Skirza. *High* 2F 169
Skitby. *Cumb* 3F 113
Skitham. *Lanc* 5D 96
Skittle Green. *Buck* 5F 51
Skroo. *Shet* 1B 172
Skulamus. *High* 1E 147
Skullomie. *High* 2G 167
Skyborry Green. *Shrp* 3E 59
Skye Green. *Essx* 3B 54
Skye of Curr. *High* 1D 151
Slack. *W Yor* 2H 91
Slackhall. *Derbs* 2E 85
Slack Head. *Cumb* 2D 97
Slackhead. *Mor* 2B 160
Slackholme End. *Linc* 3E 89
Slacks of Cairnbanno. *Abers* . .4F 161
Slack, The. *Dur* 2E 105
Slad. *Glos* 5D 48
Slade. *Swan* 4D 31
Slade End. *Oxon* 2D 36
Slade Field. *Cambs* 2C 64
Slade Green. *G Lon* 3G 39
Slade Heath. *Staf* 5D 72
Slade Hooton. *S Yor* 2C 86
Sladesbridge. *Corn* 5A 10
Slade, The. *W Ber* 5D 36
Slaggyford. *Nmbd* 4H 113
Slaidburn. *Lanc* 4G 97
Slaid Hill. *W Yor* 5F 99
Slaithwaite. *W Yor* 3A 92
Slaley. *Derbs* 5G 85
Slaley. *Nmbd* 4C 114
Slamannan. *Falk* 2B 128
Slapton. *Buck* 3H 51
Slapton. *Devn* 4E 9
Slapton. *Nptn* 1E 51
Slattock. *G Man* 4G 91
Slaugham. *W Sus* 3D 26
Slaughterbridge. *Corn* 4B 10
Slaughterford. *Wilts* 4D 34
Slawston. *Leics* 1E 63
Sleaford. *Hants* 3G 25
Sleaford. *Linc* 1H 75
Sleagill. *Cumb* 3G 103
Sleap. *Shrp* 3G 71
Sledmere. *E Yor* 3D 100
Sleightholme. *Dur* 3C 104

Sleights. *N Yor* 4F 107
Slepe. *Dors* 3E 15
Slickly. *High* 2E 169
Sliddery. *N Ayr* 3D 122
Sligachan. *High* 1C 146
Slimbridge. *Glos* 5C 48
Slindon. *Staf* 2C 72
Slindon. *W Sus* 5A 26
Slinfold. *W Sus* 2C 26
Slingsby. *N Yor* 2A 100
Slip End. *C Beds* 4A 52
Slipton. *Nptn* 3G 63
Slitting Mill. *Staf* 4E 73
Slochd. *High* 1C 150
Slockavullin. *Arg* 4F 133
Sloley. *Norf* 3E 79
Sloncombe. *Devn* 4H 11
Sloothby. *Linc* 3D 89
Slough. *Slo* 2A 38
Slough Green. *Som* 4F 21
Slough Green. *W Sus* 3D 27
Sluggan. *High* 1C 150
Slyne. *Lanc* 3D 97
Smailholm. *Bord* 1A 120
Smallbridge. *G Man* 3H 91
Smallbrook. *Devn* 3B 12
Smallburgh. *Norf* 3F 79
Smallburn. *E Ayr* 2F 117
Smalldale. *Derbs* 3E 85
Small Dole. *W Sus* 4D 26
Smalley. *Derbs* 1B 74
Smallfield. *Surr* 1E 27
Small Heath. *W Mid* 2E 61
Small Hythe. *Kent* 2C 28
Smallrice. *Staf* 2D 72
Smallridge. *Devn* 2G 13
Smallwood Hey. *Lanc* 5C 96
Smallworth. *Norf* 2C 66
Smannell. *Hants* 2B 24
Smardale. *Cumb* 4A 104
Smarden. *Kent* 1C 28
Smarden Bell. *Kent* 1C 28
Smart's Hill. *Kent* 1G 27
Smeatharpe. *Devn* 1F 13
Smeeth. *Kent* 2E 29
Smeeth, The. *Norf* 4E 77
Smeeton Westerby. *Leics* 1D 62
Smeircleit. *W Isl* 7C 170
Smerral. *High* 5D 168
Smestow. *Staf* 1C 60
Smethwick. *W Mid* 2E 61
Smirisary. *High* 1A 140
Smisby. *Derbs* 4H 73
Smitham Hill. *Bath* 1A 22
Smith End Green. *Worc* 5B 60
Smithfield. *Cumb* 3F 113
Smith Green. *Lanc* 4D 97
Smithies, The. *Shrp* 1A 60
Smithincott. *Devn* 1D 12
Smith's Green. *Essx* 3F 53
Smithstown. *High* 1G 155
Smithton. *High* 4B 158
Smithwood Green. *Suff* 5B 66
Smithy Bridge. *G Man* 3H 91
Smithy Green. *Ches E* 3B 84
Smithy Lane Ends. *Lanc* 3C 90
Smockington. *Warw* 2B 62
Smoogro. *Orkn* 7C 172
Smythe's Green. *Essx* 4C 54
Snaigow House. *Per* 4H 143
Snailbeach. *Shrp* 5F 71
Snailwell. *Cambs* 4F 65
Snainton. *N Yor* 1D 100
Snaith. *E Yor* 2G 93
Snape. *N Yor* 1E 99
Snape. *Suff* 5F 67
Snape Green. *Lanc* 3B 90
Snapper. *Devn* 3F 19
Snarestone. *Leics* 5H 73
Snarford. *Linc* 2H 87
Snargate. *Kent* 3D 28
Snave. *Kent* 3E 28
Sneachill. *Worc* 5D 60
Snead. *Powy* 1F 59
Snead Common. *Worc* 4B 60
Sneaton. *N Yor* 4F 107
Sneatonthorpe. *N Yor* 4G 107
Snelland. *Linc* 2H 87
Snelston. *Derbs* 1F 73
Snetterton. *Norf* 1B 66
Snettisham. *Norf* 2F 77
Snibston. *Leics* 4B 74
Sniseabhal. *W Isl* 5C 170
Snitter. *Nmbd* 4E 121
Snitterby. *Linc* 1G 87
Snitterfield. *Warw* 5G 61
Snitton. *Shrp* 3H 59
Snodhill. *Here* 1G 47
Snodland. *Kent* 4A 40
Snods Edge. *Nmbd* 4D 114
Snowdonia. *Gwyn* 2G 69
Snowshill. *Glos* 2F 49
Snow Street. *Norf* 2C 66
Snydale. *W Yor* 3E 93
Soake. *Hants* 1E 17
Soar. *Carm* 3G 45
Soar. *Devn* 5C 8
Soar. *Gwyn* 3C 80
Soar. *IOA* 3C 80
Soar. *Powy* 2C 46
Soberton. *Hants* 1E 16
Soberton Heath. *Hants* 1E 16

Sockbridge. *Cumb* 2F 103
Sockburn. *Darl* 4A 106
Sodom. *Den* 3C 82
Sodom. *Shet* 5G 173
Soham. *Cambs* 3E 65
Soham Cotes. *Cambs* 3E 65
Solas. *W Isl* 1D 170
Soldon Cross. *Devn* 1D 10
Soldridge. *Hants* 3E 25
Solent Breezes. *Hants* 2D 16
Sole Street. *Kent* 4A 40
 (nr. Meopham)
Sole Street. *Kent* 1E 29
 (nr. Waltham)
Solihull. *W Mid* 3F 61
Sollers Dilwyn. *Here* 5G 59
Sollers Hope. *Here* 2B 48
Sollom. *Lanc* 3C 90
Solva. *Pemb* 2B 42
Somerby. *Leics* 4E 75
Somerby. *Linc* 4D 94
Somercotes. *Derbs* 5B 86
Somerford. *Dors* 3G 15
Somerford. *Staf* 5C 72
Somerford Keynes. *Glos* 2F 35
Somerley. *W Sus* 3G 17
Somerleyton. *Suff* 1G 67
Somersal Herbert. *Derbs* 2F 73
Somersby. *Linc* 3C 88
Somersham. *Cambs* 3C 64
Somersham. *Suff* 1D 54
Somerton. *Oxon* 3C 50
Somerton. *Som* 4H 21
Somerton. *Suff* 5H 65
Somerton. *Dum* 2C 112
Sompting. *W Sus* 5C 26
Sonning. *Wok* 4F 37
Sonning Common. *Oxon* 3F 37
Sonning Eye. *Oxon* 4F 37
Sookholme. *Notts* 4C 86
Sopley. *Hants* 3G 15
Sopworth. *Wilts* 3D 34
Sorbie. *Dum* 5B 110
Sordale. *High* 2D 168
Sorisdale. *Arg* 2D 138
Sorn. *E Ayr* 2E 117
Sornhill. *E Ayr* 1E 117
Sortat. *High* 2E 169
Sotby. *Linc* 3B 88
Sots Hole. *Linc* 4A 88
Sotterley. *Suff* 2G 67
Soudley. *Shrp* 1G 59
 (nr. Church Stretton)
Soudley. *Shrp* 3B 72
 (nr. Market Drayton)
Soughton. *Flin* 4E 83
Soulbury. *Buck* 3G 51
Soulby. *Cumb* 3A 104
 (nr. Appleby)
Soulby. *Cumb* 2F 103
 (nr. Penrith)
Souldern. *Oxon* 2D 50
Souldrop. *Bed* 4G 63
Sound. *Ches E* 1A 72
Sound. *Shet* 7F 173
 (nr. Lerwick)
Sound. *Shet* 6E 173
 (nr. Tresta)
Soundwell. *Bris* 4B 34
Sourhope. *Bord* 2C 120
Sourin. *Orkn* 4D 172
Sour Nook. *Cumb* 5E 113
Sourton. *Devn* 3F 11
Soutergate. *Cumb* 1B 96
South Acre. *Norf* 4H 77
Southall. *G Lon* 3C 38
South Allington. *Devn* 5D 9
South Alloa. *Falk* 4A 136
Southam. *Glos* 3E 49
Southam. *Warw* 4B 62
South Ambersham. *W Sus* 3A 26
Southampton. *Sotn* . . . . .1C 16 & 211
Southampton International Airport.
 Hants 1C 16
Southannan. *N Ayr* 4D 126
South Anston. *S Yor* 2C 86
South Ascot. *Wind* 4A 38
South Baddesley. *Hants* 3B 16
South Balfern. *Dum* 4B 110
South Ballachulish. *High* 3E 141
South Bank. *Red C* 2C 106
South Barrow. *Som* 4B 22
South Benfleet. *Essx* 2B 40
South Bents. *Tyne* 3H 115
South Bersted. *W Sus* 5A 26
Southborough. *Kent* 1G 27
Southbourne. *Bour* 3G 15
Southbourne. *W Sus* 2F 17
South Bowood. *Dors* 3H 13
South Brent. *Devn* 2D 8
South Brewham. *Som* 3C 22
South Broomage. *Falk* 1B 128
South Broomhill. *Nmbd* 4G 121
Southburgh. *Norf* 5B 78
South Burlingham. *Norf* 5F 79
Southburn. *E Yor* 4D 101
South Cadbury. *Som* 4B 22
South Carlton. *Linc* 3G 87
South Cave. *E Yor* 1C 94
South Cerney. *Glos* 2F 35
South Chard. *Som* 2G 13
South Charlton. *Nmbd* 2F 121
South Cheriton. *Som* 4B 22

South Church. *Dur* 2F 105
Southchurch. *S'end* 2D 40
South Cleatlam. *Dur* 3E 105
South Cliffe. *E Yor* 1B 94
South Clifton. *Notts* 3F 87
South Clunes. *High* 4H 157
South Cockerington. *Linc* 2C 88
South Common. *Devn* 2G 13
South Common. *E Sus* 4E 27
South Cornelly. *B'end* 3B 32
Southcott. *Devn* 1E 11
 (nr. Great Torrington)
Southcott. *Devn* 3F 11
 (nr. Okehampton)
Southcott. *Wilts* 1G 23
Southcourt. *Buck* 4G 51
South Cove. *Suff* 2G 67
South Creagan. *Arg* 4D 141
South Creake. *Norf* 2A 78
South Crosland. *W Yor* 3B 92
South Croxton. *Leics* 4D 74
South Dalton. *E Yor* 5D 100
South Darenth. *Kent* 4G 39
Southdean. *Bord* 4A 120
Southdown. *Bath* 5C 34
South Downs. *W Sus* 5D 26
South Duffield. *N Yor* 1G 93
Southease. *E Sus* 5F 27
South Elkington. *Linc* 2B 88
South Elmsall. *W Yor* 3E 93
Southend. *Arg* 5A 122
South End. *Cumb* 3B 96
Southend. *Glos* 2C 34
South End. *N Lin* 2E 94
South End. *W Ber* 4D 36
Southend (London) Airport.
 Essx 2C 40
Southend-on-Sea. *S'end* 2C 40
Southerfield. *Cumb* 5C 112
Southerhouse. *Shet* 8E 173
Southerly. *Devn* 4F 11
Southernden. *Kent* 1C 28
Southerndown. *V Glam* 4B 32
Southerness. *Dum* 4A 112
South Erradale. *High* 1G 155
Southerton. *Devn* 3D 12
Southery. *Norf* 1F 65
Southey Green. *Essx* 2A 54
South Fambridge. *Essx* 1C 40
South Fawley. *W Ber* 3B 36
South Feorline. *N Ayr* 3D 122
South Ferriby. *N Lin* 2C 94
South Field. *E Yor* 2D 94
Southfleet. *Kent* 3H 39
South Garvan. *High* 1D 141
Southgate. *Cdgn* 2E 57
Southgate. *G Lon* 1E 39
Southgate. *Norf* 3D 78
 (nr. Aylsham)
Southgate. *Norf* 2A 78
 (nr. Fakenham)
Southgate. *Swan* 4E 31
South Gluss. *Shet* 4E 173
South Godstone. *Surr* 1E 27
South Gorley. *Hants* 1G 15
South Green. *Essx* 1A 40
 (nr. Billericay)
South Green. *Essx* 4D 54
 (nr. Colchester)
South Green. *Kent* 4C 40
South Hanningfield. *Essx* 1B 40
South Harting. *W Sus* 1F 17
South Hayling. *Hants* 3F 17
South Hazelrigg. *Nmbd* 1E 121
South Heath. *Buck* 5H 51
South Heath. *Essx* 4E 54
South Heighton. *E Sus* 5F 27
South Hetton. *Dur* 5G 115
South Hiendley. *W Yor* 3D 93
South Hill. *Corn* 5D 10
South Hill. *Som* 4H 21
South Hinksey. *Oxon* 5D 50
South Hole. *Devn* 4C 18
South Holme. *N Yor* 2B 100
South Holmwood. *Surr* 1C 26
South Hornchurch. *G Lon* 2G 39
South Huish. *Devn* 4C 8
South Hykeham. *Linc* 4G 87
South Hylton. *Tyne* 4G 115
Southill. *C Beds* 1B 52
Southington. *Hants* 2D 24
South Kelsey. *Linc* 1H 87
South Kessock. *High* 4A 158
South Killingholme. *N Lin* 3E 95
South Kilvington. *N Yor* 1G 99
South Kilworth. *Leics* 2D 62
South Kirkby. *W Yor* 3E 93
South Kirton. *Abers* 3E 153
South Knighton. *Devn* 5B 12
South Kyme. *Linc* 1A 76
South Lancing. *W Sus* 5C 26
South Ledaig. *Arg* 5D 140
Southleigh. *Devn* 3F 13
South Leigh. *Oxon* 5B 50
South Leverton. *Notts* 2E 87
South Littleton. *Worc* 1F 49
South Lopham. *Norf* 2C 66
South Luffenham. *Rut* 5G 75
South Malling. *E Sus* 4F 27
South Marston. *Swin* 3G 35
South Middleton. *Nmbd* 2E 121
South Milford. *N Yor* 1E 93

South Milton. *Devn* 4D 8
South Mimms. *Herts* 5C 52
Southminster. *Essx* 1D 40
South Molton. *Devn* 4H 19
South Moor. *Dur* 4E 115
Southmoor. *Oxon* 2B 36
South Moreton. *Oxon* 3D 36
South Mundham. *W Sus* 2G 17
South Muskham. *Notts* 5E 87
South Newbald. *E Yor* 1C 94
South Newington. *Oxon* 2C 50
South Newsham. *Nmbd* 2G 115
South Newton. *N Ayr* 4H 125
South Newton. *Wilts* 3F 23
South Normanton. *Derbs* 5B 86
South Norwood. *G Lon* 4E 39
South Nutfield. *Surr* 1E 27
South Ockendon. *Thur* 2G 39
Southoe. *Cambs* 4A 64
Southolt. *Suff* 4D 66
South Ormsby. *Linc* 3C 88
Southorpe. *Pet* 5H 75
South Otterington. *N Yor* 1F 99
South Owersby. *Linc* 1H 87
Southowram. *W Yor* 2B 92
South Oxhey. *Herts* 1C 38
South Perrott. *Dors* 2H 13
South Petherton. *Som* 1H 13
South Petherwin. *Corn* 4D 10
South Pickenham. *Norf* 5A 78
South Pool. *Devn* 4D 9
South Poorton. *Dors* 3A 14
South Port. *Arg* 1H 133
Southport. *Mers* 3B 90
Southpunds. *Shet* 10F 173
South Queensferry. *Edin* 2E 129
South Radworthy. *Devn* 3A 20
South Rauceby. *Linc* 1H 75
South Raynham. *Norf* 3A 78
South Reston. *Linc* 2D 88
Southrey. *Linc* 4A 88
Southrop. *Glos* 5G 49
Southrope. *Hants* 2E 25
South Runcton. *Norf* 5F 77
South Scarle. *Notts* 4F 87
Southsea. *Port* 3E 17
South Shields. *Tyne* 3G 115
South Shore. *Bkpl* 1B 90
Southside. *Orkn* 5E 172
South Somercotes. *Linc* 1D 88
South Stainley. *N Yor* 3F 99
South Stainmore. *Cumb* 3B 104
South Stifford. *Thur* 3G 39
Southstoke. *Bath* 5C 34
South Stoke. *Oxon* 3D 36
South Stoke. *W Sus* 4B 26
South Street. *E Sus* 4E 27
South Street. *Kent* 5E 41
 (nr. Faversham)
South Street. *Kent* 4F 41
 (nr. Whitstable)
South Tawton. *Devn* 3G 11
South Thoresby. *Linc* 3D 88
South Tidworth. *Wilts* 2H 23
South Town. *Devn* 4C 12
South Town. *Hants* 3E 25
Southtown. *Norf* 5H 79
Southtown. *Orkn* 8D 172
South View. *Shet* 7E 173
Southwaite. *Cumb* 5F 113
South Walsham. *Norf* 4F 79
South Warnborough. *Hants* 2F 25
Southwater. *W Sus* 3C 26
Southwater Street. *W Sus* 3C 26
Southway. *Som* 2A 22
South Weald. *Essx* 1G 39
South Weirs. *Hants* 2A 16
Southwell. *Dors* 5B 14
Southwell. *Notts* 5D 86
South Weston. *Oxon* 2F 37
South Wheatley. *Corn* 3C 10
South Wheatley. *Notts* 2E 87
Southwick. *Hants* 2E 17
Southwick. *Nptn* 1H 63
Southwick. *Tyne* 4G 115
Southwick. *W Sus* 5D 26
Southwick. *Wilts* 1D 22
South Widcombe. *Bath* 1A 22
South Wigston. *Leics* 1C 62
South Willingham. *Linc* 2A 88
South Wingfield. *Derbs* 5A 86
South Witham. *Linc* 4G 75
Southwold. *Suff* 3H 67
South Wonston. *Hants* 3C 24
Southwood. *Norf* 5F 79
Southwood. *Som* 3A 22
South Woodham Ferrers.
 Essx 1C 40
South Wootton. *Norf* 3F 77
South Wraxall. *Wilts* 5D 34
South Zeal. *Devn* 3G 11
Soval Lodge. *W Isl* 5F 171
Sowerby. *N Yor* 1G 99
Sowerby. *W Yor* 2A 92
Sowerby Bridge. *W Yor* 2A 92
Sowerby Row. *Cumb* 5E 113
Sower Carr. *Lanc* 5C 96
Sowley Green. *Suff* 5G 65
Sowood. *W Yor* 3A 92
Sowton. *Devn* 3C 12
Soyal. *High* 4C 164

Soyland Town. W Yor 2A **92**
Spacey Houses. N Yor 4F **99**
Spa Common. Norf 2E **79**
Spalding. Linc 3B **76**
Spaldington. E Yor 1A **94**
Spaldwick. Cambs 3A **64**
Spalford. Notts 4F **87**
Spanby. Linc 2H **75**
Sparham. Norf 4C **78**
Sparhamhill. Norf 4C **78**
Spark Bridge. Cumb 1C **96**
Sparket. Cumb 2F **103**
Sparkford. Som 4B **22**
Sparkwell. Devn 3B **8**
Sparrow Green. Norf 4B **78**
Sparrowpit. Derbs 2E **85**
Sparrow's Green. E Sus 2H **27**
Sparsholt. Hants 3C **24**
Sparsholt. Oxon 3B **36**
Spartylea. Nmbd 5B **114**
Spath. Staf 2E **73**
Spaunton. N Yor 1B **100**
Spaxton. Som 3F **21**
Spean Bridge. High 5E **149**
Spear Hill. W Sus 4C **26**
Speen. Buck 2G **37**
Speen. W Ber 5C **36**
Speeton. N Yor 2F **101**
Speke. Mers 2G **83**
Speldhurst. Kent 1G **27**
Spellbrook. Herts 4E **53**
Spelsbury. Oxon 3B **50**
Spencers Wood. Wok 5F **37**
Spennithorne. N Yor 1D **98**
Spennymoor. Dur 1F **105**
Spernall. Warw 4E **61**
Spetchley. Worc 5C **60**
Spetisbury. Dors 2E **15**
Spexhall. Suff 2F **67**
Speybank. High 3C **150**
Spey Bay. Mor 2A **160**
Speybridge. High 1E **151**
Speyview. Mor 4G **159**
Spilsby. Linc 4C **88**
Spindlestone. Nmbd 1F **121**
Spinkhill. Derbs 3B **86**
Spinney Hills. Leic 5D **74**
Spinningdale. High 5D **164**
Spital. Mers 2F **83**
Spitalhill. Derbs 1F **73**
Spital in the Street. Linc 1G **87**
Spithurst. E Sus 4F **27**
Spittal. Dum 4A **110**
Spittal. E Lot 2A **130**
Spittal. High 3D **168**
Spittal. Nmbd 4G **131**
Spittal. Pemb 2D **43**
Spittalfield. Per 4A **144**
Spittal of Glenmuick. Abers . . .5H **151**
Spittal of Glenshee. Per 1A **144**
Spittal-on-Rule. Bord 3H **119**
Spixworth. Norf 4E **79**
Splatt. Corn 4C **10**
Spofforth. N Yor 4F **99**
Spondon. Derb 2B **74**
Spon End. W Mid 3H **61**
Spooner Row. Norf 1C **66**
Sporle. Norf 4H **77**
Spott. E Lot 2C **130**
Spratton. Nptn 3E **62**
Spreakley. Surr 2G **25**
Spreyton. Devn 3H **11**
Spridlington. Linc 2H **87**
Springburn. Glas 3H **127**
Springfield. Dum 3E **113**
Springfield. Fife 2F **137**
Springfield. Here 2A **158**
Springfield. W Mid 2E **61**
Springhill. Staf 5D **73**
Springholm. Dum 2F **111**
Springside. N Ayr 1C **116**
Springthorpe. Linc 2F **87**
Spring Vale. IOW 3E **16**
Spring Valley. IOM 4C **108**
Springwell. Tyne 4F **115**
Sproatley. E Yor 1E **95**
Sproston Green. Ches W 4B **84**
Sprotbrough. S Yor 4F **93**
Sproughton. Suff 1E **55**
Sprouston. Bord 1B **120**
Sprowston. Norf 4E **79**
Sproxton. Leics 3F **75**
Sproxton. N Yor 1A **100**
Sprunston. Cumb 5E **113**
Spurstow. Ches E 5H **83**
Squires Gate. Bkpl 1B **90**
Sraid Ruadh. Arg 4A **138**
Srannda. W Isl 9C **171**
Sron an t-Sithein. High 2C **140**
Sronphadruig Lodge. Per 1E **142**
Sruth Mor. W Isl 2E **170**
Stableford. Shrp 1B **60**
Stackhouse. N Yor 3H **97**
Stackpole. Pemb 5D **43**
Stackpole Elidor. Pemb 5D **43**
Stacksford. Norf 1C **66**
Stacksteads. Lanc 2G **91**
Staddiscombe. Plym 3B **8**
Staddon. Devn 2D **10**
Staden. Derbs 3E **85**
Stadhampton. Oxon 2E **36**

Stadhlaigearraidh. W Isl 5C **170**
Stafainn. High 2D **155**
Staffield. Cumb 5G **113**
Staffin. High 2D **155**
Stafford. Staf 3D **72**
Stafford Park. Telf 5B **72**
Stagden Cross. Essx 4G **53**
Stagsden. Bed 1H **51**
Stag's Head. Devn 4G **19**
Stainburn. Cumb 2B **102**
Stainburn. N Yor 5E **99**
Stainby. Linc 3G **75**
Staincliffe. W Yor 2C **92**
Staincross. S Yor 3D **92**
Staindrop. Dur 2E **105**
Staines. Surr 3B **38**
Stainfield. Linc 3H **75**
(nr. Bourne)
Stainfield. Linc 3A **88**
(nr. Lincoln)
Stainforth. N Yor 3H **97**
Stainforth. S Yor 3G **93**
Staining. Lanc 1B **90**
Stainland. W Yor 3A **92**
Stainsacre. N Yor 4G **107**
Stainton. Cumb 4E **113**
(nr. Carlisle)
Stainton. Cumb 1E **97**
(nr. Kendal)
Stainton. Cumb 2F **103**
(nr. Penrith)
Stainton. Dur 3D **104**
Stainton. Midd 3B **106**
Stainton. N Yor 5E **105**
Stainton. S Yor 1C **86**
Stainton by Langworth. Linc . . .3H **87**
Staintondale. N Yor 5G **107**
Stainton le Vale. Linc 1A **88**
Stainton with Adgarley. Cumb . .2B **96**
Stair. Cumb 2D **102**
Stair. E Ayr 2D **116**
Stairhaven. Dum 4H **109**
Staithes. N Yor 3E **107**
Stakeford. Nmbd 1F **115**
Stake Pool. Lanc 5D **96**
Stakes. Hants 2E **17**
Stalbridge. Dors 1C **14**
Stalbridge Weston. Dors 1C **14**
Stalham. Norf 3F **79**
Stalham Green. Norf 3F **79**
Stalisfield Green. Kent 5D **40**
Stallen. Dors 1B **14**
Stallingborough. NE Lin 3F **95**
Stalling Busk. N Yor 1B **98**
Stallington. Staf 2D **72**
Stalmine. Lanc 5C **96**
Stalybridge. G Man 1D **84**
Stambourne. Essx 2H **53**
Stamford. Linc 5H **75**
Stamford. Nmbd 3G **121**
Stamford Bridge. Ches W 4G **83**
Stamford Bridge. E Yor 4B **100**
Stamfordham. Nmbd 2D **115**
Stamperland. E Ren 4G **127**
Stanah. Lanc 5C **96**
Stanborough. Herts 4C **52**
Stanbridge. C Beds 3H **51**
Stanbridge. Dors 2F **15**
Stanbury. W Yor 1A **92**
Stand. N Lan 3A **128**
Standburn. Falk 2C **128**
Standeford. Staf 5D **72**
Standen. Kent 1C **28**
Standen Street. Kent 2C **28**
Standerwick. Som 1D **22**
Standford. Hants 3G **25**
Standford Bridge. Telf 3B **72**
Standingstone. Cumb 5D **112**
Standish. Glos 5D **48**
Standish. G Man 3D **90**
Standish Lower Ground.
G Man 4D **90**
Standlake. Oxon 5B **50**
Standon. Hants 4C **24**
Standon. Herts 3D **53**
Standon. Staf 2C **72**
Standon Green End. Herts 4D **52**
Stane. N Lan 4B **128**
Stanecastle. N Ayr 1C **116**
Stanfield. Norf 3B **78**
Stanford. C Beds 1B **52**
Stanford. Kent 2F **29**
Stanford Bishop. Here 5A **60**
Stanford Bridge. Worc 4B **60**
Stanford Dingley. W Ber 4D **36**
Stanford in the Vale. Oxon 2B **36**
Stanford on Avon. Nptn 3C **62**
Stanford on Soar. Notts 3C **74**
Stanford on Teme. Worc 4B **60**
Stanford Rivers. Essx 5F **53**
Stanfree. Derbs 3B **86**
Stanghow. Red C 3D **107**
Stanground. Pet 1B **64**
Stanhoe. Norf 2H **77**
Stanhope. Dur 1C **104**
Stanhope. Bord 1D **118**
Stanion. Nptn 2G **63**
Stanley. Derbs 1B **74**
Stanley. Dur 4E **115**
Stanley. Per 5A **144**
Stanley. Shrp 2B **60**

Stanley. Staf 5D **84**
Stanley. W Yor 2D **92**
Stanley Common. Derbs 1B **74**
Stanley Crook. Dur 1E **105**
Stanley Hill. Here 1B **48**
Stanlow. Ches W 3G **83**
Stanmore. G Lon 1C **38**
Stanmore. Hants 4C **24**
Stanmore. W Ber 4C **36**
Stannersburn. Nmbd 1A **114**
Stanningfield. Suff 5A **66**
Stannington. Nmbd 2F **115**
Stannington. S Yor 2H **85**
Stansbatch. Here 4F **59**
Stansfield. Suff 5G **65**
Stanshope. Staf 5F **85**
Stanstead. Suff 1B **54**
Stanstead Abbotts. Herts 4D **53**
Stansted. Kent 4H **39**
Stansted (London) Airport.
Essx . . . . .3F **53** & **216**
Stansted Mountfitchet.
Essx 3F **53**
Stanthorne. Ches W 4A **84**
Stanton. Derbs 4G **73**
Stanton. Glos 2F **49**
Stanton. Nmbd 5F **121**
Stanton. Staf 1F **73**
Stanton. Suff 3B **66**
Stanton by Bridge. Derbs 3A **74**
Stanton by Dale. Derbs 2B **74**
Stanton Chare. Suff 3B **66**
Stanton Drew. Bath 5A **34**
Stanton Fitzwarren. Swin 2G **35**
Stanton Harcourt. Oxon 5C **50**
Stanton Hill. Notts 4B **86**
Stanton in Peak. Derbs 4G **85**
Stanton Lacy. Shrp 3G **59**
Stanton Long. Shrp 1H **59**
Stanton-on-the-Wolds. Notts . . .2D **74**
Stanton Prior. Bath 5B **34**
Stanton St Bernard. Wilts 5F **35**
Stanton St John. Oxon 5D **50**
Stanton St Quintin. Wilts 4E **35**
Stanton Street. Suff 4B **66**
Stanton under Bardon. Leics . . .4B **74**
Stanton upon Hine Heath.
Shrp 3H **71**
Stanton Wick. Bath 5B **34**
Stanwardine in the Fields.
Shrp 3G **71**
Stanwardine in the Wood.
Shrp 3G **71**
Stanway. Essx 3C **54**
Stanway. Glos 2F **49**
Stanwell. Surr 3B **38**
Stanwell Moor. Surr 3B **38**
Stanwick. Nptn 3G **63**
Stanydale. Shet 6D **173**
Staoinebrig. W Isl 5C **170**
Stape. N Yor 5E **107**
Stapehill. Dors 2F **15**
Stapeley. Ches E 1A **72**
Stapenhill. Staf 3G **73**
Staple. Kent 5G **41**
Staple Cross. Devn 4D **20**
Staplecross. E Sus 3B **28**
Staplefield. W Sus 3D **27**
Staple Fitzpaine. Som 1F **13**
Stapleford. Cambs 5D **64**
Stapleford. Herts 4D **52**
Stapleford. Leics 4F **75**
Stapleford. Linc 5F **87**
Stapleford. Notts 2B **74**
Stapleford. Wilts 3F **23**
Stapleford Abbotts. Essx 1G **39**
Stapleford Tawney. Essx 1G **39**
Staplegrove. Som 4F **21**
Staplehay. Som 4F **21**
Staple Hill. S Glo 4B **34**
Staplehurst. Kent 1B **28**
Staplers. IOW 4D **16**
Stapleton. Bris 4B **34**
Stapleton. Cumb 2G **113**
Stapleton. Here 4F **59**
Stapleton. Leics 1B **62**
Stapleton. N Yor 3F **105**
Stapleton. Shrp 5G **71**
Stapleton. Som 4H **21**
Stapley. Som 1E **13**
Staploe. Bed 4A **64**
Staplow. Here 1B **48**
Star. Fife 3F **137**
Star. Pemb 1G **43**
Starbeck. N Yor 4F **99**
Starbotton. N Yor 2B **98**
Starcross. Devn 4C **12**
Stareton. Warw 3H **61**
Starkholmes. Derbs 5H **85**
Starling. G Man 3F **91**
Starling's Green. Essx 2E **53**
Starston. Norf 2E **67**
Start. Devn 4E **9**
Startforth. Dur 3D **104**
Start Hill. Essx 3F **53**
Startley. Wilts 3E **35**
Stathe. Som 4G **21**
Stathern. Leics 2E **75**
Station Town. Dur 1B **106**
Staughton Green. Cambs 4A **64**
Staughton Highway. Cambs . . .4A **64**

Staunton. Glos 3C **48**
(nr. Cheltenham)
Staunton. Glos 4A **48**
(nr. Monmouth)
Staunton in the Vale. Notts 1F **75**
Staunton on Arrow. Here 4F **59**
Staunton on Wye. Here 1G **47**
Staveley. Cumb 5F **103**
Staveley. Derbs 3B **86**
Staveley. N Yor 3F **99**
Staveley-in-Cartmel. Cumb 1C **96**
Staverton. Devn 2D **9**
Staverton. Glos 3D **49**
Staverton. Nptn 4C **62**
Staverton. Wilts 5D **34**
Stawell. Som 3G **21**
Stawley. Som 4D **20**
Staxigoe. High 3F **169**
Staxton. N Yor 2E **101**
Staylittle. Powy 1A **58**
Staynall. Lanc 5C **96**
Staythorpe. Notts 5E **87**
Stean. N Yor 2C **98**
Stearsby. N Yor 2A **100**
Steart. Som 2F **21**
Stebbing. Essx 3G **53**
Stebbing Green. Essx 3G **53**
Stedham. W Sus 4G **25**
Steel. Nmbd 4C **114**
Steel Cross. E Sus 2G **27**
Steelend. Fife 4C **136**
Steele Road. Bord 5H **119**
Steel Heath. Shrp 2H **71**
Steen's Bridge. Here 5H **59**
Steep. Hants 4F **25**
Steep Lane. W Yor 2A **92**
Steeple. Dors 4E **15**
Steeple. Essx 5C **54**
Steeple Ashton. Wilts 1E **23**
Steeple Aston. Oxon 3C **50**
Steeple Barton. Oxon 3C **50**
Steeple Bumpstead. Essx 1G **53**
Steeple Claydon. Buck 3E **51**
Steeple Gidding. Cambs 2A **64**
Steeple Langford. Wilts 3F **23**
Steeple Morden. Cambs 1C **52**
Steeton. W Yor 5C **98**
Stein. High 3B **154**
Steinmanhill. Abers 4E **161**
Stelling Minnis. Kent 1F **29**
Stembridge. Som 4H **21**
Stemster. High 2D **169**
(nr. Halkirk)
Stemster. High 2C **168**
(nr. Westfield)
Stenalees. Corn 3E **6**
Stenhill. Devn 1D **12**
Stenhouse. Edin 2F **129**
Stenhousemuir. Falk 1B **128**
Stenigot. Linc 2B **88**
Stenscholl. High 2D **155**
Stenso. Orkn 5C **172**
Stenson. Derbs 3H **73**
Stenson Fields. Derbs 2H **73**
Stenton. E Lot 2C **130**
Stenwith. Linc 2F **75**
Steòrnabhagh. W Isl 4G **171**
Stepaside. Pemb 4F **43**
Stepford. Dum 1F **111**
Stepney. G Lon 2E **39**
Steppingley. C Beds 2A **52**
Stepps. N Lan 3H **127**
Sterndale Moor. Derbs 4F **85**
Sternfield. Suff 4F **67**
Stert. Wilts 1F **23**
Stetchworth. Cambs 5F **65**
Stevenage. Herts 3C **52**
Stevenston. N Ayr 5D **126**
Steventon. Hants 2D **24**
Steventon. Oxon 2C **36**
Steventon End. Cambs 1G **53**
Stevington. Bed 5G **63**
Stewartby. Bed 1A **52**
Stewarton. Arg 4A **122**
Stewarton. E Ayr 5F **127**
Stewkley. Buck 3G **51**
Stewkley Dean. Buck 3G **51**
Stewley. Som 1G **13**
Stewton. Linc 2C **88**
Steynton. W Sus 4C **26**
Steynton. Pemb 4D **42**
Stibb. Corn 1C **10**
Stibbard. Norf 3B **78**
Stibb Cross. Devn 1E **11**
Stibb Green. Wilts 5H **35**
Stibbington. Cambs 1H **63**
Stichill. Bord 1B **120**
Sticker. Corn 3D **6**
Stickford. Linc 4C **88**
Sticklepath. Devn 3G **11**
Sticklinch. Som 3A **22**
Stickling Green. Essx 2E **53**
Stickney. Linc 5C **88**
Stiffkey. Norf 1B **78**
Stifford's Bridge. Here 1C **48**
Stileway. Som 2H **21**
Stillingfleet. N Yor 5H **99**
Stillington. N Yor 3H **99**
Stillington. Stoc T 2A **106**
Stilton. Cambs 2A **64**
Stinchcombe. Glos 2C **34**

Stinsford. Dors 3C **14**
Stiperstones. Shrp 5F **71**
Stirchley. Telf 5B **72**
Stirchley. W Mid 2E **61**
Stirling. Abers 4H **161**
Stirling. Stir . . . . . .4G **135** & **211**
Stirton. N Yor 4B **98**
Stisted. Essx 3A **54**
Stitchcombe. Wilts 5H **35**
Stithians. Corn 5B **6**
Stittenham. High 1A **158**
Stivichall. W Mid 3H **61**
Stixwould. Linc 4A **88**
Stoak. Ches W 3G **83**
Stobo. Bord 1D **118**
Stobo Castle. Bord 1D **118**
Stoborough. Dors 4E **15**
Stoborough Green. Dors 4E **15**
Stobs Castle. Bord 4H **119**
Stobswood. Nmbd 5G **121**
Stock. Essx 1A **40**
Stockbridge. Hants 3B **24**
Stockbridge. W Yor 5C **98**
Stockbury. Kent 4C **40**
Stockcross. W Ber 5C **36**
Stockdalewath. Cumb 5E **113**
Stocker's Head. Kent 5D **40**
Stockerston. Leics 1F **63**
Stock Green. Worc 5D **61**
Stocking. Here 2B **48**
Stockingford. Warw 1H **61**
Stocking Green. Essx 2F **53**
Stocking Pelham. Herts 3E **53**
Stockland. Devn 2F **13**
Stockland Bristol. Som 2F **21**
Stockleigh English. Devn 2B **12**
Stockleigh Pomeroy. Devn 2B **12**
Stockley. Wilts 5F **35**
Stocklinch. Som 1G **13**
Stockport. G Man 2D **84**
Stocksbridge. S Yor 1G **85**
Stocksfield. Nmbd 3D **114**
Stocks, The. Kent 3D **28**
Stockstreet. Essx 3B **54**
Stockton. Here 4H **59**
Stockton. Norf 1F **67**
Stockton. Shrp 1B **60**
(nr. Bridgnorth)
Stockton. Shrp 5E **71**
(nr. Chirbury)
Stockton. Telf 4B **72**
Stockton. Warw 4B **62**
Stockton. Wilts 3E **23**
Stockton Brook. Staf 5D **84**
Stockton Cross. Here 4H **59**
Stockton Heath. Warr 2A **84**
Stockton-on-Tees. Stoc T 3B **106**
Stockton on Teme. Worc 4B **60**
Stockton-on-the-Forest.
York 4A **100**
Stockwell Heath. Staf 3E **73**
Stockwood. Bris 5B **34**
Stock Wood. Worc 5E **61**
Stodmarsh. Kent 4G **41**
Stody. Norf 2C **78**
Stoer. High 1E **163**
Stoford. Som 1A **14**
Stoford. Wilts 3F **23**
Stogumber. Som 3D **20**
Stogursey. Som 2F **21**
Stoke. Devn 4C **18**
Stoke. Hants 1C **24**
(nr. Andover)
Stoke. Hants 2F **17**
(nr. South Hayling)
Stoke. Medw 3C **40**
Stoke. W Mid 3A **62**
Stoke Abbott. Dors 2H **13**
Stoke Albany. Nptn 2F **63**
Stoke Ash. Suff 3D **66**
Stoke Bardolph. Notts 1D **74**
Stoke Bliss. Worc 4A **60**
Stoke Bruerne. Nptn 1F **51**
Stoke by Clare. Suff 1H **53**
Stoke-by-Nayland. Suff 2C **54**
Stoke Canon. Devn 3C **12**
Stoke Charity. Hants 3C **24**
Stoke Climsland. Corn 5D **10**
Stoke Cross. Here 5A **60**
Stoke D'Abernon. Surr 5C **38**
Stoke Doyle. Nptn 2H **63**
Stoke Dry. Rut 1F **63**
Stoke Edith. Here 1B **48**
Stoke Farthing. Wilts 4F **23**
Stoke Ferry. Norf 1G **65**
Stoke Fleming. Devn 4E **9**
Stokeford. Dors 4D **14**
Stoke Gabriel. Devn 3E **9**
Stoke Gifford. S Glo 4B **34**
Stoke Golding. Leics 1A **62**
Stoke Goldington. Mil 1G **51**
Stokeham. Notts 3E **87**
Stoke Hammond. Buck 3G **51**
Stoke Heath. Shrp 3A **72**
Stoke Holy Cross. Norf 5E **79**
Stokeinteignhead. Devn 5C **12**
Stoke Lacy. Here 1B **48**
Stoke Lyne. Oxon 3D **50**
Stoke Mandeville. Buck 4G **51**
Stokenchurch. Buck 2F **37**
Stoke Newington. G Lon 2E **39**
Stokenham. Devn 4E **9**

Stoke on Tern. Shrp ...3A 72
Stoke-on-Trent. Stoke ...1C 72 & 211
Stoke Orchard. Glos ...3E 49
Stoke Pero. Som ...2B 20
Stoke Poges. Buck ...2A 38
Stoke Prior. Here ...5H 59
Stoke Prior. Worc ...4D 60
Stoke Rivers. Devn ...3G 19
Stoke Rochford. Linc ...3G 75
Stoke Row. Oxon ...3E 37
Stoke St Gregory. Som ...4G 21
Stoke St Mary. Som ...4F 21
Stoke St Michael. Som ...2B 22
Stoke St Milborough. Shrp ...2H 59
Stokesay. Shrp ...2G 59
Stokesby. Norf ...4G 79
Stokesley. N Yor ...4C 106
Stoke sub Hamdon. Som ...1H 13
Stoke Talmage. Oxon ...2E 37
Stoke Town. Stoke ...1C 72 & 211
Stoke Trister. Som ...4C 22
Stoke Wake. Dors ...2C 14
Stolford. Som ...2F 21
Stondon Massey. Essx ...5F 53
Stone. Buck ...4F 51
Stone. Glos ...2B 34
Stone. Kent ...3G 39
Stone. Som ...3A 22
Stone. Staf ...2D 72
Stone. Worc ...3C 60
Stonea. Cambs ...1D 64
Stoneacton. Shrp ...1H 59
Stone Allerton. Som ...1H 21
Ston Easton. Som ...1B 22
Stonebridge. N Som ...1G 21
Stonebridge. Som ...2C 22
Stonebridge. Surr ...1C 26
Stone Bridge Corner. Pet ...5B 76
Stonebroom. Derbs ...5B 86
Stonebyres. S Lan ...5B 128
Stone Chair. W Yor ...2B 92
Stone Cross. E Sus ...5H 27
Stone Cross. Kent ...2G 27
Stone-edge-Batch. N Som ...4H 33
Stoneferry. Hull ...1D 94
Stonefield. Arg ...5D 140
Stonefield. S Lan ...4H 127
Stonegate. E Sus ...3A 28
Stonegate. N Yor ...4E 107
Stonegrave. N Yor ...2A 100
Stonehall. Worc ...1D 49
Stonehaugh. Nmbd ...2A 114
Stonehaven. Abers ...5F 153
Stone Heath. Staf ...2D 72
Stone Hill. Kent ...2E 29
Stone House. Cumb ...1G 97
Stonehouse. Glos ...5D 48
Stonehouse. Nmbd ...4H 113
Stonehouse. S Lan ...5A 128
Stone in Oxney. Kent ...3D 28
Stoneleigh. Warw ...3H 61
Stoneley Green. Ches E ...5A 84
Stonely. Cambs ...4A 64
Stonepits. Worc ...5E 61
Stoner Hill. Hants ...4F 25
Stonesby. Leics ...3F 75
Stonesfield. Oxon ...4B 50
Stones Green. Essx ...3E 55
Stone Street. Kent ...5G 39
Stone Street. Suff ...2C 54
(nr. Boxford)
Stone Street. Suff ...2F 67
(nr. Halesworth)
Stonethwaite. Cumb ...3D 102
Stoneyburn. W Lot ...3C 128
Stoney Cross. Hants ...1A 16
Stoneyford. Devn ...2D 12
Stoneygate. Leic ...5D 74
Stoneyhills. Essx ...1D 40
Stoneykirk. Dum ...4F 109
Stoney Middleton. Derbs ...3G 85
Stoney Stanton. Leics ...1B 62
Stoney Stratton. Som ...3B 22
Stoney Stretton. Shrp ...5F 71
Stoneywood. Aber ...2F 153
Stonham Aspal. Suff ...5D 66
Stonnall. Staf ...5E 73
Stonor. Oxon ...3F 37
Stonton Wyville. Leics ...1E 63
Stonybreck. Shet ...1B 172
Stony Cross. Devn ...4F 19
Stony Cross. Here ...1C 48
(nr. Great Malvern)
Stony Cross. Here ...4H 59
(nr. Leominster)
Stony Houghton. Derbs ...4B 86
Stony Stratford. Mil ...1F 51
Stoodleigh. Devn ...3G 19
(nr. Barnstaple)
Stoodleigh. Devn ...1C 12
(nr. Tiverton)
Stopham. W Sus ...4B 26
Stopsley. Lutn ...3B 52
Stoptide. Corn ...1D 6
Storeton. Mers ...2F 83
Stormontfield. Per ...1D 136
Stornoway. W Isl ...4G 171
Stornoway Airport. W Isl ...4G 171
Storridge. Here ...1C 48
Storrington. W Sus ...4B 26

Storrs. Cumb ...5E 103
Storth. Cumb ...1D 97
Storwood. E Yor ...5B 100
Stotfield. Mor ...1G 159
Stotfold. C Beds ...2C 52
Stottesdon. Shrp ...2A 60
Stoughton. Leics ...5D 74
Stoughton. Surr ...5A 38
Stoughton. W Sus ...1G 17
Stoul. High ...4F 147
Stoulton. Worc ...1E 49
Stourbridge. W Mid ...2C 60
Stourpaine. Dors ...2D 14
Stourport-on-Severn. Worc ...3C 60
Stour Provost. Dors ...4C 22
Stour Row. Dors ...4D 22
Stourton. Staf ...2C 60
Stourton. Warw ...2A 50
Stourton. W Yor ...1D 92
Stourton. Wilts ...3C 22
Stourton Caundle. Dors ...1C 14
Stove. Orkn ...4F 172
Stove. Shet ...9F 173
Stoven. Suff ...2G 67
Stow. Linc ...2H 75
(nr. Billingborough)
Stow. Linc ...2F 87
(nr. Gainsborough)
Stow. Bord ...5A 130
Stow Bardolph. Norf ...5F 77
Stow Bedon. Norf ...1B 66
Stowbridge. Norf ...5F 77
Stow cum Quy. Cambs ...4E 65
Stowe. Glos ...5A 48
Stowe. Shrp ...3F 59
Stowe. Staf ...4F 73
Stowe-by-Chartley. Staf ...3E 73
Stowell. Som ...4B 22
Stowey. Bath ...1A 22
Stowford. Devn ...4E 11
(nr. Combe Martin)
Stowford. Devn ...4D 12
(nr. Exmouth)
Stowford. Devn ...4E 11
(nr. Tavistock)
Stowlangtoft. Suff ...4B 66
Stow Longa. Cambs ...3A 64
Stow Maries. Essx ...1C 40
Stowmarket. Suff ...5C 66
Stow-on-the-Wold. Glos ...3G 49
Stowting. Kent ...1F 29
Stowupland. Suff ...5C 66
Straad. Arg ...3B 126
Strachan. Abers ...4D 152
Stradbroke. Suff ...3E 67
Stradbrook. Wilts ...1E 23
Stradishall. Suff ...5G 65
Stradsett. Norf ...5F 77
Stragglethorpe. Linc ...5G 87
Stragglethorpe. Notts ...2D 74
Straid. S Ayr ...5A 116
Straight Soley. Wilts ...4B 36
Straiton. Edin ...3F 129
Straiton. S Ayr ...4C 116
Straloch. Per ...2H 143
Stramshall. Staf ...2E 73
Strang. IOM ...4C 108
Strangford. Here ...3A 48
Stranraer. Dum ...3F 109
Strata Florida. Cdgn ...4G 57
Stratfield Mortimer. W Ber ...5E 37
Stratfield Saye. Hants ...5E 37
Stratfield Turgis. Hants ...1E 25
Stratford. Glos ...2D 49
Stratford. G Lon ...2E 39
Stratford St Andrew. Suff ...4F 67
Stratford St Mary. Suff ...2D 54
Stratford sub Castle. Wilts ...3G 23
Stratford Tony. Wilts ...4G 23
Stratford-upon-Avon.
Warw ...5G 61 & 212
Strath. High ...1G 155
(nr. Gairloch)
Strath. High ...3E 169
(nr. Wick)
Strathan. High ...4D 148
(nr. Fort William)
Strathan. High ...1E 163
(nr. Lochinver)
Strathan. High ...2F 167
(nr. Tongue)
Strathan Skerray. High ...2G 167
Strathaven. S Lan ...5A 128
Strathblane. Stir ...2G 127
Strathcanaird. High ...3F 163
Strathcarron. High ...4B 156
Strathcoil. Arg ...5A 140
Strathdon. Abers ...2A 152
Strathkinness. Fife ...2G 137
Strathmashie House. High ...4H 149
Strathmiglo. Fife ...2E 136
Strathmore Lodge. High ...4D 168
Strathpeffer. High ...3G 157
Strathrannoch. High ...1F 157
Strathtay. Per ...3G 143
Strathvaich Lodge. High ...1F 157
Strathwhillan. N Ayr ...2E 123
Strathy. High ...1A 158
(nr. Invergordon)
Strathy. High ...2A 168
(nr. Melvich)

Strathyre. Stir ...2E 135
Stratton. Corn ...2C 10
Stratton. Dors ...3B 14
Stratton. Glos ...5F 49
Stratton Audley. Oxon ...3E 50
Stratton-on-the-Fosse. Som ...1B 22
Stratton St Margaret. Swin ...3G 35
Stratton St Michael. Norf ...1E 66
Stratton Strawless. Norf ...3E 78
Stravithie. Fife ...2H 137
Stream. Som ...3D 20
Streat. E Sus ...4E 27
Streatham. G Lon ...3D 39
Streatley. C Beds ...3A 52
Streatley. W Ber ...3D 36
Street. Corn ...3C 10
Street. Lanc ...4E 97
Street. N Yor ...4E 107
Street. Som ...2G 13
(nr. Chard)
Street. Som ...3H 21
(nr. Glastonbury)
Street Ash. Som ...1F 13
Street Dinas. Shrp ...2F 71
Street End. Kent ...5F 41
Street End. W Sus ...3G 17
Street Gate. Tyne ...4F 115
Streethay. Staf ...4F 73
Streethouse. W Yor ...3D 93
Streetlam. N Yor ...5A 106
Street Lane. Derbs ...1A 74
Streetly. W Mid ...1E 61
Streetly End. Cambs ...1G 53
Street on the Fosse. Som ...3A 22
Strefford. Shrp ...2G 59
Strelley. Notts ...1C 74
Strensall. York ...3A 100
Strensall Camp. York ...4A 100
Stretcholt. Som ...2F 21
Strete. Devn ...4E 9
Stretford. G Man ...1C 84
Stretford. Here ...5H 59
Strethall. Essx ...2E 53
Stretham. Cambs ...3E 65
Stretton. Ches W ...5G 83
Stretton. Derbs ...4A 86
Stretton. Rut ...4G 75
Stretton. Staf ...4C 72
(nr. Brewood)
Stretton. Staf ...3G 73
(nr. Burton upon Trent)
Stretton. Warw ...2A 84
Stretton en le Field. Leics ...4H 73
Stretton Grandison. Here ...1B 48
Stretton Heath. Shrp ...4F 71
Stretton-on-Dunsmore. Warw ...3B 62
Stretton-on-Fosse. Warw ...2H 49
Stretton Sugwas. Here ...1H 47
Stretton under Fosse. Warw ...2B 62
Stretton Westwood. Shrp ...1H 59
Strichen. Abers ...3G 161
Strines. G Man ...2D 84
Stringston. Som ...2E 21
Strixton. Nptn ...4G 63
Stroanfreggan. Dum ...5F 117
Stroat. Glos ...2A 34
Stromeferry. High ...5A 156
Stromemore. High ...5A 156
Stromness. Orkn ...7B 172
Stronachie. Per ...3C 136
Stronachlachar. Stir ...2D 134
Stronchreggan. High ...1E 141
Strone. Arg ...1C 126
Strone. High ...1H 149
(nr. Drumnadrochit)
Strone. High ...3B 150
(nr. Kingussie)
Stronenaba. High ...5E 148
Stronganess. Shet ...1G 173
Stronmilchan. Arg ...1A 134
Stronsay Airport. Orkn ...5F 172
Strontian. High ...2C 140
Strood. Kent ...2C 28
Strood. Medw ...4B 40
Strood Green. Surr ...1D 26
Strood Green. W Sus ...3B 26
(nr. Billingshurst)
Strood Green. W Sus ...2C 26
(nr. Horsham)
Strothers Dale. Nmbd ...4C 114
Stroud. Glos ...5D 48
Stroud. Hants ...4F 25
Stroud Green. Essx ...1C 40
Stroxton. Linc ...2G 75
Struan. High ...5C 154
Struan. Per ...2F 143
Struanmore. High ...5C 154
Strubby. Linc ...2D 88
Strugg's Hill. Linc ...2B 76
Strumpshaw. Norf ...5F 79
Strutherhill. S Lan ...4A 128
Struy. High ...5F 157
Stryd. IOA ...2B 80
Stryt-issa. Wrex ...1E 71
Stuartfield. Abers ...4G 161
Stubbington. Hants ...2D 16
Stubbins. Lanc ...3F 91
Stubble Green. Cumb ...5B 102
Stubb's Cross. Kent ...2D 28
Stubbs Green. Norf ...1F 67
Stubhampton. Dors ...1E 15

Stubton. Linc ...1F 75
Stubwood. Staf ...2E 73
Stuckton. Hants ...1G 15
Studham. C Beds ...4A 52
Studland. Dors ...4F 15
Studley. Warw ...4E 61
Studley. Wilts ...4E 35
Studley Roger. N Yor ...3E 99
Stuntney. Cambs ...3E 65
Stunts Green. E Sus ...4H 27
Sturbridge. Staf ...2C 72
Sturgate. Linc ...2F 87
Sturmer. Essx ...1G 53
Sturminster Marshall. Dors ...2E 15
Sturminster Newton. Dors ...1C 14
Sturry. Kent ...4F 41
Sturton. N Lin ...4C 94
Sturton by Stow. Linc ...2F 87
Sturton le Steeple. Notts ...2E 87
Stuston. Suff ...3D 66
Stutton. N Yor ...5G 99
Stutton. Suff ...2E 55
Styal. Ches E ...2C 84
Stydd. Lanc ...1E 91
Styrrup. Notts ...1D 86
Suainebost. W Isl ...1H 171
Suardail. W Isl ...4G 171
Succoth. Abers ...5B 160
Succoth. Arg ...3B 134
Suckley. Worc ...5B 60
Suckley Knowl. Worc ...5B 60
Sudborough. Nptn ...2G 63
Sudbourne. Suff ...5G 67
Sudbrook. Linc ...1G 75
Sudbrook. Mon ...3A 34
Sudbrooke. Linc ...3H 87
Sudbury. Derbs ...2F 73
Sudbury. Suff ...1B 54
Sudgrove. Glos ...5E 49
Suffield. Norf ...2E 79
Suffield. N Yor ...5G 107
Sugnall. Staf ...2B 72
Sugwas Pool. Here ...1H 47
Suisnish. High ...5E 155
Sulaisiadar. W Isl ...4H 171
Sùlaisiadar Mòr. High ...4D 155
Sulby. IOM ...2C 108
Sulgrave. Nptn ...1D 50
Sulham. W Ber ...4E 37
Sulhamstead. W Ber ...5E 37
Sullington. W Sus ...4B 26
Sullom. Shet ...4E 173
Sully. V Glam ...5E 33
Sumburgh. Shet ...10F 173
Sumburgh Airport. Shet ...10E 173
Summer Bridge. N Yor ...3E 98
Summercourt. Corn ...3C 6
Summergangs. Hull ...1E 94
Summerhill. Aber ...3G 153
Summerhill. Pemb ...4F 43
Summer Hill. W Mid ...1D 60
Summerhouse. Darl ...3F 105
Summersdale. W Sus ...2G 17
Summerseat. G Man ...3F 91
Summit. G Man ...3H 91
Sunbury. Surr ...4C 38
Sunderland. Cumb ...1C 102
Sunderland. Lanc ...4D 96
Sunderland. Tyne ...4G 115 & 212
Sunderland Bridge. Dur ...1F 105
Sundon Park. Lutn ...3A 52
Sundridge. Kent ...5F 39
Sunk Island. E Yor ...3F 95
Sunningdale. Wind ...4A 38
Sunninghill. Wind ...4A 38
Sunningwell. Oxon ...5C 50
Sunniside. Dur ...1E 105
Sunniside. Tyne ...4F 115
Sunny Bank. Cumb ...5D 102
Sunny Hill. Derb ...2H 73
Sunnyhurst. Bkbn ...2E 91
Sunnylaw. Stir ...4G 135
Sunnymead. Oxon ...5D 50
Sunnyside. S Yor ...1B 86
Sunnyside. W Sus ...2E 27
Sunton. Wilts ...1H 23
Surbiton. G Lon ...4C 38
Surby. IOM ...4B 108
Surfleet. Linc ...3B 76
Surfleet Seas End. Linc ...3B 76
Surlingham. Norf ...5F 79
Surrex. Essx ...3B 54
Sustead. Norf ...2D 78
Susworth. Linc ...4B 94
Sutcombe. Devn ...1D 10
Suton. Norf ...1C 66
Sutors of Cromarty. High ...2C 158
Sutterby. Linc ...3D 88
Sutterton. Linc ...2B 76
Sutterton Dowdyke. Linc ...2B 76
Sutton. Buck ...3B 38
Sutton. Cambs ...3D 64
Sutton. C Beds ...1C 52
Sutton. G Lon ...4D 38
Sutton. Kent ...1H 29
Sutton. Norf ...3F 79
Sutton. Notts ...2E 75
Sutton. Oxon ...5C 50
Sutton. Pemb ...3D 42
Sutton. Pet ...1H 63

Sutton. Shrp ...2B 60
(nr. Bridgnorth)
Sutton. Shrp ...2A 72
(nr. Market Drayton)
Sutton. Shrp ...3F 71
(nr. Oswestry)
Sutton. Shrp ...4H 71
(nr. Shrewsbury)
Sutton. Som ...3B 22
Sutton. S Yor ...3F 93
Sutton. Staf ...3B 72
Sutton. Suff ...1G 55
Sutton. W Sus ...4A 26
Sutton. W Sus ...4A 60
Sutton Abinger. Surr ...1C 26
Sutton at Hone. Kent ...4G 39
Sutton Bassett. Nptn ...1E 63
Sutton Benger. Wilts ...4E 35
Sutton Bingham. Som ...1A 14
Sutton Bonington. Notts ...3C 74
Sutton Bridge. Linc ...3D 76
Sutton Cheney. Leics ...5B 74
Sutton Coldfield. W Mid ...1F 61
Sutton Corner. Linc ...3D 76
Sutton Courtenay. Oxon ...2D 36
Sutton Crosses. Linc ...3D 76
Sutton cum Lound. Notts ...2D 86
Sutton Gault. Cambs ...3D 64
Sutton Grange. N Yor ...2E 99
Sutton Green. Surr ...5B 38
Sutton Howgrave. N Yor ...2F 99
Sutton in Ashfield. Notts ...5B 86
Sutton-in-Craven. N Yor ...5C 98
Sutton Ings. Hull ...1E 94
Sutton in the Elms. Leics ...1C 62
Sutton Lane Ends. Ches E ...3D 84
Sutton Leach. Mers ...1H 83
Sutton Maddock. Shrp ...5B 72
Sutton Mallet. Som ...3G 21
Sutton Mandeville. Wilts ...4E 23
Sutton Montis. Som ...4B 22
Sutton-on-Hull. Hull ...1E 94
Sutton on Sea. Linc ...2E 89
Sutton-on-the-Forest. N Yor ...3H 99
Sutton on the Hill. Derbs ...2G 73
Sutton on Trent. Notts ...4E 87
Sutton Poyntz. Dors ...4C 14
Sutton St Edmund. Linc ...4C 76
Sutton St Edmund's Common.
Linc ...5C 76
Sutton St James. Linc ...4C 76
Sutton St Michael. Here ...1A 48
Sutton St Nicholas. Here ...1A 48
Sutton Scarsdale. Derbs ...4B 86
Sutton Scotney. Hants ...3C 24
Sutton-under-Brailes. Warw ...2B 50
Sutton-under-Whitestonecliffe.
N Yor ...1G 99
Sutton upon Derwent. E Yor ...5B 100
Sutton Valence. Kent ...1C 28
Sutton Veny. Wilts ...2E 23
Sutton Waldron. Dors ...1D 14
Sutton Weaver. Ches W ...3H 83
Swaby. Linc ...3C 88
Swadlincote. Derbs ...4G 73
Swaffham. Norf ...5H 77
Swaffham Bulbeck. Cambs ...4E 65
Swaffham Prior. Cambs ...4E 65
Swafield. Norf ...2E 79
Swainby. N Yor ...4B 106
Swainshill. Here ...1H 47
Swainsthorpe. Norf ...5E 78
Swainswick. Bath ...5C 34
Swalcliffe. Oxon ...2B 50
Swalecliffe. Kent ...4F 41
Swallow. Linc ...4E 95
Swallow Beck. Linc ...4G 87
Swallowcliffe. Wilts ...4E 23
Swallowfield. Wok ...5F 37
Swallownest. S Yor ...2B 86
Swampton. Hants ...1C 24
Swanage. Dors ...5F 15
Swanbister. Orkn ...7C 172
Swanbourne. Buck ...3G 51
Swanbridge. V Glam ...5E 33
Swan Green. Ches W ...3B 84
Swanland. E Yor ...2C 94
Swanley. Kent ...4G 39
Swanmore. Hants ...1D 16
Swannington. Leics ...4B 74
Swannington. Norf ...4D 78
Swanpool. Linc ...3G 87
Swanscombe. Kent ...3G 39
Swansea. Swan ...3F 31 & 212
Swansmoor. Staf ...3E 73
Swan Street. Essx ...3B 54
Swanton Abbott. Norf ...3E 79
Swanton Morley. Norf ...4C 78
Swanton Novers. Norf ...2C 78
Swanton Street. Kent ...5C 40
Swanwick. Derbs ...5B 86
Swanwick. Hants ...2D 16
Swanwick Green. Ches E ...1H 71
Swarby. Linc ...1H 75
Swardeston. Norf ...5E 78
Swarister. Shet ...3G 173
Swarkestone. Derbs ...3A 74
Swarland. Nmbd ...4F 121
Swarraton. Hants ...3D 24
Swartha. W Yor ...5C 98
Swarthmoor. Cumb ...2B 96

Swaton—Thornton Steward

Swaton. *Linc* 2A 76
Swavesey. *Cambs* 4C 64
Sway. *Hants* 3A 16
Swayfield. *Linc* 3G 75
Swaythling. *Sotn* 1C 16
Sweet Green. *Worc* 4A 60
Sweetham. *Devn* 3B 12
Sweetholme. *Cumb* 3G 103
Sweets. *Corn* 3B 10
Sweetshouse. *Corn* 2E 7
Swefling. *Suff* 4F 67
Swell. *Som* 4G 21
Swepstone. *Leics* 4A 74
Swerford. *Oxon* 2B 50
Swettenham. *Ches E* 4C 84
Swetton. *N Yor* 2D 98
Swffryd. *Cphy* 2F 33
Swiftsden. *E Sus* 3B 28
Swilland. *Suff* 5D 66
Swillington. *W Yor* 1D 93
Swimbridge. *Devn* 4G 19
Swimbridge Newland. *Devn* 3G 19
Swinbrook. *Oxon* 4A 50
Swincliffe. *N Yor* 4E 99
Swincliffe. *W Yor* 2C 92
Swinderby. *Linc* 4F 87
Swindon. *Glos* 3E 49
Swindon. *Nmbd* 5D 121
Swindon. *Staf* 1C 60
Swindon. *Swin* 3G 35 & 212
Swine. *E Yor* 1E 95
Swinefleet. *E Yor* 2A 94
Swineford. *S Glo* 5B 34
Swineshead. *Bed* 4H 63
Swineshead. *Linc* 1B 76
Swineshead Bridge. *Linc* 1B 76
Swiney. *High* 5E 169
Swinford. *Leics* 3C 62
Swinford. *Oxon* 5C 50
Swingate. *Notts* 1C 74
Swingbrow. *Cambs* 2C 64
Swingfield Minnis. *Kent* 1G 29
Swingfield Street. *Kent* 1G 29
Swingleton Green. *Suff* 1C 54
Swinhill. *S Lan* 5A 128
Swinhoe. *Nmbd* 2G 121
Swinhope. *Linc* 1B 88
Swinister. *Shet* 3E 173
Swinithwaite. *N Yor* 1C 98
Swinmore Common. *Here* 1B 48
Swinscoe. *Staf* 1F 73
Swinside Hall. *Bord* 3B 120
Swinstead. *Linc* 3H 75
Swinton. *G Man* 4F 91
Swinton. *N Yor* 2B 100
(nr. Malton)
Swinton. *N Yor* 2E 98
(nr. Masham)
Swinton. *Bord* 5E 131
Swinton. *S Yor* 1B 86
Swithland. *Leics* 4C 74
Swordale. *High* 2H 157
Swordly. *High* 2H 167
Sworton Heath. *Ches E* 2A 84
Swyddffynnon. *Cdgn* 4F 57
Swyffrd. *Cphy* 2F 33
Swynnerton. *Staf* 2C 72
Swyre. *Dors* 4A 14
Sycharth. *Powy* 3E 70
Sychdyn. *Flin* 4E 83
Sychnant. *Powy* 3B 58
Sychtyn. *Powy* 5B 70
Syde. *Glos* 4E 49
Sydenham. *G Lon* 3E 39
Sydenham. *Oxon* 5F 51
Sydenham. *Som* 3G 21
Sydenham Damerel. *Devn* 5E 11
Syderstone. *Norf* 2H 77
Sydling St Nicholas. *Dors* 3B 14
Sydmonton. *Hants* 1C 24
Sydney. *Ches E* 5B 84
Syerston. *Notts* 1E 75
Syke. *G Man* 3G 91
Sykehouse. *S Yor* 3G 93
Sykes. *Lanc* 4F 97
Syleham. *Suff* 3E 66
Sylen. *Carm* 5F 45
Sylfaen. *Powy* 5D 70
Symbister. *Shet* 5G 173
Symington. *S Ayr* 1C 116
Symington. *S Lan* 1B 118
Symondsbury. *Dors* 3H 13
Symonds Yat. *Here* 4A 48
Synod Inn. *Cdgn* 5D 56
Syre. *High* 4G 167
Syreford. *Glos* 3F 49
Syresham. *Nptn* 1E 51
Syston. *Leics* 4D 74
Syston. *Linc* 1G 75
Sytchampton. *Worc* 4C 60
Sywell. *Nptn* 4F 63

T

Tabost. *W Isl* 6F 171
(nr. Cearsiadar)
Tabost. *W Isl* 1H 171
(nr. Suainebost)
Tachbrook Mallory. *Warw* 4H 61
Tackley. *Oxon* 3C 50
Tacleit. *W Isl* 4D 171
Tacolneston. *Norf* 1D 66
Tadcaster. *N Yor* 5G 99
Taddington. *Derbs* 3F 85
Taddington. *Glos* 2F 49
Taddiport. *Devn* 1E 11
Tadley. *Hants* 5E 36
Tadlow. *Cambs* 1C 52
Tadmarton. *Oxon* 2B 50
Tadwick. *Bath* 4C 34
Tadworth. *Surr* 5D 38
Tafarnaubach. *Blae* 4E 46
Tafarn-y-bwlch. *Pemb* 1E 43
Tafarn-y-Gelyn. *Den* 4D 82
Taff's Well. *Rhon* 3E 33
Tafolwern. *Powy* 5A 70
Taibach. *Neat* 3A 32
Tai-bach. *Powy* 3D 70
Taigh a Ghearraidh. *W Isl* 1C 170
Taigh Bhuirgh. *W Isl* 8C 171
Tain. *High* 5E 165
(nr. Invergordon)
Tain. *High* 2E 169
(nr. Thurso)
Tai-Nant. *Wrex* 1E 71
Tai'n Lon. *Gwyn* 5D 80
Tairbeart. *W Isl* 8D 171
Tairgwaith. *Neat* 4H 45
Takeley. *Essx* 3F 53
Takeley Street. *Essx* 3F 53
Talachddu. *Powy* 2D 46
Talacre. *Flin* 2D 82
Talardd. *Gwyn* 3A 70
Talaton. *Devn* 3D 12
Talbenny. *Pemb* 3C 42
Talbot Green. *Rhon* 3D 32
Taleford. *Devn* 3D 12
Talerddig. *Powy* 5B 70
Talgarreg. *Cdgn* 5D 56
Talgarth. *Powy* 2E 47
Talisker. *High* 5C 154
Talke. *Staf* 5C 84
Talkin. *Cumb* 4G 113
Talladale. *High* 1B 156
Talla Linnfoots. *Bord* 2D 118
Tallaminnock. *S Ayr* 5D 116
Tallarn Green. *Wrex* 1G 71
Tallentire. *Cumb* 1C 102
Talley. *Carm* 2G 45
Tallington. *Linc* 5H 75
Talmine. *High* 2F 167
Talog. *Carm* 2H 43
Talsarn. *Carm* 3A 46
Talsarn. *Cdgn* 5E 57
Talsarnau. *Gwyn* 2F 69
Talskiddy. *Corn* 2D 6
Talwrn. *IOA* 3D 81
Talwrn. *Wrex* 1E 71
Tal-y-bont. *Cdgn* 2F 57
Tal-y-Bont. *Cnwy* 4G 81
Tal-y-bont. *Gwyn* 3F 81
(nr. Bangor)
Tal-y-bont. *Gwyn* 3E 69
(nr. Barmouth)
Talybont-on-Usk. *Powy* 3E 46
Tal-y-cafn. *Cnwy* 3G 81
Tal-y-coed. *Mon* 4H 47
Tal-y-llyn. *Gwyn* 5G 69
Talyllyn. *Powy* 3E 46
Talysarn. *Gwyn* 5D 81
Tal-y-waenydd. *Gwyn* 1F 69
Talywain. *Torf* 5F 47
Talywern. *Powy* 5H 69
Tamerton Foliot. *Plym* 2A 8
Tamworth. *Staf* 5G 73
Tamworth Green. *Linc* 1C 76
Tandlehill. *Ren* 3F 127
Tandridge. *Surr* 5E 39
Tanerdy. *Carm* 3E 45
Tanfield. *Dur* 4E 115
Tanfield Lea. *Dur* 4E 115
Tangasdale. *W Isl* 8B 170
Tang Hall. *York* 4A 100
Tangiers. *Pemb* 3D 42
Tangley. *Hants* 1B 24
Tangmere. *W Sus* 5A 26
Tangwick. *Shet* 4D 173
Tankerness. *Orkn* 7E 172
Tankersley. *S Yor* 1H 85
Tankerton. *Kent* 4F 41
Tan-lan. *Cnwy* 4G 81
Tan-lan. *Gwyn* 1F 69
Tannach. *High* 4F 169
Tannadice. *Ang* 3D 145
Tanner's Green. *Worc* 3E 61
Tannington. *Suff* 4E 67
Tannochside. *N Lan* 3A 128
Tan Office Green. *Suff* 5G 65
Tansley. *Derbs* 5H 85
Tansley Knoll. *Derbs* 4H 85
Tansor. *Nptn* 1H 63
Tantobie. *Dur* 4E 115
Tanton. *N Yor* 3C 106
Tanvats. *Linc* 4A 88
Tanworth-in-Arden. *Warw* 3F 61
Tan-y-bwlch. *Gwyn* 1F 69
Tan-y-fron. *Cnwy* 4B 82
Tanyfron. *Wrex* 5E 83
Tan-y-goes. *Cdgn* 1C 44
Tanygrisiau. *Gwyn* 1F 69
Tan-y-pistyll. *Powy* 3C 70
Tan-yr-allt. *Den* 2C 82
Taobh a Chaolais. *W Isl* 7C 170
Taobh a Deas Loch Aineort.
W Isl 6C 170
Taobh a Ghlinne. *W Isl* 6F 171
Taobh a Tuath Loch Aineort.
W Isl 6C 170
Taplow. *Buck* 2A 38
Tapton. *Derbs* 3A 86
Tarbert. *Arg* 1E 125
(on Jura)
Tarbert. *Arg* 3G 125
(on Kintyre)
Tarbert. *W Isl* 8D 171
Tarbet. *Arg* 3C 134
Tarbet. *High* 4F 147
(nr. Mallaig)
Tarbet. *High* 4B 166
(nr. Scourie)
Tarbock Green. *Mers* 2G 83
Tarbolton. *S Ayr* 2D 116
Tarbrax. *S Lan* 4D 128
Tardebigge. *Worc* 4E 61
Tarfside. *Ang* 1D 145
Tarland. *Abers* 3B 152
Tarleton. *Lanc* 2C 90
Tarlogie. *High* 5E 165
Tarlscough. *Lanc* 3C 90
Tarlton. *Glos* 2E 35
Tarnbrook. *Lanc* 4E 97
Tarnock. *Som* 1G 21
Tarns. *Cumb* 5C 112
Tarporley. *Ches W* 4H 83
Tarpots. *Essx* 2B 40
Tarr. *Som* 3E 20
Tarrant Crawford. *Dors* 2E 15
Tarrant Gunville. *Dors* 1E 15
Tarrant Hinton. *Dors* 1E 15
Tarrant Keyneston. *Dors* 2E 15
Tarrant Launceston. *Dors* 2E 15
Tarrant Monkton. *Dors* 2E 15
Tarrant Rawston. *Dors* 2E 15
Tarrant Rushton. *Dors* 2E 15
Tarrel. *High* 5F 165
Tarring Neville. *E Sus* 5F 27
Tarrington. *Here* 1B 48
Tarsappie. *Per* 1D 136
Tarscabhaig. *High* 3D 147
Tarskavaig. *High* 3D 147
Tarves. *Abers* 5F 161
Tarvie. *High* 3G 157
Tarvin. *Ches W* 4G 83
Tasburgh. *Norf* 1E 66
Tasley. *Shrp* 1A 60
Taston. *Oxon* 3B 50
Tatenhill. *Staf* 3G 73
Tathall End. *Mil* 1G 51
Tatham. *Lanc* 3F 97
Tathwell. *Linc* 2C 88
Tatling End. *Buck* 2B 38
Tatsfield. *Surr* 5F 39
Tattenhall. *Ches W* 5G 83
Tatterford. *Norf* 3A 78
Tattersett. *Norf* 2H 77
Tattershall. *Linc* 5B 88
Tattershall Bridge. *Linc* 5A 88
Tattershall Thorpe. *Linc* 5B 88
Tattingstone. *Suff* 2E 55
Tattingstone White Horse.
Suff 2E 55
Tattle Bank. *Warw* 4F 61
Tatworth. *Som* 2G 13
Taunton. *Som* 4F 21 & 213
Taverham. *Norf* 4D 78
Taverners Green. *Essx* 4F 53
Tavernspite. *Pemb* 3F 43
Tavistock. *Devn* 5E 11
Tavool House. *Arg* 1B 132
Taw Green. *Devn* 3G 11
Tawstock. *Devn* 4F 19
Taxal. *Derbs* 2E 85
Tayinloan. *Arg* 5E 125
Taynish. *Arg* 1F 125
Taynton. *Glos* 3C 48
Taynton. *Oxon* 4H 49
Taynuilt. *Arg* 5E 141
Tayport. *Fife* 1G 137
Tay Road Bridge. *Fife* 1G 137
Tayvallich. *Arg* 1F 125
Tealby. *Linc* 1A 88
Tealing. *Ang* 5D 144
Teams. *Tyne* 3F 115
Teangue. *High* 3E 147
Teanna Machair. *W Isl* 2C 170
Tebay. *Cumb* 4H 103
Tebworth. *C Beds* 3H 51
Tedburn St Mary. *Devn* 3B 12
Teddington. *Glos* 2E 49
Teddington. *G Lon* 3C 38
Tedsmore. *Shrp* 3F 71
Tedstone Delamere. *Here* 5A 60
Tedstone Wafer. *Here* 5A 60
Teesport. *Red C* 2C 106
Teesside. *Stoc T* 2C 106
Teeton. *Nptn* 3D 62
Teffont Evias. *Wilts* 3E 23
Teffont Magna. *Wilts* 3E 23
Tegryn. *Pemb* 1G 43
Teigh. *Rut* 4F 75
Teigncombe. *Devn* 4G 11
Teigngrace. *Devn* 5B 12
Teignmouth. *Devn* 5C 12
Telford. *Telf* 4A 72
Telham. *E Sus* 4B 28
Tellisford. *Som* 1D 22
Telscombe. *E Sus* 5F 27
Telscombe Cliffs. *E Sus* 5E 27
Tempar. *Per* 3D 142
Templand. *Dum* 1B 112
Temple. *Corn* 5B 10
Temple. *Glas* 3G 127
Temple. *Midl* 4G 129
Temple Balsall. *W Mid* 3G 61
Temple Bar. *Carm* 4F 45
Temple Bar. *Cdgn* 5E 57
Temple Cloud. *Bath* 1B 22
Templecombe. *Som* 4C 22
Temple Ewell. *Kent* 1G 29
Temple Grafton. *Warw* 5F 61
Temple Guiting. *Glos* 3F 49
Templehall. *Fife* 4E 137
Temple Hirst. *N Yor* 2G 93
Temple Normanton. *Derbs* 4B 86
Temple Sowerby. *Cumb* 2H 103
Templeton. *Devn* 1B 12
Templeton. *Pemb* 3F 43
Templeton. *W Ber* 5B 36
Templetown. *Dur* 5E 115
Tempsford. *C Beds* 5A 64
Tenandry. *Per* 2G 143
Tenbury Wells. *Worc* 4H 59
Tenby. *Pemb* 4F 43
Tendring. *Essx* 3E 55
Tendring Green. *Essx* 3E 55
Tenga. *Arg* 4G 139
Ten Mile Bank. *Norf* 1F 65
Tenterden. *Kent* 2C 28
Terfyn. *Cnwy* 3B 82
Terhill. *Som* 3E 21
Terling. *Essx* 4A 54
Ternhill. *Shrp* 2A 72
Terregles. *Dum* 2G 111
Terrick. *Buck* 5G 51
Terrington. *N Yor* 2A 100
Terrington St Clement. *Norf* 3E 77
Terrington St John. *Norf* 4E 77
Terry's Green. *Warw* 3F 61
Teston. *Kent* 5B 40
Testwood. *Hants* 1B 16
Tetbury. *Glos* 2D 35
Tetbury Upton. *Glos* 2D 35
Tetchill. *Shrp* 2F 71
Tetcott. *Devn* 3D 10
Tetford. *Linc* 3C 88
Tetney. *Linc* 4G 95
Tetney Lock. *Linc* 4G 95
Tetsworth. *Oxon* 5E 51
Tettenhall. *W Mid* 1C 60
Teversal. *Notts* 4B 86
Teversham. *Cambs* 5D 65
Teviothead. *Bord* 4G 119
Tewel. *Abers* 5F 153
Tewin. *Herts* 4C 52
Tewkesbury. *Glos* 2D 49
Teynham. *Kent* 4D 40
Teynham Street. *Kent* 4D 40
Thackthwaite. *Cumb* 2F 103
Thakeham. *W Sus* 4C 26
Thame. *Oxon* 5F 51
Thames Ditton. *Surr* 4C 38
Thames Haven. *Thur* 2B 40
Thamesmead. *G Lon* 2F 39
Thamesport. *Medw* 3C 40
Thanington Without. *Kent* 5F 41
Thankerton. *S Lan* 1B 118
Tharston. *Norf* 1D 66
Thatcham. *W Ber* 5D 36
Thatto Heath. *Mers* 1H 83
Thaxted. *Essx* 2G 53
Theakston. *N Yor* 1F 99
Thealby. *N Lin* 3B 94
Theale. *Som* 2H 21
Theale. *W Ber* 4E 37
Thearne. *E Yor* 1D 94
Theberton. *Suff* 4G 67
Theddingworth. *Leics* 2D 62
Theddlethorpe All Saints.
Linc 2D 88
Theddlethorpe St Helen. *Linc* 2D 89
Thelbridge Barton. *Devn* 1A 12
Thelnetham. *Suff* 3C 66
Thelveton. *Norf* 2D 66
Thelwall. *Warr* 2A 84
Themelthorpe. *Norf* 3C 78
Thenford. *Nptn* 1D 50
Therfield. *Herts* 2D 52
Thetford. *Linc* 4A 76
Thetford. *Norf* 2A 66
Thethwaite. *Cumb* 5E 113
Theydon Bois. *Essx* 1F 39
Thick Hollins. *W Yor* 3B 92
Thickwood. *Wilts* 4D 34
Thimbleby. *Linc* 3B 88
Thimbleby. *N Yor* 5B 106
Thingwall. *Mers* 2E 83
Thirlby. *N Yor* 1G 99
Thirlestane. *Bord* 5B 130
Thirn. *N Yor* 1E 98
Thirsk. *N Yor* 1G 99
Thirtleby. *E Yor* 1E 95
Thistleton. *Lanc* 1C 90
Thistleton. *Rut* 4G 75
Thistley Green. *Suff* 3F 65
Thixendale. *N Yor* 3C 100
Thockrington. *Nmbd* 2C 114
Tholomas Drove. *Cambs* 5D 76
Tholthorpe. *N Yor* 3G 99
Thomas Chapel. *Pemb* 4F 43
Thomas Close. *Cumb* 5F 113
Thomastown. *Abers* 4E 160
Thomastown. *Rhon* 3D 32
Thompson. *Norf* 1B 66
Thomshill. *Mor* 3G 159
Thong. *Kent* 3A 40
Thongsbridge. *W Yor* 4B 92
Thoralby. *N Yor* 1C 98
Thoresby. *Notts* 3D 86
Thoresway. *Linc* 1A 88
Thorganby. *Linc* 1B 88
Thorganby. *N Yor* 5A 100
Thorgill. *N Yor* 5E 107
Thorington. *Suff* 3G 67
Thorington Street. *Suff* 2D 54
Thorlby. *N Yor* 4B 98
Thorley. *Herts* 4E 53
Thorley Street. *Herts* 4E 53
Thorley Street. *IOW* 4B 16
Thormanby. *N Yor* 2G 99
Thorn. *Powy* 4E 59
Thornaby-on-Tees. *Stoc T* 3B 106
Thornage. *Norf* 2C 78
Thornborough. *Buck* 2F 51
Thornborough. *N Yor* 2E 99
Thornbury. *Devn* 2E 11
Thornbury. *Here* 5A 60
Thornbury. *S Glo* 3B 34
Thornby. *Cumb* 4D 112
Thornby. *Nptn* 3D 62
Thorncliffe. *Staf* 5E 85
Thorncombe. *Dors* 2G 13
Thorncombe Street. *Surr* 1A 26
Thorncote Green. *C Beds* 1B 52
Thorndon. *Suff* 4D 66
Thorndon Cross. *Devn* 3F 11
Thorne. *S Yor* 3G 93
Thornehillhead. *Devn* 1E 11
Thorner. *W Yor* 5F 99
Thorne St Margaret. *Som* 4D 20
Thorney. *Notts* 3F 87
Thorney. *Pet* 5B 76
Thorney. *Som* 4H 21
Thorney Hill. *Hants* 3G 15
Thorney Toll. *Cambs* 5C 76
Thornfalcon. *Som* 4F 21
Thornford. *Dors* 1B 14
Thorngrafton. *Nmbd* 3A 114
Thorngrove. *Som* 3G 21
Thorngumbald. *E Yor* 2F 95
Thornham. *Norf* 1G 77
Thornham Magna. *Suff* 3D 66
Thornham Parva. *Suff* 3D 66
Thornhaugh. *Pet* 5H 75
Thornhill. *Cphy* 3E 33
Thornhill. *Cumb* 4B 102
Thornhill. *Derbs* 2G 85
Thornhill. *Dum* 5A 118
Thornhill. *Sotn* 1C 16
Thornhill. *Stir* 4F 135
Thornhill. *W Yor* 3C 92
Thornhill Lees. *W Yor* 3C 92
Thornhills. *W Yor* 2B 92
Thornholme. *E Yor* 3F 101
Thornicombe. *Dors* 2D 14
Thornington. *Nmbd* 1C 120
Thornley. *Dur* 1A 106
(nr. Durham)
Thornley. *Dur* 1E 105
(nr. Tow Law)
Thornley Gate. *Nmbd* 4B 114
Thornliebank. *E Ren* 4G 127
Thornroan. *Abers* 5F 161
Thorns. *Suff* 5G 65
Thornsett. *Derbs* 2E 85
Thornthwaite. *Cumb* 2D 102
Thornthwaite. *N Yor* 4D 98
Thornton. *Ang* 4C 144
Thornton. *Buck* 2F 51
Thornton. *E Yor* 5B 100
Thornton. *Fife* 4E 137
Thornton. *Lanc* 5C 96
Thornton. *Leics* 5B 74
Thornton. *Linc* 4B 88
Thornton. *Mers* 4B 90
Thornton. *Midd* 3B 106
Thornton. *Nmbd* 5F 131
Thornton. *Pemb* 4D 42
Thornton. *W Yor* 1A 92
Thornton Curtis. *N Lin* 3D 94
Thorntonhall. *S Lan* 4G 127
Thornton Heath. *G Lon* 4E 39
Thornton Hough. *Mers* 2F 83
Thornton in Craven. *N Yor* 5B 98
Thornton in Lonsdale. *N Yor* 2F 97
Thornton-le-Beans. *N Yor* 5A 106
Thornton-le-Clay. *N Yor* 3A 100
Thornton-le-Dale. *N Yor* 1C 100
Thornton le Moor. *Linc* 1H 87
Thornton-le-Moor. *N Yor* 1F 99
Thornton-le-Moors. *Ches W* 3G 83
Thornton-le-Street. *N Yor* 1G 99
Thorntonloch. *E Lot* 2D 130
Thornton Rust. *N Yor* 1B 98
Thornton Steward. *N Yor* 1D 98

Thornton Watlass. N Yor 1E 99
Thornwood Common. Essx 5E 53
Thornythwaite. Cumb 2E 103
Thoroton. Notts 1E 75
Thorp Arch. W Yor 5G 99
Thorpe. Derbs 5F 85
Thorpe. E Yor 5D 101
Thorpe. Linc 2D 89
Thorpe. Norf 1G 67
Thorpe. N Yor 3C 98
Thorpe. Notts 1E 75
Thorpe. Surr 4B 38
Thorpe Abbotts. Norf 3D 66
Thorpe Acre. Leics 3C 74
Thorpe Arnold. Leics 3E 75
Thorpe Audlin. W Yor 3E 93
Thorpe Bassett. N Yor 2C 100
Thorpe Bay. S'end 2D 40
Thorpe by Water. Rut 1F 63
Thorpe Common. S Yor 1A 86
Thorpe Common. Suff 2F 55
Thorpe Constantine. Staf 5G 73
Thorpe End. Norf 4E 79
Thorpe Fendike. Linc 4D 88
Thorpe Green. Essx 3E 55
Thorpe Green. Suff 5B 66
Thorpe Hall. N Yor 2H 99
Thorpe Hamlet. Norf 5E 79
Thorpe Hesley. S Yor 1A 86
Thorpe in Balne. S Yor 3F 93
Thorpe in the Fallows. Linc 2G 87
Thorpe Langton. Leics 1E 63
Thorpe Larches. Dur 2A 106
Thorpe Latimer. Linc 1A 76
Thorpe-le-Soken. Essx 3E 55
Thorpe le Street. E Yor 5C 100
Thorpe Malsor. Nptn 3F 63
Thorpe Mandeville. Nptn 1D 50
Thorpe Market. Norf 2E 79
Thorpe Marriott. Norf 4D 78
Thorpe Morieux. Suff 5B 66
Thorpeness. Suff 4G 67
Thorpe on the Hill. Linc 4G 87
Thorpe on the Hill. W Yor 2D 92
Thorpe St Andrew. Norf 5E 79
Thorpe St Peter. Linc 4D 89
Thorpe Salvin. S Yor 2C 86
Thorpe Satchville. Leics 4E 75
Thorpe Thewles. Stoc T 2B 106
Thorpe Tilney. Linc 5A 88
Thorpe Underwood. N Yor 4G 99
Thorpe Waterville. Nptn 2H 63
Thorpe Willoughby. N Yor 1F 93
Thorpland. Norf 5F 77
Thorrington. Essx 3D 54
Thorverton. Devn 2C 12
Thrandeston. Suff 3D 66
Thrapston. Nptn 3G 63
Thrashbush. N Lan 3A 128
Threapland. Cumb 1C 102
Threapland. N Yor 3B 98
Threapwood. Ches W 1G 71
Threapwood. Staf 1E 73
Three Ashes. Here 3A 48
Three Bridges. Linc 2D 88
Three Bridges. W Sus 2D 27
Three Burrows. Corn 4B 6
Three Chimneys. Kent 2C 28
Three Cocks. Powy 2E 47
Three Crosses. Swan 3E 31
Three Cups Corner. E Sus 3H 27
Threehammer Common. Norf . . .3F 79
Three Holes. Norf 5E 77
Threekingham. Linc 2H 75
Three Leg Cross. E Sus 2A 28
Three Legged Cross. Dors 2F 15
Three Mile Cross. Wok 5F 37
Threemilestone. Corn 4B 6
Three Oaks. E Sus 4C 28
Threlkeld. Cumb 2E 102
Threshfield. N Yor 3B 98
Thrigby. Norf 4G 79
Thringarth. Dur 2C 104
Thringstone. Leics 4B 74
Thrintoft. N Yor 5A 106
Thriplow. Cambs 1E 53
Throckenholt. Linc 5C 76
Throcking. Herts 2D 52
Throckley. Tyne 3E 115
Throckmorton. Worc 1E 49
Throop. Bour 3G 15
Throphill. Nmbd 1E 115
Thropton. Nmbd 4E 121
Throsk. Stir 4A 136
Througham. Glos 5E 49
Throughgate. Dum 1F 111
Throwleigh. Devn 3G 11
Throwley. Kent 5D 40
Throwley Forstal. Kent 5D 40
Throxenby. N Yor 1E 101
Thrumpton. Notts 2C 74
Thrumster. High 4F 169
Thrunton. Nmbd 3E 121
Thrupp. Glos 5D 48
Thrupp. Oxon 4C 50
Thrushelton. Devn 4E 11
Thrushgill. Lanc 3F 97
Thrussington. Leics 4D 74
Thruxton. Hants 2A 24
Thruxton. Here 2H 47
Thrybergh. S Yor 1B 86

Thulston. Derbs 2B 74
Thundergay. N Ayr 5G 125
Thundersley. Essx 2B 40
Thundridge. Herts 4D 52
Thurcaston. Leics 4C 74
Thurcroft. S Yor 2B 86
Thurdon. Corn 1C 10
Thurgarton. Norf 2D 78
Thurgarton. Notts 1D 74
Thurgoland. S Yor 4C 92
Thurlaston. Leics 1C 62
Thurlaston. Warw 3B 62
Thurlbear. Som 4F 21
Thurlby. Linc 3D 89
(nr. Alford)
Thurlby. Linc 4A 76
(nr. Baston)
Thurlby. Linc 4G 87
(nr. Lincoln)
Thurleigh. Bed 5H 63
Thurlestone. Devn 4C 8
Thurloxton. Som 3F 21
Thurlstone. S Yor 4C 92
Thurlton. Norf 1G 67
Thurmaston. Leics 5D 74
Thurnby. Leics 5D 74
Thurne. Norf 4G 79
Thurnham. Kent 5C 40
Thurning. Norf 3C 78
Thurning. Nptn 2H 63
Thurnscoe. S Yor 4E 93
Thursby. Cumb 4E 113
Thursford. Norf 2B 78
Thursford Green. Norf 2B 78
Thursley. Surr 2A 26
Thurso. High 2D 168
Thurso East. High 2D 168
Thurstaston. Mers 2E 83
Thurston. Suff 4B 66
Thurston End. Suff 5G 65
Thurstonfield. Cumb 4E 112
Thurstonland. W Yor 3B 92
Thurton. Norf 5F 79
Thurvaston. Derbs 2F 73
(nr. Ashbourne)
Thurvaston. Derbs 2G 73
(nr. Derby)
Thuxton. Norf 5C 78
Thwaite. Dur 3D 104
Thwaite. N Yor 5B 104
Thwaite. Suff 4D 66
Thwaite Head. Cumb 5E 103
Thwaites. W Yor 5C 98
Thwaite St Mary. Norf 1F 67
Thwing. E Yor 2E 101
Tibbermore. Per 1C 136
Tibberton. Glos 3C 48
Tibberton. Telf 3A 72
Tibberton. Worc 5D 60
Tibenham. Norf 2D 66
Tibshelf. Derbs 4B 86
Tibthorpe. E Yor 4D 100
Ticehurst. E Sus 2A 28
Tichborne. Hants 3D 24
Tickencote. Rut 5G 75
Tickenham. N Som 4H 33
Tickhill. S Yor 1C 86
Ticklerton. Shrp 1G 59
Ticknall. Derbs 3H 73
Tickton. E Yor 5E 101
Tidbury Green. W Mid 3F 61
Tidcombe. Wilts 1A 24
Tiddington. Oxon 5E 51
Tiddington. Warw 5G 61
Tiddleywink. Wilts 4D 34
Tidebrook. E Sus 3H 27
Tideford. Corn 3H 7
Tideford Cross. Corn 2H 7
Tidenham. Glos 2A 34
Tideswell. Derbs 3F 85
Tidmarsh. W Ber 4E 37
Tidmington. Warw 2A 50
Tidpit. Hants 1F 15
Tidworth. Wilts 2H 23
Tidworth Camp. Wilts 2H 23
Tiers Cross. Pemb 3D 42
Tiffield. Nptn 5D 62
Tifty. Abers 4E 161
Tigerton. Ang 2E 145
Tighnabruaich. Arg 2A 126
Tigley. Devn 2D 8
Tilbrook. Cambs 4H 63
Tilbury. Thur 3H 39
Tilbury Green. Essx 1H 53
Tilbury Juxta Clare. Essx 1A 54
Tile Hill. W Mid 3G 61
Tilehurst. Read 4E 37
Tilford. Surr 2G 25
Tilgate Forest Row. W Sus 2D 26
Tillathrowie. Abers 5B 160
Tillers Green. Glos 2B 48
Tillery. Abers 1G 153
Tilley. Shrp 3H 71
Tillicoultry. Clac 4B 136
Tillingham. Essx 5C 54
Tillington. Here 1H 47
Tillington. W Sus 3A 26
Tillington Common. Here 1H 47
Tillybirloch. Abers 3D 152
Tillyfourie. Abers 2D 152
Tilmanstone. Kent 5H 41

Tilney All Saints. Norf 4E 77
Tilney Fen End. Norf 4E 77
Tilney High End. Norf 4E 77
Tilney St Lawrence. Norf 4E 77
Tilshead. Wilts 2F 23
Tilstock. Shrp 2H 71
Tilston. Ches W 5G 83
Tilstone Fearnall. Ches W 4H 83
Tilsworth. C Beds 3H 51
Tilton on the Hill. Leics 5E 75
Tiltups End. Glos 2D 34
Timberland. Linc 5A 88
Timbersbrook. Ches E 4C 84
Timberscombe. Som 2C 20
Timble. N Yor 4D 98
Timperley. G Man 2B 84
Timsbury. Bath 1B 22
Timsbury. Hants 4B 24
Timsgearraidh. W Isl 4C 171
Timworth Green. Suff 4A 66
Tincleton. Dors 3C 14
Tindale. Cumb 4H 113
Tindale Crescent. Dur 2F 105
Tingewick. Buck 2E 51
Tingley. W Yor 2C 92
Tingrith. C Beds 2A 52
Tingwall. Orkn 5D 172
Tinhay. Devn 4D 11
Tinshill. W Yor 1C 92
Tinsley. S Yor 1B 86
Tinsley Green. W Sus 2D 27
Tintagel. Corn 4A 10
Tintern. Mon 5A 48
Tintinhull. Som 1A 14
Tintwistle. Derbs 1E 85
Tinwald. Dum 1B 112
Tinwell. Rut 5H 75
Tippacott. Devn 2A 20
Tipperty. Abers 1G 153
Tipps End. Cambs 1E 65
Tiptoe. Hants 3A 16
Tipton. W Mid 1D 60
Tipton St John. Devn 3D 12
Tiptree. Essx 4B 54
Tiptree Heath. Essx 4B 54
Tirabad. Powy 1B 46
Tircoed. Swan 5G 45
Tiree Airport. Arg 4B 138
Tirinie. Per 2F 143
Tirley. Glos 3D 48
Tirnewydd. Flin 3D 82
Tiroran. Arg 1B 132
Tirphil. Cphy 5E 47
Tirril. Cumb 2G 103
Tir-y-dail. Carm 4G 45
Tisbury. Wilts 4E 23
Tisman's Common. W Sus 2B 26
Tissington. Derbs 5F 85
Titchberry. Devn 4C 18
Titchfield. Hants 2D 16
Titchmarsh. Nptn 3H 63
Titchwell. Norf 1G 77
Tithby. Notts 2D 74
Titley. Here 5F 59
Titlington. Nmbd 3F 121
Titsey. Surr 5F 39
Titson. Corn 2C 10
Tittensor. Staf 2C 72
Tittleshall. Norf 3A 78
Titton. Worc 4C 60
Tiverton. Ches W 4H 83
Tiverton. Devn 1C 12
Tivetshall St Margaret. Norf 2D 66
Tivetshall St Mary. Norf 2D 66
Tivington. Som 2C 20
Tixall. Staf 3D 73
Tixover. Rut 5G 75
Toab. Orkn 7E 172
Toab. Shet 10E 173
Toadmoor. Derbs 5H 85
Tobermory. Arg 3G 139
Toberonochy. Arg 3E 133
Tobha-Beag. W Isl 1E 170
(on North Uist)
Tobha Beag. W Isl 5C 170
(on Sourth Uist)
Tobha Mor. W Isl 5C 170
Tobhtarol. W Isl 4D 171
Tobson. W Isl 4D 171
Tocabhaig. High 2E 147
Tocher. Abers 5D 160
Tockenham. Wilts 4F 35
Tockenham Wick. Wilts 3F 35
Tockholes. Bkbn 2E 91
Tockington. S Glo 3B 34
Tockwith. N Yor 4G 99
Todber. Dors 4D 22
Todding. Here 3G 59
Toddington. C Beds 3A 52
Toddington. Glos 2F 49
Todenham. Glos 2H 49
Todhills. Cumb 3E 113
Todmorden. W Yor 2H 91
Todwick. S Yor 2B 86
Toft. Cambs 5C 64
Toft. Linc 4H 75
Toft Hill. Dur 2E 105
Toft Monks. Norf 1G 67
Toft next Newton. Linc 2H 87
Toftrees. Norf 3A 78

Tofts. High 2F 169
Toftwood. Norf 4B 78
Togston. Nmbd 4G 121
Tokavaig. High 2E 147
Tokers Green. Oxon 4F 37
Tolastadh a Chaolais. W Isl 4D 171
Tolladine. Worc 5C 60
Tolland. Som 3E 20
Tollard Farnham. Dors 1E 15
Tollard Royal. Wilts 1E 15
Toll Bar. S Yor 4F 93
Toller Fratrum. Dors 3A 14
Toller Porcorum. Dors 3A 14
Tollerton. N Yor 3H 99
Tollerton. Notts 2D 74
Toller Whelme. Dors 2A 14
Tollesbury. Essx 4C 54
Tolleshunt D'Arcy. Essx 4C 54
Tolleshunt Knights. Essx 4C 54
Tolleshunt Major. Essx 4C 54
Tolm. W Isl 4G 171
Tolpuddle. Dors 3C 14
Tolstadh bho Thuath. W Isl 3H 171
Tolworth. G Lon 4C 38
Tomachlaggan. Mor 1F 151
Tomaknock. Per 1A 136
Tomatin. High 1C 150
Tombuidhe. Arg 3H 133
Tomdoun. High 3D 148
Tomich. High 1F 149
(nr. Cannich)
Tomich. High 1B 158
(nr. Invergordon)
Tomich. High 3D 164
(nr. Lairg)
Tomintoul. Mor 2F 151
Tomnavoulin. Mor 1G 151
Tomsléibhe. Arg 5A 140
Ton. Mon 2G 33
Tonbridge. Kent 1G 27
Tondu. B'end 3B 32
Tonedale. Som 4E 21
Tonfanau. Gwyn 5E 69
Tong. Shrp 5B 72
Tonge. Leics 3B 74
Tong Forge. Shrp 5B 72
Tongham. Surr 2G 25
Tongland. Dum 4D 111
Tong Norton. Shrp 5B 72
Tongue. High 3F 167
Tongue End. Linc 4A 76
Tongwynlais. Card 3E 33
Tonmawr. Neat 2B 32
Tonna. Neat 2A 32
Tonnau. Neat 2A 32
Ton-Pentre. Rhon 2C 32
Ton-Teg. Rhon 3D 32
Tonwell. Herts 4D 52
Tonypandy. Rhon 2C 32
Tonyrefail. Rhon 3D 32
Toot Baldon. Oxon 5D 50
Toot Hill. Essx 5F 53
Toothill. Hants 1B 16
Topcliffe. N Yor 2G 99
Topcliffe. W Yor 2C 92
Topcroft. Norf 1E 67
Topcroft Street. Norf 1E 67
Toppesfield. Essx 2H 53
Toppings. G Man 3F 91
Toprow. Norf 1D 66
Topsham. Devn 4C 12
Torbay. Torb 2F 9
Torbeg. N Ayr 3C 122
Torbothie. N Lan 3B 128
Torbryan. Devn 2E 9
Torcross. Devn 4E 9
Tore. High 3A 158
Torgyle. High 2F 149
Torinturk. Arg 3G 125
Torksey. Linc 3F 87
Torlum. W Isl 3C 170
Torlundy. High 1F 141
Tormarton. S Glo 4C 34
Tormitchell. S Ayr 5B 116
Tormore. High 3E 147
Tormore. N Ayr 2C 122
Tornagrain. High 4B 158
Tornaveen. Abers 3D 152
Torness. High 1H 149
Toronto. Dur 1E 105
Torpenhow. Cumb 1D 102
Torphichen. W Lot 2C 128
Torphins. Abers 3D 152
Torpoint. Corn 3A 8
Torquay. Torb 2F 9
Torr. Devn 3B 8
Torra. Arg 4B 124
Torran. High 4E 155
Torrance. E Dun 2H 127
Torrans. Arg 1B 132
Torranyard. E Ayr 5E 127
Torre. Som 3D 20
Torre. Torb 2E 9
Torridon. High 3B 156
Torrin. High 1D 147
Torrisdale. Arg 2B 122
Torrisdale. High 2G 167
Torrish. High 2G 165
Torrisholme. Lanc 3D 96

Torroble. High 3C 164
Torroy. High 4C 164
Tor Royal. Devn 5G 11
Torry. Aber 3G 153
Torryburn. Fife 1D 128
Torthorwald. Dum 2B 112
Tortington. W Sus 5B 26
Tortworth. S Glo 2C 34
Torvaig. High 4D 155
Torver. Cumb 5D 102
Torwood. Falk 1B 128
Torworth. Notts 2D 86
Toscaig. High 5G 155
Toseland. Cambs 4B 64
Tosside. Lanc 4G 97
Tostock. Suff 4B 66
Totaig. High 3B 154
Totardor. High 5C 154
Tote. High 4D 154
Totegan. High 2A 168
Tothill. Linc 2D 88
Totland. IOW 4B 16
Totley. S Yor 3H 85
Totnell. Dors 2B 14
Totnes. Devn 2E 9
Toton. Derbs 2B 74
Totronald. Arg 3C 138
Totscore. High 2C 154
Tottenham. G Lon 1E 39
Tottenhill. Norf 4F 77
Tottenhill Row. Norf 4F 77
Totteridge. G Lon 1D 38
Totternhoe. C Beds 3H 51
Tottington. G Man 3F 91
Totton. Hants 1B 16
Touchen-end. Wind 4G 37
Toulvaddie. High 5F 165
Towans, The. Corn 3C 4
Toward. Arg 3C 126
Towcester. Nptn 1E 51
Towednack. Corn 3B 4
Tower End. Norf 4F 77
Tower Hill. Mers 4C 90
Tower Hill. W Sus 3C 26
Towersey. Oxon 5F 51
Towie. Abers 2B 152
Towiemore. Mor 4A 160
Tow Law. Dur 1E 105
Town End. Cambs 1D 64
Town End. Cumb 4F 103
(nr. Ambleside)
Town End. Cumb 2H 103
(nr. Kirkby Thore)
Town End. Cumb 1D 96
(nr. Lindale)
Town End. Cumb 1C 96
(nr. Newby Bridge)
Town End. Mers 2G 83
Townend. W Dun 2F 127
Townfield. Dur 5C 114
Towngate. Cumb 5G 113
Towngate. Linc 4A 76
Town Green. Lanc 4B 90
Town Head. Cumb 4E 103
(nr. Grasmere)
Town Head. Cumb 3H 103
(nr. Great Asby)
Townhead. Cumb 1G 103
(nr. Lazonby)
Townhead. Cumb 1H 103
(nr. Maryport)
Townhead. Cumb 1H 103
(nr. Ousby)
Townhead. Dum 5D 111
Townhead of Greenlaw. Dum . . .3E 111
Townhill. Fife 1E 129
Townhill. Swan 3F 31
Town Kelloe. Dur 1A 106
Town Littleworth. E Sus 4F 27
Town Row. E Sus 2G 27
Towns End. Hants 1D 24
Townsend. Herts 5B 52
Townshend. Corn 3C 4
Town Street. Suff 2G 65
Town, The. IOS 1A 4
Town Yetholm. Bord 2C 120
Towthorpe. E Yor 3C 100
Towthorpe. York 4A 100
Towton. N Yor 1E 93
Towyn. Cnwy 3B 82
Toxteth. Mers 2F 83
Toynton All Saints. Linc 4C 88
Toynton Fen Side. Linc 4C 88
Toynton St Peter. Linc 4D 88
Toy's Hill. Kent 5F 39
Trabboch. E Ayr 2D 116
Traboe. Corn 4E 5
Tradespark. High 3C 158
Tradespark. Orkn 7D 172
Trafford Park. G Man 1B 84
Trallong. Powy 3C 46
Tranent. E Lot 2H 129
Tranmere. Mers 2F 83
Trantlebeg. High 3A 168
Trantlemore. High 3A 168
Tranwell. Nmbd 1E 115
Trapp. Carm 4G 45
Traquair. Bord 1F 119
Trash Green. W Ber 5E 37
Trawden. Lanc 1H 91
Trawscoed. Powy 2D 46

Trawsfynydd—Ullinish

Trawsfynydd. *Gwyn* 2G 69
Trawsgoed. *Cdgn* 3F 57
Treaddow. *Here* 3A 48
Trealaw. *Rhon* 2D 32
Treales. *Lanc* 1C 90
Trearddur. *IOA* 3B 80
Treaslane. *High* 3C 154
Treator. *Corn* 1D 6
Trebanog. *Rhon* 2D 32
Trebanos. *Neat* 5H 45
Trebarber. *Corn* 2C 6
Trebartha. *Corn* 5C 10
Trebarwith. *Corn* 4A 10
Trebetherick. *Corn* 1D 6
Treborough. *Som* 3D 20
Trebudannon. *Corn* 2C 6
Trebullett. *Corn* 5D 10
Treburley. *Corn* 5D 10
Treburrick. *Corn* 1C 6
Trebyan. *Corn* 2E 7
Trecastle. *Powy* 3B 46
Trecenydd. *Cphy* 3E 33
Trecott. *Devn* 2G 11
Trecwn. *Pemb* 1D 42
Trecynon. *Rhon* 5C 46
Tredaule. *Corn* 4C 10
Tredavoe. *Corn* 4B 4
Tredegar. *Blae* 5E 47
Trederwen. *Powy* 4E 71
Tredington. *Glos* 3E 49
Tredington. *Warw* 1A 50
Tredinnick. *Corn* 2F 7 (nr. Bodmin)
Tredinnick. *Corn* 3G 7 (nr. Looe)
Tredinnick. *Corn* 1D 6 (nr. Padstow)
Tredogan. *V Glam* 5D 32
Tredomen. *Powy* 2E 46
Tredunnock. *Mon* 2G 33
Tredustan. *Powy* 2E 47
Treen. *Corn* 4A 4 (nr. Land's End)
Treen. *Corn* 3B 4 (nr. St Ives)
Treeton. *S Yor* 2B 86
Trefaldwyn. *Powy* 1E 58
Trefasser. *Pemb* 1C 42
Trefdraeth. *IOA* 3D 80
Trefdraeth. *Pemb* 1E 43
Trefecca. *Powy* 2E 47
Trefechan. *Mer T* 5D 46
Trefeglwys. *Powy* 1B 58
Trefeitha. *Powy* 2E 46
Trefenter. *Cdgn* 4F 57
Treffgarne. *Pemb* 2D 42
Treffynnon. *Flin* 3D 82
Treffynnon. *Pemb* 2C 42
Trefil. *Blae* 4E 46
Trefilan. *Cdgn* 5E 57
Trefin. *Pemb* 1C 42
Treflach. *Shrp* 3E 71
Trefnant. *Den* 3C 82
Trefonen. *Shrp* 3E 71
Trefor. *Gwyn* 1C 68
Trefor. *IOA* 2C 80
Treforest. *Rhon* 3D 32
Trefrew. *Corn* 4B 10
Trefriw. *Cnwy* 4G 81
Tref-y-Clawdd. *Powy* 3E 59
Trefynwy. *Mon* 4A 48
Tregada. *Corn* 4D 10
Tregadillett. *Corn* 4D 10
Tregare. *Mon* 4H 47
Tregarne. *Corn* 4E 5
Tregaron. *Cdgn* 5F 57
Tregarth. *Gwyn* 4F 81
Tregear. *Corn* 3C 6
Tregeare. *Corn* 4C 10
Tregeiriog. *Wrex* 2D 70
Tregele. *IOA* 1C 80
Tregeseal. *Corn* 3A 4
Tregiskey. *Corn* 4E 6
Tregole. *Corn* 3B 10
Tregolwyn. *V Glam* 4C 32
Tregonetha. *Corn* 2D 6
Tregonhawke. *Corn* 3A 8
Tregony. *Corn* 4D 6
Tregoodwell. *Corn* 4B 10
Tregorrick. *Corn* 3E 6
Tregoss. *Corn* 2D 6
Tregowris. *Corn* 4E 5
Tregoyd. *Powy* 2E 47
Tregrehan Mills. *Corn* 3E 7
Tre-groes. *Cdgn* 1E 45
Tregullon. *Corn* 2E 7
Tregurrian. *Corn* 2C 6
Tregynon. *Powy* 1C 58
Trehafod. *Rhon* 2D 32
Trehan. *Corn* 3A 8
Treharris. *Mer T* 2E 32
Treherbert. *Rhon* 2C 32
Trehunist. *Corn* 2H 7
Trekenner. *Corn* 5D 10
Trekenning. *Corn* 2D 6
Treknow. *Corn* 4A 10
Trelales. *B'end* 3B 32
Trelan. *Corn* 5E 5
Trelash. *Corn* 3B 10
Trelassick. *Corn* 3C 6
Trelawnyd. *Flin* 3C 82
Trelech. *Carm* 1G 43
Treleddyd-fawr. *Pemb* 2B 42
Trelewis. *Mer T* 2E 32
Treligga. *Corn* 4A 10
Trelights. *Corn* 1D 6
Trelill. *Corn* 5A 10
Trelissick. *Corn* 5C 6
Trellech. *Mon* 5A 48
Trelleck Grange. *Mon* 5H 47
Trelogan. *Flin* 2D 82
Trelystan. *Powy* 5E 71
Tremadog. *Gwyn* 1E 69
Tremail. *Corn* 4B 10
Tremain. *Cdgn* 1C 44
Tremaine. *Corn* 4C 10
Tremar. *Corn* 2G 7
Trematon. *Corn* 3H 7
Tremeirchion. *Den* 3C 82
Tremore. *Corn* 2E 6
Tremorfa. *Card* 4F 33
Trenance. *Corn* 5D 4 (nr. Helston)
Trenance. *Corn* 2C 6 (nr. Newquay)
Trenance. *Corn* 1D 6 (nr. Padstow)
Trenarren. *Corn* 4E 7
Trench. *Telf* 4A 72
Trencreek. *Corn* 2C 6
Trendeal. *Corn* 3C 6
Trenear. *Corn* 5A 6
Treneglos. *Corn* 4C 10
Trenewan. *Corn* 3F 7
Trengune. *Corn* 3B 10
Trent. *Dors* 1A 14
Trentham. *Stoke* 1C 72
Trentishoe. *Devn* 2G 19
Trentlock. *Derbs* 2B 74
Treoes. *V Glam* 4C 32
Treorchy. *Rhon* 2C 32
Treorci. *Rhon* 2C 32
Tre'r-ddol. *Cdgn* 1F 57
Tre'r llai. *Powy* 5E 71
Trerulefoot. *Corn* 3H 7
Tresaith. *Cdgn* 5B 56
Trescott. *Staf* 1C 60
Trescowe. *Corn* 3C 4
Tresham. *Glos* 2C 34
Tresigin. *V Glam* 4C 32
Tresillian. *Corn* 4C 6
Tresimwn. *V Glam* 4D 32
Tresinney. *Corn* 4B 10
Treskillard. *Corn* 5A 6
Treskinnick Cross. *Corn* 3C 10
Tresmeer. *Corn* 4C 10
Tresparrett. *Corn* 3B 10
Tresparrett Posts. *Corn* 3B 10
Tressady. *High* 3D 164
Tressait. *Per* 2F 143
Tresta. *Shet* 2H 173 (on Fetlar)
Tresta. *Shet* 6E 173 (on Mainland)
Treswell. *Notts* 3E 87
Treswithian. *Corn* 3D 4
Tre Taliesin. *Cdgn* 1F 57
Trethomas. *Cphy* 3E 33
Trethosa. *Corn* 3D 6
Trethurgy. *Corn* 3E 7
Tretio. *Pemb* 2B 42
Tretire. *Here* 3A 48
Tretower. *Powy* 3E 47
Treuddyn. *Flin* 5E 83
Trevadlock. *Corn* 5C 10
Trevalga. *Corn* 3A 10
Trevalyn. *Wrex* 5F 83
Trevance. *Corn* 1D 6
Trevanger. *Corn* 1D 6
Trevanson. *Corn* 1D 6
Trevarrack. *Corn* 3B 4
Trevarren. *Corn* 2D 6
Trevarrian. *Corn* 2C 6
Trevarrick. *Corn* 4D 6
Tre-vaughan. *Carm* 3E 45 (nr. Carmarthen)
Trevaughan. *Carm* 3F 43 (nr. Whitland)
Treveighan. *Corn* 5A 10
Trevellas. *Corn* 3B 6
Trevelmond. *Corn* 2G 7
Treverva. *Corn* 5B 6
Trevescan. *Corn* 4A 4
Trevethin. *Torf* 5F 47
Trevia. *Corn* 4A 10
Trevigro. *Corn* 2H 7
Trevilley. *Corn* 4A 4
Treviscoe. *Corn* 3D 6
Trevivian. *Corn* 4B 10
Trevone. *Corn* 1C 6
Trevor. *Wrex* 1E 71
Trevor Uchaf. *Den* 1E 71
Trew. *Corn* 4D 4
Trewalder. *Corn* 4A 10
Trewarlett. *Corn* 4D 10
Trewarmett. *Corn* 4A 10
Trewassa. *Corn* 4B 10
Treween. *Corn* 4C 10
Trewellard. *Corn* 3A 4
Trewen. *Corn* 4C 10
Trewennack. *Corn* 4D 5
Trewern. *Powy* 4E 71
Trewetha. *Corn* 5A 10
Trewidland. *Corn* 2G 7
Trewint. *Corn* 3B 10
Trewithian. *Corn* 5C 6
Trewoofe. *Corn* 4B 4
Trewoon. *Corn* 3D 6
Treworthal. *Corn* 5C 6
Trewyddel. *Pemb* 1B 44
Treyarnon. *Corn* 1C 6
Treyford. *W Sus* 1G 17
Triangle. *Staf* 5E 73
Triangle. *W Yor* 2A 92
Trickett's Cross. *Dors* 2F 15
Trimdon. *Dur* 1A 106
Trimdon Colliery. *Dur* 1A 106
Trimdon Grange. *Dur* 1A 106
Trimingham. *Norf* 2E 79
Trimley Lower Street. *Suff* 2F 55
Trimley St Martin. *Suff* 2F 55
Trimley St Mary. *Suff* 2F 55
Trimpley. *Worc* 3B 60
Trimsaran. *Carm* 5E 45
Trimstone. *Devn* 2F 19
Trinafour. *Per* 2E 142
Trinant. *Cphy* 2F 33
Tring. *Herts* 4H 51
Trinity. *Ang* 2F 145
Trinity. *Edin* 2F 129
Trisant. *Cdgn* 3G 57
Triscombe. *Som* 3E 21
Trislaig. *High* 1E 141
Trispen. *Corn* 3C 6
Tritlington. *Nmbd* 5G 121
Trochry. *Per* 4G 143
Troedrhiwdalar. *Powy* 5B 58
Troedrhiwfuwch. *Cphy* 5E 47
Troedrhiwgwair. *Blae* 5E 47
Troedyraur. *Cdgn* 1D 44
Troedyrhiw. *Mer T* 5D 46
Trondavoe. *Shet* 4E 173
Troon. *Corn* 5A 6
Troon. *S Ayr* 1C 116
Troqueer. *Dum* 2A 112
Troston. *Suff* 3A 66
Trottiscliffe. *Kent* 4H 39
Trotton. *W Sus* 4G 25
Troutbeck. *Cumb* 4F 103 (nr. Ambleside)
Troutbeck. *Cumb* 2E 103 (nr. Penrith)
Troutbeck Bridge. *Cumb* 4F 103
Troway. *Derbs* 3A 86
Trowbridge. *Wilts* 1D 22
Trowell. *Notts* 2B 74
Trowle Common. *Wilts* 1D 22
Trowley Bottom. *Herts* 4A 52
Trowse Newton. *Norf* 5E 79
Trudoxhill. *Som* 2C 22
Trull. *Som* 4F 21
Trumaisgearraidh. *W Isl* 1D 170
Trumpan. *High* 2B 154
Trumpet. *Here* 2B 48
Trumpington. *Cambs* 5D 64
Trumps Green. *Surr* 4A 38
Trunch. *Norf* 2E 79
Trunnah. *Lanc* 5C 96
Truro. *Corn* 4C 6
Trusham. *Devn* 4B 12
Trusley. *Derbs* 2G 73
Trusthorpe. *Linc* 2E 89
Tryfil. *IOA* 2D 80
Trysull. *Staf* 1C 60
Tubney. *Oxon* 2C 36
Tuckenhay. *Devn* 3E 9
Tuckhill. *Staf* 2B 60
Tuckingmill. *Corn* 4A 6
Tuckton. *Bour* 3G 15
Tuddenham. *Suff* 3G 65
Tuddenham St Martin. *Suff* 1E 55
Tudeley. *Kent* 1H 27
Tudhoe. *Dur* 1F 105
Tudhoe Grange. *Dur* 1F 105
Tudorville. *Here* 3A 48
Tudweiliog. *Gwyn* 2B 68
Tuesley. *Surr* 1A 26
Tufton. *Hants* 2C 24
Tufton. *Pemb* 2E 43
Tugby. *Leics* 5E 75
Tugford. *Shrp* 2H 59
Tughall. *Nmbd* 2G 121
Tulchan. *Per* 1B 136
Tullibardine. *Per* 2B 136
Tullibody. *Clac* 4A 136
Tullich. *Arg* 2H 133
Tullich. *High* 4B 156 (nr. Lochcarron)
Tullich. *High* 1C 158 (nr. Tain)
Tullich. *Mor* 4H 159
Tullich Muir. *High* 1B 158
Tulliemet. *Per* 3G 143
Tulloch. *Abers* 5F 161
Tulloch. *High* 4D 164 (nr. Bonar Bridge)
Tulloch. *High* 5F 149 (nr. Fort William)
Tulloch. *High* 2D 151 (nr. Grantown-on-Spey)
Tulloch. *Per* 1C 136
Tullochgorm. *Arg* 4G 133
Tullybeagles Lodge. *Per* 5H 143
Tullymurdoch. *Per* 3A 144
Tullynessle. *Abers* 2C 152
Tumble. *Carm* 4F 45
Tumbler's Green. *Essx* 3B 54
Tumby. *Linc* 4B 88
Tumby Woodside. *Linc* 5B 88
Tummel Bridge. *Per* 3E 143
Tunbridge Wells, Royal. *Kent* 2G 27
Tunga. *W Isl* 4G 171
Tungate. *Norf* 3E 79
Tunley. *Bath* 1B 22
Tunstall. *E Yor* 1G 95
Tunstall. *Kent* 4C 40
Tunstall. *Lanc* 2F 97
Tunstall. *Norf* 5G 79
Tunstall. *N Yor* 5F 105
Tunstall. *Staf* 3B 72
Tunstall. *Stoke* 5C 84
Tunstall. *Suff* 5F 67
Tunstall. *Tyne* 4G 115
Tunstead. *Derbs* 3F 85
Tunstead. *Norf* 3E 79
Tunstead Milton. *Derbs* 2E 85
Tunworth. *Hants* 2E 25
Tupsley. *Here* 1A 48
Tupton. *Derbs* 4A 86
Turfholm. *S Lan* 1H 117
Turfmoor. *Devn* 2F 13
Turgis Green. *Hants* 1E 25
Turkdean. *Glos* 4G 49
Turkey Island. *Hants* 1D 16
Tur Langton. *Leics* 1E 62
Turleigh. *Wilts* 5D 34
Turlin Moor. *Pool* 3E 15
Turnant. *Here* 3G 47
Turnastone. *Here* 2G 47
Turnberry. *S Ayr* 4B 116
Turnchapel. *Plym* 3A 8
Turnditch. *Derbs* 1G 73
Turners Hill. *W Sus* 2E 27
Turners Puddle. *Dors* 3D 14
Turnford. *Herts* 5D 52
Turnhouse. *Edin* 2E 129
Turnworth. *Dors* 2D 14
Turriff. *Abers* 4E 161
Tursdale. *Dur* 1A 106
Turton Bottoms. *Bkbn* 3F 91
Turtory. *Mor* 4C 160
Turves Green. *W Mid* 3E 61
Turvey. *Bed* 5G 63
Turville. *Buck* 2F 37
Turville Heath. *Buck* 2F 37
Turweston. *Buck* 2E 50
Tushielaw. *Bord* 3F 119
Tutbury. *Staf* 3G 73
Tutnall. *Worc* 3D 61
Tutsbill. *Glos* 2A 34
Tuttington. *Norf* 3E 79
Tutts Clump. *W Ber* 4D 36
Tutwell. *Corn* 5D 11
Tuxford. *Notts* 3E 87
Twatt. *Orkn* 5B 172
Twatt. *Shet* 6E 173
Twechar. *E Dun* 2A 128
Tweedale. *Telf* 5B 72
Tweedmouth. *Nmbd* 4F 131
Tweedsmuir. *Bord* 2C 118
Twelveheads. *Corn* 4B 6
Twemlow Green. *Ches E* 4B 84
Twenty. *Linc* 3A 76
Twerton. *Bath* 5C 34
Twickenham. *G Lon* 3C 38
Twigworth. *Glos* 3D 48
Twineham. *W Sus* 3D 26
Twinhoe. *Bath* 1C 22
Twinstead. *Essx* 2B 54
Twinstead Green. *Essx* 2B 54
Twiss Green. *Warr* 1A 84
Twiston. *Lanc* 5H 97
Twitchen. *Devn* 3A 20
Twitchen. *Shrp* 3F 59
Two Bridges. *Devn* 5G 11
Two Bridges. *Glos* 5B 48
Two Dales. *Derbs* 4G 85
Two Gates. *Staf* 5G 73
Two Mile Oak. *Devn* 2E 9
Twycross. *Leics* 5H 73
Twyford. *Buck* 3E 51
Twyford. *Derbs* 3H 73
Twyford. *Dors* 1D 14
Twyford. *Hants* 4C 24
Twyford. *Leics* 4E 75
Twyford. *Norf* 3C 78
Twyford. *Wok* 4F 37
Twyford Common. *Here* 2A 48
Twyncarno. *Cphy* 5E 46
Twynholm. *Dum* 4D 110
Twyning. *Glos* 2D 49
Twyning Green. *Glos* 2E 49
Twynllanan. *Carm* 3A 46
Twyn-y-Sheriff. *Mon* 5H 47
Twywell. *Nptn* 3G 63
Tyberton. *Here* 2G 47
Tyburn. *W Mid* 1F 61
Tyby. *Norf* 3C 78
Tycroes. *Carm* 4G 45
Tycrwyn. *Powy* 4D 70
Tyddewi. *Pemb* 2B 42
Tydd Gote. *Linc* 4D 76
Tydd St Giles. *Cambs* 4D 76
Tydd St Mary. *Linc* 4D 76
Tye. *Hants* 2F 17
Tye Green. *Essx* 3F 53 (nr. Bishop's Stortford)
Tye Green. *Essx* 3A 54 (nr. Braintree)
Tye Green. *Essx* 2F 53 (nr. Saffron Walden)
Tyersal. *W Yor* 1B 92
Ty Issa. *Powy* 3D 70
Tyldesley. *G Man* 4E 91
Tyle. *Carm* 3G 45
Tyler Hill. *Kent* 4F 41
Tylers Green. *Buck* 2G 37
Tyler's Green. *Essx* 5F 53
Tylorstown. *Rhon* 2D 32
Tylwch. *Powy* 2B 58
Ty-nant. *Cnwy* 1B 70
Tyndrum. *Stir* 5H 141
Tyneham. *Dors* 4D 15
Tynehead. *Midl* 4G 129
Tynemouth. *Tyne* 3G 115
Tyneside. *Tyne* 3F 115
Tyne Tunnel. *Tyne* 3G 115
Tynewydd. *Rhon* 2C 32
Tyninghame. *E Lot* 2C 130
Tynron. *Dum* 5H 117
Ty'n-y-bryn. *Rhon* 3D 32
Tyn-y-celyn. *Wrex* 2D 70
Tyn-y-cwm. *Swan* 5G 45
Tyn-y-ffridd. *Powy* 2D 70
Tynygongl. *IOA* 2E 81
Tynygraig. *Cdgn* 4F 57
Tyn-y-groes. *Cnwy* 3G 81
Ty'n-yr-eithin. *Cdgn* 4F 57
Tyn-y-rhyd. *Powy* 4C 70
Tyn-y-wern. *Powy* 3C 70
Tyrie. *Abers* 2G 161
Tyringham. *Mil* 1G 51
Tythecott. *Devn* 1E 11
Tythegston. *B'end* 4B 32
Tytherington. *Ches E* 3D 84
Tytherington. *Som* 2C 22
Tytherington. *S Glo* 3B 34
Tytherington. *Wilts* 2E 23
Tytherleigh. *Devn* 2G 13
Tywardreath. *Corn* 3E 7
Tywardreath Highway. *Corn* 3E 7
Tywyn. *Cnwy* 3G 81
Tywyn. *Gwyn* 5E 69

U

Uachdar. *W Isl* 3D 170
Uags. *High* 5G 155
Ubbeston Green. *Suff* 3F 67
Ubley. *Bath* 1A 22
Uckerby. *N Yor* 4F 105
Uckfield. *E Sus* 3F 27
Uckinghall. *Worc* 2D 48
Uckington. *Glos* 3E 49
Uckington. *Shrp* 5H 71
Uddingston. *S Lan* 3H 127
Uddington. *S Lan* 1A 118
Udimore. *E Sus* 4C 28
Udny Green. *Abers* 1F 153
Udny Station. *Abers* 1G 153
Udston. *S Lan* 4A 128
Udstonhead. *S Lan* 5A 128
Uffcott. *Wilts* 4G 35
Uffculme. *Devn* 1D 12
Uffington. *Linc* 5H 75
Uffington. *Oxon* 3B 36
Uffington. *Shrp* 4H 71
Ufford. *Pet* 5H 75
Ufford. *Suff* 5E 67
Ufton. *Warw* 4A 62
Ufton Nervet. *W Ber* 5E 37
Ugadale. *Arg* 3B 122
Ugborough. *Devn* 3C 8
Ugford. *Wilts* 3F 23
Uggeshall. *Suff* 2G 67
Ugglebarnby. *N Yor* 4F 107
Ugley. *Essx* 3F 53
Ugley Green. *Essx* 3F 53
Ugthorpe. *N Yor* 3E 107
Uidh. *W Isl* 9B 170
Uig. *Arg* 3C 138
Uig. *High* 2C 154 (nr. Balgown)
Uig. *High* 3A 154 (nr. Dunvegan)
Uigshader. *High* 4D 154
Uisken. *Arg* 2A 132
Ulbster. *High* 4F 169
Ulcat Row. *Cumb* 2F 103
Ulceby. *Linc* 3D 88
Ulceby. *N Lin* 3E 94
Ulceby Skitter. *N Lin* 3E 94
Ulcombe. *Kent* 1C 28
Uldale. *Cumb* 1D 102
Uley. *Glos* 2C 34
Ulgham. *Nmbd* 5G 121
Ullapool. *High* 4F 163
Ullenhall. *Warw* 4F 61
Ulleskelf. *N Yor* 1F 93
Ullesthorpe. *Leics* 2C 62
Ulley. *S Yor* 2B 86
Ullingswick. *Here* 1A 48
Ullinish. *High* 5C 154

Ullock—Wall Nook

Ullock. *Cumb* 2B **102**
Ulpha. *Cumb* 5C **102**
Ulrome. *E Yor* 4F **101**
Ulsta. *Shet* 3F **173**
Ulting. *Essx* 5B **54**
Ulva House. *Arg* 5F **139**
Ulverston. *Cumb* 2B **96**
Ulwell. *Dors* 4F **15**
Umberleigh. *Devn* 4G **19**
Unapool. *High* 5C **166**
Underbarrow. *Cumb* 5F **103**
Undercliffe. *W Yor* 1B **92**
Underdale. *Shrp* 4H **71**
Underhoull. *Shet* 1G **173**
Underriver. *Kent* 5G **39**
Under Tofts. *S Yor* 2H **85**
Underton. *Shrp* 1A **60**
Underwood. *Newp* 3G **33**
Underwood. *Notts* 5B **86**
Underwood. *Plym* 3B **8**
Undley. *Suff* 2F **65**
Undy. *Mon* 3H **33**
Union Mills. *IOM* 4C **108**
Union Street. *E Sus* 2B **28**
Unstone. *Derbs* 3A **86**
Unstone Green. *Derbs* 3A **86**
Unthank. *Cumb* 5E **113** (nr. Carlisle)
Unthank. *Cumb* 5H **113** (nr. Gamblesby)
Unthank. *Cumb* 1F **103** (nr. Penrith)
Unthank End. *Cumb* 1F **103**
Upavon. *Wilts* 1G **23**
Up Cerne. *Dors* 2B **14**
Upchurch. *Kent* 4C **40**
Upcott. *Devn* 2F **11**
Upcott. *Here* 5F **59**
Upend. *Cambs* 5G **65**
Up Exe. *Devn* 2C **12**
Upgate. *Norf* 4D **78**
Upgate Street. *Norf* 1C **66**
Uphall. *Dors* 2A **14**
Uphall. *W Lot* 2D **128**
Uphall Station. *W Lot* 2D **128**
Upham. *Devn* 2B **12**
Upham. *Hants* 4D **24**
Uphampton. *Here* 4F **59**
Uphampton. *Worc* 4C **60**
Up Hatherley. *Glos* 3E **49**
Uphill. *N Som* 1G **21**
Up Holland. *Lanc* 4D **90**
Uplawmoor. *E Ren* 4F **127**
Upleadon. *Glos* 3C **48**
Upleatham. *Red C* 3D **106**
Uplees. *Kent* 4D **40**
Uploders. *Dors* 3A **14**
Uplowman. *Devn* 1D **12**
Uplyme. *Devn* 3G **13**
Up Marden. *W Sus* 1F **17**
Upminster. *G Lon* 2G **39**
Up Nately. *Hants* 1E **25**
Upottery. *Devn* 2F **13**
Uppat. *High* 3F **165**
Upper Affcot. *Shrp* 2G **59**
Upper Arley. *Worc* 2B **60**
Upper Armley. *W Yor* 1C **92**
Upper Arncott. *Oxon* 4E **50**
Upper Astrop. *Nptn* 2D **50**
Upper Badcall. *High* 4B **166**
Upper Bangor. *Gwyn* 3E **81**
Upper Basildon. *W Ber* 4D **36**
Upper Batley. *W Yor* 2C **92**
Upper Beeding. *W Sus* 4C **26**
Upper Benefield. *Nptn* 2G **63**
Upper Bentley. *Worc* 4D **61**
Upper Bighouse. *High* 3A **168**
Upper Boddam. *Abers* 5D **160**
Upper Boddington. *Nptn* 5B **62**
Upper Bogside. *Mor* 3G **159**
Upper Booth. *Derbs* 2F **85**
Upper Borth. *Cdgn* 2F **57**
Upper Boyndlie. *Abers* 2G **161**
Upper Brailes. *Warw* 2B **50**
Upper Breinton. *Here* 1H **47**
Upper Broadheath. *Worc* 5C **60**
Upper Broughton. *Notts* 3D **74**
Upper Brynamman. *Carm* 4H **45**
Upper Bucklebury. *W Ber* 5D **36**
Upper Bullington. *Hants* 2C **24**
Upper Burgate. *Hants* 1G **15**
Upper Caldecote. *C Beds* 1B **52**
Upper Canterton. *Hants* 1A **16**
Upper Catesby. *Nptn* 5C **62**
Upper Chapel. *Powy* 1D **46**
Upper Cheddon. *Som* 4F **21**
Upper Chicksgrove. *Wilts* 4E **23**
Upper Church Village. *Rhon* 3D **32**
Upper Chute. *Wilts* 1A **24**
Upper Clatford. *Hants* 2B **24**
Upper Coberley. *Glos* 4E **49**
Upper Coedcae. *Torf* 5F **47**
Upper Cokeham. *W Sus* 5C **26**
Upper Common. *Hants* 2E **25**
Upper Cound. *Shrp* 5H **71**
Upper Cudworth. *S Yor* 4D **93**
Upper Cumberworth. *W Yor* 4C **92**
Upper Cuttlehill. *Abers* 4B **160**
Upper Cwmbran. *Torf* 2F **33**
Upper Dallachy. *Mor* 2A **160**
Upper Dean. *Bed* 4H **63**
Upper Denby. *W Yor* 4C **92**
Upper Derraid. *High* 5E **159**
Upper Diabaig. *High* 2H **155**
Upper Dicker. *E Sus* 5G **27**
Upper Dinchope. *Shrp* 2G **59**
Upper Dochcarty. *High* 2H **157**
Upper Dounreay. *High* 2B **168**
Upper Dovercourt. *Essx* 2F **55**
Upper Dunsforth. *N Yor* 3G **99**
Upper Dunsley. *Herts* 4H **51**
Upper Eastern Green. *W Mid* 2G **61**
Upper Elkstone. *Staf* 5E **85**
Upper Ellastone. *Staf* 1F **73**
Upper End. *Derbs* 3E **85**
Upper Enham. *Hants* 2B **24**
Upper Farmcote. *Shrp* 1B **60**
Upper Farringdon. *Hants* 3F **25**
Upper Framilode. *Glos* 4C **48**
Upper Froyle. *Hants* 2F **25**
Upper Gills. *High* 1F **169**
Upper Glenfintaig. *High* 5E **149**
Upper Godney. *Som* 2H **21**
Upper Gravenhurst. *C Beds* 2B **52**
Upper Green. *Essx* 2E **53**
Upper Green. *W Ber* 5B **36**
Upper Green. *W Yor* 2C **92**
Upper Grove Common. *Here* 3A **48**
Upper Hackney. *Derbs* 4G **85**
Upper Hale. *Surr* 2G **25**
Upper Halliford. *Surr* 4B **38**
Upper Halling. *Medw* 4A **40**
Upper Hambleton. *Rut* 5G **75**
Upper Hardres Court. *Kent* 5F **41**
Upper Hardwick. *Here* 5G **59**
Upper Hartfield. *E Sus* 2F **27**
Upper Haugh. *S Yor* 1B **86**
Upper Hayton. *Shrp* 2H **59**
Upper Heath. *Shrp* 2H **59**
Upper Hellesdon. *Norf* 4E **79**
Upper Helmsley. *N Yor* 4A **100**
Upper Hengoed. *Shrp* 2E **71**
Upper Hergest. *Here* 5E **59**
Upper Heyford. *Nptn* 5D **62**
Upper Heyford. *Oxon* 3C **50**
Upper Hill. *Here* 5G **59**
Upper Hindhope. *Bord* 4B **120**
Upper Hopton. *W Yor* 3B **92**
Upper Horsebridge. *E Sus* 4G **27**
Upper Howsell. *Worc* 1C **48**
Upper Hulme. *Staf* 4E **85**
Upper Inglesham. *Swin* 2H **35**
Upper Kilcott. *Glos* 3C **34**
Upper Killay. *Swan* 3E **31**
Upper Kirkton. *Abers* 5E **161**
Upper Kirkton. *N Ayr* 4C **126**
Upper Knockando. *Mor* 4F **159**
Upper Knockchoilum. *High* 2G **149**
Upper Lambourn. *W Ber* 3B **36**
Upper Langford. *N Som* 1H **21**
Upper Langwith. *Derbs* 4C **86**
Upper Largo. *Fife* 3G **137**
Upper Latheron. *High* 5D **169**
Upper Layham. *Suff* 1D **54**
Upper Leigh. *Staf* 2E **73**
Upper Lenie. *High* 1H **149**
Upper Lochton. *Abers* 4E **152**
Upper Longdon. *Staf* 4E **73**
Upper Longwood. *Shrp* 5A **72**
Upper Lybster. *High* 5E **169**
Upper Lydbrook. *Glos* 4B **48**
Upper Lye. *Here* 4F **59**
Upper Maes-coed. *Here* 2G **47**
Upper Midway. *Derbs* 3G **73**
Uppermill. *G Man* 4H **91**
Upper Millichope. *Shrp* 2H **59**
Upper Milovaig. *High* 4A **154**
Upper Minety. *Wilts* 2F **35**
Upper Mitton. *Worc* 3C **60**
Upper Nash. *Pemb* 4E **43**
Upper Neepaback. *Shet* 3G **173**
Upper Netchwood. *Shrp* 1A **60**
Upper Nobut. *Staf* 2E **73**
Upper North Dean. *Buck* 2G **37**
Upper Norwood. *W Sus* 4A **26**
Upper Nyland. *Dors* 4C **22**
Upper Oddington. *Glos* 3H **49**
Upper Ollach. *High* 5E **155**
Upper Outwoods. *Staf* 3G **73**
Upper Padley. *Derbs* 3G **85**
Upper Pennington. *Hants* 3B **16**
Upper Poppleton. *York* 4H **99**
Upper Quinton. *Warw* 1G **49**
Upper Rochford. *Worc* 4A **60**
Upper Rusko. *Dum* 3C **110**
Upper Sandaig. *High* 2F **147**
Upper Sanday. *Orkn* 7E **172**
Upper Sapey. *Here* 4A **60**
Upper Seagry. *Wilts* 3E **35**
Upper Shelton. *C Beds* 1H **51**
Upper Sheringham. *Norf* 1D **78**
Upper Skelmorlie. *N Ayr* 3C **126**
Upper Slaughter. *Glos* 3G **49**
Upper Sonachan. *Arg* 1H **133**
Upper Soudley. *Glos* 4B **48**
Upper Staploe. *Bed* 5A **64**
Upper Stoke. *Norf* 5E **79**
Upper Stondon. *C Beds* 2B **52**
Upper Stowe. *Nptn* 5D **62**
Upper Street. *Hants* 1G **15**
Upper Street. *Norf* 4F **79** (nr. Horning)
Upper Street. *Norf* 4F **79** (nr. Hoveton)
Upper Street. *Suff* 2E **55**
Upper Strensham. *Worc* 2E **49**
Upper Studley. *Wilts* 1D **22**
Upper Sundon. *C Beds* 3A **52**
Upper Swell. *Glos* 3G **49**
Upper Tankersley. *S Yor* 1H **85**
Upper Tean. *Staf* 2E **73**
Upperthong. *W Yor* 4B **92**
Upperthorpe. *N Lin* 4A **94**
Upper Thurnham. *Lanc* 4D **96**
Upper Tillyrie. *Per* 3D **136**
Upperton. *W Sus* 3A **26**
Upper Tooting. *G Lon* 3D **38**
Uppertown. *Derbs* 4H **85** (nr. Ashover)
Upper Town. *Derbs* 5G **85** (nr. Bonsall)
Upper Town. *Derbs* 5G **85** (nr. Hognaston)
Upper Town. *Here* 1A **48**
Uppertown. *High* 1F **169**
Upper Town. *N Som* 5A **34**
Uppertown. *Nmbd* 2B **114**
Uppertown. *Orkn* 8D **172**
Upper Tysoe. *Warw* 1B **50**
Upper Upham. *Wilts* 4H **35**
Upper Upnor. *Medw* 3B **40**
Upper Urquhart. *Fife* 3D **136**
Upper Wardington. *Oxon* 1C **50**
Upper Weald. *Mil* 2G **51**
Upper Weedon. *Nptn* 5D **62**
Upper Wellingham. *E Sus* 4F **27**
Upper Whiston. *S Yor* 2B **86**
Upper Wield. *Hants* 3E **25**
Upper Winchendon. *Buck* 4F **51**
Upperwood. *Derbs* 5G **85**
Upper Woodford. *Wilts* 3G **23**
Upper Wootton. *Hants* 1D **24**
Upper Wraxall. *Wilts* 4D **34**
Upper Wyche. *Here* 1C **48**
Uppincott. *Devn* 2B **12**
Uppingham. *Rut* 1F **63**
Uppington. *Shrp* 5H **71**
Upsall. *N Yor* 1G **99**
Upsettlington. *Bord* 5E **131**
Upshire. *Essx* 5E **53**
Up Somborne. *Hants* 3B **24**
Upstreet. *Kent* 4G **41**
Up Sydling. *Dors* 2B **14**
Upthorpe. *Suff* 3B **66**
Upton. *Buck* 4F **51**
Upton. *Cambs* 3A **64**
Upton. *Ches W* 4G **83**
Upton. *Corn* 2C **10** (nr. Bude)
Upton. *Corn* 5C **10** (nr. Liskeard)
Upton. *Cumb* 1E **102**
Upton. *Devn* 2D **12** (nr. Honiton)
Upton. *Devn* 4D **8** (nr. Kingsbridge)
Upton. *Dors* 3E **15** (nr. Poole)
Upton. *Dors* 4C **14** (nr. Weymouth)
Upton. *E Yor* 4F **101**
Upton. *Hants* 1B **24** (nr. Andover)
Upton. *Hants* 1B **16** (nr. Southampton)
Upton. *IOW* 3D **16**
Upton. *Leics* 1A **62**
Upton. *Linc* 2F **87**
Upton. *Mers* 2E **83**
Upton. *Norf* 4F **79**
Upton. *Nptn* 4E **62**
Upton. *Notts* 3E **87** (nr. Retford)
Upton. *Notts* 5E **87** (nr. Southwell)
Upton. *Oxon* 3D **36**
Upton. *Pemb* 4E **43**
Upton. *Pet* 5A **76**
Upton. *Slo* 3A **38**
Upton. *Som* 4H **21** (nr. Somerton)
Upton. *Som* 4C **20** (nr. Wiveliscombe)
Upton. *Warw* 5F **61**
Upton. *W Yor* 3E **93**
Upton. *Wilts* 3D **22**
Upton Bishop. *Here* 3B **48**
Upton Cheyney. *S Glo* 5B **34**
Upton Cressett. *Shrp* 1A **60**
Upton Crews. *Here* 3B **48**
Upton Cross. *Corn* 5C **10**
Upton End. *C Beds* 2B **52**
Upton Grey. *Hants* 2E **25**
Upton Heath. *Ches W* 4G **83**
Upton Hellions. *Devn* 2B **12**
Upton Lovell. *Wilts* 2E **23**
Upton Magna. *Shrp* 4H **71**
Upton Noble. *Som* 3C **22**
Upton Pyne. *Devn* 3C **12**
Upton St Leonards. *Glos* 4D **48**
Upton Scudamore. *Wilts* 2D **22**
Upton Snodsbury. *Worc* 5D **60**
Upton upon Severn. *Worc* 1D **48**
Upton Warren. *Worc* 4D **60**
Upwaltham. *W Sus* 4A **26**
Upware. *Cambs* 3E **65**
Upwell. *Cambs* 5D **77**
Upwey. *Dors* 4B **14**
Upwick Green. *Herts* 3E **53**
Upwood. *Cambs* 2B **64**
Urafirth. *Shet* 4E **173**
Uragaig. *Arg* 4A **132**
Urchany. *High* 4C **158**
Urchfont. *Wilts* 1F **23**
Urdimarsh. *Here* 1A **48**
Ure. *Shet* 4D **173**
Ure Bank. *N Yor* 2F **99**
Urgha. *W Isl* 8D **171**
Urlay Nook. *Stoc T* 3B **106**
Urmston. *G Man* 1B **84**
Urquhart. *Mor* 2G **159**
Urra. *N Yor* 4C **106**
Urray. *High* 3H **157**
Usan. *Ang* 3G **145**
Ushaw Moor. *Dur* 5F **115**
Usk. *Mon* 5G **47**
Usselby. *Linc* 1H **87**
Usworth. *Tyne* 4G **115**
Utkinton. *Ches W* 4H **83**
Uton. *Devn* 3B **12**
Utterby. *Linc* 1C **88**
Uttoxeter. *Staf* 2E **73**
Uwchmynydd. *Gwyn* 3A **68**
Uxbridge. *G Lon* 2B **38**
Uyeasound. *Shet* 1G **173**
Uzmaston. *Pemb* 3D **42**

V

Valley. *IOA* 3B **80**
Valley End. *Surr* 4A **38**
Valley Truckle. *Corn* 4B **10**
Valsgarth. *Shet* 1H **173**
Valtos. *High* 2E **155**
Van. *Powy* 2B **58**
Vange. *Essx* 2B **40**
Varteg. *Torf* 5F **47**
Vatsetter. *Shet* 3G **173**
Vatten. *High* 4B **154**
Vaul. *Arg* 4B **138**
Vauld,The. *Here* 1A **48**
Vaynol. *Gwyn* 3E **81**
Vaynor. *Mer T* 4D **46**
Veensgarth. *Shet* 7F **173**
Velindre. *Powy* 2E **47**
Vellow. *Som* 3D **20**
Velly. *Devn* 4C **18**
Veness. *Orkn* 5E **172**
Venhay. *Devn* 1A **12**
Venn. *Devn* 4D **8**
Venngreen. *Devn* 1D **11**
Vennington. *Shrp* 5F **71**
Venn Ottery. *Devn* 3D **12**
Venn's Green. *Here* 1A **48**
Venny Tedburn. *Devn* 3B **12**
Venterdon. *Corn* 5D **10**
Ventnor. *IOW* 5D **16**
Vernham Dean. *Hants* 1B **24**
Vernham Street. *Hants* 1B **24**
Vernolds Common. *Shrp* 2G **59**
Verwood. *Dors* 2F **15**
Veryan. *Corn* 5D **6**
Veryan Green. *Corn* 4D **6**
Vicarage. *Devn* 4F **13**
Vickerstown. *Cumb* 3A **96**
Victoria. *Corn* 2D **6**
Vidlin. *Shet* 5F **173**
Viewpark. *N Lan* 3A **128**
Vigo. *W Mid* 5E **73**
Vigo Village. *Kent* 4H **39**
Village Bay. *High* 3B **154**
Vinehall Street. *E Sus* 3B **28**
Vine's Cross. *E Sus* 4G **27**
Viney Hill. *Glos* 5B **48**
Virginia Water. *Surr* 4A **38**
Virginstow. *Devn* 3D **11**
Vobster. *Som* 2C **22**
Voe. *Shet* 5F **173** (nr. Hillside)
Voe. *Shet* 3E **173** (nr. Swinister)
Vole. *Som* 2G **21**
Vowchurch. *Here* 2G **47**
Voxter. *Shet* 4E **173**
Voy. *Orkn* 6B **172**
Vulcan Village. *Warr* 1H **83**

W

Waberthwaite. *Cumb* 5C **102**
Wackerfield. *Dur* 2E **105**
Wacton. *Norf* 1D **66**
Wadbister. *Shet* 7F **173**
Wadborough. *Worc* 1E **49**
Wadbrook. *Devn* 2G **13**
Waddesdon. *Buck* 4F **51**
Waddeton. *Devn* 3E **9**
Waddicar. *Mers* 1F **83**
Waddingham. *Linc* 1G **87**
Waddington. *Lanc* 5G **97**
Waddington. *Linc* 4G **87**
Waddon. *Devn* 5B **12**
Wadebridge. *Corn* 1D **6**
Wadeford. *Som* 1G **13**
Wadenhoe. *Nptn* 2H **63**
Wadesmill. *Herts* 4D **52**
Wadhurst. *E Sus* 2H **27**
Wadshelf. *Derbs* 3H **85**
Wadsley. *S Yor* 1H **85**
Wadsley Bridge. *S Yor* 1H **85**
Wadswick. *Wilts* 5D **34**
Wadwick. *Hants* 1C **24**
Wadworth. *S Yor* 1C **86**
Waen. *Den* 4C **82** (nr. Bodfari)
Waen. *Den* 4D **82** (nr. Llandyrnog)
Waen. *Den* 4B **82** (nr. Nantglyn)
Waen. *Powy* 1B **58**
Waen Fach. *Powy* 4E **70**
Waen Goleugoed. *Den* 3C **82**
Wag. *High* 1H **165**
Wainfleet All Saints. *Linc* 5D **89**
Wainfleet Bank. *Linc* 5D **88**
Wainfleet St Mary. *Linc* 5D **89**
Wainhouse Corner. *Corn* 3B **10**
Wainscott. *Medw* 3B **40**
Wainstalls. *W Yor* 2A **92**
Waitby. *Cumb* 4A **104**
Waithe. *Linc* 4F **95**
Wakefield. *W Yor* 2D **92**
Wakerley. *Nptn* 1G **63**
Wakes Colne. *Essx* 3B **54**
Walberswick. *Suff* 3G **67**
Walberton. *W Sus* 5A **26**
Walbottle. *Tyne* 3E **115**
Walby. *Cumb* 3F **113**
Walcombe. *Som* 2A **22**
Walcot. *Linc* 2H **75**
Walcot. *N Lin* 2B **94**
Walcot. *Swin* 3G **35**
Walcot. *Telf* 4H **71**
Walcot. *Warw* 5F **61**
Walcote. *Leics* 2C **62**
Walcot Green. *Norf* 2D **66**
Walcott. *Linc* 5A **88**
Walcott. *Norf* 2F **79**
Walden. *N Yor* 1C **98**
Walden Head. *N Yor* 1B **98**
Walden Stubbs. *N Yor* 3F **93**
Walderslade. *Medw* 4B **40**
Walderton. *W Sus* 1F **17**
Walditch. *Dors* 3H **13**
Waldley. *Derbs* 2F **73**
Waldridge. *Dur* 4F **115**
Waldringfield. *Suff* 1F **55**
Waldron. *E Sus* 4G **27**
Wales. *S Yor* 2B **86**
Walesby. *Linc* 1A **88**
Walesby. *Notts* 3D **86**
Walford. *Here* 3F **59** (nr. Leintwardine)
Walford. *Here* 3A **48** (nr. Ross-on-Wye)
Walford. *Shrp* 3G **71**
Walford. *Staf* 2C **72**
Walford Heath. *Shrp* 4G **71**
Walgherton. *Ches E* 1A **72**
Walgrave. *Nptn* 3F **63**
Walhampton. *Hants* 3B **16**
Walkden. *G Man* 4F **91**
Walker. *Tyne* 3F **115**
Walkerburn. *Bord* 1F **119**
Walker Fold. *Lanc* 5F **97**
Walkeringham. *Notts* 1E **87**
Walkerith. *Linc* 1E **87**
Walkern. *Herts* 3C **52**
Walker's Green. *Here* 1A **48**
Walkerton. *Fife* 3E **137**
Walkerville. *N Yor* 5F **105**
Walkford. *Dors* 3H **15**
Walkhampton. *Devn* 2B **8**
Walkington. *E Yor* 1C **94**
Walkley. *S Yor* 2H **85**
Walk Mill. *Lanc* 1G **91**
Wall. *Corn* 3D **4**
Wall. *Nmbd* 3C **114**
Wall. *Staf* 5F **73**
Wallaceton. *Dum* 1F **111**
Wallacetown. *Shet* 6E **173**
Wallacetown. *S Ayr* 2C **116** (nr. Ayr)
Wallacetown. *S Ayr* 4B **116** (nr. Dailly)
Wallands Park. *E Sus* 4F **27**
Wallasey. *Mers* 1F **83**
Wallaston Green. *Pemb* 4D **42**
Wallbrook. *W Mid* 1D **60**
Wallcrouch. *E Sus* 2A **28**
Wall End. *Cumb* 1B **96**
Wallend. *Medw* 3C **40**
Wall Heath. *W Mid* 2C **60**
Wallingford. *Oxon* 3E **36**
Wallington. *G Lon* 4D **39**
Wallington. *Hants* 2D **16**
Wallington. *Herts* 2C **52**
Wallis. *Pemb* 2E **43**
Wallisdown. *Pool* 3F **15**
Walliswood. *Surr* 2C **26**
Wall Nook. *Dur* 5F **115**

Walls. *Shet* 7D **173**
Wallsend. *Tyne* 3G **115**
Wallsworth. *Glos* 3D **48**
Wall under Heywood. *Shrp* ...1H **59**
Wallyford. *E Lot* 2G **129**
Walmer. *Kent* 5H **41**
Walmer Bridge. *Lanc* 2C **90**
Walmersley. *G Man* 3G **91**
Walmley. *W Mid* 1F **61**
Walnut Grove. *Per* 1D **136**
Walpole. *Suff* 3F **67**
Walpole Cross Keys. *Norf* 4E **77**
Walpole Gate. *Norf* 4E **77**
Walpole Highway. *Norf* 4E **77**
Walpole Marsh. *Norf* 4D **77**
Walpole St Andrew. *Norf* 4E **77**
Walpole St Peter. *Norf* 4E **77**
Walsall. *W Mid* 1E **61**
Walsall Wood. *W Mid* 5E **73**
Walsden. *W Yor* 2H **91**
Walsgrave on Sowe. *W Mid* ...2A **62**
Walsham le Willows. *Suff* ...3C **66**
Walshaw. *G Man* 3F **91**
Walshford. *N Yor* 4G **99**
Walsoken. *Cambs* 4D **76**
Walston. *S Lan* 5D **128**
Walsworth. *Herts* 2B **52**
Walter's Ash. *Buck* 2G **37**
Walterston. *V Glam* 4D **32**
Walterstone. *Here* 3G **47**
Waltham. *Kent* 1F **29**
Waltham. *NE Lin* 4F **95**
Waltham Abbey. *Essx* 5D **53**
Waltham Chase. *Hants* 1D **16**
Waltham Cross. *Herts* 5D **52**
Waltham on the Wolds. *Leics* 3F **75**
Waltham St Lawrence. *Wind* 4G **37**
Waltham's Cross. *Essx* ...2G **53**
Walthamstow. *G Lon* 2E **39**
Walton. *Cumb* 3G **113**
Walton. *Derbs* 4A **86**
Walton. *Leics* 2C **62**
Walton. *Mers* 1F **83**
Walton. *Mil* 2G **51**
Walton. *Pet* 5A **76**
Walton. *Powy* 5E **59**
Walton. *Som* 3H **21**
Walton. *Staf* 3C **72**
(nr. Eccleshall)
Walton. *Staf* 2C **72**
(nr. Stone)
Walton. *Suff* 2F **55**
Walton. *Telf* 4H **71**
Walton. *Warw* 5G **61**
Walton. *W Yor* 3D **92**
(nr. Wakefield)
Walton. *W Yor* 5G **99**
(nr. Wetherby)
Walton Cardiff. *Glos* 2E **49**
Walton East. *Pemb* 2E **43**
Walton Elm. *Dors* 1C **14**
Walton Highway. *Norf* 4D **77**
Walton-in-Gordano. *N Som* ...4H **33**
Walton-le-Dale. *Lanc* 2D **90**
Walton-on-Thames. *Surr* ...4C **38**
Walton-on-the-Hill. *Staf* ...3D **72**
Walton on the Hill. *Surr* ...5D **38**
Walton-on-the-Naze. *Essx* ...3F **55**
Walton on the Wolds. *Leics* 4C **74**
Walton-on-Trent. *Derbs* ...4G **73**
Walton West. *Pemb* 3C **42**
Walwick. *Nmbd* 2C **114**
Walworth. *Darl* 3F **105**
Walworth Gate. *Darl* 2F **105**
Walwyn's Castle. *Pemb* ...3C **42**
Wambrook. *Som* 2F **13**
Wampool. *Cumb* 4D **112**
Wanborough. *Surr* 1A **26**
Wanborough. *Swin* 3H **35**
Wandel. *S Lan* 2B **118**
Wandsworth. *G Lon* 3D **38**
Wangford. *Suff* 2G **65**
(nr. Lakenheath)
Wangford. *Suff* 3G **67**
(nr. Southwold)
Wanlip. *Leics* 4D **74**
Wanlockhead. *Dum* 3A **118**
Wannock. *E Sus* 5G **27**
Wansford. *E Yor* 4E **101**
Wansford. *Pet* 1H **63**
Wanshurst Green. *Kent* ...1B **28**
Wanstead. *G Lon* 2F **39**
Wanstrow. *Som* 2C **22**
Wanswell. *Glos* 5B **48**
Wantage. *Oxon* 3C **36**
Wapley. *S Glo* 4C **34**
Wappenbury. *Warw* 4A **62**
Wappenham. *Nptn* 1E **51**
Warbleton. *E Sus* 4H **27**
Warblington. *Hants* 2F **17**
Warborough. *Oxon* 2D **36**
Warboys. *Cambs* 2C **64**
Warbreck. *Bkpl* 1B **90**
Warbstow. *Corn* 3C **10**
Warburton. *G Man* 2A **84**
Warcop. *Cumb* 3A **104**
Warden. *Kent* 3E **40**
Warden. *Nmbd* 3C **114**

Ward End. *W Mid* 2F **61**
Ward Green. *Suff* 4C **66**
Ward Green Cross. *Lanc* ...1E **91**
Wardhedges. *C Beds* 2A **52**
Wardhouse. *Abers* 5C **160**
Wardington. *Oxon* 1C **50**
Wardle. *Ches E* 5A **84**
Wardle. *G Man* 3H **91**
Wardley. *Rut* 5F **75**
Wardley. *W Sus* 4G **25**
Wardlow. *Derbs* 3F **85**
Wardsend. *Ches E* 2D **84**
Wardy Hill. *Cambs* 2D **64**
Ware. *Herts* 4D **52**
Ware. *Kent* 4G **41**
Wareham. *Dors* 4E **15**
Warehorne. *Kent* 2D **28**
Warenford. *Nmbd* 2F **121**
Waren Mill. *Nmbd* 1F **121**
Warenton. *Nmbd* 1F **121**
Wareside. *Herts* 4D **53**
Waresley. *Cambs* 5B **64**
Waresley. *Worc* 4C **60**
Warfield. *Brac* 4G **37**
Warfleet. *Devn* 3E **9**
Wargate. *Linc* 2B **76**
Wargrave. *Wok* 4F **37**
Warham. *Norf* 1B **78**
Wark. *Nmbd* 1C **120**
(nr. Coldstream)
Wark. *Nmbd* 2B **114**
(nr. Hexham)
Warkleigh. *Devn* 4G **19**
Warkton. *Nptn* 3F **63**
Warkworth. *Nptn* 1C **50**
Warkworth. *Nmbd* 4G **121**
Warlaby. *N Yor* 5A **106**
Warland. *W Yor* 2H **91**
Warleggan. *Corn* 2F **7**
Warlingham. *Surr* 5E **39**
Warmanbie. *Dum* 3C **112**
Warmfield. *W Yor* 2D **93**
Warmingham. *Ches E* 4B **84**
Warminghurst. *W Sus* 4C **26**
Warmington. *Nptn* 1H **63**
Warmington. *Warw* 1C **50**
Warminster. *Wilts* 2D **23**
Warmley. *S Glo* 4B **34**
Warmsworth. *S Yor* 4F **93**
Warmwell. *Dors* 4C **14**
Warndon. *Worc* 5C **60**
Warners End. *Herts* 5A **52**
Warnford. *Hants* 4E **24**
Warnham. *W Sus* 2C **26**
Warningcamp. *W Sus* 5B **26**
Warninglid. *W Sus* 3D **26**
Warren. *Ches E* 3C **84**
Warren. *Pemb* 5D **42**
Warrenby. *Red C* 2C **106**
Warren Corner. *Hants* 2G **25**
(nr. Aldershot)
Warren Corner. *Hants* 4F **25**
(nr. Petersfield)
Warren Row. *Wind* 3G **37**
Warren Street. *Kent* 5D **40**
Warrington. *Mil* 5F **63**
Warrington. *Warr* 2A **84**
Warsash. *Hants* 2C **16**
Warse. *High* 1F **169**
Warslow. *Staf* 5E **85**
Warsop. *Notts* 4C **86**
Warsop Vale. *Notts* 4C **86**
Warter. *E Yor* 4C **100**
Warthermarske. *N Yor* 2E **98**
Warthill. *N Yor* 4A **100**
Wartling. *E Sus* 5A **28**
Wartnaby. *Leics* 3E **74**
Warton. *Lanc* 2D **97**
(nr. Carnforth)
Warton. *Lanc* 2C **90**
(nr. Freckleton)
Warton. *Nmbd* 4E **121**
Warton. *Warw* 5G **73**
Warwick. *Warw* 4G **61**
Warwick Bridge. *Cumb* 4F **113**
Warwick-on-Eden. *Cumb* ...4F **113**
Warwick Wold. *Surr* 5E **39**
Wasbister. *Orkn* 4C **172**
Wasdale Head. *Cumb* 4C **102**
Wash. *Derbs* 2E **85**
Washaway. *Corn* 2E **7**
Washbourne. *Devn* 3E **9**
Washbrook. *Suff* 1E **54**
Wash Common. *W Ber* 5C **36**
Washerwall. *Staf* 1D **72**
Washfield. *Devn* 1C **12**
Washfold. *N Yor* 4D **104**
Washford. *Som* 2D **20**
Washford Pyne. *Devn* 1B **12**
Washingborough. *Linc* 3H **87**
Washington. *Tyne* 4G **115**
Washington. *W Sus* 4C **26**
Washington Village. *Tyne* ...4G **115**
Waskerley. *Dur* 5D **114**
Wasperton. *Warw* 5G **61**
Wasp Green. *Surr* 1E **27**
Wasps Nest. *Linc* 4H **87**
Wass. *N Yor* 2H **99**
Watchet. *Som* 2D **20**
Watchfield. *Oxon* 2H **35**
Watchgate. *Cumb* 5G **103**

Watchhill. *Cumb* 5C **112**
Watcombe. *Torb* 2F **9**
Watendlath. *Cumb* 3D **102**
Water. *Devn* 4A **12**
Water. *Lanc* 2G **91**
Waterbeach. *Cambs* 4D **65**
Waterbeach. *W Sus* 2G **17**
Waterbeck. *Dum* 2D **112**
Waterditch. *Hants* 3G **15**
Water End. *C Beds* 2A **52**
Water End. *E Yor* 1A **94**
Water End. *Essx* 1F **53**
Water End. *Herts* 5C **52**
(nr. Hatfield)
Water End. *Herts* 4A **52**
(nr. Hemel Hempstead)
Waterfall. *Staf* 5E **85**
Waterfoot. *E Ren* 4G **127**
Waterfoot. *Lanc* 2G **91**
Waterford. *Herts* 4D **52**
Water Fryston. *W Yor* 2E **93**
Waterhead. *Cumb* 4E **103**
Waterhead. *E Ayr* 3E **117**
Waterhead. *S Ayr* 5C **116**
Waterheads. *Bord* 4F **129**
Waterhouses. *Dur* 5E **115**
Waterhouses. *Staf* 5E **85**
Wateringbury. *Kent* 5A **40**
Waterlane. *Glos* 5E **49**
Waterlip. *Som* 2B **22**
Waterloo. *Cphy* 3E **33**
Waterloo. *Corn* 5B **10**
Waterloo. *Here* 1G **47**
Waterloo. *High* 1E **147**
Waterloo. *Mers* 1F **83**
Waterloo. *Norf* 4E **78**
Waterloo. *N Lan* 4B **128**
Waterloo. *Pemb* 4D **42**
Waterloo. *Per* 5H **143**
Waterloo. *Pool* 3F **15**
Waterloo. *Shrp* 2G **71**
Waterlooville. *Hants* 2E **17**
Watermead. *Buck* 4G **51**
Watermillock. *Cumb* 2F **103**
Water Newton. *Cambs* 1A **64**
Water Orton. *Warw* 1F **61**
Waterperry. *Oxon* 5E **51**
Waterrow. *Som* 4D **20**
Watersfield. *W Sus* 4B **26**
Waterside. *Buck* 5H **51**
Waterside. *Cambs* 3F **65**
Waterside. *Cumb* 5D **112**
Waterside. *E Ayr* 4D **116**
(nr. Ayr)
Waterside. *E Ayr* 5F **127**
(nr. Kilmarnock)
Waterside. *E Dun* 2H **127**
Waterstein. *High* 4A **154**
Waterstock. *Oxon* 5E **51**
Waterston. *Pemb* 4D **42**
Water Stratford. *Buck* 2E **51**
Waters Upton. *Telf* 4A **72**
Water Yeat. *Cumb* 1B **96**
Watford. *Herts* 1B **38**
Watford. *Nptn* 4D **62**
Wath. *Cumb* 4H **103**
Wath. *N Yor* 3D **98**
(nr. Pateley Bridge)
Wath. *N Yor* 2F **99**
(nr. Ripon)
Wath Brow. *Cumb* 3B **102**
Wath upon Dearne. *S Yor* ...1B **86**
Watlington. *Norf* 4F **77**
Watlington. *Oxon* 2E **37**
Watten. *High* 3E **169**
Wattisfield. *Suff* 3C **66**
Wattisham. *Suff* 5C **66**
Wattlesborough Heath. *Shrp* ...4F **71**
Watton. *Dors* 3H **13**
Watton. *E Yor* 4E **101**
Watton. *Norf* 5B **78**
Watton at Stone. *Herts* 4C **52**
Wattston. *N Lan* 2A **128**
Wattstown. *Rhon* 2D **32**
Wattsville. *Cphy* 2F **33**
Wauldby. *E Yor* 2C **94**
Waulkmill. *Abers* 4D **152**
Waun. *Powy* 4E **71**
Waunarlwydd. *Swan* 3F **31**
Waun Fawr. *Cdgn* 2F **57**
Waunfawr. *Gwyn* 5E **81**
Waungilwen. *Carm* 1H **43**
Waunlwyd. *Blae* 5E **47**
Waun-y-Clyn. *Carm* 5E **45**
Wavendon. *Mil* 2H **51**
Waverbridge. *Cumb* 5D **112**
Waverley. *Surr* 2G **25**
Waverton. *Ches W* 4G **83**
Waverton. *Cumb* 5D **112**
Wavertree. *Mers* 2F **83**
Wawne. *E Yor* 1D **94**
Waxham. *Norf* 3G **79**
Waxholme. *E Yor* 2G **95**
Wayford. *Som* 2H **13**
Way Head. *Cambs* 2D **64**
Waytown. *Dors* 3H **13**
Way Village. *Devn* 1B **12**
Wdig. *Pemb* 1D **42**
Wealdstone. *G Lon* 2C **38**
Weardley. *W Yor* 5E **99**
Weare. *Som* 1H **21**

Weare Giffard. *Devn* 4E **19**
Wearhead. *Dur* 1B **104**
Wearne. *Som* 4H **21**
Weasdale. *Cumb* 4H **103**
Weasenham All Saints. *Norf* ...3H **77**
Weasenham St Peter. *Norf* ...3A **78**
Weaverham. *Ches W* 3A **84**
Weaverthorpe. *N Yor* 2D **100**
Webheath. *Worc* 4E **61**
Webton. *Here* 2H **47**
Wedderlairs. *Abers* 5F **161**
Weddington. *Warw* 1A **62**
Wedhampton. *Wilts* 1F **23**
Wedmore. *Som* 2H **21**
Wednesbury. *W Mid* 1D **61**
Wednesfield. *W Mid* 5D **72**
Weecar. *Notts* 4F **87**
Weedon. *Buck* 4G **51**
Weedon Bec. *Nptn* 5D **62**
Weedon Lois. *Nptn* 1E **50**
Weeford. *Staf* 5F **73**
Week. *Devn* 4E **19**
(nr. Barnstaple)
Week. *Devn* 2G **11**
(nr. Okehampton)
Week. *Devn* 1H **11**
(nr. South Molton)
Week. *Devn* 2D **9**
(nr. Totnes)
Week. *Som* 3C **20**
Weeke. *Devn* 2A **12**
Weeke. *Hants* 3C **24**
Week Green. *Corn* 3C **10**
Weekley. *Nptn* 2F **63**
Week St Mary. *Corn* 3C **10**
Weel. *E Yor* 1D **94**
Weeley. *Essx* 3E **55**
Weeley Heath. *Essx* 3E **55**
Weem. *Per* 4F **143**
Weeping Cross. *Staf* 3D **72**
Weethly. *Warw* 5E **61**
Weeting. *Norf* 2G **65**
Weeton. *E Yor* 2G **95**
Weeton. *Lanc* 1B **90**
Weeton. *N Yor* 5E **99**
Weetwood Hall. *Nmbd* 2E **121**
Weir. *Lanc* 2G **91**
Welborne. *Norf* 4C **78**
Welbourn. *Linc* 5G **87**
Welburn. *N Yor* 1A **100**
(nr. Kirkbymoorside)
Welburn. *N Yor* 3B **100**
(nr. Malton)
Welbury. *N Yor* 4A **106**
Welby. *Linc* 2G **75**
Welches Dam. *Cambs* 2D **64**
Welcombe. *Devn* 1C **10**
Weld Bank. *Lanc* 3D **90**
Weldon. *Nptn* 2G **63**
Weldon. *Nmbd* 5F **121**
Welford. *Nptn* 2D **62**
Welford. *W Ber* 4C **36**
Welford-on-Avon. *Warw* ...5F **61**
Welham. *Leics* 1E **63**
Welham. *Notts* 2E **87**
Welham Green. *Herts* 5C **52**
Well. *Hants* 2F **25**
Well. *Linc* 3D **88**
Well. *N Yor* 1E **99**
Welland. *Worc* 1C **48**
Wellbank. *Ang* 5D **144**
Well Bottom. *Dors* 1E **15**
Welldale. *Dum* 3C **112**
Wellesbourne. *Warw* 5G **61**
Well Hill. *Kent* 4F **39**
Wellhouse. *W Ber* 4D **36**
Welling. *G Lon* 3F **39**
Wellingborough. *Nptn* 4F **63**
Wellingham. *Norf* 3A **78**
Wellingore. *Linc* 5G **87**
Wellington. *Cumb* 4B **102**
Wellington. *Here* 1H **47**
Wellington. *Som* 4E **21**
Wellington. *Telf* 4A **72**
Wellington Heath. *Here* ...1C **48**
Wellow. *Bath* 1C **22**
Wellow. *IOW* 4B **16**
Wellow. *Notts* 4D **86**
Wellpond Green. *Herts* 3E **53**
Wells. *Som* 2A **22**
Wellsborough. *Leics* 5A **74**
Wells Green. *Ches E* 5A **84**
Wells-next-the-Sea. *Norf* ...1B **78**
Wells of Ythan. *Abers* 5D **160**
Wellswood. *Torb* 2F **9**
Wellwood. *Fife* 1D **129**
Welney. *Norf* 1E **65**
Welsford. *Devn* 4C **18**
Welshampton. *Shrp* 2G **71**
Welsh End. *Shrp* 2H **71**
Welsh Frankton. *Shrp* 2F **71**
Welsh Hook. *Pemb* 2D **42**
Welsh Newton. *Here* 4H **47**
Welsh Newton Common. *Here* 4A **48**
Welshpool. *Powy* 5E **70**
Welsh St Donats. *V Glam* ...4D **32**
Welton. *Bath* 1B **22**
Welton. *Cumb* 5E **113**
Welton. *E Yor* 2C **94**
Welton. *Linc* 2H **87**

Welton. *Nptn* 4C **62**
Welton Hill. *Linc* 2H **87**
Welton le Marsh. *Linc* 4D **88**
Welton le Wold. *Linc* 2B **88**
Welwick. *E Yor* 2G **95**
Welwyn. *Herts* 4C **52**
Welwyn Garden City. *Herts* ...4C **52**
Wem. *Shrp* 3H **71**
Wembdon. *Som* 3F **21**
Wembley. *G Lon* 2C **38**
Wembury. *Devn* 4B **8**
Wembworthy. *Devn* 2G **11**
Wemyss Bay. *Inv* 2C **126**
Wenallt. *Cdgn* 3F **57**
Wenallt. *Gwyn* 1B **70**
Wendens Ambo. *Essx* 2F **53**
Wendlebury. *Oxon* 4D **50**
Wendling. *Norf* 4B **78**
Wendover. *Buck* 5G **51**
Wendron. *Corn* 5A **6**
Wendy. *Cambs* 1D **52**
Wenfordbridge. *Corn* 5A **10**
Wenhaston. *Suff* 3G **67**
Wennington. *Cambs* 3B **64**
Wennington. *G Lon* 2G **39**
Wennington. *Lanc* 2F **97**
Wensley. *Derbs* 4G **85**
Wensley. *N Yor* 1C **98**
Wentbridge. *W Yor* 3E **93**
Wentnor. *Shrp* 1F **59**
Wentworth. *Cambs* 3D **65**
Wentworth. *S Yor* 1A **86**
Wenvoe. *V Glam* 4E **32**
Weobley. *Here* 5G **59**
Weobley Marsh. *Here* 5G **59**
Wepham. *W Sus* 5B **26**
Wereham. *Norf* 5F **77**
Wergs. *W Mid* 5C **72**
Wern. *Gwyn* 1E **69**
Wern. *Powy* 4E **46**
(nr. Brecon)
Wern. *Powy* 4E **71**
(nr. Guilsfield)
Wern. *Powy* 4B **70**
(nr. Llangadfan)
Wern. *Powy* 3E **71**
(nr. Llanymynech)
Wernffrwd. *Swan* 3E **31**
Wernyrheolydd. *Mon* 4G **47**
Werrington. *Corn* 4D **10**
Werrington. *Pet* 5A **76**
Werrington. *Staf* 1D **72**
Wervin. *Ches W* 3G **83**
Wesham. *Lanc* 1C **90**
Wessington. *Derbs* 5A **86**
West Aberthaw. *V Glam* 5D **32**
West Acre. *Norf* 4G **77**
West Allerdean. *Nmbd* 5F **131**
West Alvington. *Devn* 4D **8**
West Amesbury. *Wilts* 2G **23**
West Anstey. *Devn* 4B **20**
West Appleton. *N Yor* 5F **105**
West Arthurlie. *E Ren* 4F **127**
West Ashby. *Linc* 3B **88**
West Ashling. *W Sus* 2G **17**
West Ashton. *Wilts* 1D **23**
West Auckland. *Dur* 2E **105**
West Ayton. *N Yor* 1D **101**
West Bagborough. *Som* 3E **21**
West Bank. *Hal* 2H **83**
West Barkwith. *Linc* 2A **88**
West Barnby. *N Yor* 3F **107**
West Barns. *E Lot* 2C **130**
West Barsham. *Norf* 2B **78**
West Bay. *Dors* 3H **13**
West Beckham. *Norf* 2D **78**
West Bennan. *N Ayr* 3D **123**
Westbere. *Kent* 4F **41**
West Bergholt. *Essx* 3C **54**
West Bexington. *Dors* 4A **14**
West Bilney. *Norf* 4G **77**
West Blackdene. *Dur* 1B **104**
West Blatchington. *Brig* 5D **27**
Westborough. *Linc* 1F **75**
Westbourne. *Bour* 3F **15**
Westbourne. *W Sus* 2F **17**
West Bowling. *W Yor* 1B **92**
West Brabourne. *Kent* 1E **29**
West Bradford. *Lanc* 5G **97**
West Bradley. *Som* 3A **22**
West Bretton. *W Yor* 3C **92**
West Bridgford. *Notts* 2C **74**
West Briggs. *Norf* 4F **77**
West Bromwich. *W Mid* 1D **61**
Westbrook. *Here* 1F **47**
Westbrook. *Kent* 3H **41**
Westbrook. *Wilts* 5E **35**
West Buckland. *Devn* 3G **19**
(nr. Barnstaple)
West Buckland. *Devn* 4C **8**
(nr. Thurlestone)
West Buckland. *Som* 4E **21**
West Burnside. *Abers* 1G **145**
West Burrafirth. *Shet* 6D **173**
West Burton. *N Yor* 1C **98**
West Burton. *W Sus* 4B **26**
Westbury. *Buck* 2E **51**
Westbury. *Shrp* 5F **71**
Westbury. *Wilts* 1D **22**
Westbury Leigh. *Wilts* 2D **22**
Westbury-on-Severn. *Glos* ...4C **48**

Westbury on Trym. Bris ... 4A 34
Westbury-sub-Mendip. Som ... 2A 22
West Butsfield. Dur ... 5E 115
West Butterwick. N Lin ... 4B 94
Westby. Linc ... 3G 75
West Byfleet. Surr ... 4B 38
West Caister. Norf ... 4H 79
West Calder. W Lot ... 3D 128
West Camel. Som ... 4A 22
West Carr. N Lin ... 4H 93
West Chaldon. Dors ... 4C 14
West Challow. Oxon ... 3B 36
West Charleton. Devn ... 4D 8
West Chelborough. Dors ... 2A 14
West Chevington. Nmbd ... 5G 121
West Chiltington. W Sus ... 4B 26
West Chiltington Common. W Sus ... 4B 26
West Chinnock. Som ... 1H 13
West Chisenbury. Wilts ... 1G 23
West Clandon. Surr ... 5B 38
West Cliffe. Kent ... 1H 29
Westcliff-on-Sea. S'end ... 2C 40
West Clyne. High ... 3F 165
West Coker. Som ... 1A 14
Westcombe. Som ... 3B 22 (nr. Evercreech)
Westcombe. Som ... 4H 21 (nr. Somerton)
West Compton. Dors ... 3A 14
West Compton. Som ... 2A 22
West Cornforth. Dur ... 1A 106
Westcot. Oxon ... 3B 36
Westcott. Buck ... 4F 51
Westcott. Devn ... 2D 12
Westcott. Surr ... 1C 26
Westcott Barton. Oxon ... 3C 50
West Cowick. E Yor ... 2G 93
West Cranmore. Som ... 2B 22
West Croftmore. High ... 2D 150
West Cross. Swan ... 4F 31
West Cullerlie. Abers ... 3E 153
West Culvennan. Dum ... 3H 109
West Curry. Corn ... 3C 10
West Curthwaite. Cumb ... 5E 113
Westdean. E Sus ... 5G 27
West Dean. W Sus ... 1G 17
West Dean. Wilts ... 4A 24
West Deeping. Linc ... 5A 76
West Derby. Mers ... 1F 83
West Dereham. Norf ... 5F 77
West Down. Devn ... 2F 19
Westdowns. Corn ... 4A 10
West Drayton. G Lon ... 3B 38
West Drayton. Notts ... 3E 86
West Dunnet. High ... 1E 169
West Ella. E Yor ... 2D 94
West End. Bed ... 5G 63
West End. Cambs ... 1D 64
West End. Dors ... 2E 15
West End. E Yor ... 3E 101 (nr. Kilham)
West End. E Yor ... 1E 95 (nr. Preston)
West End. E Yor ... 1C 94 (nr. South Cove)
West End. E Yor ... 4F 101 (nr. Ulrome)
West End. G Lon ... 2D 39
West End. Hants ... 1C 16
West End. Herts ... 5C 52
West End. Kent ... 4F 41
West End. Lanc ... 3D 96
West End. Linc ... 1C 76
West End. Norf ... 4G 79
West End. N Som ... 5H 33
West End. N Yor ... 4D 98
West End. S Glo ... 3C 34
West End. S Lan ... 5C 128
West End. Surr ... 4A 38
West End. Wilts ... 4E 23
West End. Wind ... 4G 37
West End. Worc ... 2F 49
West End Green. Hants ... 5E 37
Westenhanger. Kent ... 2F 29
Wester Aberchalder. High ... 2H 149
Wester Balgedie. Per ... 3D 136
Wester Brae. High ... 2A 158
Wester Culbeuchly. Abers ... 2D 160
Westerdale. High ... 3D 168
Westerdale. N Yor ... 4D 106
Wester Dechmont. W Lot ... 2D 128
Wester Fearn. High ... 5D 164
Westerfield. Suff ... 1E 55
Wester Galcantray. High ... 4C 158
Westergate. W Sus ... 5A 26
Wester Gruinards. High ... 4C 164
Westerham. Kent ... 5F 39
Westerleigh. S Glo ... 4B 34
Westerloch. High ... 3F 169
Wester Mandally. High ... 3E 149
Wester Quarff. Shet ... 8F 173
Wester Rarichie. High ... 1C 158
Wester Shian. Per ... 5F 143
Wester Skeld. Shet ... 7D 173
Westerton. Ang ... 3F 145
Westerton. Dur ... 1F 105
Westerton. W Sus ... 2G 17
Westerwick. Shet ... 7D 173

West Farleigh. Kent ... 5B 40
West Farndon. Nptn ... 5C 62
West Felton. Shrp ... 3F 71
Westfield. Cumb ... 2A 102
Westfield. E Sus ... 4C 28
Westfield. High ... 2C 168
Westfield. Norf ... 5B 78
Westfield. N Lan ... 2A 128
Westfield. W Lot ... 2C 128
Westfields. Dors ... 2C 14
Westfields of Rattray. Per ... 4A 144
West Firle. E Sus ... 5F 27
West Fleetham. Nmbd ... 2F 121
Westford. Som ... 1E 13
West Garforth. W Yor ... 1D 93
Westgate. Dur ... 1C 104
Westgate. Norf ... 1B 78
Westgate. N Lin ... 4A 94
Westgate on Sea. Kent ... 3H 41
West Ginge. Oxon ... 3C 36
West Grafton. Wilts ... 5H 35
West Green. Hants ... 1F 25
West Grimstead. Wilts ... 4H 23
West Grinstead. W Sus ... 3C 26
West Haddlesey. N Yor ... 2F 93
West Haddon. Nptn ... 3D 62
West Hagbourne. Oxon ... 3D 36
West Hagley. Worc ... 2C 60
West Hall. Cumb ... 3G 113
Westhall. Suff ... 2G 67
West Hallam. Derbs ... 1B 74
West Hardwick. W Yor ... 3E 93
West Harnham. Wilts ... 4G 23
West Harptree. Bath ... 1A 22
West Harting. W Sus ... 4F 25
West Harton. Tyne ... 3G 115
West Hatch. Som ... 4F 21
Westhay. Som ... 2H 21
Westhead. Lanc ... 4C 90
West Head. Norf ... 5E 77
West Heath. Hants ... 1D 24 (nr. Basingstoke)
West Heath. Hants ... 1G 25 (nr. Farnborough)
West Helmsdale. High ... 2H 165
West Hendred. Oxon ... 3C 36
West Heogaland. Shet ... 4D 173
West Heslerton. N Yor ... 2D 100
West Hewish. N Som ... 5G 33
Westhide. Here ... 1A 48
Westhill. Abers ... 3F 153
West Hill. Devn ... 3D 12
West Hill. E Yor ... 3F 101
Westhill. High ... 4B 158
West Hill. N Som ... 4H 33
West Hill. W Sus ... 2E 27
West Hoathly. W Sus ... 2E 27
West Holme. Dors ... 4D 15
Westhope. Here ... 5G 59
Westhope. Shrp ... 2G 59
West Horndon. Essx ... 2H 39
Westhorp. Nptn ... 5C 62
Westhorpe. Linc ... 2B 76
Westhorpe. Suff ... 4C 66
West Horrington. Som ... 2A 22
West Horsley. Surr ... 5B 38
West Horton. Nmbd ... 1E 121
West Hougham. Kent ... 1G 29
Westhoughton. G Man ... 4E 91
West Houlland. Shet ... 6D 173
Westhouse. N Yor ... 2F 97
Westhouses. Derbs ... 5B 86
West Howe. Bour ... 3F 15
Westhumble. Surr ... 5C 38
West Huntspill. Som ... 2G 21
West Hyde. Herts ... 1B 38
West Hynish. Arg ... 5A 138
West Hythe. Kent ... 2F 29
West Ilsley. W Ber ... 3C 36
Westing. Shet ... 1G 173
West Itchenor. W Sus ... 2G 17
West Keal. Linc ... 4C 88
West Kennett. Wilts ... 5G 35
West Kilbride. N Ayr ... 5D 126
West Kingsdown. Kent ... 4G 39
West Kington. Wilts ... 4D 34
West Knapton. N Yor ... 2C 100
West Knighton. Dors ... 4C 14
West Knoyle. Wilts ... 3D 22
West Kyloe. Nmbd ... 5G 131
Westlake. Devn ... 3C 8
West Lambrook. Som ... 1H 13
West Langdon. Kent ... 1H 29
West Langwell. High ... 3D 164
West Lavington. Wilts ... 1F 23
West Lavington. W Sus ... 4G 25
West Layton. N Yor ... 4E 105
West Leake. Notts ... 3C 74
West Learmouth. Nmbd ... 1C 120

Westleigh. Devn ... 4E 19 (nr. Bideford)
Westleigh. Devn ... 1D 12 (nr. Tiverton)
West Leigh. Devn ... 2G 11 (nr. Winkleigh)
Westleigh. G Man ... 4E 91
West Leith. Buck ... 4H 51
Westleton. Suff ... 4G 67
West Lexham. Norf ... 4H 77
Westley. Shrp ... 5F 71
Westley. Suff ... 4H 65
Westley Waterless. Cambs ... 5F 65
West Lilling. N Yor ... 3A 100
West Lingo. Fife ... 3G 137
Westlington. Buck ... 4F 51
Westlinton. Cumb ... 3E 113
West Linton. Bord ... 4E 129
West Littleton. S Glo ... 4C 34
West Looe. Corn ... 3G 7
West Lulworth. Dors ... 4D 14
West Lutton. N Yor ... 3D 100
West Lydford. Som ... 3A 22
West Lyng. Som ... 4G 21
West Lynn. Norf ... 4F 77
West Mains. Per ... 2B 136
West Malling. Kent ... 5A 40
West Malvern. Worc ... 1C 48
Westmancote. Worc ... 2E 49
West Marden. W Sus ... 1F 17
West Markham. Notts ... 3E 86
Westmarsh. Kent ... 4G 41
West Marsh. NE Lin ... 4F 95
West Marton. N Yor ... 4A 98
West Meon. Hants ... 4E 25
West Mersea. Essx ... 4D 54
Westmeston. E Sus ... 4E 27
Westmill. Herts ... 3D 52 (nr. Buntingford)
Westmill. Herts ... 2B 52 (nr. Hitchin)
West Milton. Dors ... 3A 14
Westminster. G Lon ... 3D 39
West Molesey. Surr ... 4C 38
West Monkton. Som ... 4F 21
Westmoor End. Cumb ... 1B 102
West Moors. Dors ... 2F 15
West Morden. Dors ... 3E 15
West Muir. Ang ... 2E 145 (nr. Brechin)
Westmuir. Ang ... 3C 144 (nr. Forfar)
West Murkle. High ... 2D 168
West Ness. N Yor ... 2A 100
Westness. Orkn ... 5C 172
Westnewton. Cumb ... 5C 112
West Newton. E Yor ... 1E 95
West Newton. Norf ... 3F 77
Westnewton. Nmbd ... 1D 120
West Newton. Som ... 4F 21
West Norwood. G Lon ... 3E 39
Westoe. Tyne ... 3G 115
West Ogwell. Devn ... 2E 9
Weston. Bath ... 5C 34
Weston. Ches E ... 5B 84 (nr. Crewe)
Weston. Ches E ... 3D 84 (nr. Macclesfield)
Weston. Devn ... 2E 13 (nr. Honiton)
Weston. Devn ... 4E 13 (nr. Sidmouth)
Weston. Dors ... 5B 14 (nr. Weymouth)
Weston. Dors ... 2A 14 (nr. Yeovil)
Weston. Hal ... 2H 83
Weston. Hants ... 4F 25
Weston. Here ... 5F 59
Weston. Herts ... 2C 52
Weston. Linc ... 3B 76
Weston. Nptn ... 1D 50
Weston. Notts ... 4E 87
Weston. Shrp ... 1H 59 (nr. Bridgnorth)
Weston. Shrp ... 3F 59 (nr. Knighton)
Weston. Shrp ... 3H 71 (nr. Wem)
Weston. S Lan ... 5D 128
Weston. Staf ... 3D 73
Weston. Staf ... 2G 67
Weston. W Ber ... 4B 36
Weston Bampfylde. Som ... 4B 22
Weston Beggard. Here ... 1A 48
Westonbirt. Glos ... 3D 34
Weston by Welland. Nptn ... 1E 63
Weston Colville. Cambs ... 5F 65
Westoncommon. Shrp ... 3G 71
Weston Coyney. Stoke ... 1D 72
Weston Ditch. Suff ... 3F 65
Weston Favell. Nptn ... 4E 63
Weston Green. Cambs ... 5F 65
Weston Green. Norf ... 4D 78
Weston Heath. Shrp ... 4B 72
Weston Hills. Linc ... 4B 76
Weston in Arden. Warw ... 2A 62
Westoning. C Beds ... 2A 52
Weston-in-Gordano. N Som ... 4H 33
Weston Jones. Staf ... 3B 72
Weston Longville. Norf ... 4D 78

Weston Lullingfields. Shrp ... 3G 71
Weston-on-Avon. Warw ... 5F 61
Weston-on-the-Green. Oxon ... 4D 50
Weston-on-Trent. Derbs ... 3B 74
Weston Patrick. Hants ... 2E 25
Weston Rhyn. Shrp ... 2E 71
Weston-sub-Edge. Glos ... 1G 49
Weston-super-Mare. N Som ... 5G 33
Weston Town. Som ... 2C 22
Weston Turville. Buck ... 4G 51
Weston under Lizard. Staf ... 4C 72
Weston under Penyard. Here ... 3B 48
Weston under Wetherley. Warw ... 4A 62
Weston Underwood. Derbs ... 1G 73
Weston Underwood. Mil ... 5F 63
Westonzoyland. Som ... 3G 21
West Orchard. Dors ... 1D 14
West Overton. Wilts ... 5G 35
Westow. N Yor ... 3B 100
Westown. Per ... 1E 137
West Panson. Devn ... 3D 10
West Park. Hart ... 1B 106
West Parley. Dors ... 3F 15
West Peckham. Kent ... 5H 39
West Pelton. Dur ... 4F 115
West Pennard. Som ... 3A 22
West Pentire. Corn ... 2B 6
West Perry. Cambs ... 4A 64
West Pitcorthie. Fife ... 3H 137
West Plean. Stir ... 1B 128
West Poringland. Norf ... 5E 79
West Porlock. Som ... 2B 20
Westport. Som ... 1G 13
West Putford. Devn ... 1D 10
West Quantoxhead. Som ... 2E 20
Westra. V Glam ... 4E 33
West Rainton. Dur ... 5G 115
West Rasen. Linc ... 2H 87
West Ravendale. NE Lin ... 1B 88
Westray Airport. Orkn ... 2D 172
West Raynham. Norf ... 3A 78
Westrigg. W Lot ... 3C 128
West Rounton. N Yor ... 4B 106
West Row. Suff ... 3F 65
West Rudham. Norf ... 3H 77
West Runton. Norf ... 1D 78
Westruther. Bord ... 4C 130
West Saltoun. E Lot ... 3A 130
West Sandford. Devn ... 2B 12
West Sandwick. Shet ... 3F 173
West Scrafton. N Yor ... 1C 98
West Sleekburn. Nmbd ... 1F 115
West Somerton. Norf ... 4G 79
West Stafford. Dors ... 4C 14
West Stockwith. Notts ... 1E 87
West Stoke. W Sus ... 2G 17
West Stonesdale. N Yor ... 4B 104
West Stoughton. Som ... 2H 21
West Stour. Dors ... 4C 22
West Stourmouth. Kent ... 4G 41
West Stow. Suff ... 3H 65
West Stowell. Wilts ... 5G 35
West Strathan. High ... 2F 167
West Stratton. Hants ... 2D 24
West Street. Kent ... 5D 40
West Tanfield. N Yor ... 2E 99
West Taphouse. Corn ... 2F 7
West Tarbert. Arg ... 3G 125
West Thirston. Nmbd ... 4F 121
West Thorney. W Sus ... 2F 17
West Thurrock. Thur ... 3G 39
West Tilbury. Thur ... 3A 40
West Tisted. Hants ... 4E 25
West Tofts. Norf ... 1H 65
West Torrington. Linc ... 2A 88
West Town. Bath ... 5A 34
West Town. Hants ... 3F 17
West Town. N Som ... 5H 33
West Tytherley. Hants ... 4A 24
West Tytherton. Wilts ... 4E 35
West View. Hart ... 1C 106
Westville. Notts ... 1C 74
West Walton. Norf ... 4D 76
Westward. Cumb ... 5D 112
Westward Ho!. Devn ... 4E 19
Westwell. Oxon ... 5H 49
Westwell. Kent ... 1D 28
Westwell Leacon. Kent ... 1D 28
West Wellow. Hants ... 1A 16
West Wemyss. Fife ... 4F 137
Westwick. Cambs ... 4D 64
Westwick. Dur ... 3D 104
Westwick. Norf ... 3E 79
West Wick. N Som ... 5G 33
West Wickham. Cambs ... 1G 53
West Wickham. G Lon ... 4E 39
West Williamston. Pemb ... 4E 43
West Willoughby. Linc ... 1G 75
West Winch. Norf ... 4F 77
West Winterslow. Wilts ... 3H 23
West Wittering. W Sus ... 3F 17
West Witton. N Yor ... 1C 98
Westwood. Devn ... 3D 12
Westwood. Kent ... 4H 41
Westwood. Pet ... 1A 64
Westwood. S Lan ... 4H 127
Westwood. Wilts ... 1D 22
West Woodburn. Nmbd ... 1B 114

West Woodhay. W Ber ... 5B 36
West Woodlands. Som ... 2C 22
West Woodside. Cumb ... 5E 112
Westwoodside. N Lin ... 4H 93
West Worldham. Hants ... 3F 25
West Worlington. Devn ... 1A 12
West Worthing. W Sus ... 5C 26
West Wratting. Cambs ... 5F 65
West Wycombe. Buck ... 2G 37
West Wylam. Nmbd ... 3E 115
West Yatton. Wilts ... 4D 34
West Yell. Shet ... 3F 173
West Youlstone. Corn ... 1C 10
Wetheral. Cumb ... 4F 113
Wetherby. W Yor ... 5G 99
Wetherden. Suff ... 4C 66
Wetheringsett. Suff ... 4D 66
Wethersfield. Essx ... 2H 53
Wethersta. Shet ... 5E 173
Wetherup Street. Suff ... 4D 66
Wetley Rocks. Staf ... 1D 72
Wettenhall. Ches E ... 4A 84
Wetton. Staf ... 5F 85
Wetwang. E Yor ... 4D 100
Wetwood. Staf ... 2B 72
Wexcombe. Wilts ... 1A 24
Wexham Street. Buck ... 2A 38
Weybourne. Norf ... 1D 78
Weybourne. Surr ... 2G 25
Weybread. Suff ... 2E 67
Weybridge. Surr ... 4B 38
Weycroft. Devn ... 3G 13
Weydale. High ... 2D 168
Weyhill. Hants ... 2B 24
Weymouth. Dors ... 5B 14 & 215
Weythel. Powy ... 5E 59
Whaddon. Buck ... 2G 51
Whaddon. Cambs ... 1D 52
Whaddon. Glos ... 4D 48
Whaddon. Wilts ... 4G 23
Whale. Cumb ... 2G 103
Whaley. Derbs ... 3C 86
Whaley Bridge. Derbs ... 2E 85
Whaley Thorns. Derbs ... 3C 86
Whalley. Lanc ... 1F 91
Whalton. Nmbd ... 1E 115
Wham. N Yor ... 3G 97
Whaplode. Linc ... 3C 76
Whaplode Drove. Linc ... 4C 76
Whaplode St Catherine. Linc ... 3C 76
Wharfe. N Yor ... 3G 97
Wharles. Lanc ... 1C 90
Wharley End. C Beds ... 1H 51
Wharncliffe Side. S Yor ... 1G 85
Wharram-le-Street. N Yor ... 3C 100
Wharton. Ches W ... 4A 84
Wharton. Here ... 5H 59
Whashton. N Yor ... 4E 105
Whasset. Cumb ... 1E 97
Whatcote. Warw ... 1A 50
Whateley. Warw ... 1G 61
Whatfield. Suff ... 1D 54
Whatley. Som ... 2G 13 (nr. Chard)
Whatley. Som ... 2C 22 (nr. Frome)
Whatlington. E Sus ... 4B 28
Whatmore. Shrp ... 3A 60
Whatstandwell. Derbs ... 5H 85
Whatton. Notts ... 2E 75
Whauphill. Dum ... 5B 110
Whaw. N Yor ... 4C 104
Wheatacre. Norf ... 1G 67
Wheatcroft. Derbs ... 5A 86
Wheathampstead. Herts ... 4B 52
Wheathill. Shrp ... 2A 60
Wheatley. Devn ... 3B 12
Wheatley. Hants ... 2F 25
Wheatley. Oxon ... 5D 50
Wheatley. S Yor ... 4F 93
Wheatley. W Yor ... 2A 92
Wheatley Hill. Dur ... 1A 106
Wheatley Lane. Lanc ... 1G 91
Wheatley Park. S Yor ... 4F 93
Wheaton Aston. Staf ... 4C 72
Wheatstone Park. Staf ... 5C 72
Wheddon Cross. Som ... 3C 20
Wheelerstreet. Surr ... 1A 26
Wheelock. Ches E ... 5B 84
Wheelock Heath. Ches E ... 5B 84
Wheelton. Lanc ... 2E 90
Wheldrake. York ... 5A 100
Whelford. Glos ... 2G 35
Whelpley Hill. Buck ... 5H 51
Whelpo. Cumb ... 1E 102
Whelston. Flin ... 3E 82
Whenby. N Yor ... 3A 100
Whepstead. Suff ... 5H 65
Wherstead. Suff ... 1E 55
Wherwell. Hants ... 2B 24
Wheston. Derbs ... 3F 85
Whetsted. Kent ... 1A 28
Whetstone. G Lon ... 1D 38
Whetstone. Leics ... 1C 62
Whicham. Cumb ... 1A 96
Whichford. Warw ... 2B 50
Whickham. Tyne ... 3F 115
Whiddon. Devn ... 2E 11
Whiddon Down. Devn ... 3G 11
Whigstreet. Ang ... 4D 145
Whilton. Nptn ... 4D 62

Whimble—Winton

Whimble. Devn 2D 10
Whimple. Devn 3D 12
Whimpwell Green. Norf 3F 79
Whinburgh. Norf 5C 78
Whin Lane End. Lanc 5C 96
Whinnyfold. Abers 5H 161
Whinny Hill. Stoc T 3A 106
Whippingham. IOW 3D 16
Whipsnade. C Beds 4A 52
Whipton. Devn 3C 12
Whirlow. S Yor 2H 85
Whisby. Linc 4G 87
Whissendine. Rut 4F 75
Whissonsett. Norf 3B 78
Whisterfield. Ches E 3C 84
Whistley Green. Wok 4F 37
Whiston. Mers 1G 83
Whiston. Nptn 4F 63
Whiston. S Yor 1B 86
Whiston. Staf 1E 73
(nr. Cheadle)
Whiston. Staf 4C 72
(nr. Penkridge)
Whiston Cross. Shrp 5B 72
Whiston Eaves. Staf 1E 73
Whitacre Heath. Warw 1G 61
Whitbeck. Cumb 1A 96
Whitbourne. Here 5B 60
Whitburn. Tyne 3H 115
Whitburn. W Lot 3C 128
Whitburn Colliery. Tyne 3H 115
Whitby. Ches W 3F 83
Whitby. N Yor 3F 107
Whitbyheath. Ches W 3F 83
Whitchester. Bord 4D 130
Whitchurch. Bath 5B 34
Whitchurch. Buck 3G 51
Whitchurch. Card 4E 33
Whitchurch. Devn 5E 11
Whitchurch. Hants 2C 24
Whitchurch. Here 4A 48
Whitchurch. Pemb 2C 42
Whitchurch. Shrp 1H 71
Whitchurch Canonicorum. Dors 3G 13
Whitchurch Hill. Oxon 4E 37
Whitchurch-on-Thames. Oxon 4E 37
Whitcombe. Dors 4C 14
Whitcot. Shrp 1F 59
Whitcott Keysett. Shrp 2E 59
Whiteash Green. Essx 2A 54
Whitebog. High 2B 158
Whitebridge. High 2G 149
Whitebrook. Mon 5A 48
Whitecairns. Abers 2G 153
White Chapel. Lanc 5E 97
Whitechurch. Pemb 1F 43
White Colne. Essx 3B 54
White Coppice. Lanc 3E 90
White Corries. High 3G 141
Whitecraig. E Lot 2G 129
Whitecroft. Glos 5B 48
White Cross. Corn 4D 5
(nr. Mullion)
Whitecross. Corn 1D 6
(nr. Wadebridge)
Whitecross. Falk 2C 128
White End. Worc 2C 48
Whiteface. High 5E 164
Whitefarland. N Ayr 5G 125
Whitefaulds. S Ayr 4B 116
Whitefield. Dors 3E 15
Whitefield. G Man 4G 91
Whitefield. Som 4D 20
Whiteford. Abers 1E 152
Whitegate. Ches W 4A 84
Whitehall. Devn 1E 13
Whitehall. Hants 1F 25
Whitehall. Orkn 5F 172
Whitehall. W Sus 3C 26
Whitehaven. Cumb 3A 102
Whitehaven. Shrp 3E 71
Whitehill. Hants 3F 25
Whitehill. N Ayr 4D 126
Whitehills. Abers 2D 160
Whitehills. Ang 3D 144
White Horse Common. Norf 3F 79
Whitehough. Derbs 2E 85
Whitehouse. Abers 2D 152
Whitehouse. Arg 3G 125
Whiteinch. Glas 3G 127
Whitekirk. E Lot 1B 130
White Kirkley. Dur 1D 104
White Lackington. Dors 3C 14
Whitelackington. Som 1G 13
White Ladies Aston. Worc 5D 60
White Lee. W Yor 2C 92
Whiteley. Hants 1D 16
Whiteley Bank. IOW 4D 16
Whiteley Village. Surr 4B 38
Whitemans Green. W Sus 3E 27
White Mill. Carm 3E 45
Whitemire. Mor 3D 159
Whitemoor. Corn 3D 6
Whitenap. Hants 4B 24
Whiteness. Shet 7F 173
White Notley. Essx 4A 54
Whiteoak Green. Oxon 4B 50
Whiteparish. Wilts 4H 23
White Pit. Linc 3C 88
Whiterashes. Abers 1F 153
White Rocks. Here 3H 47
White Roding. Essx 4F 53
Whiterow. High 4F 169
Whiterow. Mor 3E 159
Whiteshill. Glos 5D 48
Whiteside. Nmbd 3A 114
Whiteside. W Lot 3C 128
Whitesmith. E Sus 4G 27
Whitestaunton. Som 1F 13
Whitestone. Abers 4D 152
Whitestone. Devn 3B 12
White Stone. Here 1A 48
Whitestones. Abers 3F 161
Whitestreet Green. Suff 2C 54
Whitewall Corner. N Yor 2B 100
White Waltham. Wind 4G 37
Whiteway. Glos 4E 49
Whitewell. Lanc 5F 97
Whitewell Bottom. Lanc 2G 91
Whiteworks. Devn 5G 11
Whitewreath. Mor 3G 159
Whitfield. D'dee 5D 144
Whitfield. Kent 1H 29
Whitfield. Nptn 2E 50
Whitfield. Nmbd 4A 114
Whitfield. S Glo 2B 34
Whitford. Devn 3F 13
Whitford. Flin 3D 82
Whitgift. E Yor 2B 94
Whitgreave. Staf 3C 72
Whithorn. Dum 5B 110
Whiting Bay. N Ayr 3E 123
Whitington. Norf 1G 65
Whitkirk. W Yor 1D 92
Whitland. Carm 3G 43
Whitleigh. Plym 3A 8
Whitletts. S Ayr 2C 116
Whitley. N Yor 2F 93
Whitley. Wilts 5D 35
Whitley Bay. Tyne 2G 115
Whitley Chapel. Nmbd 4C 114
Whitley Heath. Staf 3C 72
Whitley Lower. W Yor 3C 92
Whitley Thorpe. N Yor 2F 93
Whitlock's End. W Mid 3F 61
Whitminster. Glos 5C 48
Whitmore. Dors 2F 15
Whitmore. Staf 1C 72
Whitnage. Devn 1D 12
Whitnash. Warw 4H 61
Whitney. Here 1F 47
Whitrigg. Cumb 4D 112
(nr. Kirkbride)
Whitrigg. Cumb 1D 102
(nr. Torpenhow)
Whitsbury. Hants 1G 15
Whitsome. Bord 4E 131
Whitson. Newp 3G 33
Whitstable. Kent 4F 41
Whitstone. Corn 3C 10
Whittingham. Nmbd 3E 121
Whittingslow. Shrp 2G 59
Whittington. Derbs 3B 86
Whittington. Glos 3F 49
Whittington. Lanc 2F 97
Whittington. Shrp 2F 71
Whittington. Staf 2C 60
(nr. Kinver)
Whittington. Staf 5F 73
(nr. Lichfield)
Whittington. Warw 1G 61
Whittington. Worc 5C 60
Whittington Barracks. Staf 5F 73
Whittlebury. Nptn 1E 51
Whittleford. Warw 1H 61
Whittle-le-Woods. Lanc 2D 90
Whittlesey. Cambs 1B 64
Whittlesford. Cambs 1E 53
Whittlestone Head. Bkbn 3F 91
Whitton. N Lin 2C 94
Whitton. Nmbd 4E 121
Whitton. Powy 4E 59
Whitton. Bord 2B 120
Whitton. Shrp 3H 59
Whitton. Stoc T 2A 106
Whittonditch. Wilts 4A 36
Whittonstall. Nmbd 4D 114
Whitway. Hants 1C 24
Whitwell. Derbs 3C 86
Whitwell. Herts 3B 52
Whitwell. IOW 5D 16
Whitwell. N Yor 5F 105
Whitwell. Rut 5G 75
Whitwell-on-the-Hill. N Yor 3B 100
Whitwick. Leics 4B 74
Whitwood. W Yor 2E 93
Whitworth. Lanc 3G 91
Whixall. Shrp 2H 71
Whixley. N Yor 4G 99
Whoberley. W Mid 3G 61
Whorlton. Dur 3E 105
Whorlton. N Yor 4B 106
Whygate. Nmbd 2A 114
Whyle. Here 4H 59
Whyteleafe. Surr 5E 39
Wibdon. Glos 2A 34
Wibtoft. Warw 2B 62
Wichenford. Worc 4B 60
Wichling. Kent 5D 40
Wick. Bour 3G 15
Wick. Devn 2E 13
Wick. High 3F 169
Wick. Shet 8F 173
(on Mainland)
Wick. Shet 1G 173
(on Unst)
Wick. Som 2F 21
(nr. Bridgwater)
Wick. Som 1G 21
(nr. Burnham-on-Sea)
Wick. Som 4H 21
(nr. Somerton)
Wick. S Glo 4C 34
Wick. V Glam 4C 32
Wick. W Sus 5B 26
Wick. Wilts 4G 23
Wick. Worc 1E 49
Wick Airport. High 3F 169
Wicken. Cambs 3E 65
Wicken. Nptn 2F 51
Wicken Bonhunt. Essx 2E 53
Wickenby. Linc 2H 87
Wicken Green Village. Norf 2H 77
Wickersley. S Yor 1B 86
Wicker Street Green. Suff 1C 54
Wickford. Essx 1B 40
Wickham. Hants 1D 16
Wickham. W Ber 4B 36
Wickham Bishops. Essx 4B 54
Wickhambreaux. Kent 5G 41
Wickhambrook. Suff 5G 65
Wickhamford. Worc 1F 49
Wickham Green. Suff 4C 66
Wickham Heath. W Ber 5C 36
Wickham Market. Suff 5F 67
Wickhampton. Norf 5G 79
Wickham St Paul. Essx 2B 54
Wickham Skeith. Suff 4C 66
Wickham Street. Suff 4C 66
Wick Hill. Wok 5F 37
Wicklewood. Norf 5C 78
Wickmere. Norf 2D 78
Wick St Lawrence. N Som 5G 33
Wickwar. S Glo 3C 34
Widdington. Essx 2F 53
Widdrington. Nmbd 5G 121
Widdrington Station. Nmbd 5G 121
Widecombe in the Moor. Devn 5H 11
Widegates. Corn 3G 7
Widemouth Bay. Corn 2C 10
Wide Open. Tyne 2F 115
Widewall. Orkn 8D 172
Widford. Essx 5G 53
Widford. Herts 4E 53
Widham. Wilts 3F 35
Widmer End. Buck 2G 37
Widmerpool. Notts 3D 74
Widnes. Hal 2H 83
Widworthy. Devn 3F 13
Wigan. G Man 4D 90
Wigbeth. Dors 2F 15
Wigborough. Som 1H 13
Wiggaton. Devn 3E 12
Wiggenhall St Germans. Norf 4E 77
Wiggenhall St Mary Magdalen. Norf 4E 77
Wiggenhall St Mary the Virgin. Norf 4E 77
Wiggenhall St Peter. Norf 4F 77
Wiggens Green. Essx 1G 53
Wigginton. Herts 4H 51
Wigginton. Oxon 2B 50
Wigginton. Staf 5G 73
Wigginton. York 4H 99
Wigglesworth. N Yor 4H 97
Wiggonby. Cumb 4D 112
Wiggonholt. W Sus 4B 26
Wighill. N Yor 5G 99
Wighton. Norf 1B 78
Wightwick. Staf 1C 60
Wigley. Hants 1B 16
Wigmore. Here 4G 59
Wigmore. Medw 4C 40
Wigsley. Notts 3F 87
Wigsthorpe. Nptn 2H 63
Wigston. Leics 1D 62
Wigtoft. Linc 2B 76
Wigton. Cumb 5D 112
Wigtown. Dum 4B 110
Wigtwizzle. S Yor 1G 85
Wike. W Yor 5F 99
Wilbarston. Nptn 2F 63
Wilberfoss. E Yor 4B 100
Wilburton. Cambs 3D 65
Wilby. Norf 2C 66
Wilby. Nptn 4F 63
Wilby. Suff 3E 67
Wilcot. Wilts 5G 35
Wilcott. Shrp 4F 71
Wilcove. Corn 3A 8
Wildboarclough. Ches E 4D 85
Wilden. Bed 5H 63
Wilden. Worc 3C 60
Wildern. Hants 1C 16
Wilderspool. Warr 2A 84
Wilde Street. Suff 3G 65
Wildhern. Hants 1B 24
Wildmanbridge. S Lan 4B 128
Wildmoor. Worc 3D 60
Wildsworth. Linc 1F 87
Wildwood. Staf 3D 72
Wilford. Nott 2C 74
Wilkesley. Ches E 1A 72
Wilkhaven. High 5G 165
Wilkieston. W Lot 3E 129
Wilksby. Linc 4B 88
Willand. Devn 1D 12
Willaston. Ches E 5A 84
Willaston. Ches W 3F 83
Willaston. IOM 4C 108
Willen. Mil 1G 51
Willenhall. W Mid 3A 62
(nr. Coventry)
Willenhall. W Mid 1D 60
(nr. Wolverhampton)
Willerby. E Yor 1D 94
Willerby. N Yor 2E 101
Willersey. Glos 2G 49
Willersley. Here 1G 47
Willesborough. Kent 1E 28
Willesborough Lees. Kent 1E 29
Willesden. G Lon 2D 38
Willesley. Wilts 3D 34
Willett. Som 3E 20
Willey. Shrp 1A 60
Willey. Warw 2B 62
Willey Green. Surr 5A 38
Williamscot. Oxon 1C 50
Williamsetter. Shet 9E 173
Willian. Herts 2C 52
Willingale. Essx 5F 53
Willingdon. E Sus 5G 27
Willingham. Cambs 3D 64
Willingham by Stow. Linc 2F 87
Willingham Green. Cambs 5F 65
Willington. Bed 1B 52
Willington. Derbs 3G 73
Willington. Dur 1E 105
Willington. Tyne 3G 115
Willington. Warw 2A 50
Willington Corner. Ches W 4H 83
Willisham Tye. Suff 5C 66
Willitoft. E Yor 1H 93
Williton. Som 2D 20
Willoughbridge. Staf 1B 72
Willoughby. Linc 3D 88
Willoughby. Warw 4C 62
Willoughby-on-the-Wolds. Notts 3D 74
Willoughby Waterleys. Leics 1C 62
Willoughton. Linc 1G 87
Willow Green. Worc 5B 60
Willows Green. Essx 4H 53
Willsbridge. S Glo 4B 34
Willslock. Staf 2E 73
Willsworthy. Devn 4F 11
Wilmcote. Warw 5F 61
Wilmington. Bath 5B 34
Wilmington. Devn 3F 13
Wilmington. E Sus 5G 27
Wilmington. Kent 3G 39
Wilmslow. Ches E 2C 84
Wilnecote. Staf 5G 73
Wilney Green. Norf 2C 66
Wilpshire. Lanc 1E 91
Wilsden. W Yor 1A 92
Wilsford. Linc 1H 75
Wilsford. Wilts 3G 23
(nr. Amesbury)
Wilsford. Wilts 1G 23
(nr. Devizes)
Wilsill. N Yor 3D 98
Wilsley Green. Kent 2B 28
Wilson. Here 3A 48
Wilson. Leics 3B 74
Wilsontown. S Lan 4C 128
Wilstead. Bed 1A 52
Wilsthorpe. E Yor 3F 101
Wilsthorpe. Linc 4H 75
Wilstone. Herts 4H 51
Wilton. Cumb 3B 102
Wilton. N Yor 1C 100
Wilton. Red C 3C 106
Wilton. Bord 3H 119
Wilton. Wilts 5A 36
(nr. Marlborough)
Wilton. Wilts 3F 23
(nr. Salisbury)
Wimbish. Essx 2F 53
Wimbish Green. Essx 2G 53
Wimblebury. Staf 4E 73
Wimbledon. G Lon 3D 38
Wimblington. Cambs 1D 64
Wimboldsley. Ches W 4A 84
Wimborne Minster. Dors 2F 15
Wimborne St Giles. Dors 1F 15
Wimbotsham. Norf 5F 77
Wimpole. Cambs 1D 52
Wimpstone. Warw 1H 49
Wincanton. Som 4C 22
Winceby. Linc 4C 88
Wincham. Ches W 3A 84
Winchburgh. W Lot 2D 129
Winchcombe. Glos 3F 49
Winchelsea. E Sus 4D 28
Winchelsea Beach. E Sus 4D 28
Winchester. Hants 4C 24 & 213
Winchet Hill. Kent 1B 28
Winchfield. Hants 1F 25
Winchmore Hill. Buck 1A 38
Winchmore Hill. G Lon 1E 39
Wincle. Ches E 4D 84
Windermere. Cumb 5F 103
Winderton. Warw 1B 50
Windhill. High 4H 157
Windle Hill. Ches W 3F 83
Windlesham. Surr 4A 38
Windley. Derbs 1H 73
Windmill. Derbs 3F 85
Windmill Hill. E Sus 4H 27
Windmill Hill. Som 1G 13
Windrush. Glos 4G 49
Windsor. Wind 3A 38 & 213
Windsor Green. Suff 5A 66
Windyedge. Abers 4G 153
Windygates. Fife 3F 137
Windyharbour. Ches E 3C 84
Windyknowe. W Lot 3C 128
Wineham. W Sus 3D 26
Winestead. E Yor 2G 95
Winfarthing. Norf 2D 66
Winford. IOW 4D 16
Winford. N Som 5A 34
Winforton. Here 1F 47
Winfrith Newburgh. Dors 4D 14
Wing. Buck 3G 51
Wing. Rut 5F 75
Wingate. Dur 1A 106
Wingates. G Man 4E 91
Wingates. Nmbd 5F 121
Wingerworth. Derbs 4A 86
Wingfield. C Beds 3A 52
Wingfield. Suff 3E 67
Wingfield. Wilts 1D 22
Wingfield Park. Derbs 5A 86
Wingham. Kent 5G 41
Wingmore. Kent 1F 29
Wingrave. Buck 4G 51
Winkburn. Notts 5E 86
Winkfield. Brac 3A 38
Winkfield Row. Brac 4G 37
Winkhill. Staf 5E 85
Winklebury. Hants 1E 24
Winkleigh. Devn 2G 11
Winksley. N Yor 2E 99
Winkton. Dors 3G 15
Winlaton. Tyne 3E 115
Winlaton Mill. Tyne 3E 115
Winless. High 3F 169
Winmarleigh. Lanc 5D 96
Winnal Common. Here 2H 47
Winnard's Perch. Corn 2D 6
Winnersh. Wok 4F 37
Winnington. Ches W 3A 84
Winnington. Staf 2B 72
Winnothdale. Staf 1E 73
Winscales. Cumb 2B 102
Winscombe. N Som 1H 21
Winsford. Ches W 4A 84
Winsford. Som 3C 20
Winsham. Devn 3F 19
Winsham. Som 2G 13
Winshill. Staf 3G 73
Winsh-wen. Swan 3F 31
Winskill. Cumb 1G 103
Winslade. Hants 2E 25
Winsley. Wilts 5C 34
Winslow. Buck 3F 51
Winson. Glos 5F 49
Winson Green. W Mid 2E 61
Winsor. Hants 1B 16
Winster. Cumb 5F 103
Winster. Derbs 4G 85
Winston. Dur 3E 105
Winston. Suff 4D 66
Winstone. Glos 5E 49
Winswell. Devn 1E 11
Winterborne Clenston. Dors 2D 14
Winterborne Herringston. Dors 4B 14
Winterborne Houghton. Dors 2D 14
Winterborne Kingston. Dors 3D 14
Winterborne Monkton. Dors 4B 14
Winterborne St Martin. Dors 4B 14
Winterborne Stickland. Dors 2D 14
Winterborne Whitechurch. Dors 2D 14
Winterborne Zelston. Dors 3E 15
Winterbourne. S Glo 3B 34
Winterbourne. W Ber 4C 36
Winterbourne Abbas. Dors 3B 14
Winterbourne Bassett. Wilts 4G 35
Winterbourne Dauntsey. Wilts 3G 23
Winterbourne Earls. Wilts 3G 23
Winterbourne Gunner. Wilts 3G 23
Winterbourne Monkton. Wilts 4F 35
Winterbourne Steepleton. Dors 4B 14
Winterbourne Stoke. Wilts 2F 23
Winterbrook. Oxon 3E 36
Winterburn. N Yor 4B 98
Winter Gardens. Essx 2B 40
Winterhay Green. Som 1G 13
Winteringham. N Lin 2C 94
Winterley. Ches E 5B 84
Wintersett. W Yor 3D 93
Winterton. N Lin 3C 94
Winterton-on-Sea. Norf 4G 79
Winthorpe. Linc 4E 89
Winthorpe. Notts 5F 87
Winton. Bour 3F 15

Winton. *Cumb* 3A **104**
Winton. *E Sus* 5G **27**
Wintringham. *N Yor* 2C **100**
Winwick. *Cambs* 2A **64**
Winwick. *Nptn* 3D **62**
Winwick. *Warr* 1A **84**
Wirksworth. *Derbs* 5G **85**
Wirswall. *Ches E* 1H **71**
Wisbech. *Cambs* 4D **76**
Wisbech St Mary. *Cambs* 5D **76**
Wisborough Green. *W Sus* 3B **26**
Wiseton. *Notts* 2E **86**
Wishaw. *N Lan* 4B **128**
Wishaw. *Warw* 1F **61**
Wisley. *Surr* 5B **38**
Wispington. *Linc* 3B **88**
Wissenden. *Kent* 1D **28**
Wissett. *Suff* 3F **67**
Wistanstow. *Shrp* 2G **59**
Wistanswick. *Shrp* 3A **72**
Wistaston. *Ches E* 5A **84**
Wiston. *Pemb* 3E **43**
Wiston. *S Lan* 1B **118**
Wiston. *W Sus* 4C **26**
Wistow. *Cambs* 2B **64**
Wistow. *N Yor* 1F **93**
Wiswell. *Lanc* 1F **91**
Witcham. *Cambs* 2D **64**
Witchampton. *Dors* 2E **15**
Witchford. *Cambs* 3E **65**
Witham. *Essx* 4B **54**
Witham Friary. *Som* 2C **22**
Witham on the Hill. *Linc* 4H **75**
Witham St Hughs. *Linc* 4F **87**
Withcall. *Linc* 2B **88**
Witherenden Hill. *E Sus* 3H **27**
Withergate. *Norf* 3E **79**
Witheridge. *Devn* 1B **12**
Witheridge Hill. *Oxon* 3E **37**
Witherley. *Leics* 1H **61**
Withermarsh Green. *Suff* 2D **54**
Withern. *Linc* 2D **88**
Withernsea. *E Yor* 2G **95**
Withernwick. *E Yor* 5F **101**
Withersdale Street. *Suff* 2E **67**
Withersfield. *Suff* 1G **53**
Witherslack. *Cumb* 1D **96**
Withiel. *Corn* 2D **6**
Withiel Florey. *Som* 3C **20**
Withington. *Glos* 4F **49**
Withington. *G Man* 1C **84**
Withington. *Here* 1A **48**
Withington. *Shrp* 4H **71**
Withington. *Staf* 2E **73**
Withington Green. *Ches E* 3C **84**
Withington Marsh. *Here* 1A **48**
Withleigh. *Devn* 1C **12**
Withnell. *Lanc* 2E **91**
Withnell Fold. *Lanc* 2E **90**
Withybrook. *Warw* 2B **62**
Withycombe. *Som* 2D **20**
Withycombe Raleigh. *Devn* 4D **12**
Withyham. *E Sus* 2F **27**
Withypool. *Som* 3B **20**
Witley. *Surr* 1A **26**
Witnesham. *Suff* 5D **66**
Witney. *Oxon* 4B **50**
Wittering. *Pet* 5H **75**
Wittersham. *Kent* 3D **28**
Witton. *Norf* 5F **79**
Witton. *Worc* 4D **60**
Witton Bridge. *Norf* 2F **79**
Witton Gilbert. *Dur* 5F **115**
Witton-le-Wear. *Dur* 1E **105**
Witton Park. *Dur* 1E **105**
Wiveliscombe. *Som* 4D **20**
Wivelrod. *Hants* 3E **25**
Wivelsfield. *E Sus* 3E **27**
Wivelsfield Green. *E Sus* 4E **27**
Wivenhoe. *Essx* 3D **54**
Wiveton. *Norf* 1C **78**
Wix. *Essx* 3E **55**
Wixford. *Warw* 5E **61**
Wixhill. *Shrp* 3H **71**
Wixoe. *Suff* 1H **53**
Woburn. *C Beds* 2H **51**
Woburn Sands. *Mil* 2H **51**
Woking. *Surr* 5B **38**
Wokingham. *Wok* 5G **37**
Wolborough. *Devn* 5B **12**
Woldingham. *Surr* 5E **39**
Wold Newton. *E Yor* 2E **101**
Wold Newton. *NE Lin* 1B **88**
Wolferlow. *Here* 4A **60**
Wolferton. *Norf* 3F **77**
Wolfhill. *Per* 5A **144**
Wolf's Castle. *Pemb* 2D **42**
Wolfsdale. *Pemb* 2D **42**
Wolgarston. *Staf* 4D **72**
Wollaston. *Nptn* 4G **63**
Wollaston. *Shrp* 4F **71**
Wollaston. *W Mid* 2C **60**
Wollaton. *Nott* 1C **74**
Wollerton. *Shrp* 2A **72**
Wollescote. *W Mid* 2C **60**
Wolseley Bridge. *Staf* 3E **73**
Wolsingham. *Dur* 1D **105**
Wolstanton. *Staf* 1C **72**
Wolston. *Warw* 3B **62**
Wolsty. *Cumb* 4C **112**
Wolterton. *Norf* 2D **78**

Wolvercote. *Oxon* 5C **50**
Wolverhampton.
              W Mid . . . . . . .1D **60** & **213**
Wolverley. *Shrp* 2G **71**
Wolverley. *Worc* 3C **60**
Wolverton. *Hants* 1D **24**
Wolverton. *Mil* 1G **51**
Wolverton. *Warw* 4G **61**
Wolverton. *Wilts* 3C **22**
Wolverton Common.
              Hants 1D **24**
Wolvesnewton. *Mon* 2H **33**
Wolvey. *Warw* 2B **62**
Wolvey Heath. *Warw* 2B **62**
Wolviston. *Stoc T* 2B **106**
Womaston. *Powy* 4E **59**
Wombleton. *N Yor* 1A **100**
Wombourne. *Staf* 1C **60**
Wombwell. *S Yor* 4D **93**
Womenswold. *Kent* 5G **41**
Womersley. *N Yor* 3F **93**
Wonersh. *Surr* 1B **26**
Wonson. *Devn* 4G **11**
Wonston. *Dors* 2C **14**
Wonston. *Hants* 3C **24**
Wooburn. *Buck* 2A **38**
Wooburn Green. *Buck* 2A **38**
Wood. *Pemb* 2C **42**
Woodacott. *Devn* 2D **11**
Woodale. *N Yor* 2C **98**
Woodall. *S Yor* 2B **86**
Woodbank. *Ches W* 3F **83**
Woodbastwick. *Norf* 4F **79**
Woodbeck. *Notts* 3E **87**
Woodborough. *Notts* 1D **74**
Woodborough. *Wilts* 1G **23**
Woodbridge. *Devn* 3E **13**
Woodbridge. *Dors* 1C **14**
Woodbridge. *Suff* 1F **55**
Wood Burcote. *Nptn* 1E **51**
Woodbury. *Devn* 4D **12**
Woodbury Salterton.
              Devn 4D **12**
Woodchester. *Glos* 5D **48**
Woodchurch. *Kent* 2D **28**
Woodchurch. *Mers* 2E **83**
Woodcock Heath. *Staf* 3E **73**
Woodcombe. *Som* 2C **20**
Woodcote. *Oxon* 3E **37**
Woodcote Green. *Worc* 3D **60**
Woodcott. *Hants* 1C **24**
Woodcroft. *Glos* 2A **34**
Woodcutts. *Dors* 1E **15**
Wood Dalling. *Norf* 3C **78**
Woodditton. *Cambs* 5F **65**
Woodeaton. *Oxon* 4D **50**
Wood Eaton. *Staf* 4C **72**
Wood End. *Bed* 4H **63**
Woodend. *Cumb* 5C **102**
Wood End. *Herts* 3D **52**
Woodend. *Nptn* 1E **50**
Woodend. *Staf* 3F **73**
Wood End. *Warw* 2G **61**
              (nr. Bedworth)
Wood End. *Warw* 1G **61**
              (nr. Dordon)
Wood End. *Warw* 3F **61**
              (nr. Tanworth-in-Arden)
Woodend. *W Sus* 2G **17**
Wood Enderby. *Linc* 4B **88**
Woodend Green. *Essx* 3F **53**
Woodfalls. *Wilts* 4G **23**
Woodfield. *Oxon* 3D **50**
Woodfields. *Lanc* 1E **91**
Woodford. *Corn* 1C **10**
Woodford. *Devn* 3D **9**
Woodford. *Glos* 2B **34**
Woodford. *G Lon* 1E **39**
Woodford. *G Man* 2C **84**
Woodford. *Nptn* 3G **63**
Woodford. *Plym* 3B **8**
Woodford Green. *G Lon* 1F **39**
Woodford Halse. *Nptn* 5C **62**
Woodgate. *Norf* 4C **78**
Woodgate. *W Mid* 2D **61**
Woodgate. *W Sus* 5A **26**
Woodgate. *Worc* 4D **60**
Wood Green. *G Lon* 1D **39**
Woodgreen. *Hants* 1G **15**
Woodgreen. *Oxon* 4B **50**
Wood Hall. *E Yor* 1E **95**
Woodhall. *Inv* 2E **127**
Woodhall. *Linc* 4B **88**
Woodhall. *N Yor* 5C **104**
Woodhall Spa. *Linc* 4A **88**
Woodham. *Surr* 4B **38**
Woodham Ferrers. *Essx* 1B **40**
Woodham Mortimer. *Essx* 5B **54**
Woodham Walter. *Essx* 5B **54**
Woodhaven. *Fife* 1G **137**
Wood Hayes. *W Mid* 5D **72**
Woodhead. *Abers* 2G **161**
              (nr. Fraserburgh)
Woodhead. *Abers* 5E **161**
              (nr. Fyvie)
Woodhill. *N Som* 4H **33**
Woodhill. *Shrp* 2B **60**
Woodhill. *Som* 4G **21**
Woodhorn. *Nmbd* 1G **115**
Woodhouse. *Leics* 4C **74**
Woodhouse. *S Yor* 2B **86**

Woodhouse. *W Yor* 1C **92**
              (nr. Leeds)
Woodhouse. *W Yor* 2D **93**
              (nr. Normanton)
Woodhouse Eaves. *Leics* 4C **74**
Woodhouses. *Ches W* 3H **83**
Woodhouses. *G Man* 4H **91**
              (nr. Failsworth)
Woodhouses. *G Man* 1B **84**
              (nr. Sale)
Woodhouses. *Staf* 4F **73**
Woodhuish. *Devn* 3F **9**
Woodhurst. *Cambs* 3C **64**
Woodingdean. *Brig* 5E **27**
Woodland. *Devn* 2D **9**
Woodland. *Dur* 2D **104**
Woodland Head. *Devn* 3A **12**
Woodlands. *Abers* 4E **153**
Woodlands. *Dors* 2F **15**
Woodlands. *Hants* 1B **16**
Woodlands. *Kent* 4G **39**
Woodlands. *N Yor* 4F **99**
Woodlands. *S Yor* 4F **93**
Woodlands Park. *Wind* 4G **37**
Woodlands St Mary. *W Ber* 4B **36**
Woodlane. *Shrp* 3A **72**
Woodlane. *Staf* 3F **73**
Woodleigh. *Devn* 4D **8**
Woodlesford. *W Yor* 2D **92**
Woodley. *G Man* 1D **84**
Woodley. *Wok* 4F **37**
Woodmancote. *Glos* 3E **49**
              (nr. Cheltenham)
Woodmancote. *Glos* 5F **49**
              (nr. Cirencester)
Woodmancote. *W Sus* 2F **17**
              (nr. Chichester)
Woodmancote. *W Sus* 4D **26**
              (nr. Henfield)
Woodmancott. *Worc* 1E **49**
Woodmancott. *Hants* 2D **24**
Woodmansey. *E Yor* 1D **94**
Woodmansgreen. *W Sus* 4G **25**
Woodmansterne. *Surr* 5D **39**
Woodmanton. *Devn* 4D **12**
Woodmill. *Staf* 3F **73**
Woodminton. *Wilts* 4F **23**
Woodnesborough.
              Kent 5H **41**
Woodnewton. *Nptn* 1H **63**
Woodnook. *Linc* 2G **75**
Wood Norton. *Norf* 3C **78**
Woodplumpton. *Lanc* 1D **90**
Woodrising. *Norf* 5B **78**
Woodrow. *Cumb* 5D **112**
Woodrow. *Dors* 1C **14**
              (nr. Fifehead Neville)
Woodrow. *Dors* 2C **14**
              (nr. Hazelbury Bryan)
Wood Row. *W Yor* 2D **93**
Woods Eaves. *Here* 1F **47**
Woodseaves. *Shrp* 2A **72**
Woodseaves. *Staf* 3B **72**
Woodsend. *Wilts* 4H **35**
Woodsetts. *S Yor* 2C **86**
Woodsford. *Dors* 3C **14**
Wood's Green. *E Sus* 2H **27**
Woodshaw. *Wilts* 3F **35**
Woodside. *Aber* 3G **153**
Woodside. *Brac* 3A **38**
Woodside. *Derbs* 1A **74**
Woodside. *Dum* 2B **112**
Woodside. *Dur* 2E **105**
Woodside. *Fife* 3G **137**
Woodside. *Herts* 5C **52**
Woodside. *Per* 5B **144**
Wood Stanway. *Glos* 2F **49**
Woodstock. *Oxon* 4C **50**
Woodstock Slop. *Pemb* 2E **43**
Woodston. *Pet* 1A **64**
Wood Street. *Norf* 3F **79**
Wood Street Village.
              Surr 5A **38**
Woodthorpe. *Derbs* 3B **86**
Woodthorpe. *Leics* 4C **74**
Woodthorpe. *Linc* 2D **88**
Woodthorpe. *York* 5H **99**
Woodton. *Norf* 1E **67**
Woodtown. *Devn* 4E **19**
              (nr. Bideford)
Woodtown. *Devn* 4E **19**
              (nr. Littleham)
Woodvale. *Mers* 3B **90**
Woodville. *Derbs* 4H **73**
Woodwalton. *Cambs* 2B **64**
Woodwick. *Orkn* 5C **172**
Woodyates. *Dors* 1F **15**
Woody Bay. *Devn* 2G **19**
Woofferton. *Shrp* 4H **59**
Wookey. *Som* 2A **22**
Wookey Hole. *Som* 2A **22**
Wool. *Dors* 4D **14**
Woolacombe. *Devn* 2E **19**
Woolage Green. *Kent* 1G **29**
Woolage Village. *Kent* 5G **41**
Woolaston. *Glos* 2A **34**
Woolavington. *Som* 2G **21**
Woolbeding. *W Sus* 4G **25**
Woolcotts. *Som* 3C **20**
Wooldale. *W Yor* 4B **92**
Wooler. *Nmbd* 2D **121**

Woolfardisworthy. *Devn* 4D **18**
              (nr. Bideford)
Woolfardisworthy. *Devn* 2B **12**
              (nr. Crediton)
Woolfords. *S Lan* 4D **128**
Woolgarston. *Dors* 4E **15**
Woolhampton. *W Ber* 5D **36**
Woolhope. *Here* 2B **48**
Woolland. *Dors* 2C **14**
Woollard. *Bath* 5B **34**
Woolley. *Bath* 5C **34**
Woolley. *Cambs* 3A **64**
Woolley. *Corn* 1C **10**
Woolley. *Derbs* 4A **86**
Woolley. *W Yor* 3D **92**
Woolley Green. *Wilts* 5D **34**
Woolmere Green. *Worc* 4D **60**
Woolmer Green. *Herts* 4C **52**
Woolminstone. *Som* 2H **13**
Woolpit. *Suff* 4B **66**
Woolridge. *Glos* 3D **48**
Woolscott. *Warw* 4B **62**
Woolsery. *Devn* 4D **18**
Woolsington. *Tyne* 3E **115**
Woolstaston. *Shrp* 1G **59**
Woolsthorpe By Belvoir. *Linc* . . .2F **75**
Woolsthorpe-by-Colsterworth.
              Linc 3G **75**
Woolston. *Devn* 4D **8**
Woolston. *Shrp* 2G **59**
              (nr. Church Stretton)
Woolston. *Shrp* 3F **71**
              (nr. Oswestry)
Woolston. *Som* 4B **22**
Woolston. *Sotn* 1C **16**
Woolston. *Warr* 1A **84**
Woolstone. *Glos* 2E **49**
Woolstone. *Oxon* 3A **36**
Woolston Green. *Devn* 2D **9**
Woolton. *Mers* 2G **83**
Woolton Hill. *Hants* 5C **36**
Woolverstone. *Suff* 2E **55**
Woolverton. *Som* 1C **22**
Woolwell. *Devn* 2B **8**
Woolwich. *G Lon* 3F **39**
Woonton. *Here* 5F **59**
              (nr. Kington)
Woonton. *Here* 4H **59**
              (nr. Leominster)
Wooperton. *Nmbd* 2E **121**
Woore. *Shrp* 1B **72**
Wooth. *Dors* 3H **13**
Wootton. *Bed* 1A **52**
Wootton. *Hants* 3H **15**
Wootton. *IOW* 3D **16**
Wootton. *Kent* 1G **29**
Wootton. *Nptn* 5E **63**
Wootton. *N Lin* 3D **94**
Wootton. *Oxon* 5C **50**
              (nr. Abingdon)
Wootton. *Oxon* 4C **50**
              (nr. Woodstock)
Wootton. *Shrp* 3G **59**
              (nr. Ludlow)
Wootton. *Shrp* 3F **71**
              (nr. Oswestry)
Wootton. *Staf* 3C **72**
              (nr. Eccleshall)
Wootton. *Staf* 1F **73**
              (nr. Ellastone)
Wootton Bridge. *IOW* 3D **16**
Wootton Common. *IOW* 3D **16**
Wootton Courtenay. *Som* 2C **20**
Wootton Fitzpaine. *Dors* 3G **13**
Wootton Rivers. *Wilts* 5G **35**
Wootton St Lawrence. *Hants* . . .1D **24**
Wootton Wawen. *Warw* 4F **61**
Worcester. *Worc* . . . . .5C **60** & **214**
Worcester Park. *G Lon* 4D **38**
Wordsley. *W Mid* 2C **60**
Worfield. *Shrp* 1B **60**
Work. *Orkn* 6D **172**
Workhouse Green. *Suff* 2C **54**
Workington. *Cumb* 2A **102**
Worksop. *Notts* 3C **86**
Worlaby. *N Lin* 3D **94**
Worlds End. *Hants* 1E **17**
Worldsend. *Shrp* 1G **59**
World's End. *W Ber* 4C **36**
Worlds End. *W Mid* 2F **61**
World's End. *W Sus* 4E **27**
Worle. *N Som* 5G **33**
Worleston. *Ches E* 5A **84**
Worley. *Glos* 2D **34**
Worlingham. *Suff* 1G **67**
Worlington. *Suff* 3F **65**
Worlingworth. *Suff* 4E **67**
Wormbridge. *Here* 2H **47**
Wormegay. *Norf* 4F **77**
Wormelow Tump. *Here* 2H **47**
Wormhill. *Derbs* 3F **85**
Wormingford. *Essx* 2C **54**
Worminghall. *Buck* 5E **51**
Wormington. *Glos* 2F **49**
Worminster. *Som* 2A **22**
Wormit. *Fife* 1F **137**
Wormleighton. *Warw* 5B **62**
Wormley. *Herts* 5D **52**
Wormley. *Surr* 2A **26**
Wormshill. *Kent* 5C **40**

Wormsley. *Here* 1H **47**
Worplesdon. *Surr* 5A **38**
Worrall. *S Yor* 1H **85**
Worsbrough. *S Yor* 4D **92**
Worsley. *G Man* 4F **91**
Worstead. *Norf* 3F **79**
Worsthorne. *Lanc* 1G **91**
Worston. *Lanc* 5G **97**
Worth. *Kent* 5H **41**
Worth. *W Sus* 2E **27**
Wortham. *Suff* 3C **66**
Worthen. *Shrp* 5F **71**
Worthenbury. *Wrex* 1G **71**
Worthing. *Norf* 4B **78**
Worthing. *W Sus* 5C **26**
Worthington. *Leics* 3B **74**
Worth Matravers. *Dors* 5E **15**
Worting. *Hants* 1E **24**
Wortley. *Glos* 2C **34**
Wortley. *S Yor* 1H **85**
Wortley. *W Yor* 1C **92**
Worton. *N Yor* 5C **104**
Worton. *Wilts* 1E **23**
Wortwell. *Norf* 2E **67**
Wotherton. *Shrp* 5E **71**
Wothorpe. *Nptn* 5H **75**
Wotter. *Devn* 2B **8**
Wotton. *Glos* 4D **48**
Wotton. *Surr* 1C **26**
Wotton-under-Edge. *Glos* 2C **34**
Wotton Underwood. *Buck* 4E **51**
Wouldham. *Kent* 4B **40**
Wrabness. *Essx* 2E **55**
Wrafton. *Devn* 3E **19**
Wragby. *Linc* 3A **88**
Wragby. *W Yor* 3E **93**
Wramplingham. *Norf* 5D **78**
Wrangbrook. *W Yor* 3E **93**
Wrangle. *Linc* 5D **88**
Wrangle Lowgate. *Linc* 5D **88**
Wrangway. *Som* 1E **13**
Wrantage. *Som* 4G **21**
Wrawby. *N Lin* 4D **94**
Wraxall. *N Som* 4H **33**
Wraxall. *Som* 3B **22**
Wray. *Lanc* 3F **97**
Wraysbury. *Wind* 3B **38**
Wrayton. *Lanc* 2F **97**
Wrea Green. *Lanc* 1B **90**
Wreay. *Cumb* 5F **113**
              (nr. Carlisle)
Wreay. *Cumb* 2F **103**
              (nr. Penrith)
Wrecclesham. *Surr* 2G **25**
Wrecsam.
              Wrex . . . .5F **83** & **Wrexham 214**
Wrekenton. *Tyne* 4F **115**
Wrelton. *N Yor* 1B **100**
Wrenbury. *Ches E* 1H **71**
Wreningham. *Norf* 1D **66**
Wrentham. *Suff* 2G **67**
Wrenthorpe. *W Yor* 2D **92**
Wrentnall. *Shrp* 5G **71**
Wressle. *E Yor* 1H **93**
Wressle. *N Lin* 4C **94**
Wrestlingworth. *C Beds* 1C **52**
Wretton. *Norf* 1F **65**
Wrexham. *Wrex* . . . . .5F **83** & **214**
Wrexham Industrial Estate.
              Wrex 1F **71**
Wrickton. *Shrp* 2A **60**
Wrightington Bar. *Lanc* 3D **90**
Wright's Green. *Essx* 4F **53**
Wrinehill. *Staf* 1B **72**
Wrington. *N Som* 5H **33**
Writtle. *Essx* 5G **53**
Wrockwardine. *Telf* 4A **72**
Wroot. *N Lin* 4H **93**
Wrotham. *Kent* 5H **39**
Wrotham Heath. *Kent* 5H **39**
Wroughton. *Swin* 3G **35**
Wroxall. *IOW* 4D **16**
Wroxall. *Warw* 3G **61**
Wroxeter. *Shrp* 5H **71**
Wroxham. *Norf* 4F **79**
Wroxton. *Oxon* 1C **50**
Wyaston. *Derbs* 1F **73**
Wyatt's Green. *Essx* 1G **39**
Wybers Wood. *NE Lin* 4F **95**
Wyberton. *Linc* 1C **76**
Wyboston. *Bed* 5A **64**
Wybunbury. *Ches E* 1A **72**
Wychbold. *Worc* 4D **60**
Wych Cross. *E Sus* 2F **27**
Wychnor. *Staf* 4F **73**
Wychnor Bridges. *Staf* 4F **73**
Wyck. *Hants* 3F **25**
Wyck Hill. *Glos* 3G **49**
Wyck Rissington. *Glos* 3G **49**
Wycliffe. *Dur* 3E **105**
Wycombe Marsh. *Buck* 2G **37**
Wyddial. *Herts* 2D **52**
Wye. *Kent* 1E **28**
Wyesham. *Mon* 4A **48**
Wyfold Grange. *Oxon* 3E **37**
Wyfordby. *Leics* 4E **75**
Wyke. *Devn* 3B **12**
Wyke. *Dors* 4C **22**
Wyke. *Shrp* 5A **72**
Wyke. *Surr* 5A **38**

Wyke—Zouch

Wyke. *W Yor* 2B **92**
Wyke Champflower. *Som* 3B **22**
Wykeham. *Linc* 3B **76**
Wykeham. *N Yor* 2C **100**
(nr. Malton)
Wykeham. *N Yor* 1D **100**
(nr. Scarborough)
Wyken. *Shrp* 1B **60**
Wyken. *W Mid* 2A **62**
Wyke Regis. *Dors* 5B **14**
Wyke, The. *Shrp* 5B **72**
Wykey. *Shrp* 3F **71**
Wykin. *Leics* 1B **62**
Wylam. *Nmbd* 3E **115**
Wylde Green. *W Mid* 1F **61**
Wylye. *Wilts* 3F **23**
Wymering. *Port* 2E **17**
Wymeswold. *Leics* 3D **74**
Wymington. *Bed* 4G **63**
Wymondham. *Leics* 4F **75**
Wymondham. *Norf* 5D **78**
Wyndham. *B'end* 2C **32**
Wynford Eagle. *Dors* 3A **14**
Wyng. *Orkn* 8C **172**
Wynyard Village. *Stoc T* 2B **106**
Wyre Piddle. *Worc* 1E **49**
Wysall. *Notts* 3D **74**
Wyson. *Here* 4H **59**
Wythall. *Worc* 3E **61**
Wytham. *Oxon* 5C **50**
Wythenshawe. *G Man* 2C **84**
Wythop Mill. *Cumb* 2C **102**
Wyton. *Cambs* 3B **64**
Wyton. *E Yor* 1E **95**
Wyverstone. *Suff* 4C **66**
Wyverstone Street. *Suff* 4C **66**
Wyville. *Linc* 3F **75**
Wyvis Lodge. *High* 1G **157**

Y

Yaddlethorpe. *N Lin* 4B **94**
Yafford. *IOW* 4C **16**
Yafforth. *N Yor* 5A **106**
Yalding. *Kent* 5A **40**
Yanley. *N Som* 5A **34**
Yanwath. *Cumb* 2G **103**
Yanworth. *Glos* 4F **49**
Yapham. *E Yor* 4B **100**
Yapton. *W Sus* 5A **26**
Yarburgh. *Linc* 1C **88**
Yarcombe. *Devn* 2F **13**
Yarde. *Som* 3D **20**
Yardley. *W Mid* 2F **61**
Yardley Gobion. *Nptn* 1F **51**
Yardley Hastings. *Nptn* 5F **63**
Yardley Wood. *W Mid* 2F **61**
Yardro. *Powy* 5E **58**
Yarhampton. *Worc* 4B **60**
Yarkhill. *Here* 1B **48**
Yarlet. *Staf* 3D **72**
Yarley. *Som* 2A **22**
Yarlington. *Som* 4B **22**
Yarm. *Stoc T* 3B **106**
Yarmouth. *IOW* 4B **16**
Yarnbrook. *Wilts* 1D **22**
Yarnfield. *Staf* 2C **72**
Yarnscombe. *Devn* 4F **19**
Yarnton. *Oxon* 4C **50**
Yarpole. *Here* 4G **59**
Yarrow. *Nmbd* 1A **114**
Yarrow. *Bord* 2F **119**
Yarrow. *Som* 2G **21**
Yarrow Feus. *Bord* 2F **119**
Yarrow Ford. *Bord* 1G **119**
Yarsop. *Here* 1H **47**
Yarwell. *Nptn* 1H **63**
Yate. *S Glo* 3C **34**
Yateley. *Hants* 5G **37**
Yatesbury. *Wilts* 4F **35**
Yattendon. *W Ber* 4D **36**
Yatton. *Here* 4G **59**
(nr. Leominster)
Yatton. *Here* 2B **48**
(nr. Ross-on-Wye)
Yatton. *N Som* 5H **33**
Yatton Keynell. *Wilts* 4D **34**
Yaverland. *IOW* 4E **16**
Yawl. *Devn* 3G **13**
Yaxham. *Norf* 4C **78**
Yaxley. *Cambs* 1A **64**
Yaxley. *Suff* 3D **66**
Yazor. *Here* 1H **47**
Y Bala. *Gwyn* 2B **70**
Y Bont-Faen. *V Glam* 4C **32**
Y Clun. *Neat* 5B **46**
Y Dref. *Gwyn* 2D **69**
Y Drenewydd. *Powy* 1D **58**
Yeading. *G Lon* 2C **38**
Yeadon. *W Yor* 5E **98**
Yealand Conyers. *Lanc* 2E **97**
Yealand Redmayne. *Lanc* 2E **97**
Yealand Storrs. *Lanc* 2D **97**
Yealmpton. *Devn* 3B **8**
Yearby. *Red C* 2D **106**
Yearngill. *Cumb* 5C **112**
Yearsett. *Here* 5B **60**
Yearsley. *N Yor* 2H **99**
Yeaton. *Shrp* 4G **71**
Yeaveley. *Derbs* 1F **73**
Yeavering. *Nmbd* 1D **120**
Yedingham. *N Yor* 2C **100**
Yeldersley Hollies. *Derbs* 1G **73**
Yelford. *Oxon* 5B **50**
Yelland. *Devn* 3E **19**
Yelling. *Cambs* 4B **64**
Yelsted. *Kent* 4C **40**
Yelvertoft. *Nptn* 3C **62**
Yelverton. *Devn* 2B **8**
Yelverton. *Norf* 5E **79**
Yenston. *Som* 4C **22**
Yeoford. *Devn* 3A **12**
Yeolmbridge. *Corn* 4D **10**
Yeo Mill. *Devn* 4B **20**
Yeovil. *Som* 1A **14**
Yeovil Marsh. *Som* 1A **14**
Yeovilton. *Som* 4A **22**
Yerbeston. *Pemb* 4E **43**
Yesnaby. *Orkn* 6B **172**
Yetlington. *Nmbd* 4E **121**
Yetminster. *Dors* 1A **14**
Yett. *N Lan* 4A **128**
Yett. *S Ayr* 2D **116**
Yettington. *Devn* 4D **12**
Yetts o' Muckhart. *Clac* 3C **136**
Y Fali. *IOA* 3B **80**
Y Felinheli. *Gwyn* 4E **81**
Y Fenni. *Mon* 4G **47**
Y Ferwig. *Cdgn* 1B **44**
Y Fflint. *Flin* 3E **83**
Y Ffor. *Gwyn* 2C **68**
Y Gelli Gandryll. *Powy* 1F **47**
Yielden. *Bed* 4H **63**
Yieldshields. *S Lan* 4B **128**
Yiewsley. *G Lon* 2B **38**
Yinstay. *Orkn* 6E **172**
Ynysboeth. *Rhon* 2D **32**
Ynysddu. *Cphy* 2E **33**
Ynysforgan. *Swan* 3F **31**
Ynyshir. *Rhon* 2D **32**
Ynyslas. *Cdgn* 1F **57**
Ynysmaerdy. *Rhon* 3D **32**
Ynysmeudwy. *Neat* 5H **45**
Ynystawe. *Swan* 5G **45**
Ynyswen. *Powy* 4B **46**
Ynys-wen. *Rhon* 2C **32**
Ynys y Barri. *V Glam* 5E **32**
Ynysybwl. *Rhon* 2D **32**
Ynysymaerdy. *Neat* 3G **31**
Yockenthwaite. *N Yor* 2B **98**
Yockleton. *Shrp* 4G **71**
Yokefleet. *E Yor* 2B **94**
Yoker. *Glas* 3G **127**
Yonder Bognie. *Abers* 4C **160**
Yonderton. *Abers* 5G **161**
York. *York* 4A **100** & **214**
Yorkletts. *Kent* 4E **41**
Yorkley. *Glos* 5B **48**
Yorkshire Dales. *N Yor* 2H **97**
Yorton. *Shrp* 3H **71**
Yorton Heath. *Shrp* 3H **71**
Youlgreave. *Derbs* 4G **85**
Youlthorpe. *E Yor* 4B **100**
Youlton. *N Yor* 3G **99**
Young's End. *Essx* 4H **53**
Young Wood. *Linc* 3A **88**
Yoxall. *Staf* 4F **73**
Yoxford. *Suff* 4F **67**
Yr Hob. *Flin* 5F **83**
Y Rhws. *V Glam* 5D **32**
Yr Wyddgrug. *Flin* 4E **83**
Ysbyty Cynfyn. *Cdgn* 3G **57**
Ysbyty Ifan. *Cnwy* 1H **69**
Ysbyty Ystwyth. *Cdgn* 3G **57**
Ysceifiog. *Flin* 3D **82**
Yspitty. *Carm* 3E **31**
Ystalyfera. *Neat* 5A **46**
Ystrad. *Rhon* 2C **32**
Ystrad Aeron. *Cdgn* 5E **57**
Ystradfellte. *Powy* 4C **46**
Ystradffin. *Carm* 1A **46**
Ystradgynlais. *Powy* 4A **46**
Ystradmeurig. *Cdgn* 4G **57**
Ystrad Mynach. *Cphy* 2E **33**
Ystradowen. *Carm* 4A **46**
Ystradowen. *V Glam* 4D **32**
Ystumtuen. *Cdgn* 3G **57**
Ythanbank. *Abers* 5G **161**
Ythanwells. *Abers* 5D **160**
Y Trallwng. *Powy* 5E **70**
Y Tymbl. *Carm* 4F **45**
Y Waun. *Wrex* 2E **71**

Z

Zeal Monachorum. *Devn* 2H **11**
Zeals. *Wilts* 3C **22**
Zelah. *Corn* 3C **6**
Zennor. *Corn* 3B **4**
Zouch. *Notts* 3C **74**

Safety Camera Information

More than 4000 fixed and long term road works camera locations are shown, including Gatso, Truvelo, SPECS Monitron and Redspeed camera types. Mobile camera sites and cameras on roads not included in the map specification are not shown. Camera locations are shown as accurately as the scale allows. Symbols do not indicate camera direction. Two or more cameras in close proximity are represented by a multiple camera symbol. Safety camera locations are publicised by the Safer Roads Partnership who operate them in order to encourage drivers to comply with speed limits at these sites. It is the driver's absolute responsibility to be aware of, and adhere to, speed limits at all times. Data accurate at time of printing.
Supplied by PocketGPSWorld.com

Single Camera Locations 30

This symbol shows single camera locations with their speed limit

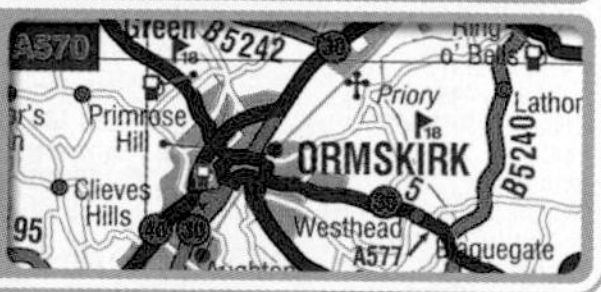

Multiple Camera Locations 70

This symbol is used where multiple cameras are sited in close proximity to each other with the same speed limit

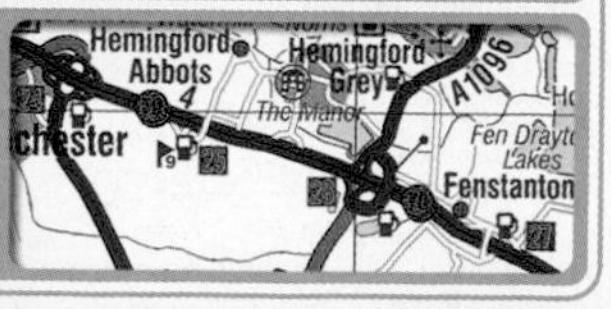

Variable MPH

Single camera
Multiple cameras

These symbols are used where variable speed limits are in force

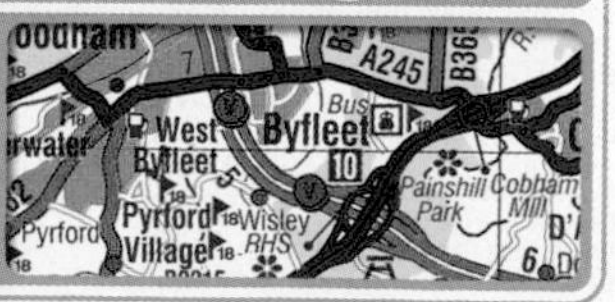

INDEX TO SELECTED PLACES OF INTEREST

(1) A strict alphabetical order is used e.g. Benmore Botanic Gdn. follows Ben Macdui but precedes Ben Nevis.

(2) Entries shown without a main map index reference have the name of the appropriate Town Plan and its page number; e.g. Ashmolean Mus. (OX1 2PH) . . . . Oxford 207
The Town Plan title is not given when this is included in the name of the Place of Interest.

(3) Entries in italics are not shown on the map but are shown with a symbol only.
Entries in italics and enclosed in brackets are not shown on the map.
Where this occurs the nearest town or village may also be given, unless that name is already included in the name of the Place of Interest.

SAT NAV POSTCODES

Postcodes (in brackets) are included as a navigation aid to assist Sat Nav users and are supplied on this basis. It should be noted that postcodes have been selected by their proximity to the Place of Interest and that they may not form part of the actual postal address.
Drivers should follow the Tourist Brown Signs when available.

ABBREVIATIONS USED IN THIS INDEX

Garden : Gdn.
Gardens : Gdns.
Museum : Mus.

National : Nat
Park : Pk.

INDEX

A

Abbeydale Industrial Hamlet (S7 2QW) 2H 85
Abbey House Mus. (LS5 3EH) 1C 92
Abbot Hall Art Gallery, Kendal (LA9 5AL) 5G 103
Abbotsbury Sub Tropical Gdns. (DT3 4LA) 4A 14
Abbotsbury Swannery (DT3 4JG) 4A 14
Abbotsford (TD6 9BQ) 1H 119
Aberdeen Maritime Mus. (AB11 5BY) 187
Aberdour Castle (KY3 0XA) 1E 129
Aberdulais Falls (SA10 8EU) 5A 46
Aberglasney Gdns. (SA32 8QH) 3F 45
Abernethy Round Tower (PH2 9RT) 2D 136
Aberystwyth Castle (SY23 1DZ) 187
Acorn Bank Gdn. & Watermill (CA10 1SP) 2H 103
Acton Burnell Castle (SY5 7PF) 5H 71
Acton Scott Historic Working Farm (SY6 6QN)
. . . . .2G 59
Adlington Hall (SK10 4LF) 2D 84
Africa Alive! (NR33 7TF) 2H 67
Aintree Racecourse (L9 5AS) 1F 83
Aira Force (CA11 0JX) 2F 103
A la Ronde (EX8 5BD) 4D 12
Alderley Edge (SK10 4UB) 3C 84
Alfriston Clergy House (BN26 5TL) 5G 27
Alloa Tower (FK10 1PP) 4A 136
Alnwick Castle (NE66 1NQ) 3F 121
Alnwick Gdn., The (NE66 1YU) 3F 121
Althorp (NN7 4HQ) 4D 62
Alton Towers (ST10 4DB) 1E 73
Amberley Mus. & Heritage Cen. (BN18 9LT) . . .4B 26
American Mus. in Britain (BA2 7BD) 5C 34
Angel of the North (NE9 6PG) 4F 115
Anglesey Abbey & Lode Mill (CB25 9EJ) 4E 65
Angus Folk Mus. (DD8 1RT) 4C 144
Animalarium at Borth (SY24 5NA) 2F 57
Anne Hathaway's Cottage (CV37 9HH) 5F 61
Antonine Wall (FK4 2AA) 2B 128
Antony (PL11 2QA) 3A 8
Appuldurcombe House (PO38 3EW) 4D 16
Arbroath Abbey (DD11 1JQ) 4F 145
Arbury Hall (CV10 7PT) 2H 61
Arbuthnott House Gdn. (AB30 1PA) 1G 145
Ardkinglas Woodland Gdns. (PA26 8BG) 2A 134
Ardnamurchan Point (PH36 4LN) 2F 139
Arduaine Gdn. (PA34 4XQ) 2E 133
Ardwell Gdns. (DG9 9LY) 5G 109
Argyll's Lodging (FK8 1EG) . . . . Stirling 211
Arley Hall & Gdns. (CW9 6NA) 2A 84
Arlington Court (EX31 4LP) 3G 19
Armadale Castle Gdns. (IV45 8RS) 3E 147
Arniston House (EH23 4RY) 4G 129
Arundel Castle (BN18 9AB) 5B 26
Arundel Wetland Centre (BN18 9PB) 5B 26
Ascot Racecourse (SL5 7JX) 4A 38
Ascott (LU7 0PT) 3G 51
Ashby-de-la-Zouch Castle (LE65 1BR) 4A 74
Ashdown Forest (TN7 4EU) 2F 27
Ashdown House (RG17 8RE) 3A 36
Ashmolean Mus. (OX1 2PH) . . . . .Oxford 207
Ashridge Estate (HP4 1LT) 4H 51
Astley Hall Mus. & Art Gallery (PR7 1NP) 3D 90
Athelhampton House (DT2 7LG) 3C 14
Attingham Pk. (SY4 4TP) 5H 71
Auchingarrich Wildlife Centre (PH6 2JE) 2G 135
Auckland Castle, Bishop Auckland (DL14 7NP)
. . . . .1F 105
Audley End House & Gdns. (CB11 4JF) 2F 53
Avebury Stone Circle (SN8 1RE) 4G 35
Avoncroft Mus. of Historic Buildings (B60 4JR)
. . . . .4D 60
Avon Valley Adventure & Wildlife Pk. (BS31 1TP)
. . . . .5B 34
Avon Valley Railway (BS30 6HD) 4B 34
Aydon Castle (NE45 5PJ) 3C 114
Ayr Racecourse (KA8 0JE) 187
Ayscoughfee Hall Mus. & Gdns. (PE11 2RA) . . .3B 76
Aysgarth Falls (DL8 3SR) 1C 98
Ayton Castle (TD14 5RD) 3F 131

B

Bachelors' Club (KA5 5RB) 2D 116
Baconsthorpe Castle (NR25 6PS) 2D 78
Baddesley Clinton (B93 0DQ) 3F 61
Bala Lake Railway (LL23 7DD) 2A 70
Ballindalloch Castle (AB37 9AX) 5F 159
Balmacara Estate (IV40 8DN) 1F 147
Balmoral Castle (AB35 5TB) 4G 151
Balvaird Castle (PH2 9PY) 2D 136
Balvenie Castle (AB55 4DH) 4H 159
Bamburgh Castle (NE69 7DF) 1F 121
Bangor Cathedral (LL57 1DN) 3E 81
Banham Zoo (NR16 2HE) 2C 66
Bannockburn Battle Site (FK7 0PL) 4G 135
Barbara Hepworth Mus. & Sculpture Gdn. (TR26 1AD)
. . . . .2C 4
Barnard Castle (DL12 8PR) 3D 104
Barnsdale Gdns. (LE15 8AH) 4G 75
Barrington Court (TA19 0NQ) 1G 13
Basildon Pk. (RG8 9NR) 4E 36
Basing House (RG24 7HB) 1E 25
Basingwerk Abbey (CH8 7GH) 3D 82
Bateman's (TN19 7DS) 3A 28
Bath Abbey (BA1 1LT) 187
Bath Assembly Rooms & Fashion Mus. (BA1 2QH)
. 187
Bath Roman Baths & Pump Room (BA1 1LZ) . .187
Battle Abbey (TN33 0AD) 4B 28
Battlefield Line Railway (CV13 0BS) 5A 74
Battle of Britain Memorial Flight Visitors Centre,
RAF Coningsby (LN4 4SY) 5B 88

Battle of Hastings Site (TN33 0AD) 4B 28
Bayham Abbey (TN3 8BE) 2H 27
Beachy Head (BN20 7YA) 5G 27
Beamish (DH9 0RG) 4F 115
Beatles Story, The (L3 4AD) . . . . .Liverpool 200
Beatrix Potter's House, Hill Top (LA22 0LF) . . .5E 103
Beaulieu Abbey (SO42 7ZN) 2B 16
Beaumaris Castle (LL58 8AP) 3F 81
Beck Isle Mus. of Rural Life (YO18 8DU) 1B 100
Bedgebury Nat. Pinetum (TN17 2SL) 2B 28
Bedruthan Steps (PL27 7UW) 2C 6
Beeston Castle & Woodland Pk. (CW6 9TX) . . .5H 83
Bekonscot Model Village & Railway (HP9 2PL)
. . . . .1A 38
Belgrave Hall Mus. & Gdns. (LE4 5PE) 5C 74
Belmont House & Gdns. (ME13 0HH) 5D 40
Belsay Hall, Castle & Gdns. (NE20 0DX) 2D 115
Belton House (NG32 2LS) 2G 75
Belvoir Castle (NG32 1PD) 2F 75
Beningbrough Hall & Gdns. (YO30 1DD) 4H 99
Benington Lordship Gdns. (SG2 7BS) 3C 52
Ben Lawers (PH15 2PA) 4D 142
Ben Lomond (FK8 3TR) 3C 134
Ben Macdui (PH22 1RB) 4D 151
Benmore Botanic Gdn. (PA23 8QU) 1C 126
Ben Nevis (PH33 6SY) 1F 141
Benthall Hall (TF12 5RX) 5A 72
Bentley Wildfowl & Motor Mus. (BN8 5AF) . . .4F 27
Berkeley Castle (GL13 9BQ) 2B 34
Berkhamsted Castle (HP4 1LJ) 5H 51
Berney Arms Windmill (NR31 9HU) 5G 79
Berrington Hall (HR6 0DW) 4H 59
Berry Pomeroy Castle (TQ9 6LJ) 2E 9
Bessie Surtees House (NE1 3JF) . . . .Newcastle 205
Beverley Minster (HU17 0DP) 1D 94
Bicton Pk. Botanical Gdns. (EX9 7BJ) 4D 12
Biddulph Grange Gdn. (ST8 7SD) 5C 84
Big Ben (SW1A 2PW) . . . . .London 203
Bignor Roman Villa (RH20 1PH) 4A 26
Big Pit: Nat. Coal Mus. (NP4 9XP) 5F 47
Binham Priory (NR21 0DQ) 1B 78
Birmingham Mus. & Art Gallery (B3 3DH) 188
Bishop's Waltham Palace (SO32 1DP) 1D 16
Black Country Living Mus., Dudley (DY1 4SQ)
. . . . .1D 60
Blackgang Chine (PO38 2HN) 5C 16
Blackhouse, The (HS2 9DB) 3F 171
Blackness Castle (EH49 7NH) 1D 128
Blackpool Pleasure Beach (FY4 1EZ) 1B 90
Blackpool Zoo (FY3 8PP) 1B 90
Blackwell, The Arts & Crafts House (LA23 3JR)
. . . . .5F 103
Blaenavon Ironworks (NP4 9RJ) 5F 47
Blaenavon World Heritage Cen. (NP4 9AS) 5F 47
Blair Castle (PH18 5TL) 2F 143
Blair Drummond Safari & Adventure Pk. (FK9 4UR)
. . . . .4G 135
Blairquhan Castle (KA19 7LZ) 4C 116
Blakeney Point (NR25 7SA) 1C 78
Blakesley Hall (B25 8RN) 2F 61
Blenheim Palace (OX20 1PX) 4C 50
Bletchley Pk. (MK3 6EB) 2G 51
Blickling Estate (NR11 6NF) 3D 78
Blists Hill Victorian Town, Telford (TF7 5DS) . .5A 72
Bluebell Railway (TN22 3QL) 3E 27
Blue John Cavern (S33 8WP) 2F 85
Blue Reef Aquarium, Bristol (BS1 5TT) 189
Blue Reef Aquarium, Hastings (TN34 3QW) . . .5C 28
Blue Reef Aquarium, Newquay (TR7 1DU) 2C 6
[Blue Reef Aquarium, Portsmouth, Southsea
(PO5 3PB)] 3E 17
Blyth Power Station, Tynemouth (NE30 4JF) . . .2G 115
Boath Doocot (IV12 5TD) 3D 158
Bocketts Farm Pk. (KT22 9BS) 5C 38
Bodelwyddan Castle (LL18 5YA) 3B 82
Bodiam Castle (TN32 5UA) 3B 28
Bodmin & Wenford Railway (PL31 1AQ) 2E 7
Bodmin Moor (PL15 7TN) 5B 10
Bodnant Gdn. (LL28 5RE) 3H 81
Bodrhyddan Hall (LL18 5SB) 3C 82
Bolingbroke Castle (PE23 4HH) 4C 88
Bolsover Castle (S44 6PR) 3B 86
Bolton Castle (DL8 4ET) 5D 104
Bolton Priory (BD23 6AL) 4C 98
Bonawe Historic Iron Furnace (PA35 1JQ) 5E 141
Bo'ness & Kinneil Railway (EH51 9AQ) 1C 128
Booth Mus. of Natural History (BN1 5AA)
. . . . .Brighton & Hove 189
Borde Hill Gdn. (RH16 1XP) 3E 27
Boscobel House (ST19 9AR) 5C 72
Boston Stump (PE21 6NQ) 1C 76
Bosworth Field Battle Site (CV13 0AB) 5A 74
Bothwell Castle (G71 8BL) 4H 127
Boughton (NN14 1BJ) .2G 63
Bowes Castle (DL12 9LG) 3C 104
Bowes Mus., The (DL12 8NP) 3D 104
Bowhill House & Country Estate (TD7 5ET) . . .2G 119
Bowood House & Gdns. (SN11 0LZ) 5E 35
Box Hill (KT20 7LF) 5C 38
Braemar Castle (AB35 5XR) 4F 151
Bramall Hall, Bramhall (SK7 3NX) 2C 84
Bramber Castle (BN44 3FJ) 4C 26
Bramham Pk. (LS23 6ND) 5G 99
Brands Hatch Motor Circuit (DA3 8NG) 4G 39
Brantwood (LA21 8AD) 5E 102
Breamore House (SP6 2DF) 1G 15
Brean Down (TA8 2RS) 1F 21
Brecon Beacons Nat. Pk. (CF44 9JG) 4B 46
Brecon Mountain Railway (CF48 2UP) 4D 46
Bressingham Steam & Gdns. (IP22 2AB) 2C 66
Brimham Rocks (HG3 4DW) 3E 98
Brindley Mill & Mus. (ST13 8FA) 5D 85
Brinkburn Priory (NE65 8AR) 5F 121

Bristol Cathedral (BS1 5TJ) 189
Bristol Zoo Gdns. (BS8 3HA) 189
Britannia Bridge (LL61 5BZ) 3E 81
British Golf Mus. (KY16 9AB) . . . . . .St Andrews 209
British Library (NW1 2DB) . . . . .London 203
British Mus. (WC1B 3DG) . . . . .London 203
Broads, The (NR3 1BQ) 5G 79
Broadway Tower (WR12 7LB) 2G 49
Brobury House Gdns. (HR6 6BS) 1G 47
Brockhampton Estate (WR6 5TB) 5A 60
Brockhole, Lake District Visitor Centre (LA23 1LJ)
. . . . .4E 103
Brodick Castle & Gdn. (KA27 8HY) 2E 123
Brodie Castle (IV36 2TE) 3D 159
Brodsworth Hall & Gdns. (DN5 7XJ) 4F 93
Brogdale (ME13 8XU) .5E 40
Bronllys Castle (LD3 0HL) 2E 47
Bronté Parsonage Mus. (BD22 8DR) 1A 92
Broseley Pipe Works (TF12 5LX) 5A 72
Brougham Castle (CA10 2AA) 2G 103
Brough Castle (CA17 4EJ) 3A 104
Broughton Castle (OX15 5EB) 2C 50
Broughton House & Gdn. (DG6 4JX) 4D 111
Brownsea Island (BH13 7EE) 4F 15
Bruce's Stone (DG7 3SQ) 2C 110
Brunel's SS Great Britain (BS1 6TY) . . . .Bristol 189
Buckfast Abbey (TQ11 0EE) 2D 8
Buckingham Palace (SW1A 1AA) . . . . .London 202
Buckland Abbey (PL20 6EY) 2A 8
Buckler's Hard Maritime Mus. (SO42 7XB) 2C 16
Buildwas Abbey (TF8 7BW) 5A 72
Bungay Castle (NR35 1DD) 2F 67
Bure Valley Railway (NR11 6BW) 3E 79
Burford House Gdns. (WR15 8HQ) 4H 59
Burghley (PE9 3JY) 5H 75
Burleigh Hall Gdns. & Mus. (YO42 2QF) 5C 100
Burns Cottage, Alloway (KA7 4PY) 3C 116
Burns House Mus. (KA5 5BZ) 2D 117
[Burrell Collection, Pollokshaws (G43 1AT)] . . .3G 127
Burton Agnes Hall (YO25 4ND) 3F 101
Burton Constable Hall (HU11 4LN) 1E 95
Bury St Edmunds Abbey (IP33 1RS) 4A 66
Buscot Pk. (SN7 8BU) 2H 35
Butser Ancient Farm (PO8 0QF) 1F 17
Butterfly & Wildlife Pk. (PE12 9LF) 3D 76
Buttertubs, The (DL11 6DR) 5B 104
Buxton Pavilion Gdns. (SK17 6XN) 3E 85
Byland Abbey (YO61 4BD) 2H 99

C

Cadair Idris (LL40 1TN) 4F 69
Cadbury World (B30 1JR) 2E 61
Caerlaverock Castle (DG1 4RU) 3B 112
Caerleon Roman Fortress (NP18 1AY) 2G 33
Caernarfon Castle (LL55 2AY) 190
Caerphilly Castle (CF83 1JD) 3E 33
Cairngorms Nat. Pk. (PH26 3HG) 3E 151
Cairnpapple Hill (EH48 4NW) 2C 128
Caister Castle & Motor Mus. (NR30 5SN) 4H 79
Caldey Island (SA70 7UH) 5F 43
Caldicot Castle (NP26 5JB) 3H 33
Caledonian Railway (DD9 7AF) 3F 145
Calke Abbey (DE73 7LE) 3A 74
Calshot Castle (SO45 1BR) 2C 16
Camber Castle (TN31 7TB) 4D 28
Cambo Sands (KY16 8QD) 2H 137
Cambridge University Botanic Gdn. (CB2 1JF) . .191
Camelot Theme Pk. (PR7 5LP) 3D 90
Camperdown Wildlife Centre (DD2 4TF) 5C 144
Canal Mus. (NN12 7SE) 5E 63
Cannock Chase (WS12 4PW) 4D 73
Cannon Hall Mus. (S75 4AT) 4C 92
Canons Ashby House (NN11 3SD) 5C 62
Canterbury Cathedral (CT1 2EH) 190
Cape Wrath (IV27 4QQ) 1C 166
Capesthorne Hall (SK11 9JY) 3C 84
Captain Cook Schoolroom Mus. (TS9 6NB) 3C 106
Cardiff Castle (CF10 3RB) 191
Cardoness Castle (DG7 2EH) 4C 110
Carew Castle & Tidal Mill (SA70 8SL) 4E 43
Carisbrooke Castle (PO30 1XY) 4C 16
Carlisle Castle (CA3 8UR) 192
Carlisle Cathedral (CA3 8TZ) 192
Carlyle's Birthplace (DG11 3DG) 2C 112
Carnasserie Castle (PA31 8RQ) 3F 133
Carn Euny Ancient Village (TR20 8RB) 4B 4
Carreg Cennen Castle & Farm (SA19 6UA) 4G 45
Carsluith Castle (DG8 7DY) 4B 110
Cartmel Priory Church (LA11 6QQ) 2C 96
Castell Coch, Tongwynlais (CF15 7JS) 3E 33
Castell Dinas Bran (LL20 8DY) 1E 70
Castell y Bere (LL36 9TP) 5F 69
Castle Acre Castle (PE32 2XB) 4H 77
Castle Acre Priory (PE32 2AA) 4H 77
Castle Campbell & Gdn. (FK14 7PP) 4B 136
Castle Drogo (EX6 6PB) 3H 11
Castle Fraser (AB51 7LD) 2E 152
Castle Howard (YO60 7DA) 2B 100
Castle Kennedy Gdns. (DG9 8SJ) 4G 109
Castle Leod (IV14 9AA) 3G 157
Castle Menzies (PH15 2JD) 4F 143
Castlerigg Stone Circle (CA12 4RN) 2D 102
Castle Rising Castle (PE31 6AH) 3F 77
Catalyst Science Discovery Centre (WA8 0DF)
. . . . .2H 83
Cawdor Castle (IV12 5RD) 4C 158
Cecil Higgins Art Gallery (MK40 3RP) . .Bedford 188
Ceramica (ST6 3DS) 1C 72

Cerne Giant (DT2 7TS) 2B 14
Chanonry Point (IV10 8SD) 3B 158
Charlecote Pk. (CV35 9ER) 5G 61
Charleston (BN8 6LL) .5F 27
Chartwell (TN16 1PS) .5F 39
Chastleton House (GL56 0SU) 3H 49
Chatsworth (DE45 1PP) 3G 85
Chavenage House (GL8 8XP) 2D 34
Cheddar Gorge (BS40 7XT) 1H 21
Chedworth Roman Villa (GL54 3LJ) 4F 49
Cheltenham Racecourse (GL50 4SH) 3E 49
Chenies Manor House & Gdns. (WD3 6ER) 1B 38
Chepstow Castle (NP16 5EZ) 2A 34
Chepstow Racecourse (NP16 6EG) 2A 34
Chesil Beach (DT3 4ED) 4B 14
Chessington World of Adventures (KT9 2NE) . . .4C 38
Chester Cathedral (CH1 2HU) 192
Chester Roman Amphitheatre (CH1 1RF) 192
Chesters Roman Fort & Mus. (NE46 4ET) 2C 114
Chester Zoo (CH2 1LH) 3G 83
Chettle House (DT11 8DB) 1E 15
Chichester Cathedral (PO19 1PX) 2G 17
Chiddingstone Castle (TN8 7AD) 1F 27
Chillingham Castle (NE66 5NJ) 2E 121
Chillingham Wild Cattle (NE66 5NJ) 2E 121
Chillington Hall (WV8 1RE) 5C 72
Chiltern Hills (RG9 6DR) 3E 37
Chiltern Open Air Mus. (HP8 4AB) 1A 38
China Clay Country Pk. (Wheal Martyn) (PL26 8XG)
. . . . .3E 6
Chirk Castle (LL14 5AF) 2E 71
Cholmondeley Castle Gdns. (SY14 8AH) 5H 83
Christchurch Castle (BH23 1BW) 3G 15
Christchurch Mansion (IP4 2BE) . . . . . .Ipswich 198
Churchill War Rooms (SW1A 2AQ) . . . .London 203
Churnet Valley Railway (ST13 7EE) 5D 85
Chysauster Ancient Village (TR20 8XA) 3B 4
Cilgerran Castle (SA43 2SF) 1B 44
Cissbury Ring (BN14 0SQ) 5C 26
Clandon Pk. (GU4 7RQ) 5B 38
Claremont Landscape Gdn. (KT10 9JG) 4C 38
Claydon (MK18 2EY) 3F 51
Clearwell Caves (GL16 8JR) 5A 48
Cleeve Abbey (TA23 0PS) 2D 20
Clevedon Court (BS21 6QU) 4H 33
Clifford's Tower (YO1 9SA) . . . . .York 214
Clifton Suspension Bridge (BS8 3PA) . . . .Bristol 189
Cliveden (SL6 0JA) 2A 38
Clouds Hill (BH20 7NQ) 3D 14
Clumber Pk. (S80 3BX) 3D 86
Clun Castle (SY7 8JR) 2E 59
Clyde Muirshiel Regional Pk. (PA10 2PZ) 3D 126
Coalbrookdale Mus. of Iron (TF8 7DQ) 5A 72
Coalport China Mus. (TF8 7HT) 5A 72
Coed y Brenin Visitor Centre (LL40 2HZ) 3G 69
Coggeshall Grange Barn (CO6 1RE) 3B 54
Coity Castle (CF35 6AU) 3C 32
Colby Woodland Gdn. (SA67 8PP) 4F 43
Colchester Castle Mus. (CO1 1TJ) 3D 54
Colchester Zoo (CO3 0SL) 3C 54
Coleridge Cottage (TA5 1NQ) 3E 21
Coleton Fishacre (TQ6 0EQ) 3F 9
Colour Experience (BD1 2JB) . . . . . . .Bradford 190
Colzium Walled Gdn. (G65 0PY) 2A 128
Combe Martin Wildlife & Dinosaur Pk. (EX34 0NG)
. . . . .2F 19
Compton Acres (BH13 7ES) 4F 15
Compton Castle (TQ3 1TA) 2E 9
Compton Verney (CV35 9HZ) 5H 61
Conisbrough Castle (DN12 3BU) 1C 86
Conishead Priory (LA12 9QQ) 2C 96
Conkers (DE12 6GA) 4H 73
Constable Burton Hall Gdns. (DL8 5LJ) 5E 105
Conwy Castle (LL32 8LD) 3G 81
Corbridge Roman Town (NE45 5NT) 3C 114
Corfe Castle (BH20 5EZ) 4E 15
Corgarff Castle (AB36 8YP) 3G 151
Corinium Mus. (GL7 2BX) 5F 49
Cornish Mines & Engines (TR15 3NP) 4A 6
Corrieshalloch Gorge (IV23 2PJ) 1E 156
Corsham Court (SN13 0BZ) 4D 35
Cotehele (PL12 6TA) 2A 8
Coton Manor Gdn. (NN6 8RQ) 3D 62
Cotswold Farm Pk. (GL54 5UG) 3G 49
Cotswold Hills (GL8 8NU) 5E 49
Cotswold Water Pk. (GL7 5TL) 2F 35
Cottesbrooke Hall & Gdns. (NN6 8PF) 3E 62
Cotton Mechanical Music Mus. (IP14 4QN) 4C 66
Coughton Court (B49 5JA) 4E 61
Courts Gdn., The (BA14 6RR) 5D 34
Coventry Cathedral (CV1 5AB) 192
Coventry Transport Mus. (CV1 1JD) 192
Cowdray House (GU29 9AL) 4G 25
Cragside (NE65 7PX) 4E 121
Craig Castle (AB54 4LP) 1B 152
Craigievar Castle (AB33 8JF) 3C 152
Craigmillar Castle (EH16 4SY) 2F 129
Craignethan Castle (ML11 9PL) 5A 128
Craigston Castle (AB53 5PX) 3E 161
Cranborne Manor Gdn. (BH21 5PS) 1F 15
Cranwell Aviation Heritage Centre (NG34 8QR)
. . . . .1H 75
Crarae Gdn. (PA32 8YA) 4G 133
Crathes Castle & Gdn. (AB31 5QJ) 4E 153
Creswell Crags (S80 3LH) 3C 86
Crewe Heritage Centre (CW1 2DD) 5B 84
Criccieth Castle (LL52 0DP) 2D 69
Crichton Castle (EH37 5XA) 3G 129
Crich Tramway Village (DE4 5DP) 5A 86
Croft Castle (HR6 9PW) 4G 59
Croft Motor Circuit (DL2 2PL) 4F 105
Cromford Mill (DE4 3RQ) 5G 85
Cromwell Mus. (PE29 3LF) 3B 64
Crookston Castle (G53 5RR) 3G 127

Croome (WR8 9JS) 1D 49
Crossraguel Abbey (KA19 8HQ) 4B 116
Croxden Abbey (ST14 5JG) 2E 73
Croxteth Hall (L12 0HB) 1G 83
Cruachan Power Station (PA33 1AN) 1H 133
Culloden Battlefield Visitor Centre (IV2 5EU) ..4B 158
Culloden Battle Site (IV2 5EU) 4B 158
Culross Palace (KY12 8JH) 1C 128
Culzean Castle (KA19 8LE) 3B 116
Curraghs Wildlife Pk. (IM7 5EA) 2C 108
Cusworth Hall (DN5 7TU) 4F 93
Cymer Abbey (LL40 2HE) 4G 69

D

Dalemain (CA11 0HB) 2F 103
Dales Countryside Mus. (DL8 3NT) 5B 104
Dallas Dhu Historic Distillery (IV36 2RR) ...1G 157
Dalmeny House (EH30 9TQ) 2E 129
Darby Houses (TF8 7DQ) 5A 72
Dartington Crystal (EX38 7AN) 1E 11
Dartington Hall Gdns. (TQ9 6EL) 2E 9
Dartmoor Nat. Pk. (TQ13 9JQ) 4F 11
Dartmoor Zoo (PL7 5DG) 3B 8
Dartmouth Castle (TQ6 0JN) 3E 9
Dartmouth Steam Railway (TQ4 6AF) 3E 9
Dawyck Botanic Gdn. (EH45 9JU) 1D 118
Deal Castle (CT14 7BA) 5H 41
Dean Castle (KA3 1XB) 1D 116
Dean Forest Railway (GL15 4ET) 5B 48
Deene Pk. (NN17 3EW) 1G 63
Deep Sea World (KY11 1JR) 1E 129
Deep, The (HU1 4DP) ....Hull 199
Delamere Forest (CW8 2JD) 3H 83
Delgatie Castle (AB53 5TD) 3E 161
Denbigh Castle (LL16 3NB) 4C 82
Devil's Dyke (BN45 7DE) 4D 26
Devil's Punch Bowl (GU26 6AB) 3G 25
Dewa Roman Experience (CH1 1NL) ....Chester 192
DH Lawrence Birthplace Mus. (NG16 3AW) ..1B 74
Dickens House Mus. (CT10 1QS) 4H 41
[Dickens World, Chatham (ME4 4LL)] 3B 40
Didcot Railway Centre (OX11 7NJ) 2D 36
Dinefwr Castle (SA19 6PF) 3G 45
Dinefwr Pk. (SA19 6RT) 3G 45
Dinorwig Power Station (Electric Mountain) (LL55 4UR) 5E 81
Dinosaur Adventure (NR9 5JW) 4D 78
Dinosaur Mus. (DT1 1EW) 3B 14
Dirleton Castle & Gdn. (EH39 5ER) 1B 130
Discovery Mus. (NE1 4JA) ....Newcastle 205
Discovery Point & RRS Discovery (DD1 4XA) ....Dundee 194
Dock Mus. (LA14 2PW) 3A 96
Doddington Hall & Gdns. (LN6 4RU) 4F 87
Doddington Place Gdns. (ME9 0BB) 5D 40
Dolaucothi Gold Mines (SA19 8RR) 2G 45
Dolbadarn Castle (LL55 4SU) 5E 81
Dolforwyn Castle (SY16 6JH) 1D 58
Domestic Fowl Trust and Honeybourne Rare Breeds (WR11 7QZ) ...1G 49
Doncaster Racecourse (DN2 6BB) 4G 93
Donington Grand Prix Collection, Castle Donington (DE74 2RP) 3B 74
Donington Pk. Motor Circuit (DE74 2RP) 3B 74
Donnington Castle (RG14 2LE) 5C 36
Dorfold Hall (CW5 8LD) 5A 84
Dorothy Clive Gdn. (TF9 4EU) 2B 72
Doune Castle (FK16 6EA) 3G 135
Dove Cottage (Wordsworth Mus.) (LA22 9SH) 4E 103
Dove Dale (DE6 1NL) 5F 85
Dover Castle (CT16 1HU) 193
Down House (BR6 7JT) 4F 39
Dozmary Pool (PL15 7TP) 5B 10
Drayton Manor Theme Pk. (B78 3TW) 5F 73
Drum Castle & Gdn. (AB31 5EY) 3E 153
Drumlanrig Castle (DG3 4AQ) 5A 118
Drummond Gdns. (PH5 2AA) 2H 135
Drusillas (BN26 5QS) 5G 27
Dryburgh Abbey (TD6 0RQ) 1H 119
Dryslwyn Castle (SA32 8JO) 3F 45
Duart Castle (PA64 6AP) 5B 140
[Dudley Zoological Gdns. & Castle (DY1 4AS)] 1D 60
Dudmaston Estate (WV15 6QN) 2B 60
Duff House & Country Gallery (AB45 3SX) ...2D 160
Duffus Castle (IV30 5RH) 2F 159
Dukeries, The (S80 3BT) 3D 86
Dumbarton Castle (G82 1JJ) 2F 127
Dunblane Cathedral (FK15 0AQ) 3G 135
Dun Carloway (HS2 9AZ) 3D 171
Duncombe Pk. (YO62 5EB) 1A 100
Dundonald Castle (KA2 9HD) 1C 116
Dundrennan Abbey (DG6 4QH) 5E 111
Dunfermline Abbey & Palace (KY12 7PE) ..1D 129
Dungeon Ghyll Force (LA22 9JY) 4D 102
Dunge Valley Rhododendron Gdns. (SK23 7RF) 3D 85
Dunham Massey (WA14 4SJ) 2B 84
Dunkeld Cathedral (PH8 0AW) 4H 143
Dunkery Beacon (TA24 7AT) 2B 20
Dunnet Head (KW14 8XS) 1D 169
Dunninald (DD10 9TD) 3G 145
Dunnottar Castle (AB39 2TL) 5F 153
Dunrobin Castle (KW10 6SF) 3F 165
Dunstaffnage Castle (PA37 1PZ) 5C 140
Dunstanburgh Castle (NE66 3TG) 2G 121
Dunster Castle (TA24 6SL) 2C 20
Dunvegan Castle (IV55 8WF) 4B 154
Durdle Door (BH20 5PU) 4D 14
Durham Cathedral (DH1 3EH) 194
Dyffryn Gdns. (CF5 6SU) 4D 32
Dylan Thomas Boathouse (SA33 4SD) 3H 43
Dyrham Pk. (SN14 8ER) 4C 34

E

Eagle Heights Wildlife Pk. (DA4 0JB) 4G 39
Easby Abbey (DL10 7JU) 4E 105
East Bergholt Place Gdn. (CO7 6UP) 2D 54
East Kent Railway (CT15 7PD) 1G 29
East Lambrook Manor Gdns. (TA13 5HH) ...1H 13
East Lancashire Railway (BL9 0EY) 2G 91
Eastnor Castle (HR8 1RD) 2C 48

East Riddlesden Hall (BD20 5EL) 5C 98
East Somerset Railway (BA4 4QP) 2B 22
Eden Project (PL24 2SG) 3E 7
Edinburgh Castle (EH1 2NG) 194
Edinburgh Zoo (EH12 6TS) 2F 129
Edzell Castle & Gdn. (DD9 7UE) 2E 145
Egglestone Abbey (DL12 9TN) 3D 104
Eilean Donan Castle (IV40 8DX) 1A 148
Elcho Castle (PH2 8QQ) 1D 136
Electric Mountain (Dinorwig Power Station) (LL55 4UR) 5E 81
Elgar Birthplace Mus. (WR2 6RH) 5C 60
Elgin Cathedral (IV30 1EL) 2G 159
Eltham Palace & Gdns. (SE9 5QE) 3F 39
Elton Hall & Gdns. (PE8 6SH) 1F 63
Ely Cathedral (CB7 4DL) 2E 65
Embsay & Bolton Abbey Steam Railway (BD23 6AF) ...4C 98
Emmetts Gdn. (TN14 6BA) 5F 39
Enginuity (TF8 7DQ) 5A 72
Epsom Downs Racecourse (KT18 5LQ) 5D 38
Erddig (LL13 0YT) 1F 71
Escot (EX11 1LU) 3D 12
Etal Castle (TD12 4TN) 1D 120
Eureka! The Nat. Children's Mus., Halifax (HX1 2NE) 2A 92
Euston Hall (IP24 2QW) 3A 66
Ewloe Castle (CH5 3BZ) 4E 83
Exbury Gdns. (SO45 1AZ) 2C 16
Exeter Cathedral (EX1 1HS) 195
Exmoor Nat. Pk. (TA22 9HL) 2A 20
Eyam Hall (S32 5QW) 4B 86
Eye Castle (IP23 7AP) 3D 66
Eynsford Castle (DA4 0AA) 4G 39

F

Fairbourne Steam Railway (LL38 2PZ) 4F 69
Fairhaven Woodland & Water Gdn. (NR13 6DZ) ...4F 79
Falkirk Wheel (FK1 4RS) 1B 128
Falkland Palace (KY15 7BU) 3E 137
Falls of Glomach (IV40 8DS) 1C 148
Falstaff Experience - Tudor World (CV37 6EE) ....Stratford 212
Farleigh Hungerford Castle (BA2 7RS) 1D 22
Farmland Mus. & Denny Abbey (CB25 9PQ) ..4D 65
Farnborough Hall (OX17 1DU) 1C 50
Farne Islands (NE68 7SY) 1G 121
Farnham Castle Keep (GU9 0AE) 2G 25
Felbrigg Hall (NR11 8PR) 2D 78
Fell Foot Pk. (LA12 8NN) 1C 96
Ferniehirst Castle (TD8 6NX) 3A 120
Ffestiniog Railway (LL49 9NF) 1F 69
Fiddleford Manor (DT10 2BU) 1D 14
Finchale Priory (DH1 5SH) 5F 115
Finchcocks (TN17 1HH) 2A 28
Finch Foundry (EX20 2NW) 3G 11
Finlaystone Country Estate (PA14 6TJ) 2E 127
Firle Place (BN8 6LP) 5F 27
Fishbourne Roman Palace & Gdns. (PO19 3QR) ...2G 17
Fitzwilliam Mus. (CB2 1RB) ....Cambridge 191
Five Sisters of Kintail (IV40 8HQ) 2B 148
Flambards Experience (TR13 0QA) 4D 4
Flamingo Land (YO17 6UX) 2B 100
Fleet Air Arm Mus. (BA22 8HT) 4A 22
Flint Castle (CH6 5PE) 3E 83
Floors Castle & Gdns. (TD5 7SF) 1B 120
Fonmon Castle (CF62 3ZN) 5D 32
Forde Abbey & Gdns. (TA20 4LU) 2G 13
Ford Green Hall (ST6 1NG) 5C 84
Forest of Dean (GL15 4SL) 5B 48
Fort George (IV2 7TD) 3B 158
Forth Bridge (EH30 9TB) 2E 129
Fountains Abbey & Studley Royal (HG4 3DY) ..3E 99
Foxfield Steam Railway (ST11 9BG) 1D 72
Foxton Locks (LE16 7RA) 2D 62
Framlingham Castle (IP13 9BP) 4E 67
Froghall Wharf (ST10 2HH) 1E 73
Furness Abbey (LA13 0PG) 2B 96
Furzey Gdns. (SO43 7GL) 1A 16
Fyne Court (TA5 2EQ) 3F 21
Fyvie Castle (AB53 8JS) 5E 161

G

Gainsborough Old Hall (DN21 2NB) 1F 87
Gainsborough's House (CO10 2EU) 1E 54
Gallery of Modern Art (G1 3AH) ....Glasgow 196
Galloway Forest Pk. (DG8 6TA) 1B 110
Galloway House Gdns. (DG8 8HF) 5B 110
Galloway Wildlife Conservation Pk. (DG6 4XX) ...4E 111
Garden House, The (PL20 7LQ) 2A 8
Gardens of the Rose (AL2 3NR) 5B 52
Gawsworth Hall (SK11 9RN) 4C 84
Gawthorpe Hall (BB12 8UA) 1G 91
Geevor Tin Mine Mus. (TR19 7EW) 3A 4
George Stephenson's Birthplace (NE41 8BP) ..3E 115
Georgian House (EH2 4DR) ....Edinburgh 194
Gilbert White's House & Gdn. (GU34 3JH) ...3F 25
Gisborough Priory (TS14 6BU) 3D 106
Gladstone Pottery Mus. (ST3 1PQ) 1D 72
Gladstone's Land (EH1 2NT) ....Edinburgh 194
Glamis Castle (DD8 1QJ) 4C 144
Glastonbury Abbey (BA6 9EL) 3A 22
Glastonbury Tor (BA6 8BG) 3A 22
Glenarn (G84 8LL) 1D 126
Glenbuchat Castle (AB36 8TN) 2A 152
Glencoe Gorge (PH50 4SG) 3F 141
Glendurgan Gdn. (TR11 5JQ) 4E 5
Glenfinnan Monument (PH37 4LT) 5B 148
Glenluce Abbey (DG8 0LW) 4A 109
Glenmore Forest Pk. Visitor Centre (PH22 1QY) ...3D 150
Glenwhan Gdns. (DG9 8PH) 4A 109
Gloucester Cathedral (GL1 2EH) 196
Gloucestershire Warwickshire Railway (GL54 5DT) ...4A 49
Gloucester Waterways Mus. (GL1 2EH) 196
Glynde Place (BN8 6SX) 5F 27
Godinton House & Gdns. (TN23 3BP) 1D 28
Godolphin (TR13 9RE) 3D 4
Goodnestone Pk. Gdns. (CT3 1PL) 5G 41
Goodrich Castle (HR9 6HY) 3A 48

Goodwood House (PO18 0PX) 2G 17
Goodwood Racecourse (PO18 0PS) 1G 17
Gordale Scar (BD23 4DL) 3B 98
Grampian Transport Mus. (AB33 8AE) 2C 152
Grange at Northington, The (SO24 9TG) 3D 24
Graves Gallery (S1 1XZ) ....Sheffield 210
Graythwaite Hall Gdns. (LA12 8BA) 5E 103
Great Central Railway (LE11 1RW) 4C 74
Great Central Railway (Nottingham) (NG11 6NX) ...2C 74
Great Chalfield Manor & Gdn. (SN12 8NH) ..5D 34
Great Comp Gdn. (TN15 8QS) 5H 39
Great Dixter (TN31 6PH) 3C 28
Great North Mus.: Hancock (NE2 4PT) ....Newcastle 205
Greenbank House & Gdn. (G76 8RB) 4G 127
Greenknowe Tower (TD3 6JL) 5C 130
Gretna Green Old Blacksmith's Shop (DG16 5EA) ...3E 112
Grey Mare's Tail Waterfall (DG10 9LH) 3D 118
Greys Court (RG9 4PG) 3F 37
Grimes Graves (IP26 5DE) 1H 65
Grimsby Fishing Heritage Centre (DN31 1UZ) ..4F 95
Grimspound (PL20 6TB) 4H 11
Grimsthorpe Castle (PE10 0LZ) 3H 75
Grizedale Forest Pk. (LA22 0QJ) 5E 103
Groombridge Place Gdns. (TN3 9QG) 2G 27
Grove Mus. (M8 3UA) 2D 108
Gulliver's Dinosaur & Farm Pk. (MK15 0DT) ..2G 51
Gulliver's Matlock Bath (DE4 3PG) 5G 85
Gulliver's Milton Keynes (MK15 0DT) 204
Gulliver's Warrington (WA5 9YZ) 1H 83
Gunby Hall (PE23 5SS) 4D 88
Gwydir Castle (LL26 0PN) 4G 81

H

Haddo House (AB41 7EQ) 5F 161
Haddon Hall (DE45 1LA) 4G 85
Hadleigh Castle (SS7 2AR) 2C 40
Hadrian's Wall (NE47 6NN) 3A 114
Hailes Abbey (GL54 5PB) 2F 49
Hailes Castle (EH41 3SB) 2B 130
Hall i' th' Wood Mus. (BL1 8UA) 3F 91
Hall Place & Gdns. (DA5 1PQ) 3G 39
Hamerton Zoo Pk. (PE28 5RE) 2A 64
Ham House & Gdn. (TW10 7RS) 3C 38
Hammerwood Pk. (RH19 3QE) 2F 27
Hampden Pk. (G42 9AY) 3G 127
Hampton Court Castle & Gdns. (HR6 0PN) ...5H 59
Hampton Court Palace (KT8 9AU) 4C 38
Hanbury Hall (WR9 7EA) 4D 60
Hardknott Roman Fort (LA20 6EQ) 4D 102
Hardwick Hall (S44 5QJ) 4B 86
Hardy Monument (DT2 9HY) 4B 14
Hardy's Cottage (DT2 8QJ) 3C 14
Hare Hill (SK10 4QA) 3C 84
Harewood House (LS17 9LG) 5F 99
Harlech Castle (LL46 2YH) 2E 69
Harley Gallery (S80 3LW) 3C 86
Hartland Abbey & Gdns. (EX39 6DT) 4C 18
Harvington Hall (DY10 4LR) 3C 60
Harwich Redoubt (CO12 3NL) 2F 55
Hatchlands Pk. (GU4 7RT) 5B 38
Hatfield House (AL9 5NQ) 5C 52
Haughmond Abbey (SY4 4RW) 4H 71
Haverfordwest Castle (SA61 2BW) 3D 42
Haverfordwest Priory (SA61 1PH) 3D 42
Hawk Conservancy Trust (SP11 8DY) 2B 24
Haydock Pk. Racecourse (WA12 0HQ) 1H 83
Head of Steam - Darlington Railway Mus. (DL3 6ST) ...3F 105
Heale Gdns. (SP4 6NT) 3G 23
Heaton Hall (M25 2SW) 4G 91
Hedingham Castle (CO9 3DJ) 2A 54
Heights of Abraham (DE4 3PB) 5G 85
Hellens (HR8 2LY) 2B 48
Helmingham Hall Gdns. (IP14 6EF) 5D 66
Helmshore Mills Textile Mus. (BB4 4NP) 2F 91
Helmsley Castle (YO62 5AB) 1A 100
Helvellyn (CA12 4TP) 3E 103
[Henry Moore Institute, Leeds (LS1 3AH)] ....Leeds 199
Heptonstall Mus. (HX7 7PL) 2H 91
Hereford Cathedral (HR1 2NG) 197
Hereford Cider Mus. (HR4 0LW) 2A 48
Hergest Croft Gdns. (HR5 3EG) 5E 59
Heritage Motor Centre (CV35 0BJ) 5A 62
Herstmonceux Castle (BN27 1RN) 4H 27
Hestercombe Gdn. (TA2 8LG) 4E 21
Hever Castle & Gdns. (TN8 7NG) 1F 27
Hexham Abbey (NE46 3NB) 3C 114
Hidcote (GL55 6LR) 1G 49
High Beeches Gdns. (RH17 6HQ) 2D 27
Highclere Castle (RG20 9RN) 1C 24
Highland Folk Mus. (PH20 1AY) 4B 150
Highland Wildlife Pk. (PH21 1NL) 3D 150
Hill of Tarvit Mansionhouse & Gdns. (KY15 5PB) ...2F 137
Hill Top (LA22 0LF) 5E 103
Hinton Ampner (SO24 0LA) 4D 24
Hirsel (TD12 4LP) 5E 131
Historic Dockyard Chatham (ME4 4TZ) ....Medway 204
HMS Victory (PO1 3LJ) ....Portsmouth 209
HMS Warrior 1860 (PO1 3QX) ....Portsmouth 209
Hodnet Hall Gdns. (TF9 3NN) 3A 72
Hodsock Priory (PR5 0SH) 2E 90
Hog's Back (GU3 1AQ) 1A 26
Holburne Mus. of Art (BA2 4DB) ....Bath 187
Holdenby House Gdns. (NN6 8DJ) 4D 62
Holehird Gdns. (LA23 1NP) 4F 103
Holker Hall & Gdns. (LA11 7PL) 2C 96
Holkham (NR23 1AB) 1A 78
Hollycombe (GU30 7LP) 4G 25
Holst Birthplace Mus. (GL52 2AY) ...Cheltenham 192
Holy Jesus Hospital (NE1 2AS) .....Newcastle 205
Holyrood Abbey (EH8 8DX) ....Edinburgh 194
Hopetoun (EH30 9SL) 2D 129
Hop Farm Family Pk. (TN12 6PY) 1A 28
Houghton Hall (PE31 6TZ) 3G 77
Houghton House (MK45 2EZ) 2A 52
Houghton Lodge Gdns. (SO20 6LQ) 3B 24
House of Dun (DD10 9LQ) 3F 145
House of Manannan Mus., Peel (IM5 1TA) 3B 108

House of the Binns (EH49 7NA) 1D 128
Houses of Parliament (SW1A 0RS) ......London 203
Housesteads Roman Fort & Mus. (NE47 6NN) ...3A 114
Hoveton Hall Gdns. (NR12 8RJ) 3F 79
Hoveton Hall (YO62 4LU) 2A 100
Howick Hall Gdns. (NE66 3LB) 3G 121
Howletts Wild Animal Pk. (CT4 5EL) 5F 41
Hughenden Manor (HP14 4LA) 2G 37
Hugh Miller Mus. & Birthplace Cottage (IV11 8XA) ...2B 158
Humber Bridge (HU13 0HE) 2D 94
Hunstanton Sea Life Sanctuary (PE36 5BH) ...1F 77
Hunterian Mus. (G12 8QQ) 3G 127
Huntingtower Castle (PH1 3JL) 1C 136
Huntly Castle (AB54 4SH) 4C 160
Hurst Castle (SO41 0TP) 4B 16
Hutton-in-the-Forest (CA11 9TH) 1F 103
Hylands House & Gdns. (CM2 8WQ) 5G 53

I

Iceni Village & Mus. (PE37 8AG) 5G 77
Ickworth (IP29 5QE) 4H 65
Iford Manor (Peto Gdn.) (BA15 2BA) 1D 22
Ightham Mote (TN15 0NT) 5G 39
Ilam Pk. (DE6 2AZ) 5F 85
Ilfracombe Aquarium (EX34 9EQ) 2F 19
Imperial War Mus. Duxford (CB22 4QR) 1E 53
Imperial War Mus. London (SE1 6HZ) 203
Imperial War Mus. North, Trafford Park (M17 1TZ) ...1C 84
Inchcolm Abbey (KY3 0XR) 1E 129
Inchmahome Priory (FK8 3RD) 3E 135
Inglestone Hall (CM4 9NS) 1A 40
International Centre for Birds of Prey (GL18 1JJ) ...3C 48
Inveraray Castle (PA32 8XE) 3H 133
Inveresk Lodge Gdn. (EH21 7TE) 2G 129
Inverewe Gdn. (IV22 2LG) 5C 162
Inverlochy Castle (PH33 6TQ) 1F 141
Inverness Mus. & Art Gallery (IV2 3EB) 198
Iona (PA76 6SP) 2A 132
Iron Bridge (TF8 7JP) 5A 72
Isle Hall (CA13 0QG) 1C 102
Isle of Man Steam Railway (IM1 4LL) 4C 108
Isle of Wight Steam Railway (PO33 4DS) 4D 16
Ivinghoe Beacon (LU6 2EG) 4H 51
Izaak Walton's Cottage (ST15 0PA) 3C 72

J

Jackfield Tile Mus. (TF8 7ND) 5A 72
Jane Austen Centre (BA1 2NT) ....Bath 187
Jane Austen's House Mus. (GU34 1SD) 3F 25
Jarlshof Prehistoric & Norse Settlement (ZE3 9JN) ...1C 173
Jedburgh Abbey (TD8 6JQ) 3A 120
Jervaulx Abbey (HG4 4PH) 1D 98
JM Barrie's Birthplace (DD8 4BX) 3C 144
Jodrell Bank Discovery Centre (SK11 9DL) 3B 84
Jorvik Viking Centre (YO1 9WT) ....York 214

K

Kedleston Hall (DE22 5JH) 1H 73
Keighley & Worth Valley Railway (BD22 8NJ) ..1A 92
Kelburn Castle & Country Centre (KA29 0BE) ...4D 126
Keld Chapel (CA10 3QF) 3G 103
Kelham Island Mus. (S3 8RY) ....Sheffield 210
Kellie Castle & Gdn. (KY10 2RF) 3H 137
Kelmarsh Hall & Gdns. (NN6 9LY) 3E 63
Kelmscott Manor (GL7 3HJ) 2A 36
Kelso Abbey (TD5 7BB) 1B 120
Kelvingrove Art Gallery & Mus., Glasgow (G3 8AG) ...3G 127
Kempton Pk. Racecourse (TW16 5AE) 3C 38
Kenilworth Castle (CV8 1NE) 3G 61
Kent & East Sussex Railway (TN30 6HE) 3C 28
Kentwell (CO10 9BA) 1B 54
Kenwood House (NW3 7JR) 2D 38
Keswick Mus. & Gallery (CA12 4NF) 2D 102
Kettle's Yard (CB3 0AQ) ....Cambridge 191
Kew Gdns. (TW9 3AB) 3C 38
Kidwelly Castle (SA17 5BQ) 5E 45
Kielder Water & Forest Pk. (NE48 1QZ) 1H 113
Kiftsgate Court Gdns. (GL55 6LN) 1G 49
Kilchurn Castle (PA33 1AF) 1A 134
Kildrummy Castle (AB33 8RA) 2B 152
Killerton (EX5 3LE) 2C 12
Kilmartin Glen Prehistoric Sites (PA31 8RQ) ..4F 133
Kilmartin House Mus. (PA31 8RQ) 4F 133
Kinder Scout (S33 7ZJ) 2E 85
King's College Chapel (CB2 1TN) ....Cambridge 191
Kingston Bagpuize House & Gdn. (OX13 5AX) ..2C 36
Kingston Lacy (BH21 4EA) 2E 15
Kingston Maurward Animal Pk. & Gdns. (DT2 8PY) ...3C 14
Kinnersley Castle (HR3 6QF) 1G 47
Kinver Edge (DY7 5NP) 2C 60
Kiplin Hall (DL10 6AT) 5F 105
Kirby Hall (NN17 3EN) 1G 63
Kirby Muxloe Castle (LE9 2DH) 5C 74
Kirkham Priory (YO60 7JS) 3B 100
Kirklees Light Railway (HD8 9XJ) 3C 92
Kirkstall Abbey (LS5 3EH) 1C 92
Kirkwall Cathedral (KW15 1JF) 6D 172
Knaresborough Castle (HG5 8BB) 4F 99
Knebworth House (SG3 6PY) 3C 52
Knightshayes Court (EX16 7RQ) 1C 12
Knockhill Motor Circuit (KY12 9TF) 4C 136
Knole (TN15 0RP) 5G 39
Knoll Gdns. (BH21 7ND) 2F 15
Knowsley Safari Pk. (L34 4AN) 1G 83

L

Lacock Abbey (SN15 2LG) 5E 35
Lady Lever Art Gallery (CH62 5EQ) 2E 83
Laing Art Gallery (NE1 8AG) ....Newcastle 205
Lake District Nat. Pk. (LA9 7RL) 3E 103
Lakeside & Haverthwaite Railway (LA12 8AL) ..1C 96

Lamb House (TN31 7ES) 3D 28
Lamphey Bishop's Palace (SA71 5NT) 4E 43
Lamport Hall & Gdns. (NN6 9HD) 3E 63
Lancaster Castle (LA1 1YJ) 3D 96
Landmark Forest Adventure Pk. (PH23 3AJ) ..1D 150
Land's End (TR19 7AA) 4A 4
Lanercost Priory (CA8 2HQ) 3G 119
Langdale Pikes (LA22 9JY) 4D 102
Langley Chapel (SY5 7HU) 1H 59
Lanhydrock (PL30 5AD) 2E 7
Lappa Valley Steam Railway (TR8 5LX) 3C 6
Larmer Tree Gdns. (SP5 5PZ) 1E 15
Laugharne Castle (SA33 4SA) 3H 43
Launceston Castle (PL15 7DR) 4D 10
Launceston Steam Railway (PL15 8DA) 4D 10
Lauriston Castle (EH4 5QD) 2F 129
Lavenham Guildhall (CO10 9QZ) 1C 54
Laxey Wheel (IM4 7NL) 3D 108
Layer Marney Tower (CO5 9US) 4C 54
Leeds Castle (Kent) (ME17 1PL) 5C 40
Leeds City Mus. (LS1 3AA) 199
Legoland (SL4 4AY) 3A 38
Leighton Buzzard Railway (LU7 4TN) 3H 51
Leighton Hall (LA5 9ST) 2E 97
Leiston Abbey (IP16 4TD) 4G 67
Leith Hall (AB54 4NQ) 1C 152
Leith Hill (RH5 6LX) 1C 26
Lennoxlove House (EH41 4NZ) 2B 130
Levant Mine & Beam Engine (TR19 7SX) 3A 4
Levens Hall & Gdns. (LA8 0PD) 1D 97
Lewes Castle (BN7 1YE) 4F 27
Lichfield Cathedral (WS13 7LD) 4H 73
Life (NE1 4EP) ....Newcastle 205
Lightwater Valley (HG4 3HT) 2E 99
Lilleshall Abbey (TF10 9HW) 4B 72
Lincoln Castle (LN1 3AA) 198
Lincoln Cathedral (LN2 1PZ) 198
Lincoln Medieval Bishops' Palace (LN2 1PU) ..198
Lincolnshire Road Transport Mus. (LN6 3QT) ..4G 87
Lindisfarne (TD15 2SF) 5H 131
Lindisfarne Castle (TD15 2SH) 5H 131
Lindisfarne Priory (TD15 2RX) 5H 131
Linlithgow Palace (EH49 7AL) 2D 128
Linton Zoo (CB21 4XN) 1F 53
Little Clarendon (SP3 5DZ) 3F 23
Little Malvern Court (WR14 4JN) 1C 48
Little Moreton Hall (CW12 4SD) 5C 84
Liverpool Cathedral (L1 7AZ) 2F 83
Liverpool Metropolitan RC Cathedral (L3 5TQ) ..200
Lizard Point (TR12 7NU) 5E 5
Llanberis Lake Railway (LL55 3HB) 4E 81
Llanerchaeron (SA48 8DG) 5D 57
Llangollen Railway (LL20 7AJ) 1D 70
Llansteffan Castle (SA33 5JX) 4D 44
Llawhaden Castle (SA67 8HL) 3E 43
Llechwedd Slate Caverns (LL41 3NB) 1G 69
Llywernog Silver-Lead Mine (SY23 3AB) 2G 57
Lochalsh Woodland Gdn. (IV40 8DN) 1F 147
Loch Doon Castle (KA6 7QE) 5D 117
Lochleven Castle (KY13 8ET) 3D 136
Loch Lomond (G83 8PA) 4C 134
Loch Lomond & The Trossachs Nat. Pk. (FK8 3UA) ..2D 134
Lochmaben Castle (DG11 1JE) 1B 112
Loch Ness Exhibition Centre (IV63 6TU) 5H 157
"Locomotion" Nat. Railway Mus. Shildon (DL4 1PQ) ..2F 105
Lodge Pk. (GL54 3PP) 4G 49
Lodge RSPB Nature Reserve, The (SG19 2DL) ..1B 52
Logan Botanic Gdn. (DG9 9ND) 5F 109
Logan Fish Pond & Marine Life Centre (DG9 9NF) ..5F 109
London Dungeon (SE1 2SZ) 203
London Eye (SE1 7PB) 203
London 2012 Olympic Pk. 2E 39
London Zoo (NW1 4RY) 202
Long Cross Victorian Gdns. (PL29 3TF) 1D 6
Longleat (House, Safari & Adventure Pk.) (BA12 7NW) ..2D 22
Long Mynd (SY7 8BH) 1G 59
Longthorpe Tower (PE3 6SU) 1A 64
Longtown Castle (HR2 0LE) 3G 47
Lord Leycester Hospital & The Master's Gdn., Warwick (CV34 4BH) 4G 61
Loseley Pk. (GU3 1HS) 1A 26
Lost Gdns. of Heligan (PL26 6EN) 4D 6
Lotherton Hall (LS25 3EB) 1E 93
Loughwood Meeting House (EX13 7DU) 3F 13
[Lowry, The, Salford (M50 3AZ)] 1C 84
Ludgershall Castle (SP11 9QS) 1A 24
Ludlow Castle (SY8 1AY) 3H 59
Lullingstone Castle & World Gdn. (DA4 0JA) ..4G 39
Lullingstone Roman Villa (DA4 0JA) 4G 39
Lulworth Castle (BH20 5QS) 4D 14
Lundy Island (EX39 2LY) 2B 18
Lyddington Bede House (LE15 9LZ) 1F 63
Lydford Castle & Saxon Town (EX20 4BH) ..4F 11
Lydford Gorge (EX20 4BH) 4F 11
Lydiard House & Pk. (SN5 3PA) 3G 35
Lydney Pk. Gdns. (GL15 6BU) 5B 48
Lyme Pk. (SK12 2NX) 2D 84
Lytes Cary Manor (TA11 7HU) 4A 22
Lyveden New Bield (PE8 5AT) 2G 63

M

Macclesfield Silk Museums (SK11 6PD) 3D 84
Macduff Marine Aquarium (AB44 1SL) 2E 160
MacLellan's Castle (DG6 4JD) 4D 111
Madame Tussaud's (NW1 5LR) ....London 202
Maeshowe Chambered Cairn (KW16 3HQ) ..6C 172
MAGNA Science Adventure Centre (S60 1DX) ..1B 86
Maiden Castle (DT2 9PP) 4B 14
Major Oak (NG21 9HN) 4D 86
Malham Cove (BD23 4DJ) 3A 98
Malham Tarn (BD24 9PU) 3A 98
Malleny Gdn. (EH14 7AF) 3E 129
Malton Mus. (YO17 7LP) 2B 100
Malvern Hills (HR8 1EN) 1C 48
Manchester Art Gallery (M2 3JL) 201
M & D's (Scotland's Theme Pk.), Motherwell (ML1 3RT) 4A 128
Manderston (TD11 3PP) 4E 130
Mannington Gdns. (NR11 7BB) 2D 78
Manorbier Castle (SA70 7SY) 5E 43
Manx Electric Railway (IM2 4NR) 3D 108
Manx Mus. (IM1 3LY) 4C 108

Mapledurham House (RG4 7TR) 4E 37
Marble Hill House (TW1 2NL) 3C 38
Mar Lodge Estate (AB35 5YJ) 5E 151
Martin Mere Wetland Centre (L40 0TA) 3C 90
Marwell Wildlife (SO21 1JH) 4D 24
Marwood Hill Gdns. (EX31 4EB) 3F 19
Mary Arden's Farm (CV37 9UN) 5F 61
Mary, Queen of Scots' House (TD8 6EN) 2A 120
Mary Rose Ship & Mus. (PO1 3LX) ....
.................Portsmouth 209
Max Gate (DT1 2AB) 3C 14
Megginch Castle (PH2 7SW) 1E 137
Melbourne Hall (DE73 8EN) 3A 74
Melford Hall (CO10 9AA) 1A 120
Mellerstain House (TD3 6LG) 1H 119
Menai Suspension Bridge (LL59 5HN) 3E 81
Mendip Hills (BS40 7XS) 1H 21
Merriments Gdns. (TN19 7RA) 3B 28
Merseyside Maritime Mus. (L3 4AQ) ..Liverpool 200
Mertoun Gdns. (TD6 0EA) 1A 120
Michelham Priory (BN27 3QS) 5G 27
Middleham Castle (DL8 4QR) 1D 98
Midland Railway Centre (DE5 3QZ) 5B 86
Mid-Norfolk Railway (NR19 1DF) 5C 78
Millennium Coastal Pk. (SA15 2LG) 3D 31
Millennium Stadium (CF10 1NS) ....Cardiff 191
Milton Manor House (OX14 4EN) 2C 36
Milton's Cottage (HP8 4JH) 1A 38
Minack Theatre (TR19 6JU) 4A 4
Minsmere (IP17 3BY) 4G 67
Minterne Gdns. (DT2 7AU) 2B 14
Mirehouse (CA12 4QE) 2D 102
Misarden Pk. Gdns. (GL6 7JA) 5E 49
Mistley Towers (CO11 1ET) 2E 54
Mr Straw's House (S81 0JG) 2C 86
Mompesson House (SP1 2EL) ....Salisbury 210
Monk Bretton Priory (S71 5QE) 4D 93
Monkey Forest at Trentham (ST4 8AY) 2C 72
Monkey Sanctuary (PL13 1NZ) 2H 7
Monkey World (BH20 6HH) 4D 14
Monk's House (BN7 3HF) 5F 27
Montacute House (TA15 6XP) 1H 13
Monteviot House (TD8 6UD) 2A 120
Montgomery Castle (SY15 6HN) 1E 58
Moreton Corbet Castle, Shawbury (SY4 4DW)
...................................3H 71
Morwellham Quay (PL19 8JL) 2A 8
Moseley Old Hall, Wolverhampton (WV10 7HY)
...................................5D 72
Mother Shipton's Cave & The Petrifying Well (HG5 8DD) 4F 99
Mottisfont (SO51 0LP) 4B 24
Mount Edgcumbe House (PL10 1HZ) 3A 8
Mount Ephraim Gdns. (ME13 9TX) 4E 41
Mountfitchet Castle (CM24 8SP) 3F 53
Mount Grace Priory (DL6 3JG) 1B 100
Mount Stuart (PA20 9LR) 4C 126
Muchelney Abbey (TA10 0DQ) 4H 21
Muchelney Priest's House (TA10 0DQ) 4H 21
Mull of Kintyre (PA28 6RU) 5C 124
Muncaster Castle & Gdns. (CA18 1RQ) 5C 102
Mus. of Army Flying (SO20 8DY) 3B 24
Mus. of East Anglian Life (IP14 1DL) 5C 66
Mus. of Lakeland Life & Industry, Kendal (LA9 5AL)
...................................5G 103
Mus. of Lincolnshire Life (LN1 3LY) ....Lincoln 198
Mus. of London (EC2Y 5HN) 203
Mus. of Science & Industry (M3 4FP)
.................................Manchester 201
Mus. of Scottish Lighthouses (AB43 9DU) ..2G 161
Mus. of the Gorge (TF8 7NH) 5A 72
Mus. of the Isles (IV45 8RS) 3E 147
Mus. of the Jewellery Quarter (B18 6HA)
.................................Birmingham 188

N

Nat. Botanic Gdn. of Wales (SA32 8HG) 4F 45
Nat. Coal Mining Mus. for England (WF4 4RH)
...................................3C 92
Nat. Coracle Centre (SA38 9JL) 1C 44
Nat. Exhibition Centre (NEC) (B40 1NT) ....
.................................Manchester 201
Nat. Football Mus. (M4 3BG) ....Manchester 201
Nat. Forest, The (DE12 6HZ) 4H 73
Nat. Gallery (WC2N 5DN) ....London 203
Nat. Gallery of Scotland (EH2 2EL) ..Edinburgh 194
Nat. Glass Centre (SR6 0GL) 4H 115
Nat. Horseracing Mus. (CB8 8JL) 4F 65
Nat. Marine Aquarium (PL4 0LF) ....Plymouth 208
Nat. Maritime Mus., Greenwich (SE10 9NF) ..3E 39
Nat. Maritime Mus. Cornwall, Falmouth (TR11 3QY)
...................................5C 6
Nat. Media Mus. (BD1 1NQ) ....Bradford 190
Nat. Memorial Arboretum (DE13 7AR) 4H 73
Nat. Motorcycle Mus. (B92 0EJ) 2G 61
Nat. Motor Mus. (Beaulieu) (SO42 7ZN) 2B 16
Nat. Mus. Cardiff (CF10 3NP) 191
Nat. Mus. of Costume (DG2 8HQ) 3A 112
Nat. Mus. of Flight (EH39 5LF) 2B 130
Nat. Mus. of Rural Life Scotland (G76 9HR) ..4H 127
Nat. Mus. of Scotland (EH1 1JF) ..Edinburgh 194
Nat. Portrait Gallery (WC2H 0HE) ....London 203
Nat. Railway Mus. (YO26 4XJ) ....York 214
Nat. Roman Legion Mus., Caerleon, Caerleon (NP18 1AE) 2G 33
Nat. Sea Life Centre (B1 2HL) ....Birmingham 188
Nat. Seal Sanctuary (TR12 6UG) 4E 5
Nat. Showcaves Centre for Wales (SA9 1GJ)
...................................4B 46
Nat. Slate Mus. (LL55 4TY) 4E 81
Nat. Space Centre (LE4 5NS) 5C 74
Nat. Waterfront Mus. (SA1 3RD) ....Swansea 212
Nat. Waterways Mus. (CH65 4FW) 3G 83
Nat. Wool Mus. (SA44 5UP) 2D 44
Natural History Mus. (SW7 5BD) ....London 202
Natural History Mus. at Tring (HP23 6AP) ..4H 51
Neath Abbey (SA10 7DW) 3G 31
Nene Valley Railway (PE8 6LR) 1A 64
Ness Botanic Gdns. (CH64 4AY) 3F 83
Nessieland Castle Monster Centre (IV63 6TU)
...................................5H 157
Nether Winchendon House (HP18 0DY) 4F 51
Netley Abbey (SO31 5HB) 2C 16
New Abbey Corn Mill (DG2 8DX) 3A 112
Newark Air Mus. (NG24 2NY) 5E 87

Newark Castle (Newark-on-Trent) (NG24 1BN)
...................................5E 87
Newark Castle (Port Glasgow) (PA14 5NG) ..2E 127
Newark Pk. (GL12 7PZ) 2C 34
New Art Gallery Walsall (WS2 8LG) 1E 61
Newburgh Priory (YO61 4AS) 2H 99
Newbury Racecourse (RG14 7NZ) 5C 36
Newby Hall & Gdns. (HG4 5AE) 3F 99
Newcastle Castle (Bridgend) (CF31 4JW) 3B 32
Newcastle Upon Tyne Castle Keep (NE1 1RQ) ..205
New Forest Nat. Pk. (SO43 7BD) 2H 15
New Lanark World Heritage Site Visitor Centre (ML11 9DB) 5B 128
Newmarket Racecourse (CB8 0TG) 4F 65
Newquay Zoo (TR7 2LZ) 2C 6
Newstead Abbey (NG15 8NA) 5C 86
Nine Ladies Stone Circle (DE4 2LF) 4G 85
Norfolk Lavender (PE31 7JE) 2F 77
Norham Castle (TD15 2LL) 5F 131
Normanby Hall Mus. (DN15 9HU) 3B 94
North Downs (GU10 5QE) 5C 38
North Norfolk Railway (NR26 8RA) 1D 78
Northumberland Nat. Pk. (NE46 1BS) 1A 114
North York Moors Nat. Pk. (YO18 8RN) 5E 107
North Yorkshire Moors Railway (YO18 7AJ) ..1C 100
Norton Conyers (HG4 5EQ) 2F 99
Norton Priory Mus. & Gdns. (WA7 1SX) 2H 83
Norwich Castle Mus. & Art Gallery (NR1 3JU) ..205
Norwich Cathedral (NR1 4DH) 205
Nostell Priory (WF4 1QE) 3E 93
Nunney Castle (BA11 4LN) 2C 22
Nunnington Hall (YO62 5UY) 2A 100
Nymans (RH17 6EB) 3D 26

O

Oakham Castle (LE15 6DR) 5F 75
Oakwell Hall, Birstall (WF17 9LG) 2C 92
Oakwood Theme Pk. (SA67 8DE) 3E 43
Observatory Science Centre (BN27 1RN) 4A 28
Oceanarium (BH2 5AA) ....Bournemouth 190
Offa's Dyke (NP16 7NQ) 5A 48
Okehampton Castle (EX20 1JA) 3F 11
Old Beaupre Castle (CF71 7LT) 4D 32
Old Gorhambury House (AL3 6AH) 5B 52
Old Oswestry Hill Fort (SY10 7AA) 2E 71
Old Sarum (SP1 3SD) 3G 23
Old Wardour Castle (SP3 6RR) 4E 23
Old Winchester Hill Hill Fort (GU32 1HN) 4E 25
Olympic Pk. (London 2012) 2E 39
Orford Castle (IP12 2NF) 1H 55
Orford Ness (IP12 2NU) 1H 55
Ormesby Hall (TS7 9AS) 3C 106
Osborne House (PO32 6JX) 3D 16
Osterley Pk. & House (TW7 4RB) 3C 38
Oulton Pk. Motor Circuit (CW6 9BW) 4H 83
Our Dynamic Earth (EH8 8AS) ....Edinburgh 194
Overbeck's Mus. & Gdn. (TQ8 8LW) 5D 8
Owletts (DA12 3AP) 4A 40
Oxburgh Hall (PE33 9PS) 5G 77
Oxford Christ Church Cathedral (OX1 4JF) 207
Oxwich Castle (SA3 1LU) 4D 31
Oystermouth Castle (SA3 5TA) 4F 31

P

Packwood House (B94 6AT) 3F 61
Paignton Zoo (TQ4 7EU) 3E 9
Painshill Pk. (KT11 1JE) 5B 38
Painswick Rococo Gdn. (GL6 6TH) 4D 48
Palace of Holyroodhouse (EH8 8DX) ..Edinburgh 194
Papplewick Pumping Station (NG15 9AJ) ..5C 86
Paradise Pk. (Hayle) (TR27 4HB) 3C 4
Paradise Wildlife Pk. (EN10 7QZ) 5D 52
Parcevall Hall Gdns. (BD23 6DE) 2C 98
Parham (RH20 4HS) 4B 26
Pashley Manor Gdns. (TN5 7HE) 2B 28
Paul Corin's Magnificent Music Machines (PL14 4SH)
...................................2G 7
Paultons Pk. (SO51 6AL) 1B 16
Paxton House (TD15 1SZ) 4F 131
Paycocke's (CO6 1NS) 3B 54
Peak Cavern (S33 8WS) 2F 85
Peak District Nat. Pk. (DE45 1AE) 3F 85
Peak Rail (DE4 3NA) 4G 85
Peckover House & Gdn. (PE13 1JR) 5D 76
Peel Castle (IM5 1AB) 3B 108
Pembroke Castle (SA71 4LA) 4D 43
Pembrokeshire Coast Nat. Pk. (SA41 3XD) ..3C 42
Pencarrow (PL30 3AG) 5A 10
Pendennis Castle (TR11 4LP) 5C 6
Pendinas Roman Mus. (SE10 9NF) 2H 33
Penhow Castle (NP26 3AD) 2H 33
Penrhyn Castle (LL57 4HN) 3F 81
Penrith Castle (CA11 7JB) 2G 103
Penshurst Place & Gdns. (TN11 8DG) 1G 27
Peover Hall (WA16 9HW) 3B 84
Perth Mus. & Art Gallery (PH1 5LB) 207
Peterborough Cathedral (PE1 1XZ) 208
Peveril Castle (S33 8WQ) 2F 85
Philipps House (SP3 5HH) 3F 23
Pickering Castle (YO18 7AX) 1C 100
Picton Castle (SA62 4AS) 3E 43
Piel Castle (LA13 0QN) 3A 96
Pistyll Rhaeadr (SY10 0BZ) 3C 70
Pitmedden Gdn. (AB41 7PD) 1F 153
Pitt Rivers Mus. (OX1 3PP) ....Oxford 207
Plantasia (SA1 2AL) ....Swansea 212
Plas Brondanw Gdn. (LL48 6SW) 1F 69
Plas Newydd (Llanfairpwllgwyngyll) (LL61 6DQ)
...................................4E 81
Plas Newydd (LL20 8AW) 1E 70
Plas yn Rhiw (LL53 8AB) 3B 68
Pleasurewood Hills (NR32 5DZ) 1H 67
Poldark Mine (TR13 0ES) 5A 6
Polesden Lacey (RH5 6BD) 5C 38
Pollok House, Glasgow (G43 1AT) 3G 127
Pontcysyllte Aqueduct (LL20 7YS) 1E 71
Portchester Castle (PO16 9QW) 2E 17
Portland Castle (DT5 1AZ) 5B 14
Port Lympne Wild Animal Pk. (CT21 4PD) ..2F 29
Portsmouth Historic Dockyard (PO1 3LJ) 209
Potteries Mus. and Art Gallery (ST1 3DW) ..Stoke 211
Powderham Castle (EX6 8JQ) 4C 12
Powis Castle & Gdn. (SY21 8RF) 5E 70
Prebendal Manor House (PE8 6QG) 1H 63

Prestongrange Mus. (EH32 9RX) 2G 129
Preston Manor (BN1 6SD) 5E 27
Preston Mill & Phantassie Doocot (EH40 3DS)
...................................2B 130
Preston Tower (Northumberland) (NE67 5DH)
...................................2F 121
Prideaux Place (PL28 8RP) 1D 6
Prior Pk. Landscape Gdn. (BA2 5AH) 5C 34
Provan Hall (G34 9NJ) 3H 127
Prudoe Castle (NE42 6NA) 3D 115

Q

Quantock Hills (TA4 4AP) 3E 21
Quarry Bank Mill (DL8 3SG) 2C 84
Quebec House (TN16 1TD) 5F 39
Queen Elizabeth Country Pk. (PO8 0QE) ..1F 17
Queen Elizabeth Forest Pk. (FK8 3UZ) 4D 134
Quex House & Gdns. (CT7 0BH) 4H 41

R

Raby Castle (DL2 3AH) 2E 105
RAF Mus. Cosford (TF11 8UP) 5B 72
RAF Mus. London (NW9 5LL) 1D 38
Raglan Castle (NP15 2BT) 5H 47
Ragley (B49 5NJ) 5E 61
Ramsey Island 2B 42
Ravenglass & Eskdale Railway (CA18 1SW) ..4C 102
Raveningham Gdns. (NR14 6NS) 1F 67
Ravenscraig Castle (KY1 2AZ) 4E 137
Reculver Towers (CT6 6SX) 4G 41
Renishaw Hall & Gdns. (S21 3WB) 3B 86
Restoration House (ME1 1RF) ....Medway 204
Restormel Castle (PL22 0HN) 2F 7
Revolution House (S41 9LA) 3A 86
Rheged Centre (CA11 0DQ) 2G 103
Rheidol Power Station & Vis. Cen. (SY23 3NF)
...................................4D 57
Rhossili Bay (SA3 1PR) 4D 30
RHS Gdn. Harlow Carr (HG3 1QB) 4E 99
RHS Gdn. Hyde Hall (CM3 8ET) 1B 40
RHS Gdn. Rosemoor (EX38 8PH) 1F 11
RHS Gdn. Wisley (GU23 6QB) 5B 38
Rhuddlan Castle (LL18 5AD) 3C 82
Ribchester Roman Mus. (PR3 3XS) 1E 91
Richmond Castle (DL10 4QW) 4E 105
Rievaulx Abbey (YO62 5LB) 1H 99
Rievaulx Terrace (YO62 5LJ) 1H 99
Ripley Castle (HG3 3AY) 3E 99
Ripon Cathedral (HG4 1QT) 2F 99
River & Rowing Mus. (RG9 1BF) 3F 37
Riverside Mus., Glasgow (G3 8RS) 3G 127
Robert Burns Birthplace Mus. (KA7 4PQ) ..3C 116
Robert Burns House (DG1 2PS) ..Dumfries 193
Roche Abbey (S66 8NW) 2C 86
Rochester Castle (ME1 1SW) ....Medway 204
Rochester Cathedral (ME1 1SX) ....Medway 204
Rockbourne Roman Villa (SP6 3PG) 1G 15
Rockingham Castle (LE16 8TH) 1F 63
Rockingham Motor Speedway (NN17 5AF) ..1G 63
Rode Hall (ST7 3QP) 5C 84
Rodmarton Manor (GL7 6PF) 2E 35
Rokeby Pk. (DL12 9RZ) 3D 105
Rollright Stones (OX7 5QB) 2A 50
Roman Painted House (CT17 9AJ) ....Dover 193
Romney, Hythe & Dymchurch Railway (TN28 8PL)
...................................3E 29
Roseberry Topping (TS9 6QX) 3C 106
Rothesay Castle (PA20 0DA) 3B 126
Rothiemurchus Centre (PH22 1QH) 2D 150
Rousham House & Gdns. (OX25 4QX) 3C 50
Royal Academy of Arts (W1J 0BD) ....London 202
Royal Albert Bridge (PL12 4GT) 3A 8
Royal Armouries Mus. (LS10 1LT) ....Leeds 199
Royal Botanic Gdn. Edinburgh (EH3 5LR) ..2F 129
Royal Botanic Gdns., Kew (TW9 3AB) 3C 38
Royal Cornwall Mus. (TR1 2SJ) 4C 6
Royal Crown Derby Mus. (DE23 8JZ) 193
Royal Navy Submarine Mus. (PO12 2AS) ..3E 16
Royal Pavilion (BN1 1EE) ....Brighton & Hove 189
Royal Pump Room Mus. (HG1 2RY) ....
.................................Harrogate 197
Royal Yacht Britannia (EH6 6JJ) 2F 129
Ruddington Framework Knitters' Mus. (NG11 6HE)
...................................2C 74
Rufford Abbey (NG22 9DF) 4D 86
Rufford Old Hall (L40 1SG) 3C 90
Rufus Stone (SO43 7HN) 1A 16
Runnymede (RG18 9NA) 3A 38
Rushton Triangular Lodge (NN14 1RP) 2F 63
Russell-Cotes Art Gallery & Mus. (BH1 3AA)
.................................Bournemouth 190
Rutland County Mus. (LE15 6HW) 5F 75
Rutland Railway Mus. (LE15 7BX) 4F 75
Rutland Water (LE15 8BL) 5G 75
Rydal Mount & Gdns. (LA22 9LU) 4E 103
Ryedale Folk Mus. (YO62 6UA) 5E 107
Ryton Gdns. (CV8 3LG) 3B 62

S

Saatchi Gallery (SW3 4RY) ....London 202
Sainsbury Centre for Visual Arts (NR4 7TJ) ..5D 78
St Abb's Head (TD14 5QF) 3F 131
St Albans Cathedral (AL1 1BY) 5B 52
St Andrews Aquarium (KY16 9AS) 209
St Andrews Cathedral (KY16 9QL) 209
St Augustine's Abbey (CT1 1NP) ....Canterbury 190
St David's Cathedral & Bishop's Palace (SA62 6RD)
...................................3B 42
St Dogmaels Abbey (SA43 3JH) 1B 44
St Fagans: Nat. History Mus. (CF5 6XB) 4E 32
St Giles' Cathedral (EH1 1RE) ....Edinburgh 194
St John's Jerusalem (DA4 9HQ) 3G 39
St Mary's Cathedral, Glasgow (G4 9JB) 3G 127
St Mary's House & Gdns. (BN44 3WE) 4C 26
St Mawes Castle (TR2 5DE) 5C 6
St Michael's Mount (TR17 0HS) 4C 4
St Paul's Cathedral (EC4M 8AE) ....London 203
Salford Mus. and Art Gallery (M5 4WU) ....
.................................Manchester 201
Salisbury Cathedral (SP1 2EQ) 210
Saltaire World Heritage Village (BD18 4PL) ..1B 92
Saltram (PL7 1UH) 3B 8

Samlesbury Hall (PR5 0UP) 1E 90
Sandford Orcas Manor House (DT9 4SB) 4B 22
Sandham Memorial Chapel (RG20 9JT) 5C 36
Sandown Pk. Racecourse (KT10 9AJ) 4C 38
Sandringham (PE35 6EP) 3F 77
Sarehole Mill (B13 0BD) 2E 61
Savill Gdn., The (SL4 2HT) 3A 38
Sawley Abbey (BB7 4LE) 5G 97
Saxtead Green Post Mill (IP13 9QQ) 4E 67
Scafell Pike (CA20 1EX) 4D 102
Scampston Hall (YO17 8NG) 2C 100
Scarborough Castle (YO11 1HY) 1E 101
Science Mus. (SW7 2DD) . . . . .London 202
Scone Palace (PH2 6BD) 1D 136
Scotch Whisky Experience (EH1 2NE)
. . . . .Edinburgh 194
Scotney Castle (TN3 8JN) 2A 28
Scotstarvit Tower (KY15 5PA) 2F 137
Scottish Deer Centre (KY15 4NQ) 2F 137
[Scottish Exhibition & Conference Centre (SECC),
Glasgow (G3 8YW)] 3G 127
Scottish Fisheries Mus. (KY10 3AB) 3H 137
Scottish Industrial Railway Centre (KA6 7JF)
. . . . .4D 116
Scottish Maritime Mus. (KA12 8QE) 1C 116
Scottish Mining Mus. (EH22 4QN) 3G 129
Scottish Nat. Gallery of Modern Art, Edinburgh
(EH4 3DR) 2F 129
Scottish Nat. Portrait Gallery (EH2 1JD)
. . . . .Edinburgh 194
Scottish Parliament (EH99 1SP) . . . . .Edinburgh 194
Scottish Sea Life Sanctuary (PA37 1SE) 4D 140
Sea Life Blackpool (FY1 5AA) 188
Sea Life Brighton (BN2 1TB) . . . . . .Brighton & Hove 189
Sea Life Great Yarmouth (NR30 3AH) 196
Sea Life Loch Lomond (G83 8QL) 1E 127
Sea Life London Aquarium (SE1 7PB) 203
Sea Life Scarborough (YO12 6RP) 5H 107
Sea Life Weymouth (DT4 7SX) 4B 14
SeaQuarium, Rhyl (LL18 3AF) 2C 82
SeaQuarium, Weston-super-Mare (BS23 1BE)
. . . . .5G 33
Seaton Delaval Hall (NE26 4QR) 2G 115
Seaton Tramway (EX12 2NQ) 3F 13
Seaview Wildlife Encounter (PO34 5AP) 3E 16
Selby Abbey (YO8 4PF) 1G 93
Selly Manor (B30 2AD) .2E 61
Severn Bridge (BS35 4BL) 2A 34
Severn Valley Railway (DY12 1BG) 2B 60
Sewerby Hall & Gdns. (YO15 1EA) 3G 101
Sezincote (GL56 9AW) 2G 49
Shaftesbury Abbey Mus. & Gdns. (SP7 8JR) . . .4D 22
Shakespeare's Birthplace (CV37 6QW)
. . . . .Stratford 212
Shandy Hall (YO61 4AD) 2H 99
Shap Abbey (CA10 3NB) 3G 103
Shaw's Corner (AL6 9BX) 4B 52
Sheffield Pk. & Gdn. (TN22 3QX) 3F 27
Sheffield Winter Gdn. (S1 2PP) 210
Shepreth Wildlife Pk. (SG8 6PZ) 1D 53
Sherborne Castle (DT9 3PY) 1B 14
Sherborne Old Castle (DT9 3SA) 1B 14
Sherwood Forest (NG21 9HN) 4D 86
Shibden Hall (HX3 6XG) 2B 92
Shipton Hall (TF13 6JZ) 1H 59
Shoe Mus. (BA16 0EQ) 3H 21
Shrewsbury Castle (SY1 2AT) 210
Shugborough (ST17 0XB) 3D 73
Shute Barton (EX13 7PT) 3F 13
Shuttleworth Collection (SG18 9EP) 1B 52
Silbury Hill (SN8 1QH) .5G 35
Silverstone Motor Circuit (NN12 8TN) 1E 51
Sir Walter Scott's Courtroom (TD7 4BT) 2G 119
Sissinghurst Castle Gdn. (TN17 2AB) 2C 28
Sizergh Castle & Gdn. (LA8 8AE) 1D 97
Skara Brae Prehistoric Village (KW16 3LR) 6B 172
Skenfrith Castle (NP7 8UH) 3H 47
Skiddaw (CA12 4QE) .2D 102
Skipness Castle (PA29 6XU) 4H 125
Skipton Castle (BD23 1AW) 4B 98
Skokholm Island (SA62 3BL) 4B 42
Skomer Island (SA62 3BL) 4B 42
Sledmere House (YO25 3XG) 3D 100
Slimbridge Wetland Centre (GL2 7BT) 5C 48
Smailholm Tower (TD5 7PG) 1A 120
Smallhythe Place (TN30 7NG) 3D 28
Snaefell Mountain Railway (IM4 7NL) 3D 108
Snibston (LE67 3LN) 4B 74
Snowdon (LL55 4UL) 5F 81
Snowdonia Nat. Pk. (LL48 6LF) 2G 69
Snowdon Mountain Railway (LL55 4TY) 5F 81
Snowshill Manor & Gdn. (WR12 7JU) 2F 49
Somerleyton (NR32 5QQ) 1G 67
Sorn Castle (KA5 6HR) 2E 117
Souter Lighthouse (SR6 7NH) 3H 115

South Devon Railway (TQ11 0DZ) 2D 8
South Downs Nat. Pk. (GU29 9SB) 4F 27
South Lakes Wild Animal Pk. (LA15 8JR) 2B 96
South Tynedale Railway (CA9 3JB) 5A 114
Southwell Minster (NG25 0HD) 5E 86
Spa Valley Railway (TN2 5QY) 2G 27
Speedwell Cavern (S33 8WA) 2F 85
Speke Hall (L24 1XD) 2G 83
Spetchley Pk. Gdns. (WR5 1RR) 5C 60
Spinners Gdn. (SO41 5QE) 3B 16
Spofforth Castle (HG3 1DA) 4F 99
Sprivers Gdn. (TN12 8DR) 1A 28
Spurn Head (HU12 0UG) 3H 95
Spynie Palace (IV30 5QG) 2G 159
Squerryes (TN16 1SJ) 5F 39
Stafford Castle (ST16 1DJ) 3D 72
Stagshaw Gdn. (LA22 0HE) 4E 103
Stanage Edge (S33 0AD) 2G 85
Standen (RH19 4NE) 2E 27
Stanford Hall (LE17 6DH) 3C 62
Stansted Pk. (PO9 6DX) 4F 27
Stanway House & Fountain (GL54 5PQ) 2F 49
Stapeley Water Gdns. (CW5 7LH) 5A 84
Staunton Harold Church (LE65 1RT) 3A 74
Steam - Mus. of the Great Western Railway (SN2 2EY)
. . . . .3G 35
Stirling Castle (FK8 1EJ) 211
Stoke Pk. Pavilions (NN12 7RZ) 1F 51
Stokesay Castle (SY7 9AH) 2G 59
Stoke-sub-Hamdon Priory (TA14 6QP) 1H 13
Stonacre (ME15 8RS) 5C 40
Stonehenge (SP4 7DE) .2G 23
Stoneleigh Abbey (CV8 2LF) 3H 61
Stonor (RG9 6HF) 3F 37
Storybook Glen (AB12 5FT) 4F 153
Stott Pk. Bobbin Mill (LA12 8AX) 1C 96
Stourhead (BA12 6QD) .3C 22
Stourton House Flower Gdn. (BA12 6QF) 3C 22
Stowe House (MK18 5EH) 2E 51
Stowe Landscape Gdns. (MK18 5EH) 2E 51
Strata Florida Abbey (SY25 6BJ) 4G 57
Stratfield Saye House (RG7 2BZ) 5F 37
Strathaven Castle (ML10 6QS) 5A 128
Strathclyde Country Pk. (ML1 3ED) 4A 128
Strathspey Railway (PH22 1PY) 2D 150
Strawberry Hill, Twickenham (TW1 4ST) 3C 38
Strome Castle (IV54 8YJ) 5A 156
Sudbury Hall (DE6 5HT) 2F 73
Sudeley Castle (GL54 5JD) 3F 49
Sufton Court (HR1 4LU) 2A 48
Sulgrave Manor (OX17 2SD) 1D 50
Summerlee - Mus. of Scottish Industrial Life
(ML5 1QD) 3A 128
Sundown Adventureland (DN22 0HX) 3E 87
Sutton Hoo (IP12 3DJ) .1F 55
Sutton Pk. (YO61 1DP) .3H 99
Sutton Scarsdale Hall (S44 5UT) 4B 86
Sutton Valence Castle (ME17 3DA) 1C 28
Swaledale Mus. (DL11 6QT) 5D 104
Swallow Falls (LL24 0DH) 5G 81
Swansea RC Cathedral (SA1 2BX) 212
Sweetheart Abbey (DG2 8BU) 3A 112
Swindon & Cricklade Railway (SN25 2DA) 2G 35
Swiss Gdn. (SG18 9ER) 1B 52
Syon Pk. (TW8 8JF) 3C 38

T

Tabley House (WA16 0HB) 3B 84
Talley Abbey (SA19 7AX) 2G 45
Talyllyn Railway (LL36 9EY) 5F 69
Tamworth Castle (B79 7NA) 5G 73
Tank Mus. (BH20 6JG) .4D 14
Tantallon Castle (EH39 5PN) 1B 130
Tarn Hows (LA22 0PR) 5E 103
Tar Tunnel (TF8 7HS) 5A 72
Tate Britain (SW1P 4RG) . . . . .London 203
Tate Liverpool (L3 4BB) 200
Tate Modern (SE1 9TG) . . . . .London 203
Tate St Ives (TR26 1TG) .2C 4
Tatton Old Hall (WA16 6QN) 5B 88
Tatton Pk. (WA16 6QN) .2B 84
Tay Forest Pk. (PH17 2QG) 3C 142
Teifi Valley Railway (SA44 5TD) 1D 44
Temple Newsam (LS15 0AE) 1D 92
Tenby Castle (SA70 7BP) 4F 43
Thames Barrier (SE18 5NJ) 3F 39
Thetford Forest Pk. (IP26 5DB) 1A 66
Thetford Priory (IP24 1AZ) 2A 66
Thirlestane Castle (TD2 6RU) 5B 130
Thoresby Gallery (NG22 9EP) 3D 86
Thornham Walled Gdn. (IP23 8HH) 3D 66
Thornton Abbey & Gatehouse (DN39 6TU) 3E 94
Thorpe Pk. (KT16 8PN) 4B 38
Thorp Perrow Arboretum (DL8 2PR) 1E 99

Threave Castle (DG7 2AB) 3E 111
Threave Gdn. (DG7 1RX) 3E 111
Thrigby Hall Wildlife Gdns. (NR29 3DR) 4G 79
Thruxton Motor Circuit (SP11 8PW) 2A 24
Thursford Collection (NR21 0AS) 2B 78
Tilbury Fort (RM18 7NR) 3H 39
Tintagel Castle (PL34 0HE) 4A 10
Tintern Abbey (NP16 6SH) 5A 48
Tintinhull Gdn. (BA22 8QL) 4A 22
Titchfield Abbey (PO15 5RA) 2D 16
Tiverton Castle (EX16 6RP) 1C 12
Tolpuddle Martyrs Mus. (DT2 7EH) 3C 14
Tolquhon Castle (AB41 7LP) 1F 153
Torridon Countryside Centre (IV22 2EW) 3B 156
Totnes Castle (TQ9 5NU) .2E 9
Tower Bridge (SE1 2UP) . . . . .London 203
Tower of London, The (EC3N 4AB) 203
Towneley Hall Art Gallery & Mus. (BB11 3RQ)
. . . . .1G 91
Townend (LA23 1LB) 4F 103
Traquair House (EH44 6PW) 1F 119
Treasurer's House, Martock (TA12 6JL) 1H 13
Treasurer's House, York (YO1 7JL) 214
Trebah Gdn. (TR11 5JZ) .4E 5
Tredegar House (NP10 8YW) 3F 33
Tregrehan Gdn. (PL24 2SJ) 3E 7
Trelissick Gdn. (TR3 6QL) 5C 6
Trengwainton Gdn. (TR20 8RZ) 3B 4
Trentham Gdns. (ST4 8NF) 1C 72
Trerice (TR8 4PG) 3C 6
Tresco Abbey Gdns. (TR24 0QQ) 1A 4
Tretower Castle & Court (NP8 1RF) 3E 47
Trewithen (TR2 4DD) 4D 6
Tropical Birdland (LE9 9GN) 5B 74
Trossachs, The (FK17 8HZ) 3E 135
Tudor Merchant's House (SA70 7BX) 4F 43
Turton Tower (BL7 0HG) 3F 91
Tutbury Castle (DE13 9JF) 3G 73
Twycross Zoo (CV9 3PX) 5H 73
Ty Mawr Wybrnant (LL25 0HJ) 5G 81
Tynemouth Castle (NE30 4BZ) 3G 115
Tyntesfield (BS48 1NT) .4A 34

U

[U-Boat Story, Birkenhead (CH41 6DU)] 2F 83
Uffington White Horse (SN7 7QJ) 3B 36
Ugbrooke (TQ13 0AD) .5B 12
Upnor Castle (ME2 4XG) 3B 40
Upton House (OX15 6HT) 1B 50
Upton Castle Gdns. (SA72 4SE) 4E 43
Urquhart Castle (IV63 6XJ) 1H 149
Usher Gallery (LN2 1NN) . . . . .Lincoln 198
Usk Castle (NP15 1SD) .5G 47

V

Vale of Rheidol Railway (SY23 1PG) 3F 57
Valle Crucis Abbey (LL20 8DT) 1E 70
Valley Gdns. (SL4 2HT) .4A 38
Veddw House Gdn. (NP16 6PH) 2H 33
Verulamium Mus., St Albans (AL3 4SW) 5B 52
Victoria & Albert Mus. (SW7 2RL) . . . . .London 202
Vindolanda Roman Fort & Mus. (NE47 7JN) 3A 114
Vyne, The (RG24 9HL) .1E 25

W

Waddesdon Manor (HP18 0JH) 4F 51
Wakehurst Place (RH17 6TN) 2E 27
Walker Art Gallery (L3 8EL) . . . . .Liverpool 200
Wallington (NE61 4AR) .1D 114
Walmer Castle & Gdns. (CT14 7LJ) 1H 29
Walsingham Abbey (NR22 6BL) 2B 78
Warkworth Castle & Hermitage (NE65 0UJ) 4G 121
Warwick Castle (CV34 4QX) 4G 61
Washington Old Hall (NE38 7LE) 4G 115
Watercress Line (SO24 9JG) 3D 16
Watermouth Castle (EX34 9SL) 2F 19
Waterperry Gdns. (OX33 1JZ) 5E 51
Watersmeet (EX35 6NT) 2H 19
Weald & Downland Open Air Mus. (PO18 0EU)
. . . . .1G 17
Weaver Hall Mus. & Workhouse (CW9 8AB) 3A 84
Weaver's Cottage (PA10 2JG) 3E 127
Wedgwood Visitor Centre (ST12 9ER) 2C 72
Weir, The (HR4 7QF) 1H 47
Wells & Walsingham Light Railway (NR23 1QB)
. . . . .1B 78
Wells Cathedral (BA5 2UE) 2A 22
Welney Wetland Centre (PE14 9TN) 1E 65

Welsh Highland Heritage Railway (LL49 9DY) . . .2E 69
Welsh Highland Railway (LL54 5UP)
. . . . .Caernarfon 190
Welsh Mountain Zoo, Colwyn Bay (LL28 5UY)
. . . . .3H 81
Welshpool & Llanfair Light Railway (SY21 0SF)
. . . . .5D 70
Wembley Stadium (HA9 0WS) 2C 38
Wenlock Edge (SY7 9JH) 2G 59
Wenlock Priory (TF13 6HS) 5A 72
Wentworth Castle Gdns. (S75 3ET) 4D 92
Weobley Castle (SA3 1HB) 3D 31
Wesley Cottage (PL15 7TG) 4C 10
Westbury Court Gdn. (GL14 1PD) 4C 48
West Green House Gdn. (RG27 8JB) 1F 25
West Highland Mus. (PH33 6AJ) 1F 141
West Midland Safari & Leisure Pk. (DY12 1LF)
. . . . .3C 60
Westminster Abbey (SW1P 3PA) . . . . .London 203
Westminster RC Cathedral (SW1P 1QH)
. . . . .London 202
Westonbirt Nat. Arboretum (GL8 8QS) 3D 34
Weston Pk. (TF11 8LE) .4C 72
West Somerset Railway (TA24 5BG) 4E 21
Westwood Manor (BA15 2AF) 1D 22
West Wycombe Pk. (HP14 3AJ) 2G 37
Wetlands Animal Pk. (DN22 8SB) 2D 86
Whalley Abbey (BB7 9TN) 1F 91
Whipsnade Tree Cathedral (LU6 2LL) 4A 52
Whipsnade Zoo (LU6 2LF) 4A 52
Whitby Abbey (YO22 4JT) 3G 100
White Castle (NP7 8UD) 4G 47
Whitehorse Hill (SN7 7QJ) 3B 36
White Scar Cave (LA6 3AW) 2G 97
Whitmore Hall (ST5 5HW) 1C 72
Whitworth Art Gallery, Hulme (M15 6ER) 1C 84
Wicken Fen Nat. Nature Reserve (CB7 5YG)
. . . . .3E 65
Wicksteed Pk. (NN15 6NJ) 3F 63
Wightwick Manor & Gdns. (WV6 8EE) 1C 60
Wigmore Castle (HR6 9UJ) 4G 59
Wilberforce House Mus. (HU1 1NE) . . . . .Hull 199
Wilderhope Manor (TF13 6EG) 1H 59
Wilton House (SP2 0BJ) 3F 23
Wimbledon Lawn Tennis Mus. (SW19 5HP)
. . . . .3D 38
Wimpole Hall & Gdns. (SG8 0BW) 5C 64
Winchester Cathedral (SO23 9LS) 213
Windmill Hill (SN4 9NW) 4F 35
Windsor Castle (SL4 1NJ) .213
Wingfield Manor (DE55 7NH) 5A 86
Winkworth Arboretum (GU8 4AD) 1A 26
Witley Court & Gdns. (WR6 6JT) 4B 60
Woburn Abbey (MK17 9WA) 2H 51
Woburn Safari Pk. (MK17 9QN) 2H 51
Wolds, The (Lincolnshire) (LN8 6BL) 1B 88
Wolds, The (Yorkshire) (YO25 9EN) 4D 100
Wolfeton House (DT2 9QN) 3B 14
Wollaton Hall (NG8 2AE) 2C 74
Wolsey Cen. (ST17 0WT) 3E 73
Wolterton Pk. (NR11 7BB) 2D 78
Wolvesey Castle (SO23 9NB) . . . . .Winchester 213
Woodchester Mansion (GL10 3TS) 5D 48
Woodhenge (SP4 7AR) .2G 23
Wookey Hole (BA5 1BB) 2A 22
Woolsthorpe Manor (NG33 5PD) 3G 75
Worcester Cathedral (WR1 2LH) 214
Worcester Porcelain Mus. (WR1 2NE) 214
Worcestershire County Mus. (DY11 7XZ) 3C 60
Wordsworth House (CA13 9RX) 1C 102
Wordsworth Mus. (Dove Cottage) (LA22 9SH)
. . . . .4E 103
Wotton House Landscape Gdns. (HP18 0SB)
. . . . .4E 51
Wrest Pk. (MK45 4HR) .2A 52
Wrexham RC Cathedral (LL11 1RB) 214
Wroxeter Roman City (SY5 6PH) 5H 71
Wroxton Abbey Gdns. (OX15 6PX) 1C 50
Wylfa Visitor Centre (LL67 0DH) 1C 80
Wyre Forest (DY14 9UH) 3B 60
Wythenshawe Hall (M23 0AB) 2C 84

Y

Yarmouth Castle (PO41 0PB) 4B 16
York Art Gallery (YO1 7EW) 214
York Castle Mus. (YO1 9RY) 214
York Minster (YO1 7JN) 214
York Racecourse (YO23 1EX) 5H 99
Yorkshire Dales Nat. Pk. (BD23 5LB) 1A 98
Yorkshire Mus. (YO30 7DR) . . . . .York 214
Yorkshire Mus. of Farming (YO19 5GH) 4A 100

Limited Interchange Motorway Junctions are shown on the maps by RED junction indicators

M1

Junction 2
Northbound: No exit, access from A1 only
Southbound: No access, exit to A1 only

Junction 4
Northbound: No exit, access from A41 only
Southbound: No access, exit to A41 only

Junction 6a
Northbound: No exit, access from M25 only
Southbound: No access, exit to M25 only

Junction 17
Northbound: No access, exit to M45 only
Southbound: No exit, access from M45 only

Junction 19
Northbound: Exit to M6 only,
    access from A14 only
Southbound: Access from M6 only,
    exit to A14 only

Junction 21a
Northbound: No access, exit to A46 only
Southbound: No exit, access from A46 only

Junction 24a
Northbound: Access from A50 only
Southbound: Exit to A50 only

Junction 35a
Northbound: No access, exit to A616 only
Southbound: No exit, access from A616 only

Junction 43
Northbound: Exit to M621 only
Southbound: Access from M621 only

Junction 48
Eastbound: Exit to A1(M)
   Northbound only
Westbound: Access from A1(M) Southbound
   only

M2

Junction 1
Eastbound: Access from A2 Eastbound only
Westbound: Exit to A2 Westbound only

M3

Junction 8
Westbound: No access, exit to A303 only
Eastbound: No exit, access from A303 only

Junction 10
Northbound: No access from A31
Southbound: No exit to A31

Junction 13
Southbound: No access from A335 to M3
   leading to M27 Eastbound

M4

Junction 1
Westbound: Access from A4 Westbound only
Eastbound: Exit to A4 Eastbound only

Junction 21
Westbound: No access from M48
Eastbound: No exit to M48

Junction 23
Westbound: No exit to M48
Eastbound: No access from M48

Junction 25
Westbound: No access
Eastbound: No exit

Junction 25a
Westbound: No access
Eastbound: No exit

Junction 29
Westbound: No access, exit to A48(M) only
Eastbound: No exit, access from A48(M) only

Junction 38
Westbound: No access, exit to A48 only

Junction 39
Westbound: No exit, access from A48 only
Eastbound: No access or exit

Junction 42
Westbound: No exit to A48
Eastbound: No access from A48

M5

Junction 10
Southbound: No access, exit to A4019 only
Northbound: No exit, access from A4019 only

Junction 11a
Southbound: No exit to A417 Westbound

Junction 18a
Southbound: No exit to M49
Northbound: No access from M49

M6

Junction 3a
Eastbound: No exit to M6 TOLL
Westbound: No access from M6 TOLL

Junction 4
Northbound: No exit to M42 Northbound
    No access from M42 Southbound
Southbound: No exit to M42
    No access from M42 Southbound

Junction 4a
Northbound: No exit, access from M42
   Southbound only
Southbound: No access, exit to M42 only

Junction 5
Northbound: No access, exit to A452 only
Southbound: No exit, access from A452 only

Junction 10a
Northbound: No access, exit to M54 only
Southbound: No exit, access from M54 only

Junction 11a
Northbound: No exit to M6 TOLL
Southbound: No access from M6 TOLL

Junction 20
Northbound: No exit to M56 Eastbound
Southbound: No access from M56 Westbound

Junction 24
Northbound: No exit, access from A58 only
Southbound: No access, exit to A58 only

Junction 25
Northbound: No access, exit to A49 only
Southbound: No exit, access from A49 only

Junction 30
Northbound: No access, exit to M61
   Northbound only
Southbound: No access, exit to M61
   Southbound only

Junction 31a
Northbound: No access, exit to B6242 only
Southbound: No exit, access from B6242 only

Junction 45
Northbound: No access onto A74(M)
Southbound: No exit from A74(M)

M6 TOLL

Junction T1
Northbound: No exit
Southbound: No access

Junction T2
Northbound: No access or exit
Southbound: No access

Junction T5
Northbound: No exit
Southbound: No access

Junction T7
Northbound: No access from A5
Southbound: No exit

Junction T8
Northbound: No exit to A460 Northbound
Southbound: No exit

M8

Junction 8
Westbound: No access from M73 Southbound
Eastbound: No exit to M73 Northbound

Junction 9
Westbound: No exit, access only
Eastbound: No access, exit only

Junction 13
Westbound: No exit to M80 Northbound
Eastbound: No access from M80 Southbound

Junction 14
Westbound: No access, exit only
Eastbound: No exit, access only

Junction 16
Westbound: No access, exit only
Eastbound: No exit, access only

Junction 17
Westbound: No access, exit to A82 only
Eastbound: No exit, access from A82 only

Junction 18
Westbound: No access, exit only

Junction 19
Westbound: No access from A814 Westbound
Eastbound: No exit to A814 Eastbound

Junction 20
Westbound: No access, exit only

Junction 21
Westbound: No access, exit only
Eastbound: No access, exit only

Junction 22
Westbound: No access, exit to M77 only
Eastbound: No exit, access from M77 only

Junction 23
Westbound: No access, exit to B768 only
Eastbound: No exit, access from B768 only

Junction 25
Westbound and Eastbound:
  Exit to A739 Northbound only
  Access from A739 Southbound only

Junction 25a
Eastbound: Access only
Westbound: Exit only

Junction 28
Westbound: no access, exit to airport only
Eastbound: no exit, access from airport only

M9

Junction 1a
Northbound: No access, exit to M9 spur only
Southbound: No exit, access from M9 spur only

Junction 2
Northbound: No exit, access from B8046 only
Southbound: No exit, access to B8046 only

Junction 3
Northbound: No access, exit to A803 only
Southbound: No exit, access from A803 only

Junction 6
Northbound: No exit, access only
Southbound: No access, exit to A905 only

Junction 8
Northbound: No access, exit to M876 only
Southbound: No exit, access from M876 only

Junction with A90
Northbound: Exit onto A90 westbound only
Southbound: Access from A90 eastbound only

M11

Junction 4
Northbound: No exit, access from A406
   Eastbound only
Southbound: No access, exit to A406
   Westbound only

Junction 5
Northbound: No access, exit to A1168 only
Southbound: No exit, access from A1168 only

Junction 8a
Northbound: No access, exit only
Southbound: No exit, access only

Junction 9
Northbound: No access, exit only
Southbound: No exit, access only

Junction 13
Northbound: No access, exit only
Southbound: No exit, access only

Junction 14
Northbound: No access from A428 Eastbound
    No exit to A428 Westbound
Southbound: No exit, access from A428
    Eastbound only

M20

Junction 2
Eastbound: No access, exit to A20 only
   (access via M26 Junction 2a)
Westbound: No exit, access only
   (exit via M26 Junction 2a)

Junction 3
Eastbound: No exit, access from M26
   Eastbound only
Westbound: No access, exit to M26
   Westbound only

Junction 11a
Westbound: No exit to Channel Tunnel
Eastbound: No access from Channel Tunnel

M23

Junction 7
Southbound: No access from A23 Northbound
Northbound: No exit to A23 Southbound

Junction 10a
Northbound: No access, exit only
Southbound: No access, exit only

M25

Junction 5
Clockwise: No exit to M26 Eastbound
Anti-clockwise: No access from M26
   Westbound

Spur to A21

Southbound: No access from M26 Westbound
Northbound: No exit to M26 Eastbound

Junction 19
Clockwise: No access exit only
Anti-clockwise: No exit access only

Junction 21
Clockwise and Anti-clockwise:
  No exit to M1 Southbound
  No access from M1 Northbound

Junction 31
Southbound: No exit access only
   (exit via Junction 30)
Northbound: No access exit only
   (access via Junction 30)

M26

Junction with M25 (M25 Junc. 5)
Westbound: No exit to M25 anti-clockwise
  or spur to A21 Southbound
Eastbound: No access from M25 clockwise
  or spur from A21 Northbound

Junction with M20 (M20 Junc. 3)
Eastbound: No exit to M20 Westbound
Westbound: No access from M20 Eastbound

M27

Junction 4
Eastbound and Westbound: No exit to A33
   Southbound (Southampton)
   No access from A33 Northbound

Junction 10
Eastbound: No exit, access from A32 only
Westbound: No access, exit to A32 only

M40

Junction 3
North-Westbound: No access,
    exit to A40 only
South-Eastbound: No exit,
    access from A40 only

Junction 7
South-Eastbound: No exit, access only
North-Westbound: No access, exit only

Junction 13
South-Eastbound: No access, exit only
North-Westbound: No exit, access only

Junction 14
South-Eastbound: No access, exit only
North-Westbound: No exit, access only

Junction 16
South-Eastbound: No access, exit only
North-Westbound: No exit, access only

M42

Junction 1
Eastbound: No exit
Westbound: No access

Junction 7
Northbound: No access, exit to M6 only
Southbound: No exit, access from M6
   Northbound only

Junction 8
Northbound: No exit, access from M6
   Southbound only
Southbound: Exit to M6 Northbound only
    Access from M6 Southbound only

M45

Junction with M1 (M1 Junc. 17)
Eastbound: No exit to M1 Northbound
Westbound: No access from M1 Southbound

**Junction with A45 east
of Dunchurch**
Eastbound: No access, exit to A45 only
Westbound: No exit, access from A45
   Northbound only

M48

Junction with M4 (M4 Junc. 21)
Westbound: No access from M4 Eastbound
Eastbound: No exit to M4 Westbound

Junction with M4 (M4 Junc. 23)
Westbound: No exit to M4 Eastbound
Eastbound: No access from M4 Westbound

M53

Junction 11
Southbound and Northbound: No access from
M56 Eastbound, no exit to M56 Westbound

M56

Junction 1
Westbound: No access from M60 South-Eastbound
No access from A34 Northbound
Eastbound: No exit to M60 North-Westbound
No exit to A34 Southbound
Junction 2
Westbound: No access, exit to A560 only
Eastbound: No exit, access from A560 only
Junction 3
Westbound: No exit, access only
Eastbound: No access, exit only
Junction 4
Westbound: No access, exit only
Eastbound: No exit, access only
Junction 7
Westbound: No access, exit only
Junction 8
Westbound: No exit, access from A556 only
Eastbound: No access or exit
Junction 9
Westbound: No exit to M6 Southbound
Eastbound: No access from M6 Northbound
Junction 15
Westbound: No access from M53
Eastbound: No exit to M53

M57

Junction 3
Northbound: No exit, access only
Southbound: No access, exit only
Junction 5
Northbound: No exit, access from A580 Westbound only
Southbound: No access, exit to A580 Eastbound only

M58

Junction 1
Eastbound: No exit, access from A506 only
Westbound: No access, exit to A506 only

M60

Junction 2
Nth.-Eastbound: No access, exit to A560 only
Sth.-Westbound: No exit, access from A560 only
Junction 3
Westbound: No exit to A34 Northbound
Eastbound: No access from A34 Southbound
Junction 4
Westbound: No access from A34 Southbound
No access from M56 Eastbound
Eastbound: No exit to M56 South-Westbound
No exit to A34 Northbound
Junction 5
South-Eastbound: No access from or exit to A5103 Northbound
North-Westbound: No access from or exit to A5103 Southbound
Junction 14
Eastbound: No exit to A580
No access from A580 Westbound
Westbound: No exit to A580 Eastbound
No access from A580
Junction 16
Eastbound: No exit, access from A666 only
Westbound: No access, exit to A666 only
Junction 20
Eastbound: No access from A664
Westbound: No exit to A664
Junction 22
Westbound: No access from A62
Junction 25
South-Westbound:
No access from A560/A6017
Junction 26
North-Eastbound: No access or exit
Junction 27
North-Eastbound: No access, exit only
South-Westbound: No exit, access only

M61

Junctions 2 and 3
North-Westbound:
No access from A580 Eastbound
Sth.-Eastbound: No exit to A580 Westbound
Junction with M6 (M6 Junc. 30)
North-Westbound:
No exit to M6 Southbound
South-Eastbound:
No access from M6 Northbound

M62

Junction 23
Eastbound: No access, exit to A640 only
Westbound: No exit, access from A640 only

M65

Junction 9
Nth.-Eastbound: No access, exit to A679 only
Sth.-Westbound:
No exit, access from A679 only
Junction 11
North-Eastbound: No access, exit only
South-Westbound: No access, exit only

M66

Junction 1
Southbound: No exit, access from A56 only
Northbound: No access, exit to A56 only

M67

Junction 1
Eastbound: Access from A57 Eastbound only
Westbound: Exit to A57 Westbound only
Junction 1a
Eastbound: No access, exit to A6017 only
Westbound: No exit, access from A6017 only
Junction 2
Eastbound: No exit, access from A57 only
Westbound: No access, exit to A57 only

M69

Junction 2
North-Eastbound:
No exit, access from B4669 only
South-Westbound:
No access, exit to B4669 only

M73

Junction 1
Southbound: No exit to A74 Eastbound
Junction 2
Northbound: No access from M8 Eastbound
No exit to A89 Eastbound
Southbound: No exit to M8 Westbound
No access from A89 Westbound
Junction 3
Northbound: No exit to A80 South-Westbound
Southbound:
No access from A80 North-Eastbound

M74

Junction 1
Eastbound: No access from M8 Westbound
Westbound: No exit to M8 Westbound
Junction 3
Eastbound: No exit
Westbound: No access
Junction 3a
Eastbound: No access
Westbound: No exit
Junction 7
Southbound: No access, exit to A72 only
Northbound: No exit, access from A72 only
Junction 9
Southbound: No access, exit to B7078 only
Northbound: No access or exit
Junction 10
Southbound: No exit, access from B7078 only
Junction 11
Southbound: No access, exit to B7078 only
Northbound: No access, exit to B7078 only
Junction 12
Southbound: No exit, access from A70 only
Northbound: No access, exit to A70 only

M77

Junction with M8 (M8 Junc. 22)
Southbound: No access from M8 Eastbound
Northbound: No exit to M8 Westbound
Junction 4
Southbound: No access
Northbound: No exit
Junction 6
Southbound: No access from A77
Northbound: No exit to A77
Junction 7
Northbound: No access from A77
No exit to A77

M80

Junction 1
Northbound: No access from M8 Westbound
Southbound: No exit to M8 Eastbound

Junction 4a
Northbound: No access
Southbound: No exit
Junction 6a
Northbound: No exit
Southbound: No access
Junction 8
Northbound: No access from M876
Southbound: No exit to M876

M90

Junction 2a
Northbound: No access, exit to A92 only
Southbound: No exit, access from A92 only
Junction 7
Northbound: No exit, access from A91 only
Southbound: No access, exit to A91 only
Junction 8
Northbound: No access, exit to A91 only
Southbound: No exit, access from A91 only
Junction 10
Northbound: No access from A912
Exit to A912 Northbound only
Southbound: No exit to A912
Access from A912 Southbound only

M180

Junction 1
Eastbound: No access, exit only
Westbound: No exit, access from A18 only

M606

Junction 2
Northbound: No access, exit only

M621

Junction 2a
Eastbound: No exit, access only
Westbound: No access, exit only
Junction 4
Southbound: No exit
Junction 5
Northbound: No access, exit to A61 only
Southbound: No exit, access from A61 only
Junction 6
Northbound: No exit, access only
Southbound: No access, exit only
Junction 7
Westbound: No exit, access only
Eastbound: No access, exit only
Junction 8
Northbound: No exit, access only
Southbound: No exit, access only

M876

Junction with M80 (M80 Junc. 5)
North-Eastbound:
No access from M80 Southbound
South-Westbound: No exit to M80 Northbound
Junction 2
North-Eastbound: No access, exit only
South-Westbound: No exit, access only
Junction with M9 (M9 Junc. 8)
North-Eastbound: No exit to M9 Northbound
South-Westbound:
No access from M9 Southbound

A1(M) (Hertfordshire Section)

Junction 2
Southbound: No exit, access from A1001 only
Northbound: No access, exit only
Junction 3
Southbound: No access, exit only
Junction 5
Northbound: No exit, access only
Southbound: No access or exit

A1(M) (Cambridgeshire Section)

Junction 13a
Northbound: No exit to B1043
Southbound: No access from B1043
Junction 14
Northbound: No exit, access only
Southbound: No access, exit only

A1(M) (Leeds Section)

Junction 40
Southbound: Exit to A1 Southbound only
Junction 43
Northbound: Access from M1 Eastbound only
Southbound: Exit to M1 Westbound only

A1(M) (Durham Section)

Junction 57
Northbound: No access, exit to A66(M) only
Southbound: No exit, access from A66(M)
Junction 65
Northbound: Exit to A1 North-Westbound, and to A194(M) only
Southbound: Access from A1 South-Eastbound, and from A194(M) only

A3(M)

Junction 4
Northbound: No access, exit only
Southbound: No exit, access only

A38(M) Aston Expressway

Junction with Victoria Road, Aston
Northbound: No exit, access only
Southbound: No access, exit only

A48(M)

Junction with M4 (M4 Junc. 29)
South-Westbound: access from M4 Westbound
North-Eastbound: exit to M4 Eastbound only
Junction 29a
South-Westbound: Exit to A48 Westbound only
North-Eastbound:
Access from A48 Eastbound only

A57(M) Mancunian Way

Junction with A34 Brook Street, Manchester
Eastbound: No exit, exit to A34 Brook Street Southbound only
Westbound: No exit, access only

A58(M) Leeds Inner Ring Road

Junction with Park Lane/ Westgate
Southbound: No access, exit only

A64(M) Leeds Inner Ring Road (Continuation of A58(M))

Junction with A58 Clay Pit Lane
Eastbound: No Access
Westbound: No exit

A66(M)

Junction with A1(M) (A1(M) Junc. 57)
South-Westbound:
Exit to A1(M) Southbound only
North-Eastbound:
Access from A1(M) Northbound only

A74(M)

Junction 18
Northbound: No access
Southbound: No exit

A167(M) Newcastle Central Motorway

Junction with Camden Street
Northbound: No exit, access only
Southbound: No access or exit

A194(M)

Junction with A1(M) (A1(M) Junc. 65) and A1 Gateshead Western By-Pass
Southbound: Exit to A1(M) only
Northbound: Access from A1(M) only

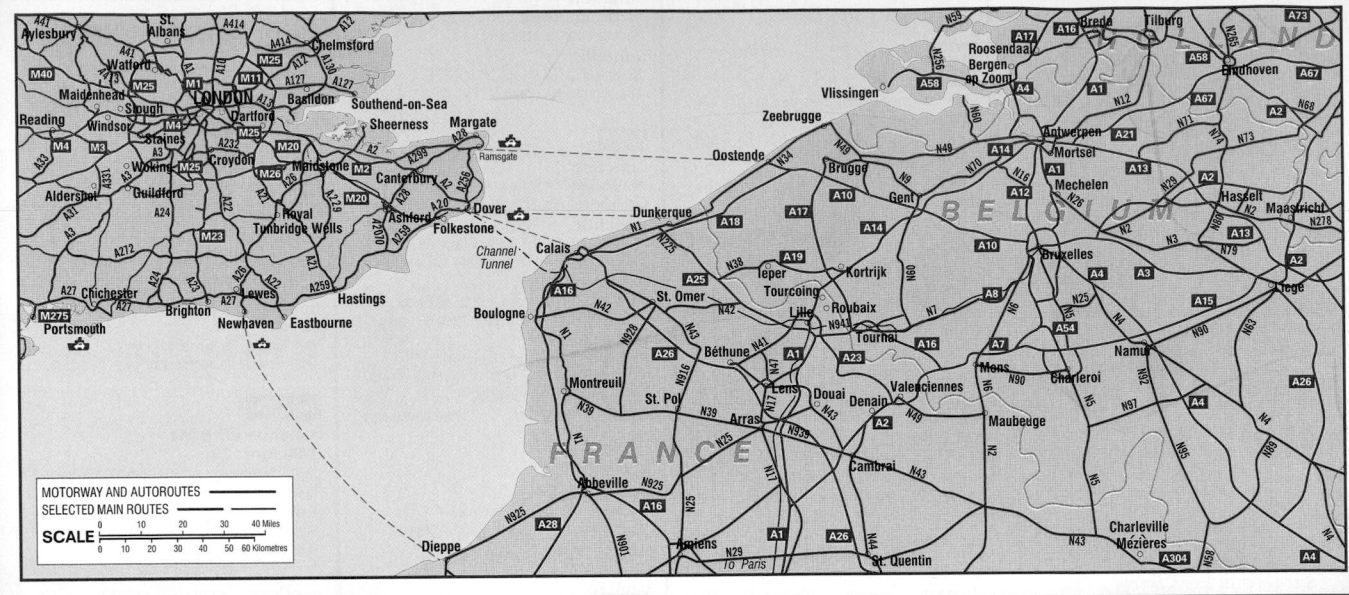

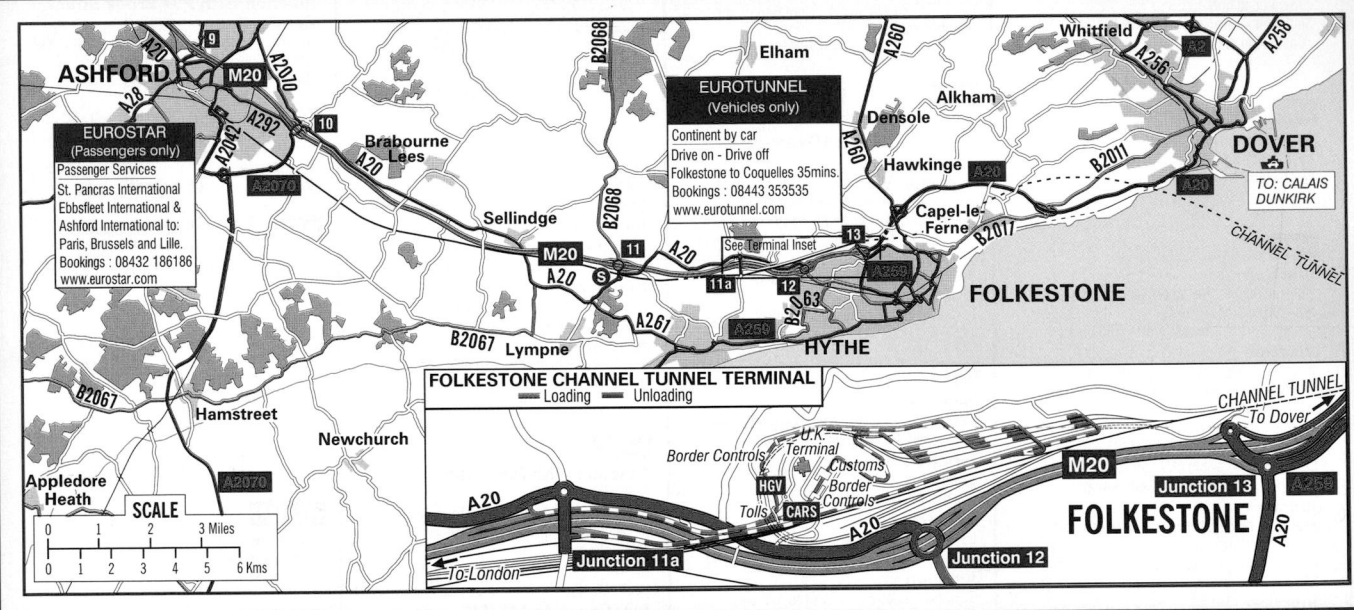

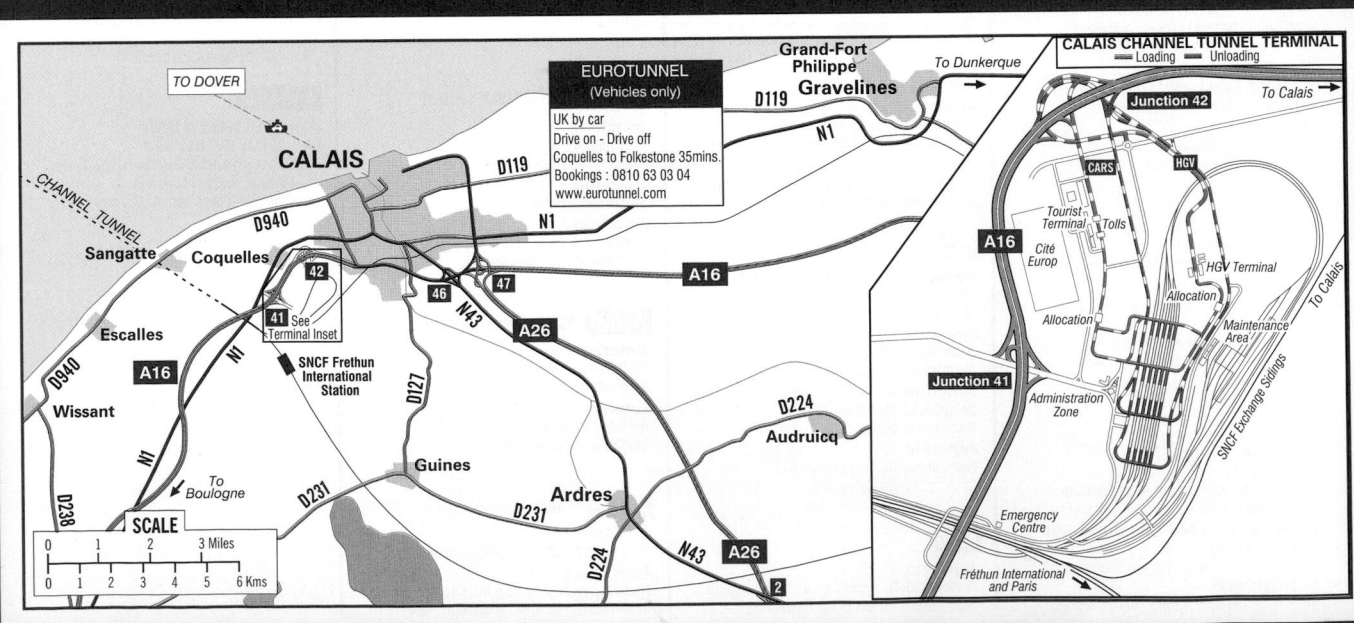